T0181122

Lecture Notes in Computer Science   10402

Commenced Publication in 1973
Founding and Former Series Editors:
Gerhard Goos, Juris Hartmanis, and Jan van Leeuwen

More information about this series at http://www.springer.com/series/7410

Jonathan Katz · Hovav Shacham (Eds.)

Advances in Cryptology – CRYPTO 2017

37th Annual International Cryptology Conference
Santa Barbara, CA, USA, August 20–24, 2017
Proceedings, Part II

 Springer

Editors
Jonathan Katz
University of Maryland
College Park, MD
USA

Hovav Shacham
UC San Diego
La Jolla, CA
USA

ISSN 0302-9743   ISSN 1611-3349 (electronic)
Lecture Notes in Computer Science
ISBN 978-3-319-63714-3   ISBN 978-3-319-63715-0 (eBook)
DOI 10.1007/978-3-319-63715-0

Library of Congress Control Number: 2017947035

LNCS Sublibrary: SL4 – Security and Cryptology

Printed on acid-free paper

This Springer imprint is published by Springer Nature
The registered company is Springer International Publishing AG
The registered company address is: Gewerbestrasse 11, 6330 Cham, Switzerland

Preface

The 37th International Cryptology Conference (Crypto 2017) was held at the University of California, Santa Barbara, USA, during August 20–24, 2017, sponsored by the International Association for Cryptologic Research.

There were 311 submissions to Crypto 2017, a substantial increase from previous years. The Program Committee, aided by nearly 350 external reviewers, selected 72 papers to appear in the program. We are indebted to all the reviewers for their service. Their reviews and discussions, if printed out, would consume about a thousand pages.

Two papers—"Identity-Based Encryption from the Diffie-Hellman Assumption," by Nico Döttling and Sanjam Garg, and "The first Collision for Full SHA-1," by Marc Stevens, Elie Bursztein, Pierre Karpman, Ange Albertini, and Yarik Markov—were honored as best papers. A third paper—"Watermarking Cryptographic Functionalities from Standard Lattice Assumptions," by Sam Kim and David J. Wu—was honored as best paper authored exclusively by young researchers.

Crypto was the venue for the 2017 IACR Distinguished Lecture, delivered by Shafi Goldwasser. Crypto also shared an invited speaker, Cédric Fournet, with the 30th IEEE Computer Security Foundations Symposium (CSF 2017), which was held jointly with Crypto.

We are grateful to Steven Myers, the Crypto general chair; to Shai Halevi, author of the IACR Web Submission and Review system; to Alfred Hofmann, Anna Kramer, and their colleagues at Springer; to Sally Vito of UCSB Conference Services; and, of course, everyone who submitted a paper to Crypto and everyone who attended the conference.

August 2017

Jonathan Katz
Hovav Shacham

Crypto 2017

The 37th IACR International Cryptology Conference

University of California, Santa Barbara, CA, USA
August 20–24, 2017

Sponsored by the *International Association for Cryptologic Research*

General Chair

Steven Myers   Indiana University, USA

Program Chairs

Jonathan Katz   University of Maryland, USA
Hovav Shacham   UC San Diego, USA

Program Committee

Masayuki Abe   NTT Secure Platform Laboratories, Japan
Shweta Agrawal   IIT Madras, India
Adi Akavia   The Academic College of Tel Aviv-Yaffo, Israel
Elena Andreeva   KU Leuven, Belgium
Mihir Bellare   UC San Diego, USA
Dan Boneh   Stanford University, USA
Elette Boyle   IDC Herzliya, Israel
Ran Canetti   Boston University, USA, and Tel Aviv University,
                        Israel
Jung Hee Cheon   Seoul National University, Korea
Dana Dachman-Soled   University of Maryland, USA
Ivan Damgård   Aarhus University, Denmark
Nico Döttling   UC Berkeley, USA
Orr Dunkelman   University of Haifa, Israel
Eiichiro Fujisaki   NTT Secure Platform Laboratories, Japan
Sergey Gorbunov   University of Waterloo, Canada
Vipul Goyal   Carnegie Mellon University, USA
Matthew Green   Johns Hopkins University, USA
Nadia Heninger   University of Pennsylvania, USA
Viet Tung Hoang   Florida State University, USA
Dennis Hofheinz   Karlsruhe Institute of Technology, Germany
Sorina Ionica   Université de Picardie, France

Tetsu Iwata	Nagoya University, Japan
Seny Kamara	Brown University, USA
Gaëtan Leurent	Inria, France
Rachel Lin	UC Santa Barbara, USA
Stefan Lucks	Bauhaus-Universität Weimar, Germany
Vadim Lyubashevsky	IBM Zurich, Switzerland
Mohammad Mahmoody	University of Virginia, USA
Payman Mohassel	Visa Research, USA
Claudio Orlandi	Aarhus University, Denmark
Elisabeth Oswald	University of Bristol, UK
Rafael Pass	Cornell University, USA
Gregory G. Rose	TargetProof LLC, USA
Christian Schaffner	University of Amsterdam and CWI and QuSoft, The Netherlands
Gil Segev	Hebrew University, Israel
Yannick Seurin	ANSSI, France
Douglas Stebila	McMaster University, Canada
Stefano Tessaro	UC Santa Barbara, USA
Mehdi Tibouchi	NTT Secure Platform Laboratories, Japan
Eran Tromer	Tel Aviv University, Israel, and Columbia University, USA
Dominique Unruh	University of Tartu, Estonia
Vassilis Zikas	Rensselaer Polytechnic Institute, USA

Additional Reviewers

Aysajan Abidin
Shashank Agrawal
Thomas Agrikola
Ali Akhavi
Gorjan Alagic
Martin Albrecht
Jacob Alperin-Sheriff
Joel Alwen
Joran van Apeldoorn
Daniel Apon
Gilad Asharov
Tomer Ashur
Nuttapong Attrapadung
Christian Badertscher
Saikrishna
  Badrinarayanan
Shi Bai
Foteini Baldimtsi
Marshall Ball

Achiya Bar-On
Razvan Barbulescu
Guy Barwell
Carsten Baum
Amin Baumeler
Fabrice Benhamouda
Daniel J. Bernstein
Jean-François Biasse
Alex Biryukov
Nir Bitansky
Olivier Blazy
Jeremiah Blocki
Andrej Bogdanov
Xavier Bonnetain
Charlotte Bonte
Carl Bootland
Christina Boura
Zvika Brakerski
Brandon Broadnax

Leon Groot Bruinderink
Benedikt Bunz
Anne Canteaut
Angelo de Caro
Ignacio Cascudo
David Cash
Wouter Castryck
Nishanth Chandran
Eshan Chattopadhyay
Binyi Chen
Jie Chen
Yilei Chen
Alessandro Chiesa
Chongwon Cho
Arka Rai Chouduhri
Heewon Chung
Kai-Min Chung
Benoit Cogliati
Aloni Cohen

Ran Cohen
Katriel Cohn-Gordon
Henry Corrigan-Gibbs
Geoffroy Couteau
Alain Couvreur
Cas Cremers
Jan Czajkowski
Wei Dai
Bernardo David
Jean Paul Degabriele
Jeroen Delvaux
Apoorvaa Deshpande
Bogdan Adrian Dina
Itai Dinur
Yevgeniy Dodis
Benjamin Dowling
Rafael Dowsley
Leo Ducas
Yfke Dulek
Tuyet Duong
Tuyet Thi Anh Duong
Fred Dupuis
Frédéric Dupuis
Alfredo Rial Duran
Sébastien Duval
Aner Moshe Ben Efraim
Maria Eichlseder
Keita Emura
Naomi Ephraim
Saba Eskandarian
Thomas Espitau
Oriol Farràs
Pooya Farshim
Sebastian Faust
Prastudy Fauzi
Nelly Fazio
Serge Fehr
Houda Ferradi
Manuel Fersch
Dario Fiore
Ben Fisch
Joseph Fitzsimons
Nils Fleischhacker
Tore Frederiksen
Rotem Arnon Friedman
Georg Fuchsbauer

Marc Fyrbiak
Tommaso Gagliardoni
Nicolas Gama
Juan Garay
Sanjam Garg
Christina Garman
Romain Gay
Peter Gazi
Alexandre Gelin
Daniel Genkin
Marios Georgiou
Benoit Gerard
Essam Ghadafi
Niv Gilboa
Dov Gordon
Rishab Goyal
Vincent Grosso
Jens Groth
Paul Grubbs
Siyao Guo
Helene Haag
Helene Haagh
Kyoohyung Han
Marcella Hastings
Carmit Hazay
Ethan Heilman
Brett Hemenway
Minki Hhan
Justin Holmgren
Akinori Hosoyamada
Yan Huang
Pavel Hubacek
Ilia Iliashenko
Vincenzo Iovino
Yuval Ishai
Joseph Jaeger
Zahra Jafragholi
Tibor Jager
Aayush Jain
Abhishek Jain
Chethan Kamath
Bhavana Kanukurthi
Angshuman Karmakar
Pierre Karpman
Stefan Katzenbeisser
Xagawa Keita

Marcel Keller
Nathan Keller
Iordanis Kerenidis
Dakshita Khurana
Andrey Kim
Dongwoo Kim
Duhyeong Kim
Eunkyung Kim
Jae-yun Kim
Jihye Kim
Jinsu Kim
Jiseung Kim
Sam Kim
Taechan Kim
Fuyuki Kitagawa
Susumu Kiyoshima
Dima Kogan
Vlad Kolesnikov
Ilan Komargodski
Venkata Koppula
Venkata Kopulla
Evgenios Kornaropoulos
Juliane Kraemer
Mukul Kulkarni
Ashutosh Kumar
Ranjit Kumaresan
Alptekin Küpçü
Lakshmi Kuppusamy
Thijs Laarhoven
Changmin Lee
Joohee Lee
Younho Lee
Nikos Leonardos
Tancrède Lepoint
Baiyu Li
Benoit Libert
Eik List
Yi-Kai Liu
Steve Lu
Yun Lu
Atul Luykx
Saeed Mahloujifar
Giulio Malavolta
Alex Malozemoff
Antonio Marcedone
Daniel P. Martin

Marco Martinoli
Daniel Masny
Takahiro Matsuda
Florian Mendel
Bart Mennink
Peihan Miao
Daniele Micciancio
Gabrielle De Micheli
Ian Miers
Andrew Miller
Kazuhiko Minematsu
Tarik Moataz
Ameer Mohammed
Hart Montgomery
Andrew Morgan
Nicky Mouha
Pratyay Mukherjee
Muhammad Naveed
María Naya-Plasencia
Kartik Nayak
Gregory Neven
Ruth Ng
Michael Nielsen
Tobias Nilges
Ryo Nishimaki
Ariel Nof
Kaisa Nyberg
Adam O'Neill
Maciej Obremski
Sabine Oechsner
Miyako Ohkubo
Rafail Ostrovsky
Daniel Page
Jiaxin Pan
Omer Paneth
Dimitris Papadopoulos
Sunno Park
Anat Paskin-Cherniavsky
Kenny Paterson
Arpita Patra
Filip Pawlega
Chris Peikert
Josef Pieprzyk
Cécile Pierrot
Krzysztof Pietrzak
Benny Pinkas

Rafael del Pino
Oxana Poburinnaya
David Pointcheval
Antigoni Polychroniadou
Raluca Ada Popa
Bart Preneel
Thomas Prest
Emmanuel Prouff
Carla Rafols
Srinivasan Raghuraman
Samuel Ranellucci
Mariana Raykova
Oded Regev
Ling Ren
Oscar Reparaz
Leo Reyzin
Silas Richelson
Matt Robshaw
Mike Rosulek
Yann Rotella
Lior Rotem
Ron Rothblum
Arnab Roy
Sujoy Sinha Roy
Olivier Ruatta
Ulrich Rührmair
Yusuke Sakai
Olivier Sanders
Yu Sasaki
Sajin Sasy
Alessandra Scafuro
Patrick Schaumont
Thomas Schneider
Peter Scholl
Gregor Seiler
Ido Shahaf
abhi shelat
Timothy Sherwood
Kyoji Shibutani
Sina Shiehian
Mark Simkin
Leonie Simpson
Maciej Skorski
Nigel Smart
Yongha Son
Fang Song

Yongsoo Song
Pratik Soni
Florian Speelman
Akshayaram Srinivasan
Martijn Stam
François-Xavier Standaert
John Steinberger
Igors Stepanovs
Noah
    Stephens-Davidowitz
Valentin Suder
Koutarou Suzuki
Björn Tackmann
Alain Tapp
Isamu Teranishi
Benjamin Terner
Aishwarya
    Thiruvengadam
Sri Aravinda Krishnan
    Thyagarajan
Yosuke Todo
Junichi Tomida
Luca Trevisan
Roberto Trifiletti
Daniel Tschudi
Nik Unger
Salil Vadhan
Margarita Vald
Luke Valenta
Kerem Varici
Srinivas Vivek Venkatesh
Muthuramakrishnan
    Venkitasubramaniam
Daniele Venturi
Damien Vergnaud
Jorge Villar
Dhinakaran
    Vinayagamurthy
Ivan Visconti
Damian Vizar
Christine van Vreedendal
Michael Walter
Mingyuan Wang
Xiao Wang
Yuyu Wang
Yohei Watanabe

Platinum Sponsor

Silver Sponsors

Contents – Part II

Quantum

Hash Functions

Lattices

Signatures

OT and ORAM

Secure Computation Based on Leaky Correlations: High Resilience Setting

Alexander R. Block$^{(\boxtimes)}$, Hemanta K. Maji, and Hai H. Nguyen

Department of Computer Science, Purdue University, West Lafayette, IN 47906, USA
{block9,hmaji,nguye245}@cs.purdue.edu

Abstract. Correlated private randomness, or correlation in short, is a fundamental cryptographic resource that helps parties compute securely over their private data. An offline preprocessing step, which is independent of the eventual secure computation, generates correlated secret shares for the parties and the parties use these shares during the final secure computation step. However, these secret shares are vulnerable to leakage attacks.

Inspired by the quintessential problem of privacy amplification, Ishai, Kushilevitz, Ostrovsky, and Sahai (FOCS 2009) introduced the concept of correlation extractors. Correlation extractors are interactive protocols that take leaky correlations as input and produce secure independent copies of oblivious transfer (OT), the building blocks of secure computation protocols. Although their initial feasibility result is resilient to linear leakage and produces a linear number of "fresh" OTs, the constants involved are minuscule. The output of this correlation extractor can be used to perform only small secure computation tasks, because the number of OTs needed to evaluate a functionality securely is roughly proportional to its circuit size. Recently, Gupta, Ishai, Maji, and Sahai (CRYPTO 2015) constructed an extractor that is resilient to 1/4 fractional leakage and has near-linear production rate. They also constructed an extractor from a large correlation that has 1/2 fractional resilience but produces only one OT, which does not suffice to compute even constant size functionalities securely.

In this paper, we show the existence of a correlation that produces n-bit shares for the parties and allows the extraction of $n^{1-o(1)}$ secure OTs, despite $n/2$ bits of leakage. The key technical idea is to embed several multiplications over a field into one multiplication over an extension field. The packing efficiency of this embedding directly translates into the production rate of our correlation extractor. Our work establishes a connection between this problem and a rich vein of research in additive combinatorics on constructing dense sets of integers that are free of arithmetic progressions, a.k.a. 3-free sets. We introduce a new combinatorial problem that suffices for our multiplication embedding, and produces concrete embeddings that beat the efficiency of the embeddings inspired by the reduction to 3-free sets.

A.R. Block, H.K. Maji and H.H. Nguyen—The research effort is supported in part by an NSF CRII Award CNS–1566499, an NSF SMALL Award CNS–1618822, and an REU CNS–1724673.

© International Association for Cryptologic Research 2017
J. Katz and H. Shacham (Eds.): CRYPTO 2017, Part II, LNCS 10402, pp. 3–32, 2017.
DOI: 10.1007/978-3-319-63715-0_1

Finally, the paper introduces a graph-theoretic measure to upperbound the leakage resilience of correlations, namely the *simple partition number*. This measure is similar in spirit to graph covering problems like the biclique partition number. If the simple partition number of a correlation is 2^λ, then it is impossible to extract even one OT if parties can perform λ-bits of leakage. We compute tight estimates of the simple partition number of several correlations that are relevant to this paper, and, in particular, show that our extractor and the extractor for the large correlation by Gupta et al. have optimal leakage resilience and (qualitatively) optimal simulation error.

1 Introduction

Secure multi-party computation [22,71] helps mutually distrusting parties to compute securely over their private data. Unfortunately, it is impossible to securely compute most functionalities in the information-theoretic plain model even against parties who honestly follow the protocol but are curious to find additional information about the other parties' private input [2,19,32,38,41–43]. However, we can securely compute any functionality if honest parties are in the majority [5,12,16,56], parties use some trusted setup [10,11,17,23,35,37,49] or correlated private randomness [15,39,44,68], or there are bounds on the computational power of the parties [22,35].

The study of secure computation using correlated private randomness, primarily initiated due to efficiency concerns, has produced several success stories, for example FairPlay [4,45], TinyOT [50] and SPDZ [18] (pronounced Speedz). These secure computation protocols offload most of the computational and cryptographic complexity to an offline preprocessing phase. During this preprocessing phase, a trusted dealer samples two shares (r_A, r_B) from the joint distribution (R_A, R_B), namely the *correlated private randomness*, or *correlation* in short, and provides the secret shares r_A to Alice and r_B to Bob. During the online secure computation phase, parties use their respective secret shares in an interactive protocol to securely compute the intended functionality. Note that the preprocessing phase is independent of the functionality or the inputs fed to the functionality by the parties.

A prominent and extremely well-studied correlation is the *random oblivious transfer correlation*, represented by ROT. It samples three bits x_0, x_1, b independently and uniformly at random, and provides the secret shares (x_0, x_1) to Alice and (b, x_b) to Bob. Note that Alice does not know the choice bit b, and Bob does not know the other bit $x_{\bar{b}}$. Intuitively, ROT is an input-less functionality that implements a randomized version of *oblivious transfer* functionality, where the sender sends (x_0, x_1) as input to the functionality and the receiver picks x_b out of the two input bits. Given m independent samples from this distribution, parties can securely compute any functionality with circuit complexity (roughly) m. For example, we can utilize the randomized self-reducibility of oblivious transfer to reimagine the GMW protocol [22] in this framework naturally.

However, the storage of the secret shares by the parties brings to fore several vulnerabilities. For instance, parties can leak additional information from the secret shares of the other parties. We emphasize that the leakage need not necessarily reveal individual bits of the other party's share. The leakage can be on the entire share and encode crucial global information that can potentially jeopardize the security of the secure computation protocol.

To address these concerns, Ishai, Kushilevitz, Ostrovsky, and Sahai [33] introduced the notion of *correlation extractors*. Correlation extractors distill leaky correlations into independent samples of the ROT correlation that are secure. That is, for each of the new samples Alice does not know Bob's choice bit and Bob does not know Alice's other bit. This problem is a direct analog of the quintessential problems of privacy amplification and randomness extraction problems in the secure computation setting. With the exception that, correlation extractors ensure security against insider attacks, i.e., the parties who perform the leakage are participants in the secure protocol itself. This additional requirement makes the task of correlation extraction significantly more challenging. It is, thus, not surprising that relatively few results are known in the field of correlation extractor construction.

For example, in the setting of privacy amplification, if Alice and Bob start with a secret n-bit random string then, in the presence of t-bits of arbitrary leakage to an eavesdropper, parties can re-establish a fresh m-bit secret key such that the advantage of the eavesdropper in guessing the secret key is roughly $2^{-\Delta} \approx 2^{-(n-t-m)}$. Intuitively, the sum of "entropy deficiency" (t), "entropy of production" (m), and "$-\log$ of the adversarial advantage" (Δ) is roughly n, the initial entropy of the secret. Analogous results also exist in the setting of randomness extraction, where we can extract nearly all of the min-entropy of a source. But similar tight extraction results are not known for correlation extractors. In fact, the task of designing correlations that simultaneously support high leakage resilience and production rate with exponential security has been elusive.

The number of the output ROT samples and their high security are crucial for the secure computation protocol. For example, protocols with exponential security can reduce the ROT production or increase the statistical security parameter only slightly to prohibitively increase the effort needed by adversaries to

	Correlation Description	Number of OTs Produced (m)	Number of Leakage bits (t)	Simulation Error (ε)	Round Complexity
IKOS [33]	$\mathsf{ROT}^{n/2}$	αn	βn	$2^{-\gamma n}$	4
GIMS [26]	$\mathsf{ROT}^{n/2}$	$n/\operatorname{poly}\log n$	$(1/4 - g)n$	$2^{-gn/m}$	2
	$\mathsf{IP}\left(\mathsf{GF}\left[2\right]^n\right)$	1	$(1/2 - g)n$	2^{-gn}	2
Our Work	$\mathsf{IP}\left(\mathbb{F}^{n/\log|\mathbb{F}|}\right)$	$n^{1-o(1)}$	$(1/2 - g)n$	2^{-gn}	2

Fig. 1. A qualitative summary of prior relevant works in correlation extractors and a comparison to our correlation extractor construction. All correlations have been normalized so that each party gets an n-bit secret share. The positive constants α, β, and γ are minuscule. And $g < 1/2$ is an arbitrary positive constant.

break them. Furthermore, the number of these ROT samples limit the size of the eventual functionality that can be securely computed, because the number of ROT samples needed to implement a functionality securely is directly proportional to its circuit size. As highlighted in [26], the initial feasibility result of Ishai et al. [33], though asymptotically linear in leakage resilience and production rate, has unsatisfactorily low resilience and production rate for realistic values of n, the size of the original share of the parties. The subsequent work of Gupta et al. [26], improves the resilience to (roughly) $n/4$ but trades-off the security of the protocol for high production rate and, consequently, achieves only negligible (and, not exponentially low) insecurity. They also consider a new correlation, namely the *inner-product correlation* where the secret shares of the parties are random n-bit binary vectors subject to the constraint that they are orthogonal to each other.[1] They construct a correlation extractor for the inner-product correlation with resilience $n/2$ and exponential security. However, it is inherently limited to producing one ROT sample as output, which is not adequate for the end goal of performing interesting secure computations. Our work shows that the inner-product correlation over an *appropriately large field* admits a correlation extractor that is resilient to $n/2$ bits of leakage, has high concrete production rate, and has exponentially high security. Figure 1 summarizes the entire preceding discussion tersely. Finally, similar to Gupta et al. [26], although our construction is stated in the information-theoretic setting, it is also relevant to the setting where computationally secure protocol generate the correlations or use the output OTs.

However, is the upper-bound of $n/2$ resilience inherent to the inner-product correlation? For example, $n/2$ samples of the ROT correlation cannot be resilient to more than $n/4$ bits of leakage. A partition argument can demonstrate this upper bound of the maximum resilience of this correlation [34]. In this partition argument, Alice emulates the generation of $n/4$ (i.e., half of $n/2$) independent samples (x_0, x_1) and (c, x_c) from the ROT correlation and sends the corresponding (c, x_c) to Bob. Moreover, Bob emulates the generation of the remaining $n/4$ samples and sends the corresponding (x_0, x_1) shares to Alice. Finally, we reimagine any correlation extractor that is resilient to $n/4$ bits of leakage and produces even one secure ROT sample as a secure ROT protocol in the plain model where Alice implements $n/4$ ROT samples, and Bob implements the remaining $n/4$ ROT samples; which is impossible. Typically, the partition argument applies to "multiple independent samples of small correlations," but its extension to one huge global correlation is not apparent.

To address this question, we introduce a new graph-theoretic measure for the maximum resilience of a correlation, namely its *simple partition number*. In particular, a correlation with simple partition number $\leqslant 2^\lambda$ cannot be resilient to λ

---

[1] The actual inner-product correlation is defined slightly differently. Parties get shares $(x_0, x_1, \ldots, x_n)$ and $(y_0, y_1, \ldots, y_n)$ such that $x_0 + y_0 = \sum_{i=1}^{n} x_i y_i$. That is, x_0 and y_0 are additive secret shares of the inner product of $(x_1, \ldots, x_n)$ and $(y_1, \ldots, y_n)$. But for intuition, it suffices to consider the correlation where the secret shares of the parties are orthogonal vectors instead.

Correlation Description	Secret Share Size (s)	Simple Partition Number (sp)	Upper Bound on the Max. Fractional Leakage (log sp/s)
$\text{ROT}^{n/2}$	n	$2^{n/4}$	$1/4$
$\text{ROLE}(\mathbb{F})^{n/2}$	$n \log |\mathbb{F}|$	$|\mathbb{F}|^{n/4}$	$1/4$
$\text{IP}(\mathbb{F}^n)$	$n \log |\mathbb{F}|$	$|\mathbb{F}|^{n/2}$	$1/2$

Fig. 2. A summary of the estimates of the simple partition number for the correlations relevant to our work.

bits of leakage (refer to Fig. 2 for a summary of these estimates). Finally, we prove the optimality of the resilience demonstrated by the correlation extractors for the inner-product correlation presented in [26] and our work. Refer to Sect. 5.7 for a discussion on how the relation between simple partition number and maximum resilience is similar to the connection between biclique partition number and Wyner's common information [69]. The existence of correlation extractors for a slightly lesser amount of leakage implies the tightness of our upper bounds on leakage resilience. Finally, we leverage the simple partition number bounds and use an averaging argument to show that the decay in simulation security with entropy gap as achieved by [26] and our correlation extractor are qualitatively optimal.

1.1 Model

This section presents the standard model of Ishai et al. [33] for correlation extractors, which subsequent works also use. We consider 2-party semi-honest secure computation in the preprocessing model. In the preprocessing step, a trusted dealer draws a sample (r_A, r_B) from the joint distribution (R_A, R_B). The joint distribution (R_A, R_B) is referred to as the correlated private randomness, and r_A and r_B, respectively, are the secret shares of Alice and Bob. The dealer provides the secret share r_A to Alice and r_B to Bob. An adversarial party can perform arbitrary t-bits of leakage on the secret share of the other party at the end of the preprocessing step. We represent this leaky correlation hybrid as $(R_A, R_B)^{[t]}$.[2]

In the leaky correlation $(R_A, R_B)^{[t]}$ hybrid, during the secure computation phase, parties perform an interactive protocol to realize their target functionality securely. No leakage occurs during the execution of the secure computation protocol. In this work, we consider the functionality that implements m independent oblivious transfers between the parties, referred to as the OT^m functionality.

Definition 1 (Correlation Extractor). *Let (R_A, R_B) be a correlated private randomness such that the secret share size of each party is n-bits.*

---

[2] That is, the functionality samples secret shares (r_A, r_B) according to the correlation (R_A, R_B). The adversarial party sends a t-bit leakage function $\mathcal{L}$ to the functionality and receives the leakage $\mathcal{L}(r_A, r_B)$ from the functionality. The functionality sends r_A to Alice and r_B to Bob. Note that the adversary does not need to know its secret share to construct the leakage function because the leakage function gets the secret shares of both parties as input.

An (n, m, t, ε)-correlation extractor for (R_A, R_B) is a two-party interactive protocol in the $(R_A, R_B)^{[t]}$ hybrid that securely implements the OT^m functionality against information-theoretic semi-honest adversaries with ε-simulation error.

1.2 Our Contribution

Our work makes a two-fold contribution regarding correlation extractors. First, we construct a highly resilient correlation extractor that produces a large number of secure OTs as output and has exponential security. Finally, we provide a general graph-theoretic measure that upper bounds the maximal resilience of any correlation.

Correlation Extraction Construction. For any field $(\mathbb{F}, +, \cdot)$, the *inner-product correlation over* $\mathbb{F}^{n+1}$, represented by $\mathsf{IP}\left(\mathbb{F}^{n+1}\right)$, is a correlation that samples random $r_A = (x_0, x_1, \ldots, x_n) \in \mathbb{F}^{n+1}$ and $r_B = (y_0, y_1, \ldots, y_n) \in \mathbb{F}^{n+1}$ such that $x_0 + y_0 = \sum_{i=1}^{n} x_i y_i$. That is, x_0 and y_0 are the additive secret shares of the inner product of $x_{[n]} := (x_1, \ldots, x_n)$ and $y_{[n]} := (y_1, \ldots, y_n)$. Gupta et al. [26] consider a special case of the inner-product correlation, where $\mathbb{F} = \mathbb{GF}[2]$. Note that each party receives $(n + 1)$ field elements as its secret share. In particular, if $\mathbb{F} = \mathbb{GF}[2^a]$, then each party gets an $a(n + 1)$-bit secret share.

Theorem 1 (High Resilience High Production Correlation Extractor). *For all constants $0 < \delta < g < 1/2$, there exists a correlation (R_A, R_B), where each party gets n-bit secret share, such that there exists a two-round (n, m, t, ε)-correlation extractor for (R_A, R_B), where $m = (\delta n)^{1-o(1)}$, $t = (1/2 - g)n$, and $\varepsilon = 2^{-(g-\delta)n/2}$.*

We use $(R_A, R_B) = \mathsf{IP}\left(\mathbb{GF}\left[2^{\delta n}\right]^{1/\delta}\right)$ in this theorem. Note that we maintain the dependence on δ explicitly in the theorem statement to enable computation of concrete efficiency. As we shall see later, this theorem achieves high production rate of $(\delta n)^{\log 10 / \log 38} \approx (\delta n)^{0.633}$ even for realistic values of n. The simulation error is exponentially low in the difference between the entropy gap gn and the parameter δn. Our construction achieves $(\delta n)^{1-o(1)}$ production asymptotically, which is close to the ideal target of δn production. Qualitatively, the decay in our simulation error is near optimal as demonstrated by Theorem 2 and Corollary 1.

The crux of our construction is the composition of two technical contributions. First, we observe that the correlation extractor for $\mathsf{IP}\left(\mathbb{GF}[2]^n\right)$ constructed by Gupta et al. [26] extends to the $\mathsf{IP}\left(\mathbb{F}^{1/\delta}\right)$ correlation, where $\mathbb{F}$ is a large field. However, in this case, instead of producing a secure OT, it produces a generalization of oblivious transfer, namely *oblivious linear-function evaluation over* $\mathbb{F}$ [68] (represented as $\mathsf{OLE}\left(\mathbb{F}\right)$). An oblivious linear-function evaluation is a 2-party functionality that takes $(A, B) \in \mathbb{F}^2$ as input from Alice and $X \in \mathbb{F}$ as input from Bob, and provides $Z = AX + B$ as output to Bob. Note that oblivious transfer is equivalent to oblivious linear-function evaluation over $\mathbb{GF}[2]$, because $x_b = (x_1 - x_0)b + x_0$, for $x_0, x_1, b \in \mathbb{GF}[2]$.

Finally, we embed m OT evaluations simultaneously into one OLE $(\mathbb{F})$ evaluation. Note that, this is *not* an asymptotic reduction. Asymptotically, there are several techniques to construct multiple copies of OT using multiple copies of OLE at a good rate. Our focus is on securely implementing multiple OT evaluations from *only one* OLE $(\mathbb{F})$ evaluation. Development of more efficient embeddings will directly improve the production rate of our construction. We demonstrate that dense sets of integers that avoid any arithmetic progressions, 3-free sets, provide such embedding of multiplications. We formulate a relaxed version of this combinatorial problem (see Fig. 5) that suffices for our embedding problem and obtain more efficient embeddings than those that are inspired by the 3-free set constructions.

We emphasize that although we state our correlation extractor for the bounded leakage model, i.e. an adversary can perform at most t-bits of leakage, it also extends to the noisy leakage setting. As long as the noise is high enough to maintain $(n - t)$ bits of (average) min-entropy in the secret share of the parties, our extractor construction remains secure.

Bound on the Maximum Resilience. The construction of Theorem 1 and the correlation extractor of Gupta et al. [26], with fractional resilience $1/2$, lead naturally to a fascinating question. Can there exist a correlation extractor for IP $(\mathbb{F}^n)$ that achieves over $1/2$ fractional resilience? In fact, more generally, can we meaningfully upper-bound the maximum leakage resilience of an arbitrary correlation?

Note that if parties obtain multiple independent samples from identical correlations, then the partition argument can be leveraged to deduce an upper bound. For example, either Alice or Bob by getting adequate information on half of the other party's secret shares can break the security of the correlation extractor protocol. As discussed earlier, this argument implies that the correlation ROT $^{n/2}$ is not resilient to $\lceil n/4 \rceil$ bits of leakage, because every ROT hides only one bit of information from each party [34]. However, this approach does not apply to correlation extractors for secret shares drawn from one large correlation, for example, IP $(\mathbb{F}^n)$. We prove the following main result.

Theorem 2 (Hardness of Correlation Extraction). *Let* $(\mathbb{F}, +, \cdot)$ *be an arbitrary field. There exists a universal constant* $\varepsilon^* > 0$ *such that, for* $(R_A, R_B) = $ IP $(\mathbb{F}^k)$, *any* $(n, 1, (n/k) \lceil (k+1)/2 \rceil, \varepsilon)$-*correlation extractor for* (R_A, R_B) *has* $\varepsilon \geqslant \varepsilon^*$, *where* $n = k \log |\mathbb{F}|$.

This result proves the optimality of the leakage resilience achieved by our extractor in Theorem 1 and the correlation extractor for IP $(\mathbb{GF}[2]^n)$ proposed by Gupta et al. [26]. In fact, a more general version of this result (using averaging arguments) shows that any $(n, 1, n/2 - gn, \varepsilon)$-correlation extractor for IP $(\mathbb{F}^k)$ has $\varepsilon \geqslant \varepsilon^* 2^{-gn}$ (see Corollary 1). This result proves the qualitative optimality of simulation error achieved by these two correlation extractors.

The technical heart of this result is a new graph-theoretic measure for maximum leakage resilience in correlations, namely *simple partition number* (see Definition 4 in Sect. 2). Theorem 2 is a consequence of precise estimation of this quantity for the IP $(\mathbb{F}^n)$ correlation. This quantity is similar in spirit to the biclique partition number of a graph [24,25], the minimum number of bicliques needed to partition the edges of a graph. Moreover, the connection of simple partition number to maximum resilience is intuitively analogous to the link between biclique partition number and Wyner's common information [69]. Section 5.7 provides details on this connection.

1.3   Prior Relevant Works

This work lies at the intersection of several fields like correlation extractors, additive combinatorics, graph covering problems, and information theory. In this section, we provide only a summary of the work on combiners and extractors. The prior relevant works related to the remaining topics are covered in appropriate sections later.

Combiners and Extractors. A closely related concept is the notion of OT combiners, which are a restricted variant of OT extractors in which the leakage is limited to local information about individual OT correlations, and there is no global leakage. The study of OT combiners was initiated by Harnik et al. [28]. Since then, there has been work on several variants and extensions of OT combiners [27,35,47,48,55]. Recently, Ishai et al. [34] constructed OT combiners with nearly optimal leakage parameters. However, combiners consider a restricted variant of leakage where the leakage function leaks only individual bits of the secret shares.

To address general leakage, Ishai, Kushilevitz, Ostrovsky, and Sahai [33], proposed the notion of correlation extractors. Their construction has a linear leakage resilience, production rate, and exponential security. However, as indicated by Gupta et al. [26], all the constants involved are minuscule. To address this concern, they [26] construct correlation extractor for ROT$^{n/2}$ that has optimal leakage resilience with only a negligible (not exponentially-low) simulation error. They also provide a correlation extractor construction from a large correlation that exhibits 1/2 leakage resilience but outputs only one OT. Our work will achieve (roughly) the best of both these constructions, i.e., fractional resilience 1/2, (near) linear production rate, and exponential security.

1.4   Technical Overview

In this section we present a brief overview of our correlation extractor construction and the graph-theoretic measure of the maximum resilience of an arbitrary correlation.

Correlation Extractor Construction. Suppose we are given $0 < \delta < g < 1/2$, and parties are in the IP $\left(\mathbb{K}^{1/\delta}\right)^{[t]}$-hybrid, where $t = (1/2 - g)n$ and $\mathbb{K} = \mathrm{GF}\left[2^{\delta n}\right]$. For $m = (\delta n)^{1-o(1)}$, we want to implement the OLE $(\mathrm{GF}\,[2])^m$

ROLE (F)	Given a field $\mathbb{F}$, Alice receives $r_A = (A, B)$ and Bob receives $r_B = (X, Z)$ such that A, B, X are independently and uniformly sampled from $\mathbb{F}$ and $Z = A \cdot X + B$.
IP ($\mathbb{F}^n$)	Given a field $\mathbb{F}$, Alice receives $r_A = (x_0, x_1, \ldots, x_{n-1})$ and Bob receives $r_B = (y_0, y_1, \ldots, y_{n-1})$ such that $x_0, \ldots, x_{n-1}, y_0, \ldots, y_{n-1}$ are randomly selected from $\mathbb{F}$, where $x_0 + y_0 = \sum_{i=1}^{n-1} x_i \cdot y_i$.

Fig. 3. A quick summary of the definitions of a few correlations that are relevant to this paper.

functionality. Figure 4 presents the outline of our correlation extractor construction. The extraction protocol π is similar to the correlation extractor of Gupta et al. [26]. Except that, in their case the inner-product correlation was over $\mathbb{GF}[2]$ instead of a large field $\mathbb{K}$. The security of the protocol is argued in Sect. 3. Our correlation extractor securely computes a sample from the ROLE ($\mathbb{K}$) correlation. The protocol ρ is the standard protocol that implements the OLE ($\mathbb{K}$) functionality in the ROLE ($\mathbb{K}$)-hybrid with perfect security. So, all that remains is to simultaneously embed OLE ($\mathbb{GF}[2]$)^m into one OLE ($\mathbb{K}$). This embedding relies on finding solutions to a combinatorial problem that is summarized in Fig. 5. Section 4 outlines the technique of choosing the inputs to the OLE ($\mathbb{K}$) functionality so that the parties can implement the OLE ($\mathbb{GF}[2]$)^m functionality with perfect security.

Ensure. Let $\mathbb{F} = \mathbb{GF}[2]$ and $\mathbb{K} = \mathbb{GF}[2^{\delta n}]$ be an extension field of $\mathbb{F}$. Let $0 < \delta < g < 1/2$.

Private Input. Let $m = (\delta n)^{1-o(1)}$. Alice has private input $(a_0, \ldots, a_{m-1}) \in \mathbb{F}^m$ and $(b_0, \ldots, b_{m-1}) \in \mathbb{F}^m$. Bob has private input $(x_0, \ldots, x_{m-1}) \in \mathbb{F}^m$.

Hybrid. Parties are in the IP $\left(\mathbb{K}^{1/\delta}\right)^{[t]}$-hybrid, where $t = (1/2 - g)n$.

Protocol.

1. Let $\pi(\mathbb{K}, 1/\delta - 1)$ be a protocol in the IP $\left(\mathbb{K}^{1/\delta}\right)^{[t]}$-hybrid that securely computes ROLE ($\mathbb{K}$) with simulation error $2^{-(g-\delta)n/2-1}$. Fig. 7 provides the details of the protocol in Section 3.
2. Let $\rho(\mathbb{K}, A^*, B^*, X^*)$ be a perfectly secure protocol for OLE ($\mathbb{K}$) in the ROLE ($\mathbb{K}$)-hybrid. The private input of Alice is $(A^*, B^*) \in \mathbb{K}^2$ and the private input of Bob is $X^* \in \mathbb{K}$. Bob obtains the output $Z^* = A^* X^* + B^*$. Fig. 8 provides the details of the protocol in Section 3.
3. The protocol $\sigma(\mathbb{K}, 1/\delta - 1, A^*, B^*, X^*)$ is the parallel composition of $\pi(\mathbb{K}, 1/\delta - 1)$ and $\rho(\mathbb{K}, A^*, B^*, X^*)$ protocol.
4. Parties run the two-round protocol $\sigma(\mathbb{K}, 1/\delta - 1, A^*, B^*, X^*)$ with Alice's private input (A^*, B^*) and Bob's private input X^*. Lemma 3 in Section 4 explains the choice of the inputs $A^*, B^*,$ and X^*.

Output Computation. Lemma 3 in Section 4 presents Bob's algorithm to compute $(z_0, \ldots, z_{m-1})$ from Z^*.

Fig. 4. For $0 < \delta < g < 1/2$, the outline of the (n, m, t, ε)-correlation extractor in the IP $\left(\mathbb{K}^{1/\delta}\right)^{[t]}$-hybrid, where $m = (\delta n)^{1-o(1)}$, $t = (1/2 - g)n$, $\varepsilon = 2^{-(g-\delta)n/2-1}$.

> *Our Combinatorial Problem.* Find S and T such that
> - S and T are ordered sets of non-negative integers of equal size.
> - The set $S + T$ represents the set of the sum of every element of S with every element in T.
> - Interpret the set $S + T$ as a matrix, where the (i,j)-th entry represents the sum of the i-th entry in S and the j-th entry in T. All entries in $S + T$ are in the range $[0,n)$, and $(S+T)_{i,i}$ is not equal to any other element in $S + T$, for $i \in \{0,\dots,|S|-1\}$.
> - Size of $|S| = |T|$ is maximum

Fig. 5. Our combinatorial problem for embedding multiple OLE over small fields into one OLE over an extension field.

Hardness of Computation Result. The starting point of this result is the observation that we know the exact characterization of the correlations which *do not* suffice to construct OT asymptotically [2,32,38,41–43], namely *simple correlations*. Constructing one OT given a single sample from a simple correlation is even more restrictive, and, hence, the hardness of computation result carries over.[3] This result holds true even when there is no leakage on (R_A, R_B). In fact, there exists a universal constant $\varepsilon^* > 0$ such that any OT protocol using any simple correlation has simulation error at least ε^*.

Intuitively, the simple partition number of a correlation (R_A, R_B), represented by $\mathsf{sp}\,(R_A, R_B)$, is the minimum Λ such that (R_A, R_B) can be "decomposed into a union of" Λ simple correlations. Section 5 formalizes this notion of decomposition. Next, we prove in Lemma 4 that for any correlation (R_A, R_B), in the presence of $t = \log \mathsf{sp}\,(R_A, R_B)$ bits of leakage, any protocol π for OT has simulation error at least ε^*. Using this result, we translate tight upper bounds on the simple partition number of relevant correlations into corresponding meaningful upper bounds on their maximum resilience. Figure 2 summarizes our results. We construct a smoother version of this technical lemma using averaging arguments, see Corollary 1. For example, if the leakage bound $t \geqslant (\log \mathsf{sp}(G)) - gn$, then any $(n, 1, t, \varepsilon)$-correlation extractor for (R_A, R_B) has $\varepsilon \geqslant \varepsilon^* \cdot 2^{-gn}$.

2   Preliminaries

We represent the set $\{1,\dots,n\}$ by $[n]$. For a vector $(x_1,\dots,x_n)$ and $S = \{i_1,\dots,i_{|S|}\} \subseteq [n]$, the set x_S represents $(x_{i_1},\dots,x_{i_{|S|}})$. In this work we work with fields $\mathbb{F} = \mathbb{GF}\,[p^a]$, where p is a prime and a is a positive integer. An extension field $\mathbb{K}$ of $\mathbb{F}$ of degree n is interpreted as the field of all polynomials of degree $< n$ and coefficients in $\mathbb{F}$.

---

[3] The problem of characterizing correlations whose single sample suffice to construct OT is a fascinating open problem that lies beyond the purview of this study.

2.1 Functionalities and Correlations

We introduce some useful functionalities and correlations.

Oblivious Transfer. Oblivious transfer, represented by OT, is a two-party functionality that takes as input $(x_0, x_1) \in \{0,1\}^2$ from Alice and $b \in \{0,1\}$ from Bob and outputs x_b to Bob.

Oblivious Linear-function Evaluation. For a field $(\mathbb{F}, +, \cdot)$, oblivious linear-function evaluation over $\mathbb{F}$, represented by OLE $(\mathbb{F})$, is a two-party functionality that takes as input $(a, b) \in \mathbb{F}^2$ from Alice and $x \in \mathbb{F}$ from Bob and outputs $z = ax + b$ to Bob. In particular, OLE refers to the OLE $(\mathbb{GF}\,[2])$ functionality. Note that OT is identical (functionally equivalent) to OLE because $x_b = (x_1 - x_0)b + x_0$.

Random Oblivious Transfer Correlation. Random oblivious transfer, represented by ROT, is a correlation that samples x_0, x_1, b uniformly and independently at random. It provides Alice the secret share $r_A = (x_0, x_1)$ and provides Bob the secret share $r_B = (b, x_b)$.

Random Oblivious Linear-function Evaluation. For a field $(\mathbb{F}, +, \cdot)$, random oblivious linear-function evaluation over $\mathbb{F}$, represented by ROLE $(\mathbb{F})$, is a correlation that samples $a, b, x \in \mathbb{F}$ uniformly and independently at random. It provides Alice the secret share $r_A = (a, b)$ and provides Bob the secret share $r_B = (x, z)$, where $z = ax + b$. In particular, ROLE refers to the ROLE $(\mathbb{GF}\,[2])$ correlation. Note that ROT and ROLE are identical (functionally equivalent) correlations.

Inner-product Correlation. For a field $(\mathbb{F}, +, \cdot)$ and $n \in \mathbb{N}$, inner-product correlation over $\mathbb{F}$ of size n, represented by IP $(\mathbb{F}^n)$, is a correlation that samples random $r_A = (x_0, \ldots, x_{n-1}) \in \mathbb{F}^n$ and $r_B = (y_0, \ldots, y_{n-1}) \in \mathbb{F}^n$ subject to the constraint that $x_0 + y_0 = \sum_{i=1}^{n-1} x_i y_i$. The secret shares of Alice and Bob are, respectively, r_A and r_B.

For $m \in \mathbb{N}$, the functionality $\mathcal{F}^m$ represents the functionality that implements m independent copies of any functionality/correlation $\mathcal{F}$.

2.2 Toeplitz Matrix Distribution

Given a field $\mathbb{F}$, the distribution $\mathbb{T}_{(k,n)}$ represents a uniform distribution over all matrices of the form $[I_{k \times k} | P_{k \times n-k}]$, where $I_{k \times k}$ is the identity matrix and $P_{k \times n-k}$ is a Toeplitz matrix with each entry in $\mathbb{F}$. The distribution $\mathbb{T}_{\perp,(k,n)}$ is the uniform distribution over all matrices of the form $[P_{n-k \times k} | I_{n-k \times n-k}]$, where $I_{n-k \times n-k}$ is the identity matrix and $P_{n-k \times k}$ is a Toeplitz matrix with each entry in $\mathbb{F}$.

2.3 Graph Representation of Correlations

We introduce a graph-theoretic representation of correlations for a more intuitive presentation.

Definition 2 (Graph of a Correlation). *Let (R_A, R_B) be the joint distribution for a correlation. The* graph of the correlation (R_A, R_B) *is the weighted bipartite graph $G = (L, R, E)$ defined as follows.*

1. *The left partite set L is the set of all possible secret shares r_A for Alice,*
2. *The right partite set R is the set of all possible secret shares r_B for Bob, and*
3. *The weight connecting the vertices r_A and r_B is the probability of sampling the shares (r_A, r_B) according to the distribution (R_A, R_B).*

In this paper, the notation (R_A, R_B) also represents the bipartite graph corresponding to it. If the correlation is a uniform distribution over a subset E of all possible edges, then we normalize the entire graph such that the weights on each edge is 1. For example, consider the correlations presented in Fig. 3. Henceforth, for the ease of presentation, we assume that the graph of a correlation is an unweighted bipartite graph. The left-most graph in Fig. 12 is the graph of the ROLE correlation.

A bipartite graph $G = (L, R, E)$ is a *biclique* if there exists $L' \subseteq L$ and $R' \subseteq R$ such that that edge-set $E(G) = L' \times R'$.

Definition 3 (Simple Graph). *A* simple graph *is a bipartite graph such that each of its connected components is a biclique.*

For example, consider the graph in Fig. 6.[4] A *simple correlation* is a correlation whose graph is simple.

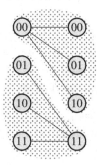

Fig. 6. A representative example of a simple graph.

Definition 4 (Simple Partition Number). *The* simple partition number *of a graph G, represented by $\mathsf{sp}(G)$, is the minimum number of simple graphs needed to partition its edges.*

Figures 12 and 13 show that the simple partition number for both ROLE $(\mathbb{GF}[2])$ and ROLE $(\mathbb{GF}[2])^2$ is 2.

In this work, we use the tensor product of bipartite graphs defined as follows.

---

[4] This definition naturally generalizes to weighted graphs. Suppose $p(r_A, r_B)$ represents the probability of jointly sampling (r_A, r_B) from the correlation (R_A, R_B). Then a simple graph has $p(r_A, r_B) = p(r_A) \cdot p(r_B)$, for every (r_A, r_B) edge with positive weight.

Definition 5 (Tensor Product Graph). *For bipartite graphs* $G = (L_G, R_G, E_G)$ *and* $H = (L_H, R_H, E_H)$ *the tensor product of* G *and* H *is the bipartite graph* $J = (L_J, R_J, E_J)$ *defined as follows.*

1. *The left partite set* $L_J := L_G \times L_H$, *the right partite set* $R_J := R_G \times R_H$, *and*
2. *The vertices* $(u, v) \in L_J$ *and* $(u', v') \in R_J$ *are connected if* $(u, u') \in E_G$ *and* $(v, v') \in E_H$.

Applying this definition recursively, we define $G^m := \overbrace{G \times \cdots \times G}^{m-\text{times}}$.

3 Extracting One OLE over a Large Field

In this section we will build some of the building blocks needed to construct the correlation extractor claimed in Theorem 1. In particular, we outline the extraction protocol that, given a leaky IP $\left(\mathbb{K}^{\eta+1}\right)^{[t]}$ correlation, realizes a secure OLE $(\mathbb{K})$ functionality.

1. First, given the IP $\left(\mathbb{K}^{\eta+1}\right)$ correlation where parties can perform t-bits of arbitrary leakage, we construct a secure sample of an ROLE $(\mathbb{K})$ correlation. This protocol $\pi(\mathbb{K}, \eta)$ is presented in Fig. 7. At the end of the protocol Alice has $(\widetilde{A}_0, \widetilde{B}_0) \in \mathbb{K}^2$ and Bob has $(\widetilde{X}_0, \widetilde{Z}_0) \in \mathbb{K}^2$, such that $\widetilde{A}_0, \widetilde{B}_0, \widetilde{X}_0$ are uniformly random elements in $\mathbb{K}$ and $\widetilde{Z}_0 = \widetilde{A}_0 \widetilde{X}_0 + \widetilde{B}_0$. The simulation error of this protocol is $\frac{1}{2}\sqrt{\frac{|\mathbb{K}|2^t}{|\mathbb{K}|^{\eta/2}}}$, refer to Lemma 2.

2. Next, starting with the private shares $(\widetilde{A}_0, \widetilde{B}_0)$ with Alice and $(\widetilde{X}_0, \widetilde{Z}_0)$ with Bob, we implement a protocol $\rho(\mathbb{K}, A^*, B^*, X^*)$. Alice has private inputs (A^*, B^*) that are arbitrary elements in $\mathbb{K}^2$. Bob has private input X^* that is an arbitrary element in $\mathbb{K}$. The protocol $\rho(\mathbb{K}, A^*, B^*, X^*)$, described in Fig. 8 is a perfectly secure protocol where Bob outputs $Z^* = A^*X^* + B^*$.

We emphasize that both $\pi(\mathbb{K}, \eta)$ and $\rho(\mathbb{K}, A^*, B^*, X^*)$ are 2-round protocols and we can compose these two protocols in parallel. The resultant protocol $\sigma(\mathbb{K}, \eta, A^*, B^*, X^*)$ is an extraction protocol that takes as input a leaky IP $\left(\mathbb{K}^{\eta+1}\right)^{[t]}$ correlation where parties can perform t-bits of arbitrary leakage and implements the ROLE $(\mathbb{K})$ functionality with simulation error $\frac{1}{2}\sqrt{\frac{|\mathbb{K}|2^t}{|\mathbb{K}|^{\eta/2}}}$. This is formalized in the following lemma and the proof is included below.

Lemma 1 (Security of Correlation Extractor). *The protocol* $\sigma(\mathbb{K}, \eta, A^*, B^*, X^*)$ *obtained by the parallel composition of the protocols* $\pi(\mathbb{K}, \eta)$ *(see Fig. 7) and* $\rho(\mathbb{K}, A^*, B^*, X^*)$ *(see Fig. 8) is a secure protocol in the* IP $\left(\mathbb{K}^{\eta+1}\right)^{[t]}$ *hybrid that implements the* OLE $(\mathbb{K})$ *functionality with simulation error at most* $\frac{1}{2}\sqrt{\frac{|\mathbb{K}|2^t}{|\mathbb{K}|^{\eta/2}}}$.

Section 4 elaborates the exact technique to choose appropriate $\mathbb{K}, \eta, A^*, B^*, X^*$ to imply Theorem 1.

3.1   Extraction of One Secure ROLE $(\mathbb{K})$ Correlation

The protocol is provided in Fig. 7. The security of the protocol is analogous to the proof in [26] that reduces to the unpredictability lemma over fields. We state this lemma in our context.

Lemma 2 (Unpredictability Lemma). *Let* $\mathcal{G} \in \left\{ \mathbb{T}_{(k,\eta+1)}, \mathbb{T}_{\perp,(k,\eta+1)} \right\}$*. Consider the following game between an honest challenger and an adversary:*

---

1. $\mathcal{H}$ *samples* $m_{[\eta]} \sim U_{\mathbb{K}^\eta}$.
2. $\mathcal{A}$ *sends a leakage function* $\mathcal{L} \colon \mathbb{K}^\eta \to \{0,1\}^t$.
3. $\mathcal{H}$ *sends* $\mathcal{L}\left(m_{[\eta]}\right)$ *to* $\mathcal{A}$.
4. $\mathcal{H}$ *samples* $x_{[k]} \sim U_{\mathbb{K}^k}$, $G \sim \mathcal{G}$, *and computes* $y_{\{0\}\cup[n]} = x \cdot G + (0, m_{[\eta]})$. $\mathcal{H}$ *sends* $(y_{[\eta]}, G)$ *to* $\mathcal{A}$. $\mathcal{H}$ *picks* $b \xleftarrow{\$} \{0,1\}$. *If* $b = 0$, *then she sends* $\mathsf{chal} = y_0$ *to* $\mathcal{A}$; *otherwise (if* $b = 1$*) then she sends* $\mathsf{chal} = u \sim U_{\mathbb{K}}$ *to* $\mathcal{A}$.
5. $\mathcal{A}$ *replies with an element* $\tilde{b} \in \{0,1\}$.

The adversary $\mathcal{A}$ *wins the game if* $b = \tilde{b}$. *For any* $\mathcal{A}$, *the advantage of the adversary is* $\leqslant \frac{1}{4}\sqrt{\frac{|\mathbb{K}|2^t}{|\mathbb{K}|^k}}$.

Similar to the security proof provided by Gupta et al. [26], the simulation error of the protocol in Fig. 7 is the bound provided by the unpredictability lemma over fields (Lemma 2). Refer to the full version of the paper [6] for a proof of correctness.

Pseudocode of the extraction protocol $\pi(\mathbb{K}, \eta)$.

Given. Alice has $(X_0, X_1, \ldots, X_\eta)$ and Bob has $(Y_0, Y_1, \ldots, Y_\eta)$ such that $X_0 + Y_0 = \sum_{i=1}^{\eta} X_i Y_i$, where $X_0, \ldots, X_\eta, Y_0, \ldots, Y_\eta \in \mathbb{K}$. For ease of presentation assume that η is odd and set $w = (\eta+1)/2$. An adversarial party can obtain arbitrary t-bit leakage on the share of the other party.

Interactive Protocol.

1. **First Round.** Bob samples a random generator matrix G from the distribution $\mathbb{T}_{w \times (\eta+1)}$ such that its elements are in $\mathbb{K}$. Let $\mathcal{C}$ be the code generated by G, and $\mathcal{C}^\perp$ be its dual code. Let H be the generator matrix for the code $\mathcal{C}^\perp$. If the first column of H is $0^{\eta+1-w}$ (i.e., all zeros), then abort the protocol. Bob picks a random codeword $(\widetilde{X}_0, \widetilde{X}_1, \ldots, \widetilde{X}_\eta) \in \mathcal{C}^\perp$ and calculates $M_{[\eta]} = Y_{[\eta]} - \widetilde{X}_{[\eta]}$. Bob sends $M_{[\eta]}$ and G to Alice.
2. **Second Round.** Alice samples a random codeword $(\widetilde{A}_0, \widetilde{A}_1, \ldots, \widetilde{A}_\eta) \in \mathcal{C}$ and a random field element $\widetilde{B}_0 \in \mathbb{K}$. Alice computes $\alpha_{[\eta]} = X_{[\eta]} + \widetilde{A}_{[\eta]}$ and $\beta = \langle X_{[\eta]}, M_{[\eta]} \rangle - \widetilde{B}_0 - X_0$. Alice sends $\alpha_{[\eta]}$ and β to Bob.

Output Computation. Alice outputs $(\widetilde{A}_0, \widetilde{B}_0)$ and Bob outputs $(\widetilde{X}_0, \widetilde{Z}_0)$, where $\widetilde{Z}_0 = -\langle \alpha_{[\eta]}, \widetilde{X}_{[\eta]} \rangle - \beta + Y_0$.

Fig. 7. Protocol to securely extract one random sample of the ROLE $(\mathbb{K})$ functionality from the leaky IP $\left(\mathbb{K}^{\eta+1}\right)^{[t]}$ correlation.

3.2   Securely Realizing OLE (𝕂) Using ROLE (𝕂) Correlation

The protocol presented in Fig. 8 is a perfectly semi-honest secure protocol for OLE (𝕂) in the ROLE (𝕂) correlation hybrid. Note that the protocols $\pi(\mathbb{K}, \eta)$ in Fig. 7 and $\rho(\mathbb{K}, A^*, B^*, X^*)$ in Fig. 8 can be composed in parallel. Let $\sigma(\mathbb{K}, \eta, A^*, B^*, X^*)$ be the parallel composition of the protocols $\pi(\mathbb{K}, \eta)$ and $\rho(\mathbb{K}, A^*, B^*, X^*)$. This completes the proof of Lemma 1.

Pseudocode of the OLE protocol $\rho(\mathbb{K}, A^*, B^*, X^*)$

Given. Alice has $(\tilde{A}_0, \tilde{B}_0)$ and Bob has $(\tilde{X}_0, \tilde{Z}_0)$, where $\tilde{A}_0, \tilde{B}_0, \tilde{X}_0$ are random elements in 𝕂 and $\tilde{Z}_0 = \tilde{A}_0 \tilde{X}_0 + \tilde{B}_0$.

Private Inputs. Alice has private input $(A^*, B^*) \in \mathbb{K}^2$ and Bob has $X^* \in \mathbb{K}$.

Interactive Protocol.

1. **First Round.** Bob sends $M' = \tilde{X}_0 - X^*$ to Alice.
2. **Second Round.** Alice sends $\alpha' = \tilde{A}_0 + A^*$ and $\beta' = \tilde{A}_0 M + B^* + \tilde{B}_0$.

Output Computation. Bob outputs $Z^* = \alpha' X^* + \beta' - \tilde{Z}_0$.

Fig. 8. Perfectly secure protocol to realize OLE (𝕂) in the ROLE (𝕂) correlation hybrid.

4   Embedding Multiple OLEs into an OLE over an Extension Field

One of the primary goals in this section is to prove the following lemma.

Lemma 3 (Embedding Multiple small OLE into a Large OLE). *Let* 𝕂 *be an extension field of* 𝔽 *of degree n. There exists a perfectly secure protocol for* OLE $(\mathbb{F})^m$ *in the* OLE (𝕂)*-hybrid that makes only one call to the* OLE (𝕂) *functionality and* $m = n^{1-o(1)}$.

Proof. Section 4.3 provides this lemma and proves Theorem 1.

4.1   Intuition of the Embedding

We illustrate the main underlying ideas of this embedding problem and our proposed solution using the representative field $\mathbb{F} = \mathrm{GF}[2]$ and its extension field $\mathbb{K} = \mathrm{GF}[2^n]$. Suppose we are provided with an oracle that takes as input $A^*, B^* \in \mathbb{K}$ from Alice and $X^* \in \mathbb{K}$ from Bob, and outputs $Z^* := A^* \cdot X^* + B^*$ to Bob. Our aim is to implement the following functionality. Alice has inputs $(a_0, \dots, a_{m-1}) \in \mathbb{F}^m$ and $(b_0, \dots, b_{m-1}) \in \mathbb{F}^m$, and Bob has inputs $(x_0, \dots, x_{m-1}) \in \mathbb{F}^m$. We want Bob to obtain $(z_0, \dots, z_{m-1}) \in \mathbb{F}^m$, where each $z_i = a_i \cdot x_i + b_i$, for $i \in \{0, \dots, m-1\}$. Intuitively, we want maximize m and embed OLE $(\mathbb{F})^m$ into one OLE (𝕂).

Preliminary Idea. Consider the following simple preliminary embedding. Let $m = \sqrt{n}$. Alice defines $A^* = a_0 + a_1\zeta + \cdots + a_{m-1}\zeta^{m-1}$, where $a_0, \ldots, a_{m-1} \in \mathbb{F}$. And, Alice defines $B^* = \sum_{i=0}^{n-1} r_i\zeta^i$, where each r_i is a random element in $\mathbb{F}$; except when $(m+1)$ divides i, then we set $r_{t(m+1)} = b_t$, for $t \in \{0, \ldots, m-1\}$. Bob defines $X^* = x_0 + x_1\zeta^m + \cdots + x_{m-1}\zeta^{(m-1)m}$, where $x_0, \ldots, x_{m-1} \in \mathbb{F}$.

Now, the parties compute $Z^* = A^*X^* + B^*$ using one oracle call to $\mathsf{OLE}(\mathbb{K})$ and Bob obtains the output Z^*. Note that the intended $z_i = a_i \cdot x_i + b_i$ is the coefficient of $\zeta^{i(m+1)}$ in Z^*, for each $i \in \{0, \ldots, m-1\}$. Coefficients of all other powers of ζ contain no information about $a_0, \ldots, a_{m-1}, b_0, \ldots, b_{m-1}$, because they are masked with random elements in $\mathbb{F}$. So, for $m = \sqrt{n}$, we have embedded $\mathsf{OLE}(\mathbb{F})^m$ into one $\mathsf{OLE}(\mathbb{K})$.

Better Embedding. Observe that $(a_0 + a_1\zeta) \cdot (x_0 + x_1\zeta) = a_0x_0 + (a_0x_1 + a_1x_0)\zeta + a_1x_1\zeta^2$. So, we can embed $\mathsf{OLE}(\mathbb{F})^2$ into one $\mathsf{OLE}(\mathbb{K})$, where $\mathbb{K}$ is an extension field of $\mathbb{F}$ of degree 3, as follows. Alice chooses $A^* = a_0 + a_1\zeta \in \mathrm{GF}\left[2^2\right]$ and $B^* = b_0 + r\zeta + b_1\zeta^2$ (where r is a random element from $\mathbb{F}$), and Bob chooses $X^* = x_0 + x_1\zeta$. Note that the coefficients of ζ^0 and ζ^2 in Z^*, respectively, correspond to $a_0x_0 + b_0$ and $a_1x_1 + b_1$. Recursively applying this idea, we can construct an embedding of $\mathsf{OLE}\left(\mathrm{GF}\left[2\right]\right)^{2^k}$ into one $\mathsf{OLE}\left(\mathrm{GF}\left[2^{3^k}\right]\right)$. Asymptotically, this scheme embeds $m = n^{\log 2/\log 3} \approx n^{0.631}$ copies of $\mathsf{OLE}(\mathrm{GF}[2])$ into one $\mathsf{OLE}(\mathrm{GF}[2^n])$.

Generalization to 3-free sets. Consider the previous solution when $n = 3^k$. Let $S = \{s_0 < s_1 < \cdots < s_{m-1}\}$ be the set of indices. The set S corresponding to the previous solution contains all integers less than 3^k whose ternary representation does not contain the digit 2. This is the famous greedy sequence of integers that does not include an arithmetic progression of length 3; namely, 3-free sets. In fact, there is nothing sacrosanct about the S chosen in the previous embedding, and *any* 3-free set suffices.

For example, let $S = \{s_0 < s_1 < \cdots < s_{m-1}\}$ be any 3-free set such that each entry is in the range $[0, n/2)$, $\mathbb{F} = \mathrm{GF}[2]$, and $\mathbb{K} = \mathrm{GF}[2^n]$. Alice prepares $A^* = \sum_{i=0}^{m-1} a_i\zeta^{s_i}$ and $B^* = \sum_{k=0}^{n-1} r_k\zeta^k$, where $r_{2s_i} = b_i$; otherwise it is a random element in $\mathbb{F}$. Bob prepares $X^* = \sum_{i=0}^{m-1} x_i\zeta^{s_i}$. Using one call to $\mathsf{OLE}(\mathbb{K})$ Bob obtains Z^*. The coefficient of ζ^{2s_i} is $a_ix_i + b_i$, because no other $s_j + s_k = 2s_i$. Now, we can embed $m = n^{1-o(1)}$ copies of $\mathsf{OLE}(\mathbb{F})$ into $\mathsf{OLE}(\mathbb{K})$ using the state-of-the-art constructions of 3-free sets [3,20]. However, this approach cannot give us $m = \Theta(n)$ due to sub-linear upper bounds on m [8,9,29,58,60,61].

New Problem. Note that although solutions to the 3-free set problem imply embeddings in our setting, our embedding problem is potentially less restrictive. For example, the solution for $m = \sqrt{n}$ presented above is not obtained by the reduction to 3-free sets. Are we missing something?

Suppose $S = (s_0, \ldots, s_{m-1})$ and $T = (t_0, \ldots, t_{m-1})$ be tuples of indices in the range $[0, n/2)$. Consider the combinatorial problem proposed in Fig. 5.

Given. Two sets S and T of size m that is a solution to the combinatorial problem presented in Fig. 5. Let $\mathbb{K}$ be an extension field of $\mathbb{F}$ of degree n.

Private input. Alice has private input $(a_0, \ldots, a_{m-1}) \in \mathbb{F}^m$ and $(b_0, \ldots, b_{m-1}) \in \mathbb{F}^m$. Bob has private input $(x_0, \ldots, x_{m-1}) \in \mathbb{F}^m$.

Hybrid. Parties are in the $\mathsf{OLE}\,(\mathbb{K})$-hybrid.

Private Input Construction.

1. Alice creates private input $A^* = \sum_{i=0}^{m-1} a_i \zeta^{s_i} \in \mathbb{K}$.
2. Alice chooses r_i, for $i \in \{0, \ldots, n-1\}$, as follows.

$$r_i = \begin{cases} b_k & \text{, if } i = s_k + t_k \text{ for some } k \in \{0, \ldots, m-1\} \\ U_{\mathbb{F}} & \text{, otherwise.} \end{cases}$$

   Alice creates private input $B^* = \sum_{i=0}^{n-1} r_i \zeta^i \in \mathbb{K}$.
3. Bob creates private input $X^* = \sum_{i=0}^{m-1} x_i \zeta^{t_i} \in \mathbb{K}$.
4. Both parties invoke the $\mathsf{OLE}\,(\mathbb{K})$ functionality with respective Alice input (A^*, B^*) and Bob input X^*. Bob receives $Z^* = A^* X^* + B^*$.

Output Decoding. Bob outputs $(z_0, \ldots, z_{m-1})$, where z_i is the coefficient of $\zeta^{s_i + t_i}$ and $i \in \{0, \ldots, m-1\}$.

Fig. 9. Embedding $\mathsf{OLE}\,(\mathbb{F})^m$ into one $\mathsf{OLE}\,(\mathbb{K})$, where $\mathbb{K}$ is an extension field of $\mathbb{F}$ of degree n.

Given S and T that are solutions to the problem in Fig. 5, Alice and Bob use the strategy explained in Fig. 9. Note that the initial solution for $m = \sqrt{n}$ indeed corresponds to the solution $S = \{0, \ldots, m-1\}$ and $T = \{0, m, \ldots, (m-1)m\}$. Restricted to $S = T$, our combinatorial problem is identical to the 3-free set problem. We numerically solve this problem for small values of n and, indeed, it produces more efficient embeddings than the embedding based on the optimal 3-free set constructions. We emphasize that we compare our solutions against the largest 3-free set computed by *exhaustive search*. We summarize our observations in Fig. 10.

4.2   Relevant Prior Work on 3-Free Sets

Our asymptotic construction for Theorem 1 relies on constructing a dense subset S of $\{0, 1, \cdots, n-1\}$ that does not contain any arithmetic progression, namely 3-free sets. Erdős and Turán introduced this problem in 1936 and presented a greedy construction with $|S| = \Omega\left(n^{\log 2/\log 3}\right) \approx n^{0.631}$. Salem and Spencer [59] showed that the surface of high-dimensional convex bodies can be embedded in the integers to construct 3-free sets of size $n^{1-o(1)}$. Later, Behrend [3] noticed that points lying on the surface of a sphere of suitable radius are a particularly good choice, and gave a construction with $|S| = \Omega\left(\frac{n}{2^{2\sqrt{2\log n}} \cdot \log^{1/4} n}\right)$. Recently, after a gap of over sixty years, Elkin [20] improved this further by a factor of $\Theta(\sqrt{\log n})$ by thickening the spheres to produce the largest known 3-free set. The proofs of Behrend [3] and Elkin [20] are constructive in nature and the sets can be constructed in poly(n) time. Although the greedy construction is asymptotically worse than these two constructions, it performs well for realistic values of n. See Fig. 11 for details.

m	$n(m)$	Solution Sets	$n'(m)$	3-free Set
1	1	$S = \{0\}$ $T = \{0\}$	1	$S = \{0\}$
2	3	$S = \{0,1\}$ $T = \{0,1\}$	3	$S = \{0,1\}$
3	7	$S = \{0,1,3\}$ $T = \{0,1,3\}$	7	$S = \{0,1,3\}$
4	9	$S = \{0,1,3,4\}$ $T = \{0,1,3,4\}$	9	$S = \{0,1,3,4\}$
5	14	$S = \{0,1,3,5,8\}$ $T = \{0,1,4,5,3\}$	17	$S = \{0,1,3,7,8\}$
6	19	$S = \{0,1,3,4,7,9\}$ $T = \{0,1,3,9,7,8\}$	21	$S = \{0,1,3,4,9,10\}$
7	24	$S = \{0,1,3,4,11,6,10\}$ $T = \{0,1,5,10,6,12,9\}$	25	$S = \{0,1,3,4,9,10,12\}$
8	27	$S = \{0,1,3,4,9,10,12,13\}$ $T = \{0,1,3,4,9,10,12,13\}$	27	$S = \{0,1,3,4,9,10,12,13\}$
9	34	$S = \{0,1,3,4,9,12,14,16,17\}$ $T = \{0,1,3,4,13,11,12,15,16\}$	39	$S = \{0,1,5,6,8,13,14,17,19\}$
10	38	$S = \{0,1,3,5,8,12,13,16,17,15\}$ $T = \{0,1,4,5,3,12,13,15,17,20\}$	47	$S = \{0,1,4,6,10,15,17,18,22,23\}$

Fig. 10. Let $\mathbb{K}$ be an extension field of $\mathbb{F}$ of degree n. Our goal is to embed m copies of OLE $(\mathbb{F})$ into one OLE $(\mathbb{K})$ using minimum n. The number $n(m)$ represents the minimum n obtained by using solutions to our combinatorial problem in Fig. 5. The number $n'(m)$ represents the minimum n obtained by using the optimum solutions to the 3-free set problem.

Roth [58] provided the first nontrivial upper bound of $O\left(\frac{n}{\log \log n}\right)$ on the size of 3-free sets. More than thirty years later, Heath-Brown [29] showed that $|S| = O\left(\frac{n}{\log^c n}\right)$, for some constant $c > 0$, and then Szemeredi [61] produced an explicit value $c = 1/20$. Bourgain [8,9] improved the upper bound by polylog factors. Currently, the best known upper bound is $O\left(\frac{n(\log \log n)^4}{\log n}\right)$ [7,60]. Nathan [46] provides a comprehensive summary for both 3-free set size constructions and upper bounds.

4.3   Generating Explicit Embedding and Proof of Theorem 1

First, we prove Lemma 3. Let $S(n)$ be a 3-free set with elements in the range $[0, n/2]$. Behrend [3] and Elkin [20] provide constructions for $S(n)$ such that $|S(n)| \geqslant n^{1-o(1)}$. Note that $S = T = S(n)$ is a solution to the combinatorial problem proposed in Fig. 5. Now, we use the protocol described in Fig. 9.

It is clear that the protocol is correct. The coefficients of all other ζ^i in Z^* are random elements in $\mathbb{F}$, if $i \neq s_k + t_k$, for all $k \in \{0, \dots, m-1\}$. It is, therefore, easy to see that this is a perfectly secure protocol for OLE $(\mathbb{F})^m$ in the OLE $(\mathbb{K})$-hybrid.

Remark. We provide a short discussion on how to pick the 3-free set S for *concrete* values of n. The greedy construction is the fastest and runs in $O(n \log n)$ time. It picks all numbers that do not have 2 in their ternary representation, and $|S(n)| = n^{\log 2/\log 3} \approx n^{0.631}$. The proofs of Behrend [3] and Elkin [20] are also

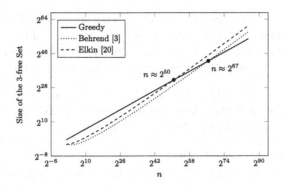

Fig. 11. A logarithmic scaled graph of the size of the 3-free sets produced by the greedy, Behrend [3], and Elkin [20] constructions.

constructive in nature and the set can be constructed in poly(n) time. However, their performance for realistic values of n are worse than the greedy algorithm.

Further, for concrete values of n, one of the solutions to our combinatorial problem generates better embeddings than the greedy solution. Note that, Fig. 10 presents a solution that enables the embedding of 10 independent OLE $(\mathbb{F})$ evaluations into one OLE $(\mathbb{K})$ evaluation, where $\mathbb{K}$ is an extension field of $\mathbb{F}$ of degree 38. Recursively applying this embedding, we embed $m = n^{\log 10/\log 38} \approx n^{0.633} \gg n^{0.631} \approx n^{\log 2/\log 3}$ independent OLE $(\mathrm{GF}[2])$ evaluations into one OLE $(\mathrm{GF}[2^n])$ evaluation.

Proof of Theorem 1. Suppose we given n, $0 < \delta < g < 1/2$, and $t = (1/2 - g)n$. Let $\mathbb{K} = \mathrm{GF}\left[2^{\delta n}\right]$ and $\mathbb{F} = \mathrm{GF}[2]$. We construct $A^*, B^*, X^* \in \mathbb{K}$ using Lemma 3 and $m \geqslant (\delta n)^{1-o(1)}$. Perform the protocol $\sigma(\mathbb{K}, 1/\delta - 1, A^*, B^*, X^*)$ in the IP $\left(\mathbb{K}^{1/\delta}\right)^{[t]}$-hybrid.[5] The simulation error is

$$\varepsilon \leqslant \frac{1}{2}\sqrt{\frac{2^{\delta n}2^t}{2^{\delta n(1/\delta - 1)/2}}} = 2^{-(g-\delta)n/2-1}$$

This is an (n, m, t, ε)-correlation extractor for the correlation IP $\left(\mathbb{K}^{1/\delta}\right)$.

5   Simple Partition Number

This section defines the simple partition number of a graph, provides estimates of this quantity for correlations relevant to our work, and proves Theorem 2.

5.1   Intuition of the Hardness of Computation Result

We know that if parties have multiple independent samples of secret shares sampled according to a simple correlation, then the parties cannot securely compute

---

[5] Recall that in the protocol $\pi(\mathbb{K}, \eta)$, all parties have share size $(\eta + 1)\log|\mathbb{K}|$.

OT [2,32,38,41–43]. Constructing one OT given a single sample from such a correlation is even more restrictive, and, hence, the hardness of computation result carries over. This result holds true even when there is no leakage on (R_A, R_B). More precisely, we import the following result that we restate in our context.

Imported Theorem 1 [43]. *Let (R_A, R_B) be a simple correlation with n-bit secret shares for each party. There exists a universal constant $\varepsilon^* > 0$, such that any $(n, 1, 0, \varepsilon)$-correlation extractor for (R_A, R_B) has $\varepsilon \geqslant \varepsilon^*$.*

Suppose (R_A, R_B) is a correlation that has simple partition number $\mathsf{sp}(G) = 2^\lambda$ and $G = G^{(1)} + \cdots + G^{(2^\lambda)}$, where each $G^{(i)}$ is a simple graph. Then we consider the leakage function $\mathcal{L}(r_A, r_B) = \ell$, where $\ell \in \{1, \ldots, 2^\lambda\}$ is the unique index such that $(r_A, r_B) \in E(G^{(\ell)})$. Note that $\mathcal{L}$ is a λ-bit leakage function and conditioned on the leakage being ℓ, for any $\ell \in \{1, \ldots, 2^\lambda\}$, the correlation $(R_A, R_B|\ell)$ is a simple correlation. So, one of the parties can break the security of any purported OT protocol where parties get secret shares sampled from the $(R_A, R_B|\ell)$ correlation. Overall, with probability half, one of the parties can break the security of any purported OT protocol where parties get secret shares sampled from the (R_A, R_B) by performing the leakage $\mathcal{L}$ described above. This technique upper-bounds the leakage resilience of (R_A, R_B) and we summarize it as follows.

Lemma 4 (Connection between Maximum Leakage Resilience and Simple Partition Number). *Let (R_A, R_B) is a correlated private randomness that provides n-bit private shares to Alice and Bob. Let G be the bipartite graph corresponding to the correlation (R_A, R_B). There exists a universal constant $\varepsilon^* > 0$ such that any $(n, 1, t, \varepsilon)$-correlation extractor for (R_A, R_B) with $t \geqslant \lceil \lg \mathsf{sp}(G) \rceil$ has $\varepsilon \geqslant \varepsilon^*$.*

We construct a smoother version of this technical lemma using averaging arguments. For example, if the leakage bound t is roughly $(\log \mathsf{sp}(G)) - gn$, then we consider a subset of simple graphs of size $\mathsf{sp}(G) \cdot 2^{-gn}$ from the set $\{G^{(1)}, \ldots, G^{(\mathsf{sp}(G))}\}$ that covers at least 2^{-gn} fraction of the edges of G. Applying the previous lemma, we can conclude that $(n, 1, t, \varepsilon)$-correlation extractor for (R_A, R_B) with $t \geqslant \lceil \log \mathsf{sp}(G) - gn \rceil$ has $\varepsilon \geqslant \varepsilon^* \cdot 2^{-gn}$.

Corollary 1 ((Smooth Version of the) Connection between Maximum Leakage Resilience and Simple Partition Number). *Let (R_A, R_B) is a correlated private randomness that provides n-bit private shares to Alice and Bob. Let G be the bipartite graph corresponding to the correlation (R_A, R_B). There exists a universal constant $\varepsilon^* > 0$ such that any $(n, 1, t, \varepsilon)$-correlation extractor for (R_A, R_B) with $t \geqslant \lceil \lg \mathsf{sp}(G) - gn \rceil$ has $\varepsilon \geqslant \varepsilon^* \cdot 2^{-gn}$.*

5.2   Relevant Prior Work on Graph Covering Problems

The graph-theoretic measure proposed in our work to measure the maximum resilience of correlations in best presented in the framework of graph covering problems. Several problems in graph theory, for example, clique partition number, biparticity, arboricity, edge-chromatic number, vertex cover number and biclique partition number, can be expressed as covering a graph with subgraphs from a family of graphs. Of these representative examples, the concept of *biclique partition number* is most relevant to our paper. For a graph G, its biclique partition number, represented by $\mathsf{bp}\,(G)$, is the minimum number of bicliques that suffice to partition it.

Refer to [40] for a comprehensive survey on graph covering problems. Motivated by network addressing problem and graph storage problem, Graham and Pollak [24,25] introduced the biclique partition problem (see also [1,63,64,70]). The celebrated Graham-Pollak Theorem states that $\mathsf{bp}\,(K_n) = (n-1)$ [25,52,62, 65,66], but all proofs are algebraic, and no purely combinatorial proof is known. In general, $\mathsf{bp}\,(G) \geqslant \max\{n_+(G), n_-(G)\}$ [25,30,52,62], where $n_+(\cdot)$ and $n_-(\cdot)$, respectively, represents the number of positive and negative eigenvalues of the adjacency matrix of the graph. Determining the $\mathsf{bp}\,(G)$ of a general graph is a hard problem [40], but it admits a trivial upper bound $\mathsf{bp}\,(G) \leqslant$ the size of the smallest vertex cover of G. Variants of this quantity have been considered recently by [14].

This quantity is closely related to the recently disproved [13,31] Alon-Saks-Seymour Conjecture [36] that $\mathsf{bp}\,(G) + 1$ colors suffice to color a graph. This conjecture can be interpreted as a generalization of the Graham-Pollak Theorem and has close relations to computational complexity [31,51,57]. In the context of this paper, intuitively, the biclique partition number is a combinatorial version of the *Wyner's Common Information* [69] that corresponds to the minimum description complexity of the information that kills the mutual information of correlations. We interpret a correlation as a weighted bipartite graph with the left-partite set being all possible values of r_A, and the right partite set being all possible values of r_B. The weight on an edge joining r_A and r_B represents the probability of jointly sampling (r_A, r_B). This graph-theoretic interpretation of correlations helps establish connections between combinatorial and information-theoretic concepts.

5.3   Relation to Leakage Resilience: Proof of Lemma 4

In this section we prove Lemma 4, i.e. the maximum leakage resilience of a correlation (R_A, R_B) is at most $\lg \mathsf{sp}\,(R_A, R_B)$.

Let G be the bipartite graph corresponding to the correlation (R_A, R_B). Let π be a $(n, 1, t, \varepsilon)$-correlation extractor for G, where $t = \lceil \log \mathsf{sp}\,(G) \rceil$. Let $G = G^{(1)} + \cdots + G^{(\mathsf{sp}(G))}$ be the simple partition of G. Define the leakage function $\mathcal{L}\colon E(G) \to \{1, \ldots, \mathsf{sp}\,(G)\}$ as follows. For $e \in E(G)$, we have $\mathcal{L}(e) = \ell$, where ℓ is the unique index in $\{1, \ldots, \mathsf{sp}\,(G)\}$ such that $e \in E(G^{(\ell)})$.

Consider an interactive protocol that runs π between Alice and Bob with secret samples drawn from the correlation G, and *both parties* receive the leakage $\mathcal{L}(r_A, r_B)$.

Note that this is identical to the interactive protocol, where the correlation G^+ that samples $\ell \in \{1, \ldots, \mathsf{sp}(G)\}$ with probability proportional to $\left| E(G^{(\ell)}) \right|$, samples $(u, v) \equiv e \xleftarrow{\$} E(G^{(\ell)})$, and provides (u, ℓ) to Alice and (v, ℓ) to Bob.

The functionality G^+ itself is simple, because each $G^{(\ell)}$ is simple. So, we can use Imported Theorem 1. Therefore, one of the parties' view cannot be simulated with less than $\varepsilon^* > 0$ simulation error when the parties follow the protocol π. Suppose, that party is Alice, without loss of generality. That is, the view of the party Alice* (to represent the semi-honest adversarial strategy) in the interactive protocol between Alice* and B incurs at least ε^* simulation error.

Now consider the case where only Alice* receives the leakage from the correlation and not Bob. The view of Alice* remains identical to the previous hybrid. Therefore, this protocol also incurs a simulation error at least ε^*

This implies that for any $(n, 1, t, \varepsilon)$-correlation extractor for (R_A, R_B), if $t \geqslant \log \mathsf{sp}(R_A, R_B)$, then $\varepsilon \geqslant \varepsilon^*$.

Intuitively, Lemma 4 can be summarized as follows. A small simple partition number of the correlated private randomness (R_A, R_B) implies a low maximum leakage-resilience of (R_A, R_B).

Proof of Corollary 1. Suppose $2^t = \mathsf{sp}(G) / 2^{gn}$ and π is an $(n, 1, t, \varepsilon)$-correlation extractor for (R_A, R_B). Now, we choose the $\mathsf{sp}(G) / (2^{gn} - 1)$ simple graphs among $\{G^{(1)}, \ldots, G^{(\mathsf{sp}(G))}\}$ that cover a subset $E' \subset E(G)$ such that $|E'| / |E(G)| \geqslant (2^{gn} - 1)^{-1}$. The leakage function $\mathcal{L}(r_A, r_B)$ outputs the index of the simple graph from which the edge $e = (r_A, r_B)$ comes, if $e \in E'$; otherwise, it returns $\bot$. Using the same proof as Lemma 4 we can conclude that the simulation error is $\varepsilon \geqslant \varepsilon^* (2^{gn} - 1)^{-1} \approx \varepsilon^* 2^{-gn}$.

5.4 Estimates of Simple Partition Number and Proof of Theorem 2

In this section we present the lemma that provides the estimates of the simple partition number of relevant correlations.

Lemma 5 (Simple Partition Number Estimates). *The following holds true for arbitrary field $\mathbb{F}$.*

1. $\mathsf{sp}(\mathsf{IP}(\mathbb{F}^n)) \leqslant |\mathbb{F}|^{\lceil (n+1)/2 \rceil}$, *and*
2. *For even n,* $\mathsf{sp}\left(\mathsf{ROLE}(\mathbb{F})^{n/2}\right) \leqslant |\mathbb{F}|^{\lceil n/4 \rceil}$.

Refer to the full version [6] for a proof of the first part. The proof outline of the second part is provided in Sect. 5.5. The simple decomposition we construct for the correlations mentioned above have an additional property. Given an edge $(r_A, r_B) \sim (R_A, R_B)$, we can efficiently compute the index of the simple graph in the decomposition that contains it. Thus, the leakage that demonstrates the upper bound of the maximal resilience in Lemma 4 is computationally efficient.

The proof of Theorem 2 is a direct application of Lemmas 4 and 5.

5.5   Subsuming the Partition Argument

In this section, using a particular example, we want to illustrate that the simple partition number is sophisticated enough to subsume partition argument based impossibility results. To begin, let us consider an example. Let (R_A, R_B) be the random oblivious linear-function evaluation over $GF[2]$. So, the correlation samples $a, b, x \in GF[2]$ independently and uniformly at random. The secret share of Alice is $r_A = (a, b)$ and the secret share of Bob is $r_B = (x, z)$, where $z = ax + b$. The secrecy of ROLE $(GF[2])$ ensures that Alice has no advantage in guessing x and Bob has no advantage in guessing a. The graph of the correlation is provided in Fig. 12. The figure presents the simple decomposition corresponding to the leakage $\ell = x - a$.

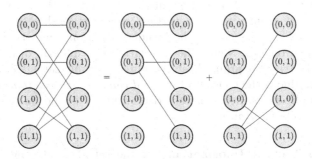

Fig. 12. The graph of the correlated private randomness ROLE $(GF[2])$ and its decomposition into two simple graphs.

Now, let us consider ROLE $(GF[2])^2$, i.e. two independent samples from the ROLE $(GF[2])$ correlation. Alice gets secret share (a_1, b_1, a_2, b_2) and Bob gets secret share (x_1, z_1, x_2, z_2), where $z_1 = a_1 x_1 + b_1$ and $z_2 = a_2 x_2 + b_2$. Suppose in the partition argument Alice implements the first correlation and Bob implements the second correlation. This implies that Alice knows x_1 and Bob knows a_2. We want to achieve this effect using only one-bit leakage that is provided to both the parties.

Given the decomposition in Fig. 12, note that we can define a two-bit leakage to achieve this. For example the first leakage bit represents $\ell_1 = x_1 - a_1$, and the second leakage bit represents $\ell_2 = x_2 - a_2$. We show in Fig. 13 that even a one-bit leakage suffices. In particular, we use $\mathcal{L}(r_A, r_B) = x_1 - a_2$. In the full version [6], we show that $\mathsf{sp}\left(\mathsf{ROLE}(\mathbb{F})^2\right) \leqslant |\mathbb{F}|$.

Using this observation and the fact that $\mathsf{sp}(G \times H) \leqslant \mathsf{sp}(G) \cdot \mathsf{sp}(H)$ (see full version [6] for the proof), Lemma 5 shows that $\mathsf{sp}(\mathsf{ROLE}(\mathbb{F})^n) \leqslant |\mathbb{F}|^{\lceil n/2 \rceil}$. This demonstrates that the simple partition number subsumes the partition argument.

5.6   Relevant Prior Work on Common Information and Assisted Common Information

We briefly introduce a few relevant information-theoretic measures for maximum resilience and maximum production rate. For a joint distribution, the mutual information $I(R_A; R_B)$ measures the distance (KL-divergence) between the joint probability distribution $p(r_A, r_B)$ and the distribution $p(r_A) \cdot p(r_B)$. The mutual information between (R_A, R_B) represents the number of bits of the secret key that the two parties can agree. The Gács-Körner [21] common information, represented by $K(R_A; R_B)$, represents the largest entropy of the common random variable that each party can generate based on their respective secret share. Intuitively, this corresponds to the number of connected components in a bipartite graph representing the correlation. The Wyner common information [69], represented by $J(R_A; R_B)$, is the minimum information that, when leaked to the eavesdropper, ensures that the parties cannot establish a secret key. This quantity roughly corresponds to the biclique partition number of a bipartite graph for the correlation, where the correlation is a uniform distribution over the edges of the bipartite graph. Prabhakaran and Prabhakaran [53,54], generalizing [67], introduced the concept of *assisted common information* that, among its various applications, helps characterize an upper bound on the number of OTs that a correlation can produce.

Relation to Mutual Information. In the setting of key-agreement, the mutual information $I(R_A; R_B)$ of a correlation (R_A, R_B) measures the length of the secret key that the two parties can agree on. We emphasize that this is a measure of production, and not a measure of resilience. For example, $I(\mathsf{IP}\,(\mathbb{GF}\,[2]^n)) = 1$. Since, secure OT implies one-bit key-agreement, mutual information is also an upper bound on the OT production that a correlation can support. However, production capacity and resilience to leakage are extremely disparate quantities. For example, in the secure computation setting, the correlation $\mathsf{IP}\,(\mathbb{GF}\,[2]^n)$ is resilient to $n/2$ bits of leakage but can only produce one OT. Additionally, mutual information significantly overestimates the maximum OT production capacity. For example, n-bit shared private key cannot produce one OT even without any leakage. However, it has n-bits of mutual information.

  We emphasize that the simple partition number is only a measure for the maximum leakage resilience of correlations in the setting of secure computation. Our measure *does not* provide any estimates on the OT production. The most relevant measure for OT production is the notion of assisted common information proposed by Prabhakaran and Prabhakaran [53,54].

5.7   Analogy of Biclique Partition Number and Wyner's Common Information

A correlation that is a biclique has no mutual-information and, hence, is useless for parties to agree on a secret key even asymptotically. In particular, one sample from a correlation that is a biclique is also useless for key-agreement.

Suppose (R_A, R_B) is an arbitrary correlation and has biclique partition complexity $\mathsf{bp}(R_A, R_B)$. Similar to Lemma 4, in the presence of $t = \log \mathsf{bp}(R_A, R_B)$ bits of leakage there is not even a one-bit secure key-agreement protocols using (R_A, R_B). The random variable J for the leakage function $\mathcal{L}(R_A, R_B)$ outputs the index of the biclique that contains the edge $e = (r_A, r_B)$.

Wyner's common information [69] is defined to be the minimum entropy random variable J that suffices to ensure $I(R_A; R_B | J) = 0$. If the bicliques that partition G have roughly equal number of edges then these two concepts are identical. Analogously, $\mathsf{sp}(R_A, R_B)$ can be interpreted as the analog for Wyner's common information in the secure computation setting.

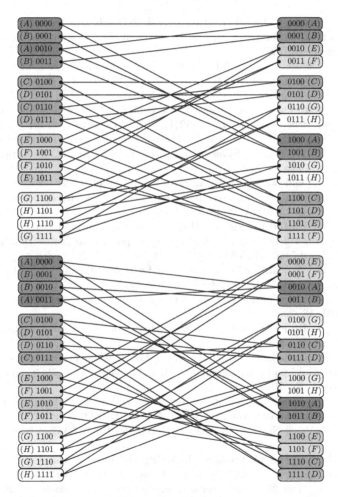

Fig. 13. A simple decomposition of $\mathsf{ROLE}\,(\mathbb{GF}\,[2])^2$, into two simple graphs. Each collection of nodes with identical shade of gray and letter represents a connected component.

However, we cannot use biclique partition number or Wyner's Common Information to meaningfully measure the resilience of a correlation against leakage in the secure computation setting. The biclique partition number $\mathsf{bp}\,(R_A, R_B)$ can be significantly higher than the simple partition number $\mathsf{sp}\,(R_A, R_B)$, which is an upper bound on the maximum resilience. For example, the biclique partition number $\mathsf{bp}\,(\mathsf{IP}\,(\mathbb{F}^n)) \approx |\mathbb{F}|^{n-1}$ while its simple partition number $\mathsf{sp}\,(\mathsf{IP}\,(\mathbb{F}^n)) \approx |\mathbb{F}|^{n/2}$ is exponentially small. This example demonstrates the non-trivial utility of the new measure introduced by us in the secure computation setting.

References

1. Babai, L., Frankl, P.: Linear Algebra Methods in Combinatorics: With Applications to Geometry and Computer Science. Department of Computer Science, University of Chicago (1992). 23
2. Beaver, D.: Perfect privacy for two-party protocols. In: Feigenbaum, J., Merritt, M. (eds.) Proceedings of DIMACS Workshop on Distributed Computing and Cryptography, vol. 2, pp. 65–77. American Mathematical Society (1989). 4, 12, 22
3. Behrend, F.A.: On sets of integers which contain no three terms in arithmetical progression. Proc. Natl. Acad. Sci. **32**(12), 331–332 (1946). 18, 19, 20, 21
4. Ben-David, A., Nisan, N., Pinkas, B.: FairplayMP: a system for secure multi-party computation. In: Ning, P., Syverson, P.F., Jha, S. (eds.) ACM CCS 08, pp. 257–266. ACM Press, October 2008. 4
5. Ben-Or, M., Goldwasser, S., Wigderson, A.: Completeness theorems for non-cryptographic fault-tolerant distributed computation (extended abstract). In: 20th ACM STOC, pp. 1–10. ACM Press, May 1988. 4
6. Block, A.R., Maji, H.K., Nguyen, H.H.: Secure computation based on leaky correlations: high resilience setting. https://www.cs.purdue.edu/homes/hmaji/papers/C:BloMajNgu17.pdf. (Full Version). 16, 24, 25
7. Bloom, T.F.: A quantitative improvement for Roth's theorem on arithmetic progressions. J. Lond. Math. Soc. **93**(3), 643–663 (2016). 20
8. Bourgain, J.: On triples in arithmetic progression. Geom. Funct. Anal. **9**(5), 968–984 (1999). 18, 20
9. Bourgain, J.: Roth's theorem on progressions revisited. J. d'Analyse Math. **104**(1), 155–192 (2008). 18, 20
10. Canetti, R., Lindell, Y., Ostrovsky, R., Sahai, A.: Universally composable two-party and multi-party secure computation. In: 34th ACM STOC, pp. 494–503. ACM Press, May 2002. 4
11. Chandran, N., Goyal, V., Sahai, A.: New constructions for UC secure computation using tamper-proof hardware. In: Smart, N. (ed.) EUROCRYPT 2008. LNCS, vol. 4965, pp. 545–562. Springer, Heidelberg (2008). doi:10.1007/978-3-540-78967-3_31. 4
12. Chaum, D., Crépeau, C., Damgård, I.: Multiparty unconditionally secure protocols (extended abstract). In: 20th ACM STOC, pp. 11–19. ACM Press, May 1988. 4
13. Cioaba, S.M., Tait, M.: More counterexamples to the Alon-Saks-Seymour and rank-coloring conjectures. Electron. J. Comb. **18**(P26), 1 (2011). 23
14. Cioabă, S.M., Tait, M.: Variations on a theme of Graham and Pollak. Discret. Math. **313**(5), 665–676 (2013). 23

15. Crépeau, C., Morozov, K., Wolf, S.: Efficient unconditional oblivious transfer from almost any noisy channel. In: Blundo, C., Cimato, S. (eds.) SCN 2004. LNCS, vol. 3352, pp. 47–59. Springer, Heidelberg (2005). doi:10.1007/978-3-540-30598-9_4. 4

16. Damgård, I., Ishai, Y.: Scalable secure multiparty computation. In: Dwork, C. (ed.) CRYPTO 2006. LNCS, vol. 4117, pp. 501–520. Springer, Heidelberg (2006). doi:10. 1007/11818175_30. 4

17. Damgård, I., Nielsen, J.B., Wichs, D.: Isolated proofs of knowledge and isolated zero knowledge. In: Smart, N. (ed.) EUROCRYPT 2008. LNCS, vol. 4965, pp. 509–526. Springer, Heidelberg (2008). doi:10.1007/978-3-540-78967-3_29. 4

18. Damgård, I., Pastro, V., Smart, N., Zakarias, S.: Multiparty computation from somewhat homomorphic encryption. In: Safavi-Naini, R., Canetti, R. (eds.) CRYPTO 2012. LNCS, vol. 7417, pp. 643–662. Springer, Heidelberg (2012). doi:10. 1007/978-3-642-32009-5_38. 4

19. Dolev, D.: The Byzantine generals strike again. J. Algorithms 3(1), 14–30 (1982). 4

20. Elkin, M.: An improved construction of progression-free sets. In: Proceedings of the Twenty-first Annual ACM-SIAM Symposium on Discrete Algorithms, pp. 886–905. Society for Industrial and Applied Mathematics (2010). 18, 19, 20, 21

21. Gács, P., Körner, J.: Common information is far less than mutual information. Probl. Control Inf. Theory 2(2), 149–162 (1973). 26

22. Goldreich, O., Micali, S., Wigderson, A.: How to play any mental game or a completeness theorem for protocols with honest majority. In: Aho, A. (ed.) 19th ACM STOC, pp. 218–229. ACM Press, May 1987. 4

23. Goyal, V., Ishai, Y., Sahai, A., Venkatesan, R., Wadia, A.: Founding cryptography on tamper-proof hardware tokens. In: Micciancio, D. (ed.) TCC 2010. LNCS, vol. 5978, pp. 308–326. Springer, Heidelberg (2010). doi:10.1007/978-3-642-11799-2_19. 4

24. Graham, R.L., Pollak, H.O.: On the addressing problem for loop switching. Bell Syst. Tech. J. 50(8), 2495–2519 (1971). 10, 23

25. Graham, R.L., Pollak, H.O.: On embedding graphs in squashed cubes. In: Alavi, Y., Lick, D.R., White, A.T. (eds.) Graph Theory and Applications. LNM, vol. 303, pp. 99–110. Springer, Heidelberg (1972). doi:10.1007/BFb0067362. 10, 23

26. Gupta, D., Ishai, Y., Maji, H.K., Sahai, A.: Secure computation from leaky correlated randomness. In: Gennaro, R., Robshaw, M. (eds.) CRYPTO 2015. LNCS, vol. 9216, pp. 701–720. Springer, Heidelberg (2015). doi:10.1007/978-3-662-48000-7_34. 6, 7, 8, 9, 10, 11, 16

27. Harnik, D., Ishai, Y., Kushilevitz, E., Nielsen, J.B.: OT-combiners via secure computation. In: Canetti, R. (ed.) TCC 2008. LNCS, vol. 4948, pp. 393–411. Springer, Heidelberg (2008). doi:10.1007/978-3-540-78524-8_22. 10

28. Harnik, D., Kilian, J., Naor, M., Reingold, O., Rosen, A.: On robust combiners for oblivious transfer and other primitives. In: Cramer, R. (ed.) EUROCRYPT 2005. LNCS, vol. 3494, pp. 96–113. Springer, Heidelberg (2005). doi:10.1007/11426639_6. 10

29. Heath-Brown, D.R.: Integer sets containing no arithmetic progressions. J. Lond. Math. Soc. (2) 35(3), 385–394 (1987). 18, 20

30. Hoffman, A.J.: Eigenvalues and partitionings of the edges of a graph. Linear Algebra Appl. 5(2), 137–146 (1972). 23

31. Huang, H., Sudakov, B.: A counterexample to the alon-saks-seymour conjecture and related problems. Combinatorica 32(2), 205–219 (2012). 23

32. Impagliazzo, R., Luby, M.: One-way functions are essential for complexity based cryptography (extended abstract). In: 30th FOCS, pp. 230–235. IEEE Computer Society Press, October/November 1989. 4, 12, 22

33. Ishai, Y., Kushilevitz, E., Ostrovsky, R., Sahai, A.: Extracting correlations. In: 50th FOCS, pp. 261–270. IEEE Computer Society Press, October 2009. 5, 6, 7, 10

34. Ishai, Y., Maji, H.K., Sahai, A., Wullschleger, J.: Single-use OT combiners with near-optimal resilience. In: 2014 IEEE International Symposium on Information Theory, Honolulu, HI, USA, 29 June–4 July 2014, pp. 1544–1548. IEEE (2014). 6, 9, 10

35. Ishai, Y., Prabhakaran, M., Sahai, A.: Founding cryptography on oblivious transfer – efficiently. In: Wagner, D. (ed.) CRYPTO 2008. LNCS, vol. 5157, pp. 572–591. Springer, Heidelberg (2008). doi:10.1007/978-3-540-85174-5_32. 4, 10

36. Kahn, J.: Recent results on some not-so-recent hypergraph matching and covering problems. DIMACS, Center for Discrete Mathematics and Theoretical Computer Science (1991). 23

37. Katz, J.: Universally composable multi-party computation using tamper-proof hardware. In: Naor, M. (ed.) EUROCRYPT 2007. LNCS, vol. 4515, pp. 115–128. Springer, Heidelberg (2007). doi:10.1007/978-3-540-72540-4_7. 4

38. Kilian, J.: Founding cryptography on oblivious transfer. In: 20th ACM STOC, pp. 20–31. ACM Press, May 1988. 4, 12, 22

39. Kilian, J.: More general completeness theorems for secure two-party computation. In: 32nd ACM STOC, pp. 316–324. ACM Press, May 2000. 4

40. Kratzke, T., Reznick, B., West, D.: Eigensharp graphs: decomposition into complete bipartite subgraphs. Trans. Am. Math. Soc. **308**(2), 637–653 (1988). 23

41. Künzler, R., Müller-Quade, J., Raub, D.: Secure computability of functions in the IT setting with dishonest majority and applications to long-term security. In: Reingold, O. (ed.) TCC 2009. LNCS, vol. 5444, pp. 238–255. Springer, Heidelberg (2009). doi:10.1007/978-3-642-00457-5_15. 4, 12, 22

42. Kushilevitz, E.: Privacy and communication complexity. In: 30th FOCS, pp. 416–421. IEEE Computer Society Press, October/November 1989. 4, 12, 22

43. Maji, H.K., Prabhakaran, M., Rosulek, M.: Complexity of multi-party computation problems: the case of 2-party symmetric secure function evaluation. In: Reingold, O. (ed.) TCC 2009. LNCS, vol. 5444, pp. 256–273. Springer, Heidelberg (2009). doi:10.1007/978-3-642-00457-5_16. 4, 12, 22

44. Maji, H.K., Prabhakaran, M., Rosulek, M.: A unified characterization of completeness and triviality for secure function evaluation. In: Galbraith, S., Nandi, M. (eds.) INDOCRYPT 2012. LNCS, vol. 7668, pp. 40–59. Springer, Heidelberg (2012). doi:10.1007/978-3-642-34931-7_4. 4

45. Malkhi, D., Nisan, N., Pinkas, B., Sella, Y.: Fairplay - secure two-party computation system. In: Blaze, M. (ed.) Proceedings of the 13th USENIX Security Symposium, San Diego, CA, USA, 9–13 August 2004, pp. 287–302. USENIX (2004). 4

46. McNew, N.: Avoiding geometric progressions in the integers, 02 May 2017. https://math.dartmouth.edu/graduate-students/works/2013-14/McNew-GradPoster Session.pdf. 20

47. Meier, R., Przydatek, B.: On robust combiners for private information retrieval and other primitives. In: Dwork, C. (ed.) CRYPTO 2006. LNCS, vol. 4117, pp. 555–569. Springer, Heidelberg (2006). doi:10.1007/11818175_33. 10

48. Meier, R., Przydatek, B., Wullschleger, J.: Robuster combiners for oblivious transfer. In: Vadhan, S.P. (ed.) TCC 2007. LNCS, vol. 4392, pp. 404–418. Springer, Heidelberg (2007). doi:10.1007/978-3-540-70936-7_22. 10

49. Moran, T., Segev, G.: David and Goliath commitments: UC computation for asymmetric parties using tamper-proof hardware. In: Smart, N. (ed.) EUROCRYPT 2008. LNCS, vol. 4965, pp. 527–544. Springer, Heidelberg (2008). doi:10.1007/978-3-540-78967-3_30. 4

50. Nielsen, J.B., Nordholt, P.S., Orlandi, C., Burra, S.S.: A new approach to practical active-secure two-party computation. In: Safavi-Naini, R., Canetti, R. (eds.) CRYPTO 2012. LNCS, vol. 7417, pp. 681–700. Springer, Heidelberg (2012). doi:10.1007/978-3-642-32009-5_40. 4

51. Nisan, N., Wigderson, A.: On rank vs. communication complexity. Combinatorica 15(4), 557–565 (1995). 23

52. Peck, G.W.: A new proof of a theorem of Graham and Pollak. Discret. Math. 49(3), 327–328 (1984). 23

53. Prabhakaran, V.M., Prabhakaran, M.: Assisted common information. In: 2010 IEEE International Symposium on Information Theory, ISIT Proceedings, Austin, Texas, USA, 13–18 June 2010, pp. 2602–2606. IEEE (2010). 26

54. Prabhakaran, V.M., Prabhakaran, M.: Assisted common information: further results. In: Kuleshov, A., Blinovsky, V., Ephremides, A. (eds.) 2011 IEEE International Symposium on Information Theory Proceedings, ISIT 2011, St. Petersburg, Russia, 31 July–5 August 2011, pp. 2861–2865. IEEE (2011). 26

55. Przydatek, B., Wullschleger, J.: Error-tolerant combiners for oblivious primitives. In: Aceto, L., Damgård, I., Goldberg, L.A., Halldórsson, M.M., Ingólfsdóttir, A., Walukiewicz, I. (eds.) ICALP 2008. LNCS, vol. 5126, pp. 461–472. Springer, Heidelberg (2008). doi:10.1007/978-3-540-70583-3_38. 10

56. Rabin, T., Ben-Or, M.: Verifiable secret sharing and multiparty protocols with honest majority (extended abstract). In: 21st ACM STOC, pp. 73–85. ACM Press, May 1989. 4

57. Razborov, A.A.: The gap between the chromatic number of a graph and the rank of its adjacency matrix is superlinear. Discret. Math. 108(1), 393–396 (1992). 23

58. Roth, K.F.: On certain sets of integers. J. Lond. Math. Soc. 1(1), 104–109 (1953). 18, 20

59. Salem, R., Spencer, D.C.: On sets of integers which contain no three terms in arithmetical progression. Proc. Natl. Acad. Sci. 28(12), 561–563 (1942). 19

60. Sanders, T.: On Roth's theorem on progressions. Ann. Math. 174, 619–636 (2011). 18, 20

61. Szemerédi, E.: Integer sets containing no arithmetic progressions. Acta Math. Hung. 56(1–2), 155–158 (1990). 18, 20

62. Tverberg, H.: On the decomposition of kn into complete bipartite graphs. J. Graph Theory 6(4), 493–494 (1982). 23

63. van Lint, J.H., Wilson, R.M.: A Course in Combinatorics. Cambridge University Press, Cambridge (2001). 23

64. Van Lint, J.H.: {0, 1,*} distance problems in combinatorics (1985). 23

65. Vishwanathan, S.: A polynomial space proof of the Graham-Pollak theorem. J. Comb. Theory Ser. A 115(4), 674–676 (2008). 23

66. Vishwanathan, S.: A counting proof of the Graham-Pollak theorem. Discret. Math. 313(6), 765–766 (2013). 23

67. Wolf, S., Wullschleger, J.: New monotones and lower bounds in unconditional two-party computation. In: Shoup, V. (ed.) CRYPTO 2005. LNCS, vol. 3621, pp. 467–477. Springer, Heidelberg (2005). doi:10.1007/11535218_28. 26

68. Wolf, S., Wullschleger, J.: Oblivious transfer is symmetric. In: Vaudenay, S. (ed.) EUROCRYPT 2006. LNCS, vol. 4004, pp. 222–232. Springer, Heidelberg (2006). doi:10.1007/11761679_14. 4, 8

32   A.R. Block et al.

69. Wyner, A.D.: The common information of two dependent random variables. IEEE
    Trans. Inf. Theory **21**(2), 163–179 (1975). 7, 10, 23, 26, 27
70. Yan, W., Yeh, Y.-N.: A simple proof of Graham and Pollak's theorem. J. Comb.
    Theory Ser. A **113**(5), 892–893 (2006). 23
71. Yao, A.C.-C.: Protocols for secure computations (extended abstract). In: 23rd
    FOCS, pp. 160–164. IEEE Computer Society Press, November 1982. 4

Laconic Oblivious Transfer and Its Applications

Chongwon Cho[1]([✉]), Nico Döttling[2]([✉]), Sanjam Garg[2]([✉]), Divya Gupta[3]([✉]),
Peihan Miao[2]([✉]), and Antigoni Polychroniadou[4]([✉])

[1] HRL Laboratories, Malibu, USA
lewisccho@gmail.com
[2] UC Berkeley, Berkeley, USA
nico.doettling@gmail.com, {sanjamg,peihan}@berkeley.edu
[3] Microsoft Research India, Bengaluru, India
dgiitd@gmail.com
[4] Cornell University, Ithaca, USA
antigonipoly@gmail.com

Abstract. In this work, we introduce a novel technique for secure computation over large inputs. Specifically, we provide a new oblivious transfer (OT) protocol with a laconic receiver. Laconic OT allows a receiver to commit to a large input D (of length M) via a short message. Subsequently, a single short message by a sender allows the receiver to learn $m_{D[L]}$, where the messages m_0, m_1 and the location $L \in [M]$ are dynamically chosen by the sender. All prior constructions of OT required the receiver's outgoing message to grow with D.

Our key contribution is an instantiation of this primitive based on the Decisional Diffie-Hellman (DDH) assumption in the common reference string (CRS) model. The technical core of this construction is a novel use of somewhere statistically binding (SSB) hashing in conjunction with hash proof systems. Next, we show applications of laconic OT to non-interactive secure computation on large inputs and multi-hop homomorphic encryption for RAM programs.

N. Döttling—Research supported by a postdoc fellowship of the German Academic Exchange Service (DAAD).

N. Döttling, S. Garg, D. Gupta and P. Miao—Research supported in part from 2017 AFOSR YIP Award, DARPA/ARL SAFEWARE Award W911NF15C0210, AFOSR Award FA9550-15-1-0274, NSF CRII Award 1464397, research grants by the Okawa Foundation, Visa Inc., and Center for Long-Term Cybersecurity (CLTC, UC Berkeley). The views expressed are those of the author and do not reflect the official policy or position of the funding agencies.

D. Gupta—Work done while at University of California, Berkeley.

A. Polychroniadou—Part of the work done while visiting University of California, Berkeley. Research supported in part the National Science Foundation under Grant No. 1617676, IBM under Agreement 4915013672, and the Packard Foundation under Grant 2015-63124.

J. Katz and H. Shacham (Eds.): CRYPTO 2017, Part II, LNCS 10402, pp. 33–65, 2017.
DOI: 10.1007/978-3-319-63715-0_2

1 Introduction

Big data poses serious challenges for the current cryptographic technology. In particular, cryptographic protocols for secure computation are typically based on Boolean circuits, where both the computational complexity and communication complexity scale with the size of the input dataset, which makes it generally unsuitable for even moderate dataset sizes. Over the past few decades, substantial effort has been devoted towards realizing cryptographic primitives that overcome these challenges. This includes works on fully-homomorphic encryption (FHE) [Gen09, BV11b, BV11a, GSW13] and on the RAM setting of oblivious RAM [Gol87, Ost90] and secure RAM computation [OS97, GKK+12, LO13, GHL+14, GGMP16]. Protocols based on FHE generally have a favorable communication complexity and are basically non-interactive, yet incur a prohibitively large computational overhead (dependent on the dataset size). On the other hand, protocols for the RAM model generally have a favorable computational overhead, but lack in terms of communication efficiency (that grows with the program running time), especially in the multi-party setting. Can we achieve the best of both worlds? In this work we make positive progress on this question. Specifically, we introduce a new tool called laconic oblivious transfer that helps to strike a balance between the two seemingly opposing goals.

Oblivious transfer (or OT for short) is a fundamental and powerful primitive in cryptography [Kil88, IPS08]. Since its first introduction by Rabin [Rab81], OT has been a foundational building block for realizing secure computation protocols [Yao82, GMW87, IPS08]. However, typical secure computation protocols involve executions of multiple instances of an oblivious transfer protocol. In fact, the number of needed oblivious transfers grows with the input size of one of the parties, which is the receiver of the oblivious transfer.[1] In this work, we observe that a two-message OT protocol, with a short message from the receiver, can be a key tool towards the goal of obtaining *simultaneous* improvements in computational and communication cost for secure computation.

1.1 Laconic OT

In this paper, we introduce the notion of laconic oblivious transfer (or laconic OT for short). Laconic OT allows an OT receiver to commit to a large input $D \in \{0,1\}^M$ via a short message. Subsequently, the sender responds with a single short message to the receiver depending on dynamically chosen two messages m_0, m_1 and a location $L \in [M]$. The sender's response message allows the receiver to recover $m_{D[L]}$ (while $m_{1-D[L]}$ remains computationally hidden). Furthermore, without any additional communication with the receiver, the sender could repeat this process for multiple choices of L. The construction we give is

---

[1] We remark that related prior works on OT extension [Bea96, IKNP03, KK13, ALSZ13] makes the number of public key operations performed during protocol executions independent of the receiver's input size. However, the communication complexity of receivers in these protocols still grows with the input size of the receiver.

secure against semi-honest adversaries, but it can be upgraded to the malicious setting in a similar way as we will discuss in Sect. 1.2 for the first application.

Our construction of laconic OT is obtained by first realizing a "mildly compressing" laconic OT protocol for which the receiver's message is factor-2 compressing, i.e., half the size of its input. We base this construction on the Decisional Diffie-Hellman (DDH) assumption. We note that, subsequent to our work, the factor-2 compression construction has been simplified by Döttling and Garg [DG17] (another alternative simplification can be obtained using [AIKW13]). Next we show that such a "mildly compressing" laconic OT can be bootstrapped, via the usage of a Merkle Hash Tree and Yao's Garbled Circuits [Yao82], to obtain a "fully compressing" laconic OT, where the size of the receiver's message is independent of its input size. The laconic OT scheme with a Merkle Tree structure allows for good properties like local verification and local updates, which makes it a powerful tool in secure computation with large inputs.

We will show new applications of laconic OT to non-interactive secure computation and homomorphic encryption for RAM programs, as briefly described below in Sects. 1.2 and 1.3.

1.2 Warm-Up Application: Non-interactive Secure Computation on Large Inputs

Can a receiver publish a (small) encoding of her large confidential database D so that any sender, who holds a secret input x, can reveal the output $f(x, D)$ (where f is a circuit) to the receiver by sending her a single message? For security, we want the receiver's encoding to hide D and the sender's message to hide x. Using laconic OT, we present the first solution to this problem. In our construction, the receiver's published encoding is independent of the size of her database, but we do not restrict the size of the sender's message.[2]

RAM Setting. Consider the scenario where f can be computed using a RAM program P of running time t. We use the notation $P^D(x)$ to denote the execution of the program P on input x with random access to the database D. We provide a construction where as before the size of the receiver's published message is independent of the size of the database D. Moreover, the size of the sender's message (and computational cost of the sender and the receiver) grows only with t and the receiver learns nothing more than the output $P^D(x)$ and the locations in D touched during the computation. Note that in all prior works on general

---

[2] We remark that solutions for this problem based on fully-homomorphic encryption (FHE) [Gen09, LNO13], unlike our result, reduce the communication cost of both the sender's and the receiver's messages to be independent of the size of D, but require additional rounds of interaction.

secure RAM computation [OS97, GKK+12, LO13, WHC+14, GHL+14, GLOS15, GLO15] the size of the receiver's message grew at least with its input size.[3]

Against Malicious Adversaries. The results above are obtained in the semi-honest setting. We can upgrade to security against a malicious sender by use of (i) non-interactive zero knowledge proofs (NIZKs) [FLS90] at the cost of additionally assuming doubly enhanced trapdoor permutations or bilinear maps [CHK04, GOS06], (ii) the techniques of Ishai et al. [IKO+11] while obtaining slightly weaker security,[4] or (iii) interactive zero-knowledge proofs but at the cost of additional interaction.

Upgrading to security against a malicious receiver is tricky. This is because the receiver's public encoding is short and hence, it is not possible to recover the receiver's entire database just given the encoding. Standard simulation-based security can be obtained by using (i) universal arguments as done by [CV12, COV15] at the cost of additional interaction, or (ii) using SNARKs at the cost of making extractability assumptions [BCCT12, BSCG+13].[5]

Other Related Work. Prior works consider secure computation which hides the input size of one [MRK03, IP07, ADT11, LNO13] or both parties [LNO13]. Our notion only requires the receiver's communication cost to be independent of the its input size, and is therefore weaker. However, these results are largely restricted to special functionalities, such as zero-knowledge sets and computing certain branching programs (which imply input-size hiding private set intersection). The general result of [LNO13] uses FHE and as mentioned earlier needs more rounds of interaction.[6]

1.3 Main Application: Multi-hop Homomorphic Encryption for RAM Programs

Consider a scenario where S (a server), holding an input x, publishes an encryption ct_0 of her private input x under her public key. Now this ciphertext is

---

[3] The communication cost of the receiver's message can be reduced to depend only on the running time of the program by allowing round complexity to grow with the running time of the program (using Merkle Hashing). Analogous to the circuit case, we remark that FHE-based solutions can make the communication of both the sender and the receiver small, but at the cost of extra rounds. Moreover, in the setting of RAM programs FHE-based solutions additionally incur an increased computational cost for the receiver. In particular, the receiver's computational cost grows with the size of its database.

[4] The receiver is required to keep the output of the computation private.

[5] We finally note that relaxing to the weaker notion of indistinguishability-based security we can expect to obtain the best of both worlds, i.e. a non-interactive solution while making only a black-box use of the adversary (a.k.a. avoiding the use of extractability assumptions). We leave this open for future work.

[6] We remark that in an orthogonal work of Hubacek and Wichs [HW15] obtain constructions where the communication cost is independent of the length of the output of the computation using indistinguishability obfuscation [GGH+13b].

passed on to a client Q_1 that homomorphically computes a (possibly private) program P_1 accessing (private) memory D_1 on the value encrypted in ct_0, obtaining another ciphertext ct_1. More generally, the computation could be performed by multiple clients. In other words, clients $Q_2, Q_3, \cdots$ could sequentially compute private programs $P_2, P_3, \cdots$ accessing their own private databases $D_2, D_3, \cdots$. Finally, we want S to be able to use her secret key to decrypt the final ciphertext and recover the output of the computation. For security, we require simulation based security for a client Q_i against a collusion of the server and any subset of the clients, and IND-CPA security for the server's ciphertext.

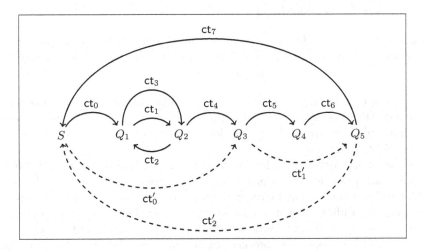

Fig. 1. Two example paths of computation on server S's ciphertexts.

Though we described the simple case above, we are interested in the general case when computation is performed in different sequences of the clients. Examples of two such computation paths are shown in Fig. 1. Furthermore, we consider the setting of persistent databases, where each client is able to execute dynamically chosen programs on the encrypted ciphertexts while using the same database that gets updated as these programs are executed.

FHE-Based Solution. Gentry's [Gen09] fully homomorphic encryption (FHE) scheme offers a solution to the above problem when circuit representations of the desired programs $P_1, P_2, \ldots$ are considered. Specifically, S could encrypt her input x using an FHE scheme. Now, the clients can publicly compute arbitrary programs on the encrypted value using a public evaluation procedure. This procedure can be adapted to preserve the privacy of the computed circuit [OPP14,DS16,BPMW16] as well. However, this construction only works for circuits. Realizing the scheme for RAM programs involves first converting the RAM program into a circuit of size at least linear in the size of the database. This linear effort can be exponential in the running time of the program for several applications of interest such as binary search.

Our Relaxation. In obtaining homomorphic encryption for RAM programs, we start by relaxing the compactness requirement in FHE.[7] Compactness in FHE requires that the size of the ciphertexts does not grow with computation. In particular, in our scheme, we allow the evaluated ciphertexts to be bigger than the original ciphertext. Gentry, Halevi and Vaikuntanathan [GHV10] considered an analogous setting for the case of circuits. As in Gentry et al. [GHV10], in our setting computation itself will happen at the time of decryption. Therefore, we additionally require that clients $Q_1, Q_2, \cdots$ first ship pre-processed versions of their databases to S for the decryption, and security will additionally require that S does not learn the access pattern of the programs on client databases. This brings us to the following question:

Can we realize multi-hop encryption schemes for RAM programs where the ciphertext grows linearly only in the running time of the computation performed on it?

We show that laconic OT can be used to realize such a multi-hop homomorphic encryption scheme for RAM programs. Our result bridges the gap between growth in ciphertext size and computational complexity of homomorphic encryption for RAM programs.

Our work also leaves open the problem of realizing (fully or somewhat) homomorphic encryption for RAM programs with (somewhat) compact ciphertexts and for which computational cost grows with the running time of the computation, based on traditional computational assumptions. Our solution for multi-hop RAM homomorphic encryption is for the semi-honest (or, semi-malicious) setting only. We leave open the problem of obtaining a solution in the malicious setting.[8]

1.4 Roadmap

We now lay out a roadmap for the remainder of the paper. In Sect. 2 we give a technical overview of this work. We introduce the notion of laconic OT formally in Sect. 3, and give a construction with factor-2 compression in Sect. 4, which can be bootstrapped to a fully compressing updatable laconic OT. We present our bootstrapping step and two applications of laconic OT in the full version of this paper [CDG+17].

---

[7] One method for realizing homomorphic encryption for RAM programs [GKP+13, GHRW14,CHJV15,BGL+15,KLW15] would be to use obfuscation [GGH+13b] based on multilinear maps [GGH13a]. However, in this paper we focus on basing homomorphic RAM computation on DDH and defer the work on obfuscation to future work.

[8] Using NIZKs alone does not solve the problem, because locations accessed during computation are dynamically decided.

2   Technical Overview

2.1   Laconic OT

We will now provide an overview of laconic OT and our constructions of this new primitive. Laconic OT consists of two major components: a hash function and an encryption scheme. We will call the hash function Hash and the encryption scheme (Send, Receive). In a nutshell, laconic OT allows a receiver R to compute a *succinct* digest digest of a large database D and a private state $\hat{D}$ using the hash function Hash. After digest is made public, anyone can non-interactively send OT messages to R w.r.t. a location L of the database such that the receiver's choice bit is $D[L]$. Here, $D[L]$ is the database-entry at location L. In more detail, given digest, a database location L, and two messages m_0 and m_1, the algorithm Send computes a ciphertext e such that R, who owns $\hat{D}$, can use the decryption algorithm Receive to decrypt e to obtain the message $m_{D[L]}$.

For security, we require sender privacy against semi-honest receiver. In particular, given an honest receiver's view, which includes the database D, the message $m_{1-D[L]}$ is computationally hidden. We formalize this using a simulation based definition. On the other hand, we do not require receiver privacy as opposed to standard oblivious transfer, namely, no security guarantee is provided against a cheating (semi-honest) sender. This is mostly for ease of exposition. Nevertheless, adding receiver privacy to laconic OT can be done in a straightforward manner via the usage of garbled circuits and two-message OT (see Sect. 3.1 for a detailed discussion).

For efficiency, we have the following requirement: First, the size of digest only depends on the security parameter and is independent of the size of the database D. Moreover, after digest and $\hat{D}$ are computed by Hash, the workload of *both* the sender and receiver (that is, the runtime of both Send and Receive) becomes essentially independent of the size of the database (i.e., depending at most polynomially on $\log(|D|)$).

Notice that our security definition and efficiency requirement immediately imply that the Hash algorithm used to compute the succinct digest must be collision resistant. Thus, it is clear that the hash function must be keyed and in our case it is keyed by a ommon reference string.

Construction at a high level. We first construct a laconic OT scheme with factor-2 compression, which compresses a 2λ-bit database to a λ-bit digest. Next, to get laconic OT for databases of arbitrary size, we bootstrap this construction using an interesting combination of Merkle hashing and garbled circuits. Below, we give an overview of each of these steps.

2.1.1   Laconic OT with Factor-2 Compression

We start with a construction of a laconic OT scheme with factor-2 compression, i.e., a scheme that hashes a 2λ-bit database to a λ-bit digest. This construction is inspired by the notion of witness encryption [GGSW13]. We will first explain the scheme based on witness encryption. Then, we show how this specific witness encryption scheme can be realized with the more standard notion of hash proof systems (HPS) [CS02]. Our overall scheme will be based on the security of Decisional Diffie-Hellman (DDH) assumption.

Construction Using Witness Encryption. Recall that a witness encryption scheme is defined for an NP-language $\mathcal{L}$ (with corresponding witness relation $\mathcal{R}$). It consists of two algorithms Enc and Dec. The algorithm Enc takes as input a problem instance x and a message m, and produces a ciphertext. A recipient of the ciphertext can use Dec to decrypt the message if $x \in \mathcal{L}$ and the recipient knows a witness w such that $\mathcal{R}(x, w)$ holds. There are two requirements for a witness encryption scheme, correctness and security. Correctness requires that if $\mathcal{R}(x, w)$ holds, then $\mathsf{Dec}(x, w, \mathsf{Enc}(x, m)) = m$. Security requires that if $x \notin \mathcal{L}$, then $\mathsf{Enc}(x, m)$ computationally hides m.

We will now discuss how to construct a laconic OT with factor-2 compression using a two-to-one hash function and witness encryption. Let $\mathsf{H} : \mathcal{K} \times \{0,1\}^{2\lambda} \to \{0,1\}^{\lambda}$ be a keyed hash function, where $\mathcal{K}$ is the key space. Consider the language $\mathcal{L} = \{(K, L, y, b) \in \mathcal{K} \times [2\lambda] \times \{0,1\}^{\lambda} \times \{0,1\} \mid \exists D \in \{0,1\}^{2\lambda} \text{ such that } \mathsf{H}(K, D) = y \text{ and } D[L] = b\}$. Let (Enc, Dec) be a witness encryption scheme for the language $\mathcal{L}$.

The laconic OT scheme is as follows: The Hash algorithm computes $y = \mathsf{H}(K, D)$ where K is the common reference string and $D \in \{0,1\}^{2\lambda}$ is the database. Then y is published as the digest of the database. The Send algorithm takes as input K, y, a location L, and two messages (m_0, m_1) and proceeds as follows. It computes two ciphertexts $\mathsf{e}_0 \leftarrow \mathsf{Enc}((K, L, y, 0), m_0)$ and $\mathsf{e}_1 \leftarrow \mathsf{Enc}((K, L, y, 1), m_1)$ and outputs $\mathsf{e} = (\mathsf{e}_0, \mathsf{e}_1)$. The Receive algorithm takes as input K, L, y, D, and the ciphertext $\mathsf{e} = (\mathsf{e}_0, \mathsf{e}_1)$ and proceeds as follows. It sets $b = D[L]$, computes $m \leftarrow \mathsf{Dec}((K, L, y, b), D, \mathsf{e}_b)$ and outputs m.

It is easy to check that the above scheme satisfies correctness. However, we run into trouble when trying to prove sender privacy. Since H compresses 2λ bits to λ bits, most hash values have exponentially many pre-images. This implies that for most values of (K, L, y), it holds that both $(K, L, y, 0) \in \mathcal{L}$ and $(K, L, y, 1) \in \mathcal{L}$, that is, most problem instances are yes-instances. However, to reduce sender privacy of our scheme to the security of witness encryption, we ideally want that if $y = \mathsf{H}(K, D)$, then $(K, L, y, D[L]) \in \mathcal{L}$ while $(K, L, y, 1 - D[L]) \notin \mathcal{L}$. To overcome this problem, we will use a somewhere statistically binding hash function that allows us to artificially introduce no-instances as described below.

Somewhere Statistically Binding Hash to the Rescue. Somewhere statistically binding (SSB) hash functions [HW15,KLW15,OPWW15] support a special key generation procedure such that the hash value information theoretically fixes certain bit(s) of the pre-image. In particular, the special key generation procedure takes as input a location L and generates a key $K^{(L)}$. Then the hash function keyed by $K^{(L)}$ will bind the L-th bit of the pre-image. That is, $K^{(L)}$ and $y = \mathsf{H}(K^{(L)}, D)$ uniquely determines $D[L]$. The security requirement for

SSB hashing is the *index-hiding* property, i.e., keys $K^{(L)}$ and $K^{(L')}$ should be computationally indistinguishable for any $L \neq L'$.

We can now establish security of the above laconic OT scheme when instantiated with SSB hash functions. To prove security, we will first replace the key K by a key $K^{(L)}$ that statistically binds the L-th bit of the pre-image. The index hiding property guarantees that this change goes unnoticed. Now for every hash value $y = \mathsf{H}(K^{(L)}, D)$, it holds that $(K, L, y, D[L]) \in \mathcal{L}$ while $(K, L, y, 1 - D[L]) \notin \mathcal{L}$. We can now rely on the security of witness encryption to argue that $\mathsf{Enc}((K^{(L)}, L, y, 1 - D[L]), m_{1-D[L]})$ computationally hides the message $m_{1-D[L]}$.

Working with DDH. The above described scheme relies on a witness encryption scheme for the language $\mathcal{L}$. We note that witness encryption for general NP languages is only known under strong assumptions such as graded encodings [GGSW13] or indistinguishability obfuscation [GGH+13b]. Nevertheless, the aforementioned laconic OT scheme does not need full power of general witness encryption. In particular, we will leverage the fact that hash proof systems [CS02] can be used to construct statistical witness encryption schemes for specific languages [GGSW13]. Towards this end, we will carefully craft an SSB hash function that is hash proof system friendly, that is, allows for a hash proof system (or statistical witness encryption) for the language $\mathcal{L}$ required above. Our construction of the HPS-friendly SSB hash is based on the Decisional Diffie-Hellman assumption and is inspired from a construction by Okamoto et al. [OPWW15].

We will briefly outline our HPS-friendly SSB hash below. We strongly encourage the reader to see Sect. 4.2 for the full construction or see [DG17] for a simplified construction.

Let $\mathbb{G}$ be a (multiplicative) cyclic group of order p generated by a generator g. A hashing key is of the form $\hat{\mathbf{H}} = g^{\mathbf{H}}$ (the exponentiation is done component-wisely), where the matrix $\mathbf{H} \in \mathbb{Z}_p^{2 \times 2\lambda}$ is chosen uniformly at random. The hash function of $\mathbf{x} \in \mathbb{Z}_p^{2\lambda}$ is computed as $\mathsf{H}(\hat{\mathbf{H}}, \mathbf{x}) = \hat{\mathbf{H}}^{\mathbf{x}} \in \mathbb{G}^2$ (where $(\hat{\mathbf{H}}^{\mathbf{x}})_i = \prod_{k=1}^{2\lambda} \hat{\mathbf{H}}_{i,k}^{x_k}$, hence $\hat{\mathbf{H}}^{\mathbf{x}} = g^{\mathbf{H}\mathbf{x}}$). The binding key $\hat{\mathbf{H}}^{(i)}$ is of the form $\hat{\mathbf{H}}^{(i)} = g^{\mathbf{A}+\mathbf{T}}$, where $\mathbf{A} \in \mathbb{Z}_p^{2 \times 2\lambda}$ is a random rank 1 matrix, and $\mathbf{T} \in \mathbb{Z}_p^{2 \times 2\lambda}$ is a matrix with zero entries everywhere, except that $\mathbf{T}_{2,i} = 1$.

Now we describe a witness encryption scheme $(\mathsf{Enc}, \mathsf{Dec})$ for the language $\mathcal{L} = \{(\hat{\mathbf{H}}, i, \hat{\mathbf{y}}, b) \mid \exists \mathbf{x} \in \mathbb{Z}_p^{2\lambda} \text{ s.t. } \hat{\mathbf{H}}^{\mathbf{x}} = \hat{\mathbf{y}} \text{ and } x_i = b\}$. $\mathsf{Enc}((\hat{\mathbf{H}}, i, \hat{\mathbf{y}}, b), m)$ first sets

$$\hat{\mathbf{H}}' = \begin{pmatrix} \hat{\mathbf{H}} \\ g^{\mathbf{e}_i^{\top}} \end{pmatrix} \in \mathbb{G}^{3 \times 2\lambda}, \hat{\mathbf{y}}' = \begin{pmatrix} \hat{\mathbf{y}} \\ g^b \end{pmatrix} \in \mathbb{G}^3,$$

where $\mathbf{e}_i \in \mathbb{Z}_p^{2\lambda}$ is the i-th unit vector. It then picks a random $\mathbf{r} \in \mathbb{Z}_p^3$ and computes a ciphertext $c = \left(\left((\hat{\mathbf{H}}')^{\top}\right)^{\mathbf{r}}, \left((\hat{\mathbf{y}}')^{\top}\right)^{\mathbf{r}} \oplus m\right)$. To decrypt a ciphertext $c = (\hat{\mathbf{h}}, z)$ given a witness $\mathbf{x} \in \mathbb{Z}_p^{2\lambda}$, we compute $m = z \oplus \hat{\mathbf{h}}^{\mathbf{x}}$. It is easy to check correctness. For the security proof, see Sect. 4.3.

2.1.2 Bootstrapping Laconic OT

We will now provide a bootstrapping technique that constructs a laconic OT scheme with arbitrary compression factor from one with factor-2 compression. Let ℓOT_{const} denote a laconic OT scheme with factor-2 compression.

Bootstrapping the Hash Function via a Merkle Tree. A binary Merkle tree is a natural way to construct hash functions with an arbitrary compression factor from two-to-one hash functions, and this is exactly the route we pursue. A binary Merkle tree is constructed as follows: The database is split into blocks of λ bits, each of which forms the leaf of the tree. An interior node is computed as the hash value of its two children via a two-to-one hash function. This structure is defined recursively from the leaves to the root. When we reach the root node (of λ bits), its value is defined to be the (succinct) hash value or digest of the entire database. This procedure defines the hash function.

The next step is to define the laconic OT algorithms Send and Receive for the above hash function. Our first observation is that given the digest, the sender can transfer specific messages corresponding to the values of the left and right children of the root (via 2λ executions of $\ell OT_{\mathsf{const}}.\mathsf{Send}$). Hence, a naive approach for the sender is to output ℓOT_{const} encryptions for the path of nodes from the root to the leaf of interest. This approach runs into an immediate issue because to compute ℓOT_{const} encryptions at any layer other than the root, the sender needs to know the value at that internal node. However, in the scheme a sender only knows the value of the root and nothing else.

Traversing the Merkle Tree via Garbled Circuits. Our main idea to make the above naive idea work is via an interesting usage of garbled circuits. At a high level, the sender will output a sequence of garbled circuits (one per layer of the tree) to transfer messages corresponding to the path from the root to the leaf containing the L-th bit, so that the receiver can traverse the Merkle tree from the root to the leaf as illustrated in Fig. 2.

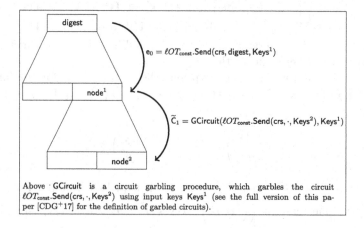

Above GCircuit is a circuit garbling procedure, which garbles the circuit $\ell OT_{\mathsf{const}}.\mathsf{Send}(\mathsf{crs}, \cdot, \mathsf{Keys}^2)$ using input keys Keys^1 (see the full version of this paper [CDG$^+$17] for the definition of garbled circuits).

Fig. 2. The bootstrapping step

In more detail, the construction works as follows: The Send algorithm outputs ℓOT_{const} encryptions using the root digest and a collection of garbled circuits, one per layer of the Merkle tree. The i-th circuit has a bit b hardwired in it, which specifies whether the path should go to the left or right child at the i-th layer. It takes as input a pair of sibling nodes ($node_0, node_1$) along the path at layer i and outputs ℓOT_{const} encryptions corresponding to nodes on the path at layer $i + 1$ w.r.t. $node_b$ as the hash value. Conceptually, the circuit computes ℓOT_{const} encryptions for the next layer.

The ℓOT_{const} encryptions at the root encrypt the input keys of the first garbled circuit. In the garbled circuit at layer i, the messages being encrypted/sent correspond to the input keys of the garbled circuit at layer $i + 1$. The last circuit takes two sibling leaves as input which contains $D[L]$, and outputs ℓOT_{const} encryptions of m_0 and m_1 corresponding to location L (among the 2λ locations).

Given a laconic OT ciphertext, which consists of ℓOT_{const} ciphertexts w.r.t. the root digest and a sequence of garbled circuits, the receiver can traverse the Merkle tree as follows. First he runs ℓOT_{const}.Receive for the ℓOT_{const} ciphertexts using as witness the children of the root, obtaining the input labels corresponding to these to be fed into the first garbled circuit. Next, he uses the input labels to evaluate the first garbled circuit, obtaining ℓOT_{const} ciphertexts for the second layer. He then runs ℓOT_{const}.Receive again for these ciphertexts using as witness the children of the second node on the path. This procedure continues till the last layer.

Security of the construction can be established using the sender security of ℓOT_{const}.Receive and simulation based security of the circuit garbling scheme.

Extension. Finally, for our RAM applications we need a slightly stronger primitive which we call *updatable laconic OT* that additionally allows for modifications/writes to the database while ensuring that the digest is updated in a consistent manner. The construction sketched in this paragraph can be modified to support this stronger notion. For a detailed description of this notion refer to Sect. 3.2.

2.2 Non-interactive Secure Computation on Large Inputs

The Circuit Setting. This is the most straightforward application of laconic OT. We will provide a non-interactive secure computation protocol where the receiver R, holding a large database D, publishes a short encoding of it such that any sender S, with private input x, can send a single message to reveal $C(x, D)$ to R. Here, C is the circuit being evaluated.

Recall the garbled circuit based approach to non-interactive secure computation, where R can publish the first message of a two-message oblivious transfer (OT) for his input D, and the sender responds with a garbled circuit for $C[x, \cdot]$ (with hardcoded input x) and sends the input labels corresponding to D via the second OT message. The downside of this protocol is that R's public message grows with the size of D, which could be substantially large.

We resolve this issue via our new primitive laconic OT. In our protocol, R's first message is the digest digest of his large database D. Next, the sender generates the garbled circuit for $C[x, \cdot]$ as before. It also transfers the labels for each location of D via laconic OT Send messages. Hence, by efficiency requirements of laconic OT, the length of R's public message is independent of the size of D. Moreover, sender privacy against a semi-honest receiver follows directly from the sender privacy of laconic OT and security of garbled circuits. To achieve receiver privacy, we can enhance the laconic OT with receiver privacy (discussed in Sect. 3.1).

The RAM Setting. This is the RAM version of the above application where S holds a RAM program P and R holds a large database D. As before, we want that (1) the length of R's first message is independent of $|D|$, (2) R's first message can be published and used by multiple senders, (3) the database is persistent for a sequence of programs for every sender, and (4) the computational complexity of both S and R per program execution grows only with running time of the corresponding program. For this application, we only achieve unprotected memory access (UMA) security against a corrupt receiver, i.e., the memory access pattern in the execution of $P^D(x)$ is leaked to the receiver. We achieve full security against a corrupt sender.

For simplicity, consider a read-only program such that each CPU step outputs the next location to be read based on the value read from last location. At a high level, since we want the sender's complexity to grow only with the running time t of the program, we cannot create a garbled circuit that takes D as input. Instead, we would go via the garbled RAM based approaches where we have a sequence of t garbled circuits where each circuit executes one CPU step. A CPU step circuit takes the current CPU state and the last bit read from the database D as input and outputs an updated state and a new location to be read. The new location would be read from the database and fed into the next CPU step. The most non-trivial part in all garbled RAM constructions is being able to compute the correct labels for the next circuit based on the value of $D[L]$, where L is the location being read. Since we are working with garbled circuits, it is crucial for security that the receiver does not learn two labels for any input wire. We solve this issue via laconic OT as follows.

For the simpler case of sender security, R publishes the short digest of D, which is fed into the first garbled circuit and this digest is passed along the sequence of garbled circuits. When a circuit wants to read a location L, it outputs the laconic OT ciphertexts which encrypt the input keys for the next circuit and use digest of D as the hash value.[9] Security against a corrupt receiver follows from the sender security of laconic OT and security of garbled circuits.

---

[9] We note that the above idea of using laconic OT also gives a conceptually very simple solution for UMA secure garbled RAM scheme [LO13]. Moreover, there is a general transformation [GHL+14] that converts any UMA secure garbled RAM into one with full security via the usage of symmetric key encryption and oblivious RAM. This would give a simplified construction of fully secure garbled RAM under DDH assumption.

To achieve security against a corrupt sender, R does not publishes digest in the clear. Instead, the labels for digest for the first circuit are transferred to R via regular OT.

Note that the garbling time of the sender as well as execution time of the receiver will grow only with the running time of the program. This follows from the efficiency requirements of laconic OT.

Above, we did not describe how we deal with general programs that also write to the database or memory. We achieve this via updatable laconic OT (for definition see Sect. 3.2), This allows for transferring the labels for updated digest (corresponding to the updated database) to the next circuit. For a formal description of our scheme for general RAM programs, see the full version of this paper [CDG+17].

2.3   Multi-hop Homomorphic Encryption for RAM Programs

Our model and problem — a bit more formally. We consider a scenario where a server S, holding an input x, publishes a public key pk and an encryption ct of x under pk. Now this ciphertext is passed on to a client Q that will compute a (possibly private) program P accessing memory D on the value encrypted in ct, obtaining another ciphertext ct'. Finally, we want that the server can use its secret key to recover $P^D(x)$ from the ciphertext ct' and $\widetilde{D}$, where $\widetilde{D}$ is an encrypted form of D that has been previously provided to S in a one-time setup phase. More generally, the computation could be performed by multiple clients $Q_1, \ldots, Q_n$. In this case, each client is required to place a pre-processed version of its database $\widetilde{D}_i$ with the server during setup. The computation itself could be performed in different sequences of the clients (for different extensions of the model, see the full version of this paper [CDG+17]). Examples of two such computation paths are shown in Fig. 1.

For security, we want IND-CPA security for server's input x. For honest clients, we want *program-privacy* as well as *data-privacy*, i.e., the evaluation does not leak anything beyond the output of the computation even when the adversary corrupts the server and any subset of the clients. We note that data-privacy is rather easy to achieve via encryption and ORAM. Hence we focus on the challenges of achieving UMA security for honest clients, i.e., the adversary is allowed to learn the database D as well as memory access pattern of P on D.

UMA secure multi-hop scheme. We first build on the ideas from non-interactive secure computation for RAM programs. Every client first passes its database to the server. Then in every round, the server sends an OT message for input x. We assume for simplicity that every client has an up-to-date digest of its own database. Next, the first client Q_1 generates a garbled program for P_1, say ct_1 and sends it to Q_2. Here, the garbled program consists of t_1 (t_1 is the running time of P_1) garbled circuits accessing D_1 via laconic OT as described in the previous application. Now, Q_2 appends its garbled program for P_2 to the end of ct_1 and generates ct_2 consisting of ct_1 and new garbled program. Note that P_2 takes the output of P_1 as input and hence, the output keys of the last

garbled circuit of P_1 have to be compatible with the input keys of the first garbled circuit of P_2 and so on. If we continue this procedure, after the last client
Q_n, we get a sequence of garbled circuits where the first t_1 circuits access D_1,
the next set accesses from D_2 and so on. Finally, the server S can evaluate the
sequence of garbled circuits given $D_1, \ldots, D_n$. It is easy to see that correctness
holds. But we have no security for clients.

The issue is similar to the issue pointed out by [GHV10] for the case of multi-
hop garbled circuits. If the client Q_{i-1} colludes with the server, then they can
learn both input labels for the garbled program of Q_i. To resolve this issue it
is crucial that Q_i re-randomizes the garbled circuits provided by Q_{i-1}. For this
we rely on re-randomizable garbled circuits provided by [GHV10], where given
a garbled circuit anyone can re-garble it such that functionality of the original
circuit is preserved while the re-randomized garbled circuit is unrecognizable
even to the party who generated it. In our protocol we use re-randomizable
garbled circuits but we stumble upon the following issue.

Recall that in the RAM application above, a garbled circuit outputs the
laconic OT ciphertexts corresponding to the input keys of the next circuit. Hence,
the input keys of the $(\tau+1)$-th circuit have to be hardwired inside the τ-th circuit.
Since all of these circuits will be re-randomized for security, for correctness we
require that we transform the hardwired keys in a manner consistent with the
future re-randomization. But for security, Q_{i-1} does not know the randomness
that will be used by Q_i.

Our first idea to resolve this issue is as follows: The circuits generated by Q_{i-1}
will take additional inputs $s_i, \ldots s_n$ which are the randomness used by future

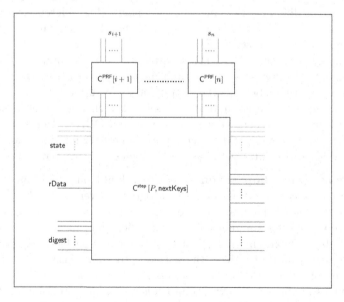

Fig. 3. One step circuit for P_i along with the attached PRF circuits generated by Q_i.

parties for their re-randomization procedure. Since we are in the non-interactive setting, we cannot run an OT protocol between clients Q_{i-1} and later clients. We resolve this issue by putting the first message of OT for s_j in the public key of client Q_j and client Q_{i-1} will send the OT second messages along with ct_{i-1}. We do not want the clients' public keys to grow with the running time of the programs, hence, we think of s_j as PRF keys and each circuit re-randomization will invoke the PRF on a unique input.

The above approach causes a subtle issue in the security proof. Suppose, for simplicity, that client Q_i is the only honest client. When arguing security, we want to simulate all the garbled circuits in ct_i. To rely on the security of re-randomization, we need to replace the output of the PRF with key s_i with uniform random values but this key is fed as input to the circuits of the previous clients. We note that this is not a circularity issue but makes arguing security hard. We solve this issue as follows: Instead of feeding in PRF keys directly to the garbled circuits, we feed in corresponding outputs of the PRF. We generate the PRF output via a bunch of PRF circuits that take the PRF keys as input (see Fig. 3). Now during simulation, we will first simulate these PRF circuits, followed by the simulation of the main circuits. We describe the scheme formally in our full version [CDG+17].

3   Laconic Oblivious Transfer

In this section, we will introduce a primitive we call *Laconic OT* (or, ℓOT for short). We will start by describing laconic OT and then provide an extension of it to the notion of updatable laconic OT.

3.1   Laconic OT

Definition 1 (Laconic OT). *A laconic OT (ℓOT) scheme syntactically consists of four algorithms* crsGen, Hash, Send *and* Receive.

- crs $\leftarrow$ crsGen(1^λ). *It takes as input the security parameter 1^λ and outputs a common reference string* crs.
- (digest, $\hat{D}$) $\leftarrow$ Hash(crs, D). *It takes as input a common reference string* crs *and a database $D \in \{0,1\}^*$ and outputs a digest* digest *of the database and a state $\hat{D}$.*
- e $\leftarrow$ Send(crs, digest, L, m_0, m_1). *It takes as input a common reference string* crs, *a digest* digest, *a database location $L \in \mathbb{N}$ and two messages m_0 and m_1 of length λ, and outputs a ciphertext* e.
- $m \leftarrow$ Receive$^{\hat{D}}$(crs, e, L). *This is a RAM algorithm with random read access to $\hat{D}$. It takes as input a common reference string* crs, *a ciphertext* e, *and a database location $L \in \mathbb{N}$. It outputs a message m.*

We require the following properties of an ℓOT scheme (crsGen, Hash, Send, Receive).

- **Correctness:** We require that it holds for any database D of size at most $M = \mathsf{poly}(\lambda)$ for any polynomial function $\mathsf{poly}(\cdot)$, any memory location $L \in [M]$, and any pair of messages $(m_0, m_1) \in \{0,1\}^\lambda \times \{0,1\}^\lambda$ that

$$
\Pr\left[m = m_{D[L]} \middle| \begin{array}{ll} \mathsf{crs} & \leftarrow \mathsf{crsGen}(1^\lambda) \\ (\mathsf{digest}, \hat{D}) & \leftarrow \mathsf{Hash}(\mathsf{crs}, D) \\ e & \leftarrow \mathsf{Send}(\mathsf{crs}, \mathsf{digest}, L, m_0, m_1) \\ m & \leftarrow \mathsf{Receive}^{\hat{D}}(\mathsf{crs}, e, L) \end{array} \right] = 1,
$$

  where the probability is taken over the random choices made by crsGen and Send.

- **Sender Privacy Against Semi-Honest Receivers:** There exists a PPT simulator ℓOTSim such that the following holds. For any database D of size at most $M = \mathsf{poly}(\lambda)$ for any polynomial function $\mathsf{poly}(\cdot)$, any memory location $L \in [M]$, and any pair of messages $(m_0, m_1) \in \{0,1\}^\lambda \times \{0,1\}^\lambda$, let $\mathsf{crs} \leftarrow \mathsf{crsGen}(1^\lambda)$ and $\mathsf{digest} \leftarrow \mathsf{Hash}(\mathsf{crs}, D)$. Then it holds that

$$
(\mathsf{crs}, \mathsf{Send}(\mathsf{crs}, \mathsf{digest}, L, m_0, m_1)) \stackrel{c}{\approx} (\mathsf{crs}, \ell\mathsf{OTSim}(D, L, m_{D[L]})) .
$$

- **Efficiency Requirement:** The length of digest is a fixed polynomial in λ independent of the size of the database; we will assume for simplicity that $|\mathsf{digest}| = \lambda$. Moreover, the algorithm Hash runs in time $|D| \cdot \mathsf{poly}(\log |D|, \lambda)$, Send and Receive run in time $\mathsf{poly}(\log |D|, \lambda)$.

Receiver Privacy. In the above definition, we do not require receiver privacy as opposed to standard oblivious transfer, namely, no security guarantee is provided against a cheating (semi-honest) sender. This is mostly for ease of exposition. We would like to point out that adding receiver privacy (i.e., standard simulation based security against a semi-honest sender) to laconic OT can be done in a straightforward way. Instead of sending digest directly from the receiver to the sender and sending e back to the receiver, the two parties compute Send together via a two-round secure 2PC protocol, where the input of the receiver is digest and the input of the sender is (L, m_0, m_1), and only the receiver obtains the output e. This can be done using standard two-message OT and garbled circuits.

Multiple executions of Send that share the same digest. Notice that since the common reference string is public (i.e., not chosen by the simulator), the sender can involve Send function multiple times while still ensuring that security can be argued from the above definition (for the case of single execution) via a standard hybrid argument.

It will be convenient to use the following shorthand notations (generalizing the above notions) to run laconic OT for every single element in a database. Let $\mathsf{Keys} = ((\mathsf{Key}_{1,0}, \mathsf{Key}_{1,1}), \ldots, (\mathsf{Key}_{M,0}, \mathsf{Key}_{M,1}))$ be a list of $M = |D|$ key-pairs, where each key is of length λ. Then we will define

$\mathsf{Send}(\mathsf{crs}, \mathsf{digest}, \mathsf{Keys})$

$= \left(\mathsf{Send}(\mathsf{crs}, \mathsf{digest}, 1, \mathsf{Key}_{1,0}, \mathsf{Key}_{1,1}), \ldots, \mathsf{Send}(\mathsf{crs}, \mathsf{digest}, M, \mathsf{Key}_{M,0}, \mathsf{Key}_{M,1})\right).$

Likewise, for a vector $\mathbf{e} = (\mathbf{e}_1, \ldots, \mathbf{e}_M)$ of ciphertexts define

$\mathsf{Receive}^{\hat{D}}(\mathsf{crs}, \mathbf{e}) = \left(\mathsf{Receive}^{\hat{D}}(\mathsf{crs}, \mathbf{e}_1, 1), \ldots, \mathsf{Receive}^{\hat{D}}(\mathsf{crs}, \mathbf{e}_M, M)\right).$

Similarly, let $\mathsf{Labels} = \mathsf{Keys}_D = (\mathsf{Key}_{1,D[1]}, \ldots, \mathsf{Key}_{M,D[M]})$, and define

$\ell\mathsf{OTSim}(\mathsf{crs}, D, \mathsf{Labels})$

$= \left(\ell\mathsf{OTSim}(\mathsf{crs}, D, 1, \mathsf{Key}_{1,D[1]}), \ldots, \ell\mathsf{OTSim}(\mathsf{crs}, D, M, \mathsf{Key}_{M,D[M]})\right).$

By the sender security for multiple executions, we have that

$$(\mathsf{crs}, \mathsf{Send}(\mathsf{crs}, \mathsf{digest}, \mathsf{Keys})) \overset{c}{\approx} (\mathsf{crs}, \ell\mathsf{OTSim}(\mathsf{crs}, D, \mathsf{Labels})).$$

3.2 Updatable Laconic OT

For our applications, we will need a version of laconic OT for which the receiver's short commitment digest to his database can be updated quickly (in time much smaller than the size of the database) when a bit of the database changes. We call this primitive supporting this functionality updatable laconic OT and define more formally below. At a high level, updatable laconic OT comes with an additional pair of algorithms SendWrite and ReceiveWrite which transfer the keys for an updated digest digest^* to the receiver. For convenience, we will define ReceiveWrite such that it also performs the write in $\hat{D}$.

Definition 2 (Updatable Laconic OT). *An updatable laconic OT (updatable ℓOT) scheme consists of algorithms* crsGen, Hash, Send, Receive *as per Definition 1 and additionally two algorithms* SendWrite *and* ReceiveWrite *with the following syntax.*

- $\mathbf{e}_w \leftarrow \mathsf{SendWrite}\left(\mathsf{crs}, \mathsf{digest}, L, b, \{m_{j,0}, m_{j,1}\}_{j=1}^{|\mathsf{digest}|}\right).$ *It takes as input the common reference string* crs, *a digest* digest, *a location* $L \in \mathbb{N}$, *a bit* $b \in \{0,1\}$ *to be written, and* $|\mathsf{digest}|$ *pairs of messages* $\{m_{j,0}, m_{j,1}\}_{j=1}^{|\mathsf{digest}|}$, *where each* $m_{j,c}$ *is of length* λ. *And it outputs a ciphertext* $\mathbf{e}_w$.
- $\{m_j\}_{j=1}^{|\mathsf{digest}|} \leftarrow \mathsf{ReceiveWrite}^{\hat{D}}(\mathsf{crs}, L, b, \mathbf{e}_w).$ *This is a RAM algorithm with random read/write access to* $\hat{D}$. *It takes as input the common reference string* crs, *a location* L, *a bit* $b \in \{0,1\}$ *and a ciphertext* $\mathbf{e}_w$. *It updates the state* $\hat{D}$ *(such that* $D[L] = b$*) and outputs messages* $\{m_j\}_{j=1}^{|\mathsf{digest}|}$.

We require the following properties on top of properties of a laconic OT scheme.

- **Correctness With Regard To Writes:** *For any database D of size at most $M = \mathsf{poly}(\lambda)$ for any polynomial function $\mathsf{poly}(\cdot)$, any memory location $L \in [M]$, any bit $b \in \{0,1\}$, and any messages $\{m_{j,0}, m_{j,1}\}_{j=1}^{|\mathsf{digest}|}$ of length λ, the following holds. Let D^* be identical to D, except that $D^*[L] = b$,*

$$
\Pr\left[
\begin{array}{l}
m'_j = m_{j,\mathsf{digest}^*_j} \\
\forall j \in [|\mathsf{digest}|]
\end{array}
\middle|
\begin{array}{rl}
\mathsf{crs} & \leftarrow \mathsf{crsGen}(1^\lambda) \\
(\mathsf{digest}, \hat{\mathsf{D}}) & \leftarrow \mathsf{Hash}(\mathsf{crs}, D) \\
(\mathsf{digest}^*, \hat{\mathsf{D}}^*) & \leftarrow \mathsf{Hash}(\mathsf{crs}, D^*) \\
\mathsf{e_w} & \leftarrow \mathsf{SendWrite}\left(\mathsf{crs}, \mathsf{digest}, L, b, \{m_{j,0}, m_{j,1}\}_{j=1}^{|\mathsf{digest}|}\right) \\
\{m'_j\}_{j=1}^{|\mathsf{digest}|} & \leftarrow \mathsf{ReceiveWrite}^{\hat{\mathsf{D}}}(\mathsf{crs}, L, b, \mathsf{e_w})
\end{array}
\right] = 1,
$$

where the probability is taken over the random choices made by crsGen and $\mathsf{SendWrite}$. Furthermore, we require that the execution of $\mathsf{ReceiveWrite}^{\hat{\mathsf{D}}}$ above updates $\hat{\mathsf{D}}$ to $\hat{\mathsf{D}}^*$. (Note that digest is included in $\hat{\mathsf{D}}$, hence digest is also updated to digest^*.)

- **Sender Privacy Against Semi-Honest Receivers With Regard To Writes:** *There exists a PPT simulator $\ell\mathsf{OTSimWrite}$ such that the following holds. For any database D of size at most $M = \mathsf{poly}(\lambda)$ for any polynomial function $\mathsf{poly}(\cdot)$, any memory location $L \in [M]$, any bit $b \in \{0,1\}$, and any messages $\{m_{j,0}, m_{j,1}\}_{j=1}^{|\mathsf{digest}|}$ of length λ, let $\mathsf{crs} \leftarrow \mathsf{crsGen}(1^\lambda)$, $(\mathsf{digest}, \hat{\mathsf{D}}) \leftarrow \mathsf{Hash}(\mathsf{crs}, D)$, and $(\mathsf{digest}^*, \hat{\mathsf{D}}^*) \leftarrow \mathsf{Hash}(\mathsf{crs}, D^*)$, where D^* is identical to D except that $D^*[L] = b$. Then it holds that*

$$
\begin{aligned}
&\left(\mathsf{crs}, \mathsf{SendWrite}(\mathsf{crs}, \mathsf{digest}, L, b, \{m_{j,0}, m_{j,1}\}_{j=1}^{|\mathsf{digest}|})\right) \\
&\stackrel{\mathrm{c}}{\approx} \left(\mathsf{crs}, \ell\mathsf{OTSimWrite}\left(\mathsf{crs}, D, L, b, \{m_{j,\mathsf{digest}^*_j}\}_{j \in [|\mathsf{digest}|]}\right)\right).
\end{aligned}
$$

- **Efficiency Requirements:** *We require that both $\mathsf{SendWrite}$ and $\mathsf{ReceiveWrite}$ run in time $\mathsf{poly}(\log|D|, \lambda)$.*

4   Laconic Oblivious Transfer with Factor-2 Compression

In this section, based on the DDH assumption we will construct a laconic OT scheme for which the hash function Hash compresses a database of length 2λ into a digest of length λ. We would refer to this primitive as laconic OT with factor-2 compression. We note that, subsequent to our work, the factor-2 compression construction has been simplified by Döttling and Garg [DG17] (another alternative simplification can be obtained using [AIKW13]). We refer the reader to [DG17] for the simpler construction and preserve the older construction here.

We will first construct the following two primitives as building blocks: (1) a somewhere statistically binding (SSB) hash function, and (2) a hash proof system that allows for proving knowledge of preimage bits for this SSB hash function. We will then present the ℓOT scheme with factor-2 compression in Sect. 4.4.

4.1 Somewhere Statistically Binding Hash Functions and Hash Proof Systems

In this section, we give definitions of somewhere statistically binding (SSB) hash functions [HW15] and hash proof systems [CS98]. For simplicity, we will only define SSB hash functions that compress 2λ values in the domain into λ bits. The more general definition works analogously.

Definition 3 (Somewhere Statistically Binding Hashing). *An SSB hash function* SSBH *consists of three algorithms* crsGen, bindingCrsGen *and* Hash *with the following syntax.*

- crs $\leftarrow$ crsGen(1^λ). *It takes the security parameter λ as input and outputs a common reference string* crs.
- crs $\leftarrow$ bindingCrsGen($1^\lambda, i$). *It takes as input the security parameter λ and an index $i \in [2\lambda]$, and outputs a common reference string* crs.
- $y \leftarrow$ Hash(crs, x). *For some domain $\mathfrak{D}$, it takes as input a common reference string* crs *and a string $x \in \mathfrak{D}^{2\lambda}$, and outputs a string $y \in \{0,1\}^\lambda$.*

We require the following properties of an SSB hash function.

- ***Statistically Binding at Position*** i: *For every $i \in [2\lambda]$ and an overwhelming fraction of* crs *in the support of* bindingCrsGen($1^\lambda, i$) *and every $x \in \mathfrak{D}^{2\lambda}$, we have that* (crs, Hash(crs, x)) *uniquely determines x_i. More formally, for all $x' \in \mathfrak{D}^{2\lambda}$ such that $x_i \neq x'_i$ we have that* Hash(crs, x') $\neq$ Hash(crs, x).
- ***Index Hiding:*** *It holds for all $i \in [2\lambda]$ that* crsGen(1^λ) $\overset{c}{\approx}$ bindingCrsGen($1^\lambda, i$), *i.e., common reference strings generated by* crsGen *and* bindingCrsGen *are computationally indistinguishable.*

Next, we define hash proof systems [CS98] that are designated verifier proof systems that allow for proving that the given problem instance in some language. We give the formal definition as follows.

Definition 4 (Hash Proof System). *Let $\mathcal{L}_z \subseteq \mathcal{M}_z$ be an NP-language residing in a universe $\mathcal{M}_z$, both parametrized by some parameter z. Moreover, let $\mathcal{L}_z$ be characterized by an efficiently computable witness-relation $\mathcal{R}$, namely, for all $x \in M_z$ it holds that $x \in \mathcal{L}_z \Leftrightarrow \exists w : \mathcal{R}(x, w) = 1$. A hash proof system* HPS *for $\mathcal{L}_z$ consists of three algorithms* KeyGen, $\mathsf{H}_{\text{public}}$ *and* $\mathsf{H}_{\text{secret}}$ *with the following syntax.*

- (pk, sk) $\leftarrow$ KeyGen($1^\lambda, z$): *Takes as input the security parameter λ and a parameter z, and outputs a public-key and secret key pair* (pk, sk).
- $y \leftarrow \mathsf{H}_{\text{public}}$(pk, x, w): *Takes as input a public key* pk, *an instance $x \in \mathcal{L}_z$, and a witness w, and outputs a value y.*
- $y \leftarrow \mathsf{H}_{\text{secret}}$(sk, x): *Takes as input a secret key* sk *and an instance $x \in M_z$, and outputs a value y.*

We require the following properties of a hash proof system.

- **Perfect Completeness:** *For every z, every $(\mathsf{pk}, \mathsf{sk})$ in the support of* $\mathsf{KeyGen}(1^\lambda, z)$*, and every $x \in \mathcal{L}_z$ with witness w (i.e., $\mathcal{R}(x, w) = 1$), it holds that*

$$\mathsf{H}_{\mathsf{public}}(\mathsf{pk}, x, w) = \mathsf{H}_{\mathsf{secret}}(\mathsf{sk}, x).$$

- **Perfect Soundness:** *For every z and every $x \in M_z \setminus \mathcal{L}_z$, let $(\mathsf{pk}, \mathsf{sk}) \leftarrow$* $\mathsf{KeyGen}(1^\lambda, z)$*, then it holds that*

$$(z, \mathsf{pk}, \mathsf{H}_{\mathsf{secret}}(\mathsf{sk}, x)) \equiv (z, \mathsf{pk}, u),$$

where u is distributed uniformly random in the range of $\mathsf{H}_{\mathsf{secret}}$. Here, $\equiv$ denotes distributional equivalence.

4.2 HPS-friendly SSB Hashing

In this section, we will construct an HPS-friendly SSB hash function that supports a hash proof system. In particular, there is a hash proof system that enables proving that a certain bit of the pre-image of a hash-value has a certain fixed value (in our case, either 0 or 1).

We start with some notations. Let $(\mathbb{G}, \cdot)$ be a cyclic group of order p with generator g. Let $\mathbf{M} \in \mathbb{Z}_p^{m \times n}$ be a matrix. We will denote by $\hat{\mathbf{M}} = g^{\mathbf{M}} \in \mathbb{G}^{m \times n}$ the element-wise exponentiation of g with the elements of $\mathbf{M}$. We also define $\hat{\mathbf{L}} = \hat{\mathbf{H}}^{\mathbf{M}} \in \mathbb{G}^{m \times k}$, where $\hat{\mathbf{H}} \in \mathbb{G}^{m \times n}$ and $\mathbf{M} \in \mathbb{Z}_p^{n \times k}$ as follows: Each element $\hat{\mathbf{L}}_{i,j} = \prod_{k=1}^n \hat{\mathbf{H}}_{i,k}^{\mathbf{M}_{k,j}}$ (intuitively this operation corresponds to matrix multiplication in the exponent). This is well-defined and efficiently computable.

Computational Assumptions. In the following, we first define the computational problems on which we will base the security of our HPS-friendly SSB hash function.

Definition 5 (The Decisional Diffie-Hellman (DDH) Problem). *Let $(\mathbb{G}, \cdot)$ be a cyclic group of prime order p and with generator g. Let a, b, c be sampled uniformly at random from $\mathbb{Z}_p$ (i.e., $a, b, c \xleftarrow{\$} \mathbb{Z}_p$). The DDH problem asks to distinguish the distributions (g, g^a, g^b, g^{ab}) and (g, g^a, g^b, g^c).*

Definition 6 (Matrix Rank Problem). *Let m, n be integers and let $\mathbb{Z}_p^{m \times n; r}$ be the set of all $m \times n$ matrices over $\mathbb{Z}_p$ with rank r. Further, let $1 \leq r_1 < r_2 \leq \min(m, n)$. The goal of the matrix rank problem, denoted as* $\mathsf{MatrixRank}(\mathbb{G}, m, n, r_1, r_2)$*, is to distinguish the distributions $g^{\mathbf{M}_1}$ and $g^{\mathbf{M}_2}$, where $\mathbf{M}_1 \xleftarrow{\$} \mathbb{Z}_p^{m \times n; r_1}$ and $\mathbf{M}_2 \xleftarrow{\$} \mathbb{Z}_p^{m \times n; r_2}$.*

In a recent result by Villar [Vil12] it was shown that the matrix rank problem can be reduced almost tightly to the DDH problem.

Theorem 1 ([Vil12] Theorem 1, simplified). *Assume there exists a PPT distinguisher $\mathcal{D}$ that solves* MatrixRank$(\mathbb{G}, m, n, r_1, r_2)$ *problem with advantage ϵ. Then, there exists a PPT distinguisher $\mathcal{D}'$ (running in almost time as $\mathcal{D}$) that solves* DDH *problem over $\mathbb{G}$ with advantage at least $\frac{\epsilon}{\lceil \log_2(r_2/r_1) \rceil}$.*

We next give the construction of an HPS-friendly SSB hash function.

Construction. Our construction builds on the scheme of Okamoto et al. [OPWW15]. We will not delve into the details of their scheme and directly jump into our construction.

Let n be an integer such that $n = 2\lambda$, and let $(\mathbb{G}, \cdot)$ be a cyclic group of order p and with generator g. Let $\mathbf{T}_i \in \mathbb{Z}_p^{2 \times n}$ be a matrix which is zero everywhere except the i-th column, and the i-th column is equal to $\mathbf{t} = (0, 1)^\top$. The three algorithms of the SSB hash function are defined as follows.

- crsGen(1^λ): Pick a uniformly random matrix $\mathbf{H} \xleftarrow{\$} \mathbb{Z}_p^{2 \times n}$ and output $\hat{\mathbf{H}} = g^{\mathbf{H}}$.
- bindingCrsGen$(1^\lambda, i)$: Pick a uniformly random vector $(w_1, w_2)^\top = \mathbf{w} \xleftarrow{\$} \mathbb{Z}_p^2$ with the restriction that $w_1 = 1$, pick a uniformly random vector $\mathbf{a} \xleftarrow{\$} \mathbb{Z}_p^n$ and set $\mathbf{A} \leftarrow \mathbf{w} \cdot \mathbf{a}^\top$. Set $\mathbf{H} \leftarrow \mathbf{T}_i + \mathbf{A}$ and output $\hat{\mathbf{H}} = g^{\mathbf{H}}$.
- Hash$(\text{crs}, \mathbf{x})$: Parse $\mathbf{x}$ as a vector in $\mathfrak{D}^n$ ($\mathfrak{D} = \mathbb{Z}_p$) and parse crs as $\hat{\mathbf{H}}$. Compute $\mathbf{y} \in \mathbb{G}^2$ as $\mathbf{y} = \hat{\mathbf{H}}^{\mathbf{x}}$. Parse $\mathbf{y}$ as a binary string and output the result.

Compression. Notice that we can get factor two compression for an input space $\{0, 1\}^{2\lambda}$ by restricting the domain to $\mathfrak{D}' = \{0, 1\} \subset \mathfrak{D}$. The input length $n = 2\lambda$, where λ is set to be twice the number of bits in the bit representation of a group element in $\mathbb{G}$. In the following we will assume that $n = 2\lambda$ and that the bit-representation size of a group element in $\mathbb{G}$ is $\frac{\lambda}{2}$.

We will first show that the distributions crsGen(1^λ) and bindingCrsGen$(1^\lambda, i)$ are computationally indistinguishable for every index $i \in [n]$, given that the DDH problem is computationally hard in the group $\mathbb{G}$.

Lemma 1 (Index Hiding). *Assume that the* MatrixRank$(\mathbb{G}, 2, n, 1, 2)$ *problem is hard. Then the distributions* crsGen(1^λ) *and* bindingCrsGen$(1^\lambda, i)$ *are computationally indistinguishable, for every $i \in [n]$.*

Proof. Assume there exists a PPT distinguisher $\mathcal{D}$ that distinguishes the distributions crsGen(1^λ) and bindingCrsGen$(1^\lambda, i)$ with non-negligible advantage ϵ. We will construct a PPT distinguisher $\mathcal{D}'$ that distinguishes MatrixRank$(\mathbb{G}, 2, n, 1, 2)$ with non-negligible advantage.

The distinguisher $\mathcal{D}'$ does the following on input $\hat{\mathbf{M}} \in \mathbb{G}^{2 \times n}$. It computes $\hat{\mathbf{H}} \in \mathbb{G}^{2 \times n}$ as element-wise multiplication of $\hat{\mathbf{M}}$ and $g^{\mathbf{T}_i}$ and runs $\mathcal{D}$ on $\hat{\mathbf{H}}$. If $\mathcal{D}$ outputs crsGen, then $\mathcal{D}'$ outputs rank 2, otherwise $\mathcal{D}'$ outputs rank 1.

We will now show that $\mathcal{D}'$ also has non-negligible advantage. Write $\mathcal{D}'$'s input as $\hat{\mathbf{M}} = g^{\mathbf{M}}$. If $\mathbf{M}$ is chosen uniformly random with rank 2, then $\mathbf{M}$ is uniform in $\mathbb{Z}_p^{2 \times n}$ with overwhelming probability. Hence with overwhelming probability, $\mathbf{M} + \mathbf{T}_i$ is also distributed uniformly random and it follows that $\hat{\mathbf{H}} = g^{\mathbf{M}+\mathbf{T}_i}$ is uniformly random in $\mathbb{G}^{2 \times n}$ which is identical to the distribution generated by crsGen(1^λ). On the other hand, if $\mathbf{M}$ is chosen uniformly random with rank 1, then there exists a vector $\mathbf{w} \in \mathbb{Z}_p^2$ such that each column of $\mathbf{M}$ can be written as $a_i \cdot \mathbf{w}$. We can assume that the first element w_1 of $\mathbf{w}$ is 1, since the case $w_1 = 0$ happens only with probability $1/p = \mathsf{negl}(\lambda)$ and if $w_1 \neq 0$ we can replace all a_i by $a_i' = a_i \cdot w_1$ and replace w_i by $w_i' = \frac{w_i}{w_1}$. Thus, we can write $\mathbf{M}$ as $\mathbf{M} = \mathbf{w} \cdot \mathbf{a}^\top$ and consequently $\hat{\mathbf{H}}$ as $\hat{\mathbf{H}} = g^{\mathbf{w} \cdot \mathbf{a}^\top + \mathbf{T}_i}$. Notice that $\mathbf{a}$ is uniformly distributed, hence $\hat{\mathbf{H}}$ is identical to the distribution generated by bindingCrsGen($1^\lambda, i$). Since $\mathcal{D}$ can distinguish the distributions crsGen(1^λ) and bindingCrsGen($1^\lambda, i$) with non-negligible advantage ϵ, $\mathcal{D}'$ can distinguish MatrixRank($\mathbb{G}, 2, n, 1, 2$) with advantage $\epsilon - \mathsf{negl}(\lambda)$, which contradicts the hardness of MatrixRank($\mathbb{G}, 2, n, 1, 2$).

A corollary of Lemma 1 is that for all $i, j \in [n]$ the distributions bindingCrsGen($1^\lambda, i$) and bindingCrsGen($1^\lambda, j$) are indistinguishable, stated as follows.

Corollary 1. *Assume the* MatrixRank($\mathbb{G}, 2, n, 1, 2$) *problem is computationally hard. Then it holds for all* $i, j \in [n]$ *that* bindingCrsGen($1^\lambda, i$) *and* bindingCrsGen($1^\lambda, j$) *are computationally indistinguishable.*

We next show that if the common reference string crs $= \hat{\mathbf{H}}$ is generated by bindingCrsGen($1^\lambda, i$), then the hash value Hash(crs, $\mathbf{x}$) is statistically binded to x_i.

Lemma 2 (Statistically Binding at Position i). *For every* $i \in [n]$, *every* $\mathbf{x} \in \mathbb{Z}_p^n$, *and all choices of* crs *in the support of* bindingCrsGen($1^\lambda, i$) *we have that for every* $\mathbf{x}' \in \mathbb{Z}_p^n$ *such that* $x_i' \neq x_i$, Hash(crs, $\mathbf{x}$) $\neq$ Hash(crs, $\mathbf{x}'$).

Proof. We first write crs as $\hat{\mathbf{H}} = g^{\mathbf{H}} = g^{\mathbf{w} \cdot \mathbf{a}^\top + \mathbf{T}_i}$ and Hash(crs, $\mathbf{x}$) as Hash($\hat{\mathbf{H}}, \mathbf{x}$) $= g^{\mathbf{y}} = g^{\mathbf{H} \cdot \mathbf{x}}$. Thus, by taking the discrete logarithm with basis g our task is to demonstrate that there exists a unique x_i from $\mathbf{H} = \mathbf{w} \cdot \mathbf{a}^\top + \mathbf{T}_i$ and $\mathbf{y} = \mathbf{H} \cdot \mathbf{x}$. Observe that

$$\mathbf{y} = \mathbf{H} \cdot \mathbf{x} = (\mathbf{w} \cdot \mathbf{a}^\top + \mathbf{T}_i) \cdot \mathbf{x} = \mathbf{w} \cdot \langle \mathbf{a}, \mathbf{x} \rangle + \mathbf{T}_i \cdot \mathbf{x}$$

$$= \begin{pmatrix} 1 \\ w_2 \end{pmatrix} \cdot \langle \mathbf{a}, \mathbf{x} \rangle + \begin{pmatrix} 0 \\ 1 \end{pmatrix} \cdot x_i,$$

where $\langle \mathbf{a}, \mathbf{x} \rangle$ is the inner product of $\mathbf{a}$ and $\mathbf{x}$. If $\mathbf{a} \neq \mathbf{0}$, then we can use any non-zero element of $\mathbf{a}$ to compute w_2 from $\mathbf{H}$, and recover x_i by computing $x_i = y_2 - w_2 \cdot y_1$; otherwise $\mathbf{a} = \mathbf{0}$, so $x_i = y_2$.

4.3   A Hash Proof System for Knowledge of Preimage Bits

In this section, we give our desired hash proof systems. In particular, we need a hash proof system for membership in a subspace of a vector space. In our proof we need the following technical lemma.

Lemma 3. *Let* $\mathbf{M} \in \mathbb{Z}_p^{m \times n}$ *be a matrix. Let* $\mathsf{colsp}(\mathbf{M}) = \{\mathbf{M} \cdot \mathbf{x} \mid \mathbf{x} \in \mathbb{Z}_p^n\}$ *be its column space, and* $\mathsf{rowsp}(\mathbf{M}) = \{\mathbf{x}^\top \cdot \mathbf{M} \mid \mathbf{x} \in \mathbb{Z}_p^m\}$ *be its row space. Assume that* $\mathbf{y} \in \mathbb{Z}_p^m$ *and* $\mathbf{y} \notin \mathsf{colsp}(\mathbf{M})$. *Let* $\mathbf{r} \xleftarrow{\$} \mathbb{Z}_p^m$ *be chosen uniformly at random. Then it holds that*

$$(\mathbf{M}, \mathbf{y}, \mathbf{r}^\top \mathbf{M}, \mathbf{r}^\top \mathbf{y}) \equiv (\mathbf{M}, \mathbf{y}, \mathbf{r}^\top \mathbf{M}, u),$$

where $u \xleftarrow{\$} \mathbb{Z}_p$ *is distributed uniformly and independently of* $\mathbf{r}$. *Here,* $\equiv$ *denotes distributional equivalence.*

Proof. For any $\mathbf{t} \in \mathsf{rowsp}(\mathbf{M})$ and $s \in \mathbb{Z}_p$, consider following linear equation system

$$\begin{cases} \mathbf{r}^\top \mathbf{M} = \mathbf{t} \\ \mathbf{r}^\top \mathbf{y} = s \end{cases}.$$

Let $\mathcal{N}$ be the left null space of $\mathbf{M}$. We know that $\mathbf{y} \notin \mathsf{colsp}(\mathbf{M})$, hence $\mathbf{M}$ has rank $\leq m - 1$, therefore $\mathcal{N}$ has dimension ≥ 1. Let $\mathbf{r}_0$ be an arbitrary solution for $\mathbf{r}^\top \mathbf{M} = \mathbf{t}$, and let $\mathbf{n}$ be a vector in $\mathcal{N}$ such that $\mathbf{n}^\top \mathbf{y} \neq \mathbf{0}$ (there must be such a vector since $\mathbf{y} \notin \mathsf{colsp}(\mathbf{M})$). Then there exists a solution $\mathbf{r}$ for the above linear equation system, that is,

$$\mathbf{r} = \mathbf{r}_0 + (\mathbf{n}^\top \mathbf{y})^{-1} \cdot (s - \mathbf{r}_0^\top \mathbf{y}) \cdot \mathbf{n},$$

where $(\mathbf{n}^\top \mathbf{y})^{-1}$ is the multiplicative inverse of $\mathbf{n}^\top \mathbf{y}$ in $\mathbb{Z}_p$. Then two cases arise: (i) column vectors of $(\mathbf{M} \ \mathbf{y})$ are full-rank, or (ii) not. In this first case, there is a unique solution for $\mathbf{r}$. In the second case the solution space has the same size as the left null space of $(\mathbf{M} \ \mathbf{y})$. Therefore, in both cases, the number of solutions for $\mathbf{r}$ is the same for every $(\mathbf{t}, s)$ pair.

As $\mathbf{r}$ is chosen uniformly at random, all pairs $(\mathbf{t}, s) \in \mathsf{rowsp}(\mathbf{M}) \times \mathbb{Z}_p$ have the same probability of occurrence and the claim follows.

Construction. Fix a matrix $\hat{\mathbf{H}} \in \mathbb{G}^{2 \times n}$ and an index $i \in [n]$. We will construct a hash proof system $\mathsf{HPS} = (\mathsf{KeyGen}, \mathsf{H_{public}}, \mathsf{H_{secret}})$ for the following language $\mathcal{L}_{\hat{\mathbf{H}},i}$:

$$\mathcal{L}_{\hat{\mathbf{H}},i} = \{(\hat{\mathbf{y}}, b) \in \mathbb{G}^2 \times \{0,1\} \mid \exists \mathbf{x} \in \mathbb{Z}_p^n \text{ s.t. } \hat{\mathbf{y}} = \hat{\mathbf{H}}^{\mathbf{x}} \text{ and } x_i = b\}.$$

Note that in our hash proof system we only enforce that a single specified bit is b, where $b \in \{0,1\}$. However, our hash proof system does not place any requirement on the value used at any of the other locations. In fact the values used at the other locations may actually be from the full domain $\mathfrak{D}$ (i.e., $\mathbb{Z}_p$). Observe that the formal definition of the language $\mathcal{L}_{\hat{\mathbf{H}},i}$ above incorporates this difference in how the honest computation of the hash function is performed and what the hash proof system is supposed to prove.

For ease of exposition, it will be convenient to work with a matrix $\hat{\mathbf{H}}' \in \mathbb{G}_p^{3 \times n}$:

$$\hat{\mathbf{H}}' = \begin{pmatrix} \hat{\mathbf{H}} \\ g^{\mathbf{e}_i^\top} \end{pmatrix},$$

where $\mathbf{e}_i \in \mathbb{Z}_p^n$ is the i-th unit vector, with all elements equal to zero except the ith one which is equal to one.

- $\mathsf{KeyGen}(1^\lambda, (\hat{\mathbf{H}}, i))$: Choose $\mathbf{r} \xleftarrow{\$} \mathbb{Z}_p^3$ uniformly at random. Compute $\hat{\mathbf{h}} = \left((\hat{\mathbf{H}}')^\top \right)^{\mathbf{r}}$. Set $\mathsf{pk} = \hat{\mathbf{h}}$ and $\mathsf{sk} = \mathbf{r}$. Output $(\mathsf{pk}, \mathsf{sk})$.
- $\mathsf{H}_{\mathsf{public}}(\mathsf{pk}, (\hat{\mathbf{y}}, b), \mathbf{x})$: Parse pk as $\hat{\mathbf{h}}$. Compute $\hat{z} = (\hat{\mathbf{h}}^\top)^{\mathbf{x}}$ and output $\hat{z}$.
- $\mathsf{H}_{\mathsf{secret}}(\mathsf{sk}, (\hat{\mathbf{y}}, b))$: Parse sk as $\mathbf{r}$ and set $\hat{\mathbf{y}}' = \begin{pmatrix} \hat{\mathbf{y}} \\ g^b \end{pmatrix}$. Compute $\hat{z} = ((\hat{\mathbf{y}}')^\top)^{\mathbf{r}}$ and output $\hat{z}$.

Lemma 4. *For every matrix $\hat{\mathbf{H}} \in \mathbb{G}^{2 \times n}$ and every $i \in [n]$, HPS is a hash proof system for the language $\mathcal{L}_{\hat{\mathbf{H}}, i}$.*

Proof. Let $\hat{\mathbf{H}} = g^{\mathbf{H}}$, $\mathbf{r} = (\mathbf{r}^*, r_3)$ where $\mathbf{r}^* \in \mathbb{Z}_p^2$. Let $\mathbf{y}' := \log_g \hat{\mathbf{y}}'$, $\mathbf{y} := \log_g \hat{\mathbf{y}}$, $\mathbf{H}' := \log_g \hat{\mathbf{H}}'$, $\mathbf{h} := \log_g \hat{\mathbf{h}}$.

For perfect correctness, we need to show that for every $i \in [n]$, every $\hat{\mathbf{H}} \in \mathbb{G}^{2 \times n}$, and every $(\mathsf{pk}, \mathsf{sk})$ in the support of $\mathsf{KeyGen}(1^\lambda, (\hat{\mathbf{H}}', i))$, if $(\hat{\mathbf{y}}, b) \in \mathcal{L}_{\hat{\mathbf{H}}, i}$ and $\mathbf{x}$ is a witness for membership (i.e., $\hat{\mathbf{y}} = \hat{\mathbf{H}}^{\mathbf{x}}$ and $x_i = b$), then it holds that $\mathsf{H}_{\mathsf{public}}(\mathsf{pk}, (\hat{\mathbf{y}}, b), \mathbf{x}) = \mathsf{H}_{\mathsf{secret}}(\mathsf{sk}, (\hat{\mathbf{y}}, b))$.

To simplify the argument, we again consider the statement under the discrete logarithm with basis g. Then it holds that

$$\log_g \left(\mathsf{H}_{\mathsf{secret}}(\mathsf{sk}, (\hat{\mathbf{y}}, b)) \right)$$
$$= \log_g \left(((\hat{\mathbf{y}}')^\top)^{\mathbf{r}} \right) = \langle \mathbf{y}', \mathbf{r} \rangle = \langle \mathbf{y}, \mathbf{r}^* \rangle + b \cdot r_3$$
$$= \langle \mathbf{H} \cdot \mathbf{x}, \mathbf{r}^* \rangle + x_i \cdot r_3 = \langle \mathbf{H}'\mathbf{x}, \mathbf{r} \rangle = \langle (\mathbf{H}')^\top \mathbf{r}, \mathbf{x} \rangle$$
$$= \langle \mathbf{h}, \mathbf{x} \rangle = \log_g \left((\hat{\mathbf{h}}^\top)^{\mathbf{x}} \right)$$
$$= \log_g \left(\mathsf{H}_{\mathsf{public}}(\mathsf{pk}, (\hat{\mathbf{y}}, b), \mathbf{x}) \right).$$

For perfect soundness, let $(\mathsf{pk}, \mathsf{sk}) \leftarrow \mathsf{KeyGen}(1^\lambda, (\hat{\mathbf{H}}', i))$. We will show that if $(\hat{\mathbf{y}}, b) \notin \mathcal{L}_{\hat{\mathbf{H}}, i}$, then $\mathsf{H}_{\mathsf{secret}}(\mathsf{sk}, (\hat{\mathbf{y}}, b))$ is distributed uniformly random in the range of $\mathsf{H}_{\mathsf{secret}}$, even given $\hat{\mathbf{H}}$, i, and pk. Again under the discrete logarithm, this is equivalent to showing that $\langle \mathbf{y}', \mathbf{r} \rangle$ is distributed uniformly random given $\mathbf{H}'$ and $\mathbf{h} = (\mathbf{H}')^\top \mathbf{r}$.

Note that we can re-write the language $\mathcal{L}_{\hat{\mathbf{H}}, i} = \{(\hat{\mathbf{y}}, b) \in \mathbb{G}^2 \times \mathbb{Z}_p \mid \exists \mathbf{x} \in \mathbb{Z}_p^n \text{ s.t. } \mathbf{H}'\mathbf{x} = \mathbf{y}'\}$. It follows that if $(\hat{\mathbf{y}}, b) \notin \mathcal{L}_{\hat{\mathbf{H}}, i}$, then $\mathbf{y}' \notin \mathsf{span}(\mathbf{H}')$. Now it follows directly from Lemma 3 that

$$\mathbf{r}^\top \mathbf{y}' \equiv u$$

given $\mathbf{H}'$ and $\mathbf{r}^\top\mathbf{H}'$, where u is distributed uniformly random. This concludes the proof.

Remark 1. While proving the security of our applications based on the above hash-proof system, we would generate $\hat{\mathbf{H}}$ to be the output of $\mathsf{bindingCrsGen}(1^\lambda, i)$ and use the property that if $(\hat{\mathbf{y}}, b) \in \mathcal{L}_{\hat{\mathbf{H}},i}$, then $(\hat{\mathbf{y}}, (1-b)) \notin \mathcal{L}_{\hat{\mathbf{H}},i}$. This follows directly from Lemma 2 (that is, $\hat{\mathbf{H}}$ and $\hat{\mathbf{y}}$ uniquely fixes x_i).

4.4 The Laconic OT Scheme

We are now ready to put the pieces together and provide our ℓOT scheme with factor-2 compression.

Construction. Let $\mathsf{SSBH} = (\mathsf{SSBH.crsGen}, \mathsf{SSBH.bindingCrsGen}, \mathsf{SSBH.Hash})$ be the HPS-friendly SSB hash function constructed in Sect. 4.2 with domain $\mathfrak{D} = \mathbb{Z}_p$. Notice that we achieve factor-2 compression (namely, compressing 2λ bits into λ bits) by restricting the domain from $\mathfrak{D}^n$ to $\{0,1\}^n$ in our laconic OT scheme. Also, abstractly let the associated hash proof system be $\mathsf{HPS} = (\mathsf{HPS.KeyGen}, \mathsf{HPS.H_{public}}, \mathsf{HPS.H_{secret}})$ for the language

$$\mathcal{L}_{\mathsf{crs},i} = \{(\mathsf{digest}, b) \in \{0,1\}^\lambda \times \{0,1\} \mid \exists D \in \mathfrak{D}^{2\lambda} : \mathsf{SSBH.Hash}(\mathsf{crs}, D) = \mathsf{digest} \text{ and } D[i] = b\}.$$

Recall that the bit-representation size of a group element of $\mathbb{G}$ is $\frac{\lambda}{2}$, hence the language defined above is the same as the one defined in Sect. 4.3.

Now we construct the laconic OT scheme $\ell OT = (\mathsf{crsGen}, \mathsf{Hash}, \mathsf{Send}, \mathsf{Receive})$ as follows.

- $\mathsf{crsGen}(1^\lambda)$: Compute $\mathsf{crs} \leftarrow \mathsf{SSBH.crsGen}(1^\lambda)$ and output crs.
- $\mathsf{Hash}(\mathsf{crs}, D \in \{0,1\}^{2\lambda})$:
    $\mathsf{digest} \leftarrow \mathsf{SSBH.Hash}(\mathsf{crs}, D)$
    $\hat{D} \leftarrow (D, \mathsf{digest})$
    Output $(\mathsf{digest}, \hat{D})$
- $\mathsf{Send}(\mathsf{crs}, \mathsf{digest}, L, m_0, m_1)$:
    Let HPS be the hash-proof system for the language $\mathcal{L}_{\mathsf{crs},L}$
    $(\mathsf{pk}, \mathsf{sk}) \leftarrow \mathsf{HPS.KeyGen}(1^\lambda, (\mathsf{crs}, L))$
    $c_0 \leftarrow m_0 \oplus \mathsf{HPS.H_{secret}}(\mathsf{sk}, (\mathsf{digest}, 0))$
    $c_1 \leftarrow m_1 \oplus \mathsf{HPS.H_{secret}}(\mathsf{sk}, (\mathsf{digest}, 1))$
    Output $\mathsf{e} = (\mathsf{pk}, c_0, c_1)$
- $\mathsf{Receive}^{\hat{D}}(\mathsf{crs}, \mathsf{e}, L)$:
    Parse $\mathsf{e} = (\mathsf{pk}, c_0, c_1)$
    Parse $\hat{D} = (D, \mathsf{digest})$, and set $b \leftarrow D[L]$.
    $m \leftarrow c_b \oplus \mathsf{HPS.H_{public}}(\mathsf{pk}, (\mathsf{digest}, b), D)$
    Output m

We will now show that ℓOT is a laconic OT protocol with factor-2 compression, i.e., it has compression factor 2, and satisfies the correctness and sender privacy requirements. First notice that $\mathsf{SSBH.Hash}$ is factor-2 compressing, so Hash also has compression factor 2. We next argue correctness and sender privacy in Lemmas 5 and 6, respectively.

Lemma 5. *Given that* HPS *satisfies the correctness property, the* ℓOT *scheme also satisfies the correctness property.*

Proof. Fix a common reference string crs in the support of crsGen(1^λ), a database string $D \in \{0,1\}^{2\lambda}$ and an index $L \in [2\lambda]$. For any crs, D, L such that $D[L] = b$, let digest = Hash(crs, D). Then it clearly holds that (digest, b) $\in \mathcal{L}_{\text{crs},L}$. Thus, by the correctness property of the hash proof system HPS it holds that

$$\text{HPS.H}_{\text{secret}}(\text{sk}, (\text{digest}, b)) = \text{HPS.H}_{\text{public}}(\text{pk}, (\text{digest}, b), D).$$

By the construction of Send(crs, digest, L, m_0, m_1), $c_b = m_b \oplus \text{HPS.H}_{\text{secret}}(\text{sk}, (\text{digest}, b))$. Hence the output m of Receive$^{\hat{D}}$(crs, e, L) is

$$
\begin{aligned}
m &= c_b \oplus \text{HPS.H}_{\text{public}}(\text{pk}, (\text{digest}, b), D) \\
&= m_b \oplus \text{HPS.H}_{\text{secret}}(\text{sk}, (\text{digest}, b)) \oplus \text{HPS.H}_{\text{public}}(\text{pk}, (\text{digest}, b), D) \\
&= m_b.
\end{aligned}
$$

Lemma 6. *Given that* SSBH *is index-hiding and has the statistically binding property and that* HPS *is sound, then the* ℓOT *scheme satisfies sender privacy against semi-honest receiver.*

Proof. We first construct the simulator ℓOTSim.

ℓOTSim(crs, $D, L, m_{D[L]}$):
    digest $\leftarrow$ SSBH.Hash(crs, D)
    Let HPS be the hash-proof system for the language $\mathcal{L}_{\text{crs},L}$
    (pk, sk) $\leftarrow$ HPS.KeyGen(1^λ, (crs, L))
    $c_0 \leftarrow m_{D[L]} \oplus \text{HPS.H}_{\text{secret}}(\text{sk}, (\text{digest}, 0))$
    $c_1 \leftarrow m_{D[L]} \oplus \text{HPS.H}_{\text{secret}}(\text{sk}, (\text{digest}, 1))$
    Output (pk, c_0, c_1)

For any database D of size at most $M = \text{poly}(\lambda)$ for any polynomial function poly($\cdot$), any memory location $L \in [M]$, and any pair of messages $(m_0, m_1) \in \{0,1\}^\lambda \times \{0,1\}^\lambda$, let crs $\leftarrow$ crsGen(1^λ) and digest $\leftarrow$ Hash(crs, D). Then we will prove that the two distributions (crs, Send(crs, digest, L, m_0, m_1)) and (crs, ℓOTSim(crs, $D, L, m_{D[L]}$)) are computationally indistinguishable. Consider the following hybrids.

- Hybrid 0: This is the real experiment, namely (crs, Send(crs, digest, L, m_0, m_1)).
- Hybrid 1: Same as hybrid 0, except that crs is generated to be binding at location L, namely crs $\leftarrow$ SSBH.bindingCrsGen($1^\lambda, L$).
- Hybrid 2: Same as hybrid 1, except that $c_{1-D[L]}$ is computed by $c_{1-D[L]} \leftarrow m_{D[L]} \oplus \text{HPS.H}_{\text{secret}}(\text{sk}, (\text{digest}, 1 - D[L]))$. That is, both c_0 and c_1 encrypt the same message $m_{D[L]}$.
- Hybrid 3: Same as hybrid 2, except that crs is computed by crs $\leftarrow$ SSBH.crsGen(1^λ). This is the simulated experiment, namely (crs, ℓOTSim(crs, $D, L, m_{D[L]}$)).

Indistinguishability of hybrid 0 and hybrid 1 follows directly from Lemma 1, as we replace the distribution of crs from $\mathsf{SSBH.crsGen}(1^\lambda)$ to $\mathsf{SSBH.bindingCrsGen}(1^\lambda, L)$. Indistinguishability of hybrids 2 and 3 also follows from Lemma 1, as we replace the distribution of crs from $\mathsf{SSBH.bindingCrsGen}(1^\lambda, L)$ back to $\mathsf{SSBH.crsGen}(1^\lambda)$.

We will now show that hybrids 1 and 2 are identically distributed. Since crs is in the support of $\mathsf{SSBH.bindingCrsGen}(1^\lambda, i)$ and $\mathsf{digest} = \mathsf{SSBH.Hash}(\mathsf{crs}, D)$, by Lemma 2 it holds that $(\mathsf{digest}, 1 - D[L]) \notin \mathcal{L}_{\mathsf{crs}, L}$. By the soundness property of the hash-proof system HPS, it holds that

$$(\mathsf{crs}, L, \mathsf{pk}, \mathsf{HPS.H}_{\mathsf{secret}}(\mathsf{sk}, (\mathsf{digest}, 1 - D[L]))) \equiv (\mathsf{crs}, L, \mathsf{pk}, u),$$

for a uniformly random u. Furthermore, $c_{D[L]}$ can be computed by $m_{D[L]} \oplus \mathsf{HPS.H}_{\mathsf{public}}(\mathsf{pk}, (\mathsf{digest}, D[L]), D)$. Hence

$$(\mathsf{crs}, L, \mathsf{pk}, m_{D[L]} \oplus \mathsf{HPS.H}_{\mathsf{secret}}(\mathsf{sk}, (\mathsf{digest}, 1 - D[L])), c_{D[L]})$$
$$\equiv (\mathsf{crs}, L, \mathsf{pk}, u, c_{D[L]})$$
$$\equiv (\mathsf{crs}, L, \mathsf{pk}, m_{1 - D[L]} \oplus \mathsf{HPS.H}_{\mathsf{secret}}(\mathsf{sk}, (\mathsf{digest}, 1 - D[L])), c_{D[L]}).$$

This concludes the proof.

5   Construction of Updatable Laconic OT

In this section, we will construct an updatable laconic OT that supports a hash function that allows for compression from an input (database) of size an arbitrary polynomial in λ to λ bits. As every updatable laconic OT protocol is also a (standard) laconic OT protocol, we will only construct the former. Our main technique in this construction, is the use of garbled circuits to bootstrap a laconic OT with factor-2 compression into one with an arbitrary compression factor.

Below in Sect. 5.1 we provide some background on the primitives needed for realizing our laconic OT construction. Then we will give the construction overview of laconic OT in Sects. 5.2. We refer the reader to our full version [CDG+17] for the full construction along with its correctness and security proofs.

5.1   Background

In this section we recall the needed background of garbled circuits and Merkle trees.

5.1.1   Garbled Circuits

Garbled circuits were first introduced by Yao [Yao82] (see Lindell and Pinkas [LP09] and Bellare et al. [BHR12] for a detailed proof and further discussion). A circuit garbling scheme GC is a tuple of PPT algorithms (GCircuit, Eval). Very roughly GCircuit is the circuit garbling procedure and Eval the corresponding evaluation procedure. Looking ahead, each individual wire w of the circuit being garbled will be associated with two labels, namely $\mathsf{key}_{w,0}, \mathsf{key}_{w,1}$.

- $\tilde{\mathsf{C}} \leftarrow \mathsf{GCircuit}\left(1^\lambda, \mathsf{C}, \{\mathsf{key}_{w,b}\}_{w\in\mathsf{inp}(\mathsf{C}),b\in\{0,1\}}\right)$: GCircuit takes as input a security parameter λ, a circuit C, and a set of labels $\mathsf{key}_{w,b}$ for all the input wires $w \in \mathsf{inp}(\mathsf{C})$ and $b \in \{0,1\}$. This procedure outputs a *garbled circuit* $\tilde{\mathsf{C}}$.
- $y \leftarrow \mathsf{Eval}\left(\tilde{\mathsf{C}}, \{\mathsf{key}_{w,x_w}\}_{w\in\mathsf{inp}(\mathsf{C})}\right)$: Given a garbled circuit $\tilde{\mathsf{C}}$ and a garbled input represented as a sequence of input labels $\{\mathsf{key}_{w,x_w}\}_{w\in\mathsf{inp}(\mathsf{C})}$, Eval outputs y.

Terminology of Keys and Labels. We note that, in the rest of the paper, we use the notation Keys to refer to both the secret values sampled for wires and the notation Labels to refer to exactly one of them. In other words, generation of garbled circuit involves Keys while computation itself depends just on Labels. Let $\mathsf{Keys} = ((\mathsf{key}_{1,0}, \mathsf{key}_{1,1}), \ldots, (\mathsf{key}_{n,0}, \mathsf{key}_{n,1}))$ be a list of n key-pairs, we denote Keys_x for a string $x \in \{0,1\}^n$ to be a list of labels $(\mathsf{key}_{1,x_1}, \ldots, \mathsf{key}_{n,x_n})$.

Correctness. For correctness, we require that for any circuit C and input $x \in \{0,1\}^m$ (here m is the input length to C) we have that:

$$\Pr\left[\mathsf{C}(x) = \mathsf{Eval}\left(\tilde{\mathsf{C}}, \{\mathsf{key}_{w,x_w}\}_{w\in\mathsf{inp}(\mathsf{C})}\right)\right] = 1$$

where $\tilde{\mathsf{C}} \leftarrow \mathsf{GCircuit}\left(1^\lambda, \mathsf{C}, \{\mathsf{key}_{w,b}\}_{w\in\mathsf{inp}(\mathsf{C}),b\in\{0,1\}}\right)$.

Security. For security, we require that there is a PPT simulator CircSim such that for any C, x, and uniformly random keys $\{\mathsf{key}_{w,b}\}_{w\in\mathsf{inp}(\mathsf{C}),b\in\{0,1\}}$, we have that

$$\left(\tilde{\mathsf{C}}, \{\mathsf{key}_{w,x_w}\}_{w\in\mathsf{inp}(\mathsf{C})}\right) \overset{c}{\approx} \mathsf{CircSim}\left(1^\lambda, \mathsf{C}, y\right)$$

where $\tilde{\mathsf{C}} \leftarrow \mathsf{GCircuit}\left(1^\lambda, \mathsf{C}, \{\mathsf{key}_{w,b}\}_{w\in\mathsf{inp}(\mathsf{C}),b\in\{0,1\}}\right)$ and $y = \mathsf{C}(x)$.

5.1.2   Merkle Tree

In this section we briefly review Merkle trees. A Merkle tree is a hash based data structure that generically extend the domain of a hash function. The following description will be tailored to the hash function of the laconic OT scheme that we will present in Sect. 5.2. Given a two-to-one hash function $\mathsf{Hash} : \{0,1\}^{2\lambda} \rightarrow \{0,1\}^\lambda$, we can use a Merkle tree to construct a hash function that compresses a database of an arbitrary (a priori unbounded polynomial in λ) size to a λ-bit string. Now we briefly illustrate how to compress a database $D \in \{0,1\}^M$ (assume for ease of exposition that $M = 2^d \cdot \lambda$). First, we partition D into strings of length 2λ; we call each string a *leaf*. Then we use Hash to compress each leaf into a new string of length λ; we call each string a *node*. Next, we bundle the new nodes in pairs of two and call these pairs *siblings*, i.e., each pair of siblings is a string of length 2λ. We then use Hash again to compress each pair of siblings into a new node of size λ. We continue the process till a single node of size λ is obtained. This process forms a binary tree structure, which we refer to as a Merkle tree. Looking ahead, the hash function of the laconic OT scheme has output $(\hat{\mathsf{D}}, \mathsf{digest})$, where $\hat{\mathsf{D}}$ is the entire Merkle tree, and digest is the root of the tree.

A Merkle tree has the following property. In order to verify that a database D with hash root digest has a certain value b at a location L (namely, $D[L] = b$), there is no need to provide the entire Merkle tree. Instead, it is sufficient to provide a path of siblings from the Merkle tree root to the leaf that contains location L. It can then be easily verified if the hash values from the leaf to the root are correct.

Moreover, a Merkle tree can be updated in the same fashion when the value at a certain location of the database is updated. Instead of recomputing the entire tree, we only need to recompute the nodes on the path from the updated leaf to the root. This can be done given the path of siblings from the root to the leaf.

5.2   Construction Overview

We will now provide an overview of our construction to bootstrap an ℓOT scheme with factor-2 compression into an updatable ℓOT scheme with an arbitrary compression factor, which can compress a database of an arbitrary (a priori unbounded polynomial in λ) size. For the full construction, see the full version of this paper [CDG+17].

Consider a database $D \in \{0, 1\}^M$ such that $M = 2^d \cdot \lambda$. Given a laconic OT scheme with factor-2 compression (denoted as ℓOT_{const}), we will first use a Merkle tree to obtain a hash function with arbitrary (polynomial) compression factor. As described in Sect. 5.1.2, the Hash function of the updatable ℓOT scheme will have an output $(\hat{D}, \text{digest})$, where $\hat{D}$ is the entire Merkle tree, and digest is the root of the tree.

In the Send algorithm, suppose we want to send a message depending on a bit $D[L]$, we will follow the natural approach of traversing the Merkle tree layer by layer until reaching the leaf containing L. In particular, L can be represented as $L = (b_1, \ldots, b_{d-1}, t)$, where $b_1, \ldots, b_{d-1}$ are bits representing the path from the root to the leaf containing location L, and $t \in [2\lambda]$ is the position within the leaf. The Send algorithm first takes as input the root digest of the Merkle tree, and it will generate a chain of garbled circuits, which would enable the receiver to traverse the Merkle tree from the root to the leaf. And upon reaching the leaf, the receiver will be able to evaluate the last garbled circuit and retrieve the message corresponding to the t-th bit of the leaf.

We briefly explain the chain of garbled circuits as follows. The chain consists of $d-1$ traversing circuits along with a reading circuit. Every traversing circuit takes as input a pair of siblings $\text{sbl} = (\text{sbl}_0, \text{sbl}_1)$ at a certain layer of the Merkle tree, chooses sbl_b which is the node in the path from root to leaf, and generates a laconic OT ciphertext (using $\ell OT_{\text{const}}.\text{Send}$) which encrypts the input keys of the next traversing garbled circuit and uses sbl_b as the hash value. Looking ahead, when the receiver evaluates the traversing circuit and obtains the laconic OT ciphertext, he can then use the siblings at the next layer to decrypt the ciphertext (by $\ell OT_{\text{const}}.\text{Receive}$) and obtain the corresponding input labels for the next traversing garbled circuit. Using the chain of traversing garbled circuits the receiver can therefore traverse from the first layer to the leaf of the Merkle tree. Furthermore, the correct keys for the first traversing circuit are sent via the ℓOT_{const} with digest (i.e., root of the tree) as the hash value.

Finally, the last traversing circuit will transfer keys for the last reading circuit to the receiver in a similar fashion as above. The reading circuit takes the leaf as input and outputs $m_{leaf[t]}$, i.e., the message corresponding to the t-th bit of the leaf. Hence, when evaluating the reading circuit, the receiver can obtain the message $m_{leaf[t]}$.

SendWrite and ReceiveWrite are similar as Send and Receive, except that (a) ReceiveWrite updates the Merkle tree from the leaf to the root, and (b) the last writing circuit recomputes the root of the Merkle tree and outputs messages corresponding to the new root. To enable (b), the writing circuit will take as input the whole path of siblings from the root to the leaf. The input keys for the writing circuit corresponding to the siblings at the $(i+1)$-th layer are transferred via the i-th traversing circuit. That is, the i-th traversing circuit transfers the keys for the $(i+1)$-th transferring circuit as well as partial keys for the writing circuit. In the actual construction, both the reading circuit and writing circuit take as input the entire path of siblings (for the purpose of symmetry).

Acknowledgement. We thank the anonymous reviewers of CRYPTO 2017 for their helpful suggestions in improving this paper. We also thank Yuval Ishai for useful discussions.

References

[ADT11] Ateniese, G., Cristofaro, E., Tsudik, G.: (If) Size matters: size-hiding private set intersection. In: Catalano, D., Fazio, N., Gennaro, R., Nicolosi, A. (eds.) PKC 2011. LNCS, vol. 6571, pp. 156–173. Springer, Heidelberg (2011). doi:10.1007/978-3-642-19379-8_10

[AIKW13] Applebaum, B., Ishai, Y., Kushilevitz, E., Waters, B.: Encoding functions with constant online rate or how to compress garbled circuits keys. In: Canetti, R., Garay, J.A. (eds.) CRYPTO 2013, Part II. LNCS, vol. 8043, pp. 166–184. Springer, Heidelberg (2013). doi:10.1007/978-3-642-40084-1_10

[ALSZ13] Asharov, G., Lindell, Y., Schneider, T., Zohner, M.: More efficient oblivious transfer and extensions for faster secure computation. In: ACM CCS 13 (2013)

[BCCT12] Bitansky, N., Canetti, R., Chiesa, A., Tromer, E.: From extractable collision resistance to succinct non-interactive arguments of knowledge, and back again. In: ITCS (2012)

[Bea96] Beaver, D.: Correlated pseudorandomness and the complexity of private computations. In: 28th ACM STOC (1996)

[BGL+15] Bitansky, N., Garg, S., Lin, H., Pass, R., Telang, S.: Succinct randomized encodings and their applications. In: 47th ACM STOC (2015)

[BHR12] Bellare, M., Hoang, V.T., Rogaway, P.: Foundations of garbled circuits. In: ACM CCS (2012)

[BPMW16] Bourse, F., Pino, R., Minelli, M., Wee, H.: FHE circuit privacy almost for free. In: Robshaw, M., Katz, J. (eds.) CRYPTO 2016, Part II. LNCS, vol. 9815, pp. 62–89. Springer, Heidelberg (2016). doi:10.1007/978-3-662-53008-5_3

[BSCG+13] Ben-Sasson, E., Chiesa, A., Genkin, D., Tromer, E., Virza, M.: SNARKs for C: verifying program executions succinctly and in zero knowledge. In: Canetti, R., Garay, J.A. (eds.) CRYPTO 2013, Part II. LNCS, vol. 8043, pp. 90–108. Springer, Heidelberg (2013). doi:10.1007/978-3-642-40084-1_6

[BV11a] Brakerski, Z., Vaikuntanathan, V.: Efficient fully homomorphic encryption from (standard) LWE. In: 52nd FOCS (2011)

[BV11b] Brakerski, Z., Vaikuntanathan, V.: Fully homomorphic encryption from ring-LWE and security for key dependent messages. In: Rogaway, P. (ed.) CRYPTO 2011. LNCS, vol. 6841, pp. 505–524. Springer, Heidelberg (2011). doi:10.1007/978-3-642-22792-9_29

[CDG+17] Cho, C., Döttling, N., Garg, S., Gupta, D., Miao, P., Polychroniadou, A.: Laconic oblivious transfer and its applications. Cryptology ePrint Archive, Report 2017/491 (2017). http://eprint.iacr.org/2017/491

[CHJV15] Canetti, R., Holmgren, J., Jain, A., Vaikuntanathan, V.: Succinct garbling and indistinguishability obfuscation for RAM programs. In: 47th ACM STOC (2015)

[CHK04] Canetti, R., Halevi, S., Katz, J.: Chosen-ciphertext security from identity-based encryption. In: Cachin, C., Camenisch, J.L. (eds.) EUROCRYPT 2004. LNCS, vol. 3027, pp. 207–222. Springer, Heidelberg (2004). doi:10.1007/978-3-540-24676-3_13

[COV15] Chase, M., Ostrovsky, R., Visconti, I.: Executable proofs, input-size hiding secure computation and a new ideal world. In: Oswald, E., Fischlin, M. (eds.) EUROCRYPT 2015, Part II. LNCS, vol. 9057, pp. 532–560. Springer, Heidelberg (2015). doi:10.1007/978-3-662-46803-6_18

[CS98] Cramer, R., Shoup, V.: A practical public key cryptosystem provably secure against adaptive chosen ciphertext attack. In: Krawczyk, H. (ed.) CRYPTO 1998. LNCS, vol. 1462, pp. 13–25. Springer, Heidelberg (1998). doi:10.1007/BFb0055717

[CS02] Cramer, R., Shoup, V.: Universal hash proofs and a paradigm for adaptive chosen ciphertext secure public-key encryption. In: Knudsen, L.R. (ed.) EUROCRYPT 2002. LNCS, vol. 2332, pp. 45–64. Springer, Heidelberg (2002). doi:10.1007/3-540-46035-7_4

[CV12] Chase, M., Visconti, I.: Secure database commitments and universal arguments of quasi knowledge. In: Safavi-Naini, R., Canetti, R. (eds.) CRYPTO 2012. LNCS, vol. 7417, pp. 236–254. Springer, Heidelberg (2012). doi:10.1007/978-3-642-32009-5_15

[DG17] Döttling, N., Garg, S.: Identity-based encryption from the diffie hellman assumption. In: Katz, J., Shacham, H. (eds.) CRYPTO 2017, Part II. LNCS, vol. 10401, pp. 537–569. Springer, Heidelberg (2017)

[DS16] Ducas, L., Stehlé, D.: Sanitization of FHE ciphertexts. In: Fischlin, M., Coron, J.-S. (eds.) EUROCRYPT 2016, Part I. LNCS, vol. 9665, pp. 294–310. Springer, Heidelberg (2016). doi:10.1007/978-3-662-49890-3_12

[FLS90] Feige, U., Lapidot, D., Shamir, A.: Multiple non-interactive zero knowledge proofs based on a single random string (extended abstract). In: 31st FOCS (1990)

[Gen09] Gentry, C.: Fully homomorphic encryption using ideal lattices. In: 41st ACM STOC (2009)

[GGH13a] Garg, S., Gentry, C., Halevi, S.: Candidate multilinear maps from ideal lattices. In: Johansson, T., Nguyen, P.Q. (eds.) EUROCRYPT 2013. LNCS, vol. 7881, pp. 1–17. Springer, Heidelberg (2013). doi:10.1007/978-3-642-38348-9_1

[GGH+13b] Garg, S., Gentry, C., Halevi, S., Raykova, M., Sahai, A., Waters, B.: Candidate indistinguishability obfuscation and functional encryption for all circuits. In: 54th FOCS (2013)

[GGMP16] Garg, S., Gupta, D., Miao, P., Pandey, O.: Secure multiparty RAM computation in constant rounds. In: Hirt, M., Smith, A. (eds.) TCC 2016, Part I. LNCS, vol. 9985, pp. 491–520. Springer, Heidelberg (2016). doi:10. 1007/978-3-662-53641-4_19

[GGSW13] Garg, S., Gentry, C., Sahai, A., Waters, B.: Witness encryption and its applications. In: 45th ACM STOC (2013)

[GHL+14] Gentry, C., Halevi, S., Lu, S., Ostrovsky, R., Raykova, M., Wichs, D.: Garbled RAM revisited. In: Nguyen, P.Q., Oswald, E. (eds.) EUROCRYPT 2014. LNCS, vol. 8441, pp. 405–422. Springer, Heidelberg (2014). doi:10. 1007/978-3-642-55220-5_23

[GHRW14] Gentry, C., Halevi, S., Raykova, M., Wichs, D.: Outsourcing private RAM computation. In: 55th FOCS (2014)

[GHV10] Gentry, C., Halevi, S., Vaikuntanathan, V.: i-hop homomorphic encryption and rerandomizable yao circuits. In: Rabin, T. (ed.) CRYPTO 2010. LNCS, vol. 6223, pp. 155–172. Springer, Heidelberg (2010). doi:10.1007/ 978-3-642-14623-7_9

[GKK+12] Gordon, S.D., Katz, J., Kolesnikov, V., Krell, F., Malkin, T., Raykova, M., Vahlis, Y.: Secure two-party computation in sublinear (amortized) time. In: ACM CCS (2012)

[GKP+13] Goldwasser, S., Kalai, Y.T., Popa, R.A., Vaikuntanathan, V., Zeldovich, N.: How to run turing machines on encrypted data. In: Canetti, R., Garay, J.A. (eds.) CRYPTO 2013, Part II. LNCS, vol. 8043, pp. 536–553. Springer, Heidelberg (2013). doi:10.1007/978-3-642-40084-1_30

[GLO15] Garg, S., Lu, S., Ostrovsky, R.: Black-box garbled RAM. In: 56th FOCS (2015)

[GLOS15] Garg, S., Lu, S., Ostrovsky, R., Scafuro, A.: Garbled RAM from one-way functions. In: 47th ACM STOC (2015)

[GMW87] Goldreich, O., Micali, S., Wigderson, A.: How to play any mental game or A completeness theorem for protocols with honest majority. In: 19th ACM STOC (1987)

[Gol87] Goldreich, O.: Towards a theory of software protection and simulation by oblivious RAMs. In: 19th ACM STOC (1987)

[GOS06] Groth, J., Ostrovsky, R., Sahai, A.: Non-interactive zaps and new techniques for NIZK. In: Dwork, C. (ed.) CRYPTO 2006. LNCS, vol. 4117, pp. 97–111. Springer, Heidelberg (2006). doi:10.1007/11818175_6

[GSW13] Gentry, C., Sahai, A., Waters, B.: Homomorphic encryption from learning with errors: conceptually-simpler, asymptotically-faster, attribute-based. In: Canetti, R., Garay, J.A. (eds.) CRYPTO 2013, Part I. LNCS, vol. 8042, pp. 75–92. Springer, Heidelberg (2013). doi:10.1007/978-3-642-40041-4_5

[HW15] Hubacek, P., Wichs, P.: On the communication complexity of secure function evaluation with long output. In: ITCS (2015)

[IKNP03] Ishai, Y., Kilian, J., Nissim, K., Petrank, E.: Extending oblivious transfers efficiently. In: Boneh, D. (ed.) CRYPTO 2003. LNCS, vol. 2729, pp. 145–161. Springer, Heidelberg (2003). doi:10.1007/978-3-540-45146-4_9

[IKO+11] Ishai, Y., Kushilevitz, E., Ostrovsky, R., Prabhakaran, M., Sahai, A.: Efficient non-interactive secure computation. In: Paterson, K.G. (ed.) EUROCRYPT 2011. LNCS, vol. 6632, pp. 406–425. Springer, Heidelberg (2011). doi:10.1007/978-3-642-20465-4_23

[IP07] Ishai, Y., Paskin, A.: Evaluating branching programs on encrypted data. In: Vadhan, S.P. (ed.) TCC 2007. LNCS, vol. 4392, pp. 575–594. Springer, Heidelberg (2007). doi:10.1007/978-3-540-70936-7_31

[IPS08] Ishai, Y., Prabhakaran, M., Sahai, A.: Founding cryptography on oblivious transfer – efficiently. In: Wagner, D. (ed.) CRYPTO 2008. LNCS, vol. 5157, pp. 572–591. Springer, Heidelberg (2008). doi:10.1007/978-3-540-85174-5_32

[Kil88] Kilian, J.: Founding cryptography on oblivious transfer. In: 20th ACM STOC (1988)

[KK13] Kolesnikov, V., Kumaresan, R.: Improved OT extension for transferring short secrets. In: Canetti, R., Garay, J.A. (eds.) CRYPTO 2013, Part II. LNCS, vol. 8043, pp. 54–70. Springer, Heidelberg (2013). doi:10.1007/978-3-642-40084-1_4

[KLW15] Koppula, V., Lewko, A.B., Waters, B.: Indistinguishability obfuscation for turing machines with unbounded memory. In: 47th ACM STOC (2015)

[LNO13] Lindell, Y., Nissim, K., Orlandi, C.: Hiding the input-size in secure two-party computation. In: Sako, K., Sarkar, P. (eds.) ASIACRYPT 2013, Part II. LNCS, vol. 8270, pp. 421–440. Springer, Heidelberg (2013). doi:10.1007/978-3-642-42045-0_22

[LO13] Lu, S., Ostrovsky, R.: How to garble RAM programs? In: Johansson, T., Nguyen, P.Q. (eds.) EUROCRYPT 2013. LNCS, vol. 7881, pp. 719–734. Springer, Heidelberg (2013). doi:10.1007/978-3-642-38348-9_42

[LP09] Lindell, Y., Pinkas, B.: A proof of security of Yao's protocol for two-party computation. J. Cryptol. 22, 161–188 (2009)

[MRK03] Micali, S., Rabin, M.O., Kilian, J.: Zero-knowledge sets. In: 44th FOCS (2003)

[OPP14] Ostrovsky, R., Paskin-Cherniavsky, A., Paskin-Cherniavsky, B.: Maliciously circuit-private FHE. In: Garay, J.A., Gennaro, R. (eds.) CRYPTO 2014, Part I. LNCS, vol. 8616, pp. 536–553. Springer, Heidelberg (2014). doi:10.1007/978-3-662-44371-2_30

[OPWW15] Okamoto, T., Pietrzak, K., Waters, B., Wichs, D.: New realizations of somewhere statistically binding hashing and positional accumulators. In: Iwata, T., Cheon, J.H. (eds.) ASIACRYPT 2015, Part I. LNCS, vol. 9452, pp. 121–145. Springer, Heidelberg (2015). doi:10.1007/978-3-662-48797-6_6

[OS97] Ostrovsky, R., Shoup, V.: Private information storage (extended abstract). In: 29th ACM STOC (1997)

[Ost90] Ostrovsky, R.: Efficient computation on oblivious RAMs. In: 22nd ACM STOC (1990)

[Rab81] Rabin, M.O.: How to exchange secrets with oblivious transfer (1981)

[Vil12] Villar, J.L.: Optimal reductions of some decisional problems to the rank problem. In: Wang, X., Sako, K. (eds.) ASIACRYPT 2012. LNCS, vol. 7658, pp. 80–97. Springer, Heidelberg (2012). doi:10.1007/978-3-642-34961-4_7

[WHC+14] Wang, X.S., Huang, Y., Chan, T.-H.H., Shelat, A., Shi, E.: Oblivious RAM for secure computation. In: ACM CCS (2014)

[Yao82] Yao, A.C.-C.: Protocols for secure computations (extended abstract). In: 23rd FOCS (1982)

Black-Box Parallel Garbled RAM

Steve Lu[1]([✉]) and Rafail Ostrovsky[2]([✉])

[1] Stealth Software Technologies, Inc., Los Angeles, USA
stevelu8@gmail.com
[2] University of California, Los Angeles, USA
rafail@cs.ucla.edu

Abstract. In 1982, Yao introduced a technique of "circuit garbling" that became a central building block in cryptography. The question of garbling general random-access memory (RAM) programs was introduced by Lu and Ostrovsky in 2013. The most recent results of Garg, Lu, and Ostrovsky (FOCS 2015) achieve a garbled RAM with black-box use of any one-way functions and poly-log overhead of data and program garbling in all the relevant parameters, including program run-time. The advantage of Garbled RAM is that large data can be garbled first, and act as persistent garbled storage (e.g. in the cloud) and later programs can be garbled and sent to be executed on this garbled database in a non-interactive manner.

One of the main advantages of cloud computing is not only that it has large storage but also that it has a large number of parallel processors. Despite multiple successful efforts on parallelizing (interactive) Oblivious RAM, the non-interactive garbling of parallel programs remained open until very recently. Specifically, Boyle, Chung and Pass in their TCC 2016-A [4] have shown how to garble PRAM programs with poly-logarithmic (parallel) overhead assuming non-black-box use of identity-based encryption (IBE). The question of whether the IBE assumption, and in particular, the non-black-box use of such a strong assumption is needed. In this paper, we resolve this question and show how to garble parallel programs, with black-box use of only one-way functions and with only poly-log overhead in the (parallel) running time. Our result works for any number of parallel processors.

Keywords: PRAM · Garbled RAM · Black-box cryptography · One-way functions · Secure computation

S. Lu – This material is based upon work supported in part by the DARPA Brandeis program.
R. Ostrovsky – Research supported in part by NSF grant 1619348, DARPA, US-Israel BSF grant 2012366, OKAWA Foundation Research Award, IBM Faculty Research Award, Xerox Faculty Research Award, B. John Garrick Foundation Award, Teradata Research Award, and Lockheed-Martin Corporation Research Award. Work done in part while consulting for Stealth Software Technologies, Inc. The views expressed are those of the authors and do not reflect position of the Department of Defense or the U.S. Government.

© International Association for Cryptologic Research 2017
J. Katz and H. Shacham (Eds.): CRYPTO 2017, Part II, LNCS 10402, pp. 66–92, 2017.
DOI: 10.1007/978-3-319-63715-0_3

1 Introduction

Yao [23] introduced a technique that allows one to "garble" a circuit into an equivalent "garbled circuit" that can be executed (once) by someone else without understanding internal circuit values during evaluation. A drawback of circuit representation (for garbling general-purpose programs) is that one can not decouple garbling encrypted data on which the program operates from the program code and inputs. Thus, to run Random Access Machine (RAM) program, one has to unroll all possible execution paths and memory usage when converting programs into circuits. For programs with multiple "if-then-else" branches, loops, etc. this often leads to an exponential blow-up, especially when operating on data which is much larger than program running time. A classic example is for a binary search over n elements, the run time of RAM program is logarithmic in n but the garbled circuit is exponentially larger as it has n size since it must touch all data items.

An alternative approach to program garbling (that does not suffer from this exponential blowup that the trivial circuit unrolling approach has) was initiated by Lu and Ostrovsky in 2013 [20], where they developed an approach that allows to separately encrypt data and separately convert a program into a garbled program without converting it into circuits first and without expanding it to be proportional to the size of data. In the Lu-Ostrovsky approach, the program garbled size and the run time is proportional to the original program run-time (times poly-log terms). The original paper required a complicated circular-security assumption but in sequence of follow-up works [11,13,14] the assumption was improved to a black-box use any one-way function with poly-logarithmic overhead in all parameters.

Circuits have another benefit that general RAM programs do not have. Specifically, the circuit model is inherently *parallelizable* - all gates at the same circuit level can be executed in parallel given sufficiently many processors. In the 1980s and 1990s a parallel model of computation was developed for general programs that can take advantage of multiple processors. Specifically, a Parallel Random Access Memory (PRAM), can take advantage of m processors, executing all of them in parallel with m parallel reads/writes. Indeed, this model was used in various Oblivious RAM papers such as in the works of Boyle, Chung, and Pass [4], as well as Chen, Lin, and Tessaro [8] in TCC 2016-A. In fact, [4] demonstrates the feasibility of garbled *parallel* RAM under the existince of Identity-based Encryption. However, constructing it from one-way functions remains open, and furthermore, to construct it in a black-box manner. The question that we ask in this paper is this:

Can we construct garbled Parallel-RAM programs with only
poly-logarithmic (parallel) overhead making only black-box use of
one-way function?

The reason this is a hard problem to answer is that now one has to garble memory in such a way that multiple garbled processor threads can read in parallel multiple garbled memory locations, which leads to complicated (garbled) interactions, and remained an elusive goal for these technical reasons. The importance of achieving such a goal in a black-box manner from minimal assumptions is motivated by the fact that almost all garbled *circuit* constructions are built in a black-box manner. Only the recent work of GLO [11], and the works of Garg et al. [10] and Miao [21] satisfies this for garbled *RAM*.

In this paper we show that our desired goal is possible to achieve. Specifically, we show a result that is tight both in terms of cryptographic assumptions and the overhead achieved (up to polylog factors): we show that any PRAM program with persistent memory can be compiled into parallel Garbled PRAM program (Parallel-GRAM) based on only a black-box use of one-way functions and with poly-log (parallel) overhead. We remark that the techniques that we develop to achieve our result significantly depart from the works of [4,11].

1.1 Problem Statement

Suppose a user has a large database D that it wants to encrypt and store in a cloud as some garbled $\tilde{D}$. Later, the user wants to encrypt several PRAM programs $\Pi_1, \Pi_2, \ldots$ where Π_i is a parallel program that requires m processors and updates $\tilde{D}$. Indeed, the user wants to garble each Π_i and ask the cloud to execute the garbled $\tilde{\Pi}$ program against $\tilde{D}$ using m processors. The programs may update/modify that encrypted database. We require *correctness* in that all garbled programs output the same output as the original PRAM program (when operated on persistent, up-to-date D.) At the same time, we require *privacy* which means that nothing but each program's running time and the output are revealed. Specifically, we require a simulator that can simulate the parallel program execution for each program, given only its run time and its output. The simulator must be able to simulate each output without knowing any future outputs. We measure the parallel efficiency in terms of garbled program size, garbled data size, and garbled running time.

1.2 Comparison with Previous Work

In the interactive setting, a problem of securely evaluating programs (as opposed to circuits) was started in the works on Oblivious RAM by Goldreich and Ostrovsky [16,17,22]. The work of non-interactive evaluation of RAM programs were initiated in the Garbled RAM work of Lu and Ostrovsky [20]. This work showed how to garble memory and program so that programs could be non-interactively and privately evaluated on persistent memory. Subsequent works on GRAM [11,13,14] improved the security assumptions, with the latest one demonstrating a fully black-box GRAM from one-way functions.

Parallel RAM. The first work on parallel Garbled RAM was initiated in the papers of Boyle, Chung and Pass [4] and Chen, Lin, and Tessaro [8] where they study it in the context of building an Oblivious Parallel RAM. Boyle et al. [4] show how to construct garbled PRAM assuming non-black-box use of identity-based encryption. That is, they use the actual code of identity-based encryption in order to implement their PRAM garbled protocol. In contrast, we achieve black-box use of one-way functions only, and while maintaining poly-logarithmic (parallel) overhead (matching classical result of Yao for circuits) for PRAM computations. One of the main reasons of why Yao's result is so influential is that it used one-way function in a black-box way. Black-box use of a one-way function is also critical because in addition to its theoretical interest, the black-box property allows implementers to use their favored instantiation of the cryptographic primitive: this could include proprietary implementations or hardware-based ones (such as hardware support for AES).

Succinct Garbled RAM. In a highly related sequence of works, researchers have also worked in the setting where the garbled programs are also *succinct* or *reusable*, so that the size of the garbled programs were independent of the running time. Following the TCC 2013 Rump Session talk of Lu and Ostrovsky, Gentry et al. [15] first presented a scheme based on a stronger notion of differing inputs obfuscation. At STOC 2015, works due to Koppula et al. [19], Canetti et al. [7], and Bitansky et al. [3], each using different machinery in clever ways, made progress toward the problem of succinct garbling using indistinguishability obfuscation. Recently, Chen et al. [9] and Canetti-Holmgren [6] achieve succinct garbled RAM from similar constructions, and the former discusses how to garble PRAM succinctly as well.

Adaptive vs Selective Security. Adaptive security has also become a recent topic of interest. Namely, the security of GRAM schemes where the adversary can adaptively choose inputs based on the garbling itself. Such schemes have recently been achieved for garbled *circuits* under one-way functions [18]. Adaptive garbled RAM has also been discovered recently, in the works of Canetti et al. [5] and Ananth et al. [1].

1.3   Our Results

In this paper, we provide the first construction of a fully black-box garbled PRAM, i.e. both the construction and the security reduction make only black-box use of any one-way function.

Main Theorem (Informal). Assuming only the existence of one-way functions, there exists a *black-box* garbled PRAM scheme, where the size of the garbled database is $\tilde{O}(|D|)$, the size of the garbled parallel program is $\tilde{O}(T \cdot m)$ where m is the number of processors needed and T is its (parallel) run time and its evaluation time is $\tilde{O}(T)$ where T is the parallel running time of program Π. Here $\tilde{O}(\cdot)$ ignores $\mathsf{poly}(\log T, \log |D|, \log m, \kappa)$ factors where κ is the security parameter.

1.4   Overview of New Ideas for Our Construction

There are several technical difficulties that must be overcome in order to construct a parallelized GRAM using only black-box access to a one-way function.

One attempt is to take the existing black-box construction of [11] and to apply all m processors in order to evaluate their garbling algorithms. However, the problem is that due to the way those circuits are packed into a node: a circuit will not learn how far a child has gone until the predecessor circuit is evaluated. So there must be some sophisticated coordination as the tree is being traversed or else parallelism will not help beyond faster evaluation of individual circuits inside the memory tree. Furthermore, circuits in the tree only accommodates a single CPU key per circuit. To take full advantage of parallelism, we have the ability to evaluate wider circuits that hold more CPU keys. However, we do not know apriori where these CPUs will read, so we must carefully balance the width of the circuit so that it is wide enough to hold all potential CPU keys that gets passed through it, yet not be too large as to impact the overhead. Indeed, the challenge is that the overhead of the storage size *cannot* depend linearly on the number of processors. We summarize the two main techniques used in our construction that greatly differentiates our new construction from all existing Garbled RAM constructions.

Garbled Label Routing. As there are now m CPUs that are evaluating per step, the garbled CPU labels that pass through our garbled memory tree must be passed along the tree so that each label reaches its according destination. At the leaf level, we want there to be no collisions between the locations so that each reach leaf emits exactly one data element encoded with one CPU's garbled labels. Looking ahead, in the concrete OPRAM scheme we will compile our solution with that of Boyle, Chung, and Pass [4], which guarantees collision-freeness and uniform access pattern. While this resolves the problem at the leaves, we must still be careful as the paths of all the CPUs will still merge at points in the tree that are only known at run-time. We employ a hybrid technique of using both parallel evaluation of wide circuits, and at some point we switch and evaluate, in parallel, a sequence of thin circuits to achieve this.

Level-dependent Circuit Width. In order to account for the multiple CPU labels being passed in at the root, we widen the circuits. Obviously, if we widen each circuit by a factor of m then this expands the garbled memory size by a prohibitively large factor of m. We do not know until run-time the number of nodes that will be visited at each level, with the exception of the root and leaves, and thus we must balance the sizes of the circuits to be not too large yet not too small. If we assume that the accesses are uniform, then we can expect the number of CPU keys a garbled memory circuit needs to hold is roughly halved at each level. Because of this, we draw inspiration from techniques derived from occupancy and concentration bounds and partition the garbled memory tree into two portions at a dividing boundary level b. This level b will be chosen so that levels above b, i.e. levels closer to the root, will have nodes which we assume will always be visited. However, we also want that the "occupancy" of CPU circuits at level b be sufficiently low that we can jump into the sequential hybrid mentioned above.

The combination of these techniques carefully joined together allows us to cut the overall garbled evaluation time and memory size so that the overhead is still poly-log.

1.5 Roadmap

In Sect. 2 we provide preliminaries and notation for our paper. We then give the full construction of our black-box garbled parallel RAM in Sect. 3. In Sect. 4 we prove that the overhead is polylogarithmic as claimed, and also provide a proof of correctness. We prove a weaker notion of security of our construction in Appendix A, show the transformation from the weaker version to full security in Appendix B and provide the full security proof in Sect. 5.

2 Preliminaries

2.1 Notation

We follow the notation of [4,11]. Let $[n]$ denote the set $\{0, \ldots, n-1\}$. For any bitstring L, we use L_i to denote the ith bit of L where $i \in [\|x\|]$ with the 0th bit being the highest order bit. We let $L_{0\ldots j-1}$ denote the j high order bits of L. We use shorthand for referring to sets of inputs and input labels of a circuit: if $\mathsf{lab} = \{\mathsf{lab}^{i,b}\}_{i \in |x|, b \in \{0,1\}}$ describes the labels for input wires of a garbled circuit, then we let lab_x denote the labels corresponding to setting the input to x, i.e. the subset of labels $\{\mathsf{lab}^{i,x_i}\}_{i \in |x|}$. We write $\bar{x}$ to denote that x is a vector of elements, with $x[i]$ being the i-th element. As we will see, half of our construction relies on the same types of circuits used in [11] and we follow their scheme of partitioning circuit inputs into separate logical colors.

2.2 PRAM: Parallel RAM Programs

We follow the definitions of [4,11]. A m parallel random-access machine is collection of m processors $\mathsf{CPU}_1, \ldots, \mathsf{CPU}_m$, having local memory of size $\log N$ which operate synchronously in parallel and can make concurrent access to a shared external memory of size N.

A PRAM *program* Π, on input N, m and input $\bar{x}$, provides instructions to the CPUs that can access to the shared memory. Each processor can be thought of as a circuit that evaluates $C^\Pi_{\mathsf{CPU}[i]}(\mathsf{state}, \mathsf{data}) = (\mathsf{state}', \mathsf{R/W}, L, z)$. These circuit steps execute until a halt state is reached, upon which all CPUs collectively output $\bar{y}$.

This circuit takes as input the current CPU state state and a block "data". Looking ahead this block will be read from the memory location that was requested for in the previous CPU step. The CPU step outputs an updated state state', a read or write bit $\mathsf{R/W}$, the next location to read/write $L \in [N]$, and a block z to write into the location ($z = \bot$ when reading). The sequence of locations and read/write values collectively form what is known as the *access pattern*, namely MemAccess $= \{(L^\tau, \text{R/W}^\tau, z^\tau, \text{data}^\tau) : \tau = 1, \ldots, t\}$, and we can consider the weak access pattern MemAccess2 $= \{L^\tau : \tau = 1, \ldots, t\}$ of just the memory locations accessed.

We work in the CRCW – concurrent read, concurrent write – model, though as we shall see, we can reduce this to a model where there are no read/write collisions. The (parallel) time complexity of a PRAM program Π is the maximum number of time steps taken by any processors to evaluate Π.

As mentioned above, the program gets a "short" input $\bar{x}$, can be thought of the initial state of the CPUs for the program. We use the notation $\Pi^D(\bar{x})$ to denote the execution of program Π with initial memory contents D and input $\bar{x}$. We also consider the case where several different parallel programs are executed sequentially and the memory persists between executions.

EXAMPLE PROGRAM EXECUTION VIA CPU STEPS. The computation $\Pi^D(\bar{x})$ starts with the initial state set as $\text{state}_0 = \bar{x}$ and initial read location $\overline{L} = \overline{0}$ as a dummy read operation. In each step $\tau \in \{0, \ldots T - 1\}$, the computation proceeds by reading memory locations $\overline{L^\tau}$, that is by setting $\overline{\text{data}^{\text{read},\tau}} :=$ $(D[L^\tau[0]], \ldots, D[L^\tau[m-1]])$ if $\tau \in \{1, \ldots T - 1\}$ and as $\overline{0}$ if $\tau = 0$. Next it executes the CPU-Step Circuit $C^\Pi_{\text{CPU}[i]}(\text{state}^\tau[i], \text{data}^{\text{read},\tau}[i]) \rightarrow (\text{state}^{\tau+1}[i], L^{\tau+1}[i], \text{data}^{\text{write},\tau+1}[i])$. Finally we write to the locations $\overline{L^\tau}$ by setting $D[L^\tau[i]] := \text{data}^{\text{write},\tau+1}[i]$. If $\tau = T - 1$ then we output the state of each CPU as the output value.

2.3   Garbled Circuits

We give a review on Garbled Circuits, primarily following the verbiage and notation of [11]. Garbled circuits were first introduced by Yao [23]. A circuit garbling scheme is a tuple of PPT algorithms (GCircuit, Eval). Very roughly GCircuit is the circuit garbling procedure and Eval the corresponding evaluation procedure. Looking ahead, each individual wire w of the circuit will be associated with two labels, namely $\text{lab}_0^w, \text{lab}_1^w$. Finally, since one can apply a generic transformation (see, e.g. [2]) to blind the output, we allow output wires to also have arbitrary labels associated with them. We also require that there exists a well-formedness test for labels which we call Test, which can trivially be instantiated, for example, by enforcing that labels must begin with a sufficiently long string of zeroes.

- $(\tilde{C}) \leftarrow \text{GCircuit}(1^\kappa, C, \{(w, b, \text{lab}_b^w)\}_{w\in\text{inp}(C), b\in\{0,1\}})$: GCircuit takes as input a security parameter κ, a circuit C, and a set of labels lab_b^w for all the input wires $w \in \text{inp}(C)$ and $b \in \{0, 1\}$. This procedure outputs a *garbled circuit* $\tilde{C}$.
- It can be efficiently tested if a set of labels is meant for a garbled circuit.
- $y = \text{Eval}(\tilde{C}, \{(w, \text{lab}_{x_w}^w)\}_{w\in\text{inp}(C)})$: Given a garbled circuit $\tilde{C}$ and a garbled input represented as a sequence of input labels $\{(w, \text{lab}_{x_w}^w)\}_{w\in\text{inp}(C)}$, Eval outputs an output y in the clear.

Correctness. For correctness, we require that for any circuit C and input $x \in \{0,1\}^n$ (here n is the input length to C) we have that:

$$\Pr\left[C(x) = \mathsf{Eval}(\tilde{C}, \{(w, \mathsf{lab}^w_{x_w})\}_{w \in \mathsf{inp}(C)})\right] = 1$$

where $\left(\tilde{C}\right) \leftarrow \mathsf{GCircuit}\left(1^\kappa, C, \{(w, b, \mathsf{lab}^w_b)\}_{w \in \mathsf{inp}(C), b \in \{0,1\}}\right)$.

Security. For security, we require that there is a PPT simulator $\mathsf{CircSim}$ such that for any C, x, and uniformly random labels $\left(\{(w, b, \mathsf{lab}^w_b)\}_{w \in \mathsf{inp}(C), b \in \{0,1\}}\right)$, we have that:

$$\left(\tilde{C}, \{(w, \mathsf{lab}^w_{x_w})\}_{w \in \mathsf{inp}(C)}\right) \stackrel{\text{comp}}{\approx} \mathsf{CircSim}\left(1^\kappa, C, C(x)\right)$$

where $\left(\tilde{C}\right) \leftarrow \mathsf{GCircuit}\left(1^\kappa, C, \{(w, \mathsf{lab}^w_b)\}_{w \in \mathsf{out}(C), b \in \{0,1\}}\right)$ and $y = C(x)$.

2.4 Oblivious PRAM

For the sake of simplicity, we let the CPU activation pattern, i.e. the processors active at each step, simply be that each processor is awake at each step and we only are concerned with the location access pattern $\mathsf{MemAccess2}$.

Definition 1. *An Oblivious Parallel RAM (OPRAM) compiler $\mathcal{O}$, is a PPT algorithm that on input $m, N \in \mathbb{N}$ and a deterministic m-processors PRAM program Π with memory size N, outputs an m-processor program Π' with memory size $\mathsf{mem}(m, N) \cdot N$ such that for any input x, the parallel running time of $\Pi'(m, N, x)$ is bounded by $\mathsf{com}(m, N) \cdot T$, where T is the parallel runtime of $\Pi(m, N, x)$, where $\mathsf{mem}(\cdot, \cdot), \mathsf{com}(\cdot, \cdot)$ denotes the memory and complexity overhead respectively, and there exists a negligible function ν such that the following properties hold:*

- *Correctness: For any $m, N \in \mathbb{N}$, and any string $x \in \{0,1\}^*$, with probability at least $1 - \nu(N)$, it holds that $\Pi(m, N, x) = \Pi'(m, N, x)$.*
- *Obliviousness: For any two PRAM programs Π_1, Π_2, any $m, N \in \mathbb{N}$, any two inputs $x_1, x_2 \in \{0,1\}^*$ if $|\Pi_1(m, N, x_1)| = |\Pi_2(m, N, x_2)|$ then $\mathsf{MemAccess2}_1$ is ν-close to $\mathsf{MemAccess2}_2$, where $\mathsf{MemAccess2}$ is the induced access pattern.*

Definition 2. *[Collision-Free]. An OPRAM compiler $\mathcal{O}$ is said to be collision free if given $m, N \in \mathbb{N}$, and a deterministic PRAM program Π with memory size N, the program Π' output by $\mathcal{O}$ has the property that no two processors ever access the same data address in the same timestep.*

REMARK. The concrete OPRAM compiler of Boyle et al. [4] will satisfy the above properties and also makes use of a convenient shorthand for inter-CPU messages. In their construction, CPUs can "virtually" communicate and coordinate with one another (e.g. so they don't access the same location) via a fixed-topology network and special memory locations. We remark that this can be emulated as a network of circuits, and will use this fact later.

2.5   Garbled Parallel RAM

We now define the extension of garbled RAM to parallel RAM programs. This primarily follows the definition of previous garbled RAM schemes, but in the parallel setting, and we refer the reader to [11,13,14] for additional details. As with many previous schemes, we have *persistent memory* in the sense that memory data D is garbled once and then many different garbled programs can be executed sequentially with the memory changes persisting from one execution to the next. We define full security and reintroduce the weaker notion of Unprotected Memory Access 2 (UMA2) in the parallel setting (c.f. [11]).

Definition 3. *A (UMA2) secure garbled* m-*parallel RAM scheme consists of four procedures (GData, GProg, GInput, GEval) with the following syntax:*

- $(\tilde{D}, s) \leftarrow$ *GData$(1^\kappa, D)$: Given a security parameter 1^κ and memory $D \in \{0,1\}^N$ as input GData outputs the garbled memory $\tilde{D}$.*
- $(\tilde{\Pi}, s^{in}) \leftarrow$ *GProg$(1^\kappa, 1^{\log N}, 1^t, \Pi, s, t_{old})$: Takes the description of a parallel RAM program Π with memory-size N as input. It also requires a key s and current time t_{old}. It then outputs a garbled program $\tilde{\Pi}$ and an input-garbling-key s^{in}.*
- $\tilde{x} \leftarrow$ *GInput$(1^\kappa, \overline{x}, s^{in})$: Takes as input $\overline{x}$ where $x[i] \in \{0,1\}^n$ for $i = 0, \ldots, m-1$ and an input-garbling-key s^{in}, outputs a garbled-input $\tilde{x}$.*
- $\tilde{y} =$ *GEval$^{\tilde{D}}(\tilde{\Pi}, \tilde{x})$: Takes a garbled program $\tilde{\Pi}$, garbled input $\tilde{x}$ and garbled memory data $\tilde{D}$ and outputs a vector of values $y[0], \ldots, y[m-1]$. We model GEval itself as a parallel RAM program with m processors that can read and write to arbitrary locations of its memory initially containing $\tilde{D}$.*

Efficiency. *We require the parallel run-time of GProg and GEval to be $t \cdot \text{poly}(\log N, \log t, \log m, \kappa)$, and the size of the garbled program $\tilde{\Pi}$ to be $m \cdot t \cdot \text{poly}(\log N, \log t, \log m, \kappa)$. Moreover, we require that the parallel run-time of GData should be $N \cdot \text{poly}(\log N, \log t, \log m, \kappa)$, which also serves as an upper bound on the size of $\tilde{D}$. Finally the parallel running time of GInput is required to be $n \cdot \text{poly}(\kappa)$.*

Correctness. *For correctness, we require that for any program Π, initial memory data $D \in \{0,1\}^N$ and input $\overline{x}$ we have that:*

$$\Pr[\text{GEval}^{\tilde{D}}(\tilde{\Pi}, \tilde{x}) = \Pi^D(\overline{x})] = 1$$

where $(\tilde{D}, s) \leftarrow$ GData$(1^\kappa, D)$, $(\tilde{\Pi}, s^{in}) \leftarrow$ GProg$(1^\kappa, 1^{\log N}, 1^t, \Pi, s, t_{old})$, $\tilde{x} \leftarrow$ GInput$(1^\kappa, \overline{x}, s^{in})$.

Security with Unprotected Memory Access 2 (Full vs UMA2). *For full or UMA2-security, we require that there exists a PPT simulator Sim such that for any program Π, initial memory data $D \in \{0,1\}^N$ and input vector $\overline{x}$, which induces access pattern MemAccess2 we have that:*

$$(\tilde{D}, \tilde{\Pi}, \tilde{x}) \overset{\text{comp}}{\approx} Sim(1^\kappa, 1^N, 1^t, \overline{y}, \text{MemAccess2})$$

where $(\tilde{D}, s) \leftarrow$ GData$(1^\kappa, D)$, $(\tilde{\Pi}, s^{in}) \leftarrow$ GProg$(1^\kappa, 1^{\log N}, 1^t, \Pi, s, t_{old})$ and $\tilde{x} \leftarrow$ GInput$(1^\kappa, \overline{x}, s^{in})$, and $\overline{y} = \Pi^D(\overline{x})$. For full security, the simulator Sim does not get MemAccess2 as input.

Security for multiple programs on persistent memory. In the case where there are multiple PRAM programs being executed in sequence, we consider the garbled memory being initially garbled and then garbled programs can then be ran on the persistent memory in sequence. That is to say, $(\tilde{D}, s) \leftarrow$ GData$(1^\kappa, D)$ is used to generate an initial garbled memory, then given programs $\Pi_1, \ldots, \Pi_u$, with running times $t_1, \ldots, t_u$ we produce garbled programs produced by $(\tilde{\Pi}_i, s_i^{in}) \leftarrow$ GProg$(1^\kappa, 1^{\log N}, 1^{t_i}, \Pi, s, \sum_{j<i} t_j)$, where the last parameter governs the sequential ordering as a program can only start running at its given time. Given inputs $(\overline{x}_1, \ldots, \overline{x}_u)$ we can produce garbled inputs $\tilde{x}_i \leftarrow$ GInput$(1^\kappa, \overline{x}_i, s_i^{in})$. Finally, we have outputs evaluated by running the programs on the persistent memory $\overline{y}_i =$ GEval$^{\tilde{D}_{i-1}}(\tilde{\Pi}_i, \tilde{x}_i)$, where $\tilde{D}_i$ is the updated persistent memory after step i. If each program induces some memory access pattern MemAccess2$_i$, then

$$(\tilde{D}, \{\tilde{\Pi}_i\}, \{\tilde{x}_i\}) \stackrel{\text{comp}}{\approx} \text{Sim}(1^\kappa, 1^N, 1^T, \{\overline{y}_i\}, \{\text{MemAccess2}_i\})$$

Similarly, for full security, the simulator Sim does not get MemAccess2 as input.

3   Construction of Black-Box Parallel GRAM

3.1   Overview

We first summarize our construction at a high level. An obvious first point to consider is to ask where the difficulty arises when attempting to parallelize the construction of Garg, Lu, and Ostrovsky (GLO) [11]. There are two main issues that go beyond that considered by GLO: first, there must be coordination amongst the CPUs so that if different CPUs want access to the same location, they don't collide, and second, the control flow is highly sequential, allowing only one CPU key to be passed down the tree per "step". In order to resolve these issues, we build up a series of steps that transform a PRAM program into an Oblivious PRAM program that satisfies nice properties, and then show how to modify the structure of the garbled memory in order to accommodate parallel accesses.

In a similar vein to previous GRAM constructions, we want to transform a PRAM program first into an Oblivious PRAM program where the memory access patterns are distributed uniformly. However, a uniform distribution of m elements would result in collisions with non-negligible probability. As such, we want an Oblivious PRAM construction where the CPUs can utilize a "virtual" inter-CPU communication to achieve collision-freeness. Looking ahead, in the concrete OPRAM scheme we are using of Boyle, Chung, and Pass (BCP) [4], this property is already satisfied, and we use this in Sect. 5 to achieve full security.

A challenge that remains is to parallelize the garbled memory so that each garbled time step can process m garbled processors in parallel assuming the evaluator has m processors. In order to pass control from one CPU step to the next, we have two distinct phases: one where the CPUs are reading from memory, and another is when the CPUs communicating amongst themselves to pass messages and coordinating. Because the latter computation can be done with an apriori fixed network of $\mathsf{polylog}(m, N)$ size, we can treat it as a small network of circuits that talk to only a few other CPUs that we can then garble (recall that in order for one CPU to talk to another when garbled, it must have the appropriate input labels hardwired, so we require low locality which is satisfied by these networks). The main technical challenge is therefore being able to read from memory in parallel.

In order to address this challenge, we first consider a solution where we widen each circuit by a factor of m so that m garbled CPU labels (or keys as we will call them) can fit into a circuit at once. This first attempt falls short for several reasons. It expands the garbled memory size by a factor of m, and although keys can be passed down the tree, there is still the issue of how fast these circuits are consumed and how it would affect the analysis of the GLO construction.

To get around the size issue, we employ a specifically calibrated size halving technique: because the m accesses are a random m subset of the N memory locations, it is expected that half the CPUs want to read to the left, and the other half to the right. Thus, as we move down the tree, the number of CPU keys a garbled memory circuit needs to hold can be roughly halved at each level. Bounding the speed of consumption is a more complex issue. A counting argument can be used to show that at level i, the probability that a particular node will be visited is $1 - \binom{N-N/2^i}{m}/\binom{N}{m}$. As $N/2^i$ and m may vary from constant to logarithmic to polynomial in N, standard asymptotic bounds might not apply, or would result in a complicated bound. Because of this, we draw inspiration from techniques derived from occupancy and concentration bounds and partition the garbled memory tree into two portions at a dividing boundary level b. This level b will be chosen so that levels above b, i.e. levels closer to the root, will have nodes which we assume will always be visited. However, we also want that at level b, the probability that within a single parallel step more than $B = \log^4(N)$ CPUs will all visit a single node is negligible.

It follows then that above level b, for each time step, one garbled circuit at each node at each level will be consumed. Below level b, the tree will fall back to the GLO setting with one major change: level $b+1$ will be the new "virtual" root of the GLO tree. We must ensure that b is sufficiently small so that this does not negatively impact the overall number of circuits. The boundary nodes at level b will output B garbled queries for each child (which includes the location and CPU keys), which will then be processed one at a time at level $b+1$. Indeed, each subtree below the nodes at level b will induce a sequence of at most B reads, where each read is performed as in GLO, all of them *sequential*, but different subtrees will be processed *in parallel*. This allows us to cut the overall garbled evaluation time down so that the parallel overhead is still poly-log. After the formal construction is given in this section, we provide a full cost analysis of this in Sect. 4, along with the proof of correctness. This construction will then be sufficient to achieve UMA2-security and se will prove in Appendix A, and as mentioned above, we show full security in Sect. 5. We now state our goal/main theorem and spend the rest of the paper providing the formal construction and proof.

Theorem (Main Theorem). *Assuming the existence of one-way functions, there exists a fully black-box secure garbled PRAM scheme for arbitrary m-processor PRAM programs. The size of the garbled database is $\tilde{O}(|D|)$, size of the garbled input is $\tilde{O}(|x|)$ and the size of the garbled program is $\tilde{O}(mT)$ and its m-parallel evaluation time is $\tilde{O}(T)$ where T is the m-parallel running time of program P. Here $\tilde{O}(\cdot)$ ignores $\mathsf{poly}(\log T, \log |D|, \log m, \kappa)$ factors where κ is the security parameter.*

3.2 Data Garbling: $(\tilde{D}, s) \leftarrow \mathsf{GData}(1^\kappa, D)$

We start by providing an informal description of the data garbling procedure, which turns out to be the most involved part of the construction. The formal description of GData is provided in Fig. 5. Before looking at the garbling algorithm, we consider several sub-circuits. Our garbled memory consists of four types of circuits and an additional table (inherited from the GLO scheme) to keep track of previously output garbled labels. As described in the overview, there will be "wide" circuits near the root that contains main CPU keys, a boundary layer at level b (to be determined later) of boundary nodes that transition wide circuits into thin circuits that are identical to those in the GLO construction. We describe the functionality of the new circuits and review the operations of the GLO style circuits.

Conceptually, the memory can be thought of as a tree of nodes, and each node contains a sequence of garbled circuits. For the circuits, which we call $\mathsf{C}^{\mathsf{wide}}$, above level b, their configuration is straightforward: for every time step, there will be one circuit at every node corresponding to that time step. Below level b, the circuits are configured as in GLO, via $\mathsf{C}^{\mathsf{node}}$ and $\mathsf{C}^{\mathsf{leaf}}$ with the difference being that there will be a fixed multiplicative factor of more circuits per node to account for the parallel reads. At level b, the circuits $\mathsf{C}^{\mathsf{edge}}$ will serve as a transition on the edge between wide and thin circuits as we describe below.

The behavior of the circuits are as follows. $\mathsf{C}^{\mathsf{wide}}$ takes as input a parallel CPU query which consists of a tuple $(\overline{\mathsf{R/W}}, \overline{L}, \overline{z}, \overline{\mathsf{cpuDKey}})$. This is interpreted as a vector of indicators to read or write, the location to read or write to, the data to write, and the key of the next CPU step for the CPU that initiated this query. On the k-th circuit of this form at a given node, the circuit has hardwired within it keys for precisely the k-th left and right child (as opposed to a window of child keys focused around $k/2$ as in the GLO circuit configuration). This circuit routes the queries to the left or right child depending on the location L and passes the (garbled) query down appropriately to exactly one left and one right child. The formal description is provided in Fig. 1.

$C^{\text{wide}}[i, k, \overline{\text{tKey}}]$

System parameters: ϵ, γ
Hardcoded parameters: $[i, k, w, \overline{\text{tKey}}]$
Input: $q = (\overline{R/W}, \overline{L}, \overline{z}, \overline{\text{cpuDKey}})$.

Set $w' := \lfloor w(\frac{1}{2} + \epsilon) \rfloor + \gamma$. Create two arrays $\overline{L^l}$ and $\overline{L^r}$ of size w' each. Partition the elements of $\overline{L}$ into those with the i-th bit set to 0 and 1, respectively, and place them into $\overline{L^l}$ and $\overline{L^r}$. If more than w' locations fall into one array, then abort and output KEY-OVERFLOW-ERROR. Fill the unused locations with $\perp$.
Set $q^l := (\overline{R/W^l}, \overline{L^l}, \overline{z^l}, \overline{\text{cpuDKey}^l})$, where $\overline{R/W^l}, \overline{z^l}$, and $\overline{\text{cpuDKey}^l}$ are induced by the partition above. Set q^r in a similar fashion.
Set $\text{outqKey}[0] := \text{tKey}[0]_{q^l}$ and $\text{outqKey}[1] := \text{tKey}[1]_{q^r}$ and output $(\text{outqKey}[0], \text{outqKey}[1])$.

Fig. 1. Formal description of the wide memory circuit.

$C^{\text{edge}}[i, k, \overline{\text{tKey}}]$

System parameters: ϵ, γ, B
Hardcoded parameters: $[i, k, w, \overline{\text{tKey}}]$
Input: $q = (\overline{R/W}, \overline{L}, \overline{z}, \overline{\text{cpuDKey}})$.

Assert $w \leq B$ otherwise abort with KEY-OVERFLOW-ERROR. Set q^l and q^r as in C^{wide}.
Note that $\overline{\text{tKey}}$ will contain $2B$ keys, corresponding to B left and B right child circuit input labels.
Let $j^\star$ denote the index of the last non-null CPU key that wants to read to the left. Set $goto^l[j] := Bk + j$ for $j < j^\star$, $goto^l[j^\star] := Bk + B - 1$ and $goto^l[j] = \perp$ for $j > j^\star$. Similarly set $goto^r$.
Set $q'[0 \ldots B - 1] := (\overline{goto^l}, \overline{R/W^l}, \overline{L^l}, \overline{z^l}, \overline{\text{cpuDKey}^l})$.
Set $q'[B \ldots 2B - 1] := (\overline{goto^r}, \overline{R/W^r}, \overline{L^r}, \overline{z^r}, \overline{\text{cpuDKey}^r})$.
Output $(\text{tKey}[0]_{q'[0]}, \ldots, \perp, \ldots, \text{tKey}[2B - 1]_{q'[2B-1]}, \ldots, \perp)$, where $\perp$ replaces a tKey value when the corresponding $goto$ is $\perp$.

Fig. 2. Formal description of the memory circuit at the edge level between wide and narrow circuits.

C^{edge} operates similarly and routes the query, but now must interface with the thin circuits below that only accept a single CPU key as input. As such, it will take as input a vector of queries and outputs labels for multiple left and right children circuits. Looking ahead, the precise number of children circuits this will execute will be determined by our analysis, but will be known and fixed in advance for GData. The formal description is provided in Fig. 2.

Finally, the remaining C^{node} and C^{leaf} behave as they did in the GLO scheme. Their formal descriptions are provided in Figs. 3 and 4. As a quick review, circuits within a node process the query L and activates either a left or a right child circuit (not both, unlike the circuits above). As such, it must also pass on information from one circuit to the subsequent on in the node, providing it information on whether it went left or right, and provides keys to an appropriate window of left and right child circuits. Finally, at the leaf level, the leaf processes the query by either outputting the stored data encoded under the appropriate

$C^{\mathsf{node}}[i, k, \mathsf{newLtKey}, \mathsf{newRtKey}, \mathsf{rKey}, \mathsf{qKey}]$

System parameters: ϵ (Will be set to $\frac{1}{\log M}$ as we will see later.)

Hardcoded parameters: $[i, k, \mathsf{newLtKey}, \mathsf{newRtKey}, \overline{\mathsf{rKey}}, \mathsf{qKey}]$

Input: (rec = (lidx, ridx, oldLKey, oldRKey, $\overline{\mathsf{tKey}}$), q = $(goto, \mathsf{R/W}, L, z, \mathsf{cpuDKey}))$.

Set $\mathsf{p} := goto$ and $\mathsf{p}' := \lfloor \left(\frac{1}{2} + \epsilon\right) k \rfloor$.

Set $\mathsf{lidx}' := \mathsf{lidx}$ and $\mathsf{ridx}' := \mathsf{ridx}$. Set $\mathsf{oldLKey}' := \mathsf{oldLKey}$ and $\mathsf{oldRKey}' := \mathsf{oldRKey}$.

Define $ins(\overline{\mathsf{tKey}}, \mathsf{newLtKey}, \mathsf{newRtKey})$ to be the function that outputs $\overline{\mathsf{tKey}}$ with a possible shift: if $\lfloor \left(\frac{1}{2} + \epsilon\right)(k+1) \rfloor > \lfloor \left(\frac{1}{2} + \epsilon\right) k \rfloor$, shift $\overline{\mathsf{tKey}}$ to the left by 1 and set $\mathsf{tKey}[\kappa-1] = \mathsf{newLtKey}, \mathsf{tKey}[2\kappa-1] = \mathsf{newRtKey}$.

We now have three cases:

1. If $k < \mathsf{p} - 1$ then we output $(\mathsf{outrKey}, \mathsf{outqKey}) := (\mathsf{rKey}_{\mathsf{rec}'}, \mathsf{qKey}_{\mathsf{q}})$, where $\mathsf{rec}' := (\mathsf{lidx}', \mathsf{ridx}', \mathsf{oldLKey}', \mathsf{oldRKey}', \overline{\mathsf{tKey}}')$ where $\overline{\mathsf{tKey}}' = ins(\overline{\mathsf{tKey}}, \mathsf{newLtKey}, \mathsf{newRtKey})$.
2. If $k \geq \mathsf{p} + \kappa$ then abort with output OVERCONSUMPTION-ERROR-I.
3. If $\mathsf{p} - 1 \leq k < \mathsf{p} + \kappa$ then:
   (a) If $L_i = 0$ then,
      i. If $\mathsf{lidx} < \mathsf{p}'$ then set $\mathsf{lidx}' := \mathsf{p}', goto' := \mathsf{p}'$ and $\mathsf{oldLKey}' := \mathsf{tKey}[0]$. Else set $\mathsf{lidx}' := \mathsf{lidx} + 1, goto' := \mathsf{lidx}'$ and if $\mathsf{lidx}' < \mathsf{p}' + \kappa$ then set $\mathsf{oldLKey}' := \mathsf{tKey}[\mathsf{lidx}' - \mathsf{p}']$ else abort with OVERCONSUMPTION-ERROR-II.
      ii. Set $\mathsf{tKey}[v] := \bot$ for all $v < \mathsf{lidx}' - \mathsf{p}'$. Set $\overline{\mathsf{tKey}}' = ins(\overline{\mathsf{tKey}}, \mathsf{newLtKey}, \mathsf{newRtKey})$.
      iii. Set $\mathsf{outqKey} := \mathsf{oldLKey}_{\mathsf{q}'}$, where $\mathsf{q}' := \mathsf{q}$ but with $goto'$ replacing $goto$.
      else
      i. If $\mathsf{ridx} < \mathsf{p}'$ then set $\mathsf{ridx}' := \mathsf{p}', goto' := \mathsf{p}'$ and $\mathsf{oldRKey}' := \mathsf{tKey}[\kappa]$. Else set $\mathsf{ridx}' := \mathsf{ridx} + 1, goto' := \mathsf{ridx}'$ and if $\mathsf{ridx}' < \mathsf{p}' + \kappa$ then set $\mathsf{oldRKey}' := \mathsf{tKey}[\kappa + \mathsf{ridx}' - \mathsf{p}']$ else abort with OVERCONSUMPTION-ERROR-II.
      ii. Set $\mathsf{tKey}[\kappa + v] := \bot$ for all $v < \mathsf{ridx}' - \mathsf{p}'$. Set $\overline{\mathsf{tKey}}' = ins(\overline{\mathsf{tKey}}, \mathsf{newLtKey}, \mathsf{newRtKey})$.
      iii. Set $\mathsf{outqKey} := \mathsf{oldRKey}_{\mathsf{q}'}$, where $\mathsf{q}' := \mathsf{q}$ but with $goto'$ replacing $goto$.
   (b) Set $\mathsf{outrKey} := \mathsf{rKey}_{\mathsf{rec}'}$ where $\mathsf{rec}' := (\mathsf{lidx}', \mathsf{ridx}', \mathsf{oldLKey}', \mathsf{oldRKey}', \overline{\mathsf{tKey}}')$ and output $(\mathsf{outrKey}, \mathsf{outqKey})$.

Fig. 3. Formal description of the nonleaf, thin memory circuit with key passing. This is identical to the node circuit in [11].

$C^{\mathsf{leaf}}[i, k, \mathsf{dKey}, \mathsf{qKey}]$

System parameters: ϵ (Will be set to $\frac{1}{\log M}$ as we will see later.)

Hardcoded parameters: $[i, k, \mathsf{dKey}, \mathsf{qKey}]$

Input: $(\mathsf{data}, \mathsf{q} = (goto, \mathsf{R/W}, L, z, \mathsf{cpuDKey}))$.

Set $\mathsf{p} := goto$ and $\mathsf{p}' := \lfloor \left(\frac{1}{2} + \epsilon\right) k \rfloor$. We now have three cases:

1. If $k < \mathsf{p} - 1$ then we output $(\mathsf{outdKey}, \mathsf{outqKey}) := (\mathsf{dKey}_{\mathsf{data}}, \mathsf{qKey}_{\mathsf{q}})$.
2. If $k \geq \mathsf{p} + \kappa$ then abort with output OVERCONSUMPTION-ERROR-I.
3. If $\mathsf{p} - 1 \leq k < \mathsf{p} + \kappa$ then: If R/W = read then output $(\mathsf{dKey}_{\mathsf{data}}, \mathsf{cpuDKey}_{\mathsf{data}})$, else if R/W = write then output $(\mathsf{dKey}_z, \mathsf{cpuDKey}_z)$.

Fig. 4. Formal description of the leaf Memory Circuit. This is identical to $C^{\mathsf{leaf}}[i, k, \mathsf{dKey}, \mathsf{qKey}]$ in [11]. See the next page for Fig. 5 describing the full GData algorithm.

The algorithm $\mathsf{GData}(1^\kappa, D)$ proceeds as follows. Without loss of generality we assume that $N = 2^d$ (where $N = |D|$) where d is a positive integer. Let m the number of parallel memory accesses. We set $\epsilon = \frac{1}{\log N}$. We set and $b = \log(m)/\log(4/3)$, $B = \log^4 N$, and $\gamma = \log^3(N)$. We set $K_{b+1} = \gamma N/m$, and for each $b < i \in [d+1]$ and set $K_i = \lfloor (\frac{1}{2} + \epsilon) K_{i-1} \rfloor + \kappa$. Set $W_0 = m$ and $W_i = \lfloor (\frac{1}{2} + \delta) W_{i-1} \rfloor + \kappa$.

1. Let $s \leftarrow \{0,1\}^\kappa$.
2. Any $\mathsf{dKey}^{d,j,k}$ needed in the computation below is obtained as $F_s(\mathsf{data}||d||j||k)$. Similarly for any i, j, k, $\mathsf{rKey}^{i,j,k} := F_s(\mathsf{rec}||i||j||k)$ and $\mathsf{qKey}^{i,j,k} := F_s(\mathsf{query}||i||j||k)$ (truncated to the correct length, as not all qKeys have the same length).
3. For all $b < i < d, j \in [2^i], k \in [K_i]$, set

$$\overline{\mathsf{tKey}}^{i,j,0} := \left\{ \underbrace{\{\mathsf{qKey}^{i+1,2j,l}\}_{l \in [\kappa]}}_{\text{left}} , \underbrace{\{\mathsf{qKey}^{i+1,2j+1,l}\}_{l \in [\kappa]}}_{\text{right}} \right\}.$$

and if $\lfloor (\frac{1}{2} + \epsilon)(k+1) \rfloor > \lfloor (\frac{1}{2} + \epsilon)(k) \rfloor$, then set

$$\mathsf{newLtKey}^{i,j,k} = \mathsf{qKey}^{i+1,2j,\lfloor (\frac{1}{2}+\epsilon)(k+1) \rfloor + \kappa - 1}$$

$$\mathsf{newRtKey}^{i,j,k} = \mathsf{qKey}^{i+1,2j+1,\lfloor (\frac{1}{2}+\epsilon)(k+1) \rfloor + \kappa - 1}$$

otherwise set $\mathsf{newLtKey}^{i,j,k} = \mathsf{newRtKey}^{i,j,k} = \perp$.
4. For all $i = b$, $j \in [2^i]$, $k \in [N/m]$, set $\overline{\mathsf{tKey}}^{i,j,k} = \{\{\mathsf{qKey}^{i+1,2j,Bk+l}\}_{l \in [B]}, \{\mathsf{qKey}^{i+1,2j+1,Bk+l}\}_{l \in [B]}\}$.
5. For all $0 \leq i < b, j \in [2^i]$, $k \in [N/m]$, set $\overline{\mathsf{tKey}}^{i,j,k} = \{\mathsf{qKey}^{i+1,2j,k}, \mathsf{qKey}^{i+1,2j+1,k}\}$.
6. For all $j \in [2^d], k \in [K_d]$, $\tilde{C}^{d,j,k} \leftarrow \mathsf{GCircuit}\left(1^\kappa, \mathsf{C}^{\mathsf{leaf}}\left[d, k, \mathsf{dKey}^{d,k,k+1}, \mathsf{qKey}^{d,j,k+1}\right], \mathsf{dKey}^{d,j,k}, \mathsf{qKey}^{d,j,k}\right)$
7. For all $b < i < d, j \in [2^i], k \in [K_i]$, $\tilde{C}^{i,j,k} \leftarrow \mathsf{GCircuit}(1^\kappa, \mathsf{C}^{\mathsf{node}}\left[i, k, \mathsf{newLtKey}^{i,j,k}, \mathsf{newRtKey}^{i,j,k}, \mathsf{rKey}^{i,j,k+1}, \mathsf{qKey}^{i,j,k+1}\right]$, $\mathsf{rKey}^{i,j,k}, \mathsf{qKey}^{i,j,k})$
8. For all $i = b, j \in [2^i], k \in [N/m]$, $\tilde{C}^{i,j,k} \leftarrow \mathsf{GCircuit}(1^\kappa, \mathsf{C}^{\mathsf{edge}}\left[i, k, W_i, \overline{\mathsf{tKey}}^{i,j,k}\right], \mathsf{qKey}^{i,j,k})$.
9. For all $0 \leq i < b, j \in [2^i], k \in [N/m]$, $\tilde{C}^{i,j,k} \leftarrow \mathsf{GCircuit}(1^\kappa, \mathsf{C}^{\mathsf{wide}}\left[i, k, W_i, \overline{\mathsf{tKey}}^{i,j,k}\right], \mathsf{qKey}^{i,j,k})$.
10. For all $j \in [2^d]$, set $\mathsf{Tab}(d, j) = \mathsf{dKey}^{d,j,0}_{D[j]}$.
11. For all $b < i \in [d], j \in [2^i]$, set $\mathsf{Tab}(i, j) := \mathsf{rKey}^{i,j,0}_{\mathsf{rec}^{i,j,0}}$, where $\mathsf{rec}^{i,j,0} := (0, 0, \mathsf{qKey}^{i+1,2j,0}, \mathsf{qKey}^{i+1,2j+1,0}, \overline{\mathsf{tKey}}^{i,j,0})$.
12. Output $\tilde{D} := \left(\left\{ \tilde{C}^{i,j,k} \right\}_{i \in [d+1], j \in [2^i], k \in [K_i]}, \{\mathsf{Tab}(i,j)\}_{b < i \in [d+1], j \in [2^i]} \right)$ and s.

Fig. 5. Formal description of GData.

CPU key, or writes data to its successor leaf circuit. This information passing is stored in a table as in the GLO scheme.

3.3 Program Garbling: $(\tilde{\Pi}, s^{in}) \leftarrow \mathsf{GProg}(1^\kappa, 1^{\log N}, 1^t, \Pi, s, t_{old})$

As we assumed, the program Π is a collision-free OPRAM program. We conceptually identify three distinct steps that are used to compute a parallel CPU step: the main CPU step itself (where each processor takes an input and state, and produces a new state and read/write request), and two types of inter-CPU communication steps that routes the appropriate read/write values before and

---

$C^{\text{step}}[t, \text{rootqKey}, \overline{\text{cpuSKey}}, \overline{\text{cpuDKey}}]$

Hardcoded parameters: $[t, \text{rootqKey}, \overline{\text{cpuSKey}}, \overline{\text{cpuDKey}}]$
Input: $(\overline{\text{state}}, \overline{\text{data}})$.

Route the appropriate data to each processor and then compute $(\text{state}'[i], \text{R/W}[i], L[i], z[i]) := C^{\Pi}_{\text{CPU}_i}(\text{state}[i], \text{data}[i])$ for each processor CPU_i. Post-process the queries so that the collision-free property is held, then set $q[i] := (\text{R/W}[i], L[i], z[i], \text{cpuDKey}[i])$ and output rootqKey_q and $\text{cpuSKey}[i]_{\text{state}'[i]}$, or a halt signal.

Fig. 6. Formal description of the step circuit.

The $\text{GProg}(1^\kappa, 1^{\log N}, 1^t, \Pi, s, t_{old})$ procedure proceeds as follows.

1. For processor i, any $\text{cpuSKey}^\tau[i]$ needed in the computation below is obtained as $F_s(\text{CPUstate}\|\tau\|i)$, and any $\text{cpuDKey}^\tau[i]$ is obtained as $F_s(\text{CPUdata}\|\tau\|i)$.
2. For $\tau = t_{old}, \dots, t_{old} + t - 1$ do:
   (a) Set $\text{qKey}^{0,0,\tau} := F_s(\text{query}\|0\|0\|\tau)$.
   (b) $\tilde{C}^\tau \leftarrow \text{GCircuit}\left(1^\kappa, C^{\text{step}}\left[\tau, \text{qKey}^{0,0,\tau}, \overline{\text{cpuSKey}}^{\tau+1}, \overline{\text{cpuDKey}}^{\tau+1}\right],\right.$
   $\left.\overline{\text{cpuSKey}}^\tau, \overline{\text{cpuDKey}}^\tau\right)$
3. Output $\tilde{\Pi} := \left(m, \{\tilde{C}^\tau\}_{\tau \in \{t_{old}, \dots, t_{old}+t-1\}}, \overline{\text{cpuDKey}}^{t_{old}}_\perp\right)$, $s^{in} = \overline{\text{cpuSKey}}^{t_{old}}$

Fig. 7. Formal description of GProg.

after memory is accessed. We compile them together as a single large circuit which we describe in Fig. 6.

Then each of the t parallel CPU steps are then garbled in sequence as with previous GRAM constructions. We provide the formal garbling of the steps in Fig. 7.

3.4 Input Garbling: $\overline{\tilde{x}} \leftarrow \text{GInput}(1^\kappa, \overline{x}, s^{in})$

Input garbling is straightforward: the inputs are treated as selection bits for the m-vector of labels. We give a formal description of GProg in Fig. 8.

3.5 Garbled Evaluation: $y \leftarrow \text{GEval}^{\tilde{D}}(\tilde{\Pi}, \tilde{x})$

The GEval procedure gets as input the garbled program $\tilde{\Pi}$ which we write as $\left(t_{old}, \{\tilde{C}^\tau\}_{\tau \in \{t_{old}, \dots, t_{old}+t-1\}}, \text{cpuDKey}\right)$, the garbled input $\tilde{x} = \overline{\text{cpuSKey}}$ and random access into the garbled database $\tilde{D} = (\{\tilde{C}^{i,j,k}\}_{i \in [d+1], j \in [2^i], k \in [K_i]},$ $\{\text{Tab}(i,j)\}_{i > b, j \in [2^i]})$ as well as m parallel processors. In order to evaluate a garbled time step τ, it evaluates every garbled circuit where $i = 0 \dots b, j \in [2^i], k = \tau$ using parallelism to evaluate the wide circuits, then it switches into evaluating $B(\frac{1}{2} + \delta) + \kappa$ sequential queries of each of the subtrees below level b as in GLO. Looking ahead, we will see that $2^b \approx m$ and so we can evaluate the different subtrees in parallel. A formal description of GEval is provided in Fig. 9.

The algorithm $\mathsf{GInput}(1^\kappa, \bar{x}, s^{in})$ proceeds as follows.

1. Parse s^{in} as $\overline{\mathsf{cpuSKey}}$ and output $\tilde{x} := (\mathsf{cpuSKey}[i]_{x[i]})$ for $i = 0 \dots m$.

Fig. 8. Formal description of GInput.

The algorithm $\mathsf{GEval}^{\tilde{D}}(\tilde{\Pi}, \tilde{x})$ proceeds as follows.

1. Parse $\tilde{\Pi}$ as $\left(t_{old}, \{\tilde{C}^\tau\}_{\tau \in \{t_{old}, \dots, t_{old}+t-1\}}, \mathsf{cpuDKey}\right)$, $\tilde{x}$ as $\mathsf{cpuSKey}$ and

   $\tilde{D}$ as $\left(\left\{\tilde{C}^{i,j,k}\right\}_{i \in [d+1], j \in [2^i], k \in [K_i]}, \{\mathsf{Tab}(i,j)\}_{i \in [d+1], j \in [2^i]}\right)$.

2. For $\tau \in \{t_{old}, \dots, t_{old}+t-1\}$ do:
   (a) Evaluate $(\overline{\mathsf{cpuSKey}}, \mathsf{qKey}^{0,0,\tau}) := \mathsf{Eval}(\tilde{C}^\tau, (\overline{\mathsf{cpuSKey}}, \mathsf{cpuDKey}))$. If an output y is produced by Eval instead, then output y and halt.
   (b) Set $i = 0, j = 0, k = \tau$.
   (c) For $i = 0 \dots b - 1, j = 0 \dots 2^i, k = \tau$, evaluate $\mathsf{qKey}^{i+1,2j,\tau}, \mathsf{qKey}^{i+1,2j+1,\tau} := \mathsf{Eval}(\tilde{C}^{i,j,k}, (\mathsf{qKey}^{i,j,\tau}))$.
   (d) Set $B' = \lfloor B(\frac{1}{2} + \delta) \rfloor + \kappa$.
   (e) For $i = b, j = 0 \dots 2^i, k = \tau$, evaluate $\mathsf{qKey}^{i+1,2j,B'\tau}, \dots, \mathsf{qKey}^{i+1,2j,B'\tau+B'-1}$, $\mathsf{qKey}^{i+1,2j+1,B'\tau}, \dots, \mathsf{qKey}^{i+1,2j+1,B'\tau+B'-1} := \mathsf{Eval}(\tilde{C}^{i,j,k}, (\mathsf{qKey}^{i,j,\tau}))$.
   (f) For $i = b + 1, j = 0 \dots 2^i, k = B'\tau \dots B'\tau + B' - 1$
       i. Set $\mathsf{qKey} = \mathsf{qKey}^{i,j,k}$, if $\mathsf{qKey} \neq \bot$, evaluate the subtree as in GLO, i.e.
       ii. Evaluate $\mathsf{outputKey} := \mathsf{Eval}(\tilde{C}^{i,j,k}, (\mathsf{Tab}(i,j), \mathsf{qKey}))$.
           A. If $\mathsf{outputKey}$ is parsed as $(\mathsf{rKey}, \mathsf{qKey}^{i',j',k'})$ for some i', j', k', then set $\mathsf{Tab}(i,j) := \mathsf{rKey}, \mathsf{qKey} := \mathsf{qKey}^{i',j',k'}, (i,j,k) = (i',j',k')$ and go to Step 2(f)ii.
           B. Otherwise, set $(\mathsf{dKey}, \mathsf{cpuDKey}[u]) := \mathsf{outputKey}$, and $\mathsf{Tab}(i,j) := \mathsf{dKey}$, where u is the appropriate CPU id.
       iii. When all subtrees finish evaluating, increment τ and go to Step 2

Fig. 9. Formal description of GEval.

4 Cost and Correctness Analysis

4.1 Overall Cost

In this section, we analyze the cost and correctness of the algorithms above, before delving into the security proof. We work with $d = \log N$, $b = \log(m)/\log(4/3)$, $\epsilon = \frac{1}{\log N}$, $\gamma = \log^3 N$, and $B = \log^4 N$. First, we observe from the GLO construction, that $|C^{\mathsf{node}}|$ and $|C^{\mathsf{leaf}}|$ are both $\mathrm{poly}(\log N, \log t, \log m, \kappa)$, and that the CPU step (with the fixed network of inter-CPU communication) is $m \cdot \mathrm{poly}(\log N, \log t, \log m, \kappa)$.

It remains to analyze the size of $|C^{\mathsf{wide}}|$ and $|C^{\mathsf{edge}}|$. Depending on the level in which these circuits appear, they may be of different sizes. Note, if we let $W_0 = m$ and $W_i = \lfloor (\frac{1}{2} + \delta) W_{i-1} \rfloor + \kappa$, then $|C^{\mathsf{wide}}|$ at level i is of size $(W_i + 2W_{i+1}) \cdot \mathrm{poly}(\log N, \log t, \log m, \kappa)$. We also note $|C^{\mathsf{edge}}|$ has size at most $3B \cdot \mathrm{poly}(\log N, \log t, \log m, \kappa) = \mathrm{poly}(\log N, \log t, \log m, \kappa)$.

We calculate the cost of the individual algorithms.

Cost of GData. The cost of the algorithm $\mathsf{GData}(1^\kappa, D)$ is dominated by the cost of garbling each circuit (the table generation is clearly $O(N) \cdot$

$\text{poly}(\log N, \log t, \log m, \kappa))$. We give a straightforward bound of $K_{b+1+i} \leq \left(\frac{1}{2} + \epsilon\right)^i (BN/m + i\kappa)$ and $W_i \leq \left(\frac{1}{2} + \epsilon\right)^i (m + i\gamma)$.

We must be careful in calculating the cost of the wide circuits, as they cannot be garbled in $\text{poly}(\log N, \log t, \log m, \kappa)$ time, seeing as how their size depends on m. Thus we require a more careful bound, and the cost of garblings of C^{node} (ignoring $\text{poly}(\log N, \log t, \log m, \kappa)$ factors) is given as

$$\sum_{i=0}^{b} 2^i N/m W_i + \sum_{i=b+1}^{d-1} 2^i K_i$$

$$\leq N/m \sum_{i=0}^{b} (1+2\epsilon)^i (m + b\gamma) + \sum_{i=0}^{d-b-2} 2^{i+b+1} K_{b+1+i}$$

$$\leq N/m e^{2b\epsilon}(m + b\gamma) + 2^{b+1} e^{2d\epsilon}(BN/m + d\kappa)$$

Plugging in the values for $d, b, \epsilon, \gamma, B$, we obtain $N \cdot \text{poly}(\log N, \log t, \log m, \kappa)$.

Cost of GProg. The algorithm $\text{GProg}(1^\kappa, 1^{\log N}, 1^t, P, s, t_{old})$ computes t values for cpuSKeys,cpuDKeys, and qKeys. It also garbles t C^{step} circuits and outputs them, along with a single cpuSKey. Since each individual operation is $m \cdot \text{poly}(\log N, \log t, \log m, \kappa)$, the overall space cost is $\text{poly}(\log N, \log t, \log m, \kappa) \cdot t \cdot m$, though despite the larger space, it can be calculated in m-parallel time $\text{poly}(\log N, \log t, \log m, \kappa) \cdot t$.

Cost of GInput. The algorithm $\text{GInput}(1^\kappa, \overline{x}, s^{in})$ selects labels of the state key based on the state as input. As such, the space cost is $\text{poly}(\log N, \log t, \log m, \kappa) \cdot m$, and again can be prepared in time $\text{poly}(\log N, \log t, \log m, \kappa)$.

Cost of GEval. For the sake of calculating the cost of GEval, we assume that it does not abort with an error (which, looking ahead, will only occur with negligible probability). At each CPU step, one circuit is evaluated per node above and including level b. At some particular level $i < b$ the circuit is wide and contains $O(W_i)$ gates (but shallow, and hence can be parallelized). From our analysis above, we know that $\sum_{i=0}^{b} 2^i W_i \leq \sum_{i=0}^{b}(1 + 2\epsilon)^i(m + b\gamma) \leq e^{2b\epsilon}(m + b\gamma)$, and can be evaluated in $\text{poly}(\log N, \log t, \log m, \kappa)$ time given m parallel processors. For the remainder of the tree, we can think of virtually spawning 2^{b+1} processes where each process sequentially performs B queries against the subtrees. The query time below level b is calculated from GLO of having amortized $\text{poly}(\log N, \log t, \log m, \kappa)$ cost, and therefore incurs $2^{b+1} \cdot B \cdot \text{poly}(\log N, \log t, \log m, \kappa)$ cost. However, $2^{b+1} \leq m$ and therefore can be parallelized down to $\text{poly}(\log N, \log t, \log m, \kappa)$ overhead.

4.2 Correctness

The arrangement of the circuits below level b follows that of the GLO scheme, and by their analysis, the errors overflow errors OVERCONSUMPTION-ERROR-I and

OVERCONSUMPTION-ERROR-II do not occur except with a negligible probability. Therefore, for correctness, we must show that KEY-OVERFLOW-ERROR never occurs except with negligible probability, both at C^{wide} and C^{edge}.

Claim. KEY-OVERFLOW-ERROR with probability negligible in N.

Proof. The only two ways this error is thrown is if a wide circuit of a parent of level i attempts to place more than W_i CPU keys into a child node at level i, or an edge circuit fails the bound $w \leq B$. We show that this cannot happen with very high probability. In order to do so, we first put a lower bound on W_i and then show that the probability that a particular query will cause a node at level i to have more than W_i CPU keys is negligible. We have that

$$W_i = (\frac{1}{2} + \epsilon)^i m + \sum_{j=0}^{i-1} (\frac{1}{2} + \epsilon)^j \gamma \geq \frac{m}{2^i} + \frac{2m\epsilon}{2^i} + \gamma$$

Our goal is to bound the probability that if we pick m random leaves that more than W_i paths from the root to those leaves go through a particular node at level i. Of course, the m random leaves are chosen to be uniformly *distinct* values, but we can bound this by performing an easier analysis where m are chosen uniformly at random with repetition.

We let X be a variable that indicates the number of paths that take a particular node at level i. We can treat X as a sum of m independent trials, and thus expect $\mu = \frac{m}{2^i}$ hits on average. We set $\delta = 2\epsilon + \frac{\gamma}{\mu}$. Then by the strong form of the Chernoff bound, we have:

$$Pr[X > W_i] \leq Pr[X > \frac{m}{2^i} + \frac{2m\epsilon}{2^i} + \gamma]$$

$$\leq Pr[X > \mu(1 + \delta)] \leq \exp\left[-\frac{\delta^2 \mu}{2 + \delta}\right]$$

$$\leq \exp\left[-\delta\mu\left(\frac{\delta}{1 + \delta}\right)\right] \leq \exp\left[-(2\epsilon\mu + \gamma)\left(\frac{2\epsilon + \gamma/\mu}{2 + 2\epsilon + \gamma/\mu}\right)\right]$$

$$\leq \exp\left[-(2\epsilon\mu + \gamma)\left(\frac{2\epsilon}{3}\right)\right] \leq \exp\left[-\frac{2}{3}(2\epsilon^2\mu + \epsilon\gamma)\right]$$

Since $\epsilon\gamma = \frac{\log^3 N}{\log N}$, this is negligible in N.

Finally, need to show that $W_b \leq B$ so that C^{edge} does not cause the error. Here, we use the *upper bound* for W_b, and assume $\log N > 4$. We calculate:

$$W_b \leq \left(\frac{1}{2} + \epsilon\right)^b (m + b\gamma) \leq \left(\frac{1}{2} + \frac{1}{4}\right)^b (m + b\gamma)$$

$$\leq \left(\frac{3}{4}\right)^{\log(m)/\log(4/3)} (m + b\gamma) \leq \frac{1}{m}(m + b\gamma)$$

$$\leq \log^4 N = B$$

$\square$

5   Main Theorem

We complete the proof of our main theorem in this section, where we combine our UMA2-secure GPRAM scheme with statistical OPRAM. First, we state a theorem from [4]:

Theorem 4 (Theorem from [4]). *There exists an activation-preserving and collision-free OPRAM compiler with polylogarithmic worst-case computational overhead and $\omega(1)$ memory overhead.*

We make the additional observation that the scheme also produces a uniformly random access pattern that always chooses m random memory locations to read from at each step, hence a program compiled under this theorem satisfies the assumption of our UMA2-security theorem. We make the following remark: REMARK ON CIRCUIT REPLENISHING As with many previous garbled RAM schemes such as [11,13,14], the garbled memory eventually becomes consumed and will needed to be refreshed as they are being consumed across multiple programs. Our garbled memory is created for N/m timesteps and for the sake of brevity we refer the reader to [12] for the details of applying such a technique.

Then, by combining Theorem 4 with Theorem 6 and Lemma 7, we obtain our main theorem.

Theorem 5 (Main Theorem). *Assuming the existence of one-way functions, there exists a fully black-box secure garbled PRAM scheme for arbitrary m-processor PRAM programs. The size of the garbled database is $\tilde{O}(|D|)$, size of the garbled input is $\tilde{O}(|x|)$ and the size of the garbled program is $\tilde{O}(mT)$ and its m-parallel evaluation time is $\tilde{O}(T)$ where T is the m-parallel running time of program P. Here $\tilde{O}(\cdot)$ ignores $\mathsf{poly}(\log T, \log|D|, \log m, \kappa)$ factors where κ is the security parameter.*

Acknowledgments. We thank Alessandra Scafuro for helpful discussions. We thank the anonymous reviewers for their useful comments.

References

1. Ananth, P., Chen, Y.-C., Chung, K.-M., Lin, H., Lin, W.-K.: Delegating RAM computations with adaptive soundness and privacy. In: Hirt, M., Smith, A. (eds.) TCC 2016. LNCS, vol. 9986, pp. 3–30. Springer, Heidelberg (2016). doi:10.1007/978-3-662-53644-5_1

2. Applebaum, B., Ishai, Y., Kushilevitz, E.: From secrecy to soundness: efficient verification via secure computation. In: Abramsky, S., Gavoille, C., Kirchner, C., Meyer auf der Heide, F., Spirakis, P.G. (eds.) ICALP 2010. LNCS, vol. 6198, pp. 152–163. Springer, Heidelberg (2010). doi:10.1007/978-3-642-14165-2_14

3. Bitansky, N., Garg, S., Lin, H., Pass, R., Telang, S.: Succinct randomized encodings and their applications. In: Servedio, R.A., Rubinfeld, R. (eds.) 47th Annual ACM Symposium on Theory of Computing, Portland, OR, USA, June 14–17, 2015, pp. 439–448. ACM Press (2015)

4. Boyle, E., Chung, K.-M., Pass, R.: Oblivious parallel RAM and applications. In: Kushilevitz, E., Malkin, T. (eds.) TCC 2016. LNCS, vol. 9563, pp. 175–204. Springer, Heidelberg (2016). doi:10.1007/978-3-662-49099-0_7

5. Canetti, R., Chen, Y., Holmgren, J., Raykova, M.: Adaptive succinct garbled RAM or: how to delegate your database. In: Hirt, M., Smith, A. (eds.) TCC 2016. LNCS, vol. 9986, pp. 61–90. Springer, Heidelberg (2016). doi:10.1007/978-3-662-53644-5_3

6. Canetti, R., Holmgren, J.: Fully succinct garbled RAM. In: Sudan, M. (ed.) ITCS 2016: 7th Innovations in Theoretical Computer Science, Cambridge, MA, USA, January 14–16, 2016, pp. 169–178. Association for Computing Machinery (2016)

7. Canetti, R., Holmgren, J., Jain, A., Vaikuntanathan, V.: Succinct garbling and indistinguishability obfuscation for RAM programs. In: Servedio, R.A., Rubinfeld, R. (eds.) 47th Annual ACM Symposium on Theory of Computing, Portland, OR, USA, June 14–17, 2015, pp. 429–437. ACM Press (2015)

8. Chen, B., Lin, H., Tessaro, S.: Oblivious parallel RAM: improved efficiency and generic constructions. In: Kushilevitz, E., Malkin, T. (eds.) TCC 2016. LNCS, vol. 9563, pp. 205–234. Springer, Heidelberg (2016). doi:10.1007/978-3-662-49099-0_8

9. Chen, Y.-C., Chow, S.S.M., Chung, K.-M., Lai, R.W.F., Lin, W.-K., Zhou, H.-S.: Cryptography for parallel RAM from indistinguishability obfuscation. In: Sudan, M. (ed.) ITCS 2016: 7th Innovations in Theoretical Computer Science, Cambridge, MA, USA, January 14–16, 2016, pp. 179–190. Association for Computing Machinery (2016)

10. Garg, S., Gupta, D., Miao, P., Pandey, O.: Secure multiparty RAM computation in constant rounds. In: Hirt, M., Smith, A. (eds.) TCC 2016. LNCS, vol. 9985, pp. 491–520. Springer, Heidelberg (2016). doi:10.1007/978-3-662-53641-4_19

11. Garg, S., Lu, S., Ostrovsky, R.: Black-box garbled RAM. In: Guruswami, V. (ed.) 56th Annual Symposium on Foundations of Computer Science, Berkeley, CA, USA, October 17–20, 2015, pp. 210–229. IEEE Computer Society Press (2015)

12. Garg, S., Lu, S., Ostrovsky, R.: Black-box garbled RAM. Cryptology ePrint Archive, Report 2015/307 (2015). http://eprint.iacr.org/2015/307

13. Garg, S., Lu, S., Ostrovsky, R., Scafuro, A.: Garbled RAM from one-way functions. In: Servedio, R.A., Rubinfeld, R. (ed.) 47th Annual ACM Symposium on Theory of Computing, Portland, OR, USA, June 14–17, 2015, pp. 449–458. ACM Press (2015)

14. Gentry, C., Halevi, S., Lu, S., Ostrovsky, R., Raykova, M., Wichs, D.: Garbled RAM revisited. In: Nguyen, P.Q., Oswald, E. (eds.) EUROCRYPT 2014. LNCS, vol. 8441, pp. 405–422. Springer, Heidelberg (2014). doi:10.1007/978-3-642-55220-5_23

15. Gentry, C., Halevi, S., Raykova, M., Wichs, D.: Outsourcing private RAM computation. In: 55th Annual Symposium on Foundations of Computer Science, Philadelphia, PA, USA, October 18–21, 2014, pp. 404–413. IEEE Computer Society Press (2014)

16. Goldreich, O.: Towards a theory of software protection and simulation by oblivious RAMs. In: Aho, A. (ed.) 19th Annual ACM Symposium on Theory of Computing, New York City, NY, USA, May 25–27, 1987, pp. 182–194. ACM Press (1987)

17. Goldreich, O., Ostrovsky, R.: Software protection and simulation on oblivious RAMs. J. ACM **43**(3), 431–473 (1996)

18. Hemenway, B., Jafargholi, Z., Ostrovsky, R., Scafuro, A., Wichs, D.: Adaptively secure garbled circuits from one-way functions. In: Robshaw, M., Katz, J. (eds.) CRYPTO 2016. LNCS, vol. 9816, pp. 149–178. Springer, Heidelberg (2016). doi:10.1007/978-3-662-53015-3_6

19. Koppula, V., Lewko, A.B., Waters, B.: Indistinguishability obfuscation for turing machines with unbounded memory. In: Servedio, R.A., Rubinfeld, R. (ed.) 47th Annual ACM Symposium on Theory of Computing, Portland, OR, USA, June 14–17, 2015, pp. 419–428. ACM Press (2015)

20. Lu, S., Ostrovsky, R.: How to Garble RAM programs? In: Johansson, T., Nguyen, P.Q. (eds.) EUROCRYPT 2013. LNCS, vol. 7881, pp. 719–734. Springer, Heidelberg (2013). doi:10.1007/978-3-642-38348-9_42

21. Miao, P.: Cut-and-choose for garbled RAM. Cryptology ePrint Archive, Report 2016/907 (2016). http://eprint.iacr.org/2016/907

22. Ostrovsky, R.: Efficient computation on oblivious RAMs. In: 22nd Annual ACM Symposium on Theory of Computing, Baltimore, MD, USA, May 14–16, 1990, pp. 514–523. ACM Press (1990)

23. Yao, A.C.-C.: Protocols for secure computations (extended abstract). In: 23rd Annual Symposium on Foundations of Computer Science, Chicago, Illinois, November 3–5, 1982, pp. 160–164. IEEE Computer Society Press (1982)

A   UMA2-security Proof

In this section we state and prove our main technical contribution on fully black-box garbled parallel RAM that leads to our full theorem. Below, we provide our main technical theorem:

Theorem 6 (UMA2-security). *Let F be a PRF and* (GCircuit, Eval, CircSim) *be a circuit garbling scheme, both of which can be built from any one-way function in black-box manner. Then our construction* (GData, GProg, GInput, GEval) *is a UMA2-secure garbled PRAM scheme for m-processor uniform parallel access programs running in total time $T < N/m$ making only black-box access to the underlying OWF.*

Proof.
    Informally, at a high level, we can describe our proof as follows. We know that below level b, the circuits can all be properly simulated due to the fact they are constructed identically to that of GLO (except there are simply more circuits). On the other hand, circuits above this level have no complex parent-to-child wiring, i.e. for each time step, every parent contains exactly the keys for its two children at that time step and not any other time step. Furthermore, circuits within a node above level b do not communicate to each other. Thus, simulating these circuits are straightforward: at time step t_{old}, simulate the root circuit $\tilde{C}^{0,0,\tau}$ then simulate the next level down $\tilde{C}^{1,0,\tau}$ and $\tilde{C}^{1,1,\tau}$ and so forth.
    The formal analysis is as follows. Since we are proving UMA2-security, we know ahead of time the number of time steps, the access locations, and hence the exact circuits that will be executed and in which order. Of course, we are evaluating circuits in parallel, but as we shall see, whenever we need to resolve the ordering of two circuits are being executed in parallel, we will already be working in a hybrid in which they are independent of one another, and hence we can arbitrarily assign an order (lexicographically). Let CircSim be the garbled circuit simulator, and let U be the total number of circuits that will be evaluated

in the real execution. We show how to construct a simulator Sim and then give a series of hybrids $\hat{H}^0, H^0, \ldots, H^U, \hat{H}^U$ such that the first hybrid outputs the $(\tilde{D}, \tilde{\Pi}, \tilde{x})$ of the is the real execution and the last hybrid is the output of Sim, which we will define. The construction will have a similar structure of previous garbling hybrid schemes, and for the circuits below level b we use the same analysis as in [11], but still the proof will require new analysis for circuits above level b. H^0 is the real execution with the PRF F replaced with a uniform random function (where previously evaluated values are tabulated). Since the PRF key is not used in evaluation, we immediately obtain $\hat{H}^0 \overset{\text{comp}}{\approx} H^0$.

Consider the sequence of circuits that would have been evaluated given MemAccess. This sequence is entirely deterministic and therefore we let $S_1, \ldots, S_U$ be this sequence of circuits, e.g. $S_1 = \tilde{C}^0$ (the first parallel CPU step circuit), $S_2 = \tilde{C}^{0,0,0}$ (the first root circuit), $\ldots$ H^u simulates the first u of these circuits, and generates all other circuits as in the real execution.

Hybrid Definition: $(\tilde{D}, \tilde{\Pi}, \tilde{x}) \leftarrow H^u$

The hybrid H^u proceeds as follows: For each circuit not in $S_1, \ldots, S_u$, generate it as you would in the real execution (note that GData can generate circuits using only, and for each circuit $S_u, \ldots, S_1$ (in that order) we simulate the circuit using CircSim by giving it as output what it would have generated in the real execution or what was provided as the simulated input labels. Note that this may use information about the database D and the inputs $\tilde{x}$, and our goal is to show that at the very end, Sim will not need this information.

We now show $H^{u-1} \overset{\text{comp}}{\approx} H^u$. Either S_u is a circuit in the tree, in which case let i be its level, or else S_u is a CPU step circuit. We now analyze the possible cases:

1. $i = 0$: In a root node, the only circuit that holds its qKey is the previous step node, which would have already been simulated, so the output of CircSim is indistinguishable from a real garbling.
2. $0 < i \leq b$: In a wide or edge node, the only circuit that holds its qKey is the parent circuit from the same time step. Since this was previously evaluated and simulated, we can again simulate this circuit with CircSim.
3. $i = b + 1$: In the level below the edge node, the circuits are arranged as in the root of the GLO construction. However, the qKey and rKey inputs for these circuits now can either come from the parent (edge circuit) or a predecessor thin circuit in the same level. These can be handled in batches of B, sequentially, because every node still has a distinct parent that holds its qKey (that will never be passed on to subsequent parents, as edge circuits do not pass information from one to the next), as well as its immediate predecessor which will already have been simulated. Thus, again we can invoke CircSim.

4. $i > b + 1$: Finally, these nodes all behave as in the GLO construction, and it similarly follows by the analysis of their construction, these nodes can all also be simulated.

In the final case, if S_u is a CPU step circuit, then only the CPU circuit of the previous time step has its $\overline{\text{cpuSKey}}$. On the other hand, its $\overline{\text{cpuDKey}}$ originated from the previous CPU step, but was passed down the entire tree. Due to the way we order the circuits, we ensure that all parallel steps have been completed before this circuit is evaluated, and this ensures that any circuit that passed a cpuDKey as a value have already been simulated in an earlier hybrid. Thus, any distinguisher of H^{u-1} and H^u can again be used to distinguish between the output of CircSim and a real garbling.

After the course of evaluation, there will be of course unevaluated circuits in the final hybrid $\hat{H}^U$. As with [11], we use the same circuit encryption technique (see Appendix B in [12] for a formal proof) and encrypt these circuits so that partial inputs of a garbled circuit reveal nothing about the circuit.

Therefore, our simulator $\text{Sim}(1^\kappa, 1^N, 1^t, \overline{y}, 1^D, \text{MemAccess} = \{L^\tau, z^{\text{read},\tau}, z^{\text{write},\tau}\}_{\tau=0,\ldots,t-1})$ can output the distribution $\hat{H}^U$ without access to D or $\overline{x}$. We see this as follows: the simulator, given MemAccess can determine the sequence $S_1, \ldots, S_U$. The simulator starts by first replacing all circuits that won't be evaluated by replacing them with encryptions of zero. It then simulates the S_u in reverse order, starting with simulating S_U using the output $\overline{y}$, and then working backwards simulates further ones ensuring that their output is set to the appropriate inputs.

□

B   UMA2 to Full Security

In this section, we describe how to achieve multi-program full security from UMA2 security by applying a Oblivious PRAM scheme. We mention that this transformation is an adaptation of the UMA2-to-full transformation of the GLO solution into PRAM setting. As such, we will paraphrase much of the proof found in [12] though in the context of parallel programs.

Lemma 7. *Assume there exists a UMA2-secure Garbled PRAM scheme for programs with uniform memory access, and a statistically secure ORAM scheme with uniform memory access that protects the access pattern but not necessarily the contents of memory. Then there exists a fully secure Garbled Parallel RAM scheme.*

Proof. We note that although we consider uniform memory access, we do not require the memory access to be strictly uniform, c.f. [12] for a discussion on leveled uniformity. Thus, we focus on the simpler case of uniform access and the proof extends to the current setting of statistical Oblivious PRAM. We show the existence of such a GPRAM scheme by explicitly constructing the new GPRAM scheme in a black-box manner as follows. Let (GData, GProg, GInput, GEval) be a

UMA2-secure GPRAM and let $(\mathsf{OData}, \mathsf{OProg})$ be an Oblivious PRAM scheme. We construct a new GPRAM scheme $(\widehat{\mathsf{GData}}, \widehat{\mathsf{GProg}}, \widehat{\mathsf{GInput}}, \widehat{\mathsf{GEval}})$ as follows:

- $\widehat{\mathsf{GData}}(1^\kappa, D)$: Execute $(D^*) \leftarrow \mathsf{OData}(1^\kappa, D)$ then $(\tilde{D}, s) \leftarrow \mathsf{GData}(1^\kappa, D^*)$. Output $\widehat{D} = \tilde{D}$ and $\widehat{s} = s$. Note that OData does not require a key as it is a statistical scheme.
- $\widehat{\mathsf{GProg}}(1^\kappa, 1^{\log N}, 1^t, \Pi, \widehat{s}, t_{old})$: Execute $\Pi^* \leftarrow \mathsf{OProg}(1^\kappa, 1^{\log N}, 1^t, \Pi)$ followed by $(\tilde{\Pi}, s^{in}) \leftarrow \mathsf{GProg}(1^\kappa, 1^{\log N'}, 1^{t'}, \Pi^*, \widehat{s}, t_{old}')$, where the primed variables are the growth in size due to the Oblivious PRAM transformation. Output $\widehat{\Pi} = \tilde{\Pi}$, $\widehat{s^{in}} = s^{in}$.
- $\widehat{\mathsf{GInput}}(1^\kappa, \overline{x}, \widehat{s^{in}})$: Note that $\overline{x}$ is a valid (parallel) input for the oblivious program Π^*. Execute $\tilde{x} \leftarrow \mathsf{GInput}(1^\kappa, \overline{x}, \widehat{s^{in}})$, and output $\widehat{x} = \tilde{x}$.
- $\widehat{\mathsf{GEval}}^{\widehat{D}}(\widehat{\Pi}, \widehat{x})$: Execute $\overline{y} \leftarrow \mathsf{GEval}^{\widehat{D}}(\widehat{\Pi}, \widehat{x})$ and output $\overline{y}$.

We now prove that $(\widehat{\mathsf{GData}}, \widehat{\mathsf{GProg}}, \widehat{\mathsf{GInput}}, \widehat{\mathsf{GEval}})$ is a fully secure Garbled PRAM scheme. Suppose $\Pi_1, \ldots, \Pi_u$ are a sequence of programs with running times $t_1, \ldots, t_u$, and let $T_j = \sum_{i<j} t_i$ denote the sum of the running times of the first $j - 1$ programs. Let $D \in \{0,1\}^N$ be any initial memory data, let $\overline{x}_1, \ldots, \overline{x}_u$ be inputs and $(\overline{y}_1, \ldots, \overline{y}_u)$ be the outputs of the sequential execution of the programs on D. Let $(\widehat{D}_0, \widehat{s}) \leftarrow \widehat{\mathsf{GData}}(1^\kappa, D)$, and for $i = 1 \ldots u$: $(\widehat{\Pi}_i, \widehat{s_i^{in}}) \leftarrow \widehat{\mathsf{GProg}}(1^\kappa, 1^{\log N}, 1^{t_i}, \Pi_i, \widehat{s}, T_i)$, $\widehat{x}_i \leftarrow \widehat{\mathsf{GInput}}(1^\kappa, \overline{x}_i, \widehat{s_i^{in}})$. Finally, we consider the sequential execution of the garbled programs for $i = 1 \ldots u$: $\overline{y}_i' \leftarrow \widehat{\mathsf{GEval}}^{\widehat{D}_{i-1}}(\widehat{\Pi}_i, \widehat{x}_i)$ which updates the garbled database to $\widehat{D}_i$.

Correctness. We argue that

$$\Pr[(\overline{y}_1', \ldots, \overline{y}_u') = (\overline{y}_1, \ldots, \overline{y}_u)] = 1.$$

This follows directly from our underlying evaluation algorithms: $\widehat{\mathsf{GEval}}$ executes the underlying GPRAM scheme for evaluation, the correctness of the underlying scheme guarantees that $(\overline{y}_1', \ldots, \overline{y}_u') = (\Pi_1^*(\overline{x}_1), \ldots, \Pi_u^*(\overline{x}_u))^{D^*}$. Then by the correctness of the underlying OPRAM scheme, $(\Pi_1^*(\overline{x}_1), \ldots, \Pi_u^*(\overline{x}_u))^{D^*} = (\Pi_1(x_1), \ldots, \Pi_u(x_u))^D = (\overline{y}_1, \ldots, \overline{y}_u)$.

Security. For any programs $\Pi_1, \ldots, \Pi_u$, database D, and inputs $\overline{x}_1, \ldots, \overline{x}_u$, let

$$\mathrm{REAL}^{D, \{\Pi_i, \overline{x}_i\}} = (\widehat{D}_0, \widehat{\Pi}_i, \widehat{x}_i{}_{i=1}^u)$$

We show how to construct a simulator Sim such that for all $D, \{\Pi_i, \overline{x}_i\}$, we have that $\mathrm{REAL}^{D, \{\Pi_i, \overline{x}_i\}} \overset{comp}{\approx} \mathsf{Sim}(1^\kappa, 1^N, \{1^{t_i}, \overline{y}_i\})$. We let OSim be the Oblivious PRAM simulator, and USim be the simulator for the UMA2-secure GPRAM scheme. We describe Sim as follows.

1. Compute $(N', \mathsf{MemAccess}) \leftarrow \mathsf{OSim}(1^\kappa, 1^N, \{1^{t_i}, \overline{y}_i\}_{i=1}^u)$. We note that we run a multi-program OPRAM simulator which then statistically simulates $\mathsf{MemAccess}$ across all programs though not D^* (only its size).

2. Compute $(\tilde{D}, \{\tilde{\Pi}_i, \tilde{x}_i\}_{i=1}^u) \leftarrow \mathsf{USim}(1^\kappa, 1^{N'}, \{1^{t'_i}, \overline{y}_i\}_{i=1}^u, \mathsf{MemAccess})$, where as before, the primed variables are the expanded ones resulting from applying OPRAM.

3. Output $(\widehat{D}_0, \widehat{\Pi}_i, \widehat{x}_{i i=1}^u) = (\tilde{D}, \{\tilde{\Pi}_i, \tilde{x}_i\}_{i=1}^u)$.

We show that the simulated output is computationally indistinguishable from the real distribution. For any $D, \{\Pi_i, \overline{x}_i\}$, we define a series of hybrid distributions $\mathbf{Hyb}_0, \mathbf{Hyb}_1, \mathbf{Hyb}_2$ with $\mathbf{Hyb}_0$ being the real distribution, $\mathbf{Hyb}_2$ being the simulated distribution, and argue that for $j = 0, 1$ we have $\mathbf{Hyb}_j \overset{comp}{\approx} \mathbf{Hyb}_{j+1}$.

- $\mathbf{Hyb}_0$: This is the real distribution $\mathrm{REAL}^{D, \Pi_i, \overline{x}_i}$.
- $\mathbf{Hyb}_1$: Use the correctly generated (D^*) from $\widehat{\mathsf{GData}}$ and Π_i^* from $\widehat{\mathsf{GProg}}$ and execute $(\Pi_1^*(\overline{x}_1), \ldots$
  $, \Pi_u^*(\overline{x}_u))^{D^*}$ to obtain $\{\overline{y}_i\}$ and a sequence of memory accesses $\mathsf{MemAccess}$. Run $(\tilde{D}, \{\tilde{\Pi}_i, \tilde{x}_i\}_{i=1}^u) \leftarrow \mathsf{USim}(1^\kappa, 1^{N'}, \{1^{t'_i}, \overline{y}_i\}_{i=1}^u, \mathsf{MemAccess})$ and output $(\widehat{D}_0, \widehat{\Pi}_i, \widehat{x}_{i i=1}^u) = (\tilde{D}, \{\tilde{\Pi}_i, \tilde{x}_i\}_{i=1}^u)$.
- $\mathbf{Hyb}_2$: This is the simulated distribution $\mathsf{Sim}(1^\kappa, 1^N, \{1^{t_i}, \overline{y}_i\}_{i=1}^u)$.

We now demonstrate indistiguishability.

$\mathbf{Hyb}_0 \overset{comp}{\approx} \mathbf{Hyb}_1$: Let $\mathcal{A}$ be a PPT distinguisher between these two hybrids for some $D, \{\Pi_i, \overline{x}_i\}$. By way of contradiction, we demonstrate an algorithm $\mathcal{B}$ that breaks the UMA2-security of the underlying GPRAM scheme. First, $\mathcal{B}$ runs $(D^*) \leftarrow \mathsf{OData}(1^\kappa, D), \Pi_i^* \leftarrow \mathsf{OProg}(1^\kappa, 1^{\log N}, 1^{t_i}, \Pi_i)$ and declares $D^*, \{\Pi_i^*, \overline{x}_i)\}$ as the challenge database, programs and inputs for the UMA2-security GRAM game. The UMA2-security challenger then outputs $(\tilde{D}', \{\tilde{\Pi}_i', \tilde{x}_i'\})$ and $\mathcal{B}$ must output a guess whether it is real or simulated. $\mathcal{B}$ sets $(\widehat{D}', \{\widehat{\Pi}_i', \widehat{x}_i'\}l) = (\tilde{D}', \{\tilde{\Pi}_i', \tilde{x}_i'\}_{i=1}^u)$ and internally invokes this as the challenge to $\mathcal{A}$. $\mathcal{B}$ then outputs the same guess as $\mathcal{A}$.

Observe that if the UMA2-challenger outputs real values, then $(\widehat{D}', \{\widehat{\Pi}_i', \widehat{x}_i'\})$ is distributed identically as if it were generated from $\mathbf{Hyb}_0$, and if the UMA challenger outputs simulated values, then $(\widehat{D}', \{\widehat{\Pi}_i', \widehat{x}_i'\}_{i=1}^u)$ is distributed identically as if it were generated from $\mathbf{Hyb}_1$. Therefore, $\mathcal{A}$ distinguishes with the same probability as $\mathcal{B}$, which is negligible by the UMA2-security of the underlying GPRAM scheme.

$\mathbf{Hyb}_1 \overset{comp}{\approx} \mathbf{Hyb}_2$:Let $\mathcal{A}$ be a PPT distinguisher between these two hybrids for some $D, \{\Pi_i, \overline{x}_i\}$. Again, by way of contradiction, $\mathcal{B}$ that breaks the security of the underlying OPRAM scheme that proceeds as follows. First, $\mathcal{B}$ announces $D, \{\Pi_i, \overline{x}_i\}$ as the challenge database, programs, and inputs for the OPRAM security game. The OPRAM challenger then outputs a challenge memory access pattern for the programs ($\mathsf{MemAccess}'$) which can be real or simulated. Then, $\mathcal{B}$ computes $(y_1, \ldots, y_u) = (\Pi_1(\overline{x}_1), \ldots, \Pi_u(\overline{x}_u))^D$ and runs the UMA2-simulator $(\tilde{D}', \{\tilde{\Pi}_i', \tilde{x}_i'\}_{i=1}^u) \leftarrow \mathsf{USim}(1^\kappa, 1^{N'}, \{1^{t'_i}, \overline{y}_i\}, \mathsf{MemAccess}')$. Next, $\mathcal{B}$ sets $(\widehat{D}', \{\widehat{\Pi}_i', \widehat{x}_i'\}_{i=1}^u) = (\tilde{D}', \{\tilde{\Pi}_i', \tilde{x}_i'\}_{i=1}^u)$ and passes this to $\mathcal{A}$. $\mathcal{B}$ then outputs the same guess as $\mathcal{A}$.

Observe that if the OPRAM challenger outputs the real values, then the tuple $(\widehat{D}', \{\widehat{\Pi}'_i, \widehat{x}'_i\})$ is distributed identically as if it were generated from $\mathbf{Hyb}_1$, and alternatively, if the OPRAM challenger outputs simulated values, then $(\widehat{D}', \{\widehat{\Pi}'_i, \widehat{x}'_i\})$ is distributed identically as if it were generated from $\mathbf{Hyb}_2$. Therefore, $\mathcal{A}$ distinguishes with the same probability as $\mathcal{B}$, which is negligible by the security of the underlying OPRAM scheme.   □

Foundations II

Non-Malleable Codes for Space-Bounded Tampering

Sebastian Faust[1(✉)], Kristina Hostáková[1], Pratyay Mukherjee[2],
and Daniele Venturi[3]

[1] Ruhr-Universität Bochum, Bochum, Germany
sebastian.faust@gmail.com
[2] Visa Research, Palo Alto, USA
[3] Sapienza University of Rome, Rome, Italy

Abstract. Non-malleable codes—introduced by Dziembowski, Pietrzak and Wichs at ICS 2010—are key-less coding schemes in which mauling attempts to an encoding of a given message, w.r.t. some class of tampering adversaries, result in a decoded value that is either identical or unrelated to the original message. Such codes are very useful for protecting arbitrary cryptographic primitives against tampering attacks against the memory. Clearly, non-malleability is hopeless if the class of tampering adversaries includes the decoding and encoding algorithm. To circumvent this obstacle, the majority of past research focused on designing non-malleable codes for various tampering classes, albeit assuming that the adversary is unable to decode. Nonetheless, in many concrete settings, this assumption is not realistic.

In this paper, we explore one particular such scenario where the class of tampering adversaries naturally includes the decoding (but not the encoding) algorithm. In particular, we consider the class of adversaries that are restricted in terms of memory/space. Our main contributions can be summarized as follows:

- We initiate a general study of non-malleable codes resisting space-bounded tampering. In our model, the encoding procedure requires large space, but decoding can be done in small space, and thus can be also performed by the adversary. Unfortunately, in such a setting it is impossible to achieve non-malleability in the standard sense, and we

S. Faust and K. Hostáková—Funded by the Emmy Noether Program FA 1320/1-1 of the German Research Foundation (DFG).

P. Mukherjee—Part of this work was done when the author was a Post-doctoral Employee at University of California, Berkeley, supported in part from DARPA/ARL SAFEWARE Award W911NF15C0210, AFOSR Award FA9550-15-1-0274, NSF CRII Award 1464397, AFOSR YIP Award and research grants by the Okawa Foundation and Visa Inc. The views expressed are those of the author and do not reflect the official policy or position of the funding agencies.

D. Venturi—Partially supported by the European Unions Horizon 2020 research and innovation programme, under grant agreement No. 644666, and by CINI Cybersecurity National Laboratory within the project FilieraSicura: Securing the Supply Chain of Domestic Critical Infrastructures from Cyber Attacks (www.filierasicura. it), funded by CISCO Systems Inc. and Leonardo SpA.

J. Katz and H. Shacham (Eds.): CRYPTO 2017, Part II, LNCS 10402, pp. 95–126, 2017.
DOI: 10.1007/978-3-319-63715-0_4

need to aim for slightly weaker security guarantees. In a nutshell, our main notion (dubbed *leaky space-bounded non-malleability*) ensures that this is the best the adversary can do, in that space-bounded tampering attacks can be simulated given a small amount of leakage on the encoded value.

– We provide a simple construction of a leaky space-bounded non-malleable code. Our scheme is based on any Proof of Space (PoS)— a concept recently put forward by Ateniese *et al.* (SCN 2014) and Dziembowski *et al.* (CRYPTO 2015)—satisfying a variant of soundness. As we show, our paradigm can be instantiated by extending the analysis of the PoS construction by Ren and Devadas (TCC 2016-A), based on so-called stacks of localized expander graphs.

– Finally, we show that our flavor of non-malleability yields a natural security guarantee against memory tampering attacks, where one can trade a small amount of leakage on the secret key for protection against space-bounded tampering attacks.

1 Introduction

Non-malleable codes (NMC) [21] were originally proposed by Dziembowski, Pietrzak and Wichs [21] in 2010 and have since been studied intensively by the research community (see, e.g., [1,10,13,25,26,33,35] for some examples). Non-malleable codes are an extension of the concept of error correction and detection and can guarantee the integrity of a message in the presence of tampering attacks when error correction/detection may not be possible. Informally, a non-malleable code (Encode, Decode) guarantees that a codeword modified via an algorithm A, from some class $\mathcal{A}$ of allowed tampering attacks,[1] either encodes the original message, or a completely unrelated value. Notice that non-malleable codes do not need to correct or detect errors. This relaxation enables us to design codes that resist much broader tampering classes $\mathcal{A}$ than what is possible to achieve for error correcting/detecting codes. As an illustrative example, it is trivial to construct non-malleable codes for the class of constant tampering functions; that is, e.g., functions that replace the codeword by a different but valid codeword. Clearly, the output of a constant tampering function is independent of the original encoded message, and hence satisfies the non-malleability property. On the other hand, it is impossible to achieve error correction/detection against such tampering classes, as by definition valid codewords do not contain errors.

Applications of non-malleable codes. The fact that non-malleable codes can be built for broader tampering classes makes them particularly attractive as a mechanism for protecting the memory of physical devices from tampering attacks [3,8]. To protect a cryptographic functionality $\mathcal{F}$ against tampering with respect to a class of attacks $\mathcal{A}$ applied to a secret key κ that is stored in memory, we can proceed as follows. Instead of storing κ directly in memory, we use a non-malleable code for $\mathcal{A}$, and store the codeword $c \leftarrow \mathsf{Encode}(\kappa)$.

---

[1] Sometimes, the tampering algorithms are also called tampering functions.

Thus, each time when $\mathcal{F}$ wants to access κ, we first decode $\tilde{\kappa} = \mathsf{Decode}(c)$, and, only if $\mathsf{Decode}(c) \neq \perp$, we run $\mathcal{F}(\tilde{\kappa}, \cdot)$ on any input of our choice. Intuitively, as long as the adversary can only apply tampering attacks from the class $\mathcal{A}$, non-malleability of $(\mathsf{Encode}, \mathsf{Decode})$ guarantees that any tampering results into a key that is unrelated to the original key, and hence the output of $\mathcal{F}$ does not reveal information about the original secret key. For further discussion on the application of non-malleable codes to tamper resilience we refer the reader to [21].

The tampering class $\mathcal{A}$. It is impossible to have codes that are non-malleable for *all* possible (efficient) tampering algorithms A. For instance, if $\mathcal{A}$ contains the composition of Encode and Decode, then given a codeword c the adversary can apply a tampering algorithm A that first decodes c to get the encoded value x; then, e.g., it flips the first bit of x to obtain $\tilde{x}$, and re-encodes $\tilde{x}$. Clearly, such an attack results into $\tilde{x}$ that is related to the original value x, and non-malleability is violated. A major research direction is hence to design non-malleable codes for broad classes of tampering attacks that exclude the above obvious attacks. Prominent examples are bit-wise tampering [21], where the adversary can modify each bit of the codeword individually, split-state tampering [2], where the codeword consists of two (possibly large) parts that can be tampered with individually, and tampering functions with bounded complexity [27].

All the above mentioned classes of attacks have in common that the Decode algorithm is not part of $\mathcal{A}$. Indeed, if we want to achieve non-malleability, then we must have that $\mathsf{Decode} \notin \mathcal{A}$, as otherwise the following attack becomes possible. Let A be the tampering algorithm that first decodes the codeword c to get the encoded value x, and then, depending on the first bit b of x, it overwrites c with c_b, where $\mathsf{Decode}(c_0) \neq \mathsf{Decode}(c_1)$. In this work, we aim at codes that achieve a weaker security guarantee than standard non-malleability, but for the first time can protect the security of cryptographic functionalities $\mathcal{F}$ with respect to a class of tampering attacks $\mathcal{A}$ with $\mathsf{Decode} \in \mathcal{A}$.

On the importance of $\mathsf{Decode} \in \mathcal{A}$. Besides being an obvious extension of the class of tampering attacks for which we can design non-malleable codes (albeit achieving a weaker security guarantee, which we will outline in Sect. 1.1), allowing that $\mathsf{Decode} \in \mathcal{A}$ has some important advantages for cryptographic applications, as emphasized by the following example. Consider a physical device storing an encoded key $\mathsf{Encode}(\kappa)$ in memory, and implementing a cryptographic functionality $\mathcal{F}$. If the device attempts to implement the cryptographic functionality $\mathcal{F}$, then whenever it is executed, it has to run the Decode function to recover the original secret key κ before running $\mathcal{F}(\kappa, \cdot)$. Suppose that a malicious piece of software A, e.g., a virus, infects the device and attempts to learn information about the secret key κ. Clearly, once A infects the device, it may use the resources available on the device itself, which in particular have to be sufficient to run the Decode algorithm. Hence, if we view the virus A as the tampering algorithm, to maintain the functionality of the device (which in particular requires to run Decode) and at the same time to allow the virus A to control the resources of attacked device, it is necessary that Decode $\in \mathcal{A}$.[2] Our main contribution is to design non-malleable codes that can guarantee meaningful security in the above described setting. We provide more details on our results in the next section.

1.1 Our Contribution

Leaky non-malleable codes. The standard non-malleability property guarantees that decoding the tampered codeword reveals nothing about the original encoded message x. Formally, this is modelled by a simulation-based argument, where we consider the following tampering experiment. First, the message x gets encoded to $c \leftarrow$ Encode(x) and the adversary can apply a tampering algorithm $A \in \mathcal{A}$ resulting in a modified codeword $\tilde{c}$; the output of the tampering experiment is then defined as Decode$(\tilde{c})$. Roughly speaking, non-malleability is guaranteed if we can construct an (efficient) simulator S that can produce a distribution that is (computationally) indistinguishable from the output of the tampering experiment, without having access to x; the simulator is typically allowed to return a special symbol same* to signal that (it believes) the adversarial tampering did not modify the encoded message.

As explained above, if Decode $\in \mathcal{A}$, then the above notion is trivially impossible to achieve, since the adversary can easily learn $O(\log k)$ bits, where k is the size of the message.[3] In this work, we introduce a new notion that we call *leaky non-malleability*, which models the fact that, when $A \in \mathcal{A}$, the adversary is allowed to learn some (bounded) amount of information about the message x. Formally, we give the simulator S additional access to a leakage oracle; more concretely, this means that in order to simulate the output of the tampering experiment, S can specify a leakage function $L : \{0,1\}^k \to \{0,1\}^\ell$ and receive $L(x)$.[4] Clearly, if $\ell = k$, then the simulation is trivial, and hence our aim is to design codes where ℓ is as close as possible to the necessary bound of $O(\log k)$. Notice that, due to the allowed leakage, our notion of leaky non-malleability makes most sense when the message x is sampled from a distribution of high min-entropy. But, indeed, this is the case in the main application of NMC, where the goal is to protect a secret key of a cryptographic scheme; and in fact, as we show at the end of the paper, leaky non-malleability still allows to guarantee protection against memory tampering in many interesting cases.

---

[2] In particular, when resources are measured by space as considered in this work, assuming that running Decode requires more space than what is available on the device would imply assuming a trusted part of memory that the virus cannot exploit, which seems unnatural.

[3] For instance, the adversary may just guess the first $O(\log k)$ bits of the message and replace c with c_u (where $u \in \{0,1\}^{O(\log k)}$) depending on whether its guess was correct; this attack succeeds with non-negligible probability.

[4] Although, later in the paper, we define leaky non-malleability only for the case of space-bounded tampering, we point out that this weaker security guarantee makes sense for arbitrary tampering classes $\mathcal{A}$.

Modelling space-bounded tampering adversaries. In the above application with the virus, we allow the virus to use all resources of the device when it tampers with the codeword. Of course, this means that the virus is limited in the *amount of space* it can use. We exploit this observation by putting forward the notion of non-malleable codes that resist adversaries operating in bounded space. That is, in contrast to earlier works on NMC, we do not require any independence of the tampering (like, e.g., in the split-state model), nor the fact that tampering comes from a restricted complexity class. Instead, we allow arbitrary efficient tampering attacks that can globally modify the codeword, as long as the attacks operate in the space available on the device. Since the lower bounds in space complexity are notoriously hard, we follow earlier works [4,18–20] that argue about space-bounded adversaries (albeit in a different setting), using the random oracle methodology and its connection to graph pebbling games.

Let us provide some more details on our model. Our setting follows the earlier work of Dziembowski, Kazana and Wichs [19,20] and considers a "big adversary" B that has unlimited space (though runs in PPT) and creates "small adversaries" A (e.g., viruses) that it sends to the device. On the device, A can use the available space to modify the codeword in some arbitrary way. We emphasize that A has no granular restrictions, and hence can read the entire codeword. Moreover, it can follow an arbitrary efficient (PPT) tampering strategy. The only restriction is that A has to operate in bounded space. Both adversaries A and B have access to a random oracle $\mathcal{H}$. After A has finished its tampering attack, we proceed as in the normal NMC experiment, i.e., we decode the modified codeword and output the result. We further strengthen our definition by allowing the adversary to repeat the above attack multiple times, which is sometimes referred to as continuous tampering [25,33]. We note that, as in [33], we require an a-priori fixed upper bound on the number of viruses A that B can adaptively choose.

Technical overview of our construction. Our construction is based on Proofs of Space (a.k.a. PoS), introduced in [4,18]. First, let us recall the notion of PoS briefly. In a PoS protocol, a prover P proves that "it has sufficient space" available to a space-bounded verifier V. Using the Fiat-Shamir [29] transformation, the entire proof can be presented by π_{id} for some identity *id*. The verifier can verify the pair (id, π_{id}) within bounded space (say s). The soundness guarantee is that a cheating prover, with overwhelming probability, can not produce a correct proof unless it uses a large amount of space. Our NMC construction encodes a value $x \in \{0,1\}^k$ by setting $id := x$ and then computing the proof π_{id}. Hence, the codeword is $c = (x, \pi_x)$. Decoding is done just by running the verification procedure of the PoS.

Now, if the codeword is stored in an s-bounded device, then decoding is possible within the available space whereas encoding is not – in particular, even if the adversary can obtain x, it can not re-encode to a related value, say $(x+1, \pi_{x+1})$, as guaranteed by the soundness of the underlying PoS.[5] We stress that our

---

[5] Notice that since the space-bounded attacker A is able to decode anyway, we do not aim to hide x in c.

soundness requirement is slightly different than the existing PoS constructions, as we require some form of "extractability" from the PoS: Given an honestly generated pair (x, π_x), if the space-bounded virus can compute a valid pair $(x', \pi_{x'})$ where $x' \neq x$, then one can efficiently extract x' from the set of random oracle queries that the big adversary made before installing the virus. Our put differently, the only way to compute a valid proof is to overwrite (x, π_x) with a valid pair $(x', \pi_{x'})$ "pre-computed" by the big adversary.

To formally prove the leaky non-malleability of our construction, we need to show that the output of the tampering experiment can be simulated given only "limited" leakage on x. For simplicity, let us explain how this can be done for one tampering query. Intuitively this is possible because the big adversary can hard-code at most polynomially many (say q) correct pairs $\{x_i, \pi_{x_i}\}_{i \in [q]}$ into the virus. Now, since any such $x_i \neq x$ can be efficiently "extracted" from the random oracle queries made by B prior to choosing the virus, $\log(q)$ bits of leakage are sufficient to compute the exact x_i from the list $\{x_i\}_{i \in [q]}$.[6] For multiple adaptive tampering queries things get more complicated. Nonetheless, we are able to show that each such query can be simulated by logarithmic leakage.

We emphasize that our encoding scheme is deterministic for a fixed choice of the random oracle. In particular, the only randomness comes from the random oracle itself. Also, in the security proof, we do not require to program the random oracle in the on-line phase of the security reduction, in that the random oracle can just be fixed at the beginning of the security game.[7] We concretely instantiate our construction by adapting the PoS protocol from Ren and Devadas [40], that uses so-called stacks of localized expander graphs.

Applications: Trading leakage for tamper resilience. One may ask if our notion of leaky non-malleability is useful for the original application of tamper protection. In Sect. 7 we show that cryptographic primitives which remain secure if the adversary obtains some bounded amount of leakage from the key, can naturally be protected against tampering attacks using our new notion of leaky non-malleability. Since there is a large body of work on bounded leakage-resilient cryptographic primitives, including signature schemes, symmetric and public key encryption [16, 22, 23, 32, 34, 38, 39], and many more, our transformation protects these primitives against any efficient space-bounded tampering attack.

1.2   Additional Related Work

Only very few works consider non-malleable codes for global tampering functions [5]. Very related to our attack model are in particular the works of

---

[6] In slightly more detail, the set $\{x_i\}_{i \in [q]}$ can be extracted by the simulator outside the leakage oracle as it does not depend on x, so the simulator can just ask for the index of the exact x_i to later reconstruct x_i in full.

[7] Since adaptive (i.e. on-line) programming is not required, for all practical purposes our construction can be instantiated by standard hash functions like SHA-1. However, our proof crucially relies on the ability of the simulator to control the random oracle (albeit non adaptively), in order to make the "extraction" work.

Dziembowski, Kazana and Wichs [19,20]. In these works, the authors also consider a setting where a so-called "big-adversary" infects a machine with a space-bounded "small adversary". Using techniques from graph pebbling, the authors show how to construct one-time computable functions [20] and leakage resilient key evolution schemes [19] when the "small adversary" has to operate in bounded space.

The flavor of non-malleable codes in which there is an a-priory upper bound on the total number of tampering queries, without self-destruct, was originally considered in [9]. This concept has a natural application to the setting of bounded tamper resilience (see, e.g., [14,15,24]).

For other related works on non-malleable codes and its applications we refer to [37].

2 Preliminaries

2.1 Notation

For a string x, we denote its length by $|x|$; if $\mathcal{X}$ is a set, $|\mathcal{X}|$ represents the number of elements in $\mathcal{X}$. When x is chosen randomly in $\mathcal{X}$, we write $x \leftarrow \mathcal{X}$. When A is an algorithm, we write $y \leftarrow \mathsf{A}(x)$ to denote a run of A on input x and output y; if A is probabilistic, then y is a random variable and $\mathsf{A}(x; r)$ denotes a run of A on input x and randomness r. An algorithm A is *probabilistic polynomial-time* (PPT) if A is probabilistic and for any input $x, r \in \{0,1\}^*$ the computation of $\mathsf{A}(x; r)$ terminates in at most a polynomial (in the input size) number of steps. We often consider algorithms $\mathsf{A}^{\mathcal{O}(\cdot)}$, with access to an oracle $\mathcal{O}(\cdot)$.

We denote with $\lambda \in \mathbb{N}$ the security parameter. A function $\nu : \mathbb{N} \to [0,1]$ is negligible in the security parameter (or simply negligible), denoted $\nu(\lambda) \in \mathrm{negl}(\lambda)$, if it vanishes faster than the inverse of any polynomial in λ, i.e. $\nu(\lambda) = \lambda^{-\omega(1)}$. A function $\mu : \mathbb{N} \to \mathbb{R}$ is a polynomial in the security parameter, written $\mu(\lambda) \in \mathrm{poly}(\lambda)$, if, for an arbitrary constant $c > 0$, we have $\mu(\lambda) \in O(\lambda^c)$.

2.2 Coding Schemes

We recall the standard notion of a coding scheme for binary messages.

Definition 1 (Coding scheme). *A (k, n)-code $\Pi = (\mathsf{Init}, \mathsf{Encode}, \mathsf{Decode})$ is a triple of algorithms specified as follows: (i) The (randomized) generation algorithm Init takes as input $\lambda \in \mathbb{N}$ and returns public parameters $\omega \in \{0,1\}^*$; (ii) The (randomized) encoding algorithm Encode takes as input hard-wired public parameters $\omega \in \{0,1\}^*$ and a value $x \in \{0,1\}^k$, and returns a codeword $c \in \{0,1\}^n$; (iii) The (deterministic) decoding algorithm Decode takes as input hard-wired public parameters $\omega \in \{0,1\}^*$ and a codeword $c \in \{0,1\}^n$, and outputs a value in $\{0,1\}^k \cup \{\bot\}$, where $\bot$ denotes an invalid codeword.*

We say that Π satisfies correctness if for all $\omega \in \{0,1\}^*$ output by $\mathsf{Init}(1^\lambda)$ and for all $x \in \{0,1\}^k$, $\mathsf{Decode}_\omega(\mathsf{Encode}_\omega(x)) = x$ with overwhelming probability over the randomness of the encoding algorithm.

In this paper we will be interested in modelling coding schemes where there is an explicit bound on the space complexity required to decode a given codeword.

Definition 2 (Time/space-bounded algorithm). *Let* A *be an algorithm. For any* $s, t \in \mathbb{N}$ *we say that* A *is* s-*space bounded and* t-*time bounded (or simply* (s, t)-*bounded) if at any time during its execution the entire state of* A *can be described by at most* s *bits and* A *runs for at most* t *time-steps.*

For such algorithms we have $s_A \le s$ *and* $t_A \le t$ *(with the obvious meaning). We often omit the time parameter and simply say that* A *is* s-*bounded, which means that* A *is an* s-*bounded polynomial-time algorithm. Given an input* $x \in \{0, 1\}^n$, *and an initial configuration* $\sigma \in \{0, 1\}^{s-n}$, *we write* $(y, \tilde{\sigma}) := A(x; \sigma)$ *for the output* y *of* A *including its final configuration* $\tilde{\sigma} \in \{0, 1\}^{s-n}$. *The class of all* s-*space bounded deterministic polynomial-time algorithms is denoted by* $\mathcal{A}^s_{space}$.

We stress that, similarly to previous works [19, 20], in case A is modelled as a Turing machine, we count the length of the input tape and the position of all the tape heads within the space bound s. However we emphasize that, although A is space-bounded, we allow to hard-wire auxiliary information of arbitrary polynomial length in its description that is not accounted for in the space-bound. Intuitively, a coding scheme can be decoded in bounded space if the decoding algorithm is space bounded.

Definition 3 (Space-bounded decoding). *Let* $\Pi = (\mathsf{Init}, \mathsf{Encode}, \mathsf{Decode})$ *be a* (k, n)-*code, and* $d \in \mathbb{N}$. *We call* Π *a* (k, n)-*code with* d-*bounded decoding, if for all* ω *output by* $\mathsf{Init}(1^\lambda)$ *the decoding algorithm* $\mathsf{Decode}_\omega(\cdot)$ *is* d-*bounded.*

Notice that we do not count the length of the public parameters in the space bound; this is because the value ω is hard-coded into the description of the encoding and decoding algorithms.

3   Non-Malleability in Bounded Space

3.1   Space-Bounded Tampering

The standard way of formalizing the non-malleability property is to require that, for any "allowed adversary"[8] A, tampering with an honestly computed target encoding of some value $x \in \{0, 1\}^k$, there exists an efficient simulator S that is able to emulate the outcome of the decoding algorithm on the tampered codeword, without knowing x. The simulator is allowed to return a special symbol same*, signalling that (it believes) the adversary did not modify the value x contained in the original encoding.

Below, we formalize non-malleability in the case where the set of allowed adversaries consists of all efficient s-bounded algorithms, for some parameter

---

[8] The adversary is often referred to as the "tampering function"; however, for our purposes, it is more convenient to think of the tampering function as an algorithm.

$s \in \mathbb{N}$ (cf. Definition 2). However, since we are particularly interested in decoding algorithms that are d-bounded for some value $d \leq s$, the standard notion of non-malleability is impossible to achieve, as in such a case the algorithm A can simply decode the tampered codeword and leak some information on the encoded message via tampering (see also the discussion in Sect. 3.2). To overcome this obstacle, we will give the simulator S some extra-power, in that S will additionally be allowed to obtain some limited amount of information on x in order to simulate the view of A. To capture this, we introduce an oracle $\mathcal{O}_{\text{leak}}^{\ell,x}$ that can be queried in order to retrieve up-to ℓ bits of information about x.

Definition 4 (Leakage oracle). *A leakage oracle $\mathcal{O}_{\text{leak}}^{\ell,x}$ is a stateful oracle that maintains a counter* ctr *that is initially set to* 0. *The oracle is parametrized by a string $x \in \{0,1\}^k$ and a value $\ell \in \mathbb{N}$. When $\mathcal{O}_{\text{leak}}^{\ell,x}$ is invoked on a polynomial-time computable leakage function L, the value $L(x)$ is computed, its length is added to* ctr, *and if* ctr $\leq \ell$, *then $L(x)$ is returned; otherwise, $\perp$ is returned.*

Since our main construction is in the random oracle model (a.k.a. ROM), we will define space-bounded non-malleability explicitly for this setting. Recall that in the ROM a hash function $\mathcal{H}(\cdot)$ is modelled as an external oracle implementing a random function, which can be queried by all algorithms (including the adversary); in the simulation, the simulator S simulates the random oracle. We introduce the notion of a tampering oracle, which essentially corresponds to repeated (adaptive) tampering with a target n-bit codeword, using at most s bits of total space. Below, we consider that the total space of length s is split into two parts: (i) Persistent space of length p, that also stores the codeword of length n, and that is never erased by the oracle; and (ii) Transient (or non-persistent) space, of length $s - p$, that is erased by the oracle after every tampering. Looking ahead, in our tampering application (cf. Sect. 7), the persistent space corresponds to the user's hard-drive (storing arbitrary data), while the transient space corresponds to the transient memory available on the device.

Definition 5 (Space-bounded tampering oracle). *A space-bounded tampering oracle $\mathcal{O}_{\text{cnm}}^{\Pi,x,\omega,s,p}$ is a stateful oracle parameterized by a (k,n)-code $\Pi = (\text{Init}^{\mathcal{H}}, \text{Encode}^{\mathcal{H}}, \text{Decode}^{\mathcal{H}})$, a string $x \in \{0,1\}^k$, public parameters $\omega \in \{0,1\}^*$, and values $s, p \in \mathbb{N}$ (with $s \geq p \geq n$). The oracle has an initial state $, := (c, \sigma)$, where $c \leftarrow \text{Encode}_\omega^{\mathcal{H}}(x)$, and $\sigma := \sigma_0 || \sigma_1 := 0^{p-n} || 0^{s-p}$. Hence, upon input a deterministic algorithm $A \in \mathcal{A}_{\text{space}}^s$, the output of the oracle is defined as follows.*

$Oracle\ \mathcal{O}_{\text{cnm}}^{\Pi,x,\omega,s,p}(\mathsf{A}):$
$\overline{Parse\ \mathsf{st} = (c, \sigma_0, \sigma_1)}$
$Let\ (\tilde{c}, \tilde{\sigma}_0, \tilde{\sigma}_1) := \mathsf{A}^{\mathcal{H}}(c; \sigma_0 || \sigma_1)$
$Return\ \tilde{x} := \text{Decode}_\omega^{\mathcal{H}}(\tilde{c})$
$Update\ := (\tilde{c}, \tilde{\sigma}_0, 0^{s-p}).$

Notice that in the definition above we put space restrictions only on the tampering algorithm A. The oracle itself is space unbounded. In particular, this means that even if the decoding algorithm requires more space than s, the oracle is well defined. Moreover, this allows us to assume that the auxiliary persistent space $\tilde{\sigma}_0$ is never erased/overwritten by the oracle.

Furthermore, each algorithm A takes as input a codeword $\tilde{c}$ which is the result of the previous tampering attempt. In the literature, this setting is sometimes called persistent continuous tampering [33]. However, a closer look into our setting reveals that the model is actually quite different. Note that, the auxiliary persistent space σ_0 (that is the persistent space left after storing the codeword) can be used to copy parts of the original encoding, that thus can be mauled multiple times. (In fact, as we show in Sect. 3.2, if $p = 2n$, the above oracle actually allows for non-persistent tampering as considered in [25,33]).

In the definition of non-malleability we will require that the output of the above tampering oracle can be simulated given only ℓ bits of leakage on the input x. We formalize this through a simulation oracle, which we define below.

Definition 6 (Simulation oracle). *A simulation oracle* $\mathcal{O}_{\mathrm{sim}}^{S_2,\ell,x,s,\omega}$ *is an oracle parametrized by a stateful PPT algorithm* S_2, *values* $\ell, s \in \mathbb{N}$, *some string* $x \in \{0,1\}^k$, *and public parameters* $\omega \in \{0,1\}^*$. *Upon input a deterministic algorithm* $A \in \mathcal{A}_{\mathrm{space}}^s$, *the output of the oracle is defined as follows.*

$Oracle\ \mathcal{O}_{\mathrm{sim}}^{S_2,\ell,x,s,\omega}(A) :$
$\rule{5cm}{0.4pt}$
$Let\ \tilde{x} \leftarrow S_2^{\mathcal{O}_{\mathrm{leak}}^{\ell,x}(\cdot)}(1^\lambda, \omega, A)$
$If\ \tilde{x} = \mathsf{same}^\star,\ set\ \tilde{x} = x$
$Return\ \tilde{x}.$

We are now ready to define our main notion.

Definition 7 (Space-bounded continuous non-malleability). *Let* $\mathcal{H}$ *be a hash function modelled as a random oracle, and let* $\Pi = (\mathsf{Init}^{\mathcal{H}}, \mathsf{Encode}^{\mathcal{H}}, \mathsf{Decode}^{\mathcal{H}})$ *be a* (k,n)-code. *For parameters* $\ell, s, p, \theta, d \in \mathbb{N}$, *with* $s \geq p \geq n$, *we say that* Π *is an* ℓ-leaky (s,p)-space-bounded θ-continuously non-malleable code with d-bounded decoding *((ℓ, s, p, θ, d)-SP-NMC for short) in the ROM, if it satisfies the following conditions.*

- **Space-bounded decoding:** *The decoding algorithm* $\mathsf{Decode}^{\mathcal{H}}$ *is* d-bounded.
- **Non-malleability:** *For all PPT distinguishers* D, *there exists a PPT simulator* $S = (S_1, S_2)$ *such that for all values* $x \in \{0,1\}^k$ *there is a negligible function* $\nu : \mathbb{N} \rightarrow [0,1]$ *satisfying*

$$\left| \Pr\left[\mathsf{D}^{\mathcal{H}(\cdot), \mathcal{O}_{\mathrm{cnm}}^{\Pi,x,\omega,s,p}(\cdot)}(\omega) = 1 : \omega \leftarrow \mathsf{Init}^{\mathcal{H}}(1^\lambda) \right] \right.$$

$$\left. - \Pr\left[\mathsf{D}^{S_1(\cdot), \mathcal{O}_{\mathrm{sim}}^{S_2,\ell,x,s,\omega}(\cdot)}(\omega) = 1 : \omega \leftarrow \mathsf{Init}^{S_1}(1^\lambda) \right] \right| \leq \nu(\lambda),$$

where D *asks at most* θ *queries to* $\mathcal{O}_{\mathrm{cnm}}$. *The probability is taken over the choice of the random oracle* $\mathcal{H}$, *the sampling of the initial state for the oracle* $\mathcal{O}_{\mathrm{cnm}}$, *and the random coin tosses of* D *and* $S = (S_1, S_2)$.

Intuitively, in the above definition algorithm S_1 takes care of simulating random oracle queries, whereas S_2 takes care of simulating the answer to tampering queries. Typically, S_1 and S_2 are allowed to share a state, but we do not explicitly write this for simplifying notation. For readers familiar with the notion of non-malleable codes in the common reference string model (see, e.g., [25,35]), we note that the simulator is not required to program the public parameters (but is instead allowed to program the random oracle).[9]

Remark 1. Note that we consider the space-bounded adversary A as deterministic; this is without loss of generality, as the distinguisher D can always hard-wire the "best randomness" directly into A. Also, A does not explicitly take the public parameters ω as input; this is also without loss of generality, as D can always hard-wire ω in the description of A.

3.2 Achievable Parameters

We now make a few remarks on our definition of space-bounded non-malleability, and further investigate for which range of the parameters s (total space available for tampering), p (persistent space available for tampering), θ (number of adaptive tampering queries), d (space required for decoding), and ℓ (leakage bound), our notion is achievable. Let $\Pi = (\text{Init}^{\mathcal{H}}, \text{Encode}^{\mathcal{H}}, \text{Decode}^{\mathcal{H}})$ be a (k, n)-code in the ROM.[10] First, note that leaky space-bounded non-malleability is trivial to achieve whenever $\ell = k$ (or $\ell = k - \varepsilon$, for $\varepsilon \in O(\log \lambda)$); this is because, for such values of the leakage bound, the simulator can simply obtain the input message

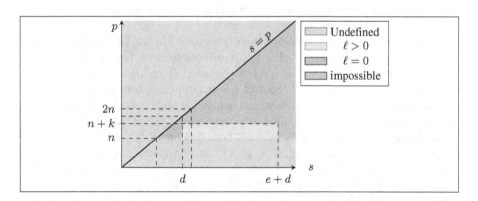

Fig. 1. Possible values for the parameters $s, p \in \mathbb{N}$ in the definition of leaky space-bounded non-malleability, for fixed values of k, n, d (assuming $d < 2n$); in the picture, "impossible" means for $\theta \geq k$ and for non-trivial values of ℓ, and e is the space bound for the encoding algorithm.

---

[9] However, we stress that in the proof of our code construction (cf. Sect. 6), we do not need adaptive random oracle programming.

[10] The discussion below applies also to codes not relying on random oracles.

$x \in \{0,1\}^k$, in which case the security guarantee becomes useless. Second, the larger the values of s and θ, the larger is the class of tampering attacks and the number of tampering attempts that the underlying code can tolerate. So, the challenge is to construct coding schemes tolerating a large space bound in the presence of "many" tampering attempts, using "small" leakage.

An important feature that will be useful for characterizing the range of achievable parameters in our definition is the so-called *self-destruct capability*, which determines the behavior of the decoding algorithm after an invalid codeword is ever processed. In particular, a code with the self-destruct capability is such that the decoding algorithm always outputs $\perp$ after the first $\perp$ is ever returned (i.e., after the first invalid codeword is ever decoded). Such a feature, which was already essential in previous works studying continuously non-malleable codes [11,12,25], can be engineered by enabling the decoding function to overwrite the entire memory content with a fixed string, say the all-zero string if a codeword is decoded to $\perp$.

Depending on the self-destruct capability being available or not, we have the following natural observations:

- If Π is not allowed to self-destruct, it is impossible to achieve space-bounded non-malleability, for non-trivial values of ℓ, whenever $\theta \geq n$ (for any $s \geq p \geq n$, and any $d \in \mathbb{N}$). This can be seen by considering the deterministic algorithm $\mathsf{A}^i_{\mathsf{aux}_i}$ (for some $i \in [n]$) that overwrites the first $i-1$ bits of the input codeword with the values $\mathsf{aux}_i := (c[1], \ldots, c[i-1])$, and additionally sets the i-th bit to 0 (leaving the other bits unchanged). Using such an algorithm, a PPT distinguisher D can guess the bit $c[i]$ of the target codeword to be either 0 (in case the tampering oracle returned the input message x) or 1 (in case the tampering oracle returned a value different from x, namely $\perp$). Hence, D returns 1 if and only if $\mathsf{Decode}^{\mathcal{H}}_\omega(c) = x$.

  The same attack was already formally analyzed in [12] (generalizing a previous attack by Gennaro et al. [31]); it suffices to note here that the above attack can be mounted using $s = n$ bits of space (which are needed for processing the input encoding), and requires $\theta = n$ tampering attempts.

- Even if Π is allowed to self-destruct, whenever $s \geq d$ and $p \geq n + \theta - 1$, leaky space-bounded non-malleability requires $\ell \geq \theta$. This can be seen by considering the following attack. An s-bounded algorithm $\mathsf{A}^1_{c_0,c_1}$, with hardwired two valid encodings $c_0, c_1 \in \{0,1\}^n$ of two *distinct* messages $x_0, x_1 \in \{0,1\}^k$ does the following: (i) Decodes c obtaining x (which requires $d \leq s$ bits of space); (ii) Stores the first $\theta - 1$ bits of x in the persistent storage $\tilde{\sigma}_0$; (iii) If the θ-th bit of x is one, it replaces c with $\tilde{c} = c_1$, else it replaces c with $\tilde{c} = c_0$. During the next tampering query, D can specify an algorithm $\mathsf{A}^2_{c_0,c_1}$ that overwrites the target encoding with either c_0 or c_1 depending on the first[11] bit of $\tilde{\sigma}_0$ being zero or one, and so on until the first $\theta - 1$ bits of

---

[11] Recall that the tampering oracle of Definition 5 initializes the persistent space σ_0 used by the current tampering algorithm, with the corresponding final state $\tilde{\sigma}_0$ returned by the previous tampering algorithm.

x are leaked. So in total, it is able to leak at least θ bits of x (including the θ-th bit of x leaked by A^1).

- The previous attack clearly implies that it is impossible to achieve leaky space-bounded non-malleability, for non-trivial values of ℓ, whenever $s \geq d$, $\theta = k$, and $p \geq n + k - \varepsilon$, for $\varepsilon \in O(\log \lambda)$. A simple variant of the above attack, where essentially D aims at leaking the target encoding c instead of the input x, yields a similar impossibility result whenever $s \geq p$, $d \in \mathbb{N}$, $\theta = n$, and $p \geq 2n - \varepsilon$, for $\varepsilon \in O(\log \lambda)$.

The above discussion is summarized in the following theorem (see also Fig. 1 for a pictorial representation).

Theorem 1. *Let $\ell, s, p, \theta, d, k, n \in \mathbb{N}$ be functions of the security parameter $\lambda \in \mathbb{N}$. The following holds:*

(i) *No (k,n)-code Π without the self-destruct capability can be an (ℓ, s, p, θ, d)-SP-NMC for $d \in \mathbb{N}$, $s \geq p \geq n$ and $\ell = n - \mu$, where $\mu \in \omega(\log \lambda)$.*

(ii) *For any $1 \leq \theta < k$, if Π is a (k,n)-code (with or without the self-destruct capability) that is an (ℓ, s, p, θ, d)-SP-NMC for $d \in \mathbb{N}$, $s \geq d$ and $p \geq n + \theta - 1$, then $\ell \geq \theta$.*

(iii) *No (k,n)-code Π (even with the self-destruct capability) can be an (ℓ, s, p, θ, d)-SP-NMC for $d \in \mathbb{N}$, $\ell = n - \mu$, with $\mu \in \omega(\log \lambda)$, where, for $\varepsilon \in O(\log \lambda)$,*

$$s \geq d \qquad\qquad \theta \geq k \qquad\qquad p \geq n + k - \varepsilon$$
$$or\ s \geq p \qquad\qquad \theta \geq n \qquad\qquad p \geq 2n - \varepsilon.$$

Remark 2. We emphasize that our coding scheme (cf. Sect. 6) does *not* rely on any self-destruct mechanism, and achieves $\theta \approx k/\log \lambda$ for non-trivial values of the leakage parameter. This leaves open the question to construct a code relying on the self-destruct capability, that achieves security for any $\theta \in \text{poly}(\lambda)$ and for non-trivial leakage, with parameters s, p, d consistent with the above theorem. We leave this as an interesting direction for future research.

4   Building Blocks

4.1   Random Oracles

All our results are in the random oracle model (ROM). Therefore we first discuss some basic conventions and definitions related to random oracles. First, recall that in the ROM, at setup, a hash function $\mathcal{H}$ is sampled uniformly at random, and all algorithms, including the adversary, are given oracle access to $\mathcal{H}$ (unless stated otherwise). For instance, we let $\Pi = (\mathsf{Init}^{\mathcal{H}}, \mathsf{Encode}^{\mathcal{H}}, \mathsf{Decode}^{\mathcal{H}})$ be a coding scheme in the ROM. Second, without loss of generality, we will always consider a random oracle $\mathcal{H}$ with a type $\mathcal{H} : \{0,1\}^* \to \{0,1\}^{n\pi}$.

We emphasize that unlike many other proofs in the ROM, we will not need the *full programmability* of random oracles. In fact, looking ahead, in the security proof of our code construction from Sect. 6, we can just assume that the random oracle is *non-adaptively programmable* as defined in [6]. [12] The basic idea is that the simulator/reduction samples a partially defined "random-looking function" at the beginning of the security game, and uses that function as the random oracle $\mathcal{H}$. In particular, by fixing a function ahead of time, the reduction fixes all future responses to random oracle calls—this is in contrast to programmable random oracles, which allow the simulator to choose random values adaptively in the game, and also to program the output of the oracle in a convenient manner.

For any string x, and any random oracle $\mathcal{H}$, we use the notation $\mathcal{H}_x$ to denote the specialized random oracle that accepts only inputs with prefix equal to x. We additionally make the following conventions:

- **Query Tables.** Random oracle queries are stored in query tables. Let $\mathcal{Q}_{\mathcal{H}}$ be such a table. $\mathcal{Q}_{\mathcal{H}}$ is initialized as $\mathcal{Q}_{\mathcal{H}} := \emptyset$. Hence, when $\mathcal{H}$ is queried on a value u, a new tuple $(I(u), u, \mathcal{H}(u))$ is appended to the table $\mathcal{Q}_{\mathcal{H}}$ where $I : \{0,1\}^* \rightarrow \{0,1\}^{O(\log \lambda)}$ is an injective function that maps each input u to a unique identifier, represented in bits. Clearly, for any tuple $(i, u, \mathcal{H}(u))$ we have that $I^{-1}(i) = u$.
- **Input Field.** Let $\mathcal{Q}_{\mathcal{H}} = ((i_1, u_1, v_1), \cdots, (i_q, u_q, v_q))$ be a query table. The input field $\mathcal{IP}_{\mathcal{Q}_{\mathcal{H}}}$ of $\mathcal{Q}_{\mathcal{H}}$ is defined as the tuple $\mathcal{IP}_{\mathcal{Q}_{\mathcal{H}}} = (u_1, \ldots, u_q)$.

4.2   Merkle Commitments

A Merkle commitment is a special type of commitment scheme[13] exploiting so-called hash trees [36]. Intuitively, a Merkle commitment allows a sender to commit to a vector of N elements $\mathbf{z} := (z_1, \ldots, z_N)$ using $N - 1$ invocations of a hash function. At a later point, the sender can open any of the values z_i, by providing a succinct certificate of size logarithmic in N.

Definition 8 (Merkle commitment). *A $(k, n_{\mathsf{cm}}, N, n_{\mathsf{op}}, \nu_{\mathsf{mt}})$-Merkle commitment scheme (or MC scheme) in the ROM is a tuple of algorithms $(\mathsf{MGen}^{\mathcal{H}}, \mathsf{MCommit}^{\mathcal{H}}, \mathsf{MOpen}^{\mathcal{H}}, \mathsf{MVer}^{\mathcal{H}})$ described as follows.*

- $\mathsf{MGen}^{\mathcal{H}}(1^{\lambda})$: *On input the security parameter, the randomized algorithm outputs public parameters $\omega_{\mathsf{cm}} \in \{0,1\}^*$.*
- $\mathsf{MCommit}^{\mathcal{H}}_{\omega_{\mathsf{cm}}}(\mathbf{z})$: *On input the public parameters and an N-tuple $\mathbf{z} = (z_1, \ldots, z_N)$, where $z_i \in \{0,1\}^k$, this algorithm outputs a commitment $\psi \in \{0,1\}^{n_{\mathsf{cm}}}$.*
- $\mathsf{MOpen}^{\mathcal{H}}_{\omega_{\mathsf{cm}}}(\mathbf{z}, i)$: *On input the public parameters, a vector $\mathbf{z} = (z_1, \ldots, z_N) \in \{0,1\}^{kN}$, and $i \in [N]$, this algorithm outputs an opening $(z_i, \phi) \in \{0,1\}^{n_{\mathsf{op}}}$.*
- $\mathsf{MVer}^{\mathcal{H}}_{\omega_{\mathsf{cm}}}(i, \psi, (z, \phi))$: *On input the public parameters, an index $i \in [N]$, and a commitment/opening pair $(\psi, (z, \phi))$, this algorithm outputs a decision bit.*

We require the following properties to hold.

---

[12] In [6], the authors show that such random oracles are equivalent to non-programmable ones, as defined in [30].

[13] Commitment schemes typically also have *hiding*, which ensures that the commitment does not reveal any information about the committed string. Looking ahead, we will commit to a public string and hence hiding is not needed in our case.

Correctness: *For all* $\mathbf{z} = (z_1, \ldots, z_N) \in \{0,1\}^{kN}$, *and all* $i \in [N]$, *we have that*

$$\Pr\left[\mathsf{MVer}^{\mathcal{H}}_{\omega_{cm}}(i, \psi, (z_i, \phi)) = 1 : \begin{array}{l} \omega_{cm} \leftarrow \mathsf{MGen}^{\mathcal{H}}(1^\lambda); \\ \psi \leftarrow \mathsf{MCommit}^{\mathcal{H}}_{\omega_{cm}}(\mathbf{z}) \\ (z_i, \phi) \leftarrow \mathsf{MOpen}^{\mathcal{H}}_{\omega_{cm}}(\mathbf{z}, i) \end{array}\right] = 1$$

Binding: *For all* $\mathbf{z} = (z_1, \ldots, z_N) \in \{0,1\}^{kN}$, *for all* $i \in [N]$, *and all PPT adversaries* A, *we have* $\Pr[\mathbf{G}^{\mathsf{bind}}_{\mathsf{A},\mathbf{z},i}(\lambda) = 1] \leq \nu_{\mathsf{mt}}$, *where the game* $\mathbf{G}^{\mathsf{bind}}_{\mathsf{A},\mathbf{z},i}(\lambda)$ *is defined as follows:*

Game $\mathbf{G}^{\mathsf{bind}}_{\mathsf{A},\mathbf{z},i}$:

1. *Sample* $\omega_{cm} \leftarrow \mathsf{MGen}^{\mathcal{H}}(1^\lambda)$.
2. *Let* $(\psi, (z', \phi')) \leftarrow \mathsf{A}^{\mathcal{H}}_{\omega_{cm}}(\mathbf{z}, i)$.
3. *Let* $(z_i, \phi_i) := \mathsf{MOpen}^{\mathcal{H}}_{\omega_{cm}}(\mathbf{z}, i)$.
4.
   Output 1 *if and only if all of the following conditions are satisfied :*
   (a) $\mathsf{MVer}^{\mathcal{H}}_{\omega_{cm}}(i, \psi, (z', \phi')) = 1$.
   (b) $\mathsf{MVer}^{\mathcal{H}}_{\omega_{cm}}(i, \psi, (z_i, \phi_i)) = 1$.
   (c) $z' \neq z_i$.

The standard hash-tree construction due to Merkle [36] gives us a $(k, k, N, O(k \log(N)), \mathsf{negl}(k))$-Merkle Commitment.

4.3 Graph Pebbling and Labeling

Throughout this paper $G = (V, E)$ is considered to be a directed acyclic graph (DAG), where V is the set of vertices and E is the set of edges of the graph G. Without loss of generality we assume that the vertices of G are ordered lexicographically and are represented by integers in $[N]$, where $N = |V|$. Vertices with no incoming edges are called *input vertices* or *sources*, and vertices with no outgoing edges are called *output vertices* or *sinks*. We denote $\Gamma^-(v)$, the set of all predecessors of the vertex v. Formally, $\Gamma^-(v) = \{w \in V : (w, v) \in E\}$.

In this section we briefly explain the concept of graph labeling and its connection to the abstract game called graph pebbling which has been introduced in [17]. For more details we refer to previous literature in, e.g., [4,17,18,40]. We follow conventions from [40] and will use results from the same. Sometimes for completeness we will use texts verbatim from the same paper.

Labeling of a graph. Let $\mathcal{H} \colon \{0,1\}^* \to \{0,1\}^{n_{\mathcal{H}}}$ be a random oracle. The $\mathcal{H}$-labeling of a graph G is a function which assigns a label to each vertex in the graph; more precisely, it is a function $\mathsf{label} \colon V \to \{0,1\}^{n_{\mathcal{H}}}$ which maps each vertex $v \in V$ to a bit string $\mathsf{label}(v) := \mathcal{H}(q_v)$, where we denote by $\{v^{(1)}, \ldots, v^{(d)}\} = \Gamma^-(v)$ and let

$$q_v := \begin{cases} v & \text{if } v \text{ is an input vertex,} \\ v \parallel \mathsf{label}(v^{(1)}) \parallel \ldots \parallel \mathsf{label}(v^{(d)}) & \text{otherwise.} \end{cases}$$

An algorithm $\mathsf{A}^{\mathcal{H}}$ labels a subset of vertices $W \subseteq V$ if it computes label(W). Specifically, $\mathsf{A}^{\mathcal{H}}$ labels the graph G if it computes label(V).

Additionally, for $m \leq |V|$, we define the $\mathcal{H}$-labeling of the graph G with m faults[14] as a function label$: V \to \{0,1\}^{n_{\mathcal{H}}}$ such that, for some subset of vertices $M \subset V$ of size m, it holds label$(v) = \mathcal{H}(q_v)$ for every $v \in V \setminus M$, and label$(v) \neq \mathcal{H}(q_v)$ for every $v \in M$. Sometimes we refer to labeling with faults as partial labeling. The following lemma appeared in form of a discussion in [40]. It is based on an observation previously made in [18].

Lemma 1 ([40, Sect. 5.2]). *Let $\mathsf{A}^{\mathcal{H}}$ be an (s,t)-bounded algorithm which computes the labeling of a DAG G with $m \in \mathbb{N}$ faults. Then there exists an $(s + m \cdot n_{\mathcal{H}}, t)$-bounded algorithm $\tilde{\mathsf{A}}^{\mathcal{H}}$ that computes the labeling of G without faults but gets m correct labels to start with (they are initially stored in the memory of $\tilde{\mathsf{A}}^{\mathcal{H}}$ and sometimes called initial labels).*

Intuitively the above lemma follows because the algorithm $\tilde{\mathsf{A}}^{\mathcal{H}}$ can overwrite the additional space it has, once the initial labels stored there are not needed.

Pebbling game. The pebbling of a DAG $G = (V, E)$ is defined as a single-player game. The game is described by a sequence of pebbling configurations $\mathbf{P} = (P_0, \ldots, P_T)$, where $P_i \subseteq V$ is the set of pebbled vertices after the i-th move. In our model, the initial configuration P_0 does not need to be empty. The rules of the pebbling game are the following. During one move (translation from P_i to P_{i+1}), the player can place one pebble on a vertex v if v is an input vertex or if all predecessors of v already have a pebble. After placing one pebble, the player can remove pebbles from arbitrary many vertices.[15] We say that the sequence $\mathbf{P}$ pebbles a set of vertices $W \subseteq V$ if $W \subseteq \bigcup_{i \in [0,T]} P_i$.

The time complexity of the pebbling game $\mathbf{P}$ is defined as the number of moves $t(\mathbf{P}) := T$. The space complexity of $\mathbf{P}$ is defined as the maximal number of pebbles needed at any pebbling step; formally, $s(\mathbf{P}) := \max_{i \in [0,T]}\{|P_i|\}$.

Ex-post-facto pebbling. Let $\mathsf{A}^{\mathcal{H}}$ be an algorithm that computes the (partial) $\mathcal{H}$-labeling of a DAG G. The ex-post-facto pebbling bases on the transcript of the graph labeling. It processes all oracle queries made by $\mathsf{A}^{\mathcal{H}}$ during the graph labeling (one at a time and in the order they were made). Informally, every oracle query of the form q_v, for some $v \in V$, results in placing a pebble on the vertex v in the ex-post-facto pebbling game. This provides us a link between labeling and pebbling of the graph G. The formal definition follows.

Let $\mathcal{H}: \{0,1\}^* \to \{0,1\}^{n_{\mathcal{H}}}$ be a random oracle and $\mathcal{Q}_{\mathcal{H}}$ a table of all random oracle calls made by $\mathsf{A}^{\mathcal{H}}$ during the graph labeling. Then we define the *ex-post-facto pebbling* $\mathbf{P}$ *of the graph G* as follows:

---

[14] One can also define an analogy of faults in the pebbling game by adding a second kind of pebbles. These pebbles are called *red pebbles* in [18] and *wild cards* in [4].

[15] Similar to [40] in our model we assume that removing pebbles is for free as it does not involve any oracle query.

- The initial configuration P_0 contains every vertex $v \in V$ such that $\mathsf{label}(v)$ has been used for some oracle query (e.g. some query of the form $\mathcal{H}(\cdots \|\mathsf{label}(v)\| \cdots))$ at some point in the transcript but the query q_v is not listed in the part of the transcript preceding such query.
- Assume that the current configuration is P_i, for some $i \geq 0$. Then find the next unprocessed oracle query which is of the form q_v, for some vertex v, and define P_{i+1} as follows:
  1. Place a pebble on the vertex v.
  2. Remove all *unnecessary* pebbles. A pebble on a vertex v is called unnecessary if $\mathsf{label}(v)$ is not used for any future oracle query, or if the query q_v is listed in the succeeding part of the transcript before $\mathsf{label}(v)$ is used in an argument of some other query later. Intuitively, either $\mathsf{label}(v)$ is never used again, or $\mathsf{A}^{\mathcal{H}}$ anyway queries q_v before it is used again.

The lemma below appeared in several variations in the literature (see, for example, [4, 17, 40]), depending on the definition of graph pebbling.

Lemma 2 (Labeling Lemma). *Let G be a DAG. Consider an (s, t)-bounded adversary $\mathsf{A}^{\mathcal{H}}$ which computes the $\mathcal{H}$-labeling of the graph G. Also assume that $\mathsf{A}^{\mathcal{H}}$ does not guess any correct output of $\mathcal{H}$ without querying it. Then the ex-post facto pebbling strategy $\mathbf{P}$ described above pebbles the graph G, and the complexity of $\mathbf{P}$ is $s(\mathbf{P}) \leq \frac{s}{n_{\mathcal{H}}}$ and $t(\mathbf{P}) \leq t$.*

Proof. By definition of ex-post-facto pebbling, it is straightforward to observe that if $\mathsf{A}^{\mathcal{H}}$ computes the $\mathcal{H}$-labeling of the graph G, then the ex-post-facto pebbling $\mathbf{P}$ pebbles the graph. Since we assume that the adversary does not guess the correct label, the only way $\mathsf{A}^{\mathcal{H}}$ can learn the label of the vertex v is by querying the random oracle. The bound on $t(\mathbf{P})$ is immediate. Again, by definition of the ex-post-facto pebbling, there is no unnecessary pebble at any time. Thus, the number of required pebbles is equal to the maximum number of labels that $\mathsf{A}^{\mathcal{H}}$ needs to store at once. Hence, the space bound follows directly from the fact that each label consists of $n_{\mathcal{H}}$ bits and that the algorithm $\mathsf{A}^{\mathcal{H}}$ is s-space bounded.

Localized expander graphs. A (μ, α, β)-bipartite expander, for $0 < \alpha < \beta < 1$, is a DAG with μ sources and μ sinks such that any $\alpha\mu$ sinks are connected to at least $\beta\mu$ sources. We can define a DAG $G'_{\mu, k_G, \alpha, \beta}$ by stacking k_G ($\in \mathbb{N}$) bipartite expanders. Informally, stacking means that sinks of the i-th bipartite expander are sources of the $i+1$-st bipartite expander. It is easy to see that such a graph has $\mu(k_G + 1)$ nodes which are partitioned into $k_G + 1$ sets (which we call layers) of size μ. A Stack of Localized Expander Graphs (SoLEG) is a DAG $G_{\mu, k_G, \alpha, \beta}$ obtained by applying the transformation called *localization* (see [7, 40] for a definition) on each layer of the graph $G'_{\mu, k_G, \alpha, \beta}$.

We restate two lemmas about pebbling complexity of SoLEG from [40]. The latter appeared in [40] in form of a discussion.

Lemma 3 ([40, Theorem 4]). *Let $G_{\mu, k_G, \alpha, \beta}$ be a SoLEG where $\gamma := \beta - 2\alpha > 0$. Let $\mathbf{P} = (P_0, \ldots, P_{t(\mathbf{P})})$ be a pebbling strategy that pebbles at least $\alpha\mu$ output* *vertices of the graph $G_{\mu,k_G,\alpha,\beta}$ which were not initially pebbled, where the initial pebbling configuration is such that $|P_0| \leq \gamma\mu$, and the space complexity of $\mathbf{P}$ is bounded by $s(\mathbf{P}) \leq \gamma\mu$. Then the time complexity of $\mathbf{P}$ has the following lower bound: $t(\mathbf{P}) \geq 2^{k_G}\alpha\mu$.*

Lemma 4 ([40, **Sect. 5.2**]. *Let $G_{\mu,k_G,\alpha,\beta}$ be a SoLEG and $\mathcal{H}: \{0,1\}^* \rightarrow \{0,1\}^{n_{\mathcal{H}}}$ be a random oracle. There exists a polynomial time algorithm $\mathsf{A}^{\mathcal{H}}$ that computes the $\mathcal{H}$-labeling of the graph $G_{\mu,k_G,\alpha,\beta}$ in $\mu n_{\mathcal{H}}$-space.*

5   Non-Interactive Proofs of Space

5.1   NIPoS Definition

A proof of space (PoS) [4,18] is a (possibly interactive) protocol between a prover and a verifier, in which the prover attempts to convince the verifier that it used a considerable amount of memory or disk space in a way that can be easily checked by the verifier. Here, "easily" means with a small amount of space and computation; a PoS with these characteristics is sometimes called a proof of transient space [40]. A non-interactive PoS (NIPoS) is simply a PoS where the proof consists of a single message, sent by the prover to the verifier; to each proof, it is possible to associate an identity.

Intuitively, a NIPoS should meet two properties known as completeness and soundness. Completeness says that a prover using a sufficient amount of space will always be accepted by the verifier. Soundness, on the other hand, ensures that if the prover invests too little space, it has a hard time to convince the verifier. A formal definition follows below.

Definition 9 (Non-interactive proof of space). *For parameters $s_P, s_V, s, t, k, n \in \mathbb{N}$, with $s_V \leq s < s_P$, and $\nu_{pos} \in (0,1)$, an $(s_P, s_V, s, t, k, n, \nu_{pos})$-non-interactive proof of space scheme (NIPoS for short) in the ROM consists of a tuple of PPT algorithms $(\mathsf{Setup}^{\mathcal{H}}, \mathsf{P}^{\mathcal{H}}, \mathsf{V}^{\mathcal{H}})$ with the following syntax.*

- *$\mathsf{Setup}^{\mathcal{H}}(1^{\lambda})$: This is a randomized polynomial-time (in λ) algorithm with no space restriction. It takes as input the security parameter and it outputs public parameters $\omega_{pos} \in \{0,1\}^*$.*
- *$\mathsf{P}^{\mathcal{H}}_{\omega_{pos}}(id)$: This is a probabilistic polynomial-time (in λ) algorithm that is s_P-bounded. It takes as input an identity $id \in \{0,1\}^k$ and hard-wired public parameters ω_{pos}, and it returns a proof of space $\pi \in \{0,1\}^n$.*
- *$\mathsf{V}^{\mathcal{H}}_{\omega_{pos}}(id, \pi)$: This algorithm is s_V-bounded and deterministic. It takes as input an identity id, hard-wired public parameters ω_{pos}, and a candidate proof of space π, and it returns a decision bit.*

We require the following properties to hold.

Completeness: *For all $id \in \{0,1\}^k$, we have that*

$$\Pr\left[\mathsf{V}^{\mathcal{H}}_{\omega_{pos}}(id, \pi) = 1 : \omega_{pos} \leftarrow \mathsf{Setup}^{\mathcal{H}}(1^{\lambda}); \pi \leftarrow \mathsf{P}^{\mathcal{H}}_{\omega_{pos}}(id)\right] = 1,$$

where the probability is taken over the randomness of algorithms Setup and P, and over the choice of the random oracle.

Extractability: *There exists a polynomial-time deterministic algorithm* K *(the knowledge extractor) such that for any probabilistic polynomial-time algorithm* B, *and for any* $id \in \{0,1\}^k$, *we have*

$$\Pr[\mathbf{G}^{\mathsf{ext}}_{\mathsf{B},id}(\lambda) = 1] \leq \nu_{\mathsf{pos}},$$

where the experiment $\mathbf{G}^{\mathsf{ext}}_{\mathsf{B},id}(\lambda)$ *is defined as follows:*

$Game\ \mathbf{G}^{\mathsf{ext}}_{\mathsf{B},id}(\lambda)$:

1. *Sample* $\omega_{\mathsf{pos}} \leftarrow \mathsf{Setup}^{\mathcal{H}}(1^\lambda)$ *and* $\pi \leftarrow \mathsf{P}^{\mathcal{H}}_{\omega_{\mathsf{pos}}}(id)$.
2. *Let* $\mathsf{A} \leftarrow \mathsf{B}^{\mathcal{H}}(\omega_{\mathsf{pos}}, id, \pi)$ *and* $\{id_i\}_{i \in [q]} := \mathsf{K}(\omega_{\mathsf{pos}}, \mathcal{Q}_{\mathcal{H}}(\mathsf{B}))$.
3. *Let* $(\tilde{id}, \tilde{\pi}) := \mathsf{A}^{\mathcal{H}}(id, \pi)$.
4. *Output* 1 *if and only if* $\mathsf{V}^{\mathcal{H}}_{\omega_{\mathsf{pos}}}(\tilde{id}, \tilde{\pi}) = 1$ *and* $\tilde{id} \notin \{id_i\}_{i \in [q]} \cup \{id\}$

where A *is an* (s, t)-*bounded deterministic algorithm,* $q \in \mathrm{poly}(\lambda)$, *the set* $\mathcal{Q}_{\mathcal{H}}(\mathsf{B})$ *contains the sequence of queries of* B *to* $\mathcal{H}$ *and the corresponding answers, and where the probability is taken over the coin tosses of* Setup, B, P, *and over the choice of the random oracle.*

Roughly, the extractability property requires that no space-bounded adversary is able to modify an honestly computed proof π for identity id into an accepting proof $\tilde{\pi}$ for an identity $\tilde{id} \neq id$. Moreover, this holds true even if A is chosen adaptively (possibly depending on the public parameters, the identity id, and a corresponding valid proof π) by a PPT algorithm B with unbounded space. Since, however, B can compute offline an arbitrary polynomial number of valid proofs (id_i, π_i), what the definition requires is that no (B, A) is able to yield a valid pair $(\tilde{id}, \tilde{\pi})$ for an $\tilde{id}$ different than id that the knowledge extractor K cannot predict by just looking at B's random oracle queries. It is easy to see that such an extractability requirement constitutes a stronger form of soundness, as defined, e.g., in [4,40].

5.2 NIPoS Construction

We now give a NIPoS construction that is essentially a non-interactive variant of the PoS constructions of [40] that is in turn based on [4]. In particular, we show that it satisfies the stronger form of soundness which we call extractability. In addition, we formalize the security analysis given in [40] with concrete parameters that may be of independent interest.

The construction is built from the following ingredients:

- A random oracle $\mathcal{H} : \{0,1\}^* \rightarrow \{0,1\}^{n_{\mathcal{H}}}$.
- A graph $G_{\mu,k_G,\alpha,\beta}$ from the family of SoLEG (cf. Sect. 4.3), where α, β are constants in $(0,1)$ such that $2\alpha < \beta$. By definition of such a graph, the number of nodes is given by $N = \mu(k_G + 1)$. The in-degree d depends on $\gamma = \beta - 2\alpha$, and it is hence constant.[16]

---

[16] As recommended in [40] we will typically work with $0.7 \leq \gamma \leq 0.9$ to get loosely $40 < d < 200$.

Without loss of generality we assume that the vertices of $G_{\mu,k_G,\alpha,\beta}$ are ordered lexicographically and are represented by integers in $[N]$. For simplicity we also assume that N is a power of 2, and that $\log(N)$ divides $n_{\mathcal{H}}$.

- A $(n_{\mathcal{H}}, n_{\mathsf{cm}}, N, n_{\mathsf{op}}, \nu_{\mathsf{mt}})$-Merkle commitment scheme $(\mathsf{MGen}^{\mathcal{H}}, \mathsf{MCommit}^{\mathcal{H}}, \mathsf{MOpen}^{\mathcal{H}}, \mathsf{MVer}^{\mathcal{H}})$ (cf. Sect. 4.2).

Our construction is formally described in Fig. 2. Let us here just briefly explain the main ideas. The setup algorithm chooses a graph $G_{\mu,k_G,\alpha,\beta}$ from the family of SoLEG. Given an identity id, the prover first computes the $\mathcal{H}_{id}$-labeling of the graph $G_{\mu,k_G,\alpha,\beta}$ and commits to the resulting string using the Merkle commitment scheme. Then τ vertices of the graph are randomly chosen. For each challenged vertex v, the prover computes and outputs the opening for

---

NIPoS Construction

$\mathsf{Setup}^{\mathcal{H}}(1^{\lambda})$: On input the security parameter λ, generate the public parameters $\omega_{\mathsf{cm}} \leftarrow \mathsf{MGen}^{\mathcal{H}}(1^{\lambda})$ for the Merkle commitment. Consider the graph $G_{\mu,k_G,\alpha,\beta}$; recall that the number of nodes of $G_{\mu,k_G,\alpha,\beta}$ is given by $N = \mu(k_G + 1)$ and the in-degree is $d \in O(1)$. Output $\omega_{\mathsf{pos}} = (G_{\mu,k_G,\alpha,\beta}, \omega_{\mathsf{cm}})$.

$\mathsf{P}^{\mathcal{H}}_{\omega_{\mathsf{pos}}}(id)$: On input an identity $id \in \{0,1\}^k$, and the public parameters $\omega_{\mathsf{pos}} = (G_{\mu,k_G,\alpha,\beta}, \omega_{\mathsf{cm}})$, proceed as follows.

1. Generate a $\mathcal{H}_{id}$-labeling of $G_{\mu,k_G,\alpha,\beta}$. Denote the labeling by $\mathbf{z} = (z_1,\ldots,z_N)$, where each $z_i \in \{0,1\}^{n_{\mathcal{H}}}$.
2. Generate a commitment of $\mathbf{z}$, i.e. $\psi \leftarrow \mathsf{MCommit}^{\mathcal{H}}_{\omega_{\mathsf{cm}}}(\mathbf{z})$ where $\psi \in \{0,1\}^{n_{\mathsf{cm}}}$.
3. Compute $\rho := \mathcal{H}(id, \psi)$. Using ρ as the randomness, pick τ vertices $\mathbf{v} = (v_1, v_2, \ldots, v_\tau)$ by setting $\mathbf{v} := \rho$ for $\tau = n_{\mathcal{H}}/\log(N)$, where each $v_i \in [N]$.
4. For each vertex $v_i \in \mathbf{v}$:
   (a) Compute the opening $(z_{v_i}, \phi_i) := \mathsf{MOpen}^{\mathcal{H}}_{\omega_{\mathsf{cm}}}(\mathbf{z}, v_i)$, for $(z_{v_i}, \phi_i) \in \{0,1\}^{n_{\mathsf{op}}}$.
   (b) Let $\Gamma^-(v_i) = (u_1^{(i)}, \ldots, u_d^{(i)})$ where each $u_j^{(i)} \in [N]$. Compute the opening corresponding to each $u_j^{(i)} \in \Gamma^-(v_i)$, i.e. $(z_{u_j^{(i)}}, \phi_j^{(j)}) := \mathsf{MOpen}^{\mathcal{H}}_{\omega_{\mathsf{cm}}}(\mathbf{z}, u_j^{(i)})$.
   (c) Define $\pi_i := \left((z_{v_i}, \phi_i), (z_{u_1^{(i)}}, \phi_1^{(i)}), \cdots, (z_{u_d^{(i)}}, \phi_d^{(i)}) \right) \in \{0,1\}^{n_{\mathsf{op}}(d+1)}$.
5. Output $\pi := (\psi, (\pi_1, \ldots, \pi_\tau)) \in \{0,1\}^n$ as a proof of space for id.

$\mathsf{V}^{\mathcal{H}}_{\omega_{\mathsf{pos}}}(id, \pi)$: On input the public parameters $\omega_{\mathsf{pos}} = (G_{\mu,k_G,\alpha,\beta}, \omega_{\mathsf{cm}})$, an identity $id \in \{0,1\}^k$, and a candidate proof of space $\pi \in \{0,1\}^n$, it first parses π as $(\psi, (\pi_1, \cdots, \pi_\tau))$, and computes $\rho := \mathcal{H}(id, \psi)$. Using ρ as the randomness, pick τ vertices $\mathbf{v} = (v_1, v_2, \ldots, v_\tau)$ by setting $\mathbf{v} := \rho$ for $\tau = n_{\mathcal{H}}/\log(N)$, where each $v_i \in [N]$ (exactly as the prover did). Hence, it proceeds as follows for each $i \in [\tau]$:

1. Parse $\pi_i := ((w_i, \phi_i), (w_1^{(i)}, \phi_1^{(i)}), \ldots, (w_d^{(i)}, \phi_d^{(i)}))$ and then:
   (a) Check that $w_i = \mathcal{H}(id, v_i, w_1^{(i)}, \ldots w_d^{(i)})$.
   (b) Check that $\mathsf{MVer}^{\mathcal{H}}_{\omega_{\mathsf{cm}}}(v_i, \psi, (w_i, \phi_i)) = 1$.
   (c) Let $\Gamma^-(v_i) := (u_1^{(i)}, \ldots, u_d^{(i)})$; for each $j \in [d]$ check that $\mathsf{MVer}^{\mathcal{H}}_{\omega_{\mathsf{cm}}}(u_j^{(i)}, \psi, (w_j^{(i)}, \phi_j^{(i)})) = 1$.
2. If the above checks succeed for all $i \in [\tau]$, then output 1, else output 0.

Fig. 2. Our NIPoS construction.

this vertex as well as opening for all its predecessors. The verifier gets as input the identity, a commitment, and $\tau(d+1)$ openings, where d is the degree of the graph. It firstly verifies the consistency of all the openings with respect to the commitment. Secondly, it checks the local correctness of the $\mathcal{H}_{id}$-labeling.

The completeness of our scheme relies on the correctness of the underlying commitment scheme. The extractability will follow from the pebbling complexity of the graph $G_{\mu,k_G,\alpha,\beta}$ and the binding property of the commitment scheme. In particular, we prove the following statement:

Theorem 2. *Let* $\mathcal{H} : \{0,1\}^* \to \{0,1\}^{n_{\mathcal{H}}}$ *be a random oracle,* $G_{\mu,k_G,\alpha,\beta}$ *be a SoLEG with* $N = \mu(k_G + 1)$ *nodes and* d *in-degree, and* $(\mathsf{MGen}^{\mathcal{H}}, \mathsf{MCommit}^{\mathcal{H}},$ $\mathsf{MOpen}^{\mathcal{H}}, \mathsf{MVer}^{\mathcal{H}})$ *be a* $(n_{\mathcal{H}}, n_{\mathsf{cm}}, N, n_{\mathsf{op}}, \nu_{\mathsf{mt}})$-*Merkle commitment. Let* $s, t \in \mathbb{N}$ *be such that, for some* $\delta \in [0, \beta - 2\alpha)$*, we have* $t < 2^{k_G}\alpha\mu$ *and* $s \leq \delta\mu n_{\mathcal{H}}$*. Then, the NIPoS scheme described in Fig. 2 is a* $(s_{\mathsf{P}}, s_{\mathsf{V}}, s, t, k, n, \nu_{\mathsf{pos}})$-*NIPoS for any* $k \in \mathbb{N}$*, as long as:*

$$s_{\mathsf{P}} \geq k + n_{\mathcal{H}}(\mu + \log(N) + 1) + n$$

$$s \geq s_{\mathsf{V}} \geq k + n + n_{\mathcal{H}}$$

$$n = n_{\mathsf{cm}} + n_{\mathsf{op}}(d+1)(n_{\mathcal{H}}/\log(N))$$

$$\nu_{\mathsf{pos}} \leq \exp\left(\frac{-n_{\mathcal{H}}\mu(\gamma - \delta)}{N\log(N)}\right) + \frac{n_{\mathcal{H}}(d+1)\nu_{\mathsf{mt}}}{\log(N)} + \frac{|\mathcal{Q}_{\mathcal{H}}(\mathsf{A})|}{2^{n_{\mathcal{H}}}},$$

where $\mathcal{Q}_{\mathcal{H}}(\mathsf{A})$ *are the random oracle queries asked by* A *and* $\gamma = \beta - 2\alpha$*.*

The formal proof appears in the full version. We provide some intuitions here. The adversary wins the game only if all the checked vertices have a correct $\mathcal{H}_{\tilde{id}}$-label. By the binding property of the underlying Merkle commitment scheme this means that the adversary A has to compute a partial $\mathcal{H}_{\tilde{id}}$-labeling of the graph $G_{\mu,k_G,\alpha,\beta}$. Since $\tilde{id}$ is not extractable from the query table of $\mathcal{Q}_{\mathcal{H}}(\mathsf{B})$ of the adversary B and it is not equal to id, the adversary A does not get any $\mathcal{H}_{\tilde{id}}$ label "for free" and hence, it has to compute the labeling on its own. By Lemma 3, however, the labeling of the graph $G_{\mu,k_G,\alpha,\beta}$ requires either a lot of space or a lot of time neither of which the (s,t)-bounded adversary A has. Instead of computing all the labels correctly via random oracle calls, the adversary A can assign labels of some vertices to an arbitrary value which does not need to be computed and stored. However, if such partial labeling consists of too many faults, the probability that at least one of the faulty vertices will be checked is high. Consequently, a winning adversary can not save a lot of recourses by computing only a partial labeling of the graph.

Using the parameters from Theorem 2 we obtain the following corollary.

Corollary 1. *Let* $\lambda \in \mathbb{N}$ *be a security parameter. Let* $\mathcal{H} : \{0,1\}^* \to \{0,1\}^{n_{\mathcal{H}}}$ *be a random oracle,* $G_{\mu,k_G,\alpha,\beta}$ *be a SoLEG with* $N = \mu(k_G + 1)$ *nodes and* $d = O(1)$

in-degree, and $(\mathsf{MGen}^{\mathcal{H}}, \mathsf{MCommit}^{\mathcal{H}}, \mathsf{MOpen}^{\mathcal{H}}, \mathsf{MVer}^{\mathcal{H}})$ *be a* $(n_{\mathcal{H}}, n_{\mathsf{cm}}, N, n_{\mathsf{op}}, \nu_{\mathsf{mt}})$-*Merkle commitment such that:*

$$n_{\mathcal{H}} = \lambda^2 \qquad \gamma = \beta - 2\alpha \in (0,1) \qquad k_G = \lambda - 1 \qquad \mu = \lambda^3$$
$$n_{\mathsf{cm}} = \lambda^2 \qquad n_{\mathsf{op}} = O(\lambda^2 \log(\lambda)) \qquad \nu_{\mathsf{mt}} \in \mathrm{negl}(\lambda).$$

Then, for any $\delta \in (0,\gamma)$, *the scheme described in* Fig. 2 *is a* $(s_{\mathsf{P}}, s_{\mathsf{V}}, s, t, k, n, \nu_{\mathsf{pos}})$-*NIPoS, for* $t \in \mathrm{poly}(\lambda)$ *and*

$$k = O(\lambda^4) \qquad\qquad s_{\mathsf{P}} = O(\lambda^5) \qquad s_{\mathsf{V}} = O(\lambda^4)$$
$$n = O(\lambda^4) \quad O(\lambda^4) \le s \le \delta \cdot \lambda^5 \quad \nu_{\mathsf{pos}} \le \exp\left(\frac{-(\gamma - \delta)\lambda}{\log(\lambda)}\right) + \mathrm{negl}(\lambda) \in \mathrm{negl}(\lambda)$$

6   Our Coding Scheme

6.1   Code Construction

Let $(\mathsf{Setup}^{\mathcal{H}}, \mathsf{P}^{\mathcal{H}}, \mathsf{V}^{\mathcal{H}})$ be a NIPoS in the ROM where $\mathcal{H} : \{0,1\}^* \to \{0,1\}^{n_{\mathcal{H}}}$ denotes the random oracle for some $n_{\mathcal{H}} \in \mathrm{poly}(\lambda)$. We define a (k,n)-coding scheme $\Pi = (\mathsf{Init}^{\mathcal{H}}, \mathsf{Encode}^{\mathcal{H}}, \mathsf{Decode}^{\mathcal{H}})$ as follows.

$\mathsf{Init}^{\mathcal{H}}(1^\lambda)$: Given as input a security parameter λ, it generates the public parameters for the NIPoS as $\omega_{\mathsf{pos}} \leftarrow \mathsf{Setup}^{\mathcal{H}}(1^\lambda)$, and outputs $\omega := \omega_{\mathsf{pos}}$.

$\mathsf{Encode}_\omega^{\mathcal{H}}(x)$: Given as input the public parameters $\omega = \omega_{\mathsf{pos}}$ and a message $x \in \{0,1\}^k$, it runs the prover to generate the proof of space $\pi \leftarrow \mathsf{P}_{\omega_{\mathsf{pos}}}^{\mathcal{H}}(x)$ using the message x as identity. Then it outputs $c := (x, \pi) \in \{0,1\}^n$ as a codeword.

$\mathsf{Decode}_\omega^{\mathcal{H}}(c)$: Given a codeword c, it first parses c as (x, π). Then it runs the verifier $b := \mathsf{V}_{\omega_{\mathsf{pos}}}^{\mathcal{H}}(x, \pi)$. If $b = 1$ it outputs x, otherwise it outputs $\perp$.

Theorem 3. *Let* λ *be a security parameter. Suppose that* $(\mathsf{Setup}^{\mathcal{H}}, \mathsf{P}^{\mathcal{H}}, \mathsf{V}^{\mathcal{H}})$ *is a* $(s_{\mathsf{P}}, s_{\mathsf{V}}, s, k_{\mathsf{pos}}, n_{\mathsf{pos}}, \mathrm{negl}(\lambda))$-*NIPoS. Then, for any* $p \in \mathbb{N}$ *such that* $k_{\mathsf{pos}} + n_{\mathsf{pos}} \le p \le s$ *and* $\theta \in \mathrm{poly}(\lambda)$, *the* (k,n)-*code* $\Pi = (\mathsf{Init}^{\mathcal{H}}, \mathsf{Encode}^{\mathcal{H}}, \mathsf{Decode}^{\mathcal{H}})$ *defined above is an* $(\ell, s, p, \theta, s_{\mathsf{V}})$-*SP-NMC in the ROM, where*

$$k = k_{\mathsf{pos}} \qquad\qquad n = k_{\mathsf{pos}} + n_{\mathsf{pos}} \qquad\qquad \ell = \theta \cdot O(\log \lambda).$$

Recall that, in our definition of non-malleability, the parameter s represents the space available for tampering, which is split into two components: p bits of persistent space, which includes the n bits necessary for storing the codeword and which is never erased, and $s - p$ bits of transient space that is erased after each tampering query.

Also, note that the above statement shows a clear tradeoff between the parameter θ (controlling the number of allowed tampering queries) and the leakage bound ℓ. Indeed, the larger θ, the more leakage we need, until the security guarantee becomes empty; this tradeoff is consistent with Theorem 1 (see also Fig. 1), as we know that leaky space-bounded non-malleability, for non-trivial values of ℓ, is impossible for $p \approx n + k$, whenever $\theta \ge k$.

6.2   Proof of Security

The correctness of the coding scheme is guaranteed by the perfect completeness of the NIPoS. Moreover, since the decoding algorithm simply runs the verifier of the NIPoS, it is straightforward to observe that decoding is s_V bounded.

Auxiliary algorithms. We start by introducing two auxiliary algorithms that will be useful in the proof. Recall that, by extractability of the NIPoS, there exists a deterministic polynomial-time algorithm K such that, given the public parameters ω_{pos} and a table of RO queries $\mathcal{Q}_{\mathcal{H}}$, returns a set of identities $\{id_i\}_{i \in [q]}$, for some $q \in \mathrm{poly}(\lambda)$. We define the following algorithms that use K as a subroutine.

Algorithm Find$(\omega_{pos}, id, \mathcal{Q}_{\mathcal{H}})$: Given a value $id \in \{0,1\}^{k_{pos}}$, it first runs K to obtain $\{id_i\}_{i \in [q]} := \mathsf{K}(\omega_{pos}, \mathcal{Q}_{\mathcal{H}})$. If there exists an index $i \in [q]$ such that $id = id_i$, then it returns the string str := bit$(i)\|01$,[17] where the function bit$(\cdot)$ returns the binary representation of its input. Otherwise, the algorithm returns the flag 1^ℓ. Clearly, $\ell = \lceil \log(q) \rceil + 2$.

Algorithm Reconstruct$(\omega_{pos}, \mathsf{str}, \mathcal{Q}_{\mathcal{H}})$: On receiving an ℓ-bit string str and a RO query table $\mathcal{Q}_{\mathcal{H}}$, it works as follows depending on the value of str:

- If str $= 0^\ell$, output the symbol same*.
- If str $= 1^\ell$, output the symbol $\perp$.
- If str $= a\|01$, set $i := \mathsf{bit}^{-1}(a)$. Hence, run algorithm K to get the set $\{id_i\}_{i \in [q]} := \mathsf{K}(\omega_{pos}, \mathcal{Q}_{\mathcal{H}})$; in case $i \in [q]$, output the value $x := id_i$, otherwise output $\perp$.
- Else, output $\perp$.

Constructing the simulator. We now describe the simulator $\mathsf{S}^{\mathsf{D}} = (\mathsf{S}_1^{\mathsf{D}}, \mathsf{S}_2^{\mathsf{D}})$, depending on a PPT distinguisher D.[18] A formal description of the simulator is given in Fig. 3; we provide some intuitions below.

Informally, algorithm S_1 simulates the random oracle $\mathcal{H}$ by sampling a random key $\chi \leftarrow \{0,1\}^{n_{key}}$ for a pseudorandom function (PRF) $\mathsf{PRF}_\chi : \{0,1\}^* \to \{0,1\}^{n_{\mathcal{H}}}$; hence, it defines $\mathcal{H}(u) := \mathsf{PRF}_\chi(u)$ for any $u \in \{0,1\}^*$.[19] S_2 receives the description of the RO (i.e., the PRF key χ) from S_1, and for each tampering query A_i from D it asks a leakage query L_i to its leakage oracle. The leakage query hard-codes the description of the simulated RO, the table $\mathcal{Q}_{\mathcal{H}}(\mathsf{D})$ consisting of all RO queries asked by D (until this point), and the code of all tampering algorithms $\mathsf{A}_1, \cdots, \mathsf{A}_i$. Thus, L_i first encodes the target message x to generate a codeword c, applies the composed function $\mathsf{A}_i \circ \mathsf{A}_{i-1} \circ \cdots \circ \mathsf{A}_1$ on c to generate the tampered codeword $\tilde{c}_i$, and decodes $\tilde{c}_i$ obtaining a value $\tilde{x}_i$. Finally, the leakage function signals whether $\tilde{x}_i$ is equal to the original message x, to $\perp$, or to some of

---

[17] Looking ahead, in the simulation we use the strings 0^ℓ and 1^ℓ as flags; therefore, appending 01 to str ensures that str is never misinterpreted as those flags.

[18] In the rest of the proof we drop the superscript D, and just let $\mathsf{S} = (\mathsf{S}_1, \mathsf{S}_2)$.

[19] Such a PRF can be instantiated using any PRF with fixed domain, and then applying the standard Merkle-Damgård transformation to extend the input domain to arbitrary-length strings.

the identities the extractor K would output given the list of D's RO queries (as defined in algorithm Find). Upon receiving the output from the leakage oracle, S_2 runs Reconstruct and outputs whatever this algorithm returns.

Some intuitions. Firstly, note that in the real experiment the random oracle is a truly random function, whereas in the simulation random oracle queries are answered using a PRF. However, using the security of the PRF, we can move to a mental experiment that is exactly the same as the simulated game, but replaces the PRF with a truly random function.

Secondly, a closer look at the algorithms Find and Reconstruct reveals that the only case in which the simulation strategy goes wrong is when the tampered codeword $\tilde{c}_i$ is valid, but the leakage corresponding to the output of Find provokes a $\perp$ by Reconstruct for some $i \in [\theta]$. We denote this event as FAIL. We prove that FAIL occurs exactly when the adversary D violates the extractability property of the underlying NIPoS, which happens only with negligible probability.

To simplify the notation in the proof, let us write

$$\mathsf{D}^{\mathrm{cnm}} := \mathsf{D}^{\mathcal{H}(\cdot), \mathcal{O}_{\mathrm{cnm}}^{\Pi, x, \omega, s, p}(\cdot)}, \quad \mathsf{D}^{\mathrm{sim}'} := \mathsf{D}^{\mathcal{H}(\cdot), \mathcal{O}_{\mathrm{sim}}^{\mathsf{S}_2, \ell, x, s, \omega}(\cdot)}, \quad \mathsf{D}^{\mathrm{sim}} := \mathsf{D}^{\mathsf{S}_1(\cdot), \mathcal{O}_{\mathrm{sim}}^{\mathsf{S}_2, \ell, x, s, \omega}(\cdot)}$$

to denote the interaction in the real, resp. mental, resp. simulated experiment.

Simulator S = $(\mathsf{S}_1, \mathsf{S}_2)$

1. Let $\mathsf{PRF}_\chi : \{0,1\}^* \to \{0,1\}^{n\mathcal{H}}$ be a PRF. The simulator S_1 samples a uniform random key $\chi \leftarrow \{0,1\}^{n_{\mathrm{key}}}$ and defines $\mathcal{H} := \mathsf{PRF}_\chi$. The query table $\mathcal{Q}_{\mathcal{H}}(\mathsf{D})$ that stores RO queries from D is initially empty.
2. For $i \in [\theta]$ the simulator does the following:
   (a) S_1 simulates the random oracle queries made by D, before A_i is chosen, and updates the table $\mathcal{Q}_{\mathcal{H}}(\mathsf{D})$ accordingly.
   (b) On receiving the adversary A_i, the simulator S_2 queries its leakage oracle $\mathcal{O}_{\mathrm{leak}}^{\ell, x}$ with $L : \{0,1\}^k \to \{0,1\}^\ell$ (where $\ell = O(\log(\lambda))$) described as follows:
      Description of L:
      – L is hard-coded with the description of $\mathcal{H}$ (i.e., with PRF_χ), the table $\mathcal{Q}_{\mathcal{H}}(\mathsf{D})$, the code of $(\mathsf{A}_1, \mathsf{A}_2, \ldots, \mathsf{A}_i)$, and the code of the knowledge extractor K of the NIPoS.
      – Produce the codeword $c \leftarrow \mathsf{Encode}_\omega^{\mathcal{H}}(x)$ and initialize the auxiliary space $\sigma := 0^{s-n}$.
      – Let $\tilde{\mathsf{A}}_i := \mathsf{A}_i \circ \mathsf{A}_{i-1} \circ \cdots \circ \mathsf{A}_1$. Run $\tilde{\mathsf{A}}_i$ to get $(\tilde{c}, \tilde{\sigma}) := \tilde{\mathsf{A}}_i(c; \sigma)$.
      – Compute $\tilde{x} := \mathsf{Decode}_\omega^{\mathcal{H}}(\tilde{c})$. If $\tilde{x} = \perp$, output the flag 1^ℓ, else, if $\tilde{x} = x$, output the flag 0^ℓ; otherwise run $\mathsf{str}_{\tilde{x}} := \mathsf{Find}(\omega, \tilde{x}, \mathcal{Q}_{\mathcal{H}}(\mathsf{D}))$ and output $\mathsf{str}_{\tilde{x}}$.
      – All other oracle queries that are not asked by D (e.g., queries made by A_j, or while running Encode etc.) are simulated internally.
   (c) On receiving an ℓ-bit string str from L, simulator S_2 runs $\tilde{x} \leftarrow \mathsf{Reconstruct}(\omega, \mathsf{str}_{\tilde{x}}, \mathcal{Q}_{\mathcal{H}}(\mathsf{D}))$ and outputs $\tilde{x}$.

Fig. 3. Description of the simulator S = $(\mathsf{S}_1, \mathsf{S}_2)$

Formal analysis. Consider an adversary D which makes θ queries to $\mathcal{O}_{\text{cnm}}$. By Definition 7, we need to prove that the simulator $\mathsf{S}^{\mathsf{D}} = (\mathsf{S}_1^{\mathsf{D}}, \mathsf{S}_2^{\mathsf{D}})$ defined in Fig. 3 is such that, for all values $x \in \{0,1\}^k$, there is a negligible function $\nu : \mathbb{N} \to [0,1]$ satisfying

$$\left| \Pr\left[\mathsf{D}^{\text{cnm}}(\omega) = 1 \colon \omega \leftarrow \mathsf{Init}^{\mathcal{H}}(1^\lambda) \right] - \Pr\left[\mathsf{D}^{\text{sim}}(\omega) = 1 \colon \omega \leftarrow \mathsf{Init}^{\mathsf{S}_1}(1^\lambda) \right] \right| \leq \nu(\lambda).$$

A straightforward reduction to the pseudorandomness of the PRF yields:

$$\left| \Pr\left[\mathsf{D}^{\text{sim}}(\omega) = 1 \colon \omega \leftarrow \mathsf{Init}^{\mathsf{S}_1}(1^\lambda) \right] - \Pr[\mathsf{D}^{\text{sim}'}(\omega) = 1 \colon \omega \leftarrow \mathsf{Init}^{\mathcal{H}}(1^\lambda)] \right| \leq \nu'(\lambda),$$

where $\nu' : \mathbb{N} \to [0,1]$ is a negligible function.

Let us now fix some arbitrary $x \in \{0,1\}^k$. For every $i \in [\theta]$, we recursively define the event NotExtr_i as:

$$\text{NotExtr}_i := \neg\text{NotExtr}_{i-1} \wedge \mathsf{Decode}_\omega^{\mathcal{H}}(\tilde{c}) \notin \{\bot, x\}$$
$$\wedge \; \mathsf{Find}(\omega, \mathsf{Decode}_\omega^{\mathcal{H}}(\tilde{c}), \mathcal{Q}_{\mathcal{H}}(\mathsf{D})) = 1^\ell,$$

where NotExtr_0 is an empty event that never happens and $(\tilde{c}, \tilde{\sigma}) := \widetilde{\mathsf{A}}_i(c, \sigma)$ for $\widetilde{\mathsf{A}}_i := \mathsf{A}_i \circ \mathsf{A}_{i-1} \circ \cdots \circ \mathsf{A}_1$. In other words, the event NotExtr_i happens when A_i is the first adversary that tampers to a valid codeword of a message $\tilde{x} \neq x$ which is not extractable from $\mathcal{Q}_{\mathcal{H}}(\mathsf{D})$. In addition, we define the event

$$\text{Fail} := \bigvee_{i \in [\theta]} \text{NotExtr}_i.$$

Now, we can bound the probability that D succeeds as follows:

$$\left| \Pr\left[\mathsf{D}^{\text{cnm}}(\omega) = 1\right] - \Pr\left[\mathsf{D}^{\text{sim}'}(\omega) = 1\right] \right| \tag{1}$$
$$\leq \left| \Pr\left[\mathsf{D}^{\text{cnm}}(\omega) = 1 \mid \neg\text{Fail}\right] - \Pr\left[\mathsf{D}^{\text{sim}'}(\omega) = 1 \mid \neg\text{Fail}\right] \right| \cdot \Pr[\neg\text{Fail}]$$
$$+ \left| \Pr\left[\mathsf{D}^{\text{cnm}}(\omega) = 1 \mid \text{Fail}\right] - \Pr\left[\mathsf{D}^{\text{sim}'}(\omega) = 1 \mid \text{Fail}\right] \right| \cdot \Pr[\text{Fail}]$$
$$\leq \left| \Pr\left[\mathsf{D}^{\text{cnm}}(\omega) = 1 \mid \neg\text{Fail}\right] - \Pr\left[\mathsf{D}^{\text{sim}'}(\omega) = 1 \mid \neg\text{Fail}\right] \right| + \Pr[\text{Fail}],$$

where in the above equations the probability is taken also on the sampling of $\omega \leftarrow \mathsf{Init}^{\mathcal{H}}(1^\lambda)$. We complete the proof by showing the following two claims.

Claim. Event Fail happens with negligible probability.

Proof. Assume that for some $x \in \{0,1\}^k$ adversary D provokes the event Fail with non-negligible probability. This implies that there is at least one index $j \in [\theta]$ such that event NotExtr_j happens with non-negligible probability. We construct an efficient algorithm B running in game $\mathsf{G}_{\mathsf{B},x}^{\text{ext}}(\lambda)$, that attempts to break the extractability of the NIPoS:

Algorithm $B_D^{\mathcal{H}}$:

1. Receive as input $\omega_{\mathsf{pos}} \leftarrow \mathsf{Setup}^{\mathcal{H}}(1^\lambda)$, $x \in \{0,1\}^{k_{\mathsf{pos}}}$, and $\pi \leftarrow \mathsf{P}_{\omega_{\mathsf{pos}}}^{\mathcal{H}}(x)$.
2. Assign $(c,\sigma) := (x||\pi, 0^{s-n})$, $\mathcal{Q}_{\mathcal{H}}(\mathsf{D}) := \emptyset$, and define $\mathsf{A} := \mathsf{Id}$, where $\mathsf{Id}\colon \{0,1\}^s \to \{0,1\}^s$ is the identity function.
3. For $i \in [\theta]$ proceed as follows:
   (a) Answer random oracle queries made by D, before A_i is chosen, by querying $\mathcal{H}$ in game $\mathbf{G}_{B,x}^{\mathsf{ext}}(\lambda)$ and forwarding the answers to D; in addition, store these queries in the table $\mathcal{Q}_{\mathcal{H}}(\mathsf{D})$.
   (b) On receiving A_i, set $\mathsf{A} := \mathsf{A} \circ \mathsf{A}_i$ and run $(\tilde{c}, \tilde{\sigma}) := \mathsf{A}_i(c;\sigma)$.
   (c) Compute $\tilde{x} := \mathsf{Decode}_\omega^{\mathcal{H}}(\tilde{c})$ and run $\mathsf{str}_{\tilde{x}} := \mathsf{Find}(\omega, \tilde{x}, \mathcal{Q}_{\mathcal{H}}(\mathsf{D}))$. If $\mathsf{str}_{\tilde{x}} = 1^\ell$ and $\tilde{x} \neq \bot$, then output A and stop. Otherwise send $\tilde{x}$ to D and let $(c,\sigma) := (\tilde{c}, \tilde{\sigma}_0 || 0^{s-p})$, where $\tilde{\sigma}_0 || \tilde{\sigma}_1 := \tilde{\sigma}$.

We observe that B perfectly simulates the view of $\mathsf{D}^{\mathsf{sim}'}$. So, if there exists at least one $j \in [\theta]$ for which $\mathrm{NOTEXTR}_j$ happens, B wins the game $\mathbf{G}_{B,x}^{\mathsf{ext}}(\lambda)$.

Therefore we have that $\Pr[\mathbf{G}_{D,x}^{\mathsf{ext}}(\lambda) = 1] \geq \Pr[\exists j \in [\theta] : \mathrm{NOTEXTR}_j]$ which, combined with the extractability of NIPoS, completes the proof.

Claim. $\left| \Pr\left[\mathsf{D}^{\mathsf{cnm}}(1^\lambda) = 1 \mid \neg\mathrm{FAIL} \right] - \Pr\left[\mathsf{D}^{\mathsf{sim}'}(1^\lambda) = 1 \mid \neg\mathrm{FAIL} \right] \right| = 0$

Proof. By inspection of the simulator's description it follows that, conditioning on event FAIL not happening, the simulation oracle using S_2 yields a view that is identical to the one obtained when interacting with the tampering oracle. The claim follows.

Combining the above two claims together with Eq. (1), we obtain that

$$\left| \Pr\left[\mathsf{D}^{\mathsf{cnm}}(\omega) = 1 : \omega \leftarrow \mathsf{Init}^{\mathcal{H}}(1^\lambda) \right] - \Pr\left[\mathsf{D}^{\mathsf{sim}'}(\omega) = 1 : \omega \leftarrow \mathsf{Init}^{\mathsf{S}_1}(1^\lambda) \right] \right|$$

is negligible, as desired.

It remains to argue about the size of leakage. To this end, it suffices to note that the simulator S_2 receives $O(\log(\lambda))$ bits of leakage for every $i \in [\theta]$. Thus, the total amount of leakage is $\theta \cdot O(\log(\lambda))$, exactly as stated in the theorem.

6.3   Concrete Instantiation and Parameters

Instantiating Theorem 3 with our concrete NIPoS from Corollary 1, and using bounds from Theorem 1, we obtain the following corollaries. The first corollary provides an upper bound on the number of tolerated tampering queries at the price of a high (but still non-trivial) leakage parameter.

Corollary 2. *For any $\gamma, \delta, \varepsilon \in (0,1)$, there exists an explicit construction of a (k,n)-code in the ROM that is a $(\gamma \cdot k, s, p, \theta, \Theta(\lambda^4))$-SP-NMC, where*

$$k = \Theta(\lambda^4) \qquad n = \Theta(\lambda^4) \qquad \Theta(\lambda^4) \leq p \leq s = \delta\lambda^5 \qquad \theta = \Theta(\lambda^{4-\varepsilon}).$$

The second corollary yields a smaller number of tolerated tampering queries with optimal (logarithmic) leakage parameter.

Corollary 3. *For any $\delta \in (0,1)$, there exists an explicit construction of a (k,n)-code in the ROM that is an $(O(\log \lambda), s, p, \theta, O(\lambda^4))$-SP-NMC, where*

$$k = O(\lambda^4) \qquad n = O(\lambda^4) \qquad O(\lambda^4) \le p \le s = \delta\lambda^5 \qquad \theta = O(1).$$

7   Trading Leakage for Tamper-Proof Security

We revise the standard application of non-malleable codes to obtain protection against memory tampering attacks. The main idea, put forward in [21], is very simple. Let $\mathcal{F}$ be an arbitrary functionality, initialized with "secret key" κ; instead of storing κ, we store an encoding c of κ, computed via a non-malleable code. Hence, whenever we have to run $\mathcal{F}$, we decode c obtaining a value $\tilde{\kappa}$ which we use to evaluate the functionality on any chosen input. It is not too hard to show that this idea yields security against tampering attacks against the secret key, for the same class of adversaries supported by the non-malleable code.

This methodology, also known as "tamper simulatability", has been explored in several variants [13, 25, 26, 35]. Here, we propose yet another variant where the above compiler is instantiated using a leaky space-bounded continuously non-malleable code; this yields security in a model where it is possible to "trade" security against space-bounded memory tampering, with some bits of leakage on the secret key, an idea already explored in a related line of research [28].

7.1   Leaky Tamper Simulatability

Let $\mathcal{F} : \{0,1\}^k \times \{0,1\}^{k_{\text{in}}} \to \{0,1\}^{k_{\text{out}}}$ be a randomized functionality, taking as input a secret value $\kappa \in \{0,1\}^k$ and a string $m \in \{0,1\}^{k_{\text{in}}}$, and producing a value $y \leftarrow \mathcal{F}(\kappa, m) \in \{0,1\}^{k_{\text{out}}}$. For simplicity, we consider the case of stateless functionalities where the value κ is never updated during the computation; an extension to the case of stateful functionalities is immediate, along the lines of previous work [21, 25, 35]. We note, however, that since updating the value κ requires execution of the encoding algorithm (which uses a lot of space), considering only stateless functionalities is natural in our model.

Given a non-malleable code Π, the hardened functionality corresponding to $\mathcal{F}$ is defined below. For consistency with the rest of the paper, we state the definition in the ROM.

Definition 10 (Hardened functionality). *Consider a functionality $\mathcal{F} : \{0,1\}^k \times \{0,1\}^{k_{\text{in}}} \to \{0,1\}^{k_{\text{out}}}$, and let $\Pi = (\text{Init}^{\mathcal{H}}, \text{Encode}^{\mathcal{H}}, \text{Decode}^{\mathcal{H}})$ be a (k,n)-code in the ROM. For parameters $s, p \in \mathbb{N}$, with $s \ge p \ge n$, the (s,p)-memory hardened functionality $\hat{\mathcal{F}}(\Pi, s, p)$ corresponding to $\mathcal{F}$ consists of algorithms $(\text{Setup}^{\mathcal{H}}, \text{Run}^{\mathcal{H}})$ with the following syntax.*

- *$\text{Setup}^{\mathcal{H}}(1^\lambda, s, \kappa)$: Upon input the security parameter $\lambda \in \mathbb{N}$, sample $\omega \leftarrow \text{Init}^{\mathcal{H}}(1^\lambda)$, let $c \leftarrow \text{Encode}_\omega^{\mathcal{H}}(\kappa)$, and set $\mathcal{M} := c||0^{p-n}||0^{s-p}$. Output $(\omega, \mathcal{M})$.*

– $\mathsf{Run}_\omega^{\mathcal{H}}(\mathcal{M}, m)$: *Parse* $\mathcal{M} := c||\sigma_0||\sigma_1$ *and let* $\tilde{\kappa} = \mathsf{Decode}_\omega^{\mathcal{H}}(c)$. *If* $\tilde{\kappa} = \bot$, *set* $\tilde{y} = \bot$; *else, run* $\tilde{y} \leftarrow \mathcal{F}(\tilde{\kappa}, m)$. *Update* $\mathcal{M} := c||\sigma_0||0^{s-p}$ *and output* $(\tilde{y}, \mathcal{M})$.

It follows by correctness of the encoding scheme that, for all inputs, $\hat{\mathcal{F}}(\Pi, s, p)$ computes exactly the same functionality as $\mathcal{F}$. Notice that the hardened functionality corresponding to $\mathcal{F}$ has p bits of persistent storage (i.e., n bits for storing the secret encoding and $p - n$ bits for auxiliary data); the remaining $s - p$ bits represent transient storage that is needed for decoding the codeword and running the original functionality with the obtained key (this memory is erased after each evaluation).

In case there is not enough transient space to decode or to run the original functionality, an external memory must be used. Thus, we get a natural trade-off between the amount of auxiliary data that can be stored on the device and the class of functionalities that can be executed without using an external memory.

Tampering experiment. To define security, we consider an s-bounded adversary that tampers with the memory content of the hardened functionality. This is done via the experiment described below, which is executed by a PPT algorithm D, and is parametrized by an (s, p)-memory hardened functionality $\hat{\mathcal{F}}(\Pi, s, p)$, a key $\kappa \in \{0, 1\}^k$, a parameter $\theta \in \mathbb{N}$, and security parameter $\lambda \in \mathbb{N}$.

Experiment **TamperInteract**$(\mathsf{D}, \hat{\mathcal{F}}(\Pi, s, p), \kappa, \theta, \lambda)$:

1. Run $(\omega, \mathcal{M}) \leftarrow \mathsf{Setup}^{\mathcal{H}}(1^\lambda, s, \kappa)$ and give ω to D.
2. D can run the following commands (in an arbitrary order):
   – $\langle \mathsf{Tamper}, \mathsf{A} \in \mathcal{A}_{\text{space}}^s \rangle$: Parse $\mathcal{M} := c||\sigma_0||\sigma_1$. Let $(\tilde{c}, \tilde{\sigma}_0, \tilde{\sigma}_1) = \mathsf{A}(c; \sigma_0||\sigma_1)$, and update $\mathcal{M} := \tilde{c}||\tilde{\sigma}_0||\tilde{\sigma}_1$. This command can be run for at most θ times.
   – $\langle \mathsf{Execute}, m \in \{0, 1\}^{k_{in}} \rangle$: Execute $(\tilde{y}, \mathcal{M}) \leftarrow \mathsf{Run}_\omega^{\mathcal{H}}(\mathcal{M}, m)$, and return $\tilde{y}$. This command can be executed an arbitrary polynomial number of times.
   – $\langle \mathsf{RO}, u \in \{0, 1\}^* \rangle$: Return $v = \mathcal{H}(u)$. This command can be executed an arbitrary polynomial number of times.
3. D outputs a bit as a function of its view.

Leaky simulation. Intuitively, a non-malleable code is ℓ-leaky tamper simulatable if the above tampering experiment can be simulated with black-box access to the original functionality $\mathcal{F}$, plus ℓ bits of leakage on the secret key. This is formalized in the experiment described below, which is executed by a PPT algorithm D and is parametrized by a functionality $\mathcal{F}$, a PPT simulator S, a value $\ell \in \mathbb{N}$, an initial key $\kappa \in \{0, 1\}^k$, a parameter $\theta \in \mathbb{N}$, and security parameter $\lambda \in \mathbb{N}$.

Experiment **BBLeak**$(\mathsf{D}, \mathcal{F}, \mathsf{S}, \ell, \kappa, \theta, \lambda)$:

1. The simulator S, which is given black-box access to $\mathcal{F}(\kappa, \cdot)$ and oracle access to $\mathcal{O}_{\text{leak}}^{\ell, \kappa}(\cdot)$, emulates the entire view of D. In particular:

- It takes care of simulating the public parameters and answering (polynomially many) random oracle queries;
- It needs to answer (at most θ) tampering queries and (polynomially many) execute queries.

2. D outputs a bit as a function of its view.[20]

Definition 11 (Leaky tamper simulatability). *Let $\ell, s, p, \theta, k, n \in \mathbb{N}$ be functions of the security parameter $\lambda \in \mathbb{N}$, with $s \geq p \geq n$. A (k,n)-code Π is ℓ-leaky (s,p)-space θ-tamper simulatable in the ROM, if for all PPT distinguishers D there exists a PPT simulator S such that for all functionalities $\mathcal{F}$, and for all $\kappa \in \{0,1\}^k$, there is a negligible function $\nu : \mathbb{N} \to [0,1]$ for which*

$$\Big| \Pr \Big[\textbf{TamperInteract}(\mathsf{D}, \hat{\mathcal{F}}(\Pi, s, p), \kappa, \theta, \lambda) = 1 \Big]$$
$$- \Pr \big[\textbf{BBLeak}(\mathsf{D}, \mathcal{F}, \mathsf{S}, \ell, \kappa, \theta, \lambda) = 1 \big] \Big| \leq \nu(\lambda).$$

7.2 Analysis

In the following theorem, the proof of which appears in the full version, we show the correspondence between leaky non-malleable and leaky tamper simulatable codes.

Theorem 4. *Let Π be an ℓ-leaky (s,p)-space-bounded θ-continuously non-malleable code in the ROM. Then, Π is also ℓ-leaky (s,p)-space θ-tamper simulatable in the ROM.*

Informally, Theorem 4 states that every functionality $\mathcal{F}$ that is resistant to ℓ bits of leakage on the secret key can be protected against memory tampering by an ℓ-leaky non-malleable code.

References

1. Aggarwal, D., Dodis, Y., Kazana, T., Obremski, M.: Non-malleable reductions and applications. In: STOC, pp. 459–468 (2015)
2. Aggarwal, D., Dodis, Y., Lovett, S.: Non-malleable codes from additive combinatorics. In: STOC, pp. 774–783 (2014)
3. Anderson, R., Kuhn, M.: Tamper resistance: a cautionary note. In: WOEC. USENIX Association, Berkeley (1996)
4. Ateniese, G., Bonacina, I., Faonio, A., Galesi, N.: Proofs of space: when space is of the essence. In: Abdalla, M., Prisco, R. (eds.) SCN 2014. LNCS, vol. 8642, pp. 538–557. Springer, Cham (2014). doi:10.1007/978-3-319-10879-7_31
5. Ball, M., Dachman-Soled, D., Kulkarni, M., Malkin, T.: Non-malleable codes for bounded depth, bounded fan-in circuits. In: Fischlin, M., Coron, J.-S. (eds.) EUROCRYPT 2016. LNCS, vol. 9666, pp. 881–908. Springer, Heidelberg (2016). doi:10.1007/978-3-662-49896-5_31

---

[20] Typically, the simulator is restricted to run the black-box functionality on the very same inputs on which the distinguisher specifies its execute queries.

6. Bhattacharyya, R., Mukherjee, P.: Non-adaptive programmability of random oracle. Theor. Comput. Sci. **592**, 97–114 (2015)
7. Boneh, D., Corrigan-Gibbs, H., Schechter, S.: Balloon hashing: a memory-hard function providing provable protection against sequential attacks. In: Cheon, J.H., Takagi, T. (eds.) ASIACRYPT 2016. LNCS, vol. 10031, pp. 220–248. Springer, Heidelberg (2016). doi:10.1007/978-3-662-53887-6_8
8. Boneh, D., DeMillo, R.A., Lipton, R.J.: On the importance of eliminating errors in cryptographic computations. J. Cryptology **14**(2), 101–119 (2001)
9. Chattopadhyay, E., Goyal, V., Li, X.: Non-malleable extractors and codes, with their many tampered extensions. In: ACM STOC, pp. 285–298 (2016)
10. Cheraghchi, M., Guruswami, V.: Capacity of non-malleable codes. In: Innovations in Theoretical Computer Science, pp. 155–168 (2014)
11. Coretti, S., Dodis, Y., Tackmann, B., Venturi, D.: Non-malleable encryption: simpler, shorter, stronger. In: Kushilevitz, E., Malkin, T. (eds.) TCC 2016. LNCS, vol. 9562, pp. 306–335. Springer, Heidelberg (2016). doi:10.1007/978-3-662-49096-9_13
12. Coretti, S., Maurer, U., Tackmann, B., Venturi, D.: From single-bit to multi-bit public-key encryption via non-malleable codes. In: Dodis, Y., Nielsen, J.B. (eds.) TCC 2015. LNCS, vol. 9014, pp. 532–560. Springer, Heidelberg (2015). doi:10. 1007/978-3-662-46494-6_22
13. Dachman-Soled, D., Liu, F.-H., Shi, E., Zhou, H.-S.: Locally decodable and updatable non-malleable codes and their applications. In: Dodis, Y., Nielsen, J.B. (eds.) TCC 2015. LNCS, vol. 9014, pp. 427–450. Springer, Heidelberg (2015). doi:10. 1007/978-3-662-46494-6_18
14. Damgård, I., Faust, S., Mukherjee, P., Venturi, D.: The chaining lemma and its application. In: Information Theoretic, Security, pp. 181–196 (2015)
15. Damgård, I., Faust, S., Mukherjee, P., Venturi, D.: Bounded tamper resilience: How to go beyond the algebraic barrier. J. Cryptology **30**(1), 152–190 (2017)
16. Dodis, Y., Yu, Y.: Overcoming weak expectations. In: Sahai, A. (ed.) TCC 2013. LNCS, vol. 7785, pp. 1–22. Springer, Heidelberg (2013). doi:10.1007/ 978-3-642-36594-2_1
17. Dwork, C., Naor, M., Wee, H.: Pebbling and proofs of work. In: Shoup, V. (ed.) CRYPTO 2005. LNCS, vol. 3621, pp. 37–54. Springer, Heidelberg (2005). doi:10. 1007/11535218_3
18. Dziembowski, S., Faust, S., Kolmogorov, V., Pietrzak, K.: Proofs of space. In: Gennaro, R., Robshaw, M. (eds.) CRYPTO 2015. LNCS, vol. 9216, pp. 585–605. Springer, Heidelberg (2015). doi:10.1007/978-3-662-48000-7_29
19. Dziembowski, S., Kazana, T., Wichs, D.: Key-evolution schemes resilient to space-bounded leakage. In: Rogaway, P. (ed.) CRYPTO 2011. LNCS, vol. 6841, pp. 335–353. Springer, Heidelberg (2011). doi:10.1007/978-3-642-22792-9_19
20. Dziembowski, S., Kazana, T., Wichs, D.: One-time computable self-erasing functions. In: Ishai, Y. (ed.) TCC 2011. LNCS, vol. 6597, pp. 125–143. Springer, Heidelberg (2011). doi:10.1007/978-3-642-19571-6_9
21. Dziembowski, S., Pietrzak, K., Wichs, D.: Non-malleable codes. In: Innovations in Computer, Science, pp. 434–452 (2010)
22. Faonio, A., Nielsen, J.B., Venturi, D.: Mind your coins: fully leakage-resilient signatures with graceful degradation. In: Halldórsson, M.M., Iwama, K., Kobayashi, N., Speckmann, B. (eds.) ICALP 2015. LNCS, vol. 9134, pp. 456–468. Springer, Heidelberg (2015). doi:10.1007/978-3-662-47672-7_37
23. Faonio, A., Nielsen, J.B., Buus, J., Venturi, D.: Fully leakage-resilient signatures revisited: graceful degradation, noisy leakage, and construction in the bounded-retrieval model. Theor. Comput. Sci. **660**, 23–56 (2017)

24. Faonio, A., Venturi, D.: Efficient public-key cryptography with bounded leakage and tamper resilience. In: Cheon, J.H., Takagi, T. (eds.) ASIACRYPT 2016. LNCS, vol. 10031, pp. 877–907. Springer, Heidelberg (2016). doi:10.1007/978-3-662-53887-6_32
25. Faust, S., Mukherjee, P., Nielsen, J.B., Venturi, D.: Continuous non-malleable codes. In: Lindell, Y. (ed.) TCC 2014. LNCS, vol. 8349, pp. 465–488. Springer, Heidelberg (2014). doi:10.1007/978-3-642-54242-8_20
26. Faust, S., Mukherjee, P., Nielsen, J.B., Venturi, D.: A tamper and leakage resilient von neumann architecture. In: Katz, J. (ed.) PKC 2015. LNCS, vol. 9020, pp. 579–603. Springer, Heidelberg (2015). doi:10.1007/978-3-662-46447-2_26
27. Faust, S., Mukherjee, P., Venturi, D., Wichs, D.: Efficient non-malleable codes and key derivation for poly-size tampering circuits. IEEE Trans. Inf. Theory 62(12), 7179–7194 (2016)
28. Faust, S., Pietrzak, K., Venturi, D.: Tamper-proof circuits: how to trade leakage for tamper-resilience. In: Aceto, L., Henzinger, M., Sgall, J. (eds.) ICALP 2011. LNCS, vol. 6755, pp. 391–402. Springer, Heidelberg (2011). doi:10.1007/978-3-642-22006-7_33
29. Fiat, A., Shamir, A.: How to prove yourself: practical solutions to identification and signature problems. In: Odlyzko, A.M. (ed.) CRYPTO 1986. LNCS, vol. 263, pp. 186–194. Springer, Heidelberg (1987). doi:10.1007/3-540-47721-7_12
30. Fischlin, M., Lehmann, A., Ristenpart, T., Shrimpton, T., Stam, M., Tessaro, S.: Random oracles with(out) programmability. In: Abe, M. (ed.) ASIACRYPT 2010. LNCS, vol. 6477, pp. 303–320. Springer, Heidelberg (2010). doi:10.1007/978-3-642-17373-8_18
31. Gennaro, R., Lysyanskaya, A., Malkin, T., Micali, S., Rabin, T.: Algorithmic tamper-proof (atp) security: theoretical foundations for security against hardware tampering. In: Naor, M. (ed.) TCC 2004. LNCS, vol. 2951, pp. 258–277. Springer, Heidelberg (2004). doi:10.1007/978-3-540-24638-1_15
32. Hazay, C., López-Alt, A., Wee, H., Wichs, D.: Leakage-resilient cryptography from minimal assumptions. In: Johansson, T., Nguyen, P.Q. (eds.) EUROCRYPT 2013. LNCS, vol. 7881, pp. 160–176. Springer, Heidelberg (2013). doi:10.1007/978-3-642-38348-9_10
33. Jafargholi, Z., Wichs, D.: Tamper detection and continuous non-malleable codes. In: Dodis, Y., Nielsen, J.B. (eds.) TCC 2015. LNCS, vol. 9014, pp. 451–480. Springer, Heidelberg (2015). doi:10.1007/978-3-662-46494-6_19
34. Katz, J., Vaikuntanathan, V.: Signature schemes with bounded leakage resilience. In: Matsui, M. (ed.) ASIACRYPT 2009. LNCS, vol. 5912, pp. 703–720. Springer, Heidelberg (2009). doi:10.1007/978-3-642-10366-7_41
35. Liu, F.-H., Lysyanskaya, A.: Tamper and leakage resilience in the split-state model. In: Safavi-Naini, R., Canetti, R. (eds.) CRYPTO 2012. LNCS, vol. 7417, pp. 517–532. Springer, Heidelberg (2012). doi:10.1007/978-3-642-32009-5_30
36. Merkle, R.C.: Method of providing digital signatures. US Patent 4309569, 5 January 1982
37. Mukherjee, P.: Protecting cryptographic memory against tampering attack. Ph.D thesis, Aarhus University (2015)
38. Naor, M., Segev, G.: Public-key cryptosystems resilient to key leakage. SIAM J. Comput. 41(4), 772–814 (2012)

39. Nielsen, J.B., Venturi, D., Zottarel, A.: Leakage-resilient signatures with graceful degradation. In: Krawczyk, H. (ed.) PKC 2014. LNCS, vol. 8383, pp. 362–379. Springer, Heidelberg (2014). doi:10.1007/978-3-642-54631-0_21

40. Ren, L., Devadas, S.: Proof of space from stacked expanders. In: Hirt, M., Smith, A. (eds.) TCC 2016. LNCS, vol. 9985, pp. 262–285. Springer, Heidelberg (2016). doi:10.1007/978-3-662-53641-4_11

Four-Round Concurrent Non-Malleable Commitments from One-Way Functions

Michele Ciampi[1]([⊠]), Rafail Ostrovsky[2], Luisa Siniscalchi[1], and Ivan Visconti[1]

[1] DIEM, University of Salerno, Fisciano, Italy
{mciampi,lsiniscalchi,visconti}@unisa.it
[2] UCLA, Los Angeles, USA
rafail@cs.ucla.edu

Abstract. How many rounds and which assumptions are required for *concurrent* non-malleable commitments? The above question has puzzled researchers for several years. Pass in [TCC 2013] showed a lower bound of 3 rounds for the case of black-box reductions to falsifiable hardness assumptions with respect to polynomial-time adversaries. On the other side, Goyal [STOC 2011], Lin and Pass [STOC 2011] and Goyal et al. [FOCS 2012] showed that one-way functions (OWFs) are sufficient with a constant number of rounds. More recently Ciampi et al. [CRYPTO 2016] showed a 3-round construction based on subexponentially strong one-way permutations.

In this work we show as *main result* the first 4-round concurrent non-malleable commitment scheme assuming the existence of any one-way function.

Our approach builds on a new security notion for argument systems against man-in-the-middle attacks: *Simulation-Witness-Independence*. We show how to construct a 4-round one-many simulation-witnesses-independent argument system from one-way functions. We then combine this new tool in parallel with a weak form of non-malleable commitments constructed by Goyal et al. in [FOCS 2014] obtaining the main result of our work.

1 Introduction

Commitment schemes are a fundamental primitive in Cryptography. Here we consider the intriguing question of constructing round-efficient schemes that remain secure even against man-in-the-middle (MiM) attacks: non-malleable (NM) commitments [12].

Non-malleable commitments. The round complexity of commitment schemes in the stand-alone setting is nowadays well understood. Non-interactive commitments can be constructed assuming the existence of 1-to-1 one-way functions (OWFs) [18]; 2-round commitments can be constructed assuming the existence of OWFs only. Moreover non-interactive commitments do not exist if one relies on the black-box use of OWFs only [33].

© International Association for Cryptologic Research 2017
J. Katz and H. Shacham (Eds.): CRYPTO 2017, Part II, LNCS 10402, pp. 127–157, 2017.
DOI: 10.1007/978-3-319-63715-0_5

Instead, the round complexity of NM commitments[1] after 25 years of research remains a fascinating open question, in particular when taking into account the required computational assumptions. The original construction of [12] required a logarithmic number of rounds and the sole use of OWFs. Then, through a long sequence of very exciting positive results [1,19,22,29–31,41–46,50], the above open question has been in part solved obtaining a constant-round[2] (even concurrent) NM commitment scheme by using any OWF in a black-box fashion. On the negative side, Pass proved that NM commitments require at least 3 rounds [40][3] when security is proved through a black-box reduction to polynomial-time hardness assumptions.

Breaking the multiple rewind-slot barrier. The above papers left open the question of achieving (concurrent) non-malleable commitments with optimal round complexity. A main common issue for round-efficient non-malleable commitments is that typically a security proof requires some simulation on the left and extraction on the right that should not interfere with each other. Indeed, a known paradigm introduced by Pass [39] proposes to have in a protocol multiple potential rewind slots so that extraction and simulation can both be run in 2 independent sequential steps. On the negative side, the use of multiple rewind slots increases the round complexity of the protocol (i.e., two rewind slots require at least 5 rounds).

More recently the multiple rewind-slot technique has been bypassed in [25] but only for the (simpler) one-one case (i.e., just one sender and one receiver). In particular, Goyal et al. [25] showed a *one-one* 4-round NM commitment scheme based on OWFs only. The more recent work of Goyal et al. [23,24] exploited the use of the NM codes in the split-state model to show a 3-round one-one NM commitment scheme based on the black-box use of any 1-to-1 OWF that is secure against super-polynomial time adversaries[4]. Ciampi et al. [6] obtained concurrent non-malleability in 3 rounds starting from any one-one non-malleable (and extractable) commitment scheme, but their security proof crucially relies on the existence of one-way permutations secure against subexponential-time adversaries. Assumptions against super-polynomial time adversaries allow to avoid multiple rewind slots even in presence of polynomially many sessions since the security proof can rely on straight-line simulation/extraction[5].

---

[1] In this paper we will consider only NM commitments w.r.t. commitments. For the case of NM w.r.t. decommitments see [2,9,21,37,43,45].

[2] The construction of [22] can be compressed to 6 rounds (see [25]).

[3] If instead one relies on non-standard assumptions or trusted setups (e.g., using trusted parameters, working in the random oracle model, relying on the existence of NM OWFs) then there exist non-interactive NM commitments [10,38].

[4] While [23,24] only claimed one-one non-malleability, the difficulty of achieving concurrent non-malleability was discussed in [6] where Ciampi et al. showed an explicit successful concurrent man-in-the-middle for the preliminary eprint version of [24].

[5] Hardness assumptions against subexponential-time adversaries were already used in [41,46,50] to improve the round-complexity of NM commitments.

1.1 Our Results

In this paper we break the multiple-slot barrier for concurrent NM commitments by showing a 4-round scheme based on the sole existence of OWFs. While previous work relied on having either (1) stronger assumptions or (2) multiple rewind slots or (3) limited concurrency, in this work we introduce new techniques that allow to have just one rewind slot, minimal hardness assumptions and full concurrency.

More specifically we give the following four contributions.

Non-malleable commitments w.r.t. non-aborting adversaries. We prove that a subprotocol of [25] is a 4-round statistically binding concurrent NM commitment scheme from OWFs (resp. a 3-round perfectly binding concurrent NM commitment scheme from 1-to-1 OWFs), if the adversary is restricted to playing well-formed commitments in the right sessions when receiving well formed commitments from the left sessions. We refer to this weaker security notion as concurrent weak non-malleability (wNM).

Simulation-Witness-Independence. We define a new security notion for argument systems w.r.t. man-in-the-middle attacks that we refer to as simulation-witness-independence (SimWI). This security notion seemingly is not implied by previous notions as simulation-extractability/soundness and strong non-malleable witness indistinguishability.

4-Round One-Many SimWI from OWFs. We then construct a 4-round one-many SimWI argument of knowledge for some specific languages by relying on OWFs only. This construction circumvents the major problem caused by the need of rewinding on the left to simulate and on the right to extract when there is only one available rewind slot.

Concurrent wNM + One-Many SimWI ⇒ 4-Round Concurrent NM Commitments. We present our new paradigm consisting in combining the above two notions in a protocol that runs in parallel the concurrent wNM commitment scheme and the one-many SimWI argument of knowledge. Therefore as main result of this work we upgrade concurrent wNM to full-fledged concurrent non-malleability without any penalization in rounds and assumptions.

We now discuss in more details each of the above 4 contributions.

Weak Non-Malleable Commitments. We define commitment schemes enjoying a limited form of non-malleability[6].

Informally, we say that a commitment scheme is weak non-malleable (wNM) if it is non-malleable w.r.t. adversaries that never commit to $\perp$ when receiving honestly computed commitments. This form of non-malleability is significantly

---

[6] We remark that Goyal in [19] defined a weaker notion of non-malleable commitments (non-malleability w.r.t. replacement) that also had the goal to deal with commitments of $\perp$. While the goal is similar to our definition, the actual formulation is quite different.

weaker than full-fledged non-malleability. Indeed, a full-fledged MiM $\mathcal{A}$ can for instance maul as follows: $\mathcal{A}$ creates a commitment of m_0 making use of messages computed by the sender in the left session so that if the sender commits to m_0 then the commitment of $\mathcal{A}$ is a well formed commitment of m_0, while instead if the sender commits to $m_1 \neq m_0$ then the commitment of $\mathcal{A}$ is not well formed and therefore corresponds to $\perp$. Such attacks can be explicitly instantiated as shown in [6] where a generalization of the above $\mathcal{A}$ is used to prove that a preliminary version of the scheme of [24] is not concurrent non-malleable.

While by itself the wNM guarantee is certainly unsatisfying as protection against MiM attacks, the design of a wNM commitment scheme can be an easier task and schemes with such light non-malleability flavor might exist with improved round complexity, efficiency and complexity assumptions compared to schemes achieving full-fledged non-malleability.

We show that a protocol due to [25] is a 4-round statistically binding concurrent wNM commitment scheme requiring OWFs only (resp., a 3-round perfectly binding concurrent wNM commitment scheme requiring 1-to-1 OWFs only). Moreover their protocol can be instantiated to be public coin. The security proof consists of some pretty straightforward observations on top of various useful lemmas already proven in [25]. Our contribution on wNM commitments therefore consists in (1) introducing and formalizing this notion; (2) observing the existence of a secure construction in previous work; (3) using it as one of the two main building blocks of our paradigm allowing to obtain 4-round concurrent (full-fledged) NM commitments from OWFs. For lack of space we postpone further details on wNM commitments to the full version (see [5]) so that in this work we can give more details on the more interesting results of this work (i.e., the definition and construction of SimWI, and the new paradigm for concurrent NM commitments). A formal definition of weak NM commitments can be found in Sect. 2.3 (see Definition 5). The proof that a scheme proposed in [25] satisfies this notion can be found in the full version (see [5]).

Simulation-Witness-Independence. We introduce a new security notion against MiM attacks to argument systems. We call our security notion *simulation-witness-independence* (SimWI) since it has similarities both with simulation extractability/soundness (see [43,48]) and with (strong) non-malleable witness indistinguishability [32,36] (sNMWI, NMWI). For simplicity we will discuss now the case of one prover and one verifier only, however our formal definition, construction and application will focus on the one-many case (i.e., up to 1 prover and polynomially many verifiers).

The 1st security flavor that our notion tries to capture is the concept that the view of a MiM in the real game should be simulatable. Therefore we will have an experiment corresponding to the real game where the MiM plays with a honest prover and a honest verifier, and an experiment corresponding to the simulated game that simply consists of the output of a stand-alone simulator that emulates the prover and runs the code of honest verifiers when interacting internally with the MiM[7].

While the above 1st security flavor guarantees that the statements proven by the MiM in the real-world experiment and in the simulated experiment are indistinguishable, there still is no guarantee that the MiM is unable to prove in the two experiments statements that are associated to witnesses belonging to distinguishable distributions. In other words, as 2nd flavor we want to capture the independence of the witnesses associated to the statements proven by the MiM with respect to the fact that the actual witness in the left session is used (this is the case of the real game) or is not used (this is the case of the simulated game). In order to avoid any ambiguity on which witness is associated to a statement, we associate to an $\mathcal{NP}$ language a non-negative integer γ. More precisely, for any $\mathcal{NP}$ language L we consider a non-negative integer γ such that for any $x \in L$ all witnesses of x have the same first γ bits[8]. The reason why we assign such a value γ to every $\mathcal{NP}$ language is that it fixes in some non-ambiguous way the input for the distinguisher of SimWI (indeed the input will be the first γ bits of any witness) and at same time the prefix of all the witnesses of an instance can be recovered by extracting any witness.

The above 2nd flavor makes our security definition non-trivial. Indeed standard zero knowledge is clearly insufficient against MiM attacks and the definition has strong connections with the (hard to achieve) concept of committed message in NM commitments[9]. One might think that some heavy machinery could already imply our new notion. However, by taking into account all subtleties of the definitions it turns out that SimWI is seemingly not implied by simulation extractability, simulation soundness and sNMWI/NMWI. We stress that our goal is to get a *one-many* *4*-round construction under minimal assumptions.

Comparison with simulation extractability and simulation soundness.
Simulation extractability requires the simulator to output a transcript and witnesses for the statements appearing in the right sessions of the transcript.

Simulation soundness requires the MiM to fail in proving false statements when receiving simulated proofs of false statements.

SimWI requires the simulator to output a transcript that includes statements proven in right sessions. The distribution of the instance/witness pairs associated to those statements is required to be indistinguishable from the distribution of the instance/witness pairs associated to the statements proved by the MiM

---

[7] There is nothing surprising so far, this is just the concept of zero knowledge naturally augmented by extending the simulator with the behavior of honest verifiers to feed the MiM with messages belonging to the right sessions too.

[8] Note that when $\gamma = 0$ the 2nd security flavor is cancelled and SimWI becomes equivalent to zero knowledge. Furthermore when γ is equal to the largest witness size then we are considering languages in $\mathcal{UP}$.

[9] We stress that the main goal of this work is to construct 4-round concurrent NM commitments from OWFs, and we will achieve it by making use of SimWI. As such, to avoid circularity, we can not use concurrent NM commitments to construct SimWI.

in the real game. In simulation extractability there is no requirement on the witness given in output by the simulator beyond being valid witnesses. Simulation soundness does not have any requirement on the witnesses associated to the statements proven by the MiM.

Comparison with sNMWI/NMWI. sNMWI considers two indistinguishable distributions of instance/witnesses pairs. Very informally, the requirement of sNMWI/NMWI is that the instance/witness pairs associated to the arguments given by the MiM in the right sessions be independent of the distribution from which the instance/witness pair of the argument given to the MiM in the left session has been sampled.

SimWI requires the existence of a simulator while instead sNMWI/NMWI only considers experiments where the actual prover plays.

One-Many SimWI From OWFs in 4 Rounds (i.e., in Just One Rewind Slot!). As discussed above, SimWI is an interesting security notions w.r.t. MiM attacks and similarly to all previous non-malleability notions is certainly non-trivial to achieve, especially when considering (1) the one-many case (2) only four rounds (i.e., one rewind slot) and (3) minimal assumptions. In this work we show how to construct a 4-round one-many SimWI argument of knowledge (AoK) from OWFs, therefore avoiding multiple rewind slots.

A common approach to construct 4-round zero-knowledge arguments (even without non-malleability requirements) relies on the FLS/FS paradigm [14,15]. First there is a subprotocol useful to extract a trapdoor from the adversarial verifier. Then there is a witness-indistinguishable proof of knowledge (WIPoK) where the prover proves knowledge of either a witness for the statement or of the trapdoor. In order to save rounds the two subprotocols are parallelized.

The above common approach fails in presence of MiM attacks. The reason is that the MiM adversary can attack the witness indistinguishability (WI) of the WIPoK received in the left session in order to prove his statements in the right sessions. Using such a MiM to contradict the WI of the WIPoK is problematic since one should extract some useful information from the right session but this would require also to rewind the challenger of the WI of the WIPoK on the left.

We bypass the above difficulty as follows. Instead of relying on the WI of the WIPoK that requires two messages played by the challenger, we propose a construction where we essentially break the interactive challenger of WI into two non-interactive challengers. We implement this idea by relying on: (1) instance-dependent trapdoor commitments (IDTCom) and (2) special honest-verifier zero knowledge (special HVZK). More in details, let $(\pi_1, \pi_2, \pi_3, \pi_4)$ be the transcript of a delayed-input[10] 4-round special HVZK adaptive-input proof of knowledge (PoK). We require the prover to send an IDTCom com of π_2 that is opened, sending the opening dec, only in the last round, when π_4 is sent. The actual transcript therefore becomes $(\pi_1, \text{com}, \pi_3, (\pi_2, \text{dec}, \pi_4))$.

---

[10] By *delayed-input* we mean that the statement will be known only at the last round. The delayed-input property has been critically used in the past (e.g., [11,27,51]) and very recently (e.g., [6–8,16,26,34]), since it helps in improving the round complexity of external protocols.

Consider now an experiment where the trapdoor is known and π_2 can be opened arbitrarily. If the output of the experiment deviates from the original one, we will have a reduction to the trapdoorness of the IDTCom. The reduction is not problematic since the challenger of the trapdoorness is non-interactive, sending a pair (commitment, decommitment) that is either computed using the regular procedure or through the use of the trapdoor. Next, in another experiment we can replace the prover of the PoK with the special HVZK simulator that will compute π_2 and π_4 after having as input π_1 and π_3. Again, the output of this experiment will not deviate from the previous one otherwise we can show an adversary for the special HVZK property. The reduction again is not problematic since the challenger of special HVZK is non-interactive.

We implement the trapdoor-extraction subprotocol through OWFs by using as trapdoor knowledge of two signatures under the same public key sent by the verifier in the 1st round. The verifier will send a signature of one message (chosen by the prover) in the 3rd round (with this approach we follow previous ideas of [3,4,11,20]). We will use a delayed-input special HVZK adaptive-input PoK where the prover proves knowledge of either a witness for the statement or of signatures of messages. The IDTCom will have the public key of the signature scheme as instance, therefore the simulator after having extracted the signatures will be able to equivocate the commitments. The security proof presents one more caveat. Once the simulator rewinds on the left to obtain the trapdoor it is not clear how to argue that the extraction from the right is meaningful since the extractor might simply obtain the same trapdoor. More specifically, the adversary might be able to equivocate on the right, therefore the extractor of the PoK would fail, and the best we can get from such a binding violation is the trapdoor of the IDTCom played in the right session. This does not give any contradiction since the trapdoor of the right session had to be already known in order to answer twice (before and after the rewind) in the right session to the MiM. We resolve this problem by relying on a specific proof approach where while the initial transcript is generated by the simulator, when the extractions are played in the right sessions, the transcript of the left session is re-completed by running the prover of the special HVZK PoK. The reason why in this case the extraction on the right will succeed is that if we extract the trapdoor from the right session then this will also happen in the real game where the trapdoor is never used. In turn it would break the security of the signature scheme.

Caveat: adaptive-input selection. We will give a formal definition that allows the MiM to select the instance/witness pair for the left session only at the end, while the MiM must fix the statement for a right session already when playing his first round in that session. Our construction satisfies this notion and even a more important form of adaptiveness. We allow the MiM to specify the statement in the last round of a right session, as long as the witness is already fixed when playing his first round in that session. The reason why we prove such more sophisticated form of adaptive-input selection is that it is required in our application for concurrent NM commitments. Ideally one would like to satisfy the best possible adaptive-input selection, in order to make this new primitive useful in a broader range of applications. However we can not prove our construction secure with fully adaptive-input selection since we are not able to extract the witness from a MiM selecting a new statement (with possibly a new witness) in the last round of a right session. Indeed we would end up having a certain statement in the transcript of the simulator and then a witness for another statement obtained through rewinds. This would negatively affect our proof approach.

4-Round Concurrent NM Commitments from OWFs. We solve the problem left open by [25] by showing a 4-round concurrent NM commitment scheme relying on OWFs only. The new paradigm that we propose to obtain concurrent non-malleability consists in combining in parallel a 4-round public-coin concurrent wNM commitment scheme from OWFs Π_0, and a one-many 4-round SimWI argument of knowledge from OWFs Π_1.

The new paradigm. Π_0 is run in order to commit to the message m. Π_1 is instead used to prove knowledge of a valid message and randomness explaining the transcript of Π_0. The power of the new approach consists in using the above two tools that are in perfect synergy to defeat a concurrent MiM attack. The idea of the security proof is now quite simple. Since any one-many NM commitment is also many-many[11] NM, we focus the following discussion on the one-many case.

In the 1st experiment (the real game RG0) the sender commits to m_0. Clearly there can not be a commitment to $\bot$ on the right otherwise the soundness of Π_1 is contradicted. Symmetrically there is an experiment RG1 where the sender commits to m_1 and there is no commitment to $\bot$ on the right. Then we consider an hybrid game H0 where the simulator of one-many SimWI of Π_1 is used. Observe that if (by contradiction) the distribution of the messages committed on the right changes w.r.t. RG0 we have that also the distribution of the witnesses corresponding to the statements proved in Π_1 on the right changes. However this clearly violates SimWI. Therefore it must still be the case that a commitment played on the right corresponds to $\bot$ with negligible probability only. Symmetrically, there is an experiment H1 that is indistinguishable from RG1 and such that commitments played on the right are well formed (i.e., different from $\bot$). Therefore we can conclude that RG0 is indistinguishable from RG1 by noticing that H0 is indistinguishable from H1. Indeed, both H0 and H1 guarantee that the messages committed by the adversary on the right correspond to $\bot$ with negligible probability only. Summing up, a detectable deviation from H0 to H1 implies a contradiction of the concurrent wNM of Π_0[12]. This observation concludes the high-level overview of the security proof. However, some remarks are in order.

---

[11] A many-many NM commitment scheme can be also indicate as a concurrent NM commitment scheme. In the rest of the paper we use the term concurrent.

[12] This reduction needs extra help, see Remark 2 below.

Remark 1: the required adaptive-input flavor. As specified in the previous section, our 4-round one-many SimWI AoK Π_1 is fully adaptive on the left but instead on the right requires the witness to be fixed already in the first round of the MiM. The statements instead can be decided in the last round also in the right sessions. The flexibility with the statement is important since Π_0 is completed only in the last round and the entire transcript of Π_0 is part of the statement of Π_1. The lack of flexibility on the witness in the right sessions forces us to add one more requirement to Π_0. We need that message and randomness are already fixed in the 2nd round of Π_0, since they will be the witness for Π_1. This property is satisfied by the construction of [25] that we prove to be concurrent wNM in the full version (see [5]).

Remark 2: on the need of public coins in Π_0. In a reduction we will have to simulate the last round of the receiver of Π_0 without knowing the randomness he used to compute the previous round. Obviously public coins are easy to simulate.

1.2   3-Round Concurrent Non-Malleable Commitments

The work of Ciampi et al. [6] relied on subexponentially strong one-way permutations and the existence of any 3-round one-one non-malleable commitment scheme Π. In this work we propose a different approach for 3-round one-one non-malleable commitments that instead can start with a limited form of non-malleability enjoyed by both a subprotocol of [25] and a subprotocol of [24] (therefore we can instantiate our result in two completely different ways). The result of Ciampi et al. [6] can still be instantiated using our 3-round one-one non-malleable commitment scheme that we present in this work. Therefore our work combined with the one of [6] gives the first 3-round concurrent non-malleable commitment scheme from falsifiable assumptions[13].

Our 3-round one-one non-malleable commitment scheme combines some ideas of [6] along with the concept of weak non-malleable commitment. In particular we start with a scheme that is one-one non-malleable only against synchronous adversaries that do not commit to $\bot$. As we discuss in the paper, both a subprotocol of [25] and a subprotocol of [24] satisfy this security property. Considering this notion we construct a compiler that, on input a 3-round synchronous weak one-one NM commitment scheme, gives as output a 3-round extractable one-one NM commitment scheme assuming OWPs secure against subexponential-time adversaries. This can then be used inside [6] to get 3-round concurrent non-malleable commitments from subexponential one-way permutations.

---

[13] We stress that after our results were publicly available, a construction for 3-round one-one non-malleable commitments with the black-box use of one-to-one one-way functions secure against quasi-polynomial-time adversaries was announced in [23]. Their work revisited the primitives that instantiated their prior construction [24] based on 1–1 OWFs that appeared before this work and before [6].

1.3   The New State of the Art

In Table 1 we summarize the new state of the art.

Table 1. Comparison with recent positive results from the oldest to the newest.

Paper		No. rounds	Assumption	Concurrency
Goyal/Lin and Pass	STOC 2011	≥ 6	OWFs	Yes
Goyal et al.	FOCS 2012	≥ 6	BB OWFs	Yes
Goyal et al.	FOCS 2014	4	OWFs	No
This work + Ciampi et al.	CRYPTO 2016	3	Subexp OWPs	Yes
This work (main result)		4	OWFs	Yes
Goyal et al.	STOC 2016[a]	3	BB quasi-poly 1–1 OWFs	No

[a]The need of super-polynomial time hardness assumptions appeared in December 2016 [23].

2   Definitions and Tools

2.1   Preliminaries

We denote the security parameter by λ and use "|" as concatenation operator (i.e., if a and b are two strings then by $a|b$ we denote the concatenation of a and b). For a finite set Q, $x \leftarrow Q$ sampling of x from Q with uniform distribution. We use the abbreviation PPT that stays for probabilistic polynomial time. We use poly$(\cdot)$ to indicate a generic polynomial function and $\mathbb{N}$ to denote the set of positive integer. We use the notation s^t to denote the first t-bits of a string s. A *polynomial-time relation* Rel (or *polynomial relation*, in short) is a subset of $\{0,1\}^* \times \{0,1\}^*$ such that membership of (x, w) in Rel can be decided in time polynomial in $|x|$. For $(x, w) \in$ Rel, we call x the *instance* and w a *witness* for x. For a polynomial-time relation Rel, we define the $\mathcal{NP}$-language L_{Rel} as $L_{\mathsf{Rel}} = \{x | \exists w : (x, w) \in \mathsf{Rel}\}$. Analogously, unless otherwise specified, for an $\mathcal{NP}$-language L we denote by Rel_L the corresponding polynomial-time relation (that is, Rel_L is such that $L = L_{\mathsf{Rel}_L}$). Let A and B be two interactive probabilistic algorithms. We denote by $\langle A(\alpha), B(\beta) \rangle(\gamma)$ the distribution of B's output after running on private input β with A using private input α, both running on common input γ. Typically, one of the two algorithms receives 1^λ as input. A *transcript* of $\langle A(\alpha), B(\beta) \rangle(\gamma)$ consists of the messages exchanged during an execution where A receives a private input α, B receives a private input β and both A and B receive a common input γ. Moreover, we will refer to the *view* of A (resp. B) as the messages it received during the execution of $\langle A(\alpha), B(\beta) \rangle(\gamma)$, along with its randomness and its input.

Definition 1 (Proof/argument system). *A pair of* PPT *interactive algorithms* $\Pi = (\mathcal{P}, \mathcal{V})$ *constitutes a* proof system *(resp., an* argument system*) for an* $\mathcal{NP}$*-language L, if the following conditions hold:*

Completeness: *For every* $x \in L$ *and* w *such that* $(x, w) \in \mathsf{Rel_L}$*, it holds that:* $Prob\left[\ \langle \mathcal{P}(w), \mathcal{V} \rangle(x) = 1\ \right] = 1.$

Soundness: *For every interactive (resp.,* PPT *interactive) algorithm* $\mathcal{P}^\star$*, there exists a negligible function* ν *such that for every* $x \notin L$ *and every* z*:* $Prob\left[\ \langle \mathcal{P}^\star(z), \mathcal{V} \rangle(x) = 1\ \right] < \nu(|x|).$

A proof/argument system $\Pi = (\mathcal{P}, \mathcal{V})$ for an $\mathcal{NP}$-language L, enjoys *delayed-input* completeness if $\mathcal{P}$ needs x and w only to compute the last round and $\mathcal{V}$ needs x only to compute the output. Before that, $\mathcal{P}$ and $\mathcal{V}$ run having as input only the size of x. The notion of delayed-input completeness was defined in [8]. An interactive protocol $\Pi = (\mathcal{P}, \mathcal{V})$ is *public coin* if, at every round, $\mathcal{V}$ simply tosses a predetermined number of coins (random challenge) and sends the outcome to the prover. We say that the transcript τ of an execution $b = \langle \mathcal{P}(z), \mathcal{V} \rangle(x)$ is *accepting* if $b = 1$.

Definition 2 (Special Honest-Verifier Zero Knowledge (Special HVZK)). *Consider a public-coin proof/argument system* $\Pi = (\mathcal{P}, \mathcal{V})$ *for an* $\mathcal{NP}$*-language L where the verifier sends m messages of length* $\ell_1, \ldots, \ell_m$*. We say that* Π *is Special HVZK if there exists a PPT simulator algorithm* $\mathcal{S}$ *that on input any* $x \in L$*, security parameter* 1^λ *and any* $c_1 \in \{0, 1\}^{\ell_1}, \ldots, c_m \in \{0, 1\}^{\ell_m}$*, outputs a transcript for proving* $x \in L$ *where* $c_1, \ldots, c_m$ *are the messages of the verifier, such that the distribution of the output of* $\mathcal{S}$ *is computationally indistinguishable from the distribution of a transcript obtained when* $\mathcal{V}$ *sends* $c_1, \ldots, c_m$ *as challenges and* $\mathcal{P}$ *runs on common input* x *and any* w *such that* $(x, w) \in \mathsf{Rel_L}$*.*

In this paper we consider the notion of proof/argument of knowledge (PoK/AoK) defined in [29]. Furthermore we consider the *adaptive-input* PoK/AoK property for all the protocols that enjoy delayed-input completeness. Adaptive-input PoK/AoK ensures that the PoK/AoK property still holds when a malicious prover can choose the statement adaptively at the last round. We consider the 3-round public-coin Special HVZK PoK proposed by Lapidot and Shamir [28], that we denote by LS. LS enjoys delayed-input completeness since the inputs for both $\mathcal{P}$ and $\mathcal{V}$ are needed only to play the last round, and only the length of the instance is needed earlier. LS also enjoys adaptive-input PoK. In particular we use a 4-round delayed-input special HVZK adaptive-input AoK that is a variant of LS [13] that relies on OWFs only. The additional round is indeed needed to instantiate the commitment scheme used in LS under any OWF.

2.2 2-Round Instance-Dependent Trapdoor Commitments

Here we define a special commitment scheme based on an $\mathcal{NP}$-language L where sender and receiver also receive as input an instance x. While correctness and computational hiding hold for any x, we require that statistical binding holds for $x \notin L$ and knowledge of a witness for $x \in L$ allows to equivocate. Finally, we require that a commitment along with two different openings allows to compute the witness for $x \in L$. We recall that $\hat{L}$ denotes the language that includes L and all well formed instances that are not in L.

Definition 3. *Let 1^λ be the security parameter, L be an $\mathcal{NP}$-language and Rel_L be the corresponding $\mathcal{NP}$-relation. A triple of PPT algorithms $\mathsf{TC} = (\mathsf{Sen}, \mathsf{Rec}, \mathsf{TFake})$ is a 2-Round Instance-Dependent Trapdoor Commitment scheme if the following properties hold.*

Correctness. *In the 1st round, Rec on input 1^λ and $x \in \hat{L}$ outputs ρ. In the 2nd round Sen on input the message m, 1^λ, ρ and $x \in L$ outputs $(\mathsf{com}, \mathsf{dec})$. We will refer to the pair (ρ, com) as the commitment of m. Moreover we will refer to the execution of the above two rounds including the exchange of the corresponding two messages as the commitment phase. Then Rec on input m, x, com, dec and the private coins used to generate ρ in the commitment phase outputs 1. We will refer to the execution of this last round including the exchange of dec as the decommitment phase. Notice that an adversarial sender Sen^* could deviate from the behavior of Sen when computing and sending com and dec for an instance $x \in \hat{L}$. As a consequence Rec could output 0 in the decommitment phase. We will say that dec is a valid decommitment of (ρ, com) to m for an instance $x \in \hat{L}$, if Rec outputs 1.*

Hiding. *Given a PPT adversary $\mathcal{A}$, consider the following hiding experiment $\mathsf{ExpHiding}^b_{\mathcal{A},\mathsf{TC}}(\lambda, x)$ for $b = 0, 1$ and $x \in \hat{L}_R$:*

*   *On input 1^λ and x, $\mathcal{A}$ outputs a message m, along with ρ.*
*   *The challenger on input x, m, ρ, b works as follows: if $b = 0$ then it runs Sen on input m, x and ρ, obtaining a pair $(\mathsf{com}, \mathsf{dec})$, otherwise it runs TFake on input x and ρ, obtaining a pair $(\mathsf{com}, \mathsf{aux})$. The challenger outputs com.*
*   *$\mathcal{A}$ on input com outputs a bit b' and this is the output of the experiment.*

We say that hiding holds if for any PPT adversary $\mathcal{A}$ there exist a negligible function ν, s.t.:

$$\left| Prob\left[\, \mathsf{ExpHiding}^0_{\mathcal{A},\mathsf{TC}}(\lambda, x) = 1 \,\right] - Prob\left[\, \mathsf{ExpHiding}^1_{\mathcal{A},\mathsf{TC}}(\lambda, x) = 1 \,\right] \right| < \nu(\lambda).$$

Special Binding. *There exists a PPT algorithm that on input a commitment (ρ, com), the private coins used by Rec to compute ρ, and two valid decommitments $(\mathsf{dec}, \mathsf{dec}')$ of (ρ, com) to two different messages m and m' w.r.t. an instance $x \in L$, outputs w s.t. $(x, w) \in \mathsf{Rel}_L$ with overwhelming probability.*

Trapdoorness. *For any PPT adversary $\mathcal{A}$ there exist a negligible function ν, s.t. for all $x \in L$ it holds that:*

$$\left| Prob\left[\, \mathsf{ExpCom}_{\mathcal{A},\mathsf{TC}}(\lambda, x) = 1 \,\right] - Prob\left[\, \mathsf{ExpTrapdoor}_{\mathcal{A},\mathsf{TC}}(\lambda, x) = 1 \,\right] \right| < \nu(\lambda)$$

where $\mathsf{ExpCom}_{\mathcal{A},\mathsf{TC}}(\lambda, x)$ and $\mathsf{ExpTrapdoor}_{\mathcal{A},\mathsf{TC}}(\lambda, x)$ are defined below[14].

---

[14] We assume w.l.o.g. that $\mathcal{A}$ is stateful.

$\mathsf{ExpCom}_{\mathcal{A},\mathsf{TC}}(\lambda, x)$:
- *On input* 1^λ *and* x, $\mathcal{A}$ *outputs* (ρ, m).
- *Sen on input* 1^λ, x, m *and* ρ, *outputs* $(\mathsf{com}, \mathsf{dec})$.

$\mathsf{ExpTrapdoor}_{\mathcal{A},\mathsf{TC}}(\lambda, x)$:
- *On input* 1^λ *and* x, $\mathcal{A}$ *outputs* (ρ, m).
- *TFake on input* 1^λ, x *and* ρ, *outputs* $(\mathsf{com}, \mathsf{aux})$.
- *TFake on input* tk *s.t.* $(x, \mathsf{tk}) \in \mathsf{Rel}_\mathsf{L}$, x, ρ, com, aux *and* m *outputs* dec.

- $\mathcal{A}$ *on input* $(\mathsf{com}, \mathsf{dec})$ *outputs a bit* b *and this is the output of the experiment.*

- $\mathcal{A}$ *on input* $(\mathsf{com}, \mathsf{dec})$ *outputs a bit* b *and this is the output of the experiment.*

2.3 Non-Malleable Commitments

Here we follow [31]. Let $\Pi = (\mathsf{Sen}, \mathsf{Rec})$ be a statistically binding commitment scheme and let λ be the security parameter. Consider MiM adversaries that are participating in left and right sessions in which $\mathsf{poly}(\lambda)$ commitments take place. We compare between a MiM and a simulated execution. In the MiM execution the adversary $\mathcal{A}$, with auxiliary information z, is simultaneously participating in $\mathsf{poly}(\lambda)$ left and right sessions. In the left sessions the MiM adversary $\mathcal{A}$ interacts with $\mathsf{Sen}_1, \ldots, \mathsf{Sen}_{\mathsf{poly}(\lambda)}$ receiving commitments to values $m_1, \ldots, m_{\mathsf{poly}(\lambda)}$ using identities $\mathsf{id}_1, \ldots, \mathsf{id}_{\mathsf{poly}(\lambda)}$ of its choice. In the right session $\mathcal{A}$ interacts with $\mathsf{Rec}_1, \ldots, \mathsf{Rec}_{\mathsf{poly}(\lambda)}$ attempting to commit to a sequence of related values $\tilde{m}_1, \ldots, \tilde{m}_{\mathsf{poly}(\lambda)}$ again using identities of its choice $\tilde{\mathsf{id}}_1, \ldots, \tilde{\mathsf{id}}_{\mathsf{poly}(\lambda)}$. If any of the right commitments is invalid, or undefined, its value is set to $\bot$. For any i such that $\tilde{\mathsf{id}}_i = \mathsf{id}_j$ for some j, set $\tilde{m}_i = \bot$ (i.e., any commitment where the adversary uses the same identity of one of the honest senders is considered invalid). Let $\mathsf{mim}_\Pi^{\mathcal{A}, m_1, \ldots, m_{\mathsf{poly}(\lambda)}}(z)$ denote a random variable that describes the values $\tilde{m}_1, \ldots, \tilde{m}_{\mathsf{poly}(\lambda)}$ and the view of $\mathcal{A}$, in the above experiment. In the simulated execution, an efficient simulator S directly interacts with $\mathsf{Rec}_1, \ldots, \mathsf{Rec}_{\mathsf{poly}(\lambda)}$. Let $\mathsf{sim}_\Pi^S(1^\lambda, z)$ denote the random variable describing the values $\tilde{m}_1, \ldots, \tilde{m}_{\mathsf{poly}(\lambda)}$ committed by S, and the output view of S; whenever the view contains in the i-th right session the same identity of any of the identities of the left sessions, then m_i is set to $\bot$.

In all the paper we denote by $\tilde{\delta}$ a value associated with the right session (where the adversary $\mathcal{A}$ plays with a receiver) where δ is the corresponding value in the left session. For example, the sender commits to v in the left session while $\mathcal{A}$ commits to $\tilde{v}$ in the right session.

Definition 4. (Concurrent NM commitment scheme [31]). *A commitment scheme is concurrent NM with respect to commitment (or a many-many NM commitment scheme) if, for every* PPT *concurrent MiM adversary* $\mathcal{A}$, *there exists a* PPT *simulator* S *such that for all* $m_i \in \{0,1\}^{\mathsf{poly}(\lambda)}$ *for* $i = 1, \ldots, \mathsf{poly}(\lambda)$ *the following ensembles are computationally indistinguishable:*
$$\{\mathsf{mim}_\Pi^{\mathcal{A}, m_1, \ldots, m_{\mathsf{poly}(\lambda)}}(z)\}_{z \in \{0,1\}^*} \approx \{\mathsf{sim}_\Pi^S(1^\lambda, z)\}_{z \in \{0,1\}^*}.$$

As in [31] we also consider relaxed notions of concurrent non-malleability: one-many and one-one NM commitment schemes. In a one-many NM commitment scheme, $\mathcal{A}$ participates in one left and polynomially many right sessions. In a one-one (i.e., a stand-alone secure) NM commitment scheme, we consider only adversaries $\mathcal{A}$ that participate in one left and one right session. We will make use of the following proposition of [31].

Proposition 1. *Let* (Sen, Rec) *be a one-many NM commitment scheme. Then,* (Sen, Rec) *is also a concurrent (i.e., many-many) NM commitment scheme.*

We say that a commitment is valid or well formed if it can be decommitted to a message $m \neq \bot$. Following [29] we say that a MiM is *synchronous* if it "aligns" the left and the right sessions; that is, whenever it receives message i on the left, it directly sends message i on the right, and vice versa.

2.4 New Definitions: Weak NM and SimWI

Definition 5 (*weak* **NM commitment scheme**). *A commitment scheme is* weak *one-one (resp., one-many) non-malleable if it is a one-one (resp., one-many) NM commitment scheme with respect to MiM adversary that when receiving a well formed commitment in the left session, except with negligible probability computes well formed commitments (i.e., the computed commitments can be opened to messages $\neq \bot$) in the right sessions.*

In the rest of the paper, following [25], we assume that identities are known before the protocol begins, though strictly speaking this is not necessary, as the identities do not appear in the protocol until after the first committer message. The MiM can choose his identity adversarially as long as it differs from the identities used by honest senders. As already observed in previous work, when the identity is selected by the sender the id-based definitions guarantee non-malleability as long as the MiM does not behave like a proxy (an unavoidable attack). Indeed the sender can pick as identity the public key of a signature scheme signing the transcript. The MiM will have to use a different identity or to break the signature scheme.

Simulation-witness-independence (SimWI) for L^γ. We define SimWI for an $\mathcal{NP}$ language L associating to the language a non-negative integer γ. Roughly speaking all witnesses of an instance have in common the first γ bits, and this property holds for all instances of L. More formally we will consider γ as a non-negative integer such that for any $x \in L$ it holds that any witness w of x can be parsed as $w = \alpha|\beta$, where $|\alpha| = \gamma$, and α is the same for all witnesses of x. In order to easy the notation, we will note denote by L^γ the $\mathcal{NP}$ language having the above prefix γ. We will say that L^γ is a γ-prefix language meaning that for any instance x of L^γ all witnesses of x have the same first γ bits.

When defining SimWI we will consider the one-many case since this is what we will use in the next part of the paper. Adapting the definition to the one-one case and to the fully concurrent case is straightforward.

Discussion on adaptive-input selection and black-box simulation. Since our definition considers a real game where the MiM plays with at most one prover and polynomially many verifiers, and a simulated game that consists of an execution of a stand-alone simulator, a natural definition would require the indistinguishability of the two games for any $x \in L^\gamma$, giving to the prover as input also a witness. This definition however would be difficult to use when the argument of knowledge is played as a subprotocol of a larger protocol, especially if it is played in parallel with other subprotocols and the adversary contributes in selecting the statement for the left session. More specifically applications require a security definition that features a delayed-input property so that players start the protocol with the common input that is still undefined, and that will be defined later potentially with the contribution of the adversary. Therefore in our definition we will allow the adversary to explicitly select the statement, and as such the adversary will provide also the witness for the prover. The simulated game however will filter out the witness so that the simulator will receive only the instance. This approach strictly follows the one of [49] where adaptive-input selection is explicitly allowed and managed in a similar way. As final remark, our definition will require the existence of a black-box simulator since a non-black-box simulator could retrieve from the code of the adversary the witness for the adaptively generated statement. The non-black-box simulator could then run the honest prover procedure, therefore canceling completely the security flavor of the simulation paradigm.

For simplicity we now give the formal definition with non-delayed inputs.

Definition. Let $\Pi = (\mathcal{P}, \mathcal{V})$ be an argument system for a γ-prefix language L^γ and let Rel_{L^γ} be the corresponding witness relation. Consider a PPT MiM adversary $\mathcal{A}$ that is simultaneously participating in one left session and $\mathsf{poly}(\lambda)$ right sessions. When the execution starts, all parties receive as a common input the security parameter 1^λ then $\mathcal{A}$ chooses the statement $x \in L^\gamma$ and witness w s.t. $(x, w) \in \mathsf{Rel}_{L^\gamma}$ and sends them to $\mathcal{P}$, furthermore $\mathcal{A}$ receives as auxiliary input $z \in \{0, 1\}^\star$.

In the left session an honest prover $\mathcal{P}$ interacting with $\mathcal{A}$ proves the membership of x in L^γ. In the $\mathsf{poly}(\lambda)$ right sessions, $\mathcal{A}$ proves the membership in L^γ of instances $\tilde{x}_1, \ldots, \tilde{x}_{\mathsf{poly}(\lambda)}$ of his choice to the honest verifiers $\mathcal{V}_1, \ldots, \mathcal{V}_{\mathsf{poly}(\lambda)}$. For simplicity, in this definition we consider an adversary $\mathcal{A}$ that chooses the statement to be proved in the 1st round that he plays in every right sessions[15].

Let $\{\mathsf{wimim}_\Pi(1^\lambda, z)\}_{\lambda \in \mathbb{N}, z \in \{0,1\}^\star}$ be a random variable that describes the following 3 values: (1) the view of $\mathcal{A}$ in the above experiment, (2) the output of $\mathcal{V}_i$ for $i = 1, \ldots, \mathsf{poly}(\lambda)$ and (3) the first γ bits $\tilde{w}_1^\gamma, \ldots, \tilde{w}_{\mathsf{poly}(\lambda)}^\gamma$ of the corresponding witnesses $\tilde{w}_1, \ldots, \tilde{w}_{\mathsf{poly}(\lambda)}$ w.r.t. the instances $\tilde{x}_1, \ldots, \tilde{x}_{\mathsf{poly}(\lambda)}$ that are part of $\mathcal{A}$'s view except that $\tilde{w}_i^\gamma = \bot$ if $\mathcal{V}_i$ did not output 1, with $i = 1, \ldots, \mathsf{poly}(\lambda)$.

---

[15] Our construction will satisfy a much stronger notion where in the left session $\mathcal{A}$ can choose statement and witness in the last round, while in the right sessions $\mathcal{A}$ can choose the statement in the very last round, as long as the witness is already fixed in the second round.

Let $\{\mathsf{sim}_\Pi^S(1^\lambda, z)\}_{\lambda \in \mathbb{N}, z \in \{0,1\}^*}$ be a random variable that describes the following 3 values: (1) and (2) correspond to the output of $\mathcal{S}$, (3) consists of the first γ bits $\tilde{w}_1^\gamma, \ldots, \tilde{w}_{\mathsf{poly}(\lambda)}^\gamma$ of the corresponding witnesses $\tilde{w}_1, \ldots, \tilde{w}_{\mathsf{poly}(\lambda)}$ w.r.t. the instances $\tilde{x}_1, \ldots, \tilde{x}_{\mathsf{poly}(\lambda)}$ that appear in the MiM view of the output of $\mathcal{S}$ except that $w_i^\gamma = \bot$ if $b_i = 0$. The output of $\mathcal{S}$ is composed by the following two values: (1) a MiM view and (2) bits $b_1, \ldots, b_{\mathsf{poly}(\lambda)}$.

$\mathcal{S}$ has black-box access to $\mathcal{A}$ and has the goal to emulate the prover without having a witness, while perfectly emulating the verifiers of the right sessions. Therefore $\mathcal{S}$ rewinds only when playing as prover[16] and every instance/witness pair (x, w) given in output by $\mathcal{A}$ is replaced by $(x, \bot)$ and then returned to $\mathcal{S}$ (i.e., the simulator runs without the witness w for the instance x chosen by $\mathcal{A}$).

Definition 6 (SimWI). *An argument system $\Pi = (\mathcal{P}, \mathcal{V})$ for a γ-prefix language L^γ with witness relation Rel_{L^γ} is SimWI if there exists an expected polynomial-time simulator $\mathcal{S}$ such that for every MiM adversary $\mathcal{A}$ that participates in one left session and $\mathsf{poly}(\lambda)$ right sessions the ensembles $\{\mathsf{wimim}_\Pi(1^\lambda, z)\}_{\lambda \in \mathbb{N}, z \in \{0,1\}^*}$ and $\{\mathsf{sim}_\Pi^S(1^\lambda, z)\}_{\lambda \in \mathbb{N}, z \in \{0,1\}^*}$ are computationally indistinguishable over λ.*

3   4-Round One-Many SimWI from OWFs

We now show our construction of a 4-round argument of knowledge SWI $=$ ($\mathcal{P}^{\mathsf{swi}}, \mathcal{V}^{\mathsf{swi}}$) for the γ-prefix language L^γ that is one-many SimWI and can be instantiated using any OWF. We will need the following tools:

1. a signature scheme $\Sigma = (\mathsf{Gen}, \mathsf{Sign}, \mathsf{Ver})$;
2. a 2-round IDTC scheme $\mathsf{TC}_\Sigma = (\mathsf{Sen}_\Sigma, \mathsf{Rec}_\Sigma, \mathsf{TFake}_\Sigma)$ for the following $\mathcal{NP}$-language

$$L_\Sigma = \big\{ \mathsf{vk} : \exists \; (\mathsf{msg}_1, \mathsf{msg}_2, \sigma_1, \sigma_2) \text{ s.t. } \mathsf{Ver}(\mathsf{vk}, \mathsf{msg}_1, \sigma_1) = 1$$
$$\text{AND } \mathsf{Ver}(\mathsf{vk}, \mathsf{msg}_2, \sigma_2) = 1 \text{ AND } \mathsf{msg}_1 \neq \mathsf{msg}_2 \big\};$$

3. a 4-round delayed-input public-coin Special HVZK (Definition 2) proof system LS $= (\mathcal{P}, \mathcal{V})$ for the γ-prefix language L^γ that is adaptive-input PoK for the corresponding relation Rel_{L^γ}.

Let $x \in L^\gamma$ be the statement that $\mathcal{P}^{\mathsf{swi}}$ wants to prove, and w a witness s.t. $(x, w) \in \mathsf{Rel}_{L^\gamma}$. The high-level idea of our protocol is depicted in Fig. 1. In the

---

[16] The motivation behind this definitional choice is that $\mathcal{S}$ is supposed to be an extended zero-knowledge simulator that takes care also of the honest behavior of the verifiers since $\mathcal{A}$ expects to play with them. Instead allowing $\mathcal{S}$ to have any behavior on the right would hurt the power of SimWI in composing in parallel with other protocols. Indeed if $\mathcal{S}$ rewinds on the right as verifier, it would in turn rewind also the left player of the external protocol that is played in parallel. This would hurt the security of the overall scheme whenever the external protocol is not resettably secure. We will indeed compose a SimWI AoK with a weak NM commitment scheme that is not resettably secure.

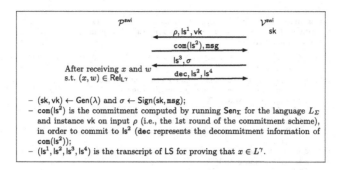

Fig. 1. 4-Round SimWI AoK SWI from OWFs.

1st round the verifier $\mathcal{V}^{swi}$ computes and sends the 1st round ls^1 of LS, computes a pair of signature and verification keys $(\mathsf{sk}, \mathsf{vk})$, sends the verification key vk to $\mathcal{P}^{swi}$ and computes and sends the 1st round ρ of TC_Σ by running Rec_Σ on input 1^λ and the instance $\mathsf{vk} \in L_\Sigma$. Then $\mathcal{P}^{swi}$ on input x, w and the received 1st round, computes the 2nd round ls^2 of LS and runs Sen_Σ on input 1^λ, vk, ρ and message ls^2 thus obtaining a pair $(\mathsf{com}, \mathsf{dec})$. $\mathcal{P}^{swi}$ sends com and a random message msg to $\mathcal{V}^{swi}$. In the 3rd round $\mathcal{V}^{swi}$ sends the 3rd round ls^3 of LS and a signature σ (computed using sk) of the message msg. In the last round $\mathcal{P}^{swi}$ verifies whether or not σ is a valid signature for msg. If σ is a valid signature, then $\mathcal{P}^{swi}$, using x, w and ls^3, computes the 4th round ls^4 of LS and sends dec, ls^2 and ls^4 to $\mathcal{V}^{swi}$. At this point $\mathcal{V}^{swi}$ outputs 1 iff Rec_Σ on input $\mathsf{vk}, \mathsf{com}, \mathsf{dec}, \mathsf{ls}^2$ accepts $(\mathsf{ls}^2, \mathsf{dec})$ as a decommitment of com and the transcript for LS is accepting for $\mathcal{V}$ with respect to the instance x. We remark that to execute LS the instance is not needed until the last round but the instance length is required from the onset of the protocol.

Figure 2 describes in details our SimWI AoK SWI.

Theorem 1. *Assuming OWFs,* $\mathsf{SWI} = (\mathcal{P}^{swi}, \mathcal{V}^{swi})$ *is a 4-round one-many SimWI AoK for γ-prefix languages.*

We divide the security proof in three parts, proving that SWI enjoys delayed-input completeness, adaptive-input AoK and SimWI. Before that, we recall that LS can be constructed from OWFs (see Sect. 2.1) as well as Σ using [47]. We also observe that if Σ relies on OWFs, then also TC_Σ can be constructed from OWFs (see the full version [5]).

Delayed-Input Completeness. The completeness follows directly from the completeness of LS, the correctness of TC_Σ and the validity of Σ. We observe that, due to the delayed-input property of LS, the statement x (and the respective witness w) are used by $\mathcal{P}^{swi}$ only to compute the last round. Therefore SWI enjoys delayed-input completeness.

Adaptive-Input Argument of Knowledge. In order to prove that SWI enjoys adaptive-input AoK for Rel_{L^γ}, we need to show an efficient extractor E that outputs the witnesses for the statements proved by an adversarial prover $\mathcal{P}^{swi\star}$.

Common input: security parameter λ, instance $x \in L^\gamma$, instance length ℓ.
Input to $\mathcal{P}^{\mathsf{swi}}$: w s.t. $(x, w) \in \mathsf{Rel}_{\mathsf{L}^\gamma}$, with x, w available only in the 4th round.
Commitment phase:

1. $\mathcal{V}^{\mathsf{swi}} \to \mathcal{P}^{\mathsf{swi}}$
   1.1. Run $(\mathsf{sk}, \mathsf{vk}) \leftarrow \mathsf{Gen}(1^\lambda)$.
   1.2. Run $\mathcal{V}$ on input 1^λ and ℓ thus obtaining the 1st round ls^1 of LS.
   1.3. Run Rec_Σ on input 1^λ and vk thus obtaining ρ.
   1.4. Send $(\mathsf{vk}, \mathsf{ls}^1, \rho)$ to $\mathcal{P}^{\mathsf{swi}}$.
2. $\mathcal{P}^{\mathsf{swi}} \to \mathcal{V}^{\mathsf{swi}}$
   2.1. Run $\mathcal{P}$ on input 1^λ, ℓ and ls^1 thus obtaining the 2nd round ls^2 of LS.
   2.2. Run Sen_Σ on input 1^λ, vk, ρ and message ls^2 to compute the pair $(\mathsf{com}, \mathsf{dec})$.
   2.3. Pick a message $\mathsf{msg} \leftarrow \{0, 1\}^\lambda$.
   2.4. Send $(\mathsf{com}, \mathsf{msg})$ to $\mathcal{V}^{\mathsf{swi}}$.
3. $\mathcal{V}^{\mathsf{swi}} \to \mathcal{P}^{\mathsf{swi}}$
   3.1. Run $\mathcal{V}$ thus obtaining the 3rd round ls^3 of LS.
   3.2. Run $\mathsf{Sign}(\mathsf{sk}, \mathsf{msg})$ thus obtaining a signature σ of the message msg.
   3.3. Send (ls^3, σ) to $\mathcal{P}^{\mathsf{swi}}$.
4. $\mathcal{P}^{\mathsf{swi}} \to \mathcal{V}^{\mathsf{swi}}$
   4.1. If $\mathsf{Ver}(\mathsf{vk}, \mathsf{msg}, \sigma) \neq 1$ then abort, continue as follows otherwise.
   4.2. Run $\mathcal{P}$ on input x, w and ls^3 thus obtaining the 4th round ls^4 of LS.
   4.3. Send $((\mathsf{dec}, \mathsf{ls}^2), \mathsf{ls}^4)$ to $\mathcal{V}^{\mathsf{swi}}$.
5. $\mathcal{V}^{\mathsf{swi}}$: output 1 iff the following conditions are satisfied.
   5.1. Rec_Σ on input $\mathsf{vk}, \mathsf{com}, \mathsf{dec}, \mathsf{ls}^2$ accepts $(\mathsf{ls}^2, \mathsf{dec})$ as a decommitment of com.
   5.2. $(\mathsf{ls}^1, \mathsf{ls}^2, \mathsf{ls}^3, \mathsf{ls}^4)$ is accepting for $\mathcal{V}$ with respect to the instance x.

Fig. 2. 4-Round SimWI AoK SWI from OWFs.

E simply runs ExtLS, the adaptive-input PoK extractor of LS, in every right session, and outputs what ExtLS outputs. More precisely E internally runs and interacts with a SWI prover $\mathcal{P}^{\mathsf{swi}}$ as $\mathcal{V}_i^{\mathsf{swi}}$ does, but acting as a proxy between $\mathcal{P}^{\mathsf{swi}\star}$ and ExtLS w.r.t. the messages of LS (for $i = 1, \ldots, \mathsf{poly}(\lambda)$). The important observation is that E could fail if the following event NoExt happens with non-negligible probability: $\mathcal{P}^{\mathsf{swi}\star}$ opens the commitment (ρ, com) to a different ls^2 during the rewinds. Indeed, in this case ExtLS could fail in obtaining a witness. We prove the following claim.

Claim 1. There exists a negligible function ν such that $\mathsf{Prob}[\, \mathsf{NoExt}\,] < \nu(\lambda)$.

Proof. The proof is by contradiction, more specifically we now show an adversary $\mathcal{A}^\Sigma$ that extracts two signatures for two different messages in order to break the signature scheme Σ when $\mathsf{Prob}[\, \mathsf{NoExt}\,]$ is non-negligible in λ.

If two decommitments of (com, ρ) w.r.t. two different messages ($\mathsf{ls}^{2'}$ and ls^2) are shown by $\mathcal{P}^{\mathsf{swi}\star}$ in the last round of SWI, $\mathcal{A}^\Sigma$ can extract two different signatures for two different messages by using the special binding of TC_Σ. More precisely, let vk be the verification key given by the challenger of the signature scheme, then our adversary $\mathcal{A}^\Sigma$ works as follows.

For all $i \in \{1, \ldots, \mathsf{poly}(\lambda)\} - \{j\}$, $\mathcal{A}^\Sigma$ interacts in the i-th session against $\mathcal{P}^{\mathsf{swi}\star}$ as $\mathcal{V}_i^{\mathsf{swi}}$ would do. Instead in the j-th session $\mathcal{A}^\Sigma$ runs as E would do, using vk to compute the first round, and the oracle $\mathsf{Sign}(\mathsf{sk}, \cdot)$ to compute a signature σ of a message m sent by $\mathcal{A}^\Sigma$ in the second round. Since we are assuming (by contradiction) that during the rewinds from the 4th round to the 3rd round the commitment (ρ, com) (sent in the second round by $\mathcal{P}^{\mathsf{swi}\star}$) is opened in more than one way, then, by using the special binding of TC_Σ, $\mathcal{A}^\Sigma$ extracts and outputs two signatures for two different messages. We conclude this proof with the following two observations. First, the signature oracle $\mathsf{Sign}(\mathsf{sk}, \cdot)$ is called only once since, by construction of E, the second round is played by $\mathcal{P}^{\mathsf{swi}\star}$ only once. Second, the extractor E is an expected polynomial-time algorithm while $\mathcal{A}^\Sigma$ must be a strict polynomial-time algorithm. This mean that the execution E has to be truncated. Obviously the running time of the extraction procedure can be truncated to a sufficiently long value so that with non-negligible probability the truncated extraction procedure will still yield the event NoExt to happened and this is sufficient for $\mathcal{A}^\Sigma$ to break the signature scheme[17].

SimWI. In order to prove that SWI is SimWI (Definition 6) for any γ-prefix language L^γ we prove the following lemma.

Lemma 1. $\{\mathsf{wimim}_{\mathsf{SWI}}(1^\lambda, z)\}_{\lambda \in \mathbb{N}, z \in \{0,1\}^\star} \approx \{\mathsf{sim}_{\mathsf{SWI}}^{\mathcal{S}^{\mathsf{swi}}}(1^\lambda, z)\}_{\lambda \in \mathbb{N}, z \in \{0,1\}^\star}.$

Proof. Here we actually prove something stronger. Indeed we prove the security of SWI considering a MiM adversary $\mathcal{A}^{\mathsf{swi}}$ that has additional power both in the left and in the right sessions. More precisely in the left session $\mathcal{A}^{\mathsf{swi}}$ can choose the statement to be proved (and the related witness) in the third round. That is, in the last round that goes from $\mathcal{A}^{\mathsf{swi}}$ to $\mathcal{P}^{\mathsf{swi}}$.

Also, in all right sessions $\mathcal{A}$ fixes a family of statements in the second round, and then adaptively picks the statement to be proved from that family in the last round. In this way the MiM adversary has the power to adaptively choose the statement to be proved in the last round of every right session conditioned on belonging to the already fixed family, that has to be fixed in the second round. In the rest of the paper we will refer to a SimWI protocol that is secure also in this setting as *adaptive-input* SimWI.

We start by showing the simulator $\mathcal{S}^{\mathsf{swi}}$ and giving an overview of the entire proof. The simulator is described in Fig. 3. Roughly, $\mathcal{S}^{\mathsf{swi}}$ interacts against $\mathcal{A}^{\mathsf{swi}}$ in both the left and right sessions. In the left session $\mathcal{S}^{\mathsf{swi}}$ runs TFake_Σ to compute and send a commitment com. $\mathcal{S}^{\mathsf{swi}}$ then rewinds $\mathcal{A}^{\mathsf{swi}}$ from the 3rd to the 2nd round, in order to obtain two valid signatures σ_1, σ_2 for two different messages $(\mathsf{msg}_1, \mathsf{msg}_2)$. This informations constitute the trapdoor tk for TC_Σ. After that tk is computed, $\mathcal{S}^{\mathsf{swi}}$ comes back to the main thread execution. Upon receiving ls^3 and x in the 3rd round from $\mathcal{A}^{\mathsf{swi}}$, $\mathcal{S}^{\mathsf{swi}}$ computes an accepting transcript for LS $(\mathsf{ls}^1, \mathsf{ls}^2, \mathsf{ls}^3, \mathsf{ls}^4)$ running the Special HVZK simulator of LS on input ls^1, received in the 1st round from $\mathcal{A}^{\mathsf{swi}}$, and (x, ls^3). In the last round computes, by using tk, the decommitment information $(\mathsf{dec}, \mathsf{ls}^2)$ for com, and sends $(\mathsf{dec}, \mathsf{ls}^2, \mathsf{ls}^4)$ to $\mathcal{A}^{\mathsf{swi}}$. In the i-th right session, for $i = 1, \ldots, \mathsf{poly}(\lambda)$, $\mathcal{S}^{\mathsf{swi}}$ acts as $\mathcal{V}_i^{\mathsf{swi}}$ would do against $\mathcal{A}^{\mathsf{swi}}$. When the execution against $\mathcal{A}^{\mathsf{swi}}$ ends, $\mathcal{S}^{\mathsf{swi}}$ outputs the view of $\mathcal{A}^{\mathsf{swi}}$.

---

[17] The same arguments are used in [17]. The same standard argument about truncating the execution of an expected polynomial-time algorithm is used in another proofs but for simplicity we will not repeat this discussion.

In the security proof we denote by $\{\text{wimim}_{\mathcal{H}_i}(1^\lambda, z)\}_{\lambda \in \mathbb{N}, z \in \{0,1\}^*}$ the random variable describing (1) the view of $\mathcal{A}^{\text{swi}}$, (2) the output of $\mathcal{V}_i^{\text{swi}}$ for $i = 1, \ldots, \text{poly}(\lambda)$, (3) the first γ-bits $\tilde{w}_1^\gamma, \ldots, \tilde{w}_{\text{poly}(\lambda)}^\gamma$ of the corresponding witnesses $\tilde{w}_1, \ldots, \tilde{w}_{\text{poly}(\lambda)}$ w.r.t. the instances $\tilde{x}_1, \ldots, \tilde{x}_{\text{poly}(\lambda)}$ that appear in $\mathcal{A}^{\text{swi}}$'s view except that $\tilde{w}_i^\gamma = \perp$ if $\mathcal{V}_i^{\text{swi}}$ rejected, with $i = 1, \ldots, \text{poly}(\lambda)$[18].

The proof makes use of the following main hybrid experiments.

- The 1st hybrid experiment is $\mathcal{H}_1(1^\lambda, z)$. In this hybrid in the left session $\mathcal{P}^{\text{swi}}$ interacts with $\mathcal{A}^{\text{swi}}$ in order to prove the validity of the instance x using the witness w, while in the right sessions $\mathcal{V}_i^{\text{swi}}$ interacts with $\mathcal{A}^{\text{swi}}$ for $i = 1, \ldots, \text{poly}(\lambda)$. We want to prove that in the i-th right session $\mathcal{A}^{\text{swi}}$ does not

---

Common input: security parameters λ and instance length ℓ.
Internal simulation of the left session:

1. Upon receiving $(\text{vk}, \text{ls}^1, \rho)$ from $\mathcal{A}^{\text{swi}}$:
   1.1. Run TFake_Σ on input 1^λ, vk, ρ to compute the pair (com, aux).
   1.2. Pick a message $\text{msg}_1 \leftarrow \{0,1\}^\lambda$.
   1.3. Send $(\text{com}, \text{msg}_1)$ to $\mathcal{A}^{\text{swi}}$.
2. Upon receiving $(\text{ls}^3, \sigma_1, x, \perp)$ from $\mathcal{A}^{\text{swi}}$:
   2.1. If $\text{Ver}(\text{vk}, \text{msg}_1, \sigma) \neq 1$ then abort, continue as follows otherwise.
   2.2. Repeat Step 1.3, 1.2 and follow-up right session message up to λ/p times[a] in order to obtain a signature σ_2 of a random message $\text{msg}_2 \neq \text{msg}_1$. Abort in case of failure in obtaining σ_2 in such λ/p attempts otherwise return to the main thread.
   2.3. Run the Special HVZK simulator of LS on input $(x, \text{ls}^1, \text{ls}^3)$ in order to obtain $(\text{ls}^2, \text{ls}^4)$.
   2.4. Run TFake_Σ on input $\text{tk} = (\text{msg}_1, \text{msg}_2, \sigma_1, \sigma_2)$, vk, ρ, com, aux and ls^2 to compute dec.
   2.5. Send $((\text{dec}, \text{ls}^2), \text{ls}^4)$ to $\mathcal{A}^{\text{swi}}$.

Internal simulation of the right sessions:

1. For $i = 1, \ldots, \text{poly}(\lambda)$ acts as $\mathcal{V}_i^{\text{swi}}$ would do against $\mathcal{A}^{\text{swi}}$.

Output: When the execution against $\mathcal{A}^{\text{swi}}$ ends, outputs the view of $\mathcal{A}^{\text{swi}}$ and the bits $b_1, \ldots, b_{\text{poly}(\lambda)}$ where, for $i = 1, \ldots, \text{poly}(\lambda)$, $b_i = 0$ iff $\mathcal{V}_i^{\text{swi}}$ is rejecting, $b_i = 1$ otherwise[b].

---

[a] We refer with p as the probability that $\mathcal{A}^{\text{swi}}$ sends in the Step 2 a valid signature for a randomly chosen message.
[b] Of course, if $\mathcal{A}^{\text{swi}}$ ends during the step 2.2 the simulator continues to work until that step is completed.

Fig. 3. The SimWI $\mathcal{S}^{\text{swi}}$ for SWI.

---

[18] To ease the notation sometimes we will refer to $\{\text{wimim}_{\mathcal{H}_i}(1^\lambda, z)\}_{\lambda \in \mathbb{N}, z \in \{0,1\}^*}$ using just $\text{wimim}_{\mathcal{H}_i}(1^\lambda, z)$.

prove any false instance $\tilde{x}_i$ for any $i = 1, \ldots, \mathsf{poly}(\lambda)$[19]. This property follows immediately from the adaptive-input AoK of SWI. We observe that in this case it is crucial that SWI is adaptive-input AoK, because we are considering an adversary $\mathcal{A}^{\mathsf{swi}}$ that can choose the instance to be proved in the last round of every right session.

- The 2nd hybrid experiment is $\mathcal{H}_2(1^\lambda, z)$ and differs from $\mathcal{H}_1(1^\lambda, z)$ in the way the commitment com and the decommitment information dec are computed in the left session. More precisely, $\mathcal{P}^{\mathsf{swi}}$ runs TFake_Σ to compute a commitment (ρ, com), and subsequently to compute a decommitment of (ρ, com) to the value ls^2 (we remark that no trapdoor is needed to run TFake_Σ in order to compute (ρ, com)). In more details, this experiment rewinds the adversary $\mathcal{A}^{\mathsf{swi}}$ from the 3rd to the 2nd round of the left session to extract two signatures σ_1, σ_2 of two different messages $(\mathsf{msg}_1, \mathsf{msg}_2)$ and uses them as trapdoor to run TFake_Σ. The indistinguishability between $\mathsf{wimim}_{\mathcal{H}_1}(1^\lambda, z)$ and $\mathsf{wimim}_{\mathcal{H}_2}(1^\lambda, z)$ comes from the hiding and the trapdoorness of TC_Σ.

- The 3rd hybrid experiment is $\mathcal{H}_3(1^\lambda, z)$ and differs from $\mathcal{H}_2(1^\lambda, z)$ in the way the transcript for LS is computed. In more details the Special HVZK simulator $\mathcal{S}$ of LS is used to compute the messages ls^2 and ls^4 instead of using the honest procedure $\mathcal{P}^{\mathsf{swi}}$. The indistinguishability between $\mathsf{wimim}_{\mathcal{H}_2}(1^\lambda, z)$ and $\mathsf{wimim}_{\mathcal{H}_3}(1^\lambda, z)$ comes from the Special HVZK of LS. We observe that the security proof ends with this hybrid experiment because $\mathsf{wimim}_{\mathcal{H}_3}(1^\lambda, z) \equiv \mathsf{sim}_{\mathsf{SWI}}^{\mathcal{S}^{\mathsf{swi}}}(1^\lambda, z)$.

A formal proof is given in the full version (see [5]).

4   4-Round Concurrent NM Commitment Scheme

Our construction makes use of an adaptive-input SimWI AoK $\mathsf{SWI} = (\mathcal{P}^{\mathsf{swi}}, \mathcal{V}^{\mathsf{swi}})$ combined with a weak concurrent NM commitment scheme Π_{wom}. For our propose we consider a weak NM commitment scheme that with overwhelming probability any well-formed commitment can be opened to only one message. We recall that the weak concurrent NM commitment scheme of [25] enjoys this property when instantiated with Naor's commitment scheme [35].

We now consider the following language L based on the weak NM commitment scheme $\Pi_{\mathsf{wom}} = (\mathsf{Sen}_{\mathsf{wom}}, \mathsf{Rec}_{\mathsf{wom}})$:

$$L = \big\{ (\tau, \mathsf{id}) : \exists\ (m, \mathsf{dec})\ \text{s.t.}\ \mathsf{Rec}_{\mathsf{wom}}\ \text{on input}$$
$$(m, \mathsf{dec}, \mathsf{id})\ \text{accepts}\ m\ \text{as decommitment of}\ \tau \big\}$$

and the corresponding relation Rel_L.

We now use $\mathsf{SWI} = (\mathcal{P}^{\mathsf{swi}}, \mathcal{V}^{\mathsf{swi}})$ to upgrade a 4-round public-coin concurrent weak NM commitment scheme Π_{wom} with the property that after the second round there is at most one valid message, to a concurrent NM commitment

---

[19] When we refer to a *proved instance* $\tilde{x}_i$ we implicitly assume that $\mathcal{V}_i^{\mathsf{swi}}$ is accepting, with $i = 1, \ldots, \mathsf{poly}(\lambda)$.

scheme. We will be able to invoke the security of SWI, since the language L is a γ-prefix language with overwhelming probability with $\gamma = |m|$. In fact, given an instance (τ, id) of L all the witnesses $w_1, \ldots, w_n$ of (τ, id) have the form $m|\text{dec}_i$ for $i = 1, \ldots, n$ (i.e., all witnesses have the same prefix m). Consider a SimWI AoK for L. Let m be the message that NM4Sen wants to commit and id be the id for this session. The high-level idea of our protocol is depicted in Fig. 4.

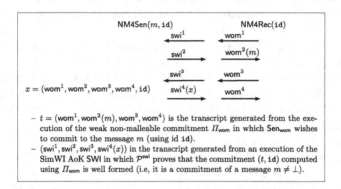

Fig. 4. 4-round concurrent NM commitment scheme from OWFs.

In the 1st round the receiver NM4Rec computes and sends the 1st round swi^1 of SWI and the 1st round wom^1 of Π_{wom} using as input the id. Then NM4Sen on input id, the message m and the received 1st round, computes the 2nd round wom^2 of Π_{wom} in order to commit to the message m, using id, furthermore he obtains dec_{wom} s.t. $(m, \text{dec}_{\text{wom}})$ constitutes the decommitment information[20]. Moreover NM4Sen computes and sends the 2nd round swi^2 of SWI. In the 3rd round NM4Rec sends the 3rd round wom^3 of Π_{wom} and the 3rd round swi^3 of SWI. In the last round NM4Sen computes the 4th round wom^4 of Π_{wom}. Furthermore, NM4Sen, using $(\text{wom}^1, \text{wom}^2, \text{wom}^3, \text{wom}^4, \text{id})$ as instance and $(m, \text{dec}_{\text{wom}})$ as a witness, computes the 4th round swi^4 of SWI and sends $\text{wom}^4, \text{swi}^4$ to NM4Rec. At this point NM4Rec accepts the commitment (i.e., the transcript of the protocol generated so far) iff the transcript for SWI is accepting for $\mathcal{V}^{\text{swi}}$ with respect to the instance $(\text{wom}^1, \text{wom}^2, \text{wom}^3, \text{wom}^4, \text{id})$. The decommitment phase of our scheme simply corresponds to the decommitment phase of Π_{wom}.

As described before, $\text{SWI} = (\mathcal{P}^{\text{swi}}, \mathcal{V}^{\text{swi}})$ is used by NM4Sen to prove knowledge of a message and randomness consistent with the transcript computed using Π_{wom}. To execute SWI the instance is not needed until the last round.

Figure 5 describes in details our 4-round concurrent NM commitment scheme Π_{NM4Com}.

Theorem 2. *Assuming OWFs, $\Pi_{\text{NM4Com}} = (\text{NM4Sen}, \text{NM4Rec})$ is a 4-round concurrent NM commitment scheme.*

---

[20] In order to match the adaptive-input selection satisfied by SWI, message and randomness explaining the entire transcript are already fixed in this round.

Common input: security parameter λ, instance length ℓ, NM4Sen's identity $\text{id} \in \{0,1\}^{\lambda}$.
Input to NM4Sen: $m \in \{0,1\}^{\text{poly}\{\lambda\}}$.
Commitment phase:

1. NM4Rec → NM4Sen
   1.1. Run Rec_{wom} on input 1^{λ}, id thus obtaining the 1st round wom^1 of Π_{wom}.
   1.2. Run $\mathcal{V}^{\text{swi}}$ on input 1^{λ} and ℓ thus obtaining the 1st round swi^1 of SWI.
   1.3. Send $(\text{swi}^1, \text{wom}^1)$ to NM4Sen.
2. NM4Sen → NM4Rec
   2.1. Run $\mathcal{P}^{\text{swi}}$ on input 1^{λ}, ℓ and swi^1 thus obtaining the 2nd round swi^2 of SWI.
   2.2. Run Sen_{wom} on input 1^{λ}, id, wom^1 and the message m thus obtaining the 2nd round wom^2 of Π_{wom} and dec_{wom} s.t. $(m, \text{dec}_{\text{wom}})$ constitutes the decommitment information.
   2.3. Send $(\text{swi}^2, \text{wom}^2)$ to NM4Rec.
3. NM4Rec → NM4Sen
   3.1. Run Rec_{wom} on input wom^2 thus obtaining the 3rd round wom^3 of Π_{wom}.
   3.2. Run $\mathcal{V}^{\text{swi}}$ on input swi^2 thus obtaining the 3rd round swi^3 of SWI.
   3.3. Send $(\text{wom}^3, \text{swi}^3)$ to NM4Sen.
4. NM4Sen → NM4Rec
   4.1. Run Sen_{wom} on input wom^3 thus obtaining the 4th round wom^4 of Π_{wom}.
   4.2. Set $x = (\text{wom}^1, \text{wom}^2, \text{wom}^3, \text{wom}^4, \text{id})$ and $w = (m, \text{dec}_{\text{wom}})$ with $|x| = \ell$. Run $\mathcal{P}^{\text{swi}}$ on input x, w and swi^3 thus obtaining the 4th round swi^4 of SWI.
   4.3. Send $(\text{wom}^4, \text{swi}^4)$ to NM4Rec.
5. NM4Rec : Set $x = (\text{wom}^1, \text{wom}^2, \text{wom}^3, \text{wom}^4, \text{id})$ and accept the commitment iff $(\text{swi}^1, \text{swi}^2, \text{swi}^3, \text{swi}^4)$ is accepting for $\mathcal{V}^{\text{swi}}$ with respect to the instance x.

Decommitment phase:

1. NM4Sen → NM4Rec: Send $(m, \text{dec}_{\text{wom}})$ to NM4Rec.
2. NM4Rec: accept m as the committed message if and only if Rec_{wom}, on input $(m, \text{dec}_{\text{wom}})$, accepts m as the committed message of $(\text{wom}^1, \text{wom}^2, \text{wom}^3, \text{wom}^4, \text{id})$.

Fig. 5. 4-round Concurrent NM Commitments Π_{NM4Com} from OWFs.

The 4-round concurrent NM commitment scheme $\Pi_{\text{NM4Com}} = (\text{NM4Sen},$ NM4Rec) relies on OWFs, because the adaptive-input SimWI AoK SWI can be constructed using OWFs only (see Theorem 1). Furthermore Π_{wom} can be instantiated using the weak one-one non-malleable commitment scheme of [25] that is proved to be weak concurrent non-malleable in the full version of our work (see [5]). Note that this construction relies on OWFs and has also the additional property that we require (i.e. after the second round the only valid message and the corresponding decommitment informations are fixed). The security proof is divided in two parts. In the 1st part we prove that Π_{NM4Com} is indeed a commitment scheme. In the second part we prove that Π_{NM4Com} is a one-many NM commitment scheme, and then we go from one-many to concurrent non-malleability by using Proposition 1.

Lemma 2. $\Pi_{\text{NM4Com}} = (\text{NM4Sen}, \text{NM4Rec})$ *is a statistically binding computationally hiding commitment scheme.*

Proof. **Correctness.** The correctness follows directly from the delayed-input completeness of SWI and the correctness of Π_{wom}.

Statistically Binding. Observe that the message given in output in the decommitment phase of Π_{NM4Com} is the message committed using Π_{wom}. Moreover the decommitment of Π_{NM4Com} coincides with the decommitment of Π_{wom}. Since Π_{wom} is statistically binding then so is Π_{NM4Com}.

Computationally Hiding. Computational hiding follows immediately from Lemma 3.

Lemma 3. *For all* $m \in \{0,1\}^{\mathsf{poly}(\lambda)}$ $\{\mathsf{mim}_{\Pi_{\mathsf{NM4Com}}}^{\mathcal{A}_{\mathsf{NMCom}},m}(z)\}_{z\in\{0,1\}^*} \approx \{\mathsf{sim}_{\Pi_{\mathsf{NM4Com}}}^{S^{\mathsf{NM4Com}}}$ $(1^\lambda, z)\}_{z\in\{0,1\}^*}.$

We denote by $\{\mathsf{mim}_{\mathcal{H}_i^m}^{\mathcal{A}^{\mathsf{NM4Com}},m}(z)\}_{z\in\{0,1\}^*}$ the random variable describing the view of the MiM $\mathcal{A}^{\mathsf{NM4Com}}$ combined with the values that it commits in the $\mathsf{poly}(\lambda)$ right sessions in hybrid $\mathcal{H}_i^m(z)$.

As required by the definition, we want to show that the distribution of the real game experiment (i.e., the view of the MiM $\mathcal{A}^{\mathsf{NM4Com}}$ when playing with NM4Sen committing m along with the messages committed in the right sessions) and the one of the output of a simulator are computationally indistinguishable. We start by showing the simulator S^{NM4Com} and giving an overview of the entire proof. The simulator is described in Fig. 6.

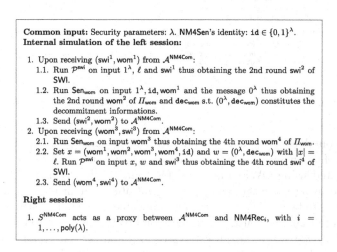

Common input: Security parameters: λ. NM4Sen's identity: $\mathsf{id} \in \{0,1\}^\lambda$.
Internal simulation of the left session:

1. Upon receiving $(\mathsf{swi}^1, \mathsf{wom}^1)$ from $\mathcal{A}^{\mathsf{NM4Com}}$:
   1.1. Run $\mathcal{P}^{\mathsf{swi}}$ on input 1^λ, ℓ and swi^1 thus obtaining the 2nd round swi^2 of SWI.
   1.2. Run $\mathsf{Sen}_{\mathsf{wom}}$ on input 1^λ, id, wom^1 and the message 0^λ thus obtaining the 2nd round wom^2 of Π_{wom} and $\mathsf{dec}_{\mathsf{wom}}$ s.t. $(0^\lambda, \mathsf{dec}_{\mathsf{wom}})$ constitutes the decommitment informations.
   1.3. Send $(\mathsf{swi}^2, \mathsf{wom}^2)$ to $\mathcal{A}^{\mathsf{NM4Com}}$.
2. Upon receiving $(\mathsf{wom}^3, \mathsf{swi}^3)$ from $\mathcal{A}^{\mathsf{NM4Com}}$:
   2.1. Run $\mathsf{Sen}_{\mathsf{wom}}$ on input wom^3 thus obtaining the 4th round wom^4 of Π_{wom}.
   2.2. Set $x = (\mathsf{wom}^1, \mathsf{wom}^2, \mathsf{wom}^3, \mathsf{wom}^4, \mathsf{id})$ and $w = (0^\lambda, \mathsf{dec}_{\mathsf{wom}})$ with $|x| = \ell$. Run $\mathcal{P}^{\mathsf{swi}}$ on input x, w and swi^3 thus obtaining the 4th round swi^4 of SWI.
   2.3. Send $(\mathsf{wom}^4, \mathsf{swi}^4)$ to $\mathcal{A}^{\mathsf{NM4Com}}$.

Right sessions:

1. S^{NM4Com} acts as a proxy between $\mathcal{A}^{\mathsf{NM4Com}}$ and $\mathsf{NM4Rec}_i$, with $i = 1, \ldots, \mathsf{poly}(\lambda)$.

Fig. 6. The simulator S^{NM4Com} of Π_{NM4Com}.

– The 1st hybrid experiment is $\mathcal{H}_1^m(z)$. In this hybrid in the left session NM4Sen commits to m, while in the right sessions $\mathsf{NM4Rec}_i$ interacts with $\mathcal{A}^{\mathsf{NM4Com}}$ for $i = 1, \ldots, \mathsf{poly}(\lambda)$. We prove that in the i-th right session $\mathcal{A}^{\mathsf{NM4Com}}$ does not commit to a message $\tilde{m}_i = \perp$ for any $i = 1, \ldots, \mathsf{poly}(\lambda)$. The proof follows immediately from the adaptive-input AoK of SWI. We observe that in this case it is crucial that SWI is adaptive-input AoK, because the theorem proved by $\mathcal{A}^{\mathsf{NM4Com}}$ are fully specified only in the last round of every right session. Clearly we have that $\mathsf{mim}_{\Pi_{\mathsf{NM4Com}}}^{\mathcal{A}^{\mathsf{NM4Com}},m}(z) = \mathsf{mim}_{\mathcal{H}_1^m}^{\mathcal{A}^{\mathsf{NM4Com}},m}(z)$.

- The 2nd hybrid experiment is $\mathcal{H}_2^m(z)$ and differs from $\mathcal{H}_1^m(z)$ in the way the transcript of SWI is computed. In this hybrid the simulator $\mathcal{S}^{\mathsf{swi}}$ of SWI is used to compute the transcript of SWI. The indistinguishability between $\mathsf{mim}_{\mathcal{H}_1^m}^{\mathcal{A}^{\mathsf{NM4Com}},m}(z)$ and $\mathsf{mim}_{\mathcal{H}_2^m}^{\mathcal{A}^{\mathsf{NM4Com}},m}(z)$ comes from the adaptive-input SimWI property of SWI. It is important to observe that we can properly rely on the adaptive-input SimWI property of SWI since the committed message in $\varPi_{\mathsf{wom}}$ is fixed in the second round. Therefore also the family of statement $\mathcal{X}_w = \{x : (x,w) \in \mathsf{Rel}_\mathsf{L} \text{ or } x \notin L\}$ proved using SWI is implicitly fixed in the second round. Moreover we can rely on the security of SWI because the language L is a γ-prefix language for $= |m|$. Indeed, all witnesses of any instance of L have the same prefix (i.e., the committed message m). Therefore when using the simulator of SWI we are guaranteed that the distribution of the first γ bits of the witnesses corresponding to the statements proven by the adversary in the right sessions of SWI does not change. In turn, this implies that the distribution of the committed messages in the right sessions does not change since each message committed in a session is in the first γ bits of any witness corresponding to the statement proven in SWI in that session.

We also consider the hybrid experiments $\mathcal{H}_1^0(z)$, $\mathcal{H}_2^0(z)$, that are the same hybrid experiments described above with the difference that $\varPi_{\mathsf{wom}}$ is used to commit to a message 0^λ instead of m. From the same arguments described above we have that $\mathsf{mim}_{\mathcal{H}_1^0}^{\mathcal{A}^{\mathsf{NM4Com}},m}(z) \approx \mathsf{mim}_{\mathcal{H}_2^0}^{\mathcal{A}^{\mathsf{NM4Com}},m}(z)$ and that in the i-th right session of $\mathcal{H}_1^0(z)$ $\mathcal{A}^{\mathsf{NM4Com}}$ commits to a message $\tilde{m}_i = \bot$ with negligible probability (for any $i = 1, \ldots, \mathsf{poly}(\lambda)$). We also observe that $\mathsf{mim}_{\mathcal{H}_1^0}^{\mathcal{A}^{\mathsf{NM4Com}},m}(z) = \mathsf{sim}_{\varPi_{\mathsf{NM4Com}}}^{\mathcal{S}^{\mathsf{NM4Com}}}(1^\lambda, z)$.

The only thing that remains to argue to complete the proof is that the view of $\mathcal{A}^{\mathsf{NM4Com}}$, along with messages committed in the right sessions of the execution of $\mathcal{H}_2^m(z)$, is indistinguishable from the view of $\mathcal{A}^{\mathsf{NM4Com}}$ along with the messages committed in the right sessions of $\mathcal{H}_2^0(z)$. This is actually ensured by the weak concurrent non-malleability of $\varPi_{\mathsf{wom}}$. Indeed, from the arguments given above, in both $\mathcal{H}_2^m(z)$ and $\mathcal{H}_2^0(z)$ the adversary $\mathcal{A}^{\mathsf{NM4Com}}$ commits to a message $\tilde{m}_i = \bot$ with negligible probability for $i = 1, \ldots, \mathsf{poly}(\lambda)$. Therefore we can use this $\mathcal{A}^{\mathsf{NM4Com}}$ to construct and adversary $\mathcal{A}^{\mathsf{wom}}$ that breaks the weak concurrent non-malleability of $\varPi_{\mathsf{wom}}$. Roughly speaking, let $m, 0^\lambda$ be the challenge messages, then $\mathcal{A}^{\mathsf{wom}}$ works as following against the challenger $\mathcal{C}^{\mathsf{wom}}$. In the left session acts as a proxy for all the messages of $\varPi_{\mathsf{wom}}$ between $\mathcal{C}^{\mathsf{wom}}$ and $\mathcal{A}^{\mathsf{NM4Com}}$ and executes the simulator $\mathcal{S}^{\mathsf{swi}}$ of SWI in parallel. In the i-th right session $\mathcal{A}^{\mathsf{wom}}$ interacts as $\mathsf{Rec}_{\mathsf{wom},i}$ would do w.r.t. the messages of $\varPi_{\mathsf{wom}}$ and as $\mathcal{V}_i^{\mathsf{swi}}$ for the messages of SWI, for all $i = 1, \ldots, \mathsf{poly}(\lambda)$. The distinguisher that break the concurrent weak non-malleability of $\varPi_{\mathsf{wom}}$ runs $\mathcal{D}^{\mathsf{NM4Com}}$ (that exists by contradiction) that distinguishes $\mathsf{mim}_{\mathcal{H}_2^0}^{\mathcal{A}^{\mathsf{NM4Com}},m}(z)$ from $\mathsf{mim}_{\mathcal{H}_2^m}^{\mathcal{A}^{\mathsf{NM4Com}},m}(z)$, and outputs what $\mathcal{D}^{\mathsf{NM4Com}}$ outputs.

A caveat that we have to address in this reduction is due to the rewinds made by $\mathcal{S}^{\mathsf{swi}}$ in the left session in order to compute the transcript of SWI. Indeed a rewind made in the left session could affect the reduction rewinding also the receivers of Π_{wom} involved in the reduction. More precisely could happen that in a session $j \in \{1, \ldots, \text{poly}(\lambda)\}$ the third round of Π_{wom} has to be played multiple times because of the multiple values $\text{w\~om}_j^2$ received in the j-th right session. We can avoid this problem by sending a random string as a third round of Π_{wom}. In this way for the first value $\text{w\~om}_j^2$ received from $\mathcal{A}^{\text{NM4Com}}$ the reduction interacts with the receiver of Π_{wom} and for all the other values the reduction sends a random string. This is the reason why in our construction we require Π_{wom} to be public coin. One additional issue is the following. The simulator of SWI could rewind the entire left session during the reduction, therefore requiring to compute a new commitment of m for the protocol Π_{wom}. Since we are assuming that Π_{wom} is weak concurrent non-malleable, the reduction can request to receive multiple commitments for the same message. A formal proof is given in the full version (see [5]).

5   3-Round NM Commitments from Strong OWPs

In addition to the definition of NM commitments given in Sect. 2.3, in this section we consider also a synchronous NM commitment scheme secure against a sub-exponential time adversary. The definitions follow below.

5.1   Synchronous NM Commitment Scheme

Definition 7 (*synchronous* NM commitment scheme). *A commitment scheme is* synchronous one-one (resp., one-many) non-malleable *if it is one-one (resp., one-many) NM with respect to synchronous MiM adversaries.*

We also consider the definition of a NM commitment scheme secure against a MIM $\mathcal{A}$ running in time bounded by $T = 2^{\lambda^\alpha}$ for some positive constant $\alpha < 1$. In this case we will say that a commitment scheme is T-non-malleable. We will also say that an NM commitment scheme is $\tilde{T}$-breakable to specify that an algorithm which runs in time $\tilde{T} = 2^{\lambda^\beta}$, for some positive constant $\beta < 1$, can maul the committed message.

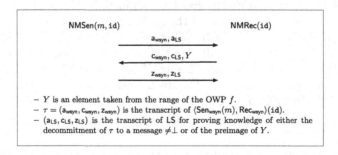

- Y is an element taken from the range of the OWP f.
- $\tau = (\text{a}_{\text{wsyn}}, \text{c}_{\text{wsyn}}, \text{z}_{\text{wsyn}})$ is the transcript of $\langle \text{Sen}_{\text{wsyn}}(m), \text{Rec}_{\text{wsyn}} \rangle (\text{id})$.
- $(\text{a}_{\text{LS}}, \text{c}_{\text{LS}}, \text{z}_{\text{LS}})$ is the transcript of LS for proving knowledge of either the decommitment of τ to a message $\neq \bot$ or of the preimage of Y.

Fig. 7. Informal description of our 3-round NM commitment scheme Π_{NMCom}.

5.2   3-Round NM Commitment Scheme: $\Pi_{\mathsf{NMCom}} = (\mathsf{NMSen}, \mathsf{NMRec})$

Our construction is based on a compiler that takes as input a 3-round synchronous weak one-one NM commitment scheme $\Pi_{\mathsf{wsyn}} = (\mathsf{Sen}_{\mathsf{wsyn}}, \mathsf{Rec}_{\mathsf{wsyn}})$, a OWP f, a WI adaptive PoK for $\mathcal{NP}$ LS, and outputs a 3-round extractable one-one NM commitment scheme $\Pi_{\mathsf{NMCom}} = (\mathsf{NMSen}, \mathsf{NMRec})$ Figs. 7 and 8.

In order to construct our compiler we consider the following tools:

1. a OWP f that is secure against PPT adversaries and that is $\tilde{T}_f$-breakable;
2. a 3-round one-one synchronous weak NM commitment scheme $\Pi_{\mathsf{wsyn}} = (\mathsf{Sen}_{\mathsf{wsyn}}, \mathsf{Rec}_{\mathsf{wsyn}})$ that is T_{wsyn}-hiding/NM, and $\tilde{T}_{\mathsf{wsyn}}$-breakable;
3. the LS PoK LS $= (\mathcal{P}, \mathcal{V})$ for the language

$$L = \big\{(a, c, z, Y, \mathsf{id}) : \exists\, (m, \mathsf{dec}, y) \text{ s.t. } (\mathsf{Rec}_{\mathsf{wsyn}} \text{ on input } (a, c, z, m, \mathsf{dec}, \mathsf{id})$$
$$\text{accepts } m \neq \bot \text{ as a decommitment of } (a, c, z, \mathsf{id}) \text{ OR } Y = f(y))\big\}$$

that is T_{LS}-WI for the corresponding relation $\mathsf{Rel}_{\mathsf{L}}$.

Let λ be the security parameter of our scheme. We use w.l.o.g. λ also as security parameter for the one-wayness of f with respect to polynomial-time adversaries. We consider the following hierarchy of security levels: $\tilde{T}_f \ll T_{\mathsf{wsyn}} \ll \tilde{T}_{\mathsf{wsyn}} = \sqrt{T_{\mathsf{LS}}} \ll T_{\mathsf{LS}}$ where by "$T \ll T'$" we mean that "$T \cdot \mathsf{poly}(\lambda) < T'$".

Common input: security parameters: λ, $(\lambda_{\mathsf{wsyn}}, \lambda_{\mathsf{LS}}, \ell) = \mathsf{Params}(\lambda)$, $\mathsf{id} \in \{0,1\}^\lambda$.
Input to NMSen: $m \in \{0,1\}^{\mathsf{poly}\{\lambda\}}$.
Commitment phase:

1. NMSen $\to$ NMRec
   1.1. Run $\mathsf{Sen}_{\mathsf{wsyn}}$ on input $1^{\lambda_{\mathsf{wsyn}}}$, id and m thus obtaining the 1st round $\mathsf{a}_{\mathsf{wsyn}}$ of Π_{wsyn}.
   1.2. Run $\mathcal{P}$ on input $1^{\lambda_{\mathsf{LS}}}$ and ℓ thus obtaining the 1st round a_{LS} of LS.
   1.3. Send $(\mathsf{a}_{\mathsf{wsyn}}, \mathsf{a}_{\mathsf{LS}})$ to NMRec.
2. NMRec $\to$ NMSen
   2.1. Run $\mathsf{Rec}_{\mathsf{wsyn}}$ on input id and $\mathsf{a}_{\mathsf{wsyn}}$ thus obtaining the 2nd round $\mathsf{c}_{\mathsf{wsyn}}$ of Π_{wsyn}.
   2.2. Run $\mathcal{V}$ on input a_{LS} thus obtaining the 2nd round c_{LS} of LS.
   2.3. Pick a random $Y \in \{0,1\}^\lambda$.
   2.4. Send $(\mathsf{c}_{\mathsf{wsyn}}, \mathsf{c}_{\mathsf{LS}}, Y)$ to NMSen.
3. NMSen $\to$ NMRec
   3.1. Run $\mathsf{Sen}_{\mathsf{wsyn}}$ on input $\mathsf{c}_{\mathsf{wsyn}}$ thus obtaining the 3rd round $\mathsf{z}_{\mathsf{wsyn}}$ of Π_{wsyn} and the decommitment information $\mathsf{dec}_{\mathsf{wsyn}}$.
   3.2. Set $x = (\mathsf{a}_{\mathsf{wsyn}}, \mathsf{c}_{\mathsf{wsyn}}, \mathsf{z}_{\mathsf{wsyn}}, Y, \mathsf{id})$ and $w = (m, \mathsf{dec}_{\mathsf{wsyn}}, \bot)$ with $|x| = \ell$. Run $\mathcal{P}$ on input x, w, and c_{LS} thus obtaining the 3rd round z_{LS} of LS.
   3.3. Send $(\mathsf{z}_{\mathsf{wsyn}}, \mathsf{z}_{\mathsf{LS}})$ to NMRec.
4. NMRec: Set $x = (\mathsf{a}_{\mathsf{wsyn}}, \mathsf{c}_{\mathsf{wsyn}}, \mathsf{z}_{\mathsf{wsyn}}, Y, \mathsf{id})$ and abort iff $(\mathsf{a}_{\mathsf{LS}}, \mathsf{c}_{\mathsf{LS}}, \mathsf{z}_{\mathsf{LS}})$ is not accepted by $\mathcal{V}$ for $x \in L$.

Decommitment phase:

1. NMSen $\to$ NMRec: Send $(\mathsf{dec}_{\mathsf{wsyn}}, m)$ to NMRec.
2. NMRec: accept m as the committed message if and only if $\mathsf{Rec}_{\mathsf{wsyn}}$ on input $(m, \mathsf{dec}_{\mathsf{wsyn}})$ accepts m as a committed message of $(\mathsf{a}_{\mathsf{wsyn}}, \mathsf{c}_{\mathsf{wsyn}}, \mathsf{z}_{\mathsf{wsyn}}, \mathsf{id})$.

Fig. 8. 3-round NM commitment scheme Π_{NMCom}.

Now, similarly to [6,46], we define different security parameters, one for each tool involved in the security proof to be consistent with the hierarchy of security levels defined above. Given the security parameter λ of our scheme, we will make use of the following security parameters: (1) λ for the OWP f; (2) λ_{wsyn} for the synchronous weak one-one NM commitment scheme; (3) λ_{LS} for LS. A formal proof of the following theorem is given in the full version (see [5]).

Theorem 3. *Suppose there exists a synchronous weak one-one NM commitment scheme and OWPs, both secure against subexponential-time adversaries, then Π_{NMCom} is an extractable one-one NM commitment scheme.*

Acknowledgments. We thank Vipul Goyal, and Silas Richelson for remarkable discussions on [24]. We thank Giuseppe Persiano and Alessandra Scafuro for several discussions on delayed-input protocols. We also thank to an anonymous reviewer of CRYPTO 2017 for suggesting prefix languages for SimWI. Research supported in part by "GNCS - INdAM", EU COST Action IC1306, NSF grants 1065276, 1118126 and 1136174, US-Israel BSF grant 2008411, OKAWA Foundation Research Award, IBM Faculty Research Award, Xerox Faculty Research Award, B. John Garrick Foundation Award, Teradata Research Award, and Lockheed-Martin Corporation Research Award. This material is based upon work supported in part by DARPA Safeware program. The views expressed are those of the authors and do not reflect the official policy or position of the Department of Defense or the U.S. Government. The work of 1st, 3rd and 4th authors has been done in part while visiting UCLA.

References

1. Barak, B.: Constant-round coin-tossing with a man in the middle or realizing the shared random string model. In: 43rd Symposium on Foundations of Computer Science (FOCS 2002), pp. 345–355 (2002)
2. Cao, Z., Visconti, I., Zhang, Z.: Constant-round concurrent non-malleable statistically binding commitments and decommitments. In: Nguyen, P.Q., Pointcheval, D. (eds.) PKC 2010. LNCS, vol. 6056, pp. 193–208. Springer, Heidelberg (2010). doi:10.1007/978-3-642-13013-7_12
3. Chung, K.-M., Ostrovsky, R., Pass, R., Venkitasubramaniam, M., Visconti, I.: 4-round resettably-sound zero knowledge. In: Lindell, Y. (ed.) TCC 2014. LNCS, vol. 8349, pp. 192–216. Springer, Heidelberg (2014). doi:10.1007/978-3-642-54242-8_9
4. Chung, K., Pass, R., Seth, K.: Non-black-box simulation from one-way functions and applications to resettable security. In: Symposium on Theory of Computing Conference, STOC 2013, pp. 231–240. ACM (2013)
5. Ciampi, M., Ostrovsky, R., Siniscalchi, L., Visconti, I.: 4-round concurrent non-malleable commitments from one-way functions. Cryptology ePrint Archive, Report 2016/621 (2016). http://eprint.iacr.org/2016/621
6. Ciampi, M., Ostrovsky, R., Siniscalchi, L., Visconti, I.: Concurrent non-malleable commitments (and more) in 3 rounds. In: Robshaw, M., Katz, J. (eds.) CRYPTO 2016. LNCS, vol. 9816, pp. 270–299. Springer, Heidelberg (2016). doi:10.1007/978-3-662-53015-3_10

7. Ciampi, M., Persiano, G., Scafuro, A., Siniscalchi, L., Visconti, I.: Improved OR-composition of sigma-protocols. In: Kushilevitz, E., Malkin, T. (eds.) TCC 2016. LNCS, vol. 9563, pp. 112–141. Springer, Heidelberg (2016). doi:10.1007/978-3-662-49099-0_5

8. Ciampi, M., Persiano, G., Scafuro, A., Siniscalchi, L., Visconti, I.: Online/offline OR composition of sigma protocols. In: Fischlin, M., Coron, J.-S. (eds.) EUROCRYPT 2016. LNCS, vol. 9666, pp. 63–92. Springer, Heidelberg (2016). doi:10.1007/978-3-662-49896-5_3

9. Dachman-Soled, D., Malkin, T., Raykova, M., Venkitasubramaniam, M.: Adaptive and concurrent secure computation from new adaptive, non-malleable commitments. In: Sako, K., Sarkar, P. (eds.) ASIACRYPT 2013. LNCS, vol. 8269, pp. 316–336. Springer, Heidelberg (2013). doi:10.1007/978-3-642-42033-7_17

10. Damgård, I., Groth, J.: Non-interactive and reusable non-malleable commitment schemes. In: Proceedings of the 35th Annual ACM Symposium on Theory of Computing, San Diego, CA, USA, 9–11 June 2003, pp. 426–437 (2003)

11. Crescenzo, G., Persiano, G., Visconti, I.: Constant-round resettable zero knowledge with concurrent soundness in the bare public-key model. In: Franklin, M. (ed.) CRYPTO 2004. LNCS, vol. 3152, pp. 237–253. Springer, Heidelberg (2004). doi:10.1007/978-3-540-28628-8_15

12. Dolev, D., Dwork, C., Naor, M.: Non-malleable cryptography (extended abstract). In: Proceedings of the 23rd Annual ACM Symposium on Theory of Computing, New Orleans, Louisiana, USA, 5–8 May 1991, pp. 542–552 (1991)

13. Feige, U.: Alternative models for zero knowledge interactive proofs. Master's thesis, Weizmann Institute of Science, Rehovot, Israel. Ph.D. thesis (1990)

14. Feige, U., Lapidot, D., Shamir, A.: Multiple non-interactive zero knowledge proofs based on a single random string (extended abstract). In: 31st Annual Symposium on Foundations of Computer Science, St. Louis, Missouri, USA, 22–24 October 1990, vol. I, pp. 308–317. IEEE Computer Society (1990)

15. Feige, U., Shamir, A.: Witness indistinguishable and witness hiding protocols. In: Proceedings of the Twenty-second Annual ACM Symposium on Theory of Computing, STOC 1990, New York, NY, USA, pp. 416–426. ACM (1990)

16. Garg, S., Mukherjee, P., Pandey, O., Polychroniadou, A.: The exact round complexity of secure computation. In: Fischlin, M., Coron, J.-S. (eds.) EUROCRYPT 2016. LNCS, vol. 9666, pp. 448–476. Springer, Heidelberg (2016). doi:10.1007/978-3-662-49896-5_16

17. Goldreich, O., Krawczyk, H.: On the composition of zero-knowledge proof systems. SIAM J. Comput. 25(1), 169–192 (1996)

18. Goldreich, O., Levin, L.A.: A hard-core predicate for all one-way functions. In: Proceedings of the 21st Annual ACM Symposium on Theory of Computing, Seattle, Washington, USA, 14–17 May 1989, pp. 25–32 (1989)

19. Goyal, V.: Constant round non-malleable protocols using one way functions. In: Proceedings of the 43rd ACM Symposium on Theory of Computing, STOC 2011, San Jose, CA, USA, 6–8 June 2011, pp. 695–704 (2011)

20. Goyal, V., Jain, A., Ostrovsky, R., Richelson, S., Visconti, I.: Constant-round concurrent zero knowledge in the bounded player model. In: Sako, K., Sarkar, P. (eds.) ASIACRYPT 2013. LNCS, vol. 8269, pp. 21–40. Springer, Heidelberg (2013). doi:10.1007/978-3-642-42033-7_2

21. Goyal, V., Khurana, D., Sahai, A.: Breaking the three round barrier for non-malleable commitments. In: 57th IEEE Annual Symposium on Foundations of Computer Science, FOCS 2016. IEEE (2016)

22. Goyal, V., Lee, C., Ostrovsky, R., Visconti, I.: Constructing non-malleable commitments: a black-box approach. In: 53rd Annual IEEE Symposium on Foundations of Computer Science, FOCS 2012, pp. 51–60 (2012)
23. Goyal, V., Pandey, O., Richelson, S.: Textbook non-malleable commitments. Cryptology ePrint Archive, Report 2015/1178 (2015). http://eprint.iacr.org/2015/1178. Accessed 29 Dec 2016
24. Goyal, V., Pandey, O., Richelson, S.: Textbook non-malleable commitments. In: Proceedings of the 48th Annual ACM SIGACT Symposium on Theory of Computing, STOC 2016, pp. 1128–1141 (2016)
25. Goyal, V., Richelson, S., Rosen, A., Vald, M.: An algebraic approach to non-malleability. In: 55th IEEE Annual Symposium on Foundations of Computer Science, FOCS 2014, pp. 41–50 (2014)
26. Hazay, C., Venkitasubramaniam, M.: On the power of secure two-party computation. In: Robshaw, M., Katz, J. (eds.) CRYPTO 2016. LNCS, vol. 9815, pp. 397–429. Springer, Heidelberg (2016). doi:10.1007/978-3-662-53008-5_14
27. Katz, J., Ostrovsky, R.: Round-optimal secure two-party computation. In: Franklin, M. (ed.) CRYPTO 2004. LNCS, vol. 3152, pp. 335–354. Springer, Heidelberg (2004). doi:10.1007/978-3-540-28628-8_21
28. Lapidot, D., Shamir, A.: Publicly verifiable non-interactive zero-knowledge proofs. In: Menezes, A.J., Vanstone, S.A. (eds.) CRYPTO 1990. LNCS, vol. 537, pp. 353–365. Springer, Heidelberg (1991). doi:10.1007/3-540-38424-3_26
29. Lin, H., Pass, R.: Constant-round non-malleable commitments from any one-way function. In: Proceedings of the 43rd ACM Symposium on Theory of Computing, STOC 2011, pp. 705–714. ACM (2011)
30. Lin, H., Pass, R.: Constant-round nonmalleable commitments from any one-way function. J. ACM **62**(1), 5:1–5:30 (2015)
31. Lin, H., Pass, R., Venkitasubramaniam, M.: Concurrent non-malleable commitments from any one-way function. In: Canetti, R. (ed.) TCC 2008. LNCS, vol. 4948, pp. 571–588. Springer, Heidelberg (2008). doi:10.1007/978-3-540-78524-8_31
32. Lin, H., Pass, R., Venkitasubramaniam, M.: A unified framework for concurrent security: universal composability from stand-alone non-malleability. In: Proceedings of the 41st Annual ACM Symposium on Theory of Computing, STOC 2009, Bethesda, MD, USA, 31 May – 2 June 2009, pp. 179–188 (2009)
33. Mahmoody, M., Pass, R.: The curious case of non-interactive commitments – on the power of black-box vs. non-black-box use of primitives. In: Safavi-Naini, R., Canetti, R. (eds.) CRYPTO 2012. LNCS, vol. 7417, pp. 701–718. Springer, Heidelberg (2012). doi:10.1007/978-3-642-32009-5_41
34. Mittelbach, A., Venturi, D.: Fiat–Shamir for highly sound protocols is instantiable. In: Zikas, V., Prisco, R. (eds.) SCN 2016. LNCS, vol. 9841, pp. 198–215. Springer, Cham (2016). doi:10.1007/978-3-319-44618-9_11
35. Naor, M.: Bit commitment using pseudorandomness. J. Cryptology **4**(2), 151–158 (1991)
36. Ostrovsky, R., Persiano, G., Visconti, I.: Constant-round concurrent non-malleable zero knowledge in the bare public-key model. In: Aceto, L., Damgård, I., Goldberg, L.A., Halldórsson, M.M., Ingólfsdóttir, A., Walukiewicz, I. (eds.) ICALP 2008. LNCS, vol. 5126, pp. 548–559. Springer, Heidelberg (2008). doi:10.1007/978-3-540-70583-3_45
37. Ostrovsky, R., Persiano, G., Visconti, I.: Simulation-based concurrent non-malleable commitments and decommitments. In: Reingold, O. (ed.) TCC 2009. LNCS, vol. 5444, pp. 91–108. Springer, Heidelberg (2009). doi:10.1007/978-3-642-00457-5_7

38. Pandey, O., Pass, R., Vaikuntanathan, V.: Adaptive one-way functions and applications. In: Wagner, D. (ed.) CRYPTO 2008. LNCS, vol. 5157, pp. 57–74. Springer, Heidelberg (2008). doi:10.1007/978-3-540-85174-5_4

39. Pass, R.: Bounded-concurrent secure multi-party computation with a dishonest majority. In: Proceedings of the 36th Annual ACM Symposium on Theory of Computing, Chicago, IL, USA, 13–16 June 2004, pp. 232–241. ACM (2004)

40. Pass, R.: Unprovable security of perfect NIZK and non-interactive Non-malleable Commitments. In: Sahai, A. (ed.) TCC 2013. LNCS, vol. 7785, pp. 334–354. Springer, Heidelberg (2013). doi:10.1007/978-3-642-36594-2_19

41. Pass, R., Rosen, A.: Bounded-concurrent secure two-party computation in a constant number of rounds. In: 44th Symposium on Foundations of Computer Science (FOCS 2003), Proceedings, pp. 404–413. IEEE Computer Society (2003)

42. Pass, R., Rosen, A.: Concurrent non-malleable commitments. In: Proceedings of the FOCS 2005, pp. 563–572 (2005)

43. Pass, R., Rosen, A.: New and improved constructions of non-malleable cryptographic protocols. In: Proceedings of the 37th Annual ACM Symposium on Theory of Computing, Baltimore, MD, USA, 22–24 May 2005, pp. 533–542. ACM (2005)

44. Pass, R., Rosen, A.: Concurrent nonmalleable commitments. SIAM J. Comput. **37**(6), 1891–1925 (2008)

45. Pass, R., Rosen, A.: New and improved constructions of nonmalleable cryptographic protocols. SIAM J. Comput. **38**(2), 702–752 (2008)

46. Pass, R., Wee, H.: Constant-round non-malleable commitments from subexponential one-way functions. In: Gilbert, H. (ed.) EUROCRYPT 2010. LNCS, vol. 6110, pp. 638–655. Springer, Heidelberg (2010). doi:10.1007/978-3-642-13190-5_32

47. Rompel, J.: One-way functions are necessary and sufficient for secure signatures. In: Proceedings of the 22nd Annual ACM Symposium on Theory of Computing, pp. 387–394 (1990)

48. Sahai, A.: Non-malleable non-interactive zero knowledge and adaptive chosen-ciphertext security. In: Proceedings of the FOCS 1999, pp. 543–553. IEEE Computer Society (1999)

49. De Santis, A., Di Crescenzo, G., Ostrovsky, R., Persiano, G., Sahai, A.: Robust non-interactive zero knowledge. In: Kilian, J. (ed.) CRYPTO 2001. LNCS, vol. 2139, pp. 566–598. Springer, Heidelberg (2001). doi:10.1007/3-540-44647-8_33

50. Wee, H.: Black-box, round-efficient secure computation via non-malleability amplification. In: 51st Annual IEEE Symposium on Foundations of Computer Science, FOCS 200, pp. 531–540. IEEE Computer Society (2010)

51. Yung, M., Zhao, Y.: Generic and practical resettable zero-knowledge in the bare public-key model. In: Naor, M. (ed.) EUROCRYPT 2007. LNCS, vol. 4515, pp. 129–147. Springer, Heidelberg (2007). doi:10.1007/978-3-540-72540-4_8

Distinguisher-Dependent Simulation in Two Rounds and its Applications

Abhishek Jain[1], Yael Tauman Kalai[2], Dakshita Khurana[3(✉)], and Ron Rothblum[4]

[1] Department of Computer Science, Johns Hopkins University, Baltimore, USA
abhishek@cs.jhu.edu
[2] Microsoft Research, Cambridge, USA
yaelism@gmail.com
[3] Department of Computer Science, UCLA, Los Angeles, USA
dakshita@cs.ucla.edu
[4] Department of Computer Science, MIT, Cambridge, USA
rothblum@gmail.com

Abstract. We devise a novel simulation technique that makes black-box use of the adversary as well as the distinguisher. Using this technique we construct several round-optimal protocols, many of which were previously unknown even using non-black-box simulation techniques:
- Two-round witness indistinguishable (WI) arguments for NP from different assumptions than previously known.
- Two-round arguments and three-round arguments of knowledge for NP that achieve strong WI, witness hiding (WH) and distributional weak zero knowledge (WZK) properties in a setting where the instance is only determined by the prover in the last round of the interaction. The soundness of these protocols is guaranteed against adaptive provers.
- Three-round two-party computation satisfying input-indistinguishable security as well as a weaker notion of simulation security against malicious adversaries.
- Three-round extractable commitments with guaranteed correctness of extraction from polynomial hardness assumptions.

Our three-round protocols can be based on DDH or QR or N^{th} residuosity and our two-round protocols require quasi-polynomial hardness of the same assumptions. In particular, prior to this work, two-round WI arguments for NP were only known based on assumptions such as the existence of trapdoor permutations, hardness assumptions on bilinear maps, or the existence of program obfuscation; we give the first construction based on (quasi-polynomial) DDH or QR or N^{th} residuosity.

Our simulation technique bypasses known lower bounds on black-box simulation [Goldreich-Krawcyzk'96] by using the distinguisher's output in a meaningful way. We believe that this technique is likely to find additional applications in the future.

A. Jain—Supported in part by a DARPA/ARL Safeware Grant W911NF-15-C-0213.
R. Rothblum—Partially supported by the grants: NSF MACS - CNS-1413920, DARPA IBM - W911NF-15-C-0236 and SIMONS Investigator award Agreement Dated 6-5-12.

J. Katz and H. Shacham (Eds.): CRYPTO 2017, Part II, LNCS 10402, pp. 158–189, 2017.
DOI: 10.1007/978-3-319-63715-0_6

1 Introduction

The notion of zero-knowledge (ZK) proofs [38] is fundamental to cryptography. Intuitively, zero-knowledge proofs guarantee that the proof of a statement does not reveal anything beyond the validity of the statement. This seemingly paradoxical requirement is formalized via the *simulation* paradigm, namely, by requiring the existence of an efficient simulator that simulates the view of a malicious verifier, without access to any witness for the statement.

Over the years, ZK proofs (and arguments) have been integral to the design of numerous cryptographic protocols, most notably general-purpose secure computation [36], as well as specific tasks such as coin-tossing, equivocal and/or extractable commitments and non-malleable protocols [25]. Even protocols satisfying weaker notions of ZK such as strong witness indistinguishability and witness hiding (WH) [29], are typically constructed only via a ZK protocol[1]. In particular, the round complexity of ZK determines the round complexity of known constructions for these tasks.

Goldreich and Krawcyzk (GK) [35] established that three round ZK arguments for NP with black-box simulation do not exist for languages outside BPP. Furthermore, all known non-black-box simulation techniques [3] require more than three rounds.[2] This has acted as a barrier towards achieving round-efficient protocols for many of the aforementioned tasks. In this work, we investigate the possibility of overcoming this barrier.

(When) Is ZK Necessary? ZK proofs are typically used to enforce "honest behaviour" for participants of a cryptographic protocol. The zero-knowledge property additionally ensures privacy of the inputs of honest parties. However, many applications of ZK described above do not themselves guarantee simulation-based security but only weaker indistinguishability-based security. As such, it is not immediately clear whether the "full" simulation power of ZK is necessary for such applications.

For example, *strong witness indistinguishability* requires that for two indistinguishable statement distributions $\mathcal{X}_1, \mathcal{X}_2$, a proof (or argument) for statement $x_1 \leftarrow \mathcal{X}_1$ must be indistinguishable from a proof (or argument) for statement $x_2 \leftarrow \mathcal{X}_2$. All known constructions of strong witness indistinguishable protocols rely on ZK arguments with standard simulation – and therefore end up requiring at least as many rounds as ZK arguments. Similar issues arise in constructing input-hiding/input-indistinguishable secure computation, witness hiding arguments and proofs, and extractable (or other sophisticated) commitment schemes. However, it is unclear whether ZK is actually *necessary* in these settings.

This raises the question of whether it is possible to devise "weaker" simulation strategies in three rounds or less that can be used to recover several applications of ZK. In this work, we implement such a black-box simulation strategy in only *two* rounds.

---

[1] The work of Bitansky and Paneth [10] constructing 3 round witness-hiding and weak zero-knowledge from variants of auxiliary-input point obfuscation, is an exception.

[2] Here we only refer to *explicit* simulation, and not non-explicit simulation via knowledge assumptions [5,41].

Distinguisher-Dependent Simulation. Our starting observation is that for any cryptographic protocol that only aims to achieve indistinguishability-based security, the security reduction has access to an efficient *distinguisher*. In such scenarios, one can hope to argue security via a (weaker) simulation strategy that potentially makes use of the distinguisher in a non-trivial manner.

The idea of distinguisher-dependent simulation is not new and has previously been studied in the context of interactive proofs, where it is referred to as weak zero knowledge (WZK) [28][3]. Informally, WZK says that any bit of information that can be learned by the verifier by interacting with the prover can be simulated given only the instance. As such, WZK suffices for many applications of ZK, and in particular, implies meaningful weaker notions such as WH and WI [29].

The immediate question is whether distinguisher-dependent simulation can be realized in three rounds or less. At first, the answer seems to be negative since the lower bound of GK also extends to WZK (this was already noted in [10]).

A key insight in our work is that in many applications of ZK proofs, the statement being proven is chosen by the prover from a (public) distribution. Suppose that the proof system is *delayed-input* [48], namely, where the instance and witness are only required for computing the last prover message. In this case, it is to an honest prover's advantage to reveal the instance to the verifier only in the last round. This does not violate correctness due to the delayed input property, but "weakens" a malicious verifier, and in particular, ensures that a malicious verifier's messages are independent of the instance. Interestingly, we observe that the lower bound of GK no longer holds in this case[4].

At a high-level, this is because in this setting, a simulator may be able to learn non-trivial information about the distinguisher's behavior by observing its output on different samples created using possibly different instances from the same distribution. This observation is, in fact, not limited to delayed-input proofs and extends to a large class of important two-party functionalities including coin-tossing, generating common reference strings and oblivious PRFs.

This observation opens doors to the possibility of constructing proof systems and secure computation in three rounds or less with meaningful simulation-based and indistinguishability-based security guarantees.

A New Black-box Simulation Technique. We devise a new distinguisher-dependent black-box simulation technique that only requires two-rounds of communication. Roughly, we show that a single bit of information (of whether the proof is accepted or rejected by the distinguisher) can be used to learn information about the (possibly) malicious verifier and distinguisher, in a bit-by-bit fashion, and that this information can later be used to efficiently simulate the proof.

---

[3] Recall that standard ZK requires that for any adversarial verifier, there exists a simulator that can produce a view that is indistinguishable from the real one to every distinguisher. WZK relaxes this notion by reversing the order of quantifiers, and allowing the simulator to depend on the distinguisher.

[4] Indeed, the GK proof strategy crucially uses a verifier that chooses its protocol message as a function of the instance. See Sect. 1.2 for further discussion.

We remark that the ability to learn a bit of information based on whether the protocol execution is accepted or rejected has in the past been viewed as a source of insecurity in cryptographic protocols. For example, in the delegation of computation schemes of [18,33], an adversarial prover can successfully cheat if it is able to observe the verifier's output over multiple executions. For similar reasons, special care is taken to prevent "input-dependent aborts" in the design of many secure computation protocols.

In this work, we turn this apparent weakness into a positive by using it to devise a new black-box simulation strategy. Using this strategy, we obtain several new results on proof systems and secure computation. Most of our results were previously unknown even using non-black-box simulation techniques.

Our Setting. In order to prove privacy, we must sometimes restrict ourselves to a setting where the prover has the *flexibility* to sample instances and witnesses in the last round of the argument. More specifically, our simulator will require knowledge of any witnesses that are fixed (implicitly or explicitly) before the last message is sent; however, it will not require knowledge of witnesses fixed in the last round.

1.1 Our Results

We now proceed to describe our results. We start with our results on interactive proof systems and then describe their applications to secure two-party computation and extractable commitment schemes. All of these results rely on our new black-box simulation strategy.

I. Delayed-Input Interactive Proofs. We study two and three round *delayed-input* interactive proof systems where the instance to be proven can be chosen by the prover in the last round, and soundness holds even against adaptive cheating provers who choose the instance depending upon the verifier's message. First studied by [48], delayed-input protocols have found numerous applications over the years in the design of round-efficient cryptographic protocols for a variety of tasks such as secure computation [31,44,47], resettable security [24,60], non-malleable commitments [20,58], improved Σ-protocols [21,22,50], and so on.

In the context of establishing various privacy notions, we consider both *adaptive* verifiers, who receive the instance at the beginning of the protocol, and hence may choose their message based on this instance, and *non-adaptive* verifiers, who receive the instance only in the last round of the protocol, and hence their message is independent of the instance. As we discuss later, guaranteeing privacy against non-adaptive verifiers suffices for many natural applications of delayed-input proof systems.

(I). TWO ROUND ARGUMENT SYSTEMS. Our first contribution is a two-round delayed-input argument system that achieves witness-indistinguishability (WI) against *adaptive* verifiers, and strong WI, witness hiding (WH) and distributional weak zero-knowledge (WZK) against *non-adaptive* verifiers.

Theorem 1 (Informal). *Assuming the existence of two-round oblivious transfer that is secure against malicious PPT receivers and quasi-polynomial time semi-honest senders, there exists a two-round delayed-input interactive argument system for* NP *with adaptive soundness and the following privacy guarantees:*

– *WI against adaptive verifiers.*
– *Strong WI, WH and distributional WZK against non-adaptive verifiers.*

Oblivious transfer (OT) protocols as required in the above theorem can be constructed based on quasi-polynomial hardness of Decisional Diffie-Hellman (DDH) [51] or N'th Residuosity or Quadratic Residuosity [43,45].

Comparison with Prior Work. If we know an a priori super-polynomial bound on the hardness of the language, then two-round WH can be obtained from two-round ZK with super-polynomial time simulators (SPS) [53]. However, no constructions of two-round WH or distributional WZK for NP against non-uniform verifiers were previously known. (We refer the reader to Sect. 1.3 for a more thorough discussion.)

WI proofs in two rounds (or less) were previously only known based on either trapdoor permutations[5] [27], or the decision linear assumption on bilinear groups [40], or indistinguishability obfuscation [11]. Our result in Theorem 1 substantially adds to the set of standard assumptions that suffice for two-round WI. We remark that unlike previous protocols, our WI protocol is not publicly verifiable.

Privacy Amplification via Round Compression. We obtain Theorem 1 by "compressing" any Σ-protocol[6] [23] into a two-round private-coin argument using OT. Our compiler follows the approach of [1,46], except that we use a maliciously secure OT as opposed to a computational PIR [17].

Interestingly, our approach of compressing a Σ-protocol into a two-round argument results in amplifying its privacy guarantees. Indeed, standard Σ-protocols are not known to be WZK. Furthermore, [42,54] proved that such protocols cannot be proven WH using black-box reductions.

Avoiding NP Reductions. An added benefit of our approach is that given a Σ-protocol for a language L, we obtain a two-round private-coin argument system with the security guarantees stated in Theorem 1 for the same language L, *without* using expensive NP reductions. To the best of our knowledge, no such two-round argument system was previously known.

(II). THREE ROUND ARGUMENTS OF KNOWLEDGE. Our second contribution is a three-round delayed-input interactive *argument of knowledge* system that achieves WH and distributional WZK against non-adaptive verifiers. This protocol uses only polynomial assumptions, but requires an extra round.

---

[5] Presently, the only known candidates for trapdoor permutations are based on factoring or indistinguishability obfuscation [12,32].

[6] Very roughly, a Σ-protocol is a three round protocol that is honest verifier zero-knowledge, and has a strong soundness guarantee. We refer the reader to Definition 1.

Theorem 2 (Informal). *Assuming the existence of two-round oblivious transfer (OT) that is secure against malicious PPT receivers and semi-honest PPT senders, as well as dense cryptosystems, there exists a three-round interactive argument of knowledge for NP that achieves soundness against adaptive (unbounded) provers and Strong WI, WH and distributional WZK against non-adaptive PPT verifiers.*

Comparison with Prior Work. Three-round ZK arguments are known either based on non-standard "knowledge assumptions" [5,41], or against adversaries with *bounded* non-uniformity [7,9]. In this work, we consider security against adversaries with non-uniform advice of arbitrarily large polynomial length, based on standard cryptographic assumptions. Prior to our work, three-round WH and WZK arguments for NP were known from non-black-box techniques that rely on auxiliary input point obfuscation assumptions [10]. These protocols, unlike ours, guarantee privacy also against adaptive verifiers. However, some of their underlying assumptions have recently been shown to be implausible [6,14]. (See Sect. 1.3 for a more detailed discussion.)

II. Secure Two-Party Computation. We next study two-party computation against malicious adversaries in the plain model without trusted setup assumptions. In this setting, the state of the art result is due to Katz and Ostrovsky [47] who constructed a four-round protocol for general functions in the setting where only one party receives the output. We refer to the output recipient as the *receiver* and the other party as the *sender*.

As an application of our new simulation technique, we obtain two new results on two-party computation in *three* rounds. Our first result achieves input-indistinguishable security [49] against malicious receivers, while our second result achieves distinguisher-dependent simulation security against malicious receivers. In both of these results, we achieve standard simulation security against malicious senders. We elaborate on these results below.

(I). THREE ROUND INPUT-INDISTINGUISHABLE COMPUTATION. The notion of input-indistinguishable computation (IIC) was introduced by Micali, Pass and Rosen [49] as a weakening of standard simulation-based security notion for secure computation while still providing meaningful security. (See also [30,52]). Roughly, input-indistinguishable security against malicious receivers guarantees[7] that for any function f and a pair of inputs (x_1, x_2) for the sender, a malicious receiver cannot distinguish whether the sender's input is x_1 or x_2 as long as the receiver's "implicit input" y in the execution is such that $f(x_1, y) = f(x_2, y)$.[8]

We construct the first three-round IIC protocol for general functions based on polynomial hardness assumptions. In fact, our protocol achieves standard simulation-based security against malicious senders and input-indistinguishable security against malicious receivers.

---

[7] Security against malicious senders can be defined analogously.

[8] The formal security definition of IIC is much more delicate, and we refer the reader to the technical sections for details.

Theorem 3 (Informal). *Assuming the existence of two-round oblivious transfer that is secure against malicious PPT receivers and semi-honest PPT senders, along with dense cryptosystems, there exists a three-round secure two-party computation protocol for general functions between a sender and a receiver, where only the receiver obtains the output, with standard simulation security against malicious senders and input-indistinguishable security against malicious receivers.*

(II). THREE ROUND TWO-PARTY COMPUTATION WITH DISTINGUISHER DEPENDENT SIMULATION. We also consider a weak simulation-based security notion for two-party computation that is defined analogously to distributional WZK by allowing the simulator to depend (non-uniformly) upon the distinguisher and the distribution over the public input to the adversary. We refer to this as distributional distinguisher-dependent simulation secure two-party computation. While this generalizes the notion of distributional WZK, it also implies distinguisher-dependent simulation security for all functionalities where the honest party's input can be efficiently sampled (without the need for non-uniform advice) even if the input of the malicious party and any common input is already fixed.

We show that the same protocol as in Theorem 3 also satisfies distributional distinguisher-dependent security for all functionalities. In particular, we obtain three round distinguisher-dependent simulation secure two party computation for inherently distributional functionalities such as coin-tossing, generating common *reference* strings and oblivious PRFs.

Theorem 4 (Informal). *Assuming the existence of two-round oblivious transfer that is secure against malicious PPT receivers and semi-honest PPT senders, as well as dense cryptosystems, there exists a three-round protocol for secure two-party computation for any function between a sender and receiver, where only the receiver obtains the output, with standard simulation security against a malicious sender and distributional distinguisher-dependent simulation security against a malicious receiver. This implies distinguisher-dependent simulation secure two-party computation for any function where the sender's input can be efficiently sampled even if the receiver's input (and any common input) is already fixed.*

A Two-round Protocol. We also remark that our three-round two-party computation protocol can be downgraded to a two-round protocol that achieves distributional distinguisher-dependent simulation security or input-indistinguishable security against malicious receivers and quasi-polynomial time simulation security against malicious senders (or polynomial-time simulation security against semi-honest senders).

Outputs for Both Parties. Theorems 3 and 4 consider the case where only one party, namely the receiver, learns the output. As observed in [47], such a protocol can be easily transformed into one where both parties receive the output by computing a modified functionality that outputs signed values. Now the output recipient can simply forward the output to the other party who accepts it only if the signature verifies.

This adds a round of communication, making the protocol four rounds in total. Because we consider distinguisher-dependent simulation security (or input-indistinguishable security), this bypasses the lower bound of [47] who proved that coin-tossing cannot be realized with standard simulation-based security in less than five rounds when both parties receive output.

III. Extractable Commitments. We finally discuss application of our techniques to *extractable* commitments. A commitment scheme is said to be extractable if there exists a PPT extractor that can extract the committed value with *guaranteed correctness of extraction*. In particular, if the commitment is not "well-formed" (i.e., not computed honestly), then the extractor must output $\perp$, while if the commitment is well-formed, then the extractor must output the correct committed value. Extractable commitments are very useful in the design of advanced cryptographic protocols, in particular, to facilitate the extraction of the adversary's input in tasks such as secure computation, non-malleable commitments, etc.

A standard way to construct extractable commitment schemes is to "compile" a standard commitment scheme with a ZKAoK, namely, by having a committer commit to its value using a standard commitment and additionally give a ZKAoK to prove knowledge of the decommitment value. The soundness property of ZKAoK guarantees the well-formedness of commitment, which in turn guarantees correctness of extraction of the committed value using the AoK extractor for ZKAoK, while the ZK property preserves the hiding of the underlying commitment. This approach yields a four round extractable commitment scheme starting from any four round ZKAoK. However, in the absence of three-round ZKAoK, constructing three-round extractable commitments from *polynomial* hardness assumptions have so far proven to be elusive.[9]

The main challenge here is to enforce honest behavior on a malicious committer, while at the same time guaranteeing privacy for honest committers. Indeed, natural variations of the above approach (e.g., using weaker notions such as WIPOK that are known in three rounds) seem to only satisfy one of these two requirements, but not both.

As an application of Theorem 2, we construct the first three-round extractable commitment scheme based on standard polynomial-time hardness assumptions.

Theorem 5 (Informal). *Assuming the existence of two-round oblivious transfer that is secure against malicious PPT receivers and semi-honest PPT senders, as well as dense cryptosystems, there exists a three-round extractable commitment scheme.*

---

[9] All known constructions of three-round extractable commitments from polynomial-hardness assumptions (such as [55,56]) only satisfy a weak extraction property where either the extractor outputs (with non-negligible probability) a non $\perp$ value when the commitment is not well-formed, or it fails to output the correct value when the commitment is well-formed. It is, however, possible to construct extractable commitments using quasi-polynomial hardness [39] or using three round zero-knowledge with super-polynomial simulation [53].

Roughly, our construction of extractable commitments follows the same app-roach as described above. Our main observation is that the hiding property of the extractable commitment can be argued if the AoK system satisfies a *strong* WI property (instead of requiring full-fledged ZK).

1.2   Discussion

Non-adaptive Verifiers. Our results on distributional WZK, WH and strong WI are w.r.t. non-adaptive verifiers who learn the statement in the last round of the protocol. To the best of our knowledge, privacy against non-adaptive verifiers has not been studied before, and therefore, it is natural to ask whether it is a meaningful notion of privacy.

We argue that privacy against non-adaptive verifiers is very useful. Our main observation is that in many applications of delayed-input proof systems, the verifier is already non-adaptive, or can be made non-adaptive by design. Two concrete examples follow:

- We construct a three-round extractable commitment scheme by combining a standard commitment with a three-round delayed-input strong WIAoK of correctness of the committed value, that achieves security against non-adaptive verifiers. By sending the commitment in the last round, we auto-matically make the verifier non-adaptive.
- In secure computation using garbled circuits (GCs) [59], a malicious sender must prove correctness of its GC. In this case, the instance (i.e., the GC) can simply be sent together with the last prover message, which automati-cally makes the verifier non-adaptive. This does not affect the security of the receiver if the proof system achieves adaptive soundness (which is true for our constructions). Indeed, our construction uses exactly this approach.

We anticipate that the notion of privacy against non-adaptive verifiers will find more applications in the future.

Bypassing GK and GO Lower Bounds. We now elaborate on the reasons why we are able to bypass the lower bounds of [35,37]. The black-box impossi-bility result of [35] for three-round ZK crucially uses an adaptive verifier. More specifically, they consider a verifier that has a random seed to a pseudo-random function hard-wired into it, and for any instance and first message sent by the prover, it uses its PRF seed, to answer honestly with fresh-looking randomness. It is then argued that a black-box simulator can be used to break soundness. Very roughly, this is because a cheating prover can simply run the black-box simulator; if the simulator rewinds the verifier, then the cheating prover answers it with a random message on behalf of the verifier. This proof also extends to WZK because any query made by the simulator to the distinguisher can simply be answered with "reject."

Note, however, that in the non-adaptive setting, the verifier is not allowed to generate different messages for different instances, and hence the simulator has more power than a cheating prover, since it can fix the first message of the prover and then test whether the distinguisher accepts or not with various instances and various third round messages. Indeed, we exploit exactly this fact to design a distinguisher-dependent simulator for our protocols.

We next explain why we are able to overcome the lower bound of [37] for two-round ZK. A key argument in the proof of [37] is that no (possibly non-black-box) simulator can simulate the prover's message for a false statement (even when the protocol is privately verifiable). For ZK, this is argued by setting the verifier's auxiliary input to be an honestly generated first message and providing the corresponding private randomness to the distinguisher, who is chosen *after* the simulator. Now, if the simulator succeeds, then we can break soundness of the protocol. However, in WZK, since the distinguisher is fixed in advance, the above approach does not work. In particular, if the distinguisher is given the private randomness then the simulator is given it as well (and hence can simulate), and otherwise, the simulator can succeed by simulating a rejecting transcript.

1.3   Related Work

Concurrent Work. Concurrent to our work, Badrinarayanan et al. [2] construct protocols that are similar to our two-round protocols. However their focus is on super-polynomial simulation, whereas we focus on polynomial time distinguisher-dependent simulation. They also give other instantiations of two-round OT, which can be combined with our results to obtain two-round delayed-input distributional weak zero-knowledge from additional assumptions.

Proof Systems. We mention two related works on two-round ZK proofs that overcome the lower bound of [37] in different ways. A recent work of [19] constructs a two-round (T, t, ϵ)-ZK proof system for languages in statistical zero-knowledge, where roughly, (T, t, ϵ) ZK requires the existence of a simulator that simulates the view of the verifier for any distinguisher running in time t and distinguishing probability ϵ. The running time T of the simulator depends upon t and ϵ. In another recent work, [9] construct a two-round ZK argument system against verifiers with auxiliary inputs of a priori bounded size.

Three-round ZK proofs are known either based on non-standard "knowledge assumptions" [5,41], or against adversaries that receive auxiliary inputs of a priori bounded size [7,9]. In contrast, in this work, we consider security against adversaries with non-uniform advice of arbitrarily polynomial size, based on standard cryptographic assumptions.

Finally, we discuss WI, WH and WZK in three rounds. While three round WI is known from injective one-way functions [29], WH and WZK are non-trivial to realize even in three rounds. In particular, [42] proved a lower bound for three-round public-coin WH w.r.t. a natural class of black-box reductions. More recently, [54] extended their result to rule out all black-box reductions. Presently, the only known constructions of three-round WH and WZK for NP require either "knowledge assumptions" [5,41], or rely on the assumption of auxiliary-input point obfuscation (AIPO) and auxiliary-input multi-bit point obfuscation (AIMPO), respectively, with an additional "recognizability" property [10]. For general auxiliary inputs, however, AIMPO was recently proven to be impossible w.r.t. general auxiliary inputs [14], assuming the existence of indistinguishability obfuscation [4]. Further, one of the assumptions used by [10] to build recognizable AIPO, namely, strong DDH assumption [15], was recently shown to be impossible w.r.t. general auxiliary inputs [6], assuming the existence of virtual grey-box obfuscation [8].

Secure Computation. Katz and Ostrovsky [47] constructed a four-round two-party computation protocol for general functions where only one party receives the output. A recent work of Garg et al. [31] extends their result to the simultaneous-message model to obtain a four-round protocol where both parties receive the outputs.

The notion of input-indistinguishable computation (IIC) was introduced by Micali, Pass and Rosen [49] as a weakening of standard simulation-based security notion for secure computation while still providing meaningful security. (See also [30,52].) We provide the first three-round protocol that provides input-indistinguishable security.

A recent work of Döttling et al. [26] constructs a two-round two-party computation protocol for oblivious computation of cryptographic functionalities. They consider semi-honest senders and malicious receivers, and prove game-based security against the latter. We remark that our three-round two-party computation protocol can be easily downgraded to a two-round protocol that achieves weak simulation security against malicious receivers and super-polynomial time simulation security against malicious senders (or polynomial-time simulation against semi-honest senders). We note that our result is incomparable to [26], because we consider a restricted class of distributions (such as product distributions), albeit any functionality, whereas [26] considers the class of cryptographic functionalities.

1.4   Organization

The rest of this paper is organized as follows. We begin with an overview of our techniques in Sect. 2. In Sect. 3, we describe important relevant preliminaries including Σ-protocols and oblivious transfer. In Sect. 4, we recall definitions of adaptive soundness, witness indistinguishability, distributional weak-ZK and witness hiding against non-adaptive verifiers. In Sect. 5, we describe our two-round protocol, which uses any Σ-protocol with a special structure, together with 2-message OT. In the same section, we describe how to modify our protocol so as to rely on *any* Σ-protocol, and also show how to base security on polynomial hardness assumptions at the cost of adding an extra round. Due to lack of space, we defer additional details of our three round protocols and their applications to the full version of the paper.

2   Technical Overview

We now give an overview of our main ideas and techniques.

2.1 Argument Systems

We construct a two-round argument system, which we prove is both witness indistinguishable (against all malicious verifiers), and is distributional ϵ-weak zero-knowledge (against non-adaptive malicious verifiers). Our protocol makes use of two components:

- Any Σ-protocol consisting of three messages (a, e, z) that is secure against unbounded provers,
- Any two-message oblivious transfer protocol, denoted by $(\mathsf{OT}_1, \mathsf{OT}_2)$, which is secure against malicious PPT receivers, and malicious senders running in time at most $2^{|z|}$. For receiver input b and sender input messages (m_0, m_1), we denote the two messages of the OT protocol as $\mathsf{OT}_1(b)$ and $\mathsf{OT}_2(m_0, m_1)$. We note that $\mathsf{OT}_2(m_0, m_1)$ also depends on the message $\mathsf{OT}_1(b)$ sent by the receiver. For the sake of simplicity, we omit this dependence from the notation.

For simplicity, throughout most of the paper, we assume that the Σ-protocol is a parallel repetition of Σ-protocols with a single-bit challenge and constant soundness[10]. Namely, we assume that the Σ-protocol contains three messages, denoted by (a, e, z) and that these messages can be parsed as $a = (a_1, \ldots, a_\kappa)$, $e = (e_1, \ldots, e_\kappa)$, and $z = (z_1, \ldots, z_\kappa)$, where for each $i \in [\kappa]$, the triplet (a_i, e_i, z_i) are messages corresponding to an underlying Σ-protocol with a single-bit challenge (i.e., where $e_i \in \{0, 1\}$). We denote by f_1 and f_2 the functions that satisfy $a_i = f_1(x, w; r_i)$ and $z_i = f_2(x, w, r_i, e_i)$, for answers provided by the honest prover, and where r_i is uniformly chosen randomness.

We show how to convert any such Σ-protocol into a two-round protocol (P, V) using OT. Our transformation is essentially the same as the one suggested by Aeillo et. al. [1], and used by Kalai and Raz [46], to reduce rounds in interactive protocols, except that we use an OT scheme rather than a computational PIR scheme (since as opposed to [1,46] we are not concerned with compressing the length of the messages). Specifically, given any such Σ-protocol and OT protocol, our two-round protocol (P, V), proceeds as follows.

- For $i \in [\kappa]$, V picks $e_i \xleftarrow{\$} \{0, 1\}$, and sends $\mathsf{OT}_{1,i}(e_i)$ in parallel. Each e_i is encrypted with a fresh OT instance.
- For $i \in [\kappa]$, P computes $a_i = f_1(x, w; r_i), z_i^{(0)} = f_2(x, w, r_i, 0), z_i^{(1)} = f_2(x, w, r_i, 1)$. The prover P then sends $a_i, \mathsf{OT}_{2,i}(z_i^{(0)}, z_i^{(1)})$ in parallel for all $i \in [\kappa]$.
- The verifier V recovers $z_i^{(e_i)}$ from the OT, and accepts if and only if for every $i \in [\kappa]$, the transcript $(a_i, e_i, z_i^{(e_i)})$ is an accepting transcript of the underlying Σ-protocol.

Soundness. It was proven in [46] that such a transformation from any public-coin interactive proof to a two-round argument preserves soundness against PPT

---

[10] We later describe how garbled circuits can be used in order to modify our construction to work with any Σ-protocol.

provers. We extend their proof to show that the resulting two-round protocol also satisfies *adaptive* soundness, i.e., is sound against cheating provers that may adaptively choose some instance x as a function of the verifier message.

To prove soundness, we rely on the following special-soundness property of Σ-protocols: There exists a polynomial-time algorithm A that given any instance x of some NP language L with witness relation R_L, and a pair of accepting transcripts $(a, e, z), (a, e', z')$ for x with the same first prover message, where $e \neq e'$, outputs w such that $w \in R_L(x)$. In particular, this means that for any $x \notin L$, for any fixed message a, there exists at most *one* unique value of receiver challenge e, for which there exists z such that (a, e, z) is an accepting transcript (as otherwise the algorithm A would output a witness $w \in R_L(x)$, which is impossible).

Going back to our protocol – suppose a cheating prover, on input the verifier message $\mathsf{OT}_1(e^*)$, outputs $x^* \notin L$, together with messages $a^*, \mathsf{OT}_2(z^*)$, such that the verifier accepts with non-negligible probability. Since, for any $x^* \notin L$ and any a^*, there exists at most one unique value of receiver challenge e, for which there exists a z that causes the verifier to accept – intuitively, this means that a^* encodes the receiver challenge e^*.

Thus, for fixed a^*, a reduction can enumerate over all possible values of z (corresponding to all possible e), and check which single e results in an accepting transcript. Then, this would allow a reduction to break receiver security of the oblivious transfer. Since such a reduction would require time at least $2^{|z|}$, we need the underlying oblivious transfer to be $2^{|z|}$-secure (or, sub-exponentially secure). If z can be scaled down to be of size poly-logarithmic in the security parameter, we can rely on an oblivious transfer protocol which is quasi-polynomially secure against malicious receivers.

A New Extraction Technique for Proving Weaker Notions of Zero-Knowledge. We now proceed to describe our main ideas for proving the privacy guarantees of our protocol. For simplicity, consider a single repetition of the protocol outlined above. That is, consider a protocol where the verifier picks a random **bit** $e \xleftarrow{\$} \{0, 1\}$ and sends $r = \mathsf{OT}_1(e)$ to the prover. The prover then sends $a, \mathsf{OT}_2(z^{(0)}, z^{(1)})$ to the verifier, where $(a, z^{(0)}, z^{(1)})$ are computed similarly as before.

By the security of the underlying OT scheme against malicious receivers (see Definition 2 and discussion therein), the following holds: For any malicious verifier (i.e. malicious receiver of the OT scheme) there exists a (possibly inefficient) simulator that interacts with an ideal OT functionality and is able to simulate the view of the verifier. This means that for any PPT distinguisher $\mathcal{D}_\mathcal{V}$ (that obtains as input the view of the verifier and additional auxiliary information), its output distribution when the prover sends $(a, \mathsf{OT}_2(z^{(0)}, z^{(1)}))$ is indistinguishable from one of the following:

- Its output distribution when the prover sends $(a, \mathsf{OT}_2(z^{(0)}, z^{(0)}))$ (implicitly corresponding to receiver choice bit 0).
- Its distribution output when the prover sends $(a, \mathsf{OT}_2(z^{(1)}, z^{(1)}))$ (implicitly corresponding to receiver choice bit 1).

Suppose the message of the verifier, $\mathsf{OT}_1(e)$ is generated independently of the instance x, and suppose that the instance x is generated according to some distribution $\mathcal{D}$. Then an extractor $\mathcal{E}$, given the message $\mathsf{OT}_1(e)$, can guess e (if the distinguisher "knows" e), up to ϵ-error in time $\mathsf{poly}(1/\epsilon)$, as follows: The extractor will generate $\mathsf{poly}(1/\epsilon)$ many instance-witness pairs $(x, w) \in R_L$, where each x is distributed independently from $\mathcal{D}$ ($\mathcal{E}$ will have these instance-witness pairs hardwired if they are hard to sample). Then for each such instance-witness pair the extractor will generate $(a, z^{(0)}, z^{(1)})$, and will observe the distinguisher's output corresponding to the prover's message $(a, \mathsf{OT}_2(z^{(0)}, z^{(0)}))$, $(a, \mathsf{OT}_2(z^{(1)}, z^{(1)}))$, and $(a, \mathsf{OT}_2(z^{(0)}, z^{(1)}))$. If the distinguisher cannot distinguish between these three distributions then the extractor outputs $\perp$ (indicating that the distinguisher does not know e). If the extractor outputs $\perp$, the distinguisher is (distributionally) insensitive to the prover's response, so we can behave as if it was approximated to 0.

However, if the distinguisher can distinguish between $(a, \mathsf{OT}_2(z^{(0)}, z^{(1)}))$ and $(a, \mathsf{OT}_2(z^{(b)}, z^{(b)}))$, then the distinguisher will guess $e = 1 - b$. In this way, the extractor can approximate (up to ϵ-error) whether the implicit receiver choice bit is 0 or 1, while running in time $\mathsf{poly}(1/\epsilon)$. This idea forms the basis of our new extraction technique.

Witness Indistinguishability. Since witness indistinguishability is known to compose under parallel repetition, it suffices to prove WI for a single repetition of the protocol outlined above. In fact, we will try to prove something even stronger.

As explained above, there exists a distinguisher-dependent simulator $\mathsf{Sim}_{\mathcal{D}_V}$, that, given a fixed receiver message r, can try to approximate the verifier's implicit challenge bit e, by observing the distinguisher's output corresponding to various sender messages, up to error ϵ. Once $\mathsf{Sim}_{\mathcal{D}_V}$ has successfully extracted the verifier's challenge, it can use the honest-verifier zero-knowledge simulator of the underlying Σ-protocol.

Of course, to even begin the extraction process, $\mathsf{Sim}_{\mathcal{D}_V}$ needs to observe the output of the distinguisher on $(a, \mathsf{OT}_2(z^{(0)}, z^{(1)}))$. However, even computing $(a, \mathsf{OT}_2(z^{(0)}, z^{(1)}))$ correctly, requires access to a witness! This is because a correctly compute tuple $(a, z^{(0)}, z^{(1)})$ actually *encodes a witness*.

In the case of witness indistinguishability, this is not a problem – since an "intermediate" simulator for witness indistinguishability has access to both witnesses in question, and therefore *can* generate valid messages $(a, \mathsf{OT}_2(z^0, z^1))$ using both witnesses. It can use these transcripts to learn the verifier's challenge bit, and then use the bit it learned, to generate a simulated transcript for the same receiver message r (where the simulated transcript uses neither of the two witnesses). We mainly rely on OT security to show that the distinguisher $\mathcal{D}_V$ cannot distinguish between the view generated by such a simulator $\mathsf{Sim}_{\mathcal{D}_V}$ and the real view of the verifier, when he interacts with an honest prover that uses only one of the witnesses.

There are additional subtleties in the proof, for instance, in ensuring that the extracted values when the simulator uses one particular witness for learning, do not contradict the values extracted when it uses the other witness. We refer the reader to Sect. 5.3 for a detailed proof.

Distributional Weak Zero-Knowledge. We prove that the same protocol satisfies distributional weak zero-knowledge against non-adaptive verifiers (which can also be easily seen to imply witness-hiding against non-adaptive verifiers). Distributional weak zero-knowledge is a "distributional" relaxation of the standard notion of zero-knowledge where the simulator is additionally allowed to depend on the distribution of instances, and on the distinguisher. This notion roughly requires that for every distribution $\mathcal{X}$ over instances, every verifier V and distinguisher $\mathcal{D}_V$ that obtains the view of V, every $\epsilon = \frac{1}{\mathsf{poly}(\kappa)}$ for some polynomial $\mathsf{poly}(\cdot)$, there exists a simulator $\mathsf{Sim}_{\mathcal{D}_V}$ that runs in time $\mathsf{poly}(1/\epsilon)$ and outputs a view, such that the distinguisher $\mathcal{D}_V$ has at most ϵ-advantage in distinguishing the real view of V from the simulated view.

Fix the first message of the verifier (since the verifier is non-adaptive, this is fixed independently of the instance). The simulator $\mathsf{Sim}_{\mathcal{D}_V}$ obtains as (non-uniform) advice, $\mathsf{poly}(1/\epsilon)$ *randomly chosen* instance-witness pairs from the distribution in question.[11] It then uses these pairs together with the extraction strategy $\mathcal{E}$ described above, to "learn" an approximation to the verifier's implicit challenge string in the fixed verifier message. However, distributional weak zero-knowledge is not known to be closed under parallel composition. Therefore, we modify the simple extraction strategy described previously for a single repetition, so as to extract *all* bits of the verifier's challenge, while still remaining efficient in $\mathsf{poly}(1/\epsilon)$.

This is done inductively: at any time-step $i \in [\kappa]$, the simulator $\mathsf{Sim}_{\mathcal{D}_V}$ has extracted an approximation for the first $(i-1)$ bits of the verifier's challenge, and is now supposed to extract the ith bit. At a high level, the extraction strategy of $\mathsf{Sim}_{\mathcal{D}_V}$ is as follows:

- It generates a "fake" output for the first $(i-1)$ parallel repetitions as follows: for $j \in [i-1]$, if the jth bit of the verifier's challenge was approximated to 0, respond with $a_j, (z_j^0, z_j^0)$ in the jth repetition (and similarly, if it was approximated to 1, respond with $a_j, (z_j^1, z_j^1)$).
- For all $j \in [i+1, \kappa]$ it responds honestly with $a_j, (z_j^0, z_j^1)$ in the jth repetition.
- With outputs for all $j < i$ set to "fake" according to approximated challenge, and for all $j > i$ set to honest, at $j = i$, $\mathsf{Sim}_{\mathcal{D}_V}$ uses the extraction strategy $\mathcal{E}$ described above. That is, for $j = i$, it sets the output to $a_i, (z_i^0, z_i^1), a_i, (z_i^0, z_i^0)$, and $a_i, (z_i^1, z_i^1)$, and checks whether the output of the distinguisher when given inputs corresponding to $a_i, \mathsf{OT}_{2,i}(z_i^0, z_i^1)$ is close to its output when given inputs corresponding to $a_i, \mathsf{OT}_{2,i}(z_i^0, z_i^0)$ or to $a_i, \mathsf{OT}_{2,i}(z_i^i, z_i^i)$. It uses this to approximate the ith bit of the verifier's challenge.

Via an inductive hybrid argument, we prove that with high probability, the approximation computed by $\mathsf{Sim}_{\mathcal{D}_V}$ has at most $\Theta(\epsilon)$-error when $\mathsf{Sim}_{\mathcal{D}_V}$ runs in

---

[11] In most cryptographic applications, and in all our applications, it is possible for the simulator to efficiently sample random instance-witness pairs from the distribution on its own, without the need for any non-uniform advice.

time $\mathsf{poly}(1/\epsilon)$. Once $\mathsf{Sim}_{\mathcal{D}_V}$ has successfully extracted the verifier's challenge, it can use the honest-verifier zero-knowledge simulator of the underlying Σ-protocol as before.

Note that in order to perform extraction, the simulator is required to generate various $a_i, \mathsf{OT}_{2,i}(z_i^0, z_i^1)$ tuples, which it does using the instance-witness pairs it sampled or obtained as advice. $\mathsf{Sim}_{\mathcal{D}_V}$ then uses the challenge it extracted to generate fake proofs for various other $x \leftarrow \mathcal{X}$. Non-adaptivity of the verifier ensures that the simulator can, for a fixed verifier messages, generate proofs for several other statements in the distribution while observing the output of the distinguisher. We refer the reader to Sect. 5.4 for a complete proof.

Three Round Protocols from Polynomial Hardness Assumptions. We also describe how quasi-polynomial assumptions can be avoided at the cost of an extra round. The need for quasi-polynomial assumptions in our two-round protocols is to guarantee soundness: roughly, we require that a cheating prover should be unable to "maul" the receiver's challenge while providing his message. In the two-round setting, this is achieved by ensuring (via complexity leveraging) that the security of receiver OT message is stronger than the security of the prover's response. Three rounds, however, give an opportunity to *rewind* and extract the value inside the prover's message, while relying on (polynomial) hiding of the receiver OT message.

We assume here that the first round of the Σ-protocol consists of commitments to certain values, and the third round consists of decommitments to a subset of these commitments, together with additional auxiliary information (for instance, the Blum protocol for Graph Hamiltonicity satisfies this requirement). We modify the protocol to have the prover send extractable commitments (instead of standard commitments) to commit to the values needed for the first round of the Σ-protocol.

Consider a PPT cheating prover that generates a proof for $x \notin L$. A reduction can obtain the receiver OT message externally as an encryption of some n-bit challenge, and then extract the values committed by the prover. Because the underlying Σ-protocol is special-sound against unbounded provers, any accepting proof for $x \notin L$, will allow recovering the receiver challenge directly by observing the values committed by the prover. We must, however, ensure that adding such extractable commitments does not harm privacy – since our simulator is required to generate several actual proofs before it is able to output a simulated proof. To accomplish this, we design a special kind of (weakly) extracting commitments, details of which can be found in Sect. 5.7. We note here that over-extraction suffices, in particular, we only care about extracting the values committed by provers that generate accepting transcripts.

2.2 Applications

We now describe some applications of our proof systems. As a first step, we describe a transformation from our three-round distributional WZK argument system to an *argument of knowledge*[12] (that retains the distributional weak ZK/strong WI property against non-adaptive verifiers).

Weak ZK/Strong WI Argument of Knowledge. We begin with the following simple idea for a distributional weak ZKAoK, for instances $x \leftarrow \mathcal{X}$: Let us use a delayed-input witness indistinguishable adaptive proof of knowledge (WIPoK), for instance the Lapidot-Shamir proof [48], to prove the following statement:

Either $x \in L$, OR, $\exists$ randomness r such that $c = \mathsf{com}(1^\kappa; r)$.

Here, the commitment string c is also chosen and sent in the last round, together with instance x. Furthermore, to ensure that a (cheating) prover indeed uses the witness for $x \in L$, the prover must also give a weak ZK proof, for the same string c that $\exists r$ such that $c = \mathsf{com}(0^\kappa; r)$. The argument of knowledge property of this protocol now follows from the proof of knowledge property of WIPoK, the soundness of the weak ZK argument, and the statistical binding property of the commitment scheme. Specifically, by adaptive soundness of the weak ZK proof, c must indeed be constructed as a commitment to 0^κ; moreover, by the statistical binding property of the commitment scheme, the same string c cannot be a commitment to 1^κ. Therefore, the only possible witness that can be extracted from the WIPoK is indeed a witness for the instance x.

To prove weak ZK/strong WI property for the same protocol, we would ideally like to have the following sequence of hybrid arguments: First, we start simulating the weak ZK proof, by observing the output of the distinguisher on several different instances from the distribution $\mathcal{X}$, while using correct witnesses for these instances. We then use the information learned to simulate the weak ZK proof for c obtained externally in the main transcript. Since the string c is not used in the main thread at all, we change it so that $\mathsf{com}(0^\kappa; r)$ for uniformly random r. Next, we must begin using (c, r) as witnesses in the WIPoK, instead of using the witness for x.

It is in this step that there arises a subtle issue, because of the way our simulator works. In each experiment, before it can generate a simulated proof, it must first generate several real proofs for other random instances. We require the WIPoK to maintain witness indistinguishability, *even when the simulator provides multiple proofs for different instances using the same first two messages.* This is in general, not true for proof systems such as Lapidot-Shamir [48]. This is also not as strong a requirement as resettable-WI [16] since the verifier's message is fixed and remains the same for all proofs.

We refer to this property as *reusable* WI and construct an adaptively sound argument of knowledge satisfying this property. The argument of knowledge works by the prover sending two three-round extractable commitments (with "over" extraction) [55,56] to random strings, encrypting the witness with each of these strings using standard private key encryption, and sending a three-round delayed-input reusable WI argument (this does not need to be an argument

---

[12] Despite using a variant of extractable commitments, the three-round argument described in the previous section not a standard AoK in the delayed-input setting.

of knowledge, and could be instantiated with a ZAP, or with our three round arguments) to establish that one of the two commitments is a valid extractable commitment, and the corresponding ciphertext correctly encrypts the witness. The use of private key encryption gives us the additional desired property of reusability.

Extractable Commitments. Given the weak ZK argument of knowledge, our construction of three-round extractable commitments simply consists of sending a non-interactive statistically binding commitment to the message in the last round, together with a (distributional) weak ZK argument of knowledge to establish knowledge of the committed message and randomness. The weak ZK property helps prove hiding of this scheme, while the proof of knowledge property guarantees correct polynomial-time extraction, with overwhelming probability. We refer the reader to the full version for details.

Three Round, Two Party, Input-Indistinguishable Secure Computation. We begin by considering the following two-round protocol for two-party computation: The receiver generates OT messages corresponding to his inputs, together with the first message of a two-round weak ZK argument. Then, the sender generates garbled circuits corresponding to his own input labels, together with the second message of the two-round weak ZK argument.

This protocol already satisfies input-indistinguishable security against malicious receivers, as well as distinguisher-dependent security against malicious receivers, when an honest sender's input is sampled from some public distribution. Even though our weak ZK proof guarantees hiding against malicious receivers, security is not immediate. Indeed, we must first *extract* an adversarial receiver's input from his OT messages, and weak ZK does not help with that. Thus, apart from simulating the weak ZK, we must use our extraction strategy in this context, in order to (distributionally) learn the receiver's input.

In the full version, we describe applications of our techniques to obtaining input-indistinguishable secure computation, as well as distributional distinguisher-dependent secure computation in three rounds from polynomial assumptions. In particular, we also note that a large class of functionalities such as coin tossing, generating common *reference* strings, oblivious PRFs, etc. (that we call *independent-input functions*) are distributional by definition, and can be realized with distinguisher-dependent polynomial simulation security in three rounds.

3   Preliminaries

Throughout this paper, we will use κ to denote the security parameter, and $\mathsf{negl}(\kappa)$ to denote any function that is asymptotically smaller than $\frac{1}{\mathsf{poly}(\kappa)}$ for any polynomial $\mathsf{poly}(\cdot)$.

Definition 1 (Σ-protocols). *Let $L \in \mathsf{NP}$ with corresponding witness relation R_L, and let x denote an instance with corresponding witness $w(x)$. A protocol*

$\Pi = (P, V)$ *is a Σ-protocol for relation R_L if it is a three-round public-coin protocol, and the following requirements hold:*

- **Completeness:** $\Pr[\langle P(x, w(x)), V(x)\rangle = 1] = 1 - \mathsf{negl}(\kappa)$, *assuming P and V follow the protocol honestly.*
- **Special Soundness:** *There exists a polynomial-time algorithm A that given any x and a pair of accepting transcripts $(a, e, z), (a, e', z')$ for x with the same first prover message, where $e \neq e'$, outputs w such that $w \in R_L(x)$.*
- **Honest verifier zero-knowledge:** *There exists a probabilistic polynomial time simulator S_Σ such that*

$$\{S_\Sigma(x, e)\}_{x \in L, e \in \{0,1\}^\kappa} \approx_c \{\langle P(x, w(x)), V(x, e)\rangle\}_{x \in L, e \in \{0,1\}^\kappa}$$

where $S_\Sigma(x, e)$ denotes the output of simulator S upon input x and e, and $\langle P(x, w(x)), V(x, e)\rangle$ denotes the output transcript of an execution between P and V, where P has input (x, w), V has input x and V's random tape (determining its query) is e.

Definition 2 (Oblivious Transfer). *Oblivious transfer is a protocol between two parties, a sender S with messages (m_0, m_1) and receiver R with input a choice bit b, such that R obtains output m_b at the end of the protocol. We let $\langle S(m_0, m_1), R(b)\rangle$ denote an execution of the OT protocol with sender input (m_0, m_1) and receiver input bit b. It additionally satisfies the following properties.*

Receiver Security. *For any sender S^*, all auxiliary inputs $z \in \{0,1\}^*$, and all $(b, b') \in \{0,1\}$, $\mathsf{View}_{S^*}(\langle S^*(z), R(b)\rangle) \approx_c \mathsf{View}_{S^*}(\langle S^*(z), R(b')\rangle)$.*

Sender Security. *This is defined using the real-ideal paradigm, and requires that for all auxiliary inputs $z \in \{0,1\}^*$, every distribution on the inputs (m_0, m_1) and any adversarial receiver R^*, there exists a (possibly unbounded) simulator Sim_{R^*} that interacts with an ideal functionality $\mathcal{F}_{\mathsf{ot}}$ on behalf of R^*. Here $\mathcal{F}_{\mathsf{ot}}$ is an oracle that obtains the inputs (m_0, m_1) from the sender and b from the Sim_{R^*} (simulating the malicious receiver), and outputs m_b to Sim_{R^*}. Then $\mathsf{Sim}_{R^*}^{\mathcal{F}_{\mathsf{ot}}}$ outputs a receiver view V_{Sim} that is computationally indistinguishable from the real view of the malicious receiver $\mathsf{View}_{R^*}(\langle S(m_0, m_1, z), R^*\rangle)$.*

We will make use of **two-message** oblivious-transfer protocols with security against malicious receivers and semi-honest senders. Such protocols have been constructed based on the DDH assumption [51], and a stronger variant of smooth-projective hashing, which can be realized from DDH as well as the Nth-residuosity and Quadratic Residuosity assumptions [43,45]. Such protocols can also be based on indistinguishability obfuscation (iO) together with one-way functions [57].

We will use the following sender security property in our protocols (which is implied by the definition of sender security in Definition 2 above). For any fixed first message generated by a malicious receiver R^*, we require that either of the following statements is true:

- For all m_0, m_1, $\mathsf{View}_{R^*}\langle S(m_0, m_1, z), R^*\rangle) \approx_c \mathsf{View}_{R^*}(\langle S(m_0, m_0, z), R^*\rangle)$
- Or, for all m_0, m_1, $\mathsf{View}_{R^*}(\langle S(m_0, m_1, z), R^*\rangle) \approx_c \mathsf{View}_{R^*}(\langle S(m_1, m_1, z), R^*\rangle)$

This follows from the (unbounded) simulation property, i.e., there exists a simulator that extracts some receiver input b from the first message of R^*, sends it to the ideal functionality, obtains m_b and generates an indistinguishable receiver view. Then, by the definition of sender security, the simulated view must be close to both $\mathsf{View}_{R^*}(\langle S(m_0, m_1, z), R^* \rangle)$, and $\mathsf{View}_{R^*}(\langle S(m_b, m_b, z), R^* \rangle)$.

We also note that all the aforementioned instantiations of two-message oblivious-transfer are additionally secure against *unbounded* malicious receivers.

4 Definitions

4.1 Proof Systems

Delayed-Input Interactive Protocols. An n-round delayed-input interactive protocol (P, V) for deciding a language L with associated relation R_L proceeds in the following manner:

- At the beginning of the protocol, P and V receive the size of the instance and execute the first $n - 1$ rounds.
- At the start of the last round, P receives an input $(x, w) \in R_L$ and V receives x. Upon receiving the last round message from P, V outputs 1 or 0.

An execution of (P, V) with instance x and witness w is denoted as $\langle P, V \rangle (x, w)$. Whenever clear from context, we also use the same notation to denote the output of V.

Delayed-Input Interactive Arguments. An n-round delayed-input interactive argument for a language L must satisfy the standard notion of completeness as well as *adaptive soundness*, where the soundness requirement holds even against malicious PPT provers who choose the statement adaptively, depending upon the first $n - 1$ rounds of the protocol.

Definition 3 (Delayed-Input Interactive Arguments). *An n-round delayed-input interactive protocol (P, V) for deciding a language L is an interactive argument for L if it satisfies the following properties:*

- **Completeness:** *For every $(x, w) \in R_L$,*

$$\Pr[\langle P, V \rangle (x, w) = 1] \geq 1 - \mathsf{negl}(\kappa),$$

  where the probability is over the random coins of P and V.
- **Adaptive Soundness:** *For every $z \in \{0, 1\}^*$, every PPT prover P^* that chooses $x \in \{0, 1\}^\kappa \setminus L$ adaptively, depending upon the first $n - 1$ rounds,*

$$\Pr[\langle P^*(z), V \rangle (x) = 1] \leq \mathsf{negl}(\kappa),$$

  where the probability is over the random coins of V.

Witness Indistinguishability. A proof system is witness indistinguishable if for any statement with at least two witnesses, proofs computed using different witnesses are indistinguishable.

Definition 4 (Witness Indistinguishability). *A delayed-input interactive argument (P, V) for a language L is said to be* witness-indistinguishable *if for every non-uniform PPT verifier V^*, every $z \in \{0,1\}^*$, and every sequence (x, w_1, w_2) such that $w_1, w_2 \in R_L(x)$, the following two ensembles are computationally indistinguishable:*

$$\{\langle P, V^*(z)\rangle(x, w_1)\} \text{ and } \{\langle P, V^*(z)\rangle(x, w_2)\}$$

Non-adaptive Distributional Weak Zero Knowledge. Zero knowledge (ZK) requires that for any adversarial verifier, there exists a simulator that can produce a view that is indistinguishable from the real one to *every* distinguisher. Weak zero knowledge (WZK) relaxes the standard notion of ZK by reversing the order of quantifiers, and allowing the simulator to depend on the distinguisher.

We consider a variant of WZK, namely, distributional WZK [28,34], where the instances are chosen from some hard distribution over the language. Furthermore, we allow the simulator's running time to depend upon the distinguishing probability of the distinguisher. We refer to this as distributional ϵ-WZK, which says that for every distinguisher D with distinguishing probability ϵ (where ϵ is an inverse polynomial) there exists a simulator with running time polynomial in ϵ. This notion was previously considered in [19,28].

We define distributional ϵ-WZK property against *non-adaptive* malicious verifiers that receive the instance only in the last round of the protocol.

Definition 5 (Non-adaptive Distributional ϵ-Weak Zero Knowledge). *A delayed-input interactive argument (P, V) for a language L is said to be* distributional ϵ-weak zero knowledge against non-adaptive verifiers *if for every efficiently samplable distribution $(\mathcal{X}_\kappa, \mathcal{W}_\kappa)$ on R_L, i.e., $\mathsf{Supp}(\mathcal{X}_\kappa, \mathcal{W}_\kappa) = \{(x, w) : x \in L \cap \{0,1\}^\kappa, w \in R_L(x)\}$, every non-adaptive PPT verifier V^*, every $z \in \{0,1\}^*$, every PPT distinguisher $\mathcal{D}$, and every $\epsilon = 1/\mathsf{poly}(\kappa)$, there exists a simulator $\mathcal{S}$ that runs in time $\mathsf{poly}(\kappa, \epsilon)$ such that:*

$$\left| \Pr_{(x,w) \leftarrow (\mathcal{X}_\kappa, \mathcal{W}_\kappa)} \left[\mathcal{D}(x, z, \mathsf{View}_{V^*}[\langle P, V^*(z)\rangle(x, w)] = 1 \right] \right.$$

$$\left. - \Pr_{(x,w) \leftarrow (\mathcal{X}_\kappa, \mathcal{W}_\kappa)} \left[\mathcal{D}(x, z, \mathcal{S}^{V^*, D}(x, z)) = 1 \right] \right| \leq \epsilon(\kappa),$$

where the probability is over the random choices of (x, w) as well as the random coins of the parties.

Non-adaptive Witness Hiding. Let L be an NP language and let $(\mathcal{X}, \mathcal{W})$ be a distribution over the associated relation R_L. A proof system is witness hiding w.r.t. $(\mathcal{X}, \mathcal{W})$ if for any $(x, w) \leftarrow (\mathcal{X}, \mathcal{W})$, a proof for x is "one-way" in the sense that no verifier can extract a witness for x from its interaction with the prover. Note that in order for WH to be non-trivial, it is necessary that $(\mathcal{X}, \mathcal{W})$ be a "hard" distribution.

Below, we define witness hiding property against *non-adaptive* malicious verifiers that receive the instance only in the last round of the protocol.

Definition 6 (Hard Distributions). *Let $(\mathcal{X}, \mathcal{W}) = (\mathcal{X}_\kappa, \mathcal{W}_\kappa)_{\kappa \in \mathbb{N}}$ be an efficiently samplable distribution on R_L, i.e., $\mathsf{Supp}(\mathcal{X}_\kappa, \mathcal{W}_\kappa) = \{(x, w) : x \in L \cap \{0,1\}^\kappa, w \in R_L(x)\}$. We say that $(\mathcal{X}, \mathcal{W})$ is hard if for any poly-size circuit family $\{C_\kappa\}$, it holds that:*

$$\Pr_{(x,w) \leftarrow (\mathcal{X}_\kappa, \mathcal{W}_\kappa)} \left[C_\kappa(x) \in R_L(x) \right] \leq \mathsf{negl}(\kappa).$$

Definition 7 (Non-adaptive Witness Hiding). *A delayed-input interactive argument (P, V) for a language L is said to be witness hiding against non-adaptive verifiers w.r.t. a hard distribution $(\mathcal{X}_\kappa, \mathcal{W}_\kappa)$ if for every non-adaptive PPT verifier V^*, every $z \in \{0,1\}^*$, it holds that:*

$$\Pr_{(x,w) \leftarrow (\mathcal{X}_\kappa, \mathcal{W}_\kappa)} \left[\langle P, V^*(z) \rangle(x) \in R_L(x) \right] \leq \mathsf{negl}(\kappa).$$

Non-adaptive Strong Witness Indistinguishability

Definition 8 (Non-adaptive Strong Witness Indistinguishability). *A delayed-input interactive argument (P, V) for a language L is said to be strong witness indistinguishable against non-adaptive verifiers w.r.t. a pair of indistinguishable distributions $(\mathcal{X}_{1,\kappa}, \mathcal{W}_{1,\kappa}), (\mathcal{X}_{2,\kappa}, \mathcal{W}_{2,\kappa})$ if for every non-adaptive PPT verifier V^*, every $z \in \{0,1\}^*$, it holds that:*

$$\left| \Pr_{(x,w) \leftarrow (\mathcal{X}_{1,\kappa}, \mathcal{W}_{1,\kappa})} \left[\mathcal{D}(x, z, \mathsf{View}_{V^*}[\langle P, V^*(z) \rangle(x, w)]) = 1 \right] \right.$$

$$\left. - \Pr_{(x,w) \leftarrow (\mathcal{X}_{2,\kappa}, \mathcal{W}_{2,\kappa})} \left[\mathcal{D}(x, z, \mathsf{View}_{V^*}[\langle P, V^*(z) \rangle(x, w)]) = 1 \right] \right| \leq \mathsf{negl}(\kappa).$$

Remark 1. A non-adaptive distributional weak ZK argument of knowledge is an argument of knowledge that satisfies the distributional weak ZK property against non-adaptive verifiers. Similarly, a non-adaptive strong WI argument of knowledge is an argument of knowledge that satisfies the strong WI property against non-adaptive verifiers. Finally, a non-adaptive witness hiding argument of knowledge can be defined similarly as an argument of knowledge that satisfies the witness hiding property against non-adaptive verifiers.

5 Two Round Argument Systems

5.1 Construction

We show how to use two-message malicious-secure oblivious transfer (OT) to convert any three-message Σ-protocol according to Definition 1, into a two-message argument system. We then prove soundness of the resulting argument system, assuming sub-exponential security of oblivious transfer. We also prove that this protocol is witness indistinguishable, satisfies distributional weak zero-knowledge, strong WI and witness hiding against non-adaptive verifiers.

Let $\mathsf{OT} = (\mathsf{OT}_1, \mathsf{OT}_2)$ denote a two-message bit oblivious transfer protocol according to Definition 2. Let $\mathsf{OT}_1(b)$ denote the first message of the OT protocol with receiver input b, and let $\mathsf{OT}_2(m_0, m_1)$ denote the second message of the OT protocol with sender input bits m_0, m_1.

Let $\Sigma = (a, e, z)$ denote the three messages of a Σ-protocol. For most of this paper, we consider Σ-protocols that are a parallel composition of individual protocols with a single-bit challenge and constant soundness, i.e., the Σ-protocol contains three messages, denoted by (a, e, z) and that these messages can be parsed as $a = (a_1, \ldots, a_\kappa)$, $e = (e_1, \ldots, e_\kappa)$, and $z = (z_1, \ldots, z_\kappa)$, where for each $i \in [\kappa]$, the triplet (a_i, e_i, z_i) are messages corresponding to an underlying Σ-protocol with a single-bit challenge (i.e., where $e_i \in \{0, 1\}$). We denote by f_1 and f_2 the functions that satisfy $a_i = f_1(x, w; r_i)$ and $z_i = f_2(x, w, r_i, e_i)$, where r_i is uniformly chosen randomness.

Examples of such Σ-protocols are the parallel Blum proof of Graph Hamiltonicity [13], and the Lapidot-Shamir [48] three round WI proof. By a Karp reduction to Graph Hamiltonicity, there exists such a Σ-protocol for all of NP.

5.2   Adaptive Soundness

The protocol in Fig. 1 compiles a three-round public coin proof to a two-round argument using oblivious transfer. Kalai-Raz [46] proved that such a compiler, applied to any public-coin proof system preserves soundness. Specifically, the following theorem in [46] proves (static) soundness of the above protocol, assuming sub-exponential oblivious transfer.

Imported Theorem 1. *(Rephrased) Let $\Sigma = (a, e, z)$ denote a Σ-protocol, and let $\ell = \mathsf{poly}(\kappa, s)$ be the size of z, where κ is the security parameter, and s is an upper bound on the length of allowed instances. Assuming the existence of an oblivious transfer protocol secure against probabilistic senders running in time at most 2^ℓ, the protocol in Fig. 1 is sound.*

Witness Indistinguishable and Weak Distributional Zero-Knowledge Argument

Prover Input: Instance $x \in L$, witness w such that $R_L(x, w) = 1$.
Verifier Input: Instance x, language L.

- **Verifier Message:** The verifier picks challenge $e \xleftarrow{\$} \{0, 1\}^\kappa$ for the Σ-protocol, and for $i \in [\kappa]$, sends $\mathsf{OT}_{1,i}(e_i)$ in parallel. Each bit e_i is encrypted with a fresh OT instance.
- **Prover Message:** For $i \in [\kappa]$, the prover sends a_i, $\mathsf{OT}_{2,i}(z_i^0, z_i^1)$ in parallel.
- **Verifier Output:** The verifier V recovers z_i as the output of OT_i for $i \in [\kappa]$, and outputs accept if for all $i \in [\kappa]$, $(a_i, e_i, z_i)_{i \in [\kappa]}$ is an accepting transcript of the underlying Σ-protocol.

Fig. 1. Two round argument system for NP

We observe that the proof in Kalai-Raz [46] can be extended to prove adaptive soundness, i.e., soundness against malicious provers that can adaptively choose $x \notin L$ based on the verifier's input message.

Lemma 1. *Let $\Sigma = (a, e, z)$ denote a Σ-protocol, and let ℓ be the size of z. Assuming the existence of an oblivious transfer protocol secure against probabilistic senders running in time at most 2^ℓ, the protocol in Fig. 1 is adaptively sound.*

Proof. We will use a prover that breaks soundness to break sub-exponential receiver security of the underlying oblivious transfer. The reduction samples two random challenge strings e_0, e_1 and reduction sends them to an external OT challenger. The external OT challenger picks $b \xleftarrow{\$} \{0, 1\}$, and outputs $\mathsf{OT}_1(e_{i,b})$ for $i \in [\kappa]$, which the reduction forwards to the cheating prover P^*.

P^* outputs $x \notin L$, together with messages a_i, $\mathsf{OT}_2(z_i^0, z_i^1)$ for $i \in [\kappa]$. Next, the reduction R does a brute-force search over all possible values of z, checking whether (a, e_0, z) is an accepting transcript for any $z \in \{0, 1\}^\ell$ and whether (a, e_1, z') is an accepting transcript for any $z' \in \{0, 1\}^\ell$.

Suppose a cheating prover breaks soundness with probability $p = \frac{1}{\mathsf{poly}(\kappa)}$ over the randomness of the experiment. Since the reduction chooses prover messages e_0, e_1 uniformly at random, with probability p, the prover P^* outputs a_i^*, $\mathsf{OT}_2(z_i^0, z_i^1)$ for $i \in [\kappa]$ that cause the verifier to accept.

Thus, with probability p, R finds at least one z such that (a^*, e_b, z) is an accepting transcript.

Since $e_{\bar{b}}$ was picked uniformly at random and independent of e_b, we argue that with at most $\mathsf{negl}(\kappa)$ probability, R finds one or more z' such that $(a^*, e_{\bar{b}}, z')$ is an accepting transcript. Note that with probability $1 - 2^{-\kappa}$, we have that $e_b \neq e_{\bar{b}}$. By special-soundness of the underlying Σ-protocol, if there exists z' such that $(a^*, e_{\bar{b}}, z')$ is an accepting transcript, conditioned on $e_b \neq e_{\bar{b}}$, this would allow obtaining a witness w from (a, e_b, z) and $(a, e_{\bar{b}}, z')$, which is a contradiction since $x \notin L$.

Therefore, if R finds z such that (a^*, e_b, z) is an accepting transcript, R outputs e_b as its guess for the first OT message, and this guess is correct with probability at least $p - \mathsf{negl}(\kappa)$. Since R runs in time 2^ℓ and guesses the OT message with non-negligible probability, this is a contradiction to the security of OT against 2^ℓ-time malicious senders.

Observing the Verifier's output. The protocol is not sound when the prover is allowed to generate a-priori unbounded arguments using the same verifier message, as an adaptive function of the *verifier's accept/reject outputs on prior arguments*. Looking ahead, such a prover can use the simulation strategy from Sect. 5.4 to explicitly break soundness.

However, the protocol is sound when the prover is only allowed to generate an *a-priori bounded* arguments that adaptively depend on the verifier's accept/reject outputs on prior arguments. This can be ensured via simply having the verifier output a longer challenge string – to obtain adaptive soundness for B executions, the protocol requires the verifier to generate $e \xleftarrow{\$} \{0,1\}^{\kappa \cdot B}$, and encrypt it using $\kappa \cdot B$ OT instances. The prover uses the first κ instances for the first argument, the second set of κ instances for the second, and so forth. It is easy to see then that the argument of Lemma 1 easily extends to the bounded execution case.

5.3   Witness Indistinguishability

We have the following theorem, the proof of which can be found in the full version of the paper.

Theorem 6. *Assuming two-round oblivious transfer (OT) secure against malicious PPT receivers, the two-round protocol in Fig. 1 is witness-indistinguishable against PPT verifiers.*

Recall that witness indistinguishability (WI) is closed under parallel composition [29], therefore it suffices to prove WI for a single repetition (i.e., for some $i \in [\kappa]$) of the protocol in Fig. 1. Our proof proceeds via a sequence of hybrid arguments, where, in an intermediate hybrid, we construct a distinguisher-dependent simulator, that learns (using both witnesses w_1 and w_2), an approximation for the verifier's challenge e. Upon learning the challenge, the simulator uses the honest-verifier ZK property to generate a simulated proof, without using any of the witnesses.

5.4   Distributional Weak Zero Knowledge

In this section, we have the following theorem:

Theorem 7. *Assuming oblivious transfer (OT) secure against malicious PPT receivers, the protocol in Fig. 1 is distributional weak zero-knowledge against non-adaptive verifiers.*

Proof. (Overview) The proof of weak zero-knowledge is more involved that WI, because weak ZK is not closed under parallel composition. We develop an inductive analysis and a simulation strategy that learns the receiver's challenge bit-by-bit.

Fix any PPT V^*, any distinguisher $\mathcal{D}$, any distribution $(\mathcal{X}, \mathcal{W}, \mathcal{Z})$, and any $\epsilon > 0$. We construct a simulator Sim_ϵ that obtains non-uniform advice z, $p_\epsilon = \mathrm{poly}(1/\epsilon)$ random instance-witness samples $(x_1^*, w_1^*), (x_2^*, w_2^*), \ldots (x_{p_\epsilon}^*, w_{p_\epsilon}^*)$ from the distribution $(\mathcal{X}, \mathcal{W})$. Or, if the distribution $(\mathcal{X}, \mathcal{W})$ is efficiently samplable, Sim_ϵ samples $(x_1^*, w_1^*), (x_2^*, w_2^*), \ldots (x_{p_\epsilon}^*, w_{p_\epsilon}^*)$ these on its own.

At a high level, the simulator uses these instances to approximately-learn the verifier's challenge string e (call this approximation e_{approx}), and then generates a transcript corresponding to a random $x \sim \mathcal{X}$, by using the honest-verifier ZK simulation strategy of the underlying Σ-protocol, corresponding to verifier challenge e_{approx}. Our simulation strategy can be found, together with the complete proof, in the full version of the paper.

5.5   Strong Witness Indistinguishability

We note that the simulator's learning is monotone for two distributions, i.e., given two distributions $\mathcal{X}_1, \mathcal{X}_2$, then the view generated by a simulator Sim_ϵ that learns using samples from both distributions, $\mathcal{X}_1 \cup \mathcal{X}_2$, but outputs the simulation for a sample from $\mathcal{X}_1$, is indistinguishable from the view generated by a simulator Sim_ϵ that learns using samples from only $\mathcal{X}_1$ and then outputs the simulation for a sample from $\mathcal{X}_1$.

In other words, learning using additional distributions can only provide "more" information to the simulator. This observation coupled with the proof of weak ZK, directly implies strong witness indistinguishability, when the instances are sampled either from distribution $\mathcal{X}_1$ or from (an indistinguishable) distribution $\mathcal{X}_2$. This is because, the simulator can learn (in all hybrids) using instances from $\mathcal{X}_1 \cup \mathcal{X}_2$, and use these to simulate external samples generated according to either $\mathcal{X}_1$ or $\mathcal{X}_2$.

Corollary 8. *Assuming oblivious transfer (OT) secure against malicious PPT receivers, the protocol in Fig. 1 is strong witness-indistinguishable against non-adaptive verifiers.*

5.6   Witness Hiding

It is easy to see that distributional weak zero-knowledge implies witness hiding. Suppose there exists a distribution $\mathcal{X}_\kappa$ and a PPT verifier V^* with auxiliary input z, that interacts with prover P. P samples random $X \sim \mathcal{X}_\kappa$ together with some witness $W(X)$ and generates a proof for V^* – such that V^* outputs a witness for $X \in \mathcal{X}$ with probability $\gamma = \frac{1}{\mathsf{poly}(\kappa)}$ for some polynomial $\mathsf{poly}(\cdot)$. Then, by the distributional weak zero-knowledge property, there exists a non-uniform simulator Sim_ϵ that uses V^* to output a witness for $X \sim \mathcal{X}$ with probability at least $\gamma - \epsilon$. Setting $\epsilon = \frac{\gamma}{2}$, we obtain a non-uniform polynomial size circuit $(\mathsf{Sim}_\epsilon, V^*)$ that outputs a witness for $X \sim \mathcal{X}$ with probability at least $\gamma/2$, which is a contradiction to the assumption in Definition 7. This implies the following corollary.

Corollary 9. *Assuming two-message oblivious transfer (OT) secure against malicious PPT receivers, the protocol in Fig. 1 is witness-hiding against non-adaptive verifiers.*

5.7   Extensions

In this section, we sketch some simple extensions of our main results.

Two Round WI and Distributional WZK from *any* Σ-Protocol. So far, we assumed that the Σ-protocol contains three messages, denoted by (a, e, z) and that these messages can be parsed as $a = (a_1, \ldots, a_\kappa)$, $e = (e_1, \ldots, e_\kappa)$, and $z = (z_1, \ldots, z_\kappa)$, where for each $i \in [\kappa]$, the triplet (a_i, e_i, z_i) are messages corresponding to an underlying Σ-protocol with a single-bit challenge (i.e., where $e_i \in \{0,1\}$). We denote by f_1 and f_2 the functions that satisfy $a_i = f_1(x, w; r_i)$ and $z_i = f_2(x, w, r_i, e_i)$, where r_i is uniformly chosen randomness.

However, there is a large class of Σ-protocols that do not have this special structure. In Fig. 2, we describe how any Σ-protocol can be compiled into 2-message WI and 2-message distributional weak ZK, assuming 2-message malicious-secure OT and garbled circuits. Our protocol is described in Fig. 2.

Witness Indistinguishable and Distributional Weak Zero-Knowledge Argument
Prover Input: Instance $x \in L$, witness w such that $R_L(x, w) = 1$.
Verifier Input: Instance x, language L.

- **Verifier Message:** The verifier picks challenge $e \xleftarrow{\$} \{0,1\}^\kappa$ for the Σ-protocol, and for $i \in [\kappa]$, sends $\mathsf{OT}_{1,i}(e_i)$ in parallel. Each e_i is encrypted with a fresh OT instance.
- **Prover Message:** The prover samples a, and then constructs a garbled circuit $\mathsf{GC}(a, \cdot)$ for a function that on input e (the verifier challenge), outputs the corresponding message z of the underlying Σ-protocol. Let $(\mathsf{label}_i^0, \mathsf{label}_i^1)_{i \in [\kappa]}$ denote the labels of the garbled circuit. The prover sends a, $\mathsf{GC}(a, \cdot)$, together with $\mathsf{OT}_{2,i}(\mathsf{label}_i^0, \mathsf{label}_i^1)$ for all $i \in [\kappa]$.
- **Verifier Output:** The verifier V recovers z as the output of the garbled circuit on the labels obtained via OT, and outputs accept if (a, e, z) is an accepting transcript of the underlying Σ-protocol.

Fig. 2. Two round argument system for NP from any Σ-protocol

Three Round Protocols from Polynomial Assumptions. Our three round protocol from polynomial assumptions is described in Fig. 3. We denote the three messages of a Σ-protocol by (a, e, z), and assume that the Σ-protocol is a parallel repetition of protocols with a single bit receiver challenge. We further

---

Witness Indistinguishable and Distributional Weak Zero-Knowledge
Prover Input: Instance $x \in L$, witness w such that $R_L(x, w) = 1$.
Verifier Input: Instance x, language L.

- **Prover Message:** Pick $r_1, r_2, r_1', r_2' \xleftarrow{\$} \{0,1\}^*$, send $c_1 = \mathsf{com}(r_1; r_1'), c_2 = \mathsf{com}(r_2; r_2')$ using non-interactive statistically binding commitment com. Also, send wi_1 as the first message of the WI argument.
- **Verifier Message:** Pick challenge $e \xleftarrow{\$} \{0,1\}^\kappa$ for the Σ-protocol, and for $i \in [\kappa]$, send $\mathsf{OT}_{1,i}(e_i)$ in parallel. Each e_i is encrypted with a fresh OT instance. Additionally send $\tilde{r} \xleftarrow{\$} \{0,1\}^*$, and send wi_2 as the second message of the WI argument.
- **Prover Message:** Send r_1, r_2 with wi_3 as the third message of the WI argument proving that $\exists r_1'$ such that $c_1 = \mathsf{com}(r_1; r_1')$ OR $\exists r_2'$ such that $c_2 = \mathsf{com}(r_2; r_2')$. Set $\mathsf{pk}_1 = r_1 \oplus \tilde{r}, \mathsf{pk}_2 = r_2 \oplus \tilde{r}$ as public keys for a dense cryptosystem.
  Define $\mathsf{commit}(M; R) = \mathsf{enc}_{\mathsf{pk}_1}(M; s_1), \mathsf{enc}_{\mathsf{pk}_2}(M; s_2)$ and $R = s_1 \| s_2$, which is decommitted by revealing R. For $i \in [\kappa]$, and send $\mathsf{commit}(h_i), \mathsf{OT}_{2,i}(z_i^0, z_i^1)$ in parallel using the scheme commit. The decommitment information in z_i^0, z_i^1 corresponding to any commitment, only consists of the randomness R used to generate the commitment using commit.
- **Verifier Output:** The verifier V recovers z_i as the output of OT_i for $i \in [\kappa]$, and outputs accept if $(a_i, e_i, z_i)_{i \in [\kappa]}$ is an accepting transcript of the underlying Σ-protocol, according to the commitment scheme commit.

Fig. 3. Three round argument system for NP

assume that a consists of a string of commitments, and z contains decommitment information for some of these commitments. We denote the ith set of commitments (in the ith parallel repetition of the Σ-protocol) by $a_i = \mathsf{commit}(h_i)$. We will implement this commitment differently in our protocol in Fig. 3. We let com denote a non-interactive statistically binding commitment scheme, and let $\mathsf{wi} = (\mathsf{wi}_1, \mathsf{wi}_2, \mathsf{wi}_3)$ denote the messages of a 3-message delayed-input WI argument for NP. We also assume the existence of dense cryptosystems which are known based on DDH, QR, RSA, etc.

Theorem 10. *There exists a 3-message argument that satisfies distributional weak zero-knowledge, strong witness indistinguishability, witness hiding and witness indistinguishability against non-adaptive malicious verifiers, assuming either polynomially-hard DDH, N^{th}-residuosity or Quadratic Residuosity.*

The proof of soundness, and privacy against malicious verifiers, of the scheme in Fig. 3 is deferred to the full version of the paper.

References

1. Aiello, W., Bhatt, S., Ostrovsky, R., Rajagopalan, S.R.: Fast verification of any remote procedure call: short witness-indistinguishable one-round proofs for NP. In: Montanari, U., Rolim, J.D.P., Welzl, E. (eds.) ICALP 2000. LNCS, vol. 1853, pp. 463–474. Springer, Heidelberg (2000). doi:10.1007/3-540-45022-X_39
2. Badrinarayanan, S., Garg, S., Ishai, Y., Sahai, A., Wadia, A.: Two-message witness indistinguishability and secure computation in the plain model from new assumptions. IACR Cryptology ePrint Archive 2017/433 (2017). http://eprint.iacr.org/2017/433
3. Barak, B.: How to go beyond the black-box simulation barrier. In: FOCS, pp. 106–115 (2001)
4. Barak, B., Goldreich, O., Impagliazzo, R., Rudich, S., Sahai, A., Vadhan, S., Yang, K.: On the (Im)possibility of obfuscating programs. In: Kilian, J. (ed.) CRYPTO 2001. LNCS, vol. 2139, pp. 1–18. Springer, Heidelberg (2001). doi:10.1007/3-540-44647-8_1
5. Bellare, M., Palacio, A.: The knowledge-of-exponent assumptions and 3-round zero-knowledge protocols. In: Franklin, M. (ed.) CRYPTO 2004. LNCS, vol. 3152, pp. 273–289. Springer, Heidelberg (2004). doi:10.1007/978-3-540-28628-8_17
6. Bellare, M., Stepanovs, I., Tessaro, S.: Contention in cryptoland: obfuscation, leakage and UCE. In: Kushilevitz, E., Malkin, T. (eds.) TCC 2016. LNCS, vol. 9563, pp. 542–564. Springer, Heidelberg (2016). doi:10.1007/978-3-662-49099-0_20
7. Bitansky, N., Brakerski, Z., Kalai, Y., Paneth, O., Vaikuntanathan, V.: 3-message zero knowledge against human ignorance. In: Hirt, M., Smith, A. (eds.) TCC 2016. LNCS, vol. 9985, pp. 57–83. Springer, Heidelberg (2016). doi:10.1007/978-3-662-53641-4_3
8. Bitansky, N., Canetti, R.: On strong simulation and composable point obfuscation. In: Rabin, T. (ed.) CRYPTO 2010. LNCS, vol. 6223, pp. 520–537. Springer, Heidelberg (2010). doi:10.1007/978-3-642-14623-7_28
9. Bitansky, N., Canetti, R., Paneth, O., Rosen, A.: On the existence of extractable one-way functions. In: Symposium on Theory of Computing, STOC 2014, New York, 31 May–03 June 2014, pp. 505–514 (2014)

10. Bitansky, N., Paneth, O.: Point obfuscation and 3-round zero-knowledge. In: Cramer, R. (ed.) TCC 2012. LNCS, vol. 7194, pp. 190–208. Springer, Heidelberg (2012). doi:10.1007/978-3-642-28914-9_11

11. Bitansky, N., Paneth, O.: ZAPs and non-interactive witness indistinguishability from indistinguishability obfuscation. In: Dodis, Y., Nielsen, J.B. (eds.) TCC 2015. LNCS, vol. 9015, pp. 401–427. Springer, Heidelberg (2015). doi:10.1007/978-3-662-46497-7_16

12. Bitansky, N., Paneth, O., Wichs, D.: Perfect structure on the edge of chaos. In: Kushilevitz, E., Malkin, T. (eds.) TCC 2016. LNCS, vol. 9562, pp. 474–502. Springer, Heidelberg (2016). doi:10.1007/978-3-662-49096-9_20

13. Blum, M.: How to prove a theorem so no one else can claim it. In: Proceedings of the International Congress of Mathematicians, pp. 1444–1451 (1987)

14. Brzuska, C., Mittelbach, A.: Indistinguishability obfuscation versus multi-bit point obfuscation with auxiliary input. In: Sarkar, P., Iwata, T. (eds.) ASIACRYPT 2014. LNCS, vol. 8874, pp. 142–161. Springer, Heidelberg (2014). doi:10.1007/978-3-662-45608-8_8

15. Canetti, R.: Towards realizing random oracles: hash functions that hide all partial information. In: Kaliski, B.S. (ed.) CRYPTO 1997. LNCS, vol. 1294, pp. 455–469. Springer, Heidelberg (1997). doi:10.1007/BFb0052255

16. Canetti, R., Goldreich, O., Goldwasser, S., Micali, S.: Resettable zero-knowledge (extended abstract). In: Proceedings of the Thirty-Second Annual ACM Symposium on Theory of Computing, Portland, OR, USA, 21–23 May 2000, pp. 235–244 (2000)

17. Chor, B., Goldreich, O., Kushilevitz, E., Sudan, M.: Private information retrieval. In: 36th Annual Symposium on Foundations of Computer Science, Milwaukee, Wisconsin, 23–25 October 1995, pp. 41–50 (1995)

18. Chung, K.-M., Kalai, Y., Vadhan, S.: Improved delegation of computation using fully homomorphic encryption. In: Rabin, T. (ed.) CRYPTO 2010. LNCS, vol. 6223, pp. 483–501. Springer, Heidelberg (2010). doi:10.1007/978-3-642-14623-7_26

19. Chung, K.-M., Lui, E., Pass, R.: From weak to strong zero-knowledge and applications. In: Dodis, Y., Nielsen, J.B. (eds.) TCC 2015. LNCS, vol. 9014, pp. 66–92. Springer, Heidelberg (2015). doi:10.1007/978-3-662-46494-6_4

20. Ciampi, M., Ostrovsky, R., Siniscalchi, L., Visconti, I.: Concurrent non-malleable commitments (and more) in 3 rounds. In: Robshaw, M., Katz, J. (eds.) CRYPTO 2016. LNCS, vol. 9816, pp. 270–299. Springer, Heidelberg (2016). doi:10.1007/978-3-662-53015-3_10

21. Ciampi, M., Persiano, G., Scafuro, A., Siniscalchi, L., Visconti, I.: Improved OR-composition of sigma-protocols. In: Kushilevitz, E., Malkin, T. (eds.) TCC 2016. LNCS, vol. 9563, pp. 112–141. Springer, Heidelberg (2016). doi:10.1007/978-3-662-49099-0_5

22. Ciampi, M., Persiano, G., Scafuro, A., Siniscalchi, L., Visconti, I.: Online/Offline or composition of sigma protocols. In: Fischlin, M., Coron, J.-S. (eds.) EUROCRYPT 2016. LNCS, vol. 9666, pp. 63–92. Springer, Heidelberg (2016). doi:10.1007/978-3-662-49896-5_3

23. Cramer, R., Damgård, I., Schoenmakers, B.: Proofs of partial knowledge and simplified design of witness hiding protocols. In: Desmedt, Y.G. (ed.) CRYPTO 1994. LNCS, vol. 839, pp. 174–187. Springer, Heidelberg (1994). doi:10.1007/3-540-48658-5_19

24. Crescenzo, G., Persiano, G., Visconti, I.: Constant-round resettable zero knowledge with concurrent soundness in the bare public-key model. In: Franklin, M. (ed.) CRYPTO 2004. LNCS, vol. 3152, pp. 237–253. Springer, Heidelberg (2004). doi:10. 1007/978-3-540-28628-8_15

25. Dolev, D., Dwork, C., Naor, M.: Non-malleable cryptography (extended abstract). In: Proceedings of the 23rd Annual ACM Symposium on Theory of Computing, New Orleans, Louisiana, USA, 5–8 May 1991, pp. 542–552 (1991)

26. Döttling, N., Fleischhacker, N., Krupp, J., Schröder, D.: Two-Message, oblivious evaluation of cryptographic functionalities. In: Robshaw, M., Katz, J. (eds.) CRYPTO 2016. LNCS, vol. 9816, pp. 619–648. Springer, Heidelberg (2016). doi:10. 1007/978-3-662-53015-3_22

27. Dwork, C., Naor, M.: Zaps and their applications. In: 41st Annual Symposium on Foundations of Computer Science, FOCS 2000, Redondo Beach, California, USA, 12–14 November 2000, pp. 283–293 (2000)

28. Dwork, C., Naor, M., Reingold, O., Stockmeyer, L.J.: Magic functions. In: 40th Annual Symposium on Foundations of Computer Science, FOCS 1999, New York, NY, USA, 17–18 October 1999, pp. 523–534 (1999)

29. Feige, U., Shamir, A.: Witness indistinguishable and witness hiding protocols. In: Proceedings of the 22nd Annual ACM Symposium on Theory of Computing, Baltimore, Maryland, USA, 13–17 May 1990, pp. 416–426 (1990)

30. Garg, S., Goyal, V., Jain, A., Sahai, A.: Concurrently secure computation in constant rounds. In: Pointcheval, D., Johansson, T. (eds.) EUROCRYPT 2012. LNCS, vol. 7237, pp. 99–116. Springer, Heidelberg (2012). doi:10.1007/978-3-642-29011-4_8

31. Garg, S., Mukherjee, P., Pandey, O., Polychroniadou, A.: The exact round complexity of secure computation. In: Fischlin, M., Coron, J.-S. (eds.) EUROCRYPT 2016. LNCS, vol. 9666, pp. 448–476. Springer, Heidelberg (2016). doi:10.1007/978-3-662-49896-5_16

32. Garg, S., Pandey, O., Srinivasan, A., Zhandry, M.: Breaking the sub-exponential barrier in obfustopia. In: Coron, J.-S., Nielsen, J.B. (eds.) EUROCRYPT 2017. LNCS, vol. 10212, pp. 156–181. Springer, Cham (2017). doi:10.1007/978-3-319-56617-7_6

33. Gennaro, R., Gentry, C., Parno, B.: Non-interactive verifiable computing: outsourcing computation to untrusted workers. In: Rabin, T. (ed.) CRYPTO 2010. LNCS, vol. 6223, pp. 465–482. Springer, Heidelberg (2010). doi:10.1007/978-3-642-14623-7_25

34. Goldreich, O.: A uniform-complexity treatment of encryption and zero-knowledge. J. Cryptol. 6(1), 21–53 (1993)

35. Goldreich, O., Krawczyk, H.: On the composition of zero-knowledge proof systems. SIAM J. Comput. 25(1), 169–192 (1996)

36. Goldreich, O., Micali, S., Wigderson, A.: How to play ANY mental game. In: STOC (1987)

37. Goldreich, O., Oren, Y.: Definitions and properties of zero-knowledge proof systems. J. Cryptol. 7(1), 1–32 (1994)

38. Goldwasser, S., Micali, S., Rackoff, C.: The knowledge complexity of interactive proof-systems. In: STOC, pp. 291–304 (1985)

39. Goyal, V., Pandey, O., Richelson, S.: Textbook non-malleable commitments. In: Wichs, D., Mansour, Y. (eds.) Proceedings of the 48th Annual ACM SIGACT Symposium on Theory of Computing, STOC 2016, Cambridge, MA, USA, 18–21 June 2016, pp. 1128–1141. ACM (2016). doi:10.1145/2897518.2897657

40. Groth, J., Ostrovsky, R., Sahai, A.: Non-interactive zaps and new techniques for NIZK. In: Dwork, C. (ed.) CRYPTO 2006. LNCS, vol. 4117, pp. 97–111. Springer, Heidelberg (2006). doi:10.1007/11818175_6

41. Hada, S., Tanaka, T.: On the existence of 3-round zero-knowledge protocols. In: Krawczyk, H. (ed.) CRYPTO 1998. LNCS, vol. 1462, pp. 408–423. Springer, Heidelberg (1998). doi:10.1007/BFb0055744

42. Haitner, I., Rosen, A., Shaltiel, R.: On the (Im)possibility of arthur-merlin witness hiding protocols. In: Reingold, O. (ed.) TCC 2009. LNCS, vol. 5444, pp. 220–237. Springer, Heidelberg (2009). doi:10.1007/978-3-642-00457-5_14

43. Halevi, S., Kalai, Y.T.: Smooth projective hashing and two-message oblivious transfer. J. Cryptol. **25**(1), 158–193 (2012)

44. Hazay, C., Venkitasubramaniam, M.: On the power of secure two-party computation. In: Robshaw, M., Katz, J. (eds.) CRYPTO 2016. LNCS, vol. 9815, pp. 397–429. Springer, Heidelberg (2016). doi:10.1007/978-3-662-53008-5_14

45. Kalai, Y.T.: Smooth projective hashing and two-message oblivious transfer. In: Cramer, R. (ed.) EUROCRYPT 2005. LNCS, vol. 3494, pp. 78–95. Springer, Heidelberg (2005). doi:10.1007/11426639_5

46. Kalai, Y.T., Raz, R.: Probabilistically checkable arguments. In: Halevi, S. (ed.) CRYPTO 2009. LNCS, vol. 5677, pp. 143–159. Springer, Heidelberg (2009). doi:10.1007/978-3-642-03356-8_9

47. Katz, J., Ostrovsky, R.: Round-optimal secure two-party computation. In: Franklin, M. (ed.) CRYPTO 2004. LNCS, vol. 3152, pp. 335–354. Springer, Heidelberg (2004). doi:10.1007/978-3-540-28628-8_21

48. Lapidot, D., Shamir, A.: Publicly verifiable non-interactive zero-knowledge proofs. In: Menezes, A.J., Vanstone, S.A. (eds.) CRYPTO 1990. LNCS, vol. 537, pp. 353–365. Springer, Heidelberg (1991). doi:10.1007/3-540-38424-3_26

49. Micali, S., Pass, R., Rosen, A.: Input-indistinguishable computation. In: 2006 47th Annual IEEE Symposium on Foundations of Computer Science (FOCS 2006), pp. 367–378, October 2006

50. Mittelbach, A., Venturi, D.: Fiat-shamir for highly sound protocols is instantiable. In: Proceedings of the 10th International Conference on Security and Cryptography for Networks, SCN 2016, Amalfi, Italy, 31 August–2 September 2016, pp. 198–215 (2016)

51. Naor, M., Pinkas, B.: Efficient oblivious transfer protocols. In: Proceedings of the Twelfth Annual Symposium on Discrete Algorithms, 7–9 January 2001, Washington, DC, USA, pp. 448–457 (2001)

52. Ostrovsky, R., Persiano, G., Visconti, I.: On input indistinguishable proof systems. In: Esparza, J., Fraigniaud, P., Husfeldt, T., Koutsoupias, E. (eds.) ICALP 2014. LNCS, vol. 8572, pp. 895–906. Springer, Heidelberg (2014). doi:10.1007/978-3-662-43948-7_74

53. Pass, R.: Simulation in quasi-polynomial time, and its application to protocol composition. In: Biham, E. (ed.) EUROCRYPT 2003. LNCS, vol. 2656, pp. 160–176. Springer, Heidelberg (2003). doi:10.1007/3-540-39200-9_10

54. Pass, R.: Limits of provable security from standard assumptions. In: Proceedings of the 43rd ACM Symposium on Theory of Computing, STOC 2011, San Jose, CA, USA, 6–8 June 2011, pp. 109–118 (2011)

55. Prabhakaran, M., Rosen, A., Sahai, A.: Concurrent zero knowledge with logarithmic round-complexity. In: Proceedings of the 43rd Symposium on Foundations of Computer Science (FOCS 2002), Vancouver, BC, Canada, 16–19 November 2002, pp. 366–375 (2002)

56. Rosen, A.: A note on constant-round zero-knowledge proofs for NP. In: Naor, M. (ed.) TCC 2004. LNCS, vol. 2951, pp. 191–202. Springer, Heidelberg (2004). doi:10. 1007/978-3-540-24638-1_11

57. Sahai, A., Waters, B.: How to use indistinguishability obfuscation: deniable encryption, and more. In: Shmoys, D.B. (ed.) Symposium on Theory of Computing, STOC 2014, New York, NY, USA, 31 May–03 June 2014, pp. 475–484. ACM (2014). doi:10.1145/2591796.2591825

58. Wee, H.: Black-box, round-efficient secure computation via non-malleability amplification. In: 51th Annual IEEE Symposium on Foundations of Computer Science, FOCS 2010, Las Vegas, Nevada, USA, 23–26 October 2010, pp. 531–540 (2010)

59. Yao, A.C.: How to generate and exchange secrets (extended abstract). In: 27th Annual Symposium on Foundations of Computer Science, Toronto, Canada, 27–29 October 1986, pp. 162–167 (1986)

60. Yung, M., Zhao, Y.: Generic and practical resettable zero-knowledge in the bare public-key model. In: Naor, M. (ed.) EUROCRYPT 2007. LNCS, vol. 4515, pp. 129–147. Springer, Heidelberg (2007). doi:10.1007/978-3-540-72540-4_8

Obfuscation II

Incremental Program Obfuscation

Sanjam Garg[1]($\boxtimes$) and Omkant Pandey[2]

[1] University of California, Berkeley, USA
sanjamg@berkeley.edu
[2] Stony Brook University, Stony Brook, NY, USA

Abstract. Recent advances in program obfuscation suggest that it is possible to create software that can provably safeguard secret information. However, software systems usually contain large executable code that is updated multiple times and sometimes very frequently. Freshly obfuscating the program for every small update will lead to a considerable efficiency loss. Thus, an extremely desirable property for obfuscation algorithms is *incrementality*: small changes to the underlying program translate into small changes to the corresponding obfuscated program.

We initiate a thorough investigation of *incremental program obfuscation*. We show that the strong simulation-based notions of program obfuscation, such as "virtual black-box" and "virtual grey-box" obfuscation, cannot be incremental (according to our efficiency requirements) even for very simple functions such as point functions. We then turn to the indistinguishability-based notions, and present two security definitions of varying strength — namely, a weak one and a strong one. To understand the overall strength of our definitions, we formulate the notion of *incremental best-possible obfuscation* and show that it is equivalent to our strong indistinguishability-based notion.

Finally, we present constructions for incremental program obfuscation satisfying both our security notions. We first give a construction achieving the weaker security notion based on the existence of general purpose indistinguishability obfuscation. Next, we present a generic transformation using *oblivious RAM* to amplify security from weaker to stronger, while maintaining the incrementality property.

1 Introduction

Program obfuscation is the process of transforming a computer program into an "unintelligible" one while preserving its functionality. Barak et al. [BGI+12] formulated several notions for program obfuscation, and demonstrated that the strongest form of obfuscation, called *virtual black-box* (VBB) obfuscation, is

S. Garg—Research supported in part from AFOSR YIP Award, DARPA/ARL SAFEWARE Award W911NF15C0210, AFOSR Award FA9550-15-1-0274, NSF CRII Award 1464397, research grants by the Okawa Foundation, Visa Inc., and Center for Long-Term Cybersecurity (CLTC, UC Berkeley). The views expressed are those of the author and do not reflect the official policy or position of the funding agencies.

© International Association for Cryptologic Research 2017
J. Katz and H. Shacham (Eds.): CRYPTO 2017, Part II, LNCS 10402, pp. 193–223, 2017.
DOI: 10.1007/978-3-319-63715-0_7

impossible in general. The recent work of Garg et al. [GGH+13b] presents an obfuscation mechanism for general programs that achieves the notion of *indistinguishability obfuscation* based on assumptions on multilinear maps [GGH13a]. Indistinguishability obfuscation, or IO, is a weaker form of obfuscation than VBB; nevertheless, it results in best possible obfuscation [GR07].

The feasibility of general purpose obfuscation, in principle, allows the creation of software that can provably safeguard secret information, e.g., cryptographic keys, proprietary algorithms, and so on. A typical software, however, can be quite complex with millions of lines of executable code [IB]. Once installed, it may go through frequent updates, e.g., when new features are added or security vulnerabilities are discovered. If cryptographic obfuscation is used to protect the software, it must be possible to quickly update the *obfuscated* software when new updates become available. In particular, if the original program is large, the obfuscating it from scratch for every new update would be prohibitive. Furthermore, in various client-server settings, where the obfuscated software resides on a networked machine, transmitting the entire (updated) software would be a bottleneck. Ideally, the effort to update the obfuscated program should only be proportional to the changes made to the original unobfuscated program.

These issues are not unique to program obfuscation and analogous problems have been considered in several other settings. Bellare, Goldreich and Goldwasser [BGG94] introduced and developed the notion of incremental cryptography, first in the context of hashing and digital signatures. The idea is that, once we have signed a document D, signing new versions of D should be rather quick. For example, if we only flip a single bit of D, we should be able to update the signature in time polynomial in $\log|D|$ (instead of $|D|$) and the security parameter λ. Incrementality is an attractive feature to have for many cryptographic primitive such as encryption, signatures, hash functions, and so on [BGG95, Mic97, Fis97a, BM97, BKY01, MPRS12].

If we want to obfuscate large programs that are frequently updated, then it is crucial to have *incremental* program obfuscation. Although, current program obfuscation methods are prohibitively slow for application to large programs. However as it becomes more efficient, it is clear that incrementality will be essential for deployment of obfuscation of large programs. This line of investigation is particularly important because of its relevance to the deployment (as opposed to security) of obfuscated software.

1.1 Our Contributions

In this work, we initiate the study of *incremental* program obfuscation. Here we ask what is the right security definition for incremental program obfuscation and if it can be realized. In this work, we show that enhancing obfuscation with incrementality must come at the some degradation in security. In contrast on the positive side, we realize the *best possible* incremental obfuscation. More specifically, our incremental obfuscation method hides as much about the original program as any other incremental obfuscation of a given size. Our results are generic in the sense that starting with a general purpose obfuscation method for circuit, Turing Machines or RAM programs, we obtain general purpose incremental obfuscation for the same class of programs. Next we provide more details.

Modeling incremental obfuscation. We model an incremental obfuscation method by an obfuscation procedure and an Update procedure. In this setting, a large program P is obfuscated and placed on a remote machine in the obfuscated form $\widetilde{P}$. Update can query any bit of the obfuscated program $\widetilde{P}$. The input to Update is a set S of indices, indicating which bits of P should be "updated." For every index $i \in S$, there is an associated update *operation* $f_i : \{0,1\} \to \{0,1\}$ to be performed on the ith bit of P; the set of these operations is denoted by $F_S = \{f_i\}_{i \in S}$. The output of Update consists of a set $\widetilde{S}$ indicating the bits of $\widetilde{P}$ to be updated; for every $i \in \widetilde{S}$ there is an associated bit b_i indicating the updated value.

The *incrementality* of an obfuscation scheme, denoted Δ, is defined to be the *running time* of Update in the worst case with respect to *singleton* sets S. This is a robust measure since it tells us how bad Update can be when we just want to update one bit.[1]

An important observation is that the Update cannot be a public algorithm, since otherwise, one can "tamper" with the $\widetilde{P}$ and potentially recover the entire P. Therefore, Update must require a *secret key*, generated at the time of obfuscation of P, to be able to make updates.

In this work, we require that the size of the updated obfuscated program should be the same as the fresh obfuscation of the new (updated) program. Further strengthening this requirement: we require that an updated obfuscation of a program should look *computationally indistinguishable* from a freshly generated obfuscation of the new program. We actually achieve statistical indistinguishability, and refer to this property as *pristine updates*. These requirements are crucial for various applications.

Lower bound for incremental VBB *and* VGB *obfuscation.* We show that incrementality significantly interferes with the security an obfuscation method can offer. More specifically, we show that for the family of point functions, every incremental VBB obfuscation scheme must have incrementality $\Delta \in \Omega(n/\log n)$ where n is the size of the point function program. In fact, our result holds also for the weaker notion of *virtual grey box* (VGB) obfuscation, introduced by Bitanksy and Canetti [BC10]. VGB obfuscation, like VBB, is a simulation-based notion of security but it allows the simulator to be unbounded; it only requires that the

---

[1] Another natural way to define incrementality is the running time of Update for S, divided by $|S|$ in the worst case, taken over all (S, F_S). For our constructions, the single bit measure obtains the same parameters for this alternative definition. Because for larger sets S, one can simply apply Update one by one for each index in S, and still achieve same incrementality. Therefore, for simplicity, we use the simpler single bit measure. We note that for correctness and security the intermediate one bit changes may not make sense and this definitional notion is just to simplify how we measure efficiency.

number of queries made by the simulator to the black-box program should be polynomial. This further strengthens our result.

Our lower bound proceeds by proving that every incremental VGB (and hence VBB) scheme must "leak" the Hamming distance between the obfuscated and updated programs. Therefore, no generic compiler can preserve obfuscation quality and provide low incrementality at the same time.

Interestingly, our negative result holds even if only one update is made to the obfuscated point function. This is somewhat surprising since point-functions are inherently related to deterministic encryption [BS16] for which incremental schemes are known for single updates [MPRS12].

Positive results for indistinguishability obfuscation. Our lower bound motivates us to look more deeply into the definitions for incremental indistinguishability obfuscation, or IIO. We aim to obtain high flexibility in addition to as strong security as possible.

With this goal, we consider an obfuscated program $\widetilde{P}$ which is continually updated over time, by applying the Update algorithm to the previous obfuscation. This results in a sequence of obfuscated programs $\widetilde{P}, \widetilde{P}^1, \ldots, \widetilde{P}^t$ where $\widetilde{P}^i$ is obtained from $\widetilde{P}^{i-1}$ using Update. Since the adversary can view the entire sequence of obfuscated programs, this suggests the following natural definition: for every pair of programs (P_0, P_1) and every sequence of increments (or updates) $I = (S_1, \ldots, S_t)$ of arbitrary polynomial size sets S_i and for arbitrary polynomial t, the distributions $X_0 := (\widetilde{P}_0, \widetilde{P}_0^1, \ldots, \widetilde{P}_0^t)$ and $X_1 := (\widetilde{P}_1, \widetilde{P}_0^1, \ldots, \widetilde{P}_1^t)$ should be computationally indistinguishable provided that P_0^i and P_1^i are functionally equivalent for every i where P_b^i is the program corresponding to $\widetilde{P}_b^i$ for every $b \in \{0, 1\}$.

We use this definition as the default definition of IIO. We present an IIO scheme for the class of all circuits with incrementality $\mathsf{poly}(\lambda, \log |P|)$, assuming the existence of IO for the same class.

Increment-privacy and "best possible" incremental obfuscation. The IIO definition does not necessarily hide the sequence I of increments. Indeed, by looking at the sequence of updated programs, an adversary might be able to recover which bits were updated at each time step. For many application this could be a serious issue. For example, if $\widetilde{P}$ is updated to fix a security vulnerability in P, by looking at which bits were updated, a hacker might be able to discover the vulnerability; it can then exploit other machines where the program is still awaiting update.

Even more importantly, since IIO may leak the sequence I, it is unlikely to achieve our desired "best possible" incremental obfuscation. We therefore consider a strengthened definition which hides the sequence I, and call it *increment-private* IIO. More specifically, we consider two sequences I_0, I_1 where I_0 is applied to $\widetilde{P}_0$ and I_1 to $\widetilde{P}_1$. As before, we require that the resulting obfuscation sequences should look indistinguishable provided that the underlying programs are functionally equivalent at every time step.

With the goal of realizing obfuscation satisfying this security notion, we show a transformation which converts any IIO scheme into increment-private IIO scheme without affecting its incrementality too much. Our transformation is obtained by combining IIO with *oblivious RAM* (ORAM) programs [GO96].

Finally, in an effort to better understand what is the strongest possible incremental obfuscation, we define the notion of *best possible incremental obfuscation*, or IBPO. For example, our lower bound for VGB/VBB obfuscations demonstrates that any incremental scheme must leak the size of incremental updates that take place. It is important to understand if this is all that is leaked. Our IBPO notion essentially captures all the information that can leak by an incremental obfuscation. Interestingly, we are able to show that increment-private IIO and IBPO are equivalent! That is, hiding the sequence suffices for best possible obfuscation. This is further evidence that increment-private IIO is the right notion to target.

In all of our constructions we work with the *sequential* and *non-adaptive* model of updates — i.e., the updates are not adversarially chosen based on the previously provided obfuscations. In most settings for software updates, the updates are not adversarial since they come from the software provider. The non-adaptive definition suffices for such applications. However, the adaptive definition might be desirable in other settings, for example if the adversary can influence the choice of updates, e.g., through insider attacks. We do not consider this notion in this work. Our results, however, easily extend to non-sequential setting which will be discussed towards the end.

Other applications. Besides being interesting in its own right, incremental obfuscation can be seen as a natural tool to enhance applications of obfuscation with incrementality properties. For example, one can very easily enhance the functional encryption scheme of Garg et al. [GGH+13b] in a way such that secret keys have incrementality properties. In functional encryption an encrypter can encrypt a message m in such a way that a secret key sk_C, parameterized by the circuit C, can be used to learn $C(m)$. Using our incremental obfuscation we can realize incremental functional encryption, where given a secret key for sk_C one can quickly provide new secret keys for incremental changes in C.

1.2 An Overview of Our Approach

In this section we provide an overview of our constructions. We begin with a systematic exploration, and show how to achieve the basic IIO definition first. We then show how to compile this construction with ORAM to obtain increment-privacy without sacrificing incrementality. For concreteness, we view the program P as a boolean circuit C.

A common approach for obfuscating a general circuit C relies on the Naor-Yung "two-key paradigm" [NY90]: C is encrypted twice to get ciphertexts (e_1, e_2) which are then "hardwired" into a low-depth circuit for which candidate obfuscation is known.

Suppose that we are given IO for the class of all circuits. We will follow the two-key paradigm to obtain IIO. Specifically, we will obfuscate a special circuit

C^* using IO which will internally evaluate C. However, we cannot hardwire either C or the value (e_1, e_2) in C^* since even if the values (e_1, e_2) support incrementality, the IO may not.

One option is to provide $e = (e_1, e_2)$ as an explicit input to C^*. C^* can obtain C by decrypting, say e_1, and evaluate it as required. If e_1, e_2 are bitwise encryptions of C, the scheme is also incremental: changing any bit only requires changing the corresponding ciphertexts in e.

In order to make sure that the scheme is secure, C^* must only accept "authorized" values of e. This can be accomplished, for example, by signing e *entirely* after every update. C^* will verify the signature on the updated e before performing the computation. This is indeed a promising approach, however, observe that now the signature must also be incremental since it would be a part of the obfuscation. Unfortunately, this is a big problem since incremental signatures are usually not injective. Consequently, there can exist multiples messages corresponding to the same signature; the existence of such messages is not quite compatible with IO techniques.

Nevertheless, it is a promising approach and it is possible to make it work based on the existence of *(public-coin) differing-inputs obfuscation* (pc-dIO) [ABG+13, BCP14, IPS15]. Our goal is to obtain a feasibility result based on the existence of IO alone, since pc-dIO, due to its extractability flavor, is viewed as a very strong assumption [GGHW14, BP15b].

SSB hash and Merkle trees. A powerful technique to avoid the pc-dIO in many settings is the *somewhere statistically binding* (SSB) hash technique based on Merkle trees. It was introduced by Hubaceck and Wichs [HW15], and is very similar in spirit to the *positional accumulators* of Koppula, Lewko, and Waters [KLW15].

At a high level, the approach considers hash functions which can be generated to be statistically binding at a chosen location. These functions are collisions-resistant, and functions generated for different locations are computationally indistinguishable. Such functions can be constructed from a variety of assumptions, including IO [HW15, KLW15, OPWW15].

Coming back to our construction, we will use the SSB hash functions based on Merkle trees presented in [HW15]. This hash has incrementality property, and consists of two values (h, T) where T is the Merkle tree and h is the root of T. Unfortunately, the SSB hash technique cannot be applied in a black-box manner to all settings. It has to be properly adapted to every setting.

We show how to apply this technique in our setting. More specifically, we take the following high level steps:

1. We encrypt the circuit twice, bit-by-bit, as before to obtain $e = (e_1, e_2)$. We then apply a quickly updatable SSB Hash to e to obtain (h, T). The value h is then "signed."
2. In fact, ordinary signatures are too rigid for our needs. Instead, we use non-interactive zero-knowledge (NIZK) proofs to give proofs that h does not have some special structure.

3. The full obfuscation will include IO of a circuit C^* which has a secret-key sk_1 hardwired for decrypting e_1 and evaluating the resulting circuit on inputs of interest if all NIZK proofs verify.
4. As new updates arrive, values e, h, T are easily updated, as well as the proofs since they only depend on h and not e, T.
5. We then rely on the combined power of SSB-hash functions and NIZK proofs to design a sequence of hybrids such that the signatures exist only for the specified sequence in question. We further use NIZK proofs, SSB hash, and the power of IO to slowly reach a point in hybrid experiments where there is exactly one value e^* that will be accepted by the obfuscated program. At this point, we will able to encrypt the circuits from the other sequence—again, this step is performed one-by-one for each location in the sequence.

We note that executing this strategy is rather involved, and we heavily rely on manipulations via NIZK proofs to complete the security proof.

Increment-privacy via ORAM. To amplify security to increment-private IIO, we rely on two techniques: ORAM programs and the two-key paradigm [NY90]. In more detail, to obfuscate a circuit C, we first apply a statistically-secure ORAM scheme to C twice, to obtain two independent encodings of C, say C_1^*, C_2^*. Next we generate a circuit P that has (C_1^*, C_2^*), and secret information to decode one of them hardcoded in it. The program P, on input x, decodes one of the encoded circuits and outputs the evaluation of the decoded circuit on input x. Having defined P, we now obfuscate P using any IIO scheme (which only satisfies the weaker definition). The resulting obfuscation is our *increment-private* IIO.

At a high level, this works because incremental changes in C can be reduced to corresponding changes in the ORAM encodings of C, and hence the program P. However, since P is encoded using our IIO scheme, this preserves incrementality up to logarithmic factors. At the same time, the use of ORAM ensures the privacy of incremental updates.

We remark that, although the underlying ideas behind this transformation are simple, the proof is not as simple as one would hope for. In particular, to be able to successfully rely on the security of IIO, the obfuscated program needs a little more "guidance" to perform its task so that the hybrids will go through.

1.3   Related Work

Patchable Obfuscation. An interesting variant of IIO–called Patachable Obfuscation (PO)—was considered in [AJS17]. In PO, one aims to release a "short patch" which can update a previously obfuscated program. There are several fundamental differences between these two works. A crucial difference between IIO and PO is that in PO, the "patch" is allowed to take *linear* time (i.e., proportional to the size of the obfuscated program) *even if* the actual change is only a single bit in the underlying program. Indeed this is the case with the constructions of [AJS17]. In contrast, IIO requires that the time to update the obfuscated program must only depend on the time to update the plain, unobfuscated program. Our constructions achieve this form of efficiency. On the flip side, PO can maintain a short concise description of the patch even if the final change will be large; IIO does not require concise description and depends on the final change.

The primary reason for this difference is the fundamental difference in how the two works formulate the updates: while our work views them as a small *set* of bit positions that need to be updated, [AJS17] views them as a small *program* that updates the bits as it processes the entire obfuscated code. Due this fundamental difference in problem formulation, the two works employ completely different methods. Our IIO constructions are obtained by relying only on standard, polynomially-hard assumptions but achieve only non-adaptive security. In contrast, the results of [AJS17] require the underlying primitives to be sub-exponentially secure but achieve adaptive security.

Finally, the stringent requirement on running time of updates in our work sheds light on the lower bounds for other notions of obfuscations such as VBB/VGB-obfuscation. We additionally develop the notion of *best possible incremental obfuscation* and develop generic tools using ORAM to achieve this notion. [AJS17] do not consider these issues or rely on ORAM techniques in any way. On the flip side, the method in [AJS17] can expand the input length of the obfuscated program which is not considered in our work.

Other related work. The concept of incremental cryptography was put forward by Bellare, Goldreich, and Goldwasser [BGG94], as a different type of efficiency measure for cryptographic schemes. They considered the case of hashing and signing, and presented discrete-logarithm based constructions for incremental collision-resistant hash functions and signatures, that support block replacement operation. Soon after, Bellare et al. [BGG95] also developed constructions for block insertion and deletion, and further issues such as tamper-proof updates, privacy of updates, and incrementality in symmetric encryption were also considered.

Subsequently, Fischlin [Fis97a] presented an incremental signature schemes supporting insertion/deletion of blocks, and tamper-proof updates, and proved a $\Omega(\sqrt{n})$ lower bound in [Fis97b] on the signature size of schemes that support substitution and replacement operations (the bound can be improved to $\Omega(n)$ in certain special cases). The case of hashing was revisited by Bellare and Micciancio [BM97] who provided new constructions for the same based on discrete logarithms and lattices. Buonanno, Katz, and Yung [BKY01] considered the issue of incrementality in symmetric unforgeable encryption and suggested three modes of operations for AES achieving this notion.

Mironov, Pandey, Reingold, and Segev [MPRS12] study incrementality in the context of deterministic public-key encryption. They prove a similar lower bound on the incrementality of such schemes, and present constructions with optimal incrementality.

The task of constructing cryptographic primitives in the complexity class NC^0 can be viewed as a dual of incremental cryptography where the focus is on *output locality* instead of input locality. Applebaum, Ishai, and Kushilevitz [AIK06] resolved this question in the affirmative for public-key encryption, and argue impossibility of the same for constant *input* locality [AIK06, Sect. 1.1].

Barak et al. [BGI+12] formulated the notion of program obfuscation and proved strong negative results for VBB obfuscation. The connection between zero-knowledge and code obfuscation was first observed and studied by Hada [Had00]. VBB obfuscation for special classes of functions such as point functions were first considered by Wee [Wee05] (and Canetti [Can97]); subsequently, constructions for more functions were achieved such as proxy re-encryption, encrypted signatures, hyperplanes, conjunctions, and so on [LPS04, HRSV07, Had10, CRV10, BR13]. Goldwasser and Kalai extended the negative results for VBB obfuscation in the presence of auxiliary inputs [GK05] which were further extended by Bitansky et al. [BCC+14].

The notion of *best possible obfuscation* was put forward by Goldwasser and Rothblum [GR07], who also prove its equivalence to indistinguishability obfuscation (for efficient obfuscators). Bitansky and Canetti [BC10] formulated the notion of *virtual grey box* (VGB) obfuscation which is a simulation based notion; it was further explored in [BCKP14].

The first positive result for indistinguishability obfuscation was first achieved in the breakthrough work of [GGH+13b], and further improved in [BGK+14]. In the idealized "generic encodings" model VBB-obfuscation for all circuits were presented in [CV13, BR14, BGK+14, AB15]. These results often involve a "bootstrapping step" which was improved by Applebaum [App14]. Further complexity-theoretic results appear in recent works of Barak et. al. [BBC+14] and Komargodski et al. [KMN+14]. Obfuscation in alternative models such as the hardware token model were considered in [GIS+10, BCG+11].

Sahai and Waters [SW14] developed powerful techniques for using indistinguishability obfuscation to construct several (old and new) cryptographic primitives. Since then, IO has been successfully applied to achieve several new results, e.g., [HSW14, BZ14, MO14, PPS15, CLP15, HW15, BP15a, BPW16, AS16]. The equivalence of IO and functional encryption [BSW11, O'N10] was recently established by Ananth and Jain [AJ15] and Bitanksy and Vaikuntanathan [BV15].

Differing input obfuscation (diO) was studied by Ananth et. al. [ABG+13] and Boyle et al. [BCP14], and subsequently used to construct obfuscation for Turing machines. After various implausibility results [GGHW14, BP15b], Ishai, Pandey, and Sahai put forward the improved notion of public-coin differing-inputs obfuscation and recovered several original applications of diO. Indistinguishability obfuscation for bounded-input Turing machines and RAM programs were presented in [BGL+15, CHJV15] and for bounded-space programs in [KLW15].

The notion of oblivious RAM programs was put forward by Goldreich and Ostrovsky [Gol87, Ost90, GO96]. Several improved constructions and variations of ORAM programs are now known [SCSL11, SvDS+13, LO13, CLP14, BCP16].

2 Definitions and Preliminaries

In this section we recall the definitions of some standard cryptographic schemes which will be used in our constructions. For concreteness, we adopt the family of polynomial-sized circuits are model of computation for describing programs. Our definitions, constructions, and results apply to Turing machines and RAM programs as well. We will bring up these models when appropriate.

From here on, unless specified otherwise, λ always denotes the security parameter. We assume familiarity with standard cryptographic primitives, specifically *public-key encryption* (PKE), *non-interactive zero-knowledge proofs* (NIZK, recalled in Sect. 2.4), *perfectly binding commitments*, and *computational indistinguishability*.

2.1 Indistinguishability Obfuscators

Definition 1 (Indistinguishability Obfuscator (IO)). *A uniform PPT machine $\mathcal{O}$ is called an* indistinguishability obfuscator *for a circuit class $\{\mathcal{C}_\lambda\}$ if the following conditions are satisfied:*

- Correctness: *For all security parameters $\lambda \in \mathbb{N}$, for all $C \in \mathcal{C}_\lambda$, for all inputs x, we have that*

$$\Pr[\widetilde{C}(x) = C(x) : \widetilde{C} \leftarrow \mathcal{O}(\lambda, C)] = 1.$$

- Indistinguishability: *For any (not necessarily uniform) PPT distinguisher D, there exists a negligible function α such that the following holds: For all security parameters $\lambda \in \mathbb{N}$, for all pairs of circuits $C_0, C_1 \in \mathcal{C}_\lambda$, we have that if $C_0(x) = C_1(x)$ for all inputs x, then*

$$\left| \Pr\left[D(\mathcal{O}(\lambda, C_0)) = 1 \right] - \Pr\left[D(\mathcal{O}(\lambda, C_1)) = 1 \right] \right| \le \alpha(\lambda).$$

2.2 Somewhere Statistically Binding Hash

We recall the definition of somewhere statistically binding (SSB) hash from [HW15, OPWW15].

Definition 2 (SSB Hash). *A somewhere statistically binding (SSB) hash consists of PPT algorithms* (Gen, H) *and a polynomial $\ell(\cdot, \cdot)$ denoting the output length.*

- $hk \leftarrow \mathsf{Gen}(1^\lambda, 1^s, L, i)$: *Takes as input a security parameter λ, a block-length s, an input-length $L \le 2^\lambda$ and an index $i \in [L]$ (in binary) and outputs a public hashing key hk. We let $\Sigma = \{0,1\}^s$ denote the block alphabet. The output size is $\ell = \ell(\lambda, s)$ and is independent of the input-length L.*
- $H_{hk} : \Sigma^L \to \{0,1\}^\ell$: *A deterministic poly-time algorithm that takes as input $x = (x[0], \ldots, x[L-1]) \in \Sigma^L$ and outputs $H_{hk}(x) \in \{0,1\}^\ell$.*

We require the following properties:

Index Hiding: We consider the following game between an attacker $\mathcal{A}$ and a challenger:

- The attacker $\mathcal{A}(1^\lambda)$ chooses parameters $1^s, L$ and two indices $i_0, i_1 \in [L]$.
- The challenger chooses a bit $b \leftarrow \{0, 1\}$ and sets $hk \leftarrow \mathsf{Gen}(1^\lambda, 1^s, L, i)$.
- The attacker $\mathcal{A}$ gets hk and outputs a bit b'. We require that for any PPT attacker $\mathcal{A}$ we have that $|\Pr[b = b'] - \frac{1}{2}| \leq \mathsf{negl}(\lambda)$ in the above game.

Somewhere Statistically Binding: We say that hk is *statistically binding for an index* $i \in [L]$ if there do not exist any values $x, x' \in \Sigma^L$ where $x[i] \neq x'[i]$ such that $H_{hk}(x) = H_{hk}(x')$. We require that for any parameters s, L and any integer $i \in [L]$ we have:

$$\Pr[hk \text{ is statistically binding for index } i: hk \leftarrow \mathsf{Gen}(1^\lambda, 1^s, L, i)] \geq 1 - \mathsf{negl}(\lambda).$$

We say the hash is perfectly binding if the above probability is 1.

Merkle SSB Hash. For concreteness, we work with a specific instantiation of SSB Hash based on Merkle trees (and fully homomorphic encryption) given in [HW15]. The has values from this construction have the form (h, T) where T is the Merkle tree and h is the root of T. This construction has the *incrementality* or "quick update" property: small changes to the underlying value only require $\mathsf{poly}(\lambda, \log n)$ changes to (h, T) where n is the length of the string. Constructions with same properties can be based on a variety of assumptions including IO alone [OPWW15, KLW15].

2.3   Oblivious RAM

We review the notion of ORAM programs from [Gol87, Ost90, GO96]. Constructions of ORAM are provided by the same papers as well. ORAM can be thought of as a compiler that encodes the memory into a special format such that the sequence of **read** and **write** operations into this memory do not reveal the actual access pattern. We recall basic definitions here and refer the reader to [GO96] for more details.

Syntax. A *Oblivious RAM* scheme consists of two procedures (OData, OAccess) with syntax:

- $(D^*, s) \leftarrow \mathsf{OData}(1^\lambda, D)$: Given a security parameter λ and memory $D \in \{0, 1\}^m$ as input, OData outputs the encoded memory D^* and the encoding key s.
- $d \leftarrow \mathsf{OAccess}^{D^*}(1^\lambda, s, \ell, v)$: OAccess takes as input the security parameter λ and the encoding key s. Additionally, it takes as input a location $\ell \in [m]$ and a value $v \in \{\bot, 0, 1\}$. If $v = \bot$ then this procedure outputs d, the value stored at location ℓ in D. If $v \in \{0, 1\}$ the the procedure writes the value v to location ℓ in D. OAccess has oracle access (read and write) to D^* and changes made to it are preserved from one execution of OAccess to another.

Efficiency. We require that the run-time of OData should be $m \cdot \mathsf{polylog}(m) \cdot \mathsf{poly}(\lambda)$, and the run-time of OAccess should be $\mathsf{poly}(\lambda) \cdot \mathsf{polylog}(m)$.

Correctness. Let $\ell_1, \ldots, \ell_t$ be locations accessed on memory D of size m and let $v_1, \ldots, v_t \in \{0, 1, \bot\}$. Then we require that on sequential executions of $d_i = \mathsf{OAccess}^{D^*}(1^\lambda, s, \ell_i, v_i)$ we have that for each $i \in \{1, \ldots t\}$ such that $v_i \neq \bot$ output d_i the correct and the latest value stored in location ℓ_i of D.

Security. For security, we require that for any sequence of access locations $\ell_1, \ldots, \ell_t$ and $\ell'_1, \ldots, \ell'_t$, in $D \in \{0, 1\}^m$, we have that:

$$\mathsf{MemAccess} \approx \mathsf{MemAccess}'$$

where MemAccess and MemAccess' correspond to the access pattern on D^* during the sequential execution of the $\mathsf{OAccess}^{D^*}$ on input locations $\ell_1, \ldots, \ell_t$ and $\ell'_1, \ldots, \ell'_t$ respectively and $\approx$ denotes computational indistinguishability.

2.4 Non-interactive Zero-Knowledge Proofs

We recall the definitions of non-interactive zero-knowledge proofs, taken verbatim from [GOS06].

Let R be an efficiently computable binary relation. For pairs $(x, w) \in R$ we call x the statement and w the witness. Let L be the language consisting of statements in R.

A non-interactive proof system [BFM88, FLS99, GOS06] for a relation R consists of a common reference string generation algorithm K, a prover P and a verifier V. We require that they all be probabilistic polynomial time algorithms, *i.e.*, we are looking at *efficient prover* proofs. The common reference string generation algorithm produces a common reference string σ of length $\Omega(\lambda)$. The prover takes as input (σ, x, w) and produces a proof π. The verifier takes as input (σ, x, π) and outputs 1 if the proof is acceptable and 0 otherwise. We call (K, P, V) a non-interactive proof system for R if it has the completeness and statistical-soundness properties described below.

PERFECT COMPLETENESS. A proof system is complete if an honest prover with a valid witness can convince an honest verifier. Formally we require that for all $(x, w) \in R$, for all $\sigma \leftarrow K(1^\lambda)$ and $\pi \leftarrow P(\sigma, x, w)$ we have that $V(\sigma, x, \pi) = 1$.

STATISTICAL SOUNDNESS. A proof system is sound if it is infeasible to convince an honest verifier when the statement is false. For all (even unbounded) adversaries $\mathcal{A}$ we have

$$\Pr\left[\sigma \leftarrow K(1^\lambda); (x, \pi) \leftarrow \mathcal{A}(\sigma) : V(\sigma, x, \pi) = 1 : x \notin L\right] = \mathsf{negl}(\lambda).$$

COMPUTATIONAL ZERO-KNOWLEDGE [FLS99]. A proof system is computational zero-knowledge if the proofs do not reveal any information about the witnesses to a bounded adversary. We say a non-interactive proof (K, P, V) is computational zero-knowledge if there exists a polynomial time simulator $\mathcal{S} = (\mathcal{S}_1, \mathcal{S}_2)$, such that for all non-uniform polynomial time adversaries $\mathcal{A}$ with oracle access to the prover or the simulator for queries $(x, w) \in R$. Simulator is not provided with the witness w.

$$\Pr\left[\sigma \leftarrow K(1^\lambda) : \mathcal{A}^{P(\sigma,\cdot,\cdot)}(\sigma) = 1\right] \approx \Pr\left[(\sigma,\tau) \leftarrow \mathcal{S}_1(1^\lambda) : \mathcal{A}^{\mathcal{S}_2(\tau,\cdot)}(\sigma) = 1\right].$$

3   Modeling Incremental Obfuscation

In this section, we provide the definitions for incremental program obfuscation. As noted before, for concreteness, we describe our definitions for circuits. The definitions for Turing machines (TM) and RAM programs are obtained by simply replacing circuits with TM/RAMs. We start by providing indistinguishability-based definitions. Let us first set up some notation.

There are four operations we can perform on a bit b: $\mathsf{set}(b) = 1, \mathsf{reset}(b) = 0, \mathsf{flip}(b) = 1 - b$ and $\mathsf{id}(b) = b$; denote by $\mathsf{OP} = \{\mathsf{set}, \mathsf{reset}, \mathsf{flip}, \mathsf{id}\}$ the set of these operations. An *incremental change* to a string x of length n consists of specifying an (ordered) subset $S \subseteq [n]$ of indices of x along with an (ordered) set of corresponding changes $F_S = \{f_i\}_{i \in S}$ (where $f_i \in \mathsf{OP}, \forall i \in S$). When we want to be explicit about F_S, we denote the incremental change by (S, F_S).

For a string x, $F_S(x)$ denotes the string x' such that $x'[i] = f_i(x[i])$ for every $i \in S$ and $x'[i] = x[i]$ otherwise. A sequence I of many updates is an ordered sequence of updates $I = ((S_1, F_{S_1}), \ldots, (S_t, F_{S_t}))$ When dealing with a sequence, we write $F_I(x)$ to denote the sequence of *strings* $(x^1, \ldots, x^t)$ where x^j is defined recursively as $x^j := F_{S_j}(x^{j-1})$ for all $j \in [t]$ and $x^0 = x$.

If C is a circuit, represented as a binary string, I is a sequence of t updates to C, and x is an input string, we write $F_I(C)(x)$ to denote the sequence $(C^1(x), \ldots, C^t(x))$ where $(C^1, \ldots, C^t) \stackrel{\mathrm{def}}{=} F_I(C)$.

3.1   Incremental Indistinguishability Obfuscation

As discussed earlier, our first definition, called IIO, simply requires that for every sequence of updates I, if I produces two functionally equivalent circuit sequences, then the updated sequence of obfuscated circuits corresponding to I should look indistinguishable. This is the weaker definition.

Definition 3 (Incremental Indistinguishability Obfuscator (IIO)). *A pair of uniform PPT machines $(\mathcal{O}, \mathsf{Update})$ is called an* incremental indistinguishability *obfuscator for a circuit class $\{\mathcal{C}_\lambda\}$ if the following conditions are satisfied:*

- Syntax: $\mathcal{O}$ *takes as input a security parameter λ and a circuit $C \in \mathcal{C}_\lambda$; it outputs an obfuscated circuit $\widetilde{C}$ and a secret key sk (for making updates).* Update *takes as input the secret-key sk, an incremental change (S, F_S), and oracle access to $\widetilde{C}$; it outputs an incremental change $(\widetilde{S}, F_{\widetilde{S}})$ for the circuit $\widetilde{C}$.*

- Correctness: *For all security parameters $\lambda \in \mathbb{N}$, for all $C^0 \in \mathcal{C}_\lambda$, for all $t \in \mathbb{N}$, for all sequences of incremental changes $I = (S_1, \ldots, S_t)$ defining the circuit sequence $F_I(C) = (C^1, \ldots, C^t)$, and for all inputs x, we have that*

$$\Pr\left[\bigwedge_{j=0}^{t}\left(\widetilde{C}^j(x) = C^j(x)\right) : \begin{array}{l} (\widetilde{C}^0, sk) \leftarrow \mathcal{O}(\lambda, C^0) \\ (\widetilde{C}^1, \ldots, \widetilde{C}^t) \leftarrow \mathsf{Update}^{\widetilde{C}^0}(sk, I) \end{array}\right] = 1.$$

  where $\mathsf{Update}^{\widetilde{C}^0}(sk, I)$ denotes the (recursively computed) sequence $(\widetilde{C}^1, \ldots, \widetilde{C}^t)$ as follows: for every $j \in [t]$ define $(\widetilde{S}_j, F_{\widetilde{S}_j}) \leftarrow \mathsf{Update}^{\widetilde{C}^{j-1}}(sk, S_j)$ and then $\widetilde{C}^j = F_{\widetilde{S}_j}\left(\widetilde{C}^{j-1}\right)$.
- Incrementality: *There is a fixed polynomial $\mathsf{poly}(\cdot, \cdot)$, independent of the class $\mathcal{C}_\lambda$, such that the running time of $\mathsf{Update}^{\widetilde{C}}(sk, (\{i\}, F_{\{i\}}))$ over all possible values of $(\lambda, \widetilde{C}, (\{i\}, F_{\{i\}}), sk)$ is at most $\Delta(\lambda) = \mathsf{poly}(\lambda, \lg|\widetilde{C}|)$. The incrementality of the scheme is defined to be $\Delta(\lambda)$.*
- Indistinguishability: *For any (not necessarily uniform) PPT distinguisher D, there exists a negligible function α such that the following holds: For all security parameters $\lambda \in \mathbb{N}$, for all pairs of circuits $C_0, C_1 \in \mathcal{C}_\lambda$, for every polynomial t and for every sequence I of t updates we have that if $C_0(x) = C_1(x)$ and $F_I(C_0)(x) = F_I(C_1)(x)$ for all inputs x, then*

$$\left|\Pr\left[D(\mathsf{Expt}(\lambda, C_0, C_1, I, 0)) = 1\right] - \Pr\left[D(\mathsf{Expt}(\lambda, C_0, C_1, I, 1)) = 1\right]\right| \leq \alpha(\lambda).$$

  where distribution $\mathsf{Expt}(\lambda, C_0, C_1, I, b)$ outputs as follows: sample $(\widetilde{C}_b, sk) \leftarrow \mathcal{O}(\lambda, C_b)$, sample sequence $(\widetilde{C}_b^1, \ldots, \widetilde{C}_b^t) \leftarrow \mathsf{Update}^{\widetilde{C}_b}(sk, I)$, and output $(I, C_0, C_1, \widetilde{C}_b, \widetilde{C}_b^1, \ldots, \widetilde{C}_b^t)$.

The above definition does not necessarily hide the sequence I from the adversary. Our next definition, called *increment-private* IIO hides the sequence of updates as well. Informally, it states that if update sequences I_0, I_1 produce functionally equivalent circuit sequences, then the sequence of updated obfuscations hides whether I_0 or I_1 was used for making updates.

Definition 4 (Increment-private IIO). *A pair of uniform PPT machines $(\mathcal{O}, \mathsf{Update})$ is called a* sequence hiding *incremental indistinguishability obfuscator for a circuit class $\{\mathcal{C}_\lambda\}$ if it satisfies the* syntax, correctness *and* incrementality *properties (as in Definition 3) and the following* sequence-hiding indistinguishability *property:*

- Increment-private indistinguishability: *For any (not necessarily uniform) PPT distinguisher D, there exists a negligible function α such that the following holds: For all security parameters $\lambda \in \mathbb{N}$, for all pairs of circuits $C_0, C_1 \in \mathcal{C}_\lambda$, for every polynomial t and for all pairs of update sequences I_0, I_1 of length t we have that if $C_0(x) = C_1(x)$ and $F_{I_0}(C_0)(x) = F_{I_1}(C_1)(x)$ for all inputs x, then*

$$\left|\Pr\left[D(\mathsf{Expt}(\lambda, C_0, C_1, I_0, I_1, 0)) = 1\right] - \Pr\left[D(\mathsf{Expt}(\lambda, C_0, C_1, I_0, I_1, 1)) = 1\right]\right| \leq \alpha(\lambda).$$

where distribution $\mathsf{Expt}(\lambda, C_0, C_1, I_0, I_1, b)$ *outputs as follows: sample* $(\widetilde{C}_b, sk) \leftarrow \mathcal{O}(\lambda, C_b)$, *sample sequence* $(\widetilde{C}_b^1, \ldots, \widetilde{C}_b^t) \leftarrow \mathsf{Update}^{\widetilde{C}_b}(sk, I_b)$, *and output* $(I_0, I_1, C_0, C_1, \widetilde{C}_b, \widetilde{C}_b^1, \ldots, \widetilde{C}_b^t)$.

Finally, we define the following *pristine updates* property which is desirable but not implied by above definitions: updated obfuscation of a circuit should be statistically close to its fresh obfuscation.

Definition 5 (Pristine updates). *An incremental indistinguishability obfuscator* $(\mathcal{O}, \mathsf{Update})$ *for a circuit class* $\{\mathcal{C}_\lambda\}$ *has* pristine updates *if there exists a negligible function* α *such that* $\forall \lambda \in \mathbb{N}$, $\forall C \in \mathcal{C}_\lambda$, *and* $\forall (S, F_S)$, *the statistical distance between distributions* $\{\widetilde{C} : (\widetilde{C}, sk) \leftarrow \mathcal{O}(\lambda, C)\}$ *and* $\{\widetilde{C}' : (\widetilde{C}, sk) \leftarrow \mathcal{O}(\lambda, C), (\widetilde{S}, F_{\widetilde{S}}) \leftarrow \mathsf{Update}^{\widetilde{C}}(sk, (S, F_S)), \widetilde{C}' = F_{\widetilde{S}}(\widetilde{C})$ *is at most* $\alpha(\lambda)$.

3.2   Incremental **VGB** and **VBB** Obfuscation

The simulation based definitions are defined analogously, but require the existence of a simulator.

Definition 6 (Incremental VGB/VBB Obfuscator). *A pair of uniform PPT machines* $(\mathcal{O}, \mathsf{Update})$ *is called an* incremental VGB obfuscator *for a circuit class* $\{\mathcal{C}_\lambda\}$ *if it satisfies the* syntax, correctness *and* incrementality *properties (as in Definition 3) and the following VGB security property:*

For any (not necessarily uniform) PPT (single bit) adversary A, there exists a simulator S, a polynomial q, and a negligible function α, such that the following holds: For all security parameters $\lambda \in \mathbb{N}$, for all circuits $C \in \mathcal{C}_\lambda$, for every polynomial t and for every sequence I of t updates, we have that,

$$\left| \Pr\left[A(\widetilde{C}, \widetilde{C}^1, \ldots, \widetilde{C}^t) = 1 \right] - \Pr\left[\mathcal{S}^{C[q(\lambda)], F_I(C)[q(\lambda)]}(1^\lambda, 1^{|C|}) = 1 \right] \right| \le \alpha(\lambda).$$

where $(\widetilde{C}, sk) \leftarrow \mathcal{O}(\lambda, C)$, $(\widetilde{C}^1, \ldots, \widetilde{C}^t) \leftarrow \mathsf{Update}^{\widetilde{C}}(sk, I)$, *and notation* $C[q(\lambda)]$ *(resp., $F_I(C)[q(\lambda)]$) represents at most q oracle calls to C (resp., every circuit in $(C, F_I(C))$).*

If S is polynomial time in λ, we say that $(\mathcal{O}, \mathsf{Update})$ is incremental VBB obfuscator for $\{\mathcal{C}_\lambda\}$.

4   Our Construction

In this section, we present our basic construction which satisfies IIO notion. Let:

- (G, E, D) be a PKE scheme for bits with ciphertext length ℓ_e,
- (Gen, H) be an SSB hash with alphabet $\Sigma = \{0, 1\}^{\ell_e}$ and output length ℓ,
- $\mathcal{O}$ be an IO scheme for all circuits,
- (K, P, V) be a NIZK proof system for NP
- com be a non-interactive perfectly binding string commitment scheme

The component algorithms of our IIO scheme ($\mathsf{IncO}, \mathsf{Update}$) are described in Figs. 1, 2 and 3.

Algorithm $\mathsf{IncO}(1^\lambda, C)$ proceeds as follows:

1. Sample $(pk_1, sk_1) \leftarrow K(1^\lambda)$ and $(pk_2, sk_2) \leftarrow G(1^\lambda)$.
2. Generate $e = (e_1, e_2)$ where e_1, e_2 are *bit-wise* encryptions of C, i.e., $e_1 = (e_{1,1}, \ldots, e_{1,|C|})$ and $e_2 = (e_{2,1}, \ldots, e_{2,|C|})$ where $e_{1,i} \leftarrow E(pk_1, C[i])$, $e_{2,i} \leftarrow E(pk_2, C[i])$, for every $i \in [|C|]$.
3. Sample $hk \leftarrow \mathsf{Gen}(1^\lambda, 1^{\ell_e}, |e|, 0)$ and $\sigma \leftarrow K(1^\lambda)$
4. Generate $c_1 \leftarrow \mathsf{com}(1^\ell; \omega_1), c_2 \leftarrow \mathsf{com}(1^\ell; \omega_2), c_3 \leftarrow \mathsf{com}(0^\ell \| 1^\ell; \omega_3)$
5. Compute $(h, T) = H_{hk}(e)$, where h is the root node of the (Merkle) tree T.
6. Choose a random r and compute the proof $\pi_h \leftarrow P(\sigma, (h, r, c_1, c_2, c_3), w)$ for relation R using witness $w = (1^\ell, 1^\ell, 0^\ell \| 1^\ell, \omega_1, \omega_2, \omega_3)$ where $((h, r, c_1, c_2, c_3), (h', u, t_1 \| t_2, \omega_1, \omega_2, \omega_3)) \in R$ iff:
   (a) $c_1 = \mathsf{com}(h'; \omega_1), c_2 = \mathsf{com}(u; \omega_2), c_3 = \mathsf{com}(t_1 \| t_2; \omega_3), t_1 \leq r \leq t_2$, AND
   (b) EITHER $(h \neq h' \wedge r \neq u)$ OR $(h = h' \wedge r = u)$
7. Compute obfuscation $\widetilde{P}_{hk, \sigma, c_1, c_2, c_3, sk_1} \leftarrow \mathcal{O}\left(1^\lambda, P_{hk, \sigma, c_1, c_2, c_3, sk_1}\right)$ where $P_{hk, \sigma, c_1, c_2, c_3, sk_1}$ is described in figure 2. The size of $P_{hk, \sigma, c_1, c_2, c_3, sk_1}$ is padded to a value Q defined later.
8. Let $\widetilde{C} := \left(e, h, T, r, \pi_h, \widetilde{P}_{hk, \sigma, c_1, c_2, c_3, sk_1}\right)$ and $uk := (pk_1, hk, c_1, c_2, c_3, \sigma, w)$; output $(\widetilde{C}, uk)$.

Evaluation of $\widetilde{C}$ on input x is obtained by evaluating $\widetilde{P}_{hk, \sigma, c_1, c_2, c_3, sk_1}$ on input (e, r, π_h, x).

Fig. 1. Description of IncO

Circuit $P_{hk, \sigma, c_1, c_2, c_3, sk_1}$ computes as follows on input (e, v, π, x):

1. Compute $(h, T) = H_{hk}(e)$ and verify that $V(\sigma, (h, v, c_1, c_2, c_3), \pi) = 1$. Output $\bot$ if verification fails.
2. Otherwise, parse e as (e_1, e_2), compute $C = D(sk_1, e_1)$, and output $C(x)$.

Fig. 2. Description of $P_{hk, \sigma, c_1, c_2, c_3, sk_1}$

Algorithm $\mathsf{Update}^{C, \widetilde{C}}(uk, S)$ computes (oracle access to C is made via $\widetilde{C}$) as follows:

Parse the update key as $uk = (pk_1, hk, c_1, c_2, c_3, \sigma, w)$ where $w = (1^\ell, 1^\ell, 1^\ell, \omega_1, \omega_2, \omega_3)$. For every index $i \in S$ do the following:

1. Access the bit $C[i]$, and corresponding ciphertexts $e_{1,i}$ and $e_{2,i}$ from e (which is part of $\widetilde{C}$).
2. Generate updated ciphertexts $e'_{1,i} \leftarrow E(pk_1, 1 - C[i])$ and $e'_{2,i} \leftarrow E(pk_2, 1 - C[i])$. Let e' denote the string e when $e_{1,i}$ is replaced with $e'_{1,i}$ and $e_{2,i}$ is replaced with $e'_{2,i}$.
3. Define $(h', T') = H_{hk}(e')$, and let S' be the set of indices where e, e' differ. Run the (incremental) update algorithm to get $S'' \leftarrow \mathsf{HashUpdate}^{e, h, T}(S')$.
4. Access h and compute h' using the knowledge of S''. Access v and set $v' = v + 1$. Compute the new proof $\pi_{h'} \leftarrow P(\sigma, (h', v', c_1, c_2, c_3), w)$.
5. Output the set of indices where $(e', h', T', v', \pi_{h'})$ differ from (e, h, T, v, π_h).

Fig. 3. Description of Update.

Theorem 1. *Scheme* $(\mathsf{Inc}\mathcal{O}, \mathsf{Update})$ *is an* IIO *scheme for all circuits.*

Proof. It is easy to verify the correctness and incrementality of this scheme. It is also easy to see that the scheme satisfies the pristine updates property.

We show that it satisfies the indistinguishability property. Fix any two circuits (C_0, C_1), and any sequence I of any polynomial many incremental updates, say t updates. We need to show that $\mathsf{Expt}(\lambda, C_0, C_1, I, 0) \equiv_c \mathsf{Expt}(\lambda, C_0, C_1, I, 0)$.

$\mathcal{H}_1$: Same as $\mathsf{Expt}(\lambda, C_0, C_1, I, 0)$. For convenience, let us define $C_0^0 = C_0$ and $C_1^0 = C_1$.

Recall that the output of this experiment is $(I, C_0^0, C_1^0, \widetilde{C}_0^0, \widetilde{C}_0^1, \ldots, \widetilde{C}_0^t)$ where $\widetilde{C}_0^i$ is of the form $(e^i, h^i, T^i, r^i, \pi_{h^i}, \widetilde{P}_{hk,\sigma,c_1,c_2,c_3,sk_1})$ and $e^i = (e_1^i, e_2^i)$ represents two (bitwise) encryptions of C_0^i under keys pk_1 and pk_2 respectively.

$\mathcal{H}_{1.5}$: Same as $\mathcal{H}_1$ except that the CRS σ and all NIZK proofs are obtained from the simulator, i.e., values $(\sigma, \pi_{h^1}, \ldots, \pi_{h^t})$ are sampled using the simulator. The distinguishing advantage from $\mathcal{H}_1$ is at most $t\delta_{\mathsf{nizk}}$.

$\mathcal{H}_2$: This hybrid tests $|r + t| \leq \ell$ (i.e., $r + t \leq 2^\ell - 1$), and if so, it sets c_3 to be a commitment to $t_1 \| t_2$ for $t_1 = r$ and $t_2 = r + t$, instead of $0^\ell \| 1^\ell$, and continues as $\mathcal{H}_2$. If the test fails, it aborts.

The advantage in distinguishing $\mathcal{H}_2$ and $\mathcal{H}_3$ is at most $\delta_{\mathsf{com}} + t2^{-\ell}$ where δ_{com} is the distinguishing advantage for com. This is because of the following: value $r + t > 2^\ell$ for a randomly chosen r if and only if $r \in [2^\ell - t, 2^\ell]$ which happens with probability $t2^{-\ell}$; if the test succeeds, the hybrids differ only in commitment c_3.

This hybrid ensures that there are no valid proofs other than the $t + 1$ proofs that are given as part of the obfuscation and the updates.

$\mathcal{H}_{2.5}$: Same as $\mathcal{H}_2$ except that the CRS σ and all NIZK proofs $(\pi_{h^1}, \ldots, \pi_{h^t})$ are now generated normally using the appropriate witness (instead of being simulated). Note that the hybrid indeed does have the appropriate witnesses to complete this step normally, and the distinguishing advantage from $\mathcal{H}_2$ is at most $t\delta_{\mathsf{nizk}}$.

$\mathcal{H}_3$: This hybrid is identical to $\mathcal{H}_{2.5}$ except that it generates the components $\{e_2^i\}$ by (bitwise) encrypting the sequence of circuits corresponding C_1, namely $\{C_1^i\}$ (instead of $\{C_0^i\}$) for every $i \in [t]$. That is, for ever $i \in [t]$, it computes $\widetilde{C}_0^i$ to be of the form $(e^i, h^i, T^i, \pi_{h^i}, \widetilde{P}_{hk,\sigma,c_1,c_2,c_3,sk_1})$ as before where $e^i = (e_1^i, e_2^i)$ and e_1^i is a bitwise encryption of C_0^i under pk_1 obtained via updates but e_2^i is a bitwise encryption of C_1^i under pk_2 (also obtained via updates).

The advantage in distinguishing $\mathcal{H}_{2.5}$ and $\mathcal{H}_3$ is at most $t \cdot |C_0| \cdot \delta_{\mathsf{pke}}$ where δ_{pke} denotes the advantage in breaking the security of PKE scheme. This claim is straightforward.

$\mathcal{H}_4$: Identical to $\mathcal{H}_3$ except that instead of obfuscating circuit $P_{hk,\sigma,c_1,c_2,c_3,sk_1}$, it obfuscates the following circuit $P2_{hk,\sigma,c_1,c_2,c_3,sk_2}$[2], padded to the size Q:

---

[2] See step 7, Fig. 1. Note that this obfuscation is generated only once and never changes during the updates.

Circuit $P2_{hk,\sigma,c_1,c_2,c_3,sk_2}(e,v,\pi,x)$:

1. Compute $(h,T) = H_{hk}(e)$ and verify that $V(\sigma,(h,v,c_1,c_2,c_3),\pi) = 1$. Output $\perp$ if verification fails.
2. Otherwise, parse e as (e_1,e_2), compute $C = D(sk_2,e_2)$, and output $C(x)$.

Let δ_4 denote the distinguishing advantage of any polynomial time distinguisher between $\mathcal{H}_4$ and $\mathcal{H}_3$. From lemma 1, $\delta_4 \leq 4t^2|C_0| \cdot (\delta_{ssb} + \delta_{nizk} + \delta, + \delta_{IO})$ where quantities $\delta_{ssb}, \delta_{nizk}$, and δ_{IO} denote the distinguishing advantage for SSB hash, NIZK proofs, and IO respectively.

$\mathcal{H}_5$: Same as $\mathcal{H}_4$ except that it generates ciphertexts e_1^i to now encrypt C_1^i (instead of C_0^i) $\forall i \in [t]$. That is, for every $i \in [t]$, it computes $\widetilde{C}_0^i$ to be of the form $(e^i, h^i, T^i, \pi_{h^i}, \widetilde{P2}_{hk,\sigma,c_1,c_2,c_3,sk_2})$ where $e^i = (e_1^i, e_2^i)$ and e_1^i, e_2^i are (bitwise) encryptions of C_1^i under pk_1, pk_2 respectively. Note that these encryptions are actually obtained via updates.

The distinguishing advantage between $\mathcal{H}_5$ and $\mathcal{H}_4$ is at most $t|C_0|\delta_{pke}$. This is straightforward.

$\mathcal{H}_6$: Same as $\mathcal{H}_5$ except that it obfuscates circuit $P_{hk,\sigma,c_1,c_2,c_3,sk_1}$ (which uses sk_1 and decrypts from e_1, see Fig. 2) instead of $P2_{hk,\sigma,c_1,c_2,c_3,sk_2}$.

Let δ_6 denote the distinguishing advantage between $\mathcal{H}_6$ and $\mathcal{H}_5$. We claim that $\delta_6 \leq 4t^2|C_0| \cdot (\delta_{ssb} + \delta_{nizk} + \delta, + \delta_{IO})$. The proof is identical to that of lemma 1 and omitted.

$\mathcal{H}_7$: Same as $\mathcal{H}_6$ but now c_3 is switched back to a commitment of $0^\ell\|1^\ell$ instead of $t_1\|t_2$. Recall that $t_1 = r, t_2 = r + t$.

The distinguishing advantage between $\mathcal{H}_7$ and $\mathcal{H}_6$ is at most $\delta, + t2^{-\ell}$ (as argued in $\mathcal{H}_2$).

Observe that $\mathcal{H}_7$ is the same as experiment $\mathsf{Expt}(\lambda, C_0, C_1, I, 1)$. The total distinguishing advantage is thus bounded by $O(t^2 \cdot |C_0| \cdot (\delta_{pke} + \delta_{nizk} + \delta_{ssb} + \delta, + 2^{-\ell}))$ which is negligible.

Lemma 1. $\delta_4 \leq 4t^2|C_0| \cdot (\delta_{ssb} + \delta_{nizk} + \delta, + \delta_{IO})$.

Proof. The lemma is proven by focusing on one of the t locations in the sequence at a time, and use the properties of SSB hash, to slowly reach a point where there is a unique value of e corresponding to the hash value at this location. All values prior to this location will use sk_2 and e_2, whereas those after it will use sk_1, e_1.

More precisely, we describe t hybrids $\mathcal{G}_1, \ldots, \mathcal{G}_t$ where hybrid $\mathcal{G}_j$ will use sk_2 on inputs with value v if $r \leq v < r + j$, and sk_1 if $r + j \leq v \leq r + t$. Note that v is always in the range $[r, r + t]$ in this hybrid. To prove that $\mathcal{G}_{j-1}$ and $\mathcal{G}_j$ are indistinguishable, we will design another $4 + 2|C_0|$ hybrids where we will first ensure the uniqueness of (j, h^j) and then perform SSB hash translation to move to $\mathcal{G}_j$.

Formally, define $\mathcal{G}_0$ to be the same as $\mathcal{H}_3$, and for $j \in [t]$ define hybrid $\mathcal{G}_j$ as follows: it is identical to $\mathcal{G}_{j-1}$ except that it obfuscates the circuit $P_{hk,\sigma,c_1,c_2,c_3,r,sk_1,sk_2,j}$ described in Fig. 4 (instead of $P_{hk,\sigma,c_1,c_2,c_3,r,sk_1,sk_2,j-1}$).[3]

---

[3] Note that the only difference between these two circuits are values j and $j-1$, and this obfuscation is performed only *once* throughout the whole sequence.

Circuit $P_{hk,\sigma,c_1,c_2,c_3,r,sk_1,sk_2,j}(e,v,\pi,x)$:

1. Compute $(h,T) = H_{hk}(e)$ and verify that $V(\sigma,(h,v,c_1,c_2,c_3),\pi) = 1$.
   Output $\perp$ if verification fails.
2. Otherwise, parse e as (e_1,e_2) and compute C as follows:
   If $r \leq v \leq r+j$, set $C = D(sk_2,e_2)$;
   If $r+j < v \leq r+t$, set $C = D(sk_1,e_1)$.
3. Output $C(x)$.

Fig. 4. Description of $P_{hk,\sigma,c_1,c_2,c_3,sk_1,j}$

Note that r was chosen uniformly in step 6 of the construction and the size of $P_{hk,\sigma,c_1,c_2,c_3,r,sk_1,sk_2,j}$ is padded to the value Q before obfuscation.

Let ε_j denote the distinguishing advantage between $\mathcal{G}_j$ and $\mathcal{G}_{j-1}$. Observe that $\mathcal{G}_t$ is the same as $\mathcal{H}_4$ and $\delta_4 \leq \sum_j \varepsilon_j$. We now prove that $\varepsilon_j \leq 4t|C_0| \cdot (\delta_{ssb} + \delta_{nizk} + \delta_, + \delta_{IO})$.

Consider the following hybrids:

$\mathcal{G}_{j:1}$: Same as $\mathcal{G}_{j-1}$ except that the CRS σ and all NIZK proofs are obtained from the simulator, i.e., values $(\sigma, \pi_{h^1}, \ldots, \pi_{h^t})$ are sampled using the simulator. The distinguishing advantage from $\mathcal{G}_{j-1}$ is at most $t\delta_{nizk}$.

$\mathcal{G}_{j:2}$: Same as $\mathcal{G}_{j:1}$ except that commitments c_1 and c_2 are changed as follows. Let e^j denote the encryptions corresponding to the j-th update in the sequence, and let $h^j = H_{hk}(e^j)$. Then, c_1 is set to be a commitment to h^j and c_2 a commitment to $r+j$: $c_1 =, (h^j; \omega_1), c_2 =, (r+j; \omega_2)$. The distinguishing advantage from $\mathcal{G}_{j:1}$ is at most $\delta_,$.

$\mathcal{G}_{j:3}$: Same as $\mathcal{G}_{j:2}$ except that the CRS σ and all NIZK proofs $(\pi_{h^1}, \ldots, \pi_{h^t})$ are now generated normally using the appropriate witness (instead of being simulated). Note that the hybrid indeed does have the appropriate witnesses to complete this step normally, and the distinguishing advantage from $\mathcal{G}_{j:2}$ is at most $t\delta_{nizk}$.

At this point, for location j, there exists only one value of h^j that can produce convincing proofs (from the soundness of NIZK). Next, we will use the SSB hash to reach a point where only the string e^j will be accepted by the obfuscated circuit as the valid input corresponding to hash h^j. We do this in a series of $2|C_0|$ hybrids corresponding to the $2|C_0|$ encryptions occurring in $e^j = (e_1^j, e_2^j)$.

Formally, for every $m = 1, \ldots, 2|C_0|$, we define two hybrids $\mathcal{G}_{j:3}^{m:1}, \mathcal{G}_{j:3}^{m:2}$ below. Let e_m^* denote the string which identical to e^j in the first m blocks, each of length ℓ_e, and 0 everywhere else. For convention, let $\mathcal{G}_{j:3}^{0:2}$ be the same as $\mathcal{G}_{j:3}$. Then:

$\mathcal{G}_{j:3}^{m:1}$: Same as $\mathcal{G}_{j:3}^{m-1:2}$ except that it makes hk to be binding at m, i.e., $hk \leftarrow \mathsf{Gen}(1^\lambda, 1^{\ell_e}, |e|, m)$.

$\mathcal{G}_{j:3}^{m:2}$: Let us recall that we started with hybrid $\mathcal{G}_{j-1}$ which obfuscates the circuit $P_{hk,\sigma,c_1,c_2,c_3,sk_1,sk_2,j-1}$. This hybrid proceeds just like $\mathcal{G}_{j:3}^{m:1}$ except that it obfuscates the circuit $P_{hk,\sigma,c_1,c_2,c_3,sk_1,sk_2,j-1}^{m,e_m^*}$ described below.

Circuit $P^{m,e_m^*}_{hk,\sigma,c_1,c_2,c_3,sk_1,sk_2,j-1}(e,v,\pi,x)$:
1. If the first m blocks of e and e_m^* are not the same, output $\bot$.
2. Otherwise output $P_{hk,\sigma,c_1,c_2,c_3,sk_1,sk_2,j-1}(e,v,\pi,x)$ (see Fig. 4).

The distinguishing advantage between $\mathcal{G}^{m-1:2}_{j:3}$ and $\mathcal{G}^{m:1}_{j:3}$ is at most δ_{ssb}, and between $\mathcal{G}^{m:1}_{j:3}$ and $\mathcal{G}^{m:2}_{j:3}$ is at most δ_{IO}.

When $m=2|C_0|$, the circuit $P^{m,e_m^*}_{hk,\sigma,c_1,c_2,c_3,sk_1,sk_2,j}$ accepts only $e^*_{2|C_0|} = e^j$ as the input for location j in the sequence and all other inputs are rejected. We can now safely change this program to use sk_2 to decrypt e^j_2 at location j (instead of e^j_1). More precisely, we consider the hybrid:

$\mathcal{G}_{j:4}$ Same as $\mathcal{G}^{2|C_0|:2}_{j:3}$ except that it obfuscates a circuit which, in location j, decrypts from e^j_2. More precisely, it obfuscates the following circuit:

Circuit $P^{e^j}_{hk,\sigma,c_1,c_2,c_3,sk_1,sk_2,j-1}(e,v,\pi,x)$:
1. If $e \neq e^j$, output $\bot$.
2. Otherwise output $P_{hk,\sigma,c_1,c_2,c_3,sk_1,\underline{sk_2,j}}(e,v,\pi,x)$ (see Fig. 4).

The distinguishing advantage from previous hybrid is at most δ_{IO}.

Our goal is now to get rid of the first condition, so that we switch back to only obfuscating $P_{hk,\sigma,c_1,c_2,c_3,sk_1,sk_2,j}$. This is performed by simply reversing the steps in m hybrids. Furthermore, we also reverse the changes made in the commitment in a sequence of 3 hybrids by considering the reverse of hybrids $\mathcal{G}_{j:3}, \mathcal{G}_{j:2}, \mathcal{G}_{j:1}$. The resulting hybrid would essentially be identical to $\mathcal{G}_j$. We omit these details.

The total distinguishing advantage between $\mathcal{G}_j$ and $\mathcal{G}_{j-1}$ is bounded by the sum of all advantages, which is at most $4t|C_0|(\delta_, + \delta_{nizk} + \delta_{ssb} + \delta_{IO})$. This completes the proof.

Size Q: The value of Q is defined to be the size of the program $P^{e^j}_{hk,\sigma,c_1,c_2,c_3,sk_1,sk_2,j-1}$ described above (for any value of j, say $j=1$).

Construction for Turing machines and RAM programs. As mentioned earlier, our constructions are quite independent of the underlying model of computation. For example, to obtain construction for the class of bounded-input Turing machines, we use the same construction as in Fig. 1 except that the obfuscator $\mathcal{O}$ for circuits in (step 7) will now be an obfuscator for the class of bounded-input Turing machines since the program in Fig. 2 will now be a bounded-input Turing machine. Likewise, we also obtain constructions for RAM programs and unbounded-input Turing machines assuming the existence of IO for the same. This gives us the following theorem.

Theorem 2. *If there exists indistinguishability obfuscation for a class of programs* $\mathcal{P} = \{P_\lambda\}$ *modeled as either boolean circuits, or (bounded/unbounded input) Turing machines, or RAM programs, then there exists incremental indistinguishability obfuscation (IIO, Definition 3) for* $\mathcal{P}$.

5   Amplifying Security to Increment-Private IIO

In this section, we present our (black-box) transformation which transform an IIO scheme (Definition 3) into an increment-private IIO scheme (Definition 4). As before, for concreteness, we present our transformation for circuits, but it works for Turing machines and RAM programs as well. Our transformation preserves the *pristine updates* property as well (Definition 5).

As discussed in the overview, the construction consists of applying the ORAM encoding on the given circuit twice. These encodings are then hardwired into a program, along with the secret information for decoding only *one* of the two ORAM encodings. This is essentially the two-key paradigm [NY90] implemented with ORAM. The resulting program is then obfuscated using the given IIO scheme. In addition to the encodings and secret information, the program is also provided with a bit b as well as some more information which tells the program which ORAM encoding to pick for evaluation. This is helpful in designing the hybrid experiments.

Our construction. Let $(\mathcal{O}, \mathsf{Update})$ be an IIO scheme for the class of all circuits. Let $(\mathsf{OData}, \mathsf{OAccess})$ be an oblivious RAM scheme as described in Sect. 2.3. Our new scheme consists of algorithms $(\mathcal{O}', \mathsf{Update}')$ described in Fig. 5.[4]

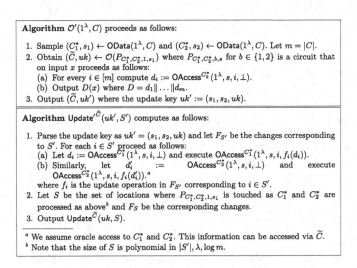

Algorithm $\mathcal{O}'(1^\lambda, C)$ proceeds as follows:

1. Sample $(C_1^*, s_1) \leftarrow \mathsf{OData}(1^\lambda, C)$ and $(C_2^*, s_2) \leftarrow \mathsf{OData}(1^\lambda, C)$. Let $m = |C|$.
2. Obtain $(\widetilde{C}, uk) \leftarrow \mathcal{O}(P_{C_1^*, C_2^*, 1, s_1})$ where $P_{C_1^*, C_2^*, b, s}$ for $b \in \{1, 2\}$ is a circuit that on input x proceeds as follows:
   (a) For every $i \in [m]$ compute $d_i := \mathsf{OAccess}^{C_b^*}(1^\lambda, s, i, \bot)$.
   (b) Output $D(x)$ where $D = d_1 \| \dots \| d_m$.
3. Output $(\widetilde{C}, uk')$ where the update key $uk' := (s_1, s_2, uk)$.

Algorithm $\mathsf{Update}'^{\widetilde{C}}(uk', S')$ computes as follows:

1. Parse the update key as $uk' = (s_1, s_2, uk)$ and let $F_{S'}$ be the changes corresponding to S'. For each $i \in S'$ proceed as follows:
   (a) Let $d_i := \mathsf{OAccess}^{C_1^*}(1^\lambda, s, i, \bot)$ and execute $\mathsf{OAccess}^{C_1^*}(1^\lambda, s, i, f_i(d_i))$.
   (b) Similarly, let $d'_i := \mathsf{OAccess}^{C_2^*}(1^\lambda, s, i, \bot)$ and execute $\mathsf{OAccess}^{C_2^*}(1^\lambda, s, i, f_i(d'_i))$.[a]
   where f_i is the update operation in $F_{S'}$ corresponding to $i \in S'$.
2. Let S be the set of locations where $P_{C_1^*, C_2^*, 1, s_1}$ is touched as C_1^* and C_2^* are processed as above[b] and F_S be the corresponding changes.
3. Output $\mathsf{Update}^{\widetilde{C}}(uk, S)$.

---
[a] We assume oracle access to C_1^* and C_2^*. This information can be accessed via $\widetilde{C}$.
[b] Note that the size of S is polynomial in $|S'|, \lambda, \log m$.

Fig. 5. Description of $\mathcal{O}'$ and Update'.

Theorem 3. *Scheme* $(\mathcal{O}', \mathsf{Update}')$ *is increment-private IIO for all circuits (Definition 4).*

---
[4] We emphasize that even though our scheme uses ORAM, program $P_{C_1^*, C_2^*, s, b}$ in Fig. 5 is still only a *circuit* and not a "RAM" program.

Proof. The correctness and the pristine updates property of our construction follows directly from the correctness and the pristine updates property of the underlying IIO scheme. We argue the increment-private indistinguishability property of our construction.

We have to show that for any (not necessarily uniform) PPT distinguisher D, there exists a negligible function α such that the following holds: For all security parameters $\lambda \in \mathbb{N}$, for all pairs of circuits $C_0, C_1 \in \mathcal{C}_\lambda$, for every polynomial t and for all pairs of update sequences I_0, I_1 of length t we have that if $C_0(x) = C_1(x)$ and $F_{I_0}(C_0)(x) = F_{I_1}(C_1)(x)$ for all inputs x, then

$$\left| \Pr\left[D(\mathsf{Expt}(\lambda, C_0, C_1, I_0, I_1, 0)) = 1 \right] - \Pr\left[D(\mathsf{Expt}(\lambda, C_0, C_1, I_0, I_1, 1)) = 1 \right] \right| \le \alpha(\lambda).$$

where distribution $\mathsf{Expt}(\lambda, C_0, C_1, I_0, I_1, b)$ outputs as follows: (1) Sample $(C_1^*, s_1) \leftarrow \mathsf{OData}(1^\lambda, C_b)$ and $(C_2^*, s_2) \leftarrow \mathsf{OData}(1^\lambda, C_b)$. (2) Sample $(\widetilde{C}, sk) \leftarrow \mathcal{O}(\lambda, P_{C_1^*, C_2^*, 1, s_1})$ and the sequence $(\widetilde{C}^1, \ldots, \widetilde{C}^t) \leftarrow \mathsf{Update}^{\widetilde{C}}(sk, J)$, and output $(I_0, I_1, C_0, C_1, \widetilde{C}, \widetilde{C}^1, \ldots, \widetilde{C}^t)$. Here $J = (S_1, \ldots, S_t)$ is obtained from $I_b = (S'_{b,1}, \ldots S'_{b,t})$ as follows (also described in Fig. 5). For each $j \in \{1, \ldots t\}$, set $S'_b = S'_{b,j}$ and proceed as follows.

1. $F_{S'_b}$ be the changes corresponding to S'_b. For each $i \in S'_b$ proceed as follows:
   (a) Let $d_i := \mathsf{OAccess}^{C_1^*}(1^\lambda, s, i, \bot)$ and execute $\mathsf{OAccess}^{C_1^*}(1^\lambda, s, i, f_i(d_i))$.
   (b) Similarly, let $d'_i := \mathsf{OAccess}^{C_2^*}(1^\lambda, s, i, \bot)$ and execute $\mathsf{OAccess}^{C_2^*}(1^\lambda, s, i, f_i(d'_i))$.
2. Let S be the set of locations where $P_{C_1^*, C_2^*, 1, s_1}$ is touched as C_1^* and C_2^* are processed as above[5] and F_S be the corresponding changes.
3. Output $\mathsf{Update}^{\widetilde{C}}(uk, S)$ as S_j.

To prove the claim, consider the following sequence of hybrids:

$\mathcal{H}_1$: This hybrid corresponds to the output of the experiment $\mathsf{Expt}(\lambda, C_0, C_1, I_0, I_1, 0)$ as above.

$\mathcal{H}_2$: In this hybrid we change Step 5 in the experiment above. In particular we instead of changing stored value to $f_i(d_i)$ we always set it to zero. More formally, the procedure is changed as follows.
   (a) $F_{S'_b}$ be the changes corresponding to S'_b. For each $i \in S'_0$ proceed as follows:
       i, Let $d_i := \mathsf{OAccess}^{C_1^*}(1^\lambda, s, i, \bot)$ and execute $\mathsf{OAccess}^{C_1^*}(1^\lambda, s, i, f_i(d_i))$.
       ii. Similarly, let $d'_i := \mathsf{OAccess}^{C_2^*}(1^\lambda, s, i, \bot)$ and execute $\mathsf{OAccess}^{C_2^*}(1^\lambda, s, i, 0)$.
   (b) Let S be the set of locations where $P_{C_1^*, C_2^*, 1, s_1}$ is touched as C_1^* and C_2^* are processed as above and F_S be the corresponding changes.

---

[5] Note that the size of S is polynomial in $|S'|, \lambda, \log m$.

(c) Output $\mathsf{Update}^{\widetilde{C}}(uk, S)$ as S_j.

Indistinguishability follows from the security of the IIO scheme. Here we use the property that any changes made to C_2^* do not affect the functionality of the program $P_{C_1^*, C_2^*, 1, s_1}$.

$\mathcal{H}_3$: In this hybrid we again change Step 5 in the experiment above. In particular, we make changes to C_2^* at locations S_1' instead of S_0'. As in $\mathcal{H}_1$ we still set these locations to zero when the change is made. More formally:

(a) $F_{S_b'}$ be the changes corresponding to S_b'. For each $i \in S_0'$ and $k \in S_1'$ proceed as follows:

    i. Let $d_i := \mathsf{OAccess}^{C_1^*}(1^\lambda, s, i, \perp)$ and execute $\mathsf{OAccess}^{C_1^*}(1^\lambda, s, i, f_i(d_i))$.

    ii. Similarly, let $d_k' := \mathsf{OAccess}^{C_2^*}(1^\lambda, s, k, \perp)$ and execute $\mathsf{OAccess}^{C_2^*}(1^\lambda, s, k, 0)$.

(b) Let S be the set of locations where $P_{C_1^*, C_2^*, 1, s_1}$ is touched as C_1^* and C_2^* are processed as above and F_S be the corresponding changes.

(c) Output $\mathsf{Update}^{\widetilde{C}}(uk, S)$ as S_j.

Indistinguishability follows from the security of the oblivious RAM scheme (as in Sect. 2.3).

$\mathcal{H}_4$: In this hybrid we change how C_2^* is generated and the changes that are made while the increments are performed. More formally:

We generate (C_2^*, s_2) by executing $\mathsf{OData}(1^\lambda, C_1)$. Additionally the increments are not set using I_1 instead of I_0 as follows:

(a) $F_{S_b'}$ be the changes corresponding to S_b'. For each $i \in S_0'$ and $k \in S_1'$ proceed as follows:

    i. Let $d_i := \mathsf{OAccess}^{C_1^*}(1^\lambda, s, i, \perp)$ and execute $\mathsf{OAccess}^{C_1^*}(1^\lambda, s, i, f_i(d_i))$.

    ii. Similarly, let $d_k' := \mathsf{OAccess}^{C_2^*}(1^\lambda, s, k, \perp)$ and execute $\mathsf{OAccess}^{C_2^*}(1^\lambda, s, k, f_k(d_k'))$.

(b) Let S be the set of locations where $P_{C_1^*, C_2^*, 1, s_1}$ is touched as C_1^* and C_2^* are processed as above and F_S be the corresponding changes.

(c) Output $\mathsf{Update}^{\widetilde{C}}(uk, S)$ as S_j.

Indistinguishability follows from the security of the IIO scheme. Here we use the property that any changes made to C_2^* do not affect the functionality of the program $P_{C_1^*, C_2^*, 1, s_1}$.

$\mathcal{H}_5$: In this hybrid instead of outputting an obfuscation of $P_{C_1^*, C_2^*, 1, s_1}$ we output and obfuscation of $P_{C_1^*, C_2^*, 2, s_2}$.

Indistinguishability follows from the security of the IIO scheme. Here we use the property that for all x we have that $C_0(x) = C_1(x)$ and $F_{I_0}(C_0)(x) = F_{I_1}(C_1)(x)$. This in particular implies that $P_{C_1^*, C_2^*, 1, s_1}(x) = P_{C_1^*, C_2^*, 2, s_2}(x)$ and $F_J(P_{C_1^*, C_2^*, 1, s_1})(x) = F_J(P_{C_1^*, C_2^*, 2, s_2})(x)$ where $J = (S_1, \ldots S_t)$ as obtained in the previous hybrid.

Observe that at this point we can reverse the hybrids presented above and obtain the distribution $\mathsf{Expt}(\lambda, C_0, C_1, I_0, I_1, 1)$. This proves our claim.

As before, this transformation is not specific to circuits. In particular, if $(\mathcal{O}, \mathsf{Update})$ is a scheme for Turing machines or RAM programs, then $(\mathcal{O}', \mathsf{Update}')$ is increment-private IIO for the same model. Thus, our transformation, together with Theorem 2, gives the following result.

Theorem 4. *If there exists indistinguishability obfuscation for a class of programs* $\mathcal{P} = \{P_\lambda\}$ *modeled as either boolean circuits, or (bounded/unbounded input) Turing machines, or RAM programs, then there exists* increment-private *indistinguishability obfuscation (Definition 4) for* $\mathcal{P}$.

6   The Lower Bound

Point functions. Let $\mathcal{I}_n = \{I_x\}_{x \in \{0,1\}^n}$ denote the family of point functions for points in $\{0,1\}^n$ where n is a (potentially large) polynomial in λ. Function I_x takes as input $y \in \{0,1\}^n$ and outputs 1 if $y = x$ and 0 otherwise.

VBB obfuscation schemes for $\mathcal{I}_n$ are known to exist [Wee05, Can97, BS16] under standard assumptions such as variants of one-way permutation or DDH. We show that even for a family as simple as $\mathcal{I}_n$, *incremental* VBB obfuscation (corresponding to our efficiency requirements) does not exist. In fact, we rule this out even for VGB obfuscation, which is weaker than VBB; this strengthens our result.

More specifically, we show that the update algorithm of every incremental VGB obfuscation for $\mathcal{I}_n$ must change $\Omega(n/\log n)$ bits for a large fraction of functions $I_x \in \mathcal{I}_n$ even if only *one* bit changes in x.

Theorem 5. *Every* VGB *obfuscation scheme for* $\mathcal{I}_n$ *must have incrementality* $\Delta \in \Omega(n/\log n)$.

Proof. Let $(\mathcal{O}, \mathsf{Update})$ be a VGB obfuscation scheme for $\mathcal{I}_n$ with incrementality Δ. Let λ be the security parameter so that $n = n(\lambda) \geq \lambda$ is a polynomial determining the length of points in $\mathcal{I}_n$, and Δ is a function of λ.

The proof proceeds by showing that incrementality "leaks" Hamming distance between updated obfuscations, which, by definition, cannot be leaked by VGB obfuscation. Formally, define the following two distributions:

- $\mathcal{D}_1$: Obtain obfuscations for programs I_x and $I_{x'}$ for a random x by obfuscating I_x and updating it for $I_{x'}$ where x, x' differ in only one position, say first. I.e., sample $x \leftarrow \{0,1\}^n$, $\widetilde{I}_x \leftarrow \mathcal{O}(I_x)$, $\widetilde{I}_{x'} \leftarrow \mathsf{Update}^{\widetilde{I}_x}(1^\lambda, uk, \{1, \mathsf{flip}\})$, and output $(\widetilde{I}_x, \widetilde{I}_{x'})$.
- $\mathcal{D}_2$: Return obfuscations of two random points y_1, y_2 through update. I.e., sample y_1, y_2 uniformly, and obtain $\widetilde{I}_{y_1} \leftarrow \mathcal{O}(I_{y_1})$. Let δ denote the set of locations where y_1, y_2 differ corresponding to the function flip. Then, obtain $\widetilde{I}_{y_2} \leftarrow \mathsf{Update}^{\widetilde{I}_{y_1}}(1^\lambda, \delta)$.

Next, define the following adversarial algorithm:

Algorithm A: on input two strings $(\widetilde{I}_1, \widetilde{I}_2)$, A outputs 1 if the Hamming distance between $\widetilde{I}_1, \widetilde{I}_2$ is at most Δ; otherwise A outputs 0.

By definition of VGB security, there exists a simulator S, a polynomial q, and a negligible function α such that S can simulate the output of A (on any two obfuscated circuits) by making at most q queries to the corresponding circuits. Note that this simulator S cannot distinguish the two cases above as it is only give oracle access to the programs.

Let us consider the output of A on input $(\widetilde{I}_x, \widetilde{I}_{x'})$ sampled from $\mathcal{D}_1$. Due to the incrementality of the scheme, these inputs differ in at most Δ locations, and hence A outputs 1 with probability 1.

Next, consider the output of A on input $(\widetilde{I}_{y_1}, \widetilde{I}_{y_2})$ sampled from $\mathcal{D}_2$. We note that for any choice of randomness of the obfuscator the Hamming distance between $\widetilde{I}_{y_1}, \widetilde{I}_{y_2}$ cannot be less than than the $\Omega(n/\log n)$. More formally, for a choice of random coins, the obfuscator is an injective function from 2^n points to an obfuscation of m bits were $m = n^c$ for constant c. Then we claim that the two obfuscations (for random y_1 and y_2) differ by at least $\Omega(n/\log n)$ bits. If this was not the case then we could encode the two random points x_1, x_2 in $o(2n)$ bits which is impossible. In particular, we could perform the encoding by giving x_1 and the update of obfuscation from x_1 to x_2. If the hamming distance between the obfuscations of x_1 and x_2 is $t = o(n/\log n)$ then we have that this change can be encoded in $\log \binom{m}{t}$ which is at most $\log((n^c)^t) < c.o(n/\log n).\log n < o(n)$. Therefore, we conclude that $\Delta \in \Omega(n/\log n)$.

7   Best Possible Incremental Obfuscation

Our lower bound on the incrementality of VGB/VBB obfuscations demonstrates that any incremental scheme must leak the size of incremental updates that take place. An interesting question is if this is all that is leaked. In particular, we investigate the possibility of realizing weaker simulation-based notions which allow for leakage of the size of the incremental updates.

However, a notion along these lines leaves a lot unexplained. For example, it is not clear if such an effort would yield a meaningful notion for general programs. Motivated by such issues and inspired by the notion of "best possible obfuscation" [GR07] for the *single use* setting, we define the notion of "best possible incremental obfuscation" or IBPO.

Definition 7 (Incremental Best Possible Obfuscator (IBPO). *A pair of uniform PPT machines $(\mathcal{O}, \mathsf{Update})$ is called an* incremental BPO obfuscator *for a circuit class $\{\mathcal{C}_\lambda\}$ if it satisfies the* syntax, correctness *and* incrementality *properties (as in Definition 3) and the following best possible obfuscation property:*

For any (not necessarily uniform) PPT adversaries A, there exists a simulator S and a negligible function α, such that the following holds: For all security parameters $\lambda \in \mathbb{N}$, for all pairs of circuits $C_1, C_2 \in \mathcal{C}_\lambda$ (with $|C_1| = |C_2|$), for every polynomial t and for all pairs of update sequences I_0, I_1 (with $S_{0,i} = S_{1,i}$ for each $i \in \{1, \ldots, t\}$) of length t we have that if $C_0(x) = C_1(x)$ and $F_{I_0}(C_0)(x) = F_{I_1}(C_1)(x)$ for all inputs x, then

$$\left| \Pr\left[A(\widetilde{C}_0, \widetilde{C}_0^1, \ldots, \widetilde{C}_0^t) = 1 \right] - \Pr\left[\mathcal{S}(C_1, I_1) = 1 \right] \right| \le \alpha(\lambda)$$

where $(\widetilde{C}_0, sk) \leftarrow \mathcal{O}(\lambda, C_0)$, and $(\widetilde{C}_0^1, \ldots, \widetilde{C}_0^t) \leftarrow \mathsf{Update}^{\widetilde{C}_0}(sk, I_0)$.

Informally, this definition guarantees that any information that can be efficiently obtained from the obfuscation $\widetilde{C}_0$ along with the obfuscation increments $\widetilde{C}_0^1, \ldots, \widetilde{C}_0^t$, can also be extracted efficiently (i.e., simulated) from any equivalent circuit of a similar size C_1 and corresponding equivalent updates I_1 of similar size. We now prove the following theorem.

Theorem 6. $(\mathcal{O}, \mathsf{Update})$ *is* incremental BPO *obfuscator for a circuit class* $\{\mathcal{C}_\lambda\}$ *if and only if it is* increment-private IIO *obfuscator for* $\{\mathcal{C}_\lambda\}$.

Proof Sketch: We need to prove that an IBPO scheme is also a *increment-private* IIO scheme and the other way around. We start with the first direction.

By the definition of best possible obfuscation we have that the distributions $A(\widetilde{C}_0, \widetilde{C}_0^1, \ldots, \widetilde{C}_0^t)$ and $\mathcal{S}(C_1, I_1)$ are close. Similarly the distributions $A(\widetilde{C}_1, \widetilde{C}_1^1, \ldots, \widetilde{C}_1^t)$ and $\mathcal{S}(C_1, I_1)$ are close. In the above expressions for $b \in \{0, 1\}$, $(\widetilde{C}_b, sk_b) \leftarrow \mathcal{O}(\lambda, C_b)$, and $(\widetilde{C}_b^1, \ldots, \widetilde{C}_b^t) \leftarrow \mathsf{Update}^{\widetilde{C}_b}(sk_b, I_b)$. These two facts together imply that the distributions $A(\widetilde{C}_0, \widetilde{C}_0^1, \ldots, \widetilde{C}_0^t)$ and $A(\widetilde{C}_1, \widetilde{C}_1^1, \ldots, \widetilde{C}_1^t)$ are close, implying that $(\mathcal{O}, \mathsf{Update})$ is a *increment-private* incremental indistinguishability obfuscator.

Next we sketch the argument for the other direction. Our simulator $\mathcal{S}$ on input C_1, I_1 computes $(\widetilde{C}_1, sk_1) \leftarrow \mathcal{O}(\lambda, C_1)$, and $(\widetilde{C}_1^1, \ldots, \widetilde{C}_1^t) \leftarrow \mathsf{Update}^{\widetilde{C}_1}(sk_1, I_1)$ and outputs $(\widetilde{C}_1, \widetilde{C}_1^1, \ldots, \widetilde{C}_1^t)$. The indistinguishability of this from obfuscation of C_0 and obfuscation increments for I_0 follows directly from the security of *increment-private* incremental indistinguishability. $\qquad \square$

8   Extensions and Future Work

We discuss three possible extensions of our results: *non-sequential* model of updates, *adaptive* updates, and new types of update operations and other refinements.

Non-sequential updates. In our current model, an update at time step i is applied to the obfuscation at time step $i-1$. A more flexible approach would be to allow the update to any obfuscation that is previously present in the history. This results in a "tree like" structure for updates instead of the "line" for sequential updates. This model is interesting for situations where the copies of software reside on several remote machines and may be updated at different times.

Our constructions can be easily adapted for this setting as well. Specifically, in our basic IIO construction, instead of choosing r at random, let it be an encryption of a random value. The update algorithm will simply encrypt a fresh value each time (instead of adding 1 to the previous value). All other operations are performed as before.

The key observation is that, since the values are now encrypted, sequential values look indistinguishable from random. Therefore, in the security proof, we will first change the random values to sequential, and then proceed exactly as before. Note that the the obfuscated program does not need to know the values in the encryption, and hence does not need the secret key. Only the update algorithm needs the secret key. The proof now additionally uses the semantic security of encryption (along with NIZK proofs as before) to switch to sequential values.

Adaptive updates. As mentioned earlier, our constructions do not achieve adaptive security where future updates are chosen adversarially based on previous obfuscations. We leave this as an interesting open problem.

More general updates, and other refinements. We did not consider updates which may *increase the size* of the underlying programs. In many settings, the size of the program would likely increase after updates. Likewise, we also did not explore other refinements such as tamper-proof security (where the obfuscation to be updated may not be "correct" due to tampering by the adversary). It would be interesting to explore these directions in future.

Acknowledgements. We are thankful to the anonymous reviewers of CRYPTO 2017 for their helpful comments.

References

[AB15]   Applebaum, B., Brakerski, Z.: Obfuscating circuits via composite-order graded encoding. In: Dodis, Y., Nielsen, J.B. (eds.) TCC 2015. LNCS, vol. 9015, pp. 528–556. Springer, Heidelberg (2015). doi:10.1007/978-3-662-46497-7_21

[ABG+13] Ananth, P., Boneh, D., Garg, S., Sahai, A., Zhandry, M.: Differing-inputs obfuscation and applications. IACR Cryptology ePrint Archive (2013). http://eprint.iacr.org/2013/689.pdf

[AIK06] Applebaum, B., Ishai, Y., Kushilevitz, E.: Cryptography in NC^0. SIAM J. Comput. **36**(4), 845–888 (2006)

[AJ15]   Ananth, P., Jain, A.: Indistinguishability obfuscation from compact functional encryption. In: Gennaro, R., Robshaw, M. (eds.) CRYPTO 2015. LNCS, vol. 9215, pp. 308–326. Springer, Heidelberg (2015). doi:10.1007/978-3-662-47989-6_15

[AJS17] Ananth, P., Jain, A., Sahai, A.: Patchable obfuscation: IO for evolving software. In: Eurocrypt, pp. 244–256 (2017). Preliminary Eprint Report 2015/1084. eprint.iacr.org/2015/1084

[App14] Applebaum, B.: Bootstrapping obfuscators via fast pseudorandom functions. In: Sarkar, P., Iwata, T. (eds.) ASIACRYPT 2014. LNCS, vol. 8874, pp. 162–172. Springer, Heidelberg (2014). doi:10.1007/978-3-662-45608-8_9

[AS16] Ananth, P., Sahai, A.: Functional encryption for turing machines. In: Kushilevitz, E., Malkin, T. (eds.) TCC 2016. LNCS, vol. 9562, pp. 125–153. Springer, Heidelberg (2016). doi:10.1007/978-3-662-49096-9_6

[BBC+14] Barak, B., Bitansky, N., Canetti, R., Kalai, Y.T., Paneth, O., Sahai, A.: Obfuscation for evasive functions. In: Lindell, Y. (ed.) TCC 2014. LNCS, vol. 8349, pp. 26–51. Springer, Heidelberg (2014). doi:10.1007/978-3-642-54242-8_2

[BC10] Bitansky, N., Canetti, R.: On strong simulation and composable point obfuscation. In: Rabin, T. (ed.) CRYPTO 2010. LNCS, vol. 6223, pp. 520–537. Springer, Heidelberg (2010). doi:10.1007/978-3-642-14623-7_28

[BCC+14] Bitansky, N., Canetti, R., Cohn, H., Goldwasser, S., Kalai, Y.T., Paneth, O., Rosen, A.: The impossibility of obfuscation with auxiliary input or a universal simulator. In: Garay, J.A., Gennaro, R. (eds.) CRYPTO 2014. LNCS, vol. 8617, pp. 71–89. Springer, Heidelberg (2014). doi:10.1007/978-3-662-44381-1_5

[BCG+11] Bitansky, N., Canetti, R., Goldwasser, S., Halevi, S., Kalai, Y.T., Rothblum, G.N.: Program obfuscation with leaky hardware. In: Lee, D.H., Wang, X. (eds.) ASIACRYPT 2011. LNCS, vol. 7073, pp. 722–739. Springer, Heidelberg (2011). doi:10.1007/978-3-642-25385-0_39

[BCKP14] Bitansky, N., Canetti, R., Kalai, Y.T., Paneth, O.: On virtual grey box obfuscation for general circuits. In: Garay, J.A., Gennaro, R. (eds.) CRYPTO 2014. LNCS, vol. 8617, pp. 108–125. Springer, Heidelberg (2014). doi:10.1007/978-3-662-44381-1_7

[BCP14] Boyle, E., Chung, K.-M., Pass, R.: On extractability (a.k.a. Differing-Inputs) obfuscation. In: TCC (2014). Preliminary version on Eprint 2013. http://eprint.iacr.org/2013/650.pdf

[BCP16] Boyle, E., Chung, K.-M., Pass, R.: Oblivious parallel RAM. In: TCC (2016)

[BFM88] Blum, M., Feldman, P., Micali, S.: Non-interactive zero-knowledge and its applications (Extended Abstract). In: STOC, pp. 103–112 (1988)

[BGG94] Bellare, M., Goldreich, O., Goldwasser, S.: Incremental cryptography: the case of hashing and signing. In: CRYPTO, pp. 216–233 (1994)

[BGG95] Bellare, M., Goldreich, O., Goldwasser, S.: Incremental cryptography and application to virus protection. In STOC, pp. 45–56 (1995)

[BGI+12] Barak, B., Goldreich, O., Impagliazzo, R., Rudich, S., Sahai, A., Vadhan, S.P., Yang, K.: On the (im)possibility of obfuscating programs. J. ACM 59(2), 6 (2012)

[BGK+14] Barak, B., Garg, S., Kalai, Y.T., Paneth, O., Sahai, A.: Protecting obfuscation against algebraic attacks. In: Nguyen, P.Q., Oswald, E. (eds.) EUROCRYPT 2014. LNCS, vol. 8441, pp. 221–238. Springer, Heidelberg (2014). doi:10.1007/978-3-642-55220-5_13

[BGL+15] Bitansky, N., Garg, S., Lin, H., Pass, R., Telang, S.: Succinct randomized encodings and their applications. In: STOC, pp. 439–448 (2015)

[BKY01] Buonanno, E., Katz, J., Yung, M.: Incremental unforgeable encryption. In: Matsui, M. (ed.) FSE 2001. LNCS, vol. 2355, pp. 109–124. Springer, Heidelberg (2002). doi:10.1007/3-540-45473-X_9

[BM97] Bellare, M., Micciancio, D.: A new paradigm for collision-free hashing: incrementality at reduced cost. In: Fumy, W. (ed.) EUROCRYPT 1997. LNCS, vol. 1233, pp. 163–192. Springer, Heidelberg (1997). doi:10.1007/3-540-69053-0_13

[BP15a] Bitansky, N., Paneth, O.: ZAPs and non-interactive witness indistinguishability from indistinguishability obfuscation. In: Dodis, Y., Nielsen, J.B. (eds.) TCC 2015. LNCS, vol. 9015, pp. 401–427. Springer, Heidelberg (2015). doi:10.1007/978-3-662-46497-7_16

[BP15b] Boyle, E., Pass, R.: Limits of extractability assumptions with distributional auxiliary input (2015). Preliminary version. http://eprint.iacr.org/2013/703.pdf

[BPW16] Bitansky, N., Paneth, O., Wichs, D.: Perfect structure on the edge of chaos. In: Kushilevitz, E., Malkin, T. (eds.) TCC 2016. LNCS, vol. 9562, pp. 474–502. Springer, Heidelberg (2016). doi:10.1007/978-3-662-49096-9_20

[BR13] Brakerski, Z., Rothblum, G.N.: Obfuscating conjunctions. In: Canetti, R., Garay, J.A. (eds.) CRYPTO 2013. LNCS, vol. 8043, pp. 416–434. Springer, Heidelberg (2013). doi:10.1007/978-3-642-40084-1_24

[BR14] Brakerski, Z., Rothblum, G.N.: Virtual black-box obfuscation for all circuits via generic graded encoding. In: Lindell, Y. (ed.) TCC 2014. LNCS, vol. 8349, pp. 1–25. Springer, Heidelberg (2014). doi:10.1007/978-3-642-54242-8_1

[BS16] Bellare, M., Stepanovs, I., Obfuscation, P.-F.: A framework and generic constructions. In: TCC (2016). Preliminary version at IACR Eprint Report 2015/703. http://eprint.iacr.org/2015/703.pdf

[BSW11] Boneh, D., Sahai, A., Waters, B.: Functional encryption: definitions and challenges. In: Ishai, Y. (ed.) TCC 2011. LNCS, vol. 6597, pp. 253–273. Springer, Heidelberg (2011). doi:10.1007/978-3-642-19571-6_16

[BV15] Bitansky, N., Vaikuntanathan, V.: Indistinguishability obfuscation from functional encryption. In: FOCS (2015)

[BZ14] Boneh, D., Zhandry, M.: Multiparty key exchange, efficient traitor tracing, and more from indistinguishability obfuscation. In: Garay, J.A., Gennaro, R. (eds.) CRYPTO 2014. LNCS, vol. 8616, pp. 480–499. Springer, Heidelberg (2014). doi:10.1007/978-3-662-44371-2_27

[Can97] Canetti, R.: Oracles, towards realizing random: hash functions that hide all partial information. In: CRYPTO, pp. 455–469 (1997)

[CHJV15] Canetti, R., Holmgren, J., Jain, A., Vaikuntanathan, V.: Indistinguishability obfuscation of iterated circuits and RAM programs. In: STOC (2015)

[CLP14] Chung, K.-M., Liu, Z., Pass, R.: Statistically-secure ORAM with õ(log² n) overhead. In: ASIACRYPT, pp. 62–81 (2014)

[CLP15] Chung, K.-M., Lin, H., Pass, R.: Constant-round concurrent zero-knowledge from indistinguishability obfuscation. In: Gennaro, R., Robshaw, M. (eds.) CRYPTO 2015. LNCS, vol. 9215, pp. 287–307. Springer, Heidelberg (2015). doi:10.1007/978-3-662-47989-6_14

[CRV10] Canetti, R., Rothblum, G.N., Varia, M.: Obfuscation of hyperplane membership. In: Micciancio, D. (ed.) TCC 2010. LNCS, vol. 5978, pp. 72–89. Springer, Heidelberg (2010). doi:10.1007/978-3-642-11799-2_5

[CV13] Canetti, R., Vaikuntanathan, V.: Obfuscating branching programs using black-box pseudo-free groups. IACR Cryptology ePrint Archive 2013:500 (2013)

[Fis97a] Fischlin, M.: Incremental cryptography and memory checkers. In: Fumy, W. (ed.) EUROCRYPT 1997. LNCS, vol. 1233, pp. 393–408. Springer, Heidelberg (1997). doi:10.1007/3-540-69053-0_27

[Fis97b] Fischlin, M.: Lower bounds for the signature size of incremental schemes. In: FOCS, pp. 438–447(1997)

[FLS99] Feige, L., Shamir, A.: Multiple noninteractive zero knowledge proofs under general assumptions. SIAM J. Comput. **29**, 1–28 (1999)

[GGH13a] Garg, S., Gentry, C., Halevi, S.: Candidate multilinear maps from ideal lattices. In: Johansson, T., Nguyen, P.Q. (eds.) EUROCRYPT 2013. LNCS, vol. 7881, pp. 1–17. Springer, Heidelberg (2013). doi:10.1007/978-3-642-38348-9_1

[GGH+13b] Garg, S., Gentry, C., Halevi, S., Raykova, M., Sahai, A., Waters, B.: Candidate indistinguishability obfuscation and functional encryption for all circuits. In: FOCS, pp. 40–49 (2013)

[GGHW14] Garg, S., Gentry, C., Halevi, S., Wichs, D.: On the implausibility of differing-inputs obfuscation and extractable witness encryption with auxiliary input. In: Garay, J.A., Gennaro, R. (eds.) CRYPTO 2014. LNCS, vol. 8616, pp. 518–535. Springer, Heidelberg (2014). doi:10.1007/978-3-662-44371-2_29

[GIS+10] Goyal, V., Ishai, Y., Sahai, A., Venkatesan, R., Wadia, A.: Founding cryptography on tamper-proof hardware tokens. In: Micciancio, D. (ed.) TCC 2010. LNCS, vol. 5978, pp. 308–326. Springer, Heidelberg (2010). doi:10.1007/978-3-642-11799-2_19

[GK05] Goldwasser, S., Kalai, Y.T.: On the impossibility of obfuscation with auxiliary input. In: FOCS, pp. 553–562 (2005)

[GO96] Goldreich, O., Ostrovsky, R.: Software protection and simulation on oblivious RAMs. J. ACM **43**(3), 431–473 (1996)

[Gol87] Goldreich, O.: Towards a theory of software protection and simulation by oblivious RAMs. In: STOC, pp. 182–194 (1987)

[GOS06] Groth, J., Ostrovsky, R., Sahai, A.: Perfect non-interactive zero knowledge for NP. In: Vaudenay, S. (ed.) EUROCRYPT 2006. LNCS, vol. 4004, pp. 339–358. Springer, Heidelberg (2006). doi:10.1007/11761679_21

[GR07] Goldwasser, S., Rothblum, G.N.: On best-possible obfuscation. In: Vadhan, S.P. (ed.) TCC 2007. LNCS, vol. 4392, pp. 194–213. Springer, Heidelberg (2007). doi:10.1007/978-3-540-70936-7_11

[Had00] Hada, S.: Zero-knowledge and code obfuscation. In: Okamoto, T. (ed.) ASIACRYPT 2000. LNCS, vol. 1976, pp. 443–457. Springer, Heidelberg (2000). doi:10.1007/3-540-44448-3_34

[Had10] Hada, S.: Secure obfuscation for encrypted signatures. In: Gilbert, H. (ed.) EUROCRYPT 2010. LNCS, vol. 6110, pp. 92–112. Springer, Heidelberg (2010). doi:10.1007/978-3-642-13190-5_5

[HRSV07] Hohenberger, S., Rothblum, G.N., Shelat, A., Vaikuntanathan, V.: Securely obfuscating re-encryption. In: Vadhan, S.P. (ed.) TCC 2007. LNCS, vol. 4392, pp. 233–252. Springer, Heidelberg (2007). doi:10.1007/978-3-540-70936-7_13

[HSW14] Hohenberger, S., Sahai, A., Waters, B.: Replacing a random oracle: full domain hash from indistinguishability obfuscation. In: Nguyen, P.Q., Oswald, E. (eds.) EUROCRYPT 2014. LNCS, vol. 8441, pp. 201–220. Springer, Heidelberg (2014). doi:10.1007/978-3-642-55220-5_12

[HW15] Hubacek, P., Wichs, D.: On the communication complexity of secure function evaluation with long output. In: ITCS, pp. 163–172 (2015)

[IB] Information is Beautiful. http://www.informationisbeautiful.net/visualizations/million-lines-of-code

[IPS15]   Ishai, Y., Pandey, O., Sahai, A.: Public-coin differing-inputs obfusca-
          tion and its applications. In: Dodis, Y., Nielsen, J.B. (eds.) TCC 2015.
          LNCS, vol. 9015, pp. 668–697. Springer, Heidelberg (2015). doi:10.1007/
          978-3-662-46497-7_26

[KLW15]   Koppula, V., Lewko, A.B., Waters, B.: Indistinguishability obfuscation for
          turing machines with unbounded memory. In: STOC (2015)

[KMN+14] Komargodski, I., Moran, T., Naor, M., Pass, R., Rosen, A., Yogev, E.: One-
          way functions and (im)perfect obfuscation. In: FOCS, pp. 374–383 (2014)

[LO13]   Lu, S., Ostrovsky, R.: Distributed oblivious RAM for secure two-party com-
          putation. In: Sahai, A. (ed.) TCC 2013. LNCS, vol. 7785, pp. 377–396.
          Springer, Heidelberg (2013). doi:10.1007/978-3-642-36594-2_22

[LPS04]   Lynn, B., Prabhakaran, M., Sahai, A.: Positive results and techniques for
          obfuscation. In: Cachin, C., Camenisch, J.L. (eds.) EUROCRYPT 2004.
          LNCS, vol. 3027, pp. 20–39. Springer, Heidelberg (2004). doi:10.1007/
          978-3-540-24676-3_2

[Mic97]   Micciancio, D., Structures, O.D.: Applications to cryptography. In: STOC,
          pp. 456–464 (1997)

[MO14]   Marcedone, A., Orlandi, C.: Obfuscation ⇒ (IND-CPA security !⇒ circular
          security). In: Proceedings of the 9th International Conference on Security
          and Cryptography for Networks, SCN 2014, Amalfi, Italy, 3–5 September
          2014, pp. 77–90 (2014)

[MPRS12] Mironov, I., Pandey, O., Reingold, O., Segev, G.: Incremental deterministic
          public-key encryption. In: Pointcheval, D., Johansson, T. (eds.) EURO-
          CRYPT 2012. LNCS, vol. 7237, pp. 628–644. Springer, Heidelberg (2012).
          doi:10.1007/978-3-642-29011-4_37

[NY90]   Naor, M., Yung, M.: Public-key cryptosystems provably secure against cho-
          sen ciphertext attacks. In: STOC, pp. 427–437 (1990)

[O'N10]   O'Neill, A.: Definitional issues in functional encryption. Cryptology ePrint
          Archive, Report 2010/556 (2010)

[OPWW15] Okamoto, T., Pietrzak, K., Waters, B., Wichs, D.: New realizations of
          somewhere statistically binding hashing and positional accumulators. In:
          Iwata, T., Cheon, J.H. (eds.) ASIACRYPT 2015. LNCS, vol. 9452, pp.
          121–145. Springer, Heidelberg (2015). doi:10.1007/978-3-662-48797-6_6

[Ost90]   Ostrovsky, R.: Efficient computation on oblivious RAMs. In: STOC, pp.
          514–523 (1990)

[PPS15]   Pandey, O., Prabhakaran, M., Sahai, A.: Obfuscation-based non-black-box
          simulation and four message concurrent zero knowledge for NP. In: Dodis,
          Y., Nielsen, J.B. (eds.) TCC 2015. LNCS, vol. 9015, pp. 638–667. Springer,
          Heidelberg (2015). doi:10.1007/978-3-662-46497-7_25

[SCSL11] Shi, E., Chan, T.-H.H., Stefanov, E., Li, M.: Oblivious RAM with
          $O((\log N)^3)$ worst-case cost. In: Lee, D.H., Wang, X. (eds.) ASIACRYPT
          2011. LNCS, vol. 7073, pp. 197–214. Springer, Heidelberg (2011). doi:10.
          1007/978-3-642-25385-0_11

[SvDS+13] Stefanov, E., van Dijk, M., Shi, E., Fletcher, C.W., Ren, L., Xiangyao, Y.,
          Devadas, S.: Path ORAM: an extremely simple oblivious RAM protocol.
          In: ACM CCS, pp. 299–310 (2013)

[SW14]   Sahai, A., Waters, B.: How to use indistinguishability obfuscation: deniable
          encryption, and more. In: STOC, pp. 475–484 (2014)

[Wee05]   Wee, H.: On obfuscating point functions. In: STOC, pp. 523–532 (2005)

From Obfuscation to the Security of Fiat-Shamir for Proofs

Yael Tauman Kalai[1](✉), Guy N. Rothblum[2], and Ron D. Rothblum[3]

[1] Microsoft Research, Cambridge, USA
yaelism@gmail.com
[2] Weizmann Institute of Science, Rehovot, Israel
[3] MIT, Cambridge, USA

Abstract. The Fiat-Shamir paradigm [CRYPTO'86] is a heuristic for converting three-round identification schemes into signature schemes, and more generally, for collapsing rounds in constant-round public-coin interactive protocols. This heuristic is very popular both in theory and in practice, and its security has been the focus of extensive study.

In particular, this paradigm was shown to be secure in the Random Oracle Model. However, in the plain model, the results shown were mostly negative. In particular, the heuristic was shown to be *insecure* when applied to *computationally sound* proofs (also known as arguments). Moreover, recently it was shown that even in the restricted setting where the heuristic is applied to interactive *proofs* (as opposed to arguments), its soundness cannot be proven via a black-box reduction to any so-called *falsifiable* assumption.

In this work, we give a *positive result* for the security of this paradigm in the *plain model*. Specifically, we construct a hash function for which the Fiat Shamir paradigm is *secure* when applied to proofs (as opposed to arguments), assuming the existence of a sub-exponentially secure indistinguishability obfuscator, the existence of an exponentially secure input-hiding obfuscator for the class of multi-bit point functions, and the existence of a sub-exponentially secure one-way function.

More generally, we construct a hash family that is *correlation intractable* (under the computational assumptions above), solving an open problem originally posed by Canetti, Goldreich and Halevi (JACM, 2004), under the above assumptions.

In addition, we show that our result resolves a long-lasting open problem in about zero-knowledge proofs: It implies that there does not exist a public-coin constant-round zero-knowledge proof with negligible soundness (under the assumptions stated above).

1 Introduction

In 1986, Fiat and Shamir [FS86] proposed a general method for converting any three-round identification (ID) scheme into a signature scheme. This method quickly gained popularity both in theory and in practice, since known ID schemes (in which a sender *interactively* identifies himself to a receiver) are significantly

© International Association for Cryptologic Research 2017
J. Katz and H. Shacham (Eds.): CRYPTO 2017, Part II, LNCS 10402, pp. 224–251, 2017.
DOI: 10.1007/978-3-319-63715-0_8

simpler and more efficient than known signature schemes, and thus this heuristic gives an efficient and easy way to implement digital signature schemes.

The Fiat-Shamir method is both simple and intuitive: The public key of the signature scheme consists of a pair (pk, H), where pk is a public key corresponding to the underlying ID scheme, and H is a hash function chosen at random from a hash family. To sign a message m, compute a triplet (α, β, γ), such that $\beta = H(\alpha, m)$ and (α, β, γ) is an accepting transcript of the ID scheme with respect to pk.

The main question is:

Is the Fiat-Shamir heuristic sound?

Namely, for what hash function families is the signature scheme, obtained by applying the Fiat-Shamir heuristic to a secure ID scheme, secure against adaptive chosen message attacks?

The intuition for why the heuristic may be sound, is that if H looks like a truly random function, and if all the adversary (i.e., impersonator) can do is use H in a black-box manner, then interacting with H is similar to interacting with the real verifier. This intuition was formalized by Pointcheval and Stern [PS96], and by followup works [OO98, AABN02], who proved that the Fiat-Shamir heuristic is sound in the so-called *Random Oracle Model* (ROM) – when the hash function is modeled by a random oracle [BR93], assuming the underlying ID scheme is sound against passive impersonation attacks.

This led to the belief that if a 2-round protocol, obtained by applying the Fiat-Shamir paradigm, is insecure, then it must be the case that the hash family used is not "secure enough", and the hope was that there exists another hash family that is sufficiently secure. These positive results (in the ROM), together with the popularity and importance of the Fiat-Shamir heuristic, led many researchers to try to prove the security of this paradigm in the plain model (without resorting to random oracles). Unfortunately, these attempts led mainly to negative results.

Goldwasser and Kalai [GK03] proved a negative result, by constructing a (contrived) 3-round public-coin ID scheme, for which the resulting signature scheme obtained by applying the Fiat-Shamir heuristic, is insecure, no matter which hash family is used.

Extending the Fiat-Shamir Heuristic. The Fiat-Shamir heuristic can be used outside the regime of ID and signature schemes. It can be used to convert any constant-round public-coin proof system into a two-round proof system, as follows: In the first round, the verifier sends a hash function H, where H is chosen at random from a hash family; in the second round, the prover sends the entire transcript of the interactive protocol, where the verifier's messages are computed by applying H to the communication so far.

The first work to extend the Fiat-Shamir paradigm to this regime, was the work of Micali [Mic94] on CS-proofs. We note that in this regime, the importance of the Fiat-Shamir heuristic stems from the fact that latency, caused by sending messages back and forth, is often a bottleneck in running cryptographic protocols [MNPS04, BDNP08].

The main question about this (extended) heuristic is therefore:

Is the two-message proof system obtained by applying the Fiat-Shamir heuristic, to a constant-round proof system, sound?

Namely, does there exist an explicit hash family, for which is it infeasible for a (computationally bounded) cheating prover, given an input outside the language and a random function H from the family, to generate an accepting transcript for the original interactive protocol (where each verifier-message is computed by applying H to the communication so far).

Barak [Bar01] gave the first negative result in the "plain model", by constructing a constant-round public-coin protocol, such that for any hash family $\mathcal{H}$, the resulting 2-round protocol, obtained by applying the Fiat-Shamir heuristic to this interactive protocol with respect to $\mathcal{H}$, is not sound.[1] However, the interactive protocol constructed in [Bar01] has only computational soundness, and thus is an *argument system* (as opposed to a proof). This gave rise to the following question:

*Is the Fiat-Shamir method secure when applied to interactive **proofs** (as opposed to arguments)?*

Namely, does there exist an explicit hash family for which the transformation, when applied to an *information-theoretically sound* interactive proof, produces a (computationally) sound two-message argument system?

In this work, we give a positive answer to this final question (under strong computational assumptions). Before we present our results in detail, we describe previous works which attempted to answer this question.

Barak, Lindell and Vadhan [BLV06] presented a security property for the Fiat-Shamir hash function which, if realized, would imply the soundness of the Fiat-Shamir paradigm applied to any constant-round public-coin interactive proof system.[2] However, they left open the problem of realizing this security definition under standard hardness assumptions (or under any assumption beyond simply assuming that the definition holds for a given hash function).

Dodis, Ristenpart and Vadhan [DRV12] showed that under specific assumptions regarding the existence of robust randomness condensers for seed-dependent sources, the definitions of [BLV06] can be realized. However, the question of constructing such suitable robust randomness condensers was left open by [DRV12].

On the other hand, Bitansky et al. [BDG+13] gave a negative result. They showed that that soundness of the Fiat-Shamir paradigm, even when applied to

---

[1] We note that the work of [GK03] is a followup work to [Bar01], and builds upon its techniques.

[2] Loosely speaking, a hash family $\{h_s\}$ is said to have this security property if for every probabilistic polynomial time adversary $\mathcal{A}$, that is given a random seed s and outputs an element in the domain of h_s, the random variable $h_s(\mathcal{A}(s))$ conditioned on $\mathcal{A}(s)$ has almost full min entropy.

interactive proofs, cannot be proved via a black-box reduction to any so-called *falsifiable* assumption, a notion defined by Naor [Nao03]).[3,4]

Correlation Intractable Hash Functions. Our results can be cast more generally in the language of *correlation intractability*, a notion defined in the seminal work of Canetti, Goldreich and Halevi [CGH04].

Roughly speaking, a correlation intractable function family is one for which it is infeasible to find input-output pairs that satisfy some "rare" relation. More precisely, a binary relation R is said to be *evasive* if for every value x only negligible fraction of the y values satisfy $(x, y) \in R$. A function family $F = \{f_s\}$ is correlation intractable if for every evasive relation R it is computationally hard, given a description of a random function $f_s \in F$, to find a value x such that $(x, f_s(x)) \in R$.

It was shown in [CGH04] that there does not exist a correlation intractable hash family whose seeds are shorter than the input length. The question of whether there exists a correlation intractable function family whose seeds are larger than the input, remained open. Very recently, [CCR15] construct a function family that is correlation intractable with respect to all relations that are computable in a-priori bounded polynomial complexity (under computational assumptions).

In this work, we construct a correlation intractable hash family with respect to *all* relations (under computational assumptions). We provide a more detailed comparison between our work and that of [CCR15] after we present our result more formally, below.

1.1 Our Results

In this work, we construct a hash family, and prove that the Fiat-Shamir paradigm is *sound* w.r.t. this hash family, when applied to interactive proofs (as opposed to arguments). We also show that the family is correlation intractable. Both results are shown under the following three cryptographic assumptions:

1. The existence of 2^n-secure indistinguishability obfuscation iO, where 2^n is the domain size of the functions being obfuscated.[5]

---

[3] The formalization of a falsifiable assumption, given in [BDG+13], is similar to the formalization given in [GW11], and differs slightly from the formalization given in [Nao03].

[4] Our assumptions (see Sect. 1.1), which deal with exponential-time (rather than polynomial-time) adversaries, are inherently not falsifiable. Note that [BDG+13] allow an unbounded challenger, but restrict to polynomial-time attackers. In the context of obfuscation, the attacker is the algorithm trying to *break* the security of the obfuscation. We assume hardness against super polynomial-time attackers, and thus our assumptions do not fall into the category ruled out by Bitansky *et al.*

[5] This assumption has been made in many previous works on iO and is referred to as sub-exponential iO, since the security parameter can be polynomially larger than n (which makes 2^n sub-exponential in the security parameter).

Recently, several constructions of iO obfuscation were proposed, starting with the work of Garg *et al.* [GGH+13]. However, to date, none of these constructions are known to be provably secure under what is known as a complexity assumption [GK16] or more generally a falsifiable assumption [Nao03]. We mention that [GLSW14] provided a construction and proved its security under the subgroup elimination assumption, which is a complexity assumption (and in particular is a falsifiable assumption). However, this assumption has been refuted in all candidate multi-linear groups.

2. The existence of 2^n-secure puncturable pseudo-random function (PRF) family $\mathcal{F}$, where 2^n is the domain size.

Puncturable PRFs were defined in [BW13, BGI14, KPTZ13]. The PRF family of [GGM86] is a puncturable PRF family, and thus 2^n-secure puncturable PRFs can be constructed from any sub-exponentially secure one-way function.

3. The existence of an exponentially secure input-hiding obfuscation hideO for the class of multi-bit point functions $\{\mathcal{I}_{n,k}\}$.

The class $\{\mathcal{I}_{n,k}\}$ consists of functions of the form $I_{\alpha,\beta}$ where $|\alpha| = n$ and $|\beta| = k$, and where $I_{\alpha,\beta}(x) = \beta$ for $x = \alpha$ and $I_{\alpha,\beta}(x) = 0$ otherwise. An obfuscation for this class is said to be input-hiding with T-security if any *poly-size* adversary that is given an obfuscation of a *random* function $I_{\alpha,\beta}$ in this family, guesses α with probability at most T^{-1}. Note that we assume hardness for a distribution where the value β may be correlated with α and furthermore, it may be computationally difficult to find β from α.

For our construction we require T that is roughly equal to $2^n \cdot \mu$, where μ is the soundness error of the underlying proof system. For example, if we start off with an interactive proof with soundness error 2^{-n^ϵ} (where n is an upper bound the length of prover messages), then we require roughly $T = 2^{n-n^\epsilon}$. For constructing correlation intractable functions, μ is the "evasiveness" of the relation R. That is, for every value x, the fraction of y's satisfying $(x, y) \in R$ is at most μ.

This assumption was considered in [CD08, BC14], who also provided a candidate construction based on a strong variant of the DDH assumption (we elaborate on this in Sect. 2.4).[6] See further discussion on various notions of point function obfuscation in [BS16].

We emphasize that we *do not* assume security of the multi-bit point function obfuscation with *auxiliary input*. Indeed, security with auxiliary input is known to be problematic, and, as was shown by Brzuska and Mittelbach [BM14], if iO obfuscation exists then multi-bit point function obfuscation with auxiliary inputs does not exist. We do not allow auxiliary information, and we only assume *input-hiding* (against exponential-time adversaries) for a *random* function from the family (rather than black-box worst-case).

---

[6] While DDH (and even discrete log) can be broken in time less than 2^n (even in the generic group model - e.g., by the baby-step giant-step algorithm), this does not imply a non-trivial *polynomial-time* attack (i.e., one with success probability greater than poly$(n)/2^n$).

Theorem 1 *[(Informally Stated, see Theorem 4)]. Under the assumptions above, for any constant-round public-coin interactive proof Π, the resulting 2-message argument Π^{FS}, obtained by applying the Fiat-Shamir paradigm to Π with the function family $iO(\mathcal{F})$, is sound.*

This theorem provides a general-purpose transformation for reducing interaction in interactive proof systems. Beyond our primary motivation of studying the security of the Fiat-Shamir transformation (and its implications to zero-knowledge proofs), the secure transformation can also serve as an avenue for obtaining new public-coin 2-message argument systems (often referred to as publicly-verifiable non-interactive arguments). For example, it can be applied to the interactive proofs of [RRR16] to obtain arguments for bounded-space polynomial-time computations, with small communication and almost-linear-time verification. We note, however, that prior works [BGL+15] have shown how to construct such arguments for general polynomial-time computations using subexponential iO and one-way functions (without the need for multi-bit point function obfuscation). Nonetheless, one advantage of Theorem 1 is that it can be applied to *any* interactive proof, which may give more efficient arguments for specific languages in P and for languages outside of P.

Cast in the language of correlation intractability, we prove:

Theorem 2 *[(Informally Stated)]. Under the assumptions above, the function family $iO(\mathcal{F})$ is correlation intractable.*

Here and throughout this work $iO(\mathcal{F})$ refers to an iO obfuscation of a program that computes the PRF, using a hardwired random seed.

Remark 1. Although outside the scope of this paper, we note that this transformation from interactive proofs to 2-message arguments preserves some secrecy guarantees.

In particular, it is easy to see that the Fiat-Shamir paradigm always preserves witness indistinguishability. Namely, if the underlying interactive proof is witness indistinguishable then the resulting 2-message argument, obtained by applying the Fiat-Shamir method with respect to *any* function family, is also witness indistinguishability. Loosely speaking, this follows from the fact that witness indistinguishability is defined to hold with respect to any cheating (poly-size) verifier.

Moreover, we claim that the Fiat-Shamir paradigm, applied with our function family $iO(\mathcal{F})$, preserves honest-verifier zero-knowledge. Loosely speaking, this (non-trivial) claim follows from the following argument: To simulate the 2-message argument with respect to some input x, first use the simulator for the interactive proof to obtain a simulated transcript $(m_1, r_1, \ldots, m_c, r_c, m_{c+1})$. Note that this transcript may not be consistent with any hash function from the family. To obtain a simulated transcript for the 2-message argument, we simulate the verifier as sending the iO of a randomly chosen PRF function $f_s \leftarrow \mathcal{F}$, punctured at the points $m_1, (m_1, r_1, m_2), \ldots, (m_1, r_1, \ldots, m_{c_1}, r_{c-1}, m_c)\}$, and hardwire the values $r_1, r_2 \ldots, r_c$ for these points (respectively). Standard iO techniques can be used to argue that this obfuscated circuit is indistinguishable from $iO(f_s)$.

As we discuss next, Theorem 1 settles a long lasting open problem about zero-knowledge proofs.

Impossibility of Constant-Round Public-Coin Zero-Knowledge. Hada and Tanaka [HT98] and Dwork *et al.* [DNRS99] observed an intriguing connection between the security of the Fiat-Shamir paradigm and the existence of certain zero-knowledge protocols. In particular, if there exists a constant-round public-coin zero-knowledge proof for a language outside BPP, then the Fiat-Shamir paradigm is not secure when applied to this zero-knowledge proof.[7] Intuitively, this follows from the following observation: Consider the cheating verifier that behaves exactly like the Fiat-Shamir hash function. The fact that the protocol is zero-knowledge implies that there exists a simulator who can simulate the view in an indistinguishable manner. Thus, for elements in the language the simulator generates accepting transcripts. The simulator cannot distinguish between elements in the language and elements outside the language (since the simulator runs in poly-time and the language is outside of BPP). In addition, the protocol is public-coin, which implies that the simulator knows whether the transcript is accepted or not. Hence, it must be the case that the simulator also generates accepting transcripts for elements that are not in the language, which implies that the Fiat-Shamir paradigm is not secure.

Thus, Theorem 1, combined with [DNRS99, Theorem 5.4] implies the following corollary.

Corollary 1. *Under the assumptions above, there does not exist a constant-round public-coin zero-knowledge proof with negligible soundness for languages outside* BPP*.*

We emphasize that the above negative result not only rule out black-box simulation, but also rules out *non-black-box* simulation. Moreover, as pointed out by [DNRS99], this negative result actually rules out even extremely weak notions of zero-knowledge which they call *ultra weak zero knowledge* (see [DNRS99, Sect. 5]).

In particular, this corollary implies that (under the assumptions above) *parallel repetition of Blum's Hamiltonicity protocol for* NP [Blu87] *is not zero-knowledge.* Previously it was not known whether (in general) parallel repetition preserves zero-knowledge. Our result shows that it does not (under the assumptions above).

The existence of constant-round public-coin zero-knowledge proofs has been a long-standing open question (see, e.g., [GO94, GK96, KPR98, Ros00, CKPR02, BLV06, BGGL01, BL04, Rey01]). For *black-box* zero-knowledge proofs (which means that the simulator only uses the verifier as a black-box), the work of Goldreich and Krawczyk [GK96] ruled out constant-round public-coin protocols

---

[7] We note that this is how Barak [Bar01] obtained his negative result. He constructed a constant-round public-coin zero-knowledge argument.

(for languages outside of BPP). It is known, however, that non black-box techniques can be quite powerful in the context of zero-knowledge [Bar01]. Under the assumptions stated above, our work rules out *any* constant-round public-coin zero knowledge proof (even non black-box ones).

We note that even for those who are skeptical about the obfuscation assumptions we make, this corollary implies that finding a constant-round public-coin zero-knowledge proof requires overcoming technical barriers, and in particular requires disproving the existence of sub-exponentially secure iO obfuscation, or the existence of exponentially secure input-hiding obfuscation for the class of multi-bit point functions (or, less likely, disproving the existence of sub-exponential OWF).

Comparison to Concurrent Works

Comparison to [CCR15]. As mentioned above, in a concurrent and independent work, Canetti *et al.* [CCR15] construct a correlation intractable function family that withstands all relations computable in a-priori bounded polynomial complexity. More specifically, they construct a function family that is correlation intractable with respect to all evasive relations that can be computed in time p, for any a priori polynomial p, where the size of the functions in the family grows with p.

We note that this result does not have any implications to the security of the Fiat-Shamir paradigm, since to prove the security of this paradigm we need a correlation intractable ensemble for relations that cannot be computed in polynomial time. Moreover, we note that since the size of the functions grow with p, leveraging techniques do not seem to apply here.

As mentioned above, our result on the security of the Fiat-Shamir paradigm can be cast more generally in the language of *correlation intractability*. In particular, the hash family that we construct, and with which we prove the security of the Fiat-Shamir paradigm, is correlation intractable (with respect to all relations) under our assumption stated above.

In terms of the assumptions used, [CCR15] assume the existence of sub-exponentially secure indistinguishability obfuscation, the existence of a sub-exponentially secure puncturable PRF family, and the existence of input-hiding obfuscation for the class of evasive functions [BBC+14]. Comparing to the assumptions we make in this work, we also make the first two assumptions. However, we assume input-hiding obfuscation only for multi-bit point functions (a significantly smaller family compared to general evasive functions). On the other hand, we require an exponentially secure input-hiding obfuscation, whereas their work only needs polynomial-time hardness of the input-hiding obfuscation.

Comparison with [MV16]. In an additional independent and concurrent work, Mittelbach and Venturi [MV16] showed a hash function for which the Fiat-Shamir is secure for a very *particular* class of protocols. The class of protocols that they consider in itself does not include any previously-studied protocols. However, [MV16] show an additional transformation for 3 message protocols (on top of Fiat-Shamir) that works when the first message in the underlying

3-message protocol is *independent* (as a function) of the input. Mittelbach and Venturi also show that their transformation, which is based on indistinguishability obfuscation, maintains zero-knowledge, and can be used to obtain signature schemes and NIZKs.

In contrast to [MV16], our primary motivation and goal is showing that the Fiat-Shamir transformation can be used to reduce interaction while preserving soundness. Reducing the interaction in cryptographic protocols and particularly showing that the Fiat-Shamir transform can be proved sound has been a central and widely-studied question in the cryptographic literature. We emphasize that the [MV16] result does *not* yield a method for reducing rounds while preserving soundness.[8]

1.2 Overview

Throughout this overview we focus on proving the security of the Fiat-Shamir paradigm, when applied to 3-round public-coin interactive proofs. The more general case, of any constant number[9] of rounds, is then proved by induction on the number of rounds (we refer the reader to Sect. 4 for details). Consider any 3-round proof Π for a language L. Denote the transcript by (α, β, γ) where α is the first message sent by the prover, β is the random message sent by the verifier, and γ is the final message sent by the prover. Fix any $x \notin L$. The fact that Π is a sound proof means that for every α, for most of the verifier's messages β, there does not exist γ that makes the verifier accept.

The basic idea stems from the original intuition for why the Fiat-Shamir is secure, which is that if we use a hash function H that looks like a truly random function, then all the prover can do is use H in a black-box manner, in which case interacting with H is similar to interacting with the real verifier, and hence security follows.

The first idea that comes to mind is to choose the hash function randomly from a pseudo-random function (PRF) family. However, the security guarantee of a PRF is that given only *black-box* access to a random function f in the PRF family, one cannot distinguish it from a truly random function. No guarantees are given if the adversary is given a succinct circuit for computing f.

Obfuscation to the Rescue. A natural next step is to try to obfuscate f, in the hope that whatever can be learned given the obfuscation of f can also be learned from black-box access to f. However, this requires virtual-black-box (VBB) security, and VBB obfuscation is known not to exist [BGI+12]. Moreover, there are

---

[8] Indeed, for the class of protocols that [MV16] support, reducing to 2 rounds while preserving soundness (but not necessarily zero-knowledge) is straightforward: Since the prover's first message is not a function of the input, the verifier can compute the prover's first message α for it, and sends α (together with the coins used to generate it) to the prover.

[9] The Fiat Shamir paradigm refers to constant round protocols. Indeed, there are interactive proofs with a super-constant number of rounds (and negligible soundness error) for which the Fiat Shamir paradigm is insecure.

specific PRF families for which VBB obfuscation is impossible [BGI+12]. Further obstacles to VBB obfuscation of PRFs and, more generally, functions with high pseudo-entropy (w.r.t. auxiliary input) are given in [GK05, BCC+14]. Given these obstacles to achieving VBB obfuscation, could we hope to prove security using relaxed notions of obfuscation, such as iO obfuscation? The question is:

Is iO obfuscation strong enough to prove the security of the Fiat-Shamir paradigm?

It is well known that iO obfuscation is *not* strong enough to prove the security of the Fiat-Shamir paradigm when applied to computationally sound interactive *arguments*. Indeed the Fiat-Shamir paradigm is known be insecure when applied to arguments as opposed to proofs.[10] In contrast, we show that iO obfuscation (together with additional assumptions) is strong enough to prove security when the Fiat-Shamir paradigm is applied to interactive *proofs* (rather than arguments).

For proving security of the Fiat-Shamir paradigm for *proofs*, consider a cheating prover for the transformed protocol Π^{FS}, who receives the obfuscation $iO(f_s)$ of a pseudo-random function f_s. Since f_s is a PRF, we know that there will only be a small set Bad_s of inputs α (corresponding to the prover's first message in the proof Π), for which the communication prefix $(\alpha, f_s(\alpha))$ can lead the verifier in the interactive proof to accept (i.e. α's for which there exists γ s.t. $(\alpha, f(\alpha), \gamma)$ is an accepting transcript).

To show the security of the resulting protocol, we now want to claim that the obfuscation *hides* this (small) set Bad_s of inputs, and that a cheating prover P^* cannot find any input $\alpha \in \mathsf{Bad}_s$. Note, however, that iO obfuscation only guarantees that one cannot distinguish between the obfuscation of two functionally equivalent circuits of the same size, and it does not give any hiding guarantees.

Puncturable PRFs to the Rescue? As mentioned above, iO obfuscation does not immediately seem to give any hiding guarantees. Nonetheless, starting with the beautiful work of Sahai and Waters [SW14], iO has proved remarkably powerful in the construction of a huge variety of cryptographic primitives. A basic technique used in order to get a hiding guarantee from iO obfuscation, as pioneered in [SW14], is to use it with a puncturable PRF family.

A puncturable PRF family is a PRF family that allows the "puncturing" of the seed at any point α in the domain of f. Namely, for any point α in the domain, and for any seed s of the PRF, one can generate a "punctured" seed, denoted by $s\{\alpha\}$. This seed allows the computation of f_s anywhere in the domain, except at point α, with the security guarantee that for a random seed s chosen independently of α, the element $f_s(\alpha)$ looks (computationally) random given $(s\{\alpha\}, \alpha)$. The security of iO obfuscation guarantees that one cannot distin-

---

[10] More specifically, the insecurity is in the sense that there exist contrived interactive arguments such that for any hash family $\mathcal{H}$, applying the Fiat-Shamir paradigm with the hash family $\mathcal{H}$, results in an insecure 2-round protocol [Bar01, GK03].

guish between $iO(s)$ and $iO(s\{\alpha\}, \alpha, f_s(\alpha))$,[11] which together with the security of the puncturable PRF, implies that one cannot distinguish between $iO(s)$ and $iO(s\{\alpha\}, \alpha, u)$ for a truly random output u. Thus, we managed to use iO, together with the puncturing technique, to generate a circuit for computing f_s that hides the value of $f_s(\alpha)$. We emphasize that this technique crucially relies on the fact that the punctured point α is independent of the seed s, and hence as a result $f_s(\alpha)$ is computationally random.

It is natural to try and use obfuscated puncturable PRFs to show security of the Fiat-Shamir paradigm. Consider the following naive (and flawed) analysis, which loosely speaking proceeds in three steps: Suppose that there exists a poly-size cheating prover P^* that convinces the verifier to accept $x \notin L$. Recall that we denote transcripts by (α, β, γ). The (statistical) soundness of Π implies that for every α, for most of the verifier's messages β, there does not exist γ that makes the verifier accept. For any function f consider the (evasive) relation $R = \{(\alpha, \beta) : \exists \gamma \text{ s.t. } V(x, \alpha, \beta, \gamma) = 1\}$. Suppose that the cheating prover P^*, given $iO(s)$, outputs α such that $(\alpha, f_s(\alpha)) \in R$, with non-negligible probability.

1. Puncture the PRF at a random point α^* s.t. $\alpha^* \in \mathsf{Bad}_s$, and send the obfuscation of $iO(s\{\alpha^*\}, \alpha^*, f_s(\alpha^*))$ to the cheating prover P^*. Note that this does not change the functionality.
   Therefore, we can use the (sub-exponential) security of iO to argue that the cheating prover P^* cannot tell where we punctured the PRF, and still succeeds with non-negligible probability. In particular, taking M to be the expected number of α's such that $(\alpha, f_s(\alpha)) \in R$, we have that P^* outputs α^* with probability $\approx 1/M$ (up to poly(n) factors).[12]
2. Next, we want to use the (sub-exponential) security of the puncturable PRF to argue that the cheating prover P^* cannot distinguish between $(s\{\alpha^*\}, \alpha^*, f_s(\alpha^*))$ and $(s\{\alpha^*\}, \alpha^*, \beta^*)$ where (α^*, β^*) is random in R. Thus, given $iO(s\{\alpha^*\}, \alpha^*, \beta^*)$ the cheating prover P^* still outputs α^* with probability $\approx 1/M$ (up to poly(n) factors).
3. In the final step, we argue that α^* is close to uniform (for an appropriate modification of the original protocol) and independent of s. Thus, given $iO(s\{\alpha^*\}, \alpha^*, \beta^*)$, the cheating prover P^* outputs α^* with probability $\approx 1/M$ (up to poly(n) factors), where α^* is close to truly random. We want to argue that this contradicts the (sub-exponential) security of iO.

Unfortunately, the argument sketched above is doubly-flawed. In particular, the arguments in Step (2) and Step (3) are simply false. In Step (2) we start with a distribution where f_s is punctured at a point α^* for which $(\alpha^*, f_s(\alpha^*))$ is not (computationally) random, and in fact *the choice of α^* depends on the seed s*. We want to argue that this is indistinguishable from the case where we pick

---

[11] We use $(s\{\alpha\}, \alpha, f_s(\alpha))$ to denote the circuit that on input α outputs the hardwired value $f_s(\alpha)$, and on any other input $x \neq \alpha$ computes $f_s(x)$ using the punctured seed $s\{\alpha\}$.

[12] We think of n as polynomially related to the security parameter, where 2^n is the domain size of f_s.

(α^*, β^*) randomly in R, and then puncture at α^*. It is not a-priori clear why the puncturable PRF or iO would guarantee this indistinguishability. Indeed, the functions generated by these two distributions can be distinguished with some advantage by simply counting the number of input-output pairs that are in R.

Nevertheless, in our analysis (see Lemma 1) we manage to argue that the cheating prover P^*, given $iO(s\{\alpha^*\}, \alpha^*, \beta^*)$ where (α^*, β^*) is random in R, still outputs α^* with probability significantly higher than $1/2^n$ (i.e., significantly higher than guessing). Indeed, P^* still outputs α^* with probability $\approx 1/M$ (up to poly(n) factors).

We next move to the flaw in Step (3). The problem here is that puncturing at the point α^* *does not at all hide* α^*. It is also not clear whether the iO obfuscation of the punctured seed hides α^*.

Input-Hiding Obfuscation to the Rescue. We overcome this hurdle by using an exponentially secure input-hiding obfuscation to hide the punctured point.

Namely, we replace $iO(s\{\alpha^*\}, \alpha^*, \beta^*)$ with $iO(s, \text{hideO}(\alpha^*, \beta^*))$, where hideO is an exponentially secure input hiding obfuscator, and where we did not change the functionality of the circuit; i.e. the circuit on input x first runs $\text{hideO}(\alpha^*, \beta^*)$ to check if $x = \alpha^*$; if so it outputs β^* and otherwise it outputs $f_s(x)$. The security of iO implies that $P^*(iO(s, \text{hideO}(\alpha^*, \beta^*)))$ outputs α^* with probability $1/M$ (up to poly(n) factors).

It remains to note that s is independent of (α^*, β^*), and hence we conclude that there exists a poly-size adversary that given $\text{hideO}(\alpha^*, \beta^*)$ outputs α^* with probability $1/M$ (up to poly(n) factors). In the last step we replace the distribution of (α^*, β^*) with a distribution where α^* is chosen uniformly at random from $\{0, 1\}^n$ and β^* is chosen at random such that $(\alpha^*, \beta^*) \in R$ and prove that still there exists a poly-size adversary that given $\text{hideO}(\alpha^*, \beta^*)$ (where (α^*, β^*) is according to the new distribution) outputs α^* with probability $1/M$ (up to poly(n) factors). This contradicts the exponential security of the input-hiding obfuscator hideO.

Remark 2. We note that the input-hiding obfuscator *was only used in the security analysis*. It plays no role in the construction itself. This is similar to some other recent uses of indistinguishability obfuscation in the literature.

We note that the idea of using input-hiding obfuscation to hide the punctured point, was also used in [BM14]. However, as opposed to this work, they relied on the obfuscation being secure against auxiliary inputs.

2 Preliminaries

2.1 Indistinguishability

Definition 1. *For any function $T : \mathbb{N} \to \mathbb{N}$ and for any function $\mu : \mathbb{N} \to [0, 1]$, we say that $\mu = negl(T)$ if for every constant $c > 0$ there exists $K \in \mathbb{N}$ such that for every $k \geq K$,*

$$\mu(k) \leq T(k)^{-c}.$$

Definition 2. *Two distribution families* $\mathcal{X} = \{\mathcal{X}_\kappa\}_{\kappa \in \mathbb{N}}$ *and* $\mathcal{Y} = \{\mathcal{Y}_\kappa\}_{\kappa \in \mathbb{N}}$ *are said to be T-indistinguishable (denoted by $\mathcal{X} \overset{T}{\approx} \mathcal{Y}$) if for every circuit family $D = \{D_\kappa\}_{\kappa \in \mathbb{N}}$ of size $poly(T(\kappa))$,*

$$Adv_D^{\mathcal{X},\mathcal{Y}}(T) \overset{def}{=} |\Pr[D(x) = 1] - \Pr[D(y) = 1]| = negl(T(\kappa)),$$

where the probabilities are over $x \leftarrow \mathcal{X}_\kappa$ and over $y \leftarrow \mathcal{Y}_\kappa$.

2.2   Puncturable PRFs

Our construction uses a *puncturable* pseudo-random function (PRF) family [BW13, BGI14, KPTZ13, SW14] that is 2^n-secure (where n is the input length); see the definitions below.

Definition 3 (T-Secure PRF [GGM86]). *Let $m = m(\kappa)$, $n = n(\kappa)$ and $k = k(\kappa)$ be functions of the security parameter κ. A PRF family is an ensemble $\mathcal{F} = \{\mathcal{F}_\kappa\}_{\kappa \in \mathbb{N}}$ of function families, where $\mathcal{F}_\kappa = \{f_s : \{0,1\}^n \rightarrow \{0,1\}^k\}_{s \in \{0,1\}^m}$. The PRF $\mathcal{F}$ is T-secure, for $T = T(\kappa)$, if for every $poly(T)$-size (non-uniform) adversary Adv:*

$$\left| Adv^{f_s}(1^\kappa) - Adv^{f}(1^\kappa) \right| = negl(T(\kappa)),$$

where f_s is a random function in $\mathcal{F}_\kappa$, generated using a uniformly random seed $s \in \{0,1\}^{m(\kappa)}$, and f is a truly random function with domain $\{0,1\}^n$ and range $\{0,1\}^k$.

We use 2^n-secure PRF families in our construction (for $k = poly(n)$). We can construct such PRFs assuming subexponentially hard one-way functions by taking the seed length m to be a sufficiently large polynomial in n. Observe that, since the entire truth table of the function can be constructed in time $poly(n) \cdot 2^n$, we get that 2^n-security implies that the entire truth table of a PRF f_s is indistinguishable from a uniformly random truth table.[13]

Definition 4 (T-Secure Puncturable PRF [SW14]). *A T-secure family of PRFs (as in Definition 3) is* puncturable *if there exist PPT procedures* puncture *and* eval *such that*

1. *Puncturing a PRF key $s \in \{0,1\}^m$ at a point $r \in \{0,1\}^n$ gives a punctured key $s\{r\}$ that can still be used to evaluate the PRF at any point $r' \neq r$*

$$\forall r \in \{0,1\}^n, r' \neq r : \Pr_{s, s\{r\} \leftarrow \mathsf{puncture}(s,r)} [\mathsf{eval}(s\{r\}, r') = f_s(r')] = 1$$

---

[13] The fact that subexponential OWF yield PRFs for which distinguishing the entire truth table from a random truth table the truth table of a random function has been previously noted in the literature, most notably by Razborov and Rudich [RR97] in their work on natural proofs.

2. *For any fixed $r \in \{0,1\}^n$, given a punctured key $s\{r\}$, the value $f_s(r)$ is pseudorandom:*

$$(s\{r\}, r, f_s(r)) \overset{T(\kappa)}{\approx} (s\{r\}, r, u),$$

where $s\{r\}$ is obtained by puncturing a random seed $s \in \{0,1\}^{m(\kappa)}$ at the point r, and u is uniformly random in $\{0,1\}^k$.

We note that the GGM-based construction of PRFs gives a construction of 2^n-secure puncturable PRFs from any subexponentially hard one-way function [GGM86, HILL99].

2.3 Indistinguishability Obfuscation

Our construction uses an indistinguishability obfuscator iO with 2^{-n} security. A candidate construction was first given in the work of Garg *et al.* [GGH+13].

Definition 5 (*T*-secure Indistinguishability Obfuscator [BGI+12]).
    Let $T : \mathbb{N} \to \mathbb{N}$ be a function. Let $\mathbb{C} = \{\mathbb{C}_n\}_{n \in \mathbb{N}}$ be a family of polynomial-size circuits, where $\mathbb{C}_n$ is a set of boolean circuits operating on inputs of length n. Let iO be a PPT algorithm, which takes as input a circuit $C \in \mathbb{C}_n$ and a security parameter $\kappa \in \mathbb{N}$, and outputs a boolean circuit iO(C) (not necessarily in $\mathbb{C}$).
    iO is a T-secure indistinguishability obfuscator for $\mathbb{C}$ if it satisfies the following properties:

1. Preserving Functionality: *For every $n, \kappa \in \mathbb{N}$, $C \in \mathbb{C}_n$, $x \in \{0,1\}^n$:*

$$(iO(C, 1^\kappa))(x) = C(x).$$

2. Indistinguishable Obfuscation: *For every two sequences of circuits $\{C_n^1\}_{n \in \mathbb{N}}$ and $\{C_n^2\}_{n \in \mathbb{N}}$, such that for every $n \in \mathbb{N}$, $|C_n^1| = |C_n^2|$, $C_n^1 \equiv C_n^2$, and $C_n^1, C_n^2 \in \mathbb{C}_n$, and for every polynomially-bounded function $m : \mathbb{N} \to \mathbb{N}$ it holds that:*

$$\left(1^\kappa, iO(C_{m(\kappa)}^1, 1^\kappa)\right) \overset{T(\kappa)}{\approx} \left(1^\kappa, iO(C_{m(\kappa)}^2, 1^\kappa)\right).$$

2.4 Input-Hiding Obfuscation

An input-hiding obfuscator for a class of circuits $\mathbb{C}$, as defined by Barak *et al.* [BBC+14], has the security guarantee that given an obfuscation of a randomly drawn circuit in the family $\mathbb{C}$, it is hard for an adversary to find an accepting input. In our work, we consider input-hiding obfuscation for the class of multi-bit point functions. A multi-bit point function $I_{x,y}$ is defined by an input $x \in \{0,1\}^n$, and an output $y \in \{0,1\}^k$. $I_{x,y}$ outputs y on input x, and 0 on all other inputs. Informally, we assume that given the obfuscation of $I_{x,y}$ for a uniformly random x and an arbitrary y, it is hard for an adversary to recover x.

Definition 6 (T-secure Input-Hiding Obfuscator [BBC+14]). *Let* $T :$ $\mathbb{N} \to \mathbb{N}$ *be a function, and let* $\mathbb{C} = \{\mathbb{C}_n\}_{n \in \mathbb{N}}$ *be a family of poly-size circuits, where* $\mathbb{C}_n$ *is a set of boolean circuits operating on inputs of length* n. *A PPT obfuscator* hideO *is a T-secure input-hiding obfuscator for* $\mathbb{C}$, *if it satisfies the preserving functionality requirement of Definition 5, as well as the following security requirement. For every poly-size (non-uniform) adversary Adv and all sufficiently large* n,

$$\Pr_{C \leftarrow \mathbb{C}_n, \text{hideO}} [C(Adv(\text{hideO}(C))) \neq 0] \leq T^{-1}(n).$$

We emphasize that (unlike other notions of T-security used in this work), we only allow the adversary for a T-secure input hiding obfuscation to run in polynomial time. Nevertheless, depending on the function T, the definition of T-secure input hiding is quite strong. In particular, for the typical case of proof-systems with soundness 2^{n^ϵ} (where $\epsilon > 0$ is a constant) we will assume input-hiding obfuscation for $T = 2^{n-n^\epsilon}$, which means that a polynomial-time adversary can only do sub-exponentially better than the trivial attack that picks random inputs until it finds an accepting input (this attack succeeds with probability $\text{poly}(n)/2^n$). This is also why we do not separate the security parameter from the input length (the adversary can always succeed with probability 2^{-n}, assuming there exists an accepting input).

We assume input-hiding obfuscation for the class of multi-bit point functions (see above), where the point x is drawn uniformly at random, and the output y is arbitrary. In particular, we do not assume that the collection $\mathbb{C}$ of pairs (x, y) can be sampled efficiently, only that its marginal distribution on x is uniform.

Assumption 3 (T-secure Input-Hiding for Multi-Bit Point Functions). *Let* $T, k : \mathbb{N} \to \mathbb{N}$ *be functions. An obfuscator* hideO *is a T-secure input-hiding obfuscator for* (n, k)-*multi-bit point functions if for every collection* $\mathbb{C}$ *as below,* hideO *is a T-secure input-hiding obfuscator for* $\mathbb{C}$. *In the collection* $\mathbb{C}$, *for every* $n \in \mathbb{N}$, *every function* $I_{x,y} \in \mathbb{C}_n$ *has* $x \in \{0,1\}^n, y \in \{0,1\}^{k(n)}$, *and the marginal distribution of a random draw from* $\mathbb{C}_n$ *on* x *is uniform.*

The assumption is strong in that we do not assume that a random function in $\mathbb{C}$ can be sampled efficiently, or that the output y is an efficient function of the input x. This assumption was studied in [CD08, BC14]. A candidate construction (in the standard model) was provided in [CD08]. Loosely speaking, their construction is an extension of the point function obfuscation of Canetti [Can97], where the obfuscation of $I_{x,y}$ consists of a pair of the form (r, r^x), together with k pairs of the form $(r_i, r_i^{\alpha_i})$ where $\alpha_i = x$ if $y_i = 1$ and is uniformly random otherwise. It was proved in [BC14] that this construction is secure in the generic group model, where the inversion probability is at most $\text{poly}(n) \cdot 2^{-n}$.

2.5   Interactive Proofs and Arguments

An interactive proof, as introduced by Goldwasser, Micali and Rackoff [GMR89], is a protocol between two parties, a computationally unbounded prover and a polynomial-time verifier. Both parties have access to an input x and the prover tries to convince the verifier that $x \in L$. Formally an interactive proof is defined as follows:

Definition 7 (Interactive Proof [GMR89]). *An r-message interactive proof for the language L is an r-message protocol between the verifier V, which is polynomial-time, and a prover P, which is computationally unbounded. We require that the following two conditions hold:*

- **Completeness**: *For every $x \in L$, if V interacts with P on common input x, then V accepts with probability at least $2/3$.*
- **Soundness**: *For every $x \notin L$ and every (computationally unbounded) cheating prover strategy $\tilde{P}$, the verifier V accepts when interacting with $\tilde{P}$ with probability at most $1/3$.*

We say that an interactive-proof is public-coin if all messages sent from V to P consist of fresh random coins tosses. Also, recall that the constants $1/3$ and $2/3$ are arbitrary and can be amplified by (e.g., parallel) repetition.

Interactive Arguments. An interactive argument is defined similarly to an interactive proof except that the soundness condition is only required to hold for cheating provers that run in polynomial time. We also require that the honest prover run in polynomial-time, given the witness as an auxiliary input.

Definition 8 (Interactive Argument). *An r-message argument for the language $L \in$ NP is an r-message protocol between a verifier V and a prover P, both of which are polynomial-time algorithms. We require that the following two conditions hold:*

- **Completeness**: *There exists a negligible function negl such that for every $x \in L$, if V interacts with P on common input x, where P is given in addition an NP witness w for $x \in L$, then V accepts with probability at least $1 - negl(|x|)$.*
- **Soundness**: *For every polynomial-size cheating prover strategy $\tilde{P}$ and for every $x \notin L$, the verifier V accepts when interacting with $\tilde{P}$ on common input x, with probability at most $negl(|x|)$.*

We remark that in contrast to Definition 7, here we require negligible completeness and soundness errors. This is because parallel repetition does not necessarily decrease the soundness error for interactive arguments [BIN97]. We further remark that it is common to add a security parameter to the definition of argument systems so as to allow obtaining strong security guarantees even for short inputs. For simplicity of notations however we refrain from introducing a security parameter and note that better security guarantees for short inputs can be simply obtained by padding the input.

2.6 The Fiat-Shamir Paradigm

In this section, we recall the Fiat-Shamir paradigm. For the sake of simplicity of notation, we describe this paradigm when applied to 3-round (as opposed to arbitrary constant round) public-coin protocols. Let $\Pi = (P, V)$ be a 3-round public-coin proof system for an NP language L. We denote its transcripts by (α, β, γ), where β are the messages sent by the verifier, and α, γ are the messages sent by the prover. We denote by n the length of α (i.e., $\alpha \in \{0, 1\}^n$), and we denote by k the length of β (i.e., $\beta \in \{0, 1\}^k$). We assume that $k \le \mathrm{poly}(n)$ (since otherwise we can just pad).

Let $\{\mathcal{H}_n\}_{n \in \mathbb{N}}$ be an ensemble of hash functions, such that for every $n \in \mathbb{N}$ and for every $h \in \mathcal{H}_n$,

$$h : \{0, 1\}^n \to \{0, 1\}^k.$$

We define Π^{FS}, with respect to the hash family $\mathcal{H}$ to be the 2-round protocol obtained by applying the Fiat-Shamir transformation to Π using $\mathcal{H}$. A formal presentation of the "collapsed" protocol $\Pi^{\mathsf{FS}} = (P^{\mathsf{FS}}, V^{\mathsf{FS}})$ is in Fig. 1.

Remark 3. We emphasize that our main result is that the Fiat-Shamir paradigm *in its original formulation* (as presented in Fig. 1) is secure when applied to interactive proofs and when using a *particular hash function* (based on the assumption mentioned above).

Protocol $\Pi^{\mathsf{FS}}(1^n, x)$ for an NP Language L

Prover's Input: Statement x and a witness w for $x \in L$.
Verifier's Input: Statement x.
$V^{\mathsf{FS}} \to P^{\mathsf{FS}}$: The verifier V^{FS} chooses a random $h \leftarrow \mathcal{H}_n$, and sends h to the prover P^{FS}.
$P^{\mathsf{FS}} \to V^{\mathsf{FS}}$: The prover P^{FS} simulates an execution with the prover P of Π in the following way:
  - Choose a random tape for P and continue the emulation of (P, V) by running P. Let $\alpha \in \{0, 1\}^n$ be the first message sent by P in Π.
  - Compute $h(\alpha) = \beta$.
  - Continue the emulation of P assuming P received β as the second message from V^{FS}. Let γ be the third message sent by P.
  Send (α, β, γ) to the verifier V^{FS}.
Verification: The verifier V^{FS} accepts if and only if:
  - $h(\alpha) = \beta$.
  - V accepts the transcript (α, β, γ).

Fig. 1. Collapsing a 3-round Protocol $\Pi = (P, V)$ into a 2-round Protocol $\Pi^{\mathsf{FS}} = (P^{\mathsf{FS}}, V^{\mathsf{FS}})$ using $\mathcal{H}$

3 Security of Fiat-Shamir for 3-Message Proofs

We show an instantiation of the Fiat-Shamir paradigm that is sound when it is applied to interactive proofs (as opposed to arguments). Taking n to be a bound on the message lengths of the prover in Π, our instantiation assumes the existence of a 2^n-secure indistinguishability obfuscation scheme iO, a 2^n-secure puncturable PRF family $\mathcal{F}$, and a 2^n-secure input-hiding obfuscation for the class of multi-bit point functions $\mathcal{I}_{n,k}$.

For clarity of exposition, we first show that our instantiation is secure for 3-round public-coin interactive proofs. This is the regime for which the Fiat-Shamir paradigm was originally suggested. We then build on the proof for the 3-message case (or rather the 4-message case, see below), and prove security for any constant number of rounds.

Theorem 4 (Fiat-Shamir for 3-message Proofs). *Let Π be a public-coin 3-message interactive proof system with negligible soundness error. Let n be an upper bound on the input length and the length of the prover's messages and let $k \leq poly(n)$ be an upper bound on the length of the verifier's messages.*

Assume the existence of a 2^n-secure puncturable PRF family $\mathcal{F}$, the existence of a 2^n-secure Indistinguishability Obfuscation iO, and the existence of a secure input-hiding obfuscation for the class of multi-bit point functions $\{\mathcal{I}_{n,k}\}$ with security $T = 2^n \cdot negl(n)$.

Then, the resulting 2-round argument Π^{FS}, obtained by applying the Fiat-Shamir paradigm (see Fig. 1) to Π with the function family iO($\mathcal{F}$), is secure.

(Recall that we defined iO($\mathcal{F}$) as the iO obfuscation of a program that computes the PRF, using a hardwired random seed.)

In Sect. 4 we prove the security of the Fiat-Shamir paradigm when applied to any constant round interactive proof. To prove the general (constant round) case, we need to rely on a more general (and more technical) variation of Theorem 4. First, we rely on the security of the Fiat-Shamir paradigm for any 4-round interactive proof Π where the first message is sent by the verifier. In the transformed protocol Π^{FS}, the first message of the verifier consists of the first message as in Π, along with a Fiat-Shamir hash function, which will be applied to the prover's first message. In addition, in the generalized theorem we allow the verifier in the original protocol Π to run in time $2^{O(n)}$.

We state the generalized theorem below.

Theorem 5 (Theorem 4, more General Statement). *Let Π be a 4-message public-coin interactive proof system, where the first message is sent by the verifier. Let n be an upper bound on the input length[14] and the lengths of the prover's messages, let $k \leq poly(n)$ be a bound on the verifier's messages, let $\mu(n) = negl(n)$ be the soundness error[15] error, and assume that the verifier runs in time at most $2^{O(n)}$.*

---

[14] We remark that the reason we bound the input length is solely because we use a simplified definition of argument system that does not have a security parameter, and we are aiming for argument systems with soundness that is negligible in the *input length*.

[15] Since parallel repetition decreases the soundness error of interactive *proofs* at an exponential rate, we may assume without loss of generality that the soundness error is negligible in n.

Assume the existence of a 2^n-secure puncturable PRF family $\mathcal{F}$, the existence of a 2^n-secure Indistinguishability Obfuscation iO, and the existence of a input-hiding obfuscation for the class of multi-bit point functions $\{\mathcal{I}_{n,k}\}$ that is T-secure for every $T = 2^n \cdot \mu/\nu$, where ν is any non-negligible function.

Then the resulting 2-round argument Π^{FS}, obtained by applying the Fiat-Shamir paradigm[16] to Π with the function family iO$(\mathcal{F})$, is secure.

We remark that $\mu \cdot 2^n \cdot \text{poly}(n)$ is a shorthand for a function T such that for every $c > 0$ and all sufficiently large $n \in \mathbb{N}$ it holds that $T(n) \geq \mu(n) \cdot 2^n \cdot n^c$.

Proof (Proof of Theorem 5). Fix any 4-round interactive proof $\Pi = (P, V)$ as claimed in the theorem statement. Let $\mu = \text{negl}(n)$ be the soundness error of Π.

Suppose for the sake of contradiction that there exists a poly-size cheating prover P^* who breaks the soundness of the protocol Π^{FS} with respect to some $x^* \notin L$ with non-negligible probability ν. We will use P^* to eventually break the security of the input-hiding obfuscation, while using along the way the soundness of Π as well as the security of the PRF $\mathcal{F}$ and Indistinguishability Obfuscator iO.

There must exist a choice for the verifier's first message τ in Π, such that the following two conditions hold: (*i*) Even conditioned on the first part of the first message in Π^{FS} being τ, the cheating prover P^* still breaks the soundness of the protocol Π^{FS} on x^* with probability at least $(\nu/2)$, and (*ii*) even conditioned on the first message in Π being τ, the original protocol Π still has soundness error at most $(2\mu/\nu)$. Such a τ must exist because at least a $(\nu/2)$-fraction of the messages must satisfy condition (*i*) (otherwise P^* cannot break Π^{FS} with total probability ν), and the fraction that do not satisfy condition (*ii*) must be smaller than $(\nu/2)$ (otherwise the soundness of Π is smaller than μ).

Fix the verifier's first message to always be τ (both in the original and in the transformed protocols). We have that:

$$\Pr_{s,\text{iO}} \left[P^*(\tau, \text{iO}(s)) = (\alpha, \gamma) \text{ s.t. } V(x^*, \tau, \alpha, f_s(\alpha), \gamma) = 1 \right] \geq \nu/2, \qquad (3.1)$$

where iO(s) refers to the iO obfuscation of a random function f_s from the family $\mathcal{F}$.

The relaxed verifier and its properties. To obtain a contradiction, we analyze a relaxed verifier V' (which is only used in the security analysis). The relaxed verifier accepts a transcript (α, β, γ) if the original verifier V would accept, or if the first $\lceil \log(\nu/(2\mu)) \rceil$ bits of β are all 0 (where recall that μ is the soundness

---

[16] For 4-message proofs, the same paradigm as in Fig. 1 is used, except that the verifier also sends its first message from the base proof-system (i.e., a random string) in the first round.

error of Π).[17] In particular, whenever V accepts, the relaxed verifier V' also accepts, and so:

$$\Pr_{s,\text{iO}} \left[P^*(\tau, \text{iO}(s)) = (\alpha, \gamma) \text{ s.t. } V'(x^*, \tau, \alpha, f_s(\alpha), \gamma) = 1 \right] \geq \nu/2. \qquad (3.2)$$

We take μ' to be the soundness of the interactive proof (P, V') (after τ is fixed), which runs the relaxed verifier. Observe that by a union bound

$$\mu' \leq (2\mu/\nu) + 2^{-\lceil \log(\nu/(2\mu)) \rceil} \leq 4\mu/\nu,$$

(in particular if μ is negligible, then so is μ').
We define:

$$\mathsf{ACC} = \left\{ (\alpha, \beta) : \exists \gamma \text{ s.t. } V'(x^*, \tau, \alpha, \beta, \gamma) = 1 \right\}$$

Observe that membership in ACC can be computed in time $2^n \cdot \text{poly}(n) = 2^{O(n)}$ by enumerating over all γ's and running V'. Equation (3.2) implies that there exists a poly-size adversary $\mathcal{A}$ (that just outputs the first part of P^*'s output) such that:

$$\Pr_{s,\text{iO}} \left[\mathcal{A}(\text{iO}(s)) \text{ outputs some } \alpha \text{ s.t. } (\alpha, f_s(\alpha)) \in \mathsf{ACC} \right] \geq \nu/2. \qquad (3.3)$$

Using Eq. (3.3) we prove our main lemma.

Lemma 1.

$$\Pr_{s,\alpha^*,u^*,\text{iO}} \left[\mathcal{A}(\text{iO}(s\{\alpha^*\}, \alpha^*, u^*)) = \alpha^* \mid (\alpha^*, u^*) \in \mathsf{ACC} \right] \geq 2^{-n+2} \cdot \nu/\mu'$$

where α^* and u^* are uniformly distributed (in $\{0,1\}^n$ and $\{0,1\}^k$, respectively) and $\text{iO}(s\{\alpha^*\}, \alpha^*, u^*)$ refers to an iO obfuscation of the program that contains the seed s punctured at the point α^*, and on input α first checks if $\alpha = \alpha^*$ and if so outputs u^* and otherwise outputs $f_s(\alpha)$.

Proof. We prove the lemma by analyzing the probability that the event

$$\left(\mathcal{A}(\text{iO}(s\{\alpha^*\}, \alpha^*, u^*)) = \alpha^* \right) \wedge \left((\alpha^*, u^*) \in \mathsf{ACC} \right)$$

occurs.

By the exponential hardness of the puncturable PRF, and the fact that membership in ACC is computable in $2^{O(n)}$ time, we have that

---

[17] In the original protocol Π, it may be the case that different messages α sent by the prover can lead the verifier to accept with different probabilities. E.g., some specific α's may lead the verifier to accept with probability μ and others with probability 0. This presents a technical difficulty later in the proof and so we construct the relaxed verifier V' so that every string α leads it to accept with roughly the same probability (up to a small multiplicative constant) without increasing the soundness error by too much.

$$\Pr_{s,\alpha^*,u^*,\text{iO}}\left[\begin{array}{c}\mathcal{A}(\text{iO}(s\{\alpha^*\},\alpha^*,u^*))=\alpha^*\\ \wedge \\ (\alpha^*,u^*)\in\text{ACC}\end{array}\right]\geq \Pr_{s,\alpha^*,\text{iO}}\left[\begin{array}{c}\mathcal{A}(\text{iO}(s\{\alpha^*\},\alpha^*,f_s(\alpha^*)))=\alpha^*\\ \wedge \\ (\alpha^*,f_s(\alpha^*))\in\text{ACC}\end{array}\right]-2^{-2n}.$$
(3.4)

Further applying the exponential hardness of the iO scheme (and the fact that membership in ACC can be decided in $2^{O(n)}$ time), we get that:

$$\Pr_{s,\alpha^*,u^*,\text{iO}}\left[\begin{array}{c}\mathcal{A}(\text{iO}(s\{\alpha^*\},\alpha^*,u^*))=\alpha^*\\ \wedge \\ (\alpha^*,u^*)\in\text{ACC}\end{array}\right]\geq \Pr_{s,\alpha^*,\text{iO}}\left[\begin{array}{c}\mathcal{A}(\text{iO}(s))=\alpha^*\\ \wedge \\ (\alpha^*,f_s(\alpha^*))\in\text{ACC}\end{array}\right]-2\cdot 2^{-2n}.$$
(3.5)

Using elementary probability theory, we have that:

$$\Pr_{s,\alpha^*,\text{iO}}\left[\begin{array}{c}\mathcal{A}(\text{iO}(s))=\alpha^*\\ \wedge \\ (\alpha^*,f_s(\alpha^*))\in\text{ACC}\end{array}\right]=\Pr_{s,\alpha^*,\text{iO}}\left[\bigcup_\alpha((\mathcal{A}(\text{iO}(s))=\alpha^*)\wedge((\alpha^*,f_s(\alpha^*))\in\text{ACC})\wedge(\alpha^*=\alpha))\right]$$

$$=\sum_\alpha\Pr_{s,\alpha^*,\text{iO}}\left[((\mathcal{A}(\text{iO}(s))=\alpha)\wedge((\alpha,f_s(\alpha))\in\text{ACC})\wedge(\alpha^*=\alpha))\right]$$

$$=2^{-n}\sum_\alpha\Pr_{s,\text{iO}}\left[(\mathcal{A}(\text{iO}(s))=\alpha)\wedge((\alpha,f_s(\alpha))\in\text{ACC})\right]$$

$$=2^{-n}\Pr_{s,\text{iO}}\left[\mathcal{A}(\text{iO}(s))\text{ outputs some }\alpha\text{ s.t. }(\alpha,f_s(\alpha))\in\text{ACC}\right]$$

$$\geq 2^{-n}\cdot\nu/2$$

where the last inequality is by Eq. (3.3). Thus, we have that:

$$\Pr_{s,\alpha^*,u^*,\text{iO}}\left[\begin{array}{c}\mathcal{A}(\text{iO}(s\{\alpha^*\},\alpha^*,u^*))=\alpha^*\\ \wedge \\ (\alpha^*,u^*)\in\text{ACC}\end{array}\middle| s\right]\geq \frac{1}{4}\cdot 2^{-n}\cdot\nu.$$

By the soundness of the underlying proof-system, it holds thats $\Pr_{\alpha^*,u^*}[(\alpha^*,u^*)\in\text{ACC}]\leq\mu'$ (since otherwise a cheating prover could violate soundness by just sending a random α^*).[18]

Let $\zeta=\Pr_{s,\alpha^*,u^*,\text{iO}}\left[\mathcal{A}(\text{iO}(s\{\alpha^*\},\alpha^*,u^*))=\alpha^*\middle|(\alpha^*,u^*)\in\text{ACC}\right]$. Then, by definition of conditional probability we have that

$$\zeta=\frac{\Pr_{s,\alpha^*,u^*,\text{iO}}\left[\begin{array}{c}\mathcal{A}(\text{iO}(s\{\alpha^*\},\alpha^*,u^*))=\alpha^*\\ \wedge \\ (\alpha^*,u^*)\in\text{ACC}\end{array}\right]}{\Pr_{\alpha^*,u^*}[(\alpha^*,u^*)\in\text{ACC}]}\geq\frac{1}{4}\cdot 2^{-n}\cdot\nu/\mu',$$

and the lemma follows.

---

[18] It may at first seem odd that we only use the soundness of the underlying proof-system with respect to a cheating prover that just sends a random message α^*. Recall however that here we consider the *relaxed* verifier who, by design, has a (roughly) similar acceptance probability given any string α.

We are now ready to use (and break) our input-hiding obfuscator hideO. Lemma 1, together with the 2^n-security of the iO implies that

$$\Pr_{s,\alpha^*,u^*,\text{iO}} \left[\mathcal{A}(\text{iO}(s, \text{hideO}(\alpha^*, u^*))) = \alpha^* \, \middle| \, (\alpha^*, u^*) \in \text{ACC} \right] \geq \frac{1}{4} \cdot 2^{-n} \cdot \nu/\mu' - 2^{-n}$$

$$\geq \frac{1}{8} \cdot 2^{-n} \cdot \nu/\mu',$$

$$(3.6)$$

where α^* and u^* are uniformly distributed and $\text{iO}(s, \text{hideO}(\alpha^*, u^*))$ refers to the iO obfuscation of the program that contains a seed s for a PRF (in its entirety), and the input-hiding obfuscation $\text{hideO}(\alpha^*, u^*)$ of a multi-bit point function that on input α^* outputs u^*. The program uses the input-hiding obfuscation to check if its input equals α^*, and if so outputs the same value as $\text{hideO}(\alpha^*, u^*)$. Otherwise the program behaves like the PRF.

Equation (3.6) is almost what we want. Namely, an adversary that given access to $\text{hideO}(\alpha^*, u^*)$ produces α^* with probability $\omega(\text{poly}(n)/2^n)$ (since ν is inverse polynomial and μ is a negligible function). The only remaining problem is that the distribution of (α^*, u^*) is not quite what we need. More specifically, in Eq. (3.6) (α^*, u^*) are distributed uniformly conditioned on $(\alpha^*, u^*) \in \text{ACC}$, whereas we need for the marginal distribution of α to be uniform in order to break the hideO obfuscation. Using the properties of the *relaxed* verifier, we show that these two distributions are actually closely related.

We define the following two distributions. The distribution $\mathcal{T}_1$ is obtained by jointly picking a pair (α, β) uniformly from ACC (this is the distribution from which (α^*, u^*) are sampled from in Eq. (3.6)). $\mathcal{T}_2$ is the distribution obtained by picking a uniformly random $\alpha \in \{0,1\}^n$ and then a random β conditioned on $(\alpha, \beta) \in \text{ACC}$ (i.e. the marginal distribution on α is uniform). For $\alpha^* \in \{0,1\}^n$, $\beta^* \in \{0,1\}^k$, we use $\mathcal{T}_1[\alpha^*, \beta^*]$ and $\mathcal{T}_2[\alpha^*, \beta^*]$ to denote the probability of the pair (α^*, β^*) by $\mathcal{T}_1$ and by $\mathcal{T}_2$ (respectively).

Proposition 1. *For any $\alpha^* \in \{0,1\}^n$ and $\beta^* \in \{0,1\}^k$:*

$$\mathcal{T}_2[\alpha^*, \beta^*] \geq \frac{1}{4} \mathcal{T}_1[\alpha^*, \beta^*]$$

Proof. For every α^* denote by:

$$S_{\alpha^*} = \{\beta^* \in \{0,1\}^k : (\alpha^*, \beta^*) \in \text{ACC}\}.$$

By construction of the relaxed verifier V', we know that for every $\alpha \in \{0,1\}^n$ it holds that

$$\frac{\mu}{\nu} \leq \frac{|S_\alpha|}{2^k} \leq \frac{4\mu}{\nu}.$$

In particular, for any $\alpha, \alpha^* \in \{0,1\}^n$:

$$|S_\alpha| \geq \frac{1}{4} |S_{\alpha^*}|.$$

Now we have that:

$$T_1[\alpha^*, \beta^*] = \frac{1}{\sum_{\alpha \in \{0,1\}^n} |S_\alpha|} \leq \frac{4}{\sum_{\alpha \in \{0,1\}^n} |S_{\alpha^*}|} = \frac{4}{2^n \cdot |S_{\alpha^*}|} = 4 \cdot T_2[\alpha^*, \beta^*] \tag{3.7}$$

In particular, drawing by T_2 rather than T_1 can only decrease the success probability of $\mathcal{A}$ by a multiplicative factor of 4. Moreover, when drawing by T_2, the marginal distribution on α^* *is* uniform. Thus Proposition 1 and Eq. (3.6) imply that there exists a poly-size adversary $\mathcal{A}$, such that

$$\Pr_{(\alpha^*, u^*) \leftarrow T_2, \text{hideO}} [\mathcal{A}(\text{hideO}(\alpha^*, u^*)) = \alpha^*] \geq \frac{1}{32} \cdot \frac{\nu}{\mu' \cdot 2^n}$$

where α^* drawn by T_2 *is* uniformly random. Since ν is a non-negligible function and $\mu' = O(\mu/\nu)$, this contradicts the security of the input-hiding obfuscation hideO.

4 Security of Fiat-Shamir for Multi-round Proofs

In this section we show a secure instantiation of the Fiat-Shamir methodology for transforming any constant-round interactive proof into a 2-round computationally-sound argument. We assume for the sake of simplicity, and without loss of generality, that the verifier always sends the first message, and thus consider interactive protocols with an even number of rounds. Namely, for any constant $c \geq 2$, we consider a $2c$-round interactive proof $\Pi = (P, V)$. We assume without loss of generality that all of the prover's messages are of the same length, and denote this length by n (i.e. $\forall i, \alpha_i \in \{0,1\}^n$). Similarly, we assume without loss of generality that all of the verifier's messages are of the same length, and denote this length by k (i.e. $\forall i, \beta_i \in \{0,1\}^k$). We assume without loss of generality that $k \leq n$. All these assumptions are only for the simplicity of notations, and can be easily achieved by padding.

For every $i \in [c-1]$, let $\{\mathcal{F}_n^{(i)}\}_{n \in \mathbb{N}}$ be an ensemble of hash functions, such that for every $n \in \mathbb{N}$ and for every $f^{(i)} \in \mathcal{F}_n$,

$$f^{(i)} : \{0,1\}^{i \cdot (n+k)} \to \{0,1\}^k.$$

We assume without loss of generality that there exists a polynomial p such that for every $i \in [c-1]$ and for every $n \in \mathbb{N}$,

$$\mathcal{F}_n^{(i)} = \{f_s^{(i)}\}_{s \in \{0,1\}^{p(n)}}.$$

We define Π^{FS} to be the 2-round protocol obtained by applying the multi-round Fiat-Shamir transformation to Π using $(\text{iO}(f_{s_1}^{(1)}), \ldots, \text{iO}(f_{s_{c-1}}^{(c-1)}))$, where $f_{s_i}^{(i)} \leftarrow \mathcal{F}_n^{(i)}$ for every $i \in [c-1]$. The security of Π^{FS} is shown in Theorem 6 below.

Theorem 6 (Fiat-Shamir Transform for Multi-Round Interactive Proofs). *Let* $\mu : \mathbb{N} \to [0,1]$ *be a function. Assume the existence of a* 2^n*-secure puncturable PRF family* $\mathcal{F}$*, assume the existence of a* 2^n*-secure Indistinguishability Obfuscation, and assume the existence of an input-hiding obfuscation for the class of multi-bit point functions* $\{\mathcal{I}_{n,k}\}$ *that is* T*-secure for any* $T = 2^n \cdot \mu/\nu$*, where* ν *is any non-negligible function.*

Then for any constant $c \in \mathbb{N}$ *such that* $c \geq 2$*, and any* $2c$*-round interactive proof* Π *with soundness* μ*, the resulting* 2*-round argument* Π^{FS}*, obtained by applying the multi-round Fiat-Shamir transformation to* Π *with the function family* $\mathrm{iO}(\mathcal{F})$*, is secure.*

Proof. The proof is by induction on $c \in \mathbb{N}$, for $c \geq 2$. The base case $c = 2$ follows immediately from Theorem 4. Suppose the theorem statement is true for $< c$ rounds, and we will prove that it is true for c rounds.

To this end, fix any $2c$-round interactive proof Π for proving membership in a language L. Suppose for the sake of contradiction that Π^{FS} is not secure. Namely, there exists a poly-size cheating prover P^* and there exists $x^* \notin L$ such that P^* succeeds in convincing the verifier of Π^{FS} that $x^* \in L$ with non-negligible probability. We assume without loss of generality that P^* is deterministic.

Consider the following protocol Ψ for proving membership in L, which consists of $2c - 2$ rounds: In the first round the verifier chooses the first message that it would have sent in Π, which we denote by β_0. In addition, it chooses a random seed $s_1 \leftarrow \{0,1\}^{p(n)}$, and sends to the prover the pair $(\beta_0, \mathrm{iO}(f_{s_1}^{(1)}))$. Then, the prover chooses $(\alpha_1, \beta_1, \alpha_2)$ such that $\beta_1 = f_{s_1}^{(1)}(\alpha_1)$, and such that α_1 and α_2 are chosen as in Π. It sends $(\alpha_1, \beta_1, \alpha_2)$ to the verifier. Then the prover and verifier continue to execute the protocol Π interactively, conditioned on $(\beta_0, \alpha_1, \beta_1, \alpha_2)$. Finally, the verifier accepts if and only if the verifier of Π would have accepted the resulting transcript and $\beta_1 = f_{s_1}^{(1)}(\alpha_1)$.

Consider the protocol Ψ_{P^*}, in which we fix the first message from the prover in Ψ to be the message $(\alpha_1, \beta_1, \alpha_2)$ generated by P^* in Π^{FS}. If Ψ_{P^*} is a sound proof then, by our induction hypothesis $(\Psi_{P^*})^{\mathsf{FS}}$ is sound. However, note that P^* can be trivially converted into a cheating prover that breaks the soundness of $(\Psi_{P^*})^{\mathsf{FS}}$, contradicting our induction hypothesis that the Fiat-Shamir transformation is sound for interactive proofs with $2(c-1)$ rounds (with the function family $\mathrm{iO}(\mathcal{F})$). Thus, it must be the case that Ψ_{P^*} is not a sound proof. Namely, there exists a (possibly inefficient) cheating prover P^{**}, an element $x^* \notin L$, and a polynomial q, such that P^{**} convinces the verifier of Ψ_{P^*} to accept x^* with probability $\geq 1/q(\kappa)$ for infinitely many $\kappa \in \mathbb{N}$.

Consider the 4-round protocol Φ, which consists of the first 4 rounds of Π, denoted by $(\beta_0, \alpha_1, \beta_1, \alpha_2)$. Given a transcript $(\beta_0, \alpha_1, \beta_1, \alpha_2)$ the verifier of Φ accepts if and only if there exists a strategy of the (cheating) prover of Π that causes the verifier of Π to accept with probability $\geq 1/q(\kappa)$ conditioned on the first 4-rounds of Π being $(\beta_0, \alpha_1, \beta_1, \alpha_2)$. Note that the verifier of Φ runs in time $\mathrm{poly}(2^{c(n+k)}) = 2^{O(n)}$. The statistical soundness of Π implies that Φ is also statistically sound. Note however that Φ^{FS} is not computationally sound. To see this, consider a poly-size cheating prover for Φ^{FS} that sends the message

$(\alpha_1, \beta_1, \alpha_2)$ that P^* sends in Π. By the fact that Ψ_{P*} is not sound (since P^{**} breaks its soundness), the verifier of Φ^{FS} will accept $x^* \notin L$. This is in contradiction to Theorem 5 (where we used the fact that Theorem 5 holds even for verifiers running in time $2^{O(n)}$).

Acknowledgments. We thank an anonymous reviewer for suggesting, and allowing us to use, a significant simplification to our original proof. We also thank the reviewers for their useful comments and especially for pointing out an error in a previous version of the proof of Theorem 6.

This work was done in part while the authors were visiting the Simons Institute for the Theory of Computing, supported by the Simons Foundation and by the DIMACS/Simons Collaboration in Cryptography through NSF grant #CNS-1523467.

The third author was also partially supported by the grants: NSF MACS - CNS-1413920, DARPA IBM - W911NF-15-C-0236, SIMONS Investigator award Agreement Dated 6-5-12 and DARPA NJIT - W911NF-15-C-0226.

References

[AABN02] Abdalla, M., An, J.H., Bellare, M., Namprempre, C.: From identification to signatures via the fiat-shamir transform: minimizing assumptions for security and forward-security. In: Knudsen, L.R. (ed.) EUROCRYPT 2002. LNCS, vol. 2332, pp. 418–433. Springer, Heidelberg (2002). doi:10.1007/3-540-46035-7_28

[Bar01] Barak, B.: How to go beyond the black-box simulation barrier. In: FOCS, pp. 106–115 (2001)

[BBC+14] Barak, B., Bitansky, N., Canetti, R., Kalai, Y.T., Paneth, O., Sahai, A.: Obfuscation for evasive functions. In: Lindell, Y. (ed.) TCC 2014. LNCS, vol. 8349, pp. 26–51. Springer, Heidelberg (2014). doi:10.1007/978-3-642-54242-8_2

[BC14] Bitansky, N., Canetti, R.: On strong simulation and composable point obfuscation. J. Cryptol. **27**(2), 317–357 (2014)

[BCC+14] Bitansky, N., Canetti, R., Cohn, H., Goldwasser, S., Kalai, Y.T., Paneth, O., Rosen, A.: The impossibility of obfuscation with auxiliary input or a universal simulator. In: Garay, J.A., Gennaro, R. (eds.) CRYPTO 2014. LNCS, vol. 8617, pp. 71–89. Springer, Heidelberg (2014). doi:10.1007/978-3-662-44381-1_5

[BDG+13] Bitansky, N., Dachman-Soled, D., Garg, S., Jain, A., Kalai, Y.T., López-Alt, A., Wichs, D.: Why "Fiat-Shamir for Proofs" lacks a proof. In: Sahai, A. (ed.) TCC 2013. LNCS, vol. 7785, pp. 182–201. Springer, Heidelberg (2013). doi:10.1007/978-3-642-36594-2_11

[BDNP08] Ben-David, A., Nisan, N., Pinkas, B.: Fairplaymp: a system for secure multi-party computation. In: ACM Conference on Computer and Communications Security, pp. 257–266 (2008)

[BGGL01] Barak, B., Goldreich, O., Goldwasser, S., Lindell, Y.: Resettably-sound zero-knowledge and its applications. In: 42nd Annual Symposium on Foundations of Computer Science, FOCS 2001, 14–17 October 2001, Las Vegas, Nevada, USA, pp. 116–125 (2001)

[BGI+12] Barak, B., Goldreich, O., Impagliazzo, R., Rudich, S., Sahai, A., Vadhan, S.P., Yang, K.: On the (im)possibility of obfuscating programs. J. ACM **59**(2), 6 (2012)

[BGI14]   Boyle, E., Goldwasser, S., Ivan, I.: Functional signatures and pseudorandom functions. In: Krawczyk, H. (ed.) PKC 2014. LNCS, vol. 8383, pp. 501–519. Springer, Heidelberg (2014). doi:10.1007/978-3-642-54631-0_29

[BGL+15] Bitansky, N., Garg, S., Lin, H., Pass, R., Telang, S.: Succinct randomized encodings and their applications. In: Proceedings of the Forty-Seventh Annual ACM on Symposium on Theory of Computing, STOC 2015, Portland, OR, USA, June 14–17, 2015, pp. 439–448 (2015)

[BIN97]   Bellare, M., Impagliazzo, R., Naor, M.: Does parallel repetition lower the error in computationally sound protocols? In: 38th Annual Symposium on Foundations of Computer Science, FOCS 1997, Miami Beach, Florida, USA, October 19–22, 1997, pp. 374–383 (1997)

[BL04]   Barak, B., Lindell, Y.: Strict polynomial-time in simulation and extraction. SIAM J. Comput. 33(4), 738–818 (2004)

[Blu87]   Blum, M.: How to prove a theorem so no one else can claim it. In: Proceedings of the International Congress of Mathematicians, pp. 1444–1451 (1987)

[BLV06]   Barak, B., Lindell, Y., Vadhan, S.P.: Lower bounds for non-black-box zero knowledge. J. Comput. Syst. Sci. 72(2), 321–391 (2006)

[BM14]   Brzuska, C., Mittelbach, A.: Indistinguishability obfuscation versus multibit point obfuscation with auxiliary input. In: Sarkar, P., Iwata, T. (eds.) ASIACRYPT 2014. LNCS, vol. 8874, pp. 142–161. Springer, Heidelberg (2014). doi:10.1007/978-3-662-45608-8_8

[BR93]   Bellare, M., Rogaway, P.: Random oracles are practical: a paradigm for designing efficient protocols. In: ACM Conference on Computer and Communications Security, pp. 62–73 (1993)

[BS16]   Bellare, M., Stepanovs, I.: Point-function obfuscation: a framework and generic constructions. In: Kushilevitz, E., Malkin, T. (eds.) TCC 2016. LNCS, vol. 9563, pp. 565–594. Springer, Heidelberg (2016). doi:10.1007/978-3-662-49099-0_21

[BW13]   Boneh, D., Waters, B.: Constrained pseudorandom functions and their applications. In: Sako, K., Sarkar, P. (eds.) ASIACRYPT 2013. LNCS, vol. 8270, pp. 280–300. Springer, Heidelberg (2013). doi:10.1007/978-3-642-42045-0_15

[Can97]   Canetti, R.: Towards realizing random oracles: hash functions that hide all partial information. In: Kaliski, B.S. (ed.) CRYPTO 1997. LNCS, vol. 1294, pp. 455–469. Springer, Heidelberg (1997). doi:10.1007/BFb0052255

[CCR15]   Canetti, R., Chen, Y., Reyzin, L.: On the correlation intractability of obfuscated pseudorandom functions. IACR Cryptology ePrint Archive, 2015:334 (2015)

[CD08]   Canetti, R., Dakdouk, R.R.: Obfuscating point functions with multibit output. In: Smart, N. (ed.) EUROCRYPT 2008. LNCS, vol. 4965, pp. 489–508. Springer, Heidelberg (2008). doi:10.1007/978-3-540-78967-3_28

[CGH04]   Canetti, R., Goldreich, O., Halevi, S.: The random oracle methodology, revisited. J. ACM 51(4), 557–594 (2004)

[CKPR02] Canetti, R., Kilian, J., Petrank, E., Rosen, A.: Black-box concurrent zero-knowledge requires (almost) logarithmically many rounds. SIAM J. Comput. 32(1), 1–47 (2002)

[DNRS99] Dwork, C., Naor, M., Reingold, O., Stockmeyer, L.J.: Magic functions. In: FOCS, pp. 523–534 (1999)

[DRV12] Dodis, Y., Ristenpart, T., Vadhan, S.: Randomness condensers for efficiently samplable, seed-dependent sources. In: Cramer, R. (ed.) TCC 2012. LNCS, vol. 7194, pp. 618–635. Springer, Heidelberg (2012). doi:10.1007/978-3-642-28914-9_35

[FS86] Fiat, A., Shamir, A.: How to prove yourself: practical solutions to identification and signature problems. In: Odlyzko, A.M. (ed.) CRYPTO 1986. LNCS, vol. 263, pp. 186–194. Springer, Heidelberg (1987). doi:10.1007/3-540-47721-7_12

[GGH+13] Garg, S., Gentry, C., Halevi, S., Raykova, M., Sahai, A., Waters, B.: Candidate indistinguishability obfuscation and functional encryption for all circuits. In: 54th Annual IEEE Symposium on Foundations of Computer Science, FOCS 2013, 26–29 October, 2013, Berkeley, CA, USA, pp. 40–49 (2013)

[GGM86] Goldreich, O., Goldwasser, S., Micali, S.: How to construct random functions. J. ACM 33(4), 792–807 (1986)

[GK96] Goldreich, O., Krawczyk, H.: On the composition of zero-knowledge proof systems. SIAM J. Comput. 25(1), 169–192 (1996)

[GK03] Goldwasser, S., Kalai, Y.T.: On the (in)security of the fiat-shamir paradigm. In: FOCS, pp. 102–113 (2003)

[GK05] Goldwasser, S., Kalai, Y.T.: On the impossibility of obfuscation with auxiliary input. In: FOCS, pp. 553–562 (2005)

[GK16] Goldwasser, S., Tauman Kalai, Y.: Cryptographic assumptions: a position paper. In: Kushilevitz, E., Malkin, T. (eds.) TCC 2016. LNCS, vol. 9562, pp. 505–522. Springer, Heidelberg (2016). doi:10.1007/978-3-662-49096-9_21

[GLSW14] Gentry, C., Lewko, A.B., Sahai, A., Waters, B.: Indistinguishability obfuscation from the multilinear subgroup elimination assumption. IACR Cryptology ePrint Archive 2014:309 (2014)

[GMR89] Goldwasser, S., Micali, S., Rackoff, C.: The knowledge complexity of interactive proof systems. SIAM J. Comput. 18(1), 186–208 (1989)

[GO94] Goldreich, O., Oren, Y.: Definitions and properties of zero-knowledge proof systems. J. Cryptol. 7(1), 1–32 (1994)

[GW11] Gentry, C., Wichs, D.: Separating succinct non-interactive arguments from all falsifiable assumptions. In: STOC, pp. 99–108 (2011)

[HILL99] Håstad, J., Impagliazzo, R., Levin, L.A., Luby, M.: A pseudorandom generator from any one-way function. SIAM J. Comput. 28(4), 1364–1396 (1999)

[HT98] Hada, S., Tanaka, T.: On the existence of 3-round zero-knowledge protocols. In: Krawczyk, H. (ed.) CRYPTO 1998. LNCS, vol. 1462, pp. 408–423. Springer, Heidelberg (1998). doi:10.1007/BFb0055744

[KPR98] Kilian, J., Petrank, E., Rackoff, C.: Lower bounds for zero knowledge on the internet. In: 39th Annual Symposium on Foundations of Computer Science, FOCS 1998, November 8–11, 1998, Palo Alto, California, USA, pp. 484–492 (1998)

[KPTZ13] Kiayias, A., Papadopoulos, S., Triandopoulos, N., Zacharias, T.: Delegatable pseudorandom functions and applications. In: ACM CCS, pp. 669–684 (2013)

[Mic94] Micali, S.: CS proofs. In: FOCS, pp. 436–453 (1994)

[MNPS04] Malkhi, D., Nisan, N., Pinkas, B., Sella, Y.: Fairplay - secure two-party computation system. In: USENIX Security Symposium, pp. 287–302 (2004)

[MV16] Mittelbach, A., Venturi, D.: Fiat–shamir for highly sound protocols is instantiable. In: Zikas, V., Prisco, R. (eds.) SCN 2016. LNCS, vol. 9841, pp. 198–215. Springer, Cham (2016). doi:10.1007/978-3-319-44618-9_11

[Nao03] Naor, M.: On cryptographic assumptions and challenges. In: Boneh, D. (ed.) CRYPTO 2003. LNCS, vol. 2729, pp. 96–109. Springer, Heidelberg (2003). doi:10.1007/978-3-540-45146-4_6

[OO98] Ohta, K., Okamoto, T.: On concrete security treatment of signatures derived from identification. In: Krawczyk, H. (ed.) CRYPTO 1998. LNCS, vol. 1462, pp. 354–369. Springer, Heidelberg (1998). doi:10.1007/BFb0055741

[PS96] Pointcheval, D., Stern, J.: Security proofs for signature schemes. In: Maurer, U. (ed.) EUROCRYPT 1996. LNCS, vol. 1070, pp. 387–398. Springer, Heidelberg (1996). doi:10.1007/3-540-68339-9_33

[Rey01] Reyzin, L.: Zero-Knowledge with Public Keys. Ph.D. thesis, MIT (2001)

[Ros00] Rosen, A.: A note on the round-complexity of concurrent zero-knowledge. In: Bellare, M. (ed.) CRYPTO 2000. LNCS, vol. 1880, pp. 451–468. Springer, Heidelberg (2000). doi:10.1007/3-540-44598-6_28

[RR97] Razborov, A.A., Rudich, S.: Natural proofs. J. Comput. Syst. Sci. **55**(1), 24–35 (1997)

[RRR16] Reingold, O., Rothblum, G.N., Rothblum, R.D.: Constant-round interactive proofs for delegating computation. In: Proceedings of the 48th Annual ACM SIGACT Symposium on Theory of Computing, STOC 2016, Cambridge, MA, USA, June 18–21, 2016, pp. 49–62 (2016)

[SW14] Sahai, A., Waters, B.: How to use indistinguishability obfuscation: deniable encryption, and more. In: STOC, pp. 475–484 (2014)

Indistinguishability Obfuscation for Turing Machines: Constant Overhead and Amortization

Prabhanjan Ananth[1(✉)], Abhishek Jain[2], and Amit Sahai[3]

[1] University of California Los Angeles, Los Angeles, USA
prabhanjan@cs.ucla.edu
[2] Johns Hopkins University, Baltimore, USA
abhishek@cs.jhu.edu
[3] University of California Los Angeles, Los Angeles, USA
sahai@cs.ucla.edu

Abstract. We study the asymptotic efficiency of indistinguishability obfuscation ($i\mathcal{O}$) on two fronts:

- **Obfuscation size:** Present constructions of indistinguishability obfuscation ($i\mathcal{O}$) create obfuscated programs where the size of the obfuscated program is at least a multiplicative factor of security parameter larger than the size of the original program.

  In this work, we construct the first $i\mathcal{O}$ scheme for (bounded-input) Turing machines that achieves only a *constant* multiplicative overhead in size. The constant in our scheme is, in fact, 2.

- **Amortization:** Suppose we want to obfuscate an arbitrary polynomial number of (bounded-input) Turing machines $M_1, \ldots, M_n$. We ask whether it is possible to obfuscate $M_1, \ldots, M_n$ using a *single* application of an $i\mathcal{O}$ scheme for a circuit family where the size of any circuit is *independent* of n as well the size of any Turing machine M_i.

  In this work, we resolve this question in the affirmative, obtaining a new bootstrapping theorem for obfuscating arbitrarily many Turing machines.

In order to obtain both of these results, we develop a new template for obfuscating Turing machines that is of independent interest and likely to find applications in future. The security of our results rely on the existence of sub-exponentially secure $i\mathcal{O}$ for circuits and re-randomizable encryption schemes.

P. Ananth—This work was partially supported by grant #360584 from the Simons Foundation and the grants listed under Amit Sahai.

A. Jain—Supported in part by DARPA/ARL Safeware Grant W911NF-15-C-0213.

A. Sahai—Research supported in part from a DARPA/ARL SAFEWARE award, NSF Frontier Award 1413955, NSF grants 1619348, 1228984, 1136174, and 1065276, BSF grant 2012378, a Xerox Faculty Research Award, a Google Faculty Research Award, an equipment grant from Intel, and an Okawa Foundation Research Grant. This material is based upon work supported by the Defense Advanced Research Projects Agency through the ARL under Contract W911NF-15-C-0205. The views expressed are those of the authors and do not reflect the official policy or position of the Department of Defense, the National Science Foundation, or the U.S. Government.

J. Katz and H. Shacham (Eds.): CRYPTO 2017, Part II, LNCS 10402, pp. 252–279, 2017.
DOI: 10.1007/978-3-319-63715-0_9

1 Introduction

The notion of indistinguishability obfuscation ($i\mathcal{O}$) [10] guarantees that given two equivalent programs M_0 and M_1, their obfuscations are computationally indistinguishable. The first candidate for general-purpose $i\mathcal{O}$ was given by Garg et al. [31]. Since their work, $i\mathcal{O}$ has been used to realize numerous advanced cryptographic tasks, such as functional encryption [31], deniable encryption [54], software watermarking [27] and PPAD hardness [13], that previously seemed beyond our reach.

Over the last few years, research on $i\mathcal{O}$ constructions has evolved in two directions. The first line of research concerns with developing $i\mathcal{O}$ candidates with stronger security guarantees and progressively weaker reliance on multilinear maps [30], with the goal of eventually building it from standard cryptographic assumptions. By now, a large sequence of works (see, e.g., [3–5,8,9,14,20,31, 33,38,48,50,52,56]) have investigated this line of research. The works of [33,50] constitute the state of the art in this direction, where [50] give a construction of $i\mathcal{O}$ for circuits from a concrete assumption on constant-degree multilinear maps, while [33] gives an $i\mathcal{O}$ candidate in a weak multilinear map model [51] that resists all known attacks on multilinear maps [17,26,28,29,35,51].

Another line of research concerns with building $i\mathcal{O}$ candidates with improved efficiency in a *generic* manner. The goal here is to develop bootstrapping theorems for $i\mathcal{O}$ that achieve greater efficiency when obfuscating different classes of programs. This started with the work of Garg et al. [31], which showed, roughly speaking, that $i\mathcal{O}$ for functions computed by branching programs implies $i\mathcal{O}$ for functions computed by general boolean circuits. While this first bootstrapping theorem achieved $i\mathcal{O}$ for all polynomial-time circuits, it still left open the question of obfuscating natural representations of the original program (for example, Turing machines).

Last year, this question was addressed in multiple works [12,23,47] showing that $i\mathcal{O}$ for circuits implies $i\mathcal{O}$ for Turing Machines with bounded-length inputs (see also [2,21,22,25] for extensions). Moving to the Turing Machine model yields significant efficiency improvements over the circuit model since the size of a Turing Machine may be much smaller than the corresponding circuit size. Importantly, it also achieves per-input running time, as opposed to incurring worst-case running time that is inherent to the circuit model of computation.

Our Work. In this work, we continue the study of bootstrapping mechanisms for $i\mathcal{O}$ to achieve further qualitative and quantitative gains in the asymptotic efficiency of obfuscation. We note that despite the recent advances, existing mechanisms for general-purpose $i\mathcal{O}$ remain highly inefficient and incur large polynomial overhead in the size of the program being obfuscated. We seek to improve the state of affairs on two fronts:

- *Size Efficiency:* First, we seek to develop obfuscation mechanisms where the size of an obfuscated program incurs only a small overhead in the size of the program being obfuscated.

- *Amortization:* Second, we seek to develop i$\mathcal{O}$ amortization techniques, where a single expensive call to an obfuscation oracle (that obfuscates programs of a priori fixed size) can be used to obfuscate arbitrarily many programs.

We expand on each of our goals below. Below, we restrict our discussion to Turing machine obfuscation, which is the main focus of this work.

I. Size Efficiency of i$\mathcal{O}$. All known mechanisms for i$\mathcal{O}$ yield obfuscated programs of size polynomial in the size of the underlying program and the security parameter, thus incurring a multiplicative overhead of at least the security parameter in the size of the underlying program.[1] The works of [1,18,45] achieve these parameters by relying on (public-coin) differing inputs obfuscation [10,45]. In contrast, [2,12,21–23,25,47] only rely upon i$\mathcal{O}$ for circuits; however, these works are restricted to programs with bounded-length inputs, and as such incur overhead of $\mathrm{poly}(\lambda, |M|, L)$, where L is the bound on the input length.

In this work, we ask the question:

> Is it possible to realize general-purpose i$\mathcal{O}$ with
> *constant multiplicative overhead* in program size?

More precisely, we ask whether it is possible to obfuscate bounded-input Turing Machines such that the resulting machine is of size $c \cdot |M| + \mathrm{poly}(\lambda, L)$, where c is a universal constant and L is the input length bound.

Achieving constant multiplicative overhead has been a major goal in many areas of computer science, from constructing asymptotically good error correcting codes, to encryption schemes where the size of the ciphertext is linear in the size of the plaintext. To the best of our knowledge, however, this question in the context of program obfuscation has appeared to be far out of reach in the context of basing security on i$\mathcal{O}$ itself.[2]

II. i$\mathcal{O}$ Amortization. We next consider the case of obfuscating *multiple* Turing machines. Since known circuit obfuscation mechanisms are inefficient not just in terms of obfuscation size but also the obfuscation time, we would like to minimize the use of circuit obfuscation for obfuscating multiple Turing machines. We ask the following question:

> Is it possible to obfuscate arbitrarily many Turing machines by using a *single* invocation to an i$\mathcal{O}$ obfuscator for circuits of *a priori fixed* polynomial size?

---

[1] For the case of circuits, the recent work of [14] gives an i$\mathcal{O}$ construction where the obfuscated circuit incurs only a constant overhead in the size of the underlying circuit but polynomial dependence on the depth of the circuit. While our focus is on Turing machine obfuscation, our results also yield improvements for circuit obfuscation. We refer the reader to Sect. 1.4 for a comparison of our results with [14].

[2] We observe that using (public-coin) differing input obfuscation, a variant of the construction given by [1,18,45] where FHE is combined with hybrid encryption, can yield constant multiplicative overhead. However, the plausibility of differing input obfuscation has come under scrutiny [11,32]. Thus, in this work, we focus only on achieving i$\mathcal{O}$ with constant multiplicative overhead from the existence of i$\mathcal{O}$ (without constant multiplicative overhead) itself.

More precisely, let O be an $i\mathcal{O}$ obfuscator for circuits of a fixed polynomial size. Then, we want the ability to obfuscate multiple Turing machines $M_1, \ldots, M_n$ for an unbounded polynomial n, by making a single invocation to O. As above, we study this question for Turing machines with an a priori fixed input length bound L, and allow O to depend on L.

Note that a successful resolution of this question will yield an *amortization* phenomenon where arbitrarily many Turing machines can be obfuscated using (relatively) less expensive cryptographic primitives and only a single expensive invocation to a circuit obfuscator.

Bounded-input vs Unbounded-input Turing machines. We note that if we could build $i\mathcal{O}$ for Turing machines with *unbounded* input length, then both of our aforementioned questions become moot. This is because one could simply obfuscate a universal Turing machine and pass on the actual machine that one wishes to obfuscate as an (encrypted) input. The state of the art in $i\mathcal{O}$ research, however, is still limited to Turing machines with *bounded* input length. In this case, the above approach does not work since the size of the obfuscation for bounded-input TMs grows polynomially in the input length bound.

In a recent work, [49] provide a transformation from output compressing randomized encodings for TMs to $i\mathcal{O}$ for unbounded-input TMs. However, no construction (with a security reduction) is presently known for such randomized encodings. In particular, in the same work, [49] show that such randomized encodings, in general, do not exist.

1.1 Our Results

I. $i\mathcal{O}$ with Constant Multiplicative Overhead. Our first result is a construction of $i\mathcal{O}$ for Turing machines with bounded input length where the size of obfuscation of a machine M is only $2|M| + \mathrm{poly}(\lambda, L)$, where L is the input length bound. Our construction is based on sub-exponentially secure $i\mathcal{O}$ for general circuits and one-way functions.

Theorem 1 (Informal). *Assuming sub-exponentially secure $i\mathcal{O}$ for general circuits and sub-exponentially secure re-randomizable encryption schemes, there exists an $i\mathcal{O}$ for Turing Machines with bounded input length such that the size of the obfuscation of a Turing machine M is $2 \cdot |M| + \mathrm{poly}(\lambda, L)$, where L is an input length bound.*

Re-randomizable encryption schemes can be based on standard assumptions such as DDH and learning with errors.

In order to obtain this result, we develop a new template for obfuscating Turing machines starting from indistinguishability obfuscation for circuits. An obfuscation of Turing machine M in our template comprises of:

- A reusable encoding of M.
- An obfuscated input encoder circuit, that takes as input x and produces an encoding of x. This encoding is then decoded, together with the (reusable) encoding of M, to recover $M(x)$.

Our template exhibits two salient properties: (a) the reusable encoding of M is constructed from standard cryptographic primitives, *without any use of* iO. (b) The size of the input encoder circuit is *independent* of M. In contrast, prior templates for iO for Turing machines comprised of a single obfuscated encoder circuit that contains M hardwired in its description, and therefore depends on the size of M.

We use the above template to reduce the problem of construction of iO for Turing machines with constant multiplicative overhead in size to the problem of constructing reusable TM encodings with constant multiplicative overhead in size. We defer discussion on the security properties associated with the reusable encoding scheme to the technical overview (Sect. 1.2). As we discuss next, our template enables some new applications.

II. A Bootstrapping Theorem for Obfuscating Multiple Programs. We now state our second result. Using our new template for Turing machine obfuscation, we show how to obfuscate $N = \text{poly}(\lambda)$ Turing machines $M_1, \ldots, M_N$, for any polynomial N, using just a single invocation to an obfuscated circuit where the circuit size is independent of N and the size of each M_i and only depends on the security parameter and an input length bound L for every TM M_i. At a high level, this can be achieved by combining the input encoder circuits corresponding to the N machines into a *single* circuit whose size is independent of N.

Theorem 2 (Informal). *Let* iO_{ckt} *be an indistinguishability obfuscation for circuits scheme for a class of circuits* $\mathcal{C}_{\lambda,L}$*. There exists an indistinguishability obfuscation scheme* iO_{tm} *for Turing machines with input length bound* L*, where any polynomial number of Turing machines can be simultaneously obfuscated by making a single call to* iO_{ckt}*.*

We emphasize that in order to obtain the above result, we crucially rely on the two aforementioned salient properties of our template. Indeed, it is unclear how to use the prior works [12,23,47] to obtain the above result.

We remark that the above bootstrapping theorem, combined with the fact that the reusable TM encodings in our template for TM obfuscation achieve constant overhead in size, implies the following useful corollary:

Corollary 1. *Assuming sub-exponentially secure* iO *for general circuits and sub-exponentially secure re-randomizable encryption schemes, there exists an* iO *scheme for Turing Machines with bounded input length such that the total size of the obfuscations of* N *Turing machines* $M_1, \ldots, M_N$ *is* $2\Sigma_i |M_i| + \text{poly}(\lambda, L)$*, where* L *is an input length bound.*[3]

We refer the reader to Sect. 1.3 for a brief discussion on how we obtain Theorem 2.

III. Subsequent work: Patchable iO. In a subsequent work [6], the same authors show how to use our template to construct patchable iO. This notion allows

---

[3] Note that, in contrast, a naive (direct) use of Theorem 1 would yield a result where the total size is $2\Sigma_i |M_i| + N \cdot \text{poly}(\lambda, L)$.

for updating obfuscation of a Turing machine M to an obfuscation of another machine M' with the help of patches that are privately-generated. Apart from being a natural extension to $i\mathcal{O}$, many applications of $i\mathcal{O}$ can be obtained from this primitive using extremely simple transformations. At a high level, the reason why our template finds use in their work is because they effectively reduce the problem of patchable $i\mathcal{O}$ to building a patchable reusable encoding scheme. However, their work has to deal with several conceptual issues that arise specifically in the context of patching. We refer the reader to [6] for more details.

IV. Other Applications. Our result on $i\mathcal{O}$ for TMs with constant overhead in size can be applied in many applications of $i\mathcal{O}$ to achieve commensurate efficiency gains. Below we highlight some of these applications.

Functional Encryption with Constant Overhead. Plugging in our $i\mathcal{O}$ in the functional encryption (FE) scheme of Waters [55],[4] we obtain an FE scheme for Turing machines where the size of a function key for a Turing machine M with input length bound L is only $c \cdot |M| + \mathrm{poly}(\lambda, L)$ for some constant c. Further, the size of a ciphertext for any message x is only $c' \cdot |x| + \mathrm{poly}(\lambda)$ for some constant c'.[5]

The size of the function keys can be further reduced by leveraging the recent result of [7] who construct adaptively secure FE for TMs with *unbounded* length inputs, based on $i\mathcal{O}$ and one-way functions. Instantiating their FE construction with our $i\mathcal{O}$ and the above discussed FE scheme, we obtain the *first* construction of an (adaptively secure) FE scheme where the size of a function key for an unbounded length input TM M is only $c \cdot |M| + \mathrm{poly}(\lambda)$ for some constant c.

Reusable Garbled Turing Machines with Constant Overhead. By applying the transformations of De Caro et al. [24] and Goldwasser et al. [39] on the above FE scheme, we obtain the *first* construction of Reusable Garbled TM scheme where both the machine encodings and input encodings incur only constant multiplicative overhead in the size of the machine and input, respectively. Specifically, the encoding size of a machine M is $c \cdot |M| + \mathrm{poly}(\lambda)$, while the encoding size of an input x is $c_1 \cdot |x| + c_2 |M(x)| + \mathrm{poly}(\lambda)$ for some constants c, c_1, c_2.

Previously, Boneh et al. [15] constructed reusable garbled *circuits* with additive overhead in either the circuit encoding size, or the input encoding size (but not both simultaneously).

1.2   Technical Overview: New Template for Succinct $i\mathcal{O}$

We now provide an overview of the main ideas underlying our results. We start by motivating and explaining our new template for succinct $i\mathcal{O}$ and then explain how we build succinct $i\mathcal{O}$ with constant overhead in size. Next, in Sect. 1.3, we explain how we obtain our bootstrapping theorem for obfuscating arbitrarily many Turing machine.

---

[4] [55] presents two FE schemes: the first one only handles post-challenge key queries, while the second one allows for both pre-challenge and post-challenge key queries. We only consider the instantiation of the first scheme with our $i\mathcal{O}$.

[5] The construction of [55] already achieves the second property.

We start by recalling the common template for constructing $i\mathcal{O}$ for Turing machines (TM) used in all the prior works in the literature [12,22,23,25,47]. Similar to these works, we focus on the restricted setting of TMs with inputs of a priori bounded length. For simplicity of discussion, however, we will ignore this restriction in this section.

Prior template for succinct $i\mathcal{O}$. [12,23,47] reduce the problem of obfuscating Turing machines to the problem of obfuscating circuits. This is achieved in the following two steps:

1. *Randomized encoding for TMs.* The first step is to construct a randomized encoding (RE) [43] for Turing machines using $i\mathcal{O}$ for circuits.
2. *From RE to $i\mathcal{O}$.* The second step consists of obfuscating the encoding procedure of RE (constructed in the first step). Very roughly, to obfuscate a machine M, we simply obfuscate a circuit $C_{M,K}$ that has the machine M and a PRF key K hardwired. On any input x, circuit C_M outputs a "fresh" RE of $M(x)$ using randomness $\mathsf{PRF}_K(x)$. To recover $M(x)$, the evaluator simply executes the decoding algorithm of RE.

Following [12,23,47], all of the subsequent works on succinct $i\mathcal{O}$ [22,25] follow the above template.[6]

Shortcomings of the prior template. However, as we discuss now, this template is highly problematic for achieving our goal of $i\mathcal{O}$ with constant multiplicative overhead in size.

- First, note that since the obfuscation of machine M corresponds to obfuscating a circuit that has machine M hardwired, in order to achieve constant overhead in the size of M, we would require the underlying circuit obfuscator to already satisfy the constant overhead property!
- Furthermore, since the description of circuit C_M includes the encoding procedure of the RE, we would require the RE scheme constructed in the first step to not only achieve constant overhead in size, but also in *encoding time*. In particular, we would require that the *running time* of the RE encode procedure on input (M, x) has only a constant multiplicative overhead in $|M| + |x|$. We stress that this is a much more serious issue. Indeed, ensuring that the running time has only a constant multiplicative overhead in the input size is in general a hard problem for many cryptographic primitives (see [44] for discussion).

Towards that end, we devise a new template for constructing $i\mathcal{O}$ for TMs which is more amenable to our goal of $i\mathcal{O}$ with constant overhead in size.

A new template for succinct $i\mathcal{O}$: Starting ideas. Our first idea is to modify the above template in such a manner that the obfuscated circuit does not contain machine M anymore. Instead, the machine M is encoded separately.

---

[6] We note that the above template also works for obfuscating RAM programs if we start with an RE for RAM in the first step.

Specifically, in our modified template, obfuscation of a machine M consists of two components:

- An encoding $\widetilde{M}$ of the machine M using an encoding key sk.
- Obfuscation of the "input encoder", i.e., a circuit $C'_{sk,K}$ that has hardwired in its description the encoding key sk and a PRF key K. On any input x, $C'_{sk,K}$ computes an input encoding $\tilde{x}$ using sk and randomness $\mathsf{PRF}_K(x)$.

To evaluate the obfuscation of M on an input x, the evaluator first executes the obfuscated circuit to obtain an encoding $\tilde{x}$. It then decodes $(\widetilde{M}, \tilde{x})$ to obtain $M(x)$.

A few remarks are in order: first, note that the above template requires a *decomposable* RE where a machine M and an input x can be encoded separately using an encoding key sk. Second, the RE scheme must be *reusable*, i.e., given an encoding $\widetilde{M}$ of M and multiple input encodings $\tilde{x}_1, \ldots, \tilde{x}_n$ (computed using the same encoding key sk) for any n, it should be possible to decode $(\widetilde{M}, \tilde{x}_i)$ to obtain $M(x_i)$ for every $i \in [n]$.

It is easy to verify the correctness of the above construction. Now, let us see why this template is more suitable for our goal. Observe that if the (reusable) encoding of M has constant overhead in size, then the obfuscation scheme also achieves the same property. Crucially, we do not need the RE scheme to achieve constant overhead in encoding time.

At this point, it seems that we have reduced the problem of $i\mathcal{O}$ for TMs with constant size overhead to the problem of reusable RE with constant size overhead. This intuition, unfortunately, turns out to be misleading. The main challenge arises in proving security of the above template. Very briefly, we note that following [37,38,52], prior works on succinct $i\mathcal{O}$ use a common "input-by-input" proof strategy to argue the security of their construction. Recall that the obfuscation of a TM M in these works corresponds to obfuscation of the circuit $C_{M,K}$ described earlier. Then, in order to implement the "input-by-input" proof strategy, it is necessary that the PRF key K supports *puncturing* [16,19, 46,54]. Note, however, that in our new template, obfuscation of M consists of a reusable encoding of M and obfuscation of circuit $C'_{sk,K}$ described above. Then, implementing a similar proof strategy for our template would require the encoding key sk of the reusable RE (that is embedded in the circuit $C'_{sk,K}$) to also support puncturing. However, the standard notion of reusable RE [39] does not support key puncturing, and therefore, does not suffice for arguing security of the above construction.

Oblivious Evaluation Encodings. Towards that end, our next idea is to develop an "iO-friendly" notion of reusable RE that we refer to as *oblivious evaluation encodings* (OEE). Our definition of OEE is specifically tailored to facilitate a security proof of the construction discussed above.

In an OEE scheme, instead of encoding a single machine, we allow encoding of two machines M_0 and M_1 together using an encoding key sk. Further, an input

x is encoded together with a "choice" bit b using sk. The decode algorithm, on input encodings of (x, b) and (M_0, M_1), outputs $M_b(x)$.[7]

An OEE scheme also comes equipped with two *key puncturing* algorithms:

- *Input puncturing*: On input an encoding key sk and input x, it outputs a punctured encoding key sk_x^{inp}. This punctured key allows for computation of encodings of $(x', 0)$ and $(x', 1)$ for all inputs $x' \neq x$. The security property associated with it is as follows: for any input x, given a machine encoding of (M_0, M_1) s.t. $M_0(x) = M_1(x)$ and a punctured key sk_x^{inp}, no PPT adversary should be able to distinguish between encodings of $(x, 0)$ and $(x, 1)$.
- *(Choice) Bit puncturing*: On input an encoding key sk and bit b, it outputs a punctured encoding key sk_b^{bit}. This punctured key allows for computation of encodings of (x, b) for all x. The security property associated with it is as follows: for any machine pair (M_0, M_1), given a punctured key sk_0^{bit}, no PPT adversary should be able to distinguish encoding of (M_0, M_0) from (M_0, M_1). (The security for punctured key sk_1^{bit} can be defined analogously.)

Finally, we say that an OEE scheme achieves constant multiplicative overhead in size if the size of machine encoding of any pair (M_0, M_1) is $|M_0| + |M_1| +$ poly(λ). Further, similar to reusable RE, we require that the size of the input encoding of x is poly$(\lambda, |x|)$ and in particular, independent of the size of $|M_0|$ and $|M_1|$.

$i\mathcal{O}$ **for TMs from OEE.** We now describe our modified template for constructing $i\mathcal{O}$ for TMs where reusable RE is replaced with OEE. An obfuscation of a machine M consists of two components: (a) An OEE TM encoding of (M, M) generated using an OEE secret key sk. (b) Obfuscation of the OEE input encoder, i.e., a circuit $C_{sk,K}$ that on input x outputs an OEE input encoding of $(x, 0)$ using the OEE key sk and randomness generated using the PRF key K. To evaluate the obfuscated machine on an input x, an evaluator first computes encoding of $(x, 0)$ using the obfuscated $C_{sk,K}$ and then decodes $(x, 0)$ and (M, M), using the OEE decode algorithm, to obtain $M(x)$.

To prove security, we need to argue that obfuscations of two equivalent machines M_0 and M_1 are computationally indistinguishable. For the above construction, this effectively boils down to transitioning from a hybrid where we give out a machine encoding of (M_0, M_0) to one where we give out a machine encoding of (M_1, M_1). We achieve this by crucially relying on the security of the key puncturing algorithms. Very roughly, we first use the punctured key sk_0^{bit} to transition from (M_0, M_0) to (M_0, M_1) and then later, we use sk_1^{bit} to transition from (M_0, M_1) to (M_1, M_1). In between these steps, we rely on punctured keys sk_x^{inp}, for every input x (one at a time), to transition from a hybrid where the (obfuscated) input encoder produces encodings corresponding to bit $b = 0$ to one where $b = 1$.

Now, note that if we instantiate the above construction with an OEE scheme that achieves constant overhead in size, then the resulting obfuscation scheme

---

[7] An informed reader might find some similarities between OEE and oblivious transfer. Indeed, the name for our primitive is inspired by oblivious transfer.

also satisfies the same property *even* if the obfuscation of circuit $C_{sk,K}$ has polynomial overhead in size. Here, note that it is crucial that we require that the size of the OEE input encodings to be independent of $|M_0|$ and $|M_1|$. Thus, in order to achieve our goal of $i\mathcal{O}$ for TMs with constant size overhead, the remaining puzzle piece is a construction of OEE with constant overhead in size. Our main technical contribution is to provide such a construction.

Construction of OEE: Initial Challenges. A natural approach towards constructing OEE is to start with known constructions of reusable RE for TMs. We note that the only known approach in the literature for constructing reusable RE for TMs is due to [36]. In their approach, for every input, a "fresh" instance of a single-use RE for TMs [7,12,22,23,25,47] is computed on the fly. However, as discussed at the beginning of this section, in order to achieve constant overhead in size, such an approach would require that the single-use RE achieves constant overhead in *encoding time*, which is a significantly harder problem. Therefore, this approach is ill suited to our goal.

In light of the above, we start from the (single-use) RE construction of Koppula et al. [47] and use the ingredients developed in their work to build all the properties necessary for an OEE scheme with constant overhead in size. Indeed, the work of KLW forms the basis of all known subsequent constructions of randomized encodings for TMs/ RAMs [2,21,22,25] that do not suffer from space bound restrictions (unlike [12,23]); therefore, it is a natural starting point for our goal.

We start by recalling the RE construction of KLW. We only provide a simplified description, omitting several technical details. An RE encoding of (M, x) has two components:

- Authenticated Hash Tree: the first component consists of a verifiable hash tree[8] computed on an encryption of the input tape initialized with TM M. The root of the hash tree is authenticated using a special signature.
- Obfuscated Next Step Function: The second component is an obfuscated circuit of the next step function of $U_x(\cdot)$, where U_x is a universal TM that takes as input a machine M and produces $M(x)$. The hash key, signing and verification keys and decryption key are hardwired inside this obfuscated circuit. It takes as input an encrypted state, an encrypted symbol on the tape along with a proof of validity that consists of authentication path in the hash tree and the signature on the root. Upon receiving such an input, it first checks input validity using the hash key and the signature verification key. It then decrypts the state and the symbol using the decryption key. Next, it executes the next step of the transition function. It then re-encrypts the new state and the new symbol. Using the old authentication path, it recomputes the new authentication path and a fresh signature on the root. Finally, it outputs the new signed root.

---

[8] [47] uses a special hash tree called positional accumulator. For this high-level overview, one can think of it as a "iO-friendly" Merkle hash tree. We refer the reader to the technical sections for further details.

A reader familiar with [47] will notice that in the above discussion, we have flipped the roles of the machine and the input. First, it is easy to see that these two presentations are equivalent. More importantly, this specific presentation is crucial to our construction of OEE because by flipping the roles of the machine and the input, we are able to leverage the inherent asymmetry in the machine encoding and input encoding in KLW. This point will become more clear later in this section.

The security proof of KLW, at a high level, works by authenticating one step of the computation at a time. In particular, this idea is implemented using a recurring hybrid where for any execution step i of $U_x(M)$, the obfuscated circuit *only accepts a unique input and all other inputs are rejected*. This unique input is a function of the parameters associated with the hashing scheme, signature scheme and the encryption scheme. We call such hybrids *unique-input accepting hybrids*. Such hybrids have, in fact, been used in other $i\mathcal{O}$-based constructions as well.[9]

Using the above template, we discuss initial ideas towards constructing an OEE scheme. In the beginning, we restrict our attention to achieving reusability with constant overhead. Later, we will discuss how to achieve the key puncturing properties later.

Challenge #1: Reusability. A natural first idea to achieve reusability is to have the first component in the above construction to be the machine encoding and the second component to be the input encoding. To argue security, lets consider a simple case when the adversary is given a machine encoding of M and two input encodings of x_1 and x_2. A natural first approach is to argue the security of M on x_1 first and then argue the security of M on x_2. The hope here is that we can reuse the (single-use) security proof of KLW separately for x_1 and x_2. This, however, doesn't work because the unique-accepting hybrids corresponding to input x_1 would be incompatible with the computation of M on x_2 (and vice versa). An alternate idea would be to employ *multi-input accepting hybrids* instead of unique-input accepting hybrids, where the obfuscated next step function, for a given i, accepts a fixed set of multiple inputs and rejects all other inputs. However, this would mean that we can only hardwire an a priori fixed number of values in the obfuscated circuit which would then put a bound on the number of input encodings that can be issued. Hence this direction is also not feasible.

In order to resolve the above difficulty, we modify the above template. For any input x, to generate an input encoding, we generate fresh parameters of the hashing, signature and the encryption schemes. We then generate the obfuscated circuit of the next step function of $U_x(\cdot)$ with all the parameters (including the freshly generated ones) hardwired inside it. The machine encoding of M, however, is computed with respect to parameters that are decided at the OEE setup

---

[9] For example, Hubacek and Wichs [42] consider a scenario where the obfuscated circuit accepts pre-images of the hash function as input. In order to use $i\mathcal{O}$ security, they use a special hash function (SSB hash) that is programmed to accept only one input on a special index.

time. At this point it is not clear why correctness should hold: the parameters associated with encodings of x and M are independently generated.

To address this, we introduce a *translation* mechanism that translates machine encoding of M with respect to one set of parameters into another machine encoding of M w.r.t to a different set of parameters. In more detail, every input encoding will be equipped with a freshly generated translator. A translator, associated with an encoding of x, takes as input a machine encoding of M, computed using the parameters part of OEE setup, checks for validity and outputs a new encoding of M corresponding to the fresh parameters associated with the encoding of x. For now, the translator can be thought of as an obfuscated circuit that has hardwired inside it the old and the new parameters. Later we discuss its actual implementation.

Finally, a word about security. Roughly speaking, due to the use of fresh parameters for every input, we are able to reduce security to the one-input security of KLW.

Challenge #2: Constant Overhead. While the above high level approach tackles reusability, it does not yet suffice for achieving constant multiplicative overhead in the size of the machine encodings. Recall that the machine encoding consists of an encryption of the machine along with the hash tree and a signature on the root. We first observe that the hashing algorithm is public and hence, it is not necessary to include the hash tree as part of the input encoding; instead the input encoding can just consist of an encryption of the machine, root of the hash tree and a signature on it. The decoder can reconstruct the hash tree and proceed as before. We can then use an encryption scheme with constant overhead in size to ensure that the encryption of M only incurs constant overhead in size. Note, however, that such an encryption scheme should also be compatible with hash tree computation over it.

While one might envision constructing such a scheme, a bigger issue is the size of the translator. In fact, the size of the translator, as described above, is polynomial in the input length, which corresponds to the size of the machine encoding. It therefore invalidates the efficiency requirement of OEE on the size of input encodings.

One plausible approach to overcome this problem might be to not refresh the encryption of M and in fact just translate the signature associated with the root of the hash tree into a different signature. This would mean that the decryption key associated with the encryption of M would be common among all the input encodings. However, in the security proof, this conflicts with the unique-input accepting hybrids as discussed earlier.

Construction of OEE: Our Approach. The main reason why the above solution does not work is because the machine M is in an encrypted form. Suppose we instead focus on the weaker goal of achieving *authenticity* without privacy. That is, we guarantee the correctness of computation against dishonest evaluators but not hide the machine. Our crucial observation is that the above high level template sans encryption of the machine is already a candidate solution for achieving this weaker security goal. An astute reader would observe that this setting resembles attribute based encryption [41,53] (ABE). Indeed in order to build OEE, our first step is to build an ABE scheme for TMs where the key size incurs a constant multiplicative overhead in the original machine length. We achieve this goal by using the ideas developed above. We then provide a *generic* reduction to transform such an ABE scheme into an OEE scheme satisfying constant multiplicative overhead in size. We now explain our steps in more detail.

ABE for TMs. Recall that in an ABE scheme, an encryption of an attribute, message pair (x, m) can be decrypted using a secret key corresponding to a machine M to recover m only if $M(x) = 1$. An ABE scheme is said to have a constant multiplicative overhead in size if the size of key of M is $c|M| + \text{poly}(\lambda)$ for a constant c. Here, note that neither x nor M are required to be hidden.

The starting point of our construction of ABE is the *message hiding encoding* (MHE) scheme of KLW. An MHE scheme is effectively a "privacy-free" RE scheme, and therefore, perfectly suited for our goal of constructing an ABE scheme. More concretely, an MHE encoding of a tuple (M, x, msg), where M is a TM and x is an input to M, allows one to recover msg iff $M(x) = 1$. On the efficiency side, computing the encoding of (M, x, msg) should take time independent of the time to compute M on x. The important point to note here is that only msg needs to be hidden from the adversary and in particular, it is not necessary to hide the computation of M on x.

The construction of MHE follows along the same lines as the RE construction of KLW with the crucial difference that the machine M (unlike the RE construction) is not encrypted. Following the above discussion, this has the right template from which we can build our ABE scheme. Using KLW's template and incorporating the ideas we developed earlier, we sketch the construction of ABE below. This is an oversimplified version and several intricate technical details are omitted.

- Generate secret key sk, verification key vk of a special signature scheme (termed as splittable signature scheme in [47]). Generate a hash key hk of a verifiable hash tree. The public key consists of (vk, hk) and the secret key is sk.
- ABE key of a machine M is computed by first computing a hash tree on M using hk. The root of the hash tree rt is then signed using sk to obtain σ. Output (M, σ). Note that $|\sigma| = \text{poly}(\lambda)$ and thus, the constant multiplicative overhead property is satisfied.
- ABE encryption of (x, msg) is computed by first computing an obfuscated circuit of the next step function of $U_{x,\text{msg}}(\cdot)$. We have $U_{x,\text{msg}}$ to be a circuit that takes as input circuit C and outputs msg if $C(x) = 1$. The parameters hardwired in this obfuscated circuit contains (among other parameters) (sk', vk') of a splittable signature scheme where (sk', vk') is sampled afresh. In addition, it consists of a *signature translator* SignProg, that we introduced earlier. This signature translator takes as input a pair (rt, σ). Upon receiving such an input, it first verifies the validity of the signature w.r.t vk and then outputs a signature on rt w.r.t sk' if the verification succeeds. Otherwise it outputs $\perp$.

The final output of the encryption algorithm is the obfuscated circuit along with the signature translator.

To argue security, we need to rely on the underlying security of message hiding encodings. Unlike several recent constructions that use KLW, thanks to the modularization of our approach, we are able to reduce the security of our construction to the security of MHE construction of KLW. We view this as a positive step towards reducing the "page complexity" of research works in this area.

Construction of OEE from ABE for TMs. One of the main differences between OEE and ABE is that OEE guarantees privacy of computation while ABE only offers authenticity. Therefore, we need to employ a privacy mechanism in order to transform ABE into an OEE scheme. A similar scenario was encountered by Goldwasser et al. [39] in a different context. Their main goal was to obtain single-key FE for circuits from ABE for circuits while we are interested in constructing OEE, which has seemingly stronger requirements than FE, from ABE for Turing machines. Nevertheless, we show how their techniques will be useful to develop a basic template of our construction of OEE.

As a starting point, we encode the pair of machines (M_0, M_1) by first encrypting them together. Since we perform computation on the machines, the encryption scheme we use is fully homomorphic [34]. In the input encoding of (x, b), we encrypt the choice bit b using the same public key. To evaluate (M_0, M_1) on (x, b), we execute the homomorphic evaluation function. Notice, however, that the output is in encrypted form. We need to provide additional capability to the evaluator to decrypt the output (and nothing else). One way around is that the input encoding algorithm publishes a garbling of the FHE decryption algorithm. But the input encoder must somehow convey the garbled circuit wire keys, corresponding to the output of the FHE evaluation, to the evaluator.

This is where ABE for TMs comes to the rescue. Using ABE, we can ensure that the evaluator gets *only* the wire keys corresponding to the output of the FHE evaluation. Once this is achieved, the garbled circuit that is provided as part of the input encoding can then be evaluated to obtain the decrypted output. We can then show that the resulting OEE scheme has constant multiplicative overhead if the underlying ABE scheme also satisfies this property.

While the above high level idea is promising, there are still some serious issues. The first issue is that we need to homomorphically evaluate on Turing machines as against circuits. This can be resolved by using the powers-of-two evaluation technique from the work of [40]. The second and the more important question is: what are the punctured keys? The input puncturing key could simply be the ABE public key and the FHE public key-secret key pair. The choice bit puncturing key, however, is more tricky. Note that setting the FHE secret key to be the punctured key will ensure correctness but completely destroy the security. To resolve this issue, we use the classic two-key technique: we encrypt machines M_0 and M_1 using two different FHE public keys. The choice bit puncturing key is set to be one of the FHE secret keys depending on which bit needs to be punctured.

1.3   Technical Overview: Boostrapping Theorem

We now explain how our template for Turing machine obfuscation can be used to obtain Theorem 2. Suppose that we wish to obfuscate N Turing machines $M_1, \ldots, M_N$ for $N = \text{poly}(\lambda)$.

Using our template discussed above, a starting idea towards obtaining Theorem 2 is as follows. Let K_1 and K_2 be keys for two puncturable PRF families. The obfuscation of $M_1, \ldots, M_N$ consists of the following parts:

- N different OEE TM encodings $(\widetilde{M_1, M_1}), \ldots, (\widetilde{M_N, M_N})$ where each $(\widetilde{M_i, M_i})$ is computed using an encoding key sk_i that is generated using randomness $PRF_{K_1}(i)$.
- Obfuscation of a "joint" input encoder circuit C_{K_1, K_2} that contains K_1 and K_2 hardwired in its description. It takes as input a pair (x, i) and performs the following steps: (a) Compute an OEE encoding key sk_i "on-the-fly" by running the OEE setup algorithm using randomness $\mathsf{PRF}_{K_1}(i)$. (b) Compute and output an OEE input encoding $\widetilde{(x, 0)}_i$ for the ith machine using the key sk_i and fresh randomness $\mathsf{PRF}_{K_2}(i, x)$.

Then security of the above construction can be argued using a straightforward hybrid argument using the puncturing properties of the PRF.

The above idea, however, does not immediately yield Theorem 2. The problem is that the OEE input encoding $\widetilde{(x, 0)}_i$ itself contains obfuscated programs. Therefore, the circuit C_{K_1, K_2} (described above) itself needs to make queries to a circuit obfuscation scheme.

We resolve the above problem in the following manner. Recall from above that an OEE input encoding in our scheme consists of two components: a garbled circuit and an ABE ciphertext. An ABE ciphertext, in turn, consists of obfuscations of two circuits. Lets refer to these circuits as C_1^{sub} and C_2^{sub}. Then, our idea is to simply "absorb" the functionality of C_1^{sub} and C_2^{sub} within C_{K_1, K_2}. In more detail, we consider a modified input encoder circuit C'_{K_1, K_2} that works in three modes: (a) In mode 1, it takes as input (x, i) and simply outputs the garbled circuit component of the input encoding $\widetilde{(x, 0)}_i$. (b) In mode 2, it takes an input for circuit C_1^{sub} and produces its output. (c) In mode 3, it takes an input for circuit C_2^{sub} and produces its output.

With the above modification, obfuscation of $M_1, \ldots, M_N$ now consists of N different OEE TM encodings $(\widetilde{M_1, M_1}), \ldots, (\widetilde{M_N, M_N})$ and obfuscation of the modified input encoder circuit C'_{K_1, K_2}. Crucially, this process only involves a *single* invocation of the circuit obfuscation scheme for the circuit family $\{C'_{K_1, K_2}\}$, where the size of C'_{K_1, K_2} is independent of N as well as the size of any M_i. This gives us Theorem 2.

1.4   Related Work

In a recent work, [14] give a construction of $i\mathcal{O}$ for circuits where the size of obfuscation of a circuit C with depth d and inputs of length L is $2 \cdot C + \text{poly}(\lambda, d, L)$.

Their construction relies on (sub-exponentially secure) $i\mathcal{O}$ for circuits with polynomial overhead and the learning with errors assumption.

While we focus on the Turing machine model in this work, we note that our construction can be easily downgraded to the case of circuits to obtain an $i\mathcal{O}$ scheme where the size of obfuscation of a circuit C with inputs of length L is $2 \cdot C + \mathrm{poly}(\lambda, L)$. In particular, it does not grow with the circuit depth beyond the dependence on the circuit size. Our construction requires (sub-exponentially secure) $i\mathcal{O}$ for circuits with poly overhead and re-randomizable encryption schemes.

2   Attribute-Based Encryption for TMs with Additive Overhead

In an attribute-based encryption (ABE) scheme, a message m can be encrypted together with an attribute x such that an evaluator holding a decryption key corresponding to a predicate P can recover m if and only if $P(x) = 1$. Unlike most prior works on ABE that model predicates as circuits, in this work, following [40], we model predicates as Turing machines with inputs of arbitrary length. We only consider the setting where the adversary can receive only one decryption key. We refer to this as 1-key ABE.

Below, we start by providing definition of 1-key ABE for TMs. In Sect. 2.2, we present our construction. The proof of security of this construction can be found in the full version. Finally, in Sect. 2.3, we extend our 1-key ABE construction to build two-outcome ABE for TMs.

2.1   Definition

A 1-key ABE for Turing machines scheme, defined for a class of Turing machines $\mathcal{M}$, consists of four PPT algorithms, 1ABE = (1ABE.Setup, 1ABE.KeyGen, 1ABE.Enc, 1ABE.Dec). We denote the associated message space to be MSG. The syntax of the algorithms is given below.

- **Setup, 1ABE.Setup(1^λ):** On input a security parameter λ in unary, it outputs a public key-secret key pair (1ABE.PP, 1ABE.SK).
- **Key Generation, 1ABE.KeyGen(1ABE.SK, M):** On input a secret key 1ABE.SK and a TM $M \in \mathcal{M}$, it outputs an ABE key 1ABE.sk_M.
- **Encryption, 1ABE.Enc(1ABE.PP, x, msg):** On input the public parameters 1ABE.PP, attribute $x \in \{0,1\}^*$ and message msg $\in$ MSG, it outputs the ciphertext 1ABE.CT$_{(x,\mathsf{msg})}$.
- **Decryption, 1ABE.Dec(1ABE.sk_M, 1ABE.CT$_{(x,\mathsf{msg})}$):** On input the ABE key 1ABE.sk_M and encryption 1ABE.CT$_{(x,\mathsf{msg})}$, it outputs the decrypted result out.

Correctness. The correctness property dictates that the decryption of a ciphertext of (x, msg) using an ABE key for M yields the message msg if $M(x) = 1$. In formal terms, the output of the decryption procedure 1ABE.Dec(1ABE.sk_M, 1ABE.CT$_{(x,\mathsf{msg})}$) is (always) msg if $M(x) = 1$, where

- $(1\mathsf{ABE.SK}, 1\mathsf{ABE.PP}) \leftarrow 1\mathsf{ABE.Setup}(1^\lambda)$,
- $1\mathsf{ABE}.sk_M \leftarrow 1\mathsf{ABE.KeyGen}(1\mathsf{ABE.SK}, M \in \mathcal{M})$ and,
- $1\mathsf{ABE.CT}_{(x,\mathsf{msg})} \leftarrow 1\mathsf{ABE.Enc}(1\mathsf{ABE.PP}, x, \mathsf{msg})$.

Security. The security framework we consider is identical to the indistinguishability based security notion of ABE for circuits except that (i) the key queries correspond to Turing machines instead of circuits and (ii) the adversary is only allowed to make a single key query. Furthermore, we only consider the setting when the adversary submits both the challenge message pair as well as the key query at the beginning of the game itself. We term this *weak selective security.* We formally define this below.

The security is defined in terms of the following security experiment between a challenger and a PPT adversary. We denote the challenger by Ch and the adversary by $\mathcal{A}$.

$\underline{\mathsf{Expt}_{\mathcal{A}}^{1\mathsf{ABE}}(1^\lambda, b)}$:

1. $\mathcal{A}$ sends to Ch a tuple consisting of a Turing machine M, an attribute x and two messages $(\mathsf{msg}_0, \mathsf{msg}_1)$. If $M(x) = 1$ then the experiment is aborted.
2. The challenger Ch replies to $\mathcal{A}$ with the public key, decryption key of M, the challenge ciphertext; $\big(1\mathsf{ABE.PP}, 1\mathsf{ABE}.sk_M, 1\mathsf{ABE.CT}_{(x,\mathsf{msg}_b)}\big)$, where the values are computed as follows:
   - $(1\mathsf{ABE.PP}, 1\mathsf{ABE.SK}) \leftarrow 1\mathsf{ABE.Setup}(1^\lambda)$,
   - $1\mathsf{ABE}.sk_M \leftarrow 1\mathsf{ABE.KeyGen}(1\mathsf{ABE.SK}, M)$
   - $1\mathsf{ABE.CT}_{(x,\mathsf{msg}_b)} \leftarrow 1\mathsf{ABE.Enc}(1\mathsf{ABE.PP}, x, \mathsf{msg}_b)$.
3. The experiment terminates when the adversary outputs the bit b'.

We say that a 1-key ABE for TMs scheme is weak-selectively secure if any PPT adversary can guess the challenge bit only with negligible probability.

Definition 1. *A 1-key attribute based encryption for TMs scheme is said to be* **weak-selectively secure** *if there exists a negligible function* $\mathsf{negl}(\lambda)$ *such that for every PPT adversary* $\mathcal{A}$,

$$\Big| \Pr[0 \leftarrow \mathsf{Expt}_{\mathcal{A}}^{1\mathsf{ABE}}(1^\lambda, 0)] - \Pr[0 \leftarrow \mathsf{Expt}_{\mathcal{A}}^{1\mathsf{ABE}}(1^\lambda, 1)] \Big| \leq \mathsf{negl}(\lambda)$$

Remark 1. Henceforth, we will omit the term "weak-selective" when referring to the security of ABE schemes.

1-Key Attribute Based Encryption for TMs with Additive Overhead. We say that a 1-key attribute based encryption for TMs scheme achieves additive overhead property if the size of an ABE key for a TM M is only $|M| + \mathrm{poly}(\lambda)$. More formally,

Definition 2. *A 1-key attribute based encryption for TMs scheme,* $1\mathsf{ABE}$, *defined for a class of Turing machines* $\mathcal{M}$, *satisfies additive overhead property if* $|1\mathsf{ABE}.sk_M| = |M| + \mathrm{poly}(\lambda)$, *where* $(1\mathsf{ABE.SK}, 1\mathsf{ABE.PP}) \leftarrow 1\mathsf{ABE.Setup}(1^\lambda)$ *and* $1\mathsf{ABE}.sk_M \leftarrow 1\mathsf{ABE.KeyGen}(1\mathsf{ABE.SK}, M \in \mathcal{M})$.

2.2 Construction of 1-Key ABE

We now present our construction of 1-key ABE for TMs. We begin with a brief overview.

Overview. Our construction uses three main primitives imported from [47] – namely, positional accumulators, splittable signatures and iterators.

The setup first generates the setup of the splittable signatures scheme to yield $(\mathsf{SK_{tm}}, \mathsf{VK_{tm}}, \mathsf{VK_{rej}})$. The rejection-verification key $\mathsf{VK_{rej}}$ will be discarded. $(\mathsf{SK_{tm}}, \mathsf{VK_{tm}})$ will be the master signing key-verification key pair. The setup also generates accumulator and iterator parameters.

The signing key $\mathsf{SK_{tm}}$ will be the ABE secret key and the rest of the parameters form the public key. To generate an ABE key of M, first compute the accumulator storage of M. Then sign the accumulator value of M using $\mathsf{SK_{tm}}$ to obtain σ. Output the values M, σ and accumulator value[10].

An ABE encryption of (x, msg) is an obfuscation of the next step function that computes $U_x(\cdot)$ (universal circuit with x hardcoded in it) one step at a time. Call this obfuscated circuit N. Embedded into this obfuscated circuit are accumulator and iterator parameters, part of the public parameters. In addition, it has a PRF key K_A used to generate fresh splittable signature instantiations. In order for this to be compatible with the master signing key, a signature translator is provided as part of the ciphertext. This translator circuit, which will be obfuscated, takes as input message, a signature verifiable using $\mathsf{VK_{tm}}$ and produces a new signature with respect to parameters generated using K_A. Call this obfuscated circuit S. The ciphertext consists of (N, S).

Construction. We will use the following primitives in our construction:

1. A puncturable PRF family denoted by F.
2. A storage accumulator scheme based on $i\mathcal{O}$ and one-way functions that was constructed by [47]. We denote it by Acc = (SetupAcc, EnforceRead, EnforceWrite, PrepRead, PrepWrite, VerifyRead, WriteStore, Update). Let Σ_{tape} be the associated message space with accumulated value of size ℓ_{Acc} bits.
3. An iterators scheme denoted by Itr =(SetupItr, ItrEnforce, Iterate). Let $\{0,1\}^{2\lambda + \ell_{\mathsf{Acc}}}$ be the associated message space with iterated value of size ℓ_{Itr} bits.
4. A splittable signatures scheme denoted by SplScheme = (SetupSpl, SignSpl, VerSpl, SplitSpl, SignSplAbo). Let $\{0,1\}^{\ell_{\mathsf{Itr}} + \ell_{\mathsf{Acc}} + 2\lambda}$ be the associated message space.

Our Scheme. We now describe our construction of a 1-key ABE scheme 1ABE = (1ABE.Setup, 1ABE.KeyGen, 1ABE.Enc, 1ABE.Dec) for the Turing machine family $\mathcal{M}$. Without loss of generality, the start state of every Turing machine in $\mathcal{M}$ is denoted by q_0. We denote the message space for the ABE scheme as MSG.

1ABE.Setup(1^λ): On input a security parameter λ, it first executes the setup of splittable signatures scheme to compute $(\mathsf{SK_{tm}}, \mathsf{VK_{tm}}, \mathsf{VK_{rej}}) \leftarrow \mathsf{SetupSpl}(1^\lambda)$.

---

[10] In this construction, the key generation also outputs an iterator value.

Next, it executes the setup of the accumulator scheme to obtain the values $(\mathsf{PP}_{\mathsf{Acc}}, \widetilde{w}_0, \widetilde{store}_0) \leftarrow \mathsf{SetupAcc}(1^\lambda)$. It then executes the setup of the iterator scheme to obtain the public parameters $(\mathsf{PP}_{\mathsf{ltr}}, v_0) \leftarrow \mathsf{SetupItr}(1^\lambda)$.

It finally outputs the following public key-secret key pair,

$$\Big(1\mathsf{ABE.PP} = (\mathsf{VK}_{\mathsf{tm}}, \mathsf{PP}_{\mathsf{Acc}}, \widetilde{w}_0, \widetilde{store}_0, \mathsf{PP}_{\mathsf{ltr}}, v_0), 1\mathsf{ABE.SK} = (1\mathsf{ABE.PP}, \mathsf{SK}_{\mathsf{tm}})\Big)$$

$\underline{1\mathsf{ABE.KeyGen}(\mathsf{SK}_{\mathsf{tm}}, M \in \mathcal{M})}$: On input a master secret key $1\mathsf{ABE.SK} = (1\mathsf{ABE.PP}, \mathsf{SK}_{\mathsf{tm}})$ and a Turing machine $M \in \mathcal{M}$, it executes the following steps:

1. Parse the public key $1\mathsf{ABE.PP}$ as $(\mathsf{VK}_{\mathsf{tm}}, \mathsf{PP}_{\mathsf{Acc}}, \widetilde{w}_0, \widetilde{store}_0, \mathsf{PP}_{\mathsf{ltr}}, v_0)$.
2. **Initialization of the storage tree**: Let $\ell_{\mathsf{tm}} = |M|$ be the length of the machine M. For $1 \le j \le \ell_{\mathsf{tm}}$, compute $\widetilde{store}_j = \mathsf{WriteStore}(\mathsf{PP}_{\mathsf{Acc}}, \widetilde{store}_{j-1}, j-1, M_j)$, $aux_j = \mathsf{PrepWrite}(\mathsf{PP}_{\mathsf{Acc}}, \widetilde{store}_{j-1}, j-1)$, $\widetilde{w}_j = \mathsf{Update}(\mathsf{PP}_{\mathsf{Acc}}, \widetilde{w}_{j-1}, M_j, j-1, aux_j)$, where M_j denotes the jth bit of M. Set the root $w_0 = \widetilde{w}_{\ell_{\mathsf{tm}}}$.
3. **Signing the accumulator value**: Generate a signature on the message $(v_0, q_0, w_0, 0)$ by computing $\sigma_0 \leftarrow \mathsf{SignSpl}(\mathsf{SK}_{\mathsf{tm}}, \mu = (v_0, q_0, w_0, 0))$, where q_0 is the start state of M.

It outputs the ABE key $1\mathsf{ABE.}sk_M = (M, w_0, \sigma_{\mathsf{tm}}, v_0, \widetilde{store}_0)$.

[Note: The key generation does not output the storage tree $store_0$ but instead it just outputs the initial store value $\widetilde{store}_0$. As we see later, the evaluator in possession of M, $\widetilde{store}_0$ and $\mathsf{PP}_{\mathsf{Acc}}$ can reconstruct the tree $store_0$.]

$\underline{1\mathsf{ABE.Enc}(1\mathsf{ABE.PP}, x, \mathsf{msg})}$: On input a public key $1\mathsf{ABE.PP} = (\mathsf{VK}_{\mathsf{tm}}, \mathsf{PP}_{\mathsf{Acc}}, \widetilde{w}_0, \widetilde{store}_0, \mathsf{PP}_{\mathsf{ltr}}, v_0)$, attribute $x \in \{0,1\}^*$ and message $\mathsf{msg} \in \mathsf{MSG}$, it executes the following steps:

1. Sample a PRF key K_A at random from the family F.
2. **Obfuscating the next step function**: Consider a universal Turing machine $U_x(\cdot)$ that on input M executes M on x for at most 2^λ steps and outputs $M(x)$ if M terminates, otherwise it outputs $\perp$. Compute an obfuscation of the program NxtMsg described in Fig. 1, namely $N \leftarrow i\mathcal{O}(\mathsf{NxtMsg}\{U_x(\cdot), \mathsf{msg}, \mathsf{PP}_{\mathsf{Acc}}, \mathsf{PP}_{\mathsf{ltr}}, K_A\})$. NxtMsg is essentially the next message function of the Turing machine $U_x(\cdot)$ – it takes as input a TM M and outputs $M(x)$ if it halts within 2^λ else it outputs $\perp$. In addition, it performs checks to validate whether the previous step was correctly computed. It also generates authentication values for the current step.
3. Compute an obfuscation of the program $S \leftarrow (\mathsf{SignProg}\{K_A, \mathsf{VK}_{\mathsf{tm}}\})$ where $\mathsf{SignProg}$ is defined in Fig. 2. The program $\mathsf{SignProg}$ takes as input a message-signature pair and outputs a signature with respect to a different key on the same message.

It outputs the ciphertext $1\mathsf{ABE.CT} = (N, S)$.

```
                          Program NxtMsg

Constants: Turing machine $U_x = \langle Q, \Sigma_{\text{tape}}, \delta, q_0, q_{\text{acc}}, q_{\text{rej}} \rangle$, message msg, Public
parameters for accumulator PP_Acc, Public parameters for Iterator PP_Itr, Puncturable
PRF key $K_A \in \mathcal{K}$.

Input: Time $t \in [T]$, symbol sym_in $\in \Sigma_{\text{tape}}$, position pos_in $\in [T]$, state st_in $\in Q$,
accumulator value $w_{in} \in \{0,1\}^{\ell_{\text{Acc}}}$, Iterator value $v_{in}$, signature $\sigma_{in}$, accumulator proof
$\pi$, auxiliary value $aux$.
```

1. **Verification of the accumulator proof:**
   – If VerifyRead(PP_Acc, w_{in}, sym_in, pos_in, π) = 0 output ⊥.
2. **Verification of signature on the input state, position, accumulator and iterator values:**
   – Let $F(K_A, t-1) = r_A$. Compute $(SK_A, VK_A, VK_{A,\text{rej}}) = \text{SetupSpl}(1^\lambda; r_A)$.
   – Let $m_{in} = (v_{in}, st_{in}, w_{in}, pos_{in})$. If VerSpl(VK_A, m_{in}, σ_{in}) = 0 output ⊥.
3. **Executing the transition function:**
   – Let $(st_{out}, sym_{out}, \beta) = \delta(st_{in}, sym_{in})$ and $pos_{out} = pos_{in} + \beta$.
   – If $st_{out} = q_{\text{rej}}$ output ⊥.
   – If $st_{out} = q_{\text{acc}}$ output msg.
4. **Updating the accumulator and the iterator values:**
   – Compute $w_{out} = \text{Update}(PP_{Acc}, w_{in}, sym_{out}, pos_{in}, aux)$. If $w_{out} = Reject$, output
     ⊥.
   – Compute $v_{out} = \text{Iterate}(PP_{Itr}, v_{in}, (st_{in}, w_{in}, pos_{in}))$.
5. **Generating the signature on the new state, position, accumulator and iterator values:**
   – Let $F(K_A, t) = r'_A$. Compute $(SK'_A, VK'_A, VK'_{A,\text{rej}}) \leftarrow \text{SetupSpl}(1^\lambda; r'_A)$.
   – Let $m_{out} = (v_{out}, st_{out}, w_{out}, pos_{out})$ and $\sigma_{out} = \text{SignSpl}(SK'_A, m_{out})$.
6. Output $sym_{out}, pos_{out}, st_{out}, w_{out}, v_{out}, \sigma_{out}$.

Fig. 1. Program NxtMsg

```
                          Program SignProg

Constants: PRF key $K_A$ and verification key VK_tm.
Input: Message $y$ and a signature $\sigma_{\text{tm}}$.
```

1. If VerSpl(VK_tm, y, σ_{tm}) = 0 then output ⊥.
2. Execute the pseudorandom function on input 0 to obtain $r_A \leftarrow F(K, 0)$.
   Execute the setup of splittable signatures scheme to compute $(SK_0, VK_0) \leftarrow \text{SetupSpl}(1^\lambda; r_A)$.
3. Compute the signature $\sigma_0 \leftarrow \text{SignSpl}(SK_0, y)$.
4. Output σ_0.

Fig. 2. Program SignProg

1ABE.Dec(1ABE.sk_M, 1ABE.CT): On input the ABE key 1ABE.sk_M = $(M, w_0, \sigma_{\text{tm}}, v_0, \widetilde{store_0})$ and a ciphertext 1ABE.CT $= (N, S)$, it first executes the obfuscated program $S(y = (v_0, q_0, w_0, 0), \sigma_{\text{tm}})$ to obtain σ_0. It then executes the following steps.

1. **Reconstructing the storage tree:** Let $\ell_{\text{tm}} = |M|$ be the length of the TM M. For $1 \leq j \leq \ell_{\text{tm}}$, update the storage tree by computing, $\widetilde{store_j} = \text{WriteStore}(PP_{Acc}, \widetilde{store_{j-1}}, j-1, M_j)$. Set $store_0 = \widetilde{store_{\ell_{\text{tm}}}}$.
2. **Executing N one step at a time:** For $i = 1$ to 2^λ,
   (a) Compute the proof that validates the storage value $store_{i-1}$ (storage value at $(i-1)^{th}$ time step) at position pos_{i-1}. Let $(sym_{i-1}, \pi_{i-1}) \leftarrow \text{PrepRead}(PP_{Acc}, store_{i-1}, pos_{i-1})$.

(b) Compute the auxiliary value, $aux_{i-1} \leftarrow$ PrepWrite(PP$_{\mathsf{Acc}}$, $store_{-1}$, pos$_{i-1}$).

(c) Run the obfuscated next message function. Compute out $\leftarrow$ $N(i, \mathsf{sym}_{i-1}, \mathsf{pos}_{i-1}, \mathsf{st}_{i-1}, w_{i-1}, v_{i-1}, \sigma_{i-1}, \pi_{i-1}, aux_{i-1})$. If out $\in$ MSG $\cup$ $\{\bot\}$, output out.
Else parse out as $(\mathsf{sym}_{w,i}, \mathsf{pos}_i, \mathsf{st}_i, w_i, v_i, \sigma_i)$.

(d) Compute the storage value, $store_i \leftarrow$ WriteStore(PP$_{\mathsf{Acc}}$, $store_{i-1}$, pos$_{i-1}$, $\mathsf{sym}_{w,i}$).

This completes the description of the scheme. The correctness of the above scheme follows along the same lines as the message hiding encoding scheme of Koppula et al. For completeness, we give a proof sketch below.

Lemma 1. 1ABE *satisfies the correctness property of an ABE scheme.*

Proof sketch. Suppose 1ABE.CT is a ciphertext of message msg w.r.t an attribute x and 1ABE.sk_M is an ABE key for a machine M. We claim that in the ith iteration of the decryption of 1ABE.CT using 1ABE.sk_M, the storage corresponds to the work tape of the execution of $M(x)$ at the ith time step, denoted by $W_{t=i}$.[11] Once we show this, the lemma follows.

We prove this claim by induction on the total number of steps in the TM execution. The base case corresponds to 0th time step when the iterations haven't begun. At this point, the storage corresponds to the description of the machine M which is exactly $W_{t=0}$ (work tape at time step 0). In the induction hypothesis, we assume that at time step $i-1$, the storage contains the work tape $W_{t=i-1}$. We need to argue for the case when $t=i$. To take care of this case, we just need to argue that the obfuscated next step function computes the ith step of the execution of $M(x)$ correctly. The correctness of obfuscated next step function in turn follows from the correctness of iO and other underlying primitives.

Remark 2. In the description of Koppula et al., the accumulator and the iterator algorithms also take the time bound T as input. Here, we set $T = 2^\lambda$ since we are only concerned with Turing machines that run in time polynomial in λ.

Additive overhead. Let 1ABE.$sk_M = (M, w_0, \sigma_{\mathsf{tm}}, v_0, \widetilde{store_0})$ be an ABE key generated as the output of 1ABE.KeyGen(1ABE.SK, $M \in \mathcal{M}$). From the efficiency property of accumulators, we have that $|w_0|$ and $|\widetilde{store_0}|$ simply polynomials in the security parameter λ. The signature σ_{tm} on the message w_0 is also of length polynomial in the security parameter. Lastly, the iterator parameter v_0 is also only polynomial in the security parameter. Thus, the size of 1ABE.sk_M is $|M| + \mathrm{poly}(\lambda)$.

The proof of security can be found in the full version.

---

[11] To be more precise, the storage in the KLW construction is a tree with the jth leaf containing the value of the jth location in the work tape $W_{t=i}$.

2.3   1-Key Two-Outcome ABE for TMs

Goldwasser et al. [39] proposed the notion of 1-key two-outcome ABE for circuits as a variant of 1-key attribute based encryption for circuits where a pair of secret messages are encoded as opposed to a single secret message. Depending on the output of the predicate, exactly one of the messages is revealed and the other message remains hidden. That is, given an encryption of a single attribute x and two messages $(\mathsf{msg}_0, \mathsf{msg}_1)$, the decryption algorithm on input an ABE key $\mathsf{TwoABE}.sk_M$, outputs msg_0 if $M(x) = 0$ and msg_1 otherwise. The security guarantee then says that if $M(x) = 0$ (resp., $M(x) = 1$) then the pair $(\mathsf{TwoABE}.sk_M, \mathsf{TwoABE}.\mathsf{CT}_{(x,\mathsf{msg}_0,\mathsf{msg}_1)})$, reveal no information about msg_1 (resp., msg_0).

We adapt their definition to the case when the predicates are implemented as Turing machines instead of circuits. We give a formal definition and a simple construction of this primitive in the full version.

3   Oblivious Evaluation Encodings

In this section, we define and construct *oblivious evaluation encodings* (OEE). This is a strengthening of the notion of machine hiding encodings (MHE) introduced in [47]. Very briefly, machine hiding encodings are essentially randomized encodings (RE), except that in MHE, the machine needs to be hidden whereas in RE, the input needs to be hidden. More concretely, an MHE scheme for Turing machines has an encoding procedure that encodes the output of a Turing machine M and an input x. This is coupled with a decode procedure that decodes the output $M(x)$. The main efficiency requirement is that the encoding procedure should be much "simpler" than actually computing M on x. The security guarantee states that the encoding does not reveal anything more than $M(x)$.

We make several changes to the notion of MHE to obtain our definition of OEE. First, we require that the machine and the input can be encoded *separately*. Secondly, the machine encoding takes as input two Turing machines (M_0, M_1) and outputs a joint encoding. Correspondingly, the input encoding now also takes as input a bit b in addition to the actual input x, where b indicates which of the two machines M_0 or M_1 needs to be used. The decode algorithm on input an encoding of (M_0, M_1) and (x, b), outputs $M_b(x)$. In terms of security, we require the following two properties to be satisfied:

- Any PPT adversary should not be able to distinguish encodings of (M_0, M_0) and (M_0, M_1) (resp., (M_1, M_1) and (M_0, M_1)) even if the adversary is given a *punctured* input encoding key that allows him to encode inputs of the form $(x, 0)$ (resp., $(x, 1)$).
- Any PPT adversary is unable to distinguish the encodings of $(x, 0)$ and $(x, 1)$ even given an oblivious evaluation encoding (M_0, M_1), where $M_0(x) = M_1(x)$ and another type of punctured input encoding key that allows him to generate input encodings of $(x', 0)$ and $(x', 1)$ for all $x' \neq x$.

3.1 Definition

Syntax. We describe the syntax of a oblivious evaluation encoding scheme OEE below. The class of Turing machines associated with the scheme is $\mathcal{M}$ and the input space is $\{0,1\}^*$. Although we consider inputs of arbitrary lengths, during the generation of the parameters we place an upper bound on the running time of the machines which automatically puts an upper bound on the length of the inputs.

- OEE.Setup(1^λ): It takes as input a security parameter λ and outputs a secret key OEE.sk.
- OEE.TMEncode(OEE.sk, M_0, M_1): It takes as input a secret key OEE.sk, a pair of Turing machines $M_0, M_1 \in \mathcal{M}$ and outputs a joint encoding $\widetilde{(M_0, M_1)}$.
- OEE.InpEncode(OEE.sk, x, b): It takes as input a secret key OEE.sk, an input $x \in \{0,1\}^*$, a choice bit b and outputs an input encoding $\widetilde{(x, b)}$.
- OEE.Decode($(\widetilde{M_0, M_1}), \widetilde{(x, b)}$): It takes as input a joint Turing machine encoding $\widetilde{(M_0, M_1)}$, an input encoding $\widetilde{(x, b)}$, and outputs a value z.

In addition to the above main algorithms, there are four helper algorithms.

- OEE.puncInp(OEE.sk, x): It takes as input a secret key OEE.sk, input $x \in \{0,1\}^*$ and outputs a punctured key OEE.sk$_x$.
- OEE.pIEncode(OEE.sk$_x$, x', b): It takes as input a punctured secret key OEE.sk$_x$, an input $x' \neq x$, a bit b and outputs an input encoding $\widetilde{(x', b)}$.
- OEE.puncBit(OEE.sk, b): It takes as input a secret key OEE.sk, an input bit b and outputs a key OEE.sk_b.
- OEE.pBEncode(OEE.sk_b, x): It takes as input a key OEE.sk_b, an input x and outputs an input encoding $\widetilde{(x, b)}$.

Correctness. We say that an OEE scheme is correct if it satisfies the following three properties:

1. *Correctness of Encode and Decode:* For all $M_0, M_1 \in \mathcal{M}$, $x \in \{0,1\}^*$ and $b \in \{0,1\}$,
$$\text{OEE.Decode}\Big((\widetilde{M_0, M_1}), \widetilde{(x, b)}\Big) = M_b(x),$$
where   (i)
OEE.sk $\leftarrow$ OEE.Setup(1^λ), (ii) $(\widetilde{M_0, M_1}) \leftarrow$ OEE.TMEncode(OEE.sk, M_0, M_1) and, (iii) $\widetilde{(x, b)} \leftarrow$ OEE.InpEncode(OEE.sk, x, b).

2. *Correctness of Input Puncturing:* For all $M_0, M_1 \in \mathcal{M}$, $x, x' \in \{0,1\}^*$ such that $x' \neq x$ and $b \in \{0,1\}$,
$$\text{OEE.Decode}\Big((\widetilde{M_0, M_1}), \widetilde{(x', b)}\Big) = M_b(x'),$$
where
(i) OEE.sk $\leftarrow$ OEE.Setup(1^λ); (ii) $(\widetilde{M_0, M_1}) \leftarrow$ OEE.TMEncode(OEE.sk, M_0, M_1) and, (iii) $\widetilde{(x', b)} \leftarrow$ OEE.pIEncode(OEE.puncInp(OEE.sk, x), x', b).

3. *Correctness of Bit Puncturing:* For all $M_0, M_1 \in \mathcal{M}$, $x \in \{0,1\}^*$ and $b \in \{0,1\}$,

$$\text{OEE.Decode}\left((\widetilde{M_0, M_1}), \widetilde{(x,b)}\right) = M_b(x),$$

where
(i) $\text{OEE.sk} \leftarrow \text{OEE.Setup}\left(1^\lambda\right)$, (ii) $(\widetilde{M_0, M_1}) \leftarrow \text{OEE.TMEncode}(\text{OEE.sk}, M_0, M_1)$ and, (iii) $\widetilde{(x,b)} \leftarrow \text{OEE.pBEncode}\left(\text{OEE.puncBit}\left(\text{OEE.sk}, b\right), x\right)$.

Efficiency. We require that an OEE scheme satisfies the following efficiency conditions. Informally, we require that the Turing machine encoding (resp., input encoding) algorithm only has a logarithmic dependence on the time bound. Furthermore, the running time of the decode algorithm should take time proportional to the computation time of the encoded Turing machine on the encoded input.

1. The running time of $\text{OEE.TMEncode}(\text{OEE.sk}, M_0 \in \mathcal{M}, M_1 \in \mathcal{M})$ is a polynomial in $(\lambda, |M_0|, |M_1|)$, where $\text{OEE.sk} \leftarrow \text{OEE.Setup}(1^\lambda)$.
2. The running time of $\text{OEE.InpEncode}(\text{OEE.sk}, x \in \{0,1\}^*, b)$ is a polynomial in $(\lambda, |x|)$, where $\text{OEE.sk} \leftarrow \text{OEE.Setup}(1^\lambda)$.
3. The running time of $\text{OEE.Decode}((\widetilde{M_0, M_1}), \widetilde{(x,b)})$ is a polynomial in $(\lambda, |M_0|, |M_1|, |x|, t)$, where $\text{OEE.sk} \leftarrow \text{OEE.Setup}(1^\lambda)$, $(\widetilde{M_0, M_1}) \leftarrow \text{OEE.TMEncode}(\text{OEE.sk}, M_0 \in \mathcal{M}, M_1 \in \mathcal{M})$, $\widetilde{(x,b)} \leftarrow \text{OEE.InpEncode}(\text{OEE.sk}, x \in \{0,1\}^*, b)$ and t is the running time of the Turing machine M_b on x.

Indistinguishability of Encoding Bit. We describe security of encoding bit as a multi-stage game between an adversary $\mathcal{A}$ and a challenger.

- *Setup:* $\mathcal{A}$ chooses two Turing machines $M_0, M_1 \in \mathcal{M}$ and an input x such that $|M_0| = |M_1|$ and $M_0(x) = M_1(x)$. $\mathcal{A}$ sends the tuple (M_0, M_1, x) to the challenger.
  The challenger chooses a bit $b \in \{0,1\}$ and computes the following: (a) $\text{OEE.sk} \leftarrow \text{OEE.Setup}(1^\lambda)$, (b) machine encoding $(\widetilde{M_0, M_1}) \leftarrow \text{OEE.TMEncode}(\text{OEE.sk}, M_0, M_1)$, (c) input encoding $\widetilde{(x,b)} \leftarrow \text{OEE.InpEncode}(\text{OEE.sk}, x, b)$, and (d) punctured key $\text{OEE.sk}_x \leftarrow \text{OEE.puncInp}(\text{OEE.sk}, x)$. Finally, it sends the following tuple to $\mathcal{A}$:

$$\left((\widetilde{M_0, M_1}), \widetilde{(x,b)}, \text{OEE.sk}_x\right).$$

- *Guess:* $\mathcal{A}$ outputs a bit $b' \in \{0,1\}$.

The advantage of $\mathcal{A}$ in this game is defined as $\text{adv}_{\text{OEE}_1} = \Pr[b' = b] - \frac{1}{2}$.

Definition 3 (Indistinguishability of encoding bit). *An OEE scheme satisfies indistinguishability of encoding bit if there exists a neglible function* $\text{negl}(\cdot)$ *such that for every PPT adversary* $\mathcal{A}$ *in the above security game,* $\text{adv}_{\text{OEE}_1} = \text{negl}(\lambda)$.

Indistinguishability of Machine Encoding. We describe security of machine encoding as a multi-stage game between an adversary $\mathcal{A}$ and a challenger.

– *Setup*: $\mathcal{A}$ chooses two Turing machines $M_0, M_1 \in \mathcal{M}$ and a bit $c \in \{0,1\}$ such that $|M_0| = |M_1|$. $\mathcal{A}$ sends the tuple (M_0, M_1, c) to the challenger.

The challenger chooses a bit $b \in \{0,1\}$ and computes the following: (a) OEE.sk $\leftarrow$ OEE.Setup(1^λ), (b) $(\widetilde{\mathsf{TM}_1, \mathsf{TM}_2}) \leftarrow$ OEE.TMEncode(OEE.sk, $\mathsf{TM}_1, \mathsf{TM}_2$), where $\mathsf{TM}_1 = M_0, \mathsf{TM}_2 = M_{1 \oplus b}$ if $c = 0$ and $\mathsf{TM}_1 = M_{0 \oplus b}, \mathsf{TM}_2 = M_1$ otherwise, and (c) OEE.sk$_c$ $\leftarrow$ OEE.puncBit(OEE.sk, c). Finally, it sends the following tuple to $\mathcal{A}$:

$$\left((\widetilde{\mathsf{TM}_1, \mathsf{TM}_2}), \mathsf{OEE.sk}_c \right).$$

– *Guess*: $\mathcal{A}$ outputs a bit $b' \in \{0,1\}$.

The advantage of $\mathcal{A}$ in this game is defined as $\mathsf{adv} = \Pr[b' = b] - \frac{1}{2}$.

Definition 4 (Indistinguishability of machine encoding). *An OEE scheme satisfies indistinguishability of machine encoding if there exists a negligible function* $\mathsf{negl}(\cdot)$ *such that for every PPT adversary $\mathcal{A}$ in the above security game,* $\mathsf{adv}_{\mathrm{OEE}_2} = \mathsf{negl}(\lambda)$.

OEE with Constant Multiplicative Overhead. The efficiency property in OEE dictates that the output length of the Turing machine encoding algorithm is a polynomial in the size of the Turing machine. We can restrict this condition further by requiring that the Turing machine encoding is only *linear* in the Turing machine size. We term the notion of OEE that satisfies this property as *OEE with constant multiplicative overhead.*

Definition 5 (OEE with constant multiplicative overhead). *An oblivious evaluation encoding scheme for a class of Turing machines $\mathcal{M}$ is said to have constant multiplicative overhead if its Turing machine encoding algorithm* OEE.TMEncode *on input* (OEE.sk, M_0, M_1) *outputs an encoding* $(\widetilde{M_0, M_1})$ *such that* $|(\widetilde{M_0, M_1})| = c \cdot (|M_0| + |M_1|) + \mathsf{poly}(\lambda)$, *where c is a constant > 0.*

References

1. Ananth, P., Boneh, D., Garg, S., Sahai, A., Zhandry, M.: Differing-inputs obfuscation and applications. IACR Cryptology ePrint Archive 2013:689 (2013)
2. Ananth, P., Chen, Y.-C., Chung, K.-M., Lin, H., Lin, W.-K.: Delegating RAM computations with adaptive soundness and privacy. In: Hirt, M., Smith, A. (eds.) TCC 2016. LNCS, vol. 9986, pp. 3–30. Springer, Heidelberg (2016). doi:10.1007/978-3-662-53644-5_1
3. Ananth, P., Gupta, D., Ishai, Y., Sahai, A.: Optimizing obfuscation: avoiding barrington's theorem. In: ACM CCS (2014)
4. Ananth, P., Jain, A.: Indistinguishability obfuscation from compact functional encryption. In: Gennaro, R., Robshaw, M. (eds.) CRYPTO 2015. LNCS, vol. 9215, pp. 308–326. Springer, Heidelberg (2015). doi:10.1007/978-3-662-47989-6_15

5. Ananth, P., Jain, A., Sahai, A.: Achieving compactness generically: indistinguishability obfuscation from non-compact functional encryption. IACR Cryptology ePrint Archive 2015:730 (2015)

6. Ananth, P., Jain, A., Sahai, A.: Patchable indistinguishability obfuscation: $i\mathcal{O}$ for evolving software. In: Coron, J.-S., Nielsen, J.B. (eds.) EUROCRYPT 2017. LNCS, vol. 10212, pp. 127–155. Springer, Cham (2017). doi:10.1007/978-3-319-56617-7_5

7. Ananth, P., Sahai, A.: Functional encryption for turing machines. In: Kushilevitz, E., Malkin, T. (eds.) TCC 2016. LNCS, vol. 9562, pp. 125–153. Springer, Heidelberg (2016). doi:10.1007/978-3-662-49096-9_6

8. Applebaum, B., Brakerski, Z.: Obfuscating circuits via composite-order graded encoding. In: Dodis, Y., Nielsen, J.B. (eds.) TCC 2015. LNCS, vol. 9015, pp. 528–556. Springer, Heidelberg (2015). doi:10.1007/978-3-662-46497-7_21

9. Barak, B., Garg, S., Kalai, Y.T., Paneth, O., Sahai, A.: Protecting obfuscation against algebraic attacks. In: Nguyen, P.Q., Oswald, E. (eds.) EUROCRYPT 2014. LNCS, vol. 8441, pp. 221–238. Springer, Heidelberg (2014). doi:10.1007/978-3-642-55220-5_13

10. Barak, B., Goldreich, O., Impagliazzo, R., Rudich, S., Sahai, A., Vadhan, S.P., Yang, K.: On the (im)possibility of obfuscating programs. J. ACM **59**(2), 6 (2012)

11. Bellare, M., Stepanovs, I., Waters, B.: New negative results on differing-inputs obfuscation. In: Fischlin, M., Coron, J.-S. (eds.) EUROCRYPT 2016. LNCS, vol. 9666, pp. 792–821. Springer, Heidelberg (2016). doi:10.1007/978-3-662-49896-5_28

12. Bitansky, N., Garg, S., Lin, H., Pass, R., Telang, S.: Succinct randomized encodings and their applications. In: STOC (2015)

13. Bitansky, N., Paneth, O., Rosen, A.: On the cryptographic hardness of finding a nash equilibrium. In: FOCS, pp. 1480–1498 (2015)

14. Bitansky, N., Vaikuntanathan, V.: Indistinguishability obfuscation from functional encryption. In: FOCS (2015)

15. Boneh, D., Gentry, C., Gorbunov, S., Halevi, S., Nikolaenko, V., Segev, G., Vaikuntanathan, V., Vinayagamurthy, D.: Fully key-homomorphic encryption, arithmetic circuit ABE and compact garbled circuits. In: Nguyen, P.Q., Oswald, E. (eds.) EUROCRYPT 2014. LNCS, vol. 8441, pp. 533–556. Springer, Heidelberg (2014). doi:10.1007/978-3-642-55220-5_30

16. Boneh, D., Waters, B.: Constrained pseudorandom functions and their applications. In: Sako, K., Sarkar, P. (eds.) ASIACRYPT 2013. LNCS, vol. 8270, pp. 280–300. Springer, Heidelberg (2013). doi:10.1007/978-3-642-42045-0_15

17. Boneh, D., Wu, D.J., Zimmerman, J.: Immunizing multilinear maps against zeroizing attacks. IACR Cryptology ePrint Archive 2014:930 (2014)

18. Boyle, E., Chung, K.-M., Pass, R.: On extractability obfuscation. In: Lindell, Y. (ed.) TCC 2014. LNCS, vol. 8349, pp. 52–73. Springer, Heidelberg (2014). doi:10.1007/978-3-642-54242-8_3

19. Boyle, E., Goldwasser, S., Ivan, I.: Functional signatures and pseudorandom functions. In: Krawczyk, H. (ed.) PKC 2014. LNCS, vol. 8383, pp. 501–519. Springer, Heidelberg (2014). doi:10.1007/978-3-642-54631-0_29

20. Brakerski, Z., Rothblum, G.N.: Virtual black-box obfuscation for all circuits via generic graded encoding. In: Lindell, Y. (ed.) TCC 2014. LNCS, vol. 8349, pp. 1–25. Springer, Heidelberg (2014). doi:10.1007/978-3-642-54242-8_1

21. Canetti, R., Chen, Y., Holmgren, J., Raykova, M.: Adaptive succinct garbled RAM or: how to delegate your database. In: Hirt, M., Smith, A. (eds.) TCC 2016. LNCS, vol. 9986, pp. 61–90. Springer, Heidelberg (2016). doi:10.1007/978-3-662-53644-5_3

22. Canetti, R., Holmgren, J.: Fully succinct garbled RAM. In: ITCS (2016)

23. Canetti, R., Holmgren, J., Jain, A., Vaikuntanathan, V.: Indistinguishability obfuscation of iterated circuits and RAM programs. In: STOC (2015)
24. Caro, A., Iovino, V., Jain, A., O'Neill, A., Paneth, O., Persiano, G.: On the achievability of simulation-based security for functional encryption. In: Canetti, R., Garay, J.A. (eds.) CRYPTO 2013. LNCS, vol. 8043, pp. 519–535. Springer, Heidelberg (2013). doi:10.1007/978-3-642-40084-1_29
25. Chen, Y.-C., Chow, S.S.M., Chung, K.-M., Lai, R.W.F., Lin, W.-K., Zhou, H.-S.: Computation-trace indistinguishability obfuscation and its applications. In: ITCS (2016)
26. Cheon, J.H., Han, K., Lee, C., Ryu, H., Stehlé, D.: Cryptanalysis of the multilinear map over the integers. In: Oswald, E., Fischlin, M. (eds.) EUROCRYPT 2015. LNCS, vol. 9056, pp. 3–12. Springer, Heidelberg (2015). doi:10.1007/978-3-662-46800-5_1
27. Cohen, A., Holmgren, J., Nishimaki, R., Vaikuntanathan, V., Wichs, D.: Watermarking cryptographic capabilities. In: STOC, pp. 1115–1127 (2016)
28. Coron, J.-S., Gentry, C., Halevi, S., Lepoint, T., Maji, H.K., Miles, E., Raykova, M., Sahai, A., Tibouchi, M.: Zeroizing without low-level zeroes: New MMAP attacks and their limitations. In: CRYPTO (2015)
29. Coron, J.-S., Lepoint, T., Tibouchi, M.: Cryptanalysis of two candidate fixes of multilinear maps over the integers. IACR Cryptology ePrint Archive 2014:975 (2014)
30. Garg, S., Gentry, C., Halevi, S.: Candidate multilinear maps from ideal lattices. In: Johansson, T., Nguyen, P.Q. (eds.) EUROCRYPT 2013. LNCS, vol. 7881, pp. 1–17. Springer, Heidelberg (2013). doi:10.1007/978-3-642-38348-9_1
31. Garg, S., Gentry, C., Halevi, S., Raykova, M., Sahai, A., Waters, B.: Candidate indistinguishability obfuscation and functional encryption for all circuits. In: FOCS (2013)
32. Garg, S., Gentry, C., Halevi, S., Wichs, D.: On the implausibility of differing-inputs obfuscation and extractable witness encryption with auxiliary input. In: Garay, J.A., Gennaro, R. (eds.) CRYPTO 2014. LNCS, vol. 8616, pp. 518–535. Springer, Heidelberg (2014). doi:10.1007/978-3-662-44371-2_29
33. Garg, S., Miles, E., Mukherjee, P., Sahai, A., Srinivasan, A., Zhandry, M.: Secure obfuscation in a weak multilinear map model. In: Hirt, M., Smith, A. (eds.) TCC 2016. LNCS, vol. 9986, pp. 241–268. Springer, Heidelberg (2016). doi:10.1007/978-3-662-53644-5_10
34. Gentry, C.: Fully homomorphic encryption using ideal lattices. In: STOC, pp. 169–178 (2009)
35. Gentry, C., Halevi, S., Maji, H.K., Sahai, A.: Zeroizing without zeroes: Cryptanalyzing multilinear maps without encodings of zero. IACR Cryptology ePrint Archive 2014:929 (2014)
36. Gentry, C., Halevi, S., Raykova, M., Wichs, D.: Outsourcing private ram computation. In: FOCS. IEEE (2014)
37. Gentry, C., Lewko, A., Waters, B.: Witness encryption from instance independent assumptions. In: Garay, J.A., Gennaro, R. (eds.) CRYPTO 2014. LNCS, vol. 8616, pp. 426–443. Springer, Heidelberg (2014). doi:10.1007/978-3-662-44371-2_24
38. Gentry, C., Lewko, A.B., Sahai, A., Waters, B.: Indistinguishability obfuscation from the multilinear subgroup elimination assumption. In: FOCS (2015)
39. Goldwasser, S., Kalai, Y.T., Popa, R.A., Vaikuntanathan, V., Zeldovich, N.: Reusable garbled circuits and succinct functional encryption. In: STOC (2013)

40. Goldwasser, S., Kalai, Y.T., Popa, R.A., Vaikuntanathan, V., Zeldovich, N.: How to run turing machines on encrypted data. In: Canetti, R., Garay, J.A. (eds.) CRYPTO 2013. LNCS, vol. 8043, pp. 536–553. Springer, Heidelberg (2013). doi:10.1007/978-3-642-40084-1_30
41. Goyal, V., Pandey, O., Sahai, A., Waters, B.: Attribute-based encryption for fine-grained access control of encrypted data. In: ACM CCS, pp. 89–98 (2006)
42. Hubáček, P., Wichs, D.: On the communication complexity of secure function evaluation with long output. In: ITCS, pp. 163–172 (2015)
43. Ishai, Y., Kushilevitz, E.: Randomizing polynomials: a new representation with applications to round-efficient secure computation. In: FOCS, pp. 294–304 (2000)
44. Ishai, Y., Kushilevitz, E., Ostrovsky, R., Sahai, A.: Cryptography with constant computational overhead. In: ACM STOC (2008)
45. Ishai, Y., Pandey, O., Sahai, A.: Public-coin differing-inputs obfuscation and its applications. In: Dodis, Y., Nielsen, J.B. (eds.) TCC 2015. LNCS, vol. 9015, pp. 668–697. Springer, Heidelberg (2015). doi:10.1007/978-3-662-46497-7_26
46. Kiayias, A., Papadopoulos, S., Triandopoulos, N., Zacharias, T.: Delegatable pseudorandom functions and applications. In: ACM CCS (2013)
47. Koppula, V., Lewko, A.B., Waters, B.: Indistinguishability obfuscation for turing machines with unbounded memory. In: STOC (2015)
48. Lin, H.: Indistinguishability obfuscation from constant-degree graded encoding schemes. In: Fischlin, M., Coron, J.-S. (eds.) EUROCRYPT 2016. LNCS, vol. 9665, pp. 28–57. Springer, Heidelberg (2016). doi:10.1007/978-3-662-49890-3_2
49. Lin, H., Pass, R., Seth, K., Telang, S.: Output-compressing randomized encodings and applications. In: Kushilevitz, E., Malkin, T. (eds.) TCC 2016. LNCS, vol. 9562, pp. 96–124. Springer, Heidelberg (2016). doi:10.1007/978-3-662-49096-9_5
50. Lin, H., Vaikuntanathan, V.: Indistinguishability obfuscation from DDH-like assumptions on constant-degree graded encodings. In: FOCS (2016)
51. Miles, E., Sahai, A., Zhandry, M.: Annihilation attacks for multilinear maps: cryptanalysis of indistinguishability obfuscation over GGH13. In: Robshaw, M., Katz, J. (eds.) CRYPTO 2016. LNCS, vol. 9815, pp. 629–658. Springer, Heidelberg (2016). doi:10.1007/978-3-662-53008-5_22
52. Pass, R., Seth, K., Telang, S.: Indistinguishability obfuscation from semantically-secure multilinear encodings. In: Garay, J.A., Gennaro, R. (eds.) CRYPTO 2014. LNCS, vol. 8616, pp. 500–517. Springer, Heidelberg (2014). doi:10.1007/978-3-662-44371-2_28
53. Sahai, A., Waters, B.: Fuzzy identity-based encryption. In: Cramer, R. (ed.) EUROCRYPT 2005. LNCS, vol. 3494, pp. 457–473. Springer, Heidelberg (2005). doi:10.1007/11426639_27
54. Sahai, A., Waters, B.: How to use indistinguishability obfuscation: deniable encryption, and more. In: ACM STOC (2014)
55. Waters, B.: A punctured programming approach to adaptively secure functional encryption. In: Gennaro, R., Robshaw, M. (eds.) CRYPTO 2015. LNCS, vol. 9216, pp. 678–697. Springer, Heidelberg (2015). doi:10.1007/978-3-662-48000-7_33
56. Zimmerman, J.: How to obfuscate programs directly. In: Oswald, E., Fischlin, M. (eds.) EUROCRYPT 2015. LNCS, vol. 9057, pp. 439–467. Springer, Heidelberg (2015). doi:10.1007/978-3-662-46803-6_15

Quantum

Quantum Security of NMAC and Related Constructions
PRF Domain Extension Against Quantum attacks

Fang Song[1]([⊠]) and Aaram Yun[2]([⊠])

[1] Portland State University, Portland, USA
fang.song@pdx.edu
[2] Ulsan National Institute of Science and Technology (UNIST), Ulsan, Korea
aaramyun@unist.ac.kr

Abstract. We prove the security of NMAC, HMAC, AMAC, and the cascade construction with fixed input-length as *quantum-secure* pseudorandom functions (PRFs). Namely, they are indistinguishable from a random oracle against any polynomial-time quantum adversary that can make quantum superposition queries. In contrast, many blockcipher-based PRFs including CBC-MAC were recently broken by quantum superposition attacks.

Classical proof strategies for these constructions do not generalize to the quantum setting, and we observe that they sometimes even fail completely (e.g., the universal-hash then PRF paradigm for proving security of NMAC). Instead, we propose a direct hybrid argument as a new proof strategy (both classically and quantumly). We first show that a quantum-secure PRF is secure against key-recovery attacks, and remains secure under random leakage of the key. Next, as a key technical tool, we extend the oracle indistinguishability framework of Zhandry in two directions: we consider distributions on *functions* rather than strings, and we also consider a relative setting, where an additional oracle, possibly correlated with the distributions, is given to the adversary as well. This enables a hybrid argument to prove the security of NMAC. Security proofs for other constructions follow similarly.

Keywords: Cascade construction · NMAC · HMAC · Augmented cascade · AMAC · PRF domain extension · Quantum query · Quantum security · Post-quantum cryptography

1 Introduction

After Shor proposed his celebrated quantum algorithm for solving integer factorization and discrete logarithms efficiently, it became apparent that once practical quantum computers become reality, a large part of public-key cryptography, including elliptic curve cryptography and RSA, will be completely broken. Therefore, research in *post-quantum cryptography* has been emerging: new cryptographic algorithms are designed which can still run on conventional classical computers, but their security holds against potential quantum attacks.

© International Association for Cryptologic Research 2017
J. Katz and H. Shacham (Eds.): CRYPTO 2017, Part II, LNCS 10402, pp. 283–309, 2017.
DOI: 10.1007/978-3-319-63715-0_10

There are two possible approaches for modeling quantum attacks in post-quantum cryptography. One is to assume a quantum attacker who has only quantum computational capabilities. In other words, a classical attacker who has a quantum computer in its garage. Such an attacker can run quantum algorithms, but its interaction with the environment remains classical. In such an adversarial model, while some important classical proof techniques do not carry over such as rewinding [16,19], there are also many examples of existing security proofs that go through relatively easily as long as we switch to hardness assumptions which are not broken by quantum computers [14].

On the other hand, we can be more conservative, and design cryptographic schemes secure against quantum attackers who have not only quantum computational capabilities, but are also capable of interacting quantumly with the environment. In other words, such an attacker can access the cryptographic primitive under attack in quantum *superposition*. Such a scheme would be secure not only now, but also in the far future when quantum computing and quantum networking technologies become prevalent and ubiquitous, and could be also used as a subprotocol in larger quantum computing protocols. We take this adversarial model in this work and refer to this security notion as *quantum security* [20].

Proving quantum security is notoriously challenging. Classically, when an adversary has access to an oracle, each query examines only one point in the domain of the oracle, and that fact is often used crucially in classical security proofs. On the other hand, when an adversary can make superposed queries, each query can potentially probe all points in the input domain in superposition. Therefore, for example, one cannot perform lazy sampling when simulating such an oracle. In fact, there are schemes which are secure classically but fail to be quantum-secure. For example, Kuwakado and Morii showed that three-round Luby-Rackoff cipher [10] and Even-Mansour cipher [11] do not have quantum security, even though they are secure classically.

Later in a series of works [5,6,20], the quantum security of several basic primitives, such as PRFs, MACs and signatures, was proved. However one important question was still largely unclear, as Boneh and Zhandry noted [6]:

> Can we construct a quantum-secure PRF for a large domain from a quantum-secure PRF for a small domain? In particular, do the CBC-MAC or NMAC constructions give quantum-secure PRFs?

Unfortunately, in Crypto 2016, Kaplan et al. showed that many popular MACs and authenticated encryption schemes are not quantum-secure [9]. For example, CBC-MAC is shown to be insecure when the adversary is allowed to make quantum queries, even when the underlying blockcipher is quantum-secure, and the number of blocks are fixed. Since it is known that a quantum-secure PRF is also quantum-secure as a MAC [5], this shows that CBC-MAC is not a quantum-secure PRF, and the same is true for many other blockcipher-based MACs attacked in the paper. Similar results were independently discovered by Santoli and Schaffner in [13]. This brings us to the basic question:

Is domain extension for PRFs possible in the quantum setting?

1.1 Our Contributions

In this paper, we give a positive answer to this question. Our discovery is that NMAC and related schemes like HMAC, AMAC, and the (fixed-length) cascade construction are quantum-secure as PRFs. Together with results in [9], our work provides almost a complete picture on the PRF domain extension problem in the quantum world. We highlight some of our main proof ideas and contributions, followed by a gentle technical overview.

- **A general framework for oracle-indistinguishability of function distributions.** All constructions consist of iterated evaluations of the basic PRF, and the output from previous round is used as the *key* to determine the PRF in the next round. This is essentially giving multiple PRF oracles $F(k_i, \cdot)$ with independent keys k_i to the adversary. Luckily since the number of oracles is polynomially bounded classically (i.e., number of adversary's queries), this does not give the adversary more power by a simple hybrid argument relating to the standard PRF indistinguishability. However, when we allow quantum-accessible oracles, in effect, the adversary can query in quantum superposition exponentially many PRF oracles each with an independently random key. Our first technical contribution shows that, the standard notion of quantum-secure PRF implies this seemingly stronger notion, which enables us to prove security of the cascade construction (for fixed-length inputs) already. More generally we view this as *oracle-indistinguishability* of distributions over *functions*. Therefore we extend Zhandry's work to this setting and show equivalence between ordinary and oracle indistinguishability. We further generalize it, for applications in NMAC for example, to the setting that some additional oracle possibly dependent on the two distributions under consideration is also given to the adversary (we call this relative oracle-indistinguishability).
- **Direct hybrid argument for NMAC and variants.** NMAC and other variants can be viewed as "encrypted" version of the cascade construction by evaluating the output from cascade by another function (e.g., PRF under an independent key). Classical security proofs usually proceed by reducing to some property of its inner cascade. For example the famous "hash-then-PRF" paradigm states that the composition of a *(computationally) almost universal hash function* with a *PRF* gives a secure PRF with larger domain. Bellare [1] shows that the cascade construction is indeed computationally almost universal, and the composition theorem implies that NMAC is a secure PRF immediately. However, it is easy to see that this would not work in the quantum world; there are many universal hash functions with nontrivial periods, and if we start with such a periodic universal hash function, any hash-then-PRF construction inherits that period, which can be detected efficiently by quantum Fourier sampling. Therefore, one cannot prove the quantum security of hash-then-PRF constructions by relying solely on the (computationally almost) universality and the PRF security. Another approach by Gaži, Pietrzak, and Rybár [7] proves the security of NMAC by reducing it to the security of the cascade construction against *prefix-free* queries. However the notion of

prefix-free does not have a natural counterpart in the regime of quantum superposition queries. Instead, we prove the security of NMAC by a direct hybrid argument based on our relative oracle-indistinguishability framework for function distributions. We stress that this also provides an alternative (and cleaner in our opinion) proof for *classical security* as well.

- **Further properties of quantum-secure PRFs.** In proving the security of these constructions, we also give further characterizations and strengthened properties of PRFs. Specifically, we show that a quantum-secure PRF is also secure against key-recovery attacks, and in addition a PRF remains indistinguishable from a random oracle even if the PRF key is leaked in some restricted way. While the corresponding classical results are more or less straightforward, they face considerable difficulties to carry through quantumly. We hence demonstrate more examples and tools of quantum proof techniques where classical security can be "lifted" to quantum security.

Technical Overview. NMAC is a construction producing a variable-input-length PRF NMAC$[f]$, given a secure PRF $f : \{0,1\}^c \times \{0,1\}^b \to \{0,1\}^c$ (with $b \geq c$)[1]. Here, the first input argument is the key $k \in \{0,1\}^c$, the second input argument is the message block $x \in \{0,1\}^b$, and the output $f(k,x) = y \in \{0,1\}^c$ has the same bit length as the key. NMAC turns this f into a PRF with the key length of $2c$, the output length of c, and the unbounded input length by

$$\mathsf{NMAC}[f]((k_1, k_2), x_1 \ldots x_l) := f(k_2, \mathsf{Casc}[f](k_1, x_1 \ldots x_l) \| 0^{b-c}),$$

where $\mathsf{Casc}[f]$ is the *cascade construction* given as

$$\mathsf{Casc}[f](k, x_1 \ldots x_l) = f(\ldots f(f(k, x_1), x_2), \ldots, x_l).$$

To explain our methods, first let us discuss the cascade construction. It is well-known that the cascade construction would not be a secure PRF if messages of variable lengths are allowed. For example, an adversary may query $y = \mathsf{Casc}[f](k, x_1) = f(k, x_1)$, and compute $f(y, x_2) = \mathsf{Casc}[f](k, x_1 x_2)$, then query $\mathsf{Casc}[f](k, x_1 x_2)$ to check if the queried oracle is $\mathsf{Casc}[f]$ or a true random function. To prevent such an *extension attack*, one obvious way is to fix the number of blocks. More generally, one can prove security against prefix-free adversaries, who never make queries m and m' where m is a proper prefix of m'. In fact, the cascade construction is proved to be secure in this sense in [4]. To achieve full security, one would process the output of the cascade construction further, and this would give us schemes like NMAC/HMAC or AMAC.

Quantum security of fixed-length cascade. For quantum security, there seems no natural analogue of prefix-freeness in presence of quantum superposed

---

[1] To be precise, the definition of NMAC given here is a simplified version which is not exactly the same as the original definition given in [3], which for example can handle messages whose lengths are not divisible by the block length b. However, the differences do not affect the security, so previous works on NMAC, like [1,7], also analyzed this simplified version.

queries. Instead, we consider fixed-input-length cascade $\mathsf{Casc}_l[f]$, processing messages of total block length l, for arbitrary but fixed l.

It is easy to observe that, when $b = 1$, the l-fold cascade $\mathsf{Casc}_l[f]$ is the same as the Goldreich-Goldwasser-Micali construction [8] of a PRF out of a secure PRG. Zhandry in [20] proved that if the underlying PRG is secure against polynomial-time quantum adversaries, then the GGM construction remains quantum-secure. In fact, a PRG is equivalent to a PRF with a polynomial-size domain, therefore Zhandry's proof almost immediately applies to $\mathsf{Casc}_l[f]$ with such a small-sized PRF f. But, to remove the small-domain restriction, we need more work.

To get a sense of the general difficulty of proving quantum security, we briefly review the classical GGM proof. Roughly speaking, two hybrid arguments are used to construct a distinguisher for the underlying PRG from a distinguisher for the GGM construction; one hybrid argument is over the bit-length of the message inputs of the GGM PRF, and the other is over the individual queries made by the adversary. When trying to adapt the classical proof to quantum security, the first hybrid is not at all problematic, but the second hybrid is not usable; since the adversary in general makes many superposed queries which examine all bitstrings of the given length, the fact that only polynomially-many bitstrings are examined by queries of the adversary is no longer true in the quantum setting.

Zhandry resolves this, by observing that the second hybrid is in fact not necessary, and instead the first hybrid can be carried out by relying on the *oracle security* of the underlying PRG. Suppose D is a distribution on a set $\mathcal{Y}$. Let us define $D^{\mathcal{X}}$ as a distribution of functions of form $\mathcal{X} \to \mathcal{Y}$ where for each $x \in \mathcal{X}$, a function value $y \in \mathcal{Y}$ is chosen independently according to D. Then, two distributions D_1 and D_2 are said to be *oracle-indistinguishable*, if $D_1^{\mathcal{X}}$ and $D_2^{\mathcal{X}}$ are indistinguishable for all $\mathcal{X}$. We also say that a PRG G is *oracle-secure*, if its output distribution is oracle-indistinguishable from the uniform random distribution. This notion expresses indistinguishability of possibly exponentially many independent samples from the PRG (indexed by each $x \in \mathcal{X}$) and possibly exponentially many uniform random numbers, and oracle indistinguishability together with the first hybrid argument gives the security proof of GGM, both classically and quantumly. In the classical case, the oracle indistinguishability can be proved via a hybrid argument over the total number of adversarial queries, since at most polynomially many of the samples will be examined by the adversary. On the other hand, in the quantum case, a completely different approach is needed, which is given by Zhandry's "small-range distributions".

Returning to the cascade construction, we need to work with PRFs instead of PRGs. We may follow the same outline of the proof for the GGM construction, except we need oracle security of PRFs. Hence, we adapt the notion of oracle indistinguishability to function distributions. When D is a distribution of functions of form $\mathcal{X} \to \mathcal{Y}$, then for any set $\mathcal{Z}$, we define $D^{\mathcal{Z}}$ as the distribution of functions of form $f : \mathcal{Z} \times \mathcal{X} \to \mathcal{Y}$, sampled by choosing $f(z) \leftarrow D$ independently for each $z \in \mathcal{Z}$. (Note that we are using the 'currying' isomorphism here, regarding f as $f : \mathcal{Z} \to \mathcal{Y}^{\mathcal{X}}$.) Then, the oracle indistinguishability of D_1 and D_2

can be defined as indistinguishability of $D_1^{\mathcal{Z}}$ and $D_2^{\mathcal{Z}}$ for every set $\mathcal{Z}$. We prove oracle security of secure PRFs also by the small-range distributions.

Quantum security of NMAC. We prove the security of NMAC by a direct hybrid argument, adapting the hybrid argument for the cascade construction, rather than reducing to some property of the inner cascade in the classical literature. We start by the standard procedure of swapping the outer instance of the PRF f with a random oracle H; now the modified scheme is $H(\mathsf{Casc}[f](k, x_1 \ldots x_l)) = H(f(\ldots f(f(k, x_1), x_2), \ldots, x_l))$. Using a hybrid argument, we would like to repeatedly swap inner instances of the PRF f with true random functions, until only the true random function remains. However, we need a stronger security notion for the PRF f to do this: while the random oracle H prevents the fatal extension attack, still, queries of different block lengths would leak some information on the inner state of PRF instances. In particular, an adversary can make a single-block query x to obtain $H(f(k, x))$, and make a zero-block query to obtain $H(k)$. Here, the hash value $H(k)$ of the secret key k is leaked by the random oracle H, and this prevents using the indistinguishability of the PRF f. What we need is that $f(k, \cdot)$ should remain pseudorandom even when $H(k)$ is leaked and the random oracle H is accessible. We call this property the *security under random leakage*. Nonetheless, we prove that a quantum-secure PRF remains quantum-secure under random leakage, and therefore we do not need to impose this additional condition on a PRF.

To carry out the hybrid argument, however, we need another augmentation to the oracle indistinguishability: while our NMAC security proof itself is in the standard model, a random oracle H is introduced during the security proof, and the PRF security under random leakage is inherently a security notion in the (quantum) random oracle model. Hence we introduce and study oracle indistinguishability of function distributions, *relative to a random oracle H*. The function distributions may be in general dependent on the random oracle H, and an adversary always in addition has access to H to attack indistinguishability or oracle indistinguishability. The tools we introduced so far are enough to enable us to complete the hybrid argument and prove quantum security of NMAC finally.

Quantum security of augmented cascade and AMAC. In [2], Bellare, Bernstein, and Tessaro prove PRF security of AMAC. In fact, they analyze ACSC, which is the *augmented cascade*. We can say that ACSC is to AMAC as NMAC is to HMAC. In ACSC, the output of the usual cascade construction $\mathsf{Casc}[f]$ is further processed by a keyless output transform Out, which is typically truncation: $\mathsf{Out}(b_1 \ldots b_c) = b_1 \ldots b_r$ for some $r < c$. They show that the augmented cascade is a secure PRF, if f is secure under Out-leakage, that is, $f(k, \cdot)$ remains pseudorandom even when $\mathsf{Out}(k)$ is leaked. In this paper, using oracle indistinguishability of functions, we also prove that ACSC is quantum-secure if f is secure under Out-leakage.

Organization. Sect. 2 introduces basic notations and definitions. We develop our technical tool of oracle distribution for function distributions in Sect. 3.

Combined with the further properties of PRFs we establish in Sect. 4, we prove quantum security of NMAC and other constructions in Sect. 5.

2   Preliminaries

2.1   Notations and Conventions

In this paper, all constructions and security notions are *implicitly* asymptotic: many quantities and objects are parametrized by the main security parameter λ, but for simplicity, we will often omit writing the dependency on λ explicitly. Although it is in reality a family of sets $\{\mathcal{X}_\lambda\}_\lambda$, we write it simply as $\mathcal{X}_\lambda$, or even just $\mathcal{X}$. Similarly, a function $f : \mathcal{X} \to \mathcal{Y}$ in such a case is really a family $\{f_\lambda : \mathcal{X}_\lambda \to \mathcal{Y}_\lambda\}_\lambda$ of functions. We also omit the size input 1^λ from arguments of polynomial-time computable functions.

A quantity $p = p(\lambda)$ is *polynomially bounded*, if $p(\lambda) = O(\lambda^d)$ for some $d > 0$. We denote this as $p(\lambda) = poly(\lambda)$, or even, $p = poly()$. Similarly, a quantity $\epsilon = \epsilon(\lambda)$ is *negligible*, if $\epsilon(\lambda) \le 2^{-\omega(\log \lambda)}$. We denote this as $\epsilon(\lambda) = negl(\lambda)$, or even, $\epsilon = negl()$.

If D is a distribution, then $x \leftarrow D$ means x is sampled according to D. Also, if $\mathcal{X}$ is a set, then $x \leftarrow \mathcal{X}$ means that x is sampled from $\mathcal{X}$ uniform randomly.

For any $r \in \mathbb{N}$, we define $[r] := \{0, 1, \ldots, r - 1\}$.

Let $\mathcal{X}$ and $\mathcal{Y}$ be two sets. We denote by $\mathcal{Y}^\mathcal{X}$ the set of all functions from $\mathcal{X}$ to $\mathcal{Y}$. We sometimes call it the *function space* from $\mathcal{X}$ to $\mathcal{Y}$.

In this paper, we are mostly interested in quantum security. Unless explicitly mentioned otherwise, by an *adversary*, we always mean a polynomial-time quantum algorithm which may have access to some oracles, to which it can make polynomially many quantum superposed queries. Similarly, when we mention 'security', unless it is in a context describing previous works and comparing them with ours, it means quantum security. On the other hand, by an 'algorithm', we always mean a classical algorithm, unless mentioned otherwise.

2.2   I.i.d Samples of Functions

Following Zhandry [20], we introduce the notation $D^\mathcal{X}$ as follows.

Definition 2.1 (Indexed family of i.i.d. samples). *Let D be a probability distribution over a set $\mathcal{Y}$, and let $\mathcal{X}$ be another set. Then, we denote by $D^\mathcal{X}$ the probability distribution over $\mathcal{Y}^\mathcal{X}$, defined such that, f is sampled according to $D^\mathcal{X}$ if and only if $f(x)$ is sampled according to D, independently for each $x \in \mathcal{X}$.*

In other words, if $f \leftarrow D^\mathcal{X}$, then $\{f(x)\}_{x \in \mathcal{X}}$ is an indexed family of i.i.d. samples, where each $f(x)$ is distributed according to D.

Suppose D is a distribution over $\mathcal{Y}^\mathcal{X}$. Since $\mathcal{Y}^\mathcal{X}$ itself is just a set, the previous definition is applicable. Let us clarify this as the following definition.

Definition 2.2 (Indexed family of i.i.d. samples of functions). *Let D be a probability distribution over $\mathcal{Y}^{\mathcal{X}}$, and let $\mathcal{Z}$ be another set. We define the distribution $D^{\mathcal{Z}}$ of functions $f \in (\mathcal{Y}^{\mathcal{X}})^{\mathcal{Z}}$ as in Definition 2.1; if f is sampled according to $D^{\mathcal{Z}}$, then $f(z) \in \mathcal{Y}^{\mathcal{X}}$ is sampled according to D, independently for each $z \in \mathcal{Z}$.*

Then, evaluating $f(z) \in \mathcal{Y}^{\mathcal{X}}$ on $x \in X$ will give a value $f(z)(x) = y \in \mathcal{Y}$. Considering the 'currying' isomorphism $(\mathcal{Y}^{\mathcal{X}})^{\mathcal{Z}} \cong \mathcal{Y}^{\mathcal{Z} \times \mathcal{X}}$, we may regard $D^{\mathcal{Z}}$ as a distribution over $\mathcal{Y}^{\mathcal{Z} \times \mathcal{X}}$, writing $f(z, x)$, instead of $f(z)(x)$. We will use the two perspectives interchangeably.

In this paper, although our results are *not* in the quantum random oracle model, during the security proofs, we mostly work in the quantum random oracle model. In other words, all players, including the adversary, are given oracle access to a uniform random function $H : \mathcal{A} \to \mathcal{B}$, and various constructions depend on H. Therefore, we need to consider the case when a distribution D over $\mathcal{Y}^{\mathcal{X}}$ depends on H, that is, D and the uniform distribution of H are both marginal distributions of a joint distribution. Therefore, we give a definition of $D^{\mathcal{Z}}$, relative to a random oracle H:

Definition 2.3 (Indexed family of relative i.i.d. samples of functions). *Let $H : \mathcal{A} \to \mathcal{B}$ be a random oracle, that is, a uniform random function in $\mathcal{B}^{\mathcal{A}}$. And let D be a probability distribution over $\mathcal{Y}^{\mathcal{X}}$ which depends on H, and let $\mathcal{Z}$ be another set. We define the distribution $D_H^{\mathcal{Z}}$ relative to H as follows. To jointly sample f from $D_H^{\mathcal{Z}}$ and also a particular $h : \mathcal{A} \to \mathcal{B}$ as realization of the random variable H, first sample $h \leftarrow \mathcal{B}^{\mathcal{A}}$ uniform randomly, and form $D|h$, which is the conditional distribution of D conditioned on the event $H = h$. Finally, sample $f \leftarrow (D|h)^{\mathcal{Z}}$. When the dependence on the random oracle H is clear, we abuse the notation and simply write $D^{\mathcal{Z}}$, instead of $D_H^{\mathcal{Z}}$.*

In other words, when we are in the quantum random oracle model, at first a function h is sampled uniformly, as a realization of the random variable H. When a distribution D is dependent on H, then sampling $f \leftarrow D^{\mathcal{Z}}$ means that, $f(z)$ is independently sampled from $D|h$, for each $z \in \mathcal{Z}$.

2.3   Various Security Notions of PRFs

First, let us define the syntax of the pseudorandom function as follows:

Definition 2.4 (Pseudorandom function). *A pseudorandom function (PRF) is a polynomial-time computable function f of form $f : \mathcal{K} \times \mathcal{X} \to \mathcal{Y}$. We call the sets $\mathcal{K}$, $\mathcal{X}$, $\mathcal{Y}$ as the key space, the domain, and the codomain of f, respectively.*

The domain of a PRF may be of fixed size or arbitrarily large. For a blockcipher, $\mathcal{X}$ would be $\{0,1\}^n$ for some n. On the other hand, for HMAC, the domain $\mathcal{X}$ is the set of all bitstrings, or bitstrings up to some large fixed length.

In this paper, we are concerned with polynomial-time quantum adversaries who can make quantum superposed queries to their oracles. Therefore, our standard definition of PRF security is as follows:

Definition 2.5 (Quantum security of PRF). *Let $f : \mathcal{K} \times \mathcal{X} \to \mathcal{Y}$ be a PRF. We say that f is secure, if for any adversary A, we have the following:*

$$\mathbf{Adv}_f^{\mathsf{prf}}(A) := \left| \mathbf{Pr}[A^{f(k,\cdot)}() = 1] - \mathbf{Pr}[A^{\rho}() = 1] \right| = negl(),$$

where $k \leftarrow \mathcal{K}$, $\rho \leftarrow \mathcal{Y}^{\mathcal{X}}$ are uniformly and independently random.

That is, sampling $k \leftarrow \mathcal{K}$ and letting F as $F(x) := f(k,x)$, any quantum adversary cannot distinguishing F from a true random function $\rho : \mathcal{X} \to \mathcal{Y}$.

Here, $\mathbf{Adv}_f^{\mathsf{prf}}(A)$ is the *advantage* of A in distinguishing $f(k, \cdot)$ from ρ, and if f is a secure PRF, then the advantage is negligible for any adversary A.

Sometimes, we may want less than the full PRF security against distinguishing attack, and only require the following:

Definition 2.6 (Security of PRF against key recovery). *Let $f : \mathcal{K} \times \mathcal{X} \to \mathcal{Y}$ be a PRF. We say that f is secure against key recovery, if for any adversary A, we have the following:*

$$\mathbf{Adv}_f^{\mathsf{prf-kr}}(A) := \mathbf{Pr}[A^{f(k,\cdot)}() = k] = negl(),$$

where $k \leftarrow \mathcal{K}$ is uniformly random.

Classically, it is well known, and indeed trivial to prove that a secure PRF is also secure against key recovery. However, in the quantum world, it is less trivial than classically. We discuss this more in Sect. 4.

Finally, let us present a stronger security notion for PRF, which will be crucial later when we prove the security of NMAC.

Definition 2.7 (Security of PRF under random leakage). *Let $f : \mathcal{K} \times \mathcal{X} \to \mathcal{Y}$ be a PRF. We say that f is secure under random leakage, if for any set $\mathcal{W}$ and any adversary A, we have the following:*

$$\mathbf{Adv}_f^{\mathsf{prf-rl}}(A) := \left| \mathbf{Pr}[A^{f(k,\cdot),H}(H(k)) = 1] - \mathbf{Pr}[A^{\rho,H}(w) = 1] \right| = negl(),$$

where $k \leftarrow \mathcal{K}, w \leftarrow \mathcal{W}, H \leftarrow \mathcal{W}^{\mathcal{K}}, \rho \leftarrow \mathcal{Y}^{\mathcal{X}}$ are uniform, independent random.

The above notion is related to the leakage-resilient cryptography. Here, the PRF key k is leaked once, via the leakage function $H(\cdot)$. But, this leakage is very weak; the adversary does not choose H, which is just a random oracle.

2.4 NMAC and Related Constructions

In this subsection, we give definitions of NMAC and other hash-based PRFs which we study in this paper.

Cascade construction. Suppose that $f : \mathcal{K} \times \mathcal{X} \to \mathcal{K}$ is a PRF where the codomain is the same as the key space $\mathcal{K}$. We define the *l-fold cascade* of f, denoted by $\mathsf{Casc}_l[f] : \mathcal{K} \times \mathcal{X}^l \to \mathcal{K}$, as follows: given $k \in \mathcal{K}$ and $x_1, \ldots, x_l \in \mathcal{X}$, we define a sequence of values $y_0, \ldots, y_l \in \mathcal{K}$, recursively.

$$y_0 := k,$$
$$y_i = f(y_{i-1}, x_i), \qquad \text{for } i = 1, \ldots, l.$$

Then, the cascade PRF is given as the last value y_l.

$$\mathsf{Casc}_l[f](k, x_1 \ldots x_l) := y_l.$$

In other words,

$$\mathsf{Casc}_l[f](k, x_1 \ldots x_l) = f(\ldots f(f(k_1, x_1), x_2), \ldots, x_l).$$

From the definition of $\mathsf{Casc}_l[f]$, we see $\mathsf{Casc}_0[f] : \mathcal{K} \times \mathcal{X}^0 \to \mathcal{K}$ is given as

$$\mathsf{Casc}_0[f](k, \epsilon) = k,$$

where $\epsilon \in \mathcal{X}^0$ is the empty string of length 0.

NMAC. Suppose that $f : \mathcal{K} \times \mathcal{X} \to \mathcal{K}$ is a PRF where the codomain is the same as the key space $\mathcal{K}$. Here, we assume that $|\mathcal{K}| \leq |\mathcal{X}|$. The *NMAC* of f, denoted by $\mathsf{NMAC}[f] : \mathcal{K}^2 \times \mathcal{X}^* \to \mathcal{K}$ is defined as

$$\mathsf{NMAC}[f]((k_1, k_2), x_1 \ldots x_m) := f(k_2, \mathsf{pad}(\mathsf{Casc}_m[f](k_1, x_1 \ldots x_m))),$$

where $\mathsf{pad} : \mathcal{K} \to \mathcal{X}$ is a simple injective 'padding function'. Typically, when $\mathcal{X} = \{0,1\}^b$ and $\mathcal{K} = \{0,1\}^c$, then $\mathsf{pad}(k) = k \| 0^{b-c}$, but the choice of pad does not affect the security of NMAC.

Augmented cascade. Let $f : \mathcal{K} \times \mathcal{X} \to \mathcal{K}$ be a PRF where the codomain is the same as the key space $\mathcal{K}$, and let $\mathsf{Out} : \mathcal{K} \to \mathcal{Y}$ be an unkeyed function. Then, the *augmented cascade* $\mathsf{ACSC}[f, \mathsf{Out}] : \mathcal{K} \times \mathcal{X}^* \to \mathcal{Y}$ is

$$\mathsf{ACSC}[f, \mathsf{Out}](k, x_1 \ldots x_m) := \mathsf{Out}(\mathsf{Casc}_m[f](k, x_1 \ldots x_m)).$$

2.5   Implementing Oracles

Here, we are going to discuss which function distributions can be 'efficiently implemented'. One possible answer is the following:

Definition 2.8. *Let D be a function distribution over $\mathcal{Y}^{\mathcal{X}}$. We say that D is efficiently samplable, if there exists a set $\mathcal{R}$ and a polynomial-time deterministic algorithm $D.\mathsf{eval} : \mathcal{R} \times \mathcal{X} \to \mathcal{Y}$, such that sampling $f \in \mathcal{Y}^{\mathcal{X}}$ according to the distribution D can be done by sampling $r \leftarrow \mathcal{R}$ and defining f by $f(x) := D.\mathsf{eval}(r, x)$. We also require that $\log |\mathcal{R}| = \mathrm{poly}()$.*

In other words, we may sample a function $f \leftarrow D$, by sampling $r \leftarrow \mathcal{R}$.

One typical example of an efficiently samplable distribution is PRF_f over $\mathcal{Y}^{\mathcal{X}}$ of a PRF $f : \mathcal{K} \times \mathcal{X} \to \mathcal{Y}$. Here, $\mathcal{R} = \mathcal{K}$, and $\mathsf{PRF}_f.\mathsf{eval} = f$.

Zhandry shows that in fact we can efficiently 'implement' function distributions which are not necessarily efficiently samplable. One such example is the uniform distribution over $\mathcal{Y}^{\mathcal{X}}$. While it is not efficiently samplable in the above sense, still, given any adversary A making at most q quantum superposed queries, it is possible to implement the uniform distribution for the adversary A perfectly. This is due to Theorem 3.1 of [21]. Here, we give a slightly extended version as follows, whose proof we defer to the full version of our paper [15], due to page limitation.

Theorem 2.9. *Let A be an adversary having oracle access to $O_1, \ldots, O_t$, and makes at most q_i quantum queries to $O_i \in \mathcal{Y}_i^{\mathcal{X}_i}$ for $i = 1, \ldots, t$. If we draw O_i from any joint distribution for $i = 1, \ldots, t$, then for every v, the quantity $\mathbf{Pr}[A^{O_1, \ldots, O_t}() = v]$ is a linear combination of the quantities*

$$\mathbf{Pr}[\forall i \in \{1, \ldots, t\}, \forall j \in \{1, \ldots, 2q_i\}, O_i(x_j^{(i)}) = y_j^{(i)}]$$

for all possible settings of the values $x_j^{(i)} \in \mathcal{X}$ and $y_j^{(i)} \in \mathcal{Y}$.

Hence if D, D' are distributions over $\mathcal{Y}^{\mathcal{X}}$ which are $2q$-wise equivalent, i.e.,

$$\mathbf{Pr}_{O \leftarrow D}[\forall i \in \{1, ..., 2q\}, O(x_i) = y_i] = \mathbf{Pr}_{O \leftarrow D'}[\forall i \in \{1, ..., 2q\}, O(x_i) = y_i],$$

for any distinct $x_1, \ldots, x_{2q} \in \mathcal{X}$ and any $y_1, \ldots, y_{2q} \in \mathcal{Y}$, then when A makes at most q queries to its oracle, for any output value v of A, we have

$$\mathbf{Pr}_{O \leftarrow D}[A^O() = v] = \mathbf{Pr}_{O \leftarrow D'}[A^O() = v].$$

In particular, for any adversary making at most q quantum queries, the uniform random function $\mathsf{U} \in \mathcal{Y}^{\mathcal{X}}$ can be efficiently 'implemented' by any $2q$-wise independent function family. We use the following standard fact (for example, see p. 72 of [18]):

Proposition 2.10. *For every n, m, k, there exists a family of k-wise independent functions $\mathcal{H} = \{h : \{0,1\}^n \to \{0,1\}^m\}$ such that, choosing a function h from $\mathcal{H}$ takes $k \cdot \max\{n, m\}$ random bits, and evaluating $h \in \mathcal{H}$ takes time $poly(n, m, k)$.*

Therefore, implementing a uniform distribution in $\mathcal{Y}^{\mathcal{X}}$ for any adversary making q quantum queries requires sampling $2q \cdot \max\{\log |\mathcal{X}|, \log |\mathcal{Y}|\}$ bits, and answering one query takes time $poly(\log |\mathcal{X}|, \log |\mathcal{Y}|, q)$.

Let us propose the following definition which captures both efficiently samplable distributions and uniform distributions.

Definition 2.11. *Let D be a function distribution over $\mathcal{Y}^{\mathcal{X}}$. We say that D is bounded samplable, if there exists a set $\mathcal{R}^{(q)}$ for each q and a polynomial-time deterministic algorithm $D.eval : 1^* \times \bigcup_q \mathcal{R}^{(q)} \times \mathcal{X} \to \mathcal{Y}$ such that, if we sample $f \in \mathcal{Y}^{\mathcal{X}}$ according to the distribution D, and sample $f' \in \mathcal{Y}^{\mathcal{X}}$ by sampling $r \leftarrow \mathcal{R}^{(q)}$ and defining f' by $f'(x) := D.eval(1^q, r, x)$, then two random functions f and f' are $2q$-wise equivalent. Also, we require that $\log |\mathcal{R}^{(q)}| = poly(\lambda, q)$.*

If D is bounded samplable, then a function f can be sampled according to D by sampling $r \leftarrow \mathcal{R}^{(q)}$, and it can be evaluated by $f(x) = D.eval(1^q, r, x)$. The resulting distribution may not be identical to D, but would be enough to 'fool' any adversary making at most q queries. The following lemma is obvious.

Lemma 2.12. *For any $\mathcal{X}, \mathcal{Y}$, the uniform distribution over $\mathcal{Y}^{\mathcal{X}}$ is bounded samplable.*

Moreover, we can see from Theorem 2.9 that, when A has access to several oracles $O_1, \ldots, O_t$ sampled according to $D_1, \ldots, D_t$, and if they are *independent*, then if the distributions D_i are all bounded samplable, then they can be 'implemented' separately: sampling $f_i \leftarrow D_i$ can be done by sampling $r_i \leftarrow \mathcal{R}_i^{(q)}$, and letting $f_i(x) = D_i.eval(1^{q_i}, r_i, x)$ for all $i = 1, \ldots, t$, since we have

$$\mathbf{Pr}[\forall i \in \{1, \ldots, t\}, \forall j \in \{1, \ldots, 2q_i\}, O_i(x_j^{(i)}) = y_j^{(i)}]$$
$$= \prod_{i=1}^{t} \mathbf{Pr}[\forall j \in \{1, \ldots, 2q_i\}, O_i(x_j^{(i)}) = y_j^{(i)}]$$

Let $H : \mathcal{A} \to \mathcal{B}$ be a random oracle, that is, a uniform random function. For our purpose, we need to 'relativize' the efficient samplability and the bounded samplability, with respect to H. First, let us give the following definitions.

Definition 2.13. *Let $H : \mathcal{A} \to \mathcal{B}$ be a random oracle, and let D_i be a distribution over $\mathcal{Y}_i^{\mathcal{X}_i}$, for $i = 1, \ldots, t$. We say that $D_1, \ldots, D_t$ are conditionally independent relative to H, if for any $h \in \mathcal{B}^{\mathcal{A}}$, the distributions $D_1, \ldots, D_t$ are independent, conditioned on the event that $H = h$.*

Definition 2.14. *Let $H : \mathcal{A} \to \mathcal{B}$ be a random oracle, and let D, D' be distributions over $\mathcal{Y}^{\mathcal{X}}$. We say that D, D' are k-wise equivalent relative to H, if*

$$\mathbf{Pr}_{O \leftarrow D}[\forall i \in \{1, \ldots, k\}, O(x_i) = y_i \mid H = h]$$
$$= \mathbf{Pr}_{O \leftarrow D'}[\forall i \in \{1, \ldots, k\}, O(x_i) = y_i \mid H = h],$$

for any distinct $x_1, \ldots, x_k \in \mathcal{X}$, any $y_1, \ldots, y_k \in \mathcal{Y}$, and any $h \in \mathcal{B}^{\mathcal{A}}$.

Then, we are ready to define relative versions of efficient samplability and bounded samplability as follows.

Definition 2.15. *Let $H : \mathcal{A} \to \mathcal{B}$ be a random oracle, and let D be a distribution over $\mathcal{Y}^{\mathcal{X}}$. We say that D is efficiently samplable relative to H, if there exists a set $\mathcal{R}$ and a polynomial-time deterministic oracle algorithm $D.eval^H : \mathcal{R} \times \mathcal{X} \to \mathcal{Y}$ such that sampling $f \in \mathcal{Y}^{\mathcal{X}}$ according to D can be done by sampling $r \leftarrow \mathcal{R}$ and defining f by $f(x) := D.eval^H(r, x)$. We also require that $\log |\mathcal{R}| = poly()$.*

Definition 2.16. *Let $H : \mathcal{A} \to \mathcal{B}$ be a random oracle, and let D be a distribution over $\mathcal{Y}^{\mathcal{X}}$. We say that D is bounded samplable relative to H, if there exists a set $\mathcal{R}^{(q)}$ for each q, and a polynomial-time deterministic oracle algorithm $D.eval^H : 1^* \times \bigcup_q \mathcal{R}^{(q)} \times \mathcal{X} \to \mathcal{Y}$ such that, if we sample $f \in \mathcal{Y}^{\mathcal{X}}$*

according to D, and sample $f' \in \mathcal{Y}^{\mathcal{X}}$ by sampling $r \leftarrow \mathcal{R}^{(q)}$ and defining f'
by $f'(x) := D.eval^H(1^q, r, x)$, then f and f' are $2q$-wise equivalent relative to H.
We also require that $\log |\mathcal{R}^{(q)}| = poly(\lambda, q)$.

We have the following lemma about 'relative implementation' of an oracle.

Lemma 2.17. *Let $H : \mathcal{A} \to \mathcal{B}$ be a random oracle, and let D be a distribution*
over $\mathcal{Y}^{\mathcal{X}}$. Suppose D is bounded samplable relative to H, and suppose an adver-
sary $A^{O,H}$ makes at most q queries to O, and at most q_H queries to H. Let
D' be the distribution of function O sampled by sampling $r \leftarrow \mathcal{R}^{(q)}$ and letting
$O(x) := D.eval^H(1^q, r, x)$. Then, we have

$$\mathbf{Pr}_{O \leftarrow D}[A^{O,H}() = v] = \mathbf{Pr}_{O \leftarrow D'}[A^{O,H}() = v],$$

for any possible output value v of A.

Lemma 2.17 is an extension of the previous result that, if a distribution
D is bounded samplable, then for each adversary A, we can implement D to
completely fool A. This time, Lemma 2.17 says that if D is bounded samplable
relative to a random oracle H, then for any adversary A, we can implement D
to completely fool A, even when D is dependent on H and A also has access
to H. The proof can be done by simple arguments using conditional probability.
Due to page limitation, we defer the proof to the full version of this paper [15].

Similar to the non-relative case, if $D_1, \ldots, D_t$ are all distributions bounded
samplable relative to H, and if they are conditionally independent relative to H,
then it is easy to see that we can implement each oracle O_i sampled from D_i
separately, which will fool any adversary which has oracle access to not only
$O_1, \ldots, O_t$, but also to the random oracle H.

Let us give another lemma, to be used later. Note that the definition of the
distribution $D^{\mathcal{Z}}$ and its dependence on H is given in Definition 2.3.

Lemma 2.18. *Suppose that D is an efficiently samplable distribution over $\mathcal{Y}^{\mathcal{X}}$*
relative to a random oracle $H : \mathcal{A} \to \mathcal{B}$. If $\mathcal{Z}$ is any set, then $D^{\mathcal{Z}}$ is bounded
samplable relative to H.

Lemma 2.18 is generalization of the following: if D is an efficiently samplable
distribution over a set $\mathcal{Y}$, then Zhandry points out in [21] that the distribution
$D^{\mathcal{X}}$ can be 'constructed' for any set $\mathcal{X}$: if $\mathcal{R}$ is the randomness space for sampling
D, and if $y = f(r)$ is the element of $\mathcal{Y}$ sampled using randomness $r \in \mathcal{R}$, then we
can implement $O \leftarrow D^{\mathcal{X}}$ by first implementing a random function $\rho \in \mathcal{R}^{\mathcal{X}}$ and
then letting $O(x) = f(\rho(x))$. In our terminology, the distribution $D^{\mathcal{X}}$ is bounded
samplable.

Lemma 2.18 says that, when we form $D^{\mathcal{Z}}$ from an efficiently samplable distribution D of functions (relative to a random oracle H), the result is analogous:
the distribution $D^{\mathcal{Z}}$ is bounded samplable (relative to H). The proof is similar,
but the fact that we are dealing with functions, and also relative to a random
oracle, makes this slightly more complex. Again, we defer the proof to the full
version of this paper [15].

3   Relative Oracle Indistinguishability of Functions

In this paper, we are primarily interested in distributions of functions. We also consider the case where these distributions may be dependent on a random oracle $H : \mathcal{A} \to \mathcal{B}$, and the adversary has access to H as well.

Zhandry [20] defines "oracle indistinguishability" of two distributions D_1, D_2 over a set $\mathcal{Y}$. We adapt this notion to our case, giving the following definitions.

Definition 3.1 (Relative indistinguishability of functions). *Let* $H : \mathcal{A} \to \mathcal{B}$ *be a random oracle, and let* D_1, D_2 *be two distributions on* $\mathcal{Y}^{\mathcal{X}}$*, which are conditionally independent relative to* H*. Then, we say that* D_1 *and* D_2 *are indistinguishable relative to* H*, if for any adversary* A*, the distinguishing advantage*

$$\mathbf{Adv}^{\mathsf{rel\text{-}dist}}_{D_1, D_2, H}(A) := \left| \mathbf{Pr}_{O \leftarrow D_1} \left[A^{O,H}() = 1 \right] - \mathbf{Pr}_{O \leftarrow D_2} \left[A^{O,H}() = 1 \right] \right|$$

is negligible.

Definition 3.2 (Relative oracle indistinguishability of functions). *Let* $H : \mathcal{A} \to \mathcal{B}$ *be a random oracle, and let* D_1, D_2 *be two distributions over* $\mathcal{Y}^{\mathcal{X}}$*, which are conditionally independent relative to* H*. We say that* D_1 *and* D_2 *are oracle-indistinguishable relative to* H*, if, for any set* $\mathcal{Z}$*, and any adversary* A*, we have the following:*

$$\mathbf{Adv}^{\mathsf{oracle\text{-}rel\text{-}dist}}_{D_1, D_2, \mathcal{Z}, H}(A) := \left| \mathbf{Pr}_{O \leftarrow D_1^{\mathcal{Z}}} \left[A^{O,H}() = 1 \right] - \mathbf{Pr}_{O \leftarrow D_2^{\mathcal{Z}}} \left[A^{O,H}() = 1 \right] \right|$$

is negligible.

Note that, when $\mathcal{A}$ and $\mathcal{B}$ are singleton sets, the random oracle H is trivial, and we obtain non-relativized definitions of the above. Moreover we are only interested in the case when D_1 and D_2 are conditionally independent relative to H, which would make sense since these are definitions of indistinguishability in the quantum random oracle model.

The following is our main result regarding oracle indistinguishability.

Theorem 3.3. *Let* $H : \mathcal{A} \to \mathcal{B}$ *be a random oracle, and let* D_1, D_2 *be two function distributions over* $\mathcal{Y}^{\mathcal{X}}$ *for some* $\mathcal{X}, \mathcal{Y}$*. Suppose that both* $D_1^{\mathcal{Z}}$ *and* $D_2^{\mathcal{Z}}$ *are bounded samplable relative to* H*, for any set* $\mathcal{Z}$*. Further, suppose that* D_1 *and* D_2 *are conditionally independent relative to* H*, and indistinguishable relative to* H*. Then, they are oracle-indistinguishable relative to* H*.*

Concretely, for any adversary $A^{O,H}$ *making at most* q *queries to* O *and at most* q_H *queries to* H*, we can construct an adversary* $A_{\mathsf{rd}}^{O',H}$ *satisfying*

$$\mathbf{Adv}^{\mathsf{oracle\text{-}rel\text{-}dist}}_{D_1, D_2, \mathcal{Z}, H}(A) < 12 q^{3/2} \sqrt{\mathbf{Adv}^{\mathsf{rel\text{-}dist}}_{D_1, D_2, H}(A_{\mathsf{rd}})}.$$

Moreover, $A_{\mathsf{rd}}^{O',H}$ *makes at most* $2q$ *queries to* O' *and* $q_H + 2(q_{e_1} + q_{e_2})q$ *queries to* H*. Here,* q_{e_i} *is the maximum number of queries to* H *needed by one invocation to the evaluation algorithm* $D_i^{\mathcal{Z}}.\mathsf{eval}^H()$*, for* $i = 1, 2$*, respectively.*

Theorem 3.3 says that, if two function distributions are indistinguishable (relative to H), and if they satisfy some additional conditions, then they are also oracle-indistinguishable (relative to H).

Our proof of Theorem 3.3 proceeds similarly as Zhandry's proof of the corresponding result in [20]. Therefore, we are going to defer the complete proof to the full version of this paper [15], but here let us describe some outline of the proof.

To prove oracle indistinguishability of indistinguishable distributions over a set, Zhandry uses 'small-range distribution' [20], given as follows.

Definition 3.4. *Given a distribution D on $\mathcal{Y}$, we define $\mathrm{SR}_r^D(\mathcal{X})$ as the following distribution on functions $O \in \mathcal{Y}^{\mathcal{X}}$:*

- *For each $i \in [r]$, sample a value $y_i \in \mathcal{Y}$ according to the distribution D.*
- *For each $x \in \mathcal{X}$, sample a uniform random $i \in [r]$ and set $O(x) = y_i$.*

This can be applied to a distribution D over $\mathcal{Y}^{\mathcal{X}}$: since $\mathcal{Y}^{\mathcal{X}}$ is just a set, surely we may talk about a small-range distribution for D. Let us make this explicit:

Definition 3.5. *Given a function distribution D on $\mathcal{Y}^{\mathcal{X}}$, we define the small-range distribution $\mathrm{SR}_r^D(\mathcal{Z})$ as the following distribution on functions $O \in \mathcal{Y}^{\mathcal{Z} \times \mathcal{X}}$:*

- *For each $i \in [r]$, sample a function $f_i \in \mathcal{Y}^{\mathcal{X}}$ according to the distribution D.*
- *For each $z \in \mathcal{Z}$, sample a uniform random $i \in [r]$ and set $O(z) = f_i$.*

Following Definition 2.3, when D depends on the random oracle H, we interpret $\mathrm{SR}_r^D(\mathcal{Z})$ as follows:

Definition 3.6. *Given a function distribution D on $\mathcal{Y}^{\mathcal{X}}$ depending on a random oracle $H : \mathcal{A} \to \mathcal{B}$, we define the small-range distribution $\mathrm{SR}_r^D(\mathcal{Z})$ as follows. To jointly sample O from $\mathrm{SR}_r^D(\mathcal{Z})$ and also a particular $h : \mathcal{A} \to \mathcal{B}$ as realization of the random variable H, first sample $h \leftarrow \mathcal{B}^{\mathcal{A}}$ uniform randomly, and form $D|h$. Then,*

- *For each $i \in [r]$, sample a function $f_i \in \mathcal{Y}^{\mathcal{X}}$ according to $D|h$.*
- *For each $z \in \mathcal{Z}$, sample a uniform random $i \in [r]$ and set $O(z) = f_i$.*

Then, we have the following theorem.

Theorem 3.7. *Let $H : \mathcal{A} \to \mathcal{B}$ be a random oracle, and let D be a function distribution over $\mathcal{Y}^{\mathcal{X}}$ which is not necessarily independent from H. Suppose that A is an adversary making at most q queries to an oracle $O \in \mathcal{Y}^{\mathcal{X}}$, and at most q_H queries to the random oracle H. Then, we have*

$$\left| \mathbf{Pr}_{O \leftarrow \mathrm{SR}_r^D(\mathcal{Z})}[A^{O,H}() = 1] - \mathbf{Pr}_{O \leftarrow D^{\mathcal{Z}}}[A^{O,H}() = 1] \right| < \frac{16q^3}{r},$$

for any $r > 0$, and any set $\mathcal{Z}$.

Remark 3.8. Note that Theorem 3.7 holds, whether D is bounded samplable or not. The bound in the theorem does not depend on q_H either.

Just like the corresponding result in [20], Theorem 3.7 says that the distribution $D^{\mathcal{Z}}$, which is the distribution of an exponentially many independent samples of D indexed by $\mathcal{Z}$ is, in fact, indistinguishable from similar collection of samples, this time duplicated from only r independent samples. Theorem 3.7 also says that the result holds regardless of dependence to a random oracle H. We give the complete proof in the full version of this paper [15].

In the classical cases, we can prove oracle indistinguishability of two indistinguishable distributions by a hybrid argument over the adversarial queries: even though $O \leftarrow D^{\mathcal{Z}}$ can be considered as a collection of exponentially many independent samples of D, if a classical adversary A makes q queries $z_1, \ldots, z_q$, then all A examines are $O(z_1), \ldots, O(z_q) \leftarrow D$, and these can be swapped to samples from another indistinguishable distribution D' one by one.

On the other hand, in the quantum case, each query can be superposed, so the previous approach would not work. Small-range distribution solves this: once we switch to a small-range distribution of size r, then only r independent samples from a distribution D are involved, and they can be swapped to samples from another indistinguishable distribution D' one by one, and the resulting small-range distribution can be once again switched to $D'^{\mathcal{Z}}$. Hence, the proof of Theorem 3.3 is again a standard hybrid argument, which we defer to the full version of this paper [15].

4   Security Against Key Recovery and Security Under Random Leakage

In this section, we characterize further properties about a quantum-secure PRF, which will be useful later (to establish quantum security of NMAC for example). We first show that a secure PRF is also secure against key recovery. Using this, we prove that a secure PRF is secure under random leakage as well. This further enables us to study oracle security under random leakage for PRFs.

4.1   Security of PRFs Against Key Recovery

First, we have the following theorem:

Theorem 4.1. *Let $f : \mathcal{K} \times \mathcal{X} \to \mathcal{Y}$ be a secure PRF. Suppose that both the domain and the codomain of f are superpolynomially large: $|\mathcal{X}|, |\mathcal{Y}| \geq 2^{\omega(\log \lambda)}$. Then, f is also secure against key recovery.*

Concretely, for any adversary $A^{f(k,\cdot)}$ making at most q queries to $f(k, \cdot)$ with uniform random $k \leftarrow \mathcal{K}$, we can construct an adversary A_{d} that makes at most $q + 1$ queries such that

$$\mathbf{Adv}_f^{\mathsf{prf\text{-}kr}}(A) \leq \mathbf{Adv}_f^{\mathsf{prf}}(A_{\mathsf{d}}) + \frac{1}{|\mathcal{Y}|} + \frac{4q}{\sqrt{|\mathcal{X}|}}.$$

Classically, it is easy to prove that a secure PRF f is also secure against key recovery: if A is a classical key recovery attacker, then using A, we can construct a PRF distinguisher B: B^O runs A^O, while answering any query of A by its own query. In the end, if A outputs a candidate k, then B uses this k to determine whether O is a true random function ρ or a PRF instance $f(k, \cdot)$, by choosing an unqueried point $z \in \mathcal{X}$ and see if

$$f(k, z) = O(z).$$

If $O(\cdot) = f(k, \cdot)$ and if A correctly found the key k, then the above equation holds. On the other hand, if $O = \rho$, then $O(z)$ is uniform random, independent from $f(k, z)$, so the probability that $f(k, z) = O(z)$ is only $1/|\mathcal{Y}|$. This difference in probability can be used to distinguish the two cases.

On the other hand, if A is a quantum adversary, the case when $O(\cdot) = f(k, \cdot)$ is essentially the same as in the classical case. However, we may not apply the classical argument when O is a truly random function since the notion of "unqueried" point no longer makes sense under quantum (e.g., uniform superposition) queries. Therefore, we need a different approach in the quantum world. We defer the proof of Theorem 4.1 to the full version of this paper [15], due to page limitation. Note that it is possible to employ a coarse counting argument to prove key-recovery security, which works against both classical and quantum attacks. But it relies on specific settings of keyspace, domain and codomain, and the bound is typically not as tight as what our strategy can prove.

4.2 Security of PRFs Under Random Leakage

We show next that random leakage of the PRF key does not compromise the security of a PRF.

Theorem 4.2. *Let $f : \mathcal{K} \times \mathcal{X} \to \mathcal{Y}$ be a secure PRF, with $\mathcal{X}$ and $\mathcal{Y}$ superpolynomially large. Then, f is also secure under random leakage.*

Concretely, for any adversary $A^{O,H}$ making at most q queries to O and q_H queries to H, we can construct adversaries A_{kr} and A_d such that

$$\mathbf{Adv}_f^{\mathsf{prf\text{-}rl}}(A) \le 2q_H \sqrt{\mathbf{Adv}_f^{\mathsf{prf\text{-}kr}}(A_{kr})} + \mathbf{Adv}_f^{\mathsf{prf}}(A_d).$$

Here, both A_{kr} and A_d make at most q oracle queries.

To prove Theorem 4.2, we are going to use the following lemma of Unruh.

Lemma 4.3 (One-Way to Hiding Lemma of) *[17]). Let $H : \mathcal{X} \to \mathcal{Y}$ be a random oracle. Consider an adversary A making at most q queries to H. Let B be an adversary that on input x does the following: pick $i \leftarrow \{1, \dots, q\}$ and $y \leftarrow \mathcal{Y}$, run $A^H(x, y)$ until (just before) the ith query, then measure the ith query in the computational basis, and output the outcome. (When A makes less than i queries, B outputs $\perp \notin \mathcal{X}$.) Then, we have*

$$\left| \mathbf{Pr}_{x \leftarrow \mathcal{X}}[A^H(x, H(x)) = 1] - \mathbf{Pr}_{\substack{x \leftarrow \mathcal{X} \\ y \leftarrow \mathcal{Y}}}[A^H(x, y) = 1] \right| \le 2q\sqrt{\mathbf{Pr}_{x \leftarrow \mathcal{X}}[B^H(x) = x]}.$$

Now, we are ready to prove Theorem 4.2:

Proof. Let $f : \mathcal{K} \times \mathcal{X} \to \mathcal{Y}$ be a secure PRF. To show that f is secure under random leakage, we need to show that for any set $\mathcal{W}$ and any adversary A, the advantage $\mathbf{Adv}_f^{\text{prf-rl}}(A)$ is negligible. Suppose A makes at most q queries to O, and at most q_H queries to H. Then,

$$\begin{aligned}
\mathbf{Adv}_f^{\text{prf-rl}}(A) &= \left| \mathbf{Pr}[A^{f(k,\cdot),H}(H(k)) = 1] - \mathbf{Pr}[A^{\rho,H}(w) = 1] \right| \\
&\leq \left| \mathbf{Pr}[A^{f(k,\cdot),H}(H(k)) = 1] - \mathbf{Pr}[A^{f(k,\cdot),H}(w) = 1] \right| \\
&\quad + \left| \mathbf{Pr}[A^{f(k,\cdot),H}(w) = 1] - \mathbf{Pr}[A^{\rho,H}(w) = 1] \right|.
\end{aligned}$$

It suffices to bound both terms. First, let us bound

$$\left| \mathbf{Pr}[A^{f(k,\cdot),H}(H(k)) = 1] - \mathbf{Pr}[A^{f(k,\cdot),H}(w) = 1] \right|.$$

Let us define the algorithm $A_1^H(k, w)$ as follows: it runs $A^{O,H}(w)$ while any H-query is answered by H-query of A_1 itself, and any O-query $|x\rangle$ is answered by $|x\rangle|f(k, x)\rangle$. And when $A^{O,H}(w)$ eventually halts with an output v, $A_1^H(k, w)$ outputs v and halts.

So,

$$\begin{aligned}
A_1^H(k, H(k)) &= A^{f(k,\cdot),H}(H(k)), \\
A_1^H(k, w) &= A^{f(k,\cdot),H}(w).
\end{aligned}$$

From Lemma 4.3, we have

$$\begin{aligned}
&\left| \mathbf{Pr}[A^{f(k,\cdot),H}(H(k)) = 1] - \mathbf{Pr}[A^{f(k,\cdot),H}(w) = 1] \right| \\
&= \left| \mathbf{Pr}[A_1^H(k, H(k)) = 1] - \mathbf{Pr}[A_1^H(k, w) = 1] \right| \\
&\leq 2q_H \sqrt{\mathbf{Pr}[B_1^H(k) = k]},
\end{aligned}$$

where the algorithm $B_1^H(k)$ can be described as follows: B_1 picks $i \leftarrow \{1, \ldots, q_H\}$, $w \leftarrow \mathcal{W}$, and runs $A_1^H(k, w) = A^{f(k,\cdot),H}(w)$ until the ith H-query, then measure the ith query and output the outcome.

Now, using A, we construct an adversary A_{kr} mounting key recovery attack on f. The algorithm A_{kr} has oracle access to $f(k, \cdot)$ for uniform random $k \leftarrow \mathcal{K}$, and A_{kr} works as follows: A_{kr} picks $i \leftarrow \{1, \ldots, q_H\}$, $w \leftarrow \mathcal{W}$, and runs $A^{f(k,\cdot),H}(w)$, while implementing $H : \mathcal{K} \to \mathcal{W}$ by a $2q_H$-wise independent function, until the ith H-query, then measure the ith query and output the outcome.

By construction, we have $\mathbf{Pr}[A_{\text{kr}}^{f(k,\cdot)}() = k] = \mathbf{Pr}[B_1^H(k) = k]$. Therefore,

$$\left| \mathbf{Pr}[A^{f(k,\cdot),H}(H(k)) = 1] - \mathbf{Pr}[A^{f(k,\cdot),H}(w) = 1] \right| \leq 2q_H \sqrt{\mathbf{Adv}_f^{\text{prf-kr}}(A_{\text{kr}})}.$$

Note that the adversary A_{kr} makes at most q queries to its oracle $f(k, \cdot)$.

Next, let us bound

$$\left| \mathbf{Pr}[A^{f(k,\cdot),H}(w) = 1] - \mathbf{Pr}[A^{\rho,H}(w) = 1] \right|.$$

This is straightforward: using A, we construct an adversary A_d attacking PRF security of f. The algorithm A_d has oracle access to O, which can be $f(k, \cdot)$ or a true random function ρ. Now, the algorithm A_d works as follows: A_d picks $w \leftarrow \mathcal{W}$, and runs $A^{O,H}(w)$, answering any O-query of A by an O-query of itself, and implementing $H : \mathcal{K} \rightarrow \mathcal{W}$ by a $2q_H$-wise independent function. When A halts and outputs a value v eventually, A_d also halts and outputs v.

By construction, we have

$$\left| \mathbf{Pr}[A^{f(k,\cdot),H}(w) = 1] - \mathbf{Pr}[A^{\rho,H}(w) = 1] \right|$$
$$= \left| \mathbf{Pr}[A_\mathsf{d}^{f(k,\cdot)}() = 1] - \mathbf{Pr}[A_\mathsf{d}^{\rho}() = 1] \right| = \mathbf{Adv}_f^{\mathsf{prf}}(A_\mathsf{d}).$$

The adversary A_d also makes at most q queries. This proves the theorem. □

4.3 Oracle-Secure PRF Under Random Leakage

In order to prove security of NMAC, we are going to use the notion of oracle security under random leakage, which we define as follows.

Definition 4.4 (Oracle security under random leakage). *Let* $f : \mathcal{K} \times \mathcal{X} \rightarrow \mathcal{Y}$ *be a PRF. We say that* f *is* oracle-secure under random leakage, *if for any sets* $\mathcal{W}, \mathcal{Z}$, *the following holds for any adversary* A:

$$\mathbf{Adv}_{f,\mathcal{Z},\mathcal{W}}^{\mathsf{os\text{-}rl}}(A) := \left| \mathbf{Pr}[A^{O_0,H}() = 1] - \mathbf{Pr}[A^{O_1,H}() = 1] \right| = negl()$$

where the oracles O_0, O_1 *are defined as*

$$O_0(z, x) := (H(\kappa(z)), f(\kappa(z), x)),$$
$$O_1(z, x) := (\rho_1(z), \rho_2(z, x)),$$

and $H \leftarrow \mathcal{W}^{\mathcal{K}}, \kappa \leftarrow \mathcal{K}^{\mathcal{Z}}, \rho_1 \leftarrow \mathcal{W}^{\mathcal{Z}}, \rho_2 \leftarrow \mathcal{Y}^{\mathcal{Z} \times \mathcal{X}}$ *are chosen uniform randomly, and independently.*

We can show that any secure PRF f is also oracle-secure under random leakage:

Theorem 4.5. *Let* $f : \mathcal{K} \times \mathcal{X} \rightarrow \mathcal{Y}$ *be a secure PRF, with* $\mathcal{X}$ *and* $\mathcal{Y}$ *superpolynomially large. Then,* f *is also oracle-secure under random leakage.*

Concretely, for any adversary $A^{O,H}$ *making at most* q *queries to* O *and at most* q_H *queries to* H, *we can construct an adversary* A_rl *such that*

$$\mathbf{Adv}_{f,\mathcal{Z},\mathcal{W}}^{\mathsf{os\text{-}rl}}(A) < 12q^{3/2}\sqrt{\mathbf{Adv}_f^{\mathsf{prf\text{-}rl}}(A_\mathsf{rl})},$$

where $A_\mathsf{rl}^{O,H}$ *makes at most* $2q$ *queries to* O, *and* $q_H + 2q$ *queries to* H.

Proof. Consider the distribution PRFRL_f over $(\mathcal{W} \times \mathcal{Y})^{\mathcal{X}}$ which is efficiently samplable relative to H: the randomness space $\mathcal{R}$ is just the key space $\mathcal{K}$ of f, and the evaluation algorithm is given by $\mathsf{PRFRL}_f.eval^H(k, x) := (H(k), f(k, x))$.

Consider another distribution RU over $(\mathcal{W} \times \mathcal{Y})^{\mathcal{X}}$ of f defined by $f(x) := (w, \rho(x))$, where $w \leftarrow \mathcal{W}$ and $\rho \leftarrow \mathcal{Y}^{\mathcal{X}}$ are chosen uniform randomly and independently.

It is clear that the oracle security of f under random leakage is merely restatement of the oracle indistinguishability of PRFRL_f and RU relative to H.

Since f is secure, we may use Theorem 4.2 to show that f is secure under random leakage, and this is equivalent to indistinguishability of PRFRL_f and RU relative to H. Therefore, we are going to use Theorem 3.3 to show that the two are oracle-indistinguishable relative to H.

By construction, PRFRL_f and RU are independent, and since PRFRL_f is efficiently samplable relative to H, $\mathsf{PRFRL}_f^{\mathcal{Z}}$ is bounded samplable relative to H for any set $\mathcal{Z}$, due to Lemma 2.18. Then, the only thing remaining to be proved to invoke Theorem 3.3 is that $\mathsf{RU}^{\mathcal{Z}}$ is bounded samplable for any set $\mathcal{Z}$. But this is to prove that the distribution of the oracle $O_1(z, x) = (\rho_1(z), \rho_2(z, x))$ is bounded samplable, which is now trivially true.

Concretely, for any adversary A attacking oracle security under random leakage of f making at most q queries to O and q_H queries to H, by Theorem 3.3, we have

$$\mathbf{Adv}^{\mathsf{os\text{-}rl}}_{f, \mathcal{Z}, \mathcal{W}}(A) = \mathbf{Adv}^{\mathsf{oracle\text{-}rel\text{-}dist}}_{\mathsf{PRFRL}_f, \mathsf{RU}, \mathcal{Z}, H}(A)$$
$$< 12q^{3/2}\sqrt{\mathbf{Adv}^{\mathsf{rel\text{-}dist}}_{\mathsf{PRFRL}_f, \mathsf{RU}, H}(A_{\mathsf{rd}})},$$

for some adversary $A_{\mathsf{rd}}^{O', H}$ attacking indistinguishability of PRFRL_f and RU relative to H, which makes at most $2q$ queries to O' and $q_H + 2(1 + 0)q$ queries to H, since 1 call to H is required to implement $\mathsf{PRFRL}_f^{\mathcal{Z}}$, and 0 calls to H are required to implement $\mathsf{RU}^{\mathcal{Z}}$.

Now we can trivially turn A_{rd} into A_{rl} attacking security of f under random leakage: $A_{\mathsf{rl}}^{O, H}(w) := A_{\mathsf{rd}}^{w \| O', H}()$, satisfying $\mathbf{Adv}^{\mathsf{rel\text{-}dist}}_{\mathsf{PRFRL}_f, \mathsf{RU}, H}(A_{\mathsf{rd}}) = \mathbf{Adv}^{\mathsf{prf\text{-}rl}}_f(A_{\mathsf{rl}})$. Like A_{rd}, $A_{\mathsf{rl}}^{O, H}$ makes at most $2q$ queries to O and $q_H + 2q$ queries to H. □

5 Security of NMAC and Other Constructions

In this section, we prove the PRF security of cascade, NMAC, HMAC, augmented cascade, and AMAC, using ingredients we have developed so far.

5.1 Security of the Cascade

The cascade construction is not secure when queries of different block lengths are allowed. However, if we fix the total number l of blocks for all messages, then it becomes a quantum-secure PRF. Since its proof is a simpler version of that of NMAC, we only state the theorem below and refer the readers to the proof of NMAC in Sect. 5.2.

Theorem 5.1 (Security of the cascade construction). *Let* $f : \mathcal{K} \times \mathcal{X} \to \mathcal{K}$ *be a secure PRF. Then,* $\mathsf{Casc}_l[f]$ *is a secure PRF, for any fixed* l.

Concretely, for any adversary A *of* $\mathsf{Casc}_l[f]$ *making at most* q *oracle queries, we can construct an adversary* A_d *making at most* $4q$ *oracle queries, such that*

$$\mathbf{Adv}^{\mathsf{prf}}_{\mathsf{Casc}_l[f]}(A) \leq 34lq^{3/2}\sqrt{\mathbf{Adv}^{\mathsf{prf}}_f(A_\mathsf{d})}.$$

5.2   Security of NMAC

We are now ready to prove the security of NMAC as a quantum PRF.

Theorem 5.2 (NMAC security). *Let* $f : \mathcal{K} \times \mathcal{X} \to \mathcal{K}$ *be a secure PRF. Then,* $\mathsf{NMAC}[f]$ *is a secure PRF.*

Concretely, for any adversary A *of* $\mathsf{NMAC}[f]$ *making at most* q *oracle queries, where each message has at most* l *message blocks, we can construct adversaries* A_d, A_rl, *such that*

$$\mathbf{Adv}^{\mathsf{prf}}_{\mathsf{NMAC}[f]}(A) \leq \mathbf{Adv}^{\mathsf{prf}}_f(A_\mathsf{d}) + 34(l+1)q^{3/2}\sqrt{\mathbf{Adv}^{\mathsf{prf\text{-}rl}}_f(A_\mathsf{rl})}.$$

Moreover, A_d^O *makes at most* q *queries to* O, *and* $A_\mathsf{rl}^{O,H}$ *makes at most* $4q$ *queries to* O, *and at most* $6q$ *queries to* H.

Proof. Let A be an adversary making at most q oracle queries, where each message has at most l message blocks. We are going to define a sequence of games, where in each game, A has access to an oracle O. The only difference between the games is how the oracle O is defined.

Here's our first game N.

Game N : In this game, the oracle O is given exactly as $\mathsf{NMAC}[f]$: first, $k_1, k_2 \leftarrow \mathcal{K}$ are picked uniform randomly and independently. Then, for any message $x_1 \ldots x_j$ of j-blocks $(j = 0, 1, \ldots, l)$, the oracle O is defined as

$$O(x_1 \ldots x_j) = f(k_2, \mathsf{pad}(f(\ldots f(f(k_1, x_1), x_2), \ldots, x_j))).$$

In the next game G_0, the outer instance of the PRF f is swapped with a random function $H : \mathcal{K} \to \mathcal{K}$.

Game G_0: In this game, the oracle O is given as follows: first, $k \leftarrow \mathcal{K}$, $H \leftarrow \mathcal{K}^\mathcal{K}$ are picked uniform randomly and independently. Then, for any message $x_1 \ldots x_j$ of j-blocks $(j = 0, 1, \ldots, l)$, the oracle O is defined as

$$O(x_1 \ldots x_j) = H(f(\ldots f(f(k, x_1), x_2), \ldots, x_j)).$$

Continuing, for each $i = 1, \ldots, l+1$, we define games G_i as follows.

Game G_i: In this game, the oracle O is given as follows: first, $H \leftarrow \mathcal{K}^\mathcal{K}$, $R \leftarrow \mathcal{K}^{\mathcal{X}^i}$, $R_j \leftarrow \mathcal{K}^{\mathcal{X}^j}$ (for $j = 0, \ldots, i-1$) are picked uniform randomly and independently. Then, for any message $x_1 \ldots x_j$ of j-blocks $(j = 0, 1, \ldots, l)$, the oracle O is defined as

$$O(x_1 \ldots x_j) = \begin{cases} R_j(x_1 \ldots x_j) & \text{if } j = 0, \ldots, i-1, \\ H(R(x_1 \ldots x_i)) & \text{if } j = i, \\ H(f(\ldots f(R(x_1 \ldots x_i), x_{i+1}), \ldots, x_j)) & \text{if } j = i+1, \ldots, l. \end{cases}$$

Note that the game G_0 is in fact a special case of the above games G_i; when $i = 0$, the definition of O in the game G_i degenerates to

$$O() = H(R()),$$
$$O(x_1 \ldots x_j) = H(f(\ldots f(R(), x_1), \ldots, x_j)),$$

where $k = R() \in \mathcal{K}$ serves as the secret key in the game G_0.

Also, let's take a special look at the final game G_{l+1}: we have

$$O() = R_0(),$$
$$O(x_1) = R_1(x_1),$$
$$\vdots$$
$$O(x_1 \ldots x_l) = R_l(x_1 \ldots x_l).$$

Therefore, in the game G_{l+1}, the oracle O is a true random function defined over the domain $\bigcup_{i=0}^{l} \mathcal{X}^i$.

For any game G and an adversary A, let $G(A)$ be the final output of A when A is executed in the game G. We see that

$$\begin{aligned} \mathbf{Adv}^{\mathsf{prf}}_{\mathsf{NMAC}[f]}(A) &= |\mathbf{Pr}[N(A) = 1] - \mathbf{Pr}[G_{l+1}(A) = 1]| \\ &\leq |\mathbf{Pr}[N(A) = 1] - \mathbf{Pr}[G_0(A) = 1]| \\ &\quad + |\mathbf{Pr}[G_0(A) = 1] - \mathbf{Pr}[G_{l+1}(A) = 1]|. \end{aligned}$$

First, it is easy to see that

$$|\mathbf{Pr}[N(A) = 1] - \mathbf{Pr}[G_0(A) = 1]| \leq \mathbf{Adv}^{\mathsf{prf}}_f(A_{\mathsf{d}}),$$

for some adversary A_{d} attacking the PRF security of f; we can construct the adversary A_{d}^O distinguishing $f(k, \cdot)$ and $\rho \leftarrow \mathcal{K}^{\mathcal{X}}$ as follows: the adversary A_{d}^O picks $k' \leftarrow \mathcal{K}$, and runs A. For any query $x_1 \ldots x_j$ of A (for $j \leq l$), return

$$O(\mathsf{pad}(f(\ldots f(f(k', x_1), x_2), \ldots, x_j))).$$

When A eventually halts with an output v, A_{d} also halts with v.

Now, when $O(x) = f(k, x)$ for $k \leftarrow \mathcal{K}$, the query $x_1 \ldots x_j$ is answered by $\mathsf{NMAC}[f]$, and when $O = \rho \leftarrow \mathcal{K}^{\mathcal{X}}$, then the function $H(k) := O(\mathsf{pad}(k))$ is a true random function uniformly random over $\mathcal{K}^{\mathcal{K}}$. In this case, the query of the adversary A is answered exactly like in the game G_0. In fact,

$$\mathbf{Adv}^{\mathsf{prf}}_f(A_{\mathsf{d}}) = |\mathbf{Pr}[N(A) = 1] - \mathbf{Pr}[G_0(A) = 1]|.$$

Next, we are going to construct an adversary $A_{\text{os-rl}}$ attacking the oracle security of f under random leakage, with respect to the set $\mathcal{X}^{l-1}$ and the random oracle $H : \mathcal{K} \to \mathcal{K}$. The adversary $A_{\text{os-rl}}^{O',H}$ can be described as follows.

1. $A_{\text{os-rl}}$ has access to two oracles O', H, where $H : \mathcal{K} \to \mathcal{K}$ is a random oracle, and the oracle $O' : \mathcal{X}^{l-1} \times \mathcal{X} \to \mathcal{K} \times \mathcal{K}$ is either $O_0'(z,x) = (H(\kappa(z)), f(\kappa(z), x))$ or $O_1'(z,x) = (\rho_1(z), \rho_2(z,x))$, for uniform random and independent $\kappa \leftarrow \mathcal{K}^{\mathcal{X}^{l-1}}$, $\rho_1 \leftarrow \mathcal{K}^{\mathcal{X}^{l-1}}$, and $\rho_2 \leftarrow \mathcal{K}^{\mathcal{X}^{l-1} \times \mathcal{X}}$. Let us parse O' into two parts and let $O'(z,x) = (O^{(1)}(z), O^{(2)}(z,x))$. Here, $O^{(1)} : \mathcal{X}^{l-1} \to \mathcal{K}$ and $O^{(2)} : \mathcal{X}^{l-1} \times \mathcal{X} \to \mathcal{K}$.
2. $A_{\text{os-rl}}$ picks a uniform random $i \leftarrow \{0, \dots, l\}$. Also, $A_{\text{os-rl}}$ implements independent uniform random functions $R_j \leftarrow \mathcal{K}^{\mathcal{X}^j}$ using bounded samplability, for $j = 0, \dots, i-1$.
3. $A_{\text{os-rl}}$ runs the adversary A until it halts, while answering any query $x_1 \dots x_j$ of A (for $j = 0, 1, \dots, l$) as $O(x_1 \dots x_j)$, which is defined as follows:

$$O(x_1 \dots x_j)$$
$$= \begin{cases} R_j(x_1 \dots x_j) & \text{if } j = 0, \dots, i-1, \\ O^{(1)}(0^{l-i-1} x_1 \dots x_i) & \text{if } j = i, \\ H(f(\dots f(O^{(2)}(0^{l-i-1} x_1 \dots x_i, x_{i+1}), x_{i+2}), \dots, x_j)) & \text{if } j = i+1, \dots, l. \end{cases}$$

In the above, $0 \in \mathcal{X}$ is an arbitrarily fixed element of $\mathcal{X}$.

4. Eventually, when A halts with an output v, $A_{\text{os-rl}}$ also halts, outputting v.

We remark that $A_{\text{os-rl}}$ makes at most two O'-queries and two H-queries to answer one query of A (for computing and uncomputing). Since A makes at most q oracle queries, $A_{\text{os-rl}}$ makes at most $2q$ queries to O' and $2q$ queries to H.

Now, conditioned on the event that a specific i is chosen on line 2, if the oracle O' is given as $O_0'(z,x) = (H(\kappa(z)), f(\kappa(z), x))$, then the oracle O is given as follows:

$$O(x_1 \dots x_j)$$
$$= \begin{cases} R_j(x_1 \dots x_j) & \text{if } j = 0, \dots, i-1, \\ H(\kappa(0^{l-i-1} x_1 \dots x_i)) & \text{if } j = i, \\ H(f(\dots f(f(\kappa(0^{l-i-1} x_1 \dots x_i), x_{i+1}), x_{i+2}), \dots, x_j)) & \text{if } j = i+1, \dots, l. \end{cases}$$

We see that this oracle is identically distributed as the oracle in game G_i.

On the other hand, if the oracle O' is given as $O_1'(z,x) = (\rho_1(z), \rho_2(z,x))$, then we have:

$$O(x_1 \dots x_j)$$
$$= \begin{cases} R_j(x_1 \dots x_j) & \text{if } j = 0, \dots, i-1, \\ \rho_1(0^{l-i-1} x_1 \dots x_i) & \text{if } j = i, \\ H(f(\dots f(\rho_2(0^{l-i-1} x_1 \dots x_i, x_{i+1}), x_{i+2}), \dots, x_j)) & \text{if } j = i+1, \dots, l. \end{cases}$$

We see that this oracle is identically distributed as the oracle in game G_{i+1}.

Hence for each i, we have

$$\Pr[A_{\text{os-rl}}^{O_0',H}() = 1 \mid i] - \Pr[A_{\text{os-rl}}^{O_1',H}() = 1 \mid i]$$
$$= \Pr[G_i(A) = 1] - \Pr[G_{i+1}(A) = 1].$$

Therefore,

$$\mathbf{Adv}_{f,\mathcal{X}^{l-1},\mathcal{K}}^{\text{os-rl}}(A_{\text{os-rl}}) = \left| \Pr[A_{\text{os-rl}}^{O_0',H}() = 1] - \Pr[A_{\text{os-rl}}^{O_1',H}() = 1] \right|$$

$$= \left| \sum_{i=0}^{l} \left(\Pr[A_{\text{os-rl}}^{O_0',H}() = 1 \mid i] - \Pr[A_{\text{os-rl}}^{O_1',H}() = 1 \mid i] \right) \Pr[i] \right|$$

$$= \frac{1}{l+1} \left| \sum_{i=0}^{l} \left(\Pr[A_{\text{os-rl}}^{O_0',H}() = 1 \mid i] - \Pr[A_{\text{os-rl}}^{O_1',H}() = 1 \mid i] \right) \right|$$

$$= \frac{1}{l+1} \left| \sum_{i=0}^{l} \left(\Pr[G_i(A) = 1] - \Pr[G_{i+1}(A) = 1] \right) \right|$$

$$= \frac{1}{l+1} \left| \Pr[G_0(A) = 1] - \Pr[G_{l+1}(A) = 1] \right|.$$

We then get

$$\left| \Pr[G_0(A) = 1] - \Pr[G_{l+1}(A) = 1] \right| = (l+1)\, \mathbf{Adv}_{f,\mathcal{X}^{l-1},\mathcal{K}}^{\text{os-rl}}(A_{\text{os-rl}}).$$

Now, by Theorem 4.5, we have proved the theorem. □

5.3   Security of HMAC

Here let us briefly discuss the quantum security of HMAC. The security of HMAC is formally studied in [1]. There, the security of HMAC is reduced to the security of NMAC, with an additional assumption on the compression function $f : \mathcal{K} \times \mathcal{X} \to \mathcal{K}$. The assumption is that the 'dual' PRF of f, which is keyed by its data input as $f(\cdot, K)$ for $K \leftarrow \mathcal{X}$, is a secure PRF against a minor related-key attack: when the key K is chosen, the adversary may query $f(\cdot, K \oplus \mathsf{ipad})$ and $f(\cdot, K \oplus \mathsf{opad})$, and these two oracles should be indistinguishable from two independent random functions $\rho_1, \rho_2 : \mathcal{K} \to \mathcal{K}$. This reduction is still applicable to the quantum security, if we assume that the dual PRF of f is secure against the related-key attack. Hence, under this additional assumption, we can conclude that HMAC is a quantum-secure PRF.

Remark 5.3. In [12], Rötteler and Steinwandt showed that related-key attacks can be very powerful, when combined with the ability to make quantum superposed queries. Under a minor, reasonable assumption on the PRF f, if an oracle $O(\delta, x) = f(k \oplus \delta, x)$ is given to an adversary who can make quantum superposed queries, then the secret key k can be efficiently recovered. Therefore, if a quantum adversary is allowed to derive keys by XORing an arbitrary constant δ, then there exist essentially no quantum-secure PRFs against such an adversary.

However, in this case, we only need our dual PRF f to be *standard-secure* against this minor related-key attack, not quantum-secure: all we need is that the pair $(f(\mathsf{IV}, K \oplus \mathsf{ipad}), f(\mathsf{IV}, K \oplus \mathsf{opad})) \in \mathcal{K}^2$ is indistinguishable from $(k_1, k_2) \leftarrow \mathcal{K}^2$, and for this we do not need quantum security. Hence, it is a reasonable assumption to make that f is secure in the above sense.

5.4 Security of the Augmented Cascade and AMAC

We also show that the augmented cascade $\mathsf{ACSC}[f, \mathsf{Out}]$ is quantum-secure. The proof is very similar to the security proof of NMAC, but unlike the case of NMAC, we need to assume that the PRF f is secure under Out-leakage. (The security proof of NMAC also uses similar security of f under random leakage, but this can be proved from the ordinary PRF security of f.)

First, let us give the following definition, which is similar to Definition 2.7.

Definition 5.4 (Security of PRF under Out-leakage). *Let* $f : \mathcal{K} \times \mathcal{X} \to \mathcal{Y}$ *be a PRF, and* $\mathsf{Out} : \mathcal{Y} \to \mathcal{Z}$ *be an unkeyed function. We say that* f *is secure under Out-leakage, if for any adversary A, we have the following:*

$$\mathbf{Adv}^{\mathsf{prf\text{-}ol}}_{f, \mathsf{Out}}(A) := \left| \mathbf{Pr}[A^{f(k,\cdot)}(\mathsf{Out}(k)) = 1] - \mathbf{Pr}[A^{\rho}(z) = 1] \right| = negl(),$$

where $k \leftarrow \mathcal{K}, z \leftarrow \mathcal{Z}, \rho \leftarrow \mathcal{Y}^{\mathcal{X}}$ *are uniformly and independently random.*

Remark 5.5. Definition 5.4 is not exactly the same as the definition given in [2]. Their version, in our notation, would be negligibility of

$$\left| \mathbf{Pr}[A^{f(k,\cdot)}(\mathsf{Out}(k)) = 1] - \mathbf{Pr}[A^{\rho}(\mathsf{Out}(k)) = 1] \right|.$$

Definition 5.4 is, in fact, two claims combined in one: the first is that $f(k, \cdot)$ remains pseudorandom even when $\mathsf{Out}(k)$ is leaked, and the second is that $\mathsf{Out}(k)$ itself is indistinguishable from a uniform random $z \leftarrow \mathcal{Z}$, for a uniform randomly chosen $k \leftarrow \mathcal{K}$. The definition in [2] is more general, but in order to obtain a PRF, eventually an output function Out close to regular should be selected, hence two definitions are essentially the same.

Now we may state the theorem showing that $\mathsf{ACSC}[f, \mathsf{Out}]$ is quantum-secure.

Theorem 5.6 (Quantum security of ACSC). *Let* $f : \mathcal{K} \times \mathcal{X} \to \mathcal{K}$ *be a PRF, and* $\mathsf{Out} : \mathcal{K} \to \mathcal{Y}$ *be an unkeyed function. Suppose that f is secure under Out-leakage. Then,* $\mathsf{ACSC}[f, \mathsf{Out}]$ *is a secure PRF.*

Concretely, for any adversary A of $\mathsf{ACSC}[f, \mathsf{Out}]$ *making at most q oracle queries, where each message has at most l message blocks, we can construct an adversary A_{ol} making at most $4q$ queries, such that*

$$\mathbf{Adv}^{\mathsf{prf}}_{\mathsf{ACSC}[f, \mathsf{Out}]}(A) \le 34(l+1)q^{3/2} \sqrt{\mathbf{Adv}^{\mathsf{prf\text{-}ol}}_{f, \mathsf{Out}}(A_{\mathsf{ol}})}.$$

In the proof, we first use oracle security of f under Out-leakage to carry out the hybrid argument, and then relate the oracle security to the PRF security under Out-leakage, again using Theorem 3.3. In fact, the proof is almost identical to that of Theorem 5.2, and we will omit the proof.

Similar to the security of HMAC, the security of AMAC follows directly from the security of ACSC, with an additional assumption on the compression function $f : \mathcal{K} \times \mathcal{X} \to \mathcal{K}$, namely, that the dual of f, that is, $f(\cdot, K)$ for $K \leftarrow \mathcal{X}$, is a (standard-)secure PRF. This reduction is also applicable in the quantum security. Hence, with that additional assumption, we may conclude that AMAC is also quantum-secure.

Acknowledgements. We would like to thank the anonymous reviewers of Crypto 2017 for many helpful comments. The second author was supported by Samsung Research Funding Center of Samsung Electronics under Project Number SRFC-IT1601-07.

References

1. Bellare, M.: New proofs for NMAC and HMAC: security without collision-resistance. In: Dwork, C. (ed.) CRYPTO 2006. LNCS, vol. 4117, pp. 602–619. Springer, Heidelberg (2006). doi:10.1007/11818175_36

2. Bellare, M., Bernstein, D.J., Tessaro, S.: Hash-function based PRFs: AMAC and its multi-user security. In: Fischlin, M., Coron, J.-S. (eds.) EUROCRYPT 2016. LNCS, vol. 9665, pp. 566–595. Springer, Heidelberg (2016). doi:10.1007/978-3-662-49890-3_22

3. Bellare, M., Canetti, R., Krawczyk, H.: Keying hash functions for message authentication. In: Koblitz, N. (ed.) CRYPTO 1996. LNCS, vol. 1109, pp. 1–15. Springer, Heidelberg (1996). doi:10.1007/3-540-68697-5_1

4. Bellare, M., Canetti, R., Krawczyk, H.: Pseudorandom functions revisited: the cascade construction and its concrete security. In: FOCS 1996, pp. 514–523. IEEE Computer Society (1996)

5. Boneh, D., Zhandry, M.: Quantum-secure message authentication codes. In: Johansson, T., Nguyen, P.Q. (eds.) EUROCRYPT 2013. LNCS, vol. 7881, pp. 592–608. Springer, Heidelberg (2013). doi:10.1007/978-3-642-38348-9_35

6. Boneh, D., Zhandry, M.: Secure signatures and chosen ciphertext security in a quantum computing world. In: Canetti, R., Garay, J.A. (eds.) CRYPTO 2013. LNCS, vol. 8043, pp. 361–379. Springer, Heidelberg (2013). doi:10.1007/978-3-642-40084-1_21

7. Gaži, P., Pietrzak, K., Rybár, M.: The exact PRF-security of NMAC and HMAC. In: Garay, J.A., Gennaro, R. (eds.) CRYPTO 2014. LNCS, vol. 8616, pp. 113–130. Springer, Heidelberg (2014). doi:10.1007/978-3-662-44371-2_7

8. Goldreich, O., Goldwasser, S., Micali, S.: How to construct random functions. J. ACM **33**(4), 792–807 (1986)

9. Kaplan, M., Leurent, G., Leverrier, A., Naya-Plasencia, M.: Breaking symmetric cryptosystems using quantum period finding. In: Robshaw, M., Katz, J. (eds.) CRYPTO 2016. LNCS, vol. 9815, pp. 207–237. Springer, Heidelberg (2016). doi:10.1007/978-3-662-53008-5_8

10. Kuwakado, H., Morii, M.: Quantum distinguisher between the 3-round Feistel cipher and the random permutation. In: ISIT 2010, pp. 2682–2685. IEEE (2010)

11. Kuwakado, H., Morii, M.: Security on the quantum-type Even-Mansour cipher. In: ISITA 2012, pp. 312–316. IEEE (2012)
12. Rötteler, M., Steinwandt, R.: A note on quantum related-key attacks. Inf. Process. Lett. **115**(1), 40–44 (2015)
13. Santoli, T., Schaffner, C.: Using Simon's algorithm to attack symmetric-key cryptographic primitives. Quantum Inf. Comput. **17**(1&2), 65–78 (2017)
14. Song, F.: A note on quantum security for post-quantum cryptography. In: Mosca, M. (ed.) PQCrypto 2014. LNCS, vol. 8772, pp. 246–265. Springer, Cham (2014). doi:10.1007/978-3-319-11659-4_15
15. Song, F., Yun, A.: Quantum security of NMAC and related constructions. Cryptology ePrint Archive, Report 2017/509, full version of this paper (2017). http://eprint.iacr.org/2017/509
16. Unruh, D.: Quantum proofs of knowledge. In: Pointcheval, D., Johansson, T. (eds.) EUROCRYPT 2012. LNCS, vol. 7237, pp. 135–152. Springer, Heidelberg (2012). doi:10.1007/978-3-642-29011-4_10
17. Unruh, D.: Revocable quantum timed-release encryption. J. ACM **62**(6), 49:1–49:76 (2015)
18. Vadhan, S.P.: Pseudorandomness. Foundations and trends® in theoretical computer science. Theoret. Comput. Sci. **7**(1–3), 1–336 (2012)
19. Watrous, J.: Zero-knowledge against quantum attacks. SIAM J. Comput. **39**(1), 25–58 (2009)
20. Zhandry, M.: How to construct quantum random functions. In: FOCS 2012, pp. 679–687. IEEE Computer Society (2012)
21. Zhandry, M.: Secure identity-based encryption in the quantum random oracle model. In: Safavi-Naini, R., Canetti, R. (eds.) CRYPTO 2012. LNCS, vol. 7417, pp. 758–775. Springer, Heidelberg (2012). doi:10.1007/978-3-642-32009-5_44

Quantum Non-malleability and Authentication

Gorjan Alagic and Christian Majenz[✉]

QMATH, Department of Mathematical Sciences,
University of Copenhagen, Copenhagen, Denmark
galagic@gmail.com, majenz@math.ku.dk

Abstract. In encryption, non-malleability is a highly desirable property: it ensures that adversaries cannot manipulate the plaintext by acting on the ciphertext. In [6], Ambainis et al. gave a definition of non-malleability for the encryption of quantum data. In this work, we show that this definition is too weak, as it allows adversaries to "inject" plaintexts of their choice into the ciphertext. We give a new definition of quantum non-malleability which resolves this problem. Our definition is expressed in terms of entropic quantities, considers stronger adversaries, and does not assume secrecy. Rather, we prove that *quantum non-malleability implies secrecy*; this is in stark contrast to the classical setting, where the two properties are completely independent. For unitary schemes, our notion of non-malleability is equivalent to encryption with a two-design (and hence also to the definition of [6]).

Our techniques also yield new results regarding the closely-related task of quantum authentication. We show that "total authentication" (a notion recently proposed by Garg et al. [18]) can be satisfied with two-designs, a significant improvement over the eight-design construction of [18]. We also show that, under a mild adaptation of the rejection procedure, both total authentication and our notion of non-malleability yield quantum authentication as defined by Dupuis et al. [16].

1 Introduction

Background. In its most basic form, encryption ensures secrecy in the presence of eavesdroppers. Besides secrecy, another desirable property is *non-malleability*, which guarantees that an active adversary cannot modify the plaintext by manipulating the ciphertext. In the classical setting, secrecy and non-malleability are independent: there are schemes which satisfy secrecy but are malleable, and schemes which are non-malleable but transmit the plaintext in the clear. If both secrecy and non-malleability is desired, then pairwise-independent permutations provide information-theoretically perfect (one-time) security [20]. In the computational security setting, non-malleability can be achieved by MACs, and ensures chosen-ciphertext security for authenticated encryption.

In the setting of quantum information, encryption is the task of transmitting quantum states over a completely insecure quantum channel. Information-theoretic secrecy for quantum encryption is well-understood. Non-malleability, on the other hand, has only been studied in one previous work, by Ambainis,

J. Katz and H. Shacham (Eds.): CRYPTO 2017, Part II, LNCS 10402, pp. 310–341, 2017.
DOI: 10.1007/978-3-319-63715-0_11

Bouda and Winter [6]. Their definition (which we will call ABW-non-malleability, or ABW-NM) requires that the scheme satisfies secrecy, and that the "effective channel" Dec ∘ Λ ∘ Enc of any adversary Λ amounts to either the identity map or replacement by some fixed state. In the case of unitary schemes, ABW-NM is equivalent to encrypting with a unitary two-design. Unitary two-designs are a natural quantum analogue of pairwise-independent permutations, and can be efficiently constructed in a number of ways (see, e.g., [10,14].)

While quantum non-malleability has only been considered by [6], the closely-related task of quantum authentication (where decryption is allowed to reject) has received significant attention (see, e.g., [2,7,11,16,18].) The widely-adopted definition of Dupuis, Nielsen and Salvail asks that the averaged effective channel of any adversary is close to a map which does not touch the plaintext [16]; we refer to this notion as DNS-authentication. Recent work by Garg, Yuen and Zhandry [18] established another notion of quantum authentication, which they call "total authentication." The notion of total authentication has two major differences from previous definitions: (i) it asks for success with high probability over the choice of keys, rather than simply on average, and (ii) it makes no demands whatsoever in the case that decryption rejects. We refer to this notion of quantum authentication as GYZ-authentication. In [18], it is shown that GYZ-authentication can be satisfied with unitary eight-designs.

This Work. In this work, we devise a new definition of non-malleability (denoted NM) for quantum encryption, improving on ABW-NM in a number of ways. First, our definition is expressed in terms of entropic quantities, which allows us to bring several quantum-information-theoretic techniques to bear (such as decoupling.) Second, we consider more powerful adversaries, which can possess side information about the plaintext. Third, we remove the possibility of a "plaintext injection" attack, whereby an adversary against an ABW-NM scheme can send a plaintext of their choice to the receiver. Finally, our definition does not demand secrecy; instead, we show that *quantum secrecy is a consequence of quantum non-malleability.* This is a significant departure from the classical case, and is analogous to the fact that quantum authentication implies secrecy [7].

The primary consequence of our work is twofold: first, encryption with unitary two-designs satisfies all of the above notions of quantum non-malleability; second, when equipped with blank "tag" qubits, the same scheme also satisfies all of the above notions of quantum authentication. A more detailed summary of the results is as follows. For schemes which have unitary encryption maps, we prove that NM is equivalent to encryption with unitary two-designs, and hence also to ABW-NM. For non-unitary schemes, we prove a characterization theorem for NM schemes that shows that NM implies ABW-NM, and provide a strong separation example between NM and ABW-NM (the aforementioned plaintext injection attack). In the case of GYZ authentication, we prove that two-designs (with tags) are sufficient, a significant improvement over the state-of-the-art, which requires eight-designs [18]. Moreover, the simulation of adversaries in this proof is efficient, in the sense of Broadbent and Wainewright [11].

Finally, we show that GYZ-authentication implies DNS-authentication, and that equipping an arbitrary NM scheme with tags yields DNS-authentication.

We remark that, after the initial version of our results was submitted, an independent work of C. Portmann gave an alternative proof that GYZ-authentication can be satisfied by the 2-design scheme [26].

1.1 Summary of Contributions

In the following, all schemes are symmetric-key encryption schemes for quantum data, in the information-theoretic security setting.

Quantum Non-malleability. We begin with non-malleability, in both the perfect setting (Sect. 3) and the approximate setting (Sect. 4).

1. **New definition of non-malleability.** We give a new definition of quantum non-malleability (NM), in terms of the information gain of an adversary's *effective attack* on the plaintext. The quantum registers are: plaintext A, ciphertext C, user's reference R, and adversary's side information B.

Definition 1.1 (NM, informal). *A scheme is non-malleable (NM) if for any* ϱ_{ABR} *and any attack* $\Lambda_{CB \to C\tilde{B}}$, *the effective attack* $\tilde{\Lambda}_{AB \to A\tilde{B}}$ *satisfies*

$$I(AR : \tilde{B})_{\tilde{\Lambda}(\varrho)} \leq I(AR : B)_{\varrho} + h(p_=(\Lambda, \varrho)).$$

The binary entropy term is necessary because adversaries can always simply record whether they disturbed the ciphertext (see Definition 3.4).

2. **Results on non-malleability.** Our first result is an alternative characterization of NM, in terms of the form of the effective map $\tilde{\Lambda}$.

Theorem 1.2 (informal). *A scheme is NM if and only if, for any attack* $\Lambda_{CB \to C\tilde{B}}$, *there exist maps* $\Lambda'_{B \to \tilde{B}}$, $\Lambda''_{B \to \tilde{B}}$ *such that the effective attack satisfies*

$$\tilde{\Lambda} = \mathrm{id}_A \otimes \Lambda' + \frac{1}{|C|^2 - 1} \left(|C| \langle D_K(\mathbb{1}_C) \rangle - \mathrm{id} \right)_A \otimes \Lambda''.$$

The fact that NM implies ABW-NM is an immediate corollary. The new definition is strictly stronger than ABW-NM: we give a scheme which is secure under ABW-NM but insecure under NM. This scheme is in fact susceptible to a powerful attack, whereby a simple adversary can replace the output of decryption with a plaintext of the adversary's choice. On the other hand, if we restrict our attention to schemes where the encryption maps are unitary, then we are able to show the following.

Theorem 1.3 (informal). *Let* Π *be a scheme such that encryption* E_k *is unitary for all keys k. Then Π is NM if and only if $\{E_k\}_k$ is a two-design.*

By the results of [6], we conclude that NM and ABW-NM are in fact equivalent for unitary schemes. Finally, we show that NM implies secrecy.

Theorem 1.4 (informal). *Quantum non-malleability implies secrecy.*

3. **Authentication from non-malleability.** Our final result in the setting of non-malleability shows that, by adding a "tag" space to the plaintext (as in the Clifford scheme [2]), we can turn an NM scheme into an authentication scheme as defined in [16]. More precisely, given an encryption scheme $\Pi = \{E_k\}$, we define Π_t^{tag} to be a new scheme whose encryption is $\varrho \mapsto E_k(\varrho_A \otimes |0\rangle\langle 0|_B^{\otimes t}) E_k^\dagger$, and whose decryption rejects unless B measures to $|0^t\rangle$.

Theorem 1.5 (informal). *Let $\Pi = \{E_k\}$ be an encryption scheme. If Π is NM, then Π_t^{tag} is 2^{2-t}-DNS-authenticating.*

Quantum Authentication. Our results on quantum authentication are summarized as follows. We note that, strictly speaking, our definitions of authentication deviate slightly from the original versions [16,18], in that decryption outputs a reject symbol in place of the plaintext (rather than setting an auxiliary bit to "reject.") This adaptation is convenient for reasons we will return to later.

1. **GYZ implies DNS.** First, we show that GYZ-authentication implies DNS-authentication. We remark that this is not trivial: on one hand, GYZ strengthens DNS by requiring high probability of success (rather than success on-average); on the other hand, in the reject case GYZ requires nothing while DNS makes rather stringent demands. Nonetheless, we show the following.

Theorem 1.6 (informal). *Let Π be an encryption scheme. If Π is ε-GYZ-authenticating, then it is also $O(\sqrt{\varepsilon})$-DNS-authenticating.*

2. **GYZ is achievable with 2-designs.** Next, we show that GYZ-authentication is achieved with a "tagged" two-design scheme. The analysis of [18] required eight-designs for the same construction.

Theorem 1.7 (informal). *Let $\Pi = \{E_k\}_k$ be a 2^{-t}-approximate 2-design scheme. Then Π_t^{tag} is $2^{-\Omega(t)}$-GYZ-authenticating.*

3. **GYZ authentication from non-malleability.** As a straightforward consequence of Theorems 1.3 and 1.7, we finally record that tagging a unitary non-malleable scheme results in a GYZ-authenticating scheme.

Corollary 1.8 (informal). *There exists a constant $r > 0$ such that the following holds. If Π is a unitary $\Omega(2^{-rn})$-NM scheme for n-qubit messages, and $t = \text{poly}(n)$, then Π_t^{tag} is $2^{-\Omega(\text{poly}(n))}$-GYZ-authenticating.*

A sufficiently strong NM scheme can be constructed via the ϵ-approximate version of Theorem 1.3 (see Theorem 4.5 and Remark 2.3 below.)

The remainder of the paper is structured as follows. In Sect. 2, we review some basic facts regarding quantum states, registers, and channels, and recall several useful facts about unitary designs. In Sect. 3, we consider the exact setting, beginning with perfect secrecy and then continuing to perfect non-malleability (NM) and the relevant new results; we also discuss the relationship to ABW-NM in detail. We continue in Sect. 4 with the approximate setting, again beginning with secrecy and then continuing to approximate non-malleability. We end with the new results on quantum authentication, in Sect. 4.2.

2   Preliminaries

2.1   Quantum States, Registers, and Channels

We assume basic familiarity with the formalism of quantum states, operators, and channels. We denote quantum registers (i.e., systems and their subsystems) with capital Latin letters, e.g., A, B, C. The Hilbert space corresponding to system A is denoted by $\mathcal{H}_A$. For a register A, we denote the dimension of $\mathcal{H}_A$ by $|A|$. We emphasize that, in this work, all Hilbert spaces will be finite-dimensional.

The space operators on $\mathcal{H}_A$ is denoted $\mathcal{B}(\mathcal{H}_A)$. We say that a quantum state is classical if it is diagonal in the standard (i.e., computational) basis. We denote the adjoint of an operator $X \in \mathcal{B}(\mathcal{H})$ by $X^\dagger$ and its transpose with respect to the computational basis by X^T. Where necessary, we will write a quantum state $\varrho \in \mathcal{B}(\mathcal{H}_A \otimes \mathcal{H}_B \otimes \mathcal{H}_C)$ as ϱ_{ABC} to emphasize that the state is a multipartite state over registers A, B, and C. When such a state has already been defined, we will write reduced states by omitting the traced-out registers, e.g., $\varrho_A := \mathrm{Tr}_{BC}[\varrho_{ABC}]$. We single out some special states which will appear frequently. Fix two systems S, S' with $|S| = |S'|$. We let

$$|\phi^+\rangle_{SS'} = |S|^{-1/2} \sum_i |ii\rangle_{SS'} \qquad \text{and} \qquad \phi^+_{SS'} = |\phi^+\rangle\langle\phi^+|_{SS'}$$

denote the maximally entangled state on the bipartite system SS' (expressed as a pure state on the left, and as a density operator on the right.) Furthermore, we let $\Pi^-_{SS'} = \mathbb{1}_{SS'} - \phi^+_{SS'}$ and $\tau^-_{SS'} = \Pi^-_{SS'}/(|S|^2 - 1)$. We also set $\tau_S = \mathbb{1}_S/|S|$ to be the maximally mixed state on S.

We denote the von Neumann entropy of a state ϱ_A by $H(A)_\varrho$, and the joint entropy of ϱ_{AB} by $H(AB)_\varrho$. We recall that the quantum mutual information of ϱ_{AB} is defined by

$$I(A : B)_\varrho := H(A)_\varrho + H(B)_\varrho - H(AB)_\varrho.$$

The quantum conditional mutual information of ϱ_{ABC} is defined by

$$I(A : B|C)_\varrho := H(AC)_\varrho + H(BC)_\varrho - H(ABC)_\varrho - H(C)_\varrho.$$

These quantities are nonnegative [21] and satisfy a chain rule:

$$I(A : BC|D)_\varrho = I(A : B|D)_\varrho + I(A : C|BD)_\varrho.$$

We remark that the above also holds for trivial D. Together with the Stinespring dilation theorem [27], non-negativity [22] and the chain rule imply the data processing inequality

$$I(A : \tilde{B}|C)_{\Lambda(\varrho)} \leq I(A : B|C)_\varrho ,$$

when Λ is a CPTP (completely-positive, trace-preserving) map from $\mathcal{B}(\mathcal{H}_B)$ to $\mathcal{B}(\mathcal{H}_{\tilde{B}})$. An important special case is where $B = B_1 B_2$ and $\Lambda = \mathrm{Tr}_{B_2}$ discards the contents of B_2.

We will refer to valid transformations between quantum states as channels, or CPTP maps. We will sometimes also consider trace-non-increasing completely-positive (CP) maps. When necessary, we will emphasize the input and output spaces of a map $\Lambda : \mathcal{B}(\mathcal{H}_A \otimes \mathcal{H}_B) \to \mathcal{B}(\mathcal{H}_C)$ by writing $\Lambda_{AB \to C}$. We denote the identity channel on, e.g., register A by $\mathrm{id}_{A \to A}$ (or simply id_A) and the channel from register A to A' with constant output $\sigma_{A'}$ by $\langle \sigma \rangle_{A \to A'}$. When composing operators on many registers, and if the context allows, we will elide tensor products with the identity operator. So, for example, with Λ as above we may write $\tau_{CD} = \Lambda \varrho_{ABD}$ in place of $\tau_{CD} = (\Lambda \otimes \mathrm{id}_D)\varrho_{ABD}$.

A standard tool in this setting is the Choi-Jamiołkowski (CJ) isomorphism [12,19]. Let $\Xi_{A \to B} : \mathcal{B}(\mathcal{H}_A) \to \mathcal{B}(\mathcal{H}_B)$ be a linear operator. Then its CJ matrix is defined as

$$(\eta_\Xi)_{BA'} = \Lambda_{A \to B}(\phi^+_{AA'}). \tag{2.1}$$

The linear operator mapping Ξ to η_Ξ is an isomorphism of vector spaces and η_Ξ is positive semidefinite iff Ξ is CP. Moreover $\Xi_{A \to B}$ is TP iff $(\eta_\Xi)_{A'} = \tau_A$. The inverse of the CJ isomorphism is given by the equation

$$\Xi_{A \to B}(X_A) = |A|\mathrm{Tr}_{A'} \left[X_{A'}^T (\eta_\Xi)_{BA'} \right] . \tag{2.2}$$

We denote the swap operator by $F : |i\rangle \otimes |j\rangle \mapsto |j\rangle \otimes |i\rangle$.

Lemma 2.1 (Swap trick [17]). *For matrices A and B, $\mathrm{Tr}[AB] = \mathrm{Tr}[FA \otimes B]$.*

We will make frequent use of the trace norm $\|\cdot\|_1$, the operator norm $\|\cdot\|_\infty$, and the diamond norm $\|\Lambda_{A \to B}\|_\diamond := \max_{\varrho_{AA'}} \|\Lambda_{A \to B} \otimes \mathrm{id}_{A'}(\varrho_{AA'})\|_1$; here the max is taken over all pure quantum states $\varrho_{AA'}$ and $\mathcal{H}_A \cong \mathcal{H}_{A'}$. Recall that the Hölder inequality for operators states that, for any two operators X and Y,

$$\mathrm{Tr}[XY] \leq \|XY\|_1 \leq \|X\|_1 \|Y\|_\infty . \tag{2.3}$$

2.2 Unitary Designs

We now recall the definition of unitary t-design, and some relevant variants. We begin by considering three different types of "twirls."

1. For a finite subset $D \subset U(\mathcal{H})$ of the unitary group on some finite dimensional Hilbert space $\mathcal{H}$, let

$$T_D^{(t)}(X) = \frac{1}{|D|} \sum_{U \in D} U^{\otimes t} X \left(U^\dagger \right)^{\otimes t} \tag{2.4}$$

be the associated t-twirling channel. If we take the entire unitary group (rather than just a finite subset), then we get the Haar t-twirling channel

$$\mathcal{T}_{\mathsf{Haar}}^{(t)}(X) = \int U^{\otimes t} X \left(U^{\dagger}\right)^{\otimes t} \mathrm{d}U. \tag{2.5}$$

2. We define the U-$\overline{U}$ twirl with respect to finite $\mathrm{D} \subset \mathrm{U}(\mathcal{H})$ by

$$\overline{\mathcal{T}}_{\mathrm{D}}(X) = \frac{1}{|\mathrm{D}|} \sum_{U \in \mathrm{D}} \left(U \otimes \overline{U}\right) X \left(U \otimes \overline{U}\right)^{\dagger}. \tag{2.6}$$

The analogous U-$\overline{U}$ Haar twirling channel is denoted by $\overline{\mathcal{T}}_{\mathsf{Haar}}$.

3. The third notion is called a channel twirl, and is defined in terms of U-$\overline{U}$-twirling. Given a channel Λ, let η_{Λ} be the CJ state of Λ. The channel twirl $\mathcal{T}_{\mathrm{D}}^{ch}(\Lambda)$ of Λ is defined to be the channel whose CJ state is $\overline{\mathcal{T}}_{\mathrm{D}}(\eta_{\Lambda})$.

Next, we define the three corresponding notions of designs.

Definition 2.2. *Let $\mathrm{D} \subset \mathrm{U}(\mathcal{H})$ be a finite set. We define the following.*

- *If $\left\|\mathcal{T}_{\mathrm{D}}^{(t)} - \mathcal{T}_{\mathsf{Haar}}^{(t)}\right\|_{\diamond} \leq \delta$ holds, then D is a δ-approximate t-design.*
- *If $\left\|\overline{\mathcal{T}}_{\mathrm{D}} - \overline{\mathcal{T}}_{\mathsf{Haar}}\right\|_{\diamond} \leq \delta$ holds, then D is a δ-approximate U-$\overline{U}$-twirl design.*
- *If $\left\|\mathcal{T}_{\mathrm{D}}^{ch}(\Lambda) - \mathcal{T}_{\mathsf{Haar}}^{ch}(\Lambda)\right\|_{\diamond} \leq \delta$ holds for all CPTP maps Λ, then D is a δ-approximate channel-twirl design.*

For all three of the above, the case $\delta = 0$ is called an "exact design" (or simply "design".) All three notions of design are equivalent in the exact case. In the approximate case they are still connected, but there are some nontrivial costs in the approximation quality (See [23], Lemma 2.2.14, and an additional easy lemma proven in the full version [3]).

It is well-known that ε-approximate t-designs on n qubits can be generated by random quantum circuits of size polynomial in n, t and $\log(1/\varepsilon)$ [10]. In particular, the size of these circuits is polynomial even for exponentially-small choices of ε. We emphasize this observation as follows.

Remark 2.3. *Fix a polynomial t in n. Then, for any $\varepsilon > 0$, a random n-qubit quantum circuit consisting of $\mathrm{poly}(n, \log(1/\varepsilon))$ gates (from a universal set) satisfies every notion of ϵ-approximate t-design in Definition 2.2.*

For exact designs, we point out two important constructions. First, the prototypical example of a unitary one-design on n qubits is the n-qubit Pauli group. For exact unitary two-designs, the standard example is the Clifford group, which is the normalizer of the n-qubit Pauli group. Alternatively, the Clifford group is generated by circuits from the gate set $\{H, P, \mathrm{CNOT}\}$. It is well-known that one can efficiently generate exact unitary two-designs on n-qubits by building appropriate circuits from this gate set, using $O(n^2)$ random bits [1,14].

3   The Zero-Error Setting

We begin with the zero-error. In the case of secrecy, zero-error means that schemes cannot leak any information whatsoever. In the case of non-malleability, zero-error means that the adversary cannot increase their correlations with the secret by even an infinitesimal amount (except by trivial means; see below).

3.1   Perfect Secrecy

We begin with a definition of symmetric-key quantum encryption. Our formulation treats rejection during decryption in a slightly different manner from previous literature.

Definition 3.1 (Encryption scheme). *A symmetric-key quantum encryption scheme (QES) is a triple (τ_K, E, D) consisting of a classical state $\tau_K \in \mathcal{B}(\mathcal{H}_K)$ and a pair of channels*

$$E : \mathcal{B}(\mathcal{H}_A \otimes \mathcal{H}_K) \longrightarrow \mathcal{B}(\mathcal{H}_C \otimes \mathcal{H}_K)$$
$$D : \mathcal{B}(\mathcal{H}_C \otimes \mathcal{H}_K) \longrightarrow \mathcal{B}((\mathcal{H}_A \oplus \mathbb{C}|\bot\rangle) \otimes \mathcal{H}_K)$$

satisfying $[D \circ E](\cdot \otimes |k\rangle\langle k|) = (\mathrm{id}_A \oplus 0_\bot) \otimes |k\rangle\langle k|$ *for all k.*

The Hilbert spaces $\mathcal{H}_A$, $\mathcal{H}_C$ and $\mathcal{H}_K$ are implicitly given by the triple (τ_K, E, D). The state $|\bot\rangle$ is an error flag that allows the decryption map to report an error. For notational convenience when dealing with these schemes, we set

$$E_k = E(\cdot \otimes |k\rangle\langle k|) \qquad\qquad E_K = \mathrm{Tr}_K E(\cdot \otimes \tau_K)$$
$$D_k = D(\cdot \otimes |k\rangle\langle k|) \qquad\qquad D_K = \mathrm{Tr}_K D(\cdot \otimes \tau_K).$$

We will often slightly abuse notation by referring to decryption maps D_k as maps from C to A; in fact, the output space of D_k is really the slightly larger space $\bar{A} := A \oplus \mathbb{C}|\bot\rangle$.

It is natural to define secrecy in the quantum world in terms of quantum mutual information. However, instead of asking for the ciphertext to be uncorrelated with the plaintext as in the classical case, we ask for the ciphertext to be uncorrelated from any reference system.

Definition 3.2 (Perfect secrecy). *A QES (τ_K, E, D) satisfies information - theoretic secrecy (ITS) if, for any Hilbert space $\mathcal{H}_B$ and any $\varrho_{AB} \in \mathcal{B}(\mathcal{H}_A \otimes \mathcal{H}_B)$, setting $\sigma_{CBK} = E(\varrho_{AB} \otimes \tau_K)$ implies $I(C : B)_\sigma = 0$.*

We note that, for perfect ITS, adding side information is unnecessary: the definition already implies that the ciphertext is in product with *any* other system. In particular, if the adversary has some auxiliary system E in their possession, then $I(B : CE)_\sigma = I(B : E)_\sigma$. Several definitions of secrecy for symmetric-key quantum encryption have appeared in the literature, but the above formulation appears to be new. It can be shown that ITS is equivalent to perfect indistin-guishability of ciphertexts (IND). The latter notion is a special case of an early indistinguishability-based definition of Ambainis et al. [5].

In many situations it makes sense to restrict ourselves to QES that have identical plaintext and ciphertext spaces; due to correctness, this is equivalent to unitarity.

Definition 3.3 (Unitary scheme). *A QES (τ_K, E, D) is called unitary if the encryption and decryption maps are controlled unitaries, i.e., if there exists $V = \sum_k U_A^{(k)} \otimes |k\rangle\langle k|_K$ such that $E(X) = VXV^\dagger$.*

It is straightforward to prove that, for unitary schemes, ITS is equivalent to the statement that the encryption maps $\{E_k\}$ form a unitary 1-design. Note that unitarity of E_k and correctness imply unitarity of D_k.

3.2   A New Notion of Non-malleability

Definition. We consider a scenario involving a user Alice and an adversary Mallory. The scenario begins with Mallory preparing a tripartite state ϱ_{ABR} over three registers: the plaintext A, the reference R, and the side-information B. The registers A and R are given to Alice, while Mallory keeps B. Alice then encrypts A into a ciphertext C and then transmits (or stores) it in the open. Mallory now applies an attack map

$$\Lambda : \mathcal{B}(\mathcal{H}_C \otimes \mathcal{H}_B) \to \mathcal{B}(\mathcal{H}_C \otimes \mathcal{H}_{\tilde{B}}).$$

Mallory keeps the (transformed) side-information $\tilde{B}$ and returns C to Alice. Finally, Alice decrypts C back to A, and the scenario ends. We are now interested in measuring the extent to which Mallory was able to increase her correlations with Alice's systems A and R. This can be understood by analyzing the mutual information $I(AR : \tilde{B})_{\tilde{\Lambda}(\varrho)}$ where $\tilde{\Lambda}_{AB \to A\tilde{B}}$ is the *effective channel* corresponding to Mallory's attack (Fig. 1):

$$\tilde{\Lambda} = \mathrm{Tr}_K(D \circ \Lambda \circ E)((\cdot) \otimes \tau_K). \tag{3.1}$$

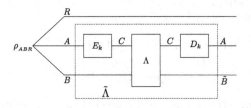

Fig. 1. The quantum non-malleability scenario.

We point out one way in which Mallory can always increase these correlations, regardless of the structure of the encryption scheme. First, she flips a coin b, and records the outcome in B. If $b = 1$, she replaces the contents of C with some fixed state σ_C, and otherwise she leaves C untouched. One then sees that Mallory's correlations have increased by $h(p_=(\Lambda, \varrho))$, where h denotes binary entropy and $p_=$ is a defined as follows.

$$p_=(\Lambda, \varrho) = \operatorname{Tr}\left[(\phi_{CC'}^+ \otimes \mathbb{1}_{\tilde{B}})\Lambda(\phi_{CC'}^+ \otimes \varrho_B)\right]. \tag{3.2}$$

This quantity is the inner product between the identity map and the map $\Lambda((\,\cdot\,) \otimes \varrho_B)$, expressed in terms of CJ states. Intuitively, it measures the probability with which Mallory chooses to apply the identity map; taking the binary entropy then gives us the information gain resulting from recording this choice.

We are now ready to define information-theoretic quantum non-malleability. Stated informally, a scheme is non-malleable if Mallory can only implement the attacks described above.

Definition 3.4 (Non-malleability). *A QES (τ_K, E, D) is non-malleable (NM) if for any state ϱ_{ABR} and any CPTP map $\Lambda_{CB \to C\tilde{B}}$, we have*

$$I(AR : \tilde{B})_{\tilde{\Lambda}(\varrho)} \leq I(AR : B)_\varrho + h(p_=(\Lambda, \varrho)). \tag{3.3}$$

One might justifiably wonder if the term $h(p_=(\Lambda, \varrho))$ is too generous to the adversary. However, as we showed above, every scheme is vulnerable to an attack which gains this amount of information. This term also appears (somewhat disguised) in the classical setting. In fact, if a classical encryption scheme satisfies Definition 3.4 against classical adversaries, then it also satisfies classical information-theoretic non-malleability as defined in [20].

Definition 3.4 directly generalizes the classical information-theoretic definition from [20]. In some settings, it might be preferable to have a definition which characterizes the set of effective attack channels as was done in [6]. As it turns out, NM can be defined in this way.

Theorem 3.7 (Non-malleability, alternative form). *A QES(τ, E, D) is NM if and only if for any attack $\Lambda_{CB \to C\tilde{B}}$, the effective map $\tilde{\Lambda}_{AB \to A\tilde{B}}$ has the form*

$$\tilde{\Lambda} = \operatorname{id}_A \otimes \Lambda'_{B \to \tilde{B}} + \frac{1}{|C|^2 - 1}\left(|C|^2 \langle D_K(\tau)\rangle - \operatorname{id}\right)_A \otimes \Lambda''_{B \to \tilde{B}} \tag{3.4}$$

where $\Lambda' = \operatorname{Tr}_{CC'}[\phi_{CC'}^+ \Lambda(\phi_{CC'}^+ \otimes (\cdot))]$ and $\Lambda'' = \operatorname{Tr}_{CC'}[\Pi_{CC'}^- \Lambda(\phi_{CC'}^+ \otimes (\cdot))]$.

The proof of this theorem is postponed to the results section below (proof sketch) and the appendix.

Finally, as we will show in later sections, Definition 3.4 implies ABW-NM (see Definition 3.8), and schemes satisfying Definition 3.4 are sufficient for building quantum authentication under the strongest known definitions.

Non-malleability Implies Secrecy. In the classical case, non-malleability is independent from secrecy: the one-time pad is secret but malleable, and non-malleability is unaffected by appending the plaintext to each ciphertext. In the quantum case, on the other hand, we can show that NM implies secrecy. This is analogous to the fact that "quantum authentication implies encryption" [7].

Proposition 3.5. *Let (τ_K, E, D) be an NM QES. Then (τ_K, E, D) is ITS.*

Proof. Let B, ϱ_{AB}, and $\sigma_{CBK} = E(\varrho_{AB} \otimes \tau_K)$ be as in the definition of ITS (Definition 3.2). We first rename B to R. We then consider the non-malleability property in the following special-case scenario. The initial side-information register is empty, the final side-information register $\tilde{B}$ satisfies $\mathcal{H}_{\tilde{B}} \cong \mathcal{H}_C$, and the adversary map $\Lambda_{C \to C\tilde{B}}$ is defined as follows. Note that the "ciphertext-extraction" map $\Theta_{C \to C\tilde{B}} = \mathrm{id}_{C \to \tilde{B}}(\cdot) \otimes \tau_C$ has CJ state $\eta^{\Theta}_{CC'\tilde{B}} = \phi^+_{C'\tilde{B}} \otimes \tau_C$. We choose Λ so that its CJ state satisfies

$$\eta^{\Lambda}_{CC'\tilde{B}} = \frac{d^2}{d^2 - 1} \Pi^-_{CC'} \eta^{\Theta}_{CC'\tilde{B}} \Pi^-_{CC'}. \tag{3.5}$$

Applying the above projection to the CJ state of Θ ensures that Λ will have $p_=(\Lambda) = 0$ (note: $p_=(\Theta) > 0$.)

Direct calculation of the $C'\tilde{B}$ marginal of the CJ state of Λ yields

$$\eta^{\Lambda}_{C'\tilde{B}} = \frac{d^2 - 2}{d^2 - 1} \phi^+_{C'\tilde{B}} + \frac{1}{d^2 - 1} \tau_{C'} \otimes \tau_{\tilde{B}}. \tag{3.6}$$

This implies that the output $\sigma_{AR\tilde{B}} = \tilde{\Lambda}_{A \to A\tilde{B}}(\varrho_{AB})$ of the effective channel $\tilde{\Lambda}$ will satisfy

$$\sigma_{\tilde{B}R} = \frac{d^2 - 2}{d^2 - 1} \gamma_{\tilde{B}R} + \frac{1}{d^2 - 1} \tau_{\tilde{B}} \otimes \varrho_R, \tag{3.7}$$

where $\gamma_{CR} = (E_K)_{A \to C}(\varrho_{AR})$ and we used the fact that $\mathcal{H}_{\tilde{B}} \cong \mathcal{H}_C$. By non-malleability, we have

$$I(\tilde{B} : R)_{\sigma} + I(\tilde{B} : A|R)_{\sigma} = I(\tilde{B} : AR)_{\sigma} = 0. \tag{3.8}$$

In particular, $I(\tilde{B} : R)_{\sigma} = 0$ and thus $\sigma_{\tilde{B}R} = \sigma_{\tilde{B}} \otimes \varrho_R$. It follows by Eq. (3.7) that

$$\gamma_{\tilde{B}R} = \frac{d^2 - 1}{d^2 - 2} \left(\sigma_{\tilde{B}} - \frac{1}{d^2 - 1} \tau_{\tilde{B}} \right) \otimes \varrho_R, \tag{3.9}$$

i.e., $\gamma_{\tilde{B}R}$ is a product state. This is precisely the definition of information-theoretic secrecy. □

Characterization of Non-malleable Schemes. Next, we provide a characterization of non-malleable schemes. First, we show that unitary schemes are equivalent to encryption with a unitary 2-design.

Theorem 3.6. *A unitary QES (τ_K, E, D) is NM if and only if $\{E_k\}_{k \in K}$ is a unitary 2-design.*

This fact is particularly intuitive when the 2-design is the Clifford group, a well-known exact 2-design. In that case, a Pauli operator acting on only one ciphertext qubit will be "propagated" (by the encryption circuit) to a completely random Pauli on all plaintext qubits. The plaintext is then maximally mixed, and the adversary gains no information. The Clifford group thus yields a perfectly non-malleable (and perfectly secret) encryption scheme using $O(n^2)$ bits of key [1].

It will be convenient to prove Theorem 3.6 as a consequence of our general characterization theorem, which is as follows.

Theorem 3.7. *Let* (τ, E, D) *be a QES. Then* (τ, E, D) *is NM if and only if, for any attack* $\Lambda_{CB \to C\tilde{B}}$, *the effective map* $\tilde{\Lambda}_{AB \to A\tilde{B}}$ *has the form*

$$\tilde{\Lambda} = \mathrm{id}_A \otimes \Lambda'_{B \to \tilde{B}} + \frac{1}{|C|^2 - 1} \left(|C|^2 \langle D_K(\tau) \rangle - \mathrm{id} \right)_A \otimes \Lambda''_{B \to \tilde{B}} \quad (3.10)$$

where $\Lambda' = \mathrm{Tr}_{CC'}[\phi^+_{CC'} \Lambda(\phi^+_{CC'} \otimes (\cdot))]$ *and* $\Lambda'' = \mathrm{Tr}_{CC'}[\Pi^-_{CC'} \Lambda(\phi^+_{CC'} \otimes (\cdot))]$.

We remark that the forward direction holds even if (τ, E, D) only fulfills the NM condition (Eq. (3.3)) against adversaries with empty side-information B. The proof of Theorem 3.7 (with this strengthening) is sketched below. The full proof is somewhat technical and can be found in Appendix B. More precisely, we prove the stronger Theorem B.3, which implies the above by setting $\varepsilon = 0$.

Proof sketch. The first implication, i.e. NM implies Eq. (3.10), is best proven in the Choi-Jamiołkowski picture. Here, any QES defines a map

$$\mathcal{E}_{CC' \to AA'} = \frac{1}{|K|} \sum_k D_k \otimes E_k^T, \quad (3.11)$$

where the transpose E_k^T is the map whose Kraus operators are the transposes of the Kraus operators of E_k (in the standard basis). Our goal is to prove that this map essentially acts like the $U\bar{U}$-twirl. We decompose the space $\mathcal{H}_C^{\otimes 2}$ as

$$\mathcal{H}_C^{\otimes 2} = \mathbb{C}|\phi+\rangle \oplus \mathrm{supp}\Pi^- \quad (3.12)$$

which induces a decomposition of

$$\mathcal{B}(\mathcal{H}_C^{\otimes 2}) = \mathbb{C}|\phi^+\rangle\langle\phi^+| \oplus \left\{ |\phi^+\rangle\langle v| \, \middle| \, \langle\phi^+ \mid v\rangle = 0 \right\}$$

$$\oplus \left\{ |v\rangle\langle\phi^+| \, \middle| \, \langle\phi^+ \mid v\rangle = 0 \right\} \oplus \left\{ X \in B \, \middle| \, \langle\phi^+|X = X|\phi^+\rangle = 0 \right\}. \quad (3.13)$$

On the first and last direct summands, the correct behavior of $\mathcal{E}$ is easy to show: the first one corresponds to the identity, and the last one to the non-identity channels Λ with $p_=(\Lambda) = 0$. For the remaining two spaces, we employ Lemma A.3 which shows that the encryption map of any valid encryption scheme has the form of appending an ancillary mixed state and then applying an isometry. Evaluating $\mathcal{E}(|\phi+\rangle\langle v|)$ for $\langle\phi^+ \mid v\rangle = 0$ reduces to evaluating the adjoint of the average encryption map, $E_K^\dagger$, on traceless matrices. It is, however, easy to verify that

$$\mathrm{Tr}_A \mathcal{E}_{CC' \to AA'}(\sigma_C \otimes (\cdot)_{C'}) = (E_K^T)_{C' \to A'}$$

for any σ_C. This can be used to prove $E_K = \langle \tau_C \rangle$ by observing that $\langle\phi^+|_{CC'} \sigma_C \otimes \varrho_{C'} |\phi^+\rangle_{CC'} = \mathrm{Tr}(\sigma_C \varrho_C)$, so for rank-deficient ϱ we can calculate $\mathcal{E}_{CC' \to AA'}(\sigma_C \otimes (\cdot)_{C'})$ using what we have already proven.

The other direction is proven by a simple application of Lemma A.2. □

The fact that NM is equivalent to 2-designs (for unitary schemes) is a straightforward consequence of the above.

Proof. (of Theorem 3.6) First, assume (τ_K, E, D) is a unitary NM QES with $E_k = U_k(\cdot)U_k^\dagger$. Then it has $|C| = |A|$, and $D_K(\tau_C) = \tau_A$, so the conclusion of Theorem 3.7 in this case (i.e., Eq. (3.10)) is exactly the condition for $\{U_k\}$ to be an exact channel twirl design and therefore an exact 2-design. If (τ_K, E, D), on the other hand, is a unitary QES and $\{U_k\}$ is a 2-design, then Eq. (3.10) holds and the scheme is therefore NM according to Theorem 3.7. $\qquad\square$

Relationship to ABW Non-malleability. Ambainis, Bouda and Winter give a different definition of non-malleability, expressed in terms of the effective maps that an adversary can apply to the plaintext by acting on the ciphertext produced from encrypting with a random key [6]. According to their definition, a scheme is non-malleable if the adversary can only apply maps from a very restricted class *when averaging over the key, and without giving side information to the active adversary.* Let us recall their definition here.

First, given a QES (τ_K, E, D), we define the set $S := \{D_K(\sigma_C) \,|\, \sigma_C \in \mathcal{B}(\mathcal{H}_C)\}$ consisting of all valid average decryptions. We then define the class C_A^S of all "replacement channels". This is the set of CPTP maps belonging to the space

$$\mathrm{span}_{\mathbb{R}}\{\mathrm{id}_A, (X \mapsto \mathrm{Tr}(X)\sigma_A) : \sigma_A \in S\}. \tag{3.14}$$

We then make the following definition, which first appeared in [6].

Definition 3.8 (ABW non-malleability). *A QES (τ_K, E, D) is ABW-non-malleable (ABW-NM) if it is ITS, and for all channels $\Lambda_{C \to C}$, we have*

$$\mathrm{Tr}_K\left[D_{CK \to AK} \circ \Lambda_{C \to C} \circ E_{AK \to CK}(\cdot \otimes \tau_K)\right] \in C_A^S. \tag{3.15}$$

As indicated in [6], an approximate version of Eq. (3.15) is obtained by considering the diamond-norm distance between the effective channel and the set C_A^S; this implies the possibility of an auxiliary reference system, which is denoted R in NM. We emphasize that this reference system is not under the control of the adversary. In particular, ABW-NM does not allow for adversaries which maintain *and actively use* side information about the plaintext system.

Another notable distinction is that [6] includes a secrecy assumption in the definition of an encryption scheme; under this assumption, it is shown that a unitary QES is ABW-NM if and only if the encryption unitaries form a 2-design. By our Theorem 3.6, we see that NM and ABW-NM are equivalent in the case of unitary schemes. So, in that case, ABW-NM actually ensures a much stronger security notion than originally considered by the authors of [6].

In the general case, NM is strictly stronger than ABW-NM. First, by comparing the conditions of Definition 3.8 to Eq. (3.10), we immediately get the following corollary of Theorem 3.7.

Corollary 3.9. *If a QES satisfies NM, then it also satisfies ABW-NM.*

Second, we give a separation example which shows that ABW-NM is highly insecure; in fact, it allows the adversary to "inject" a plaintext of their choice into the ciphertext. This is insecure even under the classical definition of information-theoretic non-malleability of [20]. We now describe the scheme and this attack.

Example 3.10. *Suppose (τ_K, E, D) is a QES that is both NM and ABW-NM. Define a modified scheme (τ_K, E', D'), with enlarged ciphertext space $\mathcal{H}_{C'} = \mathcal{H}_C \oplus \mathcal{H}_{\hat{A}}$ (where $\mathcal{H}_{\hat{A}} \cong \mathcal{H}_A$) and encryption and decryption defined by*

$$E'(X) = E(X)_C \oplus 0_{\hat{A}}$$
$$D'(X) = D_{CK \to AK}(\Pi_C X \Pi_C) + \mathrm{id}_{\hat{A}K \to AK}(\Pi_{\hat{A}} X \Pi_{\hat{A}}).$$

Then (τ_K, E', D') is ABW-NM but not NM.

While encryption ignores $\mathcal{H}_{\hat{A}}$, decryption measures if we are in C or $\hat{A}$ and then decrypts (in the first case) or just outputs the contents (in the second case.) This is a dramatic violation of NM: set $\mathcal{H}_{\tilde{B}} \cong \mathcal{H}_A$, trivial B and R, and

$$\Lambda_{C' \to C'\tilde{B}}(X) = \mathrm{Tr}(X)0_C \oplus |\phi^+\rangle\langle\phi^+|_{\hat{A}\tilde{B}}; \tag{3.16}$$

it follows that, for all ϱ,

$$I(AR : \tilde{B})_{\tilde{\Lambda}(\varrho)} = 2\log|A| \gg h(|C'|^{-2}) = h(p_=(\Lambda, \varrho)). \tag{3.17}$$

Now let us show that (τ, E', D') is still ABW-NM. Let $\Lambda_{C' \to C'}$ be an attack, i.e., an arbitrary CPTP map. Then the effective plaintext map is

$$\tilde{\Lambda}_{A \to A} = D \circ \Lambda_{C \to C}^C \circ E + \Lambda_{C \to A}^{\hat{A}} \circ E, \tag{3.18}$$

where $\Lambda^C(X_C) = \Pi_C \Lambda(X_C \oplus 0_{\hat{A}})\Pi_C$ and $\Lambda^{\hat{A}}(X_C) = \mathrm{id}_{\hat{A} \to A}(\Pi_{\hat{A}} \Lambda(X_C \oplus 0_{\hat{A}})\Pi_{\hat{A}})$. Since (τ, E, D) is ITS (Proposition 3.5), there exists a fixed state ϱ_C^0 such that $E_K(\varrho_A) = \varrho_C^0$ for all ϱ_A. Since (τ, E, D) is ABW-NM, we also know that

$$\mathrm{Tr}_K \circ D \circ \Lambda_{C \to C}^C \circ E = \tilde{\Lambda}_1 \in C_A^S,$$

with $S = \{D_K(\sigma_C) \,|\, \sigma_C \in \mathcal{B}(\mathcal{H}_C)\}$. We therefore get

$$\tilde{\Lambda}_{A \to A} = \tilde{\Lambda}_1 + \langle\Lambda^{\hat{A}}(\varrho_C^0)\rangle \in C_A^{S'}, \tag{3.19}$$

with $S' = \{D_K'(\sigma_{C'}) \,|\, \sigma_{C'} \in \mathcal{B}(\mathcal{H}_{C'})\}$. This is true because S' contains all constant maps, as $D_K'(0_C \oplus \varrho_{\hat{A}}) = \varrho_A$.

4   The Approximate Setting

We now consider the case of approximate non-malleability. Approximate schemes are relevant for several reasons. First, an approximate scheme with negligible error can be more efficient than an exact one: the most efficient construction of an exact 2-design requires a quantum circuit of $O(n \log n \log\log n)$ gates [13], where approximate 2-designs can be achieved with linear-length circuits [14]. Second, in practice, absolutely perfect implementation of all quantum gates is too much to expect—even with error-correction. Third, when passing to authentication one must allow for errors, as it is always possible for the adversary to escape detection (with low probability) by guessing the secret key.

For all these reasons, it is important to understand what happens when the perfect secrecy and perfect non-malleability requirements are slightly relaxed. In this section, we show that our definitions and results are stable under such relaxations, and prove several additional results for quantum authentication. We begin with the approximate-case analogue of perfect secrecy.

Definition 4.1 (Approximate secrecy). *Fix $\varepsilon > 0$. A QES (τ_K, E, D) is ε-approximately secret (ε-ITS) if, for any $\mathcal{H}_B$ and any ϱ_{AB}, setting $\sigma_{CBK} = E(\varrho_{AB} \otimes \tau_K)$ implies $I(C : B)_\sigma \leq \varepsilon$.*

Analogously to the exact case, unitary schemes satisfying approximate secrecy are equivalent to approximate one-designs (see the full version of this article [3]).

4.1 Approximate Non-malleability

Definition. We now define a natural approximate-case analogue of NM, i.e., Definition 3.4. Let us briefly recall the context. The malleability scenario is described by systems A, C, B and R (respectively, plaintext, ciphertext, side-information, and reference), an initial tripartite state ϱ_{ABR}, and an attack channel $\Lambda_{CB \to C\tilde{B}}$. Given this data, we have the effective channel $\tilde{\Lambda}_{AB \to A\tilde{B}}$ defined in Eq. (3.1) and the "unavoidable attack" probability $p_=(\Lambda, \varrho)$ defined in Eq. (3.2). The new definition now simply relaxes the requirement on the increase of the adversary's mutual information.

Definition 4.2 (Approximate non-malleability). *A QES (τ_K, E, D) is ε-non-malleable (ε-NM) if for any state ϱ_{ABR} and any CPTP map $\Lambda_{CB \to C\tilde{B}}$, we have*

$$I(AR : \tilde{B})_{\tilde{\Lambda}(\varrho)} \leq I(AR : B)_\varrho + h(p_=(\Lambda, \varrho)) + \varepsilon. \qquad (4.1)$$

We record the approximate version of Proposition 3.5, i.e., non-malleability implies secrecy. The proof is a straightforward adaptation of the exact case.

Proposition 4.3. *Let (τ_K, E, D) be an ε-NM QES. Then (τ_K, E, D) is 2ε-ITS.*

Non-malleability with Approximate Designs. Continuing as before, we now generalize the characterization theorems of non-malleability (Theorems 3.6 and 3.7) to the approximate case.

Theorem 4.4. *Let (τ, E, D) be a QES with ciphertext dimension $|C| = 2^m$ and $r > 0$ a sufficiently large constant. Then the following holds:*

1. If (τ, E, D) is 2^{-rm}-NM, then for any attack $\Lambda_{CB \to C\tilde{B}}$, the effective map $\tilde{\Lambda}_{AB \to A\tilde{B}}$ is $2^{-\Omega(m)}$-close (in diamond norm) to

$$\tilde{\Lambda}^{\text{exact}}_{AB \to A\tilde{B}} = \text{id}_A \otimes \Lambda'_{B \to \tilde{B}} + \frac{1}{|C|^2 - 1} \left(|C|^2 \langle D_K(\tau) \rangle - \text{id} \right)_A \otimes \Lambda''_{B \to \tilde{B}},$$

with Λ', Λ'' as in Theorem 3.7.

2. Suppose that $\log |R| = O(2^m)$, where R is the reference register in Definition 4.2. Then there exists a constant r, such that if every attack $\Lambda_{CB \to C\tilde{B}}$ results in an effective map that is 2^{-rm}-close to $\tilde{\Lambda}^{\text{exact}}$, then the scheme is $2^{-\Omega(m)}$-NM.

This theorem is proven with explicit constants in Appendix B as Theorem B.3. The condition on R required for the second implication is necessary, as the relevant mutual information can at worst grow proportional to the logarithm of the dimension according to the Alicki-Fannes inequality. This is not a very strong requirement, as it should be relatively easy for the honest parties to put a bound on their total memory.

Next, we record the corollary which states that, for unitary schemes, approximate non-malleability is equivalent to encryption with an approximate 2-design. The proof proceeds as in the exact case, now starting from Theorem 4.4.

Theorem 4.5. Let $\Pi = (\tau_K, E, D)$ be a unitary QES for n-qubit messages and $f : \mathbb{N} \to \mathbb{N}$ a function that grows at most exponential. Then there exists a constant $r > 0$ such that

1. If $\{E_k\}$ is a $\Omega(2^{-rn})$-approximate 2-design and $\log |R| \le f(n)$, then Π is $2^{-\Omega(n)}$-NM.
2. If Π is $\Omega(2^{-rn})$-NM, then $\{E_k\}_{k \in K}$ is a $2^{-\Omega(n)}$-approximate 2-design.

Relationship to Approximate ABW. Recall that, in Sect. 3.2, we discussed the relationship between our notion of exact non-malleability and that of Ambainis et al. [6] (i.e., ABW-NM.) As we now briefly outline, our conclusions carry over to the approximate case without any significant changes.

As described in Eq. (3") of [6], one first relaxes the notion of ABW-NM appropriately by requiring that the containment (3.15) in Definition 3.8 holds up to ε error in the diamond-norm distance. In the unitary case, both definitions are equivalent to approximate 2-designs (by the results of [6], and our Theorem 4.5). In the case of general schemes, the plaintext injection attack described in Example 3.10 again shows that approximate ABW-NM is insufficient, and that approximate NM is strictly stronger.

4.2 Authentication

Definitions. Our definitions of authentication will be faithful to the original versions in [16,18], with one slight modification. When decryption rejects, our encryption schemes (Definition 3.1) output $\perp$ in the plaintext space, rather than setting an auxiliary qubit to a "reject" state. These definitions are equivalent in the sense that one can always set an extra qubit to "reject" conditioned on the plaintext being $\bot$ (or vice-versa). Nonetheless, as we will see below, this mild change has some interesting consequences.

We begin with the definition of Dupuis, Nielsen and Salvail [16], which demands that the effective average channel of the attacker ignores the plaintext.

Definition 4.6 (DNS Authentication [16]). *A QES (τ_K, E, D) is called ε-DNS-authenticating if, for any CPTP-map $\Lambda_{CB \to CB'}$, there exists CP-maps $\Lambda^{acc}_{B \to \tilde{B}}$ and $\Lambda^{rej}_{B \to \tilde{B}}$ such that $\Lambda^{acc} + \Lambda^{rej}$ is[1] TP, and for all ϱ_{AB} we have*

$$\left\| \operatorname{Tr}_K D(\Lambda(E(\varrho_{AB} \otimes \tau_K))) - (\Lambda^{acc}(\varrho_{AB}) + |\bot\rangle\langle\bot| \otimes \Lambda^{rej}(\varrho_B)) \right\|_1 \leq \varepsilon. \quad (4.2)$$

An alternative definition was recently given by Garg, Yuen and Zhandry [18]. It asks that, *conditioned on acceptance*, with high probability the effective channel is close to a channel which ignores the plaintext.

Definition 4.7 (GYZ Authentication [18]). *A QES (τ_K, E, D) is called ε-GYZ-authenticating if, for any CPTP-map $\Lambda_{CB \to CB'}$, there exists a CP-map $\Lambda^{acc}_{B \to \tilde{B}}$ such that for all ϱ_{AB}*

$$\left\| \Pi_{acc} D(\Lambda(E(\varrho_{AB} \otimes \tau_K))) \Pi_{acc} - \Lambda^{acc}(\varrho_{AB}) \otimes \tau_K \right\|_1 \leq \varepsilon. \quad (4.3)$$

Here Π_{acc} is the acceptance projector, i.e. projection onto $\mathcal{H}_A$ in $\mathcal{H}_A \oplus \mathbb{C}|\bot\rangle$.

A peculiar aspect of the original definition in [18] is that it does not specify the outcome in case of rejection, and is thus stated in terms of trace non-increasing maps. Of course, all realistic quantum maps must be CPTP; this means that the designer of the encryption scheme must still declare what to do with the contents of the plaintext register after decryption. Our notion of decryption makes one such choice (i.e., output $\bot$) which seems natural.

GYZ Authentication Implies DNS Authentication. A priori, the relationship between Definition 2.2 in [16] and Definition 8 in [18] is not completely clear. On one hand, the latter is stronger in the sense that it requires success with high probability (rather than simply on average.) On the other hand, the former makes the additional demand that the ciphertext is untouched even if we reject. As we now show, GYZ-authentication in fact implies DNS-authentication.

Theorem 4.8. *Let (τ, E, D) be ε-totally authenticating for sufficiently small ε. Then it is $O(\sqrt{\varepsilon})$-DNS authenticating.*

---

[1] Note that there is a typographic error in [11,16] at this point of the definition. In those papers, the two effective maps are asked to sum to the identity (instead of just a TP map), which is impossible for many obvious choices of Λ.

Proof. Let $\Lambda_{CB \to C\tilde{B}}$ be a CPTP map and $\varepsilon \le 62^{-2}$. By Definition 4.7 there exists a CP map $\Lambda'_{B \to \tilde{B}}$ such that for all states ϱ_{AB},

$$\|\Pi_a D(\Lambda(E(\varrho_{AB} \otimes \tau_K))) \Pi_a - \Lambda'(\varrho_{AB} \otimes \tau_K)))\|_1 \le \varepsilon. \tag{4.4}$$

Assume for simplicity that $D = M_\perp \circ D$, where $M_\perp$ measures the rejection symbol versus the rest. (otherwise we can define a new decryption map that way.) Define the CP maps

$$\Lambda^{(1)}_{AB \to \tilde{B}} = \operatorname{Tr}_A \Pi_a \tilde{\Lambda}(\cdot) \qquad \Lambda^{(2)}_{AB \to \tilde{B}} = \langle \perp |_A \tilde{\Lambda}(\cdot) | \perp \rangle_A$$

$$\Lambda''_{B \to \tilde{B}} = \operatorname{Tr}_C \Lambda(E_K(\tau_A) \otimes (\cdot)).$$

By Theorem 15 in [18] we have

$$|E_K(\varrho_{ABR}) - E_K(\tau_A) \otimes \varrho_{BR}\|_1 \le 14\sqrt{\varepsilon}, \tag{4.5}$$

which implies that

$$\|\operatorname{Tr}_A \otimes \Lambda'' - \operatorname{Tr}_C \circ \Lambda \circ E_K\|_\diamond \le \hat{\varepsilon} := 14\sqrt{\varepsilon}. \tag{4.6}$$

Note that

$$\operatorname{Tr}_C \circ \Lambda \circ E_K = \operatorname{Tr}_{CK} \circ \Lambda \circ E((\cdot) \otimes \tau_K)$$
$$= \operatorname{Tr}_{AK} \circ D \circ \Lambda \circ E((\cdot) \otimes \tau_K) = \operatorname{Tr}_A \circ \tilde{\Lambda}. \tag{4.7}$$

On the other hand, we also have that, by Eq. (4.4),

$$\left\|\operatorname{Tr}_A \circ \tilde{\Lambda} - \operatorname{Tr}_A \otimes \Lambda' - \Lambda^{(2)}\right\| \le \left\|\operatorname{Tr}_A \left(\Pi_a \tilde{\Lambda}(\cdot)\right) - \Lambda'\right\|_\diamond \le \varepsilon \tag{4.8}$$

Combining Eqs. (4.6), (4.7) and (4.8), we get

$$\left\|\Lambda^{(2)} - \operatorname{Tr}_A \otimes (\Lambda'' - \Lambda')\right\|_\diamond \le \varepsilon + \hat{\varepsilon}. \tag{4.9}$$

Now observe that

$$[\operatorname{Tr}_A \otimes (\Lambda' - \Lambda'')_{B \to \tilde{B}}] \circ \Xi_{A \to A} = \operatorname{Tr}_A \otimes (\Lambda' - \Lambda'')_{B \to \tilde{B}} \tag{4.10}$$

For all CPTP maps $\Xi_{A \to A}$. We define $\Lambda'''_{B \to \tilde{B}} = \Lambda^{(2)}(\tau_A \otimes (\cdot))$ and calculate

$$\left\|\Lambda^{(2)} - \operatorname{Tr}_A \otimes \Lambda'''\right\|_\diamond \le \left\|\Lambda^{(2)} - \operatorname{Tr}_A \otimes (\Lambda'' - \Lambda')\right\|_\diamond$$
$$+ \left\|\operatorname{Tr}_A \otimes (\Lambda'' - \Lambda') - \operatorname{Tr}_A \otimes \Lambda'''\right\|_\diamond,$$

by the triangle inequality for the diamond norm. Continuing with the calculation,

$$\left\|\Lambda^{(2)} - \operatorname{Tr}_A \otimes \Lambda'''\right\|_\diamond \le \varepsilon + \hat{\varepsilon} + \left\|\operatorname{Tr}_A \otimes (\Lambda'' - \Lambda') - \operatorname{Tr}_A \otimes \Lambda'''\right\|_\diamond$$
$$= \varepsilon + \hat{\varepsilon} + \left\|\left[\operatorname{Tr}_A \otimes (\Lambda'' - \Lambda') - \Lambda^{(2)}\right] \circ \langle \tau_A \rangle_{A \to A}\right\|_\diamond$$
$$\le 2(\varepsilon + \hat{\varepsilon}) = 28\sqrt{\varepsilon} + 2\varepsilon. \tag{4.11}$$

The first inequality above is Eq. (4.9). The first equality is just a rewriting of the definition of Λ''', and the second equality is Eq. (4.10). Finally, the last inequality is due to Eq. (4.9) and the fact that the diamond norm is submultiplicative.

We have almost proven security according to Definition 4.6, as we have shown $\tilde{\Lambda}$ to be close in diamond norm to $\mathrm{id}_A \otimes \Lambda' + \langle|\perp\rangle\langle\perp|\rangle \otimes \Lambda'''$. However, $\Lambda' + \Lambda'''$ is only approximately TP; more precisely, we have that for all ϱ_{ABR},

$$|\mathrm{Tr}(\Lambda' + \Lambda''')(\varrho_{ABR}) - 1| \leq 28\sqrt{\varepsilon} + 3\varepsilon \tag{4.12}$$

by the triangle inequality. We therefore have to modify $\Lambda' + \Lambda''$ so that it becomes TP, while keeping the structure required for DNS authentication. Let $M_B = (\Lambda' + \Lambda''')^\dagger(1_{\tilde{B}})$. (4.12). Defining the CP-map $\mathcal{M}(X) = M^{-1/2}XM^{-1/2}$ and noting it is well-behaved for small ε, it follows from a straightforward calculation (see the full version [3] of this article for details) that

$$\left\|\tilde{\Lambda}_{AB\to A\tilde{B}} - \mathrm{id}_A \otimes \Lambda^{\mathrm{acc}}_{B\to\tilde{B}} - \perp \otimes \Lambda^{\mathrm{rej}}_{B\to\tilde{B}}\right\|_\diamond \leq O(\sqrt{\varepsilon}). \tag{4.13}$$

with $\lambda^{\mathrm{acc}} = \Lambda' \circ \mathcal{M}$ and $\Lambda^{\mathrm{rej}} = \Lambda'' \circ \mathcal{M}$.   □

Achieving GYZ Authentication with Two-Designs. In [18], the authors provide a scheme for their notion of authentication based on unitary eight-designs. We now show that, in fact, an approximate 2-design suffices. This implies that the well-known Clifford scheme (see e.g. [11,15]) satisfies the strong security of Definition 4.7. We remark that our proof is inspired by the reasoning based on Schur's lemma used in results on decoupling [8,9,17,24].

Theorem 4.9. *Let* $\mathrm{D} = \{U_k\}_k$ *be a δ-approximate unitary 2-design on $\mathcal{H}_C$. Let* $\mathcal{H}_C = \mathcal{H}_A \otimes \mathcal{H}_T$ *and define*

$$E_k(X_A) = U_k\left(X_A \otimes |0\rangle\langle0|_T\right)(U_k)^\dagger$$
$$D_k(Y_C) = \langle0|_T(U_k)^\dagger YU_k|0\rangle_T + \mathrm{Tr}((1_T - |0\rangle\langle0|_T)(U_k)^\dagger YU_k)|\perp\rangle\langle\perp|.$$

Then the QES (τ_K, E, D) is $4(1/|T| + 3\delta)^{1/3}$-GYZ-authenticating.

Remark 4.10. *The following proof uses the same simulator as the proof for the 8-design scheme in [18], called "oblivious adversary" there. The construction exhibited there is efficient given that the real adversary is efficient.*

Proof. To improve readability, we will occasionally switch between adding subscripts to operators (indicating which spaces they act on) and omitting these subscripts. We begin by remarking that it is sufficient to prove the GYZ condition (specifically, Eq. 4.3) for pure input states and isometric adversary channels. Indeed, for a general state ϱ_{AB} and a general map $\Lambda_{CB\to C\tilde{B}}$, we may let ϱ_{ABR} and $V_{CB\to C\tilde{B}E}$ be the purification and Stinespring dilation, respectively.

We then simply observe that the trace distance decreases under partial trace (see e.g. [25]). Let ϱ_{AB} be a pure input state and

$$\Lambda_{CB \to C\tilde{B}}(X_{CB}) = V_{CB \to C\tilde{B}} X_{CB} V_{CB \to C\tilde{B}}^{\dagger}$$

an isometry. We define the corresponding "ideal" channel Γ_V, and the corresponding "real, accept" channel Φ_k, as follows:

$$(\Gamma_V)_{B \to \tilde{B}} = \frac{1}{|C|} \mathrm{Tr}_C V \text{ and}$$

$$(\Phi_k)_{AB \to A\tilde{B}} = \langle 0|_T (U_k)_C^{\dagger} V_{CB \to C\tilde{B}} U_k |0\rangle_T. \tag{4.14}$$

Note that for any matrix M with $\|M\|_{\infty} \leq 1$, the map $\Lambda_M(X) = M^{\dagger} X M$ is completely positive and trace non-increasing. We have

$$\|\Gamma_V\|_{\infty} \leq \frac{1}{|C|} \sum_i \|\langle i|V|i\rangle\|_{\infty} \leq 1. \tag{4.15}$$

We start by bounding the expectation of $\|((\Gamma_V)_{B \to \tilde{B}} - (\Phi_k)_{AB \to A\tilde{B}})|\varrho\rangle_{AB}\|_2^2$, as follows. To simplify notation, we set $\sigma_{ABT} := |\varrho\rangle\langle\varrho|_{AB} \otimes |0\rangle\langle 0|_T$ to be the tagged state corresponding to plaintext (and side information) ϱ_{AB}.

$$\frac{1}{|K|} \sum_k \|(\Gamma_V - \Phi_k)|\varrho\rangle\|_2^2 = \frac{1}{|K|} \sum_k \langle\varrho|(\Gamma_V - \Phi_k)^{\dagger}(\Gamma_V - \Phi_k)|\varrho\rangle$$

$$= \frac{1}{|K|} \sum_k \mathrm{Tr}\left[\sigma_{ABT}(U_k)^{\dagger} V^{\dagger} U_k |0\rangle\langle 0|(U_k)^{\dagger} V U_k\right]$$

$$- 2\frac{1}{|K|} \sum_k \mathrm{Tr}\left[\sigma_{ABT}(U_k)^{\dagger} V^{\dagger} U_k \Gamma_V\right] + \langle\varrho| (\Gamma_V)^{\dagger} \Gamma_V |\varrho\rangle. \tag{4.16}$$

First we bound the second term, using the fact that Γ_V only acts on B.

$$\frac{1}{|K|} \sum_k \mathrm{Tr}\left[\sigma_{ABT}(U_k)^{\dagger} V^{\dagger} U_k \Gamma_V\right] = \frac{1}{|K|} \sum_k \mathrm{Tr}\left[U_k \sigma_{ABT}(U_k)^{\dagger} V^{\dagger} \Gamma_V\right]$$

$$= \int \mathrm{Tr}\left[(U\sigma_{ABT}U^{\dagger} + \Delta) V^{\dagger}\Gamma_V\right] \geq \int \mathrm{Tr}\left[U\sigma_{ABT}U^{\dagger}V^{\dagger}\Gamma_V\right] - \delta$$

$$= \int \mathrm{Tr}\left[\sigma_{ABT}U^{\dagger}V^{\dagger}U\Gamma_V\right] - \delta = \langle\varrho| (\Gamma_V)^{\dagger} \Gamma_V |\varrho\rangle - \delta. \tag{4.17}$$

In the above, the operator Δ is the "error" operator in the δ-approximate 2-design. The second equality above follows from $\|\Delta\|_1 \leq \delta$ and the fact that a 2-design is also a 1-design; the inequality follows from Hölder's inequality, and the last step follows from Schur's lemma.

The first term of the RHS of Eq. (4.16) can be simplified as follows. We will begin by applying the swap trick (Lemma 2.1) $\mathrm{Tr}[XY] = \mathrm{Tr}[FX \otimes Y]$ in the second line below. The swap trick is applied to register CC', with the operators X and Y defined as indicated below.

$$\frac{1}{|K|} \sum_k \text{Tr}\Big[\sigma_{ABT} \underbrace{(U_k)^\dagger_C V^\dagger_{C\tilde{B}\to CB}(U_k)_C |0\rangle\langle 0|_T}_{X} \underbrace{(U_k)^\dagger_C V_{CB\to C\tilde{B}}(U_k)_C}_{Y}\Big]$$

$$= \frac{1}{|K|} \sum_k \text{Tr}\Big[(\sigma_{ABT} \otimes |0\rangle\langle 0|_{T'})\, (U_k^{\otimes 2})_{CC'} V^\dagger_{C\tilde{B}\to CB} V_{C'B\to C'\tilde{B}} (U_k^{\otimes 2})^\dagger_{CC'} F_{CC'} \Big]$$

$$= \frac{1}{|K|} \sum_k \text{Tr}\Big[(U_k^{\otimes 2})^\dagger_{CC'} (\sigma_{ABT} \otimes |0\rangle\langle 0|_{T'})\, (U_k^{\otimes 2})_{CC'} V^\dagger_{C\tilde{B}\to CB} V_{C'B\to C'\tilde{B}} F_{CC'} \Big]$$

$$\leq \int \text{Tr}\Big[(U^{\otimes 2})^\dagger_{CC'} (\sigma_{ABT} \otimes |0\rangle\langle 0|_{T'})\, U^{\otimes 2}_{CC'} V^\dagger_{C\tilde{B}\to CB} V_{C'B\to C'\tilde{B}} F_{CC'} \Big] + \delta$$

$$= \int \text{Tr}\Big[(\sigma_{ABT} \otimes |0\rangle\langle 0|_{T'})\, U^{\otimes 2}_{CC'} V^\dagger_{C\tilde{B}\to CB} V_{C'B\to C'\tilde{B}} (U^{\otimes 2})^\dagger_{CC'} F_{CC'} \Big] + \delta. \tag{4.18}$$

The inequality above follows the same way as in Eq. 4.17. Let $d = |C|$.

An easy representation-theoretic calculation (see the Full version [3] for details) shows that

$$\int U^{\otimes 2} V^\dagger_{C\tilde{B}\to CB} V_{C'B\to C'\tilde{B}} (U^{\otimes 2})^\dagger \, dU = \mathbb{1}_{CC'} \otimes R^{\mathbb{1}}_B + F_{CC'} \otimes R^F_B, \tag{4.19}$$

where we have set

$$R^{\mathbb{1}}_B = \frac{1}{d(d^2-1)}\Big(d^3 \Gamma^\dagger_V \Gamma_V - d\mathbb{1} \Big) = \frac{1}{(d^2-1)}\Big(d^2 \Gamma^\dagger_V \Gamma_V - \mathbb{1} \Big)$$

$$R^F_B = \frac{1}{d(d^2-1)}\Big(d^2 \mathbb{1} - d^2 \Gamma^\dagger_V \Gamma_V \Big) = \frac{d}{(d^2-1)}\Big(\mathbb{1} - \Gamma^\dagger_V \Gamma_V \Big).$$

plugging (4.19) into (4.18) and using Lemma 2.1 again, we get

$$\int \text{Tr}\Big[(\sigma_{ABT} \otimes |0\rangle\langle 0|_{T'})\, U^{\otimes 2}_{CC'} V^\dagger_{C\tilde{B}\to CB} V_{C'B\to C'\tilde{B}} (U^{\otimes 2})^\dagger_{CC'} F_{CC'} \Big]$$

$$= \text{Tr}\Big[(\sigma_{ABT} \otimes |0\rangle\langle 0|_{T'})\, (\mathbb{1}_{CC'} \otimes R^{\mathbb{1}}_{B^2\to\tilde{B}^2} + F_{CC'} \otimes R^F_{B^2\to\tilde{B}^2}) F_{CC'} \Big]$$

$$= \text{Tr}\Big[|\varrho\rangle\langle\varrho|_B\, (R^{\mathbb{1}}_B + |A| R^F_B) \Big]$$

$$= \text{Tr}\Big[|\varrho\rangle\langle\varrho|_B\, \Big(\frac{d(d-|A|)}{d^2-1}\Big(\Gamma^\dagger_V \Gamma_V \Big)_B + \frac{d|A|-1}{d^2-1}\mathbb{1}_B \Big) \Big]. \tag{4.20}$$

Now recall that $d = |A||T|$. Using the fact that $(a-1)/(b-1) \leq a/b$ for $b \geq a$, we can give a bound as follows.

$$\text{Tr}\Big[|\varrho\rangle\langle\varrho|\, \Big(\frac{d(d-|A|)}{d^2-1}\Big(\Gamma^\dagger_V \Gamma_V \Big) + \frac{d|A|-1}{d^2-1}\mathbb{1} \Big) \Big]$$

$$= \frac{d|A|(|T|-1)}{d^2-1}\langle\varrho| \Big(\Gamma^\dagger_V \Gamma_V \Big) |\varrho\rangle + \frac{d|A|-1}{d^2-1}$$

$$\leq \langle\varrho| \Big(\Gamma^\dagger_V \Gamma_V \Big) |\varrho\rangle + \frac{1}{|T|}. \tag{4.21}$$

Putting everything together, we arrive at

$$\frac{1}{|K|} \sum_k \|(\Gamma_V - \Phi_k)|\varrho\rangle\|_2^2 \le \frac{1}{|T|} + 3\delta. \tag{4.22}$$

By Markov's inequality this implies

$$\mathbb{P}\left[\|(\Gamma_V - \Phi_k)|\varrho\rangle\|_2^2 > \alpha\left(\frac{1}{|T|} + 3\delta\right)\right] \le \frac{1}{\alpha} \tag{4.23}$$

which is equivalent to

$$\mathbb{P}\left[\|(\Gamma_V - \Phi_k)|\varrho\rangle\|_2 > \alpha^{1/2}\left(\frac{1}{|T|} + 3\delta\right)^{1/2}\right] \le \frac{1}{\alpha}, \tag{4.24}$$

where the probability is taken over the uniform distribution on D. Choosing $\alpha = (1/|T| + 3\delta)^{-1/3}$ this yields

$$\mathbb{P}\left[\|(\Gamma_V - \Phi_k)|\varrho\rangle\|_2 > \left(\frac{1}{|T|} + 3\delta\right)^{1/3}\right] \le \left(\frac{1}{|T|} + 3\delta\right)^{1/3}. \tag{4.25}$$

Let $S \subset D$ be such that $|S|/|D| \ge 1 - (1/|T| + 3\delta)^{1/3}$ and $\|(\Gamma_V - \Phi_k)|\varrho\rangle\|_2 \le (1/|T| + 3\delta)^{1/3}$ for all $U_k \in S$. Using the easy-to-verify inequality $\||\psi\rangle\langle\psi| - |\phi\rangle\langle\phi|\|_1 \le 2\||\psi\rangle - |\phi\rangle\|_2$, we can bound

$$\frac{1}{|K|} \sum_{U_k \in \mathcal{D}} \left\|\Phi_k|\varrho\rangle\langle\varrho|(\Phi_k)^\dagger - \Gamma_V|\varrho\rangle\langle\varrho|\Gamma_V^\dagger\right\|_1$$

$$\le \frac{1}{|S|} \sum_{U_k \in S} \left\|\Phi_k|\varrho\rangle\langle\varrho|(\Phi_k)^\dagger - \Gamma_V|\varrho\rangle\langle\varrho|\Gamma_V^\dagger\right\|_1 + 2\left(\frac{1}{|T|} + 3\delta\right)^{1/3}$$

$$\le \frac{2}{|S|} \sum_{U_k \in S} \|(\Gamma_V - \Phi_k)|\varrho\rangle\|_2 + 2|T|^{-1/3}$$

$$\le 4\left(\frac{1}{|T|} + 3\delta\right)^{1/3}. \tag{4.26}$$

This completes the proof for pure states and isometric adversary channels. As noted above, the general case follows.   □

As an example, one may set $|T| = 2^s$ (i.e. s tag qubits) and take an approximate unitary 2-design of accuracy 2^{-s}. The resulting scheme would then be $\Omega(2^{-s/3})$-GYZ-authenticating.

A straightforward corollary of the above result is that, in the case of unitary schemes, adding tags to non-malleable schemes results in GYZ authentication. We leave open the question of whether this is the case for general (not necessarily unitary) schemes.

Corollary 4.11. *Let (τ, E, D) be a 2^{-rn}-non-malleable unitary QES with plaintext space A. Define a new scheme (τ, E', D') with plaintext space A' where $A = TA'$ and*

$$E'(X) = E(X \otimes |0\rangle\langle 0|_T)$$
$$D'(Y) = \langle 0|_T D(Y)|0\rangle_T + \operatorname{Tr}\left[(\mathbb{1}_T - |0\rangle\langle 0|_T)D(Y)\right]|\perp\rangle\langle\perp|.$$

Then there is a constant $r > 0$ such that (τ, E', D') is $2^{-\Omega(n)}$-GYZ-authenticating if $|T| = 2^{\Omega(n)}$.

The proof is a direct application of Theorem 4.5 (approximate non-malleability is equivalent to approximate 2-design) and Theorem 4.9 (approximate 2-designs suffice for GYZ authentication.) We emphasize that, by Remark 2.3, exponential accuracy requirements can be met with polynomial-size circuits.

DNS Authentication from Non-malleability. We end with a theorem concerning the case of general (i.e., not necessarily unitary) schemes. We show that adding tags to a non-malleable scheme results in a DNS-authenticating scheme. In this proof we will denote the output system of the decryption map by $\overline{A}$ to emphasize that it is A enlarged by the reject symbol.

Theorem 4.12. *Let r be a sufficiently large constant, and let (τ, E, D) be an 2^{-rn}-NM QES with n qubit plaintext space A, and choose an integer d dividing $|A|$. Then there exists a decomposition $A = TA'$ and a state $|\psi\rangle_T$ such that $|T| = d$ and the scheme (τ, E', D') defined by*

$$E^t(X) = E(X \otimes |\psi\rangle\langle\psi|_T)$$
$$D^t(Y) = \langle\psi|_T D(Y)|\psi\rangle_T + \operatorname{Tr}\left[(\mathbb{1}_T - |\psi\rangle\langle\psi|_T)D(Y)\right]|\perp\rangle\langle\perp|.$$

is $(4/|T|) + 2^{-\Omega(n)}$-DNS-authenticating.

Proof. We prove the statement for $\varepsilon = 0$ for simplicity, the general case follows easily by employing Theorem 4.4 instead of Theorem 3.7.

By Theorem 3.7, for any attack map $\Lambda_{CB \to C\tilde{B}}$, the effective map is equal to

$$\tilde{\Lambda}_{AB \to \overline{A}\tilde{B}} = \operatorname{id}_A \otimes \Lambda'_{B \to \tilde{B}} + \frac{1}{|C|^2 - 1}\left(|C|^2\langle D_K(\tau_C)\rangle - \operatorname{id}\right)_{\overline{A}} \otimes \Lambda''_{B \to \tilde{B}} \quad (4.27)$$

for CP maps Λ' and Λ'' whose sum is TP. The effective map under the tagged scheme is therefore

$$\tilde{\Lambda}^t_{A'B \to \overline{A}'\tilde{B}} = \langle\psi|_T \tilde{\Lambda}_{AB \to \overline{A}\tilde{B}}((\cdot) \otimes \psi_T)|\psi\rangle_T$$
$$+ \operatorname{Tr}\left[(\mathbb{1}_T - \psi_T)\tilde{\Lambda}_{AB \to \overline{A}\tilde{B}}((\cdot) \otimes \psi_T)\right]|\perp\rangle\langle\perp|$$
$$= (\operatorname{id}_{A'})_{A' \to \overline{A}'} \otimes \Lambda'_{B \to \tilde{B}}$$
$$+ \left(|C|^2\langle(\langle\psi|_T D_K(\tau_C)|\psi\rangle_T)_{A'} \oplus \beta|\perp\rangle\langle\perp|\rangle - \operatorname{id}_{A'}\right)_{A \to \overline{A}'} \otimes \frac{\Lambda''_{B \to \tilde{B}}}{|C|^2 - 1}$$

with $\beta = \mathrm{Tr}\left[(\mathbb{1} - \psi)_T D_K(\tau_C)\right]$. We would like to say that, unless the output is the reject symbol, the effective map on A is the identity. We do not know, however, what $D_K(\tau_C)$ looks like. Therefore we apply a standard reasoning that if a quantity is small *in expectation*, then there exists at least one small instance. We calculate the expectation of $\mathrm{Tr}\langle\psi|_T D_K(\tau_C)|\psi\rangle_T$ when the decomposition $A = TA'$ is drawn at random according to the Haar measure,

$$\int \mathrm{Tr}\langle\psi|U_A^\dagger D_K(\tau_C)U_A|\psi\rangle_T \mathrm{d}U_A = \mathrm{Tr}\left[\left(\int U_A|\psi\rangle_T \otimes \mathbb{1}_{A'}\psi U_A^\dagger \mathrm{d}U_A\right)D_K(\tau_C)\right]$$

$$= \frac{\mathrm{Tr}\mathbb{1}_A}{\mathrm{Tr}\Pi_{\mathrm{acc}}}\mathrm{Tr}\Pi_{\mathrm{acc}}D_K(\tau_C)$$

$$\leq 1/|T|. \qquad (4.28)$$

Hence there exists at least one decomposition $A = TA'$ and a state $|\psi\rangle_T$ such that $\hat{\gamma} := \mathrm{Tr}\langle\psi|_T D_K(\tau_C)|\psi\rangle_T \leq 1/|T|$. Define $\gamma = \max(\hat{\gamma}, |C|^{-2})$. For the resulting primed scheme, let

$$\Lambda_{\mathrm{rej}} := \frac{(1-\gamma)|C|^2}{|C|^2 - 1}\Lambda'' \qquad \text{and} \qquad \Lambda_{\mathrm{acc}} = \Lambda' + \frac{\gamma|C|^2 - 1}{|C|^2 - 1}\Lambda''.$$

We calculate the diamond norm difference between the real effective map an the ideal effective map,

$$\left\|\tilde{\Lambda}^t - \mathrm{id}\otimes\Lambda_{\mathrm{acc}} - \langle|\perp\rangle\langle\perp|\rangle\otimes\Lambda_{\mathrm{rej}}\right\|_\diamond$$

$$\leq \left\|\mathrm{id}\otimes\Lambda' + \frac{1}{|C|^2-1}(|C|^2\langle(\langle\psi|D_K(\tau)|\psi\rangle)\rangle - \mathrm{id})\otimes\Lambda'' - \mathrm{id}\otimes\Lambda_{\mathrm{acc}}\right\|_\diamond$$

$$+ \left\||\langle|\perp\rangle\rangle\langle\perp|\otimes(1-\hat{\gamma})|C|^2\Lambda''/(|C|^2 - 1) - \langle|\perp\rangle\langle\perp|\rangle\otimes\Lambda_{\mathrm{rej}}\right\|_\diamond$$

$$\leq (1 + |C|^{-2})(|T|^{-1} + 2|C|^{-2})$$

$$= |T|^{-1}(1 + (|A'||T|)^{-2})(1 + 2|A'|^{-2})$$

$$\leq 4|T|^{-1} \qquad (4.29)$$

as desired. □

Acknowledgments. The authors would like to thank Anne Broadbent, Alexander Müller-Hermes, Frédéric Dupuis and Christopher Portmann for helpful discussions. G.A. and C.M. acknowledge financial support from the European Research Council (ERC Grant Agreement 337603), the Danish Council for Independent Research (Sapere Aude) and VILLUM FONDEN via the QMATH Centre of Excellence (Grant 10059).

References

1. Aaronson, S., Gottesman, D.: Improved simulation of stabilizer circuits. Phys. Rev. A **70**, 052328 (2004). doi:10.1103/PhysRevA.70.052328
2. Aharonov, D., Ben-Or, M., Eban, E.: Interactive proofs for quantum computations. In: Innovations in Computer Science - ICS 2010, Proceedings, Tsinghua University, Beijing, China, 5–7 January 2010, pp. 453–469 (2010)

3. Alagic, G., Majenz, C.: Quantum non-malleability and authentication. CoRR, abs/1610.04214 (2016). http://arxiv.org/abs/1610.04214

4. Alicki, R., Fannes, M.: Continuity of quantum conditional information. J. Phys. A: Math. Gen. **37**(5), L55 (2004)

5. Ambainis, A., Mosca, M., Tapp, A., De Wolf, R.: Private quantum channels. In: Proceedings of the FOCS 2000, pp. 547–553 (2000)

6. Ambainis, A., Bouda, J., Winter, A.: Nonmalleable encryption of quantum information. J. Math. Phys. **50**(4), 042106 (2009)

7. Barnum, H., Crépeau, C., Gottesman, D., Smith, A., Tapp, A.: Authentication of quantum messages. In: The 43rd Annual IEEE Symposium on Foundations of Computer Science, 2002, Proceedings, pp. 449–458. IEEE (2002)

8. Berta, M., Christandl, M., Renner, R.: The quantum reverse shannon theorem based on one-shot information theory. Commun. Math. Phys. **306**(3), 579–615 (2011)

9. Berta, M., Brandao, F.G.S.L., Majenz, C., Wilde, M.M.: Deconstruction and conditional erasure of quantum correlations. arXiv preprint arXiv:1609.06994 (2016)

10. Brandao, F.G.S.L., Harrow, A.W., Horodecki, M.: Local random quantum circuits are approximate polynomial-designs. arXiv preprint arXiv:1208.0692 (2012)

11. Broadbent, A., Wainewright, E.: Efficient simulation for quantum message authentication. arXiv preprint arXiv:1607.03075 (2016)

12. Choi, M.-D.: Completely positive linear maps on complex matrices. Linear Algebra Appl. **10**(3), 285–290 (1975)

13. Cleve, R., Leung, D., Liu, L., Wang, C.: Near-linear constructions of exact unitary 2-designs. Quantum Inf. Comput. **16**(9&10), 0721–0756 (2016)

14. Dankert, C., Cleve, R., Emerson, J., Livine, E.: Exact and approximate unitary 2-designs and their application to fidelity estimation. Phys. Rev. A **80**(1), 012304 (2009)

15. Dupuis, F., Nielsen, J.B., Salvail, L.: Secure two-party quantum evaluation of unitaries against specious adversaries. In: Rabin, T. (ed.) CRYPTO 2010. LNCS, vol. 6223, pp. 685–706. Springer, Heidelberg (2010). doi:10.1007/978-3-642-14623-7_37

16. Dupuis, F., Nielsen, J.B., Salvail, L.: Actively secure two-party evaluation of any quantum operation. In: Safavi-Naini, R., Canetti, R. (eds.) CRYPTO 2012. LNCS, vol. 7417, pp. 794–811. Springer, Heidelberg (2012). doi:10.1007/978-3-642-32009-5_46

17. Dupuis, F., Berta, M., Wullschleger, J., Renner, R.: One-shot decoupling. Commun. Math. Phys. **328**(1), 251–284 (2014)

18. Garg, S., Yuen, H., Zhandry, M.: New security notions and feasibility results for authentication of quantum data. arXiv preprint arXiv:1607.07759 (2016)

19. Jamiołkowski, A.: Linear transformations which preserve trace and positive semidefiniteness of operators. Rep. Math. Phys. **3**(4), 275–278 (1972)

20. Kawachi, A., Portmann, C., Tanaka, K.: Characterization of the relations between information-theoretic non-malleability, secrecy, and authenticity. In: Fehr, S. (ed.) ICITS 2011. LNCS, vol. 6673, pp. 6–24. Springer, Heidelberg (2011). doi:10.1007/978-3-642-20728-0_2

21. Lieb, E.H., Ruskai, M.B.: A fundamental property of quantum-mechanical entropy. Phy. Rev. Lett. **30**(10), 434 (1973a)

22. Lieb, E.H., Ruskai, M.B.: Proof of the strong subadditivity of quantum-mechanical entropy. J. Math. Phy. **14**(12), 1938–1941 (1973b)

23. Low, R.A.: Pseudo-randomness and learning in quantum computation. arXiv preprint arXiv:1006.5227 (2010)

24. Majenz, C., Berta, M., Dupuis, F., Renner, R., Christandl, M.: Catalytic decoupling of quantum information. arXiv preprint arXiv:1605.00514 (2016)
25. Nielsen, M.A., Chuang, I.L.: Quantum Computation and Quantum Information. Cambridge University Press, New York (2010)
26. Portmann, C.: Quantum authentication with key recycling. ArXiv e-prints, October 2016
27. Stinespring, W.F.: Positive functions on c*-algebras. Proc. Am. Math. Soc. **6**(2), 211–216 (1955)

A   Technical lemmas

In the following we state some technical Lemmas that we need in this article. The proofs can be found in the full version [3].

Lemma A.1. *Let* $X_{A \to B} \in L(\mathcal{H}_A, \mathcal{H}_B)$ *be a linear operator from A to B. Then*

$$X_{A \to B} |\phi^+\rangle_{AA'} = \sqrt{\frac{|B|}{|A|}} X^T_{B' \to A'} |\phi^+\rangle_{BB'}. \tag{A.1}$$

The next group of lemmas is concerned with entropic quantities.

Lemma A.2. *Let* $\Lambda^{(i)}_{A \to A'}$ *be CPTP maps and* $\Lambda^{(i)}_{B \to B'}$, $i = 1, ..., k$ *CP maps for* $i = 1, ..., k$ *such that* $\sum_i \Lambda^{(i)}_{B \to B'}$ *is trace preserving. Let* $\Lambda^{(i)}_{AB \to A'B'} = \Lambda^{(i)}_{A \to A'} \otimes \Lambda^{(i)}_{B \to B'}$ *and define the CPTP maps*

$$\Lambda_{AB \to A'B'C} = \sum_{i=1}^{k} \Lambda^{(i)}_{AB \to A'B'} \otimes |i\rangle\langle i|_C \text{ and}$$

$$\Lambda'_{B \to B'C} = \sum_{i=1}^{k} \Lambda^{(i)}_{B \to B'} \otimes |i\rangle\langle i|_C. \tag{A.2}$$

Then

$$I(A' : B')_{\Lambda(\varrho)} \leq I(A : B)_\varrho + H(C|A)_{\Lambda'(\varrho)} \leq I(A : B)_\varrho + H(C)_{\Lambda(\varrho)} \tag{A.3}$$

for any quantum state ϱ_{AB}.

The final lemma characterizes CPTP maps that are invertible on their image such that the inverse is CPTP as well.

Lemma A.3. *Let* (τ_K, E, D) *be a QES. Then the encryption maps have the structure*

$$(E_k)_{A \to C} = (V_k)_{A\hat{C} \to C} \left((\cdot) \otimes \sigma^{(k)}_{\hat{C}} \right) (V_k)^\dagger_{A\hat{C} \to C}, \tag{A.4}$$

and the decryption maps hence must have the form

$$(D_k)_{C \to A} = \mathrm{Tr}_{\hat{C}} \left[\Pi_{\mathrm{supp}\sigma^k} (V_k)^\dagger_{A\hat{C} \to C} (\cdot) (V_k)_{A\hat{C} \to C} \right]$$

$$+ \left(\hat{D}_k \right)_{C \to A} \left[\left(\mathbb{1}_C - \Pi^{\mathrm{valid}}_k \right) (\cdot) \left(\mathbb{1}_C - \Pi^{\mathrm{valid}}_k \right) \right] \tag{A.5}$$

for some quantum states $\sigma_{\hat{C}}^{(k)}$, isometries $(V_k)_{C\to A\hat{C}}$, and some CPTP map $\hat{D}_k$. Here, $\Pi_k^{\text{valid}} = (V_k)_{A\hat{C}\to C}\, \Pi_{\text{supp}\sigma^k}\, (V_k)_{A\hat{C}\to C}^{\dagger}$ is the projector onto the space of valid ciphertexts.

B   Proof of characterization theorem

This section is dedicated to proving the characterization theorem for non-malleable QES, i.e., Theorem 4.4. We begin with two preparatory lemmas.

Lemma B.1. *For any QES (τ, E, D) the map $\mathcal{E} := |K|^{-1}\sum_k D_k \otimes E_k^T$ satisfies*

$$\mathcal{E}\left(|\phi^+\rangle\langle\phi^+|_{CC'}(X_C \otimes \mathrm{id}_{C'})\right) = \frac{|A|}{|C|}|\phi^+\rangle\langle\phi^+|_{AA'}(E_K^{\dagger}(X) \otimes \mathrm{id}_{A'})$$

This lemma is a consequence of the correctness condition and is proven in the full version [3] of this article.

Lemma B.2. *Suppose (τ_K, E, D) satisfies Definition 4.2 for trivial B. Then $\mathcal{E} := |K|^{-1}\sum_k D_k \otimes E_k^T$ satisfies*

$$\left\|\mathcal{E}(X) - \frac{|A|}{|C|}\left[\langle\phi^+|X|\phi^+\rangle|\phi^+\rangle\langle\phi^+| \right.\right.$$
$$\left.\left. + \mathrm{Tr}\left(\Pi^- X\right)\frac{1}{|C|^2-1}\left(|C|^2 D_K(\tau_C)_A \otimes \tau_{A'} - \phi_{AA'}^+\right)\right]\right\|_{\diamond}$$
$$\leq 2\sqrt{2\varepsilon}|A|\left(2\sqrt{|A|}|C| + 1\right). \tag{B.1}$$

Proof. It follows directly from the fact that (τ_K, E, D) is a QES together with Lemma A.1 that

$$\mathcal{E}(\phi_{CC'}^+) = \frac{|A|}{|C|}\phi_{AA'}^+. \tag{B.2}$$

Let $\Lambda_{C\to C\tilde{B}_1}^{(i)}$, $i = 0,1$ be two attack maps such that $\eta_{\Lambda^{(i)}}|\phi^+\rangle = 0$ for $i = 0,1$ and define

$$\Lambda_{C\to C\tilde{B}_1\tilde{B}_2} = \frac{1}{2}\sum_{i=0,1}|i\rangle\langle i|_{\tilde{B}_2} \otimes \Lambda^{(i)}.$$

The ε-NM property implies

$$I(AA' : \tilde{B}_1\tilde{B}_2)_{\eta_{\tilde{\Lambda}}} \leq \varepsilon,$$

and therefore, using Pinsker's inequality,

$$\left\|\frac{1}{2}\sum_{i=0,1}|i\rangle\langle i|_{\tilde{B}} \otimes (\eta_{\tilde{\Lambda}^{(i)}})_{CC'\tilde{B}_1}\right.$$
$$\left. - \frac{1}{4}\left(\sum_{i=0,1}|i\rangle\langle i|_{\tilde{B}} \otimes (\eta_{\tilde{\Lambda}^{(i)}})_{\tilde{B}_1}\right) \otimes \left(\sum_{i=0,1}(\eta_{\tilde{\Lambda}^{(i)}})_{CC'}\right)\right\|_1 \leq \sqrt{2\varepsilon}. \tag{B.3}$$

Observe that

$$
\begin{aligned}
\eta_{\tilde{A}} &= \frac{1}{|K|} \sum_k D_k \circ \Lambda \circ E_k(\phi^+_{AA'}) \\
&= \frac{|C|}{|A|} \frac{1}{|K|} \sum_k \left(D_k \otimes E_k^T \right) \circ \Lambda(\phi^+_{CC'}) \\
&= \frac{|C|}{|A|} \mathcal{E} \circ \Lambda(\phi^+_{CC'}).
\end{aligned}
\tag{B.4}
$$

Setting $(\eta_{\Lambda^{(0)}})_{CC'\tilde{B}_1} = \tau^-_{CC'} \otimes (\eta_{\Lambda^{(1)}})_{\tilde{B}_1}$, we get

$$
\begin{aligned}
\eta_{\tilde{A}^{(0)}} &= \frac{|C|}{|A|} \mathcal{E}(\tau^-) \otimes (\eta_{\Lambda^{(1)}})_{\tilde{B}_1} \\
&= \frac{|C|}{|A|} \frac{1}{|C|^2 - 1} \left(|C|^2 \mathcal{E}(\tau_{CC'}) - \mathcal{E}(\phi^+_{CC'}) \right) \otimes (\eta_{\Lambda^{(1)}})_{\tilde{B}_1} \\
&= \frac{1}{|C|^2 - 1} \left(|C|^2 D_K(\tau_C) \otimes \tau_A - \phi^+_{AA'} \right) \otimes (\eta_{\Lambda^{(1)}})_{\tilde{B}_1}.
\end{aligned}
\tag{B.5}
$$

and therefore

$$
\left\| \frac{1}{|C|^2 - 1} \left(|C|^2 D_K(\tau_C) \otimes \tau_A - \phi^+_{AA'} \right) \otimes (\eta_{\Lambda^{(1)}})_{\tilde{B}_1} - \frac{|C|}{|A|} \mathcal{E} \left((\eta_{\Lambda^{(1)}})_{CC'\tilde{B}_1} \right) \right\|_1
$$
$$
\leq 2\sqrt{2\varepsilon}
\tag{B.6}
$$

for all $\Lambda^{(1)}$. For any state $\varrho_{CC'\tilde{B}_1}$ with $\varrho_{CC'\tilde{B}} |\phi^+\rangle_{CC'} = 0$, we define the state

$$
\varrho'_{CC'\tilde{B}_1\tilde{B}_2} \frac{1}{C} \left(|0\rangle\langle 0|_{\tilde{B}_2} \otimes \varrho_{CC'\tilde{B}_1} \right.
$$
$$
\left. + |1\rangle\langle 1|_{\tilde{B}_2} \otimes \left[((\mathbb{1}_C - \varrho_C) \otimes V_{C'}) \phi^+ ((\mathbb{1}_C - \varrho_C) \otimes V_{C'}) \right] \otimes \varrho_{\tilde{B}_2} \right).
\tag{B.7}
$$

Here, V is a unitary such that $\mathrm{Tr}(\mathbb{1}_C - \varrho_C)V_C^T = 0$. It is easy to see that such a unitary always exists, the existence is equivalent to the fact that any $|C|$-tuple of real numbers is the ordered list of side lengths of a polygon in the complex plain. Note that $\varrho'_{CC'\tilde{B}_1\tilde{B}_2}|\phi^+\rangle_{CC'} = 0$, and $\varrho'_{C'} = \tau_{C'}$. Together with the triangle inequality, Eq. (B.6) implies therefore that

$$
\frac{1}{|C|} \left\| \frac{|C|}{|A|} \mathcal{E}(\varrho) - \frac{1}{|C|^2 - 1} \left(|C|^2 D_K(\tau_C) \otimes \tau_A - \phi^+_{AA'} \right) \otimes \varrho_{\tilde{B}_1} \right\|_1
$$
$$
+ \left\| \frac{|C|}{|A|} \mathcal{E} \left[((\mathbb{1}_C - \varrho_C) \otimes V_{C'}) \phi^+ ((\mathbb{1}_C - \varrho_C) \otimes V_{C'}) \right] \right.
$$
$$
\left. - \frac{|C| - 1}{|C|} \frac{1}{|C|^2 - 1} \left(|C|^2 D_K(\tau_C) \otimes \tau_A - \phi^+_{AA'} \right) \right\|_1 \leq 2\sqrt{2\varepsilon},
$$

i.e. in particular

$$\left\|\frac{|C|}{|A|}\mathcal{E}(\varrho) - \frac{1}{|C|^2 - 1}\left(|C|^2 D_K(\tau_C) \otimes \tau_A - \phi_{AA'}^+\right) \otimes \varrho_{\tilde{B}_1}\right\|_1 \leq 2\sqrt{2\varepsilon}|C|.$$

As ϱ was arbitrary we have proven that

$$\left\|\frac{|C|}{|A|}\mathcal{E} - \left\langle\frac{1}{|C|^2 - 1}\left(|C|^2 D_K(\tau_C) \otimes \tau_A - \phi_{AA'}^+\right)\right\rangle\right\|_\diamond \leq 2\sqrt{2\varepsilon}|C|. \qquad (B.8)$$

The only fact that is left to show is, that $\|\mathcal{E}(|\phi^+\rangle\langle v|)\|_1$ is small for all normalized $|v\rangle$ such that $\langle\phi^+ \mid v\rangle = 0$. To this end, observe that $\mathrm{Tr}_A \circ \mathcal{E}(\sigma_C \otimes (\cdot)_{C'}) = E_K^T$ for all quantum states σ_C. Let ϱ_C be any quantum state that does not have full rank, note that such states span all of $\mathcal{B}(\mathcal{H}_C)$, and for hermitian operators there exists a decomposition into such operators that saturates the triangle inequality. Taking a quantum state σ_C such that $\langle\phi^+|\varrho \otimes \sigma|\phi^+\rangle = \frac{1}{|C|}\mathrm{Tr}\varrho_C\sigma_C^T = 0$ (the first equality is the mirror Lemma A.1), we have

$$\left\|\mathcal{E}(\varrho \otimes \sigma) - \frac{|A|}{|C|}\frac{1}{|C|^2 - 1}\left(|C|^2 D_K(\tau_C) \otimes \tau_A - \phi_{AA'}^+\right)\right\|_1 \leq 2\sqrt{2\varepsilon}|A|$$

according to what we have already proven. Using inequality (B.8) we arrive at

$$\left\|E_K^\dagger(X) - \frac{|A|}{|C|}\tau_A \mathrm{Tr}(X)\right\|_1 \leq 2\sqrt{2\varepsilon}|A|\|X\|_1 \qquad (B.9)$$

For Hermitian matrices X and therefore

$$\left\|E_K^\dagger(X) - \frac{|A|}{|C|}\tau_A \mathrm{Tr}(X)\right\|_1 \leq 4\sqrt{2\varepsilon}|A|\|X\|_1 \qquad (B.10)$$

For arbitrary X. We can write $|v\rangle_{CC'} = X_C|\phi^+\rangle_{CC'}$ for some traceless matrix X_C. Now we calculate

$$\begin{aligned}
\|\mathcal{E}(|\phi^+\rangle\langle v|_{CC'})\|_1 &= \left\|\frac{|A|}{|C|}|\phi^+\rangle\langle\phi^+|_{AA'}\left(E_K^\dagger(X^\dagger)\right)_A\right\|_1 \\
&= \frac{|A|}{|C|}\left\|\left(E_K^\dagger(X)\right)_A|\phi^+\rangle_{AA'}\right\|_2 \\
&= \frac{\sqrt{|A|}}{|C|}\left\|E_K^\dagger(X)\right\|_2 \\
&\leq \frac{\sqrt{|A|}}{|C|}\left\|E_K^\dagger(X)\right\|_1 \\
&\leq \frac{|A|^{3/2}}{|C|}4\sqrt{2\varepsilon}\|X\|_1 \\
&\leq 4\sqrt{2\varepsilon}|A|^{3/2}. \qquad (B.11)
\end{aligned}$$

The first equation is Lemma B.1, the second and third equations are easily verified, the first inequality is a standard norm inequality, the second inequality is Eq. (B.10), and the last inequality follows from the normalization of $|v\rangle$. By the Schmidt decomposition, we get a stabilized version of this inequality,

$$\left\| \mathcal{E}(|\phi^+\rangle_{CC'}|\alpha\rangle_{\tilde{B}_1}\langle v|_{CC'\tilde{B}_1}) \right\|_1 \leq 2\sqrt{2\varepsilon}|A|^{3/2}, \tag{B.12}$$

for all $|\alpha\rangle_{\tilde{B}_1}$ and all $|v\rangle_{CC'\tilde{B}}$ such that $\langle\phi^+ \mid v\rangle = 0$. Combining everything we arrive at

$$\left\| \mathcal{E}(X) - \frac{|A|}{|C|} \left[\langle\phi^+|X|\phi^+\rangle|\phi^+\rangle\langle\phi^+| \right. \right.$$
$$\left. \left. + \operatorname{Tr}\left(\Pi^- X\right) \frac{1}{|C|^2 - 1} \left(|C|^2 D_K(\tau_C)_A \otimes \tau_{A'} - \phi^+_{AA'}\right) \right] \right\|_\diamond$$
$$\leq 2\sqrt{2\varepsilon}|A| \left(4\sqrt{|A|} + 1\right). \tag{B.13}$$

$\square$

We are now ready to prove the characterization theorem Theorem 4.4 in the ε-approximate setting (including the exact case, Theorem 3.7 by setting $\varepsilon = 0$.)

Theorem B.3 (Precise version of Theorem 4.4). *Let* $\Pi = (\tau, E, D)$ *be a QES.*

1. *If* Π *is* ε-*NM, then any attack map* $\Lambda_{CB\to C\tilde{B}}$ *results in an effective map* $\tilde{\Lambda}_{AB\to A\tilde{B}}$ *fulfilling*

$$\left\| \tilde{\Lambda}_{AB\to A\tilde{B}} - \tilde{\Lambda}^{\text{exact}}_{AB\to A\tilde{B}} \right\|_\diamond \leq 2\sqrt{2\varepsilon}|A|^4|C| \left(4\sqrt{|A|} + 1\right), \tag{B.14}$$

where

$$\tilde{\Lambda}^{\text{exact}}_{AB\to A\tilde{B}} = \operatorname{id}_A \otimes \Lambda'_{B\to\tilde{B}} + \frac{1}{|C|^2 - 1}\left(|C|^2 \langle D_K(\tau)\rangle - \operatorname{id}\right)_A \otimes \Lambda''_{B\to\tilde{B}},$$

with $\Lambda' = \operatorname{Tr}_{CC'}[\phi^+_{CC'}\Lambda(\phi^+_{CC'} \otimes (\cdot))]$ *and* $\Lambda'' = \operatorname{Tr}_{CC'}[\Pi^-_{CC'}\Lambda(\phi^+_{CC'} \otimes (\cdot))]$.
2. *Conversely, if for a scheme all effective maps fulfill Eq. (B.14) with the right hand side replaced by* ε, *then it is* $5\varepsilon(\log(|A|) + r) + 3h(\varepsilon)$-*NM, where* r *is a bound on the size of the honest user's side information.*

Proof. We start with *1*. We want to bound the diamond norm distance between the effective map $\tilde{\Lambda}$ resulting from an attack Λ and the idealized effective map $\tilde{\Lambda}^{\text{exact}}$. Let

$$|\psi\rangle_{AA'BB'} = \sum_{i=0}^{|A|^2-1} \sqrt{p_i}|\alpha_i\rangle_{AA'} \otimes |\beta_i\rangle_{BB'}$$

be an arbitrary pure state given in its Schmidt decomposition across the biparti-
tion AA' vs. BB'. We can Write $|\alpha_i\rangle_{AA'} = X_{A'}^{(i)}|\phi^+\rangle$ for some matrices $X^{(i)}$ sat-
isfying $\|X^{(i)}\|_\infty \le |A|$. We calculate the action of $\tilde{\Lambda}$ on $|\alpha_i\rangle\langle\alpha_j|_{AA'} \otimes |\beta_i\rangle\langle\beta_j|_{BB'}$,

$$
\tilde{\Lambda}^{\text{exact}}_{AB \to A\tilde{B}}(|\alpha_i\rangle\langle\alpha_j|_{AA'} \otimes |\beta_i\rangle\langle\beta_j|_{BB'}) = X_{A'}^{(i)}\Big(|\phi^+\rangle\langle\phi^+|_{AA'} \otimes \Lambda'_{B \to \tilde{B}}(|\beta_i\rangle\langle\beta_j|_{BB'})
$$

$$
+ \frac{1}{|C|^2 - 1}\left(|C|^2 D_K(\tau)_A \otimes \tau_{A'} - |\phi^+\rangle\langle\phi^+|_{AA'}\right) \otimes \Lambda''_{B \to \tilde{B}}(|\beta_i\rangle\langle\beta_j|_{BB'})\Big)X_{A'}^{(j)}.
$$

$$(\text{B.15})$$

In a similar way we get

$$
\begin{aligned}
&\tilde{\Lambda}_{AB \to A\tilde{B}}(|\alpha_i\rangle\langle\alpha_j|_{AA'} \otimes |\beta_i\rangle\langle\beta_j|_{BB'}) \\
&= X_{A'}^{(i)}\tilde{\Lambda}_{AB \to A\tilde{B}}(|\phi^+\rangle\langle\phi^+|_{AA'} \otimes |\beta_i\rangle\langle\beta_j|_{BB'})X_{A'}^{(i)} \\
&= \frac{|C|}{|A|}X_{A'}^{(i)}\mathcal{E}_{CC' \to AA'} \circ \Lambda_{CB \to \tilde{C}\tilde{B}}(|\phi^+\rangle\langle\phi^+|_{CC'} \otimes |\beta_i\rangle\langle\beta_j|_{BB'})X_{A'}^{(i)}.
\end{aligned}
$$

$$(\text{B.16})$$

Using Lemma B.2 we bound

$$
\begin{aligned}
&\left\|\left(\tilde{\Lambda}_{AB \to A\tilde{B}} - \tilde{\Lambda}^{\text{exact}}_{AB \to A\tilde{B}}\right)(|\alpha_i\rangle\langle\alpha_j|_{AA'} \otimes |\beta_i\rangle\langle\beta_j|_{BB'})\right\|_1 \\
&= \left\|X_{A'}^{(i)}\left(\tilde{\Lambda}_{AB \to A\tilde{B}} - \tilde{\Lambda}^{\text{exact}}_{AB \to A\tilde{B}}\right)(|\phi^+\rangle\langle\phi^+|_{AA'} \otimes |\beta_i\rangle\langle\beta_j|_{BB'})X^{(j)}\right\|_1 \\
&\le \left\|X^{(i)}\right\|_\infty\left\|X^{(j)}\right\|_\infty\left\|\left(\tilde{\Lambda}_{AB \to A\tilde{B}} - \tilde{\Lambda}^{\text{exact}}_{AB \to A\tilde{B}}\right)(|\phi^+\rangle\langle\phi^+|_{AA'} \otimes |\beta_i\rangle\langle\beta_j|_{BB'})\right\|_1 \\
&= \left\|X^{(i)}\right\|_\infty\left\|X^{(j)}\right\|_\infty\left\|\frac{|C|}{|A|}\mathcal{E}_{CC' \to AA'} \circ \Lambda_{CB \to \tilde{C}\tilde{B}}(|\phi^+\rangle\langle\phi^+|_{CC'} \otimes |\beta_i\rangle\langle\beta_j|_{BB'})\right. \\
&\quad\quad \left. - \tilde{\Lambda}^{\text{exact}}_{AB \to A\tilde{B}}(|\phi^+\rangle\langle\phi^+|_{AA'} \otimes |\beta_i\rangle\langle\beta_j|_{BB'})\right\|_1 \\
&\le 2\sqrt{2\varepsilon}|A|^2|C|\left(4\sqrt{|A|} + 1\right).
\end{aligned}
$$

$$(\text{B.17})$$

The inequalities result from applying Hölder's inequality twice, and Lemma B.2,
respectively. Using the triangle inequality we get

$$
\begin{aligned}
&\left\|\left(\tilde{\Lambda}_{AB \to A\tilde{B}} - \tilde{\Lambda}^{\text{exact}}_{AB \to A\tilde{B}}\right)(|\psi\rangle\langle\psi|_{AA'BB'})\right\|_1 \\
&\le 2\sqrt{2\varepsilon}|A|^2|C|\left(4\sqrt{|A|} + 1\right)\sum_{i,j=0}^{|A|^2 - 1}\sqrt{p_i p_j} \\
&\le 2\sqrt{2\varepsilon}|A|^4|C|\left(4\sqrt{|A|} + 1\right).
\end{aligned}
$$

$$(\text{B.18})$$

As $|\psi\rangle$ was arbitrary, we have proven

$$
\left\|\tilde{\Lambda}_{AB \to A\tilde{B}} - \tilde{\Lambda}^{\text{exact}}_{AB \to A\tilde{B}}\right\|_\diamond \le 2\sqrt{2\varepsilon}|A|^4|C|\left(4\sqrt{|A|} + 1\right).
$$

$$(\text{B.19})$$

Now let us prove 2. Let $\Lambda_{CB \to C\tilde{B}}$ again be an arbitrary attack map, and assume that the resulting effective map is ε-close to $\tilde{\Lambda}^{\text{exact}}_{AB \to A\tilde{B}}$. Observe that $p^=(\Lambda, \varrho) = \operatorname{Tr}\Lambda'(\varrho_B)$.

By the Alicki-Fannes inequality [4] and Lemma A.2, this implies

$$I(AR : \tilde{B})_{\tilde{\Lambda}(\varrho)} \leq I(AR : B)_\varrho + h(p^=(\Lambda, \varrho)) + 5\varepsilon \log(|A||R|) + 3h(\varepsilon) \qquad \text{(B.20)}$$

with the help of Lemma A.2. $\square$

New Security Notions and Feasibility Results for Authentication of Quantum Data

Sumegha Garg[1]([✉]), Henry Yuen[2], and Mark Zhandry[1]

[1] Princeton University, Princeton, USA
sumeghag@cs.princeton.edu, mzhandry@princeton.edu
[2] UC Berkeley, Berkeley, USA
hyuen@cs.berkeley.edu

Abstract. We give a new class of security definitions for authentication in the quantum setting. These definitions capture and strengthen existing definitions of security against quantum adversaries for both *classical* message authentication codes (MACs) as well as full quantum state authentication schemes. The main feature of our definitions is that they precisely *characterize* the effective behavior of any adversary when the authentication protocol accepts, including correlations with the key. Our definitions readily yield a host of desirable properties and interesting consequences; for example, our security definition for full quantum state authentication implies that the entire secret key can be re-used if the authentication protocol succeeds.

Next, we present several protocols satisfying our security definitions. We show that the classical Wegman-Carter authentication scheme with 3-universal hashing is secure against superposition attacks, as well as adversaries with quantum side information. We then present conceptually simple constructions of full quantum state authentication.

Finally, we prove a lifting theorem which shows that, as long as a protocol can securely authenticate the maximally entangled state, it can securely authenticate any state, even those that are entangled with the adversary. Thus, this shows that protocols satisfying a fairly weak form of authentication security automatically satisfy a stronger notion of security (in particular, the definition of Dupuis et al. (2012)).

1 Introduction

Authenticating messages is a fundamental operation in classical cryptography. A sender Alice wishes to send a message m over an insecure channel to a receiver Bob, with the guarantee that the message was not tampered with in transit. To accomplish this, Alice appends a "signature" σ to m using a shared secret key k and sends the message/signature pair (m, σ) to Bob. Bob receives some potentially altered pair (m', σ'), and then verifies that σ' is a valid signature of m' under key k. If verification passes, Bob accepts m', and if verification fails, Bob ignores the message and discards it. A secure authentication protocol guarantees the following: even if the adversary has arbitrarily tampered with the communication channel, as long as the adversary does not know the secret

© International Association for Cryptologic Research 2017
J. Katz and H. Shacham (Eds.): CRYPTO 2017, Part II, LNCS 10402, pp. 342–371, 2017.
DOI: 10.1007/978-3-319-63715-0_12

key k, then either Bob rejects with high probability, or the message he receives is m. Such a (symmetric key) authentication protocol is usually referred to as a Message Authentication Code (MAC). As long as k is only used to authenticate a single message, information-theoretic security can be achieved: no adversary – even a computationally unbounded one – can modify the message without detection [WC81].

Just as authentication is a fundamental operation in classical cryptography, it will continue to be an important tool in the coming age of quantum computers. In this work, we investigate authentication in the quantum setting, and consider quantum attacks on both *classical* authentication protocols, as well as full-fledged *quantum* protocols for authenticating quantum data. What kinds of security guarantees can we hope for in the quantum setting? Various notions of security for authentication schemes against quantum attacks have been considered in the literature. However, as we will discuss below, these existing definitions do not fully capture security properties we would expect of a secure authentication scheme.

The contribution of our paper is three-fold: first, we present new security definitions for authentication in a quantum setting that strengthen previous definitions and address their limitations. Second, we prove interesting consequences of our stronger security definition for quantum authentication, such as information-theoretic key recycling and an easy protocol for quantum key distribution. Finally, we prove that several natural authentication protocols satisfy our security definitions.

1.1 Quantum Attacks on Classical Protocols

A recent series of works [BDF+11, DFNS13, BZ13a, BZ13b, Zha12, KLLNP16] have studied quantum superposition attacks on classical cryptosystems. In the setting of MACs, an adversary in such an attack is able to trick the sender into signing a superposition of messages.[1] That is, the sender computes the map $|m\rangle \mapsto |m, \sigma_m\rangle$ in superposition, where σ_m is the signature on m. The adversary chooses some message superposition $\sum_m \alpha_m |m\rangle$, and the sender then applies the map, giving the adversary $\sum_m \alpha_m |m, \sigma_m\rangle$. At this point, it is unclear what the security definition should actually be. The usual classical security notion asks that an adversary, after seeing a signed message, cannot produce a different message with a valid signature. The natural way to translate this into our setting is to require that the adversary, after seeing a signed superposition, cannot produce a different forged quantum state with valid signature. For classical

---

[1] One motivation for studying superposition attacks comes from the "Frozen Smart-Card" example [GHS15]: real-world classical authentication systems are frequently implemented on small electronic devices such as RFID tags or a smart-cards. A determined and sophisticated attacker in possession of such a smart-card could try to perform a quantum "side-channel attack" on it: he places the device in a very low temperature environment, and attempts to query the device in quantum superposition. One would like to guarantee that even then the attacker is unable to, say, extract the secret key.

authentication schemes, this goal is unfortunately impossible. The adversary can tamper with the signed state by measuring the entire state in the standard basis, obtaining the pair (m, σ_m) with probability $|\alpha_m|^2$. Then (m, σ_m) will pass verification, but will be very different from the signed state the adversary received. If the adversary can change the message state, what sort of guarantees can we hope for?

Boneh and Zhandry [BZ13a] give the first definition of security for classical authentication against superposition attacks. They argue that, at a minimum, the adversary given a single signed superposition should only be able to produce a single signed message; he should not be able to simultaneously produce two valid signed messages (m, σ_m) and $(m', \sigma_{m'})$ for $m \neq m'$. Note that in the classical setting, this requirement is equivalent to the traditional MAC security definition, so it appears to be a reasonable requirement for any quantum security notion. More generally, given q signed states, the Boneh-Zhandry definition says that the adversary should not be able to produce $q + 1$ distinct valid signed messages.

However, the Boneh-Zhandry definition has some unsatisfying properties. For example, consider the case where the sender only signs messages that start with the email address of some intended recipient, say, bob@gmail.com. Suppose the adversary tricks the sender into a signing a superposition of messages that all begin with bob@gmail.com, but then manipulates the signed superposition into a different superposition that includes valid signed messages that *do not* start with bob@gmail.com. Clearly, this is an undesirable outcome. Unfortunately, the Boneh-Zhandry definition does not rule out such attacks — it only disallows an adversary from producing $q + 1$ valid signed messages when given q signed superpositions. The situation illustrated here, however, is that the adversary is given *one* signed superposition, and now wants to produce *one* valid signed message that was not part of the original superposition.

Along similar lines, suppose an adversary tricks the sender into signing a uniform superposition on messages, and then produces a classical signed message (m, σ). From the sender's perspective, each message has weight $\frac{1}{|\mathcal{M}|}$, where $\mathcal{M}$ is the message space. The sender cannot prevent the adversary from measuring the message state to produce (m, σ) for a random m. However, it is reasonable to insist as a security requirement that the adversary cannot bias the output of this measurement to obtain, say, (m^*, σ_{m^*}) with probability much higher than $\frac{1}{|\mathcal{M}|}$. Again, Boneh and Zhandry's definition does not preclude such a biasing, since the adversary only ever obtains a single signed message. Thus, the Boneh-Zhandry definition does not capture natural non-malleability properties one would hope for from an authentication scheme in the quantum setting.

Boneh and Zhandry's definition suffers from these weaknesses because it only considers what types of outputs the adversary can produce, ignoring the relationships between the output and the original signed state. In the classical setting, the two approaches are actually equivalent, but in the quantum setting this is not the case.

1.2   Quantum Authentication of Quantum Data

We turn to the setting of schemes for authenticating quantum states. Barnum et al. [BCG+02] was the first to study this, and they present a definition of non-interactive quantum authentication where, conditioned on the protocol succeeding, the sender has effectively teleported a quantum state to the receiver (provided that the probability of success is not too small). They then give a scheme (called the *purity testing scheme*) which attains this definition. Interestingly, they also show that quantum state authentication also implies quantum state *encryption*.[2] Subsequent works [BCG+06, ABE10, DNS12, BW16] presented some stronger security definitions that we will discuss momentarily.

Roughly speaking, a (private-key) quantum authentication scheme is a pair of keyed quantum operations $(\mathsf{Auth}_k, \mathsf{Ver}_k)$, where k is a secret key shared by the sender and receiver, where Auth_k is a map that takes in a quantum message state ρ, and outputs an authenticated state σ. The map Ver_k is a verification operation that takes in a (possibly) tampered state $\widetilde{\sigma}$ and outputs a state $\widetilde{\rho}$, along with a flag ACC or REJ indicating whether the verification succeeded or failed. These maps are such that for all input states ρ and all keys k, we have $\mathsf{Ver}_k(\mathsf{Auth}_k(\rho)) = \rho \otimes |\mathrm{ACC}\rangle\langle\mathrm{ACC}|$.

Informally, Barnum et al. define a secure authentication scheme to be such that, for all adversaries $\mathcal{O}$, either the receiver rejects the state $\mathsf{Ver}_k(\mathcal{O}(\mathsf{Auth}_k(\rho)))$ with high probability, or it is close to the original state ρ. However it has the shortcoming that it does not consider the possibility that the adversary is *entangled* with the original message ρ, and thus may act on the entanglement to tamper with the state in an undetectable manner. Thus, the security definition of [BCG+02] is not *composable*.

In many situations we would like to use authentication not as a stand along task, but as a primitive in a larger protocol – indeed, quantum authentication *has* been used as a primitive in schemes for delegated quantum computation, e.g., [ABE10, BGS13]. Here, the "adversary" (which may be other components of the protocol) may generate the inputs to the authentication scheme, and thus be entangled with the message that is supposed to be authenticated. If an authentication scheme satisfied a composable security definition, then we may use the security of the authentication primitive in a black box manner to argue the proper functioning of the larger protocol.

Correlations between final state and the key -
Recently, several works [HLM16, DNS12, BW16] have proposed composable security definitions for quantum authentication – that is, they handle adversaries with quantum side information. However, their security definitions do not explicitly consider *correlations* between the key and the final state of the protocol.

Suppose Alice sends Bob the authenticated state $\sigma_k = \mathsf{Auth}_k(\rho)$ using key k. Bob receives a (possibly tampered) state $\widetilde{\sigma}_k$, and proceeds to verify the authentication. Let τ_k denote Bob's state *conditioned* on successful verification. Roughly

---

[2] By contrast, in the classical setting, message authentication does *not* imply message encryption.

speaking, the security definitions of [BCG+02, DNS12, BW16] refers to the *average* state $\mathbb{E}_k \tau_k$; in particular, it states that $\mathbb{E}_k \tau_k$ is close to the original state ρ. This statement does not by itself imply that τ_k is close to the original state ρ *with high probability* over k. In other words, the state of the key is traced out in their security definitions.

Later, we will show how taking into account the correlations between the key and the final state of the protocol yields interesting consequences – such as the ability to reuse the key upon successful verification.

2 Our Contributions

In this work, we address the above limitations by giving new security notions for authentication in the quantum setting. More generally, we present an abstract framework of security for both classical and quantum authentication schemes that not only captures existing security definitions (such as the Boneh-Zhandry definition for classical protocols or the Barnum et al. definition of quantum state authentication), but also is more demanding in that it strongly *characterizes* the (effective) behavior of an adversary. In particular, the adversary may have access to quantum side information with the message state that is being authenticated. The characterization of the adversary's admissable actions is what allows us to easily deduce many desirable security properties (such as unforgeability, key reuse, and more). Furthermore, we will show that various natural authentication protocols satisfy our security definitions.

Our abstract security framework follows the simulation paradigm in classical cryptography. In our framework, one first defines a class $\mathscr{A}$ of *ideal adversaries*. Intuitively, ideal adversaries are those that cannot be avoided in a real execution of an ideal authentication protocol, such as those that discard messages, or ones that carry out actions explicitly allowed by the protocol. For example, in the case of classical protocols, one can define the class of ideal adversaries to be ones that "behave classically" on the message state – that is, they're restricted to measurements in the computational basis. In the case of quantum authentication, an ideal adversary can *only* act on the side information, but otherwise acts as the identity on the authenticated message.

An authentication protocol P satisfies our security definition with respect to the class $\mathscr{A}$ if the behavior of any adversary (not necessarily ideal) in the protocol P can be approximately simulated by an ideal adversary in $\mathscr{A}$. We take the most general notion of simulation possible: the joint state of the secret key, the message state after the receiver's verification procedure, and the quantum side information held by the adversary *conditioned on successful verification* must be indistinguishable from the same joint state arising from the actions of *some* ideal adversary from the class $\mathscr{A}$. Since our notion of simulation is so general, this implies that our security definitions satisfy security under *sequential composition*; that is, the authentication protocols that realize our security definition can be securely composed with arbitrary cryptographic protocols in a sequential fashion.

We now discuss how security for both classical authentication schemes and fully quantum authentication protocols can be defined in this framework.

2.1 A New Security Definition for Classical Authentication

The Boneh-Zhandry definition focuses on what classical signed messages an adversary can produce, treating the superposition access to the sender as a tool to mount stronger attacks. Here, we instead think of a classical protocol giving rise to a weak form of authentication of quantum messages, where a superposition is authenticated by classically signing each message in the superposition. That is, a state $\sum_m \alpha_m |m\rangle$ is authenticated as the state $\sum_m \alpha_m |m, \sigma_m\rangle$. The state is similarly verified in superposition by running the classical verification algorithm in superposition.

More generally, we think of the protocol acting on message states that may be entangled with an adversary. For example, the sender could sign the $\mathcal{M}$ part of the state $\sum_m \alpha_m |m\rangle^{\mathcal{M}} \otimes |\varphi_m\rangle^{\mathcal{Z}}$, where the adversary has control of the $|\varphi_m\rangle^{\mathcal{Z}}$ states. The signed state then would become $\sum_m \alpha_m |m, \sigma_m\rangle^{\mathcal{M}\mathcal{T}} \otimes |\varphi_m\rangle^{\mathcal{Z}}$. Signing mixed states can also be expressed in this way, simply by purifying the mixture. By thinking of the protocol in this way, we are able to give security definitions that actually consider the relationship between the sender's signed state and the final state the adversary produces.

Clearly, such a classical scheme cannot fully protect the quantum state. An adversary could, for example measure (m, σ_m), or any subset of bits of the state, and keep the result of such a measurement in his own private space. This would not be detected by the classical verification procedure, but the final message would have been changed.

Our security definition for classical protocols says that, roughly, an arbitrary adversary can be simulated by an ideal adversary that can only do the following: perform some (partial) measurement of the message in the computational basis, and controlled on the outcome of the partial measurement, perform some quantum operation on his own private qubits. We also extend the definition to handle side information the adversary may have about the message state; for example, the adversary may possess the purification of the message state. Thus, our definition is essentially the best one could hope for, since it disallows the adversary from doing anything other than operations that are trivially possible on *any* classical protocol.

Our definition readily implies the Boneh-Zhandry security definition for one-time MACs, and does not suffer from the weakness of their definition[3]. Finally, we show that the classical Wegman-Carter MAC that uses three-universal hashing is sufficient for achieving this strong security definition. This improves on Boneh-Zhandry in two ways, as they show that *four*-wise independence gives their weaker security notion.

---

[3] One limitation of our definition is that we consider the signature registers as being initialized by the signer. Boneh and Zhandry, in contrast, allow the registers to be initialized by the adversary, with the signature being XORed into the registers.

2.2 Definitions for Quantum Authentication

We next turn to quantum protocols for authenticating quantum messages. For general quantum protocols, the adversary can always do the following. He can always act non-trivially on his own private workspace – the verification procedure can never detect this. Otherwise, he can forward the authenticated state as is, without recording any information about the state, or he can send junk to the receiver. Our strongest definition of security – which we call *total authentication* – says that this is essentially all an adversary can do in a secure quantum authentication protocol. In other words, a real adversary in a total authentication protocol can be approximated by an ideal adversary that behaves trivially on the authenticated state.

As mentioned above, prior works have put forth composable security definitions for quantum authentication [DNS12,BW16], who consider quantum side information held by the adversary. Our definition builds upon these definitions: not only do we consider side information about the plaintext state, we also allow the receiver's view to include the authentication key as well as whatever information the adversary may learn about the key. The ideal adversary must approximate the real adversary, even considering the entire key. In contrast, existing definitions trace out the key — either partially or entirely — and therefore do not directly consider *arbitrary* information the adversary may learn about the key. Our security definition of total authentication thus rules out the possibility of the adversary learning significant information about the key. This fact has interesting consequences:

1. **Key reuse.** For example, our definition immediately implies that, upon successful verification by the receiver, the key can actually be completely recycled to authenticate a new message. This is because, upon successful verification, the key is essentially independent of the adversary and can therefore be used again in the same protocol. This is in contrast to the classical setting: in general keys cannot be recycled without computational assumptions. Furthermore, no prior definition for authentication of quantum data directly implies key re-usability, and no prior protocol for quantum messages gets full key re-usability upon successful verification.

   Previous works have explored partial key reuse in various quantum protocols [OH05,DPS05,HLM16]. However, to our knowledge, our work is the first to establish that the *entire key* can be recycled upon successful verification.[4]

2. **A simple quantum key distribution protocol.** Our definition also gives a conceptually simple quantum key distribution (QKD) protocol[5]. Alice prepares a maximally entangled state, chooses a random key k, and authenticates half the state with the key. She then sends the authenticated half to Bob,

---

[4] The work of Dåmgard et al. [DPS05] argue that the key can be recycled entirely when authenticating *classical messages*, but their protocol does not appear to extend to handling quantum messages.

[5] The observation that quantum authentication implies a form of QKD is due to Charlie Bennett and also observed by Gottesman [Got02].

keeping the unauthenticated half to herself. When Bob receives the state, he sends a "received" message back to Alice, who then sends the key k to Bob. Bob verifies the state using the key. Even though the adversary eventually sees the authentication key k, he does not know the key when he intercepts the quantum state, and must therefore interact with the state without the key. If Bob's verification passes, it implies, roughly, that the adversary could not have tampered with the state (by the security of total authentication); in particular, the adversary could not have learned any information about the maximally entangled state. Therefore, Alice and Bob measure their halves of the maximally entangled state and obtain a shared key that is unknown to the eavesdropper. If Bob's verification rejects, the two try again. Though this is not a practical QKD scheme (because any tampering by the adversary would cause Alice and Bob to abort), it is conceptually very simple and illustrates the power of our definitions.

A protocol satisfying total authentication. We exhibit a protocol meeting our strong security notion. We present an authentication scheme based on *unitary designs*, which are efficiently sampleable distributions over unitary matrices that behave much like the uniform distribution over unitaries when only considering low degree moments.

Total authentication with key leakage. We also give a definition of *total authentication with key leakage*. This is a notion of security where the real adversary can be simulated by an ideal trivial adversary that only acts on its own private workspace, *but in a manner that may depend on the key.* This is a slightly weaker notion of security than total authentication, but it still implies simple QKD and some amount of key reuse. We note that the work of [HLM16] essentially shows that the Barnum et al. protocol satisfies total authentication with (minor) key leakage. We also give a simple protocol that achieves this, based on the *classical* Wegman-Carter authentication scheme.

A lifting theorem. Finally, we prove an intriguing *equivalence* between a very weak form of authentication security and a stronger notion. Specifically, this weak form of authentication security only guarantees that an authentication scheme is able to authenticate a *single state*: a Bell state. Furthermore, this Bell state is unentangled with the adversary, and the security guarantee holds with the key traced out (i.e. correlations with the key are not kept track of).

We prove a *lifting theorem* that "lifts" this weak security to a much stronger one that shows the same authentication scheme, when augmented with a Pauli randomization step, is actually secure when authenticating *arbitrary* messages, which might be entangled with the adversary! This stronger security notion still traces out the key, so it does not achieve total authentication. Nonetheless, we find it conceptually very interesting that such a lifting theorem holds.

We believe that our work contributes to broadening our understanding of *what security definitions are possible* for various primitives in the quantum world. In classical cryptography an eavesdropper can be correlated with the secret key simply by copying the ciphertext; thus it does not make sense for a security definition to keep track of the correlations between an adversary's private memory and the key. Our results demonstrate that it *is* meaningful to do so in the quantum setting. This is the motivation behind the name "total authentication": protocols satisfying total authentication are achieving the "best possible" security *within the framework used for the definition.*

2.3   Subsequent Work

Subsequent to the initial posting of our work, there have been several very interesting developments in quantum authentication. Portman [Por17] uses the Abstract Cryptography (AC) framework to model quantum authentication with key recycling. He shows that the Barnum et al. [BCG+02] is secure in this setting, thus demonstrating that the Barnum et al. protocol satisfies complete key recycling. Moreover, he shows that authentication based on unitary 2-designs is secure with key recycling; our analysis requires 8-designs to demonstrate key recycling. Alagic and Majenz [AM16] independently show that total authentication can be achieved with unitary 2-designs. Fehr and Salvail [FS16] examine quantum authentication of *classical* messages and demonstrate a scheme that admits key recycling as well.

Outline. In the next section we cover some preliminaries and notation. In Sect. 4 we formally present the fundamental security definitions used in our paper. In Sects. 5.1 and 5.2 we present several properties satisfied by our definitions. In Sect. 6, we analyze the security of the Wegman-Carter MAC with 3-universal hashing within our security framework. In Sect. 7 we present and analyze the Auth-QFT-Auth scheme. In Sect. 8 we present and analyze the unitary design scheme. In Sect. 9 we prove the lifting theorem.

3   Preliminaries

3.1   Notation

Quantum information. We assume basic familiarity with quantum computing concepts, such as states, measurements, and unitary operations. We will use calligraphic letters to denote Hilbert spaces, such as $\mathcal{H}$, $\mathcal{M}$, $\mathcal{T}$, $\mathcal{K}$, and so on. We write $S(\mathcal{H})$ to denote the set of unit vectors in $\mathcal{H}$. For two Hilbert spaces $\mathcal{H}$ and $\mathcal{M}$, we write $L(\mathcal{H}, \mathcal{M})$ to denote the set of matrices that map $\mathcal{H}$ to $\mathcal{M}$. We abbreviate $L(\mathcal{H}, \mathcal{H})$ as simply $L(\mathcal{H})$. The following are important subsets of $L(\mathcal{H})$ that we'll use throughout this paper.

- $D(\mathcal{H})$ denotes the set of *density matrices* on $\mathcal{H}$; that is, positive semidefinite operators on $\mathcal{H}$ with unit trace.
- $D_{\leq}(\mathcal{H})$ denotes the set of *subnormalized* density matrices on $\mathcal{H}$; that is, positive semidefinite operators on $\mathcal{H}$ with trace at most one.
- $U(\mathcal{H})$ denotes the set of unitary matrices acting on $\mathcal{H}$. For an integer N, we will also write $U(N)$ to denote the set of all $N \times N$ complex unitary matrices.

Another important class of operators are *isometries*: these are like unitaries, except that they can append ancilla qubits. We say that a map $V \in L(\mathcal{H}, \mathcal{M})$ is an isometry if for all vectors $|\psi\rangle \in \mathcal{H}$, $\||V|\psi\rangle\| = \||\psi\rangle\|$. Note that this requires $\dim(\mathcal{M}) \geq \dim(\mathcal{H})$. We will let $J(\mathcal{H}, \mathcal{M})$ denote the set of isometries in $L(\mathcal{H}, \mathcal{M})$.

We use $\mathbb{I}$ to denote the identity matrix. For a Hilbert space $\mathcal{H}$, we let $|\mathcal{H}|$ denote the dimension of $\mathcal{H}$.

We will typically decorate states and unitaries with superscripts to denote which spaces they act on. For example, let $\mathcal{Y}$ and $\mathcal{Z}$ be two Hilbert spaces. Let $U \in U(\mathcal{Y})$ and let $V \in U(\mathcal{Y} \otimes \mathcal{Z})$. Then when we write the product $U^{\mathcal{Y}} V^{\mathcal{YZ}}$ we mean the operator $(U^{\mathcal{Y}} \otimes \mathbb{I}^{\mathcal{Z}}) V^{\mathcal{YZ}}$; we will often omit mention of the identity unitary when it is clear from context.

Another convention is the implicit partial trace. For example, let $\rho^{\mathcal{KM}} \in D(\mathcal{K} \otimes \mathcal{M})$. Then $\rho^{\mathcal{M}} = \mathrm{Tr}_{\mathcal{K}}(\rho^{\mathcal{KM}})$. Additionally, given a pure state $|\rho\rangle$, we will let ρ denote the rank one density matrix $|\rho\rangle\langle\rho|$.

Superoperators. In this paper we will consider *superoperators*, which are linear maps that act on a vector space of linear maps. For Hilbert spaces $\mathcal{H}$ and $\mathcal{M}$, let $T(\mathcal{H}, \mathcal{M})$ denote the set of all linear maps that take elements of $L(\mathcal{H})$ to $L(\mathcal{M})$. While superoperators can be very general, we will focus on superoperators $\mathcal{O} \in T(\mathcal{H}, \mathcal{M})$ that are *completely positive* and *trace non-increasing*, which have the following characterization: there exists an alphabet Σ and set of matrices (not necessarily Hermitian) $\{A_a\}_{a \in \Sigma} \subset L(\mathcal{H}, \mathcal{M})$ such that

1. $\mathcal{O}(X) = \sum_{a \in \Sigma} A_a X A_a^\dagger$ for all $X \in L(\mathcal{H})$, and
2. $\sum_{a \in \Sigma} A_a^\dagger A_a \preceq \mathbb{I}^{\mathcal{H}}$.

For the rest of this paper, when we speak of superoperators, we will always mean completely positive, trace non-increasing superoperators. Although the definition of superoperators is rather abstract, they capture general quantum operations on arbitrary quantum states, including post-selection, as demonstrated by Stinespring's dilation theorem[6]:

Theorem 1 (Stinespring's dilation theorem). *A map $\mathcal{O} \in T(\mathcal{H}, \mathcal{M})$ is a completely positive, trace non-increasing superoperator if and only if there exists auxiliary Hilbert spaces $\mathcal{Z}, \mathcal{Z}'$, an isometry $V \in J(\mathcal{H} \otimes \mathcal{Z}, \mathcal{M} \otimes \mathcal{Z}')$, and a projector Π acting on $\mathcal{M} \otimes \mathcal{Z}'$ such that for all density matrices $\rho \in D(\mathcal{H})$, we have*

$$\mathcal{O}(\rho) = \mathrm{Tr}_{\mathcal{Z}'}(\Pi V \rho V^\dagger \Pi).$$

Matrix norms and distance measures. We will make use of several matrix norms and distance measures in this paper.

Given a (not necessarily unit) vector $|\psi\rangle \in \mathcal{H}$, we use $\||\psi\rangle\|_2$ to denote the Euclidean norm of $|\psi\rangle$.

---

[6] A seasoned veteran of quantum information may notice that this departs slightly from the convention in quantum information theory where physically realizable quantum operations are CPTP maps. Here the difference is that we consider maps that can possibly *decrease* the trace of an operator, which corresponds to post-selection.

The most important matrix norm is the *trace norm* of a linear operator X, defined to be $\|X\|_1 = \mathrm{Tr}(\sqrt{X^\dagger X})$. Correspondingly, the *trace distance* between density matrices ρ, σ is defined to be $\|\rho - \sigma\|_1$. The operational significance of the trace distance is that $\|\rho - \sigma\|_1$ is proportional to the maximum bias with which one can distinguish between ρ and σ using any quantum operation.

The next norm we will make use of is the *Frobenius norm* of a linear operator X, which is defined to be $\|X\|_2 = \sqrt{\mathrm{Tr}(X^\dagger X)}$. A useful property of the Frobenius norm is that $\|X\|_2 = \sqrt{\sum_{ij} |X_{ij}|^2}$, where the sum is over all the matrix entries of X (with respect to any basis).

The *operator norm* (also known as the *spectral norm*) of an operator $X \in L(\mathcal{H})$ is defined to be $\|X\|_\infty = \sup_{|v\rangle \in S(\mathcal{H})} \|X|v\rangle\|_2$, where the supremum is over all unit vectors in $\mathcal{H}$.

Fact 2. *Let* $|\psi\rangle, |\theta\rangle \in S(\mathcal{H})$. *Then*

$$\|\psi - \theta\|_1 \leq 2\||\psi\rangle - |\theta\rangle\|_2$$

where recall that $\psi = |\psi\rangle\langle\psi|$ *and* $\theta = |\theta\rangle\langle\theta|$.

Proof. It is well known that $\|\psi - \theta\|_1 \leq 2\sqrt{1 - |\langle\psi|\theta\rangle|^2}$ (see, e.g., [NC10]). But now notice that $1 - x^2 \leq 2(1 - x)$ for all x. Therefore the trace distance is at most $2\sqrt{2(1 - |\langle\psi|\theta\rangle|)} \leq 2\||\psi\rangle - |\theta\rangle\|_2$.

3.2   Basic Definitions for Authentication

Spaces. We let $\mathcal{K}$ denote the **key space**, $\mathcal{M}$ denote the **message space**, $\mathcal{Y}$ denote the **authenticated space**, and $\mathcal{F}$ denote the **flag space**. The flag space $\mathcal{F}$ is a two-dimensional Hilbert space spanned by orthogonal states $|\mathrm{ACC}\rangle$ and $|\mathrm{REJ}\rangle$. The space $\mathcal{Z}$ is the **private space of the adversary**. We will let $\mathcal{S}$ denote the registers held by the sender and receiver that, during the execution of the authentication protocol, are not communicated nor acted upon by the sender, receiver, or adversary.

Authentication scheme. An authentication scheme is a pair of keyed superoperators Auth, Ver where

– Auth_k for $k \in \mathcal{K}$ is a superoperator mapping $\mathrm{D}(\mathcal{M})$ to $\mathrm{D}(\mathcal{Y})$.
– Ver_k for $k \in \mathcal{K}$ is a superoperator mapping $\mathrm{D}(\mathcal{Y})$ to $\mathrm{D}(\mathcal{M} \otimes \mathcal{F})$.

satisfying the correctness requirements that for any quantum state $\rho \in \mathrm{D}(\mathcal{M})$, for all keys $k \in \mathcal{K}$, $\mathsf{Ver}_k(\mathsf{Auth}_k(\rho)) = \rho \otimes |\mathrm{ACC}\rangle\langle\mathrm{ACC}|$.[7]

We will also use Auth and Ver to denote the operators

$$\mathsf{Auth}(\cdot) = \sum_k |k\rangle\langle k| \otimes \mathsf{Auth}_k(\cdot) \qquad\qquad \mathsf{Ver}(\cdot) = \sum_k |k\rangle\langle k| \otimes \mathsf{Ver}_k(\cdot).$$

---

[7] One can also discuss schemes where the correctness requirements hold *approximately* (e.g., the state $\mathsf{Ver}_k(\mathsf{Auth}_k(\rho))$ is within trace distance δ of $\rho \otimes |\mathrm{ACC}\rangle\langle\mathrm{ACC}|$); using this correctness condition does not significantly affect the discussion in this paper.

Some simplifying assumptions. This definition of authentication scheme is more general than we need in this paper. Throughout this work, we shall work with a simplified model of authentication schemes: first, we will assume that Auth_k behaves as an isometry taking $\mathcal{M}$ to $\mathcal{Y}$ (i.e. it isn't probabilistic). Let $\mathcal{V}_k$ denote the subspace of the Hilbert space $\mathcal{Y}$ that is the image of Auth_k, let $\Pi_{\mathcal{V}_k}$ denote the projector onto the space $\mathcal{V}_k$, and let Auth_k^{-1} denote the inverse isometry that maps $\mathcal{V}_k$ to $\mathcal{M}$. In this case, a canonical way to define the Ver_k superoperator is as follows:

$$\rho \mapsto \left(\mathsf{Auth}_k^{-1} \circ \Pi_{\mathcal{V}_k}\right)(\rho) \otimes |\mathrm{ACC}\rangle\langle\mathrm{ACC}|^{\mathcal{F}} + \mathrm{Tr}((\mathbb{I} - \Pi_{\mathcal{V}_k})\,\rho)\,\frac{\mathbb{I}_{\mathcal{M}}}{|\mathcal{M}|} \otimes |\mathrm{REJ}\rangle\langle\mathrm{REJ}|^{\mathcal{F}}$$

$$(1)$$

Here, $\mathsf{Auth}_k^{-1} \circ \Pi_{\mathcal{V}_k}$ denotes the operation that first applies the projection $\Pi_{\mathcal{V}_k}$ to the state, followed by the inverse isometry Auth_k^{-1}. The state $\frac{\mathbb{I}_{\mathcal{M}}}{|\mathcal{M}|}$ is the maximally mixed state on the message space. In other words, the verification procedure first checks that the received state (which resides in $\mathcal{Y}$) is supported on the subspace of valid signed states $\mathcal{V}_k$. If so, then it inverts the authentication isometry to obtain an unsigned message state, and sets the $\mathcal{F}$ register to $|\mathrm{ACC}\rangle$. Otherwise, it replaces the state with a uniformly random message state, and sets the $\mathcal{F}$ register to $|\mathrm{REJ}\rangle$.

However in this paper we are mostly concerned with the output of the Ver_k procedure in the *accepting* case. For technical convenience then, throughout this paper we will treat Ver_k as the following superoperator mapping $\mathrm{D}(\mathcal{Y})$ to $\mathrm{D}(\mathcal{M})$:

$$\mathsf{Ver}_k(\rho) = \left(\mathsf{Auth}_k^{-1} \circ \Pi_{\mathcal{V}_k}\right)(\rho).$$

In other words, it only outputs the $|\mathrm{ACC}\rangle$ part of (1), and does not output a ACC or REJ flag. Furthermore, notice that this superoperator is not trace preserving; the trace of $\mathsf{Ver}_k(\rho)$ is equal to the probability that ρ was accepted by the verification procedure defined in (1). Thus one can view Ver_k as a "filter" that only accepts states that were properly authenticated.

We stress, however, that these simplifying assumptions are not crucial to our results – it is mostly for notational convenience that we treat Ver_k as a filter.

Classical Authentication. In a classical authentication protocol, the authentication operator Auth_k is specified by a classical (reversible) function $\mathsf{Auth}_k : \mathcal{M} \mapsto \mathcal{Y}$ acting on the computational basis, run in superposition on the input state. The verification operator behaves the same as described above: Ver_k projects onto the subspace of $\mathcal{Y}$ spanned by classical strings $\mathsf{Auth}_k(m)$ for all $m \in \mathcal{M}$, and then applies the inverse map Auth_k^{-1}.

Message authentication codes. A message authentication code (or MAC) is a special type of classical authentication scheme $(\mathsf{Auth}, \mathsf{Ver})$ where for a message m, $\mathsf{Auth}_k(m) = (m, \sigma(k, m))$, where we call $\sigma(k, m)$ the *message tag*. We treat

Ver_k as an operator that projects out messages that do not have valid tags, and for messages with valid tags, Ver_k will strip the tags away:

$$\mathsf{Ver}_k = \sum_m |m\rangle\langle m, \sigma(k,m)|.$$

Adversaries. We model adversaries in the following way: the adversary prepares the initial message state $|\rho\rangle^{\mathcal{MSZ}}$, where we can assume that the adversary possesses the purification of $\rho^{\mathcal{MS}}$. After the state is authenticated with a secret key k, the adversary gets to attack the $\mathcal{YZ}$ spaces with an arbitrary completely positive trace non-increasing superoperator $\mathcal{O}$. After this attack, the state is un-authenticated with the same key k.

We don't require the superoperator $\mathcal{O}$ to be trace preserving; this is to allow adversaries to *discard* certain measurement outcomes (or, alternatively, *post-select* on measurement outcomes, without renormalizing). While this may seem to give the adversary far too much power, in our security definitions we take into account the probability of the event that the adversary post-selects on. If this probability is too small (which implies that the success probability of the protocol is too small), the security guarantees are meaningless, which is necessary. Allowing for superoperators to be trace non-preserving will help make our definitions clean to state.

A remark about the sender and receiver's private register $\mathcal{S}$. The reader may wonder why we do not allow the sender, receiver, nor adversary to act upon the $\mathcal{S}$ register during the execution of the authentication protocol. The register $\mathcal{S}$ is supposed to model entanglement the sender and receiver may keep during the protocol. The important aspect of it is that the adversary does *not* have access to this side information.

If, when analyzing the authentication scheme in the context of a larger protocol in which the sender/receiver *do* act upon the register $\mathcal{S}$, we can assume that during the authentication phase, the sender and receiver do not touch $\mathcal{S}$, but wait until the authentication protocol is over. Thus we can analyze the behavior of the authentication protocol without this action.

4 Security Framework for Quantum Authentication

We present our security definitions using the real/ideal paradigm. Let $(\mathsf{Auth}, \mathsf{Ver})$ be an authentication protocol, with key space $\mathcal{K}$, message space $\mathcal{M}$, and authenticated space $\mathcal{Y}$.

Definition 1. *Let* $(\mathsf{Auth}, \mathsf{Ver})$ *be an authentication scheme. Let* $\mathscr{A} \subseteq T(\mathcal{YZ}, \mathcal{YZ})$ *denote a set of ideal adversaries. The scheme* $(\mathsf{Auth}, \mathsf{Ver})$ ε*-reduces to* $\mathscr{A}$*-adversaries iff the following holds: for all initial message states* $|\rho\rangle^{\mathcal{MSZ}}$*, for all adversaries* $\mathcal{O} \in T(\mathcal{YZ}, \mathcal{YZ})$*, there exists an ideal adversary* $\mathcal{I} \in \mathscr{A}$ *such that the following (not necessarily normalized) states are* ε*-close in trace distance:*

- *(Real experiment)* $\mathbb{E}_k \, |k\rangle\langle k| \otimes [\mathsf{Ver}_k \circ \mathcal{O} \circ \mathsf{Auth}_k] \, (\rho^{\mathcal{MSZ}})$
- *(Ideal experiment)* $\mathbb{E}_k \, |k\rangle\langle k| \otimes [\mathsf{Ver}_k \circ \mathcal{I} \circ \mathsf{Auth}_k] \, (\rho^{\mathcal{MSZ}})$

where Auth_k acts on $\mathcal{M}$, Ver_k acts on $\mathcal{Y}$, and both act as the identity on $\mathcal{SZ}$.

Intuitively, our security definition states that for an authentication scheme $(\mathsf{Auth}, \mathsf{Ver})$ that is $\mathscr{A}$-secure, for all initial message states $\rho^{\mathcal{MSZ}}$, an *arbitrary* adversary that acts on an authenticated state $\mathsf{Auth}_k(\rho^{\mathcal{MSZ}})$ is *reduced* to an "ideal adversary" in $\mathscr{A}$; behaving differently will cause the verification procedure to abort. In other words, "all the adversary can do" is behave like some adversary in the class $\mathscr{A}$. We allow the real adversary to prepare the message state $\rho^{\mathcal{MSZ}}$ and hence, allow the ideal adversary to depend on it.

A comment about normalization. It is important that the states of the real experiment and ideal experiment are not required to have unit trace. This is because their trace corresponds to the probability that the verification procedure accepts. If the probability of acceptance is smaller than ε, then the security guarantee is vacuous. Intuitively, this corresponds to situations such as the adversary successfully guessing the secret key k, so we cannot expect any security guarantee in that setting. However, if the probability of acceptance is significantly larger than ε, then we can condition on acceptance, and still obtain a meaningful security guarantee: the distance between the (renormalized) real experiment and ideal experiments is small.

We now specialize the above definition to some important classes of ideal adversaries that we will consider in this paper. Note that for two classes of ideal adversaries $\mathscr{A}$ and $\mathscr{A}'$, if $\mathscr{A} \subset \mathscr{A}'$, then an authentication scheme reducing to $\mathscr{A}$-adversaries implies reducing to $\mathscr{A}'$-adversaries. Hence reducing to $\mathscr{A}$-adversaries is a stronger security guarantee.

4.1   Basis-Dependent Authentication

We first define a notion of security of authentication schemes that reduce to a *basis-respecting* adversary.

Definition 2 (Basis-respecting adversaries). *Let $\mathcal{B} = \{|\psi\rangle\}$ denote an orthonormal basis for $\mathcal{Y}$. Then an adversary $\mathcal{I} \in \mathrm{T}(\mathcal{YZ}, \mathcal{YZ})$ is $\mathcal{B}$-respecting iff it can be written as*

$$\mathcal{I}(\sigma) = \mathrm{Tr}_{\mathcal{Z}'}(\Pi V \sigma V^\dagger \Pi)$$

for all $\sigma \in \mathrm{D}(\mathcal{YZ})$, where Π is a projector acting on $\mathcal{ZZ}'$, and $V \in \mathrm{J}(\mathcal{YZ}, \mathcal{YZZ}')$ is an isometry that can be written as

$$V = \sum_{\psi \in \mathcal{B}} |\psi\rangle\langle\psi|^{\mathcal{Y}} \otimes V_\psi$$

where for each ψ, $V_\psi \in \mathrm{J}(\mathcal{Z}, \mathcal{ZZ}')$ is some isometry.

Without the second condition on V, by Stinespring's Dilation Theorem every superoperator can be written as $\mathcal{I}(\sigma) = \mathrm{Tr}_{\mathcal{Z}'}(\Pi V \sigma V^\dagger \Pi)$ for some choice of isometry V and projector Π. However, the second condition forces V to respect the basis $\mathcal{B}$. Intuitively, a basis-respecting adversary first performs some (partial) measurement on the $\mathcal{Y}$ register in the $\mathcal{B}$ basis, and based on the measurement outcome, performs some further isometry on the side information in $\mathcal{Z}$. When $\mathcal{B}$ is simply the computational basis, then the adversary treats the $\mathcal{Y}$ register as classical.

Definition 3 (Security relative to a basis). *Let $\mathcal{B}$ be a basis for $\mathcal{Y}$. An authentication scheme (Auth, Ver) ε-authenticates relative to basis $\mathcal{B}$ iff it ε-reduces to the class of $\mathcal{B}$-respecting adversaries.*

Intuitively, our new definition captures the "best possible" security definition for *classical* authentication protocols. With a classical protocol, the adversary can perform arbitrary measurements on the authenticated space without detection by the verification algorithm. Because measurements are now undetectable, the adversary can also perform σ-dependent operations to the auxiliary registers, where σ is the classical authenticated message observed in the authenticated registers. For example, he can copy σ into the auxiliary space. He can also now choose to abort or not depending on σ. However, he should not be able to turn σ into $\sigma' \neq \sigma$.

In Sect. 5.1, we establish consequences of our definition of basis-dependent security, including the property of unforgeability: the adversary cannot produce two valid signed messages with non-negligible probability, when given access to only one superposition. Thus, our definition subsumes the Boneh-Zhandry security definition for one-time MACs.

In Sect. 6 we show that the classical Wegman-Carter MAC where the message m is appended with $h(m)$, where $h(\cdot)$ is drawn from a three-wise independent hash family, is a scheme that authenticates relative to the computational basis.

Theorem 3. *The Wegman-Carter MAC with three-universal hashing is $O(\sqrt{|\mathcal{M}|/|\mathcal{T}|})$-authenticating relative to the computational basis, where $\mathcal{T}$ is the range of the hash family.*

4.2 Total Authentication

In this section we formally define our notion of total authentication. First, we define *oblivious adversaries*.

Definition 4 (Oblivious adversary). *An adversary $\mathcal{I} \in \mathrm{T}(\mathcal{YZ}, \mathcal{YZ})$ is oblivious iff there exists a superoperator $\mathcal{O} \in \mathrm{T}(\mathcal{Z}, \mathcal{Z})$ such that*

$$\mathcal{I}(\sigma) = (\mathbb{I}^{\mathcal{Y}} \otimes \mathcal{O})(\sigma)$$

for all $\sigma \in \mathrm{D}(\mathcal{YZ})$.

In other words, an oblivious adversary does not act at all on the authenticated message, and only acts on the auxiliary side information that it possesses about the state.

Definition 5 (Total authentication). *An authentication scheme* (Auth, Ver) ε-*totally authenticates iff it* ε-*reduces to the class of oblivious adversaries.*

[DNS12]'s security definition is similar, except it traces out the key register. Therefore, it does not keep track of potential correlations between the adversary and the key. [DNS12] considers what happens in the reject case, while total authentication only makes requirements when the verifier accepts. A subsequent work by Alagic et al. [AM16] indeed showed that total authentication implies [DNS12] with a slight modification of decryption outputting $\perp$ whenever it rejects. We will argue shortly that our definition of total authentication is strictly stronger than the definition of [DNS12]; that is, there are protocols which satisfy the security definition of [DNS12], but do not satisfy total authentication.

In Sect. 5.2 we establish a few properties of this definition. The first is that a totally authenticating scheme yields encryption of the quantum state. Barnum, et al. showed that quantum state authentication implies quantum state encryption [BCG+02]. However, they did not take into account quantum side information. We show that our definition very easily implies encryption even when the adversary may be entangled with the message state.

Then, we show how our notion of total authentication gives rise to a conceptually simple version of quantum key distribution (QKD). [HLM16] have already observed that the universal composability of the Barnum et al. protocol implies that it can be used to perform QKD as well. Thus while our application of quantum authentication to QKD is not novel, we use this as another opportunity to showcase the strength of our definition. We also show how our definition easily implies full key reuse.

In Sect. 8 we present a scheme, called the *unitary design scheme*, that achieves total authentication, and to our knowledge this is the first scheme that achieves such security.

Theorem 4. *The unitary design scheme is* $2^{-s/2}$-*totally authenticating, where* s *is the number of extra* $|0\rangle$ *qubits.*

As a consequence, this yields an authentication scheme where the key can be recycled fully, conditioned on successful verification by the receiver. In contrast, the protocol of Barnum et al. is not known to possess this property; [HLM16] showed that most of the key can be securely recycled.

4.3 Total Authentication with Key Leakage

Finally, we introduce a slight weakening of the definition of total authentication above: we consider schemes that achieve total authentication of quantum data, but incur some *key leakage*. We model this in the following way: let $\mathcal{K}'$ be such that $|\mathcal{K}'| \leq |\mathcal{K}|$. Define a *key leakage function* $\ell : \mathcal{K} \mapsto \mathcal{K}'$. If $|\mathcal{K}'|$ is strictly smaller than $|\mathcal{K}|$, then $\ell(k)$ must necessarily lose information about the key $k \in \mathcal{K}$, but it will also leak some information about it.

In a total authentication scheme with key leakage, an arbitrary adversary is reduced to an oblivious adversary (i.e., is forced to only act on the side information), but the manner in which it acts on the side information *may depend on* $\ell(k)$.

Definition 6. *Let* (Auth, Ver) *be an authentication scheme. Let* $\mathcal{K}'$ *be some domain such that* $|\mathcal{K}'| \le |\mathcal{K}|$ *and let* $\ell : \mathcal{K} \to \mathcal{K}'$ *be a key leakage function. Let* $\mathscr{A} \subseteq \mathrm{T}(\mathcal{YZ}, \mathcal{YZ})$ *denote a set of ideal adversaries. The scheme* (Auth, Ver) ε*-reduces to* $\mathscr{A}$*-adversaries with key leakage* ℓ *iff the following holds: for all initial message states* $|\rho\rangle^{\mathcal{MSZ}}$*, for all adversaries* $\mathcal{O} \in \mathrm{T}(\mathcal{YZ}, \mathcal{YZ})$*, there exists a collection of ideal adversaries* $\{\mathcal{I}_h\} \subset \mathscr{A}$*, indexed by* $h \in \mathcal{K}'$*, such that the following (not necessarily normalized) states are* ε*-close in trace distance:*

- *(Real experiment)* $\mathbb{E}_k |k\rangle\langle k| \otimes [\mathsf{Ver}_k \circ \mathcal{O} \circ \mathsf{Auth}_k] (\rho^{\mathcal{MSZ}})$
- *(Ideal experiment)* $\mathbb{E}_k |k\rangle\langle k| \otimes [\mathsf{Ver}_k \circ \mathcal{I}_{\ell(k)} \circ \mathsf{Auth}_k] (\rho^{\mathcal{MSZ}})$.

Definition 7 (Total authentication with key leakage). *Let* $\mathcal{K}'$ *be some domain such that* $|\mathcal{K}'| \le |\mathcal{K}|$ *and let* $\ell : \mathcal{K} \to \mathcal{K}'$ *be a key leakage function. An authentication scheme* (Auth, Ver) ε*-totally authenticates with key leakage* ℓ *iff it* ε*-reduces to the class of oblivious adversaries with key leakage* ℓ.

This definition may seem somewhat strange: how is an ideal adversary able to learn bits $\ell(k)$ of the key k, if it doesn't act on the authenticated part of the state at all? Of course, any adversary that learns something about the key must have acted on the authenticated state, but the point is that, conditioned on successful verification, the adversary "effectively" behaved like an oblivious adversary that had access to $\ell(k)$.

In Sect. 7 we present a very simple scheme that achieves total authentication with some key leakage: to authenticate an arbitrary quantum state ρ, first apply the classical Wegman-Carter authentication scheme on it using key k. Then, apply $H^{\otimes n}$ to all the qubits in the authenticated state (i.e. apply the quantum Fourier transform over $\mathbb{Z}_2$). Finally, apply the classical Wegman-Carter scheme again using a fresh key h. Thus, we are authenticating the state ρ in complementary bases. We call this the "Auth-QFT-Auth" scheme.

We will show that this in fact achieves total authentication (and hence encryption of the state), but at the cost of leaking the "outer key" h:

Theorem 5 (Security of the Auth-QFT-Auth scheme). *The Auth-QFT-Auth scheme is* δ*-totally authenticating with outer key leakage, where* $\delta = O(\sqrt{|\mathcal{M}|^{5/2}/|\mathcal{Y}|})$.

While this scheme leaks some bits of the outer key, it preserves the secrecy of the state ρ and the "inner key" k. Furthermore, it is much more "lightweight" than the full unitary design scheme that achieves total authentication without key leakage. It also illustrates that applying a simple classical authentication scheme in complementary bases is already enough to reduce a full quantum adversary to performing only trivial attacks. Finally, the analysis of this scheme crucially relies on the basis dependent security definition above.

We note that Hayden, Leung, and Mayers show that the authentication scheme of [BCG+02] satisfies total authentication with key leakage [HLM16], but it is unclear whether it satisfies the strongest definition of total authentication without key leakage.

4.4 A Remark About Efficiency

Recently, Broadbent and Wainewright [BW16] study the *efficiency* of simulating ideal adversaries in the security proofs of two authentication schemes, the Clifford scheme and the trap code scheme. Specifically, they show that if the adversary in the authentication protocol is a quantum computer that runs in time T, then the ideal adversary which simulates it also runs in time $O(T)$. This efficiency-preservation is important for notions of composable security.

We note that the constructions of the ideal adversary in our analysis of the Wegman-Carter scheme, the Auth-QFT-Auth scheme, and the unitary design scheme are also efficiency preserving, and hence if the arbitrary adversary runs in polynomial time, then the simulating adversary also runs in polynomial time.

4.5 Comparison with security definition in [DNS12]

Similarly to our definition, the security definition of message authentication [DNS12] implies that essentially all the adversary can do is act on its own private workspace. However, it traces out the key register, and thus it does not keep track of correlations between the adversary and the secret key. It is a natural question to ask whether the security definition of [DNS12] *implies* our definition of total authentication. Here we show that it cannot, because there are protocols that satisfy the [DNS12] definition, but not ours.[8] [AM16] gives a formal proof of the fact that any protocol satisfying total authentication satisfies [DNS12] definition (with a slight modification).

Consider a protocol (Auth, Ver) that satisfies the [DNS12] definition. Let k denote the secret key used in the protocol. Now consider the following modified protocol (Auth$'$, Ver$'$): to authenticate a message state ρ, it produces Auth$_k(\rho)$, but then appends an independently random bit b, where (k, b) is the secret key register of (Auth$'$, Ver$'$). To verify, the receiver just applies the Ver$_k$ operation, and ignores the last bit. This new protocol still satisfies the [DNS12] definition, because the extra bit b is independent of the (Auth, Ver) process, and thus final state of the protocol can be simulated by an ideal adversary that generates its own b bit – as long as we're tracing out the key. However, this protocol does not satisfy total authentication. This is because an adversary can simply copy the bit b into its private workspace; but this cannot be simulated by an ideal adversary that is unentangled with the (k, b) register.

---

[8] See Sect. 9 for a formal statement of the [DNS12] definition.

Furthermore, any authentication scheme satisfying [DNS12]'s security definition also satisfies "total authentication with key leakage" for some key leakage function ℓ and any authentication scheme satisfying "total authentication with key leakage" satisfies the key-averaged security definition (with slight modification of decryption outputting $\bot$ in reject case). Hence, these two security definitions are equivalent (up to some error).

5   Properties of Security Definitions

5.1   Properties of Basis-Dependent Authentication

Unforgeability. Our security definition of authentication schemes relative to a basis implies the standard, classical security definition of authentication schemes called EUF-CMA. Namely, this says that the adversary, after having received the authenticated message state, cannot produce two distinct authenticated message-tag pairs with non-negligible probability. This property is called **unforgeability**. Thus this shows that our security definition recovers the Boneh-Zhandry (quantum) security definition for one-time MACs.

For detailed discussion and proof, refer to the full version of the paper [GYZ16][9].

5.2   Properties of Total Authentication

Encryption. Analogous to the Barnum et al.'s [BCG+02] result that authentication implies encryption, we show that authentication when considering side information must encrypt the state, even to an adversary that may be entangled with the state. This result is compatible with Barnum et al.'s: we start from a stronger property that considers side information, and end with a stronger form of encryption that also considers side information. For proof, refer to the full version [GYZ16].

Quantum Key Distribution. As mentioned in introduction, and noticed by previous works, a total authentication scheme gives a simple method to perform quantum key distribution. For details of the protocol, refer to the full version [GYZ16].

Key Reuse. It is easy to see that our definition of total authentication implies that, conditioned on successful verification of an authentication scheme (satisfying total authentication), the key can be reused by the sender and receiver for some other purpose. This is because conditioned on acceptance, the final state of the adversary is within ε/α trace distance of being independent of the key, where α is the probability of acceptance in the authentication protocol.

---

[9] https://arxiv.org/abs/1607.07759.

6   Quantum MACs from 3-universal Hashing

In the classical setting, secure one-time MACs can be constructed via universal hashing. Let $\{h_k\}_k$ be a strongly (2-)universal hash family. Then it is well known that the classical authentication protocol $\mathsf{Auth}_k(m) = (m, h_k(m))$ is secure against classical adversaries [WC81]. Here, we show that the *same* authentication protocol is also quantum-secure, provided that the hash family $\{h_k\}_k$ satisfies the following: for all distinct m_1, m_2, m_3, the distribution of $(h_k(m_1), h_k(m_2), h_k(m_3))$ for a randomly chosen $k \in \mathcal{K}$ is uniform in $\mathcal{T}^3$. Such a family is called a 3-*universal hash family*. We will overload notation and use $k(\cdot)$ to denote the function $h_k(\cdot)$.

We note that Boneh and Zhandry showed that, when authenticating classical messages in the one-time setting, pairwise independence is sufficient to ensure that a quantum adversary cannot forge a new signed message, as long as the length of the tag is longer than the message! When the tag is shorter than the message, they showed that pairwise independence is insecure, and 3-wise independence is necessary.

Our analysis of the 3-wise independent Wegman-Carter MAC requires that, in order to obtain security against quantum side information, the message tag needs to be longer than the message. Thus it is conceivable that pairwise independence is sufficient for the same guarantee; we leave this as an open question.

Theorem 6. *Let* $\mathcal{K} = \{k\}$ *be a 3-universal hash family. Let* $\mathsf{Auth}_k(m) = (m, k(m))$ *and* Ver_k *be the corresponding verification function. Then the authentication scheme* $(\mathsf{Auth}, \mathsf{Ver})$ *is* $O(\sqrt{|\mathcal{M}|/|\mathcal{T}|})$-*authenticating relative to the computational basis.*

We first state what the implications for key length are. Suppose we wish to guarantee that the Wegman-Carter MAC is ε-authenticating relative to the computational basis, then $|\mathcal{M}|/|\mathcal{T}| \leq O(\varepsilon^2)$, which implies that $\log|\mathcal{T}| \geq \log|\mathcal{M}| + 2\log\frac{1}{\varepsilon} + O(1)$. To ensure three-wise independence, it is sufficient for the key to have length $3\log|\mathcal{M}| + 6\log\frac{1}{\varepsilon} + O(1)$.

For proof of the above theorem, refer to the full version [GYZ16][10].

7   Total Authentication (with Key Leakage) from Complementary Classical Authentication

In Sect. 6, we saw how the classical Wegman-Carter message authentication scheme is still secure even when used on a superposition of messages, and even if the adversary has access to quantum side information about the messages. Here, we will show that using the Wegman-Carter scheme as a primitive, we obtain *total quantum state authentication*, which implies encryption of the quantum state.

---

[10] https://arxiv.org/abs/1607.07759.

The quantum state authentication scheme is simple: the sender authenticates the message state using the Wegman-Carter MAC in the computational basis, and then authenticates again in the Fourier basis (using a new key). The verification procedure is the reverse of this: the receiver first checks the outer authentication, performs the inverse Fourier transform, and then checks the inner authentication. We call this the "Auth-QFT-Auth" scheme. This is pleasingly analogous to the quantum one-time pad (QOTP), which encrypts quantum data using the classical one-time pad in complementary bases. However, the QOTP does not have authentication properties. Our analysis requires the 3-wise independence property of the Wegman-Carter MAC.

There is one slight caveat: we show that Auth-QFT-Auth achieves total authentication *with key leakage*. That is, we argue that conditioned on the receiver verification succeeding, the effect of an arbitrary adversary is to have ignored the authenticated state, and only acted on the adversary's side information, in a manner that may depend on the key used for the second authentication (what we call the "outer key"). In other words, we sacrifice the secrecy of the outer key, but in exchange we get complete quantum state encryption.

7.1 The Auth-QFT-Auth Scheme

Let $|\rho\rangle^{\mathcal{M}\mathcal{Z}} = \sum_m \alpha_m |m\rangle^{\mathcal{M}} \otimes |\varphi_m\rangle^{\mathcal{Z}}$ be the initial message state, where $\mathcal{Z}$ is held by the adversary.

It will be advantageous to rewrite this state in terms of the Schmidt decomposition:

$$|\rho\rangle^{\mathcal{M}\mathcal{Z}} = \sum_z \sqrt{\lambda_z} \left(\sum_m \alpha_{zm} |m\rangle^{\mathcal{M}} \right) \otimes |\varphi_z\rangle^{\mathcal{Z}}$$

where for $z \neq z'$, we have $\langle \varphi_z | \varphi_{z'} \rangle = 0$, and the λ_z's are nonnegative numbers summing to 1. Furthermore, the dimension of the span of $\{|\varphi_z\rangle\}_z$ is at most $|\mathcal{M}|$.

The authentication scheme is the composed operation $\mathsf{Auth}_2(H^{\otimes N}(\mathsf{Auth}_1(\rho)))$, where Auth_1 is the *inner* authentication scheme that uses key k, $H^{\otimes N}$ is the quantum Fourier transform over $\mathbb{Z}_2$, and Auth_2 is the *outer* authentication that uses key h. The keys k and h are independent.

The inner authentication scheme Auth_1 maps $\mathcal{M}$ to $\mathcal{Y}_1 = \mathcal{M}\mathcal{T}_1$. We define $N = |\mathcal{Y}_1|$. H is the single-qubit Hadamard unitary, and the Fourier transform $H^{\otimes N}$ acts on $\mathcal{Y}_1$. The outer authentication scheme Auth_2 maps $\mathcal{Y}_1$ to $\mathcal{Y}_2 = \mathcal{M}\mathcal{T}_1\mathcal{T}_2$. The keys k and h live in the registers $\mathcal{K}$ and $\mathcal{H}$, respectively. The evolution of the initial message state is as follows:

1. **Inner authentication.** When the inner authentication key (henceforth called the *inner key*) is k, the state becomes

$$\sum_z \sqrt{\lambda_z} \left(\sum_m \alpha_{zm} |m, k(m)\rangle^{\mathcal{Y}_1} \right) \otimes |\varphi_z\rangle^{\mathcal{Z}}$$

2. **Fourier transform over** $\mathbb{Z}_2$: Let $\{|x\rangle\}$ be a basis for $\mathcal{Y}_1$. Then:

$$\frac{1}{\sqrt{N}}\sum_z \sqrt{\lambda_z}\left(\sum_{m,x}\alpha_{zm}(-1)^{(m,k(m))\cdot x}|x\rangle^{\mathcal{Y}_1}\right)\otimes|\varphi_z\rangle^{\mathcal{Z}}.$$

3. **Outer authentication.** The outer key is denoted by h. The final authenticated state is then

$$|\sigma_{kh}\rangle^{\mathcal{Y}_1 T_2 \mathcal{Z}} = \frac{1}{\sqrt{N}}\sum_z \sqrt{\lambda_z}\left(\sum_{m,x}\alpha_{zm}(-1)^{(m,k(m))\cdot x}|x, h(x)\rangle^{\mathcal{Y}_1 T_2}\right)\otimes|\varphi_z\rangle^{\mathcal{Z}}$$

where T_2 is the space of the tag $h(x)$.

Let

$$\sigma^{\mathcal{K}\mathcal{H}\mathcal{Y}_1 T_2 \mathcal{Z}} = \mathop{\mathbb{E}}_{kh}|kh\rangle\langle kh|^{\mathcal{K}\mathcal{H}}\otimes|\sigma_{kh}\rangle\langle\sigma_{kh}|^{\mathcal{Y}_1 T_2 \mathcal{Z}}.$$

The adversary is then given the $\mathcal{Y}_1 T_2$ registers of σ, and performs a general unitary attack V that acts on $\mathcal{Y}_1 T_2 \mathcal{Z}$:

$$\widetilde{\sigma}^{\mathcal{K}\mathcal{H}\mathcal{Y}_1 T_2 \mathcal{Z}} = V\sigma V^\dagger.$$

Let $\widetilde{\tau}^{\mathcal{K}\mathcal{H}\mathcal{M}\mathcal{Z}} = \mathsf{Ver}_1\circ\mathrm{QFT}^{-1}\circ\mathsf{Ver}_2(\widetilde{\sigma})$. Let the inner authentication scheme be the 3-wise independent hashing QMAC with tag length $\log T$, and message length $\log M$. Let the outer authentication scheme be a QMAC that ε-authenticates with respect to the computational basis.

The Auth-QFT-Auth scheme can potentially leak some bits of the outer key h, but we will show that this is the *only* thing that is leaked; otherwise, it is performs total authentication (and hence encryption).

Theorem 7 (Security of the Auth-QFT-Auth scheme). *The Auth-QFT-Auth scheme is δ-totally authenticating with outer key leakage, where $\delta = \varepsilon + O(\sqrt{|\mathcal{M}|^{3/2}/|T_1|})$.*

Firstly, we consider the key requirements. The outer authentication scheme need not be a Wegman-Carter MAC, but let's assume that it is. In order to achieve δ-total authentication, the inner MAC must be such that $|\mathcal{M}|^{3/2}/|T_1| \leq O(\delta^2)$, or in other words, $\log|T_1| \geq \frac{3}{2}\log|\mathcal{M}| + 2\log\frac{1}{\delta} + O(1)$. The key needed for the inner MAC must be at least $\frac{9}{2}\log|\mathcal{M}| + 6\log\frac{1}{\delta} + O(1)$. The "message length" that is given to the outer MAC is $\log|\mathcal{M}| + \log|T_1| \geq \frac{5}{2}\log|\mathcal{M}| + 2\log\frac{1}{\delta} + O(1)$, and thus $\log|T_2| \geq \frac{5}{2}\log|\mathcal{M}| + 4\log\frac{1}{\delta} + O(1)$. The key length for the outer MAC needs to be at least $\frac{15}{2}\log|\mathcal{M}| + 12\log\frac{1}{\delta} + O(1)$, so the total key needed is $12\log|\mathcal{M}| + 18\log\frac{1}{\delta} + O(1)$.

While the inner key can be recycled (upon successful verification), the outer key unfortunately cannot be.

Proof Sketch: We will omit mention of the sender/receiver's private space $\mathcal{S}$, and discuss how our proof generalizes to the case of non-empty $\mathcal{S}$ later. We will let

$M = |\mathcal{M}|$, $T = |\mathcal{T}_1|$, and $N = MT = |\mathcal{Y}_1|$. We will assume that $M^{3/2} \leq T$; otherwise the theorem statement is vacuous.

Suppose the outer authentication scheme was ε-secure. By definition, there exists an ideal computational basis adversary $\mathcal{I}$ such that $\|\text{Ver}_2(\widetilde{\sigma}) - \text{Ver}_2(\mathcal{I}(\sigma))\|_1 \leq \varepsilon$, where Ver_2 denotes the verification procedure for the outer authentication scheme. There exists a computational basis-respecting linear map $\Lambda \in L(\mathcal{Y}_2 \mathcal{Z})$ such that

$$\mathcal{I} : \sigma \mapsto \Lambda \sigma \Lambda^\dagger.$$

Since Λ is computational basis-respecting, we have for all (x, s, z):

$$\Lambda |x, s\rangle^{\mathcal{Y}_1 \mathcal{T}_2} \otimes |\varphi_z\rangle^{\mathcal{Z}} = |x, s\rangle^{\mathcal{Y}_1 \mathcal{T}_2} \otimes |\phi_{xsz}\rangle^{\mathcal{Z}}.$$

for some collection of (not necessarily normalized) states $\{|\phi_{xsz}\rangle\}$.

Therefore the effect of the adversary on the authenticated state (after verification) is to be close to $\mathcal{I}(\sigma) = \mathbb{E}_{k,h} |kh\rangle\langle kh| \otimes |\tau_{kh}\rangle\langle\tau_{kh}|$ where for fixed inner/outer keys k, h

$$|\tau_{kh}\rangle = \frac{1}{\sqrt{(N)}} \sum_z \sqrt{\lambda_z} \sum_{m,x} \alpha_{zm} (-1)^{(m,k(m))\cdot x} |x\rangle \otimes |\phi_{xh_xz}\rangle.$$

Thus, the final state that Bob has, after performing full (i.e. inner and outer) verification, is ε-close to

$$\mathbb{E}_{k,h} |kh\rangle\langle kh| \otimes |\mu_{kh}\rangle\langle\mu_{kh}|$$

where

$$|\mu_{kh}\rangle = \sum_z \sqrt{\lambda_z} \sum_m \left(\frac{1}{N} \sum_{x,m'} \alpha_{zm'} (-1)^{(m+m',k(m)+k(m'))\cdot x} \right) |m\rangle \otimes |\phi_{xh_xz}\rangle.$$

Then security of Auth-QFT-Auth is established if we show that for every h,

$$\mathbb{E}_k \left\| |\mu_{kh}\rangle - |\nu_h\rangle \right\|^2$$

is small, where

$$|\nu_h\rangle^{\mathcal{M}\mathcal{Z}} = \sum_z \sqrt{\lambda_z} \sum_m \alpha_{zm} |m\rangle^{\mathcal{M}} \otimes |\eta_{hz}\rangle^{\mathcal{Z}}$$

with $|\eta_{hz}\rangle^{\mathcal{Z}} = \frac{1}{N} \sum_x |\phi_{xh_xz}\rangle^{\mathcal{Z}}$. Assuming this, the next Lemma will show that there is an ideal oblivious, but outer key-dependent, adversary whose actions lead to the global state $\mathbb{E}_{kh} |kh\rangle\langle kh| \otimes |\nu_h\rangle\langle\nu_h|$.

Lemma 1 (Constructing the ideal oblivious adversary). *For all h there exists an ideal oblivious adversary $\mathcal{I}_h$ acting on $\mathcal{Z}$ only such that*

$$|\nu_h\rangle\langle\nu_h|^{\mathcal{M}\mathcal{Z}} = \mathcal{I}_h(|\rho\rangle\langle\rho|^{\mathcal{M}\mathcal{Z}}).$$

We now construct an ideal adversary $\mathcal{I}_h$, derived from the computational basis adversary $\mathcal{I}$. By definition of $\mathcal{I}$, there exists a computational basis-respecting isometry $V \in J(\mathcal{Y}_2\mathcal{Z}, \mathcal{Y}_2\mathcal{Z}\mathcal{Y}_2'\mathcal{Z}_2)$ where $\mathcal{Y}_2'$ is an auxiliary register isomorphic to $\mathcal{Y}_2$, and $\mathcal{Z}_2$ is an auxiliary qubit register, such that

$$\mathcal{I} : \sigma^{\mathcal{Y}\mathcal{Z}} \mapsto \mathrm{Tr}_{\mathcal{Y}'\mathcal{Z}_2}\left(\Pi V \sigma^{\mathcal{Y}\mathcal{Z}} V^\dagger \Pi\right).$$

Here $\Pi = P \otimes |0\rangle\langle0|^{\mathcal{Z}_2}$ for some projector P acting on $\mathcal{Z}$. Furthermore, V is computational basis respecting:

$$\Pi V |x, s\rangle^{\mathcal{Y}_2} \otimes |\varphi_z\rangle^{\mathcal{Z}} = |x, s\rangle^{\mathcal{Y}_2} \otimes |\phi_{xsz}\rangle^{\mathcal{Z}} \otimes |0\cdots0\rangle^{\mathcal{Y}_2'\mathcal{Z}_2}$$

where the $|\phi_{xsz}\rangle^{\mathcal{Z}}$ were defined above.

Now we construct the ideal general adversary $\mathcal{I}_h$ as follows:

1. First, the adversary creates the entangled state $|\Phi_h\rangle^{\mathcal{A}\mathcal{A}'} = \frac{1}{\sqrt{N}}\sum_x$ $|x, h(x)\rangle^{\mathcal{A}}|x, h(x)\rangle^{\mathcal{A}'}$ in new registers $\mathcal{A}\otimes\mathcal{A}'$, which are isomorphic to $\mathcal{Y}_2\otimes\mathcal{Y}_2$, and $\{|x\rangle\}$ is a basis for $\mathcal{Y}_1$.

2. It then applies the unitary V to half of $|\Phi_h\rangle^{\mathcal{A}\mathcal{A}'}$ that resides in $\mathcal{A}$, and the $\mathcal{Z}$ part of the input state $|\rho\rangle$.

3. The adversary measures $\mathcal{A}\mathcal{A}'\mathcal{Z}\mathcal{Z}_2$ using the projective measurement $\{Q, \mathbb{I} - Q\}$, where $Q = |\Phi_h\rangle\langle\Phi_h|^{\mathcal{A}\mathcal{A}'} \otimes \Pi$. The adversary discards the outcome corresponding to $\mathbb{I} - Q$, and leaves the state unnormalized:

$$\frac{1}{N} \sum_{z,x,m} \sqrt{\lambda_z}\alpha_{zm}|m\rangle^{\mathcal{M}} |\phi_{xsz}\rangle^{\mathcal{Z}}|\Phi\rangle^{\mathcal{A}\mathcal{A}'}|0\cdots0\rangle^{\mathcal{Y}_2'\mathcal{Z}_2}$$

4. The adversary discards the $\mathcal{A}\mathcal{A}'\mathcal{Y}_2'\mathcal{Z}_2$ registers:

$$\frac{1}{N} \sum_{z,x,m} \sqrt{\lambda_z}\alpha_{zm}|m\rangle^{\mathcal{M}} \otimes |\phi_{xsz}\rangle^{\mathcal{Z}}$$

This is precisely the state $|\nu_h\rangle$, and the $\mathcal{I}_h$ only interacts with $\mathcal{Z}$ and auxiliary registers in the adversary's control, so it is an ideal general adversary.

We bound $\mathbb{E}_k \left\|\, |\mu_{kh}\rangle - |\nu_h\rangle\right\|^2$ by $O(M^{3/2}/T)$. Refer to the full version [GYZ16] for the proof. Using Fact 2 and Jensen's inequality, $\mathbb{E}_{kh} \left\|\, |\mu_{kh}\rangle\langle\mu_{kh}| - |\nu_h\rangle\langle\nu_h|\, \right\| \leq O(\sqrt{M^{3/2}/T})$.

Thus, the final state of Bob is $\varepsilon + O(\sqrt{M^{3/2}/T})$-close to

$$\mathbb{E}_{kh} |kh\rangle\langle kh| \otimes |\nu_h\rangle\langle\nu_h| = \mathbb{E}_{kh} |kh\rangle\langle kh| \otimes \mathcal{I}_h(|\rho\rangle\langle\rho|)$$

where $\mathcal{I}_h$ are the ideal adversaries given by Lemma 1.

To conclude the theorem, we now observe that when $\mathcal{S}$ is non-empty, we can use the same analysis as above where we bundle together $\mathcal{S}$ and $\mathcal{Z}$ as a joint adversary register, and the ideal adversary given by Lemma 1 will act as the identity on the $\mathcal{S}$ register. This establishes that (Auth, Ver) is a total authentication scheme with outer key leakage.

8   Total Authentication from Approximate Unitary Designs

We now present a scheme that satisfies the strongest security definition, that of total authentication (without *any* key leakage). In particular, this implies complete reuse of the entire key. This property of complete reuse of the key was not known before; it is not known whether the entire key can be reused in the authentication scheme of Barnum et al. [BCG+02].

This scheme is based on *unitary designs*, which are in some sense the quantum analogue of *t*-wise independent hash functions: a *t*-unitary design (also simply called a *t-design*) is a distribution $\mathscr{D}$ over unitary matrices such that degree *t* polynomials cannot distinguish between a unitary drawn from $\mathscr{D}$ and a fully random unitary. For a precise definition of unitary designs and efficient constructions, please see, e.g., [BHH12].

8.1   The Unitary Design Scheme

We call this scheme the *unitary design scheme*. Let *s* be a security parameter. The input state is $|\rho\rangle^{\mathcal{MZ}}$, where the $\mathcal{Z}$ register is held by the adversary.

1. The sender Alice first appends s $|0\rangle$ qubits in an auxiliary $\mathcal{T}$ register.
2. Using her secret key k, Alice samples a random unitary U_k drawn from an (approximate) unitary *t*-design that acts jointly on $\mathcal{M} \otimes \mathcal{T}$. We will set the parameter $t = 8$.
3. Alice applies U_k to the $\mathcal{M} \otimes \mathcal{T}$ register, and sends $\mathcal{M} \otimes \mathcal{T}$ across the quantum channel to Bob.
4. Bob receives some state, and applies the inverse unitary $U_k^\dagger$ to it. He measures the last s qubits and accepts if they all measure to be 0. Otherwise he rejects.

Theorem 8. *The unitary design scheme is efficiently computable, and is $2^{-s/2}$-totally authenticating.*

This scheme is inspired by the *Clifford code authentication scheme*, first proposed by Aharonov et al. [ABE10], and further analyzed in [DNS12, BW16]. Our protocol is exactly the same, except the ensemble of unitaries, instead of being an approximate 8-design, is the *Clifford group*, which is a well-studied set of unitaries that are central to quantum error-correction, simulation, and more. It was also recently shown that the Clifford group is a 3-unitary design [Web15, Zhu15][11]. [DNS12, BW16] show that the Clifford authentication scheme is secure even against entangled adversaries; however, as mentioned before, their security guarantee does not take into account the key.

Our unitary design scheme is also very similar to the *non-malleable quantum encryption scheme* proposed by Ambainis, Bouda, and Winter [ABW09], wherein a unitary 2-design is used to encrypt a quantum state. However, non-malleable quantum encryption does not imply authentication.

---

[11] However, it is not an 8-design.

We now remark upon the key requirements of the unitary design scheme. Constructions of approximate unitary 8-designs acting on n qubits involve choosing a random quantum circuit of size $\Theta(n^2)$, and thus the randomness required is $\Theta(n^2)$ [BHH12]. This asymptotically matches the randomness requirements required of the Clifford scheme described above, but is much larger than the randomness requirements of the purity-testing-based protocol of [HLM16], which uses $\Theta(n)$ bits of key to authenticate an n-qubit quantum state.

Notation and useful lemmas. We set up some notation. We let $\mathcal{M}$ denote the message space, $\mathcal{T}$ to denote the space of the dummy zero qubits. We let $\mathcal{Y} = \mathcal{M} \otimes \mathcal{T}$. We let $M = |\mathcal{M}|$, $|\mathcal{T}| = 2^s$, and $N = M2^s = |\mathcal{Y}|$.

Let $\mathcal{E}$ be an adversary acting on $\mathcal{Y} \otimes \mathcal{Z}$. By the Stinespring representation theorem, there exists a unitary V acting on a possibly larger space $\mathcal{Y} \otimes \mathcal{Z} \otimes \mathcal{Z}'$, followed by a projection P that acts on $\mathcal{Z}\mathcal{Z}'$, followed by a partial trace over $\mathcal{Z}'$. However without loss of generality we shall simply treat this additional space $\mathcal{Z}'$ as part of $\mathcal{Z}$, and ignore the partial trace operation. Thus, the adversary's action is to perform some unitary V on $\mathcal{Y} \otimes \mathcal{Z}$, followed by a projection on P on $\mathcal{Z}$.

To analyze the behavior of this scheme, we will first analyze the case when the randomizing unitary U is drawn from the Haar measure over the unitary group $U(\mathcal{Y})$, rather from a t-design. We will show that this scheme is totally authenticating. Then, we will show that actually using a $O(1)$-unitary design will suffice.

Formally, we first prove the following lemma to get total authentication when unitary U is drawn from the Haar measure over the unitary group $U(\mathcal{Y})$.

Lemma 2. *Let $N = \dim(\mathcal{Y})$. For all $\delta > 0$, for all initial message states $|\rho\rangle^{\mathcal{M}\mathcal{Z}}$ have that*

$$\Pr_U \left(\|\Gamma_V|\rho\rangle - \Lambda_U|\rho\rangle\|_2^2 \geq 2^{-s} + \delta \right) \leq \exp(-C'N\delta^2)$$

where $\Gamma_V = \mathrm{Tr}_{\mathcal{Y}}(V)/\dim(\mathcal{Y})$, C' is a universal constant, and U is a Haar-random unitary.

Here, Γ_V would be the ideal adversary corresponding to the real adversary V.

The crucial hammer we will need is a version of *Levy's Lemma*:

Definition 8. *A function $f : U(d) \to \mathbb{R}$ is η-Lipschitz if*

$$\sup_{U_1,U_2 \in U(d)} \frac{|f(U_1) - f(U_2)|}{\|U_1 - U_2\|_2} \leq \eta.$$

Lemma 3 (Levy's Lemma [MS09]). *Let $f : U(d) \to \mathbb{R}$ be an η-Lipschitz function on the unitary group of dimension d with mean $\mathbb{E}\,f$. Then*

$$\Pr\left(|f - \mathbb{E}\,f| \geq \delta\right) \leq 4\exp\left(-\frac{Cd\delta^2}{\eta^2}\right)$$

where $C = 2/9\pi^3$ and the probability is over U drawn from the Haar measure on $U(d)$.

We define $f(U) = \|\Gamma_V|\rho\rangle - \Lambda_U|\rho\rangle\|_2^2$, and bound the average and Lipshcitz constant of f to use Levy's Lemma to prove Lemma 2. For proof details, refer to the full version [GYZ16].

We then appeal to a general derandomization result of Low [Low09] who proved that, if one establishes a measure of concentration result for a low degree polynomial f that's evaluated on a Haar-random unitary, then it still satisfies (nearly) the same measure of concentration when f is evaluated on a unitary drawn from an approximate t-design.

For detailed proof of unitary 8-designs being totally authenticating, refer to the full version [GYZ16].

9   A Lifting Theorem for Authentication

We will prove a *lifting theorem* which shows that a weak form of authentication security that doesn't take into account quantum side information actually implies stronger security against quantum side information. The initial weak form of security is very weak indeed: as long as the authentication scheme can securely authenticate a *single* state (namely, one half of the maximally entangled state), in a key-averaged manner, then we can actually obtain an authentication scheme that can authenticate all states — even those that are entangled with the adversary.

Specifically, we show that this weak authentication security implies the security definition of [DNS12], which we reproduce here:

Definition 9 ([DNS12] security definition). *An authentication scheme* (Auth, Ver) *is ε-secure according to the [DNS12] definition iff for all initial message states* $|\rho\rangle^{\mathcal{MSZ}}$, *for all adversaries* $\mathcal{O} \in \mathrm{T}(\mathcal{YZ}, \mathcal{YZ})$, *there exists an oblivious adversary* $\mathcal{I}$ *such that the following are ε-close in trace distance:*

- *(Real experiment)* $\mathbb{E}_k [\mathrm{Ver}_k \circ \mathcal{O} \circ \mathrm{Auth}_k] (\rho^{\mathcal{MSZ}})$
- *(Ideal experiment)* $\mathcal{I}(\rho^{\mathcal{MSZ}})$

where Auth$_k$ *acts on* $\mathcal{M}$, Ver$_k$ *acts on* $\mathcal{Y}$, *and both act as the identity on* $\mathcal{SZ}$.

Unlike total authentication, the key is averaged over in this security definition.

There is a minor caveat: we do not prove this implication for all authentication schemes. Instead, we prove it for authentication schemes *composed* with a Pauli randomization step. If (Auth, Ver) is an authentication scheme, we call this composed scheme Pauli + (Auth, Ver), and it behaves as follows:

The secret key for Pauli + (Auth, Ver) consists of the key k for (Auth, Ver), as well as a new, independent key k'. The procedure to authenticate a message register $\mathcal{M}$ behaves as follows: first, the key k' is used to choose a random unitary from the Pauli group that acts on the space $\mathcal{M}$. [12] We call this the

---

[12] For simplicilty let us think of $\mathcal{M}$ as $(\mathbb{C}^2)^{\otimes n}$ (i.e., n qubits). Then the Pauli group consists of all operators of the form $X^p Z^q$, where $p, q \in \{0, 1\}^n$. Here, the operator X^p is defined to be the tensor product of $X_j^{p_j}$, where X_j is the X Pauli operator acting on the j'th qubit. Z^q is defined similarly.

Pauli randomization step. Next, the key k is used to apply Auth_k to the register $\mathcal{M}$ to produce a state in the $\mathcal{Y}$ register. This is the authenticated state, which is then subject to attack by the adversary.

To un-authenticate, the Ver_k procedure is applied. Note that this is not a unitary operation, but includes the projection on the receiver's acceptance (see the Preliminaries for a discussion of this). Finally, the Pauli randomization is undone using the key k'.

Theorem 9 (Lifting weak authentication to total authentication). *Let* $(\mathsf{Auth}, \mathsf{Ver})$ *be an authentication scheme, and suppose the composed scheme* $\mathsf{Pauli} + (\mathsf{Auth}, \mathsf{Ver})$ *satisfies the following security guarantee: for all adversaries* $\mathcal{O} \in \mathrm{T}(\mathcal{Y}\mathcal{Z}, \mathcal{Y}\mathcal{Z})$*, for all adversary ancilla qubits* $|\theta\rangle^{\mathcal{Z}\mathcal{Z}'}$*, there exists an oblivious adversary* $\mathcal{I}$ *acting on* $\mathcal{Z}$ *only such that the following are ε-close in trace distance:*

- *(Real experiment)* $\mathbb{E}_{k,k'}\left[\mathsf{Pauli}_{k'}^{\dagger} \circ \mathsf{Ver}_k \circ \mathcal{O} \circ \mathsf{Auth}_k \circ \mathsf{Pauli}_{k'}\right] (|\Phi\rangle\langle\Phi|^{\mathcal{M}\mathcal{B}} \otimes |\theta\rangle\langle\theta|^{\mathcal{Z}\mathcal{Z}'})$
- *(Ideal experiment)* $|\Phi\rangle\langle\Phi|^{\mathcal{M}\mathcal{B}} \otimes \mathcal{I}(|\theta\rangle\langle\theta|^{\mathcal{Z}\mathcal{Z}'})$

where $\mathcal{B}$ is a Hilbert space isomorphic to $\mathcal{M}$, and $|\Phi\rangle^{\mathcal{M}\mathcal{B}}$ is the maximally entangled state.

Then, the composed scheme $\mathsf{Pauli} + (\mathsf{Auth}, \mathsf{Ver})$ *is a ε-secure according to the [DNS12] definition.*

For proof of the above theorem, refer to the full version [GYZ16][13].

10 Open Problems

We close with some open problems:

1. We showed that the Auth-QFT-Auth scheme achieves total authentication (with outer key leakage) when the inner authentication scheme is instantiated with the Wegman-Carter scheme using threewise-independent hashing. Can one show that Auth-QFT-Auth achieves total authentication when both inner and outer authentication schemes are *arbitrary* authentication schemes secure relative to the computational basis?
2. Under what circumstances can the key be reused in any of the protocols presented in this paper, when the receiver rejects the state? For example, we conjecture that in the unitary design protocol, much of the key can be reused.
3. Our security definitions are specific to "one-time" authentication schemes (although the key reuse properties allow multiple uses). Are there natural "many-time" versions of our security definitions?
4. Does total authentication satisfy *Universally Composable* security (as defined in [BHL+05, Unr10])?

---

[13] https://arxiv.org/abs/1607.07759.

References

[ABE10] Aharonov, D., Ben-Or, M., Eban, E.: Interactive proofs for quantum computations. In: Proceedings of Innovations in Computer Science. Tsinghua University Press (2010)

[ABW09] Ambainis, A., Bouda, J., Winter, A.: Nonmalleable encryption of quantum information. J. Math. Phys. **50**(4), 042106 (2009)

[AM16] Alagic, G., Majenz, C.: Quantum non-malleability and authentication (2016). arXiv preprint arXiv:1610.04214

[BCG+02] Barnum, H., Crépeau, C., Gottesman, D., Smith, A., Tapp, A.: Authentication of quantum messages. In: 2002 The Proceedings of the 43rd Annual IEEE Foundations of Computer Science, pp. 449–458. IEEE (2002)

[BCG+06] Ben-Or, M., Crépeau, C., Gottesman, D., Hassidim, A., Smith, A.: Secure multiparty quantum computation with (only) a strict honest majority. In: 2006 47th Annual IEEE Symposium on Foundations of Computer Science (FOCS 2006), pp. 249–260. IEEE (2006)

[BDF+11] Boneh, D., Dagdelen, Ö., Fischlin, M., Lehmann, A., Schaffner, C., Zhandry, M.: Random oracles in a quantum world. In: Lee, D.H., Wang, X. (eds.) ASIACRYPT 2011. LNCS, vol. 7073, pp. 41–69. Springer, Heidelberg (2011). doi:10.1007/978-3-642-25385-0_3

[Bee97] Beenakker, C.W.J.: Random-matrix theory of quantum transport. Rev. Mod. Phys. **69**(3), 731 (1997)

[BGS13] Broadbent, A., Gutoski, G., Stebila, D.: Quantum one-time programs. In: Canetti, R., Garay, J.A. (eds.) CRYPTO 2013. LNCS, vol. 8043, pp. 344–360. Springer, Heidelberg (2013). doi:10.1007/978-3-642-40084-1_20

[BHH12] Brandao, F.G.S.L., Harrow, A.W., Horodecki, M.: Local random quantum circuits are approximate polynomial-designs (2012). arXiv preprint arXiv:1208.0692

[BHL+05] Ben-Or, M., Horodecki, M., Leung, D.W., Mayers, D., Oppenheim, J.: The universal composable security of quantum key distribution. In: Kilian, J. (ed.) TCC 2005. LNCS, vol. 3378, pp. 386–406. Springer, Heidelberg (2005). doi:10.1007/978-3-540-30576-7_21

[BW16] Broadbent, A., Wainewright, E.: Efficient simulation for quantum message authentication (2016). arXiv preprint arXiv:1607.03075

[BZ13a] Boneh, D., Zhandry, M.: Quantum-secure message authentication codes. In: Johansson, T., Nguyen, P.Q. (eds.) EUROCRYPT 2013. LNCS, vol. 7881, pp. 592–608. Springer, Heidelberg (2013). doi:10.1007/978-3-642-38348-9_35

[BZ13b] Boneh, D., Zhandry, M.: Secure signatures and chosen ciphertext security in a quantum computing world. In: Canetti, R., Garay, J.A. (eds.) CRYPTO 2013. LNCS, vol. 8043, pp. 361–379. Springer, Heidelberg (2013). doi:10.1007/978-3-642-40084-1_21

[DFNS13] Damgård, I., Funder, J., Nielsen, J.B., Salvail, L.: Superposition attacks on cryptographic protocols. In: Padró, C. (ed.) ICITS 2013. LNCS, vol. 8317, pp. 142–161. Springer, Cham (2014). doi:10.1007/978-3-319-04268-8_9

[DNS12] Dupuis, F., Nielsen, J.B., Salvail, L.: Actively secure two-party evaluation of any quantum operation. In: Safavi-Naini, R., Canetti, R. (eds.) CRYPTO 2012. LNCS, vol. 7417, pp. 794–811. Springer, Heidelberg (2012). doi:10.1007/978-3-642-32009-5_46

[DPS05] Damgård, I., Pedersen, T.B., Salvail, L.: A quantum cipher with near optimal key-recycling. In: Shoup, V. (ed.) CRYPTO 2005. LNCS, vol. 3621, pp. 494–510. Springer, Heidelberg (2005). doi:10.1007/11535218_30

[FS16] Fehr, S., Salvail, L.: Quantum authentication and encryption with key recycling (2016). arXiv preprint arXiv:1610.05614

[GHS15] Gagliardoni, T., Hülsing, A., Schaffner, C.: Semantic security and indistinguishability in the quantum world (2015). arXiv preprint arXiv:1504.05255

[Got02] Gottesman, D.: Uncloneable encryption (2002). arXiv preprint arXiv:quant-ph/0210062

[GYZ16] Garg, S., Yuen, H., Zhandry, M.: New security notions and feasibility results for authentication of quantum data (2016). arXiv preprint arXiv:1607.07759

[HLM16] Hayden, P., Leung, D.W., Mayers, D.: The universal composable security of quantum message authentication with key recyling (2016). arXiv preprint arXiv:1610.09434

[KLLNP16] Kaplan, M., Leurent, G., Leverrier, A., Naya-Plasencia, M.: Breaking symmetric cryptosystems using quantum period finding (2016). arXiv preprint arXiv:1602.05973

[Low09] Low, R.A.: Large deviation bounds for k-designs. In: Proceedings of the Royal Society of London A: Mathematical, Physical and Engineering Sciences, vol. 465, pp. 3289–3308. The Royal Society (2009)

[MS09] Milman, V.D., Schechtman, G.: Asymptotic Theory of Finite Dimensional Normed Spaces: Isoperimetric Inequalities in Riemannian Manifolds. Springer, Heidelberg (2009)

[NC10] Nielsen, M.A., Chuang, I.L.: Quantum Computation and Quantum Information. Cambridge University Press, Cambridge (2010)

[OH05] Oppenheim, J., Horodecki, M.: How to reuse a one-time pad and other notes on authentication, encryption, and protection of quantum information. Phys. Rev. A **72**(4), 042309 (2005)

[Por17] Portmann, C.: Quantum authentication with key recycling. In: Coron, J.-S., Nielsen, J.B. (eds.) EUROCRYPT 2017. LNCS, vol. 10212, pp. 339–368. Springer, Cham (2017). doi:10.1007/978-3-319-56617-7_12

[Unr10] Unruh, D.: Universally composable quantum multi-party computation. In: Gilbert, H. (ed.) EUROCRYPT 2010. LNCS, vol. 6110, pp. 486–505. Springer, Heidelberg (2010). doi:10.1007/978-3-642-13190-5_25

[WC81] Wegman, M.N., Carter, J.L.: New hash functions and their use in authentication and set equality. J. Comput. Syst. Sci. **22**(3), 265–279 (1981)

[Web15] Webb, Z.: The clifford group forms a unitary 3-design (2015). arXiv preprint arXiv:1510.02769

[Zha12] Zhandry, M.: How to construct quantum random functions. In: Proceedings of the 53rd IEEE Symposium on Foundations of Computer Science (FOCS) (2012)

[Zhu15] Zhu, H.: Multiqubit clifford groups are unitary 3-designs (2015). arXiv preprint arXiv:1510.02619

Hash Functions

Time-Memory Tradeoff Attacks on the MTP Proof-of-Work Scheme

Itai Dinur[(✉)] and Niv Nadler

Department of Computer Science, Ben-Gurion University, Beersheba, Israel
`dinuri@cs.bgu.ac.il`

Abstract. Proof-of-work (PoW) schemes are cryptographic primitives with numerous applications, and in particular, they play a crucial role in maintaining consensus in cryptocurrency networks. Ideally, a cryptocurrency PoW scheme should have several desired properties, including efficient verification on one hand, and high memory consumption of the prover's algorithm on the other hand, making the scheme less attractive for implementation on dedicated hardware.

At the USENIX Security Symposium 2016, Biryukov and Khovratovich presented a new promising PoW scheme called MTP (Merkle Tree Proof) that achieves essentially all desired PoW properties. As a result, MTP has received substantial attention from the cryptocurrency community. The scheme uses a Merkle hash tree construction over a large array of blocks computed by a memory consuming (memory-hard) function. Despite the fact that only a small fraction of the memory is verified by the efficient verification algorithm, the designers claim that a cheating prover that uses a small amount of memory will suffer from a significant computational penalty.

In this paper, we devise a sub-linear computation-memory tradeoff attack on MTP. We apply our attack to the concrete instance proposed by the designers which uses the memory-hard function Argon2d and computes a proof by allocating 2 gigabytes of memory. The attack computes arbitrary malicious proofs using less than a megabyte of memory (about 1/3000 of the honest prover's memory) at a relatively mild penalty of 170 in computation. This is more than 55,000 times faster than what is claimed by the designers. The attack requires a one-time precomputation step of complexity 2^{64}, but its online cost is only increased by a factor which is less than 2 when spending 2^{48} precomputation time.

The main idea of the attack is to exploit the fact that Argon2d accesses its memory in a way which is determined by its previous computations. This allows to inject a small fraction of carefully selected memory blocks that manipulate Argon2d's memory access patterns, significantly weakening its memory-hardness.

Keywords: Cryptocurrency · Proof-of-work · Merkle Tree Proof · Memory-hard function · Argon2 · Time-memory tradeoff · Cryptanalysis

This research was supported in part by the Israeli Science Foundation through grant No. 573/16 and by the Lynn and William Frankel Center for Computer Science.

© International Association for Cryptologic Research 2017
J. Katz and H. Shacham (Eds.): CRYPTO 2017, Part II, LNCS 10402, pp. 375–403, 2017.
DOI: 10.1007/978-3-319-63715-0_13

1 Introduction

Proof-of-work (PoW) schemes were introduced by Dwork and Naor [9] as a computational technique to combat junk mail, or more generally, to limit access to a shared resource. The main idea is to require the user to compute a moderately hard function in order to gain access to the resource, thus preventing excessive use. Since their introduction, many PoW schemes have been proposed, and they have recently become a very popular area of research with the rise of Bitcoin [14] and cryptocurrencies in general.

In the cryptocurrency setting, PoWs play a major role in maintaining consensus among cryptocurrency network nodes about the state of the distributed blockchain ledger. The proofs are generated by miners, each proof computed over a block of recent transactions. A new transaction block propagates through the cryptocurrency network and its PoW is verified by the nodes which update their local view of the blockchain accordingly.

Since verification is performed by every node in the network in order to check that new transaction blocks are valid, slow (or resource consuming) verification could expose the nodes to denial of service attacks, and in addition, increase the risk of forks (inconsistent state among the nodes). Therefore, one of the most important properties for a PoW scheme in the cryptocurrency setting is *efficient verification* of proofs. At the same time, computing proofs should ideally be as efficient (in terms of cost) on general CPUs as it is on custom designed application-specific integrated circuits (ASICs). This is desirable to combat centralization, where the majority of mining is performed by centralized mining ASIC rigs, as it is today for Bitcoin. Indeed, mining centralization in Bitcoin is a direct result of Bitcoin's SHA-256-based ASIC-friendly PoW scheme. This concentration of power is considered by many as contradictory to Bitcoin's philosophy.

One of the main ideas to combat mining centralization is to use *memory-hard functions*. Such functions require a large amount of memory to compute and pose substantial computational penalties on algorithms that attempt to compute them with less memory. The use of memory-hard functions aims to diminish the advantage of ASICs over standard PCs, as memory-intensive operations are not much more efficient on dedicated hardware compared to general CPUs. In this context, we also mention the notion of a proof-of-space (formulated by Dziembowski et al. in [10] and independently by Ateniese et al. in [3]) that offers similar security guarantees as memory-hard functions in PoW schemes. The main conceptual difference is that an honest prover in a proof-of-space scheme generally does not have to perform a computational task (besides allocating some space), whereas in a PoW scheme based on a memory-hard function, an honest prover is required to execute some non-trivial computation besides memory allocation.[1] In the cryptocurrency setting, the difficulty of this computation is fine-tuned

---

[1] Additionally, the protocol between the prover and verifier in [10] was defined as interactive and hence unsuitable to cryptocurrencies (but this is a superficial restriction that can be lifted).

to keep the rate at which new transaction blocks arrive on the network stable (typically, every few minutes).

The most popular memory-hard function among cryptocurrencies (such as Litecoin [11]) is scrypt [16]. However, despite its memory hardness, a noticeable shortcoming of scrypt is that tuning it to use substantial memory does not provide efficient verification. As a result, scrypt (as used by Litecoin) does not consume substantial memory and thus has been shown to have a very efficient hardware implementation [8].

Very recently, at the USENIX Security Symposium, 2016, Alex Biryukov and Dmitry Khovratovich presented the MTP (Merkle Tree Proof) PoW scheme [7]. MTP is claimed to offer essentially all properties[2] desired from a cryptocurrency PoW scheme, including fast verification and ASIC-resistance. As a result, it has received substantial attention from the cryptocurrency community.

MTP uses a design that combines a memory-hard function with a Merkle hash tree [13]. This design resembles the one of [12] that also proposes to build a Merkle hash tree on top of data computed by a memory-hard function (in the form of a graph with high pebbling complexity). The MTP design is also related to the proof-of-space scheme proposed in [10] (that uses an interactive proof protocol).

The memory-hard function used by MTP (denoted by $\mathcal{F}$) receives as an input a seed I and computes an array of T blocks $X[1], X[2], \ldots, X[T]$ (for a parameter T).[3] Each block $X[i]$ is generated using the internal compression function F of $\mathcal{F}$, which takes $X[i-1]$ and $X[\phi(i)]$ as inputs. The function $\phi(i)$ is an *indexing function* (defined for $\mathcal{F}$) that outputs a block index in the range $[1, \ldots, i)$.

The prover's algorithm in MTP has two phases, where in the first phase it computes $X[1], \ldots, X[T]$ using $\mathcal{F}$ from the input seed, and stores these blocks in memory. In addition, it computes a Merkle hash tree with root Φ over $X[1], \ldots, X[T]$, effectively committing to the array's value. In the second phase, the algorithm picks an arbitrary nonce N, and accesses L blocks (for a parameter L) of $X[1], \ldots, X[T]$ at pseudo-random locations in a sequence $X[i_1], X[i_2], \ldots, X[i_L]$. In this sequence, each i_j effectively depends on Φ, N and on the values of the previous blocks in the sequence. Finally, a value Y_L (which depends on all blocks in the sequence) is computed and tested against the difficulty level of the scheme (Y_L needs to have d trailing zeros for a parameter d). Assuming the test passes for some nonce N, then $(\Phi, N, \mathcal{Z})$ is a valid proof, where $\mathcal{Z}$ contains the *openings* of $2L$ blocks $\{X[i_j - 1], X[\phi(i_j)]\}$. An opening of a block $X[i]$ is evidence that it is a leaf in the Merkle hash tree at position i. Each opening contains internal node values that allow to calculate the path from the block $X[i]$ to the Merkle hash tree root Φ.

---

[2] We only mention here the few desired properties of PoW schemes which are relevant for this paper. For a more comprehensive list, refer to [7].

[3] Blocks in the array computed by $\mathcal{F}$ should not be confused with transaction blocks in the blockchain.

Given a proof $(\Phi, N, \mathcal{Z})$, the verifier checks that the openings $\mathcal{Z}$ are valid (namely, lead to Φ), reproduces all $X[i_j] = F(X[i_j - 1], X[\phi(i_j)])$, and verifies that Y_L passes the difficulty filter.

Biryukov and Khovratovich proposed a concrete instantiation of MTP with the memory-hard function Argon2 [6] (see Fig. 1), the winner of the Password Hashing Competition [15]. Argon2 has two variants, Argon2i and Argon2d, where the first uses *data-independent indexing* while the latter uses *data-dependent indexing*. In a function with data-dependent indexing, the indexing function $\phi(i)$ depends on previously computed blocks, whereas in a function with data-independent indexing it does not. The proposed MTP instantiation uses Argon2d as $\mathcal{F}$, where $\phi(i)$ depends on the value of the previously computed block $X[i-1]$. Argon2d was shown to offer somewhat better resistance to computation-memory tradeoffs compared to Argon2i (refer to [6] for details).

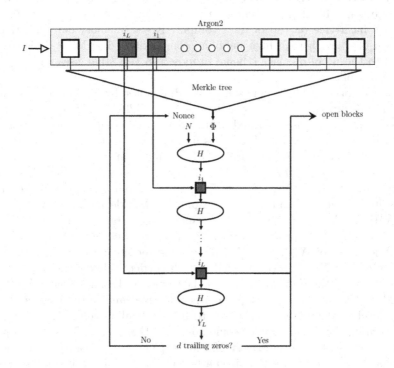

Fig. 1. The MTP PoW scheme

The concrete instantiation of MTP requires 2 gigabytes of memory and computes a proof shorter than a megabyte. Moreover, its verification algorithm requires only several hundreds of hash computations, and thus MTP provides efficient verification. MTP is memory-hard, assuming that the underlying function Argon2d is such. However, the combination of these two advantages comes at a cost, since the verification algorithm only checks part of the memory computed by the prover. This opens the door for a new type of attack on MTP, where a cheating prover computes a *malicious proof* that passes the verification algorithm, yet the computed block array contains some entries which are inconsistent with the Argon2d compression function. More specifically, there exist indexes i for which $X[i] \neq F(X[i-1], X[\phi(i)])$.

In the cryptocurrency setting, it is likely that malicious proofs will eventually be detected by fully validating nodes (which store the full blockchain) that perform additional checks on new transaction blocks beyond running the simple verification algorithm. However, typically (as in Bitcoin) most nodes in the network are SPV (Simple Payment Verification) clients that are interested in a small number of particular transactions, and only execute the efficient verification algorithm in order to check the validity of new transaction blocks. Hence malicious proofs that propagate through the network may cause it to enter an inconsistent state (namely, to fork) and result in denial of service, depending on the rate at which they arrive. While the consequences of malicious proofs depend on the specific cryptocurrency, it is important that they are not much easier to generate (in terms of cost) than honest proofs, as otherwise, attackers will have additional incentives to compute them. More specifically, it needs to be shown that MTP is *immune to cheating strategies*.

Assume that a cheater computes a malicious proof that passes verification, but is inconsistent with the internal Argon2d compression function F on some fraction ϵ of the block array $X[1], \ldots, X[T]$. Roughly speaking, the MTP designers claim that for a large ϵ, the cheater cannot efficiently produce a consistent sequence of blocks $X[i_1], X[i_2], \ldots, X[i_L]$ of length $L = 70$. More precisely, since ϵ is large, the cheater will pay a large computational penalty (of roughly $(1-\epsilon)^{-70}$) in order to produce $X[i_1], X[i_2], \ldots, X[i_{70}]$, where all blocks $X[i_j]$ are consistent $(X[i_j] = F(X[i_j - 1], X[\phi(i_j)]))$ and all pairs $\{X[i_j - 1], X[\phi(i_j)]\}$ have valid openings leading to Φ. On the other hand, when ϵ is small, $X[1], \ldots, X[T]$ are almost always consistent with F, and hence the cheater has to allocate essentially as much memory as an honest prover and there is no efficiency gain.

In this paper, we analyze the immunity of MTP against cheating strategies. Our main result shows how to compute a malicious proof much more efficiently than claimed by the designers, obtaining a sub-linear computation-memory tradeoff algorithm for a surprisingly small amount of memory. In particular, when applied to the proposed MTP instance, our attack computes a malicious proof using a fraction of about 1/3000 of the honest prover's memory (which is less than a megabyte), at a relatively mild penalty of about 173 in computation complexity. On the other hand, according to the analysis of the authors for our parameters, the cheater's computation complexity should increase by a significant factor of about 10 million. Hence our attack improves upon the analysis of [7] by a factor of more than 55,000.

The metric which is used in [7] to evaluate the computational cost of implementing an algorithm in ASICs is the *time-area product*. In this metric, the algorithm's memory requirements translate into area in hardware. Using the time-area product metric, our attack costs less than the honest prover's algorithm by a multiplicative factor of 113, improving on the analysis of [7] (in which the cheater's algorithm is more expensive by a factor of 294) by more than 33,000.

As noted above, the consequences of our attack on a cryptocurrency using MTP with Argon2d are hard to predict. However, since a cheating miner has a computational advantage of about 113 over honest miners, then such a miner can potentially overwhelm the network with malicious proofs even when possessing only a small fraction of the total computation power.

To explain the weakness of MTP, we view the computation of Argon2d as a directed acyclic graph, whose vertices are Argon2d's array blocks indexes and a directed edge connects vertex j to i if $j = i - 1$ or $j = \phi(i)$ (namely, $X[j]$ is used in computing $X[i]$). After the prover commits to the hash values of the graph vertices by computing the Merkle hash tree root, MTP challenges the prover to compute hash values of randomly chosen vertices (namely random block values). The goal of an attacker (a cheating prover) is to store only a small fraction of the vertex hash values, but still answer the challenges quickly. The ability to quickly answer random challenges on such a hash graph with limited storage strongly depends on the graph's structure. Indeed, Argon2d's graph seems to offer a very steep computation-memory tradeoff curve that forces the attacker to spend significant computation when storing a small fraction of the hash values. However, recall that since MTP does not challenge the prover on all hash values of the graph nodes, an attacker can cheat and compute a small fraction of inconsistent hash values ($X[i] \neq F(X[i - 1], X[\phi(i)])$) with substantial probability of not being caught. Moreover, since Argon2d uses data-dependent indexing, then the structure of the graph depends on hash values of its own vertices. Therefore, the attacker can exploit the inconsistent hash values and compute a manipulated graph with a much weaker computation-memory tradeoff curve compared to Argon2d.

The general outline of our attack is identical to the one considered by the MTP designers, namely, we replace Argon2d with a function which is consistent with its compression function on almost all blocks (thus using a small ϵ). However, this highly consistent function can be computed with substantially less memory compared to Argon2d at a modest sub-linear computation-memory tradeoff. This is quite surprising, as it demonstrates that although computation-memory tradeoffs for Argon2d are exponential, manipulating it in a small number of places can drastically reduce its memory-hardness.

The attack works by injecting into Argon2d's block array malicious *control blocks* that exploit in the strong way the data dependency of the indexing function of Argon2d. Control blocks significantly weaken the memory-hardness of (the slightly modified) Argon2d, allowing to compute it with a linear computation-memory tradeoff. However, this approach does not seem to lead to sub-linear computation-memory tradeoffs, which appear out of reach at first sight. Indeed, consider a significantly weakened Argon2d variant, in which we completely eliminate the indexing function component from the compression function and define $X[i] = F'(X[i-1])$ instead (for some function F').[4] If we store one out of t blocks (for some positive integer t), then a random block falls at expected distance of $(t-1)/2$ from a stored one, and its computation requires $(t-1)/2$ compression function calls on average. Therefore, the computation-memory product is reduced by $(t-1)/2t \approx 1/2$, and we cannot do much better than a linear computation-memory tradeoff even for a weak function. This simple argument shows that storing full blocks is wasteful if we aim for sub-linear computation-memory tradeoffs. To overcome this obstacle, we store a succinct representation of each control block (which is much smaller than a standard block), and these representations are essentially the only data kept in memory (besides a very small fraction of full blocks).

The control blocks in our attack are computed during a one-time precomputation phase, after which proofs can be found for arbitrary inputs. The preprocessing complexity is 2^{64}, which is challenging, yet feasible for an ambitious attacker. We stress that the preprocessing phase is very easy to parallelize and requires less than a megabyte of memory. Moreover, the online complexity of the attack is not drastically reduced when using shorter precomputation. For example, even if we spend a trivial amount of 2^{48} computations during preprocessing, our online attack costs less than the honest prover's algorithm by a factor which is larger than 60.

While the parameters of our attack are optimized for MTP when instantiated with Argon2d, it is applicable to the MTP scheme when instantiated with any memory-hard function that uses data-dependent indexing. The most natural way to avoid the attack is to use a memory-hard function with data-independent indexing (such as Argon2i). Such an instantiation of MTP resists our attack, but interestingly, it still has some undesired properties that we discuss towards the end of this paper.

The rest of this paper is organized as follows. We describe the egalitarian computing framework of [7] in Sect. 2, while the description and previous analysis of MTP is given in Sect. 3. An overview of our attack is given in Sect. 4, its details are described in Sect. 5, while in Sect. 6 we analyze the full attack. Finally, we describe extensions of the attack in Sect. 7, discuss countermeasures in Sect. 8 and conclude the paper in Sect. 9.

2 Egalitarian Computing Framework [7]

In this section, we summarize the egalitarian computing framework, as described in [7].

Given a function $\mathcal{H}$, the goal of the attacker is to minimize the cost of computing $\mathcal{H}$ on hardware (ASICs), while keeping its running time close to that of a standard implementation (typically x86). On ASICs, the memory size M translates into a certain area A and the running time T is determined by the

---

[4] The graph structure of this weakened variant is a hash chain, as the graph structure of scrypt [16].

length of the longest computational chain and memory latency.[5] The cost of the attacker in the framework is measured by the time-area product AT.

Given that the standard implementation of $\mathcal{H}$ consumes M units of memory, the attacker aims to compute $\mathcal{H}$ using only αM memory for $\alpha < 1$. Using a computation-memory tradeoff algorithm specific to $\mathcal{H}$, the attacker has to spend $C(\alpha)$ times as much computation as the standard implementation and his total running time increases by the factor $D(\alpha)$ (where $C(\alpha)$ may exceed $D(\alpha)$ since the attacker can parallelize the computation).

In order to obtain a running time of $T \cdot D(\alpha)$ (despite having to perform $C(\alpha)$ as much computation), the attacker has to place $\frac{C(\alpha)}{D(\alpha)}$ additional cores on chip. Therefore, the time-area product changes from AT to AT_α where

$$AT_\alpha = A \cdot (\alpha + \frac{\beta C(\alpha)}{D(\alpha)}) \cdot T \cdot D(\alpha) = AT(\alpha D(\alpha) + \beta C(\alpha)), \qquad (1)$$

and β is the fraction of the original memory occupied by a single computing core. There is additional cost in case of significant communication between the computing cores, but this cost is irrelevant to this paper, as our attack does not use extensive communication.

A function is defined to be *memory-hard* if any algorithm that computes it using M memory units has a computation-space tradeoff $C(\alpha)$ where $C(\cdot)$ is at least a super-linear function of $1/\alpha$.

3   Description and Previous Analysis of MTP [7]

In this section, we provide a brief description of MTP and summarize its preliminary analysis as given in its specification. For more details, refer to [7].

MTP uses as a building block a memory-hard function $\mathcal{F}$ that takes as input a password P (which may be null in the cryptocurrency setting) and a salt S. It fills T blocks of memory $X[1], X[2], \ldots, X[T]$ of a certain size, and then may overwrite them several times. However, in MTP the function $\mathcal{F}$ does not overwrite the memory.

Each block $X[i]$ is generated using the internal compression function F of $\mathcal{F}$, which takes $X[i-1]$ and $X[\phi(i)]$ as inputs, where $\phi(i)$ is an *indexing function* (defined for $\mathcal{F}$) that outputs a block index in the range $[1, \ldots, i)$.

Another building block used in MTP is a Merkle hash tree, which is described in Appendix A. MTP is defined using global parameters T, L and d (difficulty level) and a hash function H. We denote the output size of H in bytes by h.

---

[5] Note the distinction between computation complexity which is measured according to the total size of the algorithm's circuit and time complexity which is measured according to the depth of the circuit. In this paper, both complexities are measured in terms of basic function (compression function or hash function) invocations.

The prover's algorithm takes as input a challenge[6] I. The output of the algorithm is a proof $(\Phi, N, \mathcal{Z})$, as described below.

---

1. Compute $\mathcal{F}(I)$ and store the T blocks $X[1], X[2], \ldots, X[T]$ in memory.
2. Compute the root Φ of the Merkle hash tree over the blocks $X[1], X[2], \ldots, X[T]$.
3. Select nonce N.
4. Compute $Y_0 = H(\Phi, N)$.
5. For $1 \leq j \leq L$:

$$i_j = Y_{j-1} \pmod{T};$$
$$Y_j = H(Y_{j-1}, X[i_j]).$$

6. If Y_L has d trailing zeros, then output $(\Phi, N, \mathcal{Z})$ as the proof-of-work, where $\mathcal{Z}$ contains the openings (defined in Appendix A) of $2L$ blocks $\{X[i_j - 1], X[\phi(i_j)]\}$. Otherwise, go to Step 3.

In the following, we refer to Step 5 as computing a *chain* of values. The prover's algorithm requires T blocks of memory (in addition to a small amount of memory, required to compute the Merkle hash tree) and its running time is about $T + 2^d \cdot L$. The generated proof size is dominated by $\mathcal{Z}$ and is slightly more than $2L$ blocks in addition to $2L \cdot \log(T) \cdot h$ bytes for the openings.

The verifier's algorithm is given a proof $(\Phi, N, \mathcal{Z})$ as input and it outputs 'Yes' if the proof is valid, and otherwise 'No'.

---

1. Verify all block openings $\mathcal{Z}$ using Φ.
2. Compute $Y_0 = H(\Phi, N)$.
3. Compute from $\mathcal{Z}$ for $1 \leq j \leq L$:

$$i_j = Y_{j-1} \pmod{T};$$
$$X[i_j] = F(X[i_j - 1], X[\phi(i_j)]);$$
$$Y_j = H(Y_{j-1}, X[i_j]).$$

4. If Y_L has d trailing zeros, output 'Yes', otherwise output 'No'.

3.1 Previous Tradeoff analysis of MTP [7]

We summarize the previous tradeoff analysis of MTP, as described in its specification.

Denote by M the total amount of memory consumed by a standard implementation of the MTP prover's algorithm. The analysis of [7] aims to deduce the

---

[6] In the cryptocurrency setting, I depends on the hash value of the previous transaction block in the blockchain and the transactions included in the current block.

function $C'(\cdot)$ for MTP, given the function $C(\cdot)$ for the underlying memory-hard function $\mathcal{F}$. This analysis is divided into several possible cheating strategies.

Memory savings: A memory-saving prover can use αM memory for $\alpha < 1$. In [7] it is asserted that the computation penalty of such a prover is increased by $C'(\alpha) = C(\alpha)$ to $C(\alpha)(T + 2^d \cdot L)$.

Block modification: A cheater can compute a different function $\hat{\mathcal{F}} \neq \mathcal{F}$ by computing inconsistent intermediate blocks $X[i] \neq F(X[i-1], X[\phi(i)])$. If the fraction of inconsistent blocks is ϵ, then the probability that only consistent blocks are accessed in the second phase of the prover's algorithm (namely, during the L block computation starting from Φ) is

$$\gamma = (1 - \epsilon)^L.$$

Thus, the authors of [7] conclude that the cheater's time is increased by the factor $1/\gamma$.

Overall cheating penalties: A cheater can use both strategies above by storing only αT blocks and additionally allowing ϵT inconsistent blocks. According to [7], it is possible to combine to results from the analysis strategies above and conclude that the cheater makes at least

$$\frac{C(\alpha + \epsilon)(T + 2^d \cdot L)}{(1 - \epsilon)^L} \tag{2}$$

calls to the compression function F. This gives $C'(\alpha + \epsilon) = \frac{C(\alpha + \epsilon)}{(1 - \epsilon)^L}$ for a cheating prover.

Parallelism. Both the honest prover and the cheater can parallelize the computation for different nonces N. According to [7], the latency $D'(\cdot)$ of the cheater's computation for MTP will be

$$D(\alpha + \epsilon). \tag{3}$$

3.2   Instantiation of MTP

Biryukov and Khovratovich propose to instantiate MTP with the memory-hard function Argon2d [6] and the hash function Blake2 [4].

Argon2d uses a block size of 1 KB. Its T blocks are arranged in a matrix, where in MTP it is of size 4×4. A row of a matrix is called a *lane*, while a column is called a *slice*. Each of the 16 matrix entries is called a *segment*. Segments of the same slice (column) are computed in parallel, and may not reference blocks from each other. All other blocks can be referenced.

Below we describe the indexing function of Argon2d according to the 2-dimensional matrix notation. However, throughout most of this paper, we will index the memory of Argon2d as a single dimensional array for the sake of simplicity, as done in the MTP algorithm specification (the translations of indexes from the single to the 2-dimensional case and vise-versa are straightforward).

The indexing function of Argon2d for a block with index $[i][j]$ (where $i \in \{0, 1, 2, 3\}$, $j \in \{0, 1, \ldots, T/4\}$ refer to lane and block index in the lane, respectively) is defined using the value of the previous block in the same lane $X[i][j-1]$. The value of the 32 least significant bits (LSBs) of this block is denoted by $J_1 \in \{0, \ldots, 2^{32} - 1\}$ and value of the next 32 bits is denoted by J_2. If block $X[i][j]$ is in the first slice, then the lane (row) number of the indexing function value (which is denoted by l) is set to the current lane index $l = i$. Otherwise, the 2 LSBs of J_2 determine l.

Next, we compute the value of ϕ, $[l][z]$, using i, j and J_1. The details of this computation are not important for the rest of this paper and are given in Appendix B for the sake of completeness. We only note that the index z is computed using a simple function that defines a non-uniform distribution (according to the randomness of J_1) over a prefix of blocks in lane l, where more weight is placed on the larger indexes (closer to j).

The parameters of MTP selected in [7] are $T = 2^{21}$ (hence the prover's algorithm requires $2^{21} \cdot 2^{10} = 2^{31}$ bytes of RAM, or 2 gigabytes) and $L = 70$. The output of hash function Blake2 is truncated to 128 bits, and thus $h = 16$. Note that the difficulty level d is determined by the application (typically a cryptocurrency).

Previous Tradeoff Analysis for the MTP Instantiation. The tradeoff analysis for the concrete instantiation above relies on the functions $C(\cdot)$ and $D(\cdot)$ for Argon2d. Some values of these functions at specific points (taken from [6,7]) are given here[7] in Table 1.

Table 1. Time and computation penalties for Argon2d

α	$\frac{1}{2}$	$\frac{1}{3}$	$\frac{1}{4}$	$\frac{1}{5}$	$\frac{1}{6}$	$\frac{1}{7}$
$C(\alpha)$	1.5	4	20.2	344	4660	2^{18}
$D(\alpha)$	1.5	2.8	5.5	10.3	17	27

Relying on the generic MTP tradeoff analysis (summarized in Sect. 3.1), the authors of [7] plug into Eq. 1 the values of $C'(\cdot)$ for MTP (given by Eq. 2) and $D'(\cdot)$ (given by Eq. 3), obtaining

$$AT_\alpha = AT \frac{\alpha D(\alpha + \epsilon) + \beta C(\alpha + \epsilon)}{(1 - \epsilon)^L}. \tag{4}$$

---

[7] These are the best known tradeoff parameters at the time of writing.

Based on this equation, it is shown that for the concrete instance described above, the time-area product can be reduced by the factor of 12 at most, assuming that each Blake2b core occupies an equivalent of 2^{16} bytes, namely $\beta = 2^{16}/2^{31} = 2^{-15}$.

4 Overview of the Attack on MTP

In this section, we give a general overview of our improved tradeoff analysis for MTP, while pointing out where the previous analysis of [7] fails.

4.1 A Trivial Attack

We start by describing a trivial attack on MTP and a simple fix which avoids this attack with very little overhead. The attack is based on the observation that the verifier does not actually check that the proof corresponds to the particular challenge I. As a result, a cheating prover can simply replay a proof for some old challenge I' (generated for the same difficulty level d), and this proof would pass verification for the current challenge I as well. Note that in the cryptocurrency setting, storing the previously generated proofs does not prevent this attack, since not all previously generated (valid) proofs are included in the blockchain, or even reach all the nodes in the network.

In order to avoid this simple attack, we can add to the proof the opening of the first block $X[1]$. The verifier would then compute $X[1]$ directly from the challenge and check this additional opening with little added cost.

In the following, we assume that this simple countermeasure is implemented and focus on attacks which are less trivial and more difficult to counter.

4.2 Weaknesses of MTP

We describe two related weaknesses of MTP that will be exploited in our attack. These weaknesses are not specific to the use of Argon2d in MTP, and apply to MTP when instantiated with essentially any function $\mathcal{F}$ that uses data-dependent indexing.

1. A cheating prover is allowed to modify blocks so that they are inconsistent with the compression function F. Thus, the cheater may compute a function which is completely different than $\mathcal{F}$. When the compression function F uses data-dependent indexing (such as in Argon2d), the cheater can inject (potentially very few) inconsistent blocks that influence its indexing function, weakening the computation-memory tradeoff resistance of (the modified) $\mathcal{F}$, which we denote by $\hat{\mathcal{F}}$. We conclude that it is non-trivial to relate the memory-hardness of $\mathcal{F}$ to the memory-hardness of its potentially modified variant $\hat{\mathcal{F}}$ computed by the cheater to obtain a proof for MTP. More specifically, the main flaw in the analysis of [7] is in Eqs. 2 and 3, where the tradeoff functions $C(\cdot)$ and $D(\cdot)$ for $\mathcal{F}$ are used to compute the overall cheating penalties. However, the (potentially much weaker) tradeoff functions for $\hat{\mathcal{F}}$ should have been used instead.

2. The cheater can use preprocessing (which is independent of a challenge I) to speed up the online computation that begins once a challenge I is received. At first sight, it may not be clear how the cheater can benefit from preprocessing, as the function $\mathcal{F}$ has to be applied online to a challenge I whose value cannot be predicted in advance, and computations of $\mathcal{F}$ with different pseudo-random challenges are generally unrelated (especially when $\mathcal{F}$ uses data-dependent indexing). However, recall that the cheater can manipulate the function $\mathcal{F}$ and compute a different function $\hat{\mathcal{F}}$ both in preprocessing and online. In our attack, we show how to carefully choose $\hat{\mathcal{F}}$ such that the preprocessing computation is made independent of the online challenge I, but nevertheless reduces the online complexity of computing a valid proof for MTP on arbitrary challenges.

4.3   General Description of the Attack

In this section, we show how to exploit the first weakness described above in order to obtain an efficient computation-memory tradeoff for MTP. The attack is mostly independent of the specification of the compression function F of Argon2d, but makes use of its data-dependent indexing function $\phi(i)$, which depends on $X[i-1]$. Hence, the algorithm of the attack should be adjusted when applied to MTP instantiated with $\mathcal{F}$ that has a different data-dependent indexing function.

The main idea of the attack is to compute a function $\hat{\mathcal{F}}$ that has weaker computation-memory tradeoff resistance compared to $\mathcal{F}$, yet the number of consistent blocks in $\hat{\mathcal{F}}$ (with respect to the compression function F of $\mathcal{F}$) remains relatively high.

The computation of an arbitrary block $X[i+1]$ depends on $X[i]$ and $X[\phi(i+1)]$, where for Argon2d $\phi(i+1)$ depends on $X[i]$. Each one of these two blocks depends on two other previous blocks and so forth. If we store only a small fraction α of the T blocks, then computing $X[i+1]$ will require computing the hash labels (block values) for a graph of blocks with in-degree 2 of size $C(\alpha)$, which seems to be exponential in $1/\alpha$ as shown in Table 1. However, if we allow some inconsistent blocks, we can store a small subset of blocks (denoted by S) in memory and manipulate $\phi(i+1)$ by changing the value of $X[i]$ such that $X[\phi(i+1)] \in S$. Proceeding the same way, we manipulate all blocks at even indexes so that for each such block, its successor is computed using the manipulated block and another block in S (stored in memory). Unfortunately, this strategy leads to a large fraction of inconsistent blocks $\epsilon \approx 1/2$, and results in a major penalty in the second phase of the proof computation, which is roughly[8] $1/(1-\epsilon)^L$, as described in Sect. 3.1.

---

[8] The proposed instance of MTP uses $L = 70$, and hence the penalty is about $1/(1-\epsilon)^L \approx 2^{70}$.

To obtain a more efficient attack we extend the above approach by looking at $X[i+2]$ and noticing that $X[\phi(i+2)]$ depends on $X[i+1]$, which in turn, depends on $X[i]$. Therefore, we can try to compute a value for $X[i]$ such that both conditions $X[\phi(i+1)] \in S$ and $X[\phi(i+2)] \in S$ are satisfied. This strategy reduces the fraction of inconsistent blocks to $\epsilon \approx 1/3$, which is smaller than $1/2$, but still results in a significant penalty in the second phase of the proof computation.

Generalizing the above idea further, let t be a small integer (our concrete attack uses $t = 20$). We partition the T computed blocks into about T/t consecutive intervals of size t (for the sake of simplicity we assume that t divides T). The first block $X[i]$ in each interval satisfies $i \equiv 0 \pmod{t}$ and we write it as $i = s \cdot t$ for a positive $s < T/t$. Such blocks are called *control blocks* and they serve two purposes simultaneously: first, they will be the only blocks stored in memory (up to small modifications described later), and hence they make up the set S. Consequently, a control block with index s serves as a "target" for array blocks which belong to intervals with indexes larger than s, thus allowing to recompute them using little memory. Second, besides serving as a target for array blocks in later intervals, each control block ensures that the large hash label graph for each of the blocks in its own interval collapses from expected exponential size in $1/\alpha$ to a linear size. Next, we describe how this is achieved.

Control block $X[s \cdot t]$ is computed such that all $t-1$ conditions

$$X[\phi(s \cdot t + 1)] \in S_s, X[\phi(s \cdot t + 2)] \in S_s, \ldots, X[\phi(s \cdot t + t - 1)] \in S_s$$

are satisfied (see Fig. 2), where S_s contains all the previously computed control blocks (namely, $S_s = \{X[s' \cdot t] \mid 0 \le s' \le s\}$). We slightly relax the $t-1$ conditions above for s and $\ell \in \{1, 2, \ldots, t-1\}$ as follows

$$X[\phi(s \cdot t + \ell)] \in S_s \cup \{X[s \cdot t + 1], \ldots, X[s \cdot t + \ell - 1]\}. \tag{5}$$

In other words, we allow $\phi(s \cdot t + \ell)$ to fall into the range of indexes $s \cdot t + 1, \ldots, s \cdot t + \ell - 1$ (as computing $X[s \cdot t + \ell]$ requires computing earlier blocks in the interval anyway, this relaxation does not increase the complexity of computing $X[s \cdot t + \ell]$).

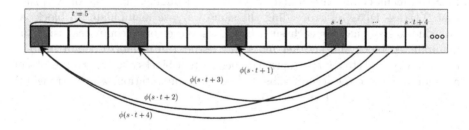

Fig. 2. Satisfying 4 conditions for $t = 5$

For an integer s and $\ell \in \{1, 2, \ldots, t-1\}$, we have

$$
\begin{aligned}
X[s \cdot t + \ell] &= F(X[s \cdot t + \ell - 1], X[\phi(s \cdot t + \ell)]) \\
&= F(F(X[s \cdot t + \ell - 2], X[\phi(s \cdot t + \ell - 1)]), X[\phi(s \cdot t + \ell)]) = \ldots \\
&= F(F(\ldots F(X[s \cdot t], X[\phi(s \cdot t + 1)]), \ldots, X[\phi(s \cdot t + \ell - 1)]), X[\phi(s \cdot t + \ell)]).
\end{aligned}
\tag{6}
$$

Given that the conditions of Eq. 5 are satisfied for any s and ℓ, then all the above $\ell + 1$ blocks are stored in memory (or fall into the same interval as $X[s \cdot t + \ell]$). Therefore, computing $X[s \cdot t + \ell]$ given only the values of control blocks with indexes $1, 2, \ldots, s$ is performed using at most ℓ calls to the compression function F as claimed (starting from $X[s \cdot t + 1] = F(X[s \cdot t], X[\phi(s \cdot t + 1)])$ and proceeding according to Eq. 6).

The full attack has two phases that correspond to the two phases of the honest prover's algorithm. In the first phase, we compute the control blocks in their natural order and simultaneously compute the Merkle hash tree over all the blocks $X[1], X[2], \ldots, X[T]$. Since the blocks are computed in their natural order, the root Φ of the Merkle hash tree can be computed on-the-fly while keeping in memory the roots of at most $\log(T)$ sub-trees, and joining them (using the hash function H) whenever possible. Overall, the memory complexity of this phase is dominated by the storage of T/t control blocks. Note that only the control blocks are inconsistent with F and hence $\epsilon = 1/t$. In the second phase of the attack, we pick arbitrary values for the nonce N and hope to find a valid proof such that the L blocks in the chain (involved in the computation of $Y_1, \ldots, Y_L$) do not fall onto the inconsistent control blocks (and Y_L has d trailing zeros as required from a valid proof).

5   Details of the Attack

We now describe our basic attack in detail and then extend and optimize it in various ways.

The First Phase. We fix a parameter $t > 3$, whose value will be specified later. The input to the first phase of the attack is the challenge I. The output of this phase is an array of control blocks CB (containing the values of about T/t control blocks) and the Merkle hash tree root Φ. In order to comply with the additional restriction imposed by the trivial attack of Sect. 4.1 (which binds the proof to I), we also compute the first $t - 1$ blocks honestly and return them. As t will be very small compared to T (e.g., $t = 20$), this tweak has negligible additional cost in memory. For the sake of simplicity, we omit the details of the Merkle hash tree computation, which it is straightforward and has negligible cost.

1. Compute the first $t - 1$ blocks $X[1], \ldots, X[t - 1]$ honestly using the compression function F, and store them in memory.
2. Initialize the control block array $CB[1, \ldots, (T/t) - 1]$. For each interval $s \in \{1, \ldots, (T/t) - 1\}$:
   (a) Initialize the 32 LSBs J_1 of the current control block value $X[s \cdot t]$ and the 2 LSBs of J_2 such that $\phi(s \cdot t + 1) = (s - 1) \cdot t$ according to the algorithm of Eq. 10 (in Appendix B). This ensures the condition of Eq. 5 (for $\ell = 1$), as the next block in the interval $X[s \cdot t + 1]$ is computed using the previous control block $X[(s - 1) \cdot t]$ (which is stored in $CB[s - 1]$).
   (b) Ensure that the remaining $t - 2$ conditions of Eq. 5 hold using exhaustive search on the control block value $X[s \cdot t]$. Namely, for values of $k = 0, 1, \ldots$ let $X[s \cdot t] = J_1 + J_2 \cdot 2^{32} + k \cdot 2^{64}$, and perform:
      i. For $\ell \in \{1, \ldots, t - 2\}$, compute

$$X[s \cdot t + \ell] = F(X[s \cdot t + \ell - 1], X[\phi(s \cdot t + \ell)]),$$

where $X[\phi(s \cdot t + \ell)])$ is stored in memory or previously computed in the interval (as the condition of Eq. 5 for the current value of ℓ was previously assured to hold).
Using J_1, J_2 for $X[s \cdot t + \ell]$, compute $\phi(s \cdot t + \ell + 1)$ and verify the condition of Eq. 5 for $\ell + 1$. If the condition does not hold, choose the next control block value by returning to Step 2(b). Otherwise, increment ℓ and continue. Once all $t - 1$ conditions of Eq. 5 hold, continue to the next step.
      ii. Store the current $X[s \cdot t]$ value in $CB[s]$, update the Merkle hash tree computation accordingly, and increment s by returning to Step 2.
3. Return the control block array CB, the first $t - 1$ blocks $X[1], \ldots, X[t - 1]$ and the Merkle hash tree root Φ.

Computational complexity analysis: The computational complexity is dominated by Step 2 which computes about T/t control blocks, all of which satisfy the $t - 1$ conditions of Eq. 5. The first condition is enforced by Step 2(a). Note the finding J_1, J_2 is trivial (as Eq. 10 in Appendix B is very simple) and this value is not changed in Step 2(b) as the value of $X[s \cdot t]$ is incremented by multiples of 2^{64}.[9]

Next, we estimate the complexity of Step 2(b), which depends on the expected number of values of k that we have to try before all remaining $t - 2$ conditions are satisfied. If the indexing function ϕ used in Argon2d was uniform over the previous indexes, then the probability for an arbitrary condition for s, ℓ in Eq. 5 to be satisfied[10] would be slightly larger than $1/t$. The reason is that at any point

---

[9] Since only the 2 LSBs of J_2 determine the lane l, we could also increment $X[s \cdot t]$ by multiples of 2^{34}.

[10] The probability is taken over the choice of J_1, J_2 in $X[s \cdot t + \ell - 1]$, which we can assume to be uniform, given that the compression function F is pseudo-random.

in the computation, we store a fraction of (at least) $1/t$ of the blocks computed in the previous intervals, and moreover, we allow ϕ of each index to land in the current interval.

However, as noted in Sect. 3.2, the indexing function of Argon2d in nonuniform and places more probability weight on larger indexes. Nevertheless, the probability of satisfying an arbitrary condition s, ℓ remains at least $1/t$. This can be easily shown by considering all previous intervals shifted by one (whose index values modulo t are $[1, 2, \ldots, t-1, 0]$). The last block in each such shifted interval is a control block stored in memory and its probability weight is at least as large as the average weight of the interval (the sum of weights divided by t). Since we also allow ϕ of each index to land in the current interval, the probability of satisfying an arbitrary condition for s, ℓ is indeed at least $1/t$.

From the analysis above (based on randomness assumptions on the compression function F), we conclude that the probability that all $t-2$ conditions in Step 2(b) are satisfied for an arbitrary value of k is at least $(1/t)^{t-2}$. Hence we expect to try at most t^{t-2} such values in this step. For each value of k, the expected number of compression function evaluations is about $1 + 1/t + (1/t)^2 + \ldots + (1/t)^{t-2}$, which is very close to 1 for the values of $t \approx 20$ we consider in this paper. We conclude that the expected complexity of Step 2(b) is about t^{t-2}, and the complexity of the algorithm is about

$$T/t \cdot t^{t-2} = T \cdot t^{t-3}. \tag{7}$$

In Appendix C, we show how to reduce this complexity by a (small) factor of about $8t/(t+8)$ by exploiting the specific Argon2d compression function.

Memory complexity analysis: The efficiency of the attack in the time-area product metric crucially depends on reducing the required storage. The memory complexity of the first phase is dominated by storing T/t control blocks. To save memory, instead of storing each full control block, we simply store the corresponding value of k computed in Step 2(b). We then easily reconstruct the control block value when we access it in the second phase of the attack. Since we expect to try t^{t-2} values of k, we require about $(t-2) \log(t)$ bits of storage on average per control block. However, we use static allocation of addresses in an array, and some blocks will require more storage than the average.

To overcome this problem, we allocate a small additional allowance of b bits per control block. The probability that these additional bits will not suffice to store k (i.e., we do not find an appropriate k after exhausting all $t^{t-2} \cdot 2^b$ possible values) is about $e^{2^{-b}}$. In our concrete analysis we use $b = 5$, which gives a negligible probability of about e^{-32} that the storage for a single block does not suffice.

We conclude that the total memory complexity of the attack in bits is about

$$T/t \cdot (b + (t-2) \log(t)). \tag{8}$$

The Second Phase. The input to the second phase of the attack is the output of the first phase, namely, an array of control blocks CB, the Merkle hash tree root Φ and the first $t-1$ blocks $X[1], \ldots, X[t-1]$. Its output is a valid (yet malicious) proof $(\Phi, N, \mathcal{Z})$. The algorithm tries different values for the nonce N until the corresponding chain of values does not access the control blocks (which are the only inconsistent blocks we have) and the last value computed in the chain Y_L has d trailing zeroes.

---

1. For nonce values $N = 0, 1, \ldots$
   (a) Compute $Y_0 = H(\Phi, N)$.
   (b) For $1 \le j \le L$:
      i. Compute $i_j = Y_{j-1} \pmod{T}$. Let $i_j = s \cdot t + \ell$, where $s \cdot t$ is the index of the control block in the interval of i_j. If $\ell = 0$ (namely, i_j is an index of an inconsistent control block), increment N by returning to Step 1. Otherwise, continue.
      ii. Compute $X[i_j] = X[s \cdot t + \ell]$, as specified in Eq. 6.
      iii. Compute $Y_j = H(Y_{j-1}, X[i_j])$ and increment j by going back to Step 1(b).
   (c) If Y_L has d trailing zeros, then output $(\Phi, N, \mathcal{Z})$ as the proof-of-work, where $\mathcal{Z}$ is the opening of $2L$ blocks $\{X[i_j - 1], X[\phi(i_j)]\}$. Otherwise, select another value for N by returning to Step 1.

Computational complexity analysis: To calculate the expected computational complexity, note that we have to compute about 2^d full chains of length L in Step 1(b) until some Y_L has d trailing zeros. Since $\epsilon = 1/t$, an arbitrary chain extends to length L with probability $(1 - 1/t)^L$, and we expect to compute $2^d \cdot (1 - 1/t)^{-L}$ chains in total. As the average length of a chain is t, the algorithm computes an expected number of $2^d \cdot t \cdot (1 - 1/t)^{-L}$ blocks $X[i_j]$.[11] The cost of computing $X[i_j]$ for $i_j = s \cdot t + \ell$ is at most ℓ, where the expected value of ℓ is $t/2$. This gives a total expected complexity of

$$2^d \cdot t^2/2 \cdot (1 - 1/t)^{-L}. \tag{9}$$

Memory complexity analysis: The memory complexity remains similar to the previous phase.

5.1 Balancing the Phases

The complexity analysis above shows that there is a tradeoff between the two phases of the attack: larger values of t decrease the value of $(1 - 1/t)^{-L}$ which is the dominant factor in Eq. 9 (for $L = 70$), and hence reduce the complexity of

---

[11] This computation shows that the analysis of the block modification cheating strategy (given in Sect. 3.1) is slightly inaccurate, since it does not take into consideration the fact that the expected chain length computed by the cheater is shorter than L.

the second phase. At the same time, larger values of t increase the complexity of the first phase (given by Eq. 7).

Besides the choice of t, another way to balance the phases is to reconsider the condition $X[\phi(s\cdot t+\ell)] \in S_s$ in Eq. 5. This condition is equivalent to $\phi(s\cdot t+\ell) \equiv 0 \pmod{t}$. Assume we relax this condition (for all values of s, but for a specific value of $\ell > 0$) to

$$\phi(s \cdot t + \ell) \in \{0, 1 \ldots, m_\ell - 1\} \pmod{t}$$

for some $2 \leq m_\ell < \ell$. This increases the probability of satisfying the condition from about $1/t$ to m_ℓ/t, reducing the expected complexity of phase 1 by a multiplicative factor of m_ℓ. On the other hand, computing $X[s \cdot t + \ell]$ requires computing $X[\phi(s\cdot t+\ell)]$, which may no longer be stored in memory. This increases the average number of compression function evaluations (units) required to compute $X[s \cdot t + \ell]$ by an additive factor of $(m_\ell - 1)/2$ (since $\phi(s \cdot t + \ell)$ is expected to land in the middle of the allowed interval of m_ℓ blocks modulo t). Moreover, the computation of all values $X[s \cdot t + \ell + 1], \ldots, X[s \cdot t + t - 1]$ also requires $X[s\cdot t+\ell]$ and hence the average computation complexity increases by $(m_\ell - 1)/2$ units for these as well. Overall, the expected computation of a block increases by an additive factor of $((m_\ell - 1)/2 \cdot (t - \ell))/t$. Therefore, it is more efficient to use this approach for large values of ℓ (which are close to the end of each interval).

For example, for $t = 20$ we can set $m_{19} = 2$, reducing the expected complexity of phase 1 by a multiplicative factor of $m_{19} = 2$, while the expected computation of a block increases by an additive factor of $((m_\ell - 1)/2 \cdot (t - \ell))/t = 1/2 \cdot (20 - 19)/20 = 1/40$. If we set $m_{18} = 2$, the expected complexity of phase 1 is also reduced by a multiplicative factor of $m_{18} = 2$, while the expected computation of a block increases by a larger additive factor of $((m_\ell - 1)/2 \cdot (t - \ell))/t = 1/2 \cdot (20 - 18)/20 = 2/40$.

Our optimized attack will use this method by relaxing the conditions for several indexes $\ell, \ldots, t - 1$ at the end of each interval (see Fig. 3), assigning them respective values of $m_\ell, m_{\ell+1}, \ldots, m_{t-1}$ (allowing their index functions to land in a larger prefix of a previous interval). To simplify the analysis, we will make sure that all $m_\ell, m_{\ell+1}, \ldots, m_{t-1}$ are smaller than ℓ (which avoids more complex recursions). In total, the expected complexity of phase 1 is reduced by a multiplicative factor of

$$\prod_{j=\ell}^{t-1} m_j,$$

while the expected computation complexity of a block in phase 2 increases by an additive factor of

$$1/2t \cdot \sum_{j=\ell}^{t-1} (m_j - 1)(t - j).$$

We note that there is also a computational penalty on phase 1 of the attack due to the additional complexity required for calculating a block when exhaustively searching for control blocks. However, in our attack we make sure that

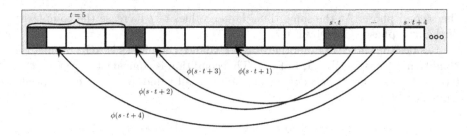

Fig. 3. Relaxing Eq. 5 by setting $m_3 = m_4 = 2$ for $t = 5$

there is a penalty only on several blocks at the end of each interval which are rarely computed compared to the other blocks.[12] In total, the overall penalty on phase 1 is negligible for the parameters we choose.

5.2   Using Preprocessing

Although we can select interesting parameters for the attack described above, it is still generally impractical in the standard cryptocurrency setting. The reason for this is that the tradeoff between the two phases forces us to spend considerable time on phase 1 in order to obtain a reasonable overall computation complexity. However, the probability of producing a valid proof in phase 1 is zero, implying that the attack is not a *progress-free* algorithm. As a result, the malicious prover (miner) has to spend significant computation on phase 1 for a certain challenge I with no chance of finding a valid proof in this phase. Once a new proof arrives on the network (which typically occurs every few minutes), this computational effort is lost.

To solve this problem, we modify the algorithm so that the first phase can be performed during preprocessing with no dependency on the challenge.[13] This is achieved by partitioning the Argon2d block array into two parts, where the first part is relatively small and will be computed honestly online using the actual challenge I. The second part contains most blocks in the block array, and we force it to be independent of the first part of the block array and the challenge. In other words, we disconnect the second part from the first, which allows us to perform the heavy control block computation during preprocessing. Details are given below.

We choose a small fraction $\delta \ll 1/t$ and leave the first δT blocks in each of the 4 lanes (rows) of Argon2d with an undetermined value during preprocessing (their value will only be determined online). In order to compute the remaining

---

[12] Moreover, computing the blocks in their natural order in phase 1 is more efficient (on average) than computing an average block, as by the time we compute block $X[i]$ we have already computed its predecessor $X[i-1]$.

[13] This modification can be easily combined with the method of balancing the phases described above, but we describe each one of them separately for the sake of simplicity.

control blocks during preprocessing with no additional cost, we have to maintain the property that at all stages, each condition given by Eq. 5 (for indexes s, ℓ) holds with probability of at least $1/t$. To achieve this, we set the $\delta T/(t-1)$ blocks that follow the δT prefix in each lane to some fixed value. We change the conditions given by Eq. 5 by allowing $X[\phi(s \cdot t + \ell)]$ to land on the fixed-value blocks, but do not allow them to land on the undetermined prefix in each lane.

Thus, we start computing the control blocks in phase 1 from index $(1 + 1/(t-1)) \cdot \delta T$ in each lane. As we cannot compute the root of the full Merkle hash tree in preprocessing, we compute the roots of all the subtrees of the known blocks and pass them to the online phase. Since there are 4 lanes, the number of such roots is at most $4\log(T)$, and they consume negligible memory (which can be reused once the Merkle hash tree computation in phase 2 is finished). Overall, the complexity of phase 1 when performed in preprocessing remains roughly the same.

During the online phase, we receive the challenge I, compute the first δT blocks in each lane honestly and finish the Merkle hash tree computation. We then execute phase 2 of the attack. Assuming that the prefix of size δT is sufficiently small, the memory complexity of the attack will be roughly as in Eq. 8. The fraction of inconsistent blocks remains (at most) $\epsilon = 1/t$, hence the computation complexity remains unchanged.

6   Analysis of the Full Attack

In this section, we analyze the full attack. Our goal is to optimize the time-area product ratio for the attack between the honest and malicious provers according to Eq. 1. While the previous sections analyzed the attack phases as a function of the parameters in symbolic form in order to maintain generality, we choose to perform the most of the analysis in this section in numerical form. The reason for this choice is that the symbolic expressions that can be derived in this section are rather complex and do not seem to provide additional insight into the attack. Hence, we favor readability over generality.

It is not obvious how to treat the preprocessing phase in the framework of Sect. 2. On one hand, a one-time precomputation should not be taken into account in Eq. 1. On the other hand, a very long preprocessing phase will render the attack impractical. Our compromise is to set a hard limit on the complexity of the preprocessing phase and then optimize the online phase with respect to the framework of Sect. 2.

Before choosing concrete parameters for the attack in order to optimize the time-area product, we argue informally that it achieves a sub-linear computation-memory tradeoff for a wide range of parameters: recall that the online phase has complexity of $2^d \cdot t^2/2 \cdot (1 - 1/t)^{-L}$. Allowing for a sufficiently long preprocessing phase, we can choose $t < L$ sufficiently large such that the term $(1 - 1/t)^{-L}$ is small and the complexity becomes roughly $2^d \cdot t^2 < 2^d \cdot L \cdot t$. This is about t times larger than honest prover's complexity (which is more than $2^d \cdot L$). In terms of memory, recall that we store a succinct representation of a $1/t$

fraction of all blocks, whereas the honest prover stores all of them. Consequently, the computation-memory product of the attacker is reduced by a factor which is proportional to c/b, where c is the memory occupied by our succinct block representation and b is the memory occupied by a full block. Namely, the attack achieves a sub-linear computation-memory tradeoff depending on the ratio c/b. Next, we show how to actually obtain such a tradeoff by choosing concrete parameters and applying the optimizations described in the previous section.

We begin by setting a hard limit of 2^{64} for the preprocessing phase. We believe that this is a reasonable complexity, as it is feasible for a motivated attacker, but does not require exceptional computing power that is available only to very resourceful attackers. This feasibility assertion is based on the fact that the preprocessing phase can be easily parallelized (exhaustive search for each control block can be performed in parallel) and requires a small amount of memory (as we show later, it requires less than one megabyte).

We now reconsider the preprocessing complexity of $T \cdot t^{t-3}$ given by Eq. 7 (without using the balancing technique of Sect. 5.1). This complexity can be slightly reduced by a factor of $8t/(t + 8)$, as shown in Appendix C. Setting $T = 2^{21}$ as fixed by the MTP instance, we conclude that we can use $t = 14$, which keeps the preprocessing complexity below the hard limit of 2^{64}. However, these parameters do not give the optimal time-area ratio, as they do not use the balancing technique. To optimize the attack, we wrote a computer program that finds the best parameters for the balancing technique of Sect. 5.1 for a given value of t, limiting the values of all m_ℓ to powers of 2 for simplicity. We then searched for the best value of t exhaustively. Next, we describe the optimal parameters.

6.1 Concrete Parameters

We use the balancing technique for $t = 20$ by setting $m_8, m_{11}, \ldots, m_{19}$ to the respective values of $2, 4, 4, 4, 4, 4, 4, 8, 8, 8, 8, 8$. These values reduce the complexity of preprocessing by a multiplicative factor of $\prod_{j=8}^{19} m_j = 2^{28}$ (from $T \cdot t^{t-3} \cdot (t + 8)/8t = 2^{21} \cdot 20^{17} \cdot 28/160 < 2^{92}$ to less than 2^{64}). We also note that these values will increase the expected computation complexity of a block in phase 2 by an additive factor of $1/2t \cdot \sum_{j=8}^{19}(m_j - 1)(t - j) = 1/40 \cdot (1 \cdot 12 + 3 \cdot (11 + 10 + 9 + 8 + 7 + 6) + 7 \cdot (5 + 4 + 3 + 2 + 1)) = 6.75$.

Memory complexity: The memory complexity of the honest prover's algorithm is T blocks, and specifically for the MTP instance we have $T = 2^{21}$ blocks which consume 2^{34} bits. According to Eq. 8, the memory complexity of the attack is $T/t \cdot (b + (t - 2)\log(t))$ bits. However, this is changed by setting $m_8, \ldots, m_{19}$ as above, since computing a block in phase 1 now requires about $20^{18} \cdot 2^{-28} < 2^{50}$ computations (and $50 + b$ bits of storage on average). Using this value, and setting $T = 2^{21}$, $b = 5$ (as specified in Sect. 5) and $t = 20$, we obtain a total memory complexity of $2^{21}/20 \cdot (50 + 5) \approx 2^{22.45}$ bits, which is less than a megabyte. Hence, the ratio between the memory complexities of the honest and the malicious provers is

$$\alpha \approx 2^{22.45-34} = 2^{-11.55} \approx 1/3000.$$

Computation complexity: Recall that the computation complexity of the honest MTP prover's algorithm is $T + 2^d \cdot L > 2^d \cdot L$. For the MTP instance considered, we have $L = 70$ giving a complexity of at least $2^d \cdot 70$.

The computation complexity of phase 2 according to Eq. 9 is $2^d \cdot t^2/2 \cdot (1 - 1/t)^{-L}$. Taking into account the balancing technique, the average computation complexity per block increases by an additive factor of 6.75 (from $t/2 = 10$ to 16.75). For $L = 70$ and $t = 20$, we obtain $2^d \cdot 16.75 \cdot 20 \cdot 36.25 \approx 2^d \cdot 12144$. Hence, the ratio between the computation complexities of the honest and the malicious provers is

$$C(\alpha) \approx (2^d \cdot 12144)/(2^d \cdot 70) \approx 173.$$

Time-area product ratio: In terms of the time-area product ratio for the attack, according to Eq. 1 we should evaluate $\alpha D(\alpha) + \beta C(\alpha)$, where $\beta = 2^{-15}$ for MTP. If we do not use any parallelism, then the total running time ratio is $D(\alpha) = C(\alpha)$ and we have

$$\alpha D(\alpha) + \beta C(\alpha) = C(\alpha)(\alpha + \beta) \approx 173(1/3000 + 2^{-15}) \approx 1/15.9.$$

In other words, the time-area product of the malicious prover is reduced by an approximate factor of 15.9.

To compute $D(\alpha)$ when using parallelism, observe that the circuit depth of the attack is increased by an expected factor of at most $(t+1)/2 = 10.5$ compared to the honest prover's algorithm.[14] This is because the expected circuit depth of computing an arbitrary block $X[i_j]$ in the chain is $(t-1)/2$ and computing the corresponding Y_j requires an additional hash function invocation (chains computed with different nonce values do not increase the circuit depth). We have

$$\alpha D(\alpha) + \beta C(\alpha) \approx 1/3000 \cdot 10.5 + 2^{-15} \cdot 173 < 1/113.$$

Consequently, the time-area product of the malicious prover is reduced by an approximate factor of 113.

6.2   Comparison with the Analysis of [7]

Plugging the parameter values of our attack $\alpha \approx 1/3000$ and $\epsilon = 1/20$ into Eq. 2 (using Table 1), we obtain that the computational penalty should increase according to the MTP designers by a factor of more than

$$C(\alpha + \epsilon) \cdot (1 - \epsilon)^{-L} = C(1/3000 + 1/20) \cdot (19/20)^{-70}$$
$$\approx 2^{5.2} \cdot C(1/19) > 2^{5.2} \cdot C(1/7) = 2^{5.2+18} = 2^{23.2},$$

---

[14] If we consider the initial computation of Argon2d by the honest prover, then $D(\alpha)$ can be even smaller.

which is about 10 million. This is more than 55,000 times as much as the 173 computational penalty we obtain. Using the actual value of $C(1/19)$ (instead of $C(1/7)$) would give a larger improvement factor.[15]

In terms of time-area product, our improvement ratio of 113 (or even the ratio of 15.9, obtained without exploiting parallelism) contradicts the claims of the MTP designers that the time-area product can be reduced by a factor of 12 at most. Moreover, plugging our parameters into Eq. 4 (using Table 1), we obtain a value which is more than

$$\beta C(\alpha + \epsilon) \cdot (1 - \epsilon)^{-L} > 2^{-15} \cdot 2^{23.2} = 2^{8.2}.$$

In other words, for our set of parameters, the time-area product of the attacker should increase by a factor of more than 294 according to [7]. As we actually reduce the time-area product by 113, we improve this analysis by a multiplicative factor which is more than 33,000. Once again, using the actual value of $C(1/19)$ (instead of $C(1/7)$) would give a larger improvement factor.

7   Extensions of the Attack

There are several possible extensions of the attack. In this section, we briefly mention two of them.

First, a natural question is how the attack behaves when changing the preprocessing complexity hard limit. Interestingly, the time-area product ratio (between the honest and malicious provers) does not drastically change when the preprocessing complexity varies in the region between 2^{48} and 2^{80}. For example, if we set the preprocessing complexity to a trivial value of 2^{48}, the time-area product ratio is still more than 60 in favor of the attacker.

Next, note that in order to detect inconsistency in the malicious proof, a verifier should (in addition to running the standard verification algorithm) compute Argon2d until the first block of the proof which in inconsistent with the Argon2d compression function. Detecting this inconsistency already involves non-trivial computation and memory. Furthermore, it is possible to further increase the amount of resources required for detection at the cost of increasing the amount of resources (namely, memory, time, or both) required for the attack.

More specifically, recall from Sect. 5.2 that we set a parameter δ which controls the number of prefix blocks that are computed honestly. So far, we assumed that $\delta \ll 1/t$, and thus this prefix can be neglected. However, we can set δ to a non-negligible value in order to force the verifier to compute more blocks to detect inconsistency. Obviously, this increases the memory complexity of the attack, but we can trade some of the memory for computation by storing only an α fraction of the prefix. As a result, we pay a computational penalty based on α according to Table 1 for these blocks. The total expected additional penalty for computing a block is multiplied by δ (since it only involves the prefix blocks).

---

[15] We do not have a concrete value of $C(1/19)$ for Argon2d, but based on the very fast growth of this function, the actual value of $C(1/19)$ should be significantly larger than $C(1/7) = 2^{18}$. Hence we expect our actual improvement ratio to be much larger than 55,000.

8   Countermeasures

In this section, we discuss possible countermeasures for the attack.

We first consider simple ad-hoc countermeasures which try to detect some "non-random" properties of the proof. For example, one may observe that many blocks in the proof depend on control blocks which have a small value and occur at indexes which have the same offset modulo some number $t > 1$. However, such countermeasures are very easy to defeat. For example, we can start the exhaustive search for each control block from a pseudo-random value which depends on its index (and is not stored in memory). To eliminate the property that all control blocks have the same value modulo some number $t > 1$, we can use variable alignment of the blocks (e.g., by introducing a slightly shorter interval every 100 intervals). This may change the cost of the attack, as we need to keep track of the control block indexes, but all the additional work can be made negligible with appropriate choice of parameters.

Next, we consider other countermeasure options which adjust the parameters of MTP. For example, we can increase the value of L. This will definitely increase the complexity of the attack, but it will also increase the complexity of the verifier's (and honest prover's) algorithm. Overall, such countermeasures do not seem reasonable, as they do not eliminate the main properties of MTP which make the attack possible and they introduce additional overhead for the honest players.

Finally, the most reasonable countermeasure is to instantiate MTP with a memory-hard function that uses data-independent indexing (such as Argon2i). This may enable computation-memory tradeoff algorithms which are somewhat more efficient (for details regarding Argon2i, refer to [1,2,6]), but it completely resists the basic form of our attack. In the following, we call such an instantiation *data-independent MTP* in short.

It is natural to ask whether the analysis given by Eq. 4 holds (even heuristically) for data-independent MTP. The answer to this question is negative and we demonstrate this by the following example: assume that two blocks X_1, Y_1 are computed as $X_1 = F(X_2, X_3)$, $Y_1 = F(Y_2, Y_3)$ and moreover, $Y_3 = X_3$ (they point to the same array index). Then, the attacker can set $Y_2 = X_2$, resulting in $Y_1 = X_1$. Altogether, the attacker introduced a single inconsistent block Y_2, but the result is that the two blocks Y_1, Y_2 do not have to be stored. This is inconsistent with Eq. 4, since α is not directly reduced (the attacker can still compute all blocks with the honest prover's complexity), but the memory complexity is reduced by a factor of 2ϵ for a fraction of ϵ inconsistent blocks.

Overall, the above property does not immediately lead to a very efficient attack, but it seems undesirable in general. To avoid this self-similarity property, it is possible to use a different compression function F_i for each index i (essentially, setting i to be another input to F), as in the HAIFA mode-of-iteration construction for hash functions [5]. However, this tweak may still not be sufficient when using a compression function which is not collision resistant. In particular, if $X_1 = F_1(X_2, X_3)$, $Y_1 = F_2(Y_2, Y_3)$, the attacker may try to find a value for Y_2 such that $X_1 = Y_1$ (even if $Y_3 \neq X_3$), resulting in a similar property as above. When basing the functions F_i on Argon2's F, finding such collisions may be very simple, as it is trivial to find collisions in its compression function (which was not designed to resist to such attacks).

It may also be possible to exploit preprocessing in computing malicious proofs for data-independent MTP. Although it is unlikely that we can split the block array into completely independent parts (as in the case of Argon2d), we can make the first part (which depends on the online challenge) sufficiently small such that only a small fraction of blocks in the second part depend on it directly. This allows to compute most of the block array during preprocessing in a way that is highly consistent with the Argon2 compression function.

From the discussion above, we conclude that the analysis of data-independent MTP is non-trivial and we leave it to future work.

9   Conclusion

In this paper, we described a new cryptanalytic computation-memory tradeoff for MTP when instantiated with a memory-hard function that uses data-dependent indexing. When applied to the instance proposed by Biryukov and Khovratovich, our attack reduces the cost of a malicious prover's algorithm by a factor of 113 compared to the honest prover's algorithm. Finally, while data-independent MTP avoids the basic form of our attack, it may still be susceptible to its extensions and we leave its concrete instantiation and analysis to future work.

References

1. Alwen, J., Blocki, J.: Efficiently computing data-independent memory-hard functions. In: Robshaw, M., Katz, J. (eds.) CRYPTO 2016. LNCS, vol. 9815, pp. 241–271. Springer, Heidelberg (2016). doi:10.1007/978-3-662-53008-5_9
2. Alwen, J., Blocki, J.: Towards practical attacks on Argon2i and balloon hashing. IACR Cryptology ePrint Archive, 2016:759 (2016). Presented at the IEEE European Symposium on Security and Privacy (2017)
3. Ateniese, G., Bonacina, I., Faonio, A., Galesi, N.: Proofs of space: when space is of the essence. In: Abdalla, M., Prisco, R. (eds.) SCN 2014. LNCS, vol. 8642, pp. 538–557. Springer, Cham (2014). doi:10.1007/978-3-319-10879-7_31
4. Aumasson, J.-P., Neves, S., Wilcox-O'Hearn, Z., Winnerlein, C.: BLAKE2: simpler, smaller, fast as MD5. In: Jacobson, M., Locasto, M., Mohassel, P., Safavi-Naini, R. (eds.) ACNS 2013. LNCS, vol. 7954, pp. 119–135. Springer, Heidelberg (2013). doi:10.1007/978-3-642-38980-1_8
5. Biham, E., Dunkelman, O.: A framework for iterative hash functions - HAIFA. IACR Cryptology ePrint Archive, 2007 (2007). http://eprint.iacr.org/2007/278
6. Biryukov, A., Dinu, D., Khovratovich, D.: Argon2: new generation of memory-hard functions for password hashing and other applications. In: IEEE European Symposium on Security and Privacy, EuroS&P 2016, Saarbrücken, Germany, 21–24 March 2016, pp. 292–302. IEEE (2016)
7. Biryukov, A., Khovratovich, D.: Egalitarian computing. In: Holz, T., Savage, S. (eds.) 25th USENIX Security Symposium, USENIX Security 2016, Austin, TX, USA, 10–12 August 2016, pp. 315–326. USENIX Association (2016)

8. Bonneau, A.N.J., Felten, E., Miller, A., Goldfeder, S.: Bitcoin and Cryptocurrency Technologies: A Comprehensive Introduction. Princeton University Press, Princeton (2016)

9. Dwork, C., Naor, M.: Pricing via processing or combatting junk mail. In: Brickell, E.F. (ed.) CRYPTO 1992. LNCS, vol. 740, pp. 139–147. Springer, Heidelberg (1993). doi:10.1007/3-540-48071-4_10

10. Dziembowski, S., Faust, S., Kolmogorov, V., Pietrzak, K.: Proofs of space. In: Gennaro, R., Robshaw, M. (eds.) CRYPTO 2015. LNCS, vol. 9216, pp. 585–605. Springer, Heidelberg (2015). doi:10.1007/978-3-662-48000-7_29

11. Lee, C.: Litecoin (2011). https://litecoin.org/

12. Mahmoody, M., Moran, T., Vadhan, S.P.: Publicly verifiable proofs of sequential work. In: Kleinberg, R.D. (ed.) Innovations in Theoretical Computer Science, ITCS 2013, Berkeley, CA, USA, 9–12 January 2013, pp. 373–388. ACM (2013)

13. Merkle, R.C.: A digital signature based on a conventional encryption function. In: Pomerance, C. (ed.) CRYPTO 1987. LNCS, vol. 293, pp. 369–378. Springer, Heidelberg (1988). doi:10.1007/3-540-48184-2_32

14. Nakamoto, S.: Bitcoin: A Peer-to-Peer Electronic Cash System (2009). https://bitcoin.org/bitcoin.pdf

15. Password Hashing Competition (2015). https://password-hashing.net/

16. Percival, C.: Stronger Key Derivation via Sequential Memory-Hard Functions (2009). http://www.tarsnap.com/scrypt/scrypt.pdf

A   Merkle Hash Trees

Merkle hash tree is a data structure proposed by Ralph Merkle in order to create digital signatures using symmetric cryptography primitives [13]. However, it has found many additional applications since its introduction.

The value of every non-leaf node in a Merkle hash tree is computed by hashing the concatenated values of its children nodes. An opening of a data block X_i is a proof that $H(X_i)$ is indeed a leaf in the tree contained in the tree at index i. The opening includes X_i itself and the values of the siblings of $H(X_i)$'s path to

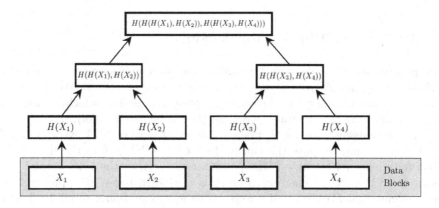

Fig. 4. Merkle hash tree

the root, which are sufficient to compute the full path. For example, the opening of X_3 in the tree of Fig. 4 contains (besides the value of X_3) the values of $H(X_4)$ and $H(H(X_1), H(X_2))$.

Assuming that the hash function H is collision resistant, the Merkle hash tree construction guarantees that it is computationally hard to open a block in more than one way.

B   The Indexing Function of Argon2d

Recall from Sect. 3.2 that given indexes i, j of a block $[i][j]$, we first compute J_1, J_2 and determine the lane of the referenced block, denoted by l. Next, we show how to compute the block index z within the lane. First, we determine the set of indexes that can be referenced given $[i][j]$ (denoted by $\mathcal{R}$) according to the following rules:

1. If l is the current lane, then $\mathcal{R}$ includes all previous blocks computed in this lane, excluding $[i][j-1]$.
2. If l is not the current lane, then $\mathcal{R}$ includes all blocks in the segments whose computation is finished in lane l. If $[i][j]$ is the first block of a segment, then the last block from $\mathcal{R}$ is excluded.

The size of $\mathcal{R}$ is denoted by $|\mathcal{R}|$. The value of J_1 determines the block index within this lane by computing (over the integers)

$$
\begin{aligned}
x &= (J_1)^2/2^{32}; \\
y &= (|\mathcal{R}| \cdot x)/2^{32}; \\
z &= |\mathcal{R}| - 1 - y.
\end{aligned}
\tag{10}
$$

The value of ϕ is $[l][z]$. Note that ϕ for $[i][j]$ defines a non-uniform distribution over the indexes of $\mathcal{R}$, where more weight is placed on the larger indexes closer to j.

C   Optimizing Phase 1 for Argon2d

In this appendix, we exploit the Argon2d compression function to optimize phase 1 of the attack (described in Sect. 5) by a factor of about $8t/(t+8)$. We start with a high-level description of the Argon2d compression function, which is sufficient to understand the optimization (more details can be found in [6]).

The compression function F takes as input 2 blocks of 1024 bytes, denoted by X and Y, and outputs the single block $G(X \oplus Y) \oplus X \oplus Y$, where G is a permutation on 1024 bytes. The permutation G views the 1024 input bytes as an 8×8 matrix A, where each entry is of size 16 bytes. It applies a 128-byte permutation P once to all 8 rows of the matrix and once to all 8 columns (altogether P is applied 16 times in G). The permutation P is the round-function of Blake2 [4], but we do not exploit its specification in the attack. In total, the main effort in computing F is in the 16 applications of the permutation P.

We now show how to reduce the expected number of invocations of P in phase 1 of the attack. Recall that in phase 1 we set the 64 LSBs of the control block to some fixed value (ensuring that $\phi(s \cdot t + 1) = (s - 1) \cdot t$). We then do an exhaustive search on the remaining bits to find a value such that all the following blocks in the current interval (with indexes $2, 3, \ldots, t - 1$ inside the interval) are also computed using previous control blocks.

The expected complexity of verifying that a control block value satisfies the constraints is about $1 + 1/t + (1/t)^2 + \ldots + (1/t)^{t-2}$, where the first term (1) in the sum stands for the first F computation (that takes as input the current control block $X[s \cdot t]$ and the previous one $X[(s - 1) \cdot t]$). Note that $X[(s - 1) \cdot t]$ never changes during the exhaustive search, while $X[s \cdot t]$ changes, but this change is limited to a single 16-byte entry[16] in the 8×8 matrix A (whose value is $X[s \cdot t] \oplus X[(s - 1) \cdot t]$) at the input of G. Therefore, 7 out of 8 rows of A never change during this computation and their value after the application of P can be computed once, stored in memory, and reused. Moreover, in order to verify the next condition (namely, compute $\phi(s \cdot t + 2)$ of the next block), we only need to compute the 64 LSBs of the output of F. Hence, after computing P on the rows, we compute P on the first column, verify the condition, and only if it is satisfied we continue (otherwise, we change $X[s \cdot t]$ and recompute $F(X[s \cdot t] \oplus X[(s - 1) \cdot t])$). The probability that the condition will not be satisfied is $(t - 1)/t$, implying that we need to apply P only twice, equivalent to $2/16 = 1/8$ full F invocations. With probability $1/t$ we continue by first finishing the computation of $F(X[s \cdot t] \oplus X[(s - 1) \cdot t])$ on the remaining 7 columns. We start computing the next invocation of $F(X[s \cdot t + 1], X[\phi(s \cdot t + 1)])$ by applying P to the 8 rows of A, and once more to the first column, giving the 64 output LSBs that allow to compute $\phi(s \cdot t + 2)$. Once again, we continue only if $\phi(s \cdot t + 2)$ satisfies the condition of Eq. 5. Thus, with probability $1/t$, we compute $7 + 8 + 1 = 16$ additional P invocations, equivalent to a single F invocation.

In total, the expected complexity of verifying a single value of the control block in the exhaustive search is optimized to $1/8 \cdot (t - 1)/t + 1/t + 1/t^2 + \ldots < 1/8 + 1/t$ invocations of F. Therefore, the total complexity of phase 1 is optimized by a factor of about $8t/(t + 8)$.

We note that additional optimizations are possible by exploiting differential properties of P. However, we do not mention such optimizations here as they are more complex and do not seem to lead to a significant advantage.

---

[16] We iterate through the 64 MSBs of the first matrix entry (the 64 LSBs are fixed) and the total computation per control block is significantly lower than 2^{64}. Hence, we do not overflow the first matrix entry.

Functional Graph Revisited: Updates on (Second) Preimage Attacks on Hash Combiners

Zhenzhen Bao[1,2], Lei Wang[1,3,4(✉)], Jian Guo[2], and Dawu Gu[1]

[1] Shanghai Jiao Tong University, Shanghai, China
baozhenzhen10@gmail.com, {wanglei_hb,dwgu}@sjtu.edu.cn
[2] Nanyang Technological University, Singapore, Singapore
guojian@ntu.edu.sg
[3] State Key Laboratory of Information Security,
Institute of Information Engineering, Chinese Academy
of Sciences, Beijing, China
[4] Westone Cryptologic Research Center, Beijing, China

Abstract. This paper studies functional-graph-based (second) preimage attacks against hash combiners. By exploiting more properties of functional graph, we find an improved preimage attack against the XOR combiner with a complexity of $2^{5n/8}$, while the previous best-known complexity is $2^{2n/3}$. Moreover, we find the first generic second-preimage attack on Zipper hash with an optimal complexity of $2^{3n/5}$.

Keywords: Hash combiner · Functional graph · XOR combiner · Zipper hash · (Second) preimage attack

1 Introduction

A cryptographic hash function $\mathcal{H} : \{0,1\}^* \rightarrow \{0,1\}^n$ maps arbitrarily long messages to n-bit digests. It is a fundamental primitive in modern cryptography and has been widely utilized in various cryptosystems. There are three *basic* security requirements on a hash function $\mathcal{H}$:

- **Collision Resistance.** It must be computationally infeasible to find two distinct messages M and M' such that $\mathcal{H}(M) = \mathcal{H}(M')$;
- **Second Preimage Resistance.** Given a message M, it must be computationally infeasible to find a message M' such that $M' \neq M$ and $\mathcal{H}(M') = \mathcal{H}(M)$;
- **Preimage Resistance.** Given a target hash digest V, it must be computationally infeasible to find a message M such that $\mathcal{H}(M) = V$.

As generic birthday attack and the brute-force attack require complexities of $2^{n/2}$ and 2^n to find a collision and a (second) preimage, respectively. It is expected that a secure hash function should provide the same security level of resistance.

© International Association for Cryptologic Research 2017
J. Katz and H. Shacham (Eds.): CRYPTO 2017, Part II, LNCS 10402, pp. 404–427, 2017.
DOI: 10.1007/978-3-319-63715-0_14

Among various approaches of designing a hash function, one is to build a hash combiner from two (or more) hash functions in order to achieve security amplification, that is the hash combiner has higher bound of security resistance than its underlying hash functions, or to achieve security robustness, that is the hash combiner is secure as long as (at least) any one of its underlying hash functions is secure. In particular, hash combiners were used in practice, e.g., in SSL [14] and TLS [2].

Concatenation combiner and XOR combiner are the two most classical hash combiners. Using two (independent) hash functions $\mathcal{H}_1$ and $\mathcal{H}_2$, the former concatenates their outputs: $\mathcal{H}_1(M)\|\mathcal{H}_2(M)$, and the latter XORs their outputs: $\mathcal{H}_1(M) \oplus \mathcal{H}_2(M)$. From a theoretical point of view, the concatenation combiner is robust with respect to collision resistance, and the XOR combiner is robust with respect to PRF and MAC in the black-box reduction model [22]. Advanced security amplification combiners and robust multi-property combiners for hash functions have been constructed [9–12]. More generally[1], cryptographers have also studied cascade constructions of two (or more) hash functions, that is to compute $\mathcal{H}_1$ and $\mathcal{H}_2$ in a sequential order. Well-known examples are Hash Twice: $\mathcal{H}_2(\mathcal{H}_1(IV, M), M)$ and Zipper Hash [25]: $\mathcal{H}_2(\mathcal{H}_1(IV, M), \overleftarrow{M})$, where $\overleftarrow{M}$ is the reversed (block) order of original message M. We regard these cascade constructions of hash functions as hash combiners in this paper.

This paper is mainly interested in combiners of *iterative* hash functions, in particular following the Merkle-Damgård construction [6,27]. An iterative hash function splits a message M into blocks $m_1, \ldots, m_\ell$ of fixed length, and processes these blocks by iterating a compression function h (or a series of compression functions) over an internal state x with an initial constant denoted as IV. Finally, the hash digest is computed by a finalization function with the bit length of M denoted as $|M|$ as input. The finalization function can be either the compression function h or another independent function. For the simplicity of description, we fix the finalization function as h in the rest of the paper, but we stress that our attacks also work in a straight forward way for the case of an independent finalization function. We mainly focus on narrow-pipe iterative hash functions, i.e., every internal state x_i ($0 \le i \le \ell$) have the same bit length with the output

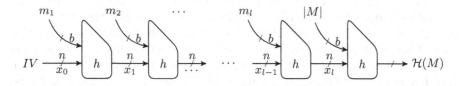

Fig. 1. Narrow-pipe Merkle-Damgård hash function

---

[1] Here we need to generalize the syntax of hash functions such that the initial value is also regarded as an input parameter.

hash digest (Fig. 1).

$$x_0 = IV \qquad x_{i+1} = h(x_i, m_{i+1}) \qquad \mathcal{H}(M) = h(x_\ell, |M|)$$

Combiners of iterative hash functions have received extensive analysis. Several generic attacks have been devised on the above combiners, which can work even with *ideal* compression functions, indicating the upper security bound of these combiners. In a seminal paper [20], Joux presents a technique to find multi-collision on an iterative hash function that has a complexity not much greater than that of finding a single collision. Based on this technique, he finds collision and preimage attacks on the concatenation combiner with complexities much lower than expected, and shows that it offers essentially the same security level with a single n-bit hash function.[2] In [24], Leurent and Wang propose an interchange structure that can break the pairwise dependency between the internal states of two iterative hash functions during computing a common message. Based on this structure, they are able to compute the two hash functions independently, and then launch a meet-in-the-middle preimage attack on the XOR combiner with a complexity exponentially lower than 2^n, more precisely $\tilde{\mathcal{O}}(2^{5n/6})$.

For combiners of cascade constructions, towards the basic security requirements, a second preimage attack on Hash twice has been published by Andreeva *et al.* in [3] with a complexity of $\mathcal{O}(2^n/L)$, where L is the block length of the challenging message. On the other hand, there is no generic attack on Zipper hash with respect to the basic security notions, which is highlighted as an *open problem* in [24]. Besides, cryptographers have also analyzed the resistance of Hash twice and Zipper hash with respect to other security notions such as multi-collision, herding attack, etc. Examples include [3,17,19,28].

Very recently Dinur in [7] publishes new generic attacks on the concatenation combiner and the XOR combiner. He finds a second preimage attack on the concatenation combiner with a complexity of optimally $2^{3n/4}$, and an improved preimage attack on the XOR combiner with a complexity of optimally $2^{2n/3}$. Differently from previous attacks on combiners in [20,24] which are mainly based on collision-finding techniques [20,21], one main technical contribution of Dinur's attacks is to exploit properties of functional graph of a random mapping. More specifically, one can fix the message input as a constant, and then turn the compression function h to an n-bit to n-bit random mapping. It has many interesting properties, and has been extensively studied and utilized in cryptography. Examples include [8,15,16,23,29–32]. Besides using known functional graph properties, Dinur finds an observation, which is essential for the complexity advantage of his attacks on those combiners. The observation is (briefly) described as follows. For two (independent) n-bit functional graphs defined by f_1 and f_2, let $\bar{x}$ and $\bar{y}$ be two iterates of depth 2^t in f_1 and f_2 respectively, that is $\bar{x}$ and $\bar{y}$ are images of 2^t iterations on f_1 and f_2 respectively. For a pair of random nodes x_r and y_r in the functional graphs defined by f_1 and f_2 respectively, compute a chain by iteratively applying f_1 and f_2 to update x_r and y_r until a maximum length of 2^t. The probability of x_r and y_r being iteratively updated to $\bar{x}$ and $\bar{y}$ at a common distance is

---

[2] In fact, Joux's attacks require that only one hash function is iterative and narrow-pipe.

2^{3t-2n}. By trying 2^{2n-3t} pairs of random x_r and y_r, one pair will be found that reaches $\bar{x}$ and $\bar{y}$, respectively, at a common distance.[3]

Lines of research of combining iterative hash functions also include the study of hash combiners with weak compression functions, *i.e.*, the attacker is given additional interfaces to receive random preimages of the compression functions [5,18,19,25], and analysis of combiners of dedicated hash functions [26]. In particular, the concatenation combiner, the XOR combiner and Zipper hash with weak compression functions have been proven in [18,25] to be indifferentiable from a random oracle with an $n/2$-bit security, indicating the lower security bound regarding basic security notions for these combiners.

1.1 Our Contributions

This paper investigates functional graph of a random mapping, and based on its properties evaluates the security of hash combiners.

We find an improved preimage attack on the XOR combiner, by exploiting the cyclic nodes in a functional graph. One main step in previous preimage attack on the XOR combiner is to search for a pair of nodes, x in functional graph of a function f_1 and y in functional graph of another function f_2, which reach to a pair of predefined nodes $\bar{x}$ of f_1 and $\bar{y}$ of f_2 at a common distance. We find that the probability of a random pair x_r and y_r reaching to $\bar{x}$ and $\bar{y}$ at a common distance can be greatly amplified, by exploiting some property of cyclic nodes as follows. When applying a function f to update a cyclic node in its functional graph iteratively, the cyclic node loops along the cycle and goes back to itself after a number of multi-cycle-length function calls. This property of cyclic nodes turns out to be very beneficial for finding a pair (x, y) that reach to $(\bar{x}, \bar{y})$ at a common distance. More specifically, $\bar{x}$ and $\bar{y}$ are predefined to be cyclic nodes within the largest components in the functional graphs of f_1 and f_2 respectively. Suppose a random pair of x_r and y_r reach to $\bar{x}$ and $\bar{y}$ at distances of d_1 and d_2 respectively. We can try correcting the distance bias $d_1 - d_2 \neq 0$, by letting $\bar{x}$ and $\bar{y}$ loop along their cycles. Note these two cycles have different lengths with an overwhelming probability, and their length are denoted as L_1 and L_2 respectively. More precisely, we search for a pair of integers i and j such that $d_1 + i \cdot L_1 = d_2 + j \cdot L_2$. Thus, the probability of a random pair (x_r, y_r) being the expected (x, y) is amplified by $\#C$ times, where $\#C$ is the maximum number of cycle loops that can be added. It contributes to improving preimage attacks on the XOR combiner. The complexity of our attack is $2^{5n/8}$, which is $2^{n/24}$ times lower than previous best-known complexity of $2^{2n/3}$ in [7]. We point out that the preimage message of our attack has a length of at least $2^{n/2}$ blocks, since the cycle length of an n-bit functional graph is $\Theta(2^{n/2})$.

Moreover, we propose functional-graph-based second preimage attacks on Zipper hash. Differently from the XOR combiner and the concatenation combiner, the two passes of Zipper hash are sequential. Moreover, the second pass

---

[3] In fact, Dinur's observation has been experimentally verified in [7], but the proof stays incomplete. More details are referred to [7, Appendix B].

processes message blocks in a reversed order. These unique specifications bring extra degrees of freedom for the attacker. In details, after being linked to an internal state of the original message in the second pass, the first few blocks of our second preimage message are fixed. Note these blocks do not include the padding block of message length. As a result, we are always able to choose a length for second preimage message that optimizes the complexity. Moreover, when looking for a pair of nodes $(\breve{x}, \breve{y})$ reaching two predefined nodes of deep iterates $(\bar{x}, \bar{y})$ at a common distance, $\breve{x}$ and $\breve{y}$ are generated with different message blocks, since the message blocks are hashed in different orders in two passes. It enables us to launch a meet-in-the-middle procedure by using Joux's multi-collision when finding a pair of nodes $(\breve{x}, \breve{y})$, then the complexity of the attack is further reduced. If message length longer than $2^{n/2}$ is allowed, the complexity of our second preimage attack on Zipper hash is $2^{3n/5}$ for $L \geq 2^{2n/5}$, and $2^n/L$ for $0 < L < 2^{2n/5}$, where L is the block length of original message. Otherwise, the complexity of our attack is $2^{5n/8}$ for $2^{3n/8} < L \leq 2^{n/2}$, and $2^n/L$ for $0 \leq L < 2^{3n/8}$. We note these attacks are the first generic second-preimage attacks on Zipper hash to our best knowledge,[4] which solve an open problem proposed in [24].

Roadmap. Section 2 describes preliminaries. In Sect. 3, we further investigate properties of functional graph. Sections 4 and 5 present (second) preimage attacks on the XOR combiner and Zipper hash, respectively. Finally, we conclude the paper in Sect. 6.

2   Preliminaries

2.1   Functional Graph

The functional graph (FG) of a random function f is defined by the successive iteration of this function. Explicitly, let f be an element of $\mathcal{F}_N$ which is the set of all mappings with a set N as both domain and range. The functional graph of f is a directed graph whose nodes are the elements $[0, \ldots, N-1]$ and whose edges are the ordered pairs $\langle x, f(x) \rangle$, for all $x \in [0, \ldots, N-1]$. If starting from any x_0 and iterating f, that is $x_1 = f(x_0), x_2 = f(x_1), \ldots$, we are going to find, before N iterations, a value x_j equal to one of $x_0, x_1, \ldots, x_{j-1}$. In this case, we say x_j is a *collision* and the path $x_0 \to x_1 \to \cdots \to x_{j-1} \to x_j$ connects to a *cycle* which describes the iteration structure of f starting from x_0. If we consider all possible starting points x_0, paths exhibit confluence and form into trees; trees grafted on cycles form components; a collection of components forms a functional graph [13].

Structure of FG has been studied for a long time, some parameters such as the number of components (*i.e.*, the number of connected components), the number

---

[4] Assuming compression functions are weak, second-peimage attacks have been published on Zipper hash [5,19].

of cyclic nodes (a node is cyclic if it belongs to a cycle), the number of terminal points (*i.e.*, nodes without preimage: $f^{-1}(x) = \emptyset$), the number of preimage points (*i.e.*, nodes with preimage), the expectation of tail length, the expectation of cycle length and rho-length have got accurate asymptotic evaluation [13], which are summarized below. A k-th iterate image point of f is an image point of the k-th iterate f^k of f.

Theorem 1 ([13]). *The expectations of parameters, number of components, number of cyclic points, number of terminal points, number of image points, and number of k-th iterate image points in a random mapping of size N have the asymptotic forms, as $N \to \infty$,*

1. *# Components $\frac{1}{2} \log N = 0.5 \cdot n$*
2. *# Cyclic nodes $\sqrt{\pi N/2} \approx 1.2 \cdot 2^{n/2}$*
3. *# Terminal nodes $e^{-1} N \approx 0.37 \cdot 2^n$*
4. *# Image points $(1 - e^{-1})N \approx 0.62 \cdot 2^n$*
5. *# k-th iterate image points $(1 - \tau_k)N$*

where the τ_k satisfies the recurrence $\tau_0 = 0$, $\tau_{k+1} = e^{-1+\tau_k}$.

Theorem 2 ([13]). *Seen from a random point (any of the N nodes in the associated functional graph is taken equally likely) in a random mapping of $\mathcal{F}_N$, the expectations of parameters tail length, cycle length, rho-length, tree size, component size, and predecessors size have the following asymptotic forms:*

1. *Tail length (λ) $\sqrt{\pi N/8} \approx 0.62 \cdot 2^{n/2}$*
2. *Cycle length (μ) $\sqrt{\pi N/8} \approx 0.62 \cdot 2^{n/2}$*
3. *Rho length ($\rho = \lambda + \mu$) $\sqrt{\pi N/2} \approx 1.2 \cdot 2^{n/2}$*
4. *Tree size $N/3 \approx 0.34 \cdot 2^n$*
5. *Component size $2N/3 \approx 0.67 \cdot 2^n$*
6. *Predecessors size $\sqrt{\pi N/8} \approx 0.62 \cdot 2^{n/2}$*

Theorem 3 ([13]). *Assuming the smoothness condition, the expected value of the size of the largest tree and the size of the largest connected component in a random mapping of $\mathcal{F}_N$, are asymptotically:*

1. *Largest tree: $0.48 \cdot 2^n$.*
2. *Largest component: $0.75782 \cdot 2^n$.*

Results from these theorems indicate that, in a random mapping, most of the points tend to be grouped together in a single giant component. This component might therefore be expected to have very tall trees and a large cycle.

2.2 XOR Combiner

The XOR combiner xors the outputs of two independent hash functions $\mathcal{H}_1$ and $\mathcal{H}_2$, *i.e.* $\mathcal{H}_1(M) \oplus \mathcal{H}_2(M)$, which is depicted in Figs. 2 and 3.

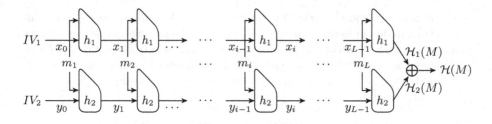

Fig. 2. The XOR combiner

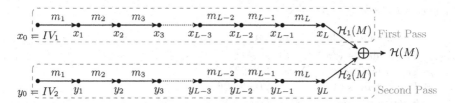

Fig. 3. Condensed graphical representation of the XOR combiner

2.3   Zipper Hash

Zipper hash is composed of two passes, denoted by $\mathcal{H}_1$ and $\mathcal{H}_2$ respectively, operating on a single message. The two passes in Zipper hash are sequential, and the second pass operates the sequence of message blocks in a reversed order. The construction is depicted in Figs. 4 and 5.

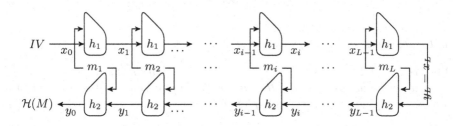

Fig. 4. The Zipper hash

2.4   Joux's Multi-collision [20]

In 2004, Joux [20] introduced multi-collisions on narrow-pipe Merkle-Damgård hash functions. Given a hash function $\mathcal{H}$, a multi-collision refers to a set of messages $\mathcal{M} = \{M_1, M_2, \ldots\}$ whose hash digests are all the same, *i.e.*, $\mathcal{H}(M_i) = \mathcal{H}(M_j)$ for any pair $M_i, M_j \in \mathcal{M}$. While the complexity is well-known to be birthday bound to find such a set when the size $|\mathcal{M}| = 2$, the

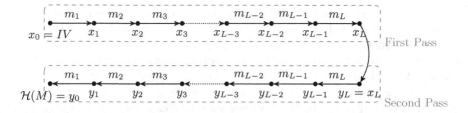

Fig. 5. Condensed graphical representation of the Zipper hash [19]

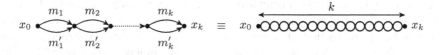

Fig. 6. Joux's multicollision structure and its condensed representation in R.H.S. [19]

computational complexity gradually approximates 2^n when the target size $|\mathcal{M}|$ increases. Utilizing the iterative nature of Merkle-Damgård structure, Joux's algorithm is able to find multi-collision of size 2^k with a complexity of $k \cdot 2^{n/2}$, i.e., a complexity not much greater than that of finding a single collision. It works as follows. Given an iterative hash function $\mathcal{H}$ with compression function h, and an initial value x_0, one finds a pair of message (m_1, m'_1) such that $h(x_0, m_1) = h(x_0, m'_1) = x_1$ with a complexity of $2^{n/2}$. The process can be repeated to find (m_i, m'_i) such that $h(x_{i-1}, m_i) = h(x_{i-1}, m'_i) = x_i$ for $i = 2, 3, \ldots, k$ iteratively, as shown in Fig. 6. It is trivial to see the message set $\mathcal{M} = \{\overline{m}_1 \| \overline{m}_2 \| \cdots \| \overline{m}_k \mid \overline{m}_i = m_i \text{ or } m'_i \text{ for } i = 1, 2, \ldots, k\}$ form a multi-collision of size 2^k, and the overall complexity is $\mathcal{O}(k \cdot 2^{n/2})$.

2.5   Expandable Message [21]

In 2005, Kelsey and Schneier [21] introduced the technique named *expandable message* to find second-preimages of Merkle-Damgård structure with a complexity of 2^{n-l}, instead of the long believed 2^n, for a given challenging message of about 2^l blocks. As depicted in Fig. 7, given a chaining value x_0 one finds a pair of message (m_1, m'_1) in time $2^{n/2}$ such that $h(x_0, m_1) = h(x_0, m'_1) = x_1$, and

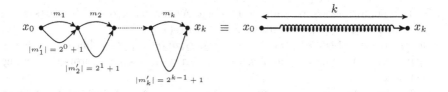

Fig. 7. The expandable message and its condensed representation in R.H.S. [19]

m_1 and m'_1 are of 1, and 2 blocks, respectively. The process can be repeated to find (m_i, m'_i) such that $h(x_{i-1}, m_i) = h(x_{i-1}, m'_i) = x_i$ for $i = 2, 3, \ldots, k$ iteratively, where m_i and m'_i are of 1, and $1 + 2^{i-1}$ blocks respectively. As a result, for each $t \in [k, k + 2^k - 1]$, there is a message of t blocks from the set $\mathcal{M} = \{\overline{m}_1 \| \overline{m}_2 \| \cdots \| \overline{m}_k \mid \overline{m}_i = m_i \text{ or } m'_i \text{ for } i = 1, 2, \ldots, k\}$. Note $h(x_0, M) = x_k$ for any $M \in \mathcal{M}$ and the overall complexity is $\mathcal{O}(k \cdot 2^{n/2} + 2^k)$. It is a special multi-collision, from which one can choose message of any desired block length in the range $[k, k + 2^k - 1]$.

Extension to Two Hash Functions [7]. Dinur extends Kelsey and Schneier's technique [21] to build simultaneous expandable message on two hash functions $\mathcal{H}_1$ and $\mathcal{H}_2$. Prior to that, Jha and Nandi propose a similar construction of an expandable message over two hash functions in the independent paper [19]. The main idea is, when building an expandable message on $\mathcal{H}_1$, to find two sets of $\mathcal{M} = \{m_i\}$ and $\mathcal{M}' = \{m'_i\}$ by Joux's multi-collision such that $h_1(x_{i-1}, m_i) = h_1(x_{i-1}, m'_i) = x_i$ for any $m_i \in \mathcal{M}$ and any $m'_i \in \mathcal{M}'$. Later, find a pair of $m_i \in \mathcal{M}$ and $m'_i \in \mathcal{M}'$ colliding on $\mathcal{H}_2$ that is $h_2(y_{i-1}, m_i) = h_2(y_{i-1}, m'_i) = y_i$. Hence, we find a pair of m_i and m'_i with carefully pre-determined lengths, colliding on both $\mathcal{H}_1$ and $\mathcal{H}_2$, with a complexity not much greater than that of finding a collision on a single hash function. The complexity is upper bounded by $L + n^2 \cdot 2^{n/2}$, where L is the maximum length that expandable message can produce. For completed description of the procedure, we refer to [7] or to Sect. 5.3 (slightly adapted due to specification of Zipper hash).

2.6   Dinur's Attack [7]

In [7], Dinur proposed second preimage attacks on the concatenation combiner and preimage attack on the XOR combiner, which are built on two independent Merkle-Damgård hash functions. In this section, we briefly describe his attack on the XOR combiner $\mathcal{H}_1(M) \oplus \mathcal{H}_2(M)$.

The attack is based on functional graph. Fix a message m, and define $f_1(x) = h_1(x, m)$ and $f_2(y) = h_2(y, m)$, where h_1 and h_2 are the compression functions of $\mathcal{H}_1$ and $\mathcal{H}_2$ respectively. In particular, it uses some special nodes, which are located deep in functional graphs defined by f_1 and f_2 and hence referred to as *deep iterates*. In other words, a deep iterate is a node that is reached after iterating f_1 (resp. f_2) many times.

Given a target hash digest V, the attack is composed of three main steps:

1. Build a simultaneous expandable message $\mathcal{M}$ for $\mathcal{H}_1$ and $\mathcal{H}_2$. It starts from the initial values (IV_1, IV_2) and ends at state $(\hat{x}, \hat{y})$.
2. Generate a set of tuples $\{(\bar{x}_1, \bar{y}_1, \bar{m}_1), (\bar{x}_2, \bar{y}_2, \bar{m}_2), \ldots\}$ such that $h_1(\bar{x}_i, \bar{m}_i) \oplus h_2(\bar{y}_i, \bar{m}_i) = V$, where $\bar{x}_i$ and $\bar{y}_i$ are chosen with a special property (being deep iterates).
3. Find a message $M_{\text{link}} = m_r \| m^d$, which links $(h_1(\hat{x}, m_r), h_2(\hat{y}, m_r))$ to some $(\bar{x}_i, \bar{y}_i)$ after iterating f_1 and f_2 by d times.

At the end, derive a message M_{L-2-d} with a block length of $L-2-d$ from the expandable message $\mathcal{M}$, and produce a preimage of V with a length L: $M = M_{L-2-d}\|M_{\text{link}}\|\bar{m}_i$.

$$(IV_1, IV_2) \xrightarrow{M_{L-2-d}} (\hat{x}, \hat{y}) \xrightarrow{M_{\text{link}}} (\bar{x}_i, \bar{y}_i) \xrightarrow{\bar{m}_i} (\mathcal{H}_1(M), \mathcal{H}_2(M)),$$

where $\mathcal{H}_1(M) \oplus \mathcal{H}_2(M) = V$ holds. The overall time complexity of Dinur's attack is optimally $2^{2n/3}$ obtained for $L = 2^{n/2}$.

The complexity advantage is gained thanks to two properties of deep iterates, which are listed below informally:

(i) it is easy to get a large set of deep iterates;
(ii) a deep iterate has a (relatively) high probability to be reached from an arbitrary starting node.

Property (i) contributes to the efficiency of Step 2, since one can find large sets of deep iterates in f_1 and f_2 independently, and then carry out a meet-in-the-middle procedure to find a set of tuples $\{(\bar{x}_i, \bar{y}_i, \bar{m}_i)\}$. Property (ii) contributes to the efficiency of Step 3. Thus, in order to estimate the complexity of the attack, it is necessary and important to study these two properties *quantitatively*.

- For property (i), $\Theta(2^t)$ iterates of depth 2^{n-t} can be collected with a complexity of 2^t by using Algorithm 1 for $t \geq n/2$;
- For property (ii), the author observes that the probability of a random pair (x_r, y_r) encountering d-th iterates $\bar{x}$ and $\bar{y}$ at a common distance (no larger than d) is $d^3/2^{2n}$, and experimentally verifies that after $2^{2n}/d^3$ trials, such a random pair (x_r, y_r) can be found [7, Sect. 3.3].

3   Functional Graph Revisited: Cyclic Node and Multi-cycles

In this section, we study a property of cyclic nodes within functional graph of a random mapping. Each cyclic node in a functional graph defined by f loops along the cycle when computed by f iteratively, and goes back to itself after a (multi-) cycle-length number of function calls. This property can be utilized to provide extra degrees of freedom, when estimating the distance of other nodes to a cyclic node in the functional graph, *i.e.*, it can be expanded to a set of discrete values by using multi-cycles. For example, let x and x' be two nodes in a component of the functional graph defined by f, x is a cyclic node, and the cycle length of the component is denoted as L. Clearly there exists a path from x' to x as they are in the same component, and the path length is denoted as d. Then we have

$$f^d(x') = x; \quad f^L(x) = x \implies f^{(d+i\cdot L)}(x') = x \quad \text{for any positive integer } i.$$

Algorithm 1. Collect $\Theta(2^t)$ iterates of depth 2^{n-t} with a complexity of 2^t, for $t \geq n/2$

```
1: procedure GEN(t)
2:      G ← ∅
3:      while |G| < 2^t do
4:          Chain ← ∅
5:          x ←_$ {0, 1, ..., 2^n − 1} \ G
6:          while true do
7:              if x ∈ G or x ∈ Chain then
8:                  G ←_merge Chain
9:                  go to line 3
10:             else
11:                 Chain ←_insert x
12:                 x ← f(x)
13:             end if
14:         end while
15:     end while
16:     output G
17: end procedure
```

Suppose it is limited to use at most t cycles. Then the distance from x' to x is expanded to a set of $t + 1$ values $\{d + i \cdot L \mid i = 0, 1, 2, ..., t\}$.

Now let us consider a special case of reaching two deep iterates from two random starting nodes: *select two cyclic nodes within the largest components in the functional graphs as the deep iterates.* More specifically, let two functional graphs be defined by f_1 and f_2. Let $\bar{x}$ and x_r be two nodes in a common largest component of functional graph defined by f_1, where $\bar{x}$ is a cyclic node. Let L_1 denote the cycle length of the component and d_1 denote the path length from x_r to $\bar{x}$. Similarly, we define notations $\bar{y}$, y_r, L_2 and d_2 in functional graph of f_2. We are interested in the probability of linking x_r to $\bar{x}$ and y_r to $\bar{y}$ at a common distance. Thanks to the usage of multiple cycles, the distance values from x_r to $\bar{x}$ and from y_r to $\bar{y}$ can be selected from two sets $\{d_1 + i \cdot L_1 \mid i = 0, 1, 2, \ldots, t\}$ and $\{d_2 + j \cdot L_2 \mid j = 0, 1, 2, \ldots t\}$, respectively. Hence, as long as there exists a pair of integers (i, j) such that $0 \leq i, j \leq t$ and $d_1 + i \cdot L_1 = d_2 + j \cdot L_2$, we get a common distance $d = d_1 + i \cdot L_1 = d_2 + j \cdot L_2$ such that

$$f_1^d(x_r) = \bar{x}, \qquad\qquad f_2^d(y_r) = \bar{y}.$$

Next, we evaluate the probability amplification of reaching $(\bar{x}, \bar{y})$ from a random pair (x_r, y_r) at the same distance. Without loss of generality, we assume $L_1 \leq L_2$. Let ΔL be $\Delta L = L_2 \mod L_1$. Then, it has that

$$d_1 + i \cdot L_1 = d_2 + j \cdot L_2 \qquad\qquad \Longrightarrow$$
$$d_1 - d_2 = j \cdot L_2 - i \cdot L_1 \qquad\qquad \Longrightarrow$$
$$(d_1 - d_2) \mod L_1 = j \cdot \Delta L \mod L_1$$

Letting j range over all integer values in internal $[0, t]$, we will collect a set of $t + 1$ values $\mathcal{S} = \{j \cdot \Delta L \mod L_1 \mid j = 0, 1, \ldots, t\}^5$. Since $d_1 = \mathcal{O}(2^{n/2})$, $d_2 = \mathcal{O}(2^{n/2})$ and $L_1 = \Theta(2^{n/2})$, it has $|d_1 - d_2| = \mathcal{O}(L_1)$, and we assume $|d_1 - d_2| < L_1$ by ignoring the constant factor. Therefore, for a randomly sampled pair (x_r, y_r) that encounter $(\bar{x}, \bar{y})$, we are able to derive a pair of (i, j) such that $d_1 + i \cdot L_1 = d_2 + j \cdot L_2$, as long as their distance bias $d_1 - d_2$ is in the set $\mathcal{S}$. In other words, we are able to *correct such a distance bias by using multi-cycles*. Thus, the probability of reaching $(\bar{x}, \bar{y})$ from a random pair (x_r, y_r) at a common distance is amplified by roughly t times, which is the maximum number of cycles used.

This property of cyclic nodes in functional graph can be utilized to improve preimage attacks on the XOR combiner, which is presented in next sections. The set $\mathcal{S}$ is referred to as the set of *correctable distance bias* hereafter.

4   Improved Preimage Attack on XOR Combiner

4.1   Attack Overview

Firstly, we recall previous preimage attack on the XOR combiner [7] introduced in Sect. 2.6. We name $(\bar{x}_i, \bar{y}_i)$'s as *target* node pairs. Clearly the larger the number of target node pairs (generated at Step 2) is, the higher the probability of a random node pair $(x_r = h_1(\hat{x}, m_r), y_r = h_2(\hat{y}, m_r))$ reaching a target node pair $(\bar{x}_i, \bar{y}_i)$ (at Step 3) at a common distance becomes. Hence, a complexity tradeoff exists between Steps 2 and 3. The optimal complexity is obtained by balancing Step 2 and Step 3.

In this section, we use cyclic nodes and multi-cycles to improve preimage attack on the XOR combiner. More specifically, if a target node pair $(\bar{x}, \bar{y})$ are both cyclic nodes within the largest components in two functional graphs respectively, the probability of a random pair $(x_r = h_1(\hat{x}, m_r), y_r = h_2(\hat{y}, m_r))$ reaching $(\bar{x}, \bar{y})$ at a common distance is amplified by $\#C$ times, the maximum number of cycles that can be used, by using the set of correctable distance bias as stated in Sect. 3. Moreover, such a probability amplification comes with almost no increase of complexity at Step 2, which leads to a new complexity tradeoff between Steps 2 and 3. Thus, the usage of cyclic nodes and multi-cycles enables us to reduce the computational complexity of preimage attacks on the XOR combiner.

Here we briefly list the *main* steps of our preimage attack on the XOR combiner.

Step A. Build a simultaneous expandable message $\mathcal{M}$ for $\mathcal{H}_1$ and $\mathcal{H}_2$ ending with $(\hat{x}, \hat{y})$.

Step B. Collect cyclic nodes within the largest components in functional graphs of $f_1 = h_1(\cdot, m)$ and $f_2 = h_2(\cdot, m)$ with a fixed m, and compute the set of correctable distance bias

$$\mathcal{S} = \{i \cdot \Delta L \mod L_1 \mid i = 0, 1, \ldots, \#C\},$$

---

^{5} With very low probability L_1 and L_2 are not co-prime, and large t will result in repeated values.

where L_1 and L_2 are cycle length of the largest components in the functional graphs of f_1 and f_2 respectively and $\Delta L = L_2 - L_1 \mod L_1$.

Step C. Find a set of tuples $\{(\bar{x}_1, \bar{y}_1, \bar{m}_1), (\bar{x}_2, \bar{y}_2, \bar{m}_2), \ldots\}$ such that $\bar{x}_i$'s and $\bar{y}_j$'s are cyclic nodes within the largest components in functional graphs of f_1 and f_2 respectively, and $h_1(\bar{x}_i, \bar{m}_i) \oplus h_2(\bar{y}_i, \bar{m}_i) = V$, where V is the target hash digest.

Step D. Find a message $M_{\text{link}} = m_r \| m^d$ that links $(\hat{x}, \hat{y})$ to some $(\bar{x}_i, \bar{y}_i)$. For each pair $(x_r = h_1(\hat{x}, m_r), y_r = h_2(\hat{y}, m_r))$ that encounters $(\bar{x}_i, \bar{y}_i)$, compute the distance difference and examine whether it belongs to $\mathcal{S}$.

Up to now, we are able to derive a message M_e from expandable message with an appropriate length, and produce a preimage message M:

$$(IV_1, IV_2) \xrightarrow{M_e} (\hat{x}, \hat{y}) \xrightarrow{M_{\text{link}}} (\bar{x}_i, \bar{y}_i) \xrightarrow{\bar{m}_i} (\mathcal{H}_1(M), \mathcal{H}_2(M)) : \mathcal{H}_1(M) \oplus \mathcal{H}_2(M) = V$$

By balancing the complexities of these steps, we obtain an optimal complexity of $2^{5n/8}$.

A completed description of attack procedure and complexity evaluation is provided in next sections (Fig. 8). We point out the length of our preimage is at least $2^{n/2}$ block long due to the usage of (multi-) cycles.

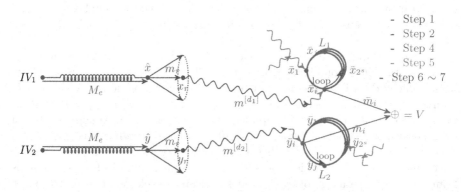

Fig. 8. Preimage attack on the XOR hash combiner $\mathcal{H}_1(M) \oplus \mathcal{H}_2(M)$

4.2   Attack Procedure

Denote by V the target hash digest. Suppose the attacker is going to produce a preimage message with a length L. The value of L will be discussed later. The attack procedure is described below.

1. Build a simultaneous expandable message structure $\mathcal{M}$ ending with a pair of state $(\hat{x}, \hat{y})$ such that for each positive integer i of an integer interval,

there is a message M_i with a block length i in $\mathcal{M}$ that links (IV_1, IV_2) to $(\hat{x}, \hat{y})$:

$$h_1^i(IV_1, M_i) = \hat{x}, \qquad\qquad h_2^i(IV_2, M_i) = \hat{y}.$$

Refer to Sect. 2.5 and [7] for more descriptions of the procedure.

2. Fix a single-block message m, and construct two n-bit to n-bit random mappings as $f_1(x) = h_1(x, m)$ and $f_2(y) = h_2(y, m)$. Repeat the cycle search several times, and find all the cyclic nodes within the largest components in the functional graphs defined by f_1 and f_2. Denote their cycle lengths as L_1 and L_2, and the two sets of cyclic nodes as $\{x_1, x_2, \ldots, x_{L_1}\}$ and $\{y_1, y_2, \ldots, y_{L_2}\}$, and store them in tables $\mathcal{T}_1$ and $\mathcal{T}_2$, respectively.

3. Without loss of generality, assume $L_1 \leq L_2$. Compute $\#C = \lfloor L/L_1 \rfloor$ as the maximum number of cycles that can be used to correct distance bias. Compute $\Delta L = L_2 \mod L_1$, and then compute the set of correctable distance bias: $\mathcal{S} = \{i \cdot \Delta L \mod L_1 \mid i = 0, 1, 2, \ldots, \#C\}$.

4. Find a set of 2^s tuples $(\bar{x}, \bar{y}, \bar{m})$ such that $h_1(\bar{x}, \bar{m}) \oplus h_2(\bar{y}, \bar{m}) = V$. The search procedure is described as follows.

   (a) Initialize a table $\mathcal{T}_3$ as empty.

   (b) Select a random single-block message $\bar{m}$.

   (c) Compute $h_1(x_i, \bar{m})$ for all x_i's in $\mathcal{T}_1$, and store them in a table $\mathcal{T}_4$.

   (d) For each y_j in $\mathcal{T}_2$, compute $h_2(y_j, \bar{m}) \oplus V$, and match it to the elements in $\mathcal{T}_4$. If it is matched to some $h_1(x_i, \bar{m})$, that is

   $$h_2(y_j, \bar{m}) \oplus V = h_1(x_i, \bar{m}) \implies h_1(x_i, \bar{m}) \oplus h_2(y_j, \bar{m}) = V,$$

   store $(x_i, y_j, \bar{m})$ in $\mathcal{T}_3$.

   (e) If $\mathcal{T}_3$ contains less than 2^s elements, goto step 4(b) and repeat the search procedure.

   Denote the stored tuples in $\mathcal{T}_3$ as $\{(\bar{x}_1, \bar{y}_1, \bar{m}_1), \ldots, (\bar{x}_{2^s}, \bar{y}_{2^s}, \bar{m}_{2^s})\}$. Moreover, $\bar{x}_i$'s and $\bar{y}_j$'s are called *target nodes* in functional graphs of f_1 and f_2 respectively.

5. Run Algorithm 1 with a parameter t to develop 2^t nodes in the functional graph of f_1 (resp. f_2), and store them in a table $\mathcal{T}_{4x}$ (resp. $\mathcal{T}_{4y}$). Moreover,

   (a) Store at each node its distance from a particular target node (say target node $\bar{x}_1$ (resp. $\bar{y}_1$), similar to phase 3 in Sect. 3.3 of [7]), together with its distance from the cycle (i.e. its height, similar to phase 3 in Sect. 5 of [32]).

   (b) Store the distance of other target nodes $\bar{x}_i$ (resp. $\bar{y}_i$) to this particular target node $\bar{x}_1$ (resp. $\bar{y}_1$) in a table $\mathcal{T}_{3x}$ (resp. $\mathcal{T}_{3y}$) by iterating f_1 (resp. f_2) along the cycle.

   (c) Thus, when the distance of a node from the particular target node and that from the cycle is known from $\mathcal{T}_{4x}$ (resp. $\mathcal{T}_{4y}$), the distances of this node from all the other target nodes can be immediately deduced from $\mathcal{T}_{3x}$ (resp. $\mathcal{T}_{3y}$). Specifically, suppose the distance of a node x_r from $\bar{x}_1$ is d_1 and its height is e_1, and suppose the distance of a target node $\bar{x}_i$ from $\bar{x}_1$ is d_i, then the distance of x_r from $\bar{x}_i$ is $d_1 - d_i$ if $d_i \leq (d_1 - e_1)$, and $L_1 - d_i + d_1$ if $d_i > (d_1 - e_1)$.

6. Find a message M_{link} that links $(\hat{x}, \hat{y})$ to a pair of target nodes $(\bar{x}_i, \bar{y}_i)$ in $\mathcal{T}_3$. We search for such a linking message among a set of special messages: $M_{\text{link}} = m_r \| m \| m \| \cdots \| m$, where m_r is a random single-block message, and m is the fixed message at Step 2. The search procedure is as follows.

   (a) Select a random m_r, and compute $x_r = h_1(\hat{x}, m_r)$ and $y_r = h_2(\hat{y}, m_r)$;

   (b) Compute a chain by iteratively applying f_1 (resp. f_2) to update x_r (resp. y_r), until either of the following two cases occurs.

   - The chain length reaches 2^{n-t}. In this case, goto step 6(a);
   - The chain encounters a node stored in $\mathcal{T}_{4x}$ (resp. $\mathcal{T}_{4y}$). Compute the distance of x_r (resp. y_r) to every target node $\bar{x}_i$ (resp. $\bar{y}_i$) as described in step 5(c), and denote it as dx_i (resp. dy_i).

   (c) Examine whether $dx_i - dy_i \bmod L_1$ is a correctable distance difference in $\mathcal{S}$. If it is, derive the corresponding j and k such that $dx_i + j \cdot L_1 = dy_i + k \cdot L_2$ holds. Let p be $p = dx_i + j \cdot L_1 = dy_j + k \cdot L_2$, and then $M_{\text{link}} = m_r \| m^p$. Otherwise, goto step 6(a).

7. Derive a message M_{L-2-p} with a block length of $L - 2 - p$ from the expandable message $\mathcal{M}$.

8. Produce a preimage M of the target hash digest V as

$$M = M_{L-2-p} \| M_{\text{link}} \| \bar{m}_i = M_{L-2-p} \| m_r \| m^p \| \bar{m}_i.$$

4.3   Attack Complexity

This subsection evaluates the attack complexity. In particular, we note that we ignore the constant and polynomial factors for the simplicity of description.

- Step 1: $L + n^2 \cdot 2^{n/2}$ (refer to Sect. 2.5);
- Step 2: $2^{n/2}$;
- Step 3: $L/L_1 \approx 2^{-n/2} \cdot L$;
- Step 4: $2^{s+n/2}$;

   One execution of the search procedure takes a complexity of $L_1 + L_2$, and contributes to $L_1 \cdot L_2$ pairs. As $L_1 \cdot L_2 = \Theta(2^n)$, one tuple can be obtained by a constant number of executions. Hence, the number of necessary executions is $\Theta(2^s)$, and the complexity of this step is $\Theta(2^{s+n/2})$.

- Step 5: $2^t + 2^{n/2}$;

   The complexity of developing 2^t nodes and computing their distance to a particular target node is 2^t (refer to Algorithm 1 and step 5(a)). The complexity to compute the distance of all the other target nodes to the particular target node is upper bounded by $2^{n/2}$ (refer to the number of cyclic nodes in Theorem 1). Hence, the complexity of this step is $2^t + 2^{n/2}$.

- Step 6: $2^{2n-t-s}/L$;

   One execution of the search procedure needs a time complexity of 2^{n-t}. Clearly a constant factor of both of the two chains encounter nodes stored in $\mathcal{T}_{4x}$ and $\mathcal{T}_{4y}$ which are of size 2^t. We mainly need to evaluate the probability of deriving a common distance for each chain. For every pair of target nodes $(\bar{x}_i, \bar{y}_i)$, the value of $dx_i - dy_i$ is equal to a correctable distance bias in $\mathcal{S}$ with a probability of $\#C \cdot 2^{-n/2} \approx L \cdot 2^{-n}$. Since there are 2^s pairs of target nodes, the success probability of each chain is $L \cdot 2^{s-n}$. Hence, the total number of chains is $2^{n-s}/L$, and the complexity of this step is $2^{n-t} \cdot 2^{n-s}/L = 2^{2n-t-s}/L$.

- Steps 7 and 8: $\mathcal{O}(L)$.

The overall complexity is computed as

$$L + 2^{s+n/2} + 2^t + 2^t + 2^{n/2} + \frac{2^{2n-t-s}}{L},$$

where the complexities of steps 2, 7 and 8 are ignored.

Now we search for parameters L, t and s that give the lowest complexity. Firstly, we balance the complexities between Step 1 and Step 6, that gives

$$L = \frac{2^{2n-t-s}}{L} \quad \Longrightarrow \quad L = 2^{n-t/2-s/2}$$

Hence, the total complexity becomes (ignoring constant factors)

$$2^{n-t/2-s/2} + 2^{s+n/2} + 2^t + 2^{n/2}.$$

By balancing the complexities, we have that setting parameters $t = 2^{5n/8}$ and $s = 2^{n/8}$ contributes to the lowest complexities: $2^{5n/8}$. In the setting, we produce a preimage message with a length of $L = 2^{n-t/2-s/2} = 2^{5n/8}$.

5   Second Preimage Attacks on Zipper Hash

In this section, we give a second preimage attack on Zipper hash, which is also applicable for *idealized* compression functions.

5.1   Attack Overview

Given a message $M = m_1 \| m_2 \| \cdots \| m_L$, the second preimage attack on Zipper hash is to find another message M' such that $\mathcal{H}_2(\mathcal{H}_1(IV, M), \overleftarrow{M}) = \mathcal{H}_2(\mathcal{H}_1(IV, M'), \overleftarrow{M'})$, where $\overleftarrow{M}$ is a message generated by reversing the order of message blocks of M (we call $\overleftarrow{M}$ the reverse of M for simplicity), *i.e.*, $\overleftarrow{M} = m_L \| m_{L-1} \| \cdots \| m_2 \| m_1$, and $\overleftarrow{M'}$ is the reverse of M'.

In contrast to the attack against XOR combiner, here we make use of a single pair of target α-nodes $(\bar{x}, \bar{y})$, that are the roots of the largest trees within the largest components in functional graphs defined by h_1 and h_2 and a fixed single-block message value m, and then proceed as follows.

Step A. Compute a multi-collision $\mathcal{M}_1$ (resp. $\mathcal{M}_2$) from $\bar{x}$ (resp. $\bar{y}$) as the starting value to an ending value denoted as $\hat{x}$ (resp. $\hat{y}$).

Step B. Build a simultaneous expandable message $\mathcal{M}_e$ across the two passes, starting from $\hat{x}$ to an ending value denoted as $\tilde{y}$.

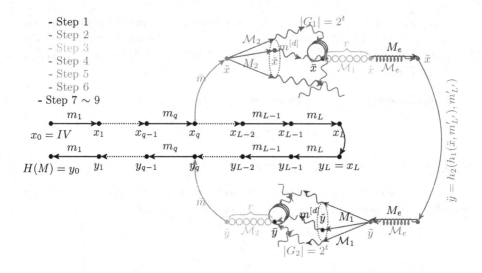

Fig. 9. Second preimage attack on Zipper hash

Step C. Find $\bar{m}$ linking $\hat{y}$ to one of the chaining values y_q of the second pass of the original message, and then compute from x_q with $\bar{m}$ to an internal value denoted as $\tilde{x}$ in the first pass.

Step D. Exploit the messages of $\mathcal{M}_2$ and $\mathcal{M}_1$ to link $\tilde{x}$ and $\tilde{y}$ to $\bar{x}$ and $\bar{y}$, respectively, at a common distance.

Finally, we just need to derive a message with a suitable length from $\mathcal{M}_e$ to contribute to a second preimage message. There are two main differences between the attack on Zipper hash and the attack on the XOR combiner in Sect. 4. One is that linking $\tilde{x}$ to $\bar{x}$ and linking $\tilde{y}$ to $\bar{y}$ can be carried out independently, resulting in a meet-in-the-middle like effect. The other is that the message length is embedded inside the expandable message $\mathcal{M}_e$, which enables us to choose the length of second preimage message to optimize the complexity. Details of the attack are presented in the next sections (Fig. 9).

5.2   Attack Procedure

In the attack procedure below, we omit the description of using multi-cycles to correct distance bias for the simplicity of description. We note that multi-cycles should be used at Steps 6 and 7, which provides extra degrees of freedom, in the case that the message length is allowed beyond the birthday bound.

1. Fix an arbitrary single-block message value m, and construct $f_1(\cdot) = h_1(\cdot, m)$ and $f_2(\cdot) = h_2(\cdot, m)$. Repeat the cycle search several times to locate the largest tree and corresponding α-node in functional graph of f_1 (resp. f_2) and denote it by $\bar{x}$ (resp. $\bar{y}$).

2. Run Algorithm 1 with a parameter t to develop 2^t nodes, compute and store their distance from $\bar{x}$ (resp. $\bar{y}$) in functional graph of f_1 (resp. f_2). Store these nodes of f_1 (resp. f_2) in the data structure G_1 (resp. G_2). The role of G_1 (resp. G_2) is to reduce the number of evaluations of f_1 (resp. f_2) to find the distance of a random starting node from the target node $\bar{x}$ (resp. $\bar{y}$) at Step 6 and Step 7. This is similar to the lookahead procedure of phase 3 in Sect. 3.3 of [7].

3. Build a Joux's multi-collision of size 2^r for h_1 (resp. h_2) starting from $\bar{x}$ (resp. $\bar{y}$) and ending at a node $\hat{x}$ (resp. $\hat{y}$). Denote the multi-collision message set by $\mathcal{M}_1$ (resp. $\mathcal{M}_2$).

4. Construct a simultaneous expandable message $\mathcal{M}_e$ across the two hash functions, which starts from the node $\hat{x}$ in the first pass and ends at a node $\tilde{y}$ in the second pass. The details of constructing such an expandable message is provided in Sect. 5.3.

5. Find a single-block $\bar{m}$ that links $\hat{y}$ to some internal state y_q of the second pass on computing the original message M. The search procedure is trivial and hence omitted. Compute $\tilde{x} = h_1(x_q, \bar{m})$.

6. For each message M_2 in $\mathcal{M}_2$,
   (a) Compute $\check{x} = h_1^r(\tilde{x}, M_2)$;
   (b) Compute a chain $\boldsymbol{x}$ by applying f_1 to update $\check{x}$ iteratively until up to a maximum length 2^{n-t} or until it hits G_1. In the latter case, compute the distance d_1 of $\check{x}$ to $\bar{x}$, and store (d_1, M_2) in a table $\mathcal{T}_1$.

7. For each message M_1 in $\mathcal{M}_1$,
   (a) Compute $\check{y} = h_2^r(\tilde{y}, M_1)$;
   (b) Compute a chain $\boldsymbol{y}$ by applying f_2 to update $\check{y}$ up to a maximum length 2^{n-t} or until it hits G_2. In the latter case, compute the distance d_2 of $\check{y}$ to $\bar{y}$, and store (d_2, M_1) in a table $\mathcal{T}_2$.

8. Find (d_1, M_2) in $\mathcal{T}_1$ and (d_2, M_1) in $\mathcal{T}_2$ with $d_1 = d_2$. The search is a meet-in-the-middle procedure to match elements between $\mathcal{T}_1$ and $\mathcal{T}_2$.

9. Derive a message M_e with a block length $L' - q - 1 - r - d_2 - r$ from $\mathcal{M}_e$, where L' is the length of the constructed second preimage. Construct a message $M' = m_1 \| m_2 \| \cdots \| m_q \| \bar{m} \| M_2 \| m^{[d_2]} \| M_1 \| M_e$ and output M' as a second preimage.

5.3   Step 4: Constructing an Expandable Message

The constructing method is similar with that proposed in [7] with slight modifications. Detailed steps are as follows and the constructing process is depicted in Fig. 10, where C is set as a constant such that $C \approx n/2 + \log(n)$:

1. $x_0' \leftarrow \hat{x}$
2. For $i \leftarrow 1, 2, \cdots, C - 1 + k$:
   (a) Build a 2^{C-1} standard Joux's multi-collision in h_1 starting from x_{i-1}', denote its final endpoint by sp_i.

(b) Compute $xp_i = h_1(sp_i, \mathbf{0})$, where $\mathbf{0}$ is an all zero message of size s blocks, where $s = i$ if $i \leq C - 1$ and $s = C2^{i-(C-1)-1}$ if $C - 1 < i \leq C - 1 + k$.

(c) Find a collision $h_1(sp_i, m_i) = h_1(xp_i, m'_i)$ with single block messages m_i, m'_i. Denote the collision by x'_i.

(d) We get a multi-collision in h_1 with 2^C messages that map x'_{i-1} to x'_i.

  i. Out of these messages, 2^{C-1} are of length b (obtained by combine one of the 2^{C-1} Joux's multi-collisions with m_i) and we denote this set of messages by SS_i, where $b = C$.

  ii. Out of these messages, 2^{C-1} are of length b (obtained by combine one of the 2^{C-1} Joux's multi-collisions with $\mathbf{0}\|m'_i$) and we denote this set of messages by SL_i, where $b = C + i$ if $i \leq C - 1$ and $b = C(2^{i-(C-1)-1} + 1)$ if $C - 1 < i \leq C - 1 + k$.

3. Denote the last collision state x'_{C-1+k} by $\ddot{x}$, and compute $\ddot{y} = h_2(h_1(\ddot{x}, m'_{L'}), m'_{L'})$, where $m'_{L'}$ is a message block padded with the length L' of the second preimage.

4. $y'_{C-1+k} \leftarrow \ddot{y}$, $MS \leftarrow \emptyset$, $ML \leftarrow \emptyset$.

5. For $i \leftarrow C - 1 + k$, $C - 1 + k - 1$, $\ldots$, 2, 1:

(a) For each $\boldsymbol{ms}_i \in SS_i$, compute $u_i = h_2(y'_i, \overleftarrow{\boldsymbol{ms}}_i)$ where $\boldsymbol{ms}_i = ms_{i,1}\|ms_{i,2}\|\ldots\|ms_{i,C-1}\|ms_{i,C}$ and $\overleftarrow{\boldsymbol{ms}}_i = ms_{i,C}\|ms_{i,C-1}\|\ldots\|ms_{i,1}$. Store each pair $(u_i, \boldsymbol{ms}_i)$ in a table U_i indexed by u_i. The final size of U_i is 2^{C-1}.

(b) For each $\boldsymbol{ml}_i \in SL_i$, compute $v_i = h_2(y'_i, \overleftarrow{\boldsymbol{ml}}_i)$ where $\boldsymbol{ml}_i = ml_{i,1}\|ml_{i,2}\|\ldots\|ml_{i,s-1}\|ml_{i,s}$ and $\overleftarrow{\boldsymbol{ml}}_i = ml_{i,s}\|ml_{i,s-1}\|\ldots\|ml_{i,1}$. Where $s = C(2^{i-(C-1)-1} + 1)$ if $C - 1 < i \leq C - 1 + k$ and $s = C + i$ if $1 \leq i \leq C - 1$. Store each pair $(v_i, \boldsymbol{ml}_i)$ in a table V_i indexed by v_i. The final size of V_i is 2^{C-1}.

(c) Find a match $u_i = v_i$ between U_i and V_i, denote the matched state by $y'_{i-1} = u_i$. Combine the corresponding message fragment $\boldsymbol{ms}_i$ indexed by y'_i with MS and $\boldsymbol{ml}_i$ indexed by y'_i with ML, i.e. $MS = \boldsymbol{ms}_i\|MS$ and $ML = \boldsymbol{ml}_i\|ML$.

Then, for any length κ lying in the appropriate range of $[C(C-1)+kC, C^2 - 1 + C(2^k + k - 1)]$, one can construct a message M_e mapping $\hat{x}$ to $\tilde{y} = y'_0$ through h_1 and h_2 by picking messages fragment either from MS or from ML as described in [7]:

1. Select the length $\kappa' \in [C(C-1), C^2 - 1]$ such that $\kappa' = \kappa \bmod C$, defining the first $C - 1$ message fragment choices: Selecting the message fragment $\boldsymbol{ms}_i$ in MS for $1 \leq i \leq C - 1$ and $i \neq \kappa' - C$; Selecting the message fragment $\boldsymbol{ml}_i$ in ML for $i = \kappa' - C$.

2. Compute $kp \leftarrow (\kappa - \kappa')/C$ which is an integer in the range of $[k, 2^k + k - 1]$ and select the final k message fragment choices as in a standard expandable message using the binary representation of $kp - k$.

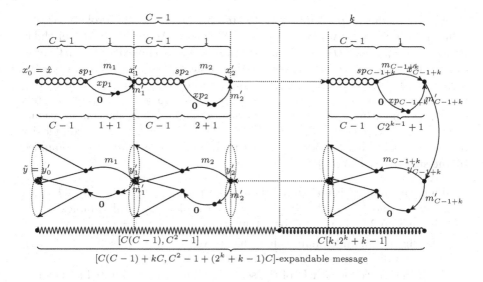

Fig. 10. Flowchart of constructing a simultaneous expandable message

5.4 Complexity of Second Preimage Attack on Zipper Hash

The computational complexity of this second preimage attack on Zipper hash are summarized as follows, where the constant and polynomial factors are ignored.

- Step 1: $2^{\frac{n}{2}}$
- Step 2: $2 \cdot 2^t$
- Step 3: $r \cdot 2^{\frac{n}{2}}$
- Step 4: $n \cdot 2^k + n^2 \cdot 2^{\frac{n}{2}+\log_2(n)} = 2^{l'} + 2^{\frac{n}{2}+2\log_2(n)+1}$
- Step 5: 2^{n-l}
- Step 6: $2^r \cdot 2^{n-t}$
- Step 7: $2^r \cdot 2^{n-t}$
- Step 8: 2^r
- Step 9: $\mathcal{O}(2^{l'})$

It is required to sample 2^{2n-3w} different starting point pairs until they simultaneously hit two α-nodes $(\bar{x}, \bar{y})$ using up to 2^w iterates in two independent functional graphs of f_1 and f_2, where w is the allowed maximum distance to reach $\bar{x}$ and $\bar{y}$, which is determined by the allowed length L' of the second preimage, and is set to be $L' - q - 2r - C(C-1) - kC$. Thus, the number of messages in $\mathcal{M}_1$ which is set to be 2^r and that in $\mathcal{M}_2$ which is also set to be 2^r should satisfy $2^r \times 2^r = 2^{2n-3w} \approx 2^{2n-3l'}$, then $2^r \approx 2^{n-\frac{3}{2}l'}$.

The computational complexity is dominated by Step 2, 4, 5, 6, 7. In Step 2, we develop 2^t nodes for each functional graph of f_1 and f_2. So it requires $2 \cdot 2^t$ function calls. In Step 4, we build a simultaneous expandable message by a slightly modified constructing method proposed in [7]. The complexity is almost the same as that in [7]. We refer to [7] for the detailed discussion on the complexity of this step. Complexity of Step 5 depends on the probability of a collision $h_2(\bar{y}, \bar{m}) = y_q$ where y_q has $L = 2^l$ choices. According to the birthday paradox, it requires $2^n/L = 2^{n-l}$ trails for a collision. Complexity of Step 6 (resp. Step 7) depends on the number of starting point $\check{x}$ (resp. $\check{y}$) and the expected number of iterates before the chain $\boldsymbol{x}$ (resp. $\boldsymbol{y}$) hits G_1 (resp. G_2). Considering that the size of G_1 (resp. G_2) is 2^t, it is expected to require 2^{n-t} iterates before a chain hits a point in G_1 starting from a random point. Thus, the computational complexity of Step 6 (resp. Step 7) is $r \cdot 2^r + 2^r \cdot 2^{n-t} = \Theta(2^r \cdot 2^{n-t})$. Complexity of Step 8 depends on numbers of entries in T_1 and T_2 which are upper bounded by the size of $\mathcal{M}_1$ and $\mathcal{M}_2$.

- When the allowed length L' of the second preimage is limited by $2^{\frac{n}{2}}$, then $2^w \approx 2^{l'}$ and $2^r = 2^{n-\frac{3}{2}w} \approx 2^{n-\frac{3}{2}l'}$. To achieve optimal complexity, we balance Step 2 and Step 6, 7 by setting $t = r + n - t \Rightarrow t = n - \frac{3}{4}l'$. We set l' to be the allowed maximum value, that is we set $2^{l'} = 2^{\frac{n}{2}} \Rightarrow 2^t = 2^{\frac{5}{8}n}$. This attack is valid and faster than 2^n as long as $l < n$.

- When the allowed length L' of the second preimage is not limited and can be greater than $2^{\frac{n}{2}}$, we utilize multi-cycles to reach $\bar{x}$ and $\bar{y}$ simultaneously as the technique used to improve preimage attack on XOR combiner in Sect. 4. In this case, we set $r = \frac{\frac{n}{2}-(l'-\frac{n}{2})}{2}$. That is because, the number of pairs $(\check{x}, \check{y})$ is 2^{2r}, and the required number of pairs to find one pair simultaneously reaching $(\bar{x}, \bar{y})$ is $2^{2n-\frac{3n}{2}}/2^{l'-\frac{n}{2}}$ when multi-cycles are used to amplify the probability of linking each pair to $(\bar{x}, \bar{y})$ at a common distance. Thus, we set $2r = 2n - \frac{3n}{2} - (l' - \frac{n}{2}) \Rightarrow r = \frac{\frac{n}{2}-(l'-\frac{n}{2})}{2}$.

  • For $\frac{3}{8}n < l \le \frac{2}{5}n$, we can set $l' = n - l$. And balance Step 2 and Step 6, 7 by setting $t = r + n - t = \frac{\frac{n}{2}-(l'-\frac{n}{2})}{2} + n - t = \frac{l}{2} + n - t \Rightarrow t = \frac{l}{4} + \frac{n}{2}$. Since $l \le \frac{2}{5}n$, one have $t = \frac{l}{4} + \frac{n}{2} \le n - l$. Thus, complexity of Step 5, i.e. 2^{n-l}, is the dominating part.

  • For $\frac{2}{5}n < l$, we set $l' = \frac{3}{5}n$ and limit $q < l' = \frac{3}{5}n$ where q is the merged point of the second message to the state chain of the original message. And balance Step 2 and Step 6, 7 by setting $t = \frac{\frac{n}{2}-(l'-\frac{n}{2})}{2} + n - t = \Rightarrow t = \frac{3}{5}n$. Thus, keep a stable complexity $2^{\frac{2}{5}n}$ for attack on messages of length $l > \frac{2}{5}n$.

A trade-off curve for these cases is shown in Fig. 11. In these attacks, length of the constructed second message L' is $2^{n/2}$ when limit on length of message is $2^{n/2}$, or $l' = n - l$ for $\frac{3}{8}n < l \le \frac{2}{5}n$ and $l' = \frac{3}{5}n$ for $\frac{2}{5}n < l$ when no limit on length of message.

Remark 1. We notice that, when $l < \frac{2}{5}n$, the complexity of this second preimage attack on Zipper hash is dominated by Step 5. Thus, in this case the strength of Zipper Hash (with each pass using Merkle-Damgård-structure compression functions) against second preimage attack is no more than that of a single pass Merkle-Damgård-structure Hash function.

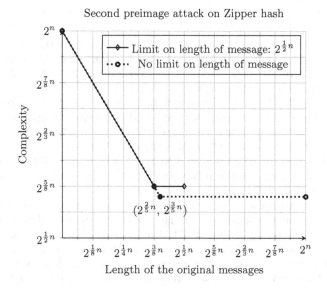

Fig. 11. Trade-offs between the message length and the complexity

5.5 Experimental Results

We have simulated the entire process of this second preimage attack on Zipper hash (simulated h_1 with chopped AES-128 and h_2 with chopped SM4-128) for $n = 24$ and $n = 32$ with $t = \frac{5}{8}n$, $r = \frac{1}{4}n + 1$. In our simulations we preformed 1000 times attack for $n = 24$ and 100 times for $n = 32$. The success probability is 0.684 for $n = 24$ and is 0.8 for $n = 32$. The number of function calls for each step in those attacks are all as expected.

6 Conclusion

In this paper, we proposed the first second-preimage attack on Zipper hash and improved preimage attack on the XOR combiner with two narrow-pipe Merkle-Damgård hash functions. These attacks are based on functional graph of a random mapping. A future work might be to further investigate properties of functional graph in order to improve generic attacks on hash combiners, e.g., reducing the complexity of generic attacks to match the lower security bounds, or shortening the length of (second) preimage messages.

Acknowledgments. Lei Wang and Dawu Gu are sponsored by National Natural Science Foundation of China (61602302, 61472250, 61672347), Natural Science Foundation of Shanghai (16ZR1416400), Shanghai Excellent Academic Leader Funds (16XD1401300). The authors would like to thank the anonymous reviewers of CRYPTO 2017 for their comments and suggestions.

References

1. Aceto, L., Damgård, I., Goldberg, L.A., Halldórsson, M.M., Ingólfsdóttir, A., Walukiewicz, I. (eds.): ICALP 2008. LNCS, vol. 5126. Springer, Heidelberg (2008)
2. Allen, C., Dierks, T.: The TLS Protocol Version 1.0. RFC 2246, January 1999. https://rfc-editor.org/rfc/rfc2246.txt
3. Andreeva, E., Bouillaguet, C., Dunkelman, O., Kelsey, J.: Herding, second preimage and trojan message attacks beyond Merkle-Damgård. In: Jacobson, M.J., Rijmen, V., Safavi-Naini, R. (eds.) SAC 2009. LNCS, vol. 5867, pp. 393–414. Springer, Heidelberg (2009). doi:10.1007/978-3-642-05445-7_25
4. Brassard, G. (ed.): CRYPTO 1989. LNCS, vol. 435. Springer, New York (1990)
5. Chen, S., Jin, C.: A second preimage attack on Zipper hash. Secur. Commun. Netw. **8**(16), 2860–2866 (2015)
6. Damgård, I.: A design principle for hash functions. In: Brassard [4], pp. 416–427
7. Dinur, I.: New attacks on the concatenation and XOR hash combiners. In: Fischlin, M., Coron, J.-S. (eds.) EUROCRYPT 2016, Part I. LNCS, vol. 9665, pp. 484–508. Springer, Heidelberg (2016). doi:10.1007/978-3-662-49890-3_19
8. Dinur, I., Leurent, G.: Improved generic attacks against hash-based MACs and HAIFA. In: Garay, J.A., Gennaro, R. (eds.) CRYPTO 2014, Part I. LNCS, vol. 8616, pp. 149–168. Springer, Heidelberg (2014). doi:10.1007/978-3-662-44371-2_9
9. Fischlin, M., Lehmann, A.: Security-amplifying combiners for collision-resistant hash functions. In: Menezes, A. (ed.) CRYPTO 2007. LNCS, vol. 4622, pp. 224–243. Springer, Heidelberg (2007). doi:10.1007/978-3-540-74143-5_13
10. Fischlin, M., Lehmann, A.: Multi-property preserving combiners for hash functions. In: Canetti, R. (ed.) TCC 2008. LNCS, vol. 4948, pp. 375–392. Springer, Heidelberg (2008). doi:10.1007/978-3-540-78524-8_21
11. Fischlin, M., Lehmann, A., Pietrzak, K.: Robust multi-property combiners for hash functions revisited. In: Aceto et al., [1], pp. 655–666
12. Fischlin, M., Lehmann, A., Pietrzak, K.: Robust multi-property combiners for hash functions. J. Cryptol. **27**(3), 397–428 (2014)
13. Flajolet, P., Odlyzko, A.M.: Random mapping statistics. In: Quisquater, J.-J., Vandewalle, J. (eds.) EUROCRYPT 1989. LNCS, vol. 434, pp. 329–354. Springer, Heidelberg (1990). doi:10.1007/3-540-46885-4_34
14. Freier, A.O., Karlton, P., Kocher, P.C.: The Secure Sockets Layer (SSL) Protocol Version 3.0. RFC 6101, August 2011. https://rfc-editor.org/rfc/rfc6101.txt
15. Guo, J., Peyrin, T., Sasaki, Y., Wang, L.: Updates on generic attacks against HMAC and NMAC. In: Garay, J.A., Gennaro, R. (eds.) CRYPTO 2014, Part I. LNCS, vol. 8616, pp. 131–148. Springer, Heidelberg (2014). doi:10.1007/978-3-662-44371-2_8
16. Hellman, M.E.: A cryptanalytic time-memory trade-off. IEEE Trans. Inf. Theory **26**(4), 401–406 (1980)
17. Hoch, J.J., Shamir, A.: Breaking the ICE – finding multicollisions in iterated concatenated and expanded (ICE) hash functions. In: Robshaw, M. (ed.) FSE 2006. LNCS, vol. 4047, pp. 179–194. Springer, Heidelberg (2006). doi:10.1007/11799313_12
18. Hoch, J.J., Shamir, A.: On the strength of the concatenated hash combiner when all the hash functions are weak. In: Aceto et al. [1], pp. 616–630
19. Jha, A., Nandi, M.: Some Cryptanalytic Results on Zipper Hash and Concatenated Hash. Cryptology ePrint Archive, Report 2015/973 (2015). http://eprint.iacr.org/2015/973

20. Joux, A.: Multicollisions in iterated hash functions. application to cascaded constructions. In: Franklin, M. (ed.) CRYPTO 2004. LNCS, vol. 3152, pp. 306–316. Springer, Heidelberg (2004). doi:10.1007/978-3-540-28628-8_19

21. Kelsey, J., Schneier, B.: Second preimages on n-bit hash functions for much less than 2^n work. In: Cramer, R. (ed.) EUROCRYPT 2005. LNCS, vol. 3494, pp. 474–490. Springer, Heidelberg (2005). doi:10.1007/11426639_28

22. Lehmann, A.: On the security of hash function combiners. Ph.D. thesis, Darmstadt University of Technology (2010)

23. Leurent, G., Peyrin, T., Wang, L.: New generic attacks against hash-based MACs. In: Sako, K., Sarkar, P. (eds.) ASIACRYPT 2013, Part II. LNCS, vol. 8270, pp. 1–20. Springer, Heidelberg (2013). doi:10.1007/978-3-642-42045-0_1

24. Leurent, G., Wang, L.: The sum can be weaker than each part. In: Oswald, E., Fischlin, M. (eds.) EUROCRYPT 2015, Part I. LNCS, vol. 9056, pp. 345–367. Springer, Heidelberg (2015). doi:10.1007/978-3-662-46800-5_14

25. Liskov, M.: Constructing an ideal hash function from weak ideal compression functions. In: Biham, E., Youssef, A.M. (eds.) SAC 2006. LNCS, vol. 4356, pp. 358–375. Springer, Heidelberg (2007). doi:10.1007/978-3-540-74462-7_25

26. Mendel, F., Rechberger, C., Schläffer, M.: MD5 is weaker than weak: attacks on concatenated combiners. In: Matsui, M. (ed.) ASIACRYPT 2009. LNCS, vol. 5912, pp. 144–161. Springer, Heidelberg (2009). doi:10.1007/978-3-642-10366-7_9

27. Merkle, R.C.: One way hash functions and DES. In: Brassard [4], pp. 428–446

28. Nandi, M., Stinson, D.R.: Multicollision attacks on some generalized sequential hash functions. IEEE Trans. Inf. Theory 53(2), 759–767 (2007)

29. van Oorschot, P.C., Wiener, M.J.: Parallel collision search with cryptanalytic applications. J. Cryptol. 12(1), 1–28 (1999)

30. Perrin, L., Khovratovich, D.: Collision spectrum, entropy loss, T-sponges, and cryptanalysis of GLUON-64. In: Cid, C., Rechberger, C. (eds.) FSE 2014. LNCS, vol. 8540, pp. 82–103. Springer, Heidelberg (2015). doi:10.1007/978-3-662-46706-0_5

31. Peyrin, T., Sasaki, Y., Wang, L.: Generic related-key attacks for HMAC. In: Wang, X., Sako, K. (eds.) ASIACRYPT 2012. LNCS, vol. 7658, pp. 580–597. Springer, Heidelberg (2012). doi:10.1007/978-3-642-34961-4_35

32. Peyrin, T., Wang, L.: Generic universal forgery attack on iterative hash-based MACs. In: Nguyen, P.Q., Oswald, E. (eds.) EUROCRYPT 2014. LNCS, vol. 8441, pp. 147–164. Springer, Heidelberg (2014). doi:10.1007/978-3-642-55220-5_9

Non-full Sbox Linearization: Applications to Collision Attacks on Round-Reduced Keccak

Ling Song[1,2,4], Guohong Liao[1,3], and Jian Guo[1(✉)]

[1] Nanyang Technological University, Singapore, Singapore
songling.alpha@gmail.com, liaogh.cs@gmail.com, ntu.guo@gmail.com
[2] State Key Laboratory of Information Security,
Institute of Information Engineering, Chinese Academy of Sciences, Beijing, China
[3] South China Normal University, Guangzhou, China
[4] Data Assurance and Communication Research Center,
Chinese Academy of Sciences, Beijing, China

Abstract. The Keccak hash function is the winner of the SHA-3 competition and became the SHA-3 standard of NIST in 2015. In this paper, we focus on practical collision attacks against round-reduced Keccak hash function, and two main results are achieved: the first practical collision attacks against 5-round Keccak-224 and an instance of 6-round Keccak collision challenge. Both improve the number of practically attacked rounds by one. These results are obtained by carefully studying the algebraic properties of the nonlinear layer in the underlying permutation of Keccak and applying linearization to it. In particular, techniques for partially linearizing the output bits of the nonlinear layer are proposed, utilizing which attack complexities are reduced significantly from the previous best results.

Keywords: Keccak · SHA-3 · Hash function · Collision · Non-full linearization · Adaptive

1 Introduction

The Keccak hash function [4] was a submission to the SHA-3 competition [19] in 2008. After four years of evaluation, it was selected as the winner of the competition in 2012. In 2015, it was formally standardized by the National Institute of Standards and Technology of the U.S. (NIST) as Secure Hash Algorithm-3 [23]. The SHA-3 family contains four main instances of the Keccak hash function with fixed digest lengths, denoted by Keccak-d with $d \in \{224, 256, 384, 512\}$, and two eXtendable-Output Functions (XOFs) SHAKE128 and SHAKE256. To promote the analysis of the Keccak hash function, the Keccak designers proposed versions with lower security levels in the Keccak Crunchy Crypto Collision and Pre-image Contest (the Keccak challenge for short) [2], for which the digest lengths are 80 and 160 bits for preimage and collision resistance, respectively. For clarity, these variants are denoted by Keccak$[r, c, n_r, d]$ with parameters r, c, n_r, d to be specified later.

© International Association for Cryptologic Research 2017
J. Katz and H. Shacham (Eds.): CRYPTO 2017, Part II, LNCS 10402, pp. 428–451, 2017.
DOI: 10.1007/978-3-319-63715-0_15

Since the KECCAK hash function was made public in 2008, it has attracted intensive cryptanalysis from the community [1, 9–16, 18, 21]. In this paper, we mainly focus on the collision resistance of KECCAK hash function, in particular those collision attacks with practical complexities. In collision attacks, the aim is to find two distinct messages which lead to the same hash digest. Up to date, the best practical collision attacks against KECCAK-224/256 is for 4 out of 24 rounds due to Dinur et al.'s work [10] in 2012. These 4-round collisions were found by combining a 1-round connector and a 3-round differential trail. The same authors gave practical collision attacks for 3-round KECCAK-384/512, and theoretical collision attacks for 5/4-round KECCAK-256/384 in [11] using internal differentials. Following the work of Dinur et al., Qiao et al. [21] further introduced 2-round connectors by adding a fully linearized round to the 1-round connectors, and gave practical collisions for 5-round SHAKE128 and two 5-round instances of the KECCAK collision challenge, as well as collision attack against 5-round KECCAK-224 with theoretical complexities. To the best of our knowledge, there exists neither practical collision attacks against 5-round KEC-CAK-224/256/384/512, nor solution for any 6-round instances of the KECCAK collision challenge.

Our Contributions. We develop techniques of non-full linearizaion for the KECCAK Sbox, upon which two major applications are found. Firstly, improved 2-round connectors are constructed and actual collisions are consequently found for 5-round KECCAK-224. Secondly, we extend the connectors to 3 rounds, and apply it to KECCAK[1440, 160, 6, 160] — a 6-round instance of the KECCAK collision challenge, which leads to the first 6-round real collision of KECCAK.

These results are obtained by combining a differential trail and a connector which links the initial state of KECCAK and the input of the trail. Our work benefits from two observations on linearization of the KECCAK Sbox, which are necessary for building connectors for more than one round. One is to linearize part (not all) of the output bits of a non-active Sbox, at most 2 binary linear equations over the input bits are needed. The other is that, for an active Sbox whose entry in the differential distribution table (DDT) is 8, 4 out of 5 output bits are already linear when the input is chosen from the solution set. Note that to restrict the input to the solution set for such an Sbox, two linear equations of input bits are required, as noted by Dinur et al. in [10]. Therefore, for both non-active and active Sboxes, 2 or less equations can be used to linearize part of the output bits. In this paper, we call it *non-full linearization*. When all output bits of an Sbox need to be linearized, *at least* three equations of input bits are required as shown in [21]. So, the non-full linearization saves degrees of freedom on Sboxes where it is applicable. With this in mind, we apply techniques of non-full linearization to the first round permutation of KECCAK-224, and successfully construct a 2-round connector with a much larger solution space, which brings the collision attack complexity against 5-round KECCAK-224 from 2^{101} down to practise. Applying techniques of non-full linearization to the second round, 3-round connectors are constructed for KECCAK for the first time. Furthermore, adaptive constructions for connectors are proposed to save degrees of freedom, and applied to KECCAK[1440,160,6,160]. In adaptive 3-round connectors, non-full linearization of the second round actually does not consume any degree of freedom, but rather it divides the solution space into subspaces of smaller sizes. This guarantees that sufficiently many message pairs that bypass the first three rounds can be generated such that a colliding pair following the latter 3-round differential trail can be found eventually.

Results obtained in this paper are listed in Table 1, compared with the best previous practical collision attacks and related theoretical attacks.

Table 1. Summary of our attacks and comparison with related works

Target	n_r Rounds	Complexity	Reference
KECCAK-512	3	Practical	[11]
KECCAK-384	3	Practical	[11]
KECCAK-256	4	Practical	[10]
SHAKE128	5	Practical	[21]
KECCAK-224	4	Practical	[10]
	5	2^{101}	[21]
	5	Practical	Sect. 6
KECCAK[1440, 160, 160]	5	Practical	[21]
	6	$2^{70.24}$	[21]
	6	Practical	Sect. 7

Organization. The rest of the paper is organized as follows. In Sect. 2, a brief description of the KECCAK family is given, followed by some notations to be used in this paper. The framework of our collision attacks is sketched in Sect. 3. We propose techniques of non-full linearization in Sect. 4. Section 5 presents GPU implementation of KECCAK for searching differential trails and collisions. Sections 6 and 7 are applications to 5-round KECCAK-224 and KECCAK[1440, 160, 6, 160], respectively. We conclude the paper in Sect. 8.

2   Description of Keccak

2.1   The Sponge Function

The sponge construction is a framework for constructing hash functions from permutations, as depicted in Fig. 1. The construction consists of three components: an underlying b-bit permutation f, a parameter r called rate and a padding rule. A hash function following this construction takes in a message M

as input and outputs a digest of d bits. Given a message M, it is first padded and split into r-bit blocks. The b-bit state is initialized to be all zeros. The sponge construction then proceeds in two phases. In the absorbing phase, each message block is XORed into the first r bits of the state, followed by application of the permutation f. This process is repeated until all message blocks are processed. Then, the sponge construction switches to the squeezing phase. In this phase, each iteration returns the first r bits of the state as output and then applies the permutation f to the current state. This repeats until all d bits digest are obtained.

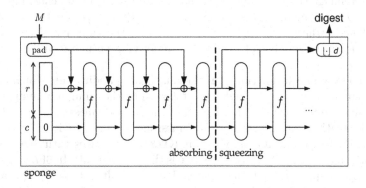

Fig. 1. Sponge construction [3].

2.2 The Keccak Hash Function

The KECCAK hash function follows the sponge construction. The underlying permutation of KECCAK is chosen from a set of seven KECCAK-f permutations, denoted by KECCAK-$f[b]$, where $b \in \{25, 50, 100, 200, 400, 800, 1600\}$ is the width of the permutation in bits. The default KECCAK employs KECCAK-$f[1600]$. The 1600-bit state can be viewed as a 3-dimensional $5 \times 5 \times 64$ array of bits, denoted as $A[5][5][64]$. Let $0 \le i, j < 5$, and $0 \le k < 64$, $A[i][j][k]$ represents one bit of the state at position (i, j, k). Defined by the designers of KECCAK, $A[*][j][k]$ is called a row, $A[i][*][k]$ is a column, and $A[i][j][*]$ is a lane.

The KECCAK-$f[1600]$ permutation has 24 rounds, each of which consists of five mappings $R = \iota \circ \chi \circ \pi \circ \rho \circ \theta$.

$$\theta: \ A[i][j][k] \leftarrow A[i][j][k] + \sum_{j'=0}^{4} A[i-1][j'][k] + \sum_{j'=0}^{4} A[i+1][j'][k-1]$$

$$\rho: \ A[i][j][k] \leftarrow A[i][j][(k+T(i,j))\%64], \text{where } T(i,j) \text{ is a predefined constant}$$

$$\pi: \ A[i][j][k] \leftarrow A[i'][j'][k], \text{where } \begin{pmatrix} i \\ j \end{pmatrix} = \begin{pmatrix} 0 & 1 \\ 2 & 3 \end{pmatrix} \begin{pmatrix} i' \\ j' \end{pmatrix}.$$

$$\chi: \ A[i][j][k] \leftarrow A[i][j][k] + ((A[i+1][j][k]+1) \cdot A[i+2][j][k]),$$

$$\iota: \ A \leftarrow A + RC_{i_r}, \text{where } RC_{i_r} \text{ is the round constants for } i_r\text{-th round.}$$

Here, '+' denotes XOR and '·' denotes logic AND. As ι plays no essential role in our attacks, we will ignore it in the rest of the paper unless otherwise stated.

2.3   Instances of Keccak and SHA-3

There are four instances KECCAK-d of the KECCAK sponge function, where c is chosen to be $2d$ and $d \in \{224, 256, 384, 512\}$. To promote cryptanalysis against KECCAK, the KECCAK design team also proposed versions with lower security levels in the KECCAK challenge, where $b \in \{1600, 800, 400, 200\}$, $(d = 80, c = 160)$ for preimage challenge and $(d = 160, c = 160)$ for collision challenge. In this paper, we follow the designers' notation KECCAK$[r, c, n_r, d]$ for the instances in the challenge, where r is the rate, $c = b - r$ is the capacity, d is the digest size, and n_r is the number of rounds the underlying permutation KECCAK-f is reduced to.

The KECCAK hash function uses the multi-rate padding rule which appends to the original message M a single bit 1 followed by the minimum number of bits 0 and a single bit 1 such that the length of the resulted message is a multiple of the block length r. Namely, the padded message $\overline{M}$ is $M\|10^*1$.

The SHA-3 standard adopts the four KECCAK instances with digest lengths $224, 256, 384$, and 512. The only difference is the padding rule. In SHA-3 standard, the message is appended '01' first. After that, the multi-rate padding is applied. In this paper, we only fucus on collision attacks against 5-round KECCAK-224 and KECCAK$[1440, 160, 6, 160]$.

2.4   Notations

In this paper, only one-block padded messages are considered for collision attacks, i.e., we choose message M such that $\overline{M} = M\|10^*1$ is one block. According to the multi-rate padding rule, the minimal number of padded bits is 2 while the minimal number of fixed padding bit p is 1. The first three mappings θ, π, ρ of the round function are linear, and we denote their composition by $L \triangleq \pi \circ \rho \circ \theta$. The nonlinear layer χ applying to each row is called an Sbox, denoted by $S(\cdot)$. The differential distribution table (DDT) is a 2-dimensional 32×32 array, where all differences are calculated with respect to bitwise XOR. δ_{in} and δ_{out} are used to denote the input and output difference of an Sbox. Then DDT $(\delta_{in}, \delta_{out})$ is the size of the solution set $\{x \mid S(x) + S(x + \delta_{in}) = \delta_{out}\}$. Let $AS(\alpha)$ denote the number of active Sboxes in the state α.

3   The Collision Attack Framework

This section gives an overview of the framework of our collision attacks, and describes our motivations after a brief review of previous works.

In our attacks, as well as two previous related works [10,21], an n_{r_1}-round connector and a high probability n_{r_2}-round differential trail are combined to find collisions for $(n_{r_1} + n_{r_2})$-round KECCAK. Here, an n_{r_1}-*round connector* is defined as a certain procedure which produces message pairs $(\overline{M}_1, \overline{M}_2)$ satisfying three requirements.

(1) The last $(c + p)$-bit difference of the initial state is zeros;
(2) The last $(c + p)$-bit value of the initial state is fixed;
(3) The output difference after n_{r_1} rounds should be fixed and equal to the input difference of the differential trail.

Given an n_{r_2}-round differential, there are two stages of our $(n_{r_1} + n_{r_2})$-round attack, as illustrated in Fig. 2 below:

– *Connecting stage.* Construct an n_{r_1}-round connector and get a subspace of messages bypassing the first n_{r_1} rounds.
– *Brute-force searching stage.* Find a colliding pair following the n_{r_2}-round differential trail from the subspace by brute force.

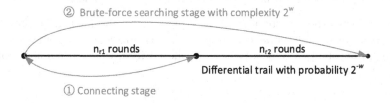

Fig. 2. Overview of $(n_{r_1} + n_{r_2})$-round collision attacks

We use χ_i to represent the nonlinear layer χ at round i. Then the first n_{r_1} rounds of KECCAK can be denoted as

$$\chi_{n_{r_1}-1} \circ L \circ \cdots \circ \chi_0 \circ L.$$

For the differential trail, we denote the differences before and after i-th round by α_i and α_{i+1}, respectively. Let $\beta_i = L(\alpha_i)$, then an n_{r_2}-round differential trail starting from the n_{r_1}-th round is of the following form

$$\alpha_{n_{r_1}} \xrightarrow{L} \beta_{n_{r_1}} \xrightarrow{\chi} \alpha_{n_{r_1}+1} \xrightarrow{L} \cdots \alpha_{n_{r_1}+n_{r_2}-1} \xrightarrow{L} \beta_{n_{r_1}+n_{r_2}-1} \xrightarrow{\chi} \alpha_{n_{r_1}+n_{r_2}}.$$

For the sake of simplicity, a differential trail can also be represented with only β_i's or α_i's. Additionally, let the weight $w_i = -\log_2 \Pr(\beta_i \to \alpha_{i+1})$. For the last round, since only the Sboxes related to the digest matter, we denote the weight and difference for those Sboxes as $w^d_{n_{r_1}+n_{r_2}-1}$ and $\alpha^d_{n_{r_1}+n_{r_2}}$, respectively.

3.1 Dinur et al.'s One-Round Connector

In [10], collisions of 4-round KECCAK-224 and KECCAK-256 are found by combining 1-round connectors and 3-round differential trails. The 1-round connector is implemented by a procedure called *target difference algorithm* which converts the construction of a 1-round connector to solving a system of linear equations. An important property used in the target difference algorithm is as follow.

Property 1. [10] Given a pair of input and output difference $(\delta_{in}, \delta_{out})$ of a KECCAK Sbox such that $\mathtt{DDT}(\delta_{in}, \delta_{out}) \neq 0$, the set of values $V = \{v \mid S(v) + S(v + \delta_{in}) = \delta_{out}\}$ forms an affine subspace.

Note that, any i-dimensional affine subspace of $\{0,1\}^5$ can be deduced from $(5-i)$ linear equations. Now, given an output difference of the first round (or the input difference of a 3-round differential trail), the target difference algorithm proceeds in two phases by adding certain linear equations.

1. Choose a subspace of input differences for each active Sbox which are required to be consistent with the $(c+p)$-bit initial difference. As noted in [10], for any non-zero output difference of a KECCAK Sbox, the set of possible input differences include at least five 2-dimensional affine subspaces.
2. Choose a subspace of input values for each active Sbox which are required to be consistent with the $(c+p)$-bit initial value by selecting an input difference from the difference subspace obtained in the previous phase.

Once a consistent system of linear equations is obtained after processing all active Sboxes, a 1-round connector succeeds and the first round now can be fulfilled automatically if messages are chosen from the solution space of the system.

3.2 Qiao et al.'s Two-Round Connector

In [21], 5-round collisions are found by combining 2-round connectors and 3-round differential trails. These 5-round collisions directly benefit from the 2-round connectors in which the first round is fully linearized. It was noted in [21] that affine subspaces of dimension up to 2 could be found such that the Sbox can be linearized.

Any affine subspace of dimension 2 requires 3 linear equations to be defined. Therefore, at least $\frac{b}{5} \times 3$ degrees of freedom are needed to linearize one full round. Note that the total number of available degrees of freedom is at most $b - (c+p)$. Hence, when the capacity is relatively small, i.e., $c < \frac{2b}{5}$ (omitting the small p), linearization of one full round is possible. Once the first round is linearized, the constraints (linear equations over the values) for the Sbox in the first round and in the second round can be united to construct 2-round connectors.

However, linearizing a full round consumes too many degrees of freedom, which leads to very small message subspaces or even makes the 2-round connector fail. To save degrees of freedom, differential trails which impose least possible conditions to the 2-round connector are more desirable. To this end, a dedicated search strategy was used [21] to find suitable differential trails of up to 4 rounds.

3.3 Directions for Improvements

It can be seen that both Dinur et al.'s original 1-round connectors and Qiao et al.'s 2-round connectors are constructed by processing a system of linear equations. A side effect of these methods, especially linearizing a full round, is a quick reduction of freedom degrees. On the other hand, connectors are possible only when there are sufficient degrees of freedom. Furthermore, the message space returned by the connector needs to be large enough, otherwise no collision can be found. For example, in the collision attack of 5-round KECCAK-224 from [21], a 2-round connector was constructed successfully, however the obtained message space has a dimension of only 2 which is far from being sufficient to find a colliding pair following the 3-round differential trail.

In [21], a 2-round connector was also constructed successfully for KECCAK[1440, 160, 6, 160], and returned a subspace with large enough messages that bypass the first two rounds. However, the complexity of the brute-force stage is $2^{70.24}$, which leaves the attack against KECCAK[1440, 160, 6, 160] impractical.

In order to find practical collisions for both 5-round KECCAK-224 and KECCAK[1440, 160, 6, 160], these remaining problems in the previous work need be solved. There are two directions to this end. The first is to save degrees of freedom and to consume only when necessary. The second is to spend more effort in faster implementations of KECCAK, for finding differential trails which impose less conditions to the connector, as well as speeding up the brute-force stage.

These are our starting point of this paper. The next four sections elaborate on our effort in these two directions which finally results in practical collisions on 5-round KECCAK-224 and KECCAK[1440, 160, 6, 160].

4   Non-full Sbox Linearization

In this section, techniques of non-full linearization are proposed to save degrees of freedom. For convenience, we introduce the techniques in the context of 2-round connectors, even though they can be applied to 3-round connectors or potentially connectors of even more rounds.

4.1   Two Observations

In the construction of a 2-round connector, there are two systems of linear equations, E_M and E_z, which are generated using Property 1. E_M is over the input value x of the nonlinear layer χ_0 of the first round, while E_z is over the input value z of the nonlinear layer χ_1 of the second round. In order to unite these two systems of linear equations to get a 2-round connector, the nonlinear layer χ_0 between them should be linearized. However, the question is whether all Sboxes of χ_0 must be fully linearized? We show below that the answer is no.

Let the output value of χ_0 be y. Then E_z can be re-expressed over y as E_y since $L \cdot (y + RC_0) = z$, where RC_0 is the round constant for the first round. Due to the diffusion of L, E_y is usually denser than E_z. Let $u = (u_0, u_1, \cdots, u_{b-1})$ be a flag vector where $u_i = 1$ $(0 \le i < b)$ if y_i is involved in E_y, otherwise $u_i = 0$. Let $U = (U_0, U_1, \cdots, U_{\frac{b}{5}-1})$ where $U_i = u_{5i}u_{5i+1}u_{5i+2}u_{5i+3}u_{5i+4}$, $0 \le i < \frac{b}{5}$. According to the definition, $0 \le U_i < 2^5$. For the i-th Sbox of χ_0, if U_i is not zero, a.k.a. some bits of the corresponding Sbox are involved in the equation system, this Sbox should be linearized for the union of the two systems of equations.

Note that, it requires at least 3 equations to fully linearize an Sbox. However, the aim of linearization is to unite the two systems of linear equations, which does not necessarily require a full linearization of all Sboxes.

With this intuition in mind, below we show two observations of the KECCAK Sbox which explain the background for the non-full linearization.

Observation 1. *For a non-active* KECCAK *Sbox, when* $U_i \neq 31$,

a. *if* $U_i = 0$, *it does not require any linearization;*
b. *if* $U_i \in \{01,\ 02,\ 04,\ 08,\ 10,\ 03,\ 06,\ 0C,\ 11,\ 18\}$ *(numbers in typewriter font are hexadecimals), at least 1 equation should be added to* E_M *to linearize the output bit(s) of the Sbox marked by* U_i;
c. *otherwise, at least 2 equations should be added to* E_M *to linearize the output bits of the Sbox marked by* U_i.

This observation comes from the algebraic relation between the input and output of χ. Suppose the 5-bit input of the Sbox is $x_0 x_1 x_2 x_3 x_4$ and the 5-bit output $y_0 y_1 y_2 y_3 y_4$. Then the algebraic normal forms of the Sbox are as follows.

$$y_0 = x_0 + (x_1 + 1) \cdot x_2,$$
$$y_1 = x_1 + (x_2 + 1) \cdot x_3,$$
$$y_2 = x_2 + (x_3 + 1) \cdot x_4,$$
$$y_3 = x_3 + (x_4 + 1) \cdot x_0,$$
$$y_4 = x_4 + (x_0 + 1) \cdot x_1.$$

Take $U_i = 01$ as an example. It indicates that y_0 should be linearized. As can be seen, the only nonlinear term in the expression of y_0 is $x_1 \cdot x_2$. Fixing the value of either x_1 or x_2 makes y_0 linear. Without loss of generality, assume the value of x_1 is fixed to be 0 or 1. When $x_1 = 0$, we have $y_0 = x_0 + x_2$; otherwise $y_0 = x_0$. When $U_i = $ 0F, it maps to 4 output bits y_0, y_1, y_2, y_3 and they should be linearized. We can fix the value of two bits x_2 and x_4 only. Once x_2 and x_4 are fixed, the nonlinear terms in the algebraic form of all y_0, y_1, y_2, y_3 will disappear. Other cases work similarly. If $U_i = $ 1F, a full linearization is required by fixing the value of any three input bits which are not cyclically continuous, e.g., (x_0, x_2, x_4).

For the nonlinear layer χ_0 of the first round, most Sboxes are active and many of them have a DDT value of 8. As noted in [21], to fully linearize those Sboxes with DDT of 8, three equations should be added to E_M for each of them. However, Observation 2 shows that two equations may be enough, and thus 1 bit degree of freedom could be saved.

Observation 2. *For a 5-bit input difference* δ_{in} *and a 5-bit output difference* δ_{out} *such that* DDT$(\delta_{in}, \delta_{out}) = 8$, *4 out of 5 output bits are already linear if the input is chosen from the solution set* $V = \{x \mid S(x) + S(x + \delta_{in}) = \delta_{out}\}$.

Take $\text{DDT}(01,01) = 8$ as an example (see Table 6 of [21]). The solution set is $V = \{10,11,14,15,18,19, \ 1C,1D\}$. We rewrite these solutions in 5-bit stings where the right most bit is the LSB as follows.

$$10 : 10000$$
$$11 : 10001$$
$$14 : 10100$$
$$15 : 10101$$
$$18 : 11000$$
$$19 : 11001$$
$$1C : 11100$$
$$1D : 11101$$

It is easy to see for the values from this set, $x_1 = 0$ and $x_4 = 1$ always hold, making y_0, y_2, y_3, y_4 linear since their algebraic forms could be rewritten as

$$y_0 = x_0 + x_2,$$
$$y_1 = (x_2 + 1) \cdot x_3,$$
$$y_2 = x_2 + x_3 + 1,$$
$$y_3 = x_3,$$
$$y_4 = 1.$$

Therefore, if the only nonlinear bit y_1 is not involved in E_y, these two equations $x_1 = 0$ and $x_4 = 1$ are enough for the union. Note that, given the input difference and the output difference, these two equations are used to restrict the input value from $\{0,1\}^5$ to the solution set and have already been included in E_M.

4.2   How to Choose β_1

In both previous works [10,21], those β_1s are chosen such that all Sboxes of $\alpha_1 = L^{-1}(\beta_1)$ are active. This is reasonable since a fully active α_1 makes it easy to find a β_0 that is compatible with α_1 and $(c+p)$-bit zero initial difference. Additionally, if full linearization is applied to every Sbox of χ_0, non-active Sboxes have no advantage over active Sboxes in saving degree of freedoms.

Now non-full linearizations are to be applied. The observations in this section demonstrate that for an Sbox less than 3 equations may be enough for the union. It is likely that non-active Sboxes have advantage over active Sboxes. To extensively exploit the non-full linearization for a larger solution space, it is better to have more non-active Sboxes. Moreover, it is interesting to note that once β_1 is chosen, we can not only calculate the number of non-active Sboxes #nonact of the first round, but also the number of non-active Sboxes which require only 1 or 2 equations for the union. Those non-active Sboxes which require only 1 equation for the union are more interesting. Let the number of them be #save. Large #nonact and #save probably lead to large message subspaces that bypass the first two rounds. However, too many non-active Sboxes will slow down the 2-round connector finding program. This problem will be further discussed when techniques of non-full linearization are applied to concrete instances in latter sections.

5   GPU Implementation of Keccak

In this section, techniques for GPU implementation of KECCAK are introduced to improve our computing capacity over CPU implementations. While one could expect a speed of order 2^{21} KECCAK-f evaluations per second on a single CPU core, we show in this section this number could increase to 2^{29} per second on NVIDIA GeForce GTX1070 graphic card. The significant speedup will benefit us in two usages: searching for differential trails among larger spaces and bruteforce search of collisions from differential trails with lower probability.

5.1   Overview of the GPU and CUDA

GPUs (Graphics Processing Unit) are intended to process the computer graphics and image originally. With more transistors for data processing, a GPU usually consists of thousands of smaller but efficient ALUs (Arithmetic Logic Unit), which can be used to process parallel tasks efficiently. So GPU computing is widely used to accelerate compute-intensive applications nowadays. From the view of hardware architecture, a GPU is comprised of several SMs (Streaming Multiprocessors), which determine the parallelization capability of GPU. In Maxwell architecture, each SM owns 128 SPs (streaming processors) — the basic processing units. Warp is the basic execution unit in SM and each warp consists of 32 threads. All threads in a warp execute the same instructions at the same time. Each thread will be mapped into a SP when it is executed.

CUDA is a general purpose parallel computing architecture and programming model that is used in Nvidia GPUs [20]. One of programming interfaces of CUDA is CUDA C/C++ which is based on standard C/C++. Here, we mainly focus CUDA C++.

5.2   Existing Implementations and Our Implementations

Guillaume Sevestre [22] implemented KECCAK in a tree hash mode, the nature of which allows each thread to run a copy of KECCAK. Unfortunately, there are no implementation details given. In [8], Pierre-Louis Gayrel et al. implemented KECCAK-f[1600] with 25 threads that calculate all 25 lanes in parallel in a warp and these threads cooperate via shared memory. One disadvantage of this strategy is bank conflict — concurrent access to shared memory of the same bank by threads from the same warp will be forced to be sequential. Besides, there are two open-source softwares providing GPU implementations of KECCAK: ccminer (ref. http://ccminer.org) and hashcat (ref. https://hashcat.net) in CUDA and OpenCL, respectively.

Having learnt from the existing works and codes, we implemented KECCAK following two different strategies: one thread for one KECCAK or one warp for one KECCAK. From experimental results, we find that one thread for one KECCAK gives a better number of KECCAK-f evaluations per second. So we adopt this strategy in this paper. More detailed techniques of implementation optimization are introduced in Appendix A.1.

5.3   Benchmark

With all the optimization techniques in mind, we implemented KECCAK-$f[1600]$ in CUDA, and have it tested on NVIDIA GeForce GTX1070 and NVIDIA GeForce GTX970 graphics cards. The hardware specifications of GTX1070 and GTX970 are given in Table 5 of Appendix A.2.

Table 2. Benchmark of our KECCAK implementations in CUDA

Target	KECCAK-f evaluations per second	GPU
KECCAK-$f[1600]v1$	$2^{28.90}$	GTX1070
KECCAK-$f[1600]v2$	$2^{29.24}$	GTX1070
KECCAK-$f[1600]v1$	$2^{27.835}$	GTX970
KECCAK-$f[1600]v2$	$2^{28.37}$	GTX970

Table 2 lists the performance. KECCAK-$f[1600]v1$ and KECCAK-$f[1600]v2$ are our implementations used to search for differential trails and to find real collisions in the bruteforce stage, respectively. The difference between the two versions is: KECCAK-$f[1600]v1$ copies all digests into global memory, and KECCAK-$f[1600]v2$ only copies the digest into global memory when the resulted digest equals to a given digest value. Both versions did not include the data transfer time. It can be seen that GTX1070 can be 2^8 times faster than a CPU core. The source codes of these two versions are available freely via http://team.crypto. sg/Keccak_GPU_V1andV2.zip.

5.4   Search for Differential Trails

We follow the strategies proposed in [21] for searching differential trails. Specifically, special differences (explained more in Appendix B) before χ of the third round β_3 are first generated by KeccakTools [6], and then extended one-round forward to check the validity for d-bit collisions. For those β_3s which are possible for collision, we extend them one round backward, and calculate the number of active Sbox AS in the extended round. A trail with small AS is desirable for connectors.

Note that all extensions should be traversed. Given a β_3, suppose there are C_1 possible one-round forward extensions and C_2 one round backward extensions. These two numbers are determined by the active Sboxes of β_3. If the number of active Sboxes is AS, then roughly $C_1 = 4^{AS}$ and $C_2 = 9^{AS}$ according to the DDT referred from Table 6 in [21]. In the search for 3-round trails of KECCAK-224, C_2 is the dominant time complexity, while for 4-round trails of KECCAK[1440, 160, 6, 160], we start from (β_3, β_4) generated by KeccakTools, and C_1 is almost as large as C_2.

With the help of the GPU implementation, the β_3s generated by KeccakTools where $C_2 \leq 2^{35}$ are traversed for finding differential trails for KECCAK-224 with AS as small as possible, and (β_3, β_4) where $C_1 \leq 3^{36}$ are explored for finding 4-round trails for KECCAK[1440, 160, 6, 160] with $w_3 + w_4 + w_5^d$ as small as possible. As a comparison, the search for differential trails in [21] only covers β_3 and (β_3, β_4) with C_1, C_2 being less than 2^{30}. In summary, the best 3-round differential trail we obtained for KECCAK-224 has $AS = 81$, and the best 4-round differential trail for KECCAK[1440, 160, 6, 160] holds with $w_3 + w_4 + w_5^d = 52$. These two trails are used in our collision attacks in the following two sections respectively. More details of the searching algorithm are given in Appendix B.

6   Application to 5-Round Keccak-224

In this section, techniques for non-full linearization are applied to 5-round KECCAK-224. Firstly, the best 3-round differential trail we found for KECCAK-224 is described. With this differential trail, an improved 2-round connector using non-full linearizations is constructed and it outputs sufficient message pairs among which collisions of 5-round KECCAK-224 are found with real examples.

6.1   3-Round Differential Trail

The information of the best 3-round differential trail we obtain is listed in Table 3 and the trail itself is displayed in Table 7. Specifically, the weight of χ_1 is 187. Once the 2-round connector succeeds and outputs an sufficiently large message space, the complexity for searching a collision is 2^{48} and can be reduced to $2^{45.62}$ if multiple trails of last two rounds are taken into account. In brief, this trail imposes 187 equations to the 2-round connector and requires a solution space of size at least $2^{45.62}$. As shown in the table, our trail is better than the one used in [21] which imposes a bit more equations to the 2-round connector.

Table 3. Differential trails for collision attacks against KECCAK-224.

No	$AS(\alpha_2\text{-}\beta_2\text{-}\beta_3\text{-}\beta_4^d)$	$w_1\text{-}w_2\text{-}w_3\text{-}w_4^d$	$w_2 + w_3 + w_4^d$	Reference
1	85- 9-10-2	190-25-20-3	48	[21]
2	81-10-10-1	187-26-20-2	48	This paper

6.2 Improved 2-Round Connector

In order to extensively exploit the non-full linearization, large #*nonact* and #*save* would be beneficial. However, too many non-active Sboxes may make it difficult or impossible to find β_0s that are compatible with the $(c + p)$-bit zero initial difference, and further make it difficult for the 2-round connector to succeed. To find a balance, values for #*nonact* and #*save* are heuristically explored. Finally, we set $10 < \#nonact \leq 30$ and $\#save \geq 16$.

Our improved 2-round connector is given as follows and the steps are visualized in Fig. 3.

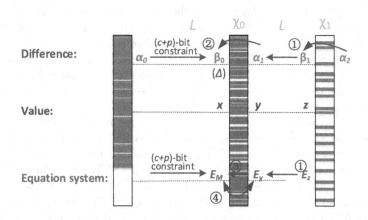

Fig. 3. Visualized 2-round connector.

The 2-Round Connector for KECCAK-*224.*

Inputs: 449-bit fixed initial value, α_2, two bound variables bnd_1, bnd_2.
Outputs: Difference Δ, a subspace of messages.

1. Randomly choose a possible input difference β_1 of χ_1 according to α_2 such that the differential $\beta_1 \rightarrow \alpha_2$ has the best probability. Calculate $\alpha_1 = L^{-1}(\beta_1)$ and #*nonact* of α_1. Construct a system of linear equations E_z over the values of the second χ using Property 1. Derive E_y from E_z using L, RC_0. Calculate U and #*save*. If $10 < \#nonact \leq 30$ and $\#save \geq 16$, go to Step 2, otherwise repeat this step.
2. Launch Dinur et al.'s target difference algorithm with β_1 and 449-bit fixed initial value. Once the algorithm succeeds, the input differences for the first two rounds are fixed and a system of linear equations E_M over the input x of χ_0 that defines a subspace is obtained, and move to Step 3. If this step fails bnd_1 times, go to Step 1, otherwise repeat this step.
3. Partially linearize the first round according to Observations 1 and 2 by adding equations to E_M. Once succeed, a smaller subspace defined by the updated E_M and the corresponding partial linear mapping of the first χ is obtained, and move to Step 4, otherwise repeat this step.

4. Unite E_M and E_y using the partial linear mapping of χ_0. Once a consistent system is obtained, go to Step 5. If this step fails bnd_2 times, go to Step 1, otherwise go to Step 3.

5. A 2-round connector is constructed successfully. Check the size of the solution space of the resulted equation system. If the size of the solution space is less than 2^{46}, go to Step 1; otherwise output difference Δ and the solution space.

6.3   Experiments and Results

Our 2-round connector succeeds in 15 core hours. The obtained subspace of messages has a size of 2^{55}, larger than the required size of 2^{46}. The number of non-active Sboxes of χ_0 is 29 and $\#save = 16$. Among the non-active Sboxes, no Sbox has $U_i = 0$, and seven Sboxes require 2 equations for the union. Among the 105 active Sboxes with DDT entry 8, 26 of them are exempted from adding an extra equation to E_M. These results confirm that the non-full linearization does save some degrees of freedom and both observations contribute to a larger message subspace that bypasses the first two rounds.

After the 2-round connector succeeds, from the message space returned by the connector, a brute-force search is needed to find a colliding message pair which follows the differential trail in latter 3 rounds. The brute-force search is implemented in CUDA and the search is done on an NVIDIA GeForce GTX1070 graphic card. The first collision is found in 21 min, which corresponds to $2^{39.90}$ message pair evaluations in the brute-force stage[1]. The actual complexity is smaller than expected by a non-negligible factor. This may be due to the possibility that there are some other differential trails missing from our collision probability calculation, or we might be just lucky. We give one instance of collision in Table 6.

7   Applications to Keccak[1440, 160, 6, 160]

In this section, 3-round connectors are firstly introduced to attack more rounds of KECCAK practically. Since one more round is covered by the connector, hence one less round needs to be fulfilled probabilistically in the bruteforce stage, resulting in lower complexities for the bruteforce search stage. This idea leads to a practical attack against KECCAK[1440, 160, 6, 160]. In the following, the differential trail used in our attack is described first, and details of 3-round connectors and experiments are given afterwards.

7.1   4-Round Differential Trail

Four-round differential trails are searched and used in the attack against KEC-CAK [1440, 160, 6, 160]. The first round of the trail is covered by the connector.

---

[1] Our experiment shows $2^{29.6}$ pairs of 5-round KECCAK could be evaluated per second on NVIDIA GeForce GTX1070 graphic card.

Namely, $\beta_2 \to \alpha_3$ is included as the last round of 3-round connector. Thus the weight of the last three rounds, namely $w_3 + w_4 + w_5^d$, determines the time complexity for the brute-force searching stage. To make the attack practical, $w_3 + w_4 + w_5^d$ should be as small as possible. So in the search for differential trails for KECCAK[1440, 160, 6, 160], our major goal is to find a 4-round trail with minimal $w_3 + w_4 + w_5^d$, which is different from the goal of searching trails for 5-round KECCAK-224. The best 4-round trail we obtained using GPU is listed in Table 4. The exact differential trail is shown in Table 9. The time complexity for the brute-force stage is 2^{52} which can be reduced to $2^{51.14}$ if we consider multiple trails starting from the same β_4. The weight of the third round is 25, indicating 25 linear equations of this round should be added to the whole equation system by surmounting the barrier of χ_1.

Table 4. Differential trails for collision attacks against KECCAK[1440, 160, 6, 160].

No	$AS(\alpha_2\text{-}\beta_2\text{-}\beta_3\text{-}\beta_4\text{-}\beta_5^d)$	$w_1\text{-}w_2\text{-}w_3\text{-}w_4\text{-}w_5^d$	$w_3 + w_4 + w_5^d$	Reference
1	145-6-6-10-14	340-15-12-22-23	57	[21]
2	127-9-8- 8-10	292-25-18-18-16	52	This paper

7.2 Adaptive 3-Round Connector

To construct 3-round connectors, a 2-round connectors is constructed first. Here, full linearizations are applied to χ_0 in the first round, since almost all (1595 $\sim$ 1600) output bits of χ_0 are involved in the equation system of latter two rounds due to the diffusion of the linear layer L. Suppose the resulted equation system of the 2-round connector over the first two rounds is E_M. Then equations for the third round are added to E_M adaptively to get 3-round connectors.

Note that, the first three rounds of KECCAK permutation is represented as

$$\chi_2 \circ L \circ \chi_1 \circ L \circ \chi_0 \circ L$$

by omitting the ι. Let the input and output of χ_0 be x and y, the input and output of χ_1 be z and y', and the input of χ_2 be z', as shown in Fig. 4. Suppose the system of equations E_M returned by the 2-round connector is

$$A \cdot x = t_0.$$

The full linear map of χ_0 is also returned and expressed as

$$L_{\chi_0} \cdot x + t_1 = y.$$

That is to say, $x = L_{\chi_0}^{-1} \cdot (y + t_1)$. Since $z = L \cdot (y + RC_0)$, now E_M can be re-expressed over z as follow.

$$
\begin{aligned}
A \cdot x &= A \cdot L_{\chi_0}^{-1} \cdot (y + t_1) \\
&= A \cdot L_{\chi_0}^{-1} \cdot (L^{-1} \cdot z + RC_0 + t_1) \\
&= t_0.
\end{aligned}
$$

Let $A' = A \cdot L_{\chi_0}^{-1} \cdot L^{-1}$ and $t'_0 = t_0 + A \cdot L_{\chi_0}^{-1} \cdot (RC_0 + t_1)$. Then an equivalent equation system E'_M of E_M is obtained as

$$A' \cdot z = t'_0. \tag{1}$$

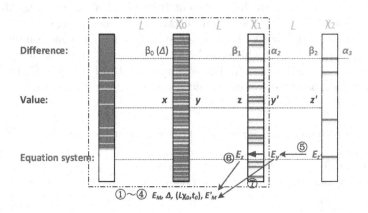

Fig. 4. Visualized 3-round connector.

With E'_M, equations of the third round, i.e., χ_2, now can be processed in the following way. Suppose the equation system $E_{z'}$ constructed using Property 1 for χ_2 is

$$D \cdot z' = t_4.$$

Since $z' = L \cdot (y' + RC_1)$, then $E_{z'}$ can be re-expressed as $E_{y'}$ over y', i.e.,

$$D \cdot L \cdot (y' + RC_1) = t_4. \tag{2}$$

Now to combine E'_M and $E_{y'}$, a linear map between z and y' is needed. Suppose using techniques of non-full linearization a couple of equations E_z,

$$B \cdot z = t_2$$

linearize y' as

$$L_{\chi_1} \cdot z + t_3 = y'. \tag{3}$$

By stacking E'_M and E_z, we get

$$\begin{bmatrix} A' & t'_0 \\ B & t_2 \end{bmatrix} \tag{4}$$

Check the consistency of system (4). If it is consistent, then the linear map (3) is valid, otherwise it is not valid. If the linear map (3) is valid, the equation system (2) for the third round now can be united, since

$$D \cdot L \cdot (y' + RC_1) = D \cdot L \cdot (L_{\chi_1} \cdot z + t_3 + RC_1)$$
$$= t_4.$$

If the consistency of the following system (5) holds, then the 3-round connector succeeds, and returns a subspace of z and β_1.

$$\begin{bmatrix} A' & t_0' \\ B & t_2 \\ D \cdot L \cdot L_{\chi_1} \, t_4 + D \cdot L \cdot (t_3 + RC_1) \end{bmatrix} \tag{5}$$

Special Sboxes of χ_1. The 3-round connector for KECCAK$[1440, 160, 6, 160]$ may not return a sufficiently large solution space due to a great consumption of degrees of freedom for linearizing χ_1, so multiple 3-round connectors are needed. Whether a 3-round connector succeeds or not depends on the consistency of (5). Note that, if (4) is consistent, (5) is consistent with high probability. However, (4) is consistent with a low probability. This is because $E_{z'}$ has a few equations, while E_z has much more. Take Trail 2 as an example, E_z has 146 equations, while $E_{z'}$ has only 25.

To make the 3-round connector succeed faster, E_z is scrutinized in depth. For an Sbox of χ_1 that should be linearized for uniting E_z with E_M', let the 5-bit input be $z_0 z_1 z_2 z_3 z_4$ and the 5-bit output $y_0' y_1' y_2' y_3' y_4'$. Suppose the value of z_0 is to be fixed to partially linearize χ_1. There are two cases for z_0. The first case is that the value of z_0 has not been fixed in E_M'. In this case both values (0 or 1) for z_0 are valid for the linearization of χ_1. The other case is that z_0 has already been fixed in E_M'. Then only the value that is consistent with E_M' is valid for the linearization. For the latter case, this Sbox is defined to be a *special Sbox*. Our idea is to spot all special Sboxes of χ_1 and always choose the valid linearization for them. For the rest Sboxes, any linearization is valid. In this way, (4) is always consistent.

For Trail 2, 125 Sboxes of χ_1 require to be linearized. The number of special Sboxes is 19. So for the rest 106 Sboxes, any linearization is valid and can be used to successfully construct sufficiently many 3-round connectors.

Algorithm of Adaptive 3-Round Connectors. In adaptive 3-round connectors, full linearizations are applied to χ_0, while non-full linearizations are used for χ_1. Each time the algorithm outputs a subspace of messages by solving (5). More subspaces of messages can be obtained by replacing the linearization of χ_1 with an unused one.

The Adaptive 3-Round Connector

Inputs: 161-bit fixed initial value, α_3, β_2 and α_2
Outputs: initial difference Δ and β_1, multiple subspaces of messages.

1. Apply *The 2-Round Connector* using the 161-bit fixed initial value and α_2. When the 2-round connector succeeds, it returns E_M, Δ, β_1 and the linear map (L_{χ_0}, t_1) with which the equivalent system E_M' can be derived.
2. Construct $E_{z'}$ using β_2 and α_3. Then deduce $E_{y'}$ from $E_{z'}$. Calculate U' for $E_{y'}$. Now the bits of y' that need to be linearized are known. Spot special Sboxes by trying all linearizations for each Sbox whose output bits are

marked by U'. After that, a list of special Sboxes and a corresponding valid linearization are obtained. Initialize a list structure for all Sboxes of χ_1 that are marked by U'. Each Sbox is a node on the list structure. For special Sboxes, the node has only one choice for the linearization, while for other Sboxes, the node contains multiple choices for the linearization.

3. Use the current linearization (L_{χ_0}, t_3) to deduce a united equation system (5). If the system (5) is consistent, solve this system, return a solution space and β_1 and go to Step 4; otherwise, shift the pointer of the list to the next linearization, go to Step 3.
4. Check whether more messages are needed or not. If yes, shift the pointer of the list to the next linearization, go to Step 3; otherwise, exit.

In brief, in 3-round adaptive connectors, the freedom degrees for linearizing the second round are reused and hence not consumed. Thus, multiple solution spaces can be generated successively if one is not enough.

7.3   Experiments and Results

The 3-round adaptive connector is applied to Trail 2 in our experiments. In the first step, the 2-round connector succeeds in 4.5 core hours and returns an E_M with 174 degrees of freedom. Every time Step 4 outputs a subspace of messages of size $2^{32} \sim 2^{35}$ which bypass the first three rounds. In order to find one colliding pair, at least $2^{51.14}$ pairs of messages are required. This could be achieved by repeating Step 3 $\sim$ 4 for $2^{16.14} \sim 2^{19.14}$ times. By running our CUDA implementation on three NVIDIA GeForce GTX970 GPUs, the first collision is found in 112 h, which equals to $2^{49.07}$ message pair evaluations[2]. An example of collision is given in Table 8.

8   Conclusions

In conclusion, we proposed two major types of techniques for saving degrees of freedom in constructing connectors: non-full linearizations and adaptive connectors. Techniques of non-full linearization avoid unnecessary consumption of degrees of freedom, and its application directly leads to practical collision attacks against 5-round KECCAK-224. Adaptive connectors are constructed in an adaptive way that some degrees of freedom are reused, hence not consumed. By combining techniques of non-full linearization and adaptive connectors, 3-round connectors are constructed successfully, resulting in a practical collision attack against KECCAK[1440, 160, 6, 160].

These two types of techniques significantly save degrees of freedom. Therefore, one potential future work is to apply these techniques to other KECCAK instances which have a tighter budget of freedom degrees, such as KECCAK[240, 160, 5, 160].

---

[2] Our experiment shows $2^{28.87}$ pairs of 5-round KECCAK could be evaluated per second on NVIDIA GeForce GTX970 graphic card.

Acknowledgement. The authors would like to thank anonymous reviewers of CRYPTO 2017 for their helpful comments and suggestions. Part of this work was supported by the National Key Basic Research Program of China (2013CB834203) the National Natural Science Foundation of China (Grants 61472417, 61472415, 61402469, 61672516, and 61572028), the Project of Science and Technology of Guangdong (2016B010125002), and the Natural Science Foundation of Guangdong (No. 2015A030313630, 2014A030313439).

References

1. Aumasson, J.P., Meier, W.: Zero-Sum distinguishers for reduced keccak-f and for the core functions of Luffa and Hamsi. In: Rump Session of Cryptographic Hardware and Embedded Systems-CHES 2009 (2009)
2. Bertoni, G., Daemen, J., Peeters, M., Van Assche, G.: Keccak crunchy crypto collision and pre-image contest. http://keccak.noekeon.org/crunchy_contest.html
3. Bertoni, G., Daemen, J., Peeters, M., Van Assche, G.: Cryptographic Sponge functions. Submission to NIST (Round 3) (2011). http://sponge.noekeon.org/CSF-0.1.pdf
4. Bertoni, G., Daemen, J., Peeters, M., Van Assche, G.: The Keccak Reference, version 3.0. http://keccak.noekeon.org
5. Bertoni, G., Daemen, J., Peeters, M., Van Assche, G.: The Keccak SHA-3 Submission. Submission to NIST (Round 3) 6(7) (2011)
6. Bertoni, G., Daemen, J., Peeters, M., Van Assche, G.: KeccakTools (2015). http://keccak.noekeon.org/
7. Canteaut, Anne (ed.): FSE 2012. LNCS, vol. 7549. Springer, Heidelberg (2012)
8. Cayrel, P.-L., Hoffmann, G., Schneider, M.: GPU implementation of the Keccak Hash function family. In: Kim, T., Adeli, H., Robles, R.J., Balitanas, M. (eds.) ISA 2011. CCIS, vol. 200, pp. 33–42. Springer, Heidelberg (2011). doi:10.1007/978-3-642-23141-4_4
9. Daemen, J., Assche, G.V.: Differential propagation analysis of keccak. In: Canteaut [7], pp. 422–441
10. Dinur, I., Dunkelman, O., Shamir, A.: New attacks on keccak-224 and keccak-256. In: Canteaut [7], pp. 442–461
11. Dinur, I., Dunkelman, O., Shamir, A.: Collision attacks on up to 5 rounds of SHA-3 using generalized internal differentials. In: Moriai, S. (ed.) FSE 2013. LNCS, vol. 8424, pp. 219–240. Springer, Heidelberg (2014). doi:10.1007/978-3-662-43933-3_12
12. Dinur, I., Dunkelman, O., Shamir, A.: Improved practical attacks on round-reduced keccak. J. Cryptol. **27**(2), 183–209 (2014)
13. Dinur, I., Morawiecki, P., Pieprzyk, J., Srebrny, M., Straus, M.: Cube attacks and cube-attack-like cryptanalysis on the round-reduced keccak sponge function. In: Oswald, E., Fischlin, M. (eds.) EUROCRYPT 2015. LNCS, vol. 9056, pp. 733–761. Springer, Heidelberg (2015). doi:10.1007/978-3-662-46800-5_28
14. Duc, A., Guo, J., Peyrin, T., Wei, L.: Unaligned rebound attack: application to keccak. In: Canteaut [7], pp. 402–421
15. Guo, J., Liu, M., Song, L.: Linear structures: applications to cryptanalysis of round-reduced KECCAK. In: Cheon, J.H., Takagi, T. (eds.) ASIACRYPT 2016. LNCS, vol. 10031, pp. 249–274. Springer, Heidelberg (2016). doi:10.1007/978-3-662-53887-6_9
16. Jean, J., Nikolic, I.: Internal differential boomerangs: practical analysis of the round-reduced Keccak-f permutation. In: Leander, G. (ed.) FSE 2015. LNCS, vol. 9054, pp. 537–556. Springer, Heidelberg (2015)

17. Murthy, G.S.: Optimal loop unrolling for GPGPU programs. Ph.D. thesis, The Ohio State University (2009)

18. Naya-Plasencia, M., Röck, A., Meier, W.: Practical analysis of reduced-round KEC-CAK. In: Bernstein, D.J., Chatterjee, S. (eds.) INDOCRYPT 2011. LNCS, vol. 7107, pp. 236–254. Springer, Heidelberg (2011). doi:10.1007/978-3-642-25578-6_18

19. NIST: SHA-3 COMPETITION (2007–2012). http://csrc.nist.gov/groups/ST/hash/sha-3/index.html

20. Nvidia, C.: CUDA C Programming Guide. Nvidia Corporation 120(18) (2011)

21. Qiao, K., Song, L., Liu, M., Guo, J.: New collision attacks on round-reduced Keccak. In: Coron, J.-S., Nielsen, J.B. (eds.) EUROCRYPT 2017. LNCS, vol. 10212, pp. 216–243. Springer, Cham (2017). doi:10.1007/978-3-319-56617-7_8

22. Sevestre, G.: Implementation of Keccak hash function in tree hashing mode on Nvidia GPU (2010). http://hgpu.org/?p=6833

23. The U.S. National Institute of Standards and Technology: SHA-3 Standard: Permutation-Based Hash and Extendable-Output Functions. Federal Information Processing Standard, FIPS 202, 5th August 2015, http://nvlpubs.nist.gov/nistpubs/FIPS/NIST.FIPS.202.pdf

24. Volkov, V.: Better performance at lower occupancy. In: Proceedings of the GPU Technology Conference, GTC, vol. 10. San Jose, CA (2010)

A   GPU Implementation

A.1   Techniques of GPU Implementation Optimization

The techniques commonly used to optimize the CUDA program include memory optimizations, execution configuration optimizations, and instruction-level parallelism (ILP).

Memory Optimizations. Usually registers have the shortest access latency compared with other memory, so keeping data in registers as much as possible improves the efficiency in general. However, dynamically indexed arrays cannot be stored in registers, so we define some variables for the 25 lanes by hand in order to have them stored in registers. Constant memory is a type of read-only memory. When it is necessary for a warp of threads read the same location of memory, constant memory is the best choice. So we store 24 round constants on it. When the threads in a warp read data which is physically adjacent to each other, texture memory provides better performance than global memory, and it reduces memory traffic as well. So we can bind input data and some frequent accessed read-only data with texture memory.

Execution Configuration. With resources like registers and shared memory limited in each graphic card, the number of threads run in each block will affect the performance since too many threads running in parallel will cause shortage of registers and shared memory allocated to each thread, while too few parallel threads reduce the overall performance directly. According to our experiments, one block with 128 threads gives the best performance.

Instruction-Level Parallelism. From [24], hashcat, and ccminer, we see that forcing adjacent instructions independent gives better performance. Without prejudice to the functions of the program, we can adjust the order of instructions to improve the efficiency of the operations. In addition, loop unrolling [17] is also a good practice to obtain ILP.

A.2   Hardware specification sheet of GPU

Table 5. The hardware specification sheet of GTX1070 and GTX970

	GTX1070	GTX970
Core clock rate	1645 MHz	1228 MHz
Multiprocessors	16	13
Regs per block	65536	65536
Total global memory	8105.06 MiB	4036.81 MiB
Bus width	256 bits	256 bits
Memory clock rate	4004 MHz	3505 MHz
L2 cache size	48 KiB	48 KiB
Shared memory per block	48 KiB	48 KiB
Total constant memory	64 KiB	64 KiB

B   Algorithm for Searching Differential Trails

Before the description of our algorithm for searching differential trails, we introduce more notations which are mainly defined by the designers of KECCAK. A state s is in the *Column Parity kernel* (CP-kernel) if $s = \theta(s)$ [5], which means θ acts as an identity and dose not diffuse any bit of the state. The differential trail in the CP-kernel has a number of rounds at most 2, as studied in [9,14,18]. Also, an n-round *trail core* (suppose starting from Round 0) is defined with $n - 1$ consecutive β_i's, $(\beta_1, \cdots, \beta_{n-1})$, which contains a set of n-round trails $\alpha_0 \xrightarrow{L} \beta_0 \xrightarrow{\chi} \alpha_1 \xrightarrow{L} \beta_1 \cdots \xrightarrow{L} \beta_{n-1} \xrightarrow{\chi} \alpha_n$ where the first round is of the minimal weight determined by $\alpha_1 = L^{-1}(\beta_1)$, and α_n is compatible with β_{n-1}. In the collision attack of 5-round KECCAK-224, actually a 4-round trail core is needed even though the first round is covered by the 2-round connector. In the attack of KECCAK[1440, 160, 6, 160], a 5-round core is required and the first two rounds of the trail are covered by 3-round connectors. We list below the steps for finding 4-round cores for KECCAK-224, and then describe the difference for KECCAK[1440, 160, 6, 160].

- Generate β_3 such that $\alpha_3 = L^{-1}(\beta_3)$ lies in CP-kernel, and that there exists a compatible α_3 in CP-kernel, using TrailCoreInKernelAtC of KeccakTools [6] where the parameter *aMaxWeight* is set to be 64. The number of such β_3 we obtained is 2347.

- For each β_3, if $C_1 \leq 2^{36}$, we traverse all possible α_4, compute β_4, and check whether the collision is possible for β_4. If yes, keep this β_3 and record this forward extension, otherwise, discard this β_3.
- For remaining β_3, if $C_2 \leq 2^{35}$, try all possible β_2 which are compatible with $\alpha_3 = L^{-1}(\beta_3)$, and compute $AS(\alpha_2)$ where $\alpha_2 = L^{-1}(\beta_3)$. If $AS(\alpha_2) \leq 86$, check whether this trail core $\beta_2, \beta_3, \beta_4$ is practical for the collision attack.

Using this algorithm, the best 4-round trail core we found for KECCAK-224 has $AS(\alpha_2) = 81$ and $w_2 + w_3 + w_4^d = 48$. In the case of KECCAK$[1440, 160, 6, 160]$, trails with one more round are searched, so the second step is adapted as follow.

- For each β_3, extend forwards for one round using KeccakFTrailExtension of KeccakTools [6] with weight up to 45. As a result, 43042 two-round cores are generated. Then for each generated two-round core, if $C_1 \leq 2^{36}$ for β_4, traverse all possible α_5 and compute β_5. Check whether there exists a α_6 such that $\alpha_6^d = 0$. If yes, record the three-round core $\beta_3, \beta_4, \beta_5$, otherwise, discard the β_3. In total, there are only 11 β_3s left for the 160-bit collision.

The best 5-round trail core we found for KECCAK$[1440, 160, 6, 160]$ has $AS(\alpha_2) = 127$ and $w_3 + w_4 + w_5^d = 52$. In order to estimate the complexity for the brute-force stage accurately, we consider all possible trails which are possible for the collision and start from the same β_3 for KECCAK-224 (β_4 for KECCAK$[1440, 160, 6, 160]$).

C Differential Trails and Collisions

In this section, we give details of differential trails used in our attacks and the obtained collisions. The 1600-bit state is displayed as a 5×5 array, ordered from left to right, where '|' acts as the separator; each lane is denoted in hexadecimal using little-endian format; '0' is replaced with '-' for differential trails.

Table 6. Collision for 5-round KECCAK-224

M_1	F49A78F0E0CBB2C0	997CF6C13F9F5E37	091EF2AE68CA026C	787A6189D311D2AB	F410786AB060476E
	A56E341B9175DDBD	ED9381C907F7DEFD	EAF49557D1F449F4	BBFDC0C22F0ED3C6	A5FCE33236960AAE
	192598A5E0B275ED	DA7C4363F554A4AE	85B14515A3040D1B	2C5E5C7DDC7E43C3	A900385251BB4F77
	DB530E201E571450	A9C981793A78152F	C55991AC63389C0F	0000000000000000	0000000000000000
	0000000000000000	0000000000000000	0000000000000000	0000000000000000	0000000000000000
M_2	C316798E019C8ECB	2EFDF516C6322BEA	B9FE8432A626B2B2	4EEA0858AF5684C2	1793DC9B8BE1EFF0
	DDF791B683238A70	E43E484F5F767DB3	6AE5AD63D1FD51DC	57C509C21AF67220	AF14D053F09C4E6C
	44E594BA9943900F	F2995743C285D101	00C055CA1502459A	013AD29EE0FFB76B	8A9B6A7750956AFF
	D200A9BD2E38993F	54583BF0DAF4D84D	E9784271C6556FFF	0000000000000000	0000000000000000
	0000000000000000	0000000000000000	0000000000000000	0000000000000000	0000000000000000
digest	9F78D9AAD557721B	8DA633A88E5FA089	97403614B9152D9D	0E1F496F	

Table 7. Differential trail used in the collision attack of 5-round KECCAK-224. The total probability is $2^{-45.62}$ considering multiple trails of the last two rounds. After collisions were obtained, we found that the trail obtained by cyclically rotating this one 22 bits to the right has a better probability of $2^{-44.59}$.

```
      -----------8----|--22------------|--2--------8----|--2-------------|--22------8-----|
      ----------------|----------------|----------------|----------------|----------------|
β2    -----------8----|----------------|-----------8----|---------8------|----------8-----| 2^-26
      -------2--------|----------------|----------------|--2----2--------|----------------|
      -------2--------|---2------------|----------------|----------------|----------------|

      ----------------|----------------|4---------------|----------------|-----------4--|--
      -------2--------|----------------|----------------|----------------|----------------|
β3    ---4------------|----------------|----------------|----------------|--------8-------| 2^-20
      ---4------------|----------------|----------------|----------------|----------------|
      -------2--------|----------------|4---------------|----------------|----4-----8-----|

      ----------------|----------------|----------------|----------------|--------------2
      ------4---------|----------------|--2-------------|----------------|-8--------------
β4    ----------------|----------------|----------------|----------------|-------8-------- 2^-2
      ----------------|--2-------------|----------------|----------------|--------------4
      1---------------|----------------|--------4-------|--------8-------|----------------
```

Table 8. Collision for the challenge instance KECCAK[1440, 160, 6, 160]

M_1	DA27ABE5B7EC359D|328A2AB4CD0E256A|00DBDEECA184390E|3843F66481C745F4|DDF83BEF39D4F594
	46BA2A960272C97A|8CC8CE3E13185558|2D7C6CC662546532|4D8DCDC25DC7F4B8|574252F43F85BF94
	BDCFA2D6B04CBDEE|208D7A02168A7596|AFE7C652F0A68792|467C04748D85916F|F1BFEAF63C4B97C3
	C2B0AAEA35887CD4|72A3D23F9D84434D|97A5D9A090590B61|BBE1EC62DBD4327E|64284BCB9BE462C5
	8843CBC8B55E106A|DD3DD96A1AC48100|00000000E9151D67|0000000000000000|0000000000000000
M_2	5A0C640730278910|32C1A7D724790C0B|8BCE75C46404A83A|7FCE23E92ECE7E31|1BEE08F9F932C785
	3969BA55EB6B17F9|E82948B06C21C6A8|AF42ACEF22202C1F|A9C1BD90BF96FB60|0F98E27C36B57BDA
	A02B26453D88C70F|5EC5F74DC919C7E6|31391D7A23A3C8DD|C0BECDAD0AC7F275|14FA28F6B2C9D390
	69F67EEAEF258217|159B7FEDCED37178|DA89C2B0291CCA7D|7BDDE79F989414AE|3088CBE192E15B4B
	138617865C48CEA9|2A917CE5E3AD1374|0000000098425E60|0000000000000000|0000000000000000
digest	602133DD97109089|611B5125914B0F05| 532B96C0

Table 9. Differential trail used in the collision attack of KECCAK[1440, 160, 6, 160]. The total probability is $2^{-76.14}$ considering multiple trails of last two rounds. The probability of last three rounds is $2^{-51.14}$.

```
      ----------------|-----8----------|-----8------4---|----------------|-----------4---
      ----------2--8|--------------2----|---------------8|--------2--8|-----------2----
β2    ----------------|-----8----------|----------------|----------------|-----8------4--- 2^-25
      ----------2----|----------------|-----8----------|--------2--8|----------------
      ----------------|----------------|----------------|----------------|----------------

      ----------------|----------------|----------------|--------1-----|----------------
      ----------------|----------------|----------------|--------1-----|----------------
β3    ----------------|----------------|----------------|----------------|---------------- 2^-18
      ------2---------|--2-------------|--2-------------|-4--------------|----------------
      ------2---------|-4--------------|--2-------------|-4--------------|----------------

      ----------------|----------------|----------------|--------8---|----------------
      --1-------------|----------------|----------------|----------------|---4------------
β4    ----------------|----------------|----------------|--------|-8-------------- 2^-18
      ----------------|----------------|----------------|--------------1-|---4------------
      ----------------|--------8---|----------------|----------------|----4-----------

      -8--------------|--------1-------|48-1---1--------|----------2-2----|-------12-4---C
      -----8--1-----|------48-1---34|4---------------|--------2--------|---4-------12--4
β5    --2----1-----|---9-------24--8|----------2-----|34-------48-1---|--------------2--- 2^-16
      ---24--8--18---|--------81------|4---------------|-----48-1---12|--1----------4--
      ---8-------24--8|---8-8--------|-24--8-418------|-------1--------|--4--------2----
```

Lattices

Gaussian Sampling over the Integers: Efficient, Generic, Constant-Time

Daniele Micciancio and Michael Walter[(✉)]

University of California, San Diego, La Jolla, USA
{daniele,miwalter}@eng.ucsd.edu

Abstract. Sampling integers with Gaussian distribution is a fundamental problem that arises in almost every application of lattice cryptography, and it can be both time consuming and challenging to implement. Most previous work has focused on the optimization and implementation of integer Gaussian sampling in the context of specific applications, with fixed sets of parameters. We present new algorithms for discrete Gaussian sampling that are both generic (application independent), efficient, and more easily implemented in constant time without incurring a substantial slow-down, making them more resilient to side-channel (e.g., timing) attacks. As an additional contribution, we present new analytical techniques that can be used to simplify the precision/security evaluation of floating point cryptographic algorithms, and an experimental comparison of our algorithms with previous algorithms from the literature.

1 Introduction

Lattice-based cryptography has gained much popularity in recent years, not only within the cryptographic community, but also in the area of computer security in both research and industry, for at least two reasons: first, many classical cryptographic primitives can be realized very efficiently using lattices, providing strong security guarantees, including conjectured security against quantum computers [4,14,40]. Second, lattices allow to build advanced schemes that go beyond classical public key encryption, like fully homomorphic encryption [8,9,16,21], identity based encryption [1,2], attribute based encryption [6,7], some forms of multilinear maps [20,26] and even some forms of program obfuscation [10]. Discrete Gaussian distributions (i.e., normal Gaussian distributions on the real line, but restricted to take integer values), play a fundamental role in lattice cryptography: Gaussian sampling is at the core of security proofs (from worst-case lattice problems) supporting both the conjectured hardness of the Learning With Errors (LWE) problem [27,37,42,43], and the tightest reductions for the Short Integer Solution (SIS) problem [30,31], which provide a theoretical foundation to the field. The use of Gaussian distributions is especially important in the context of the most advanced cryptographic applications of lattices that make use of preimage sampling [22,29,38], as the use of other distributions can easily leak information about secret keys and open cryptographic primitives to devastating attacks [35]. Even in the technically simpler context of LWE noise generation,

© International Association for Cryptologic Research 2017
J. Katz and H. Shacham (Eds.): CRYPTO 2017, Part II, LNCS 10402, pp. 455–485, 2017.
DOI: 10.1007/978-3-319-63715-0_16

where Gaussian distributions can be safely replaced by more easily samplable (e.g., uniform) distributions (see e.g. [12,30]), this requires a noticeable increase in the noise level, resulting in substantial performance degradation, and still points to discrete Gaussian distributions as the most desirable choice to achieve good performance/security trade-offs. In summary, despite continued theoretical efforts and practical attempts to replace Gaussian distributions with more implementation friendly ones, and a few isolated examples where discrete Gaussians can be avoided altogether with almost no penalty [4], the cryptography research community has been converging to accept discrete Gaussian sampling as one of the fundamental building blocks of lattice cryptography.

Gaussian sampling aside, lattice cryptography can be very attractive from an implementation standpoint, requiring only simple arithmetic operations on small integer numbers (easily fitting a computer word on commodity microprocessors), and offering ample opportunities for parallelization at the register and processor level, both in hardware and in software implementations. In this respect, discrete Gaussian sampling can often be the main hurdle in implementation/optimization efforts, and a serious bottleneck to achieve good performance in practice. As many primitives find their way into practical implementations [3,15] and lattice cryptography is considered for possible standardization as a post-quantum security solution [36], the practical aspects of discrete Gaussian sampling (including efficiency, time-memory trade-offs, side-channel resistance, etc.) have started to attract the attention of the research community, e.g., see [11,13,14,17,18,34,44,46]. However, most of these works address the problem of Gaussian sampling in the context of a specific application, and for specific values of the parameters and settings that come to define the discrete Gaussian sampling problem: the standard deviation of the Gaussian distribution, the center (mean) of the Gaussian, how these values depend on the targeted security level, and whether the values are fixed once and for all, or during key generation time, or even on a sample-by-sample basis. So, while implementation efforts have clearly demonstrated that (if properly specialized and optimized) discrete Gaussian sampling can be used in practice, it is unclear to what extent optimized solutions can be ported from one application to another, and even when this is possible, achieving good performance still seems to require a disproportionate amount of effort. Finally, achieving security against side-channel (e.g., timing) attacks has been recognized as an important problem [23,39,45], but developing constant-time implementations of Gaussian sampling without incurring major performance penalties is still a largely unsolved problem.

Our Contribution. We develop of a new discrete Gaussian sampling algorithm over the integers with a unique set of desirable properties that make it very attractive in cryptographic applications. The new algorithm

- can be used to sample efficiently from discrete Gaussian distributions with arbitrary and varying parameters (standard deviation and center), enabling its use in a wide range of applications.
- provides a time-memory trade-off, the first of its kind for sampling with varying parameters, allowing to fine-tune the performance on different platforms.

- can be split into an offline and online phase, where the offline phase can be carried out even before knowing the parameters of the requested distribution. Moreover, both phases can be implemented in constant time with only minor performance degradation, providing resilience against timing side-channel attacks.
- can be parallelized and optimized, both in hardware and software, in a largely application-independent manner.

We demonstrate the efficiency of the new algorithm both through a rigorous theoretical analysis, and practical experimentation with a prototype implementation. Our experimental results show that our new algorithms achieve generality and flexibility without sacrificing performance, matching, or even beating the online phase of previous (specialized) algorithms. See next paragraph and Sect. 6.6 for details.

A recurring problem in the analysis of Gaussian sampling (or other probabilistic algorithms involving the use of real numbers at some level), is to accurately account for how the use of floating point approximations affects performance and security. This is often a critical issue in practice, as using standard (53 bit) double precision floating point numbers offers major efficiency advantages over the use of arbitrary precision arithmetic libraries, but can have serious security implications when targeting 80 bit or 100 bit security levels. As an additional contribution, we develop new analytical tools for the accuracy/security analysis of floating point algorithms, and exemplify their use in the analysis of our new Gaussian sampling algorithm. More specifically, we propose a new notion of closeness between probability distributions (which we call the "max-log" distance), that combines the simplicity and ease of use of statistical distance (most commonly used in cryptography), with the effectiveness of Rényi and KL divergences recently used in cryptography to obtain sharp security estimates [5,40,41]. The new measure is closely related to the standard notion of relative error and the Rényi divergence of order ∞, but it is easier to define[1] and it is also a metric, i.e., it enjoys the (symmetric and triangle inequality) properties that make the statistical distance a convenient tool for the analysis of complex algorithms. Using this new metric, we show that our new algorithms can be implemented using standard (extended) double precision floating point arithmetic, and still provide a more than adequate (100 bits or higher) level of security.

Finally, we also evaluate different algorithms for discrete Gaussian sampling experimentally in a common setting. While previous surveys [19] and experimental studies [11,24] exist, they either do not provide a fair comparison or are incomplete. Somewhat surprisingly, an algorithm [25] that has gone mostly unnoticed in the cryptographic community so far, emerged as very competitive solution in our study, within the class of variable-time algorithms that can be used when timing attacks are not a concern.

---

[1] The distance between two discrete distributions $\mathcal{P}$ and $\mathcal{Q}$ (with the same support S), is simply the maximum (over $x \in S$) of $|\log \mathcal{P}(x) - \log \mathcal{Q}(x)|$.

Techniques. The main idea behind our algorithm is to reduce the general discrete Gaussian sampling problem (for arbitrary standard deviation s and center c), to the generation (and recombination) of a relatively small number of samples coming from a Gaussian distribution for a fixed and rather small value of s. Reducing the general problem to discrete Gaussian sampling for a fixed small value of s has several advantages:

- Gaussian sampling for fixed parameters can be performed more efficiently than general Gaussian sampling because the probability tables or tree traversal data structures required by the basic sampler can be precomputed. Moreover, as the standard deviation s of the basic sampler is small, these tables or data structures only require a very modest amount of memory.
- Since the parameters of the basic sampler are fixed and do not depend on the application input, the basic samples can be generated offline. The online (recombination) phase of the algorithm is very fast, as it only needs to combine a small number of basic samples.
- The online (recombination) phase of the algorithm is easily implemented in constant time, as the number of operations it performs only depends on the application parameters, and not on the actual input values or randomness. The offline phase can also be made constant time with only a minor performance penalty, observing that basic samples are always generated and used in batches. So, instead of requiring the generation of each basic sample to take a fixed amount of time, one can look at the time to generate a batch of samples in the aggregate. Since the basic samples are totally independent, their aggregate generation time is very sharply concentrated around the expectation, and can be made constant (except with negligible probability) simply by adding a small time penalty to the generation of the whole batch.
- The parameters of the basic sampler are fixed once and for all, and do not depend on the parameters of online phase and final application. This opens up the possibility of a hybrid hardware/software implementation, where the basic sampler is optimized and implemented once and for all, perhaps in hardware, and making efficient use of parallelism. The fast recombination phase is quickly executed in software by combining the samples generated by the hardware module, based on the application parameters.

The method we use to combine the basic samples extends and generalizes techniques that have been used in the implementation of Gaussian samplers before. The work most closely related to ours is [40], which generates Gaussian samples with a relatively large standard deviation s by first computing two samples x_1, x_2 with smaller standard deviation $\approx \sqrt{s}$, and then computing $kx_1 + x_2$, for $k \approx \sqrt{s}$. We improve on this basic idea in several dimensions:

- First, we use the idea recursively, obtaining x_1 and x_2 also by combining multiple samples with even smaller standard deviation. While recursion is a rather natural and simple idea, and it was already mentioned in [40], the realization that the performance benefits of using basic samples with even smaller standard deviation more than compensate the overhead associated to computing several samples is new.

- Second, we employ a convolution theorem from [30] to combine the samples (at each level of the recursion). This allows for greater flexibility in the choice of parameters, for example the number of samples to combine at each level or the choice of coefficients. This can be important in the context of side-channel attacks as demonstrated in [39].
- Finally, we generalize the algorithm to sample according to Gaussian distributions with arbitrary center as follows. Assume the center c has k binary fractional digits, i.e., $c \in \mathbb{Z}/2^k$. Then, we can use a first integer Gaussian sample (scaled by a factor 2^{-k}) to randomly round c to a center in $\mathbb{Z}/2^{k-1}$. Then, we use a second sample (scaled by $2^{-(k-1)}$) to round the new center to a coarser set $\mathbb{Z}/2^{k-2}$, and so on for k times, until we obtain a sample in $\mathbb{Z}$ as desired. Since the final output is obtained by combining a number of Gaussian samples together, the result still follows a discrete Gaussian distribution. Moreover, since the scaling factors grow geometrically, the standard deviation of the final output is (up to a small constant factor) the same as the one of the original samples.

The algorithms presented in this paper include several additional improvements and optimizations, as described below. Using different values for the standard deviation of the basic sampler, and expressing the center of the Gaussian c to a base other than 2, allows various time-memory trade-offs that can be used to fine-tune the performance of the algorithm to different platforms. The exact value of the standard deviation of the final output distribution can be finely adjusted by adding some noise to the initial center and invoking the convolution theorem of [38]. Finally, when the center of the Gaussian c is a high precision floating point number, the number of iterations (and basic samples required) can be greatly reduced by first rounding it to a coarser grid using a simple biased coin flip, and using our *max-log* metric to get sharper estimates on the number of precision bits required.

Outline. We begin by introducing some notation in Sect. 2, and a general framework for the analysis of approximate samplers in Sect. 3. In Sect. 4 we introduce our new "max-log" metric, which we will use to simplify the analysis for complex sampling algorithms. Our new sampling algorithms are presented in Sect. 5. Section 6 concludes the paper with a description of our experimental results.

2   Preliminaries

Notation. We denote the integers by $\mathbb{Z}$ and the reals by $\mathbb{R}$. Roman and Greek letters can denote elements from either set, while bold letters denote vectors over them. Occasionally, we construct vectors on the fly using the notation $(\cdot)_{i \in S}$ for some set S (or in short $(\cdot)_i$ if the set S is clear from context), where $\cdot$ is a function of i. We denote the logarithm with base 2 by log and the one with base e by ln.

Calligraphic letters are reserved for probability distributions and $x \leftarrow \mathcal{P}$ means that x is sampled from the distribution $\mathcal{P}$. For any x in the support of $\mathcal{P}$ we denote its probability under $\mathcal{P}$ by $\mathcal{P}(x)$. All distributions in this work are discrete. The statistical distance between two distributions $\mathcal{P}$ and $\mathcal{Q}$ over the same support S is defined as $\Delta_{\mathrm{SD}}(\mathcal{P}, \mathcal{Q}) = \frac{1}{2} \sum_{x \in S} |\mathcal{P}(x) - \mathcal{Q}(x)|$ and the KL-divergence as $\delta_{\mathrm{KL}}(\mathcal{P}, \mathcal{Q}) = \sum_{x \in S} \mathcal{P}(x) \ln \frac{\mathcal{P}(x)}{\mathcal{Q}(x)}$. Note that the former is a metric, while the latter is not. Pinsker's inequality bounds Δ_{SD} in terms of δ_{KL} by $\Delta_{\mathrm{SD}}(\mathcal{P}, \mathcal{Q}) \leq \sqrt{\delta_{\mathrm{KL}}(\mathcal{P}, \mathcal{Q})/2}$. A probability ensemble $\mathcal{P}_\theta$ is a family of distributions indexed by a parameter θ (which is possibly a vector). We extend any measure δ between distributions to probability ensembles as $\delta(\mathcal{P}_\theta, \mathcal{Q}_\theta) = \max_\theta \delta(\mathcal{P}_\theta, \mathcal{Q}_\theta)$. For notational simplicity, we do not make a distinction between random variables, probability distributions, and probabilistic algorithms generating them. An algorithm A with oracle access to a sampler for distribution ensemble $\mathcal{P}_\theta$ is denoted by $A^{\mathcal{P}}$, which means that it adaptively sends queries θ_i to the sampler, which returns a sample from $\mathcal{P}_{\theta_i}$. If A uses only one sample from $\mathcal{P}_\theta$, then we write $A(\mathcal{P}_\theta)$.

In this work we will occasionally encounter expressions of the form $\epsilon + O(\epsilon^2)$ for some small ϵ. In all of these cases, the constant c hidden in the asymptotic notation is much smaller than $1/\epsilon$ (say $c\epsilon \leq 2^{-30}$). So, the higher order term $O(\epsilon^2)$ has virtually no impact, neither in practice nor asymptotically, on our applications. We define $\hat{\epsilon} = \epsilon + O(\epsilon^2)$ and write $a \simeq b$ for $a = \hat{b}$, and similarly $a \lesssim b$ for $a \leq \hat{b}$. This allows us to drop the $O(\epsilon^2)$ term and avoid tracing irrelevant terms through our calculations without losing rigor, e.g. $\ln(1 + \epsilon) = \epsilon + O(\epsilon^2)$ can be written as $\ln(1 + \epsilon) \simeq \epsilon$.

For $c \in [0, 1)$ and $k \in \mathbb{Z}$ we define rounding operators $\lceil c \rceil_k = \lceil 2^k c \rceil / 2^k$ and $\lfloor c \rfloor_k = \lfloor 2^k c \rfloor / 2^k$, which round c (up or down, respectively) to a number with k fractional bits. We also define a randomized rounding operator $\lfloor c \rceil_k = \lfloor c \rfloor_k + \mathcal{B}_\alpha / 2^k$ (where $\mathcal{B}_\alpha$ is a Bernoulli random variable of parameter $\alpha = 2^k c \bmod 1$) which rounds c to either $\lceil c \rceil_k$ (with probability α) or $\lfloor c \rfloor_k$ (with probability $1 - \alpha$).

Approximations of Real Numbers. A p-bit floating point (FP) approximation $\bar{x}$ of a real x stores the p most significant bits of x together with a binary exponent. This guarantees that the relative error is bounded by $\delta_{\mathrm{RE}}(x, \bar{x}) = |x - \bar{x}|/|x| \leq 2^{-p}$. We extend the notion of relative error to any two distributions $\mathcal{P}$ and $\mathcal{Q}$

$$\delta_{\mathrm{RE}}(\mathcal{P}, \mathcal{Q}) = \max_{x \in S} \delta_{\mathrm{RE}}(\mathcal{P}(x), \mathcal{Q}(x)) = \max_{x \in S} \frac{|\mathcal{P}(x) - \mathcal{Q}(x)|}{\mathcal{P}(x)},$$

where S is the support of $\mathcal{P}$. It is straightforward to verify that $\Delta_{\mathrm{SD}}(\mathcal{P}, \mathcal{Q}) \leq \frac{1}{2}\delta_{\mathrm{RE}}(\mathcal{P}, \mathcal{Q})$. The relative error can also be used to bound the KL-divergence:

Lemma 1 (Strengthening [40, Lemma 2]). *For any two distributions $\mathcal{P}$ and $\mathcal{Q}$ with $\mu = \delta_{\mathrm{RE}}(\mathcal{P}, \mathcal{Q}) < 1$,*

$$\delta_{\mathrm{KL}}(\mathcal{P}, \mathcal{Q}) \leq \frac{\mu^2}{2(1 - \mu)^2}.$$

In particular, if $\mu \leq 1/4$, then $\delta_{\mathrm{KL}}(\mathcal{P}, \mathcal{Q}) \leq (8/9)\mu^2 < \mu^2$.

Proof. Recall that $\delta_{\mathrm{KL}}(\mathcal{P}, \mathcal{Q}) = \sum_i \mathcal{P}(i) \ln(\mathcal{P}(i)/\mathcal{Q}(i))$. For any $p, q > 0$, let $x = (p - q)/p = 1 - (q/p) < 1$, so that $\ln(p/q) = -\ln(1 - x) = x + e(x)$ with error function $e(x) = -x - \ln(1 - x)$. Notice that $e(0) = 0$, $e'(0) = 0$ and $e''(x) = 1/(1 - x)^2 \leq 1/(1 - \mu)^2$ for all $x \leq \mu$. It follows that $e(x) \leq x^2/(2(1 - \mu)^2) \leq \mu^2/(2(1 - \mu)^2)$ for all $|x| \leq \mu$, and

$$\delta_{\mathrm{KL}}(\mathcal{P}, \mathcal{Q}) = \sum_i \mathcal{P}(i) \ln \left(\frac{\mathcal{P}(i)}{\mathcal{Q}(i)} \right) \leq \sum_i \mathcal{P}(i) \cdot \left(\frac{\mathcal{P}(i) - \mathcal{Q}(i)}{\mathcal{P}(i)} + e \right) = 1 - 1 + e = e$$

where $e = \mu^2/(2(1 - \mu)^2)$. □

This is a slight improvement over [40, Lemma 2], which shows that if $\mu \leq 1/4$, then $\delta_{\mathrm{KL}}(\mathcal{P}, \mathcal{Q}) \leq 2\mu^2$. So, Lemma 1 improves the bound by a constant factor $9/4$. In fact, for $\mu \approx 0$, Lemma 1 shows that the bound can be further improved to $\delta_{\mathrm{KL}}(\mathcal{P}, \mathcal{Q}) \lesssim \frac{1}{2}\mu^2$.

Discrete Gaussians. Let $\rho(x) = \exp(-\pi x^2)$ be the Gaussian function with total mass $\int_x \rho(x) = 1$. We extend it to countable sets A by $\rho(A) = \sum_{x \in A} \rho(x)$. We write $\rho_{c,s}(x) = \rho((x - c)/s)$ for the Gaussian function centered around c and scaled by a factor s. The discrete Gaussian distribution over the integers, denoted $\mathcal{D}_{\mathbb{Z},c,s}$, is the distribution that samples $y \leftarrow \mathcal{D}_{\mathbb{Z},c,s}$ with probability $\rho_{c,s}(y)/\rho_{c,s}(\mathbb{Z})$ for any $y \in \mathbb{Z}$. Sampling from $\mathcal{D}_{\mathbb{Z},c,s}$ is computationally equivalent to sampling from $\mathcal{D}_{c+\mathbb{Z},s}$, the centered discrete Gaussian over the coset $c + \mathbb{Z}$. For any $\epsilon > 0$, the smoothing parameter [31] of the integers $\eta_\epsilon(\mathbb{Z})$ is the smallest $s > 0$ such that $\rho(s\mathbb{Z}) \leq 1 + \epsilon$. A special case of [31, Lemma 3.3] shows that the smoothing parameter satisfies

$$\eta_\epsilon(\mathbb{Z}) \leq \sqrt{\ln(2 + 2/\epsilon)/\pi}.$$

So, $\eta_\epsilon(\mathbb{Z}) < 6$ is a relatively small constant even for very small values of $\epsilon < 2^{-160}$. Another useful bound, which easily follows from Poisson summation formula [31, Lemma 2.8], is $\delta_{\mathrm{RE}}(s, \rho_{c,s}(\mathbb{Z})) \leq \delta_{\mathrm{RE}}(s, \rho_s(\mathbb{Z})) = \rho(s\mathbb{Z}) - 1$. Therefore, for any $s \geq \eta_\epsilon(\mathbb{Z})$, and $c \in \mathbb{R}$, we have

$$\delta_{\mathrm{RE}}(s, \rho_{c,s}(\mathbb{Z})) \leq \epsilon,$$

i.e., the total measure of $\rho_{c,s}(\mathbb{Z})$ approximates s. We will use the smoothing parameter to invoke the following tail bound and discrete convolution theorems.

Lemma 2 ([22, **Lemma 4.2 (ePrint)**]). *For any $\epsilon > 0$, any $s > \eta_\epsilon(\mathbb{Z})$, and any $t > 0$,*

$$\Pr_{x \leftarrow \mathcal{D}_{\mathbb{Z},c,s}}[|x - c| \geq t \cdot s] \leq 2e^{-\pi t^2} \cdot \frac{1 + \epsilon}{1 - \epsilon}.$$

Theorem 1 ([30, **Theorem 3**]). *Let Λ be an n-dimensional lattice, $\mathbf{z} \in \mathbb{Z}^m$ a nonzero integer vector, $\mathbf{s} \in \mathbb{R}^m$ with $s_i \geq \sqrt{2}\|\mathbf{z}\|_\infty \eta_\epsilon(\mathbb{Z})$ for all $i \leq m$ and $\mathbf{c}_i + \Lambda$ arbitrary cosets. Let $\mathbf{y}_i$ be independent samples from $\mathcal{D}_{\mathbf{c}_i+\Lambda,s_i}$, respectively. Then the distribution of $\mathbf{y} = \sum z_i \mathbf{y}_i$ is close to $\mathcal{D}_{Y,s}$, where $Y = \sum_i z_i \mathbf{c}_i + \gcd(\mathbf{z})\Lambda$ and $s = \sqrt{\sum_i z_i^2 s_i^2}$. In particular, if $\tilde{\mathcal{D}}_{Y,s}$ is the distribution of $\mathbf{y}$, then $\delta_{\mathrm{RE}}(\mathcal{D}_{Y,s}, \tilde{\mathcal{D}}_{Y,s}) \leq \frac{1+\epsilon}{1-\epsilon} - 1 \simeq 2\epsilon$.*

The theorem is stated in its full generality, but in this work we will only use it for the one dimensional lattice $\mathbb{Z}$ and for the case that $\mathbf{c}_i = 0$ and $\gcd(\mathbf{z}) = 1$.

Theorem 2 ([38, Theorem 1]). *Let* $\mathbf{S}_1, \mathbf{S}_2 > 0$ *be positive definite matrices, with* $\mathbf{S} = \mathbf{S}_1 + \mathbf{S}_2$ *and* $\mathbf{S}_3^{-1} = \mathbf{S}_1^{-1} + \mathbf{S}_2^{-1} > 0$. *Let* Λ_1, Λ_2 *be lattices such that* $\sqrt{\mathbf{S}_1} \geq \eta_\epsilon(\Lambda_1)$ *and* $\sqrt{\mathbf{S}_3} \geq \eta_\epsilon(\Lambda_2)$ *for some positive* $\epsilon \leq 1/2$, *and let* $\mathbf{c}_1, \mathbf{c}_2 \in \mathbb{R}^n$ *be arbitrary. Then the distribution of* $\mathbf{x}_1 \leftarrow \mathbf{x}_2 + \mathcal{D}_{\mathbf{c}_1 - \mathbf{x}_2 + \Lambda_1, \sqrt{\mathbf{S}_1}}$, *where* $\mathbf{x}_2 \leftarrow \mathcal{D}_{\mathbf{c}_2 + \Lambda_2, \sqrt{\mathbf{S}_2}}$, *is close to* $\mathcal{D}_{\mathbf{c}_1 + \Lambda_1, \sqrt{\mathbf{S}_1}}$. *In particular, if* $\tilde{\mathcal{D}}_{\mathbf{c}_1 + \Lambda_1, \sqrt{\mathbf{S}_1}}$ *is the distribution of* $\mathbf{x}_1$, *then* $\delta_{\mathrm{RE}}(\mathcal{D}_{\mathbf{c}_1 + \Lambda_1, \sqrt{\mathbf{S}_1}}, \tilde{\mathcal{D}}_{\mathbf{c}_1 + \Lambda_1, \sqrt{\mathbf{S}_1}}) \leq \left(\frac{1+\epsilon}{1-\epsilon}\right)^2 - 1 \simeq 4\epsilon$.

Again, we stated the theorem in its full generality, but we will only need it for one dimensional lattices. Accordingly, $\mathbf{S}_1$, $\mathbf{S}_2$, and $\mathbf{S}_3$ will simply be (the square of) real noise parameters s_1, s_2, s_3.

3   The Security of Approximate Samplers

Many security reductions for lattice-based cryptographic primitives assume that the primitive has access to samplers for an ideal distribution, which may be too difficult or costly to sample from, and is routinely replaced by an approximation in any concrete implementation. Naturally, if the approximation is good enough, then security with respect to the ideal distribution implies that the actual implementation (using the approximate distribution) is also secure. But evaluating how the quality of approximation directly affects the concrete security level achieved by the primitive can be a rather technical task. Traditionally, the quality of the approximation has been measured in terms of the statistical distance $\delta = \Delta_{\mathrm{SD}}$, which satisfies the following useful properties:

1. *Probability preservation:* for any event E over the random variable X we have $Pr_{X \leftarrow \mathcal{P}}[E] \geq Pr_{X \leftarrow \mathcal{Q}}[E] - \delta(\mathcal{P}, \mathcal{Q})$. This property allows to bound the probability of an event occurring under $\mathcal{P}$ in terms of the probability of the same event occurring under $\mathcal{Q}$ and the quantity $\delta(\mathcal{P}, \mathcal{Q})$. It is easy to see that this property is equivalent to the bound $\Delta_{\mathrm{SD}}(\mathcal{P}, \mathcal{Q}) \leq \delta(\mathcal{P}, \mathcal{Q})$. So the statistical distance $\delta = \Delta_{\mathrm{SD}}$ satisfies this property by definition.
2. *Sub-additivity for joint distributions:* if $(X_i)_i$ and $(Y_i)_i$ are two lists of discrete random variables over the support $\prod_i S_i$, then

$$\delta((X_i)_i, (Y_i)_i) \leq \sum_i \max_a \delta([X_i \mid X_{<i} = a], [Y_i \mid Y_{<i} = a]),$$

where $X_{<i} = (X_1, \ldots, X_{i-1})$ (and similarly for $Y_{<i}$), and the maximum is taken over $a \in \prod_{j<i} S_j$.
3. *Data processing inequality:* $\delta(f(\mathcal{P}), f(\mathcal{Q})) \leq \delta(\mathcal{P}, \mathcal{Q})$ for any two distributions $\mathcal{P}$ and $\mathcal{Q}$ and (possibly randomized) algorithm $f(\cdot)$, i.e., the measure does not increase under function application.

We call any measure that satisfies these three properties a *useful* measure. Before using such a measure to prove security, we need to define the class of generic cryptographic schemes it applies to.

Definition 1 (Standard cryptographic scheme). *We consider an arbitrary cryptographic scheme S, consisting of one or more algorithms with oracle access to a probability distribution ensemble $\mathcal{P}_\theta$, and whose security against an adversary A (also consisting of one or more algorithms) is described in terms of a game $G_{S,A}^\mathcal{P}$ defining the event that A succeeded in breaking the scheme S. The success probability of A against S (when using samples from $\mathcal{P}_\theta$) is defined as $\epsilon_A^\mathcal{P} = \Pr\{G_{S,A}^\mathcal{P}\}$. The cost of an attack A against S is defined as $t_A/\epsilon_A^\mathcal{P}$, and the bit-security of S is the minimum (over all adversaries A) of $\log(t_A/\epsilon_A^\mathcal{P})$.*

For simplicity, we assume that the running time t_A of the game $G_{S,A}^\mathcal{P}$ does not depend on the distributions $\mathcal{P}_\theta$, and that the number of calls to $\mathcal{P}_\theta$ performed during any run of the game $G_{S,A}^\mathcal{P}$ is bounded from above by t_A.

Proving security of cryptosystems using approximate samplers using properties 1 to 3 is folklore, but for completeness we give a proof in the full version [32]. The proof captures the intuition that security with respect to an ideal distribution implies security with respect to any sufficiently good approximation, and it also gives a way to establish concrete security bounds. In order to (almost) preserve κ bits of security, one needs $\delta(\mathcal{P}_\theta, \mathcal{Q}_\theta) < 2^{-\kappa}$, e.g., as obtained, using $\delta = \Delta_{\text{SD}}$ and estimating the ideal probabilities $\mathcal{Q}(x)$ with κ-bit (fixed point or floating point) approximations. Additionally, this allows us to view $\mathcal{D}_{\mathbb{Z},c,s}$ as a ts-bounded distribution without losing security. Notice that for a security parameter κ we can set t to about $\sqrt{\kappa \ln 2/\pi} \approx \eta_{2^{-\kappa}}(\mathbb{Z})$, which by Lemma 2 implies a statistical distance of less than $2^{-\kappa}$ if $s \geq \eta_\epsilon(\mathbb{Z})$. So in the rest of this work we will identify the unbounded Gaussian distribution $\mathcal{D}_{\mathbb{Z},c,s}$ with its truncation with support $\mathbb{Z} \cap [c \pm ts]$ whenever appropriate.

While using Δ_{SD} is asymptotically efficient, it has been observed that in practice it can lead to unnecessarily large memory cost and slow computations. The work of [40] showed that we can improve the security analysis of approximate distributions. Assume we have a measure δ that satisfies the following strengthening of the probability preservation property:

1.[*] *Pythagorean probability preservation* with parameter $\lambda \in \mathbb{R}$, which states that for any joint distributions $(\mathcal{P}_i)_i$ and $(\mathcal{Q}_i)_i$ over support $\prod_i S_i$, if

$$\delta(\mathcal{P}_i \mid a_i, \mathcal{Q}_i \mid a_i) \leq \lambda$$

for all i and $a_i \in \prod_{j<i} S_j$, then

$$\Delta_{\text{SD}}((\mathcal{P}_i)_i, (\mathcal{Q}_i)_i) \leq \|(\max_{a_i} \delta(\mathcal{P}_i \mid a_i, \mathcal{Q}_i \mid a_i))_i\|_2.$$

We call a measure that satisfies this property λ-*pythagorean*. A pythagorean measure additionally satisfying sub-additivity for joint distributions and the data processing inequality (i.e. properties 2 and 3) will be called λ-*efficient*. Using a pythagorean δ, we can improve the folklore security proof as follows.

Lemma 3. *Let $S^{\mathcal{P}}$ be a standard cryptographic scheme as in Definition 1 with black-box access to a probability distribution ensemble $\mathcal{P}_\theta$. If $S^{\mathcal{P}}$ is κ-bit secure and $\delta(\mathcal{P}_\theta, \mathcal{Q}_\theta) \leq 2^{-\kappa/2}$ for some $2^{-\kappa/2}$-efficient measure δ, then $S^{\mathcal{Q}}$ is $(\kappa - 3)$-bit secure.*

Proof. Towards a contradiction, assume for some adversary A we have $\frac{t_A}{\epsilon_A^{\mathcal{P}}} \geq 2^\kappa$, but $\frac{t_A}{\epsilon_A^{\mathcal{Q}}} < 2^{\kappa-3}$. Consider the hypothetical game $[G_{S,A}^{\mathcal{Q}}]^n$ (resp. $[G_{S,A}^{\mathcal{P}}]^n$) consisting of n independent copies of $G_{S,A}^{\mathcal{Q}}$ (resp. $G_{S,A}^{\mathcal{P}}$). Denote the probability of the event that A wins at least one of the n games by $\epsilon_{A^n}^{\mathcal{Q}}$ (resp. $\epsilon_{A^n}^{\mathcal{P}}$). We begin by showing that we can bound $\epsilon_{A^n}^{\mathcal{P}}$ from below in terms of $\epsilon_{A^n}^{\mathcal{Q}}$ using probability preservation and data processing inequality of Δ_{SD}:

$$\epsilon_{A^n}^{\mathcal{P}} \geq \epsilon_{A^n}^{\mathcal{Q}} - \Delta_{SD}([G_{S,A}^{\mathcal{P}}]^n, [G_{S,A}^{\mathcal{Q}}]^n) \geq \epsilon_{A^n}^{\mathcal{Q}} - \Delta_{SD}((\theta_i, \mathcal{P}_{\theta_i})_i, (\tilde{\theta}_i, \mathcal{Q}_{\tilde{\theta}_i})_i)$$

where $(\theta_i)_i$ (resp. $(\tilde{\theta}_i)_i$) is the sequence of queries made during the game $[G_{S,A}^{\mathcal{P}}]^n$ (resp. $[G_{S,A}^{\mathcal{Q}}]^n$).

Now we note that at any point during the game, conditioned on the event X_i that $(\theta_j, \mathcal{P}_{\theta_j})_{j<i}$ and $(\tilde{\theta}_j, \mathcal{Q}_{\tilde{\theta}_j})_{j<i}$ take some specific (and identical) value, the adversary behaves identically in the two games up to the point it makes the ith query. In particular, the conditional distributions $(\theta_i \mid X_i)$ and $(\tilde{\theta}_i \mid X_i)$ are identical and $\delta((\theta_i \mid X_i), (\tilde{\theta}_i \mid X_i)) = 0$. It follows by sub-additivity (for joint distributions) that

$$\delta((\theta_i, \mathcal{P}_{\theta_i} \mid X_i), (\tilde{\theta}_i, \mathcal{Q}_{\tilde{\theta}_i} \mid X_i)) \leq \delta((\theta_i \mid X_i), (\tilde{\theta}_i \mid X_i)) + \delta(\mathcal{P}_\theta, \mathcal{Q}_\theta)$$
$$\leq 0 + 2^{-\kappa/2} = 2^{-\kappa/2}.$$

This ensures that we can apply pythagorean probability preservation (Property 1^*) to obtain

$$\epsilon_{A^n}^{\mathcal{P}} \geq \epsilon_{A^n}^{\mathcal{Q}} - \sqrt{t_{A^n}} \cdot \delta(\mathcal{P}_\theta, \mathcal{Q}_\theta) \geq \epsilon_{A^n}^{\mathcal{Q}} - \sqrt{t_{A^n}} \cdot 2^{-\kappa/2} \geq \epsilon_{A^n}^{\mathcal{Q}} - \sqrt{\frac{n \cdot t_A}{2^\kappa}}. \quad (1)$$

Now we set $n = 1/\epsilon_A^{\mathcal{Q}}$ so that $\epsilon_{A^n}^{\mathcal{Q}} = 1 - (1 - \epsilon_A^{\mathcal{Q}})^n > 1 - \exp(-1)$. Substituting into (1) and using $\frac{t_A}{\epsilon_A^{\mathcal{Q}}} < 2^{\kappa-3}$ we get

$$\epsilon_{A^n}^{\mathcal{P}} > 1 - \exp(-1) - \sqrt{\frac{t_A}{2^\kappa \epsilon_A^{\mathcal{Q}}}} > 1 - \exp(-1) - 2^{-3/2} \approx 0.279.$$

Finally, to achieve a contradiction, we derive a simple upper bound. By union bound $\epsilon_{A^n}^{\mathcal{P}} \leq n \epsilon_A^{\mathcal{P}}$. Since $S^{\mathcal{P}}$ is κ-bit secure, $\epsilon_A^{\mathcal{P}} \leq t_A/2^\kappa$, which shows that

$$\epsilon_{A^n}^{\mathcal{P}} \leq \frac{n t_A}{2^\kappa} = \frac{t_A}{2^\kappa \epsilon_A^{\mathcal{Q}}} < 2^{-3} = 0.125$$

which is smaller than the lower bound. $\qquad\square$

This shows that $\delta(\mathcal{P}_\theta, \mathcal{Q}_\theta) \sim 2^{-\kappa/2}$ is sufficient to maintain κ bits of security. This type of analysis was first used in [40] for the special case of fixed distributions (i.e. θ is fixed and cannot be chosen by the adversary) and the KL-divergence $\delta = \sqrt{\delta_{\mathrm{KL}}}$, which is efficient (see e.g. [5,40] for proofs). Lemma 1, in combination with Lemma 3, shows that it is sufficient for algorithms to approximate the probabilities of the target distribution with floating point numbers of precision about half the security parameter. Interestingly, in this setting, it is important to approximate probabilities in floating point, as $\kappa/2$ bits of fixed-point precision is not secure. (See the full version [32] for an attack.)

In this work, we make use of the Theorems 1 and 2 to reduce the task of generating a specific discrete Gaussian, to generating samples from different distributions. Observe that these theorems assume access to exact samplers. In order to analyze our algorithms, we need to bound the divergence from the true distribution when applying the theorems to samples from a distribution close to the exact Gaussian distributions.

Lemma 4. *Let Δ be a useful or efficient metric. Let $A^\mathcal{P}$ be an algorithm querying a distribution ensemble $\mathcal{P}_\theta$ at most q times. Then we have*

$$\Delta(A^\mathcal{Q}, \mathcal{R}) \leq \Delta(A^\mathcal{P}, \mathcal{R}) + q \cdot \Delta(\mathcal{P}_\theta, \mathcal{Q}_\theta)$$

for any distribution $\mathcal{R}$ and any ensemble $\mathcal{Q}_\theta$.

For the proof we refer to the full version [32].

By letting A be the algorithm that performs the convolution as in Theorem 1 and applying Lemma 4 to it with $\mathcal{P}_i = \mathcal{D}_{\Lambda, \mathbf{c}_i, s_i}$ and approximate distributions $\mathcal{Q}_i = \tilde{\mathcal{D}}_{\Lambda, \mathbf{c}_i, s_i}$, we can show that convolving approximate discrete Gaussians results in good approximations of the expected discrete Gaussian. Furthermore, we can also apply Lemma 4 to Theorem 2, if we have a bound on the approximation of the second sampler for *any* center $\mathbf{c}_2$.

As an example, consider again the statistical distance Δ_{SD}. By applying Lemma 4 to the convolutions in Theorem 1 (resp. 2), the resulting approximation error satisfies:

$$\Delta_{\mathrm{SD}}(A^{\tilde{\mathcal{D}}_{\Lambda, \mathbf{c}_i, s_i}}, \mathcal{D}_{Y,s}) \lesssim 2\epsilon + \sum_i \Delta_{\mathrm{SD}}(\tilde{\mathcal{D}}_{\Lambda, \mathbf{c}_i, s_i}, \mathcal{D}_{\Lambda, \mathbf{c}_i, s_i}).$$

Conveniently, this works recursively: if we use the obtained approximate samples as input to another convolution, the loss in statistical distance is simply additive in the number of convolutions we apply. This shows that using a metric to analyze approximation errors is relatively straight-forward.

Unfortunately, Δ_{SD} is not efficient and thus requires high precision to guarantee security. While $\sqrt{\delta_{\mathrm{KL}}}$ allows to improve on that, it is not a metric and thus Lemma 4 does not apply. One can still use $\sqrt{\delta_{\mathrm{KL}}}$ to improve on the efficiency by exploiting the metric properties of Δ_{SD}, i.e. one first decomposes the statistical distance of the approximate distribution as in the previous paragraph, and then bounds the individual parts using property 3. But as we start working with more complex and recursive algorithms, this method becomes more involved. One needs to be careful to not rely on typical metric properties when analyzing algorithms using $\sqrt{\delta_{\mathrm{KL}}}$, like triangle inequality and symmetry. We found it much more convenient to use an efficient *metric* Δ. This allows to carry out the analysis using only Δ, and directly claim bit security of $-2\log\Delta(\mathcal{P}_\theta, \mathcal{Q}_\theta)$ by Lemma 3.

4 A New Closeness Metric

In this section we introduce a new measure of closeness between probability distributions which combines the ease of use of a metric with the properties of divergences that allow to obtain sharper security bounds. More specifically, we provide an efficient metric with a simple definition.

Definition 2. *The* max-log *distance between two distributions $\mathcal{P}$ and $\mathcal{Q}$ over the same support S is*

$$\Delta_{\mathrm{ML}}(\mathcal{P},\mathcal{Q}) = \max_{x\in S}|\ln\mathcal{P}(x) - \ln\mathcal{Q}(x)|.$$

For convenience, we also write $\Delta_{\mathrm{ML}}(p,q) = |\ln p - \ln q|$ for any two positive reals p and q. It is easy to see that Δ_{ML} is a metric.

Lemma 5. Δ_{ML} *is a metric, i.e., it is symmetric ($\Delta_{\mathrm{ML}}(\mathcal{P},\mathcal{Q}) = \Delta_{\mathrm{ML}}(\mathcal{Q},\mathcal{P})$), positive definite ($\Delta_{\mathrm{ML}}(\mathcal{P},\mathcal{Q}) \geq 0$ with equality if and only if $\mathcal{P} = \mathcal{Q}$), and it satisfies the triangle inequality ($\Delta_{\mathrm{ML}}(\mathcal{P},\mathcal{Q}) \leq \Delta_{\mathrm{ML}}(\mathcal{P},\mathcal{R}) + \Delta_{\mathrm{ML}}(\mathcal{R},\mathcal{Q})$).*

Proof. All properties are inherited from the infinity norm, simply by noticing that $\Delta_{\mathrm{ML}}(\mathcal{P},\mathcal{Q}) = \|f(\mathcal{P}) - f(\mathcal{Q})\|_\infty$ for some function $f(\mathcal{P}) = (\ln\mathcal{P}(x))_x$. □

In the full version [32] we proof that in the regime close to 0, Δ_{ML} is essentially equal to δ_{RE}.

Lemma 6. *For any two positive real p and q,*

$$\Delta_{\mathrm{ML}}(p,q) \leq -\ln(1-\delta_{\mathrm{RE}}(p,q)) \lesssim \delta_{\mathrm{RE}}(p,q) \tag{2}$$
$$\delta_{\mathrm{RE}}(p,q) \leq \exp(\Delta_{\mathrm{ML}}(p,q)) - 1 \lesssim \Delta_{\mathrm{ML}}(p,q). \tag{3}$$

The same bounds hold for $\Delta_{\mathrm{ML}}(\mathcal{P},\mathcal{Q})$ and $\delta_{\mathrm{RE}}(\mathcal{P},\mathcal{Q})$ for any two distributions $\mathcal{P},\mathcal{Q}$ over the same support S.

The next two lemmas prove that Δ_{ML} is an efficient metric.

Lemma 7. Δ_{ML} *satisfies the sub-additivity property (for joint distributions) and data processing inequality.*

The proof essentially follows the proof of the same properties for Δ_{SD} from [28]. For completeness we provide it in the full version [32].

Finally, we show that Δ_{ML} also satisfies the pythagorean probability preservation property for any parameter $\lambda \leq \frac{1}{3}$.

Lemma 8. *For distributions $\mathcal{P}_i$ and $\mathcal{Q}_i$ over support $\prod_i S_i$, if $\Delta_{\mathrm{ML}}(\mathcal{P}_i \mid a_i, \mathcal{Q}_i \mid a_i) \leq 1/3$ for all i and $a_i \in \prod_{j<i} S_j$, then*

$$\Delta_{\mathrm{SD}}((\mathcal{P}_i)_i, (\mathcal{Q}_i)_i) \leq \|(\max_{a_i} \Delta_{\mathrm{ML}}(\mathcal{P}_i \mid a_i, \mathcal{Q}_i \mid a_i))_i\|_2.$$

Proof. First, we observe that under the condition $\Delta_{\mathrm{ML}}(\mathcal{P}, \mathcal{Q}) \leq 1/3$, we have $\delta_{\mathrm{KL}}(\mathcal{P}, \mathcal{Q}) \leq 2\Delta_{\mathrm{ML}}(\mathcal{P}, \mathcal{Q})^2$. This can be checked using Eq. (3) as follows. Let $x = \Delta_{\mathrm{ML}}(\mathcal{P}, \mathcal{Q}) \leq 1/3$. Applying Lemma 1 with $\mu = e^x - 1$, we get

$$\delta_{\mathrm{KL}}(\mathcal{P}, \mathcal{Q}) \leq \frac{(e^x - 1)^2}{2(2 - e^x)^2} \leq 2x^2,$$

where the last inequality is implied by $(e^x - 1)(1 + 1/(2x)) \leq 1$, which can be verified using the convexity bound $e^x - 1 \leq (e^{\frac{1}{3}} - 1)3x$ (valid for $x \in [0, 1/3]$) as follows:

$$(e^x - 1) \cdot \left(1 + \frac{1}{2x}\right) \leq (e^{\frac{1}{3}} - 1) \cdot (3x + 1.5) \leq (e^{\frac{1}{3}} - 1) \cdot 2.5 \approx 0.99.$$

Now that we have established the bound $\delta_{\mathrm{KL}}(\mathcal{P}, \mathcal{Q}) \leq 2\Delta_{\mathrm{ML}}(\mathcal{P}, \mathcal{Q})^2$, we can use Pinsker's inequality and the sub-additivity of δ_{KL} (which directly follows from what is often referred to as the *chain rule*) to get

$$\Delta_{\mathrm{SD}}((\mathcal{P}_i)_i, (\mathcal{Q}_i)_i) \leq \sqrt{\delta_{\mathrm{KL}}((\mathcal{P}_i)_i, (\mathcal{Q}_i)_i)/2}$$

$$\leq \sqrt{\frac{1}{2} \sum_i \max_{a_i} \delta_{\mathrm{KL}}(\mathcal{P}_i \mid a_i, \mathcal{Q}_i \mid a_i)}$$

$$\leq \sqrt{\sum_i \max_{a_i} \Delta_{\mathrm{ML}}(\mathcal{P}_i \mid a_i, \mathcal{Q}_i \mid a_i)^2}$$

$$= \|(\max_{a_i} \Delta_{\mathrm{ML}}(\mathcal{P}_i \mid a_i, \mathcal{Q}_i \mid a_i))_i\|_2.$$

$\square$

It follows that we can instantiate Lemma 4 with Δ_{ML} to analyze the increase of approximation error if applying multiple convolutions to approximate samples. We make this explicit by reformulating Theorems 1 and 2 in terms of the max-log distance and approximate distributions (following Lemma 4), specializing them to our setting.

Corollary 1. *Let $\mathbf{z} \in \mathbb{Z}^m$ be a nonzero integer vector with $\gcd(\mathbf{z}) = 1$ and $\mathbf{s} \in \mathbb{R}^m$ with $s_i \geq \sqrt{2}\|\mathbf{z}\|_\infty \eta_\epsilon(\mathbb{Z})$ for all $i \leq m$. Let y_i be independent samples from $\tilde{\mathcal{D}}_{\mathbb{Z},s_i}$, respectively, with $\Delta_{\mathrm{ML}}(\mathcal{D}_{\mathbb{Z},s_i}, \tilde{\mathcal{D}}_{\mathbb{Z},s_i}) \leq \mu_i$ for all i. Let $\tilde{\mathcal{D}}_{\mathbb{Z},s}$ be the distribution of $y = \sum z_i y_i$. Then $\Delta_{\mathrm{ML}}(\mathcal{D}_{\mathbb{Z},s}, \tilde{\mathcal{D}}_{\mathbb{Z},s}) \lesssim 2\epsilon + \sum_i \mu_i$.*

Corollary 2. *Let $s_1, s_2 > 0$, with $s^2 = s_1^2 + s_2^2$ and $s_3^{-2} = s_1^{-2} + s_2^{-2}$. Let $\Lambda = K\mathbb{Z}$ be a copy of the integer lattice $\mathbb{Z}$ scaled by a constant K. For any c_1 and $c_2 \in \mathbb{R}$,* denote the distribution of $x_1 \leftarrow x_2 + \tilde{\mathcal{D}}_{c_1-x_2+\mathbb{Z},s_1}$, where $x_2 \leftarrow \tilde{\mathcal{D}}_{c_2+\Lambda,s_2}$, by $\tilde{\mathcal{D}}_{c_1+\mathbb{Z},s}$. If $s_1 \geq \eta_\epsilon(\mathbb{Z})$, $s_3 \geq \eta_\epsilon(\Lambda) = K\eta_\epsilon(\mathbb{Z})$, $\Delta_{\mathrm{ML}}(\mathcal{D}_{c_2+\Lambda,s_2}, \tilde{\mathcal{D}}_{c_2+\Lambda,s_2}) \leq \mu_2$ and $\Delta_{\mathrm{ML}}(\mathcal{D}_{c+\mathbb{Z},s_1}, \tilde{\mathcal{D}}_{c+\mathbb{Z},s_1}) \leq \mu_1$ for any $c \in \mathbb{R}$, then

$$\Delta_{\mathrm{ML}}(\mathcal{D}_{c_1+\mathbb{Z},s}, \tilde{\mathcal{D}}_{c_1+\mathbb{Z},s}) \lesssim 4\epsilon + \mu_1 + \mu_2.$$

Relationship to Other Measures. The max-log distance is closely related to the Rényi divergence of order ∞ and shares many of its properties, including a multiplicative probability preservation: $Pr_{X\leftarrow\mathcal{P}}[E] \geq Pr_{X\leftarrow\mathcal{Q}}[E]/\exp(\Delta_{\mathrm{ML}}(\mathcal{P},\mathcal{Q}))$ [5]. While we do not use this property in this work, a subsequent work [41] shows that this property can be used to achieve even stronger security proofs (for a different definition of bit security).

It has also been noted that the Rényi divergence is related to the notion of differential privacy. More specifically, an algorithm $A(D)$, taking a database D as input, is ϵ-differentially private if the Rényi divergence of order ∞ between the output distributions of $A(D_1)$ and $A(D_2)$ is less than ϵ for any two neighboring databases D_1 and D_2. Since *neighborhood* is often defined using a symmetric relation on the set of databases, this is equivalent to a formulation using the max-log distance. Finally, the techniques used in [41] are related to *advanced composition theorems* in the differential privacy terminology. For more details we refer the reader to [33] and references therein.

5   Sampling the Integers

In this section we describe and analyze our new algorithm to sample the discrete Gaussian distribution. The entire algorithm SAMPLEZ is presented in Algorithm 1. In Sects. 5.1 and 5.2, we analyze the sub-routines SAMPLEI and SAMPLEC, which may already be directly useful in some applications. Then, in Sect. 5.3, we analyze the full algorithm SAMPLEZ. All algorithms assume access to a base sampler SAMPLEB to approximate the distribution $\mathcal{D}_{c_i+\mathbb{Z},s_0}$, for a small and fixed set of values for the coset c_i and one fixed s_0. Any algorithm can be used as a base sampler, provided it produces distributions $\tilde{\mathcal{D}}_{c_i+\mathbb{Z},s_0}$ within a small distance $\Delta_{\mathrm{ML}}(\tilde{\mathcal{D}}_{c_i+\mathbb{Z},s_0}, \mathcal{D}_{c_i+\mathbb{Z},s_0}) \leq \mu$ from the exact Gaussian $\mathcal{D}_{c_i+\mathbb{Z},s_0}$. By Lemma 6, this is essentially equivalent to approximating the Gaussian probabilities with a relative error bound of μ. The reader is referred to Sect. 6.2 for a possible choice of SAMPLEB.

$\text{SAMPLEZ}_{b,k,\max}(c,s)$
  $x \leftarrow \text{SAMPLEI}(\max)$
  $K \leftarrow \sqrt{s^2 - \bar{s}^2}/s_{\max}$
  $c' \leftarrow \lfloor c + Kx \rceil_k$ $\text{SAMPLEI}(i)$
  $y \leftarrow \text{SAMPLEC}_{b,s_0}(c')$ **if** $i = 0$
  return y $x \leftarrow \text{SAMPLEB}_{s_0}(0)$
            return x
            $x_1 \leftarrow \text{SAMPLEI}(i-1)$
            $x_2 \leftarrow \text{SAMPLEI}(i-1)$
$\text{SAMPLEC}_b(c \in b^{-k}\mathbb{Z})$ $y = z_i x_1 + \max(1, z_i - 1)x_2$
  if $k = 0$ **return** y
   return 0
  $g \leftarrow b^{-k+1} \cdot \text{SAMPLEB}_{s_0}(b^{k-1}c)$
  return $g + \text{SAMPLEC}_b(c - g \in b^{-k+1}\mathbb{Z})$

Algorithm 1: A sampling algorithm for $\mathcal{D}_{c+\mathbb{Z},s}$ for arbitrary c and s. Definitions for z_i and s_i as in (4) and (5) and $\bar{s}$ as in (6). SAMPLEB is an arbitrary base sampler for $\mathcal{D}_{c+\mathbb{Z},s_0}$ with fixed s_0 and small number of cosets $c+\mathbb{Z}$, where $c \in \mathbb{Z}/b$.

5.1 Large Deviations

In this section we show how to efficiently sample $\mathcal{D}_{\mathbb{Z},s}$ for an arbitrarily large $s \gg \eta_\epsilon(\mathbb{Z})$ using samples from $\mathcal{D}_{\mathbb{Z},s_0}$ for some small fixed value of $s_0 \geq \sqrt{2}\eta_\epsilon(\mathbb{Z})$. For this we make use of convolution to combine the samples from the basic sampler to yield a distribution with larger noise parameter. The algorithm accomplishing this is given in Algorithm 1 as SAMPLEI.

Lemma 9. *For a given value of $s_0 \geq 4\sqrt{2}\eta_\epsilon(\mathbb{Z})$ define the following sequence of values[2] for $i > 0$:*

$$z_i = \left\lfloor \frac{s_{i-1}}{\sqrt{2}\eta} \right\rfloor \tag{4}$$

$$s_i^2 = (z_i^2 + \max((z_i - 1)^2, 1))s_{i-1}^2 \tag{5}$$

If $\Delta_{\mathrm{ML}}(\mathcal{D}_{\mathbb{Z},s_0}, \text{SAMPLEB}_{s_0}(0)) \leq \mu$, then $\Delta_{\mathrm{ML}}(\mathcal{D}_{\mathbb{Z},s_i}, \text{SAMPLEI}(i)) \leq (\mu + 2\epsilon)2^i$ and the running time of SAMPLEI is at most 2^i plus 2^i invocations of SAMPLEB. Finally, $s_i(s_0) \geq 2^{2^i}$, implying $i \leq \lceil \log \log s \rceil$ is sufficient to achieve a given target s.

We defer the proof to the full version [32].

  The algorithm SAMPLEI will overshoot the noise parameter, but in many applications (including ours further below) this is enough. In fact, for us it will not matter by how much we overshoot a given target s, as we will show in the

---

[2] Notice that the values in (4) and (5) depend both on the index i and the initial s_0, so we will write them as $z_i(s_0)$ and $s_i(s_0)$ when we need to emphasize this dependency.

following sections how to adjust the noise parameter to obtain a sample from a specific target distribution (with arbitrary center).

SAMPLECENTEREDGAUSSIAN(s)
    Select largest i such that $s_i < s$
    $x_1 \leftarrow$ SAMPLEI(i)
    $x_2 \leftarrow$ SAMPLEI(i)
$$z \leftarrow \left\lceil \frac{1}{2}\left(1 + \sqrt{2\left(\frac{s}{s_i}\right)^2 - 1}\right)\right\rceil$$
    return $zx_1 + (z-1)x_2$

Algorithm 2: A sampling algorithm for $\mathcal{D}_{\mathbb{Z},\tilde{s}}$ for some $\tilde{s}$ not much larger than s. Definition of s_i as in (5).

If all we are interested in is the centered Gaussian distribution with a specific noise parameter not much larger than a certain target width, as is the case in many applications, it is relatively easy to adapt the algorithm to get closer to the target s. One way of doing this is to adjust z_i in the top level of the recursion to yield something closer to s. This is demonstrated by Algorithm 2, for which the following corollary establishes a bound on the size of the resulting noise parameter.

Corollary 3. *If $\Delta_{\mathrm{ML}}(\text{SAMPLEI}(i), \mathcal{D}_{\mathbb{Z},s_i}) \lesssim \mu$ for the largest i such that $s_i \leq s$ and $s \geq s_0 \geq \sqrt{2}\eta_\epsilon(\mathbb{Z})$, then $\Delta_{\mathrm{ML}}(\text{SAMPLECENTEREDGAUSSIAN}(s), \mathcal{D}_{\mathbb{Z},\tilde{s}}) \lesssim 2\mu + 2\epsilon$ for some $\tilde{s}$ such that $s \leq \tilde{s} \leq \sqrt{5}s$.*

Proof. First note that $s_i < s$ implies $z \geq 2$. The choice of z and s_i now guarantees that Corollary 1 is applicable and that $(z-1)^2 + (z-2)^2 < \frac{s^2}{s_i^2} \leq z^2 + (z-1)^2$. Since $\tilde{s}^2 = (z^2 + (z-1)^2)s_i^2$ this establishes the lower bound and shows that $\tilde{s}^2 \leq \frac{z^2 + (z-1)^2}{(z-1)^2 + (z-2)^2}s^2$. The upper bound follows from the fact that the ratio $\frac{z^2 + (z-1)^2}{(z-1)^2 + (z-2)^2}$ is decreasing in z and equals 5 for $z = 2$.

The bound on the Δ_{ML} distance is immediate from Corollary 1.   □

Note that the constant $\sqrt{5}$ in Corollary 3 follows from the worst case where $z = 2$. Using a little more care in the choice of small coefficients, the bound can be improved to $\sqrt{2}$, but for a simpler exposition we omitted this optimization. However, it will not be possible to get arbitrarily close to any target s if given a fixed s_0, but if the target s is fixed we can always choose a suitable small s_0 such that the target distribution will be generated exactly.

For a fixed s_0, $z_i(s_0)$ and $s_i(s_0)$ are fixed, so one can precompute s_i and corresponding z_i for a small set of i. As Lemma 9 shows, the s_i grow very rapidly so only a very small number ($\sim \log\log s$) of precomputed values are necessary to generate extremely wide distributions. If the target s is fixed, only the coefficients z_i need to be stored.

5.2 Arbitrary Center

We now show how to sample from an arbitrary coset $c + \mathbb{Z}$ using samplers for only a small number of cosets. We assume c is given as a k digit number in base b between 0 and 1. The parameter k dictates the trade-off between running time and output precision, while the basis b determines the number of cosets the base sampler SAMPLEB needs to be able to sample from.

The idea of our new algorithm SAMPLEC (see Algorithm 1) is to round the center randomly digit by digit to finally obtain a sample from $c + \mathbb{Z}$. Every rounding operation consumes a sample from one of b cosets of $\mathbb{Z}$ (where b is a parameter). To show correctness, we iteratively use a convolution theorem.

While this process of iterative rounding increases the noise of the output distribution, this increase is minor as the following lemma shows.

Lemma 10. *Let* $2 \leq b \in \mathbb{Z}$ *be a base,* $s_0 \geq (\sqrt{(b+1)/b})\eta_\epsilon(\mathbb{Z})$ *and* $c \in b^{-k}\mathbb{Z}$. *If*

$$\Delta_{\mathrm{ML}}(\mathcal{D}_{c_i+\mathbb{Z},s_0}, \mathrm{SAMPLEB}_{s_0}(c_i)) \leq \mu$$

for all $c_i \in \mathbb{Z}/b$, *then* $\Delta_{\mathrm{ML}}(\mathrm{SAMPLEC}_b(c), \mathcal{D}_{c+\mathbb{Z},\bar{s}}) \lesssim (4\epsilon + \mu)k$ *where*

$$\bar{s} = s_0 \left(\sqrt{\sum_{i=0}^{k-1} b^{-2i}} \right). \tag{6}$$

Proof. The proof follows by induction and Corollary 2. For $k = 1$ the claim is obviously true. For $k > 1$, invoke the induction hypothesis and apply Corollary 2 with $s_1 = s_0\sqrt{\sum_{i=0}^{k-2} b^{-2i}}$, $s_2 = s_0/b^{k-1}$, $\Lambda = b^{-k+1}\mathbb{Z}$, $c_2 = b^{-k}[c]_k$ (where $[c]_k$ is the k-th digit in the b-ary expansion of c), and $c_1 = c$.

It remains to show that the conditions on the noise parameters are met. First note that $\sum_{i=0}^{k} b^{-2i} \geq 1$ for all $k \geq 1$, and so $s_1 \geq s_0 > \eta_\epsilon(\mathbb{Z})$.

Then we have

$$s_3^{-2} = s_1^{-2} + s_2^{-2} = s_0^{-2}\left(\left(\sum_{i=0}^{k-2} b^{-2i} \right)^{-1} + b^{2(k-1)} \right)$$

$$= s_0^{-2}\left(\frac{1 - b^{-2}}{1 - b^{-2(k-1)}} + b^{2(k-1)} \right) = s_0^{-2}\frac{b^{2(k-1)} - b^{-2}}{1 - b^{-2(k-1)}}$$

and so

$$s_3 = \sqrt{\frac{1 - b^{-2(k-1)}}{b^{2(k-1)} - b^{-2}}} s_0 = \frac{1}{b^{k-1}}\sqrt{\frac{1 - b^{-2(k-1)}}{1 - b^{-2k}}} s_0 = \frac{1}{b^{k-1}}\sqrt{\frac{b^{2k} - b^2}{b^{2k} - 1}} s_0$$

Note that

$$\frac{b+1}{b} \cdot \frac{b^{2k} - b^2}{b^{2k} - 1} \geq 1$$

for all $k > 1$, which shows that $s_3 \geq b^{-k+1}\eta_\epsilon(\mathbb{Z}) = \eta_\epsilon(\Lambda)$. □

The parameter b in SAMPLEC offers a trade-off between running time and number of required samplers for cosets of $\mathbb{Z}$. As most efficient samplers require storage for each coset, this is effectively a time-memory trade-off. The larger the base b, the more bits we can round at a time, but that requires more cosets. Note that the running time decreases by a logarithmic factor in b, while the storage requirement increases linearly with b.

Reducing the Number of Required Samples. Recall from the previous section that the parameter k determines the trade-off between running time and output precision: the larger k, the closer the approximation of the centers and thus the better the output distribution, but the number of required base samples and the running time grow linearly with k. We now show that by using a biased coin flip we can speed up the algorithm by a factor 2 while maintaining a good approximation.

Lemma 11. *Let $s \geq \eta_\epsilon(\mathbb{Z})$ and $b, k \in \mathbb{Z}$ such that $\tau = b^{-k} \leq (4\pi)^{-1}$. Then*

$$\Delta_{\mathrm{ML}}(\mathcal{D}_{\mathbb{Z},c,s}, \mathcal{D}_{\mathbb{Z},\lfloor c \rceil_k, s}) \lesssim \pi^2 \tau^2 + 2\epsilon = \pi^2/b^{2k} + 2\epsilon,$$

where $\mathcal{D}_{\mathbb{Z},\lfloor c \rceil_k, s}$ is the distribution of the process of computing $c' = \lfloor c \rceil_k$ and then returning a sample from $\mathcal{D}_{\mathbb{Z},c',s}$.

To prove the lemma, we first observe that linear functions can approximate the Gaussian function well on small enough intervals.

Lemma 12. *For any x_1, x_2 with $x_2 - x_1 = \tau$, $|x_1|, |x_2| \leq ts$ for some $t \geq 1$ and $x \in [x_1, x_2]$, we have*

$$\delta_{\mathrm{RE}}\left(\rho_s(x), \frac{x - x_1}{\tau}\rho_s(x_2) + \frac{x_2 - x}{\tau}\rho_s(x_1)\right) \leq \frac{\pi^2 t^2 \tau^2}{2s^2} e^{\frac{2\pi\tau t}{s}}.$$

In particular, if $\tau \leq \frac{s}{4\pi t}$, the bound on the right hand side is less than $\frac{\pi^2 t^2 \tau^2}{s^2}$.

Proof. By linear interpolation,

$$\left| \rho_s(x) - \left(\frac{x - x_1}{\tau}\rho_s(x_2) + \frac{x_2 - x}{\tau}\rho_s(x_1)\right)\right| \leq \frac{\tau^2}{8} \max_{x_1 \leq x' \leq x_2} |\rho_s''(x')|$$

Observe that

$$\rho_s''(x) = \left(\frac{2\pi x^2}{s^2} - 1\right)\frac{2\pi}{s^2}\rho_s(x)$$

implying that $\|\rho_s''(x')\| \leq \max(\frac{2\pi x'^2}{s^2}, 1)\frac{2\pi}{s^2}\rho_s(x') \leq \frac{4\pi^2 t^2}{s^2}\rho(x')$. Finally note that if $x'^2 \geq x^2$, then $\rho_s(x') \leq \rho_s(x)$. Otherwise,

$$\frac{\rho_s(x')}{\rho_s(x)} = e^{-\pi(\frac{x'^2 - x^2}{s^2})} = e^{\pi(\frac{x^2 - x'^2}{s^2})} = e^{\pi(\frac{(x-x')(x+x')}{s^2})} \leq e^{\frac{2\pi\tau t}{s}}$$

concluding the proof.   □

Proof (of Lemma 11*).* We set $t = \eta_\epsilon(\mathbb{Z})$, which allows us to treat $\mathcal{D}_{c+\mathbb{Z},s}$ as a ts-bounded distribution. If we assume that $s \geq \eta_\epsilon(\mathbb{Z})$ for some negligible ϵ, we can conclude that Lemma 12 also holds for the respective distributions, since $\rho_s(c + \mathbb{Z}) \approx s$ for any c, i.e. with $c_1 = \lfloor c \rfloor_k$ and $c_2 = \lceil c \rceil_k$:

$$\Delta_{\mathrm{ML}}(\mathcal{D}_{\mathbb{Z},c,s}, \mathcal{D}_{\mathbb{Z},\lfloor c \rceil_r,s}) = \max_x \left| \ln \frac{\mathcal{D}_{\mathbb{Z},c,s}(x)}{\mathcal{D}_{\mathbb{Z},\lfloor c \rceil_r,s}(x)} \right|$$

$$= \max_x \left| \ln \frac{\mathcal{D}_{\mathbb{Z},c,s}(x)}{\left(\frac{c_2 - c}{\tau} \mathcal{D}_{\mathbb{Z},c_1,s}(x) + \frac{c - c_1}{\tau} \mathcal{D}_{\mathbb{Z},c_2,s}(x) \right)} \right|$$

$$\leq \max_x \left| \ln \frac{\rho_s(x - c)(1 \pm \epsilon)s}{(1 \pm \epsilon)s \left(\frac{c_2 - c}{\tau} \rho_s(x - c_1) + \frac{c - c_1}{\tau} \rho_s(x - c_2) \right)} \right|$$

$$\leq \max_x \left| \Delta_{\mathrm{ML}} \left(\rho_s(x - c), \frac{c_2 - c}{\tau} \rho_s(x - c_1) + \frac{c - c_1}{\tau} \rho_s(x - c_2) \right) + \ln \frac{1 \pm \epsilon}{1 \pm \epsilon} \right|$$

$$\lesssim \max_x \delta_{\mathrm{RE}} \left(\rho_s(x - c), \frac{c_2 - c}{\tau} \rho_s(x - c_1) + \frac{c - c_1}{\tau} \rho_s(x - c_2) \right) + 2\epsilon$$

$$\leq \frac{\pi^2 t^2 \tau^2}{s^2} + 2\epsilon$$

$$\lesssim \frac{\pi^2}{b^{2k}} + 2\epsilon$$

where we used Lemmas 6 and 12.   □

In combination with SAMPLEC (cf. Algorithm 1), Lemma 11 suggests an efficient algorithm to sample from $\mathcal{D}_{\mathbb{Z},c,\bar{s}}$ for fixed s and arbitrary c:

1. write c in base b (which is a parameter of the algorithm) and divide this representation into the $k = \log_b \frac{1}{\tau}$ higher order digits (representing c_{head}) and the rest c_{tail}
2. use c_{tail} to define the bias of a Bernoulli distribution to round c_{head} either up or down
3. return SAMPLEC$_{b,s_0}(c_{\text{head}} \in b^{-k}\mathbb{Z})$.

These steps correspond to the computation of c' and the following invocation of SAMPLEC in the algorithm SAMPLEZ. The efficiency gain stems from the fact that sampling from a biased Bernoulli distribution is much cheaper than drawing samples from the discrete Gaussian. This allows us to support centers c with arbitrary precision above k with essentially no efficiency loss, since the lower order bits only define the bias of the Bernoulli distribution, which is cheap to implement.

5.3   The Full Sampler

So far we have shown how to generate samples efficiently from $\mathcal{D}_{\mathbb{Z},s_i}$ for potentially very large s_i and how to sample from $\mathcal{D}_{\mathbb{Z},c,\bar{s}}$ for arbitrary $c \in \mathbb{R}$ and a specific $\bar{s}$, both using only b samplers for $\mathcal{D}_{\mathbb{Z},c_i,s_0}$ for $c_i \in b^{-1}\mathbb{Z}$ and fixed $s_0 \geq \eta_\epsilon(\mathbb{Z})$. We now prove correctness of the full sampler, SAMPLEZ, which puts all the pieces together by leveraging Corollary 2 yet again.

Lemma 13. *Let* $b, k \in \mathbb{Z}$ *be a base and a precision parameter such that* $k > \log_b 4\pi$. *If*

- $\Delta_{\mathrm{ML}}(\mathcal{D}_{\mathbb{Z},s_{\max}}, \mathrm{SAMPLEI}(\max)) \leq \mu_i$ *and*
- $\Delta_{\mathrm{ML}}(\mathcal{D}_{c'+\mathbb{Z},\bar{s}}, \mathrm{SAMPLEC}_b(c')) \leq \mu_c$ *for any* $c' \in \mathbb{Z}/b^k$ *and some* $\bar{s} \geq \eta_\epsilon(\mathbb{Z})$,

then

$$\Delta_{\mathrm{ML}}(\mathcal{D}_{c+\mathbb{Z},s}, \mathrm{SAMPLEZ}_{b,k,\max}(c,s)) \lesssim 6\epsilon + \pi^2/b^{2k} + \mu_i + \mu_c$$

for any c *and* s *such that* $1 < s/\bar{s} \leq s_{\max}/\eta_\epsilon(\mathbb{Z})$.

Proof. By Lemmas 4 and 11, $\Delta_{\mathrm{ML}}(\mathcal{D}_{c+Kx}, \mathrm{SAMPLEC}(\lfloor c+Kx \rceil_k)) \leq \pi^2/b^{2k}+2\epsilon+\mu_c$. By correctness of SAMPLEI (Lemma 9), $\Delta_{\mathrm{ML}}(\mathcal{D}_{K\mathbb{Z},Ks_{\max}}, Kx) \leq \mu_i$ (where $x \leftarrow \mathrm{SAMPLEI}(\max)$) and by definition of K we have $s = \sqrt{(Ks_{\max})^2 + \bar{s}^2}$. Now rewrite $\mathcal{D}_{\mathbb{Z},c+Kx,\bar{s}} = c + Kx + \mathcal{D}_{-Kx-c+\mathbb{Z},\bar{s}}$ and apply Corollary 2 with $c_2 = 0$, $c_1 = c$, $x_1 = Kx$ and $x_2 = y$ to see that $\Delta_{\mathrm{ML}}(\mathcal{D}_{c+\mathbb{Z},s}, \mathrm{SAMPLEZ}_{b,k,\max}(c,s)) \lesssim 6\epsilon + \pi^2/b^{2k} + \mu_i + \mu_c$, if the conditions in the theorem are met. This can easily be seen to be true from the assumptions on s by the following calculation.

$$s_3 = \left((Ks_{\max})^{-2} + \bar{s}^{-2}\right)^{-\frac{1}{2}} = \left(\frac{1}{s^2 - \bar{s}^2} + \frac{1}{\bar{s}^2}\right)^{-\frac{1}{2}} = \left(\frac{\bar{s}^2(s^2 - \bar{s}^2)}{s^2}\right)^{\frac{1}{2}}$$

$$= \frac{\bar{s}}{s}\sqrt{s^2 - \bar{s}^2} \geq \sqrt{s^2 - \bar{s}^2}\,\eta_\epsilon(\mathbb{Z})/s_{\max} = \eta_\epsilon(K\mathbb{Z})$$

$\square$

The running time of SAMPLEZ is obvious: one invocation of SAMPLEI and one of SAMPLEC, which we analyzed in Sects. 5.1 and 5.2, resp., and a few additional arithmetic operations to calculate K and c'. It is worth noting that the computation of K, the most complex arithmetic computation of the entire algorithm, depends only on s. In many applications, for example trapdoor sampling, s is restricted to a relatively small set, which depends on the key. This means that K_s can be precomputed for the set of possible s's allowing to avoid the FP computation at very low memory cost. Finally, the algorithm may approximate the scaling factor K by a value $\tilde{K}$ such that $\delta_{\mathrm{RE}}(\tilde{K}, K) \leq \mu_K$, which results in an approximation of the distribution of width $\tilde{s} = \sqrt{(\tilde{K}s_i)^2 + \bar{s}}$ instead of s. Elementary calculations show that $\Delta_{\mathrm{ML}}(\mathcal{D}_{\mathbb{Z},c,s}, \mathcal{D}_{\mathbb{Z},c,\tilde{s}}) \lesssim 4\pi t^2 \mu_K$ which by triangle inequality adds to the approximation error.

As an example, assume we have an application, where we know that $\bar{s} \leq s \leq 2^{20} = s_{\max}$. It can be checked, that for any base b and $s_0 \geq 4\sqrt{2}\eta_\epsilon(\mathbb{Z})$, the following parameter settings for our algorithm result in

$$\Delta_{\mathrm{ML}}(\mathcal{D}_{\mathbb{Z},c,s}, \mathrm{SAMPLEZ}_{b,k,\max}(c,s)) \leq 2^{-52},$$

and thus in ≥ 100 bits of security by Lemma 3:

- $t = \eta_\epsilon(\mathbb{Z}) = 6$, which results in $\epsilon \leq 2^{-112}$
- $\mu = 2^{-60}$, the precision of the base sampler, resulting in $\mu_i \leq 2^{-55}$
- $k = \lceil 30/\log b \rceil$, which results in $\mu_c \leq 2^{-55}$ and $\pi^2/b^{2k} \leq 2^{-56}$
- $\mu_K = 2^{-64}$, the precision of calculating K, resulting in $4\pi t^2 \mu_K \leq 2^{-55}$.

5.4 Online-Offline Phase and Constant-Time Implementation

Note that a large part of the computation time during our convolution algorithm is spent in the base sampler, which is independent of the center and the noise parameter. This allows us to split the algorithm into an offline and an online phase, similar in spirit to Peikert's sampler [38], which gives rise to a number of platform dependent optimizations. The obvious approach is to simply pre-compute a number of samples for each of the b cosets and combine them in the online phase until we run out. Note that the trade-off now is not only a time-memory trade-off anymore, it is a time-memory-lifetime trade-off for the device that depends on b. Increasing b speeds up the algorithm, but requires to precompute and store samples for more cosets. While it also means that we effectively decrease the number of samples required per output sample, the latter dependence is only logarithmic, while the former is linear in b.

There are a number of other ways to exploit this structure without limiting the lifetime of the device. Most devices that execute cryptographic primitives have idle times (e.g. web servers) which can be used to restock the number of pre-computed samples. As another example, one can separate the offline phase (basic sampler) and the online phase (combination phase) into two parallel devices with a shared buffer. While the basic sampler keeps filling the buffer with samples, the online phase can combine these samples into the desired distribution. An obvious architecture for such a high performance system would implement the base sampler in a highly parallel fashion (e.g. FPGA or GPU) and the online phase on a regular CPU. This shows that in many scenarios the offline phase can be for free.

The separation of offline and online phase also allows for a straight-forward constant-time implementation with very little overhead. A general problem with sampling algorithms in this context is that the running time of the sampler can leak information about the output sample or the input, which clearly hurts security. For a fixed Gaussian, a simple mitigation strategy is to generate the samples in large batches. This approach breaks down in general when the parameters of the target distribution vary per sample and are not known in advance. In contrast, this idea can be used to implement our algorithm in constant time by generating the basic samples in batches in constant time. Note that every output sample requires the exact same number of base samples and convolutions, so the online phase lends itself naturally to a constant-time implementation.

Assume every invocation of SAMPLEZ requires q base samples and let $\hat{t}_0$ be the maximum over $c_i \in \mathbb{Z}/b$ of the expected running time (over the random coins) of the base sampler (computed either by analysis or experimentation). Consider the following algorithm.

Initialization:

- Use the base sampler to fill b buffers of size q, where the i-th buffer stores discrete Gaussian samples $\mathcal{D}_{c_i+\mathbb{Z},s_o}$ for all $c_i \in \mathbb{Z}/b$.

Query phase:

- On input c and s, call $\text{SAMPLEZ}(c, s)$, where $\text{SAMPLEB}_{s_0}(c_i)$ simply reads from the respective buffer.
- Call the base sampler q times to restock the buffers and pad the running time of this step to $T = q\hat{t}_0 + O(\sqrt{\kappa q})$.

Note that the restocking of base samples in the query phase runs in constant time with overwhelming probability, which follows from Hoeffding's inequality (the constant in the O-notation depends on the worst-case running time of the base sampler). It follows, that the query phase runs in constant time if all the arithmetic operations in SAMPLEZ are implemented in constant time and the randomized rounding operation is converted to constant time, both of which are easy to achieve.

The amortized overhead is only $O(\sqrt{\kappa/q})$, where q is the number of base samples required per output sample. This can be further reduced, if enough memory for larger buffers is available. Finally, the separation of online and offline phase into different independent systems or precomputation of the offline phase allow for an even more convenient constant-time implementation: One only needs to convert the arithmetic operations and the coin flip into constant time. This incurs only a minimal penalty in running time.

6   Applications and Comparison

We first give a short overview of existing sampling algorithms (Sect. 6.1) and select a suitable one as our base sampler, before we describe the experimental study.

6.1   Brief Survey of Existing Samplers

All of the currently known samplers can be categorized into two types[3]: rejection-based samplers and tree traversal algorithms. Table 1 summarizes the existing sampling algorithms and their properties in comparison to our work. The table does not contain a column with the running time, since this depends on a lot of factors (speed of FP arithmetic vs memory access vs randomness etc.), but for the rejection-based samplers, the rejection rate can be thought of as a measure of the running time. Tree-traversal algorithms should be thought of as much faster than rejection based samplers. A more concrete comparison on a specific platform will be given in Sects. 6.4 and 6.6.

---

[3] Technically, even rejection-based samplers can be thought of as tree traversal algorithms, but this is not as natural for them, hence our categorization.

Table 1. Comparison of Sampling Algorithms, starting with rejection-based sampler, followed by tree-traversal samplers and finally Algorithm 1. The column $\exp(\cdot)$ indicates if the algorithm requires to evaluate $\exp(\cdot)$ online. The column "Generic" refers to the property of being able to produce samples from discrete Gaussians with different parameters not known before precomputation (i.e. which may vary from query to query). The security parameter is denoted by κ.

Algorithm	Memory	Rejection rate	$\exp(\cdot)$	Generic
Rejection sampling [22]	0	$\sim .9$	Yes	Yes
Discrete ziggurat [11]	var	var	Yes	No
Bernoulli-type [14]	$O(\kappa \log s)$	$\sim .5$	No	No
Karney [25]	0	$\sim .5$	No	Yes
Knuth-Yao [18]	$O(\kappa s)$	–	No	No
Inversion sampling [38]	$O(\kappa s)$	–	No	No
Our work	var	–	No	Yes

6.2 The Base Sampler

We first consider the problem of generating samples from $\mathcal{D}_{\mathbb{Z},c,s}$ when $s = O(\eta_\epsilon(\mathbb{Z}))$ is relatively small and c is fixed. We are interested in the amortized cost of sample generation, where we want to generate a large batch of samples.

We first observe that we are sampling from a relatively narrow Gaussian distribution, so memory will not be a concern for us. Since we want to generate a large number of samples, our main criteria for the suitability of an algorithm is its expected running time. For any algorithm, this is lower bounded by the entropy of $\mathcal{D}_{\mathbb{Z},c,s}$, so a natural choice is (lazy) inversion sampling [38] or Knuth-Yao [18], since both are (close to) randomness optimal and their running time is essentially the number of random bits they consume, hence providing us with an optimal algorithm for our purpose. In fact, Knuth-Yao is a little faster than inversion sampling, so we focus on that.

6.3 Setup of Experimental Study

There are a number of cryptographic applications for our sampler, most of which use an integer sampler in one of three typical settings.

– The output distribution is the centered discrete Gaussian with fixed noise parameter. This is the case in most basic LWE based schemes, where the noise for the LWE instance is sampled using an integer sampler.
– The output distribution is the discrete Gaussian with fixed noise parameter, but varying center. This is the case in the online phase of Peikert's sampler [38]. In particular, if applied to q-ary lattices the centers are restricted to the set $\frac{1}{q}\mathbb{Z}$.

– The output distribution is the discrete Gaussian where both, the center and the noise parameter may vary for each sample. This is typically used as a subroutine for sampling from the discrete Gaussian over lattices, as the GPV sampler [22] or in the offline phase of Peikert's sampler.

The ideas presented in this work can be applied to any of these settings. In particular, the algorithms in Sect. 5 can be used to achieve new time-memory trade-offs in all three cases. The optimal trade-off is highly application specific and depends on a lot of factors, for example, the target platform (hardware vs. software), the cost of randomness (TRNGs vs. PRNGs), available memory, cost of evaluating $\exp(\cdot)$, cost of basic floating point/integer arithmetic, etc. In the following we present an experimental comparison of our algorithm to previous algorithms. Obviously, we are not able to take all factors into account, so we restrict ourselves to a comparison in a software implementation, where all algorithms use the same source of randomness (NTL's PRNG), evaluate the randomness bit by bit in order to minimize randomness consumption, and use only elementary data types during the sampling. In particular, whenever FP arithmetic is necessary or $\rho_s(\cdot)$ needs to be evaluated during the sampling, all the algorithms use only double or extended double precision. This should be sufficient since we are targeting around 100 bits of security and the arguments in Sect. 3 apply to any algorithm. We do not claim that the implementation is optimal for any of the evaluated algorithms, but it should provide a fair comparison. We instantiated our algorithms with the parameters as listed at the end of Sect. 5.3. Our implementation makes no effort towards a constant-time implementation. Even though turning Algorithm 1 into a constant-time algorithm is conceptually simple (cf. Sect. 5.4), this still requires a substantial amount of design and implementation effort, which is out of the scope of this work.

When referring to specific settings of the parameter s, we will often refer to it as multiple of $\sqrt{2\pi}$. The reason is that two slightly different definitions of $\rho_s(\cdot)$ are common in the literature and the factor $\sqrt{2\pi}$ converts between them. While we found one of them to be more convenient in the analytic part of this work, most previous experimental studies [11, 40] use the other. So this notation is for easier comparability.

6.4 Fixed Centered Gaussian

In this section we consider the simplest scenario for discrete Gaussian sampling: sampling from the centered discrete Gaussian distribution above a certain noise level. This is accomplished by Algorithm 2. Note that the parameter s_0 allows for a time memory trade-off in our setting: the larger s_0, the more memory required by our base sampler (Knuth-Yao), but the fewer the levels of recursion. More precisely, the memory requirement grows linearly with s_0, while the running time decreases logarithmically.

We compare the method in different settings to the only other adjustable time-memory trade-off known to date – the discrete Ziggurat. For our evaluation we modified the implementation of [11] to use elementary data types only during the sampling (as opposed to arbitrary precision arithmetic in the original implementation). The baseline algorithms in this setting are the Bernoulli-type sampler and Karney's algorithm, as they allow to sample from the centered discrete Gaussian quite efficiently using very little or no memory. Figure 1 shows the result of our experimental analysis for a set of representative s's. We chose the examples mostly according to the examples in [11], where we skipped the data point at $s = 10\sqrt{2\pi}$, since this is already a very narrow distribution which can be efficiently sampled using Knuth-Yao with very moderate memory requirements. Instead, we show the results for $s = 2^{14}\sqrt{2\pi}$ (chosen somewhat arbitrarily), additionally to data points close to the ones presented in [11]: $s \in \{2^5, 2^{10}, 2^{17}\}\sqrt{2\pi}$.

Figure 1 shows that the two algorithms complement each other quite nicely: while Ziggurat allows for better trade-offs in the low memory regime, using convolution achieves much better running times in the high memory regime. This suggests that Ziggurat might be the better choice for constrained devices, but recall that it requires evaluations of $\exp(\cdot)$. So if s is not too large, even for constrained devices the convolution type sampler can be a better choice (see for example [40]).

Note that the improvement gained by using more memory deteriorates in our implementation, up to the point where using more memory actually hurts the running time (see Fig. 1, bottom right). A similar effect can be observed with the discrete Ziggurat algorithm. At first sight this might be counter-intuitive, but can be easily explained with a limited processor cache size: larger memory requirement in our case means fewer cache hits, which results in more RAM accesses, which are much slower. This nicely illustrates how dependent this trade-off is on the speed of the available memory. Since fast memory is usually much more expensive than slower memory, for a given budget it is very plausible that the money is better spent on limited amounts of fast memory and using Algorithm 2 rather than implementing the full Knuth-Yao with larger and slower memory. In our specific example (Fig. 1, bottom right), this means that using a convolution of two samples generated by smaller Knuth-Yao samplers is actually faster than generating the samples directly with a large Knuth-Yao sampler.

6.5   Fixed Gaussian with Varying Center

We now turn to the second setting, where the noise parameter is still fixed but the center may vary. In order to take advantage of the fact that the noise parameter is fixed and the center in a restricted set for the online phase, Peikert suggested that "if q is reasonably small it may be worthwhile (for faster rounding) to precompute the tables of the cumulative distribution functions for all q possibilities" [38]. This might be feasible, but only for very small q and s (depending on the available memory). If not enough memory is available, there is currently no option other than falling back to Karney's algorithm or rejection sampling.

Depending on the cost of randomness, speed and amount of available memory and processor speed for arithmetic, Knuth-Yao can be significantly faster than Karney's algorithm. For example, in our prototype implementation, Knuth-Yao was up to 6 times faster, but keep in mind that this number is highly platform

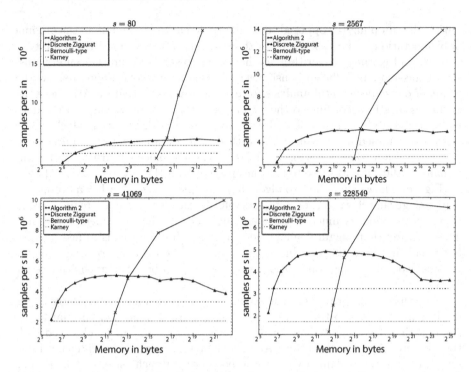

Fig. 1. Time memory trade-off for Algorithm 2 and discrete Ziggurat compared to Bernoulli-type sampling and Karney's algorithm for $s \in \{2^5, 2^{10}, 2^{14}, 2^{17}\}\sqrt{2\pi}$. Knuth-Yao corresponds to right most point of Algorithm 2.

dependent and can vary widely. Accordingly, we can afford to invoke Knuth-Yao several times, sacrificing some running time for memory savings, and still outperform Karney's algorithm. Our algorithms offer exactly this kind of trade-off. There are two ways in which we can take advantage of convolution theorems to address the challenge of having to store q Knuth-Yao samplers. The first simply consists in storing the samplers for some smaller s_0, which will reduce the required memory by a factor s/s_0. After obtaining a sample from the right coset, using only the 0-coset we can generate and add a sample from a wider distribution to obtain the correct distribution. This is very similar to Algorithm 2 with the additional step of adding a sample from the right coset, where we simply invoke Corollary 1 once more. This step will increase the running time by at most $\log_{s_0} s$ additively (cf. Lemma 9).

Note that there is a limit to this technique though, since we need $s_0 > \sqrt{2}\eta_\epsilon(\mathbb{Z})$ for the convolution to yield the correct output distribution. If s is already small, but there is not enough memory available because q is too large, this approach will fail. In this case we can use the algorithm from Sect. 5.2 to reduce the number of samplers needed to be stored. In particular, for any base b

such that[4] $\mathrm{rad}(q) \mid b$, we can cut down on the memory cost by a factor q/b, which will increase the running time by $\lceil \log_b q \rceil$. For this, we simply need to express the center c in the base b and round the digits individually using $\mathrm{SAMPLEC}_b$. For example, if q is a power of a small prime p, we can choose b to be any multiple of p. This can dramatically increase the modulus q for which we can sample fast with a given amount of memory, assuming $\mathrm{rad}(q)$ is small. As a more specific example, say q is a perfect square and let $b = \sqrt{q}$. Instead of storing q Knuth-Yao samplers and invoking one when a sample is required for a coset $\frac{1}{q}\mathbb{Z}$, we can store b samplers and randomly round each of the 2 digits of the center in base b successively. This effectively doubles the running time, but this is likely to still be much faster than Karney's algorithm (again, depending on the platform), but we reduced the amount of necessary memory by a factor $\sqrt{q}$.

Clearly, depending on the specific q, s and platform, the two techniques can be combined. The optimal trade-off depends on all three factors and has to be evaluated for each application. Our algorithms provide developers with the tools to optimize this trade-off and make the most of the available resources.

6.6 Varying Gaussian

Finally, we evaluate the practical performance of our full sampler, $\mathrm{SAMPLEZ}$. Precomputing the value K, as suggested in Sect. 5.3, made little difference in our software implementation and we show results for the algorithm that does not precompute K. The bottleneck in our algorithm is the call to $\mathrm{SAMPLEC}$, as it consumes a number of samples which depends on the base b. Again, similar to the previous section, the base b offers a time-memory trade-off, which is the target of our evaluation. We experimented with the sampler for a wide range of noise parameters s, but since our algorithm is essentially independent of s (as long as it is $\leq s_{\max}$), it is not surprising that the trade-off is essentially the same in all cases. Accordingly, we present only one exemplary result in Fig. 2. As a frame of reference, rejection sampling achieved $0.994 \cdot 10^6$ samples per second, which shows that by spending only very moderate amounts of memory ($< 1\mathrm{mb}$), our algorithm can match and outperform rejection sampling. On the other hand, Karney's algorithm achieved $3.281 \cdot 10^6$ samples per second, which seems out of reach for reasonable amounts of memory, making it the most efficient choice in this setting, if no other criteria are of concern. But we stress again that this depends highly on how efficiently Knuth-Yao can be implemented compared to Karney's algorithm on the target platform. While the running time of both, rejection sampling and Karney's algorithm depends on s, this dependence is rather weak (logarithmic with small constants) so the picture does not change much for other noise parameters.

Recall that our algorithm can be split into online and offline phase, since the base samples are independent of the target distribution. Karney's algorithm also initially samples from a Gaussian that is independent of the target distribution,

---

[4] This is the condition for $\frac{1}{q}$ being expressible as a finite number in base b.

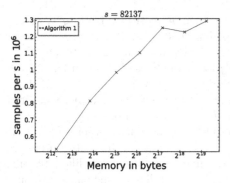
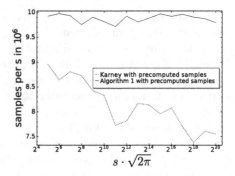

Fig. 2. Time memory trade-off Algorithm 1 for $s = 2^{15}\sqrt{2\pi}$.

Fig. 3. Performance of Algorithm 1 compared to Karney's algorithm, (online phase only).

so a similar approach can be applied. However, the trade-off is fixed and no speed-ups can be achieved by spending more memory.

We tested both algorithms, where we assumed that the offline phase is free, for a wide range of s. For this, we fixed $b = 16$ for our algorithm, which seemed to be a good choice in our setting. Note that similar to Sect. 6.4, spending more memory (and increasing b) should in theory only improve the algorithm. But if this comes at the cost of slowing down memory access due to a limited cache size, this can actually hurt performance. The results are depicted in Fig. 3. The graph allows for two interesting observations: First, our algorithm consistently outperforms Karney's algorithm in this setting. So if the offline phase can be considered to be free or a limited life-time is acceptable (cf. Sect. 5.4), our algorithm seems to be the better choice. Second, as expected, our algorithm is essentially independent of s (as long as it is $< s_{\max}$), while the performance of Karney's algorithm deteriorates as s grows. This is due to the fact that Karney's algorithm requires to sample a uniform number in $[0, s]$ during the online phase, which is logarithmic in s. This leads to a larger gap between the performance of the two algorithms as s grows, and supports the claim that our sampler allows for an efficient constant time implementation. In contrast, both Karney's algorithm and rejection sampling seem to be inherently costly to turn into constant time algorithms, due to their dependence on s and the fact that they are probabilistically rejecting samples.

In summary, we believe that there are a number of applications and target platforms, where our algorithm will be the best choice to implement a discrete Gaussian sampler.

Acknowledgment. We thank the authors of [11] for providing the source code of their implementation of different discrete Gaussian samplers, Ilya Mironov for pointing out the connection between differential privacy and the max-log distance, and the CRYPTO'17 reviewers for helpful comments. This work was sponsored by the Defense Advanced Research Projects Agency (DARPA) and the U.S. Army Research Office under contract number W911NF-15-C-0226.

References

1. Agrawal, S., Boneh, D., Boyen, X.: Efficient lattice (H)IBE in the standard model. In: Gilbert, H. (ed.) EUROCRYPT 2010. LNCS, vol. 6110, pp. 553–572. Springer, Heidelberg (2010). doi:10.1007/978-3-642-13190-5_28

2. Agrawal, S., Boneh, D., Boyen, X.: Lattice basis delegation in fixed dimension and shorter-ciphertext hierarchical IBE. In: Rabin, T. (ed.) CRYPTO 2010. LNCS, vol. 6223, pp. 98–115. Springer, Heidelberg (2010). doi:10.1007/978-3-642-14623-7_6

3. Albrecht, M.R., Cocis, C., Laguillaumie, F., Langlois, A.: Implementing candidate graded encoding schemes from ideal lattices. In: Iwata, T., Cheon, J.H. (eds.) ASIACRYPT 2015. LNCS, vol. 9453, pp. 752–775. Springer, Heidelberg (2015). doi:10.1007/978-3-662-48800-3_31

4. Alkim, E., Ducas, L., Pöppelmann, T., Schwabe, P.: Post-quantum key exchange— a new hope. In: USENIX Security (2016)

5. Bai, S., Langlois, A., Lepoint, T., Stehlé, D., Steinfeld, R.: Improved security proofs in lattice-based cryptography: using the rényi divergence rather than the statistical distance. In: Iwata, T., Cheon, J.H. (eds.) ASIACRYPT 2015. LNCS, vol. 9452, pp. 3–24. Springer, Heidelberg (2015). doi:10.1007/978-3-662-48797-6_1

6. Boyen, X.: Attribute-based functional encryption on lattices. In: Sahai, A. (ed.) TCC 2013. LNCS, vol. 7785, pp. 122–142. Springer, Heidelberg (2013). doi:10.1007/978-3-642-36594-2_8

7. Boyen, X., Li, Q.: Attribute-based encryption for finite automata from LWE. In: Au, M.-H., Miyaji, A. (eds.) ProvSec 2015. LNCS, vol. 9451, pp. 247–267. Springer, Cham (2015). doi:10.1007/978-3-319-26059-4_14

8. Brakerski, Z., Gentry, C., Vaikuntanathan, V.: (leveled) fully homomorphic encryption without bootstrapping. In: ITCS (2012)

9. Brakerski, Z., Vaikuntanathan, V.: Fully homomorphic encryption from ring-LWE and security for key dependent messages. In: Rogaway, P. (ed.) CRYPTO 2011. LNCS, vol. 6841, pp. 505–524. Springer, Heidelberg (2011). doi:10.1007/978-3-642-22792-9_29

10. Brakerski, Z., Vaikuntanathan, V., Wee, H., Wichs, D.: Obfuscating conjunctions under entropic ring LWE. In: ITCS (2016)

11. Buchmann, J., Cabarcas, D., Göpfert, F., Hülsing, A., Weiden, P.: Discrete ziggurat: a time-memory trade-off for sampling from a gaussian distribution over the integers. In: Lange, T., Lauter, K., Lisoněk, P. (eds.) SAC 2013. LNCS, vol. 8282, pp. 402–417. Springer, Heidelberg (2014). doi:10.1007/978-3-662-43414-7_20

12. Döttling, N., Müller-Quade, J.: Lossy codes and a new variant of the learning-with-errors problem. In: Johansson, T., Nguyen, P.Q. (eds.) EUROCRYPT 2013. LNCS, vol. 7881, pp. 18–34. Springer, Heidelberg (2013). doi:10.1007/978-3-642-38348-9_2

13. Du, C., Bai, G.: Towards efficient discrete Gaussian sampling for lattice-based cryptography. In: FPL (2015)

14. Ducas, L., Durmus, A., Lepoint, T., Lyubashevsky, V.: Lattice signatures and bimodal gaussians. In: Canetti, R., Garay, J.A. (eds.) CRYPTO 2013. LNCS, vol. 8042, pp. 40–56. Springer, Heidelberg (2013). doi:10.1007/978-3-642-40041-4_3

15. Ducas, L., Lyubashevsky, V., Prest, T.: Efficient identity-based encryption over NTRU lattices. In: Sarkar, P., Iwata, T. (eds.) ASIACRYPT 2014. LNCS, vol. 8874, pp. 22–41. Springer, Heidelberg (2014). doi:10.1007/978-3-662-45608-8_2

16. Ducas, L., Micciancio, D.: FHEW: bootstrapping homomorphic encryption in less than a second. In: Oswald, E., Fischlin, M. (eds.) EUROCRYPT 2015. LNCS, vol. 9056, pp. 617–640. Springer, Heidelberg (2015). doi:10.1007/978-3-662-46800-5_24

17. Ducas, L., Nguyen, P.Q.: Faster gaussian lattice sampling using lazy floating-point arithmetic. In: Wang, X., Sako, K. (eds.) ASIACRYPT 2012. LNCS, vol. 7658, pp. 415–432. Springer, Heidelberg (2012). doi:10.1007/978-3-642-34961-4_26

18. Dwarakanath, N.C., Galbraith, S.D.: Sampling from discrete Gaussians for lattice-based cryptography on a constrained device. Appl. Algebra Eng. Commun. Comput. **25**, 159–180 (2014)

19. Folláth, J.: Gaussian sampling in lattice based cryptography. Tatra Mountains Mathematical Publications (2015)

20. Garg, S., Gentry, C., Halevi, S.: Candidate multilinear maps from ideal lattices. In: Johansson, T., Nguyen, P.Q. (eds.) EUROCRYPT 2013. LNCS, vol. 7881, pp. 1–17. Springer, Heidelberg (2013). doi:10.1007/978-3-642-38348-9_1

21. Gentry, C., Halevi, S.: Implementing Gentry's fully-homomorphic encryption scheme. In: Paterson, K.G. (ed.) EUROCRYPT 2011. LNCS, vol. 6632, pp. 129–148. Springer, Heidelberg (2011). doi:10.1007/978-3-642-20465-4_9

22. Gentry, C., Peikert, C., Vaikuntanathan, V.: Trapdoors for hard lattices and new cryptographic constructions. In: STOC (2008)

23. Groot Bruinderink, L., Hülsing, A., Lange, T., Yarom, Y.: Flush, gauss, and reload - a cache attack on the BLISS lattice-based signature scheme. In: CHES (2016)

24. Howe, J., Khalid, A., Rafferty, C., Regazzoni, F., O'Neill, M.: On practical discrete Gaussian samplers for lattice-based cryptography. IEEE Transactions on Computers (2016)

25. Karney, C.F.F.: Sampling exactly from the normal distribution. ACM Trans. Math. Softw. (2016)

26. Langlois, A., Stehlé, D., Steinfeld, R.: GGHLite: more efficient multilinear maps from ideal lattices. In: Nguyen, P.Q., Oswald, E. (eds.) EUROCRYPT 2014. LNCS, vol. 8441, pp. 239–256. Springer, Heidelberg (2014). doi:10.1007/978-3-642-55220-5_14

27. Lyubashevsky, V., Peikert, C., Regev, O.: On ideal lattices and learning with errors over rings. In: Gilbert, H. (ed.) EUROCRYPT 2010. LNCS, vol. 6110, pp. 1–23. Springer, Heidelberg (2010). doi:10.1007/978-3-642-13190-5_1

28. Micciancio, D., Goldwasser, S.: Complexity of Lattice Problems: A Cryptographic Perspective. Kluwer Academic Publishers, Berlin (2002)

29. Micciancio, D., Peikert, C.: Trapdoors for lattices: simpler, tighter, faster, smaller. In: Pointcheval, D., Johansson, T. (eds.) EUROCRYPT 2012. LNCS, vol. 7237, pp. 700–718. Springer, Heidelberg (2012). doi:10.1007/978-3-642-29011-4_41

30. Micciancio, D., Peikert, C.: Hardness of SIS and LWE with small parameters. In: Canetti, R., Garay, J.A. (eds.) CRYPTO 2013. LNCS, vol. 8042, pp. 21–39. Springer, Heidelberg (2013). doi:10.1007/978-3-642-40041-4_2

31. Micciancio, D., Regev, O.: Worst-case to average-case reductions based on Gaussian measure. SIAM J. Comput. **37**, 267–302 (2007). Preliminary version in FOCS 2004

32. Micciancio, D., Walter, M.: Gaussian sampling over the integers: Efficient, generic, constant-time. Cryptology ePrint Archive, Report 2017/259 (2017). http://eprint.iacr.org/2017/259

33. Mironov, I.: Renyi differential privacy. http://arxiv.org/abs/1702.07476

34. More, S., Katti, R.: Discrete Gaussian sampling for low-power devices. In: PACRIM (2015)

35. Nguyen, P.Q., Regev, O.: Learning a parallelepiped: cryptanalysis of GGH and NTRU signatures. In: Vaudenay, S. (ed.) EUROCRYPT 2006. LNCS, vol. 4004, pp. 271–288. Springer, Heidelberg (2006). doi:10.1007/11761679_17

36. NIST: Post-quantum crypto standardization - call for proposals announcement. https://csrc.nist.gov/groups/ST/post-quantum-crypto/cfp-announce-dec2016. html

37. Peikert, C.: Public-key cryptosystems from the worst-case shortest vector problem. In: STOC (2009)

38. Peikert, C.: An efficient and parallel gaussian sampler for lattices. In: Rabin, T. (ed.) CRYPTO 2010. LNCS, vol. 6223, pp. 80–97. Springer, Heidelberg (2010). doi:10.1007/978-3-642-14623-7_5

39. Pessl, P.: Analyzing the shuffling side-channel countermeasure for lattice-based signatures. In: Dunkelman, O., Sanadhya, S.K. (eds.) INDOCRYPT 2016. LNCS, vol. 10095, pp. 153–170. Springer, Cham (2016). doi:10.1007/978-3-319-49890-4_9

40. Pöppelmann, T., Ducas, L., Güneysu, T.: Enhanced lattice-based signatures on reconfigurable hardware. In: Batina, L., Robshaw, M. (eds.) CHES 2014. LNCS, vol. 8731, pp. 353–370. Springer, Heidelberg (2014). doi:10.1007/978-3-662-44709-3_20

41. Prest, T.: Sharper bounds in lattice-based cryptography using the Rényi divergence. Cryptology ePrint Archive, Report 2017/480 (2017). http://eprint.iacr.org/2017/480

42. Regev, O.: The learning with errors problem (invited survey). In: CCC (2010)

43. Regev, O.: On lattices, learning with errors, random linear codes, and cryptography. J. ACM (2009). Preliminary version in STOC 2005

44. Roy, S.S., Reparaz, O., Vercauteren, F., Verbauwhede, I.: Compact and side channel secure discrete Gaussian sampling. Cryptology ePrint Archive, Report 2014/591 (2014). http://eprint.iacr.org/2014/591

45. Saarinen, M.J.O.: Arithmetic coding and blinding countermeasures for lattice signatures. J. Cryptogr. Eng. (2017)

46. Sinha Roy, S., Vercauteren, F., Verbauwhede, I.: High precision discrete gaussian sampling on FPGAs. In: Lange, T., Lauter, K., Lisoněk, P. (eds.) SAC 2013. LNCS, vol. 8282, pp. 383–401. Springer, Heidelberg (2014). doi:10.1007/978-3-662-43414-7_19

LPN Decoded

Andre Esser, Robert Kübler$^{(\boxtimes)}$, and Alexander May

Faculty of Mathematics, Horst Görtz Institute for IT Security,
Ruhr University, Bochum, Germany
{andre.esser,robert.kuebler,alex.may}@rub.de

Abstract. We propose new algorithms with *small memory consumption* for the Learning Parity with Noise (LPN) problem, both classically and quantumly. Our goal is to predict the hardness of LPN depending on both parameters, its dimension k and its noise rate τ, as accurately as possible both in theory and practice. Therefore, we analyze our algorithms asymptotically, run experiments on medium size parameters and provide bit complexity predictions for large parameters.

Our new algorithms are modifications and extensions of the simple Gaussian elimination algorithm with recent advanced techniques for decoding random linear codes. Moreover, we enhance our algorithms by the dimension reduction technique from Blum, Kalai, Wasserman. This results in a hybrid algorithm that is capable for achieving the best currently known run time for any fixed amount of memory.

On the asymptotic side, we achieve significant improvements for the run time exponents, both classically and quantumly. To the best of our knowledge, we provide the first quantum algorithms for LPN.

Due to the small memory consumption of our algorithms, we are able to solve for the first time LPN instances of medium size, e.g. with $k = 243, \tau = \frac{1}{8}$ in only 15 days on 64 threads.

Our algorithms result in bit complexity prediction that require relatively large k for small τ. For instance for small noise LPN with $\tau = \frac{1}{\sqrt{k}}$, we predict 80-bit classical and only 64-bit quantum security for $k \geq 2048$. For the common cryptographic choice $k = 512, \tau = \frac{1}{8}$, we achieve with limited memory classically 102-bit and quantumly 69-bit security.

Keywords: LPN key size · Information set decoding · Grover · BKW

1 Introduction

With the upcoming NIST initiative for recommending quantum-secure public key cryptosystems [1], it becomes even more urgent and mandatory to properly select cryptographic key sizes with a well-defined security level, both classically and of course also quantumly. Therefore, the cryptographic community has to establish for the most prominent hardness problems, e.g. in the areas of codes, lattices, multivariate and isogenies, predictions for solving cryptographic instances with security levels of 128 bit and above.

© International Association for Cryptologic Research 2017
J. Katz and H. Shacham (Eds.): CRYPTO 2017, Part II, LNCS 10402, pp. 486–514, 2017.
DOI: 10.1007/978-3-319-63715-0_17

The choice of key sizes has naturally been a tradeoff between efficiency and security. On the one hand, one would like to choose small parameters that allow for efficient implementations. On the other hand, one is usually quite conservative in estimating which parameters can be broken within say 2^{128} steps. While giving conservative security estimates is in general good, we believe that this practice is often disproportionate in cryptographic research.

For instance, when selecting the best algorithm, cryptographers usually completely ignore memory consumption. And quite often, the best time complexity T is only achieved with memory consumption as large as T. An example with such huge memory requirement is the Blum-Kalai-Wasserman (BKW) algorithm [7] for solving LPN. But when implementing an algorithm in practice, memory consumption is the main limiting factor. While performing 2^{60} steps is even doable on smallish computing clusters in a reasonable amount of time, getting an amount of 2^{60} of RAM is clearly out of reach. If one has to rely on additional hard disk space, the running time will increase drastically.

An Internet investigation shows that nowadays the largest supercomputers[1] have a RAM of at most 1.6 PB $< 2^{54}$ bits. Putting some safety margin, it seems to be fair to say that any algorithm with memory consumption larger than 2^{60} bits cannot be instantiated in practice. In the course of the paper we will also consider a higher safety margin of 2^{80} bits.

Hence, there is a need for finding algorithms for post-quantum problems that can be instantiated with *small memory*, in order to run them on medium size instances for an accurate extrapolation to cryptographic key sizes. For the selection of key sizes, one might safely restrict to algorithms that do not exceed a certain amount of memory, like e.g. 2^{60} bits. Belaïd et al. [5] considered a related model in which an attacker has limited LPN samples and memory. However, we do not want to limit the number of LPN samples.

Ideally, we would design algorithms whose running time benefit from any fixed amount of memory. Let us assume that we have M bits of RAM on our computing facility. The main research question is then which optimal running time can be achieved when (fully) using this amount.

Our goal is to answer this question for Learning Parity with Noise (LPN). LPN is the basis for many code-based constructions and can be seen as a special instance of Learning with Errors (LWE) [29]. In the LPN problem, one has to learn a secret $\mathbf{s} \in \mathbb{F}_2^k$ using access to an oracle that provides samples of the form $(\mathbf{a}_i, b_i)$, where $\mathbf{a}_i$ is uniformly at random from $\mathbb{F}_2^k$, and $b_i = \langle \mathbf{a}_i, \mathbf{s} \rangle + e_i$ for some error $e_i \in \{0, 1\}$ with $\Pr[e_i = 1] = \tau$. Hence, LPN is a two-parameter problem with dimension k and error rate $\tau \in [0, \frac{1}{2})$.

Naturally, the problem becomes harder with increasing k and τ. For $\tau = 0$ we can easily draw k samples with linearly independent $\mathbf{a}_i$ and solve for $\mathbf{s}$ via Gaussian elimination. This algorithm can simply be generalized to any $\tau \in [0, \frac{1}{2})$, by drawing k samples in each iteration, computing a candidate $\mathbf{s}'$, and test whether $\mathbf{s} = \mathbf{s}'$. Notice that $\mathbf{s} = \mathbf{s}'$ iff in this iteration all samples are error-free.

---

[1] E.g. the IBM 20-Petaflops cluster installed in Sequoia, Lawrence Livermore National Laboratory, California [2].

This algorithm, that we call Gauss, seems to be somewhat folklore. To the best of our knowledge it was first used in 2008 by Carrijo et al. [11], and has been e.g. analyzed in Bogos et al. [8]. The benefits of Gauss are that it consumes only small memory and performs well for small noise τ, e.g. for the currently required choice of $\tau = \frac{1}{\sqrt{k}}$ in the public key encryption schemes of Alekhnovich [3], Damgård, Park [12], Döttling, Müller-Quade, Anderson [13] and Duc, Vaudenay [14].

For constant noise τ, as used e.g. in the HB family of protocols [16,20,21] and their extensions [19,23], currently the best known algorithm is BKW, due to Blum, Kalai and Wasserman [7] with running time, memory consumption and sample complexity $2^{\mathcal{O}(k/\log k)}$. BKW has been widely studied in the cryptographic literature and there are several improvements in practice due to Fossorier et al. [15], Levieil, Fouque [24], Lyubashevsky [25], Guo, Johansson, Löndahl [18] and Zhang, Jiao, Mingsheng [30]. While BKW offers for large τ the best running time, it cannot be implemented even for medium size LPN parameters due to its huge memory consumption. But without having any experimental results, it is an error-prone process to predict security levels. This also led to some discussion about the accuracy of predictions [9].

Gauss and BKW are the starting point of our paper. We revisit both in Sect. 2, where we analyze them asymptotically and show that BKW has a very bad dependency on τ with a running time of $2^{\mathcal{O}(k/\log(\frac{k}{\tau}))}$. So even for τ as small as $\tau = \frac{1}{k}$, the running time remains $2^{\mathcal{O}(k/\log k)}$.

Another drawback of Gauss and BKW is their large sample complexity, i.e. the number of calls to an LPN oracle, which is for both algorithms as large as their running time. Since the LPN oracle is by definition classical, this prevents any possible speed-ups by quantum search techniques, e.g. by Grover search [17].

Therefore, we will first reduce the number of samples to a pool of only $n = \text{poly}(k)$ samples. Out of these n samples, we look for a set of k error-free samples similar to Gauss. The resulting algorithm Pooled Gauss (Sect. 4) has the same time and memory complexity as Gauss, while consuming far fewer samples. This immediately gives rise to a quantum version, for which we save a square root in the run time via Grover search.

Another benefit of having small sample complexity is that we can add a preprocessing step that reduces the dimension of our LPN instances via intensive use of the LPN oracle. The resulting algorithm that we call Well-Pooled Gauss (Sect. 5.1) offers a significantly reduced time complexity.

In a nutshell, Well-Pooled Gauss has a simple *preprocessing step* that decreases the LPN dimension, and then a *decoding step* via Gaussian elimination. The preprocessing step can be improved by more sophisticated dimension reduction methods such as BKW. This comes at the cost of using some memory, but we can control the required memory by adjusting the amount of dimension reduction. Altogether, this results in Algorithm Hybrid (Sect. 5.3) that for any given memory M first reduces the dimension with full memory use, and second runs Gaussian elimination on the dimension-reduced, and thus easier, LPN instance.

Another nice feature of Hybrid is that its preprocessing step allows to easily include many of the recent BKW optimizations [18,24,30].

Moreover, we are also able to improve on the decoding step by replacing Gaussian elimination with more sophisticated information set decoding algorithms, like Ball-Collision Decoding of Bernstein, Lange, Peters [6], MMT of May, Meurer, Thomae [26], BJMM of Becker et al. [4] or May-Ozerov [27]. For our purpose of decoding LPN instances, it turns out that the MMT algorithm tuned to the LPN setting performs best. The resulting algorithm that we call Well-Pooled MMT is studied in Sect. 5.4.

Table 1 provides a more detailed overview of our algorithms and results. For ease of exposition, in Table 1 we omit all small error terms in run times, like $(1 + o(1))$-factors or $\tilde{O}$-notation.

Table 1. Overview of our results, $f(\tau) := \log\left(\frac{1}{1-\tau}\right)$

Algorithm	Time	Samples	Memory	Quantum
BKW (Theorem 1)	$2^{\frac{k}{\log\left(\frac{k}{\tau}\right)}}$	=Time	=Time	Inapplicable
Gauss (Theorem 2)	$2^{f(\tau)k}$	=Time	k^2	Inapplicable
Pooled Gauss (Theorems 3 & 4)	$2^{f(\tau)k}$	k^2	k^3	$2^{\frac{f(\tau)k}{2}}$
Pooled Gauss, $\tau(k) \to 0$ (Corollary 1)	$e^{\tau k}$	k^2	k^3	$e^{\frac{\tau k}{2}}$
Well-Pooled Gauss (Theorems 5 & 6)	$2^{\frac{f(\tau)}{1+f(\tau)}k}$	=Time	k^3	$2^{\frac{f(\tau)}{2+f(\tau)}k}$
Hybrid (Theorem 7)	$2^{f(\tau)k}$ to $2^{\frac{k}{\log\left(\frac{k}{\tau}\right)}}$	=Time	k^3 to $2^{\frac{k}{\log\left(\frac{k}{\tau}\right)}}$	Applicable
Well-Pooled MMT (Sect. 5.4)	$\approx 2^{\frac{f(\frac{7}{6}\tau)}{\log\left(\frac{12}{5}\right)+f(\frac{7}{6}\tau)}}$	=Time	$< \sqrt{\text{Time}}$	Applicable [22]

2 Preliminaries and the LPN Problem

2.1 Preliminaries

Let us first fix some notation. With log we denote the binary logarithm. For a positive integer $n \in \mathbb{N}$ we define $[n] := \{1, 2, \ldots, n\}$. Let M be a set and $k \in \mathbb{N}$. Then $\binom{M}{k}$ is the set of all subsets of M of size k. In particular, $\binom{[n]}{k}$ is the set of size-k subsets of $\{1, \ldots, n\}$.

Let $A \in \mathbb{F}_2^{n \times k}$, $\mathbf{b} \in \mathbb{F}_2^k$ and $I = \{i_1, \ldots, i_\ell\} \subseteq [k]$. Then A_I consists of the rows indexed by I and $\mathbf{b}_I$ consists of the entries indexed by I, e.g.

$$A_I := \begin{pmatrix} - a_{i_1} - \\ \vdots \\ - a_{i_\ell} - \end{pmatrix} \text{ and } \mathbf{b}_I := (b_{i_1}, \ldots, b_{i_\ell})^t.$$

Let $\mathbf{v} = (v_1, \ldots, v_n) \in \mathbb{F}_2^n$. Then we call $\mathrm{wt}(\mathbf{v}) := \|\mathbf{v}\|_1 = |\{i \in [n] \mid v_i \neq 0\}|$ the Hamming weight (or just weight) of $\mathbf{v}$. A linear code $\mathcal{C}$ is a subspace of $\mathbb{F}_2^n$. If $\dim(\mathcal{C}) = k$ and $d := \min_{0 \neq c \in \mathcal{C}} \{\mathrm{wt}(c)\}$, then we call $\mathcal{C}$ an $[n, k, d]$ code.

This implies $\mathcal{C} = \mathrm{im}(G)$ for some matrices $G \in \mathbb{F}_2^{n \times k}$ with rank k. We call G a *generator matrix* of $\mathcal{C}$. For a random matrix G we call $\mathcal{C} = \mathrm{im}(G)$ a *random linear code*.

For a finite set M we write the uniform distribution on M by $\mathcal{U}(M)$. Moreover, we denote by Ber_τ the Bernoulli distribution with parameter τ, i.e., $e \sim \mathrm{Ber}_\tau$ means that we draw a 0–1 valued random variable e with $\Pr[e = 1] = \tau$.

The binomial distribution is denoted as $\mathrm{Bin}_{n,p}$ and can be seen as the sum of n independently identically distributed Ber_p variables. If $X \sim \mathrm{Bin}_{n,p}$, we have $\Pr[X = i] = \binom{n}{i} p^i (1-p)^{n-i}$. In the course of the paper we will deal with the question: Given $p = p(k)$ and $N = N(k)$, how large does the number of Bernoulli trials $n = n(k)$ have to be, such that $\Pr[X \geq N] \geq 1 - \mathrm{negl}(k)$? Here k is a security parameter and $\mathrm{negl}(k) = o(\frac{1}{\mathrm{poly}(k)}) = k^{-\omega(1)}$. We call probabilities of the form $1 - \mathrm{negl}(k)$ overwhelming.

For example, setting $n = \frac{N}{p}$ only yields $\Pr[X \geq N] \geq \frac{1}{2}$, so n has to be larger than that. How much larger it has to be is answered by

Lemma 1. *Let $X \sim \mathrm{Bin}_{n,p>0}$ and $0 \leq N \leq np$. If $n = \Theta\left(\frac{N + \log^2 k}{p}\right)$, then we have $\Pr[X \geq N] \geq 1 - k^{-\omega(1)}$.*

Proof. The Chernoff bounds give us $\Pr[X \geq N] \geq 1 - e^{-\frac{(np-N)^2}{2np}}$. If we set $n \geq \frac{N + \log^2 k + \sqrt{N \cdot \log^2 k + \log^4 k}}{p}$, for example $n = \frac{2N + \log^2 k}{p}$, we get

$$1 - e^{-\frac{(np-N)^2}{2np}} = 1 - e^{-\frac{(N + \log^2 k)^2}{4N + 2\log^2 k}} \geq 1 - e^{-\frac{N + \log^2 k}{4}} \geq 1 - e^{-\frac{\log^2 k}{4}} = 1 - k^{-\omega(1)}.$$

$\square$

For $N = 1$, Lemma 1 gives us the amount of Bernoulli trials we need, until we get a success with overwhelming probability, i.e. $\frac{\log^2 k}{p}$ suffices. One can see, that this is only slightly more than $\frac{1}{p}$, the expectation value of a geometric distributed random variable with parameter p.

2.2 The LPN Problem

Let us now formally define the LPN problem.

Definition 1. *In the $\mathrm{LPN}_{k,\tau}$ problem, for some secret $\mathbf{s} \in \mathbb{F}_2^k$ and error parameter $\tau \in [0, \frac{1}{2})$ we are given access to an oracle that provides samples of the form*

$$(\mathbf{a}_i, b_i) := (\mathbf{a}_i, \langle \mathbf{a}_i, \mathbf{s} \rangle + e_i), \text{ for } i = 1, 2, \ldots,$$

where $\mathbf{a}_i \sim \mathcal{U}(\mathbb{F}_2^k)$ and $e_i \sim \mathrm{Ber}_\tau$, independently. Our goal is to recover $\mathbf{s}$. We call b_i the corresponding label of $\mathbf{a}_i$.

Notation: *Upon asking m queries, we write* $(A, \mathbf{b}) \leftarrow \text{LPN}_{k,\tau}^m$ *meaning that* $A\mathbf{s} = \mathbf{b} + \mathbf{e}$, *where the* i^{th} *row of* $A \in \mathbb{F}_2^{m \times k}$ *and* $\mathbf{b} \in \mathbb{F}_2^m$ *present the* i^{th} *sample.*

Remark 1. We say that an algorithm A with overwhelming probability solves $\text{LPN}_{k,\tau}$ in running time T, if it *both* terminates within time T and outputs the correct $\mathbf{s}$ with probability $1 - \text{negl}(k)$. This means that A might not terminate in time T or that A might output an incorrect $\mathbf{s}'$, but we bound both events by some negligible function in k. Notice that our notion is stronger than just *expected running time* T_e, where the real running time might significantly deviate from T_e with even constant probability.

The error-free case $\text{LPN}_{k,0}$ can be easily solved by obtaining k sample $(\mathbf{a}_i, b_i)$ with linearly independent $\mathbf{a}_i$, and computing via Gaussian elimination

$$\mathbf{s} = A^{-1}\mathbf{b}. \qquad (1)$$

However, in case of errors we obtain $\mathbf{s} = A^{-1}\mathbf{b} + A^{-1}\mathbf{e}$, with an accumulated error of $A^{-1}\mathbf{e}$, where $\text{wt}(A^{-1}\mathbf{e})$ is usually large. In other words, Gaussian elimination lets the error grow too fast by adding together too many samples.

The error growth can be made precise in terms of the number n of additions via the following lemma, usually called Piling-up Lemma in the cryptographic literature.

Lemma 2 (Piling-up Lemma). *Let* $e_i \sim Ber_\tau$, $i = 1, \dots, n$ *be identically, independently distributed. Then we have* $\sum_{i=1}^n e_i \sim Ber_{\frac{1}{2} - \frac{1}{2}(1-2\tau)^n}$.

Proof. $n = 1$ is immediate. Induction over n yields

$$\Pr\left[\sum_{i=1}^n e_i = 1\right] = \Pr\left[\sum_{i=1}^{n-1} e_i = 0\right] \cdot \Pr[e_n = 1] + \Pr\left[\sum_{i=1}^{n-1} e_i = 1\right] \cdot \Pr[e_n = 0]$$

$$= \left(\frac{1}{2} + \frac{1}{2}(1 - 2\tau)^{n-1}\right)\tau + \left(\frac{1}{2} - \frac{1}{2}(1 - 2\tau)^{n-1}\right)(1 - \tau)$$

$$= \frac{1}{2} - \frac{1}{2}(1 - 2\tau)^n. \qquad \square$$

3   Revisiting Previous Work

3.1   The BKW Algorithm

Blum, Kalai and Wasserman [7] proposed a variant of Gaussian elimination, called BKW algorithm, that performs elimination of whole blocks instead of single coordinates. This results in way less additions of samples, thus controlling the error, at the cost of requiring way more initial LPN samples to perform eliminations.

The following high-level description of BKW eliminates blocks of size d in each of its $c - 1$ iterations, resulting in vectors that are sums of 2^{c-1} original samples. We describe only how to compute the first bit of $\mathbf{s}$, the other bits are analogous.

Input: $\text{LPN}_{k,\tau}$ oracle, $\tau > 0$
Output: First bit s_1 of the secret $\mathbf{s} = (s_1, \ldots, s_k)$
Choose $\varepsilon > 0$;
$c := (1 - \varepsilon) \log \left(\frac{k}{\tau} \right)$;
$d := \frac{k}{c}$;
$N := \left(c - 1 + \frac{\log^2 k}{(1-2\tau)^{2^c}} + \log^2 k \right) 2^d$;
$(A, \mathbf{b}) \leftarrow \text{LPN}_{k,\tau}^N$;
for $i = 1, \ldots, c - 1$ **do**
  foreach $j \in \mathbb{F}_2^d$ **do**
    Pick a row $\mathbf{a}_k$ of A with suffix $j|0^{(i-1)d}$ (if any); add $\mathbf{a}_k$ to all the other rows of A with suffix $j|0^{(i-1)d}$, also add corresponding labels;
    Remove the kth row from A and $\mathbf{b}$;
  end
end
$I := \{ i \in [N] \mid a_i = u_1 = (1, 0, \ldots, 0) \}$;
return $s_1 = $ the bit which is the majority of all bits in $\mathbf{b}_I$.

Algorithm 1. BKW

Blum, Kalai and Wasserman show that, for constant τ, instantiating their algorithm with blocks of size roughly $d = \frac{k}{\log k}$ and $c = \log k$ iterations while using $N = 2^{\mathcal{O}(k/\log k)}$ samples results in running time and memory complexity also $2^{\mathcal{O}(k/\log k)}$.

Since for concrete cryptographic instantiations, we are also interested in the dependence on τ and the constant hidden in the $\mathcal{O}$-notion, we give a slightly more detailed analysis in the following.

Theorem 1. *BKW solves* $\text{LPN}_{k,\tau}$ *for* $\tau > 0$ *with overwhelming success probability in time, memory and sample complexity* $2^{\frac{k}{\log\left(\frac{k}{\tau}\right)}(1+o(1))}$.

Proof. By our choice in BKW we initially start with $N := \left(c - 1 + \frac{\log^2 k}{(1-2\tau)^{2^c}} + \log^2 k \right) 2^d$ samples. Every foreach loop reduces the number of samples by at most 2^d, resulting in at least $\left(\frac{\log^2 k}{(1-2\tau)^{2^c}} + \log^2 k \right) 2^d$ samples after loop termination.

Let $\mathbf{u}_1 = (1, 0, 0, \ldots, 0)$ be the first unit vector. Among the remaining samples there will be at least $r = \frac{\log^2 k}{(1-2\tau)^{2^c}}$ samples of the form $(\mathbf{u}_1, s_1 + e)$ for some error $e \in \{0, 1\}$ with overwhelming probability according to Lemma 1. Since our r remaining samples are generated as a sum of 2^{c-1} initial samples, the Piling-up lemma (Lemma 2) yields $e \sim \text{Ber}_{\frac{1}{2} - \frac{1}{2}(1-2\tau)^{2^{c-1}}}$.

Hence, e has a bias of $\bar{b} = \frac{1}{2}(1 - 2\tau)^{2^{c-1}}$. An easy Chernoff bound argument shows that having $\bar{b}^{-2}$ samples is sufficient to obtain s_1 with constant success probability by majority vote. Since our number r is larger than $\bar{b}^{-2}$ by a factor of $\frac{\log^2 k}{4}$, we even obtain s_1 with overwhelming success probability. By repeating this process for all bits $s_1, \ldots, s_k$ a union bound shows that we lose a factor of at most k in the success probability, meaning that we can recover $\mathbf{s}$ with overwhelming success probability.

The algorithm's run time and memory consumption is (up to polynomial factors) dominated by its sample complexity, which by our choice of c, d is

$$
N = \left(c - 1 + \frac{\log^2 k}{(1 - 2\tau)^{2c}} + \log^2 k\right)2^d = 2^{\mathcal{O}(k^{1-\varepsilon}) + \frac{1}{1-\varepsilon} \cdot \frac{k}{\log(\frac{k}{\tau})}} = 2^{\frac{k}{\log(\frac{k}{\tau})}(1+o(1))}.
$$

$\square$

We would like to point out that in Theorem 1 the running time $2^{k/\log(\frac{k}{\tau})(1+o(1))}$ only very slowly decreases with τ. Notice that even for τ as small as $\Theta(\frac{1}{k})$ we still obtain a running time of $2^{\frac{1}{2}k/\log k(1+o(1))}$, while $\mathrm{LPN}_{k,\mathcal{O}(\frac{1}{k})}$ clearly can be solved in polynomial time via correcting $\mathcal{O}(1)$ errors and running Gaussian elimination.

3.2 Gauss

The following simple Algorithm 2, that we call Gauss, is the most natural extension of Gaussian elimination from Sect. 2.2, where one repeats sampling k linearly independent $\mathbf{a}_i$ until they are all error-free.

In each iteration of Gauss we simply assume error-freeness and compute a candidate secret key $\mathbf{s}' = A^{-1}\mathbf{b}$ as in Eq. (1). We take fresh samples to test our hypothesis, whether we were indeed in the error-free case and hence $\mathbf{s}' = \mathbf{s}$.

Notice that we are in the error-free case with probability $(1 - \tau)^k$. Hence, Algorithm 2 has up to polynomial factors expected running time $(\frac{1}{1-\tau})^k$, provided that Test can be carried out in polynomial time. Thus in comparison to BKW in Sect. 3.1, we obtain a much better dependence on τ. For instance for $\tau = \mathcal{O}(\frac{1}{k})$, we obtain polynomial running time, as one would expect.

Input: $\mathrm{LPN}_{k,\tau}$ oracle, τ
Output: secret $\mathbf{s}$
repeat
    repeat
        | $(A, \mathbf{b}) \leftarrow \mathrm{LPN}_{k,\tau}^k$;
    until $A \in \mathrm{GL}_k(\mathbb{F}_2)$;
    $s' := A^{-1}\mathbf{b}$;
until $\mathrm{Test}(\mathbf{s}', \tau, \frac{1}{2^k}, (\frac{1-\tau}{2})^k) = \mathrm{Accept}$;
return s';

Algorithm 2. Gauss

Basically our algorithm Test computes for sufficiently many fresh LPN sample $(A, \mathbf{b}) \leftarrow \mathrm{LPN}_{k,\tau}^m$ whether $A\mathbf{s}' + \mathbf{b}$ is closer to $\mathrm{Ber}_{m,\tau}$ or to $\mathrm{Ber}_{m,\frac{1}{2}}$ via checking whether its weight is close to τm or $\frac{m}{2}$, respectively.

We have designed Test in a flexible way that allows us to control the two-sided error probabilities Pr[Test rejects | $\mathbf{s}' = \mathbf{s}$] for rejecting the right candidate and Pr[Test accepts | $\mathbf{s}' \neq \mathbf{s}$] for accepting an incorrect $\mathbf{s}'$ via two parameters α, β. Throughout this paper, we will tune these parameters α, β to guarantee that all subsequent algorithms have overwhelming success probability $1 - \text{negl}(k)$.

Input: $\mathbf{s}'$, τ, error levels $\alpha, \beta \in (0,1]$
Output: Accept or Reject

$$m := \left(\frac{\sqrt{\frac{3}{2} \ln(\frac{1}{\alpha})} + \sqrt{\ln(\frac{1}{\beta})}}{\frac{1}{2} - \tau} \right)^2 ;$$

$(A, \mathbf{b}) \leftarrow \text{LPN}_{k,\tau}^m$;

$c := \tau m + \sqrt{3(\frac{1}{2} - \tau) \ln(\frac{1}{\alpha}) m}$;

if $\text{wt}(A\mathbf{s}' + \mathbf{b}) \leq c$ **then**
 | **return** Accept;
end
else
 | **return** Reject;
end

Algorithm 3. Test

Notice that by our definition of m in Test even an exponentially small choice of $\alpha = \beta = \frac{1}{2^k}$ leads to only $m = \Theta\left(\frac{k}{(\frac{1}{2} - \tau)^2} \right)$ samples, which is linear in k and quadratic in $(\frac{1}{2} - \tau)^{-1}$. Thus, our hypothesis test can be carried out efficiently even for exponentially small error probabilities.

Lemma 3 (Hypothesis Testing). *For any $\alpha, \beta \in (0,1]$, Test accepts the correct LPN secret $\mathbf{s}$ with probability at least $1 - \alpha$, and rejects incorrect $\mathbf{s}'$ with probability at least $1 - \beta$, using m samples in time and space $\Theta(mk)$.*

Proof. Inputting the correct $\mathbf{s}$ to Test implies, that $\text{wt}(A\mathbf{s}' + \mathbf{b}) \sim \text{Bin}_{m,\tau}$. In this case we have

$$\Pr\left[\text{wt}(A\mathbf{s}' + \mathbf{b}) \geq c\right] \overset{\text{Chernoff}}{\leq} \exp\left(-\frac{1}{3} \cdot \min\left(\frac{c}{\tau m} - 1, \left(\frac{c}{\tau m} - 1 \right)^2 \right) \cdot \tau m \right)$$
$$\leq \exp\left(-\frac{1}{3} \cdot \frac{\tau}{\frac{1}{2} - \tau} \left(\frac{c}{\tau m} - 1 \right)^2 \cdot \tau m \right) \overset{!}{=} \alpha.$$

We need that the last term is equal to α, which leads to the threshold weight of

$$c := \tau m + \sqrt{3(\frac{1}{2} - \tau) \ln\left(\frac{1}{\alpha} \right) m},$$

as defined in Test. If $\mathbf{s}' \neq \mathbf{s}$, then $\text{wt}(A\mathbf{s}' + \mathbf{b}) \sim \text{Bin}_{m,\frac{1}{2}}$. We want to upper bound the acceptance probability in this case.

$$\Pr\left[\text{wt}(A\mathbf{s}' + \mathbf{b}) \leq c\right] \overset{\text{Chernoff}}{\leq} \exp\left(-\frac{1}{2} \cdot \left(1 - \frac{2c}{m} \right)^2 \cdot \frac{m}{2} \right) \overset{!}{=} \beta$$

Using the c from above, the last equation holds, if

$$m := \left(\frac{\sqrt{\frac{3}{2} \ln \left(\frac{1}{\alpha} \right)} + \sqrt{\ln \left(\frac{1}{\beta} \right)}}{\frac{1}{2} - \tau} \right)^2 . \qquad \square$$

Remark 2. As defined, Test takes m fresh samples on every invocation for achieving independence. However, for efficiency reasons we will in practice use the same m samples for Test on every invocation. Our experiments confirm that the introduced dependencies do not noticeably affect the algorithms' performance and success probability.

Now that we are equipped with an efficient hypothesis test, we can carry out the analysis of Gauss. For ease of notation, we use for the running time soft-Theta notion $\tilde{\Theta}$ to suppress factors that are polynomial in k.

Theorem 2. *Gauss solves $LPN_{k,\tau}$ with overwhelming success probability in time and sample complexity $\tilde{\Theta} \left(\frac{1}{(1-\tau)^k} \right)$ using $\Theta(k^2)$ memory.*

Proof. We already noted that the outer repeat loop of Gauss takes an expected number of $\frac{1}{(1-\tau)^k}$ to produce a batch of k error-free LPN samples. In particular, Lemma 1 tells us that we will find an error-free batch after at most $\frac{\log^2 k}{(1-\tau)^k}$ trials with overwhelming probability.

The inner loop is executed an expected number of $\mathcal{O}(1)$ times until $A \in GL_k(\mathbb{F}_2)$. Here again, after at most $\mathcal{O}\left(\log^2 k \right)$ iterations it is ensured that we get an invertible A with overwhelming probability. This already proves the upper bound on the running time.

Since, we only have to store k samples for A of length $\Theta(k)$ each, our memory consumption is $\Theta(k^2)$. In Test we do not necessarily have to store our $m = \Theta(k)$ samples, since we can process them on the fly. However, in practice (see Remark 2) it is useful to reserve for them another $\Theta(k^2)$ memory cells.

Considering the success probability, Gauss solves $LPN_{k,\tau}$ when it rejects all false candidates $\mathbf{s}'$, and accepts the secret key $\mathbf{s}$ (if it appears). The first event happens by Lemma 3 with probability at least $1 - \beta = (\frac{1-\tau}{2})^k$ for each incorrect candidate by our choice in Gauss. The second event happens by Lemma 3 with probability at least $1 - \alpha = 1 - 2^{-k}$.

Let X be a random variable for the number of iterations of the outer loop until we are for the first time in the error-free case. Then

$$\Pr[\text{Success}] = \sum_{i=1}^{\infty} \Pr[\text{Success} \mid X = i] \cdot \Pr[X = i]$$

$$\geq \sum_{i=1}^{\infty} (1 - \beta)^{i-1} (1 - \alpha) \cdot \left(1 - (1 - \tau)^k \right)^{i-1} (1 - \tau)^k$$

$$= \frac{(1-\alpha)(1-\tau)^k}{1-(1-\beta)(1-(1-\tau)^k)}$$

$$\geq \frac{(1-\alpha)(1-\tau)^k}{\beta+(1-\tau)^k} = 1 - \mathrm{negl}(k). \qquad \square$$

Notice that Gauss' sample complexity is as large as its running time by Theorem 2. We will show in the following section that the sample complexity can be decreased to $\mathrm{poly}(k)$ without affecting the run time. This will be the starting point for further improvements.

4   LPN and Its Relation to Decoding

Let us slightly modify the Gauss algorithm from Sect. 3.2. Instead of taking in each iteration a fresh batch of k LPN samples, we initially fix a large enough pool of n samples. Then in each iteration we take k out of our pool of n samples, with linearly independent $\mathbf{a}_i$. This results in the following Algorithm 4 that we call Pooled Gauss.

Input: $\mathrm{LPN}_{k,\tau}$ oracle, τ
Output: secret $\mathbf{s}$
$n := k^2 \log^2 k$;
$(A, \mathbf{b}) \leftarrow \mathrm{LPN}_{k,\tau}^n$;
repeat
    repeat
        $I \leftarrow \mathcal{U}(\binom{[n]}{k})$;
    until $A_I \in \mathrm{GL}_k(\mathbb{F}_2)$;
    $s' := A_I^{-1} \mathbf{b}_I$;
until $\mathrm{Test}(\mathbf{s}', \tau, \frac{1}{2^k}, (\frac{1-\tau}{2})^k) = \mathrm{Accept}$;
return $\mathbf{s}'$;

Algorithm 4. Pooled Gauss

Before we analyze Pooled Gauss, we want to clarify its connection to the decoding of random linear codes. Notice that we fix a sample matrix $A \in \mathbb{F}_2^{n \times k}$ with uniformly random entries. A can be considered a generator matrix of some random linear $[n, k]$ code $\mathcal{C}$, which is the column span of $\mathcal{C}$. The secret $\mathbf{s} \in \mathbb{F}_2^k$ is a message and the label vector $\mathbf{b} \in \mathbb{F}_2^n$ is an erroneous encoding of $\mathbf{s}$ with some error vector $\mathbf{e} \in \mathbb{F}_2^n$ having components $e_i \sim \mathrm{Ber}_\tau$. Thus, decoding the codeword $\mathbf{b}$ to the original message $\mathbf{s}$ solves $\mathrm{LPN}_{k,\tau}$.

Decoding such a codeword $\mathbf{b}$ can be done by finding an error-free index set as in Pooled Gauss. In coding theory language, such an error-free index set is called an information set. Thus, our Pooled Gauss algorithm is in this language an information set decoding algorithm, namely it resembles the well-known algorithm of Prange [28] from 1962. One should notice however that as opposed to the decoding scenario, we can fix the length n of $\mathcal{C}$ ourselves.

Theorem 3. *Pooled Gauss solves* $LPN_{k,\tau}$ *with overwhelming success probability in time* $\tilde{\Theta}\left(\frac{1}{(1-\tau)^k}\right)$ *using* $\tilde{\Theta}(k^2)$ *samples and* $\tilde{\Theta}(k^3)$ *memory.*

Proof. Pooled Gauss' run time follows with the same reasoning as for Gauss' running time. The outer loop will with overwhelming probability be executed at most $\frac{\log^2 k}{(1-\tau)^k}$ times, and all other parts can be performed in time $\mathcal{O}(k^3)$. The sample complexity follows by our choice of n in Pooled Gauss. Storing n samples requires $\tilde{\Theta}(k^3)$ memory.

For the success probability, we would first like to notice that the probability for drawing k linearly independent vectors out of a pool even as small as $n' = 2k$ without replacement can easily be lower-bounded by $\frac{1}{4}$. We will see, that the pool in our algorithm will be even bigger than that in the following. Therefore, by our choice of n and similar to the reasoning in the proof of Theorem 2, the inner loop of Pooled Gauss will always find an invertible A_I with overwhelming probability. So we condition our further analysis on this event.

Let Y be the number of error-free samples in the pool of n vectors. On expectation, we have $\mathbb{E}[Y] = (1-\tau)n$. By using a Chernoff bound, we can show that we deviate by a factor of $1 - \frac{1}{k}$ from the expectation with probability at most

$$\Pr[Y \geq (1-\frac{1}{k})(1-\tau)n] \geq 1 - e^{-\frac{(1-\tau)n}{2k^2}}.$$

By our choice of $n = \omega\left(k^2 \log k\right)$ the right hand side is $1 - k^{-\omega(1)}$, which is overwhelming.

We call any pool with at least $(1-\frac{1}{k})(1-\tau)n$ error-free samples *good*. Conditioned on the event G that our pool is good, we draw a batch of k error-free samples with probability

$$p \geq \prod_{i=0}^{k-1} \frac{(1-\frac{1}{k})(1-\tau)n - i}{n} \geq \left(\frac{(1-\frac{1}{k})(1-\tau)n - k}{n}\right)^k$$

$$= (1-\frac{1}{k})^k(1-\tau)^k\left(1 - \frac{k}{n(1-\frac{1}{k})(1-\tau)}\right)^k = \Omega\left((1-\tau)^k\right).$$

Now, following the same arguments with p instead of $(1-\tau)^k$ as in Theorem 2 gives us an overwhelming probability of success. $\square$

4.1   Low-Noise LPN

Some interesting cryptographic applications require that the LPN error $e_i \sim \text{Ber}_\tau$ has an error term $\tau = \tau(k)$ depending on k. E.g. public key encryption seems to require some $\tau(k)$ as small as $\frac{1}{\sqrt{k}}$.

As a corollary from Theorem 3, we obtain that for any $\tau(k)$ that approaches 0 for $k \to \infty$, our Pooled Gauss algorithm runs – up to polynomial factors – in time $e^{\tau(k)k(1+o(1))}$. This implies that for $\tau(k) = o(\frac{1}{\log k})$ the run time of Pooled Gauss asymptotically outperforms the run time of BKW from Theorem 1.

Corollary 1 (Low Noise). *Let* $\tau(k) \overset{k\to\infty}{\longrightarrow} 0$. *Pooled Gauss solves* $LPN_{k,\tau(k)}$ *with overwhelming success probability in time* $\tilde{\Theta}\left(e^{\tau k(1+o(1))}\right)$ *using* $\tilde{\Theta}(k^2)$ *samples and* $\tilde{\Theta}(k^3)$ *memory.*

Proof. The run time statement follows by observing that

$$\left(\frac{1}{1-\tau}\right)^k = \left(\frac{1}{(1-\tau)^{\frac{1}{\tau}}}\right)^{\tau k} = \left(\frac{1}{\frac{1}{e}-o(1)}\right)^{\tau k} = (e+o(1))^{\tau k} = e^{\tau k(1+o(1))}. \quad \square$$

For small noise $\tau(k) = \Omega(\frac{1}{\sqrt{k}})$, i.e. a case that covers the mentioned encryption application above, we can also remove the error term $(1+o(1))$ in the exponent, meaning that Pooled Gauss achieves – up to polynomial factors – run time $e^{\tau(k)k}$.

Corollary 2 (Really Low Noise). *Let* $\tau(k) = \frac{1}{k^c}$ *for* $c \geq \frac{1}{2}$. *Pooled Gauss solves* $LPN_{k,\tau}$ *with overwhelming success probability in time* $\tilde{\Theta}\left(e^{k^{1-c}}\right)$, *using* $\tilde{\Theta}(k^2)$ *samples and* $\tilde{\Theta}(k^3)$ *memory.*

Proof. Since $\ln(\frac{1}{1-x}) = x + \frac{x^2}{2} + \mathcal{O}\left(x^3\right)$ for $x \in [-1,1)$ we get

$$\left(\frac{1}{1-\frac{1}{k^c}}\right)^k = e^{\ln\left(\frac{1}{1-\frac{1}{k^c}}\right)k} = e^{k^{1-c}+\frac{k^{1-2c}}{2}+\mathcal{O}\left(k^{1-3c}\right)}.$$

We see, that for $c \geq \frac{1}{2}$, the last term is in $\mathcal{O}\left(e^{k^{1-c}}\right)$ and for $c < \frac{1}{2}$ it is not. $\square$

4.2   Quantum Pooled Gauss

In a nutshell, Pooled Gauss runs until it finds an error-free batch of k LPN samples from a pool of n samples. The expected number of error-free samples in such a pool is $(1-\tau)n$. Hence, we search for an index set I in a total search space of size $\binom{n}{k}$, in which we expect $\binom{(1-\tau)n}{k}$ good index sets. Therefore, we expect

$$T = \frac{\binom{n}{k}}{\binom{(1-\tau)n}{k}}$$

iterations of Pooled Gauss until we hit an error-free batch. It is not hard to show that T equals up to a polynomial the run time from Theorem 3.

The event of hitting an error-free batch can be modeled by the function $f\colon \binom{[n]}{k} \to \{0,1\}$ that takes value $f(I) = 1$ iff I is an index set of k error-free LPN samples. More formally, we can define

$$f\colon \binom{[n]}{k} \to \{0,1\}, \; I \mapsto \begin{cases} 1_{A_I^{-1}\mathbf{b}_I=\mathbf{s}}, & A_I \in \mathrm{GL}(\mathbb{F}_2^k) \\ 0, & A_I \notin \mathrm{GL}(\mathbb{F}_2^k) \end{cases}. \tag{2}$$

Here, the characteristic function $1_{A_I^{-1}\mathbf{b}_I=\mathbf{s}}$ takes value 1 iff we compute the correct secret key $\mathbf{s}$, which is equivalent to I being an index set of k error-free LPN samples. In our algorithm `Pooled Gauss` the evaluation of $1_{A_I^{-1}\mathbf{b}_I=\mathbf{s}}$ is done by `Test`, which may err with negligible probability. But assume for a moment that we have a perfect instantiation of f.

Using f, the task of `Pooled Gauss` is to find an index set I^* among all index sets from $\binom{[n]}{k}$ such that $f(I^*) = 1$, which can be done *classically* in expected time

$$T = \frac{\binom{n}{k}}{|f^{-1}(1)|}.$$

We can now speed up `Pooled Gauss` *quantumly* by applying Boyer et al.'s [10] version of Grover search [17], which results in run time $\sqrt{T}$. It is worth to point out that Boyer et al.'s algorithm works even in our case, where we do not know the number $|f^{-1}(1)|$ of error-free index sets. All that the algorithm requires is oracle access to the function f, for which we show that this oracle access can be perfectly simulated by `Test`. This results in Algorithm 5 that we call `Quantum Pooled Gauss`.

Input: $\text{LPN}_{k,\tau}$ oracle, τ
Output: secret $\mathbf{s}$
$n := k^2 \log^2 k$;
$(A, \mathbf{b}) \leftarrow \text{LPN}_{k,\tau}^n$;
Define
$$\tilde{f} \colon \binom{[n]}{k} \to \{0,1\}, \ I \mapsto \begin{cases} \text{Test}(A_I^{-1}\mathbf{b}_I, \tau, \binom{n}{k}^{-2}, \binom{n}{k}^{-2}), & A_I \in \mathrm{GL}(\mathbb{F}_2^k), \\ 0, & A_I \notin \mathrm{GL}(\mathbb{F}_2^k) \end{cases};$$
$I^* \leftarrow \text{Grover}(\tilde{f})$;
return $\mathbf{s} = A_{I^*}^{-1}\mathbf{b}_{I^*}$;

Algorithm 5. `Quantum Pooled Gauss`

Theorem 4. *`Quantum Pooled Gauss` quantumly solves $LPN_{k,\tau}$ with overwhelming probability in time $\tilde{\Theta}\left(\left(\frac{1}{1-\tau}\right)^{\frac{k}{2}}\right)$, using $\tilde{\Theta}(k^2)$ queries and $\tilde{\Theta}(k^3)$ memory.*

Proof. According to [10], `Grover` succeeds with overwhelming success probability. Hence, the proof of Theorem 3 essentially carries over to the quantum setting.

However, it remains to show that we can safely replace oracle access to the function f as defined in Eq. (2) by `Test`, which in turn defines some function

$$\tilde{f} \colon \binom{[n]}{k} \to \{0,1\}, \ I \mapsto \begin{cases} \text{Test}(A_I^{-1}\mathbf{b}_I, \tau, \binom{n}{k}^{-2}, \binom{n}{k}^{-2}), & A_I \in \mathrm{GL}(\mathbb{F}_2^k) \\ 0, & A_I \notin \mathrm{GL}(\mathbb{F}_2^k) \end{cases}.$$

We will show that by our choice of $\alpha = \beta = \binom{n}{k}^{-2}$ with overwhelming probability $f(I) = \tilde{f}(I)$ for *all* I, i.e. we perfectly simulate f. Let us define a random variable X that counts the number of inputs in which f and $\tilde{f}$ disagree, i.e.

$$X := \left| \left\{ I \in \binom{[n]}{k} \mid \tilde{f}(I) \neq f(I) \right\} \right|.$$

Notice that $X \sim \text{Bin}_{\binom{n}{k}, \leq \alpha}$, since by Lemma 3 Test errs with probability (at most) $\alpha = \beta$ for all of the $\binom{n}{k}$ sets I. We obtain

$$\Pr[\tilde{f} = f] = \Pr[X = 0] \geq \left(1 - \frac{1}{\binom{n}{k}^2} \right)^{\binom{n}{k}} \geq 1 - \frac{1}{\binom{n}{k}},$$

where we use Bernoulli's inequality for the last step. Since we chose $n = \omega(k^2)$, we have $\binom{n}{k} \geq \left(\frac{n}{k} \right)^k = \omega(k^k)$. This implies $\Pr[\tilde{f} = f] = 1 - \text{negl}(k)$, as required.   □

Remark 3. Notice that our slight modification from Gauss to Pooled Gauss enables the use of quantum techniques. While both algorithms Gauss and Pooled Gauss achieve the same running time T, Gauss also requires (roughly) T samples. But any algorithm with sample complexity T has automatically run time lower bound $\Omega(T)$, since our LPN oracle is by Definition 1 classical and each oracle access costs $\Omega(1)$.

So while there is good motivation to reduce the number of samples, it is somewhat unsatisfactory from a cryptanalysts' point of view to make only limited use of an LPN oracle by restricting to a polynomial number of samples. In the next section, we will show how more extensive queries give rise to a better suited pool of vectors that will further speed up Pooled Gauss.

5   Decoding LPN with Preprocessing

Our idea is to add some preprocessing to Pooled Gauss that produces LPN samples with $\mathbf{a}_i$ of *smaller dimension* k' by zeroing some columns in the A-matrix. This may come at the cost of slightly increasing the noise parameter τ. This idea gives rise to the following meta algorithm Dim-Decode.

Input: $\text{LPN}_{k,\tau}$ oracle, τ
Output: secret $\mathbf{s}$
(1) *Modify:* Use a large number of samples to produce a small number of dimension-reduced samples, resulting in a new $\text{LPN}_{k',\tau'}$ instance with $k' < k$ and $\tau' \geq \tau$;
(2) *Decode:* Use a decoding algorithm to solve $\text{LPN}_{k',\tau'}$, e.g. use Pooled Gauss;
(3) *Complete:* Recover the remaining coordinates of $\mathbf{s}$, e.g. via enumeration or by iterating (1) and (2) accordingly;
                        Algorithm 6. Dim-Decode

In the following, we give different instantiations of Dim-Decode. We start by looking at techniques for the *Modify* step for dimension reduction.

5.1 Improvements Using only Polynomial Memory

Our first simple technique is to keep only those LPN samples $(\mathbf{a}, b)$ that have zeros in the last $k - k'$ coordinates of $\mathbf{a}$. We will balance the running time for steps *Modify* and *Decode* by choosing k' accordingly. This results in Algorithm 7 that we call `Well-Pooled Gauss`.

Notice that by our choice of k', `Well-Pooled Gauss` reduces the dimension to a $\frac{1}{1+\log(\frac{1}{1-\tau})}$-fraction of k. Since $\tau \in [0, \frac{1}{2})$ we have

$$\frac{1}{1 + \log(\frac{1}{1-\tau})} \in (\frac{1}{2}, 1],$$

meaning that $k' \geq \frac{k}{2}$ or in other words that `Pooled Gauss` in its first run recovers at least the first half of the bits of $\mathbf{s}$, and in its second run the remaining half.

Input: $\text{LPN}_{k,\tau}$ oracle, τ
Output: secret $\mathbf{s}$
$k' := \frac{1}{1+\log(\frac{1}{1-\tau})}k$;
Set parameters n, m as in `Pooled Gauss` for an $\text{LPN}_{k',\tau}$ instance;
(1) *Modify*
repeat

    $(\mathbf{a}, b) \leftarrow \text{LPN}_{k,\tau}$;
    if $\mathbf{a}_{\{k'+1,\ldots,k\}} = 0^{k-k'}$ **then**
      | Add $(\mathbf{a}_{\{1,\ldots,k'\}}, b)$ to sample pool;
    end

until pool contains more than $n + m$ elements;
(2) *Decode*
$(s_1, \ldots, s_{k'}) \leftarrow$ Run `Pooled Gauss` on the pool containing the first n $\text{LPN}_{k',\tau}$ samples, while taking the remaining m samples for `Test`;
(3) *Complete*
$(A, \mathbf{b}) \leftarrow \text{LPN}_{k,\tau}^{n+m}$. Reduce A's dimension to $k - k'$ using $(s_1, \ldots, s_{k'})$;
$(s_{k'+1}, \ldots, s_k) \leftarrow$ Run `Pooled Gauss` on the pool containing the first n $\text{LPN}_{k-k',\tau}$ samples, while taking the remaining m samples for `Test`;
return s;

Algorithm 7. Well-Pooled Gauss

Hence the run time of `Pooled Gauss`' first application dominates the run time of its second application. Since `Pooled Gauss`' run time depends exponentially on k, we can gain up to a square root in the running time when we reduce the dimension up to $\frac{k}{2}$.

Theorem 5 (Well-Pooled Gauss). *Well-Pooled Gauss solves $\text{LPN}_{k,\tau}$ with overwhelming probability in time and query complexity*

$$\tilde{\Theta}\left(\left(\frac{1}{(1-\tau)^k}\right)^{\frac{1}{1+\log(\frac{1}{1-\tau})}}\right)$$

using $\tilde{\Theta}(k^3)$ memory.

Proof. Pooled Gauss's first application runs in time $T := \tilde{\Theta}\left(\frac{1}{(1-\tau)^{k'}}\right)$, which is the claimed total running time. Furthermore, by Lemma 1 with overwhelming probability the run time of the *Modify* step for finding $n + m$ samples with last $k - k'$ 0-coordinates is bounded by

$$2^{k-k'}\left(n + m + \log^2 k\right) = \tilde{\Theta}\left(2^{k-k'}\right) = \tilde{\Theta}\left(2^{\left(1-\frac{1}{1+\log\left(\frac{1}{1-\tau}\right)}\right)k}\right)$$

$$= \tilde{\Theta}\left(2^{\frac{\log\left(\frac{1}{1-\tau}\right)}{1+\log\left(\frac{1}{1-\tau}\right)}k}\right) = T.$$

$\square$

5.2   Quantum Improvements with Polynomial Memory

In the quantum version of Well-Pooled Gauss, called Quantum Well-Pooled Gauss, we simply replace in Algorithm 7 the Pooled Gauss procedure by its quantum version. Notice that by Remark 3 we cannot provide a quantum version of our *Modify* step. So we cannot expect to gain another full square root by going to the quantum version of Well-Pooled Gauss.

The following theorem shows that in Quantum Well-Pooled Gauss one should take the parameter choice $k' := \frac{2}{2+\log\left(\frac{1}{1-\tau}\right)}k > \frac{2}{3}k$. The Quantum Pooled Gauss routine then runs in time

$$T := \tilde{\Theta}\left(\left(\frac{1}{1-\tau}\right)^{\frac{k'}{2}}\right).$$

Hence in comparison with Well-Pooled Gauss (Theorem 5) we gain at most an additional factor of $\frac{2}{3}$ in the exponent.

Theorem 6 (Quantum Well-Pooled Gauss). *Quantum Well-Pooled Gauss quantumly solves* $LPN_{k,\tau}$ *with overwhelming probability in time and query complexity*

$$\tilde{\Theta}\left(\left(\frac{1}{(1-\tau)^k}\right)^{\frac{1}{2+\log\left(\frac{1}{1-\tau}\right)}}\right),$$

using $\tilde{\Theta}(k^3)$ *space.*

Proof. Analogous to the proof of Well-Pooled Gauss' run time (Theorem 5), in its quantum version the run time of the first Quantum Pooled Gauss routine is $T = \tilde{\Theta}((\frac{1}{1-\tau})^{\frac{k'}{2}})$, which is the claimed total run time. T dominates the run time of the second call for Quantum Pooled Gauss, since $k' > \frac{2}{3}k$. T also upper bounds the run time of the *Modify* step, since by Lemma 1 with overwhelming probability for obtaining $n + m$ of the desired form it takes at most time

$$2^{k-k'}\left(n+m+\log^2 k\right) = \tilde{\Theta}(2^{k-k'}) = \tilde{\Theta}\left(2^{\frac{\log\left(\frac{1}{1-\tau}\right)}{2+\log\left(\frac{1}{1-\tau}\right)}k}\right) = T. \qquad \Box$$

5.3   Using Memory – Building a Bridge Towards BKW

Up to now, for instantiating Algorithm 6 in Well Pooled Gauss we made only somewhat naive use of our LPN oracle by storing only those vectors in the stream of all oracle answers that were already dimension-reduced. The reason for this was our restriction to polynomial memory consumption in order to achieve highly efficient algorithms in practice.

Optimally, we could tune our LPN algorithm by the memory that is available on our machine. Let us say, we have memory M and we are looking for the fastest algorithm that uses at most M memory cells. In this scenario, we are free to store more LPN samples and to add them until they provide us dimension-reduced samples, at the cost of a growing error $\tau' > \tau$ determined by the Piling-up Lemma (Lemma 2).

Notice that this is exactly the strategy of BKW. But as opposed to the BKW algorithm, which basically reduces the dimension k all the way down to 1, we allow – due to our constraint memory M – only limited dimension reduction down to some k'. Since afterwards, we will in Algorithm 6 resort again to a *Decoding* step, the optimal choice of k' is not determined by the size of M alone, but also by the growth of the error τ' that our decoding procedure can handle.

More precisely, the following Algorithm 8, called Hybrid, in a first step uses the naive strategy of Well-Pooled Gauss to decrease the dimension by k_1, while leaving τ unchanged. Then in a second step it uses c BKW-iterations on blocks of size d to further reduce the dimension by k_2, thereby increasing to error τ' which grows double-exponentially in c.

Hybrid instantiated with only polynomial memory leaves out all BKW-iterations and boils down to Well-Pooled Gauss. Hybrid instantiated with sufficiently memory achieves BKW's time complexity $2^{k/\log(\frac{k}{\tau})(1+o(1))}$. Thus, Hybrid provides a perfect interpolation between both algorithms.

Theorem 7 (Hybrid). *Using $\tilde{\mathcal{O}}(M)$ space, Hybrid solves $\mathrm{LPN}_{k,\tau}$ with overwhelming probability in time and query complexity $\tilde{\mathcal{O}}(M \cdot 2^{k_1})$, where k_1 is as defined in Hybrid.*

For $M = \mathrm{poly}(k)$ we get the same time, memory and sample complexity as in Well-Pooled Gauss (Theorem 5).

Choosing $M = 2^{k/\log(\frac{k}{\tau})(1+o(1))}$ gives us the complexities of BKW (Theorem 1).

Proof. For the *Decoding* step, we need $m = \tilde{\Theta}\left(\frac{1}{(\frac{1}{2}-\tau')^2}\right) = \tilde{\Theta}\left(\frac{1}{(1-2\tau)^{2^{c+1}}}\right)$ samples for the hypothesis test and $n = \mathrm{poly}(k)$ samples for the pool at the end. That's why we initially need to feed the BKW step $N = m + n + c2^d = \tilde{\Theta}\left(2^{\max\left(\frac{k_2}{c},2^c\log(\frac{1}{(1-2\tau)^2})\right)}\right)$ samples. As in Well-Pooled Gauss we can create

Input: $\mathrm{LPN}_{k,\tau}$ oracle, τ, memory M
Output: secret $\mathbf{s}$
Choose $\varepsilon > 0$;
$c := \max\left(0, \log\left(\frac{1}{\tau^{1-\varepsilon}k^{\varepsilon}}\log(M)\log(\frac{k}{\tau})\right)\right)$;
Choose $k_2 \le c\frac{k-1}{\log\left(\frac{k}{\tau}\right)}$ s.t. $\max\left(\frac{k_2}{c}, 2^c\log(\frac{1}{(1-2\tau)^2})\right) \le \log(M)$;
$d := \frac{k_2}{c}$;
$\tau' = \frac{1}{2} - \frac{1}{2}(1-2\tau)^{2^c}$;
$k_1 := \dfrac{\log\left(\frac{1}{1-\tau'}\right)(k-k_2)+2^c\log\left(\frac{1}{(1-2\tau)^2}\right)-\log M}{1+\log\left(\frac{1}{1-\tau'}\right)}$;
$k' := k - k_1 - k_2$;
Set parameters n, m as in **Pooled Gauss** for an $\mathrm{LPN}_{k',\tau'}$ instance;
(1) *Modify*
repeat
$\quad\big|\quad (\mathbf{a}, \ell) \leftarrow \mathrm{LPN}_{k,\tau}$;
$\quad\big|\quad$ **if** $\mathbf{a}_{\{k-k_1+1,\dots,k\}} = 0^{k_1}$ **then**
$\quad\big|\quad\big|\quad$ Add $(\mathbf{a}_{1,\dots,k-k_1}, b)$ to sample pool;
$\quad\big|\quad$ **end**
until pool contains more than $n + m + c2^d$ samples;
for $i = 1, \dots, c$ **do**
$\quad\big|\quad$ **foreach** $j \in \mathbb{F}_2^d$ **do**
$\quad\big|\quad\big|\quad$ Pick a row $\mathbf{a}_k$ of A with suffix $j|0^{(i-1)d}$ (if any); add $\mathbf{a}_k$ to all the other
$\quad\big|\quad\big|\quad$ rows of A with suffix $j|0^{(i-1)d}$, also add corresponding labels;
$\quad\big|\quad\big|\quad$ Remove the kth row from A and $\mathbf{b}$;
$\quad\big|\quad$ **end**
end
(2) *Decode*
$(s_1, \dots, s_{k'}) \leftarrow$ Run **Pooled Gauss** on the pool containing the first n $\mathrm{LPN}_{k',\tau'}$ samples, while taking the remaining m samples for **Test**;
(3) *Complete*
While there are still unknown bits of $\mathbf{s}$ go to (1), using the known bits of $\mathbf{s}$ to create smaller dimension samples;
return $\mathbf{s}$;

Algorithm 8. Hybrid

these samples in time $\tilde{\Theta}(N \cdot 2^{k_1})$. Therefore with overwhelming probability the *Modify* and *Decoding* steps in **Hybrid** take time $\tilde{\Theta}\left(N \cdot 2^{k_1} + N + \left(\frac{1}{1-\tau'}\right)^{k'} m\right)$

$$= \tilde{\Theta}\left(2^{k_1 + \max\left(\frac{k_2}{c}, 2^c\log(\frac{1}{(1-2\tau)^2})\right)} + 2^{\log\left(\frac{1}{1-\tau'}\right)(k-k_1-k_2)+2^c\log\left(\frac{1}{(1-2\tau)^2}\right)}\right),$$

using $\tilde{\Theta}\left(N \cdot 2^{k_1}\right)$ samples and $\tilde{\Theta}\left(N\right)$ memory. Our choice of k_1 in **Hybrid** balances both run time summands. Our choice of k_2 then gives us the stated time, sample and memory complexity. Notice that the *Complete* step takes less time, queries and memory, since here we solve smaller LPN instances.

It remains to show that Hybrid contains as special cases Well-Pooled Gauss and BKW. For some $\varepsilon > 0$, let us define similar to Hybrid

$$c(k, \tau, M) := \max\left(0, \log\left(\frac{1}{\tau^{1-\varepsilon}k^{\varepsilon}} \log\left(M\right) \log\left(\frac{k}{\tau}\right)\right)\right).$$

For the choice $M = \text{poly}(k)$ we get $c = o(1)$ and $k_2 = o(1)$, which means that we do not perform any BKW steps. Thus, Hybrid is identical to Well-Pooled Gauss. For the choice $M = 2^{(1+o(1))k/\log\left(\frac{k}{\tau}\right)}$ we obtain $c = (1-\varepsilon)\log(\frac{k}{\tau}) + o(1)$, $k_2 = k - o(1)$ and $k_1 = o(1)$, giving us the complexities of BKW from Theorem 1.   □

5.4   Using Memory – Advanced Decoding Algorithms

In the previous Sect. 5.3 we provided a time-memory tradeoff for Algorithm 6 Dim-Decode by looking at the *Modify* step only. In this section, we will focus on the *Decode* step. So far, we only used the quite naive Gauss decoding procedure, which resembles Prange's information set decoding algorithm [28]. However, within the last years there has been significant progress in information set decoding, starting with Ball-Collision Decoding [6], then followed by a series of papers, MMT [26], BJMM [4] and May-Ozerov [27], using the so-called representation technique.

In principle, one can freely choose the preferred decoding procedure in *Decode*. Our starting point was a simplified version of BJMM, but then on optimizing the BJMM parameters we found out that for the LPN instances under consideration (see Sect. 6), MMT performs actually best. Since BJMM offers asymptotically a better run time than MMT, the situation should however change for (very) large LPN dimension k. We also did not consider the Nearest Neighbor algorithm May-Ozerov, since its large polynomial run time factor currently prevents speedups in the parameter ranges that we consider.

Instantiating Dim-Decode with MMT decoding results in Algorithm 9, called Well-Pooled MMT.

Input: $\text{LPN}_{k,\tau}$ oracle, τ
Output: secret $\mathbf{s}$
Set parameters n, m as in Pooled Gauss for a $\text{LPN}_{k',\tau}$ instance;
(1) *Modify*
Use the same procedure as in Well-Pooled Gauss (Algorithm 7).
(2) *Decode*
$(s_1, \ldots, s_{k'})$ ←Run MMT on the pool containing the first n $\text{LPN}_{k',\tau}$ samples, while taking the remaining m samples for Test;
(3) *Complete*
$(A, \mathbf{b}) \leftarrow \text{LPN}_{k,\tau}^{n+m}$. Reduce A's dimension to $k - k'$ using $(s_1, \ldots, s_{k'})$;
$(s_{k'+1}, \ldots, s_k) \leftarrow$ Run MMT on the pool containing the first n $\text{LPN}_{k-k',\tau}$ samples, while taking the remaining m samples for Test;
return $\mathbf{s}$;

Algorithm 9. Well-Pooled MMT

Unfortunately, [26] does not provide a closed run time formula for MMT. Therefore, we cannot give a theorem for `Well-Pooled MMT` that provides a precise bound for the time complexity as a function of k, τ as in the previous sections. However, we are able to optimize the run time of `Well-Pooled MMT` for every fixed τ as a function of k.

Let us conjecture that `Well-Pooled MMT`'s time complexity is $2^{c(\tau)k}$. Recall from Theorem 5 that `Well-Pooled Gauss`'s time complexity is

$$\tilde{\Theta}\left(2^{\frac{\log\left(\frac{1}{(1-\tau)}\right)}{1+\log\left(\frac{1}{1-\tau}\right)}k}\right) = \tilde{\Theta}\left(2^{c'(t)k}\right).$$

We can plot both functions $c(\tau)$ and $c'(\tau)$ as a function of τ. The following graph in Fig. 1 visualizes that the run time exponent $c(\tau)$ of `Well-Pooled MMT` is smaller than the run time exponent $c'(\tau)$ of `Well-Pooled Gauss` for every $\tau \in [0, \frac{1}{2})$, as one would expect. The largest gap appears at $\tau = \frac{1}{4}$, where `Well-Pooled MMT` achieves time $2^{0.282k}$, whereas `Well-Pooled Gauss` requires time $2^{0.293k}$.

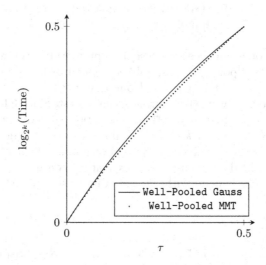

Fig. 1. `Well-Pooled Gauss` and `Well-Pooled MMT`

Remark 4. Since we do not know how to express the running time of MMT as a closed formula, a function that approximates $c(\tau)$ reasonably well is

$$\frac{\log\left(\frac{1}{1-\frac{7}{6}\tau}\right)}{\log\left(\frac{12}{5}\right) + \log\left(\frac{1}{1-\frac{7}{6}\tau}\right)}.$$

It is worth noticing that MMT, as opposed to Prange, consumes exponential memory. However, the memory consumption is still quite moderate. For the LPN instances that we considered the memory never exceeded $2^{\frac{c(\tau)k}{2}}$.

Quantumly we can also speed up our *Decode* step. Naively, i.e. just using Grover search, MMT collapses to Quantum Gauss. But using quantum random walks, one obtains a Quantum Well-Pooled MMT algorithm, as recently proposed by Kachigar and Tillich [22], that slightly outperforms Quantum Gauss.

6   Classical and Quantum Bit Security Estimates

In LPN cryptanalysis, it is currently practice to give estimated bit complexities, that is the binary logarithm of the running time, for newly developed algorithms in table form. In order to allow some comparison with existing work and to give an impression how our algorithms might perform for LPN parameters of cryptographic interest, we also give tables in the following. However, at the same time we want to express a clear warning that *all* LPN tables should be taken with care, since the given bit security levels might over- or underestimate the real performance in practice.

Therefore, we also provide experimental results in Sect. 7 on medium-size LPN parameter, which we extrapolate to cryptographic size by our asymptotic formulas. In our opinion, this is the only reliable way of predicting key sizes with good accuracy. Nevertheless, experimental results might not be possible even for medium-size parameters in some cases, e.g. when an algorithm consumes large memory or when we predict quantum running-times. Hence, performance tables are in these cases unavoidable.

Since we care about practical memory consumption in this work, we enforce upper limits on the available memory for the considered algorithms. We first consider 2^{60} bits, since that is more memory than the biggest RAM we are aware of. Second, we consider a bound of 2^{80} bits for an extra safety margin.

For these upper bounds on the memory M, we compute the bit complexities of our algorithms and compare them to the Coded-BKW [18] table from Bogos et al. [8].

The formulas we used for computing the bit complexities are available at https://github.com/Memphisd/LPN-decoded. In these formulas, we tried to take any polynomial factors into account. As in [8], the cost of the *Complete* step is not taken into account in the tables, but the cost of *Complete* would not significantly change the data.

One can see in Table 2 that for the chosen LPN parameters only 7 parameter sets can be solved with Coded-BKW within the memory limit of 2^{60}. Using instead 2^{80} bits of memory as in Table 3, Coded-BKW can be used or a larger range of instances, as one would expect.

Let us compare this to Tables 4 and 5, where we used either Hybrid, marked as bold face entries, or Well-Pooled MMT (WP MMT). Interestingly, most instances are optimally solved with Well-Pooled MMT using always less than 2^{30} bits of memory. For small memory, Hybrid collapses to Well-Pooled Gauss.

Table 2. Coded-BKW [8], $M = 2^{60}$

τ	k							
	256	384	448	512	576	640	768	1280
$\frac{1}{\sqrt{k}}$	44	55	59	-	-	-	-	-
0.05	42	54	59	-	-	-	-	-
0.125	52	-	-	-	-	-	-	-
0.25	-	-	-	-	-	-	-	-
0.4	-	-	-	-	-	-	-	-

Table 3. Coded-BKW [8], $M = 2^{80}$

τ	k							
	256	384	448	512	576	640	768	1280
$\frac{1}{\sqrt{k}}$	44	55	59	64	70	73	-	-
0.05	42	54	59	65	72	78	-	-
0.125	52	67	74	-	-	-	-	-
0.25	70	-	-	-	-	-	-	-
0.4	-	-	-	-	-	-	-	-

Table 4. WP MMT or Hybrid, $M = 2^{60}$

τ	k							
	256	384	448	512	576	640	768	1280
$\frac{1}{\sqrt{k}}$	43	49	51	52	54	56	59	70
0.05	39	48	52	56	60	64	72	108
0.125	**58**	81	91	102	113	123	144	230
0.25	**65**	**124**	153	172	192	211	250	406
0.4	**85**	**153**	**186**	**219**	**251**	**286**	**357**	584

Table 5. WP MMT or Hybrid, $M = 2^{80}$

τ	k							
	256	384	448	512	576	640	768	1280
$\frac{1}{\sqrt{k}}$	43	49	51	52	54	56	59	70
0.05	39	48	52	56	60	64	72	108
0.125	**58**	**77**	91	102	113	123	144	230
0.25	**65**	**88**	**119**	**151**	**184**	211	250	406
0.4	**76**	**122**	**154**	**186**	**219**	**251**	**318**	**576**

Table 6. Quantum Hybrid, $M = 2^{60}$

τ	k							
	256	384	448	512	576	640	768	1280
$\frac{1}{\sqrt{k}}$	33	37	39	40	42	43	46	54
0.05	30	37	40	42	45	48	53	73
0.125	56	57	63	69	75	81	93	140
0.25	**63**	89	101	112	123	135	158	248
0.4	**76**	**121**	**144**	163	181	198	234	373

Table 7. Quantum Hybrid, $M = 2^{80}$

τ	k							
	256	384	448	512	576	640	768	1280
$\frac{1}{\sqrt{k}}$	33	37	39	40	42	43	46	54
0.05	30	37	40	42	45	48	53	73
0.125	56	57	63	69	75	81	93	140
0.25	**63**	**83**	**96**	112	123	135	158	248
0.4	**73**	**100**	**122**	**144**	**165**	**187**	**232**	373

However, Well-Pooled MMT outperforms Well-Pooled Gauss for the given instances. Interestingly, most instances – especially those of cryptographic interest – are solved via Well-Pooled MMT, that is with pure decoding and *without* using the given memory.

Note that according to our predictions, 80-bit security on classical computers for $\mathrm{LPN}_{\frac{1}{\sqrt{k}},k}$ can only be achieved for $k \geq 2048$. This makes current applications of LPN for encryption quite inefficient.

Coded-BKW shows its strength for errors around $\frac{1}{8}$. However, the same techniques could be used in the *Modify* step of our Hybrid algorithm, which would result in a similar running time.

Tables 6 and 7 finally state the quantum bit security levels when taking Quantum Well-Pooled Gauss inside Hybrid. Here again, the bold marked entries are those where the optimization suggests to use BKW steps. In comparison to the classical case, these are even less instances. We see that the prominent cryptographic choice $\mathrm{LPN}_{512,\frac{1}{8}}$ offers only 69-bit security on quantum computers.

Table 8. $\tau = \frac{1}{\sqrt{k}}$			Table 9. $\tau = \frac{1}{8}$			Table 10. $\tau = \frac{1}{4}$		
k	Classic	Quantum	k	Classic	Quantum	k	Classic	Quantum
6100	**128**	91	670	**128**	84	470	**128**	105
15000	**192**	127	1060	**192**	120	610	**192**	128
26500	**256**	158	1410	**256**	152	790	**256**	162
2200	86	**64**	460	93	**64**	260	66	**64**
4300	113	**80**	630	121	**80**	370	86	**80**
15400	199	**128**	1150	208	**128**	610	192	**128**

Choice of k for security levels $128, 192, 256$ (classic) and $64, 80, 128$ (quantum)

NIST's Post-Quantum Call. NIST [1] asks for classical security levels of $128, 192, 256$ bit and quantum security levels of $64, 80, 128$ bit. Tables 8, 9 and 10 define the minimal k that fulfill these levels for τ taking values $\frac{1}{\sqrt{k}}, \frac{1}{8}, \frac{1}{4}$, respectively. The memory is constrained to $M = 2^{80}$ bits.

7 Experiments

All our implementations are available via
https://github.com/Memphisd/LPN-decoded.

Our experiments were done on a server with four 16-core-processors, allowing a parallelization of 64 threads, using $256\,\text{GB} < 2^{41}$ bit RAM.

We executed Well-Pooled Gauss and Well-Pooled MMT for $\tau = \frac{1}{8}, \frac{1}{4}$ and various k. In order to get reliable run times for $\tau = \frac{1}{8}$ and $k < 170$, respectively $\tau = \frac{1}{4}$ and $k < 100$, we averaged the run time over 30 instances. For larger k, we solved only a single instance.

The results for $\tau = \frac{1}{8}$ and $\tau = \frac{1}{4}$ are shown in Figs. 2 and 3, respectively. Here we plot the logarithm of the running time in msec as a function of k. Hence negative values mean that it takes only a fraction of a msec to solve the instance. For Well-Pooled Gauss we plotted as a comparison the asymptotic line with slope

$$\frac{\log_2(\frac{1}{1-\tau})}{1 + \log_2(\frac{1}{1-\tau})},$$

which follows from Theorem 5. For Well-Pooled MMT we numerically computed the slopes 0.177 and 0.381 for $\tau = \frac{1}{8}$ and $\tau = \frac{1}{4}$, respectively, similar to the computation in Fig. 1.

As can be seen in Figs. 2 and 3, as expected the experiments take slightly longer than the asymptotic prediction, since the asymptotic hides polynomial factors. But especially for Well-Pooled MMT large values of k are close to the asymptotic line, which means that the asymptotic quite accurately predicts the running time.

Since Well-Pooled MMT's run time includes quite large polynomials factors, due to MMT, we expected that it outperforms Well-Pooled Gauss only for large

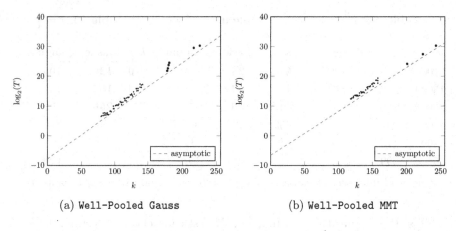

(a) Well-Pooled Gauss   (b) Well-Pooled MMT

Fig. 2. Experimental results for $\tau = \frac{1}{8}$

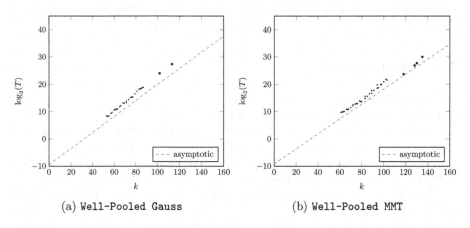

(a) Well-Pooled Gauss   (b) Well-Pooled MMT

Fig. 3. Experimental results for $\tau = \frac{1}{4}$

values of k. To our surprise, the break even point for both algorithms was only $k = 78$ for $\tau = \frac{1}{8}$, and $k = 9$ for $\tau = \frac{1}{4}$. Hence, for these error rates τ one should always prefer Well-Pooled MMT over Well-Pooled Gauss even for relatively small sizes of k.

Largest instances. The largest instances that we solved with Well-Pooled MMT were $k = 243, \tau = \frac{1}{8}$ and $k = 135, \tau = \frac{1}{4}$. Let us provide more details for these computations.

For $k = 243, \tau = \frac{1}{8}$, we first computed in almost 7 days a pool of samples $(\mathbf{a}_i, b_i)$ where the $\mathbf{a}_i$ had their last 35 coordinates equal to zero. The resulting $\text{LPN}_{208,\frac{1}{8}}$ was solved with MMT in 8 days, resulting in a total of 15 days. This recovers already 208 coordinates of $\mathbf{s}$. The *Complete* step in Well-Pooled MMT that recovers the remaining 35 coordinates took less than a second.

For $k = 135, \tau = \frac{1}{4}$, the preprocessing step on again 35 coordinates took almost 6 days, the decoding step 8 days and *Complete* less than a second, resulting in a total of 14 days. We summarize the results in Table 11.

Table 11. Solved instances

Algorithm	k	τ	Pool gen.	BKW	Decoding	Total
Well-Pooled MMT	243	0.125	6.73 d	-	8.34 d	15.07 d
Well-Pooled MMT	135	0.25	5.65 d	-	8.19 d	13.84 d
Hybrid	135	0.25	2.21 d	1.72 h	3.41 d	5.69 d
Well-Pooled Gauss	113	0.25	0.77 d	-	1.21 d	1.98 d
Well-Pooled MMT	113	0.25	1.64 h	-	2.18 h	3.82 h
Hybrid	113	0.25	0.13 h	0.98 h	0.57 h	1.68 h

Extrapolation to $k = 512$. Let $T(k, \tau)$ be the time to solve an $\text{LPN}_{k,\tau}$ instance via Well-Pooled MMT as computed numerically in Fig. 1. Then it would take us a factor of $\frac{T(512, \frac{1}{8})}{T(243, \frac{1}{8})} \approx 2^{41}$ longer to break an $\text{LPN}_{512, \frac{1}{8}}$ than an $\text{LPN}_{243, \frac{1}{8}}$ instance. For $\tau = \frac{1}{4}$ we would even need an additional factor of $\frac{T(512, \frac{1}{4})}{T(135, \frac{1}{4})} \approx 2^{113}$.

To make these kind of statements more trustworthy, we should check, if the numerically computed running times resemble the experimental data. Therefore consider the following: It took about $2^{6.4}$ times as long to solve $\text{LPN}_{135, \frac{1}{4}}$ than solving $\text{LPN}_{113, \frac{1}{4}}$ in the experiments. Using formulas, there is a gap of 2^6 between these instances, which is close to what we actually measured.

Hence, both instances seem to provide sufficient classical security, but also recall from Sect. 6 that $\text{LPN}_{512, \frac{1}{8}}$ only offers 69-bit quantum security.

Hybrid implementation. We solved $\text{LPN}_{113, \frac{1}{4}}$ in less than 2 h, which in comparison took for Well-Pooled Gauss around 2 days and for Well-Pooled MMT still almost 4 h. We were also able to solve $\text{LPN}_{135, \frac{1}{4}}$ using Hybrid in 5.69 days. In comparison, solving this instance with Well-Pooled MMT took 13.84 days.

Let us provide some more details of both computations, starting with $\text{LPN}_{113, \frac{1}{4}}$. We first computed a pool of 2^{33} samples with $k_1 = 3$ bits fixed in 8 min. BKW then eliminated $k_2 = 93$ bit in $c = 3$ iterations with block-size $d = 31$ in 56 min. This gave an $\text{LPN}_{17, \frac{255}{512}}$ instance, which Gauss solved in 9 min.

Thus, we recovered the first 17 bits of s, which we then eliminated from our pool, resulting in an $\text{LPN}_{93, \frac{1}{4}}$ instance. In a second iteration, BKW eliminated $k_2 = 78$ bit in $c = 3$ iterations with block-size $d = 26$ in 3 min. The resulting $\text{LPN}_{15, \frac{255}{512}}$ instance was solved by Gauss in 6 min.

After eliminating these further 15 bits from our pool, we are left with an $\text{LPN}_{78, \frac{1}{4}}$ instance, which was directly solved by MMT in another 19 min. The remaining $k_1 = 3$ bits were brute-forced in 125 msec.

Thus, in total it took us only 101 min to solve $\text{LPN}_{113, \frac{1}{4}}$ with Hybrid.

For solving $LPN_{135,\frac{1}{4}}$, we computed again a pool of 2^{33} samples with $k_1 = 10$ coordinates fixed in 1.47 days. BKW then eliminated $k_2 = 99$ bits in $c = 3$ iterations taking 36 min, which resulted in $2^{21.4}$ samples with $k_1 + k_2 = 109$ coordinates fixed.

This amount of samples is not yet sufficient to achieve a good success probability for solving the remaining $LPN_{26,\frac{255}{512}}$ by Gauss. In order to increase the input samples to Gauss we computed a new pool of 2^{32} samples with $k_1 = 10$ coordinates fixed in 0.74 days, and exchanged half of the samples of the bigger pool that we compute in the beginning. This altered pool of size 2^{33} was then used as input to BKW to eliminate again $k_2 = 99$ bits in $c = 3$ iterations in another 35 min. This allowed us to double the size of the input pool for Gauss while increasing the runtime only by a factor of ≈ 1.5.

After acquiring enough input samples, solving $LPN_{26,\frac{255}{512}}$ by Gauss took 3.12 days. The remaining $LPN_{109,\frac{1}{4}}$ instance could be solved by another iteration and subsequent execution of MMT in less then 7 h. In total, solving $LPN_{135,\frac{1}{4}}$ took us 5.69 days with Hybrid.

References

1. http://csrc.nist.gov/groups/ST/post-quantum-crypto/
2. https://computing.llnl.gov/?set=resources&page=SCF_resources#sequoia
3. Alekhnovich, M.: More on average case vs approximation complexity. In: 44th FOCS, pp. 298–307. IEEE Computer Society Press, October 2003
4. Becker, A., Joux, A., May, A., Meurer, A.: Decoding random binary linear codes in $2^{n/20}$: How $1 + 1 = 0$ improves information set decoding. In: Pointcheval, D., Johansson, T. (eds.) EUROCRYPT 2012. LNCS, vol. 7237, pp. 520–536. Springer, Heidelberg (2012). doi:10.1007/978-3-642-29011-4_31
5. Belaïd, S., Coron, J.-S., Fouque, P.-A., Gérard, B., Kammerer, J.-G., Prouff, E.: Improved side-channel analysis of finite-field multiplication. In: Güneysu, T., Handschuh, H. (eds.) CHES 2015. LNCS, vol. 9293, pp. 395–415. Springer, Heidelberg (2015). doi:10.1007/978-3-662-48324-4_20
6. Bernstein, D.J., Lange, T., Peters, C.: Smaller decoding exponents: ball-collision decoding. In: Rogaway, P. (ed.) CRYPTO 2011. LNCS, vol. 6841, pp. 743–760. Springer, Heidelberg (2011). doi:10.1007/978-3-642-22792-9_42
7. Blum, A., Kalai, A., Wasserman, H.: Noise-tolerant learning, the parity problem, and the statistical query model. In: 32nd ACM STOC, pp. 435–440. ACM Press, May 2000
8. Bogos, S., Tramer, F., Vaudenay, S.: On solving LPN using BKW and variants. Cryptology ePrint Archive, Report 2015/049 (2015). http://eprint.iacr.org/2015/049
9. Bogos, S., Vaudenay, S.: Observations on the LPN solving algorithm from eurocrypt'16 (2016). http://eprint.iacr.org/2016/437
10. Boyer, M., Brassard, G., Høyer, P., Tapp, A.: Tight bounds on quantum searching. arXiv preprint quant-ph/9605034 (1996)
11. Carrijo, J., Tonicelli, R., Imai, H., Nascimento, A.C.A.: A novel probabilistic passive attack on the protocols HB and HB+ (2008). http://eprint.iacr.org/2008/231
12. Damgård, I., Park, S.: How practical is public-key encryption based on LPN and ring-LPN? Cryptology ePrint Archive, Report 2012/699 (2012). http://eprint.iacr.org/2012/699

13. Döttling, N., Müller-Quade, J., Nascimento, A.C.A.: IND-CCA secure cryptography based on a variant of the LPN problem. In: Wang, X., Sako, K. (eds.) ASIACRYPT 2012. LNCS, vol. 7658, pp. 485–503. Springer, Heidelberg (2012). doi:10.1007/978-3-642-34961-4_30

14. Duc, A., Vaudenay, S.: HELEN: a public-key cryptosystem based on the LPN and the decisional minimal distance problems. In: Youssef, A., Nitaj, A., Hassanien, A.E. (eds.) AFRICACRYPT 2013. LNCS, vol. 7918, pp. 107–126. Springer, Heidelberg (2013). doi:10.1007/978-3-642-38553-7_6

15. Fossorier, M.P., Mihaljevic, M.J., Imai, H., Cui, Y., Matsuura, K.: A novel algorithm for solving the LPN problem and its application to security evaluation of the HB protocol for RFID authentication. Cryptology ePrint Archive, Report 2006/197 (2006). http://eprint.iacr.org/2006/197

16. Gilbert, H., Robshaw, M.J.B., Seurin, Y.: HB$^{\#}$: Increasing the security and efficiency of HB^{+}. In: Smart, N. (ed.) EUROCRYPT 2008. LNCS, vol. 4965, pp. 361–378. Springer, Heidelberg (2008). doi:10.1007/978-3-540-78967-3_21

17. Grover, L.K.: A fast quantum mechanical algorithm for database search. In: 28th ACM STOC, pp. 212–219. ACM Press, May 1996

18. Guo, Q., Johansson, T., Löndahl, C.: Solving LPN using covering codes. In: Sarkar, P., Iwata, T. (eds.) ASIACRYPT 2014. LNCS, vol. 8873, pp. 1–20. Springer, Heidelberg (2014). doi:10.1007/978-3-662-45611-8_1

19. Heyse, S., Kiltz, E., Lyubashevsky, V., Paar, C., Pietrzak, K.: Lapin: an efficient authentication protocol based on ring-LPN. In: Canteaut, A. (ed.) FSE 2012. LNCS, vol. 7549, pp. 346–365. Springer, Heidelberg (2012). doi:10.1007/978-3-642-34047-5_20

20. Hopper, N.J., Blum, M.: Secure human identification protocols. In: Boyd, C. (ed.) ASIACRYPT 2001. LNCS, vol. 2248, pp. 52–66. Springer, Heidelberg (2001). doi:10.1007/3-540-45682-1_4

21. Juels, A., Weis, S.A.: Authenticating pervasive devices with human protocols. In: Shoup, V. (ed.) CRYPTO 2005. LNCS, vol. 3621, pp. 293–308. Springer, Heidelberg (2005). doi:10.1007/11535218_18

22. Kachigar, G., Tillich, J.-P.: Quantum information set decoding algorithms. arXiv preprint arXiv:1703.00263 (2017)

23. Kiltz, E., Pietrzak, K., Cash, D., Jain, A., Venturi, D.: Efficient authentication from hard learning problems. In: Paterson, K.G. (ed.) EUROCRYPT 2011. LNCS, vol. 6632, pp. 7–26. Springer, Heidelberg (2011). doi:10.1007/978-3-642-20465-4_3

24. Levieil, É., Fouque, P.-A.: An improved LPN algorithm. In: Prisco, R., Yung, M. (eds.) SCN 2006. LNCS, vol. 4116, pp. 348–359. Springer, Heidelberg (2006). doi:10.1007/11832072_24

25. Lyubashevsky, V.: The parity problem in the presence of noise, decoding random linear codes, and the subset sum problem. In: Chekuri, C., Jansen, K., Rolim, J.D.P., Trevisan, L. (eds.) APPROX/RANDOM -2005. LNCS, vol. 3624, pp. 378–389. Springer, Heidelberg (2005). doi:10.1007/11538462_32

26. May, A., Meurer, A., Thomae, E.: Decoding random linear codes in $\tilde{\mathcal{O}}(2^{0.054n})$. In: Lee, D.H., Wang, X. (eds.) ASIACRYPT 2011. LNCS, vol. 7073, pp. 107–124. Springer, Heidelberg (2011). doi:10.1007/978-3-642-25385-0_6

27. May, A., Ozerov, I.: On computing nearest neighbors with applications to decoding of binary linear codes. In: Oswald, E., Fischlin, M. (eds.) EUROCRYPT 2015. LNCS, vol. 9056, pp. 203–228. Springer, Heidelberg (2015). doi:10.1007/978-3-662-46800-5_9

28. Prange, E.: The use of information sets in decoding cyclic codes. IRE Trans. Inf. Theory **8**(5), 5–9 (1962)

29. Regev, O.: On lattices, learning with errors, random linear codes, and cryptography. In: Gabow, H.N., Fagin, R. (eds.) 37th ACM STOC, pp. 84–93. ACM Press, May 2005
30. Zhang, B., Jiao, L., Wang, M.: Faster algorithms for solving LPN. In: Fischlin, M., Coron, J.-S. (eds.) EUROCRYPT 2016. LNCS, vol. 9665, pp. 168–195. Springer, Heidelberg (2016). doi:10.1007/978-3-662-49890-3_7

Signatures

Optimal Security Reductions for Unique Signatures: Bypassing Impossibilities with a Counterexample

Fuchun Guo[1]([✉]), Rongmao Chen[2], Willy Susilo[1], Jianchang Lai[1], Guomin Yang[1], and Yi Mu[1]

[1] Institute of Cybersecurity and Cryptology,
School of Computing and Information Technology, University of Wollongong,
Wollongong, NSW 2522, Australia
{fuchun,wsusilo,jl1967,gyang,ymu}@uow.edu.au
[2] College of Computer, National University
of Defense Technology, Changsha, China
chromao@nudt.edu.cn

Abstract. Optimal security reductions for unique signatures (Coron, Eurocrypt 2002) and their generalization, i.e., efficiently re-randomizable signatures (Hofheinz *et al.* PKC 2012 & Bader *et al.* Eurocrypt 2016) have been well studied in the literature. Particularly, it has been shown that under a non-interactive hard assumption, any security reduction (with or without random oracles) for a unique signature scheme or an efficiently re-randomizable signature scheme must loose a factor of at least q_s in the security model of existential unforgeability against chosen-message attacks (EU-CMA), where q_s denotes the number of signature queries. Note that the number q_s can be as large as 2^{30} in practice. All unique signature schemes and efficiently re-randomizable signature schemes are concluded to be accompanied with loose reductions from these impossibility results.

Somewhat surprisingly, in contrast to previous impossibility results (Coron, Eurocrypt 2002; Hofheinz *et al.* PKC 2012; Bader *et al.* Eurocrypt 2016), in this work we show that without changing the assumption type and security model, it is not always the case that any security reduction must loose a factor of at least q_s. As a counterexample, we propose a unique signature scheme with a tight reduction in the EU-CMA security model under the Computational Diffie-Hellman (CDH) assumption. Precisely, in the random oracle model, we can program a security reduction with a loss factor of at most $nq^{1/n}$, where n can be any integer independent of the security parameter for the scheme construction and q is the number of hash queries to random oracles. The loss factor in our reduction can be very small. Considering $n = 25$ and $q = 2^{50}$ as an example, the loss factor is of at most $nq^{1/n} = 100$ and therefore our security reduction is tight.

Notice that the previous impossibility results are derived from proofs via a so-called meta-reduction technique. We stress that instead of indicating any flaw in their meta-reduction proofs, our counterexample merely demonstrates that their given meta-reduction proofs fail to

© International Association for Cryptologic Research 2017
J. Katz and H. Shacham (Eds.): CRYPTO 2017, Part II, LNCS 10402, pp. 517–547, 2017.
DOI: 10.1007/978-3-319-63715-0_18

capture all security reductions. More precisely, we adopt a reduction called *query-based reduction*, where the reduction uses a hash query from the adversary to solve an underlying hard problem. We show that the meta-reduction proofs break down in our query-based reduction. The query-based reduction is not a new notion and it has been adopted for encryption proofs, but this work is the first seminal approach for applying query-based reduction in digital signatures.

The given counterexample in this work is of an independent interest as it implies a generic way of constructing a digital signature scheme (including unique signatures) with a tight reduction in the random oracle model from a digital signature scheme with a loose reduction. Although our proposed methodology is somewhat impractical due to the inefficiency of signature length, it introduces a completely new approach for tight proofs that is different from traditional approaches using a random salt.

Keywords: Unique signatures · Tight reduction · Impossibility · Counterexample

1   Introduction

Security reduction is the fundamental method for proving provable security in cryptosystems. In a security reduction, if there exists an efficient adversary who can break a newly proposed scheme, we prove that a generally believed-to-be-hard mathematical problem can be efficiently solvable with the help of this adversary. This, however, contradicts with the hardness assumption and hence we conclude that the proposed scheme is secure. Suppose the adversary can break a digital signature scheme in t polynomial time with a non-negligible probability ϵ. Generally speaking, a security reduction will solve an underlying hard problem in $t+T$ time with probability $\frac{\epsilon}{L}$. Here T refers to the time cost of reduction while L refers to the loss factor (or security loss), which means the success probability of reduction is $\frac{1}{L}$ only. When the loss factor is linear in the number of signature queries denoted by q_s from the adversary, the security reduction is said to be a loose reduction because the number of signature queries can be as larger as 2^{30}. When the loss factor L is constant and small, the security reduction is said to be a tight reduction. In concrete security [4,17], a tight reduction is essential for constructing an efficient scheme without increasing the security parameter to compensate the loss factor.

A significant number of digital signature schemes have been proposed in the literature. Many of them, such as [2,5,6,9,11,14,17,19], are provably secure with tight reductions. In this work, a security reduction for a signature scheme refers to a reduction from a non-interactive computational hard problem under the security model of existential unforgeability against chosen-message attacks (EU-CMA) [12]. In a security reduction, we say a signature is simulatable if the signature can be simulated by the simulator without knowing the corresponding secret (signing) key and a signature is reducible if the signature can be reduced to solve a hard problem. The difficulty of achieving a tight reduction in the literature is due to the fact that we need to program the reduction with a high success probability without knowing which messages whose signatures should be programmed as simulatable and which messages whose signatures should be programmed as reducible. To overcome this difficulty, all known signature schemes with tight reductions to date use a random salt (number) in the signature generation such that a signature of a given message can be either simulatable or reducible depending on the choice of the random salt. The simulator relies on this functionality to obtain a high success probability of reduction, especially without abortion during signature queries.

Unique signatures are one special type of digital signatures which do not use any random salt in the signature generation. The signature for each message therefore is unique. As a consequence, we cannot switch the functionality (simulatable or reducible) of each unique signature in the security reduction. Therefore, it seems any security reduction for a unique signature scheme cannot be tight. In fact, optimal security reductions for unique signatures or their generalization have been studied in [3,10,15]. They showed that it is impossible to program a better security reduction with a loss factor of less than q_s for a unique signature scheme or an efficiently re-randomizable signature scheme, where q_s is the number of signature queries. To be precise, in Eurocrypt 2002, Coron [10] described a meta-reduction proof to prove the impossibility of tight reductions for certain digital signatures including unique signatures. Coron claimed the success probability of any security reduction for a unique signature scheme cannot substantially exceed $\epsilon_{\mathcal{F}}/(eq_s)$. That is, the loss factor is of at least $e \cdot q_s$. Here e is the base of the natural logarithm and $\epsilon_{\mathcal{F}}$ is the adversary's advantage (probability) of forging a valid signature in the EU-CMA security model. Ten years later, in Eurocrypt 2012, Kakvi and Kiltz [16] found and fixed a subtle technical flaw in the Coron's impossibility result. They showed the optimal security reduction for the RSA-FDH (Full Domain Hash) signature scheme cannot be guaranteed, if public keys are not certified. In PKC 2012, Hofheinz, Jager and Knapp [15] extended the meta-reduction proof for a slightly more general signature notion, namely efficiently re-randomizable signatures. They proved and claimed that any black-box security reduction for a signature scheme with efficiently re-randomizable signatures must have a reduction loss of at least $\Omega(q_s)$; otherwise, the underlying hardness assumption is false. In Eurocrypt 2016, Bader, Jager, Li and Schäge [3] improved the impossibility result of [10,15,16] with simpler proofs and bound, where the minimum loss factor is q_s. Particularly, they introduced the notion of efficiently re-randomizable relations to overcome the subtle issue discovered by Kakvi and Kiltz [16] and further generalized the notion of efficiently re-randomizable signatures [15].

In short, the aforementioned impossibility results (Coron, Eurocrypt 2002; Hofheinz *et al.* PKC 2012; Bader *et al.* Eurocrypt 2016) have shown that *any security reduction* for a unique signature scheme or an efficiently re-randomizable signature scheme must loose a factor of q_s, which is the number of signature queries. That is, in all corresponding security reductions, the success probability of reduction is of at most $\frac{1}{q_s}$.

Our contributions. In contrast to previous impossibility results, in this work, we show that *not all security reductions* for unique signature schemes or efficiently re-randomizable signature schemes must loose a factor of q_s. As a counterexample, we construct a special unique signature scheme with a tight reduction under the Computational Diffie-Hellman (CDH) assumption in the EU-CMA security model. In our security proof with random oracles, we program the security reduction to solve the CDH problem with a loss factor of at most $nq^{\frac{1}{n}}$. Here, n is an integer decided by the scheme designer independent of the security parameter for the scheme construction and q is the number of hash queries to the random oracle. Although our loss factor is associated with q but it can be very small. Taking the example of $n = 25, q = 2^{50}$ and $q_s = 2^{30}$, the loss factor in our security reduction for the given counterexample is of $nq^{\frac{1}{n}} = 100$ only, which is significantly reduced compared to $q_s = 2^{30}$. Hence, we claim that our security reduction is a tight reduction from a non-interactive computational hard problem in the standard EU-CMA security model. We note that our unique signature scheme is the first real[1] unique signature scheme with a tight reduction.

We stress that our counterexample does not indicate any flaw in the given proofs [3,10,15]. Instead, we found their proofs fail to capture all security reductions. More precisely, in the traditional security reduction for digital signatures, the reduction uses a forged signature from the adversary that cannot be efficiently computed by the simulator to solve a computational hard problem. We call this reduction *forgery-based reduction*. The tight security reduction in our given example is completely different and we name it as *query-based reduction*, where the reduction uses one of hash queries from the adversary to solve a computational hard problem. We analyze the reason why there is a gap in the proofs of impossibilities when using the query-based reduction in Sect. 1.4. Notice that the query-based reduction is not a completely new notion because it has been used in enabling provable security for encryption under computational hard problems in the indistinguishability security model, such as the hashed ElGamal encryption scheme [1]. However, this is the first time of applying query-based reduction in proving security for digital signatures.

The given counterexample is of an independent interest in terms of exploring generic approaches for signature scheme constructions with tight reductions. It implies a methodology of constructing a digital signature scheme including unique signatures with a tight reduction in the random oracle model from a digital signature scheme with a loose reduction. Our proposed methodology has to increase the signature length by n times and hence it is somewhat impractical even taking the loss factor into account. However, we stress that our idea is theoretically interesting as it, for the first time, introduces how to obtain a tight

---

[1] Kakvi and Kiltz in [16] proposed a conceptual level FDH (Full Domain Hash) unique signature scheme with a tight reduction. The proposed RSA-FDH scheme is a unique signature, while the reduction uses a fake but indistinguishable public key in the simulation such that the simulated RSA-FDH signatures are no longer unique. We note that both real signature scheme and simulated signature scheme in our counterexample are unique signatures.

proof for digital signatures without the use of a random salt in the signature generation.

Remark 1. *The authors in [3,10,15] claimed that the impossibility of tight reductions holds for* any *security reduction. From what they have proved (i.e., given theorems), we found that their "security reduction" refers to the following two types.*

- *Any security reduction without the use of random oracles for a signature scheme.*
- *Any security reduction with random oracles for a hash-and-sign signature scheme [10], such as a full domain hash signature scheme.*

We note that our query-based reduction with random oracles is proposed to prove a unique signature scheme, whose structure is different from the hash-and-sign signature defined in [10]. Our signature scheme can be seen as a hash-and-sign structure repeated for n times. Therefore, our given example is not included in the above two types of reductions.

1.1 Overview of Our Counterexample and Security Reduction

In this section, we propose a simplified counterexample with $n = 2$ and show how to program the reduction with a loss factor of at most $2q^{\frac{1}{2}}$ under the CDH assumption in the EU-CMA security model. Here, q is the number of hash queries to the random oracle made by the adversary[2]. The given scheme and reduction can be naturally extended to a full scheme with a loss factor of $nq^{\frac{1}{n}}$, where each signature in the full signature scheme contains $n + 1$ group elements. We admit that the proposed scheme is less efficient compared to other unique signature schemes such as [7] especially with the growth of n. We emphasize that the proposed scheme is merely for demonstrating that there indeed exists a unique signature scheme with a tight reduction.

Our unique signature scheme is constructed over a pairing group $\mathbb{PG} = (\mathbb{G}, \mathbb{G}_T, p, e, g)$ with a bilinear map $e : \mathbb{G} \times \mathbb{G} \to \mathbb{G}_T$, where p is the group order of $\mathbb{G}, \mathbb{G}_T$ and g is the generator of $\mathbb{G}$. The simplified scheme is described as follows.

SysGen: The system generation algorithm takes as input a security parameter λ, it chooses a pairing group $\mathbb{PG} = (\mathbb{G}, \mathbb{G}_T, p, e, g)$ and a cryptographic hash function $H : \{0,1\}^* \to \mathbb{G}$ that will be viewed as a random oracle in the security proof. The system parameters are composed of $\mathbb{PG}$ and H.

KeyGen: The key generation algorithm randomly chooses $\alpha \in \mathbb{Z}_p$ and computes $h = g^\alpha$. The algorithm returns a public/secret key pair $(pk, sk) = (h, \alpha)$.

---

[2] For easy understanding, we assume $q^{\frac{1}{2}}$ and $q^{\frac{1}{n}}$ are both integers for the query number q and the given number n in discussions.

Sign: The signing algorithm takes as input the system parameters, a message $m \in \{0, 1\}^*$ and the secret key sk. It returns the signature Σ_m on m as

$$\Sigma_m = (\sigma_1, \sigma_2, \sigma_3) = \Big(H(m)^\alpha, \ H(m||\Sigma_m^1)^\alpha, \ H(m||\Sigma_m^2)^\alpha \Big),$$

where $\Sigma_m^i = (\sigma_1, \sigma_2, \cdots, \sigma_i)$. The final signature Σ_m is equivalent to Σ_m^3.

Verify: The verification algorithm takes as input the system parameters, a signed message (m, Σ_m) and the public key pk. It accepts the signature if and only if

$$e(\sigma_1, g) = e(H(m), h), \quad \text{and}$$
$$e(\sigma_2, g) = e(H(m||\Sigma_m^1), h), \quad \text{and}$$
$$e(\sigma_3, g) = e(H(m||\Sigma_m^2), h).$$

The structure of our unique signature is similar to the *blockchain* [8,18]. Each component σ_i in our signature scheme is a *block signature* of a given message m to be signed together with all previous block signatures. The block signature is generated using the BLS signature [7]. In this simplified scheme, each signature Σ_m is composed of three block signatures $(\sigma_1, \sigma_2, \sigma_3)$. The full unique signature scheme will be composed of $n + 1$ block signatures. We note that the block signature does not have to use the BLS signature and can be instantiated using a different unique signature from other schemes such as [20][3]. Our proposed signature scheme can also be seen as a variant of the BLS signature scheme towards a tight reduction.

For the security proof of the simplified unique signature scheme, we will program the security reduction in the random oracle model, where H is set as the random oracle. The reduction is an interaction between an adversary who can break the proposed scheme and a simulator who simulates both the real scheme and the random oracle for the adversary. Different from the forgery-based security reduction, the constructed simulator in our reduction will use one of hash queries generated by the adversary instead of a forged signature from the adversary to solve the CDH problem. Therefore, the random oracle plays the most important role in this type of reduction. The reduction is much more complex compared to that for the BLS signature scheme especially in the simulation of the random oracle. Before showing how to program the reduction, we give three preliminaries to help understanding the core of this security reduction.

In this paper, we say an adversary makes a hash query $H(x)$ to the random oracle meaning that the adversary sends x to the random oracle in order to

---

[3] We emphasize that the corresponding security reduction is different when the adopted block signature is changed. In particular, how to simulate a block signature and how to solve a hard problem are dependent on the block signature. However, the reduction method with a tight reduction is the same.

know what $H(x)$ is. Without querying $H(x)$ to the random oracle, $H(x)$ is random and unknown to the adversary, such that the adversary has no advantage in computing $H(x)^\alpha$ even it knows α. In our simplified scheme, due to the "chain" structure, the adversary who does not know the signature Σ_m of a message m must first query $H(m)$, then query $H(m||\Sigma_m^1)$, and finally query $H(m||\Sigma_m^2)$ to the random oracle. This sequence is essential because Σ_m^1 contains the block signature $H(m)^\alpha$ requiring to know $H(m)$ first, and Σ_m^2 contains the block signature $H(m||\Sigma_m^1)^\alpha$ requiring to know $H(m||\Sigma_m^1)$ first. Therefore, each signature generation is required to make three hash queries to the random oracle and these three hash queries must be made sequentially. This is the first preliminary about sequential hash queries on the same message without having its signature.

The adversary could launch hash queries associated with the same message m in the following four cases **before querying its signature or without its signature query**.

- In the first case, the adversary never queries $H(m), H(m||\Sigma_m^1), H(m||\Sigma_m^2)$ to the random oracle.
- In the second case, the adversary queries $H(m)$ only to the random oracle. That is, the adversary never queries $H(m||\Sigma_m^1), H(m||\Sigma_m^2)$ to the random oracle.
- In the third case, the adversary queries $H(m)$ and $H(m||\Sigma_m^1)$ to the random oracle. That is, the adversary never queries $H(m||\Sigma_m^2)$ to the random oracle.
- In the fourth case, the adversary queries all $H(m), H(m||\Sigma_m^1), H(m||\Sigma_m^2)$ to the random oracle. Hash queries associated with the message m^* to be forged by the adversary falls into this case. Otherwise, at least one hash value is random and unknown to the adversary, such that it cannot forge a valid signature of m^* with a non-negligible advantage.

These four cases are also summarized in Table 1. We stress that as an example, if the adversary first queries $H(m)$ to the random oracle, then queries the signature Σ_m of m to the simulator, and thereafter queries $H(m||\Sigma_m^1), H(m||\Sigma_m^2)$ to the random oracle for signature verification, we have the message m belongs to the second case not the fourth case. For a message m belonging to the third case, we note that the adversary must compute Σ_m^1 first before the hash query $H(m||\Sigma_m^1)$. For a message m belonging to the fourth case, the adversary must

Table 1. Classification of hash queries from the adversary into four cases. Each column refers to the input structure of each query, which will be used in the introduction of the third preliminary.

	Type 0	Type 1	Type 2
Case 1	–	–	–
Case 2	$H(m)$	–	–
Case 3	$H(m)$	$H(m||\Sigma_m^1)$	–
Case 4	$H(m)$	$H(m||\Sigma_m^1)$	$H(m||\Sigma_m^2)$

compute Σ_m^1 and Σ_m^2 first before the hash queries $H(m||\Sigma_m^1), H(m||\Sigma_m^2)$. To forge a valid signature, the adversary must compute $\Sigma_{m^*}^1$ and $\Sigma_{m^*}^2$ for hash queries $H(m^*), H(m^*||\Sigma_{m^*}^1), H(m^*||\Sigma_{m^*}^2)$ in order to forge the signature Σ_{m^*} of m^*. Therefore, there must exist one message belonging to the fourth case. Notice that the adversary could make hash queries associated with other messages belonging to the third case or the fourth case. In our reduction, the simulator shall use these special hash queries for reduction and these queries require the adversary to compute block signatures first. When one of block signatures is reducible, the simulator can then use the corresponding block signature to solve a computational hard problem. This is the second preliminary explaining how our query-based reduction works.

In the query-based reduction, we need to identify who (either the adversary or the simulator) **first time** submits a query to the random oracle. We note that the above four cases are only those queries first time generated and submitted by the adversary to the random oracle. Besides these hash queries, the simulator could add some other hash queries to the random oracle. Considering the above example where the adversary first queries $H(m)$ to the random oracle and then queries the signature Σ_m to the simulator. The simulator has to program hash queries $H(m||\Sigma_m^1)$ and $H(m||\Sigma_m^2)$ before the signature simulation on m, where these two queries could be made by the adversary again for the signature verification purpose. These two queries therefore are first time made by the simulator and the simulator should be able to compute Σ_m^1 and Σ_m^2. Notice that the simulator cannot solve the underlying hard problem using one hash query first time submitted to the random oracle by itself. Otherwise, the simulator can solve the hard problem without the adversary. It is therefore important to identify who first time makes a query to the random oracle and we focus on those queries first time generated by the adversary. This is the supplementary of the second preliminary.

The query input to the random oracle can be any arbitrary string adaptively chosen by the adversary. In this work, we assume the concatenation notation "$||$" will not appear within messages[4], such that it is easy for the simulator to distinguish the input structure of each query denoted by x. Furthermore, the simulator can run the pairing computation to verify the correctness of each block signature. Therefore, for each query x first time generated by the adversary, we define

---

[4] This can be done via encoding to make sure m does not contain the concatenation notation. For example, each bit $X \in \{0,1\}$ of message and block signatures will be encoded into "0X" and the concatenation notation is represented using "11" such that the whole bit string as input to the hash function looks like '$0X_10X_20X_3110X_40X_5$', where $X_1X_2X_3$ is the message and X_4X_5 is the block signature. We can force the scheme to use this encoding before hashing and signature generation. In the security proof, if a query made by the adversary does not use this encoding, this query is a query with an invalid structure and the simulator will randomly respond to the hash query because it will not be used in signature query or signature forgery.

- x is a query belonging to **Type 0** if x is equal to m without the notation "$||$".
- x is a query belonging to **Type 1** if x is equal to $m||\Sigma_m^1$ with one block signature.
- x is a query belonging to **Type 2** if x is equal to $m||\Sigma_m^2$ with two block signatures.
- x is a query belonging to **Type D** if x is different from the above three types. For example, x is equal to a message concatenated with invalid block signatures or more than two block signatures.

We define three message sets $\mathcal{M}_0, \mathcal{M}_1, \mathcal{M}_2$ during the random oracle simulation as follows to include all messages in those queries generated by the adversary and belonging to **Type 0**, **Type 1** or **Type 2**. We are not interested in queries belonging to **Type D** because they are not used for signature generations. Before the adversary starts making hash queries to the random oracle, these three message sets are initialized with empty sets. These three message sets are managed by the simulator and it adds messages into them when a query from the adversary satisfies the following conditions.

- If x is a query belonging to **Type 0**, the message m in x will be added into the message set $\mathcal{M}_0$. Let $\mathcal{M}_0 = \{m_{0,1}, m_{0,2}, \cdots, m_{0,q_0}\}$ where $|\mathcal{M}_0| = q_0$.
- If x is a query belonging to **Type 1**, the message m in x will be added into the message set $\mathcal{M}_1$. Let $\mathcal{M}_1 = \{m_{1,1}, m_{1,2}, \cdots, m_{1,q_1}\}$ where $|\mathcal{M}_1| = q_1$.
- If x is a query belonging to **Type 2**, the message m in x will be added into the message set $\mathcal{M}_2$. Let $\mathcal{M}_2 = \{m_{2,1}, m_{2,2}, \cdots, m_{2,q_2}\}$ where $|\mathcal{M}_2| = q_2$.

For easy understanding, all messages in the message sets are added sequentially. That is, $m_{i,1}$ is first added to the message set $\mathcal{M}_i$ followed by the message $m_{i,2}$.

Suppose the total number of hash queries made by the adversary is q and the adversary ever queries $H(m^*), H(m^*||\Sigma_{m^*}^1), H(m^*||\Sigma_{m^*}^2)$ for a message m^* in order to forge its signature. According to the first preliminary and Table 1, we have the following important observation

$$\mathcal{M}_2 \subseteq \mathcal{M}_1 \subseteq \mathcal{M}_0, \quad 1 \le q_2 \le q_1 \le q_0 < q.$$

The above relationship is always correct and independent of what messages are selected for hash queries, what messages are selected for signature queries and which message is selected for signature forgery. This is the third preliminary about the relationship of messages in those hash queries generated by the adversary.

Now, we are ready to describe how to program the security reduction for the simplified scheme. Suppose there exists an adversary who can break the signature scheme in the EU-CMA security model. The simulator programs the simulation as follows. Given a random instance of the CDH problem (g, g^a, g^b) under a pairing group $\mathbb{PG}$, the simulator sets $\mathbb{PG}$ as the system parameters and $h = g^a$ in the public key simulation, where the secret key $\alpha = a$ is unknown to the simulator. The simulator simulates the random oracle for H instead of giving the hash function to the adversary. During the random oracle simulation, the simulator programs the instance g^b in one of $H(x)$ such that $H(x)^\alpha$ contains[5] the CDH solution g^{ab}. For all other queries, the simulator computes $H(y)$ in the way that $H(y)^\alpha$ is computable by the simulator. The core of oracle simulation is which query should be responded using g^b. We name this query as *target query* and the corresponding message as *target message* denoted by $\hat{m}$. In our simulation, the simulator firstly chooses a random integer $c^* \in \{0,1\}$ and then it works as follows.

- If $c^* = 0$, it randomly chooses another integer $k^* \in [1, q^{1-\frac{c^*}{2}}]$, where the range is equal to $[1, q]$. In this case, the target query is the one whose message will be the k^*-th message added into the message set $\mathcal{M}_0$, if such a message exists in the message set. Otherwise, aborts. That is, the target query is

$$m_{c^*, k^*} = \hat{m}.$$

We have $H(\hat{m})$ contains g^b. When the message $\hat{m} \in \mathcal{M}_0$ also appears in the message set $\mathcal{M}_1$, it means the adversary ever submitted the following query to the random oracle

$$\hat{m} || \Sigma_{\hat{m}}^1,$$

where the block signature σ_1 in $\Sigma_{\hat{m}}$ is equal to $H(\hat{m})^\alpha$ containing the solution g^{ab} to the hard problem. That is, the simulator embeds g^b in the response to one of **Type 0** queries and will use a **Type 1** query to solve the underlying hard problem.

- If $c^* = 1$, it randomly chooses another integer $k^* \in [1, q^{1-\frac{c^*}{2}}]$ (Note: this range is different from the first case), where the range is equal to $[1, q^{\frac{1}{2}}]$. In this case, the target query is the query whose message will be the k^*-th message added into the message set $\mathcal{M}_1$, if such a message exists in the message set. Otherwise, aborts. That is, the target query is

$$m_{c^*, k^*} || \Sigma_{m_{c^*, k^*}}^1 = \hat{m} || \Sigma_{\hat{m}}^1.$$

We have $H(\hat{m} || \Sigma_{\hat{m}}^1)$ contains g^b. When the message $\hat{m} \in \mathcal{M}_1$ also appears in the message set $\mathcal{M}_2$, it means the adversary ever submitted the following query to the random oracle

$$\hat{m} || \Sigma_{\hat{m}}^2,$$

where the second block signature σ_2 in $\Sigma_{\hat{m}}^2$ is equal to $H(\hat{m} || \Sigma_{\hat{m}}^1)^\alpha$ containing the solution g^{ab} to the hard problem. That is, the simulator embeds g^b in the response to one of **Type 1** queries and will use a **Type 2** query to solve the underlying hard problem.

---

[5] The word "contain" here means that a group element can be extracted from another group element. For example, $H(x) = (g^b)^z$ where $z \in \mathbb{Z}_p^*$ is a random number chosen by the simulator. Then, we have g^{ab} can be extracted from $H(x)^\alpha$ by computing $(H(x)^\alpha)^{\frac{1}{z}}$.

We emphasize that the target message $\hat{m}$ does not have to be equal to the message m^* for the signature forgery. This is the main reason why our security reduction has a small loss factor. This completes the core of our simulation.

Now, we analyze the loss factor of our reduction. Let $\Pr[Success]$ be the success probability of reduction when the adversary can successfully forge a valid signature. According to the simulation setting, the reduction is successful when one of hash queries contains the solution to the hard problem. We claim the loss factor is of at most $2q^{\frac{1}{2}}$. A compact probability analysis is given as follows.

First, since $c^* \in \{0, 1\}$ is randomly chosen, we have

$$
\begin{aligned}
&\Pr[Success] \\
&= \Pr[Success|c^* = 0] \Pr[c^* = 0] + \Pr[Success|c^* = 1] \Pr[c^* = 1] \\
&= \frac{1}{2} \Big(\Pr[Success|c^* = 0] + \Pr[Success|c^* = 1] \Big).
\end{aligned}
$$

We calculate one of conditional probabilities only, which is decided by q_1 as follows.

- If $q_1 \geq q^{\frac{1}{2}}$, we calculate $\Pr[Success|c^* = 0]$ only where

$$
q_0 < q = q^{1-\frac{0}{2}} \quad \text{and} \quad q_1 \geq q^{\frac{1}{2}} = q^{1-\frac{1}{2}}.
$$

- Otherwise, $q_1 < q^{\frac{1}{2}}$, we calculate $\Pr[Success|c^* = 1]$ only where

$$
q_1 < q^{\frac{1}{2}} = q^{1-\frac{1}{2}} \quad \text{and} \quad q_2 \geq 1 = q^{1-\frac{2}{2}}.
$$

One can note that no matter $q_1 \geq q^{\frac{1}{2}}$ or $q_1 < q^{\frac{1}{2}}$, there exists an integer $i^* \in [0, 1]$ (i.e. $i^* \in \{0, 1\}$) such that

$$
q_{i^*} < q^{1-\frac{i^*}{2}} \quad \text{and} \quad q_{i^*+1} \geq q^{1-\frac{i^*+1}{2}}.
$$

Then, we prove $\Pr[Success|c^* = i^*] \geq 1/q^{\frac{1}{2}}$. The target query is associated with a target message from the message set $\mathcal{M}_{c^*}$, where the target message is m_{c^*,k^*} denoted by $\hat{m}$. When $c^* = i^*$, we have

$$
|\mathcal{M}_{c^*}| = q_{c^*} = q_{i^*} < q^{1-\frac{i^*}{2}} \quad \text{and} \quad k^* \in [1, q^{1-\frac{i^*}{2}}],
$$

such that each message in $\mathcal{M}_{c^*}$ will be chosen as the target message $\hat{m}$ with probability $1/q^{1-\frac{i^*}{2}}$. Furthermore, we have

$$
\mathcal{M}_{c^*+1} \subseteq \mathcal{M}_{c^*} \quad \text{and} \quad |\mathcal{M}_{c^*+1}| = q_{i^*+1} \geq q^{1-\frac{i^*+1}{2}}
$$

such that

$$
\Pr[Success|c^* = i^*] = \Pr[\hat{m} \in \mathcal{M}_{c^*} \cap \mathcal{M}_{c^*+1}] = \frac{q_{i^*+1}}{q^{1-\frac{i^*}{2}}}.
$$

Finally, we have

$$
\begin{aligned}
\Pr[Success] &= \Pr[Success|c^* = 0]\Pr[c^* = 0] + \Pr[Success|c^* = 1]\Pr[c^* = 1] \\
&\geq \Pr[Success|c^* = i^*]\Pr[c^* = i^*] \\
&= \frac{1}{2}\cdot\Pr[\hat{m}\in\mathcal{M}_{c^*}\cap\mathcal{M}_{c^*+1}] \\
&= \frac{1}{2}\cdot\frac{q_{i^*+1}}{q^{1-\frac{i^*}{2}}} \\
&\geq \frac{1}{2}\cdot\frac{q^{1-\frac{i^*+1}{2}}}{q^{1-\frac{i^*}{2}}} \\
&= \frac{1}{2q^{\frac{1}{2}}}.
\end{aligned}
$$

This completes the high level description of our security reduction for the simplified unique signature scheme where $n = 2$.

1.2   Examples

We give four simple examples to verify the success probability. In these examples, suppose $q = 9$ and the message chosen by the adversary for signature forgery is $m^* = m_3$. No matter what the adversary has queried to the random oracle, we must have all queried messages satisfy $m_3 \in \mathcal{M}_2 \subseteq \mathcal{M}_1 \subseteq \mathcal{M}_0$. According to our simulation result, we should have that the loss factor is of at most $2\cdot 9^{\frac{1}{2}} = 6$. That is, we should have

$$
\Pr[Success] \geq \frac{1}{2q^{\frac{1}{2}}} = \frac{1}{6}.
$$

Recall that messages in all message sets are in sequence and they are added according to their orders. For instance, the second and the third messages added into the message set $\mathcal{M}_1$ in the Example 2 are m_4 and m_1, respectively. Furthermore,

- A message m is added to the message set $\mathcal{M}_0$ meaning that the adversary generated and submitted the **Type 0** query $x = m$ to the random oracle.
- A message m is added to the message set $\mathcal{M}_1$ meaning that the adversary generated and submitted the **Type 1** query $x = m||\Sigma_m^1$ to the random oracle.
- A message m is added to the message set $\mathcal{M}_2$ meaning that the adversary generated and submitted the **Type 2** query $x = m||\Sigma_m^2$ to the random oracle.

If the message m under **Type 0** and **Type 1** is queried and g^b is embedded in the response to the **Type 0** query m, we can use the **Type 1** query $m||\Sigma_m^1$ to solve the underlying hard problem because Σ_m^1 is equal to $H(m)^\alpha$. Similarly, if the message m under **Type 1** and **Type 2** is queried and g^b is embedded in the response to the **Type 1** query $m||\Sigma_m^1$, we can use the **Type 2** query $m||\Sigma_m^2$ to solve the underlying hard problem because σ_2 in Σ_m^2 is equal to $H(m||\Sigma_m^1)^\alpha$ (Table 2).

Table 2. The given four examples where $q = 9$.

(a) Example 1
$\mathcal{M}_0 = \{\ m_1, m_2, m_3\ \}$
$\mathcal{M}_1 = \{\ m_1, m_2, m_3\}$
$\mathcal{M}_2 = \{\ m_1, m_2, m_3\}$

(b) Example 2
$\mathcal{M}_0 = \{\ m_1, m_2, m_3, m_4\ \}$
$\mathcal{M}_1 = \{\ m_2, m_4, m_1, m_3\}$
$\mathcal{M}_2 = \{\ m_3\}$

(c) Example 3
$\mathcal{M}_0 = \{\ m_1, m_2, m_3, m_4, m_5\}$
$\mathcal{M}_1 = \{\ m_3, m_5\ \}$
$\mathcal{M}_2 = \{\ m_5, m_3\}$

(d) Example 4
$\mathcal{M}_0 = \{\ m_1, m_2, m_3, m_4, m_5, m_6, m_7\}$
$\mathcal{M}_1 = \{\ m_3\ \}$
$\mathcal{M}_2 = \{\ m_3\}$

According to the setting of (c^*, k^*), the k^*-th message in the message set $\mathcal{M}_{c^*}$ is chosen as the target message $\hat{m} = m_{c^*, k^*}$, where g^b will be embedded in the element $H(m_{c^*, k^*} || \Sigma^{c^*}_{m_{c^*, k^*}})$. Notice that the integer k^* is randomly chosen from $[1, 9]$ when $c^* = 0$ and randomly chosen from $[1, 3]$ when $c^* = 1$. In the following examples, we only need to consider one case ($c^* = 0$ or $c^* = 1$), whose success probability is at least $1/9^{\frac{1}{2}} = 1/3$.

1. In the first example, the adversary makes the hash queries $H(m), H(m||\Sigma^1_m)$, $H(m||\Sigma^2_m)$ for messages $\{m_1, m_2, m_3\}$. When $c^* = 0$, k^* is randomly chosen from $[1, 9]$. According to the queried messages, we have the reduction is successful if $c^* = 0$ and $k^* \in \{1, 2, 3\}$, because the message m_{c^*, k^*} under **Type 0** and **Type 1** will be both queried. Since k^* is randomly chosen from $[1, 9]$, we therefore have

$$\Pr[Success] \geq \Pr[k^* \in \{1, 2, 3\}] \cdot \Pr[c^* = 0] = \frac{3}{9} \cdot \frac{1}{2} = \frac{1}{6}.$$

2. In the second example, the adversary makes the hash query $H(m)$ for messages $\{m_1, m_2, m_3, m_4\}$, the hash query $H(m||\Sigma^1_m)$ for messages $\{m_2, m_4, m_1, m_3\}$ and the hash query $H(m||\Sigma^2_m)$ for the message m_3 only. When $c^* = 0$, k^* is randomly chosen from $[1, 9]$. According to the queried messages, we have the reduction is successful if $c^* = 0$ and $k^* \in \{1, 2, 3, 4\}$, because the message m_{c^*, k^*} under **Type 0** and **Type 1** will be both queried. Since k^* is randomly chosen from $[1, 9]$, we therefore have

$$\Pr[Success] \geq \Pr[k^* \in \{1, 2, 3, 4\}] \cdot \Pr[c^* = 0] = \frac{4}{9} \cdot \frac{1}{2} \geq \frac{1}{6}.$$

3. In the third example, the adversary makes the hash query $H(m)$ for messages $\{m_1, m_2, m_3, m_4, m_5\}$, the hash queries $H(m||\Sigma^1_m), H(m||\Sigma^2_m)$ for messages $\{m_3, m_5\}$ only. When $c^* = 1$, k^* is randomly chosen from $[1, 3]$. According to the queried messages, we have the reduction is successful if $c^* = 1$ and $k^* \in \{1, 2\}$, because the message m_{c^*, k^*} under **Type 1** and **Type 2** will be both queried. Since k^* is randomly chosen from $[1, 3]$, we therefore have

$$\Pr[Success] \geq \Pr[k^* \in \{1, 2\}] \cdot \Pr[c^* = 1] = \frac{2}{3} \cdot \frac{1}{2} \geq \frac{1}{6}.$$

4. In the fourth example, the adversary makes the hash query $H(m)$ for messages $\{m_1, m_2, m_3, m_4, m_5, m_6, m_7\}$, the hash queries $H(m||\Sigma_m^1), H(m||\Sigma_m^2)$ for the message m_3 only. When $c^* = 1$, k^* is randomly chosen from $[1,3]$. According to the queried messages, we have the reduction is successful if $c^* = 1$ and $k^* = 1$, because the message m_{c^*, k^*} under **Type 1** and **Type 2** will be both queried. Since k^* is randomly chosen from $[1,3]$, we therefore have

$$\Pr[Success] \geq \Pr[k^* = 1] \cdot \Pr[c^* = 1] = \frac{1}{3} \cdot \frac{1}{2} = \frac{1}{6}.$$

1.3   Security Reduction for the Full Scheme and Other Discussions

The above reduction is programmed for the simplified unique signature scheme, where each signature is composed of three block signatures only. The reduction for the full unique signature scheme with $n+1$ block signatures is more complex but similar, which is given in Sect. 5. In the corresponding reduction, $n+1$ message sets $\mathcal{M}_0, \mathcal{M}_1, \mathcal{M}_2, \cdots, \mathcal{M}_n$ will be defined which also satisfy

$$\mathcal{M}_n \subseteq \mathcal{M}_{n-1} \subseteq \cdots \subseteq \mathcal{M}_1 \subseteq \mathcal{M}_0.$$

Similarly, we prove there exists an integer $i^* \in [0, n-1]$ such that

$$|\mathcal{M}_{i^*}| < q^{1-\frac{i^*}{n}} \text{ and } |\mathcal{M}_{i^*+1}| \geq q^{1-\frac{i^*+1}{n}}.$$

In the corresponding simulation, the random values (c^*, k^*) will be chosen from the following ranges

$$c^* \in [0, n-1], \quad k^* \in [1, q^{1-\frac{c^*}{n}}].$$

When g^b is programmed in the response to the target query $\hat{m}||\Sigma_{\hat{m}}^{i^*}$ for the message $\hat{m} \in \mathcal{M}_{i^*}$ and the target message $\hat{m}$ also appears in the message set $\mathcal{M}_{i^*+1}$ (i.e. the adversary also submits the hash query $\hat{m}||\Sigma_{\hat{m}}^{i^*+1}$ to the random oracle), we have the hash query $\hat{m}||\Sigma_{\hat{m}}^{i^*+1}$ contains the solution to the CDH problem. The success reduction requires that c^* happens to be equal to i^* mentioned above. Since $|\mathcal{M}_{i^*}| < q^{1-\frac{i^*}{n}}$ and $k^* \in [1, q^{1-\frac{i^*}{n}}]$, we have $H(m||\Sigma_m^{i^*})$ for any message m in $\mathcal{M}_{i^*}$ will be responded using g^b with probability $1/q^{1-\frac{i^*}{n}}$. Furthermore, since $\mathcal{M}_{i^*+1} \subseteq \mathcal{M}_{i^*}$ and $|\mathcal{M}_{i^*+1}| = q_{i^*+1} \geq q^{1-\frac{i^*+1}{n}}$, $\hat{m}$ can be any one of q_{i^*+1} messages within $\mathcal{M}_{i^*+1}$. Therefore, we have the success probability

$$\Pr[Success] = \sum_{i=0}^{n-1} \Pr[Success|c^* = i] \Pr[c^* = i]$$

$$\geq \Pr[Success|c^* = i^*] \Pr[c^* = i^*]$$

$$= \frac{1}{n} \cdot \frac{q_{i^*+1}}{q^{1-\frac{i^*}{n}}}$$

$$\geq \frac{1}{n} \cdot \frac{q^{1 - \frac{i^* + 1}{n}}}{q^{1 - \frac{i^*}{n}}}$$

$$= \frac{1}{n q^{\frac{1}{n}}}.$$

This completes the overview of our counterexample with a tight reduction.

Our proposed scheme can select other signature schemes to generate block signatures. The security reduction is still tight as long as only the block signature of the message $m_{c^*, k^*} \in \mathcal{M}_{c^*}$ is reducible and the block signatures of other messages are simulatable. The proposed signature structure and the reduction method towards a tight reduction are independent of the block signatures and hence are universal.

Comparison of reductions. For easy understanding of the query-based reduction, we compare it with the traditional forgery-based reduction according to the above reduction as follows.

- The forgery-based reduction utilizes a forged signature from the adversary to solve an underlying hard problem, while the query-based reduction utilizes one of hash queries from the adversary to solve an underlying hard problem.
- In the forgery-based reduction, the solution must be associated with the message of forged signature. While in the query-based reduction, the solution does not have to be related to the message for signature forgery.
- In the forgery-based reduction, the simulator cannot stop the simulation before it receives a forged signature from the adversary. While in the query-based reduction, the simulator can stop the simulation immediately after receiving a query containing the solution to the underlying hard problem.
- In the forgery-based reduction, the simulator cannot compute the forged signature from the adversary. While in the query-based reduction, the simulator can compute signatures on all messages as long as the adversary's hash queries have already contained the solution to the underlying hard problem.
- The forgery-based reduction can be with or without random oracles, while the query-based reduction must be with random oracles.

Remark 2. *In our given signature scheme, each signature comprises of three block signatures in the simplified scheme and $n + 1$ block signatures in the full signature scheme. The last block signature is not used in our security reduction, except forcing the adversary to make at least a* **Type 2** *query or a* **Type n** *query (full scheme). We note that the number of block signatures can be reduced by one if we partially adopt the forgery-based reduction. Taking the simplified scheme as an example. It will be composed of two block signatures instead of three, such that there is no* **Type 2** *query. When $c^* = 1$, g^b is programmed in the response to a* **Type 1** *query. That is, the target query is*

$$m_{c^*, k^*} || \Sigma^1_{m_{c^*, k^*}} = \hat{m} || \Sigma^1_{\hat{m}}.$$

We have that $H(\hat{m} || \Sigma^1_{\hat{m}})$ contains g^b. When the message $\hat{m} \in \mathcal{M}_1$ is chosen as the message m^* to be forged, we have the second block signature in the forged signature is $H(\hat{m}||\Sigma_{\hat{m}}^1)^{\alpha}$ which contains the solution to the CDH problem. That is, we use the forged signature to solve the underlying hard problem. We stress that this reduction is also correct. However, we do not adopt this method because it is relatively simpler to use only query-based reduction in the security proof.

1.4 The Gap in the Proofs of Impossibilities

We explain why our query-based reduction for the counterexample cannot be captured by the meta-reduction proofs [3,10,15]. Specifically, we would like to clarify the gap in the existing proofs for the impossibilities of tight reductions. We start with briefly recalling the notion of *meta-reduction*, which is the main technique adopted to derive their impossibility results. It is worth mentioning that Bader *et al.* [3] proposed a different meta-reduction to derive more generalized impossibility results. However, we note that they have the same principle. We provide more details as follows.

The meta-reduction proof for impossibilities. Roughly speaking, a meta-reduction is associated with the following three entities.

- The reducer $\mathcal{R}$ who can reduce a forged signature to solving an underlying hard problem. Let $\epsilon_{\mathcal{R}}$ be the success probability of solving the underlying hard problem.
- The real forger (adversary) $\mathcal{F}$ who is able to forge a valid signature. Let $\epsilon_{\mathcal{F}}$ be the advantage (probability) of forging a valid signature.
- The simulated forger $\overline{\mathcal{F}}$ who cannot forge a valid signature and aims to solve an underlying hard problem with the help of $\mathcal{R}$ but without the help of $\mathcal{F}$.

In the traditional security reduction, the interaction is between $\mathcal{R}$ and $\mathcal{F}$, while in the meta-reduction, the interaction is between $\overline{\mathcal{F}}$ and $\mathcal{R}$ only without the real forger. Specifically, in the meta-reduction, a simulated forger $\overline{\mathcal{F}}$ is constructed to solve a hard problem with the help of the reducer $\mathcal{R}$. Precisely, $\overline{\mathcal{F}}$ firstly asks $\mathcal{R}$ to sign a number of messages and then rewinds $\mathcal{R}$ to the state before signature queries and re-starts the security game with $\mathcal{R}$. Finally, it forges a valid signature using one of the signed message/signature pairs (say (m^*, Σ_{m^*})) obtained before the rewinding. When the simulated forger $\overline{\mathcal{F}}$ is indistinguishable from the real forger $\mathcal{F}$, the reducer $\mathcal{R}$ should be able to output a solution to the underlying hard problem with a certain probability. It has been proved in [10] that through the above meta-reduction, $\overline{\mathcal{F}}$ can obtain a solution to the underlying hard problem from the reducer $\mathcal{R}$ with a success probability at least

$$\epsilon_{\overline{\mathcal{F}}} = \epsilon_{\mathcal{R}} - \frac{\epsilon_{\mathcal{F}}}{\Omega(q_s)},$$

for q_s number of signature queries to the reducer $\mathcal{R}$.

If $\epsilon_{\overline{\mathcal{F}}}$ is positive and non-negligible, it means we can efficiently solve a hard problem using the simulated forger $\overline{\mathcal{F}}$ without the help of the real forger. This would contradict with the underlying hardness assumption. It therefore implies that $\epsilon_{\mathcal{R}}$ must be no more than $\epsilon_{\mathcal{F}}/\Omega(q_s)$ for all security reductions. Hence, the loss factor in any security reduction is of at least q_s.

The central argument in the meta-reduction requires that the simulated forger $\overline{\mathcal{F}}$ is indistinguishable from the real forger $\mathcal{F}$. To achieve this, the forged signature generated by the simulated forger must be indistinguishable from the forged signature generated by the real forger, such that $\mathcal{R}$ is convinced that it is interacting with a real forger and thus outputs a solution to the hard problem. In the literature, unique signatures [10] and efficiently re-randomizable signatures [3,15] are shown to be able to capture this indistinguishability.

The gap in the proofs. One could note that the existing work [3,10,15] implicitly claimed that the aforementioned meta-reduction works as long as the simulated forger $\overline{\mathcal{F}}$ outputs a *correctly distributed signature* (and hence indistinguishable from a real forged signature) to convince $\mathcal{R}$ that it is a real forger. In fact, this is the central argument for the existing meta-reductions in proving the impossibility results for unique signatures and their generalization. Let $\Sigma(pk, m)$ be the set of signatures Σ_m with regards to the message m and the public key pk under the system parameters. During the proofs [3,10,15], they are silently assumed that this signature set $\Sigma(pk, m)$ in the simulation is determined by pk, m and possibly by additional random oracle queries that are assumed to be efficiently computable. However, this assumption does not necessarily hold in all security reductions. In our example, each useful hash query except **Type 0** requires to compute a block signature that is not efficiently computable without knowing the signing key. Any successful (real) forger $\mathcal{F}$ must make some non-efficiently computable hash queries to the random oracle. This is the reason why the meta-reduction requiring that all hash queries are efficiently computable will fail to simulate the forger.

More precisely, as shown in our query-based reduction for the simplified scheme, a successful reduction essentially relies on the fact that the real forger must at least generate hash queries to random oracle satisfying $q_2 \geq 1$ (or $q_n \geq 1$ in the full scheme). This is guaranteed by the assumption that the real forger is able to forge a valid signature. Suppose the aforementioned meta-reduction utilizes our constructed reducer $\mathcal{R}'$. We stress that the simulated forger $\overline{\mathcal{F}}$ is not able to generate hash queries satisfying $q_2 \geq 1$. Otherwise, it will be the real forger. During the first round before rewinding, the simulated forger $\overline{\mathcal{F}}$ should make some hash queries and signature queries. When the simulated forger $\overline{\mathcal{F}}$ rewinds the interaction, it is worth noting that $\overline{\mathcal{F}}$ must rewind $\mathcal{R}'$ to the state after the hash queries. This is because if it rewinds $\mathcal{R}'$ to the state before the hash queries, all hash values before and after the rewinding will be completely different in the random oracle model and hence the simulated forger $\overline{\mathcal{F}}$ cannot use one of queried signatures to derive the forged signature. That is, all previous hash queries are not changed and the simulated forger $\overline{\mathcal{F}}$ could query more. Finally, even the simulated forger $\overline{\mathcal{F}}$ returns a valid signature indistinguishable from the one generated by the real forger, we still have that the hash queries do not satisfy the requirement of $q_2 \geq 1$. In this case, the reducer $\mathcal{R}'$ fails and the meta-reduction breaks down, because the simulated forger $\overline{\mathcal{F}}$ cannot solve an underlying hard problem.

2 Preliminaries

2.1 Definition of Digital Signatures

A digital signature scheme Sig = (SysGen, KeyGen, Sig, Verify) consists of the following four algorithms:

SysGen(1^λ). Taking as input a security parameter 1^λ, this system generation algorithm returns the system parameters *params*.

KeyGen(*params*). Taking as input the system parameters *params*, this key generation algorithm returns a public/secret key pair (pk, sk).

Sign(*params*, *sk*, *m*). Taking as input the system parameters *params*, a secret key *sk* and a message *m*, this signing algorithm returns a signature of *m* denoted by Σ_m.

Verify(*params*, *pk*, Σ_m, *m*). Taking as input the system parameters *params*, a public key *pk*, a signature Σ_m and a message *m*, this verification algorithm outputs 0 (reject) or 1 (accept).

We say that a signature is *valid* if **Verify**(*params*, *pk*, Σ_m, *m*) $= 1$ for all generated system parameters *params*, public key *pk* and any message *m*. In the rest of paper, we omit the input of the system parameters *params* in the signing algorithm and the verification algorithm unless otherwise stated explicitly.

2.2 Definition of Unique Signatures and Efficiently Re-Randomizable Signatures

Given a public key *pk* and a message *m*, we denote

$$\Sigma(pk, m) = \left\{ \Sigma_m : \ \textbf{Verify}(pk, \Sigma_m, m) = 1 \right\}$$

as the set of signatures Σ_m with regards to the message *m* and the public key *pk* under the system parameters *params*. In particular, this signature set could be associated with specific instantiations of hash functions adopted as part of system parameters. This notion was introduced in [3] to define unique signatures and re-randomizable signatures.

Definition 1 (Unique Signatures). *A signature scheme is unique if*

$$\left| \Sigma(pk, m) \right| = 1$$

holds for all public keys under the system parameters params and all messages.

Definition 2 (Efficiently Re-Randomizable Signatures). *A signature scheme is efficiently re-randomizable with t-re-randomizable, if there exists an efficient algorithm* ReRand *running in polynomial time at most t, such that for all* (pk, Σ_m, m) *under the system parameters params with* **Verify**$(pk, \Sigma_m, m) = 1$ *holds that the output distribution of*

$$\textsf{ReRand}(pk, \Sigma_m, m)$$

is identical to the uniform distribution over $\Sigma(pk, m)$.

Unique signatures are a particular case of efficiently re-randomizable signatures where

$$\mathsf{ReRand}(pk, \Sigma_m, m) = \Sigma_m.$$

Therefore, the efficiently re-randomizable signatures can be seen as the generalization of unique signatures. An important requirement of efficiently re-randomizable signatures is the uniform distribution over $\Sigma(pk, m)$. Generally speaking, efficiently re-randomizable signatures are signatures whose random salts used in signature generations can be changed uniformly without the knowledge of the secret key, such that we cannot use a random salt to switch signatures between simulatable and reducible. That is, all signatures on the same message must be either simulatable or reducible. Therefore, all efficiently re-randomizable signatures are believed to have optimal security reductions with a loss factor of at least q_s, same as unique signatures.

2.3   Security Model

We recall the notion of existential unforgeability against chosen message attacks (EU-CMA) played between a challenger and an adversary $\mathcal{A}$.

Setup: The challenger runs the SysGen algorithm to generate the system parameters $params$ and runs the KeyGen algorithm to generate a key pair (pk, sk). The system parameters and the public key pk are sent to the adversary.

Signature-Query: The adversary sequentially asks the signature of any message that is adaptively chosen by the adversary. To query the signature of m, $\mathcal{A}$ submits the message m to the challenger. The challenger runs the Sign algorithm and returns a signature Σ_m of m to the adversary.

Forgery: The adversary outputs a message m^* and the corresponding signature Σ_{m^*}. It wins the game if Σ_{m^*} is a valid signature of m^* and m^* has never been queried for its signature.

We refer to such adversary as an EU-CMA adversary and define the advantage of $\mathcal{A}$ in winning the above game as

$$\Pr\left[\mathsf{EU\text{-}CMA}^{\mathcal{F}}_{\mathsf{Sig}}\left(1^\lambda\right) \to 1\right] = \epsilon.$$

Definition 3. *We say that a signature scheme* Sig *is* (t, q_s, ϵ)*-secure in the EU-CMA security model if any PPT adversary* $\mathcal{A}$ *who runs in* t *polynomial time and makes at most* q_s *signature queries has advantage at most* ϵ *in winning the game, where* ϵ *is negligible function of the input security parameter.*

2.4   Complexity Assumption

Let $\mathbb{PG} = (\mathbb{G}, \mathbb{G}_T, p, e, g)$ be a pairing group where p is the order of the groups $\mathbb{G}, \mathbb{G}_T$, $e : \mathbb{G} \times \mathbb{G} \to \mathbb{G}_T$ is the bilinear map and g is a generator of $\mathbb{G}$. Our proposed unique signature scheme is based on the BLS signature scheme in the symmetric pairing stated in $\mathbb{PG}$. The underlying hard assumption for our scheme is the Computational Diffie-Hellman (CDH) assumption, which says it is hard to compute g^{ab} from a given instance (g, g^a, g^b) in the pairing group $\mathbb{PG}$, where a, b are unknown and uniformly chosen from the space $\mathbb{Z}_p$. The formal definition of the CDH assumption is omitted here.

3   The Full Counterexample of Unique Signature Scheme

Our full unique signature scheme is described as follows.

SysGen: The system generation algorithm takes as input a security parameter 1^λ and a small integer n. It chooses a pairing group $\mathbb{PG} = (\mathbb{G}, \mathbb{G}_T, p, e, g)$ and a cryptographic hash function $H : \{0, 1\}^* \to \mathbb{G}$ that will be viewed as a random oracle in the security proof. The system parameters $params$ are composed of $(\mathbb{PG}, H, n)$. A signature will be composed of $n + 1$ block signatures.

KeyGen: The key generation algorithm randomly chooses $\alpha \in \mathbb{Z}_p$ and computes $h = g^\alpha$. The algorithm returns a public/secret key pair $(pk, sk) = (h, \alpha)$.

Sign: The signing algorithm takes as input the system parameters $params$, a message $m \in \{0, 1\}^*$ and the secret key sk. It returns the signature Σ_m on m as

$$\Sigma_m = \left(\sigma_1, \sigma_2, \sigma_3, \cdots, \sigma_n, \sigma_{n+1} \right)$$
$$= \left(H(m)^\alpha,\ H(m||\Sigma_m^1)^\alpha,\ H(m||\Sigma_m^2)^\alpha, \cdots, H(m||\Sigma_m^{n-1})^\alpha, H(m||\Sigma_m^n)^\alpha \right),$$

where $\Sigma_m^i = (\sigma_1, \sigma_1, \cdots, \sigma_i)$ and the final signature Σ_m is equivalent to Σ_m^{n+1}.

Verify: The verification algorithm takes as input the system parameters $params$, a signed message (m, Σ_m) and the public key pk. It accepts the signature if and only if the $n + 1$ pairing computations are correct. That is, $e(\sigma_1, g) = e(H(m), h)$ and $e(\sigma_{i+1}, g) = e(H(m||\Sigma_m^i), h)$ holds for all $i = 1, 2, \cdots, n$.

4   Two Essential Lemmas for Security Reduction

Let $m \in \{0, 1\}^*$ be a message and $\mathcal{M}_0, \mathcal{M}_1, \mathcal{M}_2, \cdots, \mathcal{M}_n$ be $n + 1$ message sets defined as follows.

- The message set $\mathcal{M}_{i+1}$ is a subset of $\mathcal{M}_i$ for all $i = 0, 1, 2, \cdots, n - 1$.

$$\mathcal{M}_n \subseteq \mathcal{M}_{n-1} \subseteq \mathcal{M}_{n-2} \subseteq \cdots \subseteq \mathcal{M}_1 \subseteq \mathcal{M}_0.$$

- The set $\mathcal{M}_i$ has q_i distinct messages and is composed of $\{m_{i,1}, m_{i,2}, \cdots, m_{i,q_i}\}$.

$$\mathcal{M}_0 = \{\ m_{0,1}\ ,\ m_{0,2}\ ,\ m_{0,3}\ ,\ \cdots\ ,\ \cdots\ ,\ \cdots\ ,\ \cdots\ ,\ m_{0,q_0}\ \}$$
$$\mathcal{M}_1 = \{\ m_{1,1}\ ,\ m_{1,2}\ ,\ m_{1,3}\ ,\ \cdots\ ,\ \cdots\ ,\ \cdots\ ,\ m_{1,q_1}\ \}$$
$$\mathcal{M}_2 = \{\ m_{2,1}\ ,\ m_{2,2}\ ,\ m_{2,3}\ ,\ \cdots\ ,\ \cdots\ ,\ m_{2,q_2}\ \}$$
$$\cdots$$
$$\mathcal{M}_n = \{\ m_{n,1},\ m_{n,2}\ ,\ m_{n,3}\ ,\ \cdots\ ,\ m_{n,q_n}\ \}$$

We have the following two essential lemmas based on the above message set definitions for our security reduction. The first lemma is proposed for proving the second lemma.

Lemma 1 (Range Lemma). *Suppose $q_0 < q$ and $q_n \geq 1$. There exists an integer $i^* \in [0, n-1]$ satisfying*

$$q_{i^*} < q^{1-\frac{i^*}{n}} \quad and \quad q_{i^*+1} \geq q^{1-\frac{i^*+1}{n}}.$$

Proof of Lemma 1. We use a proof via contradiction to prove the existence of i^*. If the integer i^* does not exist, it means

$$q_i \geq q^{1-\frac{i}{n}} \quad or \quad q_{i+1} < q^{1-\frac{i+1}{n}}$$

holds for all $i = 0, 1, 2, 3, \cdots, n-1$.

For any integer $j \in [1, n-1]$, we have

- When $i = j - 1$, it means

$$q_{j-1} \geq q^{1-\frac{j-1}{n}} \quad or \quad q_j < q^{1-\frac{j}{n}}.$$

- When $i = j$, it means

$$q_j \geq q^{1-\frac{j}{n}} \quad or \quad q_{j+1} < q^{1-\frac{j+1}{n}}.$$

That is, we have

$$\left(q_{j-1} \geq q^{1-\frac{j-1}{n}} \bigvee q_j < q^{1-\frac{j}{n}} \right) \bigwedge \left(q_j \geq q^{1-\frac{j}{n}} \bigvee q_{j+1} < q^{1-\frac{j+1}{n}} \right).$$

It indicates that

If $q_j \geq q^{1-\frac{j}{n}}$ then $q_{j-1} \geq q^{1-\frac{j-1}{n}}$ for $j = n-1, n-2, n-3, \cdots, 2, 1$.

When $i = n - 1$, we also have

$$q_{n-1} \geq q^{1-\frac{n-1}{n}} \quad or \quad q_n < q^{1-\frac{n}{n}}.$$

Since $q_n < q^{1-\frac{n}{n}} = 1$ contradicts with the assumption $q_n \geq 1$, we therefore have $q_{n-1} \geq q^{1-\frac{n-1}{n}}$ and deduct

$$q_{n-2} \geq q^{1-\frac{n-2}{n}}, \quad q_{n-3} \geq q^{1-\frac{n-3}{n}}, \quad \cdots \quad q_2 \geq q^{1-\frac{2}{n}} \quad q_1 \geq q^{1-\frac{1}{n}} \quad q_0 \geq q^{1-\frac{0}{n}}.$$

The deduction $q_0 \geq q^{1-\frac{0}{n}} = q$ contradicts with the assumption $q_0 < q$. Therefore, the assumption at the beginning of the proof is wrong and hence the integer $i^* \in [0, n-1]$ exists. This completes the proof. $\qquad\square$

Lemma 2 (Probability Lemma). *Suppose $q_0 < q$ and $q_n \geq 1$. If we randomly choose two integers (c^*, k^*) satisfying $c^* \in [0, n-1]$ and $k^* \in [1, q^{1-\frac{c^*}{n}}]$, then the target message $m_{c^*, k^*} \in \mathcal{M}_{c^*}$ will appear in the message set $\mathcal{M}_{c^*+1}$ with probability at least*

$$\frac{1}{n} \cdot \frac{1}{q^{\frac{1}{n}}}$$

for any $n+1$ defined message sets $\mathcal{M}_0, \mathcal{M}_1, \mathcal{M}_2, \cdots, \mathcal{M}_n$. Here, if the chosen message $m_{c^*, k^*} \notin \mathcal{M}_{c^*}$ (the size of message set is less than k^*), we define $m_{c^*, k^*} \notin \mathcal{M}_{c^*+1}$.

Proof of Lemma 2. Let $\Pr[Success]$ be the success probability that the chosen message $m_{c^*, k^*} \in \mathcal{M}_{c^*}$ also appears in the message set $\mathcal{M}_{i^*+1}$. We are going to prove

$$\Pr[Success] \geq \frac{1}{n} \cdot \frac{1}{q^{\frac{1}{n}}}.$$

The success probability is associated with the choice of (c^*, k^*), where c^* is randomly chosen from $[0, n-1]$. Hence, we have $\Pr[c^* = i] = \frac{1}{n}$ for any $i \in [0, n-1]$. According to the setting, we have

$$\Pr[Success] = \sum_{i=0}^{n-1} \Pr[Success|c^* = i] \Pr[c^* = i] \geq \frac{1}{n} \cdot \Pr[Success|c^* = i^*],$$

where i^* is the integer defined in Lemma 1.

According to Lemma 1, we have

$$|\mathcal{M}_{i^*}| = q_{i^*} < q^{1-\frac{i^*}{n}} \quad \text{and} \quad |\mathcal{M}_{i^*+1}| = q_{i^*+1} \geq q^{1-\frac{i^*+1}{n}}.$$

When $c^* = i^*$, the target message m_{c^*, k^*} is chosen from the k^*-th message of the message set $\mathcal{M}_{i^*}$. Since $|\mathcal{M}_{i^*}| < q^{1-\frac{i^*}{n}}$ and k^* is randomly chosen from $[1, q^{1-\frac{i^*}{n}}]$, any message in $\mathcal{M}_{i^*}$ will be selected as the target message with probability $1/q^{1-\frac{i^*}{n}}$. Furthermore, since $\mathcal{M}_{i^*+1} \subseteq \mathcal{M}_{i^*}$, the success event will happen when m_{c^*, k^*} also appears in $\mathcal{M}_{i^*+1}$. There are q_{i^*+1} messages in $\mathcal{M}_{i^*+1}$ and hence we have the success probability

$$\Pr[Success] = \sum_{i=0}^{n-1} \Pr[Success|c^* = i] \Pr[c^* = i]$$

$$\geq \frac{1}{n} \cdot \Pr[Success|c^* = i^*]$$

$$= \frac{1}{n} \cdot \Pr[m_{c^*, k^*} \in \mathcal{M}_{i^*} \cap \mathcal{M}_{i^*+1}]$$

$$= \frac{1}{n} \cdot \frac{q_{i^*+1}}{q^{1-\frac{i^*}{n}}}$$

$$\geq \frac{1}{n} \cdot \frac{q^{1-\frac{i^*+1}{n}}}{q^{1-\frac{i^*}{n}}}$$

$$= \frac{1}{nq^{\frac{1}{n}}}.$$

This completes the proof. □

5   Security Proof with a Tight Reduction

In this section, we prove the proposed full unique signature scheme is secure under the CDH assumption in the EU-CMA security model with a tight reduction, where H is set as a random oracle in the security proof.

Theorem 1. *Let H be a random oracle and q be the number of queries to the random oracle. If the proposed full signature scheme can be broken with (t, q_s, ϵ) in the EU-CMA model, the CDH problem is solvable with*

$$\left(t + O(q_s n), \frac{\epsilon}{nq^{1/n}}\right).$$

Proof. Suppose there exists an adversary $\mathcal{A}$ who can break the signature scheme in the EU-CMA model. We construct a simulator $\mathcal{B}$ that uses one of hash queries generated by the adversary to solve the CDH problem. Given as input the instance (g, g^a, g^b) in the pairing group $\mathbb{PG}$, the simulator aims to compute g^{ab}. $\mathcal{B}$ interacts with the adversary as follows.

Setup: The system parameters are the pairing group $\mathbb{PG}$ and the integer n, where H is set as a random oracle controlled by the simulator. For the key pair, the simulator sets $\alpha = a$ and hence the public key $h = g^\alpha = g^a$ is available from the instance. The system parameters and the public key are sent to the adversary.

Hash-Query: We state how to simulate the random oracle here. The adversary can access the random oracle any time, such as after the signature query. We note that the random oracle simulation is the core of our proof for having a tight reduction.

Before simulating the random oracle, the simulator firstly chooses a random integer $c^* \in [0, n-1]$ and then chooses another random value k^* from the range

$$\left[1, q^{1-\frac{c^*}{n}}\right].$$

In particular, we have the range is $[1, q]$ when $c^* = 0$ and the range is $[1, q^{\frac{1}{n}}]$ when $c^* = n-1$. The size of range for k^* is dependent on the integer c^*.

Let $\mathcal{L}$ be the list which records all queries and responses. Each query and its response are stored in a tuple. For each tuple, the format is

$$(x, \; I_x, \; T_x, O_x, \; U_x, \; z_x),$$

which is explained as follows.

x refers to the query input

I_x refers to the identity either the adversary $\mathcal{A}$ or the simulator $\mathcal{B}$

T_x refers to the type of the hash query

O_x refers to the order index of the query within the same type

U_x refers to the response to x, i.e., $U_x = H(x)$

z_x refers to the secret for computing U_x.

For a query on x, if there already has a tuple $(x, I_x, T_x, O_x, U_x, z_x)$ in the list, the simulator responds with U_x. Otherwise, the simulator responds to this new query as follows.

Response of object I_x. The object I_x is to identify who first time generates and submits x to the random oracle. For easy understanding, we comprehend the query in the way that both the adversary and the simulator can query to the random oracle, although the random oracle is controlled by the simulator. If a query on x is first time generated and submitted by the adversary, we say this query is made by the adversary and set $I_x = \mathcal{A}$. Otherwise, we set $I_x = \mathcal{B}$.

Taking a new message m as the example. Suppose the adversary firstly queries $H(m), H(m||\Sigma_m^1), H(m||\Sigma_m^2)$ to the random oracle and then queries the signature of m to the simulator. Notice that the signature generation on the message m requires to know all the following values

$$H(m), \ H(m||\Sigma_m^1), \ H(m||\Sigma_m^2), \ H(m||\Sigma_m^3), \ \cdots, \ H(m||\Sigma_m^n).$$

The hash list does not record how to respond to hash queries $H(m||\Sigma_m^i)$ for all $i = 3, 4, \cdots, n$. Therefore, the simulator must add all these hash queries to the random oracle first before generating its signature. Notice that the hash queries $H(m||\Sigma_m^3), \cdots, \ H(m||\Sigma_m^n)$ could be made by the adversary again for signature verification, but they are first time generated and made by the simulator. Hence, we define

- For any $x \in \{m, \ m||\Sigma_m^1, \ m||\Sigma_m^2\}$, the corresponding I_x for x is $I_x = \mathcal{A}$.
- For any $x \in \{m||\Sigma_m^3, \cdots, m||\Sigma_m^n\}$, the corresponding I_x for x is $I_x = \mathcal{B}$.

Response of object T_x. We assume "$||$" is a concatenation notation that will never appear within messages after encoding (See the footnote in the introduction section to know how to achieve it.). The simulator can also run the verification algorithm to verify whether each block signature is correct or not. Therefore, it is easy to distinguish the input structure of all hash queries. We define $n + 2$ types of hash queries to the random oracle.

Type i. $x = m||\Sigma_m^i$. Here, Σ_m^i denotes the first i block signatures of m and i refers to any integer $i \in [0, n]$. We assume $m||\Sigma_m^0 = m$ without "$||$" in x for easy analysis.

Type D. x is a query different from the previous $n + 1$ types. For example, $x = m||R_m$ but $R_m \neq \Sigma_m^i$ for any $i \in [1, n]$, or $x = m||\Sigma_m^{i'}$ for any $i' \geq n+1$.

The object T_x is set as follows.

- If $I_x = \mathcal{B}$, then $T_x = \perp$.
- Otherwise, suppose $I_x = \mathcal{A}$. Then, the simulator can run the verification algorithm to know which type x belongs to and set

$$T_x = \begin{cases} i & \text{if } x \text{ belongs to \textbf{Type i} for any } i \in [0, n] \\ \perp & \text{otherwise } x \text{ belongs to \textbf{Type D}} \end{cases}.$$

We emphasize that T_x and O_x are used to mark "valid" queries generated by the adversary only, which will be used in signature generation. We define **Type D** is to match the truth that the adversary can generate any arbitrary string as a query to the random oracle. Notice that the last type of queries will never be used in signature generation or signature forgery.

Response of object O_x. The object O_x is set as follows.

- If $T_x = \perp$, then $O_x = \perp$.
- Otherwise, suppose $T_x = c$. Then, $O_x = k$ if x is the k-th new query added into the list $\mathcal{L}$ in those queries where $T_x = c$.

To calculate the integer k for the new query x, the simulator must count how many queries have been added in $\mathcal{L}$, where only those queries with the same T_x will be counted. We emphasize that the setting of O_x needs to know the value T_x first.

For the objects I_x, T_x and O_x on the query x, there are only three cases in all tuples in the list.

$$(I_x, T_x, O_x) = (\mathcal{A}, c, k), \ (I_x, T_x, O_x) = (\mathcal{A}, \perp, \perp), \ (I_x, T_x, O_x) = (\mathcal{B}, \perp, \perp),$$

where $c \in [0, n]$ and $k \in [1, q]$.

Response of objects (U_x, z_x). Let (I_x, T_x, O_x) be the response to the query x according to the above description. The simulator randomly chooses $z_x \in \mathbb{Z}_p$ and sets the response U_x to x according to the chosen (c^*, k^*) as follows.

$$U_x = H(x) = \begin{cases} (g^b)^{z_x} & \text{if } (T_x, O_x) = (c^*, k^*) \\ g^{z_x} & \text{otherwise} \end{cases}.$$

We use z_x to denote the secret for response to x. In the following, if the query x needs to be written as $x = m || \Sigma_m^i$, the corresponding secret will be rewritten as z_m^i.

Finally, the simulator adds the defined tuple $(x, I_x, T_x, O_x, U_x, z_x)$ for the new query x to the list. This completes the description of the hash query and its response.

For the tuple $(x, I_x, T_x, O_x, U_x, z_x)$, we have $H(x)^\alpha = U_x^a = (g^a)^{z_x}$ is computable by the simulator for any query x as long as $(T_x, O_x) \neq (c^*, k^*)$. Notice that when $(T_x, O_x) = (c^*, k^*)$, we have

$$H(x)^\alpha = U_x^a = g^{abz_x} = (g^{ab})^{z_x}.$$

For the tuple $(x, I_x, T_x, O_x, U_x, z_x)$, we use $m_{i,j}$ to denote the message in the query input x if $(T_x, O_x) = (i, j)$. We define

$$\mathcal{M}_i = \{m_{i,1}, m_{i,2}, \cdots, m_{i,q_i}\}$$

to be the message set with q_i messages, where $\mathcal{M}_i$ contains all messages in those tuples with $T_x = i$. According to the setting of oracle response, for those hash queries belonging to **Type i** for all $i \in [0, n]$, there have $n + 1$ message sets $\mathcal{M}_0, \mathcal{M}_1, \mathcal{M}_2, \cdots, \mathcal{M}_n$ at most to capture all messages in these queries.

Without knowing the signature Σ_m of m, the adversary must make hash queries $H(m), H(m||\Sigma_m^1), H(m||\Sigma_m^2), \cdots, H(m||\Sigma_m^n)$ in sequence because Σ_m^i in the query $m||\Sigma_m^i$ contains

$$H(m)^\alpha, H(m||\Sigma_m^1)^\alpha, \cdots, H(m||\Sigma_m^{i-1})^\alpha.$$

For a message before its signature query, the adversary could not query all $n+1$ hash queries for this message. Therefore, we have the following inequality and subset relationship hold.

$$q_n \le q_{n-1} \le \cdots \le q_2 \le q_1 \le q_0, \quad \mathcal{M}_n \subseteq \mathcal{M}_{n-1} \subseteq \cdots \subseteq \mathcal{M}_2 \subseteq \mathcal{M}_1 \subseteq \mathcal{M}_0.$$

All queried messages mentioned above can be described in Table 3. Suppose the adversary can finally forge a valid signature on a message m^*. The adversary must at least make the hash query $H(m^*||\Sigma_{m^*}^n)$ in order to compute $H(m^*||\Sigma_{m^*}^n)^\alpha$, which guarantees $q_n \ge 1$. Since the number of hash queries is of at most q, we have $q_0 < q$.

Table 3. Messages queried by the adversary where $T_x \ne \bot$.

$$\mathcal{M}_0 = \{m_{0,1}, m_{0,2}, m_{0,3}, \cdots, \cdots, \cdots, m_{0,q_0}\}$$
$$\mathcal{M}_1 = \{m_{1,1}, m_{1,2}, m_{1,3}, \cdots, \cdots, \cdots, m_{1,q_1}\}$$
$$\mathcal{M}_2 = \{m_{2,1}, m_{2,2}, m_{2,3}, \cdots, \cdots, m_{2,q_2}\}$$
$$\cdots$$
$$\mathcal{M}_n = \{m_{n,1}, m_{n,2}, m_{n,3}, \cdots, m_{n,q_n}\}$$

The queried messages in $n+1$ message sets fulfill the message set description in Sect. 4. Since $q_n \ge 1$ and $q_0 < q$, we have the **Range Lemma** and the **Probability Lemma** can also be applied to the above message sets, even these message sets are adaptively generated by the adversary.

Signature-Query: For a signature query on the message m that is adaptively chosen by the adversary, the simulation is described as follows.

If m is never queried to the random oracle, the simulator works as follows from $i = 1$ to $i = n + 1$, where i is increased by one for each time.

– Add a query on $m||\Sigma_m^{i-1}$ to the list (We define $m||\Sigma_m^0 = m$). According to the setting of the random oracle simulation, we have the corresponding tuple is
$$(m||\Sigma_m^{i-1}, \; \mathcal{B}, \; \bot, \; \bot, \; g^{z_m^{i-1}}, \; z_m^{i-1}).$$

– Compute the block signature σ_i as
$$\sigma_i = H(m||\Sigma_m^{i-1})^\alpha = (g^a)^{z_m^{i-1}}.$$

Notice that σ_i for all i are computable by the simulator and the signature of Σ_m is equal to $\Sigma_m^{n+1} = (\sigma_0, \sigma_1, \cdots, \sigma_{n+1})$. Therefore, the signature of m is computable by the simulator.

Suppose the message m is ever queried to the random oracle by the adversary, where the following queries associated with the message m are made by the adversary
$$m||\Sigma_m^0, \; m||\Sigma_m^1, \; m||\Sigma_m^2, \cdots, \; m||\Sigma_m^{r_m} : \; r_m \in [0, n].$$

Here, the integer r_m is adaptively decided by the adversary. Let $(x, I_x, T_x, O_x, U_x, z_x)$ be the tuple for $x = m||\Sigma_m^{r_m}$. That is, $T_x = r_m$.

– If $(T_x, O_x) = (c^*, k^*)$, the simulator aborts because
$$H(m||\Sigma_m^{r_m}) = g^{bz_x}, \quad \sigma_{r_m+1} = H(m||\Sigma_m^{r_m})^\alpha = U_x^a = (g^{bz_x})^a = (g^{ab})^{z_x},$$

which cannot be computed by the simulator and hence the simulator fails in simulating the signature for the adversary, especially the block signature σ_{r_m+1}.

– Otherwise, $(T_x, O_x) \neq (c^*, k^*)$. Then, σ_{r_m+1} is computable by the simulator because
$$H(m||\Sigma_m^{r_m}) = g^{z_x}, \quad \sigma_{r_m+1} = H(m||\Sigma_m^{r_m})^\alpha = (g^a)^{z_x}.$$

Similarly to the case that m is never queried to the random oracle, the simulator can generate and make hash queries
$$H(m||\Sigma_m^{r_m+1}), \; H(m||\Sigma_m^{r_m+2}), \cdots, H(m||\Sigma_m^n)$$

to the random oracle. Finally, it computes the signature Σ_m for the adversary.

This completes the description of signature simulation. Once the simulator generates the signature of m, it forwards the signature to the adversary. It is easy to verify that the computed signature is a valid signature.

Forgery: The adversary outputs a valid signature Σ_{m^*} on a message m^* that is not asked for a signature. Since the adversary cannot make a signature query on m^*, we have the following queries to the random oracle were made by the adversary
$$m^*||\Sigma_{m^*}^0, \; m^*||\Sigma_{m^*}^1, \; m^*||\Sigma_{m^*}^2, \; \cdots, \; m^*||\Sigma_{m^*}^n.$$

The solution to the hard problem does not have to be associated with the forged message m^*. The simulator solves the hard problem as follows.

- The simulator searches $\mathcal{L}$ to find the first tuple $(x, I_x, T_x, O_x, U_x, z_x)$ satisfying

$$(T_x, O_x) = (c^*, k^*).$$

If this tuple does not exist, abort. Otherwise, let the message m_{c^*,k^*} in this tuple be denoted by $\hat{m}$ for short. That is, $m_{c^*,k^*} = \hat{m}$ and we have $\hat{m} \in \mathcal{M}_{c^*}$. We note that $\hat{m}$ could be different from m^*. This tuple therefore is equivalent to

$$(x, I_x, T_x, O_x, U_x, z_x) = \left(\hat{m}||\Sigma_{\hat{m}}^{c^*}, \ \mathcal{A}, \ c^*, \ k^*, \ g^{bz_{\hat{m}}^{c^*}}, \ z_{\hat{m}}^{c^*}\right).$$

That is $H(\hat{m}||\Sigma_{\hat{m}}^{c^*}) = g^{bz_{\hat{m}}^{c^*}}$ contains the instance g^b.
- The simulator searches $\mathcal{L}$ to find the second tuple $(x', I_{x'}, T_{x'}, O_{x'}, U_{x'}, z_{x'})$, where x' is the query about the message $\hat{m}$ and $T_{x'} = c^* + 1$. If this tuple does not exist, abort. Otherwise, we have $\hat{m} \in \mathcal{M}_{c^*+1}$ and

$$x' = \hat{m}||\Sigma_{\hat{m}}^{c^*+1},$$

where $\Sigma_{\hat{m}}^{c^*+1}$ contains $\sigma_{c^*+1} = H(m||\Sigma_m^{c^*})^\alpha$.
- The simulator computes and outputs

$$\left(H(\hat{m}||\Sigma_{\hat{m}}^{c^*})^\alpha\right)^{\frac{1}{z_{\hat{m}}^{c^*}}} = \left(g^{abz_{\hat{m}}^{c^*}}\right)^{\frac{1}{z_{\hat{m}}^{c^*}}} = g^{ab}$$

as the solution to the CDH problem.

Analysis. This completes the description of simulation and solution. The scheme simulation is indistinguishable from the real scheme because the signing key α is simulated using the random exponent a in the instance and there is no random number in the signature simulation. The random oracle response is correct because the response U_x to each query x is computed using a random integer z_x, independent of other integers.

According to the assumption, the adversary will break the signature scheme with advantage ϵ. We have the adversary will make the hash query $H(m^*||\Sigma_{m^*}^n)$ with probability at least ϵ,[6] such that $m^* \in \mathcal{M}_n$ and hence $q_n \geq 1$. The number of hash query is q. Since $q_0 + q_1 + q_2 + \cdots + q_n = q$, we have $q_0 < q$. Therefore, the conditions of the **Probability Lemma** hold with success probability ϵ in our reduction.

The reduction is successful when the simulator does not abort in the query phase and the forgery phase. According to the setting of the simulation, we found

- The simulator aborts in the query phase when $m_{c^*,k^*} \in \mathcal{M}_{c^*}$ but $m_{c^*,k^*} \notin \mathcal{M}_{c^*+1}$, because the simulator cannot compute the queried signature on the message m_{c^*,k^*}.

---

[6] The adversary can forge a valid signature via randomly choosing group elements as the forged signature without making the corresponding hash queries. However, the success probability is less than $1/p$. The actual probability of making such a hash query is $\epsilon - 1/p$. Since $1/p$ is negligible compared to ϵ, we simplify the probability $\epsilon - 1/p$ into ϵ.

- The simulator aborts in the forgery phase when $m_{c^*,k^*} \notin \mathcal{M}_{c^*}$ because the simulator cannot embed g^b in the response to the query m_{c^*,k^*} under **Type** c^*, or when $m_{c^*,k^*} \notin \mathcal{M}_{c^*+1}$ because the solution to the CDH problem does not exist in the hash list.

Therefore, we have the reduction is successful when $m_{c^*,k^*} \in \mathcal{M}_{c^*}$ and $m_{c^*,k^*} \in \mathcal{M}_{c^*+1}$. According to the **Probability Lemma**, if $q_0 < q$ and $q_n \geq 1$, we have $\hat{m} = m_{c^*,k^*} \in \mathcal{M}_{c^*} \cap \mathcal{M}_{c^*+1}$ holds with probability $1/(nq^{\frac{1}{n}})$. Therefore, the reduction is successful and the simulator can solve the hard problem with success probability at least $\epsilon/(nq^{\frac{1}{n}})$.

The simulation time is mainly dominated by the signature simulation, where all signature computations cost $O(n \cdot q_s)$ point multiplications. Notice that the simulation time does not consider the time cost of oracle responses. This completes the proof. □

Very recently, the work of [13] showed how to find a correct solution to a computational hard problem from hash queries for encryption schemes under the indistinguishability model. The loss factor is also $nq^{\frac{1}{n}}$ with a similar chain-like structure in hash queries. However, we stress that the approaches towards tight reductions are totally different.

Remark 3. *In the above probability analysis, we use the condition that the adversary can forge a valid signature to guarantee $q_n \geq 1$, which is a desired condition in the* **Probability Lemma**. *We note that this condition is sufficient but not necessary in our reduction as long as $q_n \geq 1$ holds.*

6   Conclusion

Optimal security reductions with impossibility results of tight reductions for unique signatures and efficiently re-randomizable signatures have been well studied in the literature (Coron, Eurocrypt 2002; Hofheinz *et al.* PKC 2012; Bader *et al.*, Eurocrypt 2016). It has been proved and claimed that any security reduction for a unique signature scheme or an efficiently re-randomizable signature scheme must loose a factor of at least q_s for q_s number of signature queries under a non-interactive assumption in the EU-CMA security model. In this work, we pointed out that their optimal security reductions cannot cover all security reductions and proposed a counterexample with a tight reduction in the random oracle model. We can program the security reduction with a very small loss factor, e.g., 100, for 2^{50} hash queries to random oracles under the CDH assumption in the EU-CMA security model. We stress that our counterexample just bypasses the given proofs of optimal security reduction, because the proofs via meta-reduction break down in our query-based reduction. The given counterexample implies a new way of constructing a signature scheme with a tight reduction in the random oracle model from a signature scheme with a loose reduction. This transformation is universal and also applicable for unique signatures. This transformation method is somewhat impractical because of inefficiency due to the growth of signature length by n times. Nevertheless, this is the first method for enabling a tight proof without the use of a random salt in the signature generation.

Acknowledgment. We would like to thank Yannick Seurin for his helpful comments to improve the clarity of this paper. We would also like to thank Tibor Jager for his insightful comments especially for helping identify the gap between the proofs of impossibilities and our example. Finally, we would like to thank anonymous reviewers of CRYPTO 2017 for their insightful comments which help us improve the quality of this work. This work was partially supported by ARC Discovery Early Career Researcher Award (DECRA) DE170100641.

References

1. Abdalla, M., Bellare, M., Rogaway, P.: The oracle diffie-hellman assumptions and an analysis of DHIES. In: Naccache, D. (ed.) CT-RSA 2001. LNCS, vol. 2020, pp. 143–158. Springer, Heidelberg (2001). doi:10.1007/3-540-45353-9_12

2. Abdalla, M., Fouque, P.-A., Lyubashevsky, V., Tibouchi, M.: Tightly-secure signatures from lossy identification schemes. In: Pointcheval, D., Johansson, T. (eds.) EUROCRYPT 2012. LNCS, vol. 7237, pp. 572–590. Springer, Heidelberg (2012). doi:10.1007/978-3-642-29011-4_34

3. Bader, C., Jager, T., Li, Y., Schäge, S.: On the impossibility of tight cryptographic reductions. In: Fischlin, M., Coron, J.-S. (eds.) EUROCRYPT 2016. LNCS, vol. 9666, pp. 273–304. Springer, Heidelberg (2016). doi:10.1007/978-3-662-49896-5_10

4. Bellare, M., Rogaway, P.: The exact security of digital signatures-how to sign with RSA and rabin. In: Maurer, U. (ed.) EUROCRYPT 1996. LNCS, vol. 1070, pp. 399–416. Springer, Heidelberg (1996). doi:10.1007/3-540-68339-9_34

5. Bernstein, D.J.: Proving tight security for rabin-williams signatures. In: Smart, N. (ed.) EUROCRYPT 2008. LNCS, vol. 4965, pp. 70–87. Springer, Heidelberg (2008). doi:10.1007/978-3-540-78967-3_5

6. Blazy, O., Kakvi, S.A., Kiltz, E., Pan, J.: Tightly-secure signatures from chameleon hash functions. In: Katz, J. (ed.) PKC 2015. LNCS, vol. 9020, pp. 256–279. Springer, Heidelberg (2015). doi:10.1007/978-3-662-46447-2_12

7. Boneh, D., Lynn, B., Shacham, H.: Short signatures from the weil pairing. In: Boyd, C. (ed.) ASIACRYPT 2001. LNCS, vol. 2248, pp. 514–532. Springer, Heidelberg (2001). doi:10.1007/3-540-45682-1_30

8. Boyd, C., Carr, C.: Fair client puzzles from the bitcoin blockchain. In: Liu, J.K.K., Steinfeld, R. (eds.) ACISP 2016. LNCS, vol. 9722, pp. 161–177. Springer, Cham (2016). doi:10.1007/978-3-319-40253-6_10

9. Chevallier-Mames, B., Joye, M.: A practical and tightly secure signature scheme without hash function. In: Abe, M. (ed.) CT-RSA 2007. LNCS, vol. 4377, pp. 339–356. Springer, Heidelberg (2006). doi:10.1007/11967668_22

10. Coron, J.-S.: Optimal security proofs for PSS and other signature schemes. In: Knudsen, L.R. (ed.) EUROCRYPT 2002. LNCS, vol. 2332, pp. 272–287. Springer, Heidelberg (2002). doi:10.1007/3-540-46035-7_18

11. Goh, E., Jarecki, S., Katz, J., Wang, N.: Efficient signature schemes with tight reductions to the diffie-hellman problems. J. Cryptol. **20**(4), 493–514 (2007)

12. Goldwasser, S., Micali, S., Rivest, R.L.: A digital signature scheme secure against adaptive chosen-message attacks. SIAM J. Comput. **17**(2), 281–308 (1988)

13. Guo, F., Susilo, W., Mu, Y., Chen, R., Lai, J., Yang, G.: Iterated random oracle: a universal approach for finding loss in security reduction. In: Cheon, J.H., Takagi, T. (eds.) ASIACRYPT 2016. LNCS, vol. 10032, pp. 745–776. Springer, Heidelberg (2016). doi:10.1007/978-3-662-53890-6_25

14. Hofheinz, D., Jager, T.: Tightly secure signatures and public-key encryption. In: Safavi-Naini, R., Canetti, R. (eds.) CRYPTO 2012. LNCS, vol. 7417, pp. 590–607. Springer, Heidelberg (2012). doi:10.1007/978-3-642-32009-5_35

15. Hofheinz, D., Jager, T., Knapp, E.: Waters signatures with optimal security reduction. In: Fischlin, M., Buchmann, J., Manulis, M. (eds.) PKC 2012. LNCS, vol. 7293, pp. 66–83. Springer, Heidelberg (2012). doi:10.1007/978-3-642-30057-8_5

16. Kakvi, S.A., Kiltz, E.: Optimal security proofs for full domain hash, revisited. In: Pointcheval, D., Johansson, T. (eds.) EUROCRYPT 2012. LNCS, vol. 7237, pp. 537–553. Springer, Heidelberg (2012). doi:10.1007/978-3-642-29011-4_32

17. Katz, J., Wang, N.: Efficiency improvements for signature schemes with tight security reductions. In: Jajodia, S., Atluri, V., Jaeger, T. (eds.) CCS 2003, pp. 155–164. ACM (2003)

18. Luu, L., Narayanan, V., Zheng, C., Baweja, K., Gilbert, S., Saxena, P.: A secure sharding protocol for open blockchains. In: Weippl, E.R., Katzenbeisser, S., Kruegel, C., Myers, A.C., Halevi, S. (eds.) ACM Conference on Computer and Communications Security 2016, pp. 17–30. ACM (2016)

19. Schäge, S.: Tight proofs for signature schemes without random oracles. In: Paterson, K.G. (ed.) EUROCRYPT 2011. LNCS, vol. 6632, pp. 189–206. Springer, Heidelberg (2011). doi:10.1007/978-3-642-20465-4_12

20. Zhang, F., Safavi-Naini, R., Susilo, W.: An efficient signature scheme from bilinear pairings and its applications. In: Bao, F., Deng, R., Zhou, J. (eds.) PKC 2004. LNCS, vol. 2947, pp. 277–290. Springer, Heidelberg (2004). doi:10.1007/978-3-540-24632-9_20

Compact Structure-Preserving Signatures
with Almost Tight Security

Masayuki Abe[1]($\boxtimes$), Dennis Hofheinz[2], Ryo Nishimaki[1], Miyako Ohkubo[3],
and Jiaxin Pan[2]

[1] Secure Platform Laboratories, NTT Corporation, Tokyo, Japan
{abe.masayuki,nishimaki.ryo}@lab.ntt.co.jp
[2] Karlsruhe Institute of Technology, Karlsruhe, Germany
{dennis.hofheinz,jiaxin.pan}@kit.edu
[3] Security Fundamentals Laboratory, CSR, NICT, Tokyo, Japan
m.ohkubo@nict.go.jp

Abstract. In structure-preserving cryptography, every building block shares the same bilinear groups. These groups must be generated for a specific, a priori fixed security level, and thus it is vital that the security reduction of all involved building blocks is as tight as possible. In this work, we present the first generic construction of structure-preserving signature schemes whose reduction cost is independent of the number of signing queries. Its chosen-message security is almost tightly reduced to the chosen-plaintext security of a structure-preserving public-key encryption scheme and the security of Groth-Sahai proof system. Technically, we adapt the adaptive partitioning technique by Hofheinz (Eurocrypt 2017) to the setting of structure-preserving signature schemes. To achieve a structure-preserving scheme, our new variant of the adaptive partitioning technique relies only on generic group operations in the scheme itself. Interestingly, however, we will use non-generic operations during our security analysis. Instantiated over asymmetric bilinear groups, the security of our concrete scheme is reduced to the external Diffie-Hellman assumption with linear reduction cost in the security parameter, independently of the number of signing queries. The signatures in our schemes consist of a larger number of group elements than those in other non-tight schemes, but can be verified faster, assuming their security reduction loss is compensated by increasing the security parameter to the next standard level.

Keywords: Structure-preserving signature · Tight reduction · Adaptive partitioning

1 Introduction

BACKGROUND. A structure-preserving signature (SPS) scheme [3] is designed over bilinear groups, and features public keys, messages, and signatures that only

D. Hofheinz—Supported by DFG grants HO 4534/4-1 and HO 4534/2-2.
J. Pan—Supported by the DFG grant HO 4534/4-1.

J. Katz and H. Shacham (Eds.): CRYPTO 2017, Part II, LNCS 10402, pp. 548–580, 2017.
DOI: 10.1007/978-3-319-63715-0_19

consist of source group elements. Furthermore, signature verification only uses group membership testing and relations that can be expressed as pairing product equations. Coupled with the Groth-Sahai non-interactive proof system [29] (GS proofs for short), SPS schemes are a powerful tool in constructing a wide range of cryptographic applications. Various SPS schemes based on compact standard assumptions exist in the literature [2–4,18,28,33,35,39]. When looking at schemes from standard assumptions, the state-of-the-art scheme in [33] yields signatures as compact as consisting of six source group elements.

In this paper, we address the tightness of security proofs for SPS schemes with compact parameters, i.e., constant-size signatures and standard (non q-type) assumptions. Formally, a security reduction constructs an adversary $\mathcal{A}$ on a computational assumption out of an adversary $\mathcal{A}'$ on the security of a cryptographic scheme. If we let ϵ and t denote the success probability and runtime of $\mathcal{A}$, and ϵ' and t' the success probability and runtime of $\mathcal{A}'$, then we define the security loss of the reduction, or simply the reduction cost, as $(\epsilon't)/(\epsilon t')$ [19]. The reduction is tight if the security loss is a small constant or almost tight if it grows only (as a preferably small function) in the security parameter λ. In particular, we are concerned with the independence of the security loss from the number q_s of $\mathcal{A}'$'s signing queries in a chosen-message attack. We note that in practice, q_s can be as large as 2^{30} while λ is typically 128.

The only tightly secure SPS under compact assumptions is that by Hofheinz and Jager [32]. Their tree-based construction, however, yields unacceptably large signatures consisting of hundreds of group elements. For other SPS schemes under compact assumptions the security is proven using a hybrid argument that repeat reductions in q_s. Thus, their security loss is $\mathcal{O}(q_s)$ [2,39] or even $\mathcal{O}(q_s^2)$ [35], as shown in Table 1.

The non-tightness of security reductions does not necessarily mean the existence of a forger with reduced complexity, but the security guarantees given by non-tight reductions are quantitatively weaker than those given by tight reductions. Recovering from the security loss by increasing the security parameter is not a trivial solution when bilinear groups are involved. The security in source and target groups should be balanced, and computational efficiency is influenced by the choice of curves, pairings, and parameters such as embedding degrees, and the presence of dedicated techniques. In practice, an optimal setting for a targeted security parameter is determined by actual benchmarks, e.g., [6,23,26], and only standard security parameters such as 128, 192, and 256, have been investigated. One would thus have to hop to the next standard security level to offset the security loss in reality. Besides, we stress that increasing the security parameter for a building block in structure-preserving cryptography is more costly than usual as it results in losing efficiency in all other building blocks using the same bilinear groups. Thus, the demand for tight security is stronger in structure-preserving cryptography.

Even in ordinary (i.e. non-structure-preserving) signature schemes, most of the constructions satisfying tight security are either in the random oracle model, e.g., [1,11,21,34], rely on q-type or strong RSA assumptions, e.g., [15,40], or lead

Table 1. Object sizes and loss of security among structure-preserving signature schemes with assumptions in the standard model. Smallest possible parameters are set to parameterized assumptions. Notation (x, y) means x and y elements in $\mathbb{G}_1$ and $\mathbb{G}_2$, respectively. The $|\mathsf{M}|$, $|\sigma|$, $|pk|$ columns mean the number of messages, the number of group elements in a signature, and the number of group elements in a public key, respectively. The "Sec. Loss" column means reduction costs. The "Assumptions" column means the underlying assumptions for proving security. For HJ, parameter d limits number of signing to 2^d. Parameters q_s and λ represent number of signing queries and security parameter, respectively.

Reference	$|\mathsf{M}|$	$|\sigma|$	$|pk|$	Sec. Loss	Assumptions
HJ [32]	1	$10d + 6$	13	8	DLIN
ACDKNO [2]	$(n_1, 0)$	$(7, 4)$	$(5, n_1 + 12)$	$\mathcal{O}(q_s)$	SXDH, XDLIN$_1$
ACDKNO [2]	(n_1, n_2)	$(8, 6)$	$(n_2 + 6, n_1 + 13)$	$\mathcal{O}(q_s)$	SXDH, XDLIN$_1$
LPY [39]	$(n_1, 0)$	$(10, 1)$	$(16, 2n_1 + 5)$	$\mathcal{O}(q_s)$	SXDH, XDLIN$_2$
KPW [35]	$(n_1, 0)$	$(6, 1)$	$(0, n_1 + 6)$	$\mathcal{O}(q_s^2)$	SXDH
KPW [35]	(n_1, n_2)	$(7, 3)$	$(n_2 + 1, n_1 + 7)$	$\mathcal{O}(q_s^2)$	SXDH
JR [33]	$(n_1, 0)$	$(5, 1)$	$(0, n_1 + 6)$	$\mathcal{O}(q_s \log q_s)$	SXDH
Ours (Sect. 4.2)	$(n_1, 0)$	$(13, 12)$	$(18, n_1 + 11)$	$\mathcal{O}(\lambda)$	SXDH
Ours (Sect. 4.3)	(n_1, n_2)	$(14, 14)$	$(n_2 + 19, n_1 + 12)$	$\mathcal{O}(\lambda)$	SXDH

to large signatures and/or keys, e.g., [20,37]. Hofheinz presented the first tightly secure construction with compact signatures and keys under a standard compact assumption over bilinear groups [30]. However, his construction can only be used to sign integer messages (and not group elements or, e.g., its own public key), so it is not structure-preserving.

Table 2. Comparison of factors relevant to computational efficiency against SPS schemes having smallest signature sizes. Third column indicates number of scalar multiplications in $\mathbb{G}_1$ and $\mathbb{G}_2$ for signing. Multi-scalar multiplication is counted as 1.5. For JR, a constant pairing is included. Column "Batched" shows the number of pairings in a verification when pairing product equations are merged into one by using a batch verification technique [13].

Reference	$|\mathsf{M}|$	#(s.mult) in signing	#(PPEs)	#(Pairings)	
				Plain	Batched
KPW [35]	$(n_1, 0)$	$(6, 1)$	3	$n_1 + 11$	$n_1 + 10$
JR [33]		$(6, 1)$	2	$n_1 + 8$	$n_1 + 6$
Ours (Sect. 4.2)		$(15, 15)$	15	$n_1 + 57$	$n_1 + 16$
KPW [35]	(n_1, n_2)	$(8, 3.5)$	4	$n_1 + n_2 + 15$	$n_1 + n_2 + 14$
Ours (Sect. 4.3)		$(17.5, 16)$	16	$n_1 + n_2 + 61$	$n_1 + n_2 + 18$

OUR CONTRIBUTIONS. We propose the *first (almost) tightly secure* SPS schemes with *constant* number of group elements in signatures. Our schemes are proven secure based on standard assumptions (e.g., the symmetric external Diffie-Hellman (SXDH) assumption). Concretely, we first present a generic construction of an almost tightly secure SPS scheme from a structure-preserving public-key encryption secure against chosen-plaintext attacks and the GS proof system. With ElGamal encryption and the GS proofs over asymmetric pairing groups, we obtain concrete SPS schemes with compact signature size whose unforgeability against adaptive chosen-message attacks (UF-CMA) is reduced from the SXDH assumption with security loss of $\mathcal{O}(\lambda)$, which is independent of q_s.

The primary benefit of our tightly secure SPS schemes is their availability in structure-preserving cryptography under the current standard security level. For a system modularly built with structure-preserving building blocks, a compact and tightly secure SPS scheme has been a missing piece, since other useful building blocks, such as one-time signatures and commitments, are known to be tightly secure. Plugging in our scheme, one can increase the proven security in applications of structure-preserving cryptography such as blind signatures [3], group signatures [39], and unlinkable redactable signatures [17] used in anonymous credential systems.

The second benefit of our result is the removal of q_s from the security bound, which aims to simplify the systems design. With previous schemes, there are trade-offs among security, efficiency, and usability; if one desires stronger security guarantees without sacrificing efficiency, a rigid limitation has to be put on the number of signatures per public key, or, if more flexibility on the number of possible signatures is important in considered applications, one has to take the risk with weaker security guarantees or less efficiency. With our schemes, one no longer needs to fix q_s in advance and can focus on desirable security and permissible efficiency for the targeted system.

Nevertheless, the performance as a stand-alone signature scheme is of a concern. We summarise several parameters that dominate the space and computation costs in Tables 1 and 2. The bare numbers in the tables imply that our schemes are outperformed by those in the literature if they are used at the *same* security level. Taking the security loss into consideration, however, the tightness of our schemes offsets the difference in terms of computational complexity. We elaborate this point in the following. Though concrete complexity varies widely depending on platforms and implementations, it seems that computing a pairing in the 192-bit security level is slowed by a factor of $\delta := 6$ to 7 on ordinary personal computers [8,23] and $\delta := 9$ to 12 on processors for embedded systems [5,27,42] compared to those in the 128-bit security level. According to the number of pairings in Table 2, our scheme for bilateral messages at the 128-bit security level verifies a signature with batch verification $4.6 < \delta(n_1 + n_2 + 14)/(n_1 + n_2 + 18) < 9.3$ times faster than the KPW scheme at the 192-bit security setting for offsetting its security loss of 60 bits. Applying the same argument to the case of unilateral messages, ours in the 128-bit security level will be $2.2 < \delta(n_1 + 6)/(n_1 + 16) < 4.5$ times faster compared to the JR scheme in the 192-bit security level.

We note that the above simple argument ignores dedicated techniques for computing pairing products, e.g., [41], and costs for subtle computations. It may not be fair to ignore the concrete security loss in our schemes, which can be as large as 13 bits at the 128-bit security level, as mentioned in Sect. 4. Nevertheless, taking into account the fact that the performance gap between different security levels will be larger than those shown in the above benchmarks published previously [36] (i.e., slowdown factor δ in the above argument will be much larger), even the simple estimation is aimed to show the practical significance of tightly secure schemes.

TECHNICAL OVERVIEW. Eliminating any representation-dependent computation in the construction is a crucial technical challenge. Towards this goal, we adapt the "adaptive partitioning" technique of Hofheinz [31] (which in turn builds upon [20]) to the setting of structure-preserving signatures. Thus, in our security proof, we gradually transform the conditions necessary for a successful forgery until a valid forgery is impossible. This will require $\mathcal{O}(\lambda)$ game hops, thus leading to a security loss independent of the number of adversarial signing queries.

Concretely, in the scheme itself, we require that every valid signature must carry an (encrypted) "authentication tag" $Z = X$, where $X \in \mathbb{G}$ is a fixed group element. We will gradually transform this requirement $Z = X$ into the following combination of requirements on the authentication tag Z^* from a valid forgery:

(a) We must have $Z^* = X \cdot M^*$, where $X \in \mathbb{G}$ is a fixed random group element, and $M^* \in \mathbb{G}$ is the signed message in the forgery.
(b) Also, we must have $Z^* = X \cdot M_i$ for some previously signed message M_i.

Since we may assume $M^* \notin \{M_i\}$ in the (non-strong) existential unforgeability experiment, any attempted forgery will thus be invalid.

The key technique to establishing these modified requirements is a "partitioning argument" similar to the one from [31]. That is, in the proof, we will enforce more and more dependencies of the authentication tag Z on the *bit representation* of M. Note that this bit representation is not used in the real scheme; this would in fact be problematic in the context of structure-preserving constructions. For instance, to establish a dependence of Z on the k-th bit b_M of the bit representation of M, we proceed as follows:

1. First, we "partition" the set of all messages into two subsets, depending on b_M. This means that signatures issued by the experiment now carry (an encryption of) b_M in a special component. The reason for this partitioning is that we can now, depending on the encrypted b_M, use different verification rules.
2. We guess the encrypted bit b^* from the forgery, and change the encrypted Z in issued signatures for all $b_M \neq b^*$. (This change can be justified by setting up things such that Z can only be retrieved from a signature if the encrypted bit b is equal to b^*. If $b \neq b^*$, then Z is hidden, and can hence be modified in issued signatures.) This introduces a dependence of Z in issued signatures on b_M.

However, the encrypted bit b^* from the forgery is not necessarily identical to b_{M^*} (since this property cannot be easily enforced in a structure-preserving way). As a consequence, we cannot force the adversary to respect the additional dependencies in his forgery. Yet, we will show that we *can* force the adversary to *reuse* one $Z = X \cdot \mathsf{M}_i$ from a signing query. This leads to requirement (b) in verification forgeries, and requirement (a) will finally be enforced by a regular GS proof in signatures (that GS proof is simulated in all intermediate steps).

This line of reasoning borrows from Chen and Wee's [20] general idea of establishing tight security through a repeated partitioning of the message space (resp. identity space in an identity-based encryption scheme) into two sets, each time adjusting signatures for messages from one of the two sets in the process. However, their approach, as well as other follow-up approaches (e.g., [7,14,25,30,38]) embeds the partitioning already in the scheme (in the sense that the scheme must already contain all potentially possible "partitioning rules," for instance according to each message bit). Since these rules in the mentioned schemes are based on the message bits (or an algebraic predicate on the discrete logarithm of the message [30]), this would not lead to a structure-preserving scheme.

Instead, we adapt the "adaptive partitioning" (AP) technique of Hofheinz [31], in which the partitioning is performed dynamically, through an *encrypted* partitioning bit embedded in signatures. This allows us to separate partitioning from the way messages are bound to signatures in the scheme. We thus bind a message through an authentication tag, as mentioned above, that is more algebraic and admits structure-preserving GS proofs. The encrypted partitioning bit is fixed to a constant in the real scheme and turned into a variable only in the security proof where non-generic computations are allowed.

In adapting AP to our setting, we face two difficulties, however: the partitioning used in AP is bit-based (which is incompatible with our requirement of a structure-preserving scheme), and its complexity leads to comparatively complex schemes. More specifically, AP leads to several expensive "OR"-proofs in ciphertexts, resp. signatures. As a consequence, the (encryption) schemes in [31] are not competitive in complexity to non-tightly secure schemes, even when taking into account a potentially larger security level for non-tightly secure schemes. On the other hand, our signature schemes are carefully designed so that GS proofs in signatures are done only for less costly linear relations (except for one crucial "OR"-proof). We further use optimization techniques of Escala and Groth [24] to reduce the size of GS proofs in our instantiation.

Moreover, AP crucially relies on the bit representation of messages (resp. encryption tags that are hash values in [31]). In particular, the encryption scheme from [31] is not structure-preserving. For our purposes, we thus have to modify this technique to work with group elements instead of hash values. This leads to a very simple and clean structure-preserving signature scheme whose security proof still crucially uses the bit representation of group elements. We find this property surprising and conceptually interesting.

OPEN PROBLEMS. While being compact and tightly secure, our concrete SPS schemes contain a moderate number of group elements in a signature. We leave as an open problem to design more compact SPSes with even smaller number of group elements. Another interesting open problem is to decrease the security loss from $\mathcal{O}(\lambda)$ to $\mathcal{O}(1)$.

ORGANIZATION. The rest of the paper is organized as follows. After introducing notations, security definitions, and building blocks in Sect. 2, we present our generic construction and its security proof in Sect. 3. We discuss an instantiation over asymmetric bilinear groups in Sect. 4.

2   Preliminaries

2.1   Notations

For an integer p, define $\mathbb{Z}_p$ as the residual ring $\mathbb{Z}/p\mathbb{Z}$. If $\mathcal{B}$ is a set, then $x \xleftarrow{\$} \mathcal{B}$ denotes the process of sampling an element x from set $\mathcal{B}$ uniformly at random. All our algorithms are probabilistic polynomial time (p.p.t. for short) unless stated otherwise. If $\mathcal{A}$ is an algorithm, then $a \xleftarrow{\$} \mathcal{A}(b)$ denotes the random variable, which is defined as the output of $\mathcal{A}$ on input b. To make the randomness explicit, we use the notation $a \leftarrow \mathcal{A}(b; \rho)$ meaning that the algorithm is executed on input b and randomness ρ. Note that $\mathcal{A}$'s execution is now deterministic.

We say that a function ϵ is negligible in security parameter λ if, for all constant $c > 0$ and all sufficiently large λ, $\nu(\lambda) < \lambda^{-c}$ holds.

2.2   Pairing Groups and Diffie-Hellman Assumptions

Let PGGen be an algorithm that on input security parameter λ returns a description par $= (p, \mathbb{G}_1, \mathbb{G}_2, \mathbb{G}_T, e, G_1, G_2)$ of pairing groups, where p is a poly(λ)-bit prime, $\mathbb{G}_1$, $\mathbb{G}_2$, $\mathbb{G}_T$ are cyclic groups of order p, G_1 and G_2 are generators of $\mathbb{G}_1$ and $\mathbb{G}_2$, respectively, and $e : \mathbb{G}_1 \times \mathbb{G}_2 \to \mathbb{G}_T$ is an efficiently computable non-degenerate bilinear map. $G_T := e(G_1, G_2)$ is a generator in $\mathbb{G}_T$. Pairing group par is said to be a Type-III asymmetric pairing group if $\mathbb{G}_1 \neq \mathbb{G}_2$, and there does not exist an efficiently computable isomorphism between $\mathbb{G}_1$ and $\mathbb{G}_2$. When distinction between source groups is not important, we use $\mathbb{G}$ and G to represent $\mathbb{G}_1$ and/or $\mathbb{G}_2$, and their default generator, respectively. When a group element is given to an algorithm as an input, its membership to the intended group must be tested, but we make it implicit throughout the paper for conciseness of the description.

Our instantiation in Sect. 4 is based on the following standard assumption over asymmetric pairing groups.

Definition 1 (Decisional Diffie-Hellman assumption). The decisional Diffie-Hellman assumption (DDH$_s$) *holds relative to* PGGen *in group* $\mathbb{G}_s$ *(*$s \in \{1, 2, T\}$*) if, for all p.p.t. adversaries* $\mathcal{A}$*, advantage function*

$$\mathsf{Adv}^{\mathsf{ddh}_s}_{\mathsf{PGGen}}(\mathcal{A}) := |\Pr[\mathcal{A}(\mathsf{par}, G_s^a, G_s^b, G_s^{ab}) = 1] - \Pr[\mathcal{A}(\mathsf{par}, G_s^a, G_s^b, G_s^c) = 1]|$$

is negligible in security parameter λ, where the probability is taken over par $\xleftarrow{\$}$ PGGen$(1^\lambda), a, b, c \xleftarrow{\$} \mathbb{Z}_p$. *The SXDH assumption holds relative to* PGGen *if for all p.p.t. adversaries $\mathcal{A}$, advantage function* $\mathsf{Adv}^{\mathsf{sxdh}}_{\mathsf{PGGen}}(\mathcal{A}) := \max(\mathsf{Adv}^{\mathsf{ddh_1}}_{\mathsf{PGGen}}(\mathcal{A}),$ $\mathsf{Adv}^{\mathsf{ddh_2}}_{\mathsf{PGGen}}(\mathcal{A}))$ *is negligible.*

2.3   Structure-Preserving Signatures

Definition 2 (Structure-preserving signature scheme). *An SPS scheme* SPS *with respect to* PGGen *is a tuple of algorithms* SPS = (Gen, Sign, Ver)*:*

- *The key generation algorithm* Gen(par) *takes* par $\xleftarrow{\$}$ PGGen(1^λ) *as input and returns a public/secret key pair,* (pk, sk), *where* $pk \in \mathbb{G}^{n_{pk}}$ *for some* $n_{pk} \in$ poly(λ). *Message space* $\mathcal{M} := \mathbb{G}^n$ *for some constant* $n \in$ poly(λ) *is implicitly determined by* pk.
- *The signing algorithm* Sign(sk, M) *returns a signature* $\sigma \in \mathbb{G}^{n_\sigma}$ *for some* $n_\sigma \in$ poly(λ).
- *The deterministic verification algorithm* Ver(pk, M, σ) *solely evaluates pairing product equations and returns 1 (accept) or 0 (reject).*

(Perfect correctness). *For all* $(pk, sk) \xleftarrow{\$}$ Gen(par), *all messages* $M \in \mathcal{M}$, *and all* $\sigma \xleftarrow{\$}$ Sign(sk, M), Ver$(pk, M, \sigma) = 1$ *holds.*

Though our final goal is to achieve security against adaptive chosen-message attacks, we use the following slightly relaxed notion in the generic construction.

Definition 3 (UF-XCMA Security). *A signature scheme* SPS *is unforgeable against auxiliary chosen-message attacks (UF-XCMA-secure) for relation $\mathcal{R}$ if, for all p.p.t. adversaries $\mathcal{A}$, advantage function*

$$\mathsf{Adv}^{\mathsf{uf\text{-}xcma}}_{\mathsf{SPS}}(\mathcal{A}) := \Pr\left[\mathrm{VER}(M^*, \sigma^*) = 1 \,\middle|\, \begin{array}{l} \mathsf{par} \xleftarrow{\$} \mathsf{PGGen}(1^\lambda); \\ (M^*, \sigma^*) \xleftarrow{\$} \mathcal{A}^{\mathrm{INIT}, \mathrm{SIGN}(\cdot, \cdot)}(\mathsf{par}) \end{array}\right]$$

is negligible in security parameter λ where

- INIT *runs* $(pk, sk) \xleftarrow{\$}$ Gen(par), *initializes* $\mathcal{Q}_M$ *with* $\emptyset$, *and returns* pk *to* $\mathcal{A}$,
- SIGN(M, m) *checks if* $\mathcal{R}(M, m) = 1$, *runs* $\sigma \xleftarrow{\$}$ Sign(sk, M), *adds the* M *to* $\mathcal{Q}_M$, *and returns* σ *to* $\mathcal{A}$, *and*
- VER(M^*, σ^*) *returns 1 if* $M^* \notin \mathcal{Q}_M$ *and* $1 = $ Ver(pk, M^*, σ^*), *or returns 0, otherwise.*

As we are concerned with structure-preserving schemes, we fix $\mathcal{R}(M, m)$ to a relation that returns 1 iff $M = G^m$ where G is a generator in a group. This relation is sufficient for our purpose, that is, combining with a partial one-time signature scheme described below. By letting $\mathcal{R}$ be a constant function $\mathcal{R} = 1$, we obtain a standard notion of *unforgeability against chosen-message attacks* (UF-CMA-secure) and denote its advantage function by $\mathsf{Adv}^{\mathsf{uf\text{-}cma}}_{\mathsf{SPS}}(\mathcal{A})$. UF-XCMA is slightly stronger than unforgeability against extended random message attacks (UF-XRMA) introduced by Abe et al. [2]. While UF-XRMA is relative to a preliminary fixed algorithm that chooses messages to sign, it is the adversary that selects messages in UF-XCMA. Thus, UF-XCMA implies UF-XRMA.

FROM UF-XCMA TO UF-CMA. In this paper, we focus on constructing UF-XCMA secure structure-preserving signature and then transform it to a UF-CMA secure SPS by using a partial one-time signature (POS) scheme [2,12] in the standard way [2,35]. POS is also known as two-tier signature schemes and is a variation of one-time signatures where parts of keys are updated after every signing. Here we recall useful definitions of POS and the transform.

Definition 4 (Partial One-Time Signature Scheme [12]). *A partial one-time signature scheme* POS *with respect to* PGGen *is a set of polynomial-time algorithms* $(\mathsf{G}, \mathsf{Update}, \mathsf{S}, \mathsf{V})$ *that, for* $par \xleftarrow{\$} \mathsf{PGGen}(1^\lambda)$:

- $\mathsf{G}(par)$ *generates a long-term public key* pk *and secret key* sk, *and implicitly defines the associated message space* $\mathcal{M}_o$ *and the one-time public key space* $\mathcal{K}_{opk}$.
- $\mathsf{Update}(par)$ *takes* par *as input, and outputs a one-time key pair* (opk, osk).
- $\mathsf{S}(sk, osk, \mathsf{M})$ *outputs a signature* σ *on message* M *based on* sk *and* osk.
- $\mathsf{V}(pk, opk, \mathsf{M}, \sigma)$ *outputs 1 for acceptance or 0 for rejection.*

(Perfect correctness). *For all* $(pk, sk) \xleftarrow{\$} \mathsf{G}(par)$, *all* $(opk, osk) \xleftarrow{\$} \mathsf{Update}(par)$, *all messages* $\mathsf{M} \in \mathcal{M}$, *and all* $\sigma \xleftarrow{\$} \mathsf{S}(sk, osk, \mathsf{M})$, $\mathsf{V}(pk, opk, \mathsf{M}, \sigma) = 1$ *holds.*

POS *is structure-preserving if* pk, opk, M, *and* σ *consist only elements of* $\mathbb{G}$, *and* V *evaluates group membership testing and pairing product equations.*

We require POS to be *unforgeable against one-time non-adaptive chosen-message attacks* (OT-nCMA), which is defined as follows.

Definition 5 (OT-nCMA Security). *A POS scheme is* unforgeable against one-time non-adaptive chosen-message attacks (OT-nCMA) *if for any algorithm* $\mathcal{A}$, *the following advantage function* $\mathsf{Adv}_{\mathsf{POS}}^{\mathsf{ncma}}(\mathcal{A})$ *is negligible in* λ,

$$\mathsf{Adv}_{\mathsf{POS}}^{\mathsf{ncma}}(\mathcal{A}) := \Pr\left[\mathrm{VER}(opk^*, \mathsf{M}^*, \sigma^*) = 1 \,\middle|\, \begin{array}{l} par \xleftarrow{\$} \mathsf{PGGen}(1^\lambda); \\ (opk^*, \sigma^*, \mathsf{M}^*) \xleftarrow{\$} \mathcal{A}^{\mathrm{INIT}, \mathrm{SIGN}(\cdot)}(par) \end{array} \right]$$

where

- INIT *runs* $(pk, sk) \xleftarrow{\$} \mathsf{G}(par)$, *initializes* $\mathcal{Q}_\mathsf{M}$ *with* $\emptyset$, *and returns* pk *to* $\mathcal{A}$.
- SIGN(M) *runs* $(opk, osk) \xleftarrow{\$} \mathsf{Update}(par)$ *and* $\sigma \xleftarrow{\$} \mathsf{S}(sk, osk, \mathsf{M})$, *and then returns* (opk, σ) *to* $\mathcal{A}$, *and records* $(opk, \mathsf{M}, \sigma)$ *to the list* $\mathcal{Q}_\mathsf{M}$.
- VER($opk^*, \sigma^*, \mathsf{M}^*$) *returns 1 if there exists* $(opk^*, \mathsf{M}, \sigma) \in \mathcal{Q}_\mathsf{M}$ *and* $\mathsf{M}^* \neq \mathsf{M}$ *and* $1 = \mathsf{V}(pk, opk^*, \mathsf{M}^*, \sigma^*)$, *or returns 0, otherwise.*

Let $\mathsf{POS} := (\mathsf{G}, \mathsf{Update}, \mathsf{S}, \mathsf{V})$ be a structure-preserving partially one-time signature scheme with message space $\mathcal{M}$ and one-time public key space $\mathcal{K}_{opk}$, and $\mathsf{xSPS} := (\mathsf{Gen}', \mathsf{Sign}', \mathsf{Ver}')$ be a structure-preserving signature scheme with message space $\mathcal{K}_{opk}$. The transformed UF-CMA secure SPS scheme, $\mathsf{SPS} := (\mathsf{Gen}, \mathsf{Sign}, \mathsf{Ver})$, is defined as follows.

Gen(par):	Sign(sk, M):	Ver(pk, M, σ):
$(pk_1, sk_1) \xleftarrow{\$} \mathsf{G}(\mathrm{par})$	$(opk, osk) \xleftarrow{\$} \mathsf{Update}(\mathrm{par})$	Parse $\sigma = (opk, \sigma_1, \sigma_2)$
$(pk_2, sk_2) \xleftarrow{\$} \mathsf{Gen}'(\mathrm{par})$	$\sigma_1 \xleftarrow{\$} \mathsf{S}(sk_1, osk, \mathrm{M})$	If $\mathsf{V}(pk_1, opk, \mathrm{M}, \sigma_1) = 1$
$pk := (pk_1, pk_2)$	$\sigma_2 \xleftarrow{\$} \mathsf{Sign}'(sk_2, opk)$	$\wedge \mathsf{Ver}'(pk_2, opk, \sigma_2) = 1$
$sk := (sk_1, sk_2)$	Return $(opk, \sigma_1, \sigma_2)$	then return 1
Return (pk, sk)		Else return 0

The correctness and structure-preserving property of SPS are implied by those of POS and xSPS in a straightforward way. The following theorem ([2, Theorem 3]) states UF-CMA security of SPS.

Theorem 1. *If POS is OT-nCMA secure and xSPS is UF-XRMA secure, then SPS defined as above is UF-CMA secure. In particular, for all adversaries $\mathcal{A}$ against UF-CMA security of SPS, there exist adversaries $\mathcal{B}$ against OT-nCMA security of POS and $\mathcal{C}$ against UF-XRMA security of xSPS with running times $\mathbf{T}(\mathcal{A}) \approx \mathbf{T}(\mathcal{B}) \approx \mathbf{T}(\mathcal{C})$ and $\mathsf{Adv}_{\mathsf{SPS}}^{\mathsf{uf\text{-}cma}}(\mathcal{A}) \leq \mathsf{Adv}_{\mathsf{POS}}^{\mathsf{ncma}}(\mathcal{B}) + \mathsf{Adv}_{\mathsf{xSPS}}^{\mathsf{uf\text{-}xcma}}(\mathcal{C})$.*

2.4 Public-Key Encryption Schemes

Definition 6 (Public-key encryption). *A Public-Key Encryption scheme consists of algorithms $\mathsf{PKE} := (\mathsf{Gen_P}, \mathsf{Enc}, \mathsf{Dec})$:*

- *The key generation algorithm $\mathsf{Gen_P}(\mathrm{par})$ takes $\mathrm{par} \xleftarrow{\$} \mathsf{PGGen}(1^\lambda)$ as input and generates a pair of public and secret keys (pk, sk). Message space $\mathcal{M}$ is implicitly defined by pk.*
- *The encryption algorithm $\mathsf{Enc}(pk, \mathrm{M})$ returns a ciphertext ct.*
- *The deterministic decryption algorithm $\mathsf{Dec}(sk, \mathsf{ct})$ returns a message M.*

(Perfect correctness). For all $\mathrm{par} \xleftarrow{\$} \mathsf{PGGen}(1^\lambda)$, $(pk, sk) \xleftarrow{\$} \mathsf{Gen_P}(\mathrm{par})$, messages $\mathrm{M} \in \mathcal{M}$, and $\mathsf{ct} \xleftarrow{\$} \mathsf{Enc}(pk, \mathrm{M})$, $\mathsf{Dec}(sk, \mathsf{ct}) = \mathrm{M}$ holds.

Definition 7 (IND-mCPA Security [9]). *A PKE scheme PKE is indistinguishable against multi-instance chosen-plaintext attack (IND-mCPA-secure) if for any $q_e \geq 0$ and for all adversaries $\mathcal{A}$ with access to oracle ENC at most q_e times the following advantage function $\mathsf{Adv}_{\mathsf{PKE}}^{\mathsf{mcpa}}(\mathcal{A})$ is negligible,*

$$\mathsf{Adv}_{\mathsf{PKE}}^{\mathsf{mcpa}}(\mathcal{A}) := \left| \Pr\left[b' = b \, \middle| \, \begin{array}{l} \mathrm{par} \xleftarrow{\$} \mathsf{PGGen}(1^\lambda); (pk, sk) \xleftarrow{\$} \mathsf{Gen_P}(\mathrm{par}); \\ b \xleftarrow{\$} \{0, 1\}; b' \xleftarrow{\$} \mathcal{A}^{\mathrm{ENC}(\cdot, \cdot)}(pk) \end{array} \right] - \frac{1}{2} \right|,$$

where $\mathrm{ENC}(\mathrm{M}_0, \mathrm{M}_1)$ runs $\mathsf{ct}^* \xleftarrow{\$} \mathsf{Enc}(pk, \mathrm{M}_b)$, and returns ct^* to $\mathcal{A}$.

Some public-key encryption schemes, e.g., ElGamal encryption [22] and Linear encryption [16], are structure-preserving and satisfy IND-mCPA security with tight reductions to compact assumptions such as DDH and the Decision Linear assumption [16], respectively (cf. [32]).

2.5   The Groth-Sahai Proof System

We recall the Groth-Sahai proof system and its properties as a commit-and-prove scheme. We follow definitions by Escala and Groth in [24] in a simplified form that is sufficient for our purpose. For a given pairing group $par \xleftarrow{\$} PGGen(1^\lambda)$, the GS proof system is a non-interactive zero-knowledge proof (NIZK) system for satisfiability of a set of equations over par. Let $\mathcal{L}_{par}$ be a family of NP languages defined over par. For a language $\mathcal{L} \in \mathcal{L}_{par}$, let $R_{\mathcal{L}} := \{(x, \omega) : x \in \mathcal{L} \text{ and } \omega \in W(x)\}$ be a witness relation, where $W(x)$ is the set of witnesses for $x \in \mathcal{L}$. As our construction fixes the language in advance, it is sufficient for our purpose to define the proof system to be specific to $\mathcal{L}$ as follows.

Definition 8 (The Groth-Sahai Proof System). *The Groth-Sahai commit-and-prove system for* $par \xleftarrow{\$} PGGen(1^\lambda)$ *and* $\mathcal{L} \in \mathcal{L}_{par}$ *consists of p.p.t. algorithms* $GS := (BG, Com, P, V)$ *that:*

- $BG(par)$ *is a binding common reference string generation algorithm that outputs* **crs**.
- $Com(\mathbf{crs}, \omega; r)$ *is a commitment algorithm that outputs a commitment* c *for given witness* ω *with randomness* $r \leftarrow R_c$ *and* **crs**.
- $P(\mathbf{crs}, (x, c), (\omega, r))$ *is a prover algorithm that returns a proof* ρ *on* $(x, \omega) \in R_{\mathcal{L}} \wedge c = Com(\mathbf{crs}, \omega; r)$.
- $V(\mathbf{crs}, x, c, \rho)$ *is a deterministic verification algorithm that returns 0 (reject) or 1 (accept).*

(Perfect correctness). *For all* $par \xleftarrow{\$} PGGen(1^\lambda)$, $\mathbf{crs} \xleftarrow{\$} BG(par)$, $(x, \omega) \in R_{\mathcal{L}}$, *and* $r \in R_c$, $V(\mathbf{crs}, x, c, P(\mathbf{crs}, (x, c), (\omega, r))) = 1$ *holds, where* $c \leftarrow Com(\mathbf{crs}, \omega; r)$.

When witness ω consists of several objects and only part of them are committed to c, commitments for the remaining part of the witness is prepared by P and included in the proof.

The following properties of the GS proof system are used in this paper. For fully formal treatment, we refer to [24].

Definition 9 (Security properties of the Groth-Sahai proof system). *The following properties hold for all* $par \xleftarrow{\$} PGGen(1^\lambda)$,

- *Perfect Soundness.* *For all* $\mathbf{crs} \in BG(par)$, *all* $x \notin \mathcal{L}$, *all* c, *and all* ρ, *we have* $V(\mathbf{crs}, x, c, \rho) = 0$.

- **CRS Indistinguishability.** *There exists a algorithm* HG, *called the hiding common reference string generator that, for all adversaries* $\mathcal{A}$, *the following advantage function is negligible,*

$$\mathsf{Adv}_{\mathsf{GS}}^{\mathsf{crsind}}(\mathcal{A}) := \left| \Pr \left[b' = b \,\middle|\, \begin{array}{l} \mathsf{par} \xleftarrow{\$} \mathsf{PGGen}(1^\lambda); \\ \mathbf{crs}_0 \xleftarrow{\$} \mathsf{BG}(\mathsf{par}); (\mathbf{crs}_1, \mathsf{trap}) \xleftarrow{\$} \mathsf{HG}(\mathsf{par}); \\ b \xleftarrow{\$} \{0,1\}; b' \xleftarrow{\$} \mathcal{A}(\mathbf{crs}_b) \end{array} \right] - \frac{1}{2} \right|.$$

- **Dual-mode Commitment.** *For all* $\mathbf{crs} \in \mathsf{BG}(\mathsf{par})$, Com *is perfectly binding. Namely, for all* $w_0 \neq w_1$, *we have* $\{c_0 \leftarrow \mathsf{Com}(\mathbf{crs}, w_0; r_0)\} \bigcap \{c_1 \leftarrow \mathsf{Com}(\mathbf{crs}, w_1; r_1)\} = \emptyset$ *(where the sets are taken over* $r_0, r_1 \in \mathcal{R}_c$*).*
  For all $(\mathbf{crs}, \mathsf{trap}) \in \mathsf{HG}(\mathsf{par})$, Com *is perfectly hiding. Namely, for all* $\omega_0 \neq \omega_1$, *the following two distributions are identical:* $\{c_0 \leftarrow \mathsf{Com}(\mathbf{crs}, \omega_0; r_0)\}$ *and* $\{c_1 \leftarrow \mathsf{Com}(\mathbf{crs}, \omega_1; r_1)\}$, *where* $r_0, r_1 \in \mathcal{R}_c$.
- **Perfect Zero-knowledge.** *There exists a simulator* Sim := (SimCom, SimP) *such that, for all* $(\mathbf{crs}, \mathsf{trap}) \in \mathsf{HG}(\mathsf{par})$, *and* $(x, \omega) \in R_{\mathcal{L}}$, *the following two distributions are identical:*

$$\{(\mathsf{c}, \rho) \mid r \xleftarrow{\$} \mathcal{R}_c; \mathsf{c} \leftarrow \mathsf{Com}(\mathbf{crs}, \omega; r); \rho \xleftarrow{\$} \mathsf{P}(\mathbf{crs}, (x, \mathsf{c}), (\omega, r))\}, and$$

$$\{(\mathsf{c}', \rho') \mid (\mathsf{c}', \gamma) \xleftarrow{\$} \mathsf{SimCom}(\mathbf{crs}, \mathsf{trap}); \rho' \xleftarrow{\$} \mathsf{SimP}(\mathbf{crs}, \mathsf{trap}, \gamma)\}.$$

Since the above distributions are identical, it also holds for reused commitment and multiple adaptively chosen statements x *that involve the same witness and commitment. This implies perfect witness indistinguishability: for* ω *and* ω' *with* $(x, \omega) \in R_{\mathcal{L}}$ *and* $(x, \omega') \in R_{\mathcal{L}}$ *the following two distributions are identical:*

$$\{(\mathsf{c}, \rho) \mid r \xleftarrow{\$} \mathcal{R}_c; \mathsf{c} \leftarrow \mathsf{Com}(\mathbf{crs}, \omega; r); \rho \xleftarrow{\$} \mathsf{P}(\mathbf{crs}, x, (\omega, r))\}, and$$

$$\{(\mathsf{c}', \rho') \mid r' \xleftarrow{\$} \mathcal{R}_c; \mathsf{c}' \leftarrow \mathsf{Com}(\mathbf{crs}, \omega'; r'); \rho' \xleftarrow{\$} \mathsf{P}(\mathbf{crs}, x, (\omega', r'))\}.$$

The GS proof system is structure-preserving for proving satisfiability of linear multi-scalar multiplication equations (MSEs) and a non-linear quadratic equation (QE). Regarding security, it is known that its CRS indistinguishability is tightly reduced to the SXDH assumption (cf. Theorem 5).

3   Generic Construction

In this section, we focus on a generic construction of a UF-XCMA-secure SPS scheme, xSPS. By coupling it with an off-the-shelf structure-preserving POS scheme, we obtain a UF-CMA-secure SPS scheme via Theorem 1.

3.1   Scheme Description

Let $\mathsf{par} \xleftarrow{\$} \mathsf{PGGen}(1^\lambda)$ be a set of system parameters. We represent a source group and its generator by $\mathbb{G}$ and G, respectively. Let $\mathsf{PKE} := (\mathsf{Gen_P}, \mathsf{Enc}, \mathsf{Dec})$

Gen(par):
$\mathbf{crs}_0, \mathbf{crs}_1 \xleftarrow{\$} \mathsf{BG}(par)$; For $i = 0, 1, 2 : (pk_i, sk_i) \xleftarrow{\$} \mathsf{Gen_P}(par)$

$x_0 \xleftarrow{\$} \mathbb{Z}_p$; $x_1 := x_2 := 0 \in \mathbb{Z}_p$; $r_0, r_1, r_2, t_0, t_1, t_2, t_3 \xleftarrow{\$} \mathcal{R}_c$
$\mathbf{c}_0 \leftarrow \mathsf{Com}(\mathbf{crs}_0, x_0; r_0)$; $\mathbf{c}_1 \leftarrow \mathsf{Com}(\mathbf{crs}_0, x_1; r_1)$; $\mathbf{c}_2 \leftarrow \mathsf{Com}(\mathbf{crs}_1, x_2; r_2)$
$\mathbf{k}_0 \leftarrow \mathsf{Com}(\mathbf{crs}_1, sk_0; t_0)$; $\mathbf{k}_1 \leftarrow \mathsf{Com}(\mathbf{crs}_1, sk_1; t_1)$; $\mathbf{k}_2 \leftarrow \mathsf{Com}(\mathbf{crs}_1, sk_2; t_2)$
$\mathbf{k}_3 \leftarrow \mathsf{Com}(\mathbf{crs}_0, sk_0; t_3)$
$pk := (\mathbf{crs}_0, \mathbf{crs}_1, (pk_i, \mathbf{c}_i)_{0 \le i \le 2}, (\mathbf{k}_i)_{0 \le i \le 3})$; $sk := ((sk_i, x_i, r_i)_{0 \le i \le 2}, (t_i)_{0 \le i \le 3})$
Return (pk, sk)

Sign$(sk, \mathsf{M} \in \mathbb{G})$:
$z_0 := z_1 := x_0$; $z_2 := 0$; For $i = 0, 1, 2 : \mathsf{ct}_i \xleftarrow{\$} \mathsf{Enc}(pk_i, G^{z_i})$
$\mathsf{ins}_0 := (pk_0, \mathsf{ct}_0, \mathsf{M})$; $\mathsf{cv}_0 := (\mathbf{c}_0, \mathbf{c}_1, \mathbf{k}_3)$; $w_0 := (x_0, x_1, sk_0)$; $R_0 := (r_0, r_1, t_3)$
$\mathsf{ins}_1 := (pk_i, \mathsf{ct}_i)_{0 \le i \le 2}$; $\mathsf{cv}_1 := (\mathbf{c}_2, (\mathbf{k}_i)_{0 \le i \le 2})$; $w_1 := (x_2, (sk_i)_{0 \le i \le 2})$
$R_1 := (r_2, (t_i)_{0 \le i \le 2})$
$\rho_0 \xleftarrow{\$} \mathsf{P}(\mathbf{crs}_0, (\mathsf{ins}_0, \mathsf{cv}_0), (w_0, R_0))$ //Prove that $\mathsf{ins}_0 \in \mathcal{L}_0$ and w_0 is committed to in cv_0
$\rho_1 \xleftarrow{\$} \mathsf{P}(\mathbf{crs}_1, (\mathsf{ins}_1, \mathsf{cv}_1), (w_1, R_1))$ //Prove that $\mathsf{ins}_1 \in \mathcal{L}_1$ and w_1 is committed to in cv_1
Return $\sigma := (\mathsf{ct}_0, \mathsf{ct}_1, \mathsf{ct}_2, \rho_0, \rho_1)$

Ver(pk, M, σ):
Parse $\sigma := ((\mathsf{ct}_i)_{0 \le i \le 2}, \rho_0, \rho_1)$
$\mathsf{ins}_0 := (pk_0, \mathsf{ct}_0, \mathsf{M})$; $\mathsf{cv}_0 := (\mathbf{c}_0, \mathbf{c}_1, \mathbf{k}_3)$; $\mathsf{ins}_1 := (pk_i, \mathsf{ct}_i)_{0 \le i \le 2}$; $\mathsf{cv}_1 := (\mathbf{c}_2, \mathbf{k}_0, \mathbf{k}_1, \mathbf{k}_2)$
Return $(\mathsf{V}(\mathbf{crs}_0, \mathsf{ins}_0, \mathsf{cv}_0, \rho_0) \wedge \mathsf{V}(\mathbf{crs}_1, \mathsf{ins}_1, \mathsf{cv}_1, \rho_1))$

Languages:
$\mathcal{L}_0 := \{ (pk_0, \mathsf{ct}_0, \mathsf{M}) \mid \exists x_0, x_1 \in \mathbb{Z}_p, sk_0 \in \mathcal{SK}$ s.t.
$\qquad G^{z_0} = G^{x_0} \mathsf{M}^{x_1} \wedge G^{z_0} = \mathsf{Dec}(sk_0, \mathsf{ct}_0) \wedge (pk_0, sk_0) \in \mathsf{Gen_P}(par) \}$
$\mathcal{L}_1 := \{ (pk_i, \mathsf{ct}_i)_{0 \le i \le 2} \mid \exists x_2 \in \mathbb{Z}_p, sk_0, sk_1, sk_2 \in \mathcal{SK}$ s.t.
$\qquad ((z_0 - z_1)(x_2 - z_2) = 0) \wedge_{i=0}^{2} (G^{z_i} = \mathsf{Dec}(sk_i, \mathsf{ct}_i) \wedge (pk_i, sk_i) \in \mathsf{Gen_P}(par)) \}$

Fig. 1. Our signature scheme xSPS.

be a PKE scheme, and GS := (BG, Com, P, V) be the Groth-Sahai proof system for languages $\mathcal{L}_0$ and $\mathcal{L}_1$ defined below. Our SPS scheme xSPS := (Gen, Sign, Ver) is defined in Fig. 1.

The correctness of xSPS is implied by that of the Groth-Sahai proof system, and the structure-preserving property is implied by that of the PKE scheme and the Groth-Sahai proof system.

Remark 1 (Role of proof ρ_0). The main role is to bind a message into a signature. In the real scheme, it is just a proof of the signing key x_0 in ct_0 (and $\mathbf{c}_0$) since x_1 is fixed to 0. Yet the proof is bound to message M through randomness r_1 used for committing to x_1. In the security proof, it can be seen as an encrypted one-time message authentication code (MAC) of M and forces the adversary to reuse given signatures since, intuitively, the adversary cannot generate a new MAC for hidden keys x_0 and x_1.

Remark 2 (Role of proof ρ_1). ρ_1 is used for partitioning. It proves that two ciphertexts ct_0 and ct_1 are consistent (namely, the same plaintext is encrypted) *or* the plaintext in the ciphertext ct_2 is committed to in c_2. In the real scheme, ρ_1 proves the consistency of double encryption ct_0 and ct_1. In the security proof, ρ_1 enables us to achieve two (seemingly incompatible) functionalities under a binding mode CRS. One is forcing the adversary to use consistent ciphertexts in its forgery. A simulator guesses z_2^* in the forgery and makes $x_2 \neq z_2^*$ hold. The other is letting the simulator use inconsistent ciphertexts in a special situation achieved using a partitioning technique (see Sect. 3.2 for more details). In that situation, the simulator can make $x_2 = z_2$ hold and use a real witness of ρ_0.

Remark 3 (On the range of z_2). The range of z_2 is $\mathbb{Z}_p$ since z_2 is the plaintext of ct_2. Readers might think we should bind z_2 on $\{0, 1\}$ by using a Groth-Sahai proof since the simulator in the security proof guesses z_2^* in the forgery as explained in the previous remark. This is not the case. In fact, even if an adversary uses z_2^* such that $z_2^* \notin \{0, 1\}$, it has no advantage because the simulator uses x_2 such that $x_2 \in \{0, 1\}$ in the security proof. Value z_2 affects ρ_1. However, to make a valid forgery by using $x_2 = z_2^*$ as a witness in ρ_1, adversaries have no choice but to use $z_2^* \in \{0, 1\}$ as long as $x_2 \in \{0, 1\}$. Accordingly, we do not need to bind z_2 on $\{0, 1\}$. This intuition is implemented formally in the proof of Lemma 14.

Remark 4 (On verifying correctness of pk). Verifying correctness of commitment k_i with respect to sk_i is not necessary for achieving UF-CMA security where keys are generated honestly by definition. But it may have to be verified (once for all at the time of publishing pk) if the scheme is used in an application where signers can be corrupted at the time of key generation.

Remark 5 (On XCMA and CMA security of xSPS). We prove that xSPS is UF-XCMA for efficiency though, in fact, we can prove xSPS is UF-CMA. When we prove UF-CMA, a simulator does not have exponents of queried messages, but the simulator must generate proofs ρ_0 for $x_1 \neq 0$ under the *binding mode* crs_0 in the security proof (see Sect. 3.3 for details). This is achievable if ρ_0 is generated as a proof of "pairing product equations (PPEs)" (in both the real and simulated schemes). If the simulator has exponents, then ρ_0 is generated as a proof of "(linear) multiscalar multiplication equations", which is more efficient than that of PPEs. We not only upgrade UF-XCMA to UF-CMA but also achieve an SPS scheme for vector messages by combining our xSPS with (partial) one-time signature at very low cost [2]. Thus, we select the UF-XCMA-secure scheme. See also Sect. 4 for efficiency.

3.2 Overview of Security Proof

Our main goal is to implement an additional check of $\mathcal{A}$'s forgery $\sigma^* := (ct_0^*, ct_1^*, ct_2^*, \rho_0^*, \rho_1^*)$. We not only verify Groth-Sahai proofs, but also check $Z_0^* \in \{G^{x_0} \cdot M_i^{x_1}\}_{i=1}^{q_s}$ for $Z_0^* \leftarrow \text{Dec}(sk_0, ct_0^*)$. That is, we will force $\mathcal{A}$ to *reuse* an M_i in queried messages for Z_0^* (we will set $x_1 := 1$ to achieve this during the game transitions). With $\mathbf{crs}_0$ for ρ_0^* being in the perfect soundness mode, $\mathcal{A}$ is forced to fulfill $G^{z_0^*} = G^{x_0} \cdot \mathsf{M}^*$. This leads to a contradiction and $\mathcal{A}$ never wins.

To change the success forgery condition, we replace the value $z_0 := x_0$ in signatures of the signing oracle and the additional forgery check with a value $z_0 := \mathbf{RF}_k(\mu|_k)$ where $\mathbf{RF}_k : \{0,1\}^k \to \mathbb{Z}_p$ is truly random, and $\mu|_k$ is the k-bit prefix of a random binary encoding $\mu \in \{0,1\}^L$ of a signed message $\mathsf{M} \in \mathbb{G}$, where L is the smallest even integer that is equal to or larger than the bit size of p. Note that encoding μ appears only in the security proof (not in the real scheme). We start with $\mathbf{RF}_0(\epsilon) := x_0$ for the empty string ϵ. We will introduce more dependencies of z_0 on x_2 and z_2^* in ct_2^*.

To increase the entropy of z_0 (this will make z_0 unpredictable for M^* and force $\mathcal{A}$ to reuse z_0 from the signing oracle) and eventually set $z_0 := \mathbf{RF}_L(\mu)$, we replace $z_0 := \mathbf{RF}_k(\mu|_k)$ with $z_0 := \mathbf{RF}_{k+1}(\mu|_{k+1})$ step by step. At each step, we partition the signature space into two halves according to the $(k+1)$-th bit of μ. The partitioning bit is dynamically changed by z_2^* hidden in ct_2^*. At the beginning of the game, the simulator guesses the bit z_2^* used in a forgery and aborts if the guess is incorrect (z_2^* is accessible with the decryption key sk_2). Signature queries are created with a case distinction depending on the $(k+1)$-th bit $\mu[k+1]$ of μ. If $\mu[k+1]$ is equal to the guessed z_2^* from the forgery, nothing is changed in the signing process. However, if $\mu[k+1]$ is different from z_2^*, we use another independent random function $\mathbf{RF}_k'$ and set $z_1 := \mathbf{RF}_k'(\mu|_k)$ in the generated signature (i.e., more randomness is supplied).

Note that at this point, we want to change the encrypted values z_0, z_1 in the generated signature, while being able to decrypt the value z_0^* from the forgery (to implement the additional check mentioned above). Intuitively, we can do so since the proved statement $(z_0 - z_1)(x_2 - z_2) = 0$ guarantees a consistent double encryption with $z_0 = z_1$ precisely when $x_2 \neq z_2$. Hence, if we initially set up x_2 as $1 - z_2^*$ (using our guess for z_2^*), it is possible for the simulator to generate inconsistent double encryptions (with $z_0 \neq z_1$) whenever $\mu[k+1] = z_2 \neq z_2^*$. On the other hand, a decryption key for either z_0^* or z_1^* can be used to implement the final check on the adversary's forgery (since $z_0^* = z_1^*$). These observations enable a Naor-Yung-like double encryption argument to modify the z_0, z_1 values in all generated signatures with $\mu[k+1] \neq z_2^*$.

After the above transition is iterated, all signatures are generated with (or checked for) $z_0 := z_1 := \mathbf{RF}_L(\mu)$ for a truly random function $\mathbf{RF}_L$. At this point, we can replace z_0 and z_1 with $z_0 := z_1 := \mathbf{RF}_L(\mu) + \mathsf{m}$ since $\mathbf{RF}_L(\mu)$ is an independently and uniformly random element.

We can replace $z_0 := z_1 := \mathbf{RF}_L(\mu) + \mathsf{m}$ with $z_0 := z_1 := x + \mathsf{m}$ in a similar way to the case from $\mathbf{RF}_0(\epsilon) = x$ to $\mathbf{RF}_L(\mu)$ (see the proof for details). Thus, we can force $\mathcal{A}$ to reuse an M_i in queried messages for Z_0^*, as we explained at the beginning of this section.

3.3   Security Proof

Theorem 2. *If* PKE *is* IND-mCPA-*secure and* GS *is a Groth-Sahai proof system, then* xSPS *(defined in Sect. 3.1) is* UF-XCMA-*secure. Particularly, for all* *adversaries $\mathcal{A}$, there exist adversaries $\mathcal{B}_1$ and $\mathcal{B}_2$ with running time $\mathbf{T}(\mathcal{B}_1) \approx \mathbf{T}(\mathcal{A}) \approx \mathbf{T}(\mathcal{B}_2)$ and*

$$\mathsf{Adv}_{\mathsf{xSPS}}^{\mathsf{uf\text{-}xcma}}(\mathcal{A}) \leq (8L+6)\mathsf{Adv}_{\mathsf{GS}}^{\mathsf{crsind}}(\mathcal{B}_1) + 12L \cdot \mathsf{Adv}_{\mathsf{PKE}}^{\mathsf{mcpa}}(\mathcal{B}_2) + \frac{4Lq_s}{p},$$

where L is the smallest even integer that is equal or larger than the bit size of p.

Proof. Let $\mathcal{A}$ be an adversary against UF-XCMA security of xSPS. We prove Theorem 2 via Games G_0–G_3 defined in Fig. 2. We use AdvG_i to denote the advantage of $\mathcal{A}$ in Game G_i.

G_0 is the real attack game. We have lemmata below.

Fig. 2. Games G_0–G_3 for the proof of Theorem 2. Boxed code is only executed in the games marked in the same box style at the top right of every procedure. Non-boxed code is always run. $\mathbf{F} : \mathbb{G} \to \mathbb{Z}_p$ is a truly random function. $\mathcal{L}_0$ and $\mathcal{L}_1$ are languages defined in Sect. 3.1.

Lemma 1. $\mathrm{AdvG}_0 = \mathsf{Adv}^{\mathsf{uf\text{-}cma}}_{\mathsf{xSPS}}(\mathcal{A})$.

Lemma 2 (G_0 to G_1). *There exist adversaries $\mathcal{B}_1$ against CRS indistinguishability of GS and $\mathcal{B}_2$ against IND-mCPA security of PKE with running times $\mathbf{T}(\mathcal{A}) \approx \mathbf{T}(\mathcal{B}_1) \approx \mathbf{T}(\mathcal{B}_2)$ and $\mathrm{AdvG}_0 \leq \mathrm{AdvG}_1 + (4L + 3) \cdot \mathsf{Adv}^{\mathsf{crsind}}_{\mathsf{GS}}(\mathcal{B}_1) + 6L \cdot \mathsf{Adv}^{\mathsf{mcpa}}_{\mathsf{PKE}}(\mathcal{B}_2) + \frac{2Lq_s}{p}$.*

We prove Lemma 2 in Sect. 3.4.

Lemma 3 (G_1 to G_2). $\mathrm{AdvG}_1 = \mathrm{AdvG}_2$.

Proof. The changes in G_2 are:

- Switching x_1 from 0 to 1: since c_1 is already simulated and is independent of x_1 in G_1, pk is distributed identically in both G_1 and G_2.
- Switching Z_0 and Z_1 from $G^{\mathbf{F}(\mathsf{M}_j)}$ to $G^{\mathbf{F}(\mathsf{M}_j)} \cdot \mathsf{M}_j$: since $\mathbf{F}$ is a truly random function, $\{G^{\mathbf{F}(\mathsf{M}_j)}\}_{j=1}^{q_s}$ and $\{G^{\mathbf{F}(\mathsf{M}_j)} \cdot \mathsf{M}_j\}_{j=1}^{q_s}$ are distributed identically.

Thus, games G_1 and G_2 are identical.

Lemma 4 (G_2 to G_3). *There exist adversaries $\mathcal{B}_1$ against CRS indistinguishability of GS and $\mathcal{B}_2$ against IND-mCPA security of PKE with running times $\mathbf{T}(\mathcal{A}) \approx \mathbf{T}(\mathcal{B}_1) \approx \mathbf{T}(\mathcal{B}_2)$ and $\mathrm{AdvG}_2 \leq \mathrm{AdvG}_3 + (4L + 3) \cdot \mathsf{Adv}^{\mathsf{crsind}}_{\mathsf{GS}}(\mathcal{B}_1) + 6L \cdot \mathsf{Adv}^{\mathsf{mcpa}}_{\mathsf{PKE}}(\mathcal{B}_2) + \frac{2Lq_s}{p}$.*

After switching $z_{0,i}$ and $z_{1,i}$ from $\mathbf{F}(\mathsf{M}_i)$ to $\mathbf{F}(\mathsf{M}_i) + m_i$ in G_2, G_3 switches them from $\mathbf{F}(\mathsf{M}_i) + m_i$ to $x_0 + m_i$, which is exactly the step from G_0 to G_1, but in a reverse direction. The proof of Lemma 4 is similar to that of Lemma 2. The details are found in the full version of this paper.

Lemma 5 (G_3). $\mathrm{AdvG}_3 = 0$.

Proof. In G_3, $\mathsf{crs}_0 \xleftarrow{\$} \mathsf{BG}(\mathsf{par})$ is in the binding mode. By the perfect soundness, $Z_0^* = G^{x_0} \cdot \mathsf{M}^*$ if $\mathsf{V}(\mathsf{crs}_0, (pk_0, \mathsf{ct}_0^*, \mathsf{M}^*), (c_0, c_1, k_3), \rho_0^*) = 1$. Since $\mathsf{M}^* \notin \mathcal{Q}_\mathsf{M}$, $Z_0^* \notin \{Z_{0,j} = G^{\mathbf{F}(\mathsf{M}_j)} \cdot \mathsf{M}_j\}_{j=1}^{q_s}$ always holds and $\mathrm{VER}(\mathsf{M}^*, \sigma^*)$ outputs 0.

Summarizing Lemmata 1–5, we have Theorem 2.

3.4   From G_0 to G_1: Proof of Lemma 2

In this section, we prove Lemma 2. The proof proceeds via Games H_0–H_3 and $\mathsf{H}_{4,0}$–$\mathsf{H}_{4,L}$ defined in Fig. 4 and Fig. 3 gives an overview of the game transitions. The advantage of $\mathcal{A}$ in Game H_i is denoted by AdvH_i.

We define $\mathsf{H}_0 := \mathsf{G}_0$ and have lemmata as follows.

Lemma 6 (H_0). $\mathrm{AdvH}_0 = \mathrm{AdvG}_0$.

Lemma 7 (H_0 to H_1). $\mathrm{AdvH}_1 = \mathrm{AdvH}_0$.

Game	$\mathbf{crs_0}$	$\mathbf{crs_1}$	$z_{0,i} = z_{1,i}$	ρ_0	Additional forgery check	Reduction
H_0	B	B	x_0	real	-	$\equiv G_0$
H_1	B	B	x_0	real	$Z_0^* \in \{G^{x_0}\}_{i=1}^{q_s}$	Soundness
H_2	H	B	x_0	real	$Z_0^* \in \{G^{x_0}\}_{i=1}^{q_s}$	CRS IND
H_3	H	B	x_0	sim	$Z_0^* \in \{G^{x_0}\}_{i=1}^{q_s}$	ZK
$H_{4,0}$	H	H	$\mathbf{RF}_0(\epsilon) := x_0$	sim	$Z_0^* \in \{G^{x_0}\}_{i=1}^{q_s}$	CRS IND
$H_{4,k}$	H	H	$\mathbf{RF}_k(\mu_i|_k)$	sim	$Z_{k \bmod 2}^* \in \{G^{\mathbf{RF}_k(\mu_i|_k)}\}_{i=1}^{q_s}$	Loop
$H_{4,k+1}$	H	H	$\mathbf{RF}_{k+1}(\mu_i|_{k+1})$	sim	$Z_{(k+1) \bmod 2}^* \in \{G^{\mathbf{RF}_{k+1}(\mu_i|_{k+1})}\}_{i=1}^{q_s}$	Loop
$H_{4,L}$	H	H	$\mathbf{RF}_L(\mu_i|_L)$	sim	$Z_0^* \in \{G^{\mathbf{RF}_L(\mu_i|_L)}\}_{i=1}^{q_s}$	Loop END
G_1	H	B	$\mathbf{F}(M_i) := \mathbf{RF}_L(\mu_i|_L)$	sim	$Z_0^* \in \{G^{\mathbf{RF}_L(\mu_i|_L)}\}_{i=1}^{q_s}$	CRS IND

Fig. 3. Overview of transitions in Lemma 2. In the "$\mathbf{crs_0}$" and "$\mathbf{crs_1}$" columns, "B" (resp. "H") means that commitments are perfectly binding and proofs are perfectly sound (resp. commitments are perfectly hiding and proofs are perfectly zero-knowledge). In the "ρ_0" column, "real" (resp. "sim") means that proofs are generated by using the real witness w_0 (resp. the trapdoor trap). In the "reduction" column, we write what kind of security is used. "Soundness" (resp. "ZK") means the perfect soundness (resp. zero-knowledge) of the Groth-Sahai proof system.

Proof. In H_1, $\mathbf{crs_0} \xleftarrow{\$} \mathsf{BG}(\mathsf{par})$ is in the binding mode and the GS proof for $\mathcal{L}_0$ is perfectly sound. Then $Z_0^* = G^{x_0}$ holds if ρ_0 is accepted. Thus, H_1 and H_0 are identical.

Lemma 8 (H_1 to H_2). *There exists an adversary $\mathcal{B}$ against CRS indistinguishability with running time $\mathbf{T}(\mathcal{B}) \approx \mathbf{T}(\mathcal{A})$ and $\mathsf{Adv}_{\mathsf{GS}}^{\mathsf{crsind}}(\mathcal{B}) \geq |\mathrm{AdvH}_2 - \mathrm{AdvH}_1|$.*

Proof. Games H_2 and H_1 only differ in the distribution of $\mathbf{crs_0}$ returned by INIT, namely, $\mathbf{crs_0}$ is in the hiding or binding mode. From that, we obtain a straightforward reduction to CRS indistinguishability of GS.

Lemma 9 (H_2 to H_3). $\mathrm{AdvH}_3 = \mathrm{AdvH}_2$.

Proof. Instead of using the prover algorithm P, H_3 generates ρ_0 and relevant commitments with the zero-knowledge simulator, Sim. By the perfect zero-knowledge property, $H_3 = H_2$.

In $H_{4,0}$, we syntactically define x_0 by $\mathbf{RF}_0(\epsilon)$ which is a fixed random element from $\mathbb{Z}_p$, and we have

Lemma 10 (H_3 to $H_{4,0}$). *There exists an adversary $\mathcal{B}$ against CRS indistinguishability of GS with running time $\mathbf{T}(\mathcal{B}) \approx \mathbf{T}(\mathcal{A})$ and $\mathsf{Adv}_{\mathsf{GS}}^{\mathsf{crsind}}(\mathcal{B}) \geq |\mathrm{AdvH}_{4,0} - \mathrm{AdvH}_3|$.*

Proof. The only difference between $H_{4,0}$ and H_3 is the simulation of $\mathbf{crs_1}$, which is generated by either BG (in H_3) or HG (in $H_{4,0}$) since $\mathbf{RF}_0(\epsilon) = x_0$ and $\mu_j|_0 = \epsilon$ for all $j \in [q_s]$. From that, we obtain a straightforward reduction to CRS indistinguishability of GS.

Fig. 4. Games H_0–H_3 and $H_{4,0}$–$H_{4,L}$ for the proof of Lemma 2. $\mathbf{RF}_k : \{0,1\}^k \to \mathbb{Z}_p$ is a truly random function. $\mu_i|k$ is the first k bits of μ_i.

Lemma 11 ($H_{4,k}$ to $H_{4,k+1}$). *There exist adversaries $\mathcal{B}_1$ against CRS indistinguishability of GS and $\mathcal{B}_2$ against IND-mCPA security of PKE with running times $\mathbf{T}(\mathcal{B}_1) \approx \mathbf{T}(\mathcal{B}_2) \approx \mathbf{T}(\mathcal{A})$ and $\mathrm{AdvH}_{4,k} - \mathrm{AdvH}_{4,k+1} \le 4\mathrm{Adv}_{\mathsf{GS}}^{\mathsf{crsind}}(\mathcal{B}_1) + 6\mathrm{Adv}_{\mathsf{PKE}}^{\mathsf{mcpa}}(\mathcal{B}_2) + \frac{2q_s}{p}$.*

Proof. We define the games between $H_{4,k}$ and $H_{4,k+1}$ in Fig. 5.

Lemma 12 ($H_{4,k}$ to $H_{4,k,1}$). $\mathrm{AdvH}_{4,k,1} = \mathrm{AdvH}_{4,k}$.

Proof. In $H_{4,k,1}$, x_2 is switched from 0 to $1 - \beta$, where $\beta \xleftarrow{\$} \{0,1\}$. Though $x_2 \ne z_{2,i}$ may happen in $H_{4,k,1}$, still $z_{0,i} = z_{1,i}$ holds and hence ins_1 is in $\mathcal{L}_1$ in both games. Thus commitment $c_2 \xleftarrow{\$} \mathsf{Com}(\mathbf{crs}_1, x_2)$ and proofs ρ_1 distribute identically in both games due to the witness indistinguishability under $\mathbf{crs}_1$ generated by $\mathsf{HG}(\mathrm{par})$. Thus, $\mathrm{AdvH}_{4,k,1} = \mathrm{AdvH}_{4,k}$.

Lemma 13 ($\mathsf{H}_{4,k,1}$ **to** $\mathsf{H}_{4,k,2}$)**.** *There exists an adversary $\mathcal{B}$ against* IND-mCPA *security of* PKE *with running time* $\mathbf{T}(\mathcal{B}) \approx \mathbf{T}(\mathcal{A})$ *and* $\mathsf{Adv}^{\mathsf{mcpa}}_{\mathsf{PKE}}(\mathcal{B}) \geq |\mathrm{AdvH}_{4,k,2} - \mathrm{AdvH}_{4,k,1}|$.

Proof. In $\mathsf{H}_{4,k,2}$, ct_2 encrypts $Z_{2,i} = G^{\mu_i[k+1]}$, instead of $Z_{2,i} = G^0$. Observe that sk_2 is used only in making commitment k_2 and proof ρ_1 with $\mathbf{crs}_1$ generated by $\mathsf{HG(par)}$ in both games. Thus we can construct a straightforward reduction to bound the difference by IND-mCPA security of PKE by using perfect zero-knowledge simulator Sim for making ρ_1 and relevant commitments.

Lemma 14 ($\mathsf{H}_{4,k,2}$ **to** $\mathsf{H}_{4,k,3}$)**.** $\mathrm{AdvH}_{4,k,3} = \frac{1}{2}\mathrm{AdvH}_{4,k,2}$.

<u>INIT:</u> // $\mathsf{H}_{4,k,(1\text{-}9)}$

$(\mathbf{crs}_0, \mathsf{trap}_0) \xleftarrow{\$} \mathsf{HG(par)}$; $(\mathbf{crs}_1, \mathsf{trap}_1) \xleftarrow{\$} \mathsf{HG(par)}$
For $j = 0, 1, 2$: $(pk_j, sk_j) \xleftarrow{\$} \mathsf{Gen_P(par)}$
$x_0 \xleftarrow{\$} \mathbb{Z}_p$; $x_1 := 0 \in \mathbb{Z}_p$;
$x_2 := 0$; $\beta \xleftarrow{\$} \{0,1\}; x_2 := 1 - \beta$
For $j = 0, 1$:
  $(\mathsf{c}_j, \gamma_j) \xleftarrow{\$} \mathsf{SimCom}(\mathbf{crs}_0, \mathsf{trap}_0)$
$r_2 \xleftarrow{\$} \mathcal{R}_c$; $\mathsf{c}_2 \leftarrow \mathsf{Com}(\mathbf{crs}_1, x_2; r_2)$
For $j = 0, 1, 2$:
  $t_j \xleftarrow{\$} \mathcal{R}_c$, $\mathsf{k}_j \leftarrow \mathsf{Com}(\mathbf{crs}_1, sk_j; t_j)$
$(\mathsf{k}_3, \gamma_2) \xleftarrow{\$} \mathsf{SimCom}(\mathbf{crs}_0, \mathsf{trap}_0)$
$pk := (\mathbf{crs}_0, \mathbf{crs}_1, (pk_j, \mathsf{c}_j)_{0 \leq j \leq 2}, (\mathsf{k}_j)_{0 \leq j \leq 3})$
$sk := ((sk_j, x_j, r_j)_{0 \leq j \leq 2}, (t_j)_{0 \leq j \leq 3}))$
Return pk

<u>SIGN$(\mathsf{M}_i, \mathsf{m}_i)$:</u> // $\mathsf{H}_{4,k,(2\text{-}8)}$, $\mathsf{H}_{4,k,(4\text{-}10)}$, $\mathsf{H}_{4,k,(6\text{-}10)}$

// $(\mathsf{M}_i, \mathsf{m}_i)$ is the i-th query $(1 \leq i \leq q_s)$
// μ_i is the binary encoding of M_i
If $\mathsf{M}_i \neq G^{\mathsf{m}_i}$ then return $\perp$
$z_{2,i} := 0$; $z_{2,i} := \mu_i[k+1] \in \mathbb{Z}_p$
$z_{0,i} := \mathbf{RF}_k(\mu_i|_k)$; $z_{0,i} := \mathbf{RF}_{k+1}(\mu_i|_{k+1})$
$z_{1,i} := \mathbf{RF}_k(\mu_i|_k)$; $z_{1,i} := \mathbf{RF}_{k+1}(\mu_i|_{k+1})$
For $j = 0, 1, 2$:
  $Z_{j,i} := G^{z_{j,i}}$; $\mathsf{ct}_j \xleftarrow{\$} \mathsf{Enc}(pk_j, Z_{j,i})$
$\mathsf{ins}_0 := (pk_0, \mathsf{ct}_0, \mathsf{M})$
$\mathsf{ins}_1 := (pk_i, \mathsf{ct}_i)_{0 \leq i \leq 2}$
$\mathsf{cv}_1 := (\mathsf{c}_2, (\mathsf{k}_i)_{0 \leq i \leq 2})$
$w_1 := (x_2, (sk_i)_{0 \leq i \leq 2})$
$R_1 := (r_2, (t_i)_{0 \leq i \leq 2})$
$\rho_0 \xleftarrow{\$} \mathsf{SimP}(\mathbf{crs}_0, \mathsf{trap}_0, \mathsf{ins}_0, \gamma_0, \gamma_1, \gamma_2)$
$\rho_1 \xleftarrow{\$} \mathsf{P}(\mathbf{crs}_1, (\mathsf{ins}_1, \mathsf{cv}_1), (w_1, R_1))$
Return $\sigma := ((\mathsf{ct}_j)_{0 \leq j \leq 2}, \rho_0, \rho_1)$

<u>VER(M^*, σ^*) :</u> // $\mathsf{H}_{4,k,(1\text{-}4)}$, $\mathsf{H}_{4,k,(3\text{-}7)}$, $\mathsf{H}_{4,k,(5\text{-}6)}$, $\mathsf{H}_{4,k,(7\text{-}10)}$

Parse $\sigma^* := ((\mathsf{ct}^*_j)_{0 \leq j \leq 2}, \rho^*_0, \rho^*_1)$
$Z^*_2 \leftarrow \mathsf{Dec}(sk_2, \mathsf{ct}^*_2)$; $b \xleftarrow{\$} \{0,1\}$
ABORT $:= (Z^*_2 \in \{1, G\} \wedge Z^*_2 = G^{1-\beta}) \vee (Z^*_2 \notin \{1, G\} \wedge b = 0)$
If ABORT $= 1$ then return 0
$Z^*_{k \bmod 2} \leftarrow \mathsf{Dec}(sk_{k \bmod 2}, \mathsf{ct}^*_{k \bmod 2})$; If $Z^*_{k \bmod 2} \notin \{G^{\mathbf{RF}_k(\mu_j|_k)}\}_{j=1}^{q_s}$ then return 0
$Z^*_{1-(k \bmod 2)} \leftarrow \mathsf{Dec}(sk_{1-(k \bmod 2)}, \mathsf{ct}^*_{1-(k \bmod 2)})$; If $Z^*_{1-(k \bmod 2)} \notin \{G^{\mathbf{RF}_k(\mu_j|_k)}\}_{j=1}^{q_s}$ then return 0
$Z^*_{1-(k \bmod 2)} \leftarrow \mathsf{Dec}(sk_{1-(k \bmod 2)}, \mathsf{ct}^*_{1-(k \bmod 2)})$; If $Z^*_{1-(k \bmod 2)} \notin \{G^{\mathbf{RF}_{k+1}(\mu_j|_{k+1})}\}_{j=1}^{q_s}$
then return 0
Return $(\mathsf{M}^* \notin \mathcal{Q}_\mathsf{M}) \wedge (\mathsf{Ver}(pk, \mathsf{M}^*, \sigma^*) = 1)$

Fig. 5. Games $\mathsf{H}_{4,k,1}$–$\mathsf{H}_{4,k,10}$ for the proof of Lemma 11. $\mu[k]$ is the k-th bit of μ and $\mu|_k$ is the first k bits of μ. $\mathbf{RF}_{k+1} : \{0,1\}^{k+1} \rightarrow \mathbb{Z}_p$ is a truly random functions (defined by Eq. (2)).

Proof. In $H_{4,k,3}$, β and b are independent of adversary's view and chosen uniformly at random. c_2 perfectly hides β since $\mathbf{crs}_1$ is generated by $\mathsf{HG}(\mathsf{par})$ and the simulation of SIGN is independent of β. Thus, the event ABORT is independent of adversary's success event and

$$\Pr[\text{ABORT}] = \Pr[(z_2^* \in \{0,1\}) \wedge z_2^* = 1 - \beta] + \Pr[z_2^* \notin \{0,1\} \wedge b = 0]$$
$$= \frac{1}{2}\Pr[z_2^* \in \{0,1\}] + \frac{1}{2}(1 - \Pr[z_2^* \in \{0,1\}]) = \frac{1}{2},$$

where z_2^* is the discrete log of Z_2^* based on G and independent of b. This only halves $\mathcal{A}$'s advantage. We note that, for all accepted forgeries in Games $H_{4,k,3}$ to $H_{4,k,8}$, the following equation holds:

$$z_2^* \neq x_2. \tag{1}$$

In the following games, we define the random function:

$$\mathbf{RF}_{k+1}(\mu|_{k+1}) := \begin{cases} \mathbf{RF}_k(\mu|_k) & (\mu[k+1] = \beta) \\ \mathbf{RF}_k'(\mu|_k) & (\mu[k+1] = 1 - \beta) \end{cases}, \tag{2}$$

where $\mathbf{RF}_k$ and $\mathbf{RF}_k'$ are two independent random functions from $\{0,1\}^k \to \mathbb{Z}_p$. By the definition, we note that $\mathbf{RF}_{k+1} : \{0,1\}^{k+1} \to \mathbb{Z}_p$ is a random function.

Lemma 15 ($H_{4,k,3}$ **to** $H_{4,k,4}$)**.** *There exists an adversary $\mathcal{B}$ against* IND-mCPA *security of* PKE *with running time* $\mathbf{T}(\mathcal{B}) \approx \mathbf{T}(\mathcal{A})$ *and* $\mathsf{Adv}_{\mathsf{PKE}}^{\mathsf{mcpa}}(\mathcal{B}) \geq |\mathsf{AdvH}_{4,k,4} - \mathsf{AdvH}_{4,k,3}|$.

Proof. In game $H_{4,k,4}$, $x_2 = z_{2,i}$ holds if $\mu_i[k+1] \neq \beta$; otherwise $z_{0,i} = z_{1,i}$. If $\mu_i[k+1] = \beta$, then $z_{0,i} = z_{1,i} = \mathbf{RF}_k(\mu_i|_k)$, otherwise $x_2 = z_{2,i} = 1-\beta$ by Eq. (2). Thus, in either case, $(z_{0,i} - z_{1,i})(x_2 - z_{2,i}) = 0$ holds and $\mathsf{ins}_1 \in \mathcal{L}_1$. Another difference between $\mathsf{AdvH}_{4,k,3}$ and $H_{4,k,4}$ is that ct_1 is a ciphertext either of $Z_{1,i} = G^{\mathbf{RF}_{k+1}(\mu_i|_{k+1})}$ (in $H_{4,k,4}$) or $Z_{1,i} = G^{\mathbf{RF}_k(\mu_i|_k)}$ (in $\mathsf{AdvH}_{4,k,3}$). Moreover, sk_1 is used only for making k_1 and ρ_1 with respect to $\mathbf{crs}_1$ generated by $\mathsf{HG}(\mathsf{par})$ in both games. Thus, as well as Lemma 13, we can construct a straightforward reduction to bound this difference by IND-mCPA-security of PKE using Sim for simulating ρ_1 and relevant commitments. Lemma 15 is concluded.

Lemma 16 ($H_{4,k,4}$ **to** $H_{4,k,5}$)**.** *There exists an adversary $\mathcal{B}$ against CRS indistinguishability of* GS *with running time* $\mathbf{T}(\mathcal{B}) \approx \mathbf{T}(\mathcal{A})$ *and* $2\mathsf{Adv}_{\mathsf{GS}}^{\mathsf{crsind}}(\mathcal{B}) \geq |\mathsf{AdvH}_{4,k,5} - \mathsf{AdvH}_{4,k,4}|$.

Proof. In $H_{4,k,5}$, VER rejects a forgery if $Z_{1-(k \bmod 2)}^* \notin \{G^{\mathbf{RF}_k(\mu_j|_k)}\}_{j=1}^{q_s}$ instead of using $Z_{k \bmod 2}^*$. In these games, Eq. (1) holds and we can switch $\mathbf{crs}_1$ to be binding and argue that $Z_{k \bmod 2}^* = Z_{1-(k \bmod 2)}^*$ by $z_2^* \neq x_2$ and the perfect soundness of GS for language $\mathcal{L}_1$. More formally, we prove that via the game sequence in Fig. 6. As shown in Lemma 15, ins_1 is always in $\mathcal{L}_1$ and we can construct a straightforward reduction to show that there exists an adversary $\mathcal{B}$ against CRS indistinguishability of GS with

$$\mathsf{Adv}_{\mathsf{GS}}^{\mathsf{crsind}}(\mathcal{B}) \geq |\mathsf{AdvH}_1' - \mathsf{AdvH}_{4,k,4}|.$$

Since $\mathbf{crs}_1$ is binding in both H'_1 and H'_2, by the perfect soundness of GS and Eq. (1), $Z^*_{k\bmod 2} = Z^*_{1-(k\bmod 2)}$ holds if ρ^*_1 gets verified. Hence, the changes between H'_1 and H'_2 are only conceptual, and thus $\mathrm{AdvH}'_2 = \mathrm{AdvH}'_1$. By the CRS indistinguishability of GS, we have $\mathrm{Adv}^{\mathrm{crsind}}_{\mathsf{GS}}(\mathcal{B}) \geq |\mathrm{AdvH}'_3 - \mathrm{AdvH}'_2|$. It is clear that $\mathrm{AdvH}'_3 = \mathrm{AdvH}_{4,k,5}$

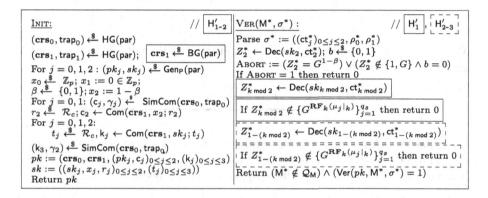

Fig. 6. Games H'_1–H'_3 for the proof of Lemma 16.

Lemma 17 ($\mathsf{H}_{4,k,5}$ to $\mathsf{H}_{4,k,6}$). *There exists an adversary $\mathcal{B}$ against IND-mCPA security of PKE with running time $\mathbf{T}(\mathcal{B}) \approx \mathbf{T}(\mathcal{A})$ and $\mathrm{Adv}^{\mathrm{mcpa}}_{\mathsf{PKE}}(\mathcal{B}) \geq |\mathrm{AdvH}_{4,k,6} - \mathrm{AdvH}_{4,k,5}|$.*

Proof. In $\mathsf{H}_{4,k,6}$, $z_{0,i} = z_{1,i}$ is used as w_1. It holds that $(z_{0,i} - z_{1,i})(x_2 - z_{2,i}) = 0$ and $\mathsf{ins}_1 \in \mathcal{L}_1$ as the case in $\mathsf{H}_{4,k,5}$. In the signing oracle of $\mathsf{H}_{4,k,6}$, ct_0 encrypts $Z_{0,i} = G^{\mathbf{RF}_{k+1}(\mu_i|_{k+1})}$ instead of $Z_{0,i} = G^{\mathbf{RF}_k(\mu_i|_k)}$. Observe that sk_0 is used only in making k_0 and ρ_1 with $\mathbf{crs}_1$ generated by $\mathsf{HG}(par)$ in both games. We thus can construct a straightforward reduction to bound the difference between $\mathsf{H}_{4,k,5}$ and $\mathsf{H}_{4,k,6}$ by IND-mCPA security using zero-knowledge simulator Sim for making ρ_1 and relevant commitments.

Lemma 18 ($\mathsf{H}_{4,k,6}$ to $\mathsf{H}_{4,k,7}$). $\mathrm{AdvH}_{4,k,6} \leq \mathrm{AdvH}_{4,k,7} + \frac{q_s}{p}$.

Proof. According to Eq. (2), the difference between $\mathsf{H}_{4,k,6}$ and $\mathsf{H}_{4,k,7}$ is that the accepted forgery with a $Z^*_{1-(k\bmod 2)}$ in either:

$$\mathcal{Z}_6 := \{G^{\mathbf{RF}_k(\mu_j|_k)}\}^{q_s}_{j=1}$$
$$= \underbrace{\{G^{\mathbf{RF}_k(\mu_j|_k)} : \mu_j[k+1] = \beta\}^{q_s}_{j=1}}_{=:S_1} \cup \{G^{\mathbf{RF}_k(\mu_j|_k)} : \mu_j[k+1] = 1-\beta\}^{q_s}_{j=1}$$

(in $\mathsf{H}_{4,k,6}$)

or

$$\mathcal{Z}_7 := \{G^{\mathbf{RF}_{k+1}(\mu_j|_{k+1})}\}_{j=1}^{q_s} = \mathcal{S}_1 \cup \{G^{\mathbf{RF}'_k(\mu_j|_k)} : \mu_j[k+1] = 1-\beta\}_{j=1}^{q_s} (\text{in } \mathsf{H}_{4,k,7}).$$

We note that, for those messages M where $\mu[k+1] = 1-\beta$ and $\mu|_k \in \mathcal{CM} := \{\mu_j|_k : \mu_j[k+1] = \beta\}_{j=1}^{q_s}$, the value $G^{\mathbf{RF}_k(\mu|_k)} \in \mathcal{S}_1$. Namely,

$$\mathcal{S}' := \mathcal{S}_1 \bigcap \{G^{\mathbf{RF}_k(\mu_j|_k)} : \mu_j[k+1] = 1-\beta\}_{j=1}^{q_s}$$
$$= \{G^{\mathbf{RF}_k(\mu_j|_k)} : \mu_j[k+1] = 1-\beta \wedge \mu_j|_k \in \mathcal{CM}\}_{j=1}^{q_s}.$$

We note that $\mathcal{S}'$ is not empty, since each element $G^{\mathbf{RF}_k(\mu_j|_k)}$ depends on k-bit prefix of μ_j. Thus, we can rewrite

$$\mathcal{Z}_6 = \mathcal{S}_1 \cup \underbrace{\{G^{\mathbf{RF}_k(\mu_j|_k)} : \mu_j[k+1] = 1-\beta \wedge \mu_j|_k \notin \mathcal{CM}\}_{j=1}^{q_s}}_{=:S_2}.$$

We define the following game $\mathsf{H}_{4,k,6'}$ between $\mathsf{H}_{4,k,6}$ and $\mathsf{H}_{4,k,7}$. $\mathsf{H}_{4,k,6'}$ simulates INIT and SIGN as in $\mathsf{H}_{4,k,6}$, but differs in simulating VER, where it only accepts forgery with $Z^*_{1-(k \bmod 2)} \in \mathcal{S}_1$. Precisely, $\mathsf{H}_{4,k,6'}$ simulates VER as follows:

- Parse $\sigma^* := ((\mathsf{ct}^*_j)_{0 \le j \le 2}, \rho^*_0, \rho^*_1)$.
- $Z^*_2 \leftarrow \mathsf{Dec}(sk_2, \mathsf{ct}^*_2)$. If $Z^*_2 \ne G^\beta$ then return 0.
- $Z^*_{1-(k \bmod 2)} \leftarrow \mathsf{Dec}(sk_{1-(k \bmod 2)}, \mathsf{ct}^*_{1-(k \bmod 2)})$. If $Z^*_{1-(k \bmod 2)} \notin \mathcal{S}_1$ then return 0.
- Return $(\mathsf{M}^* \notin \mathcal{Q}_\mathsf{M}) \wedge (\mathsf{Ver}(pk, \mathsf{M}^*, \sigma^*) = 1)$.

We note that the value $\mathbf{RF}_k(\mu|_k)$ is perfectly hidden from $\mathcal{A}$ for $\mu[k+1] = 1-\beta$ and $\mu|_k \notin \mathcal{CM}$ since $\mathcal{A}$ only learns $\mathbf{RF}'_k(\mu|_k)$ from SIGN by Eq. (2) and $\mathbf{RF}$ and $\mathbf{RF}'$ are two independent random functions. Thus, even an unbounded adversary $\mathcal{A}$ can output a value in $\mathcal{S}_2$ with probability at most q_s/p and the following holds,

$$\mathrm{AdvH}_{4,k,6} - \mathrm{AdvH}_{4,k,6'} \le \frac{q_s}{p}.$$

Compared to $\mathsf{H}_{4,k,6'}$, there are more valid forgeries in $\mathsf{H}_{4,k,7}$ and we have

$$\mathrm{AdvH}_{4,k,6'} \le \mathrm{AdvH}_{4,k,7}.$$

Thus, $\mathrm{AdvH}_{4,k,6} - \mathrm{AdvH}_{4,k,7} \le \frac{q_s}{p}$ and we conclude the lemma.

Lemma 19 ($\mathsf{H}_{4,k,7}$ to $\mathsf{H}_{4,k,8}$). $\mathrm{AdvH}_{4,k,8} = 2\mathrm{AdvH}_{4,k,7}$.

Proof. $\mathsf{H}_{4,k,8}$ accepts a forgery no matter if ABORT $= 1$ or not. By the same argument as in Lemma 14, this doubles the advantage of $\mathcal{A}$.

Note that we have stopped using sk_2 in $\mathsf{H}_{4,k,8}$. In $\mathsf{H}_{4,k,9}$, ct_2 encrypts $Z_{2,i} = G^0$ instead of $Z_{2,i} = G^{\mu_i[k+1]}$. By the same argument as Lemma 13, we have

Lemma 20 ($\mathsf{H}_{4,k,8}$ to $\mathsf{H}_{4,k,9}$). *There exists an adversary $\mathcal{B}$ against* IND-mCPA *security of* PKE *with running time* $\mathbf{T}(\mathcal{B}) \approx \mathbf{T}(\mathcal{A})$ *and* $\mathsf{Adv}^{\mathsf{mcpa}}_{\mathsf{PKE}}(\mathcal{B}) \ge |\mathrm{AdvH}_{4,k,9} - \mathrm{AdvH}_{4,k,8}|$.

Lemma 21 ($H_{4,k,9}$ to $H_{4,k,10}$). $AdvH_{4,k,10} = AdvH_{4,k,9}$.

Proof. In $H_{4,k,10}$, x_2 is switched from $1 - \beta$ to 0 and ρ_1 is generated by using P instead of Sim. Since crs_1 is generated by $HG(par)$, $c_2 \xleftarrow{\$} Com(crs_1, x_2)$ is distributed the same in both $H_{4,k,9}$ and $H_{4,k,10}$. So is ρ_1 by the perfect zero-knowledge property. Thus, $AdvH_{4,k,10} = AdvH_{4,k,19}$.

Lemma 22 ($H_{4,k,10}$ to $H_{4,k+1}$). $AdvH_{4,k+1} = AdvH_{4,k,10}$.

Proof. $H_{4,k,10}$ simulates INIT and VER the same as in $H_{4,k}$ and $z_{0,i} = z_{1,i} = RF_{k+1}(\mu_i|_{k+1})$. Thus, $AdvH_{4,k,10} = AdvH_{4,k+1}$.

From Lemmata 12 to 17, we have

$$AdvH_{4,k} - 2AdvH_{4,k,6} \le |AdvH_{4,k} - 2AdvH_{4,k,6}| \le 4Adv_{GS}^{crsind}(\mathcal{B}_1) + 5Adv_{PKE}^{mcpa}(\mathcal{B}_2).$$

From Lemmata 19 to 22, we have

$$2AdvH_{4,k,7} - AdvH_{4,k+1} \le |2AdvH_{4,k,7} - AdvH_{4,k+1}| \le Adv_{PKE}^{mcpa}(\mathcal{B}_2).$$

As $2AdvH_{4,k,6} \le 2AdvH_{4,k,7} + \frac{2q_s}{p}$ (Lemma 18), we conclude Lemma 11 as

$$AdvH_{4,k} - AdvH_{4,k+1} \le 4Adv_{GS}^{crsind}(\mathcal{B}_1) + 6Adv_{PKE}^{mcpa}(\mathcal{B}_2) + 2q_s/p.$$

We syntactically define $\mathbf{F}(M_i) := \mathbf{RF}_L(\mu_i)$ in G_1 since the binary representation of a group element is unique and have

Lemma 23 ($H_{4,L}$ to G_1). *There exists an adversary $\mathcal{B}$ against CRS indistinguishability of GS with running time $\mathbf{T}(\mathcal{B}) \approx \mathbf{T}(\mathcal{A})$ and $Adv_{GS}^{crsind}(\mathcal{B}) \ge |AdvG_1 - AdvH_{4,L}|$.*

Proof. We note that L is the smallest even integer that is equal or larger than the bit size of p (namely, $L \bmod 2 = 0$). The only difference between G_1 and $H_{4,L}$ is the simulation of crs_1, which is generated by either BG (in G_1) or HG (in $H_{4,L}$) since $\mathbf{F}(M_i) = \mathbf{RF}_L(\mu_i)$. From that, we obtain a straightforward reduction to CRS indistinguishability of GS.

Combining Lemma 6 to 11 and Lemma 23, we have $AdvG_0 \le AdvG_1 + 3Adv_{GS}^{crsind}(\mathcal{B}_1) + L \cdot (4Adv_{GS}^{crsind}(\mathcal{B}_1) + 6Adv_{PKE}^{mcpa}(\mathcal{B}_2) + \frac{2q_s}{p})$ and conclude Lemma 2.

4   Instantiation

We instantiate our generic construction in Type-III bilinear groups under the SXDH assumption. Throughout this section, we denote group elements in $\mathbb{G}_1$ with plain upper-case letters, such as X, and elements in $\mathbb{G}_2$ such letters with tilde, such as $\tilde{X}$. By G and $\tilde{G}$, we denote generators for $\mathbb{G}_1$ and $\mathbb{G}_2$, respectively. Scalar values in $\mathbb{Z}_p$ are denoted with lower-case letters. We may also put a tilde to scalar values or other objects when they are related to group elements in $\mathbb{G}_2$ in a way that is clear from the context.

We begin with optimizations in Sect. 4.1 made on top of the generic construction. We then present a concrete scheme for signing unilateral messages in Sect. 4.2 and for bilateral messages in Sect. 4.3 followed by full details of the Groth-Sahai proofs in Sect. 4.4.

4.1 ElGamal Encryption with Common Randomness

Observe that relation $(z_0 - z_1)(x_2 - z_2) = 0$ in $\mathcal{L}_1$ is a quadratic equation and it can be proved efficiently by a GS proof if z_0 and z_1 are committed in the same group and z_2 is committed in the other group. Relevant encryptions should follow the deployment of groups. We thus build the first two ciphertexts, ct_0 and ct_1 in $\mathbb{G}_1$, and ct_2 in $\mathbb{G}_2$.

To gain efficiency, we consider using the same randomness for making ct_0 and ct_1. For this to be done without spoiling the security proof, it is sufficient that one of the ciphertext ct_b is perfectly simulated given the other ciphertext ct_{1-b}. Formally, we assume that there exists a function, say SimEnc, such that, for any key pairs $(pk, sk) \xleftarrow{\$} \mathsf{Gen}_\mathsf{P}(par)$ and $(pk', sk') \xleftarrow{\$} \mathsf{Gen}_\mathsf{P}(par)$, any messages m and m' in the legitimate message space, and any randomness s, it holds that $\mathsf{Enc}(pk', m'; s) = \mathsf{SimEnc}(sk', m', \mathsf{Enc}(pk, m; s))$. In [10], Bellare et al. formally defined such a property as *reproducibility*. Given reproducible PKE and its ciphertext $\mathsf{ct}_b \xleftarrow{\$} \mathsf{Enc}(pk_b, G^{z_b}; s)$, we can compute another ciphertext $\mathsf{ct}_{1-b} \xleftarrow{\$} \mathsf{SimEnc}(sk_{1-b}, G^{z_{1-b}}, \mathsf{ct}_b)$ without knowing sk_b or s. All reduction steps with respect to the CPA security of PKE go through using SimEnc and simulated GS proofs. Precisely, we use SimEnc in Lemma 15 to compute ct_0 from given ct_1. Similar adjustment applies to Lemma 17.

As shown in [10], ElGamal encryption (EG) is reproducible. Let (y, G^y) and $(y', G^{y'}) \in \mathbb{Z}_p \times \mathbb{G}_1$ be two key pairs of ElGamal encryption. Given ciphertext $(M \cdot (G^y)^s, G^s)$ of message M with s and public key G^y, one can compute $(M' \cdot (G^s)^{y'}, G^s)$ for any M' using secret key y'. It is exactly the same ciphertext obtained from the regular encryption with common randomness s. We thus encrypt z_0 and z_1 with ElGamal encryption in $\mathbb{G}_1$ using the same randomness and removing redundant G^s. For encrypting z_2, we also use ElGamal but in $\mathbb{G}_2$. Bellare et al. show that the multi-message chosen-plaintext security for each encryption holds under the DDH assumption in respective groups, which is directly implied by the SXDH assumption [9]. We thus have:

Theorem 3. *For all adversaries $\mathcal{A}$ against IND-mCPA security of EG, there exists an adversary $\mathcal{C}$ against the SXDH assumption with running time $\mathbf{T}(\mathcal{C}) \approx \mathbf{T}(\mathcal{A})$ and $\mathsf{Adv}^{\mathsf{mcpa}}_{\mathsf{PKE}}(\mathcal{A}) \leq 2\,\mathsf{Adv}^{\mathsf{sxdh}}_{\mathsf{PGGen}}(\mathcal{C}) + \frac{1}{p}$.*

4.2 Concrete Scheme for Unilateral Messages

We present a concrete scheme, $\mathsf{SPSu1}$, for signing messages in $\mathbb{G}_1$. We use a structure-preserving one-time signature scheme, $\mathsf{POSu1}$, taken from the results of Abe et al. [2], and the SXDH-based instantiation of GS proof system. The description of $\mathsf{POSu1}$ is blended into the description of $\mathsf{SPSu1}$. For the GS proofs, however, we only show concrete relations in this section and present details of computation in Sect. 4.4.

We use notations $[x]_i$ and $[\tilde{x}]_1$ as a shorthand of $\mathsf{Com}(\mathbf{crs}_i, x)$ and $\mathsf{Com}(\widetilde{\mathbf{crs}}_1, x)$, respectively. We abuse these notations to present witnesses in a relation. It is indeed useful to keep track which CRS and which source group is used to commit to a witness. This notational convention is used in the rest of the paper.

Scheme SPSu1: Let $\text{par} := (p, \mathbb{G}_1, \mathbb{G}_2, \mathbb{G}_T, e, G, \tilde{G})$ be a description of Type-III bilinear groups generated by $\mathsf{PGGen}(1^\lambda)$.

SPSu1.Gen(par). Generates $\mathbf{crs}_0$, and $(\mathbf{crs}_1, \widetilde{\mathbf{crs}}_1)$ as shown in (13). Picks $x_0 \xleftarrow{\$} \mathbb{Z}_p$ and set $x_1 = x_2 := 0$. Generates three ElGamal keys $\tilde{Y}_0 := \tilde{G}^{y_0}$, $\tilde{Y}_1 := \tilde{G}^{y_1}$, and $Y_2 := G^{y_2}$ where $y_i \xleftarrow{\$} \mathbb{Z}_p$ for $i = 0, 1, 2$. Then computes commitments

$$[x_0]_0 := \mathsf{Com}(\mathbf{crs}_0, x_0; r_{x00}), \qquad [x_1]_0 := \mathsf{Com}(\mathbf{crs}_0, x_1; r_{x10}),$$
$$[y_0]_0 := \mathsf{Com}(\mathbf{crs}_0, y_0; r_{y00}), \qquad [\tilde{x}_2]_1 := \mathsf{Com}(\widetilde{\mathbf{crs}}_1, x_2; r_{x21}),$$
$$[y_0]_1 := \mathsf{Com}(\mathbf{crs}_1, y_0; r_{y01}), \qquad [y_1]_1 := \mathsf{Com}(\mathbf{crs}_1, y_1; r_{y11}),$$
$$[\tilde{y}_2]_1 := \mathsf{Com}(\widetilde{\mathbf{crs}}_1, y_2; r_{y21})$$

as shown in Eq. (14). Generates a persistent key pair of POSu1 by $w \xleftarrow{\$} \mathbb{Z}_p^*$, $\gamma_i \xleftarrow{\$} \mathbb{Z}_p^*$, $\tilde{G}_r := \tilde{G}^w$, and $\tilde{G}_i := \tilde{G}_r^{\gamma_i}$ for $i = 1, \dots, n_1$. Outputs pk and sk defined as $pk := (G, \tilde{G}, \mathbf{crs}_0, \mathbf{crs}_1, \widetilde{\mathbf{crs}}_1, \tilde{Y}_0, \tilde{Y}_1, Y_2, [x_0]_0, [x_1]_0, [\tilde{x}_2]_1, [y_0]_0, [y_0]_1, [y_1]_1, [\tilde{y}_2]_1, \tilde{G}_r, \tilde{G}_1, \dots, \tilde{G}_{n_1})$, and $sk := (x_0, y_0, y_1, y_2, r_{x00}, r_{x10}, r_{x21}, r_{y00}, r_{y01}, r_{y11}, r_{y21}, w, \gamma_1, \dots, \gamma_{n_1})$, where par and pk are implicitly included in pk and sk, respectively.

SPSu1.Sign(sk, M). Given sk as defined above and $\mathsf{M} =: (M_1, \dots, M_{n_1}) \in \mathbb{G}_1^{n_1}$, proceeds as follows.

– Generate one-time POSu1 key pair $\alpha \xleftarrow{\$} \mathbb{Z}_p^*$ and $\tilde{A} := \tilde{G}^\alpha$, and compute a one-time signature, (Z, R), by

$$Z := G^{\alpha - \rho w} \quad \text{and} \quad R := G^\rho \prod_{i=1}^{n_1} M_i^{-\gamma_i}, \tag{3}$$

where $w, \gamma_1, \dots, \gamma_{n_1}$ are taken from sk, and ρ is chosen uniformly from $\mathbb{Z}_p$.
– Encrypt $z_0 = z_1 := x_0$, and $z_2 := 0$ as $(\tilde{E}_{z_0}, \tilde{E}_{z_1}, \tilde{E}_s) := (\tilde{G}^{z_0} \tilde{Y}_0^s, \tilde{G}^{z_1} \tilde{Y}_1^s, \tilde{G}^s)$ and $(E_{z_2}, E_t) := (G^{z_2} Y_2^t, G^t)$, where $s, t \xleftarrow{\$} \mathbb{Z}_p$.
– Commit to z_0, z_1, and z_2 by $[z_0]_0$, $[z_0]_1$, $[z_1]_1$, and $[\tilde{z}_2]_1$, as described in Eq. (14).
– Using $\mathbf{crs}_0$, commitments $[x_0]_0$, $[x_1]_0$, and $[y_0]_0$ in pk, and default commitment $[1]_0$ computed with randomness $0 \in \mathbb{Z}_p$, as shown in Eq. (15), compute GS proofs $\rho_{0,0}$ and $\rho_{0,1}$ for relations

$$\rho_{0,0} : \tilde{G}^{[z_0]_0} (\tilde{G}^{-1})^{[x_0]_0} (\tilde{A}^{-1})^{[x_1]_0} = 1, \text{ and} \qquad \text{(linear MSE in } \mathbb{G}_2) \quad (4)$$
$$\rho_{0,1} : \tilde{E}_{z_0}^{[1]_0} (\tilde{G}^{-1})^{[z_0]_0} (\tilde{E}_s^{-1})^{[y_0]_0} = 1 \qquad \text{(linear MSE in } \mathbb{G}_2) \quad (5)$$

that correspond to clauses $\tilde{G}^{z_0} = \tilde{G}^{x_0} \cdot \tilde{\mathsf{M}}^{x_1}$ for $\tilde{\mathsf{M}} := \tilde{A}$ and $(\tilde{E}_{z_0}, \tilde{E}_s) \in \mathsf{Enc}(\tilde{Y}_0, \tilde{G}^{z_0})$ in $\mathcal{L}_0$, respectively. Correctness of ElGamal secret-key is implicit by the use of $[y_0]_0$ in pk. This completes the proof for $\mathcal{L}_0$.

– Similarly, using $(\mathbf{crs}_1, \widetilde{\mathbf{crs}}_1)$ and default commitments $[1]_1$ and $[\tilde{1}]_1$, computes GS proofs $\rho_{1,0}, \rho_{1,1}, \rho_{1,2},$ and $\rho_{1,3}$ for relations

$$\rho_{1,0} : ([\tilde{x}_2]_1 - [\tilde{z}_2]_1)([z_0]_1 - [z_1]_1) = 0, \qquad \text{(non-linear QE)} \qquad (6)$$

$$\rho_{1,1} : \tilde{E}_{z_0}^{[1]_1}(\tilde{G}^{-1})^{[z_0]_1}(\tilde{E}_s^{-1})^{[y_0]_1} = 1, \qquad \text{(linear MSE in } \mathbb{G}_2) \qquad (7)$$

$$\rho_{1,2} : \tilde{E}_{z_1}^{[1]_1}(\tilde{G}^{-1})^{[z_1]_1}(\tilde{E}_s^{-1})^{[y_1]_1} = 1, \text{ and} \qquad \text{(linear MSE in } \mathbb{G}_2) \qquad (8)$$

$$\rho_{1,3} : E_{z_2}^{[\tilde{1}]_1}(G^{-1})^{[\tilde{z}_2]_1}(E_t^{-1})^{[\tilde{y}_2]_1} = 1, \qquad \text{(linear MSE in } \mathbb{G}_1) \qquad (9)$$

that correspond to clauses in $\mathcal{L}_1$ except for the correctness of ElGamal keys that is implicitly done by the use of commitments $[y_0]_1, [y_1]_1,$ and $[\tilde{y}_2]_1$ in pk. This completes the proof for $\mathcal{L}_1$.

– Output a signature $\sigma := (\tilde{A}, Z, R, \tilde{E}_{z_0}, \tilde{E}_{z_1}, \tilde{E}_s, E_{z_2}, E_t, [z_0]_0, [z_0]_1, [z_1]_1, [\tilde{z}_2]_1, \rho_{0,0}, \rho_{0,1}, \rho_{1,0}, \rho_{1,1}, \rho_{1,2}, \rho_{1,3})$.

SPSu1.Ver(pk, M, σ). Return 1 if all the following verifications are passed. Return 0, otherwise.

– Verify signature (Z, R) of POSu1 for $\mathsf{M} = (M_1, \ldots, M_{n_1})$ with one-time key $\tilde{A}$ by

$$e(G, \tilde{A}) = e(Z, \tilde{G}) \, e(R, \tilde{G}_r) \prod_{i=1}^{n_1} e(M_i, \tilde{G}_i). \qquad (10)$$

– Verify all GS proofs $\rho_{0,0}, \rho_{0,1}, \rho_{1,0}, \rho_{1,1}, \rho_{1,2}, \rho_{1,3}$ with commitments $[z_0]_0, [z_0]_1, [z_1]_1, [\tilde{z}_2]_1,$ and ciphertext $\tilde{E}_{z_0}, \tilde{E}_{z_1}, \tilde{E}_s, E_{z_2}, E_t$ in σ, using $[x_0]_0, [x_1]_0, [y_0]_0, [\tilde{x}_2]_1, [y_0]_1, [y_1]_1, [\tilde{y}_2]_1$ in pk, as expressed in Eqs. (17) and (19). Default commitments $[1]_1$ and $[\tilde{1}]_1$ are built on-the-fly following Eq. (15).

This completes the description of SPSu1.

PERFORMANCE. In Tables 1 and 2, we summarize the performance of SPSu1. Since computational cost largely depends on available resources and implementation, we only present basic dominant parameters. In bach verification, we consider the most aggressive case where all equations are wrapped into one. See Sect. 4.4 for more details about batch verification.

SECURITY. Regarding POSu1 used in the above construction, the following statement is proven in [2].

Theorem 4 ([2]). *POSu1 is OT-nCMA secure if the DDH_2 assumption holds with respect to* PGGen. *In particular, for all polynomial-time algorithms $\mathcal{A}$ there exists a polynomial-time algorithm $\mathcal{B}$ with* $\mathbf{T}(\mathcal{A}) \approx \mathbf{T}(\mathcal{B})$ *and* $\mathsf{Adv}_{\mathsf{POSu1}}^{\mathsf{ncma}}(\mathcal{A}) \leq \mathsf{Adv}_{\mathsf{PGGen}}^{\mathsf{ddh}_2}(\mathcal{B}) + 1/p.$

With asymmetric pairing groups, CRS indistinguishability of GS proof system is tightly reduced from the SXDH assumption. Namely, the following theorem holds.

Theorem 5 ([29]). *For all adversaries $\mathcal{A}$ against CRS indistinguishability of GS, there exists an adversary $\mathcal{B}$ with running time $\mathbf{T}(\mathcal{B}) \approx \mathbf{T}(\mathcal{A})$ and $\mathsf{Adv}_{\mathsf{GS}}^{\mathsf{crsind}}(\mathcal{A}) \leq 2 \cdot \mathsf{Adv}_{\mathsf{PGGen}}^{\mathsf{sxdh}}(\mathcal{B})$.*

Combining Theorems 1, 2, 3, 4 and 5, we have the following theorem.

Theorem 6. $\mathsf{SPSu1}$ *is* $\mathsf{UF\text{-}CMA}$ *if the SXDH assumption holds with respect to* PGGen. *In particular, for any polynomial-time algorithm $\mathcal{A}$, there exists a polynomial-time algorithm $\mathcal{B}$ that runs in almost the same as $\mathcal{A}$ and*

$$\mathsf{Adv}_{\mathsf{SPSu1}}^{\mathsf{uf\text{-}cma}}(\mathcal{A}) \leq (40L + 13) \cdot \mathsf{Adv}_{\mathsf{PGGen}}^{\mathsf{sxdh}}(\mathcal{B}) + \frac{4L(q_s + 3) + 1}{p}. \qquad (11)$$

If we have $L = \log_2 p = 256$ for the targeted 128-bit security level, for instance, the security loss of $\mathsf{SPSu1}$ is approximately in 13 bits ($2^{13.3}$).

4.3 Concrete Scheme for Bilateral Messages

To sign bilateral messages $(\mathsf{M}_1, \mathsf{M}_2) \in \mathbb{G}_1^{n_1} \times \mathbb{G}_2^{n_2}$, we use $\mathsf{SPSu1}$ in the previous section to sign $\mathsf{M}_1 \in \mathbb{G}_1^{n_1}$ and combine it with another POS, say $\mathsf{POSu2}$, that signs $\mathsf{M}_2 \in \mathbb{G}_2^{n_2}$. Since a one-time public key of $\mathsf{POSu2}$ is in $\mathbb{G}_1$, it can be appended to M_1 and authenticated by $\mathsf{SPSu1}$ by extending the message space to $\mathbb{G}_2^{n_1+1}$. The signing and verification procedure of $\mathsf{POSu2}$ is analogous to $\mathsf{POSu1}$ shown in the construction of $\mathsf{SPSu1}$ with $\mathbb{G}_1$ and $\mathbb{G}_2$ interchanged. $\mathsf{POSu2}$ is $\mathsf{OT\text{-}nCMA}$ if DDH_1 holds. Therefore, for the resulting scheme, that we denote SPSb, the following theorem holds by combining Theorem 6 and Theorem 4 for $\mathsf{POSu2}$.

PERFORMANCE. Regarding the performance of SPSb, the only difference from $\mathsf{SPSu2}$ is the cost due to $\mathsf{POSu2}$. Concrete numbers obtained by inspection of the scheme are shown in Tables 1 and 2.

SECURITY. Theorem 4 holds for $\mathsf{POSu2}$ under the DDH_1 assumption. Combining it with Theorem 6, we obtain the following.

Theorem 7. SPSb *is* $\mathsf{UF\text{-}CMA}$ *if the SXDH assumption holds with respect to* PGGen. *In particular, for any polynomial-time algorithm $\mathcal{A}$, there exists an algorithm $\mathcal{B}$ with $\mathbf{T}(\mathcal{B}) \approx \mathbf{T}(\mathcal{A})$ and*

$$\mathsf{Adv}_{\mathsf{SPSb}}^{\mathsf{uf\text{-}cma}}(\mathcal{A}) \leq (40L + 14) \cdot \mathsf{Adv}_{\mathsf{PGGen}}^{\mathsf{sxdh}}(\mathcal{B}) + \frac{4L(q_s + 3) + 2}{p}. \qquad (12)$$

4.4 Specific Groth-Sahai Proofs Under SXDH

Among wide variations of relations that are provable with GS proofs, our instantiation involves only three types of relations; linear multiscalar multiplication equations (MSEs) in $\mathbb{G}_1$ and $\mathbb{G}_2$, and non-linear quadratic equations (QEs). Witnesses are committed in either $\mathbb{G}_1$ or $\mathbb{G}_2$ depending on the relations to prove. We

Table 3. Sizes and computational costs for GS proofs in the SXDH assumption setting for relations used in our construction. Default generators G and $\tilde{G}$ are *not* included in CRS. Column #(s.mult) indicates number of scalar multiplications in $\mathbb{G}_1$ and $\mathbb{G}_2$ for generating object by counting multi-scalar multiplication as 1.5. Linear MSE and non-linear QE are specific to relations in Eqs. (4) to (9).

Object	#(elements)	#(s.mult)	Verification	
			#(equations)	#(pairings)
CRS in $\mathbb{G}_1$	$(3, 0)$	$(3, 0)$	-	-
CRS in $\mathbb{G}_2$	$(0, 3)$	$(0, 3)$	-	-
Commitment $[w]$ for $w \in \mathbb{Z}_p$	$(2, 0)$	$(3, 0)$	-	-
Commitment $[\tilde{w}]$ for $w \in \mathbb{Z}_p$	$(0, 2)$	$(0, 3)$	-	-
Commitment $[b]$ for $b \in \{0, 1\}$	$(2, 0)$	$(2, 0)$	-	-
Commitment $[\tilde{b}]$ for $b \in \{0, 1\}$	$(0, 2)$	$(0, 2)$	-	-
Proof of linear MSE in $\mathbb{G}_1$	$(1, 0)$	$(1.5, 0)$	2	4
Proof of linear MSE in $\mathbb{G}_2$	$(0, 1)$	$(0, 1.5)$	2	4
Proof of non-linear QE	$(2, 2)$	$(3, 3)$	4	16

summarize the space and computation complexity in Table 3 and give details in the sequel.

CRS Generation: Our construction includes three independent common reference strings, $\mathbf{crs}_0$ and $(\mathbf{crs}_1, \widetilde{\mathbf{crs}}_1)$ generated in the binding mode as

$$\mathbf{crs}_0 := \begin{pmatrix} G & Q_0 \\ U_0 & V_0 \end{pmatrix}, \quad \mathbf{crs}_1 := \begin{pmatrix} G & Q_1 \\ U_1 & V_1 \end{pmatrix}, \quad \widetilde{\mathbf{crs}}_1 := \begin{pmatrix} \tilde{G} & \tilde{Q}_1 \\ \tilde{U}_1 & \tilde{V}_1 \end{pmatrix}, \quad (13)$$

where, for $\chi_0, \xi_0, \chi_1, \xi_1, \tilde{\chi}_1, \tilde{\xi}_1 \xleftarrow{\$} \mathbb{Z}_p^*$, $Q_i := G^{\chi_i}$, $U_i := G^{\xi_i}$, $V_i := G^{\chi_i \xi_i}$ for $i = 0, 1$ and $\tilde{Q}_1 := \tilde{G}^{\tilde{\chi}_1}$, $\tilde{U}_1 := \tilde{G}^{\tilde{\xi}_1}$, $\tilde{V}_1 := \tilde{G}^{\tilde{\chi}_1 \tilde{\xi}_1}$.

Scalar Commitments: To commit to $x \in \mathbb{Z}_p$ under $\mathbf{crs}_i$, compute

$$[x]_i := \mathsf{Com}(\mathbf{crs}_i, x; r) := (U_i^x \, G^r, (V_i \, G)^x \, Q_i^r), \quad (14)$$

where $r \in \mathbb{Z}_p$ is a fresh randomness. A default commitment of $1 \in \mathbb{Z}_p$ uses $0 \in \mathbb{Z}_p$ as a randomness, namely,

$$[1]_i := \mathsf{Com}(\mathbf{crs}_i, 1; 0) := (U_i, V_i \, G). \quad (15)$$

Commitment $[\tilde{x}]_1$ is computed analogously using elements in $\widetilde{\mathbf{crs}}_1$.

Proof of Scalar MSE: Proof $\rho_{0,0}$ for relation (4) as a linear MSE in $\mathbb{G}_1$ consists of a single element $\pi_{0,0} \in \mathbb{G}_2$ computed as

$$\pi_{0,0} := \tilde{G}^{r_{z_0}} (\tilde{G}^{-1})^{r_{x_0}} (\tilde{A}^{-1})^{r_{x_1}}, \quad (16)$$

where r_{z_0}, r_{x_0}, and r_{x_1} are random coins used to commit to z_0, x_0, x_1 by $[\tilde{z}_0]_0$, $[\tilde{x}_0]_0$, $[\tilde{x}_1]_0$, respectively. It is verified by evaluating

$$e(C_{z_0,1}, \tilde{G})\, e(C_{x_0,1}, \tilde{G}^{-1})\, e(C_{x_1,1}, \tilde{A}^{-1}) = e(G, \pi_{0,0}), \text{ and}$$
$$e(C_{z_0,2}, \tilde{G})\, e(C_{x_0,2}, \tilde{G}^{-1})\, e(C_{x_1,2}, \tilde{A}^{-1}) = e(Q_0, \pi_{0,0}), \tag{17}$$

where $(C_{\mathsf{x},1}, C_{\mathsf{x},2}) := [\mathsf{x}]_0$ for $\mathsf{x} \in \{z_0, x_0, x_1\}$, and $\tilde{G}$ and Q_0 are taken from $\mathbf{crs}_0$.

Proofs $\rho_{0,1}$, $\rho_{1,1}$, and $\rho_{1,2}$, are for linear MSEs in exactly the same form as Eq. (4). They are generated and verified in the same manner as above.

Proof of Non-linear QE: Proof $\rho_{1,0}$ for non-linear QE (6) consists of $(\theta_{1,0,1}, \theta_{1,0,2}, \pi_{1,0,1}, \pi_{1,0,2}) \in \mathbb{G}_1^2 \times \mathbb{G}_2^2$ that, $\psi \xleftarrow{\$} \mathbb{Z}_p$,

$$\theta_{1,0,1} := U_1^{z_0(r_{x_2} - r_{z_2}) - z_1(r_{x_2} - r_{z_2})}\, G^{(x_2 - z_2)(z_0 - z_1) - \psi},$$
$$\theta_{1,0,2} := (V_1 G)^{z_0(r_{x_2} - r_{z_2}) - z_1(r_{x_2} - r_{z_2})}\, Q_1^{(x_2 - z_2)(z_0 - z_1) - \psi},$$
$$\pi_{1,0,1} := \tilde{U}_1^{x_2(r_{z_0} - r_{z_1}) - z_2(r_{z_0} - r_{z_1})}\, \tilde{G}^{\psi}, \text{ and} \tag{18}$$
$$\pi_{1,0,2} := (\tilde{V}_1 \tilde{G})^{x_2(r_{z_0} - r_{z_1}) - z_2(r_{z_0} - r_{z_1})}\, \tilde{Q}_1^{\psi},$$

where r_{x} is a random coin used to commit to x. The verification evaluates

$$e(C_{z_0,1} C_{z_1,1}^{-1}, \tilde{D}_{x_2,1})\, e(C_{z_0,1} C_{z_1,1}^{-1}, \tilde{D}_{z_2,1}^{-1}) = e(G, \pi_{1,0,1})\, e(\theta_{1,0,1}, \tilde{G}),$$
$$e(C_{z_0,2} C_{z_1,2}^{-1}, \tilde{D}_{x_2,1})\, e(C_{z_0,2} C_{z_1,2}^{-1}, \tilde{D}_{z_2,1}^{-1}) = e(Q_1, \pi_{1,0,1})\, e(\theta_{1,0,2}, \tilde{G}),$$
$$e(C_{z_0,1} C_{z_1,1}^{-1}, \tilde{D}_{x_2,2})\, e(C_{z_0,1} C_{z_1,1}^{-1}, \tilde{D}_{z_2,2}^{-1}) = e(G, \pi_{1,0,2})\, e(\theta_{1,0,1}, \tilde{Q}_1), \text{ and} \tag{19}$$
$$e(C_{z_0,2} C_{z_1,2}^{-1}, \tilde{D}_{x_2,2})\, e(C_{z_0,2} C_{z_1,2}^{-1}, \tilde{D}_{z_2,2}^{-1}) = e(Q_1, \pi_{1,0,2})\, e(\theta_{1,0,2}, \tilde{Q}_1),$$

where $(C_{\mathsf{x},1}, C_{\mathsf{x},2}) := [\mathsf{x}]_1$ for $\mathsf{x} \in \{z_0, z_1\}$, $(\tilde{D}_{\mathsf{y},1}, \tilde{D}_{\mathsf{y},2}) := [\tilde{\mathsf{y}}]_1$ for $\mathsf{y} \in \{x_2, z_2\}$, and other group elements are taken from $(\mathbf{crs}_1, \tilde{\mathbf{crs}}_1)$.

Batch Verification: The number of pairing computations in Eqs. (17) and (19) can be reduced when verifying proofs $\rho_{0,0}, \rho_{0,1}, \rho_{1,0}, \rho_{1,1}, \rho_{1,2}$ and $\rho_{1,3}$ at once by batch verification. By merging pairings with respect to G, $\tilde{G}$, Q_0, Q_1, $\tilde{Q}_1$, $\tilde{A}$, $\tilde{E}_{z_0}$, $\tilde{E}_s$, $\tilde{D}_{x_2,1}$, $\tilde{D}_{x_2,2}$, $\tilde{D}_{z_2,1}$, $\tilde{D}_{z_2,2}$, $\tilde{E}_{z_1}$, E_{z_2}, and E_t, we have a single pairing product equation consisting of 15 pairings. It will be merged further with the verification equations for the POS part that includes pairings involving G and $\tilde{G}$. For SPSu1, the batch verification equation consists of $n_1 + 16$ pairings, of which $n_1 + 1$ pairings are from POSu1. For SPSb, it consists of $n_1 + n_2 + 18$ pairings, of which $n_1 + n_2 + 3$ pairings are from POSb.

References

1. Abdalla, M., Fouque, P.-A., Lyubashevsky, V., Tibouchi, M.: Tightly-secure signatures from lossy identification schemes. In: Pointcheval, D., Johansson, T. (eds.) EUROCRYPT 2012. LNCS, vol. 7237, pp. 572–590. Springer, Heidelberg (2012). doi:10.1007/978-3-642-29011-4_34

2. Abe, M., Chase, M., David, B., Kohlweiss, M., Nishimaki, R., Ohkubo, M.: Constant-size structure-preserving signatures: generic constructions and simple assumptions. J. Cryptol. **29**(4), 833–878 (2016)

3. Abe, M., Fuchsbauer, G., Groth, J., Haralambiev, K., Ohkubo, M.: Structure-preserving signatures and commitments to group elements. J. Cryptol. **29**(2), 363–421 (2016)

4. Abe, M., Groth, J., Haralambiev, K., Ohkubo, M.: Optimal structure-preserving signatures in asymmetric bilinear groups. In: Rogaway, P. (ed.) CRYPTO 2011. LNCS, vol. 6841, pp. 649–666. Springer, Heidelberg (2011). doi:10.1007/978-3-642-22792-9_37

5. Acar, T., Lauter, K., Naehrig, M., Shumow, D.: Affine pairings on ARM. In: Abdalla, M., Lange, T. (eds.) Pairing 2012. LNCS, vol. 7708, pp. 203–209. Springer, Heidelberg (2013). doi:10.1007/978-3-642-36334-4_13

6. Aranha, D.F., Fuentes-Castañeda, L., Knapp, E., Menezes, A., Rodríguez-Henríquez, F.: Implementing pairings at the 192-bit security level. In: Abdalla, M., Lange, T. (eds.) Pairing 2012. LNCS, vol. 7708, pp. 177–195. Springer, Heidelberg (2013). doi:10.1007/978-3-642-36334-4_11

7. Attrapadung, N., Hanaoka, G., Yamada, S.: A framework for identity-based encryption with almost tight security. In: Iwata, T., Cheon, J.H. (eds.) ASIACRYPT 2015. LNCS, vol. 9452, pp. 521–549. Springer, Heidelberg (2015). doi:10.1007/978-3-662-48797-6_22

8. Barreto, P.S.L.M., Costello, C., Misoczki, R., Naehrig, M., Pereira, G.C.C.F., Zanon, G.: Subgroup security in pairing-based cryptography. In: Lauter, K., Rodríguez-Henríquez, F. (eds.) LATINCRYPT 2015. LNCS, vol. 9230, pp. 245–265. Springer, Cham (2015). doi:10.1007/978-3-319-22174-8_14

9. Bellare, M., Boldyreva, A., Micali, S.: Public-key encryption in a multi-user setting: security proofs and improvements. In: Preneel, B. (ed.) EUROCRYPT 2000. LNCS, vol. 1807, pp. 259–274. Springer, Heidelberg (2000). doi:10.1007/3-540-45539-6_18

10. Bellare, M., Boldyreva, A., Staddon, J.: Randomness re-use in multi-recipient encryption schemeas. In: Desmedt, Y.G. (ed.) PKC 2003. LNCS, vol. 2567, pp. 85–99. Springer, Heidelberg (2003). doi:10.1007/3-540-36288-6_7

11. Bellare, M., Rogaway, P.: The exact security of digital signatures-how to sign with RSA and rabin. In: Maurer, U. (ed.) EUROCRYPT 1996. LNCS, vol. 1070, pp. 399–416. Springer, Heidelberg (1996). doi:10.1007/3-540-68339-9_34

12. Bellare, M., Shoup, S.: Two-Tier signatures, strongly unforgeable signatures, and Fiat-Shamir without random oracles. In: Okamoto, T., Wang, X. (eds.) PKC 2007. LNCS, vol. 4450, pp. 201–216. Springer, Heidelberg (2007). doi:10.1007/978-3-540-71677-8_14

13. Blazy, O., Fuchsbauer, G., Izabachène, M., Jambert, A., Sibert, H., Vergnaud, D.: Batch Groth-Sahai. In: Zhou, J., Yung, M. (eds.) ACNS 2010. LNCS, vol. 6123, pp. 218–235. Springer, Heidelberg (2010). doi:10.1007/978-3-642-13708-2_14

14. Blazy, O., Kiltz, E., Pan, J.: (Hierarchical) Identity-based encryption from affine message authentication. In: Garay, J.A., Gennaro, R. (eds.) CRYPTO 2014. LNCS, vol. 8616, pp. 408–425. Springer, Heidelberg (2014). doi:10.1007/978-3-662-44371-2_23

15. Boneh, D., Boyen, X.: Secure identity based encryption without random oracles. In: Franklin, M. (ed.) CRYPTO 2004. LNCS, vol. 3152, pp. 443–459. Springer, Heidelberg (2004). doi:10.1007/978-3-540-28628-8_27

16. Boneh, D., Boyen, X., Shacham, H.: Short group signatures. In: Franklin, M. (ed.) CRYPTO 2004. LNCS, vol. 3152, pp. 41–55. Springer, Heidelberg (2004). doi:10.1007/978-3-540-28628-8_3

17. Camenisch, J., Dubovitskaya, M., Haralambiev, K., Kohlweiss, M.: Composable and modular anonymous credentials: definitions and practical constructions. In: Iwata, T., Cheon, J.H. (eds.) ASIACRYPT 2015. LNCS, vol. 9453, pp. 262–288. Springer, Heidelberg (2015). doi:10.1007/978-3-662-48800-3_11

18. Chase, M., Kohlweiss, M.: A new hash-and-sign approach and structure-preserving signatures from DLIN. In: Visconti, I., Prisco, R. (eds.) SCN 2012. LNCS, vol. 7485, pp. 131–148. Springer, Heidelberg (2012). doi:10.1007/978-3-642-32928-9_8

19. Chatterjee, S., Koblitz, N., Menezes, A., Sarkar, P.: Another look at tightness II: practical issues in cryptography. Cryptology ePrint Archive, Report 2016/360 (2016). http://eprint.iacr.org/2016/360

20. Chen, J., Wee, H.: Fully, (Almost) tightly secure ibe and dual system groups. In: Canetti, R., Garay, J.A. (eds.) CRYPTO 2013. LNCS, vol. 8043, pp. 435–460. Springer, Heidelberg (2013). doi:10.1007/978-3-642-40084-1_25

21. Chevallier-Mames, B.: An efficient CDH-based signature scheme with a tight security reduction. In: Shoup, V. (ed.) CRYPTO 2005. LNCS, vol. 3621, pp. 511–526. Springer, Heidelberg (2005). doi:10.1007/11535218_31

22. ElGamal, T.: A public key cryptosystem and a signature scheme based on discrete logarithms. In: Blakley, G.R., Chaum, D. (eds.) CRYPTO 1984. LNCS, vol. 196, pp. 10–18. Springer, Heidelberg (1985). doi:10.1007/3-540-39568-7_2

23. Enge, A., Milan, J.: Implementing Cryptographic pairings at standard security levels. In: Chakraborty, R.S., Matyas, V., Schaumont, P. (eds.) SPACE 2014. LNCS, vol. 8804, pp. 28–46. Springer, Cham (2014). doi:10.1007/978-3-319-12060-7_3

24. Escala, A., Groth, J.: Fine-tuning Groth-Sahai proofs. In: Krawczyk, H. (ed.) PKC 2014. LNCS, vol. 8383, pp. 630–649. Springer, Heidelberg (2014). doi:10.1007/978-3-642-54631-0_36

25. Gay, R., Hofheinz, D., Kiltz, E., Wee, H.: Tightly CCA-secure encryption without pairings. In: Fischlin, M., Coron, J.-S. (eds.) EUROCRYPT 2016. LNCS, vol. 9665, pp. 1–27. Springer, Heidelberg (2016). doi:10.1007/978-3-662-49890-3_1

26. Granger, R., Page, D., Smart, N.P.: High security pairing-based cryptography revisited. In: Hess, F., Pauli, S., Pohst, M. (eds.) ANTS 2006. LNCS, vol. 4076, pp. 480–494. Springer, Heidelberg (2006). doi:10.1007/11792086_34

27. Grewal, G., Azarderakhsh, R., Longa, P., Hu, S., Jao, D.: Efficient implementation of bilinear pairings on ARM processors. In: Knudsen, L.R., Wu, H. (eds.) SAC 2012. LNCS, vol. 7707, pp. 149–165. Springer, Heidelberg (2013). doi:10.1007/978-3-642-35999-6_11

28. Groth, J.: Simulation-sound NIZK proofs for a practical language and constant size group signatures. In: Lai, X., Chen, K. (eds.) ASIACRYPT 2006. LNCS, vol. 4284, pp. 444–459. Springer, Heidelberg (2006). doi:10.1007/11935230_29

29. Groth, J., Sahai, A.: Efficient non-interactive proof systems for bilinear groups. SIAM J. Comput. 41(5), 1193–1232 (2012)

30. Hofheinz, D.: Algebraic partitioning: fully compact and (almost) tightly secure cryptography. In: Kushilevitz, E., Malkin, T. (eds.) TCC 2016. LNCS, vol. 9562, pp. 251–281. Springer, Heidelberg (2016). doi:10.1007/978-3-662-49096-9_11

31. Hofheinz, D.: Adaptive partitioning. In: Coron, J.-S., Nielsen, J.B. (eds.) EURO-CRYPT 2017. LNCS, vol. 10212, pp. 489–518. Springer, Cham (2017). doi:10.1007/978-3-319-56617-7_17

32. Hofheinz, D., Jager, T.: Tightly secure signatures and public-key encryption. Des. Codes Crypt. **80**(1), 29–61 (2016)

33. Jutla, C.S., Roy, A.: Improved structure preserving signatures under standard bilinear assumptions. Cryptology ePrint Archive, Report 2017/025 (2017)

34. Katz, J., Wang, N.: Efficiency improvements for signature schemes with tight security reductions. In: ACM CCS 2003, pp. 155–164. ACM Press (2003)

35. Kiltz, E., Pan, J., Wee, H.: Structure-preserving signatures from standard assumptions, revisited. In: Gennaro, R., Robshaw, M. (eds.) CRYPTO 2015. LNCS, vol. 9216, pp. 275–295. Springer, Heidelberg (2015). doi:10.1007/978-3-662-48000-7_14

36. Kim, T., Barbulescu, R.: Extended tower number field sieve: a new complexity for the medium prime case. In: Robshaw, M., Katz, J. (eds.) CRYPTO 2016. LNCS, vol. 9814, pp. 543–571. Springer, Heidelberg (2016). doi:10.1007/978-3-662-53018-4_20

37. Libert, B., Joye, M., Yung, M., Peters, T.: Concise multi-challenge CCA-secure encryption and signatures with almost tight security. In: Sarkar, P., Iwata, T. (eds.) ASIACRYPT 2014. LNCS, vol. 8874, pp. 1–21. Springer, Heidelberg (2014). doi:10.1007/978-3-662-45608-8_1

38. Libert, B., Peters, T., Joye, M., Yung, M.: Compactly hiding linear spans - tightly secure constant-size simulation-sound QA-NIZK proofs and applications. In: Iwata, T., Cheon, J.H. (eds.) ASIACRYPT 2015. LNCS, vol. 9452, pp. 681–707. Springer, Heidelberg (2015). doi:10.1007/978-3-662-48797-6_28

39. Libert, B., Peters, T., Yung, M.: Short group signatures via structure-preserving signatures: standard model security from simple assumptions. In: Gennaro, R., Robshaw, M. (eds.) CRYPTO 2015. LNCS, vol. 9216, pp. 296–316. Springer, Heidelberg (2015). doi:10.1007/978-3-662-48000-7_15

40. Schäge, S.: Tight proofs for signature schemes without random oracles. In: Paterson, K.G. (ed.) EUROCRYPT 2011. LNCS, vol. 6632, pp. 189–206. Springer, Heidelberg (2011). doi:10.1007/978-3-642-20465-4_12

41. Scott, M.: On the efficient implementation of pairing-based protocols. In: Chen, L. (ed.) IMACC 2011. LNCS, vol. 7089, pp. 296–308. Springer, Heidelberg (2011). doi:10.1007/978-3-642-25516-8_18

42. Verma, R.: Efficient implementations of pairing-based cryptography on embedded systems. Ph.D. thesis, Rochester Institute of Technology, New York, USA (2015)

Snarky Signatures: Minimal Signatures of Knowledge from Simulation-Extractable SNARKs

Jens Groth$^{(\boxtimes)}$ and Mary Maller

University College London, London, UK
{j.groth,mary.maller.15}@ucl.ac.uk

Abstract. We construct a pairing based simulation-extractable SNARK (SE-SNARK) that consists of only 3 group elements and has highly efficient verification. By formally linking SE-SNARKs to signatures of knowledge, we then obtain a succinct signature of knowledge consisting of only 3 group elements.

SE-SNARKs enable a prover to give a proof that they know a witness to an instance in a manner which is: (1) *succinct* - proofs are short and verifier computation is small; (2) *zero-knowledge* - proofs do not reveal the witness; (3) *simulation-extractable* - it is only possible to prove instances to which you know a witness, even when you have already seen a number of simulated proofs.

We also prove that any pairing based signature of knowledge or SE-NIZK argument must have at least 3 group elements and 2 verification equations. Since our constructions match these lower bounds, we have the smallest size signature of knowledge and the smallest size SE-SNARK possible.

1 Introduction

Non-Interactive Zero-Knowledge (NIZK) arguments enable a prover to convince a verifier that they know a witness to an instance being member of a language in NP, whilst revealing no information about this witness. Recent works have looked into building NIZK arguments that are efficient enough to use in scenarios where a large number of proofs need to be stored and where verifiers have limited computational resources. Such arguments are called succinct NIZK arguments, or zk-SNARKs (zero-knowledge Succinct Non-interactive Arguments of Knowledge). A weakness of zk-SNARKs is that they are, currently without exception, susceptible to man-in-the-middle attacks. As a result, any application intending to use zk-SNARKs has to take additional measures to ensure security e.g. signing the instance and proof. Conversely, schemes that do not require succinctness can take advantage of a primitive called Signatures of Knowledge (SoKs).

J. Groth—The research leading to these results has received funding from the European Research Council under the European Union's Seventh Framework Programme (FP/2007-2013)/ERC Grant Agreement n. 307937

M. Maller—Supported by a scholarship from Microsoft Research.

J. Katz and H. Shacham (Eds.): CRYPTO 2017, Part II, LNCS 10402, pp. 581–612, 2017.
DOI: 10.1007/978-3-319-63715-0_20

Signatures of knowledge [16, 17] generalise signatures by replacing the public key with an instance in an NP-language. A signer who holds a witness for the instance can create signatures, and somebody who does not know a witness for the instance cannot sign. SoKs should not reveal the witness, since this would enable others to sign with respect to the same witness. Chase and Lysyanskaya [17] therefore define signatures of knowledge to be simulatable: if you have a trapdoor associated with some public parameters, you can simulate the signature without the witness, and hence the signature cannot be disclosing information about the witness. Moreover, in the spirit of strong existential unforgeability for digital signatures, we want it to be the case that even after seeing many signatures under different instances, it should still not be possible to create a new signature unless you know a witness. Chase and Lysyanskaya capture this property through the notion of simulation-extractability where you may obtain arbitrary simulated signatures, but still not create a new signature not seen before unless you know the witness for the instance.

Both zk-SNARKs and SoKs are key building blocks in cryptographic applications, including but not limited to: ring signatures, group signatures, policy based signatures, cryptocurrencies, anonymous delegatable credentials and direct anonymous attestation [3, 5, 6, 22, 44].

Our Contribution. We construct a succinct simulation-extractable NIZK argument, or an SE-SNARK. Our construction is pairing based. Given three groups with a bilinear map $e : \mathbb{G}_1 \times \mathbb{G}_2 \mapsto \mathbb{G}_T$, our proofs consist of only 3 group elements from the source groups: 2 from $\mathbb{G}_1$ and 1 from $\mathbb{G}_2$. The proofs also have fast verification with verifiers needing to check just 2 pairing product equations.

By exploring the link between SoKs and SE-NIZK arguments, we show that our construction also yields a succinct SoK. We formally define the notions of succinct SoKs and SE-SNARKs. Then we construct SoKs from SE-NIZK arguments and collision resistant hash functions, and also prove the reverse implication that SoKs give rise to SE-NIZK arguments. Our SoK inherits the high efficiency of the SE-SNARK, in particular that it consists of only 3 group elements.

We also prove a lower bound: a pairing based SE-NIZK argument for a non-trivial language in NP must have at least 2 verification equations and 3 group elements. Due to our proof that any pairing based SoK yields a pairing based SE-NIZK (where the signature size equals the proof size and the number of verification equations are equal), this lower bound also applies to the signature size and the number of verification equations in SoKs. Our constructions are therefore optimal with respect to size and number of verification equations. We note that the lower bound improves on previous lower bounds on standard NIZK arguments by explicitly taking advantage of the simulation-extractability properties in the proof.

Our construction of an SE-NIZK argument compares well with the state of the art pairing based zk-SNARKs. Groth [36] gave a 3 element zk-SNARK, however, it is not simulation-extractable and it only has a proof of security in the generic group model. While we pay a price in computational efficiency, our simulation-extractable SNARK matches the size of Groth's zk-SNARK. We also get comparable verification complexity and unlike Groth's zk-SNARK we give a security proof based on concrete intractability assumptions instead of relying on the full generic group model. Ben-Sasson, Chiesa, Tromer, and Virza gave an 8 element zk-SNARK which is also not simulation extractable, however they do have smaller prover computation [4]. Compared to other pairing based zk-SNARKs in the literature we have both the simulation-extractability property and also better efficiency. In Table 1 we give a comparison of our simulation-extractable SNARK with these prior zk-SNARKs.

Table 1. Comparison for arithmetic circuit satisfiability with ℓ element instance, m wires, n multiplication gates. Since our work uses squarings gates, we have conservatively assumed n multiplication gates translate to $2n$ squaring gates; if a circuit natively has many squaring gates our efficiency would therefore improve compared to Groth and BCTV. Units: $\mathbb{G}$ means group elements, E means exponentiations and P means pairings.

	Groth	BCTV	This work
CRS size	$m + 2n + 3\ \mathbb{G}_1\ n + 3\ \mathbb{G}_2$	$6m + n - \ell\ \mathbb{G}_1\ m\ \mathbb{G}_2$	$m + 4n + 5\ \mathbb{G}_1\ 2n + 3\ \mathbb{G}_2$
Proof size	$2\ \mathbb{G}_1,\ 1\ \mathbb{G}_2$	$7\ \mathbb{G}_1,\ 1\ \mathbb{G}_2$	$2\ \mathbb{G}_1,\ 1\ \mathbb{G}_2$
Prover comp.	$m + 3n - \ell + 3\ E_1\ n + 1\ E_2$	$6m + n - \ell\ E_1\ m\ E_2$	$m + 4n - \ell\ E_1\ 2n\ E_2$
Verifier comp.	$\ell\ E_1,\ 3\ P$	$\ell\ E_1,\ 12\ P$	$\ell\ E_1,\ 5\ P$
Vfy Eq.	1	5	2

Our construction of a succinct signature of knowledge is the first in any computational model. This reduces the size of the signatures, albeit at the expense of having more public parameters. For applications where the public parameters need only be generated once, such as DAA and anonymous cryptocurrencies, this can be advantageous. A comparison with the most efficient prior signature of knowledge by Bernhard, Fuchsbauer and Ghadafi [6] is given in Table 2. The BFG scheme uses standard assumptions, as opposed to ours which uses knowledge extractor assumptions. It is difficult to directly compare computational efficiency since the languages are different; our work uses arithmetic circuits whereas the BFG scheme uses satisfiability of a set of pairing product equations. Therefore, we get better efficiency for arithmetic circuits and they get better efficiency for pairing product equations. However, what is clear is that we make big efficiency gains in terms of the signature size and the number of verification equations.

Techniques and Challenges. Standard definitions of signatures of knowledge [17] and simulation-extractable NIZK proofs [34] assume the ability to encrypt the witness, which can then be decrypted using a secret extraction key. However, since we are interested in having succinct signatures and proofs, we do not have space to send a ciphertext. Instead we give new definitions that use

Table 2. Comparison of signatures of knowledge schemes. We use m and n for the number of wires and multiplication gates in our arithmetic curcuit, λ refers to the security parameter; $|w|$ is the witness size and n_p is the number of pairing product equations in BFG (one can translate an arithmetic circuit to pairing product equations, in which case $n_p = n$). Size is measured in number of group elements and computation in the number of exponentiations.

	BFG	This work
Public parameters	$10 + \lambda$	$8 + 6n + m$
Signer computation	$\Omega(|w| + n_p)$	$m + 6n$
Signature size	$O(m + n_p)$	3
Verification equations	$O(n_p)$	2

non-black-box extraction. Roughly, the definitions say that given the signer's or prover's state it is possible to extract a witness if it succeds in creating a valid signature or proof.

To formalise the close link between SoKs and SE-NIZK arguments, we illustrate how to build a relation which includes the signature's message as part of the instance to be proved. Given an SE-NIZK for this relation, we build an SoK for the same relation only without the message encoded. This SoK is built solely from a collision resistant hash function and the SE-NIZK argument. The SoK is proven to be simulation-extractable directly from the definition of simulation-extractability of the NIZK argument. Once this link has been formalized, the rest of the paper focuses on how to build SE-SNARKs with optimum efficiency.

Our SE-SNARK is pairing based. The common reference string describes a bilinear group and some group elements, the proofs consist of group elements, and the verifier checks that the exponents of the proofs satisfy quadratic equations by calculating products of pairings. The underlying relation is a square arithmetic program, which is a SNARK-friendly characterisation of arithmetic circuits. Square arithmetic programs are closely related to quadratic arithmetic programs [30], but use only squarings instead of arbitrary multiplications. As suggested by Groth [36] the use of squarings give nice symmetry properties, which in our case makes it possible to check different parts of the proof against each other and hence make it intractable for an adversary to modify them without knowing a witness.

The security of our construction is based on concrete intractability assumptions. For standard knowledge soundness our strongest intractability assumption is similar to the power knowledge of exponent assumption used in [19]. To go beyond knowledge soundness to the stronger simulation-extractability property requires a stronger assumption, probably unavoidably so. We formulate the eXtended Power Knowledge of Exponent (XPKE) assumption, which assumes that an adversary cannot find elements in two source groups that have a linear relationship between each other unless it already knows what this relationship is - not even if it can query an oracle for functions of these exponents.

Finally, we rely on Groth's [36] definition of pairing based non-interactive arguments and rule out the existence of SE-NIZK arguments with 1 verification equation or 2 group elements. Groth [36] already ruled out 1 element NIZK arguments by exploiting that if there is only one group element then the verification equations are linear in the exponents and easy to fool. It is an open problem from [36] whether regular NIZK arguments can have 2 group element proofs, a more difficult problem since a pairing of two group elements gives rise to quadratic verification equations in the exponents. We show that in the case of SE-NIZK arguments 2 group elements is not possible by leveraging the simulation-extractability property to deal also with quadratic verification equations.

Related Work. Signatures of knowledge are a core ingredient in many cryptographic protocols. For example, [6,7,15,26,29,52] are DAA schemes that use SoKs. Anonymous cryptocurrencies can also be constructed using signatures of knowledge, for example Zero-Coin [44]. In order to make sufficient efficiency gains so that it could be deployed, the Zcash cryptocurrency [48] instead uses zk-SNARKs. To use zk-SNARKs, Zcash has to take extra steps to avoid malleability (MiTM) attacks. Specifically, Zcash samples a key pair for a one-time signature scheme; computes MACs to "tie" the signing key to the identities secret keys; modifies the instance to include signature verifying key and the MACs; and finally uses the signing key to sign the transaction. However, the use of succinct SoKs for cryptocurrencies would yield the same, if not better, efficiency as the use of zk-SNARKs and the resulting models would be simpler.

NIZK proofs originated with Blum, Feldman and Micali [2,12] and there has been many works making both theoretical advances and efficiency improvements [18,20,21,25,31,35,37,41]. Groth, Ostrovsky and Sahai [38] proposed the first pairing based NIZK proofs and subsequent works [34,39] have yielded efficient NIZK proofs that can be used in pairing based protocols. NIZK proofs with unconditional soundness need to be linear in the witness size. However, for NIZK arguments with computational soundness it is possible to get succinct proofs that are smaller than the size of the witness [40,43].

The practical improvements have been accompanied by theoretical works on how SNARKs compose [4,8,51] and on the necessity of using strong cryptographic assumptions when building SNARKs [1,9,11,14,32]. The latter works give methods to take SNARKs with long common reference strings and build SNARKs with common reference string size that is independent of the instance size, i.e., fully succinct SNARKs. Using these techniques on our simulation-extractable SNARK, which has a long common reference string, gives a fully succinct SE-SNARK.

Simulation-soundness of NIZK proofs was a notion introduced by Sahai [47] to capture the notion that even after seeing simulated proofs it is not possible to create a fake proof for a false instance unless copying a previous simulated proof. Combining this with proofs of knowledge, Groth [34] defined the even stronger security notion that we should be able to extract a witness from an adversary that creates a valid new proof, even if this adversary has seen many simulated proofs for arbitrary instances. Faust, Kohlweiss, Marson, and Venturi discuss how to achieve simulation soundness in the random oracle model [24]. Kosba et al. [46] discuss how to lift any zk-SNARK into a simulation-extractable one, however they do so by appending an encryption of the witness to the proof, so the result is not succinct.

Camenisch [16] coined the term signatures of knowledge to capture zero-knowledge protocols relying on techniques used in Schnorr signatures [49]. Signatures of knowledge have been used in many constructions albeit without a precise security definition. Chase and Lysyanskaya [17] gave the first formal definition of signatures of knowledge. They also broke the tight connection with Schnorr signatures and NIZK arguments based on cyclic groups and the Fiat-shamir heuristic and instead provided a general construction from simulation-sound NIZK proofs and dense public key encryption. An alternative definition of signatures of knowledge was given by Fischlin and Onete [27] which requires witness indistinguishability as opposed to full zero-knowledge.

2   Definitions

2.1   Notation

We write $y = A(x; r)$ when algorithm A on input x and randomness r, outputs y. We write $y \leftarrow A(x)$ for the process of picking randomness r at random and setting $y = A(x; r)$. We use the abbreviation PPT for probabilistic polynomial time. We also write $y \leftarrow S$ for sampling y uniformly at random from the set S. We will assume it is possible to sample uniformly at random from sets such as $\mathbb{Z}_p$. For an algorithm $\mathcal{A}$ we define $\mathsf{trans}_\mathcal{A}$ to be a list containing all of $\mathcal{A}$'s inputs and outputs, including random coins.

When considering security of our cryptographic schemes, we will assume there is an adversary $\mathcal{A}$. The security of our schemes will be parameterised by a security parameter $\lambda \in \mathbb{N}$. The intuition is that the larger the security parameter, the better security we get. For functions $f, g : \mathbb{N} \rightarrow [0; 1]$ we write $f(\lambda) \approx g(\lambda)$ if $|f(\lambda) - g(\lambda)| = \lambda^{-\omega(1)}$. We say a function f is negligible if $f(\lambda) \approx 0$ and overwhelming if $f(\lambda) \approx 1$. We will always implicitly assume all participants and the adversary know the security parameter, i.e., from their input they can efficiently compute the security parameter in unary representation 1^λ.

We use games in security definitions and proofs. A game $\mathcal{G}$ has a number of procedures including a main procedure. The main procedure outputs either 0 or 1 depending on whether the adversary succeeds or not. $\Pr[\mathcal{G}]$ denotes the probability that this output is 1.

2.2   Relations

Let $\mathcal{R}$ be a relation generator that given a security parameter λ in unary returns a polynomial time decidable relation $R \leftarrow \mathcal{R}(1^\lambda)$ in NP. For $(\phi, w) \in R$ we call ϕ the instance and w the witness. We define $\mathcal{R}_\lambda$ to be the set of possible relations $\mathcal{R}(1^\lambda)$ might output.

2.3   Hard Decisional Problems

A relation R is sampleable if there are two algorithms, Yes and No such that:

- Yes samples instances and witnesses in the relation.
- No samples instances outside the language L_R defined by the relation.

When proving our lower bounds for the efficiency of SE-NIZK arguments, we will assume the existence of sampleable relations where it is hard to tell whether an instance ϕ has been sampled by Yes or No.

Definition 2.1. *Let $\mathcal{R}$ a relation generator, and let* Yes, No *be two PPT algorithms such that for $(R, \text{aux}) \leftarrow \mathcal{R}(1^\lambda)$ we have* $\text{Yes}(R) \rightarrow (\phi, w) \in R$ *and* $\text{No}(R) \rightarrow \phi \notin L_R$, *and let $\mathcal{A}$ be an adversary. Define* $\mathbf{Adv}^{DP}_{\mathcal{R}, \text{Yes}, \text{No}, \mathcal{A}}(1^\lambda) = 2\Pr[\mathcal{G}^{DP}_{\mathcal{R}, \text{Yes}, \text{No}, \mathcal{A}}(1^\lambda)] - 1$ *where $\mathcal{G}^{DP}_{\mathcal{R}, \text{Yes}, \text{No}, \mathcal{A}}(1^\lambda)$ is given by*

$$\text{MAIN } \mathcal{G}^{DP}_{\mathcal{R}, \text{Yes}, \text{No}, \mathcal{A}}(\lambda)$$

$(R, \text{aux}) \leftarrow \mathcal{R}(1^\lambda); \ \phi_0 \leftarrow \text{No}(R); \ (\phi_1, w) \leftarrow \text{Yes}(R)$
$b \leftarrow \{0, 1\}; \ b' \leftarrow \mathcal{A}(R, \text{aux}, \phi_b)$
return 1 if $b = b'$ and else return 0

We say Yes, No *is a hard decisional problem for $\mathcal{R}$ if for all PPT adversaries $\mathcal{A}$,* $\mathbf{Adv}^{DP}_{\mathcal{R}, \text{Yes}, \text{No}, \mathcal{A}}(1^\lambda) \approx \frac{1}{2}$.

2.4   Signatures of Knowledge

Signatures of knowledge [17] (SoKs) generalise digital signatures by replacing the public key with an instance in a language in NP. If you have a witness for the instance, you can sign a message. If you do not know a witness, then you cannot sign. The notion of SoKs mimic digital signatures with strong existential unforgeability; even if you have seen many signatures on arbitrary messages under arbitrary instances, you cannot create a new signature not seen before without knowing the witness for the instance.

Signatures of knowledge are closely related to simulation-extractable NIZK arguments and previous constructions have also explored the link between SoKs and NIZK proofs. In the following, we define signatures of knowledge, simulation-extractable NIZK arguments, and give a formal proof that signatures of knowledge can be constructed from simulation-extractable NIZK arguments. When we later in the article construct compact and easy to verify SE-NIZK arguments, i.e., simulation-extractable SNARKs, we will therefore automatically obtain compact and easy to verify SoKs.

For our definition of a simulation-extractable signature of knowledge, we follow the game based definitions of Chase and Lysyanskaya [17]. However, Chase and Lysyanskaya define their relations with respect to Turing Machines, whereas in our definitions the use of Turing Machines is implicit in the relation generator. Another more important difference is that since we want compact signatures, we give a non-black-box of simulation-extractability.

Definition 2.2. *Let $\mathcal{R}$ be a relation generator and let $\{\mathcal{M}_\lambda\}_{\lambda \in \mathbb{N}}$ be a sequence of message spaces. Then the quintet of efficient algorithms* (SSetup, SSign, SVfy, SSimSetup, SSimSign) *is a simulation-extractably secure signature of knowledge scheme for $\mathcal{R}$ and $\{\mathcal{M}_\lambda\}_{\lambda \in \mathbb{N}}$ if it is correct, simulatable and simulation-extractable (defined below) and works as follows:*

- $\boldsymbol{pp} \leftarrow \mathsf{SSetup}(R)$: *the setup algorithm is a PPT algorithm which takes as input a relation $R \in \mathcal{R}_\lambda$ and returns public parameters $\boldsymbol{pp}$.*
- $\boldsymbol{\sigma} \leftarrow \mathsf{SSign}(\boldsymbol{pp}, \boldsymbol{\phi}, \boldsymbol{w}, m)$: *the signing algorithm is a PPT algorithm which takes as input the public parameters, a pair $(\boldsymbol{\phi}, \boldsymbol{w}) \in R$ and a message $m \in \mathcal{M}_\lambda$ and returns a signature $\boldsymbol{\sigma}$.*
- $0/1 \leftarrow \mathsf{SVfy}(\boldsymbol{pp}, \boldsymbol{\phi}, m, \boldsymbol{\sigma})$: *the verification algorithm is a deterministic polynomial time algorithm, which takes as input some public parameters $\boldsymbol{pp}$, an instance $\boldsymbol{\phi}$, a message $m \in \mathcal{M}_\lambda$, and a signature $\boldsymbol{\sigma}$ and outputs a 0 or a 1 depending on whether it considers the signature to be valid or not.*
- $(\boldsymbol{pp}, \boldsymbol{\tau}) \leftarrow \mathsf{SSimSetup}(R)$: *the simulated setup algorithm is a PPT algorithm which takes as input a relation $R \in \mathcal{R}_\lambda$ and returns public parameters $\boldsymbol{pp}$ and a trapdoor $\boldsymbol{\tau}$.*
- $\boldsymbol{\sigma} \leftarrow \mathsf{SSimSign}(\boldsymbol{pp}, \boldsymbol{\tau}, \boldsymbol{\phi}, m)$: *the simulated signing algorithm is a PPT algorithm which takes as input some public parameters $\boldsymbol{pp}$, a simulation trapdoor $\boldsymbol{\tau}$, and an instance $\boldsymbol{\phi}$ and returns a signature $\boldsymbol{\sigma}$.*

Perfect Correctness: A signer with a valid witness can always produce a signature that will convince the verifier.

Definition 2.3. *A signature of knowledge scheme is perfectly correct if for all $\lambda \in \mathbb{N}$, for all $R \in \mathcal{R}_\lambda$, for all $(\boldsymbol{\phi}, \boldsymbol{w}) \in R$, and for all $m \in \mathcal{M}_\lambda$*

$$\Pr[\boldsymbol{pp} \leftarrow \mathsf{SSetup}(R); \boldsymbol{\sigma} \leftarrow \mathsf{SSign}(\boldsymbol{pp}; \boldsymbol{\phi}, \boldsymbol{w}, m) : \mathsf{SVfy}(\boldsymbol{pp}, \boldsymbol{\phi}, m, \boldsymbol{\sigma}) = 1] = 1.$$

Perfect Simulatability: The verifier should learn nothing from a signature about the witness that it did not already know. The secrecy of the witness is modelled by the ability to simulate signatures without the witness. More precisely, we say the signatures of knowledge are simulatable if there is a simulator that can create good looking public parameters and signatures without the witness.

Definition 2.4. *For a signature of knowledge SoK, define* $\mathbf{Adv}_{SoK,\mathcal{A}}^{simul}(\lambda) = 2 \Pr[\mathcal{G}_{SoK,\mathcal{A}}^{simul}(\lambda)] - 1$ *where the game $\mathcal{G}_{SoK,\mathcal{A}}^{simul}$ is defined as follows*

MAIN $\mathcal{G}_{SoK,\mathcal{A}}^{simul}(\lambda)$

$R \leftarrow \mathcal{R}(1^\lambda);\ pp_0 \leftarrow \mathsf{SSetup}(R);\ (pp_1, \tau) \leftarrow \mathsf{SSimSetup}(R)$

$b \leftarrow \{0,1\};\ b' \leftarrow \mathcal{A}^{P^b_{pp_b,\tau}}(pp_b)$

return 1 if $b = b'$ and return 0 otherwise

$P^0_{pp_0,\tau}(\phi_i, w_i, m_i)$

assert $(\phi_i, w_i) \in R \ \wedge \ m_i \in \mathcal{M}_\lambda$
$\sigma_i \leftarrow \mathsf{SSign}(pp_0, \phi, w, m)$
return σ_i

$P^1_{pp_1,\tau}(\phi_i, w_i, m_i)$

assert $(\phi_i, w_i) \in R \wedge m_i \in \mathcal{M}_\lambda$
$\sigma_i \leftarrow \mathsf{SSimSign}(pp_1, \tau, \phi, m)$
return σ_i

A signature of knowledge SoK is perfectly simulatable if for any PPT adversary $\mathcal{A}$, $\mathbf{Adv}_{SoK,\mathcal{A}}^{simul}(\lambda) = \frac{1}{2}$.

Simulation-Extractability: An adversary should not be able to issue a new signature unless it knows a witness. This should hold even if the adversary gets to see signatures on arbitrary messages under arbitrary instances. We model this notion in a strong sense, by letting the adversary see simulated signatures for arbitrary messages and instances, which potentially includes false instances. Even under this strong attack model, we require that whenever the adversary outputs a valid signature not seen before, it is possible to extract a witness for the instance if you have access to the internal data of the adversary.

Definition 2.5. *For a signature of knowledge SoK, define $\mathbf{Adv}_{SoK,\mathcal{A},\chi_\mathcal{A}}^{sig\text{-}ext}(\lambda) = \Pr[\mathcal{G}_{SoK,\mathcal{A},\chi_\mathcal{A}}^{sig\text{-}ext}(\lambda)]$ where the game $\mathcal{G}_{SoK,\mathcal{A},\chi_\mathcal{A}}^{sig\text{-}ext}$ is defined as follows*

MAIN $\mathcal{G}_{SoK,\mathcal{A},\chi_\mathcal{A}}^{sig\text{-}ext}(\lambda)$

$R \leftarrow \mathcal{R}(1^\lambda);\ Q = \emptyset$
$(pp, \tau) \leftarrow \mathsf{SSimSetup}(R)$
$(\phi, m, \sigma) \leftarrow \mathcal{A}^{\mathsf{SSimSign}_{pp,\tau}}(pp)$
$w \leftarrow \chi_\mathcal{A}(\mathsf{trans}_\mathcal{A})$
assert $(\phi, w) \notin R$
assert $(\phi, m, \sigma) \notin Q$
return $\mathsf{SVfy}(pp, \phi, m, \sigma)$

$\mathsf{SSimSign}_{pp,\tau}(\phi_i, m_i)$

$\sigma_i \leftarrow \mathsf{SSimSign}(pp, \tau, \phi_i, m_i)$
$Q = Q \cup \{(\phi_i, m_i, \sigma_i)\}$
return σ_i

A signature of knowledge SoK is simulation-extractable if for any PPT adversary $\mathcal{A}$, there exists a PPT extractor $\chi_\mathcal{A}$ such that $\mathbf{Adv}_{SoK,\mathcal{A},\chi_\mathcal{A}}^{sig\text{-}ext}(\lambda) \approx 0$.

2.5 Non-interactive Zero-Knowledge Arguments of Knowledge

Definition 2.6. *Let $\mathcal{R}$ be a relation generator. A NIZK argument for $\mathcal{R}$ is a quadruple of algorithms $(\mathsf{ZSetup}, \mathsf{ZProve}, \mathsf{ZVfy}, \mathsf{ZSimProve})$, which is complete, zero-knowledge and knowledge sound (defined below) and works as follows:*

- $(\mathbf{crs}, \tau) \leftarrow \mathsf{ZSetup}(R)$: *the setup algorithm is a PPT algorithm which takes as input a relation $R \in \mathcal{R}_\lambda$ and returns a common reference string $\mathbf{crs}$ and a simulation trapdoor τ.*

- $\pi \leftarrow$ ZProve($\mathbf{crs}, \phi, \boldsymbol{w}$): *the prover algorithm is a PPT algorithm which takes as input a common reference string* $\mathbf{crs}$ *for a relation R and* $(\phi, \boldsymbol{w}) \in R$ *and returns a proof* π.
- $0/1 \leftarrow$ ZVfy($\mathbf{crs}, \phi, \pi$): *the verifier algorithm is a deterministic polynomial time algorithm which takes as input a common reference string* $\mathbf{crs}$, *an instance* ϕ *and a proof* π *and returns 0 (reject) or 1 (accept).*
- $\pi \leftarrow$ ZSimProve($\mathbf{crs}, \tau, \phi$): *the simulator is a PPT algorithm which takes as input a common reference string* $\mathbf{crs}$, *a simulation trapdoor* τ *and an instance* ϕ *and returns a proof* π.

Perfect Completeness: Perfect completeness says that given a true statement, a prover with a witness can convince the verifier.

Definition 2.7. (ZSetup, ZProve, ZVfy, ZSimProve) *is a perfectly complete argument system for* $\mathcal{R}$ *if for all* $\lambda \in \mathbb{N}$, *for all* $R \in \mathcal{R}_\lambda$ *and for all* $(\phi, \boldsymbol{w}) \in R$:

$$\Pr\left[(\mathbf{crs}, \tau) \leftarrow \mathsf{ZSetup}(R); \pi \leftarrow \mathsf{ZProve}(\mathbf{crs}, \phi, \boldsymbol{w}) : \mathsf{ZVfy}(\mathbf{crs}, \phi, \pi) = 1\right] = 1.$$

Note that the simulation trapdoor τ is kept secret and is not known to either prover or verifier in normal use of the NIZK argument, but it enables the simulation of proofs when we define zero-knowledge below.

Perfect Zero-Knowledge: An argument system has perfect zero-knowledge if it does not leak any information besides the truth of the instance. This is modelled a simulator that does not know the witness but has some trapdoor information that enables it to simulate proofs.

Definition 2.8. *For* $\mathfrak{A} = $ (ZSetup, ZProve, ZVfy, ZSimProve) *an argument system, define* $\mathbf{Adv}_{\mathfrak{A}, \mathcal{A}}^{zk}(\lambda) = 2\Pr[\mathcal{G}_{\mathfrak{A}, \mathcal{A}}^{zk}(\lambda)] - 1$ *where the game* $\mathcal{G}_{\mathfrak{A}, \mathcal{A}}^{zk}$ *is defined as follows*

MAIN $\mathcal{G}_{\mathfrak{A}, \mathcal{A}}^{zk}(\lambda)$

$R \leftarrow \mathcal{R}(1^\lambda);\ (\mathbf{crs}, \tau) \leftarrow \mathsf{ZSetup}(R)$
$b \leftarrow \{0, 1\};\ b' \leftarrow \mathcal{A}^{P_{\mathbf{crs}, \tau}^b}(\mathbf{crs})$
return 1 if $b = b'$ *and return 0 otherwise*

$P_{\mathbf{crs}, \tau}^0(\phi_i, \boldsymbol{w}_i)$

assert $(\phi_i, \boldsymbol{w}_i) \in R$
$\pi_i \leftarrow \mathsf{ZProve}(\mathbf{crs}, \phi, \boldsymbol{w})$
return π_i

$P_{\mathbf{crs}, \tau}^1(\phi_i, \boldsymbol{w}_i)$

assert $(\phi_i, \boldsymbol{w}_i) \in R$
$\pi_i \leftarrow \mathsf{ZSimProve}(\mathbf{crs}, \tau, \phi)$
return π_i

The argument system $\mathfrak{A}$ *is perfectly zero knowledge if for any PPT adversary* $\mathcal{A}$, $\mathbf{Adv}_{\mathfrak{A}, \mathcal{A}}^{zk}(\lambda) = \frac{1}{2}$.

Computational Knowledge Soundness: An argument system is computationally knowledge sound if whenever somebody produces a valid argument it is possible to extract a valid witness from their internal data.

Definition 2.9. *For* $\mathfrak{A} = (\mathsf{ZSetup}, \mathsf{ZProve}, \mathsf{ZVfy}, \mathsf{ZSimProve})$ *an argument system, define* $\mathbf{Adv}^{sound}_{\mathfrak{A},\mathcal{A},\chi_{\mathcal{A}}}(\lambda) = \Pr[\mathcal{G}^{sound}_{\mathfrak{A},\mathcal{A},\chi_{\mathcal{A}}}(\lambda)]$ *where the game* $\mathcal{G}^{sound}_{\mathfrak{A},\mathcal{A},\chi_{\mathcal{A}}}$ *is defined as follows*

$$
\begin{array}{l}
\underline{\text{MAIN } \mathcal{G}^{sound}_{\mathfrak{A},\mathcal{A},\chi_{\mathcal{A}}}(\lambda)} \\[4pt]
R \leftarrow \mathcal{R}(1^\lambda); \ (\mathbf{crs}, \boldsymbol{\tau}) \leftarrow \mathsf{ZSetup}(R) \\
(\boldsymbol{\phi}, \boldsymbol{\pi}) \leftarrow \mathcal{A}(\mathbf{crs}) \\
\boldsymbol{w} \leftarrow \chi_{\mathcal{A}}(\mathsf{trans}_{\mathcal{A}}) \\
assert \ (\boldsymbol{\phi}, \boldsymbol{w}) \notin R \\
return \ \mathsf{ZVfy}(\mathbf{crs}, \boldsymbol{\phi}, \boldsymbol{\pi})
\end{array}
$$

An argument system $\mathfrak{A}$ *is computationally knowledge sound if for any PPT adversary* $\mathcal{A}$*, there exists a PPT extractor* $\chi_{\mathcal{A}}$ *such that* $\mathbf{Adv}^{sound}_{\mathfrak{A},\mathcal{A},\chi_{\mathcal{A}}}(\lambda) \approx 0$.

Simulation-Extractability: Zero-knowledge and soundness are core security properties of NIZK arguments. However, it is conceivable that an adversary that sees a simulated proof for a false instance might modify the proof into another proof for a false instance. This scenario is actually very common in security proofs for cryptographic schemes, so it is often desirable to have some form of non-malleability that prevents cheating in the presence of simulated proofs.

Traditionally, simulation-extractability is defined with respect to a decryption key associated with the common reference string that allows the extraction of a witness from a valid proof. However, in succinct NIZK arguments the proofs are too small to encode the full witness. We will therefore instead define simulation-extractable NIZK arguments using a non-black-box extractor that can deduce the witness from the internal data of the adversary.

Definition 2.10. *Let* $\mathfrak{A} = (\mathsf{ZSetup}, \mathsf{ZProve}, \mathsf{ZVfy}, \mathsf{ZSimProve})$ *be a NIZK argument for* $\mathcal{R}$*. Define* $\mathbf{Adv}^{proof\text{-}ext}_{\mathfrak{A},\mathcal{A},\chi_{\mathcal{A}}}(\lambda) = \Pr[\mathcal{G}^{proof\text{-}ext}_{\mathfrak{A},\mathcal{A},\chi_{\mathcal{A}}}(\lambda)]$ *where the game* $\mathcal{G}^{proof\text{-}ext}_{\mathfrak{A},\mathcal{A},\chi_{\mathcal{A}}}$ *is defined as follows*

$$
\begin{array}{ll}
\underline{\text{MAIN } \mathcal{G}^{proof\text{-}ext}_{\mathfrak{A},\mathcal{A},\chi_{\mathcal{A}}}(\lambda)} & \qquad \underline{\mathsf{ZSimProve}_{\mathbf{crs},\boldsymbol{\tau}}(\boldsymbol{\phi}_i)} \\[4pt]
R \leftarrow \mathcal{R}(1^\lambda); \ Q = \emptyset & \qquad \boldsymbol{\pi}_i \leftarrow \mathsf{ZSimProve}(\mathbf{crs}, \boldsymbol{\tau}, \boldsymbol{\phi}_i) \\
(\mathbf{crs}, \boldsymbol{\tau}) \leftarrow \mathsf{ZSetup}(R) & \qquad Q = Q \cup \{(\boldsymbol{\phi}_i, \boldsymbol{\pi}_i)\} \\
(\boldsymbol{\phi}, \boldsymbol{\pi}) \leftarrow \mathcal{A}^{\mathsf{ZSimProve}_{\mathbf{crs},\boldsymbol{\tau}}}(\mathbf{crs}) & \qquad return \ \boldsymbol{\sigma}_i \\
\boldsymbol{w} \leftarrow \chi_{\mathcal{A}}(\mathsf{trans}_{\mathcal{A}}) \\
assert \ (\boldsymbol{\phi}, \boldsymbol{w}) \notin R \\
assert \ (\boldsymbol{\phi}, \boldsymbol{\pi}) \notin Q \\
return \ \mathsf{ZVfy}(\mathbf{crs}, \boldsymbol{\phi}, \boldsymbol{\pi})
\end{array}
$$

A NIZK argument $\mathfrak{A}$ *is simulation-extractable if for any PPT adversary* $\mathcal{A}$*, there exists a PPT extractor* $\chi_{\mathcal{A}}$ *such that* $\mathbf{Adv}^{proof\text{-}ext}_{\mathfrak{A},\mathcal{A},\chi_{\mathcal{A}}}(\lambda) \approx 0$.

We observe that simulation-extractability implies knowledge soundness, since the latter corresponds to a simulation-extractability adversary that is not allowed to use the simulation oracle.

Definition 2.11. *A succinct argument system is one in which the proof size is polynomial in the security parameter and the verifier's computation time is polynomial in the security parameter and the instance size.*

Terminology:

- A Succinct Non-interactive ARgument of Knowledge is a SNARK.
- A zk-SNARK is a zero-knowledge SNARK, or a succinct NIZK argument.
- A simulation-extractable NIZK argument is an SE-NIZK.
- A succinct SE-NIZK argument is an SE-SNARK.

Benign Relation Generators. Bitansky et al. [10] showed that indistinguishability obfuscation implies that there are potential auxiliary inputs to the adversary that allow it to create a valid proof in an obfuscated way such that it is impossible to extract the witness. Boyle and Pass [14] show that assuming the stronger notion of public coin differing input obfuscation there is even auxiliary inputs that defeat witness extraction for all candidate SNARKs. These counter examples, however, rely on specific input distributions for the adversary. We will therefore in the following assume the relationship generator is *benign* such that the relation (and the potential auxiliary inputs included in it) are distributed in such a way that the SNARKs we construct can be simulation extractable.

3   Signatures of Knowledge from SE-NIZKs

Signatures of knowledge and SE-NIZK arguments are closely related. We will now show how to construct a signature of knowledge scheme for messages in $\{0,1\}^*$ from an SE-NIZK argument and a public coin collision-resistant hash-function. This means that in the rest of the article we can focus our efforts on constructing succinct SE-NIZK arguments, which is a slightly simpler notion than signatures of knowledge since it does not involve a message.

We will be using collision-resistant hash-functions, where the key for the hash-function can be sampled from a source of public coins.

Definition 3.1 (Public coin collision-resistant hash-function). *We say the polynomial time algorithm $H : \{0,1\}^{\phi(\lambda)} \times \{0,1\}^* \to \{0,1\}^\lambda$, with ϕ being a polynomial in λ, is collision resistant if for all PPT adversaries $\mathcal{A}$, $\mathbf{Adv}_{\mathcal{A}}^{hash} \approx 0$ where $\mathbf{Adv}_{\mathcal{A}}^{hash}$ is given by*

$$\Pr[K \leftarrow \{0,1\}^{\phi(\lambda)}; (m_0, m_1) \leftarrow \mathcal{A}(K) : m_0 \neq m_1 \ \wedge \ H_K(m_0) = H_K(m_1)]$$

Suppose $\mathcal{R}'$ is a relation generator which, on input of a security parameter λ, outputs a relation R'. We define a corresponding relation

$$R = \{((h, \phi), \boldsymbol{w}) : h \in \{0,1\}^\lambda \ \wedge \ (\boldsymbol{\phi}, \boldsymbol{w}) \in R'\}.$$

In the following, we let $\mathcal{R}$ be the relation generator that runs $R' \leftarrow \mathcal{R}'(1^\lambda)$ and returns R as defined above. Let H be a public coin collision-resistant hash function and (ZSetup, ZProve, ZVfy, ZSimProve) be a SE-NIZK argument for $\mathcal{R}$. Then Fig. 1 describes a signature of knowledge for $\mathcal{R}'$.

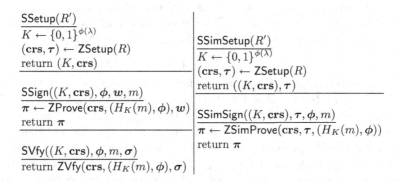

Fig. 1. SoK scheme based on collision-resistant hash-function and SE-NIZK argument.

Proposition 3.1. *If H is a public coin collision-resistant hash-function and $\mathfrak{A} = $ (ZSetup, ZProve, ZVfy, ZSimProve) is an SE-NIZK argument for $\mathcal{R}$, then the scheme (SSetup, SSign, SVfy) given in Fig. 1 is a signature of knowledge for $\mathcal{R}'$ with respect to the message space $\mathcal{M} = \{0,1\}^\lambda$.*

Proof. We shall show that the signature of knowledge is perfectly correct, perfectly simulatable and that it is simulation extractable.

<u>Perfect Correctness:</u> Suppose that $\lambda \in \mathbb{N}$, $R' \in \mathcal{R}'_\lambda$, $(\phi, w) \in R'$ and $m \in \{0,1\}^*$. Running $\boldsymbol{pp} \leftarrow \mathsf{SSetup}(R')$, $\boldsymbol{\sigma} \leftarrow \mathsf{SSign}(\boldsymbol{pp}, \phi, \boldsymbol{w}, m)$ and checking that $\mathsf{SVfy}(\boldsymbol{pp}, \phi, m, \boldsymbol{\sigma})$ outputs 1 corresponds to running $K \leftarrow \{0,1\}^{\phi(\lambda)}$, $(\mathbf{crs}, \boldsymbol{\tau}) \leftarrow \mathsf{ZSetup}(R)$, $\boldsymbol{\pi} \leftarrow \mathsf{ZProve}(\mathbf{crs}, (H_K(m), \phi), \boldsymbol{w})$ and checking that $\mathsf{ZVfy}(\mathbf{crs}, (H_K(m), \phi), \boldsymbol{\pi})$ outputs 1. As the NIZK argument is perfectly complete this check will always pass.

<u>Perfect Simulatability:</u> We show that for any PPT adversary $\mathcal{A}$ there exists a PPT adversary $\mathcal{B}$ such that $\mathbf{Adv}^{\text{simul}}_{SoK,\mathcal{A}}(\lambda) \leq \mathbf{Adv}^{\text{zk}}_{\mathfrak{A},\mathcal{B}}(1^\lambda)$ for all $\lambda \in \mathbb{N}$. Since an SE-NIZK is perfectly zero-knowledge, this implies that $\mathbf{Adv}^{\text{simul}}_{SoK,\mathcal{A}}$ is negligible in λ i.e. if $\mathcal{A}$ breaks simulatability for SoK then $\mathcal{B}$ breaks the zero-knowledge for $\mathfrak{A}$.

Let $\mathcal{A}$ be a PPT adversary against $\mathcal{G}^{\text{simul}}_{SoK,\mathcal{A}}$. Define the PPT adversary $\mathcal{B}$ that uses the output of $\mathcal{A}$ to attack the zero-knowledge of $\mathfrak{A}$ and behaves as follows:

$$
\begin{array}{ll}
\underline{\mathcal{B}^{P^b_{\mathbf{crs},\tau}}(\mathbf{crs})} & \underline{P'^b_{(K,\mathbf{crs}),\tau}(\phi_i, \boldsymbol{w}_i, m_i)} \\[4pt]
K \leftarrow \{0,1\}^{\phi(\lambda)}; & \text{assert } m_i \in \mathcal{M}_\lambda \\
b' \leftarrow \mathcal{A}^{P'^b_{(K,\mathbf{crs}),\tau}}((K, \mathbf{crs})) & \text{return } P^b_{\mathbf{crs},\tau}((H_K(m_i), \phi_i), \boldsymbol{w}_i) \\
\text{return } b' &
\end{array}
$$

We argue that if $P^b_{\mathbf{crs},\tau}$ is defined to be the oracles in $\mathcal{G}^{\mathrm{zk}}_{\mathfrak{A},\mathcal{B}}$ then $P'^b_{(K,\mathbf{crs}),\tau}$ behaves exactly as the oracles in $\mathcal{G}^{\mathrm{simul}}_{\mathrm{SoK},\mathcal{A}}$. To see this first note that if $(\phi_i, \boldsymbol{w}_i) \notin R$ then P'^b returns $\bot$. If $(\phi_i, \boldsymbol{w}_i) \in R$ then the following holds.

- when $b = 0$, $P^b_{\mathbf{crs},\tau}$ returns $\boldsymbol{\pi}_i \leftarrow \mathsf{ZProve}(\mathbf{crs}, (H_K(m_i), \phi), \boldsymbol{w}_i)$. This corresponds exactly to sampling $\boldsymbol{\sigma}_i \leftarrow \mathsf{SSign}((K, \mathbf{crs}), \phi, m_i, \boldsymbol{w}_i)$.
- when $b = 1$, $P^b_{\mathbf{crs},\tau}$ returns $\boldsymbol{\pi}_i \leftarrow \mathsf{ZSimProve}(\mathbf{crs}, \tau, (H_K(m_i), \phi))$. This corresponds exactly to sampling $\boldsymbol{\sigma}_i \leftarrow \mathsf{SSimSign}((K, \mathbf{crs}), \tau, \phi_i, m_i)$.

Hence whenever $\mathcal{A}$ succeeds at $\mathcal{G}^{\mathrm{simul}}_{\mathrm{SoK},\mathcal{A}}$, $\mathcal{B}$ succeeds at $\mathcal{G}^{\mathrm{zk}}_{\mathfrak{A},\mathcal{B}}$ and the result holds.

Simulation-Extractability: We show that for all PPT adversaries $\mathcal{A}$, there exists a PPT adversary $\mathcal{B}$ such that for all PPT extractors $\chi_\mathcal{B}$, there exists a PPT extractor $\chi_\mathcal{A}$ such that $\mathbf{Adv}^{sig-ext}_{\mathrm{SoK},\mathcal{A},\chi_\mathcal{A}}(\lambda) \leq \mathbf{Adv}^{\mathrm{proof\text{-}ext}}_{\mathfrak{A},\mathcal{B},\chi_\mathcal{B}} + \mathbf{Adv}^{\mathrm{hash}}_\mathcal{B}$ for all $\lambda \in \mathbb{N}$. By simulation-extractability of the SE-NIZK, we have that for any choice of $\mathcal{B}$, there exists a PPT $\chi_\mathcal{B}$ such that the above is negligible in λ, meaning that there exists a $\chi_\mathcal{A}$ such that $\mathbf{Adv}^{sig-ext}_{\mathrm{SoK},\mathcal{A},\chi_\mathcal{A}}(\lambda)$ is negligible in λ. In other words, we construct an adversary $\mathcal{B}$ such that if $\mathcal{A}$ breaks simulation-extractability for SoK then $\mathcal{B}$ breaks simulation extractability for $\mathfrak{A}$.

Let $\mathcal{A}$ be a PPT adversary that on input of some public parameters outputs an instance, a message and a signature. Define the PPT adversary $\mathcal{B}$ that uses $\mathcal{A}$ to attack simulation-extractability of $\mathfrak{A}$ and behaves as follows.

$\underline{\mathcal{B}^{\mathsf{ZSimProve}_{\mathbf{crs},\tau}}(\mathbf{crs})}$

$K \leftarrow \{0,1\}^{\phi(\lambda)}; Q' = \emptyset;$
$(\phi, m, \boldsymbol{\sigma}) \leftarrow \mathcal{A}^{\mathsf{SSimSign}_{(K,\mathbf{crs}),\tau}}((K, \mathbf{crs}));$
$h \leftarrow H_K(m);$
return $((h, \phi), \boldsymbol{\sigma})$

$\underline{\mathsf{SSimSign}_{(K,\mathbf{crs}),\tau}(\phi_i, m_i)}$

$h_i \leftarrow H_K(m_i);$
$\boldsymbol{\pi} \leftarrow \mathsf{ZSimProve}_{\mathbf{crs},\tau}((h_i, \phi_i));$
$Q' = Q' \cup \{(\phi_i, m_i, \boldsymbol{\pi}_i)\};$
return $\boldsymbol{\pi}_i$

Where $\mathcal{A}$ is given K as well as all of $\mathcal{B}$'s oracle responses, $\mathsf{trans}_\mathcal{B}$ contains no information that cannot be calculated in polynomial time from $\mathsf{trans}_\mathcal{A}$. We need to design an extractor $\chi_\mathcal{A}$ that uses $\chi_\mathcal{B}$'s output to break simulation-extractability for $\mathfrak{A}$. Let T be such that $\mathsf{trans}_\mathcal{B} = T(\mathsf{trans}_\mathcal{A})$. Let $\chi_\mathcal{B}$ be a PPT extractor that on input of $\mathsf{trans}_\mathcal{B}$ outputs some $\boldsymbol{w}$. Define $\chi_\mathcal{A}$ as follows.

$$\frac{\chi_\mathcal{A}(\mathsf{trans}_\mathcal{A})}{\mathsf{trans}_\mathcal{B} \leftarrow T(\mathsf{trans}_\mathcal{A});}$$
$$\text{return } \chi_\mathcal{B}(\mathsf{trans}_\mathcal{B})$$

For all PPT $\mathcal{A}$, if $\mathcal{B}$ is defined as above, then for all PPT $\chi_\mathcal{B}$, if $\chi_\mathcal{A}$ is defined as above, then $\mathcal{B}$ succeeds at $\mathcal{G}^{\mathrm{prove\text{-}ext}}_{\mathfrak{A},\mathcal{B},\chi_\mathcal{B}}$ whenever $\mathcal{A}$ succeeds at $\mathcal{G}^{\mathrm{sig\text{-}ext}}_{\mathrm{SoK},\mathcal{A},\chi_\mathcal{A}}$. To see this observe that

1. If $((\phi, h), \boldsymbol{\sigma}) \in Q$ then either $(\phi, m, \boldsymbol{\sigma}) \in Q'$ or $\mathcal{A}$ outputs some m such that $H_K(m) = H_K(m_i)$ (for m_i one of the queried messages) but $m \neq m_i$. The latter happens with negligible probability when H_K is collision resistant.
2. $(\phi, \boldsymbol{w}) \in R' \iff ((h, \phi), \boldsymbol{w}) \in R$.
3. $\mathsf{SVfy}((K, \mathbf{crs}), \phi, m, \boldsymbol{\sigma}) = \mathsf{ZVfy}(\mathbf{crs}, (H_K(m), \phi), \boldsymbol{\pi})$.

This completes the proof.   □

In the other direction, it is easy to see that an SoK scheme can be used to construct an SE-NIZK argument by using the default message $m = 0$.

Proposition 3.2. *If an SoK scheme is simulation-extractably secure for a relation generator $\mathcal{R}$ then the NIZK for the relation generator $\mathcal{R}$ described in Fig. 2 has perfect completeness, perfect zero-knowledge and is simulation-extractable.*

Proof. This holds directly from the perfect correctness, perfect simulatability and simulation-extractability of the SoK scheme.

$\mathsf{ZSetup}(R)$	$\mathsf{ZSimProve}(\boldsymbol{pp}, \boldsymbol{\tau}, \boldsymbol{\phi})$
$(\boldsymbol{pp}, \boldsymbol{\tau}) \leftarrow \mathsf{SSimSetup}(R)$	$\boldsymbol{\sigma} \leftarrow \mathsf{SSimSign}(\boldsymbol{pp}, \boldsymbol{\tau}, \boldsymbol{\phi}, 0)$
return $(\boldsymbol{pp}, \boldsymbol{\tau})$	return $\boldsymbol{\sigma}$

$\mathsf{ZProve}(\boldsymbol{pp}, \boldsymbol{\phi}, \boldsymbol{w})$	$\mathsf{ZVfy}(\boldsymbol{pp}, \boldsymbol{\phi}, \boldsymbol{\pi})$
$\boldsymbol{\sigma} \leftarrow \mathsf{SSign}(\boldsymbol{pp}, \boldsymbol{\phi}, 0, \boldsymbol{w})$	return $\mathsf{SVfy}(\mathbf{crs}, \boldsymbol{\phi}, 0, \boldsymbol{\pi})$
return $\boldsymbol{\sigma}$	

Fig. 2. SE-NIZK construction from an SoK.

4   Bilinear Groups and Assumptions

Definition 4.1. *A* bilinear group generator $\mathcal{BG}$ *takes as input a security parameter in unary and returns a bilinear group $gk = (p, \mathbb{G}_1, \mathbb{G}_2, \mathbb{G}_T, e)$ consisting of cyclic groups $\mathbb{G}_1$, $\mathbb{G}_2$, $\mathbb{G}_T$ of prime order p and a bilinear map $e : \mathbb{G}_1 \times \mathbb{G}_2 \to \mathbb{G}_T$ such that*

- *there are efficient algorithms for computing group operations, evaluating the bilinear map, deciding membership of the groups, and sampling generators of the groups;*
- *the map is bilinear, i.e., for all $G \in \mathbb{G}_1$ and $H \in \mathbb{G}_2$ and for all $a, b \in \mathbb{Z}$ we have $e(G^a, H^b) = e(G, H)^{ab}$;*
- *and the map is non-degenerate, i.e., if $e(G, H) = 1$ then $G = 1$ or $H = 1$.*

Usually bilinear groups are constructed from elliptic curves equipped with a pairing, which can be tweaked to yield a non-degenerate bilinear map. There are many ways to set up bilinear groups both as symmetric bilinear groups where $\mathbb{G}_1 = \mathbb{G}_2$ and as asymmetric bilinear groups where $\mathbb{G}_1 \neq \mathbb{G}_2$. We will be working in the asymmetric setting, in what Galbraith, Paterson and Smart [28] call the Type III setting where there is no efficiently computable non-trivial homomorphism in either direction between $\mathbb{G}_1$ and $\mathbb{G}_2$. Type III bilinear groups are the most efficient type of bilinear groups and hence the most relevant for practical applications.

4.1 Intractability Assumptions

We will now specify the intractability assumptions used to prove our pairing based SE-SNARK secure.

The eXtended Power Knowledge of Exponent Assumption

Our strongest assumption is the extended power knowledge of exponent (XPKE) assumption, which is a knowledge extractor assumption. We consider an adversary that gets access to source group elements that have discrete logarithms that are polynomials evaluated on secret random variables. The assumption then says that the only way the adversary can produce group elements in the two source groups with matching discrete logarithms, i.e., $G^a \in \mathbb{G}_1$ and $H^b \in \mathbb{G}_2$ with $a = b$, is if it knows that b is the evaluation of a known linear combination of the polynomials.

Assumption 4.1. *Let $\mathcal{A}$ be an adversary and let $\chi_{\mathcal{A}}$ be an extractor. Define*
$$\mathbf{Adv}^{XPKE}_{\mathcal{BG},d(\lambda),q(\lambda),\mathcal{A},\chi_{\mathcal{A}}}(\lambda) = \Pr[\mathcal{G}^{XPKE}_{\mathcal{BG},d(\lambda),q(\lambda),\mathcal{A},\chi_{\mathcal{A}}}(\lambda)] \text{ where } \mathcal{G}^{XPKE}_{\mathcal{BG},d(\lambda),q(\lambda),\mathcal{A},\chi_{\mathcal{A}}} \text{ is}$$
defined by

$$\text{MAIN } \mathcal{G}^{XPKE}_{\mathcal{BG},d(\lambda),q(\lambda),\mathcal{A},\chi_{\mathcal{A}}}(\lambda)$$

$$gk = (p, \mathbb{G}_1, \mathbb{G}_2, \mathbb{G}_T, e) \leftarrow \mathcal{BG}(1^\lambda);$$
$$G \leftarrow \mathbb{G}_1^*; H \leftarrow \mathbb{G}_2^*; \boldsymbol{z} \leftarrow (\mathbb{Z}_p^*)^q; Q = \emptyset$$
$$(G^a, H^b) \leftarrow \mathcal{A}^{\mathcal{O}^1_{G,\boldsymbol{z}}, \, \mathcal{O}^2_{H,\boldsymbol{z}}}(gk)$$
$$\boldsymbol{\eta} \in (\mathbb{Z}_p)^{|Q|} \leftarrow \chi_{\mathcal{A}}(\text{trans}_{\mathcal{A}});$$
$$\text{return } 1 \text{ if } a = b \text{ and } b \neq \sum_{h_j \in Q} \eta_j h_j(\boldsymbol{z})$$
$$\text{else return } 0$$

$$\frac{\mathcal{O}^1_{G,\boldsymbol{z}}(g_i)}{}$$
$$\text{assert } g_i \in \mathbb{Z}_p[Z_1, \dots Z_q]$$
$$\text{assert } \deg(g_i) \leq d$$
$$\text{return } G^{g_i(\boldsymbol{z})}$$

$$\frac{\mathcal{O}^2_{H,\boldsymbol{z}}(h_j)}{}$$
$$\text{assert } h_j \in \mathbb{Z}_p[Z_1, \dots Z_q]$$
$$\text{assert } \deg(h_j) \leq d$$
$$Q = Q \cup \{h_j\};$$
$$\text{return } H^{h_j(\boldsymbol{z})}$$

The $(d(\lambda), q(\lambda))$-XPKE assumption holds relative to $\mathcal{BG}$ if for all PPT adversaries $\mathcal{A}$, there exists a PPT algorithm $\chi_{\mathcal{A}}$ such that $\mathbf{Adv}^{XPKE}_{\mathcal{BG},d(\lambda),q(\lambda),\mathcal{A},\chi_{\mathcal{A}}}(\lambda)$ is negligible in λ.

The Computational Polynomial Assumption

The computational polynomial (Poly) assumption is related to the d-linear assumption of Escala, Herold, Kiltz, Ràfols and Villar [23]. In the univariate case, the Poly assumption says that for any $G \in \mathbb{G}_1^*$, given $G^{g_1(z)}, \dots, G^{g_I(z)}$, an adversary cannot compute $G^{g(z)}$ for a polynomial g that is linearly independent from $g_1, \dots, g_I$ - even if it knows $H^{g(z)}$ for $H \in \mathbb{G}_2^*$.

Assumption 4.2. *Let $\mathcal{A}$ be a PPT algorithm and define $\mathbf{Adv}^{Poly}_{\mathcal{BG},d(\lambda),q(\lambda),\mathcal{A}}(\lambda) = \Pr[\mathcal{G}^{Poly}_{\mathcal{BG},d(\lambda),q(\lambda),\mathcal{A}}(\lambda)]$ where $\mathcal{G}^{Poly}_{\mathcal{BG},d(\lambda),q(\lambda),\mathcal{A}}$ is defined by*

$$\text{MAIN } \mathcal{G}^{Poly}_{\mathcal{BG},d(\lambda),q(\lambda),\mathcal{A}}(\lambda)$$

$gk = (p, \mathbb{G}_1, \mathbb{G}_2, \mathbb{G}_T, e, \mathsf{aux}_{\mathcal{BG}}) \leftarrow \mathcal{BG}(1^\lambda);$
$G \leftarrow \mathbb{G}_1^*; H \leftarrow \mathbb{G}_2^*; z \leftarrow (\mathbb{Z}_p^*)^q; Q = \emptyset$
$(G^a, g(Z_1, \dots, Z_q)) \leftarrow \mathcal{A}^{\mathcal{O}^1_{G,z}, \ \mathcal{O}^2_{H,z}}(gk)$
$return \ 1 \ if \ a = g(z) \ and \ g \notin span\{Q\}$
$else \ return \ 0$

$\mathcal{O}^1_{G,z}(g_i)$	$\mathcal{O}^2_{H,z}(h_j)$
$assert \ g_i \in \mathbb{Z}_p[Z_1, \dots Z_q]$	$assert \ h_j \in \mathbb{Z}_p[Z_1, \dots Z_q]$
$assert \ \deg(g_i) \leq d$	$assert \ \deg(h_j) \leq d$
$Q = Q \cup \{g_i\};$	$return \ H^{h_j(z)}$
$return \ G^{g_i(z)}$	

The $(d(\lambda), q(\lambda))$-Poly assumption holds relative to $\mathcal{BG}$ if for all PPT adversaries $\mathcal{A}$ we have $\mathbf{Adv}^{XPKE}_{Poly,d(\lambda),q(\lambda),\mathcal{A}}(\lambda)$ is negligible in λ.

Plausibility of the assumptions

To be plausible an assumption should not be trivial to break using generic group operations. There are various ways to formalize generic group models that restrict the adversary to such operations [42,45,50]. Using the framework from [13] it is easy to show the following proposition.

Proposition 4.1. *The $(d(\lambda), q(\lambda))$-XPKE and $(d(\lambda), q(\lambda))$-Poly assumptions both hold in the generic group model.*

We will in the following construct a pairing based SE-SNARK. The simulation extractability of the SE-SNARK will rely on the XPKE and Poly assumptions. It is instructive to consider also the assumption requirements for the weaker notion of knowledge soundness of the SNARK. To prove our SNARK has standard knowledge soundness, it suffices to consider the XPKE and Poly assumptions where the adversary has non-adaptive oracle access. We can reformulate this as the adversary specifies all the polynomials it wants to query, and then submits all queries at once and gets the matching oracle responses. The non-adaptive Poly assumption is a computational target assumption [33] and is implied by the $q - \mathrm{BGDHE}_2$ assumption for sufficiently large q, which says given $G, G^x, \dots, G^{x^2 q} \in \mathbb{G}_1$ and $H, H^x, \dots, H^{x^{q-1}}, H^{x^{q+1}}, \dots, H^{x^2 q} \in \mathbb{G}_2$ it is hard to compute H^{x^q}. The non-adaptive XPKE assumption bears resemblance to the power knowledge of exponent (PKE) assumption from [19]. It is also worth noting that we only want to ensure the if the response G^a and H^b has $a = b$ then it is beceause b is some known linear combination of the queried polynomials, whereas in the only previous 3 element zk-SNARK [36] it is necessary in the proof of knowledge soundness to also consider elements where the exponent has a quadratic relationship to the queried polynomials.

To get simulation-extractability, we strengthened both the XPKE and Poly assumptions to make them interactive. We conjecture this is unavoidable, simulation extractability is interactive in nature and we do not see how to base it on non-interactive assumptions.

5   SE-SNARK

We will now construct an SE-SNARK for square arithmetic program (SAP) generators, which we define below. Any arithmetic circuit over a finite field can be efficiently converted into an SAP over the same field, see Appendix B, so this gives us SE-SNARKs for arithmetic circuit satisfiability.

Before giving our SE-SNARK, let us first provide some intuition as to why pairing based zk-SNARKs are, typically speaking, not simulation extractable. The problem is that an adversary that sees a proof is often able to modify it into a different proof for the same instance. Suppose that (A, B, C) are three of the group elements in the proof (there might be more) that satisfy the verification equations of some SNARK scheme. At least two of the proof elements must satisfy some quadratic constraint of the form

$$e(A, B) = T.$$

In the first generic attack, the adversary takes $A' = A^r$ and $B' = B^{\frac{1}{r}}$ for any value r. These new components will also satisfy the quadratic constraint. Hence, an SE-SNARK must have an additional constraint on the pairs of components that satisfy a quadratic constraint, since otherwise it is possible to forge a new proof for a previously proved statement. This is at the heart of why an SE-SNARK must have at least two verification equations. The second generic attack involves any constraint of the form

$$e(A, B) = e(C, H^\delta),$$

where H is a generator of $\mathbb{G}_2$ given in the common reference string. This constraint can also be satisfied by $A' = A$, $B' = BH^{r\delta}$, $C' = A^rC$.

To build an SE-SNARK we need to neutralize both of these generic attacks. In our scheme, we include a constraint of the form

$$e(A, B) = e(C, H)$$

as well as a linear constraint to ensure $\log_G A = \log_H B$. The CRS will be designed to contain H, G^γ and H^γ but not G. That way, if the adversary sets $B' = BH^r$, then the only possible value for A' is AG^r - which means that r must depend on γ. This in turn forces the adversary to include a factor of γ^2 in C'. By limiting the information we give the adversary about γ^2, we ensure that the adversary cannot calculate the required value of C'. The full SE-SNARK verifications then also include parts to ensure the instance is correctly incorporated.

5.1   Square Arithmetic Programs

Formally, we will be working with square arithmetic programs R that have the following description

$$R = (\mathbb{Z}_p, gk, \ell, \{u_i(X), w_i(X)\}_{i=0}^m, t(X)),$$

where the bilinear group $gk = (p, \mathbb{G}_1, \mathbb{G}_2, \mathbb{G}_T, e)$ is included as auxiliary information, $1 \le \ell \le m$, $u_i(X), w_i(X), t(X) \in \mathbb{Z}_p[X]$ and $u_i(X), w_i(X)$ have strictly lower degree than n, the degree of $t(X)$. Furthermore, suppose that the set $S = \{u_i(X) : 0 \le i \le \ell\}$ is linearly independent and that any $u_i \in S$ is also linearly independent from the set $\{u_j(X) : \ell < j \le m\}$. A square arithmetic program with such a description defines the following binary relation, where we define $s_0 = 1$,

$$
R = \left\{ (\boldsymbol{\phi}, \boldsymbol{w}) \left|
\begin{array}{l}
\boldsymbol{\phi} = (s_1, \ldots, s_\ell) \in \mathbb{Z}_p^\ell \\
\boldsymbol{w} = (s_{\ell+1}, \ldots, s_m) \in \mathbb{Z}_p^{m-\ell} \\
\\
\exists h(X) \in \mathbb{Z}_p[X], \deg(h) \le n - 2 : \\
\left(\sum_{i=0}^m s_i u_i(X) \right)^2 = \sum_{i=0}^m s_i w_i(X) + h(X) t(X)
\end{array}
\right. \right\}
$$

We say $\mathcal{R}$ is a square arithmetic program generator if it generates relations of the form given above with $p > 2^{\lambda-1}$.

5.2   The Construction

$(\mathbf{crs}, \boldsymbol{\tau}) \leftarrow \mathsf{ZSetup}(R)$:
Pick $\alpha, \beta, \gamma, x \leftarrow \mathbb{Z}_p^*$; $G \leftarrow \mathbb{G}_1^*$; $H \leftarrow \mathbb{G}_2^*$ such that $t(x) \ne 0$ and set

$$
\boldsymbol{\tau} = (R, G, H, \alpha, \beta, \gamma, x)
$$

$$
\mathbf{crs} = \left(
\begin{array}{c}
R, G^\alpha, G^\beta, G^{\gamma t(x)}, G^{\gamma t(x)^2}, G^{(\alpha+\beta)\gamma t(x)}, H, H^\beta, H^{\gamma t(x)}, \\
\left\{ G^{\gamma x^i}, H^{\gamma x^i}, G^{\gamma^2 t(x) x^i} \right\}_{i=0}^{n-1}, \\
\left\{ G^{\gamma w_i(x) + (\alpha+\beta)u_i(x)} \right\}_{i=0}^\ell, \left\{ G^{\gamma^2 w_i(x) + (\alpha+\beta)\gamma u_i(x)} \right\}_{i=\ell+1}^m
\end{array}
\right)
$$

$\boldsymbol{\pi} \leftarrow \mathsf{ZProve}(\mathbf{crs}, \boldsymbol{\phi}, \boldsymbol{w})$:
Pick $r \leftarrow \mathbb{Z}_p$ and compute $\boldsymbol{\pi} = (A, B, C)$ such that

$$
A = G^{\gamma \left(\sum_{i=0}^m s_i u_i(x) + r \cdot t(x) \right)}, \qquad B = H^{\gamma \left(\sum_{i=0}^m s_i u_i(x) + r \cdot t(x) \right)}
$$

$$
C = G^{f(\boldsymbol{w}) + r^2 \gamma^2 (t(x))^2 + r(\alpha+\beta)\gamma t(x) + \gamma^2 t(x) \left[h(x) + 2r \sum_{i=0}^m s_i u_i(x) \right]}
$$

where $f(\boldsymbol{w}) = \sum_{i=l+1}^m s_i (\gamma^2 w_i(x) + (\alpha+\beta)\gamma u_i(x))$.

$0/1 \leftarrow \mathsf{ZVfy}(\mathbf{crs}, \boldsymbol{\phi}, \boldsymbol{\pi})$:
Check that

$$
e(AG^\alpha, BH^\beta) = e(G^\alpha, H^\beta) e(G^{\varphi(\boldsymbol{\phi})}, H^\gamma) e(C, H) \tag{1}
$$

$$
e(A, H^\gamma) = e(G^\gamma, B) \tag{2}
$$

where $\varphi(\boldsymbol{\phi}) = \sum_{i=0}^\ell s_i (\gamma w_i(x) + (\alpha+\beta)u_i(x))$. Accept the proof if and only if both the tests pass.

$\boldsymbol{\pi} \leftarrow \mathsf{ZSimProve}(\boldsymbol{\tau}, \boldsymbol{\phi})$:
Pick $\mu \leftarrow \mathbb{Z}_p$ and compute $\boldsymbol{\pi} = (A, B, C)$ such that

$$
A = G^\mu, \quad B = H^\mu, \quad C = G^{\mu^2 + (\alpha+\beta)\mu - \gamma\varphi(\boldsymbol{\phi})}.
$$

5.3   Efficiency

The proof size is 2 elements in $\mathbb{G}_1$ and 1 element in $\mathbb{G}_2$. The common reference string contains a description of R (which includes the bilinear group), $m+2n+5$ elements in $\mathbb{G}_1$ and $n+3$ elements in $\mathbb{G}_2$.

Although the verifier is modelled as knowing the whole common reference string, actually it only needs to know

$$\mathbf{crs}_V =$$
$$\left(p, \mathbb{G}_1, \mathbb{G}_2, \mathbb{G}_T, e, H, G^\alpha, H^\beta, G^\gamma, H^\gamma, \{G^{\gamma w_i(x)+(\alpha+\beta)u_i(x)}\}_{i=0}^{\ell}, e(G^\alpha, H^\beta) \right).$$

Thus the verifier's common reference string only contains a description of the bilinear group $\mathcal{G}$, $\ell+3$ elements from $\mathbb{G}_1$, 3 elements from $\mathbb{G}_2$, and 1 element from $\mathbb{G}_T$.

The verification consists of checking that the proof contains 3 appropriate group elements and checking 2 pairing product equations. The verifier computes ℓ exponentiations in $\mathbb{G}_1$ (noting that $s_0 = 1$), 4 group multiplications and 5 pairings (assuming $e(G^\alpha, H^\beta)$ is precomputed in the verifier's common reference string).

The prover has to compute the polynomial $h(X)$. It depends on the relation how long time this computation takes; if it arises from an arithmetic circuit where each multiplication gate connects to a constant number of wires, the relation will be sparse and the computation will be linear in n. The prover also computes the coefficients of $\sum_{i=0}^{m} s_i u_i(X)$. Having all the coefficients, the prover does $m + 2n - \ell$ exponentiations in $\mathbb{G}_1$ and n exponentiations in $\mathbb{G}_2$.

5.4   Security Proof

Theorem 5.1. *The protocol given above is a non-interactive zero knowledge argument of knowledge with perfect completeness, perfect zero knowledge and it has simulation-extractability (implying it also has knowledge soundness) provided that the $(d(\lambda), q(\lambda))$-XPKE and $(d(\lambda), q(\lambda))$-Poly assumptions hold.*

Proof.
Perfect Completeness
Perfect completeness holds by direct verification. Given the number of variables and the length of the equations in the exponent, we have included this verification in Appendix A for completeness.

Zero-Knowledge
To see that this scheme has perfect zero knowledge, suppose that $\pi = (A, B, C)$ is a valid proof for the instance $(s_1, \ldots s_\ell)$. If A was constructed by the prover then it is uniformly random as it depends on the random element r. The element B is then completely determined by A due to the second verification equation and C is completely determined by A and B due to the first verification equation. Similarly, when A is constructed by the simulator, A is random because it

depends on the random exponent μ. The element B is then completely determined by A since it can be seen to satisfy the second verification equation and C is completely determined by A and B since it can be seen to satisfy the first verification equation. Thus, real proofs and simulated proofs have identical probability distributions.

Simulation Extractability

To show simulation extractability, we shall show that any adversary that breaks simulation extractability for our scheme can also either break the $(d(\lambda), q(\lambda))$-XPKE assumption or break the $(d(\lambda), q(\lambda))$-Poly assumption. To put this formally in terms of the games $\mathcal{G}^{\text{prove-ext}}$, $\mathcal{G}^{\text{XPKE}}$ and $\mathcal{G}^{\text{Poly}}$, we observe that the relation generator $\mathcal{R}$ corresponds to a bilinear group generator where the values ℓ, $\{u_i(X), w_i(X)\}_{i=0}^m$, $t(X)$ are auxiliary information. Formally, we will show that for all PPT adversaries $\mathcal{A}$, there exists PPT algorithms $\mathcal{B}$, $\mathcal{C}$ such that for all PPT extractors $\chi_\mathcal{B}$, there exists a PPT extractor $\chi_\mathcal{A}$ such that for all $\lambda \in \mathbb{N}$

$$\mathbf{Adv}^{\text{prove-ext}}_{\text{Arg},\mathcal{A},\chi_\mathcal{A}}(\lambda) \leq \mathbf{Adv}^{\text{XPKE}}_{\mathcal{R},d(\lambda),q(\lambda),\mathcal{B},\chi_\mathcal{B}}(\lambda) + \mathbf{Adv}^{\text{Poly}}_{\mathcal{R},d(\lambda),q(\lambda),\mathcal{C}}(\lambda) + \epsilon \quad (3)$$

where ϵ is some negligible function in λ. By the $(d(\lambda), q(\lambda))-$XPKE and the $(d(\lambda), q(\lambda))-$Poly assumption we then have that for any choice of $\mathcal{B}$, $\mathcal{C}$ there exists $\chi_\mathcal{B}$ such that the RHS of 3 is negligible in λ. Thus there exists $\chi_\mathcal{A}$ such that $\mathbf{Adv}^{\text{prove-ext}}_{\text{Arg},\mathcal{A},\chi_\mathcal{A}}$ is negligible in λ.

Choosing the algorithms $\mathcal{B}$ and $\mathcal{C}$:

To begin, we choose two PPT algorithms $\mathcal{B}$ and $\mathcal{C}$ such that whenever $\mathcal{A}$ outputs a verifying (ϕ, G^a, H^b, G^c), $\mathcal{B}$ outputs elements (G^a, H^b) such that $a = b$ and $\mathcal{C}$ outputs G^c. Both of these algorithms will run the algorithm $\mathcal{D}$ below as a sub-protocol. The PPT adversary $\mathcal{D}$ takes a bilinear group gk as input, is given access to the oracles described in $\mathcal{G}^{\text{XPKE}}$ (or $\mathcal{G}^{\text{Poly}}$), and is defined as follows.

$$\underline{\mathcal{D}^{\mathcal{O}^1_{G,z}, \mathcal{O}^2_{H,z}}(gk)}$$
$$\mathbf{crs}_{\mathbb{G}_1} = G^\alpha, G^\beta, \ldots \leftarrow \mathcal{O}^1_{G,z}\big(X_\alpha; X_\beta; X_\gamma \, t(X_x); X_\gamma^2 \, t(X_x)^2;$$
$$(X_\alpha + X_\beta) X_\gamma \, t(X_x);$$
$$\{X_\gamma X_x^i, X_\gamma^2 \, t(X_x) \, X_x^i\}_{i=0}^{n-1};$$
$$\{X_\gamma \, w_i(X_x) + (X_\alpha + X_\beta) \, u_i(X_x)\}_{i=0}^\ell;$$
$$\{X_\gamma^2 \, w_i(X_x) + (X_\alpha + X_\beta) X_\gamma \, u_i(X_x)\}_{i=\ell+1}^m\big)$$

$$\mathbf{crs}_{\mathbb{G}_2} = H^1, H^\beta, \ldots \leftarrow \mathcal{O}^2_{H,z}\big(1; X_\beta; X_\gamma \, t(X_x); \{X_\gamma X_x^i\}_{i=0}^{n-1}\big)$$
$$\mathbf{crs} = (\mathbf{crs}_{\mathbb{G}_1}, \mathbf{crs}_{\mathbb{G}_2}); \quad Q' = \emptyset;$$
$$(\phi, (G^a, H^b, G^c)) \leftarrow \mathcal{A}^{\text{ZSimProve}_{\mathbf{crs},\tau}}(\mathbf{crs})$$
$$\text{return } (G^a, H^b, G^c)$$

$$\underline{\text{ZSimProve}_{\mathbf{crs},\tau}(\phi_j)}$$
$$G^{\mu_j}, G^{\mu_j^2 + (\alpha+\beta)\mu_j - \gamma\varphi(\phi_j)} \leftarrow \mathcal{O}^1_{G,z}(X_{\mu_j}; X_{\mu_j}^2 + (X_\alpha + X_\beta) X_{\mu_j});$$
$$H^{\mu_j} \leftarrow \mathcal{O}^2_{H,z}(X_{\mu_j});$$
$$Q' = Q' \cup \{G^{\mu_j}, H^{\mu_j}, G^{\mu_j^2 + (\alpha+\beta)\mu_j - \gamma\varphi(\phi_j)}\}$$
$$\text{return } (G^{\mu_j}, H^{\mu_j}, G^{\mu_j^2 + (\alpha+\beta)\mu_j - \gamma\varphi(\phi_j)}).$$

Then the adversaries $\mathcal{B}$ and $\mathcal{C}$ are given by

$$\frac{\mathcal{B}^{\mathcal{O}^1_{G,z},\mathcal{O}^2_{H,z}}(gk)}{(G^a,H^b,G^c) \leftarrow \mathcal{D}^{\mathcal{O}^1_{G,z},\mathcal{O}^2_{H,z}}(gk)}$$
return (G^a,H^b)

$$\frac{\mathcal{C}^{\mathcal{O}^1_{G,z},\mathcal{O}^2_{H,z}}(gk)}{(G^a,H^b,G^c) \leftarrow \mathcal{D}^{\mathcal{O}^1_{G,z},\mathcal{O}^2_{H,z}}(gk)}$$
$g(\boldsymbol{X}) \leftarrow \chi_{\mathcal{C}}(\text{trans}_{\mathcal{C}})$
return $(G^c, g(\boldsymbol{X}))$

$$\frac{\mathcal{O}^1_{G,z}(g_i)}{\text{return } \mathcal{O}^1_{G,z}(g_i)} \quad \frac{\mathcal{O}^2_{H,z}(h_j)}{\text{return } \mathcal{O}^2_{H,z}(h_j)} \quad \Big| \quad \frac{\mathcal{O}^1_{G,z}(g_i)}{\text{return } \mathcal{O}^1_{G,z}(g_i)} \quad \frac{\mathcal{O}^2_{H,z}(h_j)}{\text{return } \mathcal{O}^2_{H,z}(h_j)}$$

where the algorithm $\chi_{\mathcal{C}}$ outputs $g(\boldsymbol{X})$ specified in (4).

Choosing the algorithm $\chi_{\mathcal{C}}$:
Define $\chi_{\mathcal{C}}$ such that if it receives $\text{trans}_{\mathcal{C}}$ as input and then it outputs

$$g(\boldsymbol{X}) = c_\alpha \cdot X_\alpha + c_\beta \cdot X_\beta + c_{\gamma t} \cdot X_\gamma t(X_x) + \sum_{i=0}^{n-1} \left(c_{x,i} \cdot X_x^i X_\gamma + c_{t,i} \cdot X_x^i X_\gamma^2 t(X_x)\right)$$

$$+ \sum_{i=0}^{\ell} c_i \cdot (X_\alpha + X_\beta) u_i(X_x) + \sum_{i=\ell+1}^{m} c_i (X_\gamma^2 w_i(X_x) + (X_\alpha + X_\beta) X_\gamma u_i(X_x))$$

$$+ \sum_{j=1}^{|Q'|} \left(c_{A_j} \cdot X_{\mu_j} + c_{C_j} \cdot (X_{\mu_j}^2 + (X_\alpha + X_\beta) X_{\mu_j} - X_\gamma \varphi(\phi_j))\right). \quad (4)$$

Possible $\chi_{\mathcal{B}}$ such that $\mathcal{A}$'s output verifies and $\mathcal{B}$ fails at $\mathcal{G}^{\text{XPKE}}$:
Let $\chi_{\mathcal{B}}$ be a PPT extractor for $\mathcal{B}$. If $\mathcal{A}$ were to output (ϕ, G^a, H^b, G^c) such that $\text{ZVfy}(\mathbf{crs}, G^a, H^b, G^c) = 1$, then a must equal b due to the second verification equation. Thus either $\mathcal{B}$ succeeds at $\mathcal{G}^{\text{XPKE}}_{\mathcal{R},d(\lambda),q(\lambda),\mathcal{B},\chi_{\mathcal{B}}}$ or $\chi_{\mathcal{B}}(\text{trans}_{\mathcal{B}})$ outputs

$$\boldsymbol{\eta} = \left(b_0, b_\beta, b_{\gamma,t}, \{b_{x,i}\}_{i=0}^{n-1}, \{b_j\}_{j=1}^{|Q'|}\right) \in \mathbb{Z}^{3+n+|Q'|}$$

such that

$$b = b_0 \cdot 1 + b_\beta \cdot \beta + b_{\gamma,t} \cdot \gamma t(x) + \sum_{i=0}^{n-1} b_{x,i} \cdot x^i \gamma + \sum_{j=1}^{|Q'|} b_j \cdot \mu_j.$$

Choosing the extractor $\chi_{\mathcal{A}}$:
Since $\mathcal{A}$ receives all of $\mathcal{C}$'s oracle responses and $\mathcal{C}$ does not use any random coins to calculate anything else, there is no information in $\text{trans}_{\mathcal{C}}$ that cannot be calculated from $\text{trans}_{\mathcal{A}}$. Let T be such that $T(\text{trans}_{\mathcal{A}}) = \text{trans}_{\mathcal{C}}$. Define the PPT extractor $\chi_{\mathcal{A}}$ as follows[1]

---

[1] where c_i are as in (4).

$$\chi_{\mathcal{A}}(\text{trans}_{\mathcal{A}})$$
$$\text{trans}_C \leftarrow T(\text{trans}_{\mathcal{A}})$$
$$g \in \mathbb{Z}_p[\boldsymbol{X}] \leftarrow \chi_C$$
$$\text{return } c_{\ell+1}, \ldots, c_m$$

Contrapositive - if $\mathcal{B}$ and $\mathcal{C}$ fail then $\mathcal{A}$ fails:

Suppose that $\mathcal{A}$ outputs (ϕ, G^a, H^b, G^c) with $\mathsf{ZVfy}(\mathbf{crs}, \phi, G^a, H^b, G^c) = 1$, and both $\mathcal{B}$ and $\mathcal{C}$ output 0 for $\mathcal{G}^{\text{XPKE}}_{\mathcal{R}, d(\lambda), q(\lambda), \mathcal{B}, \chi_{\mathcal{B}}}$ and $\mathcal{G}^{\text{Poly}}_{\mathcal{R}, d(\lambda), q(\lambda), \mathcal{C}}$ respectively. We shall show that either

1. $(\phi, G^a, H^b, G^c) \in Q'$;
2. the extractor $\chi_{\mathcal{A}}$ outputs a valid witness for ϕ.

Consequently, $\mathcal{A}$ fails at the $\mathcal{G}^{prove-etr}_{\text{Arg}, \mathcal{A}, \chi_{\mathcal{A}}}$ game. This suffices to show that (3) holds. We consider two cases: the case where the vector extracted by $\chi_{\mathcal{B}}$, $\boldsymbol{\eta}$, is such that $b_k \neq 0$ for some $1 \leq k \leq |Q'|$; and the case where $\boldsymbol{\eta}$ is such that $b_j = 0$ for all $1 \leq j \leq |Q'|$. In the first case we shall show that $(\phi, G^a, H^b, G^c) \in Q'$ and in the second case we shall show that $\chi_{\mathcal{A}}$ outputs a valid witness for ϕ.

Relating $\chi_{\mathcal{B}}$'s and χ_C's outputs when $\mathcal{B}$ and $\mathcal{C}$ fail:

If $\mathcal{A}$ outputs (ϕ, G^a, H^b, G^c) such that $\mathsf{ZVfy}(\mathbf{crs}, \phi, G^a, H^b, G^c) = 1$, and if both $\mathcal{B}$ and $\mathcal{C}$ fail at $\mathcal{G}^{\text{XPKE}}_{\mathcal{R}, d(\lambda), q(\lambda), \mathcal{B}, \chi_{\mathcal{B}}}$ and $\mathcal{G}^{\text{Poly}}_{\mathcal{R}, d(\lambda), q(\lambda), \mathcal{C}}$ respectively, then $\chi_{\mathcal{B}}$ and χ_C output $\boldsymbol{\eta}$ and $g(\boldsymbol{X})$ as above such that, with $b = \boldsymbol{\eta} \cdot (\mathbf{crs}_{\mathbb{G}_1}, \boldsymbol{\mu})$,

$$g(\boldsymbol{z}) = b^2 + (\alpha + \beta)b - \gamma\varphi(\phi). \tag{5}$$

If $\chi_{\mathcal{B}}$ outputs $\boldsymbol{\eta}$ with $b_k \neq 0$ then $\mathcal{A}$ outputs $(\phi, G^a, G^b, G^c) \in Q'$:

Suppose that $\chi_{\mathcal{B}}$ outputs $\boldsymbol{\eta}$ is such that $b_k \neq 0$ for some integer $1 \leq k \leq |Q'|$.

Table 3 gives lists the coefficients of the terms that must cancel out if (5) holds. The coefficients in b relating to the all but the kth simulated proofs must cancel because else b^2 would contain a term $\mu_j \mu_k$ and $\mathcal{C}$ does not query $X_{\mu_j} X_{\mu_k}$ for $j \neq k$. Thus $g(\boldsymbol{z})$ cannot contain any C_{A_j}, C_{C_j} terms for $j \neq k$. Similarly, b cannot contain any $b_\beta, b_{\gamma t}, \{b_{x,i}\}_{i=0}^{n-1}$ terms because $\mathcal{C}$ does not query X_β^2 or $X_{\mu_k} X_\gamma$. We also have that b_0 is cancelled because $\mathcal{C}$ does not query $\mathcal{O}^1_{G,z}$ on 1.

We can now use that the remaining terms in the RHS of (5) contain either a factor of γ^2, $\alpha\gamma$, $\beta\gamma$, $\gamma\mu_k$, or μ_k^2; and that none of them contain a factor of x^n. The terms involving c_α, c_β and $\{c_i\}_{i=0}^\ell$, $\{c_{x,i}\}_{i=0}^{n-1}$, c_{A_k} do not involve X_γ^2, $X_{\alpha\gamma}$, $X_{\beta\gamma}$, $X_{\gamma\mu_k}$, or $X_{\mu_k}^2$ terms, and so must cancel. The terms involving $c_{\gamma t}$, $\{c_{t,i}\}_{i=0}^{n-1}$ include the polynomial $t(X_x)$, which is a degree n polynomial, so they must cancel too. Denote the instance ϕ output by $\mathcal{A}$ as $(s_1, \ldots, s_\ell)$ and the instances that $\mathcal{A}$ queries the $\mathsf{ZSimProve}_{\mathbf{crs}, \tau}$ oracle on as $\phi_j = (s_{j1}, \ldots, s_{j\ell})$.

Table 3. Table of coefficients of terms that cancel.

Coefficients	Explanation
$\{b_j\}_{j\neq k}$, , b_β, $b_{\gamma t}$, $\{b_{x,i}\}_{i=0}^{n-1}$, b_0	b cannot contain factors of $\{\mu_j\mu_k\}_{j\neq k}$, β^2, $\mu_k\gamma$, 1
$\{c_{A_j}, c_{C_j}\}_{j\neq k}$	All terms in b involving $\{\mu_j\}_{j\neq k}$ have been cancelled
c_α, c_β, $\{c_i\}_{i=0}^{\ell}$, $\{c_{x,i}\}_{i=0}^{n-1}$, c_{A_k}	Terms in $g(\boldsymbol{X})$ must contain X_γ^2, $X_{\alpha\gamma}$, $X_{\beta\gamma}$, $X_{\gamma\mu_k}$, or $X_{\mu_k}^2$ factors
$c_{\gamma t}$, $c_{t,i}$ for $0 \leq i \leq n-1$	$g(\boldsymbol{X})$ cannot contain factor of X_x^n

The remaining terms in (5) are,

$$b_k^2 X_{\mu_k}^2 + b_k(X_\alpha + X_\beta)X_{\mu_k} - \sum_{i=0}^{\ell} s_i(X_\gamma^2 w_i(X_x) + (X_\alpha + X_\beta)X_\gamma u_i(X_x))$$

$$= \sum_{i=\ell+1}^{m} c_i(X_\gamma^2 w_i(X_x) + (X_\alpha + X_\beta)X_\gamma u_i(X_x))$$

$$+ c_{C_k}\left(X_{\mu_k}^2 + (X_\alpha + X_\beta)X_{\mu_k} - \sum_{i=0}^{\ell} s_{ki}(X_\gamma^2 w_i(X_x) + (X_\alpha + X_\beta)X_\gamma u_i(X_x))\right). \quad (6)$$

Looking separately at the terms involving $X_{\mu_k}^2$, $X_\alpha X_{\mu_k}$, and $X_\alpha X_\gamma$ yields the three simultaneous equations

1. $b_k^2 = c_{C_k}$;
2. $b_k = c_{C_k}$;
3. $\sum_{i=0}^{\ell}(s_i - c_{C_k} s_{ki})u_i(X_x) - \sum_{i=\ell+1}^{m} c_i u_i(X_x) = 0$.

Since $b_k \neq 0$, the first two equations mean that $b_k = c_{C_k} = 1$. Also, where the polynomials $\{u_i(X)\}_{i=0}^{\ell}$ are independent from each other as well as independent from the polynomials $\{u_i(X)\}_{i=\ell+1}^{m}$, the third equation gives us that $s_i = s_{ki}$ for $0 \leq i \leq \ell$ and $\sum_{i=\ell+1}^{m} C_i u_i(x) = 0$.

This is precisely the situation where $\phi = \phi_k$ and $a = \mu_k$, $b = \mu_k$, $c = \mu_k^2 + (\alpha + \beta)\mu_k - \gamma\varphi(\phi_k)$. Hence $(\phi, G^a, G^b, G^c) \in Q'$.

If $\chi_{\mathcal{B}}$ outputs η with all $b_k = 0$ then $\chi_{\mathcal{A}}$ outputs valid w:
Suppose that $\chi_{\mathcal{B}}$ outputs η is such that $b_k = 0$ for all $1 \leq j \leq |Q'|$.

Table 4 gives lists the coefficients of the terms that must cancel out if (5) holds. We have that $g(\boldsymbol{X})$ cannot contain any $\{C_{A_j}, C_{C_j}\}_{i=1}^{|Q'|}$ as b contains no terms involving $\{\mu_j\}_{j=1}^{|Q'|}$. Also, b cannot contain any b_β, b_0 terms because $\mathcal{C}$ does not query X_β^2 or 1.

We can now use that the remaining terms in the RHS of (5) contain either a factor of γ. The terms involving c_α, c_β and $\{c_i\}_{i=0}^{\ell}$ do not involve X_γ so must cancel. This means that we from the remaining coefficients in (5), dividing both sides by X_γ yields

Table 4. Table of coefficients of terms that cancel.

Coefficients	Explanation
b_β, b_0	b cannot contains factor of β^2, 1
$\{c_{A_j}, c_{C_j}\}_{j=1}^{|Q'|}$	$g(\boldsymbol{X})$ cannot contain factors of $\{X_{\mu_j}\}_{j=1}^{|Q'|}$
c_α, c_β, c_i for all $0 \le i \le \ell$	Terms in $g(\boldsymbol{X})$ must contain a factor of X_γ

$$X_\gamma \left(b_{\gamma t} t(X_x) + \sum_{i=0}^{n-1} b_{x,i} X_x^i \right)^2 + (X_\alpha + X_\beta)(b_{\gamma t} t(X_x) + \sum_{i=0}^{n-1} b_{x,i} X_x^i)$$

$$- \sum_{i=0}^{\ell} s_i (X_\gamma w_i(X_x) + (X_\alpha + X_\beta) u_i(X_x))$$

$$= c_{\gamma t} t(X_x) + \sum_{i=0}^{n-1} \left(c_{x,i} X_x^i + c_{t,i} X_x^i X_\gamma t(X_x) \right)$$

$$+ \sum_{i=\ell+1}^{m} c_i (X_\gamma w_i(X_x) + (X_\alpha + X_\beta) u_i(X_x)).$$

Looking separately at the terms involving X_γ and X_α provides the two simultaneous equations

1. $\left(\sum_{i=0}^{n-1} b_{x,i} X_x^i + b_{\gamma t} t(X_x) \right)^2 = \sum_{i=0}^{n-1} c_{t,i} X_x^i t(X_x) + \sum_{i=0}^{\ell} s_i w_i(X_x)$
$$+ \sum_{i=\ell+1}^{m} c_i w_i(X_x);$$

2. $\sum_{i=0}^{n-1} b_{x,i} X_x^i + b_{\gamma t} t(X_x) = \sum_{i=0}^{\ell} s_i u_i(X_x) + \sum_{i=\ell+1}^{m} c_i u_i(X_x).$

The first equation means that $b_{\gamma t} = 0$ because the term $b_{\gamma t}^2 t^2(X_x)$ is a degree $2n$ polynomial in X_x, whereas all other polynomials in X_x in that equation have maximum degree $2n - 1$. Set $h(X_x) = \sum_{i=0}^{n-1} c_{t,i} X_x^i$. Then these two equations ensure that the witness $\boldsymbol{w} = (c_{\ell+1}, \ldots, c_m)$ is a valid witness for ϕ. $\qquad\square$

6   Lower Bounds

Our pairing based simulation-extractable SNARK construction in Sect. 5 is optimal in the number of group elements and verification equations. In the full paper, we prove that in the generic group model it is impossible to have a pairing based SE-NIZK with just one verification equation or have proofs with just 2 group elements. Consequently, it is impossible to have a pairing based SoK with one verification equation or with 2 group elements. This stands in contrast to standard knowledge sound NIZK arguments, for which there are constructions consisting of just one verification equation [36].

Theorem 6.1. *If $\mathcal{R}$ is a relation generator with hard decision problems and* (ZSetup, ZProve, ZVfy, ZSimProve) *is a pairing based (as defined by Groth [36]) SE-NIZK for $\mathcal{R}$ then* ZVfy *must consist of at least 2 verification equations and the proofs must consist of at least 3 group elements.*

We refer to the full paper for the proof.

A   Completeness of the SE-SNARK in Sect. 5

Here we show perfect completeness of the SE-SNARK presented in Sect. 5. Suppose that

$$A = G^{\gamma\left(\sum_{i=0}^{m} s_i u_i(x) + r \cdot t(x)\right)}, \qquad B = H^{\gamma\left(\sum_{i=0}^{m} s_i u_i(x) + r \cdot t(x)\right)}$$

$$C = G^{f(w) + r^2 \gamma^2 (t(x))^2 + r(\alpha+\beta)\gamma t(x) + \gamma^2 t(x)\left[h(x) + 2r \sum_{i=0}^{m} s_i u_i(x)\right]}$$

where $f(w) = \sum_{i=l+1}^{m} s_i(\gamma^2 w_i(x) + (\alpha + \beta)\gamma u_i(x))$.

It is easy to see the second verification equation $e(A, H^\gamma) = e(G^\gamma, B)$ holds. Here we show that so does the first verification equation

$$e(AG^\alpha, BH^\beta) = e(G^\alpha, H^\beta)e(G^{\varphi(\phi)}, H^\gamma)e(C, H),$$

where $\varphi(\phi) = \sum_{i=0}^{\ell} s_i(\gamma w_i(x) + (\alpha + \beta)u_i(x))$. Taking discrete logarithms, this is equivalent to showing that

$$\left(\gamma\left(\sum_{i=0}^{m} s_i u_i(x) + r \cdot t(x)\right) + \alpha\right) \cdot \left(\gamma\left(\sum_{i=0}^{m} s_i u_i(x) + r \cdot t(x)\right) + \beta\right)$$

$$= \alpha\beta + \gamma \sum_{i=0}^{\ell} s_i \left(\gamma w_i(x) + (\alpha + \beta)u_i(x)\right) + \sum_{i=l+1}^{m} s_i(\gamma^2 w_i(x) + (\alpha + \beta)\gamma u_i(x))$$

$$+ r^2\gamma^2(t(x))^2 + r(\alpha + \beta)\gamma t(x) + \gamma^2 t(x)\left[h(x) + 2r \sum_{i=0}^{m} s_i u_i(x)\right]. \quad (7)$$

Combining the sums, the right hand side of (7) can be rewritten as

$$\alpha\beta + \gamma(\alpha + \beta)\left(\sum_{i=0}^{m} s_i(u_i(x)) + r \cdot t(x)\right)$$

$$+ \gamma^2 \left(\sum_{i=0}^{m} s_i(w_i(x) + 2r \cdot t(x)u_i(x)) + r^2(t(x))^2 + t(x)h(x)\right). \quad (8)$$

Expanding the left hand side of (7) yields

$$\alpha\beta + \gamma(\alpha + \beta)\left(\sum_{i=0}^{m} s_i u_i(x) + r \cdot t(x)\right) + \gamma^2 \left(\sum_{i=0}^{m} s_i u_i(x) + r \cdot t(x)\right)^2.$$

Since $(s_0, \ldots, s_m)$ is a valid witness for R, we have that $\left(\sum_{i=0}^{m} s_i u_i(X)\right)^2 = \sum_{i=0}^{m} s_i w_i(X) + h(X)t(X)$ for all $X \in \mathbb{Z}_p$. In particular this means that the left hand side of (7) is equal to

$$\alpha\beta + \gamma\left(\alpha + \beta\right)\left(\sum_{i=0}^{m} s_i u_i(x) + r \cdot t(x)\right)$$

$$+ \gamma^2 \left(\sum_{i=0}^{m} s_i \left(w_i(x) + 2r \cdot t(x)u_i(x)\right) + r^2(t(x))^2 + h(x)t(x)\right).$$

This is identical to the expression in (8), which gives us that the left hand side and the right hand side of (7) are equal.

B   Square Arithmetic Programs

We defined Square Arithmetic Program (SAP) relations in Sect. 5. We will now show how any arithmetic circuit with fan-in 2 gates over a finite field $\mathbb{Z}_p$ can be expressed as a SAP over the same finite field. The conversion is largely the same as the conversions described in [19,30], however we also discuss how to instantiate the trick of replacing multiplications with squarings that was mentioned in [36].

Gennaro, Gentry, Parno and Raykova [30] introduced quadratic span programs (QSPs) and quadratic arithmetic programs (QAPs). These define NP-complete languages specified by a quadratic equation over polynomials. QSPs characterise boolean circuits and QAPs characterise arithmetic circuits in a natural way. Danezis, Fournet, Groth and Kohlweiss [19] noticed that by replacing each of the constraints in QSPs with 2 other constaints, it is possible to design a square span program (SSP), which is a QSP in which the two sets of polynomials involved in the quadratic term are identical. Using this technique they were able to reduce the number of proof elements and verification equations (at the cost of a circuit with twice as many gates) by having the quadratic proof components on each side of the pairing be replicas. We use SAPs in a similar way to make the group elements A and B in our proof symmetric.

An arithmetic circuit can be described as a set of equations over the wires $s_1, \ldots, s_m$. We fix the constant $s_0 = 1$, use $s_1, \ldots, s_\ell \in \mathbb{Z}_p$ to describe the instance, and the rest of the wires $s_{\ell+1}, \ldots, s_m$ can be viewed as the (extended) witness. Generalising from the simple equations that arise in arithmetic circuit, we can consider a set of equations of the form

$$\sum_{i=0}^{m} s_i u_{i,q} \cdot \sum_{i=0}^{m} s_i v_{i,q} = \sum_{i=0}^{m} s_i w_{i,q},$$

where $u_{i,q}, v_{i,q}, w_{i,q}$ are constants in $\mathbb{Z}_p$ specifying the qth equation.

Our SAP is based on a simplification of systems of arithmetic constraints, where all multiplications are replaced with squarings. As suggested by [36], we can write a product $ab = \frac{(a+b)^2 - (a-b)^2}{4}$. A system with n multiplication constraints can therefore be rewritten as a system with at most $2n$ squaring constraints. To be precise, for each multiplication constraint $\sum_{i=0}^{m} s_i u_{i,q} \cdot \sum_{i=0}^{m} s_i v_{i,q} = \sum_{i=0}^{m} s_i w_{i,q}$ we introduce a new variable s_{m+q} and replace it with two squaring constraints

1. $\left(\sum_{i=0}^{m} s_i(u_{i,q} + v_{i,q})\right)^2 = 4\sum_{i=0}^{m} s_i w_{i,q} + s_{m+q};$
2. $\left(\sum_{i=0}^{m} s_i(u_{i,q} - v_{i,q})\right)^2 = s_{m+q}.$

Given n squaring constraints $\left\{\left(\sum_{i=0}^{m} s_i u_{i,q}\right)^2 = \sum_{i=0}^{m} s_i w_{i,q}\right\}_{q=1}^{n}$ we can now pick arbitrary distinct $r_1, \ldots, r_n \in \mathbb{Z}_p$ and define $t(x) = \prod_{q=1}^{n}(x - r_q)$. Furthermore, let $u_i(x), w_i(x)$ be degree $n-1$ polynomials such that

$$u_i(r_q) = u_{i,q} \quad \text{and} \quad w_i(r_q) = w_{i,q} \quad \text{for} \quad i = 0, \ldots, m, q = 1, \ldots, n.$$

We now have that $s_0 = 1$ and the variables $s_1, \ldots, s_m \in \mathbb{F}$ satisfy the n equations if and only if in each point $r_1, \ldots, r_q$

$$\left(\sum_{i=0}^{m} s_i u_i(r_q)\right)^2 = \sum_{i=0}^{m} s_i w_i(r_q).$$

Since $t(X)$ is the lowest degree monomial with $t(r_q) = 0$ in each point, we can reformulate this condition as

$$\left(\sum_{i=0}^{m} s_i u_i(X)\right)^2 \equiv \sum_{i=0}^{m} s_i w_i(X) \mod t(X).$$

This gives rise to a SAP as defined in Sect. 5.

Formally, we work with square arithmetic programs R that have the following description

$$R = \left(\mathbb{Z}_p, \text{aux}, \ell, \{u_i(X), w_i(X)\}_{i=0}^{m}, t(X)\right),$$

where p is a prime, aux is some auxiliary information, $1 \le \ell \le m$, $u_i(X), w_i(X), t(X) \in \mathbb{Z}_p[X]$ and $u_i(X), w_i(X)$ have strictly lower degree than n, the degree of $t(X)$. A square arithmetic program with such a description defines the following binary relation, where we define $s_0 = 1$,

$$R = \left\{ (\phi, w) \,\middle|\, \begin{array}{l} \phi = (s_1, \ldots, s_\ell) \in \mathbb{Z}_p^\ell \\ w = (s_{\ell+1}, \ldots, s_m) \in \mathbb{Z}_p^{m-\ell} \\[4pt] \left(\sum_{i=0}^{m} s_i u_i(X)\right)^2 \equiv \sum_{i=0}^{m} s_i w_i(X) \mod t(X) \end{array} \right\}.$$

We say $\mathcal{R}$ is a square arithmetic program generator if it generates relations of the form given above with $p > 2^{\lambda-1}$.

Relations can arise in many different ways in practice. It may be that the relationship generator is deterministic or it may be that it is randomized. It may be that first the prime p is generated and then the rest of the relation is built on top of the $\mathbb{Z}_p$. Or it may be that the polynomials are specified first and then a random field $\mathbb{Z}_p$ is chosen. To get maximal flexibility we have chosen our definitions to be agnostic with respect to the exact way the field and the relation is generated, the different options can all be modelled by appropriate choices of relation generators.

In our pairing-based NIZK arguments the auxiliary information aux specifies a bilinear group. It may seem a bit surprising to make the choice of bilinear group part of the relation generator but this provides a better model of settings where the relation is built on top of an already existing bilinear group. Again, there is no loss of generality in this choice, one can think of a traditional setting where the relation is chosen first and then the bilinear group is chosen at random as the special case where the relation generator works in two steps, first choosing the relation and then picking a random bilinear group. Of course letting the relation generator pick the bilinear group is another good reason that we need to assume it is benign; an appropriate choice of bilinear group is essential for security.

We use in the security proofs that the polynomials $u_0(X), \ldots, u_\ell(X)$ are linearly independent from each other and linearly independent from $u_{\ell+1}(X), \ldots, u_m(X)$. When constructing the square arithmetic program from squaring constraints, we can achieve this by introducing the constraint $s_i \cdot 1 = s_i$ for any $u_i(X)$ that is not already linearly independent. This makes $u_i(X)$ linearly independent from all the other $u_j(X)$ since $u_i(r_{m+i}) = 1$, while $u_j(r_{m+i}) = 0$ for all $j \neq i$.

Finally, we note that given the square arithmetic program defining R', we can formulate the square arithmetic program defining

$$R = \{((h, \phi), w) : \quad h \in \{0,1\}^\lambda \ \wedge \ (\phi, w) \in R'\}$$

by introducing another new variable h and adding the constraint that $h \cdot 1 = h$. This means that from a simulation-extractable NIZK for relation R, we can build a simulation extractable signature of knowledge as in Sect. 3.

Acknowledgments. We thank Vasilios Mavroudis and Markulf Kohlweiss for helpful discussions.

References

1. Abe, M., Fehr, S.: Perfect NIZK with adaptive soundness. In: Vadhan, S.P. (ed.) TCC 2007. LNCS, vol. 4392, pp. 118–136. Springer, Heidelberg (2007). doi:10.1007/978-3-540-70936-7_7

2. Bdmp, M.B., De Santis, A., Micali, S., Persiano, G.: Non-interactive zero-knowledge proof systems. SIAM J. Comput. **20**(6), 1084–1118 (1991)

3. Bellare, M., Fuchsbauer, G.: Policy-based signatures. In: Krawczyk, H. (ed.) PKC 2014. LNCS, vol. 8383, pp. 520–537. Springer, Heidelberg (2014). doi:10.1007/978-3-642-54631-0_30

4. Ben-Sasson, E., Chiesa, A., Tromer, E., Virza, M.: Scalable zero knowledge via cycles of elliptic curves. In: Garay, J.A., Gennaro, R. (eds.) CRYPTO 2014. LNCS, vol. 8617, pp. 276–294. Springer, Heidelberg (2014). doi:10.1007/978-3-662-44381-1_16

5. Benhamouda, F., Camenisch, J., Krenn, S., Lyubashevsky, V., Neven, G.: Better zero-knowledge proofs for lattice encryption and their application to group signatures. In: Sarkar, P., Iwata, T. (eds.) ASIACRYPT 2014. LNCS, vol. 8873, pp. 551–572. Springer, Heidelberg (2014). doi:10.1007/978-3-662-45611-8_29

6. Bernhard, D., Fuchsbauer, G., Ghadafi, E.: Efficient signatures of knowledge and DAA in the standard model. In: Jacobson, M., Locasto, M., Mohassel, P., Safavi-Naini, R. (eds.) ACNS 2013. LNCS, vol. 7954, pp. 518–533. Springer, Heidelberg (2013). doi:10.1007/978-3-642-38980-1_33

7. Bernhard, D., Fuchsbauer, G., Ghadafi, E., Smart, N.P., Warinschi, B.: Anonymous attestation with user-controlled linkability. Int. J. Inf. Secur. 12(3), 219–249 (2013)

8. Bitansky, N., Canetti, R., Chiesa, A., Tromer, E.: Recursive composition and bootstrapping for snarks and proof-carrying data. In: Proceedings of the Forty-Fifth Annual ACM Symposium on Theory of Computing, pp. 111–120. ACM (2013)

9. Bitansky, N., Canetti, R., Paneth, O., Rosen, A.: Indistinguishability obfuscation vs. auxiliary-input extractable functions: One must fall. IACR Cryptology ePrint Archive, 2013:641 (2013)

10. Bitansky, N., Canetti, R., Paneth, O., Rosen, A.: On the existence of extractable one-way functions. SIAM J. Comput. 45(5), 1910–1952 (2016)

11. Bitansky, N., Chiesa, A., Ishai, Y., Paneth, O., Ostrovsky, R.: Succinct non-interactive arguments via linear interactive proofs. In: Sahai, A. (ed.) TCC 2013. LNCS, vol. 7785, pp. 315–333. Springer, Heidelberg (2013). doi:10.1007/978-3-642-36594-2_18

12. Blum, M., Feldman, P., Micali, S.: Non-interactive zero-knowledge and its applications. In: Proceedings of the Twentieth Annual ACM Symposium on Theory of Computing, pp. 103–112. ACM (1988)

13. Boneh, D., Boyen, X., Goh, E.-J.: Hierarchical identity based encryption with constant size ciphertext. In: Cramer, R. (ed.) EUROCRYPT 2005. LNCS, vol. 3494, pp. 440–456. Springer, Heidelberg (2005). doi:10.1007/11426639_26

14. Boyle, E., Pass, R.: Limits of extractability assumptions with distributional auxiliary input. In: Iwata, T., Cheon, J.H. (eds.) ASIACRYPT 2015. LNCS, vol. 9453, pp. 236–261. Springer, Heidelberg (2015). doi:10.1007/978-3-662-48800-3_10

15. Brickell, E., Chen, L., Li, J.: A new direct anonymous attestation scheme from bilinear maps. In: Lipp, P., Sadeghi, A.-R., Koch, K.-M. (eds.) Trust 2008. LNCS, vol. 4968, pp. 166–178. Springer, Heidelberg (2008). doi:10.1007/978-3-540-68979-9_13

16. Camenisch, J., Stadler, M.: Efficient group signature schemes for large groups. In: Kaliski, B.S. (ed.) CRYPTO 1997. LNCS, vol. 1294, pp. 410–424. Springer, Heidelberg (1997). doi:10.1007/BFb0052252

17. Chase, M., Lysyanskaya, A.: On signatures of knowledge. In: Dwork, C. (ed.) CRYPTO 2006. LNCS, vol. 4117, pp. 78–96. Springer, Heidelberg (2006). doi:10.1007/11818175_5

18. Damgård, I.: Non-interactive circuit based proofs and non-interactive perfect zero-knowledge with preprocessing. In: Rueppel, R.A. (ed.) EUROCRYPT 1992. LNCS, vol. 658, pp. 341–355. Springer, Heidelberg (1993). doi:10.1007/3-540-47555-9_28

19. Danezis, G., Fournet, C., Groth, J., Kohlweiss, M.: Square span programs with applications to succinct NIZK arguments. In: Sarkar, P., Iwata, T. (eds.) ASIACRYPT 2014. LNCS, vol. 8873, pp. 532–550. Springer, Heidelberg (2014). doi:10.1007/978-3-662-45611-8_28

20. Santis, A., Crescenzo, G., Persiano, G.: Necessary and sufficient assumptions for non-interactive zero-knowledge proofs of knowledge for All NP relations. In: Montanari, U., Rolim, J.D.P., Welzl, E. (eds.) ICALP 2000. LNCS, vol. 1853, pp. 451–462. Springer, Heidelberg (2000). doi:10.1007/3-540-45022-X_38

21. De Santis, A., Persiano, G.: Zero-knowledge proofs of knowledge without inter-action. In: 33rd Annual Symposium on Foundations of Computer Science, 1992, Proceedings, pp. 427–436. IEEE (1992)

22. Derler, D., Slamanig, D.: Fully-anonymous short dynamic group signatures without encryption. IACR Cryptology ePrint Archive 2016:154 (2016)

23. Escala, A., Herold, G., Kiltz, E., Rafols, C., Villar, J.: An algebraic framework for diffie-hellman assumptions. J. Cryptol. **30**(1), 242–288 (2017)

24. Faust, S., Kohlweiss, M., Marson, G.A., Venturi, D.: On the non-malleability of the fiat-shamir transform. In: Galbraith, S., Nandi, M. (eds.) INDOCRYPT 2012. LNCS, vol. 7668, pp. 60–79. Springer, Heidelberg (2012). doi:10.1007/978-3-642-34931-7_5

25. Feige, U., Lapidot, D., Shamir, A.: Multiple noninteractive zero knowledge proofs under general assumptions. SIAM J. Comput. **29**(1), 1–28 (1999)

26. Feng, D.-G., Xu, J., Chen, X.-F.: An efficient direct anonymous attestation scheme with forward security. WSEAS Trans. Commun. **8**(10), 1076–1085 (2009)

27. Fischlin, M., Onete, C.: Relaxed security notions for signatures of knowledge. In: Lopez, J., Tsudik, G. (eds.) ACNS 2011. LNCS, vol. 6715, pp. 309–326. Springer, Heidelberg (2011). doi:10.1007/978-3-642-21554-4_18

28. Galbraith, S.D., Paterson, K.G., Smart, N.P.: Pairings for cryptographers. Discrete Appl. Math. **156**(16), 3113–3121 (2008)

29. Ge, H., Tate, S.R.: A direct anonymous attestation scheme for embedded devices. In: Okamoto, T., Wang, X. (eds.) PKC 2007. LNCS, vol. 4450, pp. 16–30. Springer, Heidelberg (2007). doi:10.1007/978-3-540-71677-8_2

30. Gennaro, R., Gentry, C., Parno, B., Raykova, M.: Quadratic span programs and succinct NIZKs without PCPs. In: Johansson, T., Nguyen, P.Q. (eds.) EURO-CRYPT 2013. LNCS, vol. 7881, pp. 626–645. Springer, Heidelberg (2013). doi:10.1007/978-3-642-38348-9_37

31. Gentry, C., Groth, J., Ishai, Y., Peikert, C., Sahai, A., Smith, A.D.: Using fully homomorphic hybrid encryption to minimize non-interative zero-knowledge proofs. J. Cryptol. **28**(4), 820–843 (2015)

32. Gentry, C., Wichs, D.: Separating succinct non-interactive arguments from all fal-sifiable assumptions. In: Proceedings of the Forty-Third Annual ACM Symposium on Theory of Computing, pp. 99–108. ACM (2011)

33. Ghadafi, E., Groth, J.: Towards a classification of non-interactive computational assumptions in cyclic groups. Cryptology ePrint Archive, Report 2017/343 (2017)

34. Groth, J.: Simulation-sound NIZK proofs for a practical language and constant size group signatures. In: Lai, X., Chen, K. (eds.) ASIACRYPT 2006. LNCS, vol. 4284, pp. 444–459. Springer, Heidelberg (2006). doi:10.1007/11935230_29

35. Groth, J.: Short non-interactive zero-knowledge proofs. In: Abe, M. (ed.) ASI-ACRYPT 2010. LNCS, vol. 6477, pp. 341–358. Springer, Heidelberg (2010). doi:10.1007/978-3-642-17373-8_20

36. Groth, J.: On the size of pairing-based non-interactive arguments. In: Fischlin, M., Coron, J.-S. (eds.) EUROCRYPT 2016. LNCS, vol. 9666, pp. 305–326. Springer, Heidelberg (2016). doi:10.1007/978-3-662-49896-5_11

37. Groth, J., Ostrovsky, R.: Cryptography in the multi-string model. J. Cryptol. **27**(3), 506–543 (2014)

38. Groth, J., Ostrovsky, R., Sahai, A.: New techniques for noninteractive zero-knowledge. J. ACM (JACM) **59**(3), 11 (2012)

39. Groth, J., Sahai, A.: Efficient noninteractive proof systems for bilinear groups. SIAM J. Comput. **41**(5), 1193–1232 (2012)

40. Kilian, J.: Improved efficient arguments. In: Coppersmith, D. (ed.) CRYPTO 1995. LNCS, vol. 963, pp. 311–324. Springer, Heidelberg (1995). doi:10.1007/3-540-44750-4_25

41. Kilian, J., Petrank, E.: An efficient noninteractive zero-knowledge proof system for np with general assumptions. J. Cryptol. **11**(1), 1–27 (1998)

42. Maurer, U., Wolf, S.: Lower bounds on generic algorithms in groups. In: Nyberg, K. (ed.) EUROCRYPT 1998. LNCS, vol. 1403, pp. 72–84. Springer, Heidelberg (1998). doi:10.1007/BFb0054118

43. Micali, S.: Computationally sound proofs. SIAM J. Comput. **30**(4), 1253–1298 (2000)

44. Miers, I., Garman, C., Green, M., Rubin, A.D.: Zerocoin: anonymous distributed e-cash from bitcoin. In: 2013 IEEE Symposium on Security and Privacy (SP), pp. 397–411. IEEE (2013)

45. Nechaev, V.I.: Complexity of a determinate algorithm for the discrete logarithm. Math. Notes **55**(2), 165–172 (1994)

46. Peikert, C., Vaikuntanathan, V., Waters, B.: A framework for efficient and composable oblivious transfer. In: Wagner, D. (ed.) CRYPTO 2008. LNCS, vol. 5157, pp. 554–571. Springer, Heidelberg (2008). doi:10.1007/978-3-540-85174-5_31

47. Sahai, A.: Non-malleable non-interactive zero knowledge and adaptive chosen-ciphertext security. In: 40th Annual Symposium on Foundations of Computer Science, 1999, pp. 543–553. IEEE (1999)

48. Sasson, E.B., Chiesa, A., Garman, C., Green, M., Miers, I., Tromer, E., Virza, M.: Zerocash: decentralized anonymous payments from bitcoin. In: 2014 IEEE Symposium on Security and Privacy (SP), pp. 459–474. IEEE (2014)

49. Schnorr, C.-P.: Efficient signature generation by smart cards. J. Cryptol. **4**(3), 161–174 (1991)

50. Shoup, V.: Lower bounds for discrete logarithms and related problems. In: Fumy, W. (ed.) EUROCRYPT 1997. LNCS, vol. 1233, pp. 256–266. Springer, Heidelberg (1997). doi:10.1007/3-540-69053-0_18

51. Valiant, P.: Incrementally verifiable computation or proofs of knowledge imply time/space efficiency. In: Canetti, R. (ed.) TCC 2008. LNCS, vol. 4948, pp. 1–18. Springer, Heidelberg (2008). doi:10.1007/978-3-540-78524-8_1

52. Yang, B., Yang, K., Qin, Y., Zhang, Z., Feng, D.: DAA-TZ: an efficient DAA scheme for mobile devices using ARM TrustZone. In: Conti, M., Schunter, M., Askoxylakis, I. (eds.) Trust 2015. LNCS, vol. 9229, pp. 209–227. Springer, Cham (2015). doi:10.1007/978-3-319-22846-4_13

Fast Secure Two-Party ECDSA Signing

Yehuda Lindell[(✉)]

Department of Computer Science, Bar-Ilan University, Ramat Gan, Israel
`lindell@biu.ac.il`

Abstract. ECDSA is a standard digital signature schemes that is widely used in TLS, Bitcoin and elsewhere. Unlike other schemes like RSA, Schnorr signatures and more, it is particularly hard to construct efficient threshold signature protocols for ECDSA (and DSA). As a result, the best-known protocols today for secure distributed ECDSA require running heavy zero-knowledge proofs and computing many large-modulus exponentiations for every signing operation. In this paper, we consider the specific case of two parties (and thus no honest majority) and construct a protocol that is approximately *two orders of magnitude faster* than the previous best. Concretely, our protocol achieves good performance, with a single signing operation for curve P-256 taking approximately 37 ms between two standard machine types in Azure (utilizing a single core only). Our protocol is proven secure under standard assumptions using a game-based definition. In addition, we prove security by simulation under a plausible yet non-standard assumption regarding Paillier.

1 Introduction

1.1 Background

In the late 1980s and the 1990s, a large body of research emerged around the problem of *threshold cryptography*; cf. [3,7,9,10,13,20,23,24]. In its most general form, this problem considers the setting of a private key shared between n parties with the property that any subset of t parties may be able to decrypt or sign, but any set of less than t parties can do nothing. This is a specific example of secure multiparty computation, where the functionality being computed is either decryption or signing. Note that trivial solutions like secret sharing the private key and reconstructing to decrypt or sign do not work since after the first operation the key is reconstructed, and any single party can decrypt or sign by itself from that point on. Rather, the requirement is that a subset of t parties is needed for *every* private-key operation.

Threshold cryptography can be used in applications where multiple signators are needed to generate a signature, and likewise where highly confidential documents should only be decrypted and viewed by a quorum. Furthermore, threshold cryptography can be used to provide a high level of key protection.

Y. Lindell—Much of this work was done for Dyadic Security Ltd.

J. Katz and H. Shacham (Eds.): CRYPTO 2017, Part II, LNCS 10402, pp. 613–644, 2017.
DOI: 10.1007/978-3-319-63715-0_21

This is achieved by sharing the key on multiple devices (or between multiple users) and carrying out private-key operations via a secure protocol that reveals nothing but the output. This provides key protection since an adversary needs to breach multiple devices in order to obtain the key. After intensive research on the topic in the 1990s and early 2000s, threshold cryptography received considerably less interest in the past decade. However, interest has recently been renewed. This can be seen by the fact that a number of startup companies are now deploying threshold cryptography for the purpose of key protection [25–27]. Another reason is due to the fact that ECDSA signing is used in bitcoin, and the theft of a signing key can immediately be translated into concrete financial loss. Bitcoin has a multisignature solution built in, which is based on using multiple distinct signing keys rather than a threshold signing scheme. Nevertheless, a more general solution may be obtained via threshold cryptography (for the more general t-out-of-n threshold case).

Fast threshold cryptography protocols exist for a wide variety of problems, including RSA signing and decryption, ElGamal and ECIES encryption, Schnorr signatures, Cramer-Shoup, and more. Despite the above successes, and despite the fact that DSA/ECDSA is a widely-used standard, DSA/ECDSA has resisted attempts at constructing efficient protocols for threshold signing. This seems to be due to the need to compute k and k^{-1} without knowing k. We explain this by comparing ECDSA signing to EC-Schnorr signing. In both cases, the public verification key is an elliptic curve point Q and the private signing key is x such that $Q = x \cdot G$, where G is the generator point of an EC group of order q.

EC-Schnorr signing	ECDSA signing
Choose a random $k \leftarrow \mathbb{Z}_q$	Choose a random $k \leftarrow \mathbb{Z}_q$
Compute $R = k \cdot G$	Compute $R = k \cdot G$
Compute $e = H(m\|R)$	Compute $r = r_x \bmod q$ where $R = (r_x, r_y)$
Compute $s = k - x \cdot e \bmod q$	Compute $s = k^{-1} \cdot (H(m) + r \cdot x) \bmod q$
Output (s, e)	Output (r, s)

Observe that Schnorr signing can be easily distributed since the private key x and the value k are both used in a linear equation. Thus, two parties with shares x_1, x_2 such that $Q = (x_1 + x_2) \cdot G$ can each locally choose k_1, k_2, and set $R = k_1 \cdot G + k_2 \cdot G = (k_1 + k_2) \cdot G$. Then, each can locally compute e and $s_i = k_i - x_i \cdot e \bmod q$ and send to each other, and each party can sum $s = s_1 + s_2 \bmod q$ and output a valid signature (s, e). In the case of malicious adversaries, some zero knowledge proofs are needed to ensure that R is uniformly distributed, but these are highly efficient proofs of knowledge of discrete log. In contrast, in ECDSA signing, the equation for computing s includes k^{-1}. Now, given shares k_1, k_2 such that $k_1 + k_2 = k \bmod q$ it is very difficult to compute k_1', k_2' such that $k_1' + k_2' = k^{-1} \bmod q$.

As a result, beginning with [20] and more lately in [14], two-party protocols for ECDSA signing use *multiplicative sharing* of x and of k. That is, the parties hold x_1, x_2 such that $x_1 \cdot x_2 = x \bmod q$, and in each signing operation they generate k_1, k_2 such that $k_1 \cdot k_2 = k \bmod q$. This enables them to easily compute k^{-1} since each party can locally compute $k'_i = k_i^{-1} \bmod q$, and then k'_1, k'_2 are multiplicative shares of k^{-1}. The parties can then use additively homomorphic encryption – specifically Paillier encryption [21] – in order to combine their equations. For example, P_1 can compute $c_1 = \mathsf{Enc}_{pk}((k_1)^{-1} \cdot H(m))$ and $c_2 = \mathsf{Enc}_{pk}(k_1^{-1} \cdot x_1 \cdot r)$. Then, using scalar multiplication (denoted $\odot$) and homomorphic addition (denoted $\oplus$), P_2 can compute $(k_2^{-1} \odot c_1) \oplus [(k_2^{-1} \cdot x_2) \odot c_2]$ which will be an encryption of

$$k_2^{-1} \cdot (k_1^{-1} \cdot H(m)) + k_2^{-1} \cdot x_2 \cdot (k_1^{-1} \cdot x_1 \cdot r) = k^{-1} \cdot (H(m) + r \cdot x),$$

as required. However, proving that each party worked correctly is extremely difficult. For example, the first party must prove that the Paillier encryption includes k_1^{-1} when the second party only has $R_1 = k_1 \cdot G$, it must prove that the Paillier encryptions are to values in the expected range, and more. This can be done, but it results in a protocol that is very expensive.

1.2 Our Results

As in previous protocols, we use Paillier homomorphic encryption (with a key generated by P_1), and multiplicative sharing of both the private key x and the random value k. However, we make the novel observation that if P_2 already holds a Paillier encryption c_{key} of P_1's share of the private key x_1, then P_1 need not do anything except participate in the generation of $R = k \cdot G$. Specifically, assume that the parties P_1 and P_2 begin by generating $R = k_1 \cdot k_2 \cdot G$ (this is essentially accomplished by just running a Diffie-Hellman key exchange with basic knowledge-of-discrete-log proofs which are highly efficient). Then, given $c_{key} = \mathsf{Enc}_{pk}(x_1)$, R and k_2, x_2, party P_2 can singlehandedly compute an encryption of $k_2^{-1} \cdot H(m) + k_2^{-1} \cdot r \cdot x_2 \cdot x_1$ using the homomorphic properties of Paillier encryption. This ciphertext can be sent to P_1 who decrypts and multiplies the result by k_1^{-1}. If P_2 is honest, then the result is a valid signature.

The crucial issue that must be dealt with is what happens when P_1 or P_2 is corrupted. If P_1 is corrupted, it cannot do anything since the only message that it sends P_2 is in the generation of R which is protected by an efficient zero-knowledge proof. Thus, no expensive proofs are needed. Furthermore, if P_2 is corrupted, then the only way it can cheat is by encrypting something incorrect and sending it to P_1. However, here we can utilize the fact that we are specifically computing a digital signature that can be *publicly verified*. That is, since all P_1 does is locally decrypt the ciphertext received from P_2 and multiply by k_1^{-1}, it can locally check if the signature obtained is valid. If yes, it outputs it, and if not it detects P_2 cheating. Thus, no zero-knowledge proofs are required for P_2 either (again, beyond the zero-knowledge proof in the generation of R).

As a result, we obtain a signing protocol that is extremely simple and efficient. As we show, our protocol is approximately two orders of magnitude faster than the previous best. Before proceeding, we remark that there are additional elements needed in the protocol (like P_2 adding random noise in the ciphertext it sends), but these have little effect on the efficiency.

We remark that since the security of the signing protocol rests upon the assumption that P_2 holds an encryption of x_1, which is P_1's share of the key, this must be proven in the key generation phase. Thus, the key generation phase of our protocol is more complicated than the signing phase, and includes a proof that P_1 generated the Paillier key correctly and that c_{key} is an encryption of x_1, given $R_1 = x_1 \cdot G$. This latter proof is of interest since it connects between Paillier encryption and discrete log, and we present a novel efficient proof in the paper. We remark that since key generation is run only once, having a more expensive key-generation phase is a worthwhile tradeoff. This is especially the case since it is still quite reasonable (concretely taking about 5 s between standard single-core machines in Azure, which is much faster than the key-generation phase of [14]). Furthermore, it can easily be parallelized to further bring down the cost.

DSA vs ECDSA. In this paper, we refer to ECDSA throughout and we use Elliptic curve (additive group) notation. However, our entire protocol translates easily to the DSA case, since we do nothing but standard group operations.

Caveat. The only caveat of our work is that it focuses specifically on the two-party case, whereas prior works considered general thresholds as well. The two-party case is in some ways the most difficult case (since there is no honest majority), and we therefore believe that our techniques may be useful for the general case as well. We leave this for future research.

1.3   Related Work and a Comparison of Efficiency

The first specific protocol for threshold DSA signing with proven security was presented in [13]. Their protocol works as long as more than 1/3 of the parties are honest. The two party case (where there is no honest majority) was later dealt with by [20]. The most recent protocol by [14] contains efficiency improvements for the two-party case, and improvements regarding the thresholds for the case of an honest majority.

Efficiency comparison with [14]. The previous best DSA/ECDSA threshold signing protocol is due to [14]. Their signing protocol requires the following operations by each party: 1 Paillier encryption, 5 Paillier homomorphic scalar multiplications, 5 Paillier homomorphic additions, and 46 exponentiations (the vast majority of these modulo N or N^2 for the Paillier modulus). Furthermore, they require the Paillier modulus to be greater than q^8 where q is the group order. Now, for P-256, this makes no difference since anyway a 2048-bit modulus is minimal. However, for P-384 and P-521 respectively, this requires a modulus of size 3072 and 4168 respectively, which severely slows down the computation. Regarding the key generation phase, [14] need to run a protocol for distributed key generation for Paillier. This outweighs all other computations and is very expensive for the case of malicious adversaries. (They did not implement this phase in their prototype, but the method they refer to [17] has a reported time of 15 min for generating a 2048-bit modulus for the semi-honest case alone.)

In contrast, the cost of our key-generation protocol is dominated by approximately 350 Paillier encryptions/exponentiations by each party; see Sect. 3.3 for an exact count. Furthermore, as described in Sect. 3.3, in the signing protocol, party P_1 computes 7 Elliptic curve multiplications and 1 Paillier decryption, and party P_2 computes 5 Elliptic curve multiplications and 1 Paillier encryption, 1 homomorphic scalar multiplication and 1 Paillier homomorphic addition. Furthermore, the Paillier modulus needs only to be greater than $2q^4 + q^3$, where q is the ECDSA group order. Thus, a 2048-bit modulus can be taken for P-256 and P-384, and a 2086-bit modulus only is needed for P-521. We therefore conclude that the cost of our signing protocol is approximately *two orders of magnitude* faster than their protocol.[1] This theoretical estimate is validated by our experimental results.

Experimental results and comparison. The running-time reported for the protocol of [14] for curve P-256 is approximately 12 s per signing operation between a mobile and PC. An improved optimized implementation using parallelism and *4 cores* on a 2.4 GHz machine achieves approximately 1 s per signing operation (these measurements are only for the *computation time* and do not include communication). In contrast, as we describe in Sect. 3.3, for curve P-256 our signing protocol takes approximately 37ms, using a single core (measuring the actual full running time, including communication). This validates the theoretical analysis of approximately *two orders of magnitude difference*, when taking into account the use of multiple cores. Specifically, on 4 cores, we can achieve a throughput of over 100 signatures per second, in contrast to a single signing operation for [14]. Full details of our experiments, for curves P-256, P-384 and P-521 appear in Sect. 3.3.

Finally, the key generation phase of our protocol for curve P-256 takes approximately 5 s, using a single core. In contrast, [14] requires distributed Paillier key generation which is extremely expensive, as described above.

2 Preliminaries

The ECDSA signing algorithm. The ECDSA signing algorithm is defined as follows. Let $\mathbb{G}$ be an Elliptic curve group of order q with base point (generator) G. The private key is a random value $x \leftarrow \mathbb{Z}_q$ and the public key is $Q = x \cdot G$.

The ECDSA signing operation on a message $m \in \{0,1\}^*$ is defined as follows:

1. Compute m' to be the $|q|$ leftmost bits of $SHA256(m)$, where $|q|$ is the bit-length of q
2. Choose a random $k \leftarrow \mathbb{Z}_q^*$
3. Compute $R \leftarrow k \cdot G$. Let $R = (r_x, r_y)$.

---

[1] We base this estimate on an OpenSSL speed test that puts the speed of the entire ECDSA signing operation for P-256 (which consists of one EC multiplication and more) at more than 10 times faster than a single RSA2048 private-key exponentiation. Note that for P-521 and RSA4096 the gap is even larger with the entire ECDSA signing operation being more than 30 times faster than a single RSA4096 private-key exponentiation.

4. Compute $r = r_x \bmod q$. If $r = 0$, go back to Step 2.
5. Compute $s \leftarrow k^{-1} \cdot (m' + r \cdot x) \bmod q$.
6. Output (r, s)

It is a well-known fact that for every valid signature (r, s), the pair $(r, -s)$ is also a valid signature. In order to make (r, s) unique (which will help in formalizing security), we mandate that the "smaller" of $s, -s$ is always output (where the smaller is the value between 0 and $\frac{q-1}{2}$.)

The ideal commitment functionality $\mathcal{F}_{\text{com}}$. In one of our subprotocols, we assume an ideal commitment functionality $\mathcal{F}_{\text{com}}$, formally defined in Functionality 2.1. Any UC-secure commitment scheme fulfills $\mathcal{F}_{\text{com}}$; e.g., [1,12,18]. In the random-oracle model, $\mathcal{F}_{\text{com}}$ can be trivially realized with static security by simply defining $,(x) = H(x, r)$ where $r \leftarrow \{0, 1\}^n$ is random.

FIGURE 2.1 (The Commitment Functionality $\mathcal{F}_{\text{com}}$)

Functionality $\mathcal{F}_{\text{com}}$ works with parties P_1 and P_2, as follows:

- Upon receiving (commit, sid, x) from party P_i (for $i \in \{1, 2\}$), record (sid, i, x) and send (receipt, sid) to party P_{3-i}. If some (commit, $sid, *$) is already stored, then ignore the message.
- Upon receiving (decommit, sid) from party P_i, if (sid, i, x) is recorded then send (decommit, sid, x) to party P_{3-i}.

The ideal zero knowledge functionality $\mathcal{F}_{\text{zk}}$. We use the standard ideal zero-knowledge functionality defined by $((x, w), \lambda) \rightarrow (\lambda, (x, R(x, w)))$, where λ denotes the empty string. For a relation R, the functionality is denoted by $\mathcal{F}_{\text{zk}}^R$. Note that any zero-knowledge proof of knowledge fulfills the $\mathcal{F}_{\text{zk}}$ functionality [16, Sect. 6.5.3]; non-interactive versions can be achieved in the random-oracle model via the Fiat-Shamir paradigm [11]; see Functionality 2.2 for the formal definition.

FIGURE 2.2 (The Zero-Knowledge Functionality $\mathcal{F}_{\text{zk}}^R$ for Relation R)

Upon receiving (prove, sid, x, w) from a party P_i (for $i \in \{1, 2\}$): if $(x, w) \notin R$ or sid has been previously used then ignore the message. Otherwise, send (proof, sid, x) to party P_{3-i}.

The committed non-interactive zero knowledge functionality $\mathcal{F}_{\text{com-zk}}$. In our protocol, we will have parties send commitments to non-interactive zero-knowledge proofs. We model this formally via a commit-zk functionality, denoted $\mathcal{F}_{\text{com-zk}}$, defined in Functionality 2.3. Given non-interactive zero-knowledge proofs of knowledge, this functionality is securely realized by just having the prover commit to such a proof using the ideal commitment functionality $\mathcal{F}_{\text{com}}$.

> **FIGURE 2.3 (The Committed NIZK Functionality $\mathcal{F}_{\text{com-zk}}^R$ for R)**
> Functionality $\mathcal{F}_{\text{zk}}$ works with parties P_1 and P_2, as follows:
>
> - Upon receiving (com-prove, sid, x, w) from a party P_i (for $i \in \{1,2\}$): if $(x, w) \notin R$ or sid has been previously used then ignore the message. Otherwise, store (sid, i, x) and send (proof-receipt, sid) to P_{3-i}.
> - Upon receiving (decom-proof, sid) from a party P_i (for $i \in \{1,2\}$): if (sid, i, x) has been stored then send (decom-proof, sid, x) to P_{3-i}.

Paillier encryption. Denote the public/private key pair by (pk, sk), and denote encryption and decryption under these keys by $\mathsf{Enc}_{pk}(\cdot)$ and $\mathsf{Dec}_{sk}(\cdot)$, respectively. We denote by $c_1 \oplus c_2$ the "addition" of the plaintexts in c_1, c_2, and by $a \odot c$ the multiplication of the plaintext in c by scalar a.

Security, the hybrid model and composition. We prove the security of our protocol under a game-based definition with standard assumptions (in Sect. 4), and under the simulation-based ideal/real model definition with a non-standard ad-hoc assumption (in Sect. 5). In all cases, we prove our protocols secure in a hybrid model with ideal functionalities that securely compute $\mathcal{F}_{\text{com}}, \mathcal{F}_{\text{zk}}, \mathcal{F}_{\text{com-zk}}$. The soundness of working in this model is justified in [5] (for stand-alone security) and in [6] (for security under composition). Specifically, as long as subprotocols that securely compute the functionalities are used (under the definition of [5] or [6], respectively), it is guaranteed that the output of the honest and corrupted parties when using real subprotocols is computationally indistinguishable to when calling a trusted party that computes the ideal functionalities.

3   Two-Party ECDSA

In this section, we present our protocol for distributed ECDSA signing. We separately describe the key generation phase (which is run once) and the signing phase (which is run multiple times).

Our protocol is presented in the $\mathcal{F}_{\text{zk}}$ and $\mathcal{F}_{\text{com-zk}}$ hybrid model. We use the zero-knowledge functionalities $\mathcal{F}_{\text{zk}}^{R_P}$, $\mathcal{F}_{\text{zk}}^{R_{DL}}$ and $\mathcal{F}_{\text{zk}}^{R_{PDL}}$ based on the following three different relations:

1. *Proof that a Paillier public-key was generated correctly:* define the relation

$$R_P = \{(N, (p_1, p_2)) \mid N = p_1 \cdot p_2 \text{ and } p_1, p_2 \text{ are prime}\}$$

   of valid Paillier public keys. We use the protocol described in Sect. 3.3 in the full version of [17]. The cost of this protocol is $3t$ Paillier exponentiations by each of the prover and verifier for statistical error 2^{-t}, as well as $3t$ GCD computations by the prover.
2. *Proof of knowledge of the discrete log of an Elliptic-curve point:* define the relation

$$R_{DL} = \{(\mathbb{G}, G, q, P, w) \mid P = w \cdot G\}$$

   of discrete log values (relative to the given group). We use the standard Schnorr proof for this [22].

3. *Proof of encryption of a discrete log in a Paillier ciphertext:* define

$$R_{PDL} = \{((c, pk, Q_1, \mathbb{G}, G, q), (x_1, sk)) \mid$$
$$x_1 = \mathsf{Dec}_{sk}(c) \text{ and } Q_1 = x_1 \cdot G \text{ and } x_1 \in \mathbb{Z}_q\},$$

where pk is a given Paillier public key and sk is its associated private key. (We will actually prove a slightly relaxed variant which is that completeness holds for $x_1 \in \mathbb{Z}_{q/3}$. This suffices for our needs.)

A novel contribution of our result is a highly efficient proof for relation R_{PDL}; this is of interest since it bridges between two completely different worlds (Paillier encryption and Elliptic curve groups). This proof appears in Sect. 6.

For the sake of clarity of notation, we omit the group description $(\mathbb{G}, G, q)$ within calls to the $\mathcal{F}_{zk}$ functionalities, since this is implicit. In addition, throughout, we assume that all values (Elliptic curve points) received are not equal to 0, and if zero is received then the party receiving the value aborts immediately.

3.1 Distributed Key Generation

The idea behind the distributed key generation protocol is as follows. The parties run a type of "simulatable coin tossing" in order to generate a random group element Q. This coin tossing protocol works by P_1 choosing a random x_1 and computing $Q_1 = x_1 \cdot G$, and then committing to Q_1 along with a zero-knowledge proof of knowledge of x_1, the discrete log of Q_1 (for technical reasons that will become apparent in Sect. 6, P_1 actually chooses $x \in \mathbb{Z}_{q/3}$, but this makes no difference). Then, P_2 chooses a random x_2 and sends $Q_2 = x_2 \cdot G$ along with a zero-knowledge proof of knowledge to P_1. Finally, P_1 decommits and P_2 verifies the proof. The output is the point $Q = x_1 \cdot Q_2 = x_2 \cdot Q_1$. This is fully simulatable due to the extractability and equivocality of the proof and commitment. In particular, assume that P_1 is corrupted. Then, a simulator receiving Q from the trusted party can cause the output of the coin-toss to equal Q. This is because it receives Q_1, x_1 from P_1 (who sends these values to the proof functionality) and can define the value sent by P_2 to be $Q_2 = (x_1)^{-1} \cdot Q$. Noting that $x_1 \cdot Q_2 = Q$, we have the desired property. Likewise, if P_2 is corrupted, then the simulator can commit to anything and then after seeing (Q_2, x_2) as sent to the proof functionality, it can define $Q_1 = (x_2)^{-1} \cdot Q$. The fact that the P_1 is supposed to already be committed is solved by using an equivocal commitment scheme (modeled here via the $\mathcal{F}_{com\text{-}zk}$ ideal functionality). Beyond generating Q, the protocol concludes with P_2 holding a Paillier encryption of x_1, where $Q_1 = x_1 \cdot G$. As described, this is used to obtain higher efficiency in the signing protocol, and is guaranteed via a zero-knowledge proof. See Protocol 3.1 for a full description.

PROTOCOL 3.1 (Key Generation Subprotocol KeyGen$(\mathbb{G}, g, q)$**)**

Upon joint input $(\mathbb{G}, G, q)$ and security parameter 1^n, the parties work as follows:

1. **P_1's first message:**
   (a) P_1 chooses a random $x_1 \leftarrow \mathbb{Z}_{q/3}$, and computes $Q_1 = x_1 \cdot G$.
   (b) P_1 sends (com-prove, $1, Q_1, x_1$) to $\mathcal{F}^{R_{DL}}_{\text{com-zk}}$ (i.e., P_1 sends a commitment to Q_1 and a proof of knowledge of its discrete log).
2. **P_2's first message:**
   (a) P_2 receives (proof-receipt, 1) from $\mathcal{F}^{R_{DL}}_{\text{com-zk}}$.
   (b) P_2 chooses a random $x_2 \leftarrow \mathbb{Z}_q$ and computes $Q_2 = x_2 \cdot G$.
   (c) P_2 sends (prove, $2, Q_2, x_2$) to $\mathcal{F}^{R_{DL}}_{\text{zk}}$.
3. **P_1's second message:**
   (a) P_1 receives (proof, $2, Q_2$) from $\mathcal{F}^{R_{DL}}_{\text{zk}}$. If not, it aborts.
   (b) P_1 sends (decom-proof, 1) to $\mathcal{F}^{R_{DL}}_{\text{com-zk}}$.
   (c) P_1 generates a Paillier key-pair (pk, sk) of length $\min(4 \log |q| + 2, n)$ and computes $c_{key} = \text{Enc}_{pk}(x_1)$.
   (d) P_1 sends (prove, $1, N, (p_1, p_2)$) to $\mathcal{F}^{R_P}_{\text{zk}}$, where $pk = N = p_1 \cdot p_2$.
   (e) P_1 sends (prove, $1, (c_{key}, pk, Q_1), (x_1, sk)$) to $\mathcal{F}^{R_{PDL}}_{\text{zk}}$.
4. **P_2's final check:** P_2 receives (decom-proof, $1, Q_1$) from $\mathcal{F}^{R_{DL}}_{\text{zk}}$, (proof, $1, N$) from $\mathcal{F}^{R_P}_{\text{zk}}$, and (proof, $1, (c_{key}, pk, Q_1)$) from $\mathcal{F}^{R_{PDL}}_{\text{zk}}$; if not it aborts. P_2 also checks that $pk = N$ is of length at least $\min(4 \log |q| + 2, n)$ and aborts if not.
5. **Output:**
   (a) P_1 computes $Q = x_1 \cdot Q_2$ and stores (x_1, Q).
   (b) P_2 computes $Q = x_2 \cdot Q_1$ and stores (x_2, Q, c_{key}).

3.2 Distributed Signing

The idea behind the signing protocol is as follows. First, the parties run a similar "coin tossing protocol" as in the key generation phase in order to obtain a random point R that will be used in generating the signature; after this, the parties P_1 and P_2 hold k_1 and k_2, respectively, where $R = k_1 \cdot k_2 \cdot G$. Then, since P_2 already holds a Paillier encryption of x_1 (under a key known only to P_1), it is possible for P_1 to singlehandedly compute r from $R = (r_x, r_y)$ and an encryption of $s' = (k_2)^{-1} \cdot m' + (k_2)^{-1} \cdot r \cdot x_2 \cdot x_1$; this can be carried out by P_2 since it knows all the values involved directly except for x_1 which is encrypted under Paillier. Observe that this is "almost" a valid signature since in a valid signature $s = k^{-1} \cdot m' + k^{-1} \cdot r \cdot x$ (and here $x = x_1 \cdot x_2$). Indeed, P_2 can send the encryption of this value to P_1, who can then decrypt and just multiply by $(k_1)^{-1}$. Since $k = k_1 \cdot k_2$ we have that the result is a valid ECDSA signature. The only problem with this method is that the encryption of $(k_2)^{-1} \cdot m' + (k_2)^{-1} \cdot r \cdot x_2 \cdot x_1$ may reveal information to P_1 since no reduction modulo q is carried out on the values (because Paillier works over a different modulus). In order to prevent this, we have P_2 add $\rho \cdot q$ to the value inside the encryption, where ρ is random and "large enough"; in the proof, we show that if $\rho \leftarrow \mathbb{Z}_{q^2}$, then this value is statistically close to $k_1 \cdot s$, where s is the final signature. Thus, P_1 can learn nothing more than the result (and in fact its view can be simulated). Note that since $s = k_1^{-1} \cdot s'$, it holds that $s' = k_1 \cdot s$ and so s' reveals no more information to P_1 than the signature s itself (this is due to the fact that P_1 can compute s' from the signature s and from its share k_1).

The only problem that remains is that P_2 may send an incorrect s' value to P_1. However, since we are dealing specifically with digital signatures, P_1 can verify that the result is correct before outputting it. Thus, a corrupt P_2 cannot cause P_1 to output incorrect values. However, it is conceivable that P_2 may be able to learn something from the fact that P_1 output a value or aborted. Consider, hypothetically, that P_2 could generate an encryption of a value s' so that $(k_1)^{-1} \cdot s'$ is a valid signature if $LSB(x_1) = 0$ and $(k_1)^{-1} \cdot s'$ is not a valid signature if $LSB(x_1) = 1$. In such a case, the mere fact that P_1 aborts or not can leak a single bit about P_1's private share of the key. In the proof(s) of security below, we show how we deal with this issue. See the formal definition of the signing phase in Protocol 3.2 (and a graphical representation in Fig. 1).

Offline/Online. Observe that the message to be signed is only used in P_2's second message and by P_1 to verify that the signature is valid. Thus, it is possible to run the first three steps in an offline phase. Then, when m is received, all that is required to generate a signature is for P_2 to send a single message to P_1.

Output to both parties. Observe that since the validity of the signature can be checked by P_2, it is possible for P_1 to send P_2 the signature if it verifies it and it's valid. This will not affect security at all.

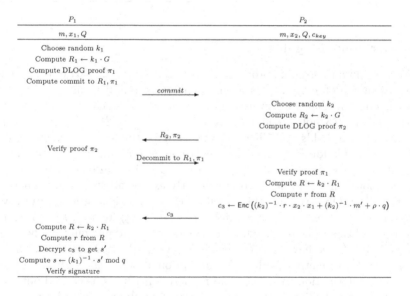

Fig. 1. The 2-Party ECDSA signing protocol

PROTOCOL 3.2 (Signing Subprotocol Sign(sid, m))

A graphical representation of the protocol appears in Fig. 1.

Inputs:
1. Party P_1 has (x_1, Q) as output from Protocol 3.1, the message m, and a unique session id sid.
2. Party P_2 has (x_2, Q, c_{key}) as output from Protocol 3.1, the message m and the session id sid.
3. P_1 and P_2 both locally compute $m' \leftarrow H_q(m)$ and verify that sid has not been used before (if it has been, the protocol is not executed).

The Protocol:
1. **P_1's first message:**
   (a) P_1 chooses a random $k_1 \leftarrow \mathbb{Z}_q$ and computes $R_1 = k_1 \cdot G$.
   (b) P_1 sends (com-prove, $sid\|1, R_1, k_1$) to $\mathcal{F}_{\text{com-zk}}^{RDL}$.
2. **P_2's first message:**
   (a) P_2 receives (proof-receipt, $sid\|1$) from $\mathcal{F}_{\text{com-zk}}^{RDL}$.
   (b) P_2 chooses a random $k_2 \leftarrow \mathbb{Z}_q$ and computes $R_2 = k_2 \cdot G$.
   (c) P_2 sends (prove, $sid\|2, R_2, k_2$) to $\mathcal{F}_{\text{zk}}^{RDL}$.
3. **P_1's second message:**
   (a) P_1 receives (proof, $sid\|2, R_2$) from $\mathcal{F}_{\text{zk}}^{RDL}$; if not, it aborts.
   (b) P_1 sends (decom-proof, $sid\|1$) to $\mathcal{F}_{\text{com-zk}}$.
4. **P_2's second message:**
   (a) P_2 receives (decom-proof, $sid\|1, R_1$) from $\mathcal{F}_{\text{com-zk}}^{RDL}$; if not, it aborts.
   (b) P_2 computes $R = k_2 \cdot R_1$. Denote $R = (r_x, r_y)$. Then, P_2 computes $r = r_x \bmod q$.
   (c) P_2 chooses a random $\rho \leftarrow \mathbb{Z}_{q^2}$ and computes $c_1 = \text{Enc}_{pk}\left(\rho \cdot q + [(k_2)^{-1} \cdot m' \bmod q]\right)$. Then, P_2 computes $v = (k_2)^{-1} \cdot r \cdot x_2 \bmod q$, $c_2 = v \odot c_{key}$ and $c_3 = c_1 \oplus c_2$.
   (d) P_2 sends c_3 to P_1.
5. **P_1 generates output:**
   (a) P_1 computes $R = k_1 \cdot R_2$. Denote $R = (r_x, r_y)$. Then, P_1 computes $r = r_x \bmod q$.
   (b) P_1 computes $s' = \text{Dec}_{sk}(c_3)$ and $s'' = (k_1)^{-1} \cdot s' \bmod q$. P_1 sets $s = \min\{s'', q - s''\}$ (this ensures that the signature is always the smaller of the two possible values).
   (c) P_1 verifies that (r, s) is a valid signature with public key Q. If yes it outputs the signature (r, s); otherwise, it aborts.

If a party aborts at any point, then it does not participate in any future Sign(sid, m) executions.

Correctness. Denoting $k = k_1 \cdot k_2$ and $x = x_1 \cdot x_2$, we have that c_3 is an encryption of $s' = \rho \cdot q + (k_2)^{-1} \cdot m' + (k_2)^{-1} \cdot r \cdot x_2 \cdot x_1 = \rho \cdot q + (k_2)^{-1} \cdot (m' + r \cdot x)$ (assuming that all is done correctly). Thus, $s = (k_1)^{-1} \cdot s' = k^{-1} \cdot (m' + rx) \bmod q$.

3.3   Efficiency and Experimental Results

We now analyze the theoretical complexity of our protocol, and describe its concrete running time based on our implementation.

Theoretical complexity – key-distribution protocol. Leaving aside the ZK proofs for now, P_1 carries out 2 Elliptic curve multiplications, 1 Paillier public-key generation and 1 Paillier encryption, and P_2 carries out two Elliptic curve multiplications. In addition, the parties run two discrete log proofs (each playing as prover once and as verifier once), and P_1 proves that N is a valid Paillier public key and runs the PDL proof described in Sect. 3.1. The cost of these proofs is as follows:

– *Discrete log:* the standard Schnorr zero-knowledge proof of knowledge for discrete log requires a single multiplication by the prover and two by the verifier.
– *Paillier public-key validity* [17]: For a statistical error of 2^{-40} this costs 120 Paillier exponentiations by each of the prover and the verifier (but 40 of these are "short"). In addition, the prover P_1 carries out 120 GCD computations.
– *PDL proof (Sect. 6):* This proof in Protocol 6.1 also involves running two executions of a range proof, and one execution of the zero-knowledge proof of Sect. 6.2. The cost is computed as follows:
   • The instructions within Protocol 6.1 for the prover P_1 cost 1 Paillier encryption, 1 Paillier (40-bit) scalar multiplication and 1 Elliptic curve multiplication. The cost for the verifier P_2 is 1 Paillier (40-bit) scalar multiplication and 2 Elliptic curve multiplications.
   • As described in the beginning of Sect. 6, each range proof is dominated by $2t$ Paillier encryptions for a statistical soundness error of 2^{-t}. Setting $t = 40$, we have 80 Paillier encryptions each.
   • The instructions within Sect. 6.2 require the prover P_1 to carry out 40 Paillier encryptions, and 40 Paillier exponentiations. The verifier P_2 computes on average 20 Paillier encryptions and 80 Paillier exponentiations.

Theoretical complexity – signing protocol. We now count the complexity of the signing protocol. We count the number of Elliptic curve multiplications and Paillier operations since this dominates the computation. As above, the zero-knowledge proof of knowledge for discrete log requires a single multiplication by the prover and two by the verifier, and ECDSA signature verification requires two multiplications. Thus, P_1 computes 7 Elliptic curve multiplications and a single Paillier decryption. In contrast, P_2 computes 5 Elliptic curve multiplications, 1 Paillier encryptions, 1 Paillier homomorphic scalar multiplication (which is a single "short" exponentiation) and one Paillier homomorphic addition (which is a single multiplication). Observe that unlike previous work, the length of the Paillier key need only be 5 times the length of the order of the Elliptic curve group (and not 8 times). Regarding rounds of communication, the protocol has only four rounds of communication (two in each direction). Thus, the protocol is very fast even on a slow network.

Implementation and running times. We implemented our protocol in C++ and ran it on Azure between two Standard_DS3_v2 instances. Although these instances have 4 cores each, we utilized a single core only with a single-thread implementation (note that key generation can be easily parallelized, if desired).

We ran our implementation on the standard NIST curves P-256, P-384 and P-521; the times for key generation and signing appear in Tables 1 and 2.

Table 1. Running times for **key generation** (average over 20 executions)

Curve	Mean time	Standard deviation
P-256	4888 ms	142
P-384	4849 ms	124
P-521	7842 ms	166

Table 2. Running times for **signing** (average over 1,000 executions)

Curve	Mean time	Standard deviation
P-256	36.8 ms	7.30
P-384	47.11 ms	1.96
P-521	78.19 ms	1.45

We remark that the size of the Paillier key has a great influence on the running time. We know this since in our initial manuscripts, our analysis required $N > q^5$ (instead of $N > 2q^4 + q^3$). This seemingly small difference meant that for P-521, the Paillier key needed to be of size 2560 (instead of 2086). For this mildly larger key, the running time was 110ms for signing and 15,776ms for key generation. This is explained by the fact that Paillier operations have cubic cost, and thus the cost *doubles* when the key size increases by just 25%.

4 Proof of Security – Game-Based Definition

4.1 Definition of Security

We begin by presenting a game-based definition for the security of a digital signature scheme $\pi = (\mathsf{Gen}, \mathsf{Sign}, \mathsf{Verify})$. This will be used when proving the security of our protocol and thus is presented for the sake of completeness and a concrete reference.

EXPERIMENT 4.1 (Expt-Sign$_{\mathcal{A},\pi}(1^n)$)

1. $(vk, sk) \leftarrow \mathsf{Gen}(1^n)$.
2. $(m^*, \sigma^*) \leftarrow \mathcal{A}^{\mathsf{Sign}_{sk}(\cdot)}(1^n, vk)$.
3. Let $\mathcal{Q}$ be the set of all m queried by $\mathcal{A}$ to its oracle. Then, the output of the experiment equals 1 if and only if $m^* \notin \mathcal{Q}$ and $\mathsf{Verify}_{vk}(m^*, \sigma^*) = 1$.

Standard security of digital signatures

Definition 4.2. *A signature scheme π is* existentially unforgeable under chosen-message attacks *if for every probabilistic polynomial-time oracle machine $\mathcal{A}$ there exists a negligible function μ such that for every n,*

$$\Pr[\text{Expt-Sign}_{\mathcal{A},\pi}(1^n) = 1] \leq \mu(n).$$

We now proceed to define security for a distributed signing protocol. In the experiment $\text{Expt-DistSign}_{\mathcal{A},\Pi}^b$, we consider $\mathcal{A}$ controlling party P_b in protocol Π for two-party signature generation. Let $\Pi_b(\cdot, \cdot)$ be a *stateful* oracle that runs the instructions of honest party P_{3-b} in protocol Π. The adversary $\mathcal{A}$ can choose which messages will be signed, and can interact with multiple instances of party P_{3-b} to concurrently generate signatures. Note that the oracle is defined so that distributed key generation is first run once, and then multiple signing protocols can be executed concurrently.

Formally, $\mathcal{A}$ receives access to an oracle that receives two inputs: the first input is a session identifier and the second is either an input or a next incoming message. The oracle works as follows:

- Upon receiving a query of the form $(0, 0)$ for the first time, the oracle initializes a machine M running the instructions of party P_{3-b} in the distributed key generation part of protocol Π. If party P_{3-b} sends the first message in the key generation protocol, then this message is the oracle reply.
- Upon receiving a query of the form $(0, m)$, if the key generation phase has not been completed, then the oracle hands the machine M the message m as its next incoming message and returns M's reply. (If the key generation phase has completed, then the oracle returns $\perp$.)
- If a query of the form (sid, m) is received where $sid \neq 0$, but the key generation phase with M has not completed, then the oracle returns $\perp$.
- If a query (sid, m) is received and the key generation phase has completed and this is the first oracle query with this identifier sid, then the oracle invokes a new machine M_{sid} running the instructions of party P_{3-b} in protocol Π with session identifier sid and input message m to be signed. The machine M_{sid} is initialized with the key share and any state stored by M at the end of the key generation phase. If party P_{3-b} sends the first message in the signing protocol, then this message is the oracle reply.
- If a query (sid, m) is received and the key generation phase has completed and this is not the first oracle query with this identifier sid, then the oracle hands M_{sid} the incoming message m and returns the next message sent by M_{sid}. If M_{sid} concludes, then the output obtained by M_{sid} is returned.

The experiment for defining security is formalized by simply providing $\mathcal{A}$ who controls party P_b with oracle access to Π_b. Adversary $\mathcal{A}$ "wins" if it can forge a signature on a message not queried in the oracle queries. Observe that $\mathcal{A}$ can run multiple executions of the signing protocol concurrently. We remark that we have considered only a single signing key; the extension to multiple different signing keys is straightforward and we therefore omit it. (This is due to the fact since signing keys are independent, one case easily simulate all executions with other keys.)

EXPERIMENT 4.3 (Expt-DistSign$^b_{\mathcal{A},\Pi}(1^n)$)

Let $\pi = (\mathsf{Gen}, \mathsf{Sign}, \mathsf{Verify})$ be a digital signature scheme.

1. $(m^*, \sigma^*) \leftarrow \mathcal{A}^{\Pi_b(\cdot, \cdot)}(1^n)$.
2. Let $\mathcal{Q}$ be the set of all inputs m such that (sid, m) was queried by $\mathcal{A}$ to its oracle as the first query with identifier sid. Then, the output of the experiment equals 1 if and only if $m^* \notin \mathcal{Q}$ and $\mathsf{Verify}_{vk}(m^*, \sigma^*) = 1$, where vk is the verification key output by P_{3-b} from the key generation phase, and Verify is as specified in π.

Security experiment for secure digital signature protocol

Definition 4.4. *A protocol Π is a* secure two-party protocol for distributed signature generation *for π if for every probabilistic polynomial-time oracle machine $\mathcal{A}$ and every $b \in \{1, 2\}$, there exists a negligible function μ such that for every n, $\Pr[\mathsf{Expt\text{-}DistSign}^b_{\mathcal{A},\Pi}(1^n) = 1] \leq \mu(n)$.*

4.2 Proof of Security

In this section, we prove that Π comprised of Protocols 3.1 and 3.2 for key generation and signing, respectively, constitutes a secure two-party protocol for distributed signature generation of ECDSA.

Theorem 4.5. *Assume that the Paillier encryption scheme is indistinguishable under chosen-plaintext attacks, and that ECDSA is existentially-unforgeable under a chosen message attack. Then, Protocols 3.1 and 3.2 constitute a secure two-party protocol for distributed signature generation of ECDSA.*

Proof. We prove the security of the protocol in the $\mathcal{F}_{\mathsf{com\text{-}zk}}, \mathcal{F}_{\mathsf{zk}}$ hybrid model. Note that if the commitment and zero-knowledge protocols are UC-secure, then this means that the output in the hybrid and real protocols is computationally indistinguishable. In particular, if $\mathcal{A}$ can break the protocol with some probability ϵ in the hybrid model, then it can break the protocol with probability $\epsilon \pm \mu(n)$ for some negligible function μ. Thus, this suffices.

We separately prove security for the case of a corrupted P_1 and a corrupted P_2. Our proof works by showing that, for any adversary $\mathcal{A}$ attacking the protocol, we construct an adversary $\mathcal{S}$ who forges an ECDSA signature in

Experiment 4.1 with probability that is negligibly close to the probability that $\mathcal{A}$ forges a signature in Experiment 4.3. Formally, we prove that if Paillier has indistinguishable encryptions under chosen-plaintext attacks, then for every PPT algorithm $\mathcal{A}$ and every $b \in \{1, 2\}$ there exists a PPT algorithm $\mathcal{S}$ and a negligible function μ such that for every n,

$$\left| \Pr[\text{Expt-Sign}_{\mathcal{S},\pi}(1^n) = 1] - \Pr[\text{Expt-DistSign}_{\mathcal{A},\Pi}^b(1^n) = 1] \right| \leq \mu(n), \quad (1)$$

where Π denotes Protocols 3.1 and 3.2, and π denotes the ECDSA signature scheme. Proving Eq. (1) suffices, since by the assumption in the theorem that ECDSA is secure, we have that there exists a negligible function μ' such that for every n, $\Pr[\text{Expt-Sign}_{\mathcal{S},\pi}(1^n) = 1] \leq \mu'(n)$. Combining this with Eq. (1), we conclude that $\Pr[\text{Expt-DistSign}_{\mathcal{A},\Pi}^b(1^n) = 1] \leq \mu(n) + \mu'(n)$ and thus Π is secure by Definition 4.4. We prove Eq. (1) separately for $b = 1$ and $b = 2$.

Proof of Eq. (1) for $b = 1$ – corrupted P_1: Let $\mathcal{A}$ be a probabilistic polynomial-time adversary in $\text{Expt-DistSign}_{\mathcal{A},\Pi}^1(n)$; we construct a probabilistic polynomial-time adversary $\mathcal{S}$ for $\text{Expt-Sign}_{\mathcal{S},\pi}(n)$. The adversary $\mathcal{S}$ essentially simulates the execution for $\mathcal{A}$, as described in the intuition behind the security of the protocol. Formally:

1. In Expt-Sign, adversary $\mathcal{S}$ receives $(1^n, Q)$, where Q is the public verification key for ECDSA.
2. $\mathcal{S}$ invokes $\mathcal{A}$ on input 1^n and simulates oracle Π for $\mathcal{A}$ in Expt-DistSignm, answering as described in the following steps:
   (a) $\mathcal{S}$ replies $\perp$ to all queries $(sid, \cdot)$ to Π by $\mathcal{A}$ before the key-generation subprotocol is concluded. $\mathcal{S}$ replies $\perp$ to all queries from $\mathcal{A}$ before it queries $(0, 0)$.
   (b) After $\mathcal{A}$ sends $(0, 0)$ to Π, adversary $\mathcal{S}$ receives $(0, m_1)$ which is P_1's first message in the key generation subprotocol (any other query is ignored). $\mathcal{S}$ computes the oracle reply as follows:
      i. $\mathcal{S}$ parses m_1 into the form $(\text{com-prove}, 1, Q_1, x_1)$ that P_1 sends to $\mathcal{F}_{\text{com-zk}}^{R_{DL}}$ in the hybrid model.
      ii. $\mathcal{S}$ verifies that $Q_1 = x_1 \cdot G$. If yes, then it computes $Q_2 = (x_1)^{-1} \cdot Q$ (using the value Q received as the verification key in experiment Expt-Sign and the value x_1 from $\mathcal{A}$'s prove message); if no, then $\mathcal{S}$ just chooses a random Q_2.
      iii. $\mathcal{S}$ sets the oracle reply of Π to be $(\text{proof}, 2, Q_2)$ and internally hands this to $\mathcal{A}$ (as if sent by $\mathcal{F}_{\text{zk}}^{R_{DL}}$).
   (c) The next message of the form $(0, m_2)$ received by $\mathcal{S}$ (any other query is ignored) is processed as follows:
      i. $\mathcal{S}$ parses m_2 into the following three messages: **(1)** (decom-proof, $sid\|1$) as $\mathcal{A}$ intends to send to $\mathcal{F}_{\text{com-zk}}^{R_{DL}}$; **(2)** (proof, $1, N, (p_1, p_2)$) as $\mathcal{A}$ intends to send to $\mathcal{F}_{\text{zk}}^{R_P}$; and **(3)** (proof, $1, (c_{key}, pk, Q_1), (x_1, r)$) as $\mathcal{A}$ intends to send to $\mathcal{F}_{\text{zk}}^{R_{PDL}}$.

    ii. $\mathcal{S}$ verifies that $pk = N = p_1 \cdot p_2$ and that the length of $pk = N$ is as specified, and generates the oracle response to be P_2 aborting if they are not correct.

    iii. Likewise, $\mathcal{S}$ generates the oracle response to be P_2 aborting if $Q_1 \neq x_1 \cdot G$ or $c_{key} \neq \mathsf{Enc}_{pk}(x_1; r)$ or $x_1 \notin \mathbb{Z}_q$.

    iv. If $\mathcal{S}$ simulates an abort, then the experiment concludes (since the honest P_2 no longer participates in the protocol and so all calls to Π_b are ignored). $\mathcal{S}$ does not output anything in this case since no verification key vk is output by P_2 in this case.

        Otherwise, $\mathcal{S}$ stores (x_1, Q, c_{key}) and the distributed key generation phase is completed.

(d) Upon receiving a query of the form (sid, m) where sid is a *new* session identifier, $\mathcal{S}$ queries its signing oracle in experiment Expt-Sign with m and receives back a signature (r, s). Using the ECDSA verification procedure, $\mathcal{S}$ computes the Elliptic curve point R. (Observe that the ECDSA verification works by constructing a point R and then verifying that this defines the same r as in the signature.) Then, queries received by $\mathcal{S}$ from $\mathcal{A}$ with identifier sid are processed as follows:

    i. The first message (sid, m_1) is processed by first parsing the message m_1 as $(\mathsf{com\text{-}prove}, sid\|1, R_1, k_1)$. If $R_1 = k_1 \cdot G$ then $\mathcal{S}$ sets $R_2 = (k_1)^{-1} \cdot R$; else it chooses R_2 at random. $\mathcal{S}$ sets the oracle reply to $\mathcal{A}$ to be the message $(\mathsf{proof}, sid\|2, R_2)$ that $\mathcal{A}$ expects to receive. (Note that the value R_2 is computed using R from the ECDSA signature and k_1 as sent by $\mathcal{A}$.)

    ii. The second message (sid, m_2) is processed by parsing the message m_2 as $(\mathsf{decom\text{-}proof}, sid\|1)$ from $\mathcal{A}$. If $R_1 \neq k_1 \cdot G$ then $\mathcal{S}$ simulates P_2 aborting and the experiment concludes (since the honest P_2 no longer participates in *any executions* of the protocol and so all calls to Π_b are ignored).

       Otherwise, $\mathcal{S}$ chooses a random $\rho \leftarrow \mathbb{Z}_{q^2}$, computes the ciphertext $c_3 \leftarrow \mathsf{Enc}_{pk}([k_1 \cdot s \bmod q] + \rho \cdot q)$, where s is the value from the signature received from $\mathcal{F}_{\mathrm{ECDSA}}$, and sets the oracle reply to $\mathcal{A}$ to be c_3.

3. Whenever $\mathcal{A}$ halts and outputs a pair (m^*, σ^*), adversary $\mathcal{S}$ outputs (m^*, σ^*) and halts.

We proceed to prove that Eq. (1) holds. First, observe that the public-key generated by $\mathcal{S}$ in the simulation with $\mathcal{A}$ equals the public-key Q that it received in experiment Expt-Sign. This is due to the fact that $\mathcal{S}$ defines $Q_2 = (x_1)^{-1} \cdot Q$ when $\mathcal{A}$ is committed to $Q_1 = x_1 \cdot G$. Thus, the public key is defined to be $x_1 \cdot Q_2 = x_1 \cdot (x_1)^{-1} \cdot Q = Q$, as required. We now proceed to show that $\mathcal{A}$'s view in the simulation by $\mathcal{S}$ is identical to its view in a real execution of Protocols 3.1 and 3.2. (Note that the view is identical when taking $\mathcal{F}_{zk}$ and $\mathcal{F}_{com\text{-}zk}$ as ideal functionalities; the real protocol is computationally indistinguishable.) This suffices since it implies that $\mathcal{A}$ outputs a pair (m^*, σ^*) that is a valid signature with the same probability in the simulation and in Expt-DistSign (otherwise, the views can be distinguished by just verifying if the output signature is correct relative to the public key). Since the public key in the simulation is the same public key that S receives in Expt-Sign, a valid forgery generated by A in Expt-DistSign constitutes a valid forgery by S in Expt-Sign. Thus, Eq. (1) follows.

In order to see that the view of A in the simulation of the key generation phase is identical to its view in a real execution of Protocol 3.1 (as in Expt-DistSign), note that the only difference between the simulation by A and a real execution with an honest P_2 is the way that Q_2 is generated: P_2 chooses a random x_2 and computes $Q_2 \leftarrow x_2 \cdot G$, whereas S computes $Q_2 \leftarrow (x_1)^{-1} \cdot Q$, where Q is the public verification key received by S in Expt-Sign. We stress that in all other messages and checks, S behaves exactly as P_2 (note that the zero-knowledge proof of knowledge of the discrete log of Q_2 is simulated by S, but in the $\mathcal{F}_{zk}, \mathcal{F}_{com-zk}$-hybrid model this is identical). Now, since Q is chosen randomly, it follows that the distributions over $x_2 \cdot G$ and $(x_1)^{-1} \cdot Q$ are *identical*. Observe finally that if P_2 does not abort then the public-key defined in both a real execution and the simulation by S equals $x_1 \cdot Q_2 = Q$. Thus, the view of A is identical and the output public key is Q.

In order to see that the view of A in the simulation of the signing phase is computationally indistinguishable to its view in a real execution of Protocol 3.2 (as in Expt-DistSign), note that the only difference between the view of A in a real execution and in the simulation is the way that c_3 is chosen. Specifically, R_2 is distributed identically in both cases due to the fact that R is randomly generated by $\mathcal{F}_{ECDSA}$ in the signature generation and thus $(k_1)^{-1} \cdot R$ has the same distribution as $k_2 \cdot G$ (this is exactly the same as in the key generation phase with Q). The zero-knowledge proofs and verifications are also identically distributed in the $\mathcal{F}_{zk}, \mathcal{F}_{com-zk}$-hybrid model. Thus, the only difference is c_3: in the simulation it is an encryption of $[k_1 \cdot s \bmod q] + \rho \cdot q$, whereas in a real execution it is an encryption of $s' = (k_2)^{-1} \cdot (m' + rx) + \rho \cdot q$, where $\rho \in \mathbb{Z}_{q^2}$ is random (we stress that all additions here are over the *integers* and not mod q, except for where it is explicitly stated in the protocol description).

We therefore prove that A's view is indistinguishable by showing that despite this difference, the values are actually *statistically close*. In order to see this, first observe that by the definition of ECDSA signing, $s = k^{-1} \cdot (m' + rx) = (k_1)^{-1} \cdot (k_2)^{-1} \cdot (m + rx) \bmod q$. Thus, $(k_2)^{-1} \cdot (m' + rx) = k_1 \cdot s \bmod q$, implying that there exists some $\ell \in \mathbb{N}$ with $0 \leq \ell < q$ such that $(k_2)^{-1} \cdot (m' + rx) = k_1 \cdot s + \ell \cdot q$. The reason that ℓ is bound between 0 and q is that in the protocol the only operations without a modular reduction are the multiplication of $[(k_2)^{-1} \cdot r \cdot x_2 \bmod q]$ by x_1, and the addition of $[(k_2)^{-1} \cdot m' \bmod q]$. This cannot increase the result by more than q^2. Therefore, the difference between the real execution and simulation with S is:

1. *Real:* the ciphertext c_3 encrypts $[k_1 \cdot s \bmod q] + \ell \cdot q + \rho \cdot q$
2. *Simulated:* the ciphertext c_3 encrypts $[k_1 \cdot s \bmod q] + \rho \cdot q$

We show that for all k_1, s, ℓ with $k_1, s, \ell \in \mathbb{Z}_q$, the above values are statistically close (for a random choice of $\rho \in \mathbb{Z}_{q^2}$). In order to see this, fix k_1, s, ℓ, and let v be a value. If $v \neq [k_1 \cdot s \bmod q] + \zeta \cdot q$ for some ζ, then neither the real or simulated values can equal v. Else, if $v = [k_1 \cdot s \bmod q] + \zeta \cdot q$ for some ζ, then there are three cases:

1. *Case $\zeta < \ell$:* in this case, v can be obtained in the simulated execution for $\rho < \ell$, but can never be obtained in a real execution.
2. *Case $\zeta > q^2 - 1$):* in this case, v can be obtained in the real execution for $\rho \geq q^2 - 1 - \ell$, but can never be obtained in a simulated execution.
3. *Case $\ell \leq \zeta < q^2 - 1$:* in this case, v can be obtained in both the real and simulated executions, with identical probability (observe that in both the real and simulated executions, ρ is chosen uniformly in $\mathbb{Z}_{q^2}$).

Recall that the statistical distance between two distributions X and Y over a domain $\mathcal{D}$ is defined to be:

$$\Delta(X, Y) = \max_{T \subseteq D} \left| \Pr[X \in T] - \Pr[Y \in T] \right|$$

Let X be the values generated in a real execution of the protocol and let Y be the values generated in the simulation with $\mathcal{S}$. Then, taking T to be set of values v for which $\zeta < \ell$, we have that $\Pr[X \in T] = 0$ whereas $\Pr[Y \in T] \leq \frac{q}{q^2} = \frac{1}{q}$ (this holds since $0 \leq \ell < q$ and $\rho \in \mathbb{Z}_{q^2}$). Thus, $\Delta(X, Y) = \frac{1}{q}$, which is negligible. (Taking T to be the set of values v for which $\zeta > q^2 - 1$ would give the same result and are both the maximum since any other values add no difference.) We therefore conclude that the distributions over c_3 in the real and simulated executions are statistically close. This proves that Eq. (1) holds for the case that $b = 1$.

Proof of Eq. (1) for $b = 2$ – corrupted P_2: We follow the same strategy as for the case that P_1 is corrupted, which is to construct a simulator $\mathcal{S}$ that simulates the view of $\mathcal{A}$ while interacting in experiment Expt-Sign. This simulation is easy to construct and similar to the case that P_1 is corrupted, with one difference. Recall that the last message from P_2 to P_1 is an encryption c_3. This ciphertext may be maliciously constructed by $\mathcal{A}$, and the simulator cannot detect this. (Formally, there is no problem for $\mathcal{S}$ to decrypt, since as will be apparent below, it generates the Paillier public key. However, this strategy will fail since in order to prove computational indistinguishability it is necessary to carry out a reduction to the security of Paillier, meaning that the simulation must be designed to work *without knowing* the corresponding private key.) We solve this problem by simply having $\mathcal{S}$ simulate P_1 aborting at some random point. That is, $\mathcal{S}$ chooses a random $i \in \{1, \dots, p(n) + 1\}$ where $p(n)$ is an upper bound on the number of queries made by $\mathcal{A}$ to Π. If $\mathcal{S}$ chose correctly, then the simulation is fine. Now, since $\mathcal{S}$'s choice of i is correct with probability $\frac{1}{p(n)+1}$, this means that $\mathcal{S}$ simulates $\mathcal{A}$'s view with probability $\frac{1}{p(n)+1}$ (note that $\mathcal{S}$ can also choose $i = p(n) + 1$, which is correct if c_3 is always constructed correctly). Thus, $\mathcal{S}$ can forge a signature in Expt-Sign with probability at least $\frac{1}{p(n)+1}$ times the probability that $\mathcal{A}$ forges a signature in Expt-DistSign.

Let $\mathcal{A}$ be a probabilistic polynomial-time adversary; $\mathcal{S}$ proceeds as follows:

1. In Expt-Sign, adversary $\mathcal{S}$ receives $(1^n, Q)$, where Q is the public verification key for ECDSA.
2. Let $p(\cdot)$ denote an upper bound on the number of queries that $\mathcal{A}$ makes to Π in experiment Expt-DistSign. Then, $\mathcal{S}$ chooses a random $i \in \{1, \ldots, p(n) + 1\}$.
3. $\mathcal{S}$ invokes $\mathcal{A}$ on input 1^n and simulates oracle Π for $\mathcal{A}$ in Expt-DistSign, answering as described in the following steps:
   (a) $\mathcal{S}$ replies $\perp$ to all queries $(sid, \cdot)$ to Π by $\mathcal{A}$ before the key-generation subprotocol is concluded. $\mathcal{S}$ replies $\perp$ to all queries from $\mathcal{A}$ before it queries $(0,0)$.
   (b) After $\mathcal{A}$ sends $(0,0)$ to Π, adversary $\mathcal{S}$ computes the oracle reply to be (proof-receipt, 1) as $\mathcal{A}$ expects to receive.
   (c) The next message of the form $(0, m_1)$ received by $\mathcal{S}$ (any other query is ignored) is processed as follows:
       i. $\mathcal{S}$ parses m_1 into the form $(\text{prove}, 2, Q_2, x_2)$ that P_2 sends to $\mathcal{F}_{\text{com-zk}}^{R_{DL}}$ in the hybrid model.
       ii. $\mathcal{S}$ verifies that Q_2 is a non-zero point on the curve and that $Q_2 = x_2 \cdot G$; if not, it simulates P_1 aborting, and halts (there is no point outputting anything since no verification key is output by P_1 in this case and so the output of Expt-DistSign is always 0).
       iii. $\mathcal{S}$ generates a valid Paillier key-pair (pk, sk), computes $c_{key} = \text{Enc}_{pk}(\tilde{x}_1)$ for a random $\tilde{x}_1 \in \mathbb{Z}_{q/3}$.
       iv. $\mathcal{S}$ sets the oracle response to $\mathcal{A}$ to be the messages $(\text{decom-proof}, 1, Q_1)$, $(\text{proof}, 1, N)$ and $(\text{proof}, 1, (c_{key}, N, Q_1))$, where $Q_1 = (x_2)^{-1} \cdot Q$ with Q as received by $\mathcal{S}$ initially.
       $\mathcal{S}$ stores (x_2, Q, c_{key}) and the key distribution phase is completed.
   (d) Upon receiving a query of the form (sid, m) where sid is a *new* session identifier, $\mathcal{S}$ computes the oracle reply to be $(\text{proof-receipt}, sid\|1)$ as $\mathcal{A}$ expects to receive, and hands it to $\mathcal{A}$.
       Next, $\mathcal{S}$ queries its signing oracle in experiment Expt-Sign with m and receives back a signature (r, s). Using the ECDSA verification procedure, $\mathcal{S}$ computes the Elliptic curve point R. Then, queries received by $\mathcal{S}$ from $\mathcal{A}$ with identifier sid are processed as follows:
       i. The first message (sid, m_1) is processed by first parsing the message m_1 as $(\text{prove}, sid\|2, R_2, k_2)$ that $\mathcal{A}$ sends to $\mathcal{F}_{\text{zk}}^{R_{DL}}$. $\mathcal{S}$ verifies that $R_2 = k_2 \cdot G$ and that R_2 is a non-zero point on the curve; otherwise, it simulates P_1 aborting. $\mathcal{S}$ computes $R_1 = (k_2)^{-1} \cdot R$ and sets the oracle reply to be $(\text{decom-proof}, sid\|, R_1)$ as if coming from $\mathcal{F}_{\text{com-zk}}^{R_{DL}}$.
       ii. The second message (sid, m_2) is processed by parsing m_2 as c_3. If this is the ith call by $\mathcal{A}$ to the oracle Π, then $\mathcal{S}$ simulates P_1 aborting (and not answering any further oracle calls). Otherwise, it continues.
4. Whenever $\mathcal{A}$ halts and outputs a pair (m^*, σ^*), adversary $\mathcal{S}$ outputs (m^*, σ^*) and halts.

As in the case that P_1 is corrupted, the public-key generated by $\mathcal{S}$ in the simulation with $\mathcal{A}$ equals the public-key Q that it received in experiment Expt-Sign.

Now, let j be the *first* call to oracle Π with (sid, c_3) where c_3 is such that P_1 does not obtain a valid signature (r, s) with respect to Q. Then, we argue that if $j = i$, then the only difference between the distribution over $\mathcal{A}$'s view in a real execution and in the simulated execution by $\mathcal{S}$ is the ciphertext c_{key}. Specifically, in a real execution $c_{key} = \mathsf{Enc}_{pk}(x_1)$ where $Q_1 = x_1 \cdot G$, whereas in the simulation $c_{key} = \mathsf{Enc}_{pk}(\tilde{x}_1)$ for a random $\tilde{x}_1$ and is independent of $Q_1 = x_1 \cdot G$.[2] Observe, however, that $\mathcal{S}$ does not use the private-key for Paillier at all in the simulation. Thus, indistinguishability of this simulation follows from a straightforward reduction to the indistinguishability of the encryption scheme, under chosen-plaintext attacks.

This proves that

$$\left| \Pr[\mathsf{Expt\text{-}Sign}_{\mathcal{S},\pi}(1^n) = 1 \mid i = j] - \Pr[\mathsf{Expt\text{-}DistSign}^2_{\mathcal{A},\Pi}(1^n) = 1] \right| \leq \mu(n),$$

and so

$$\Pr[\mathsf{Expt\text{-}DistSign}^2_{\mathcal{A},\Pi}(1^n) = 1] \leq \frac{\Pr[\mathsf{Expt\text{-}Sign}_{\mathcal{S},\pi}(1^n) = 1 \land i = j]}{\Pr[i = j]} + \mu(n)$$

$$\leq \frac{\Pr[\mathsf{Expt\text{-}Sign}_{\mathcal{S},\pi}(1^n) = 1]}{1/(p(n) + 1)} + \mu(n)$$

and so

$$\Pr[\mathsf{Expt\text{-}Sign}_{\mathcal{S},\pi}(1^n) = 1] \geq \frac{\Pr[\mathsf{Expt\text{-}DistSign}^2_{\mathcal{A},\Pi}(1^n) = 1]}{p(n) + 1} - \mu(n).$$

This implies that if $\mathcal{A}$ forges a signature in $\mathsf{Expt\text{-}DistSign}^2_{\mathcal{A},\Pi}$ with non-negligible probability, then $\mathcal{S}$ forges a signature in $\mathsf{Expt\text{-}Sign}_{\mathcal{S},\pi}$ with non-negligible probability, in contradiction to the assumed security of ECDSA.

5 Simulation Proof of Security (With a New Assumption)

There are advantages to full simulation based proofs of security (via the real/ideal paradigm). Observe that we proved the security of our protocol in Sect. 4 by simulating the view of $\mathcal{A}$ in a real execution. In fact, our simulation can be used to prove the security of our protocol under the real/ideal world paradigm except for exactly one place. Recall that when P_2 is corrupted, $\mathcal{S}$ cannot determine if c_3 is correctly constructed or not. Thus, $\mathcal{S}$ simply chooses a random point and "hopes" that the jth value c_3 generated is the first badly constructed c_3. This suffices for a game-based definition, but it does not suffice for simulation-based security definitions. Thus, in order to be able to prove our protocol using simulation, we need to be able to determine if c_3 was constructed correctly. Of course, we could add zero-knowledge proofs to the protocol, but these would be very expensive. Alternatively, we consider a rather ad-hoc but plausible assumption that suffices. The assumption is formalized in Appendix A, along with a full proof of security under this assumption.

---

[2] As before, this is true in the $\mathcal{F}_{zk}, \mathcal{F}_{com\text{-}zk}$-hybrid model; by using UC-secure protocols for $\mathcal{F}_{zk}, \mathcal{F}_{com\text{-}zk}$ the result is computationally indistinguishable.

6   Zero-Knowledge Proof for Relation R_{PDL}

6.1   The Main Zero-Knowledge Proof

In this section, we present an efficient construction of a zero-knowledge proof for the relation R_{PDL}, defined by:

$$R_{PDL} = \{((c, pk, Q_1, \mathbb{G}, G, q), (x_1, r)) \mid c = \mathsf{Enc}_{pk}(x_1; r) \text{ and } Q_1 = x_1 \cdot G \text{ and } x_1 \in \mathbb{Z}_q\}.$$

Intuitively, this relation means that c is a valid Paillier encryption of the discrete log of Q_1.

Our proof contains a new zero-knowledge protocol for proving that $c = \mathsf{Enc}_{pk}(x_1)$ and $Q_1 = x_1 \cdot G$, while calling an existing zero-knowledge protocol for proving that $x_1 \in \mathbb{Z}_q$. It is possible to prove that $x_1 \in \mathbb{Z}_q$ by using the proof of non-negativity of [19] on the ciphertext $c' = c \ominus \mathsf{Enc}_{pk}(q)$. This works, but such proofs are quite expensive. In contrast, there exist much more simple and efficient proofs if $x_1 \in \mathbb{Z}_{q/3}$ [4]. This suffices for our use since a random x_1 would be in this range anyway with probability $1/3$, and so this cannot adversely affect the security. We therefore prove that $x_1 \in \mathbb{Z}_{q/3}$ using the proof of [4]. Formally, this proof guarantees completeness when $x \in \mathbb{Z}_{q/3}$ and soundness for $x \in \mathbb{Z}_q$. This means that an honest prover will succeed in proving as long as $x \in \mathbb{Z}_{q/3}$ and a cheating prover will fail if $x \notin \mathbb{Z}_q$, except with negligible probability. We use the version of the proof as described in [2, Sect. 1.2.2]. With statistical soundness error of 2^{-t}, the cost of this proof is dominated by computing $2t$ Paillier encryptions.

The idea behind the proof that $c = \mathsf{Enc}_{pk}(x_1)$ and $Q_1 = x_1 \cdot G$ is as follows. The prover chooses a random r, and sends the verifier $r \cdot G$ along with a Paillier encryption c_r of r. Then, for a random challenge e, the prover sends $z = r + e \cdot x_1$, and proves the $c_r \oplus (e \odot c)$ encrypts the value z. The verifier checks this proof and also checks that $z \cdot G = R + e \cdot Q_1$. Now, if $c \neq \mathsf{Enc}_{pk}(x_1)$ then the probability that z will fulfill both that $z \cdot G = R + e \cdot Q_1$ and $\mathsf{Enc}_{pk}(z) = c_r \oplus (e \odot c)$ is negligible, due to the random choice of e. Intuitively, this holds since the check that $c_r \oplus (e \odot c)$ encrypts z together with the check that $z \cdot G = R + e \cdot Q_1$ ensures that the *same* x_1 is used to compute Q_1 and is encrypted in c. This is shown formally in the proof.

We remark that the above is not enough since $z = r + e \cdot x_1$ may potentially reveal information about x_1 (note that there is no modular reduction carried out here and the computation is over the integers; this is necessary since there is no mod q inside Paillier). The prover therefore also adds to z the value $\rho \cdot q$ for a large-enough random ρ, and proves that $\mathsf{Enc}_{pk}(z) - c_r \oplus (e \odot c)$ is a multiple of q. Observe that the addition of $\rho \cdot q$ makes no difference to the check of $z \cdot G = R + e \cdot Q_1$ since this is all modulo q and so $\rho \cdot q$ disappears. The proof contains additional checks regarding the size of z and more; this is needed to ensure that values are in the appropriate range so that no modulo N operations happen inside Paillier.

PROTOCOL 6.1 (Zero-Knowledge Proof for Relation R_{PDL})

Inputs: The joint statement is $(c, pk, Q_1, \mathbb{G}, G, q)$, and the prover has a witness (x_1, sk) with $x_1 \in \mathbb{Z}_{q/3}$. (Recall that the proof is that $x_1 = \mathsf{Dec}_{sk}(c)$ and $Q_1 = x_1 \cdot G$ and $x_1 \in \mathbb{Z}_q$.)

The Protocol:

1. **V's first message:** V chooses a random $e \leftarrow \mathbb{Z}_{2^t}$ and sends (commit, sid, e) to $\mathcal{F}_{\mathsf{com}}$.
2. **P's first message:** Upon receiving (receipt, sid) from $\mathcal{F}_{\mathsf{com}}$, the prover P chooses a random $r \leftarrow \mathbb{Z}_{q/3}$ and computes $c_r = \mathsf{Enc}_{pk}(r)$ and $R = r \cdot G$. Then, P sends (c_r, R) to V.
3. **V's second message:** V sends (decommit, sid) to $\mathcal{F}_{\mathsf{com}}$.
4. **P's second message:** Upon receiving (decommit, sid, e) from $\mathcal{F}_{\mathsf{com}}$, prover P chooses a random $\rho \leftarrow \mathbb{Z}_{q^2}$ and computes $z = r + e \cdot x_1 + \rho \cdot q$. Then, P sends z to V.
5. **Range-ZK phase:** P provides a zero-knowledge *proof of knowledge* that $r \in \mathbb{Z}_q$ and $x_1 \in \mathbb{Z}_q$, using the proof described above from [2, Sect. 1.2.2].
6. **Ciphertext-ZK phase:** V checks that $q^2 < z < q^3 + q^2$; if not, it aborts. Otherwise, both parties independently compute $c_q = \mathsf{Enc}_{pk}(z) \ominus c_r \ominus (e \odot c)$. Then, P provides a zero-knowledge proof that c_q is an encryption of a multiple of q under key pk under the guarantee that it is an encryption of a value between 0 and $q^3 + q^2$, as shown in Sect. 6.2.
7. **V's output:** V computes $z' = z \bmod q$ and verifies that $z' \cdot G = R + e \cdot Q_1$. V outputs 1 if and only if this holds *and* it accepted the zero-knowledge proofs of the previous steps.

Theorem 6.2. *If Paillier encryption is indistinguishable under chosen-plaintext attacks and $N > 2q^4 + q^3$, then Protocol 6.1 is a zero-knowledge proof of knowledge of the relation $\mathcal{F}_{\mathsf{zk}}^{R_{PDL}}$ in the $\mathcal{F}_{\mathsf{com}}$-hybrid model with soundness error 2^{-t}.*

Proof. We prove completeness, soundness and zero knowledge, and that the proof is a proof of knowledge. Regarding completeness, it is easy to see that if both parties follow the protocol then $q^2 < z < q^3 + q^2$. In addition, c_q is an encryption of $z - r - e \cdot x_1 = \rho \cdot q$ and thus V accepts the proof in the final step.

We now proceed to prove soundness. First, if $x_1 \notin \mathbb{Z}_q$ then V rejects due to the range-ZK phase. It thus remains to prove that V rejects unless $c = \mathsf{Enc}_{pk}(x_1; r)$ and $Q_1 = x_1 \cdot G$. Let $c = \mathsf{Enc}_{pk}(x_1; r)$ and assume that $Q_1 \neq x_1 \cdot G$.

First, consider the subcase that P sends (c_r, R) such that $c_r = \mathsf{Enc}_{pk}(r)$ and $R = r \cdot G$. It then follows that c_q as computed by V is an encryption of $v = z - r - e \cdot x_1$. If v is not a multiple of q then V outputs 0 in the ciphertext-ZK phase.[3] However, if v is a multiple of q then this implies that $z = r + e \cdot x_1 + \rho \cdot q$ for some integer ρ. Thus, $z' = r + e \cdot x_1 \bmod q$ and $z' \cdot G = r \cdot G + e \cdot x_1 \cdot G$.

---

[3] This only holds as long as the value encrypted is between 0 and $q^3 + q^2$. Now, since $x_1, r \in \mathbb{Z}_q$ as guaranteed in the range-ZK phase, and V checks that $q^2 < z < q^3 + q^2$, it follows that $z - r - e \cdot x_1$ is in the range between 0 and $q^3 + q^2$, as required.

By the assumption that $R = r \cdot G$ we have that $z' \cdot G = R + e \cdot (x_1 \cdot G) \neq R + e \cdot Q_1$ since $Q_1 \neq x_1 \cdot G$. Thus, V outputs 0.

Next, consider the subcase that $c_r = \mathsf{Enc}_{pk}(r)$ but $R \neq r \cdot G$. As before, if v is not a multiple of q then V outputs 0 and so we have that $z = r + e \cdot x_1 + \rho \cdot q$ for some integer ρ. Now, V outputs 0 unless $z' \cdot G = R + e \cdot Q_1$. Thus, V outputs 0 unless $(r + e \cdot x_1) \cdot G = R + e \cdot Q_1$, which holds if and only if $r \cdot G + e \cdot (x_1 \cdot G) = R + e \cdot Q_1$ which in turn holds if and only if $r \cdot G - R = e \cdot (Q_1 - x_1 \cdot G)$. By the assumption, $R \neq r \cdot G$ and $Q_1 \neq x_1 \cdot G$. Thus, both $r \cdot G - R$ and $Q_1 - x_1 \cdot G$ are non-zero points on the curve. Since the curve is of prime order, $Q_1 - x_1 \cdot G$ is a generator of the group and thus there exists a single w such that $w \cdot (Q_1 - x_1 \cdot G) = r \cdot G - R$. However, $e \in \mathbb{Z}_{2^t}$ is chosen uniformly at random and so the probability that equality holds is at most 2^{-t}, as required.

The fact that the proof is a proof of knowledge follows from the proof of knowledge in the range-ZK phase. In particular, it is possible to extract the value x_1 from the proof that c is an encryption of a value in $\mathbb{Z}_q$. This suffices since the fact that the extracted x_1 fulfills the conditions of the relation follows from the proof of soundness above.

Finally, we prove that the protocol is zero knowledge by constructing a simulator S. Intuitively, S can work since it can know the value of e before sending R to V^* (by extracting e from $\mathcal{F}_{\mathsf{com}}$). Let V^* be an adversarial verifier. Upon input $(c, pk, Q_1, \mathbb{G}, G, q)$, simulator S works as follows:

1. S receives $(\mathsf{commit}, sid, e)$ from V^* as it intends to send to $\mathcal{F}_{\mathsf{com}}$.
2. S chooses a random $z \in \mathbb{Z}_{q^2}$, computes $z' = z \bmod q$, and computes $R = z' \cdot G - e \cdot Q_1$. In addition, S computes $c_r = \mathsf{Enc}_{pk}(0)$.
3. S internally hands V^* the pair (c_r, R) and receives back its decommitment. If it does not decommit, then S simulates P aborting.
4. S internally hands V^* the value z it chose above.
5. S simulates the zero-knowledge proofs of the range-ZK and ciphertext-ZK phases.

We prove that the simulation is computationally indistinguishable from a real zero-knowledge proof of knowledge by constructing a hybrid simulator S' who is given the witness (x_1, r). Then, S' works in exactly the same way as S except that it computes z as the real prover does. Clearly, the only difference between the output of S and S' is in the distribution over z: S chooses z randomly in $\mathbb{Z}_{q^2}$ and S' sets $z = r + e \cdot x_1 + \rho \cdot q$ where $\rho \in \mathbb{Z}_{q^2}$ is random. We argue that these distributions over z are statistically close. In order to see this, fix $r \in \mathbb{Z}_q, e \in \mathbb{Z}_{2^t}, x_1 \in \mathbb{Z}_q$ and let $z \in \mathbb{Z}_{q^2}$ be a value. We have the following cases:

1. *Case 1 – $z < r + e \cdot x_1$:* In this case, z cannot be generated in a real execution, but can be generated in the simulation.
2. *Case 2 – $z > q^2 - 1$:* In this case, z cannot be generated in the simulation, but can be generated in a real execution (note that the maximum value of z in a real execution is $r + e \cdot x_1 + q^2 - 1$).
3. *Case 3 – $r + e \cdot x_1 \leq z \leq q^2 - 1$:* In this case, the probability that z is obtained in the simulation is exactly $1/(q^2 - 1)$ since z is randomly chosen

in $\mathbb{Z}_{q^2}$. Likewise, the probability that z is obtained in a real execution is also exactly $1/(q^2 - 1)$ since this is obtained if and only if $\rho = \frac{r+e \cdot x_1}{q}$ and ρ is randomly chosen in $\mathbb{Z}_{q^2}$.

Recall that the statistical distance between two distributions X and Y over a domain $\mathcal{D}$ is defined to be:

$$\Delta(X, Y) = \max_{T \subseteq \mathcal{D}} \left| \Pr[X \in T] - \Pr[Y \in T] \right|$$

Let X be the real execution values and let Y be the simulation values. Then, taking T to be set of values z for which $z < r + e \cdot x_1$, we have that $\Pr[X \in T] = 0$ whereas $\Pr[Y \in T] < \frac{q + 2^t \cdot q}{q^2} < \frac{1}{\sqrt{q}}$ (this holds since $0 \leq r, x_1 < q$ and $e \in \mathbb{Z}_{2^t}$ where $2^t < \sqrt{q}$). (Taking T to be the set of values z for which $z > q^2 - 1$ would give the same result and are both the maximum since any other values add no difference.) We therefore conclude that $\Delta(X, Y) < \frac{1}{\sqrt{q}}$, and so the distributions over z in the real execution and simulation are statistically close. Since the only difference between $\mathcal{S}$ and $\mathcal{S}'$ is that $\mathcal{S}$ is the simulation and $\mathcal{S}'$ generates z as in a real execution, we have that the outputs of $\mathcal{S}$ and $\mathcal{S}'$ are statistically close.

Now, the only difference between $\mathcal{S}'$ and a real execution is that the proofs in the range-ZK and ciphertext-ZK phases are simulated by $\mathcal{S}'$ and are not real proofs. However, note that the statement is correct in both cases and this is the only difference. Thus, computational indistinguishability follows from the zero knowledge property of the proofs used in these phases.

We conclude by remarking that the requirement that $N > 2q^4 + q^3$ is needed for the zero knowledge proof that c_q encrypts a multiple of q. This is because $z = r + ex_1 + \rho q$ and it is crucial that no modulo N operation takes place. Since $\rho < q^2$ we have that $\rho q < q^3$. However, in Sect. 6.2, the proof further multiplies this be q and so it can be up to q^4 (as we will see below, the guarantee is that it is less than $2q^4 + q^3$ and thus we need N to be greater than this value). This completes the proof.

It has been proven formally in [16] that any proof of knowledge securely computes the ideal zero-knowledge functionality. We therefore conclude:

Corollary 6.3. *If Paillier encryption is indistinguishable under chosen-plaintext attacks and $N > 2q^4 + q^3$, then Protocol 6.1 securely computes the functionality $\mathcal{F}_{\mathsf{zk}}^{R_{PDL}}$ in the $\mathcal{F}_{\mathsf{com}}$-hybrid model, in the presence of malicious, static adversaries.*

6.2   A Proof that c Encrypts a Multiple of q

In this section, we present a zero-knowledge proof of knowledge of the following relation R:

$$R_q = \{((pk, c, q), (sk, L)) \mid \exists w : c = \mathsf{Enc}_{sk}(L \cdot q; w))\}$$

In actuality, our proof will only be sound and zero knowledge for the case that $0 \leq L \leq q^2 + q$. We do not include this in the relation definition for simplicity.

However, formally, this is a promise problem and the guarantee that the promise holds is due to the fact that V checks that $q^2 < z < q^3 + q^2$ inside Protocol 6.1. Now, since in Protocol 6.1 we also prove that $x_1 \in \mathbb{Z}_q$ and $r \in \mathbb{Z}_q$ and we know that $e << q$, we have that $r + e \cdot x_1 < q^2$. Thus, $L = z - r - e \cdot x_1 > 0$ and no modulo N operations happens inside the Paillier subtraction. We therefore conclude that the input L to this proof is such that $0 \le L \cdot q < q^3 + q^2$, as required.

PROTOCOL 6.4 (Zero-Knowledge Proof for Relation R_q)

Inputs: The joint statement is (pk, c, q), and the prover has a witness (sk, L) and wishes to prove that c encrypts $L \cdot q$.
The parties have a joint soundness parameter t (ensuring soundness error 2^{-t}) [8].

The Protocol:

1. **P's first message:** P chooses random $r_1, \ldots, r_t \leftarrow \mathbb{Z}_{q^3}$ and $s_1, \ldots, s_t \in \{0,1\}^n$ and computes $c_i = \mathsf{Enc}_{pk}(r_i \cdot q; s_i)$ for every i. P sends $(c_1, \ldots, c_t)$ to V.
2. **V's first message:** V chooses a random $e \leftarrow \mathbb{Z}_{2^t}$ and sends e to P.
3. **P's second message:** Upon receiving e from V, prover P works as follows:
   (a) For every i such that $e_i = 0$, prover P sends r_i, s_i to V.
   (b) For every i such that $e_i = 1$, prover P sends $M_i = (L + r_i) \cdot q$ to V.
4. **Final proof:** P proves to V that for every i such that $e_i = 1$ it holds that $c \oplus c_i \ominus \mathsf{Enc}_{pk}(M_i)$ is an encryption of 0, using the zero-knowledge proof of [8].
5. **V's output:** V outputs 1 if and only if:
   (a) V accepts all zero-knowledge proofs at the end, and
   (b) For every i s.t. $e_i = 0$, it holds that $r_i < q^3$ and $c_i = \mathsf{Enc}_{pk}(r_i \cdot q; s_i)$, and
   (c) For every i s.t. $e_i = 1$, it holds that $q_i \mid M_i$ and $q^2 < M_i < 2q^4 + q^3$.

Security. We prove that if $N > 2q^4 + q^3$ and we have a promise that $L < q^2 + q$, then the protocol is a zero-knowledge proof. Completeness is straightforward (note that since $L < q^2 + q$ it holds that $(L + r_i) \cdot q < (q^3 + q^2 + q^3) \cdot q = 2q^4 + q^3$ and so M_i is in the appropriate range). We informally argue security.

We begin by proving soundness with error 2^{-t}; assume that $c = \mathsf{Enc}_{pk}(x)$ for some x that is not a multiple of q. Denote $x = L \cdot q + v$ for $1 < v < q$.

First, assume that there exists an i such that $e_i = 1$ and $c_i = \mathsf{Enc}_{pk}(r_i \cdot q)$ for some $r_i \in \mathbb{Z}_{q^3}$. In such a case, $C = c \oplus c_i \ominus \mathsf{Enc}_{pk}(M_i)$ is an encryption of $L \cdot q + v + r_i \cdot q - M_i$. Now, V accepts only if $L \cdot q + v + r_i \cdot q - M_i = 0 \bmod N$, by the soundness of the zero-knowledge proof at the end (this computation is modulo N since it happens inside the Paillier encryption). Clearly, it cannot hold that $L \cdot q + v + r_i \cdot q - M_i = 0$ (over the integers) since this would imply that $M_i = L \cdot q + r_i \cdot q + v$, but M_i is divisible by q (since otherwise V rejects) and $0 < v < q$. Furthermore, it cannot hold that $L \cdot q + v + r_i \cdot q - M_i = -N$ since this implies that $M_i = L \cdot q + v + r_i \cdot q + N$, but V checks that $M_i < 2q^4 + q^3$ and N is greater than this value. Finally, it cannot hold that $L \cdot q + v + r_i \cdot q - M_i = N$. In order to see this, note that V checks that $r_i < q^3$ and that $M_i > q^2$. Thus, $N = L \cdot q + v + r_i \cdot q - M_i$ would imply that $N < L \cdot q + q + q^4 - q^2$ and so $L \cdot q > N - q^4 + q^2 - q$. However, the promise is that $L \cdot q < q^3 + q^2$; since $N > 2q^4 + q^3$, this is a contradiction. The same arguments hold for any multiple of N and $-N$.

Thus, if the statement is incorrect, then V will reject unless for every i such that $e_i = 1$ it holds that c_i does not encrypt a value that is a multiple of q. Since V checks that c_i does encrypt a value that is a multiple of q for every i such that $e_i = 0$, it follows that a cheating prover can only succeed if it guesses the exact e before it sends $c_1, \ldots, c_t$ (observe that there is exactly one e that will enable it to cheat). However, this occurs with probability 2^{-t} only.

Regarding zero knowledge, a simulator $\mathcal{S}$ follows the honest P's instructions up to the final proof, and runs the zero-knowledge simulator for that proof. Since P doesn't use the witness until the final proof, the simulator can work in this way. Computational indistinguishability thereby follows from a straightforward reduction to the zero knowledge property of the final proof.

Acknowledgements. We would like to than Valery Osheter from Dyadic Security for the implementation of ECDSA protocol and for running the experiments.

References

1. Blazy, O., Chevalier, C., Pointcheval, D., Vergnaud, D.: Analysis and improvement of Lindell's UC-Secure commitment schemes. In: Jacobson, M., Locasto, M., Mohassel, P., Safavi-Naini, R. (eds.) ACNS 2013. LNCS, vol. 7954, pp. 534–551. Springer, Heidelberg (2013). doi:10.1007/978-3-642-38980-1_34

2. Boudot, F.: Efficient proofs that a committed number lies in an interval. In: Preneel, B. (ed.) EUROCRYPT 2000. LNCS, vol. 1807, pp. 431–444. Springer, Heidelberg (2000). doi:10.1007/3-540-45539-6_31

3. Boyd, C.: Digital multisignatures. In: Cryptography and Coding, pp. 241–246 (1986)

4. Brickell, E.F., Chaum, D., Damgård, I.B., Graaf, J.: Gradual and verifiable release of a secret (Extended Abstract). In: Pomerance, C. (ed.) CRYPTO 1987. LNCS, vol. 293, pp. 156–166. Springer, Heidelberg (1988). doi:10.1007/3-540-48184-2_11

5. Canetti, R.: Security and composition of multiparty cryptographic protocols. J. Cryptol. **13**(1), 143–202 (2000)

6. Canetti, R.: Universally composable security: a new paradigm for cryptographic protocols. In: 42nd FOCS, pp. 136–145 (2001). Full version http://eprint.iacr.org/2000/067

7. Croft, R.A., Harris, S.P.: Public-key cryptography and reusable shared secrets. In: Cryptography and Coding, pp. 189–201 (1989)

8. Damgård, I., Jurik, M.: A generalisation, a simplification and some applications of Paillier's probabilistic public-key system. In: Kim, K. (ed.) PKC 2001. LNCS, vol. 1992, pp. 119–136. Springer, Heidelberg (2001). doi:10.1007/3-540-44586-2_9

9. Desmedt, Y.: Society and group oriented cryptography: a new concept. In: Pomerance, C. (ed.) CRYPTO 1987. LNCS, vol. 293, pp. 120–127. Springer, Heidelberg (1988). doi:10.1007/3-540-48184-2_8

10. Desmedt, Y., Frankel, Y.: Threshold cryptosystems. In: Brassard, G. (ed.) CRYPTO 1989. LNCS, vol. 435, pp. 307–315. Springer, New York (1990). doi:10.1007/0-387-34805-0_28

11. Fiat, A., Shamir, A.: How to prove yourself: practical solutions to identification and signature problems. In: Odlyzko, A.M. (ed.) CRYPTO 1986. LNCS, vol. 263, pp. 186–194. Springer, Heidelberg (1987). doi:10.1007/3-540-47721-7_12

12. Fujisaki, E.: Improving practical UC-secure commitments based on the DDH assumption. In: Zikas, V., Prisco, R. (eds.) SCN 2016. LNCS, vol. 9841, pp. 257–272. Springer, Cham (2016). doi:10.1007/978-3-319-44618-9_14

13. Gennaro, R., Jarecki, S., Krawczyk, H., Rabin, T.: Robust threshold DSS signatures. In: Maurer, U. (ed.) EUROCRYPT 1996. LNCS, vol. 1070, pp. 354–371. Springer, Heidelberg (1996). doi:10.1007/3-540-68339-9_31

14. Gennaro, R., Goldfeder, S., Narayanan, A.: Threshold-optimal DSA/ECDSA signatures and an application to bitcoin wallet security. ACNS 2016, 156–174 (2016)

15. Goldreich, O.: Foundations of Cryptography: Volume 2 - Basic Applications. Cambridge University Press, New York (2004)

16. Hazay, C., Lindell, Y.: Protocols, Efficient Secure Two-Party: Techniques and Constructions. Springer, Heidelberg (2010)

17. Hazay, C., Mikkelsen, G.L., Rabin, T., Toft, T.: Efficient RSA key generation and threshold Paillier in the two-party setting. In: Dunkelman, O. (ed.) CT-RSA 2012. LNCS, vol. 7178, pp. 313–331. Springer, Heidelberg (2012). doi:10.1007/978-3-642-27954-6_20

18. Lindell, Y.: Highly-efficient universally-composable commitments based on the DDH assumption. In: Paterson, K.G. (ed.) EUROCRYPT 2011. LNCS, vol. 6632, pp. 446–466. Springer, Heidelberg (2011). doi:10.1007/978-3-642-20465-4_25

19. Lipmaa, H.: On diophantine complexity and statistical zero-knowledge arguments. In: Laih, C.-S. (ed.) ASIACRYPT 2003. LNCS, vol. 2894, pp. 398–415. Springer, Heidelberg (2003). doi:10.1007/978-3-540-40061-5_26

20. MacKenzie, P.D., Reiter, M.K.: Two-party generation of DSA signatures. Int. J. Inf. Secur. 2, 218–239 (2004). An extended abstract appeared at CRYPTO 2001

21. Paillier, P.: Public-key cryptosystems based on composite degree residuosity classes. In: Stern, J. (ed.) EUROCRYPT 1999. LNCS, vol. 1592, pp. 223–238. Springer, Heidelberg (1999). doi:10.1007/3-540-48910-X_16

22. Schnorr, C.P.: Efficient identification and signatures for smart cards. In: Brassard, G. (ed.) CRYPTO 1989. LNCS, vol. 435, pp. 239–252. Springer, New York (1990). doi:10.1007/0-387-34805-0_22

23. Shoup, V.: Practical threshold signatures. In: Preneel, B. (ed.) EUROCRYPT 2000. LNCS, vol. 1807, pp. 207–220. Springer, Heidelberg (2000). doi:10.1007/3-540-45539-6_15

24. Shoup, V., Gennaro, R.: Securing threshold cryptosystems against chosen ciphertext attack. In: Nyberg, K. (ed.) EUROCRYPT 1998. LNCS, vol. 1403, pp. 1–16. Springer, Heidelberg (1998). doi:10.1007/BFb0054113

25. Porticor. www.porticor.com

26. Dyadic Security. www.dyadicsec.com

27. Sepior. www.sepior.com

A Simulation-Based Proof of Security (Using a New Assumption)

A.1 Definition of Security

We show how to securely compute the functionality $\mathcal{F}_{\text{ECDSA}}$. The functionality is defined with two functions: key generation and signing. The key generation is called once, and then any arbitrary number of signing operations can be carried out with the generated key. The functionality is defined in Fig. A.1.

FIGURE A.1 (The ECDSA Functionality $\mathcal{F}_{\text{ECDSA}}$)

Functionality $\mathcal{F}_{\text{ECDSA}}$ works with parties P_1 and P_2, as follows:

- Upon receiving KeyGen$(\mathbb{G}, G, q)$ from both P_1 and P_2, where $\mathbb{G}$ is an Elliptic-curve group of order q with generator G:
  1. Generate an ECDSA key pair (Q, x) by choosing a random $x \leftarrow \mathbb{Z}_q^*$ and computing $Q = x \cdot G$. Choose a hash function $H_q : \{0,1\}^* \rightarrow \{0,1\}^{\lfloor \log |q| \rfloor}$, and store $(\mathbb{G}, g, q, H_q, x)$.
  2. Send Q (and H_q) to both P_1 and P_2.
  3. Ignore future calls to KeyGen.
- Upon receiving Sign(sid, m) from both P_1 and P_2, if KeyGen was already called and sid has not been previously used, compute an ECDSA signature (r, s) on m, and send it to both P_1 and P_2. (Specifically, choose a random $k \leftarrow \mathbb{Z}_q^*$, compute $(r_x, r_y) = k \cdot G$ and $r = r_x \bmod q$. Finally, compute $s \leftarrow k^{-1}(H_q(m) + rx)$ and output (r, s).)

We defined $\mathcal{F}_{\text{ECDSA}}$ using Elliptic curve (additive) group notation, although all of our protocols work for *any* prime-order group.

Security in the presence of malicious adversaries. We prove security according to the standard simulation paradigm with the real/ideal model [5,15]. We prove security in the presence of *malicious adversaries* and *static corruptions*. As is standard for the case of no honest majority, we consider security with abort meaning that a corrupted party can learn output while the honest party does not. In our definition of functionalities, we describe the instructions of the trusted party. Since we consider security with abort, the corrupted party receives output first and then sends either continue or abort to the trusted party to determine whether or not the honest party also receives output.

We remark that when all of the zero-knowledge proofs are UC secure [6], then our protocol can also be proven secure in this framework.

A.2 Background and New Assumption

In Sect. 4, we proved the security of our protocol under a game-based definition. In some sense, proving security via simulation-based definitions (following the ideal/real model paradigm) is preferable. In particular, it guarantees security under composition. Following our proof in Sect. 4.2 closely, one may observe that S is essentially a simulator for an ideal functionality that securely computes ECDSA. Indeed, S is invoked with a public-key, and can use its oracle in Expt-Sign to obtain a signature on any value it wishes. This is very similar to an ideal functionality that generates a public key and can be used to generate signatures. The only problem with the simulation strategy used in Sect. 4.2 is that in the case that P_2 is corrupted, S just guesses if c_3 is correctly constructed. Needless to say, this is not allowed in a simulation-based proof. One may be tempted to solve this problem by saying that since S generates the Paillier key-pair (pk, sk) when playing P_1, it can decrypt c_3 and check if the value is generated as expected. However, when trying to formally prove this, one needs to show a reduction to the indistinguishability of the encryption scheme (since the simulator does not know x_1 and so cannot provide $c_{key} = \mathsf{Enc}_{pk}(x_1)$). In this reduction, the simulator is given pk externally and does not know sk (see the proof of the key generation subprotocol in Sect. 4.2). Thus, in this reduction, it is not possible to decrypt c_3 and the appropriate distributions cannot be generated.

In this section, we introduce a new assumption under which it is possible to prove the full simulation-based security of Protocol 3.2 without any modifications. The assumption is non-standard, but very plausible. Consider an adversary who is given a Paillier encryption of a (high-entropy) secret value w; denote $c = \mathsf{Enc}_{pk}(w)$. Then, the adversary can always randomize c to generate an encryption c' of the same w, but without anyone but itself and the secret-key owner knowing whether c and c' encrypt the same value. In addition, the adversary can always generate an encryption c' of a plaintext value that it knows but without knowing whether c and c' encrypt the same value. Now, consider a setting where an adversary is given an oracle $\mathcal{O}_c(c')$ that outputs 1 if and only if $\mathsf{Dec}_{sk}(c') = \mathsf{Dec}_{sk}(c)$, where $c = \mathsf{Enc}_{pk}(w)$ is the challenge ciphertext, and the adversary's task is to learn w. Clearly, the adversary can use this oracle to try and guess the value encrypted in c one at a time (just guess x', compute $c' = \mathsf{Enc}_{pk}(x')$ and query $\mathcal{O}_c(c')$). However, since w has high entropy, this seems to be futile. Furthermore, it seems that the oracle $\mathcal{O}_c$ cannot help in any other way.

Extending the above a further step, the adversary can generate any *affine* function of w by choosing scalars α and β and computing $c' = \alpha \odot (\mathsf{Enc}_{pk}(\beta) \oplus c) = \mathsf{Enc}_{pk}(\alpha + \beta \cdot x)$. Then, as before, $\mathcal{A}$ tries to output w given an oracle $\mathcal{O}_c(c', \alpha, \beta)$ that outputs 1 if and only if $\mathsf{Dec}_{sk}(c') = \alpha + \beta \cdot \mathsf{Dec}_{sk}(c)$. The adversary can use this oracle to try to guess w one value at a time, but it does not seem that it can help beyond this.

In order to formally define a security experiment including such an oracle, one must consider the task of the adversary. Since w must be a high-entropy random value one cannot consider the standard indistinguishability game. Rather, one could formalize a simple task where some w is randomly chosen and the adversary is given $(pk, \mathsf{Enc}_{pk}(w))$ and oracle access to $\mathcal{O}$ above, and its task is to output w

(in entirety). This is very plausible since without the oracle it is clearly hard, and the oracle only answers queries (c', α, β) by determining if "c' encrypts $\alpha + \beta \cdot x$", which essentially gives a *single guess* on the value of w. However, requiring that the adversary output the entire w turns out to not be very helpful for us. This is due to the fact that w must maintain some property of secrecy. We therefore extend this experiment by giving the adversary either $(pk, f(w_0), \mathsf{Enc}_{pk}(w_0))$ or $(pk, f(w_0), \mathsf{Enc}_{pk}(w_1))$, where w_0, w_1 are random and f is a *one-way function*. The adversary's task is to guess which input type it received (with the input to the one-way function equal to what is encrypted or independent of it), and it is given the oracle $\mathcal{O}$ above to help it. Note that f may reveal some information about w_0 (since it is only a one-way function), but if f is somehow *unrelated* of the encryption scheme, then it still seems that this should not help very much.

For our actual experiment, we will define the one-way function to be the computation $w_0 \cdot G$ in a group where the discrete log is hard. Observe that here the one-way function is related to the discrete log problem over Elliptic curve groups, whereas the encryption is Paillier and thus seems completely unrelated. Thus, we conjecture that this problem is hard. Since we consider a group, the equality that is actually checked by the oracle is modulo q, where q is the order of the group.

Formal assumption definition. The above description leads to the following experiment. Let G be a generator of a group $\mathbb{G}$ of order q. Consider the following experiment with an adversary $\mathcal{A}$, denoted $\mathsf{Expt}_{\mathcal{A}}(1^n)$:

1. Generate a Paillier key pair (pk, sk).
2. Choose random $w_0, w_1 \in \mathbb{Z}_q$ and compute $Q = w_0 \cdot G$.
3. Choose a random bit $b \in \{0, 1\}$ and compute $c = Enc_{pk}(w_b)$.
4. Let $b' = \mathcal{A}^{\mathcal{O}_c(\cdot, \cdot, \cdot)}(pk, c, Q)$, where $\mathcal{O}_c(c', \alpha, \beta) = 1$ if and only if $Dec_{sk}(c') = \alpha + \beta \cdot w_b \bmod q$.
5. The output of the experiment is 1 if and only if $b' = b$.

We define the following:

Definition A.2. *We say that the* Paillier-EC assumption *is hard if for every probabilistic polynomial-time adversary $\mathcal{A}$ there exists a negligible function μ such that* $\Pr[\mathsf{Expt}_{\mathcal{A}}(1^n) = 1] \leq \frac{1}{2} + \mu(n)$.

The assumption in Definition A.2 is rather ad-hoc and tailored to the problem at hand. However, it is very plausible and enables us prove full simulation without modifying the protocol. In particular, an adversary for the above experiment can run the protocol simulator *and* can verify whether or not c_3 was constructed correctly. This is because c_3 is supposed to be an encryption of $\alpha + \beta \cdot x_1$ for $\alpha = (k_2)^{-1} \cdot m' \bmod q$ and $\beta = (k_2)^{-1} \cdot r \cdot x_2 \bmod q$, where the simulator knows all of the values k_2, r, x_2. Thus, the adversary can use its oracle to verify the validity of the ciphertext sent by the adversary who controls P_2. This means that the simulation can be run while interacting in this experiment, and if the result of the simulation can be distinguished from a real execution then this can be used to win the experiment.

In the full version of this paper we formally prove Theorem A.3 below. We assume only that the Paillier-EC assumption is hard, since this trivially implies that the Paillier encryption scheme is indistinguishable under chosen-plaintext attacks.

Theorem A.3. *Assume that the* Paillier-EC *assumption is hard. Then, Protocol 3.2 securely computes* $\mathcal{F}_{\text{ECDSA}}$ *in the* $(\mathcal{F}_{\text{zk}}, \mathcal{F}_{\text{com-zk}})$-*hybrid model in the presence of a malicious static adversary (under the full ideal/real definition).*

Block Ciphers

Proving Resistance Against Invariant Attacks: How to Choose the Round Constants

Christof Beierle[1]([⊠]), Anne Canteaut[2], Gregor Leander[1], and Yann Rotella[2]

[1] Horst Görtz Institute for IT Security,
Ruhr-Universität Bochum, Bochum, Germany
{christof.beierle,gregor.leander}@rub.de
[2] Inria, Paris, France
{anne.canteaut,yann.rotella}@inria.fr

Abstract. Many lightweight block ciphers apply a very simple key schedule in which the round keys only differ by addition of a round-specific constant. Generally, there is not much theory on how to choose appropriate constants. In fact, several of those schemes were recently broken using invariant attacks, i.e., invariant subspace or nonlinear invariant attacks. This work analyzes the resistance of such ciphers against invariant attacks and reveals the precise mathematical properties that render those attacks applicable. As a first practical consequence, we prove that some ciphers including Prince, Skinny-64 and Mantis7 are not vulnerable to invariant attacks. Also, we show that the invariant factors of the linear layer have a major impact on the resistance against those attacks. Most notably, if the number of invariant factors of the linear layer is small (e.g., if its minimal polynomial has a high degree), we can easily find round constants which guarantee the resistance to all types of invariant attacks, independently of the choice of the S-box layer. We also explain how to construct optimal round constants for a given, but arbitrary, linear layer.

Keywords: Block cipher · Nonlinear invariant · Invariant subspace attack · Linear layer · Round constants · Mantis · Midori · Prince · Skinny · LED

1 Introduction

One of the main topics in symmetric cryptography in recent years is lightweight cryptography. Even though it is not really clearly defined what lightweight cryptography exactly is, the main idea can be embraced as designing cryptographic primitives that put an extreme focus on performance. This in turn resulted in many new, especially block cipher, designs which achieve better performance by essentially removing any operations that are not strictly necessary (or believed to be necessary) for the security of the scheme. One particular interesting case of reducing the complexity is the design of the key schedule and the choice of round constants. Both of these are arguably the parts that we understand least and only very basic design criteria are available on how to choose a good key

© International Association for Cryptologic Research 2017
J. Katz and H. Shacham (Eds.): CRYPTO 2017, Part II, LNCS 10402, pp. 647–678, 2017.
DOI: 10.1007/978-3-319-63715-0_22

schedule or how to choose good round constants. Consequently, many of the lightweight block ciphers remove the key schedule completely. Instead, identical keys are used in the rounds and (often very simple and sparse) round constants are added on top (e.g., see LED [10], Skinny [1], Prince [2], Mantis [1], to mention a few).

However, several of those schemes were recently broken using a structural attack called invariant subspace attack [14,15], as well as the recently published generalization called nonlinear invariant attack [19]. Indeed, those attacks have been successfully applied to quite a number of recent designs including PRINT-cipher [14], Midori-64 [9,19], iSCREAM [15] and SCREAM [19], NORX v2.0 [4], Simpira v1 [17] and Haraka v.0 [12]. Both attacks, that we jointly call *invariant attacks* in this work, notably exploit the fact that these lightweight primitives have a very simple key schedule where the same round key (up to the addition of a round constant) is applied in several rounds.

It is therefore of major importance to determine whether a given primitive is vulnerable to invariant attacks. More generally, it would be interesting to exhibit some design criteria for the building blocks in a cipher which guarantee the resistance against these attacks. As mentioned above, this would shed light on the fundamental open question on how to select proper round constants.

Our Contribution. In this work, we analyze the resistance of several lightweight substitution-permutation ciphers against invariant attacks. Our framework both covers the invariant subspace attack, as well as the recently published nonlinear invariant attack. By exactly formalizing the requirements of those attacks, we are able to reveal the precise mathematical properties that render those attacks applicable. Indeed, as we will detail below, the rational canonical form of the linear layer will play a major role in our analysis. Our results show that the linear layer and the round constants have a major impact on the resistance against invariant attacks, while this type of attacks was previously believed to be mainly related to the behaviour of the S-box, see e.g., [9]. In particular, if the number of invariant factors of the linear layer is small (for instance, if its minimal polynomial has a high degree), we can easily find round constants which guarantee the resistance to all types of invariant attacks, independently of the choice of the S-box layer. In order to ease the application of our results in practice, we implemented all our findings in Sage [18] and added the source code in Appendix D.

In our framework, the resistance against invariant attacks is defined in the following sense: For each instantiation of the cipher with a fixed key, there is no function that is invariant for both the substitution layer and for the linear part of each round. This implies that any adversary who still wants to apply an invariant attack necessarily has to search for invariants over the *whole round function*, which appears to have a cost exponential in the block size in general. Indeed, all published invariant attacks we are aware of exploit weaknesses in the underlying building blocks of the round. Therefore, our notion of resistance guarantees complete security against the major class of invariant attacks, including all variants published so far.

This paper is split in two parts, a first part (Sect. 3) which can be seen as the attacker's view on the problem and a second part (Sect. 4) which reflects more on the designer's decision on how to avoid those attacks. More precisely, the first part of the paper details an algorithmic approach which enables an adversary to spot a possible weakness with respect to invariant attacks within a given cipher. For the lightweight block ciphers Skinny-64, Prince and Mantis$_7$, the 7-round version of Mantis, this algorithm is used to prove the resistance against invariant attacks.

These results come from the following observation, detailed in this first part: Let L denote the linear layer of the cipher in question and let $c_1, \ldots, c_t \in \mathbb{F}_2^n$ be the (XOR) differences between two round constants involved in rounds where the same round key is applied. Furthermore let $W_L(c_1, \ldots, c_t)$ denote the smallest L-invariant subspace of $\mathbb{F}_2^n$ that contains all $c_1, \ldots, c_t$. Then, one can guarantee resistance if $W_L(c_1, \ldots, c_t)$ covers the whole input space $\mathbb{F}_2^n$. As a direct result, we will see that in Skinny-64, there are enough differences between round constants to guarantee the full dimension of the corresponding L-invariant subspace. This directly implies the resistance of Skinny-64, and this result holds *for any reasonable choice of the S-box layer*.[1] In contrast, for Prince and Mantis$_7$, there are not enough suitable c_i to generate a subspace $W_L(c_1, \ldots, c_t)$ with full dimension. However, for both primitives, we are able to keep the security argument by also considering the S-box layer, using the fact that the dimension of $W_L(c_1, \ldots, c_t)$ is not too low in both cases.

In the second part of the paper, we provide an in-depth analysis of the impact of the round constants and of the linear layer on the resistance against invariant attacks. The first question we ask is the following:

Given the linear layer L of a cipher, what is the minimum number of round constants needed to guarantee resistance against the invariant attack, independently from the choice of the S-box?

Figure 1 shows the maximal dimension that can be reached by $W_L(c_1, \ldots, c_t)$ when t values of c_i are considered. It shows in particular that the whole input space can be covered with only $t = 4$ values in the case of Skinny-64, while 8 and 16 values are needed for Prince and Mantis respectively. This explains why, even though Prince and Mantis apply very dense round constants, the dimension does not increase rapidly for higher values of t. The observations in Fig. 1 are deduced from the *invariant factors* (or the *rational canonical form*) of the linear layer, as shown in the following theorem.

Theorem 1. *Let $Q_1, \ldots, Q_r$ be the invariant factors of the linear layer L and let $t \le r$. Then*

$$\max_{c_1, \ldots, c_t \in \mathbb{F}_2^n} \dim W_L(c_1, \ldots, c_t) = \sum_{i=1}^{t} \deg Q_i.$$

---

[1] We have to provide that the S-box has no component of degree 1. If the S-box has such a linear component, the cipher could be easily broken using linear cryptanalysis.

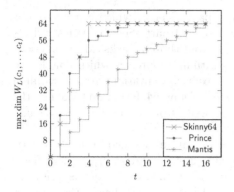
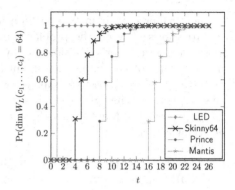

Fig. 1. For Skinny-64, Prince and Mantis, this figure shows the highest possible dimension of $W_L(c_1, \ldots, c_t)$ for t values $c_1, \ldots, c_t$ (see Theorem 1).

Fig. 2. For several lightweight ciphers, this figure shows the probability that $W_L(c_1, \ldots, c_t) = \mathbb{F}_2^n$ for uniformly random constants c_i (see Theorem 2).

For the special case of a single constant c, the maximal dimension of $W_L(c)$ is equal to the degree of the greatest invariant factor of L, i.e., the minimal polynomial of L. We will also explain how the particular round constants must be chosen in order to guarantee the best possible resistance.

As designers often choose random round constants to instantiate the primitive, we were also interested in the following question:

How many randomly chosen round constants are needed to guarantee the best possible resistance with a high probability?

We derive an exact formula for the probability that the linear subspace $W_L(c_1, \ldots, c_t)$ has full dimension for t uniformly random constants c_i. Figure 2 gives an overview of this probability for several lightweight designs.

Organization of the Paper. The principle of invariant attacks is first briefly recalled in Sect. 2. In Sect. 3, a new necessary condition is established on the functions which are both invariant for the S-box layer and for the linear parts (including the round key addition) of all rounds. This leads to a new security argument against invariant attacks. An algorithm to check whether the round constants avoid the existence of such invariants is then presented and applied to several lightweight ciphers, including Mantis7, Skinny-64 and Prince. Section 4 analyzes in more detail how the choice of the linear layer and of the round constants affects the resistance against invariant attacks. Some existing lightweight designs serve as examples to illustrate the arguments.

2   Preliminaries

By $\mathcal{B}_n$, we denote the set of all Boolean functions of n variables. The constant functions in $\mathbb{F}_2^n$ will be denoted by **0** and **1**, respectively. The *derivative of* $f \in \mathcal{B}_n$

in direction $\alpha \in \mathbb{F}_2^n$ is the Boolean function defined as $\Delta_\alpha f := x \mapsto f(x + \alpha) + f(x)$. The following terminology will be extensively used in the paper. It refers to the constant derivatives which play a major role in our work.

Definition 1. [13] *An element* $\alpha \in \mathbb{F}_2^n$ *is said to be a* linear structure *of* $f \in \mathcal{B}_n$ *if the corresponding derivative* $\Delta_\alpha f$ *is constant. The set of all linear structures of a function* f *is a linear subspace of* $\mathbb{F}_2^n$ *and is called the* linear space *of* f:

$$\mathsf{LS}(f) := \{\alpha \in \mathbb{F}_2^n \mid \Delta_\alpha f = \varepsilon, \ \varepsilon \in \{0, 1\}\}.$$

The nonlinear invariant attack was described in [19] as a distinguishing attack on block ciphers. For a block cipher E operating on an n-bit block,

$$E : \mathbb{F}_2^n \times \mathbb{F}_2^\kappa \to \mathbb{F}_2^n, \quad (x, k) \mapsto E_k(x),$$

the idea is to find a subset $\mathcal{S} \subset \mathbb{F}_2^n$ such that the partition of the input set into $\mathcal{S} \cup (\mathbb{F}_2^n \setminus \mathcal{S})$ is preserved by the cipher for as many keys k as possible, i.e.,

$$E_k(\mathcal{S}) = \mathcal{S} \text{ or } E_k(\mathcal{S}) = \mathbb{F}_2^n \setminus \mathcal{S}.$$

The special case when $\mathcal{S}$ is a linear space corresponds to the so-called *invariant subspace attacks* [14].

An equivalent formulation is obtained by considering the n-variable Boolean function g defined by $g(x) = 1$ if and only if $x \in \mathcal{S}$. Then, finding an invariant consists in finding a function $g \in \mathcal{B}_n$ such that $g + g \circ E_k$ is constant. We call such a function g an *invariant* for E_k, and we obviously focus on non-trivial invariants, i.e., on $g \notin \{0, 1\}$. In the following, for any permutation $F : \mathbb{F}_2^n \to \mathbb{F}_2^n$, we denote the set of all invariants for F by

$$\mathcal{U}(F) := \{g \in \mathcal{B}_n \mid g + g \circ F \text{ is constant}\}.$$

As observed in [19], this set is a linear subspace of $\mathcal{B}_n$. An important remark, which will be used later, is that if F has a cycle of odd length, then all $g \in \mathcal{U}(F)$ satisfy $g + g \circ F = \mathbf{0}$.

3   Proving the Absence of Invariants in Lightweight SPNs

In the whole paper, we concentrate on block ciphers which follow the specific design of substitution-permutation networks (SPNs) as depicted in Fig. 3.

Usually, the technique applied for finding invariants for the cipher consists in exploiting its iterative structure and in searching for functions which are *invariant for all constituent building blocks*. Indeed computing invariants for the round function is in general infeasible for a proper block size, typically $n = 64$ or $n = 128$. Despite the fact that all published invariant attacks we are aware of exploit invariants for all the constituent building blocks, the algorithm described in [15] searches for invariant subspaces over *the whole round function*. However, it can only be applied in the special case for finding an invariant subspace, and

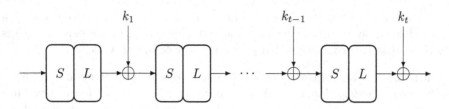

Fig. 3. SPN with S-box layer S and linear layer L. After the i-th round, one adds a round key k_i, where $(k_1, \ldots, k_t)$ is the expanded key resulting from the key schedule.

not for detecting an arbitrary invariant set, and only detects spaces of large dimension efficiently.

Therefore, we consider in the following only those invariants that are invariant under both the substitution layer S and the linear parts $\mathsf{Add}_{k_i} \circ L$ of all rounds. The linear spaces of these invariants have then a very specific structure as pointed out in the following proposition.

Proposition 1. *Let $g \in \mathcal{B}_n$ be an invariant for both $\mathsf{Add}_{k_i} \circ L$ and $\mathsf{Add}_{k_j} \circ L$ for two round keys k_i and k_j. Then $\mathsf{LS}(g)$ is a linear space invariant under L which contains $(k_i + k_j)$.*

Proof. By definition of g, there exist $\varepsilon_i, \varepsilon_j \in \mathbb{F}_2$ such that, for all $x \in \mathbb{F}_2^n$,

$$g(x) = g(L(x) + k_i) + \varepsilon_i \text{ and } g(x) = g(L(x) + k_j) + \varepsilon_j.$$

This implies that, for all $x \in \mathbb{F}_2^n$,

$$g(L(x) + k_i) + g(L(x) + k_j) = \varepsilon_i + \varepsilon_j,$$

or equivalently, by replacing $(L(x) + k_j)$ by y:

$$g(y + k_i + k_j) + g(y) = \varepsilon_i + \varepsilon_j, \ \forall y \in \mathbb{F}_2^n$$

and thus $(k_i + k_j) \in \mathsf{LS}(g)$. We then have to show that $\mathsf{LS}(g)$ is invariant under L. Let $s \in \mathsf{LS}(g)$. Then, there exists a constant $\varepsilon \in \mathbb{F}_2$ such that $g(x) = g(x+s)+\varepsilon$. Since g is an invariant for $\mathsf{Add}_{k_i} \circ L$, we deduce

$$g(L(x) + k_i) + \varepsilon_i = g(x) = g(x + s) + \varepsilon = g(L(x) + L(s) + k_i) + (\varepsilon_i + \varepsilon).$$

Finally, we set $y := L(x) + k_i$ and obtain

$$g(y) = g(y + L(s)) + \varepsilon \tag{1}$$

which completes the proof. □

Therefore, the attack requires the existence of an invariant for the substitution layer whose linear space is invariant under L and contains all differences between the round keys. The difference between two round keys, which should be contained in $\mathsf{LS}(g)$, is dependent on the initial key. However, if we consider only designs where some round keys are equal up to the addition of a round constant, we obtain that the differences between these round constants must belong to $\mathsf{LS}(g)$. Then, $\mathsf{LS}(g)$ is a linear space invariant under L which contains the differences $(\mathsf{RC}_i + \mathsf{RC}_j)$ for any pair (i, j) of rounds such that $k_i = k + \mathsf{RC}_i$ and $k_j = k + \mathsf{RC}_j$. The smallest such subspaces are spanned by the cycles of L as shown by the following lemma. We use the angle bracket notation to denote the linear span.

Lemma 1. *Let L be a linear permutation of $\mathbb{F}_2^n$. For any $c \in \mathbb{F}_2^n$, the smallest L-invariant linear subspace of $\mathbb{F}_2^n$ which contains c, denoted by $W_L(c)$, is*

$$\langle L^i(c), i \geq 0 \rangle.$$

Proof. Obviously, $\langle L^i(c), i \geq 0 \rangle$ is included in $W_L(c)$, since $W_L(c)$ is a linear subspace of $\mathbb{F}_2^n$ and is invariant under L. Moreover, we observe that $\langle L^i(c), i \geq 0 \rangle$ is invariant under L. Indeed, for any $\lambda_1, \lambda_2 \in \mathbb{F}_2$ and any (i, j),

$$L(\lambda_1 L^i(c) + \lambda_2 L^j(c)) = \lambda_1 L^{i+1}(c) + \lambda_2 L^{j+1}(c)$$

and then belongs to $\langle L^i(c), i \geq 0 \rangle$. Then, this subspace is the smallest linear subspace of $\mathbb{F}_2^n$ invariant under L which contains c. □

Let now D be a set of known differences between round keys, i.e., a subset of all $k_i + k_j = (\mathsf{RC}_i + \mathsf{RC}_j)$. We define the subset

$$W_L(D) := \sum_{c \in D} \langle L^i(c),\ i \geq 0 \rangle = \sum_{c \in D} W_L(c).$$

We then deduce from the previous observations that the invariant attack applies only if there is a non-trivial invariant g for the S-box layer such that $W_L(D) \subseteq \mathsf{LS}(g)$. A Sage code that computes the linear space $W_L(D)$ for a predefined list D is given in Appendix D (lines 31–38). It has been used for determining the dimension of $W_L(D)$ corresponding to the round constants in several lightweight ciphers.

Skinny-64. Considering the untweaked version Skinny-64-64, one observes that the round keys repeat every 16 rounds. We define

$$D := \{\mathsf{RC}_1 + \mathsf{RC}_{17}, \mathsf{RC}_2 + \mathsf{RC}_{18}, \mathsf{RC}_3 + \mathsf{RC}_{19}, \mathsf{RC}_4 + \mathsf{RC}_{20}, \mathsf{RC}_5 + \mathsf{RC}_{21}\}$$

and obtain $\dim W_L(D) = 64$.

Skinny-128. In Skinny-128, The round constants are all of the following form:

$$\begin{bmatrix} c_0 & 0 & 0 & 0 \\ c_1 & 0 & 0 & 0 \\ c_2 & 0 & 0 & 0 \\ 0 & 0 & 0 & 0 \end{bmatrix}$$

with 8-bit values $c_0 \in \{\texttt{0x00}, \ldots, \texttt{0x0f}\}$, $c_1 \in \{\texttt{0x00}, \ldots, \texttt{0x03}\}$ and $c_2 = \texttt{0x02}$. Then, as the linear layer is defined by a binary matrix, we can see that the dimension of $W_L(D)$ is at most 64, because none of the four most significant bits will be activated with any round constant.

Prince. Prince uses ten round keys k_i, $1 \leq i \leq 10$, which are all of the form $k_i = k + RC_i$. The so-called α-reflection property implies that, for any i, $k_i + k_{11-i} = \alpha$ where α is a fixed constant. We can then consider the set of (independent) round constant differences

$$D = \{\alpha, RC_1 + RC_2, RC_1 + RC_3, RC_1 + RC_4, RC_1 + RC_5\}.$$

We obtain that $\dim W_L(D) = 56$.

Mantis. As Prince, Mantis$_7$ follows the α-reflection construction. We therefore consider the following set of round constant differences:

$$D = \{\alpha, RC_1 + RC_2, RC_1 + RC_3, RC_1 + RC_4, RC_1 + RC_5, RC_1 + RC_6, RC_1 + RC_7\}$$

We obtain that $\dim W_L(D) = 42$.

Midori-64. In Midori-64, the round constants are only added to the least significant bit of each cell and the linear layer does not provide any mixing within the cells. Then $W_L(D) = \{0000, 0001\}^{16}$, and has dimension 16 only.

As the invariant attack applies only if there is a non-trivial invariant g for the S-box layer such that $W_L(D) \subseteq LS(g)$, by intuition, the attack should be harder as the dimension of $W_L(D)$ increases. In the following, we analzye the impact of the dimension of $W_L(D)$ to the applicability of the attack in detail and present a method to prove the non-existence of invariants based on this dimension.

3.1 The Simple Case

We first consider a simple case, that is when the dimension of $W_L(D)$ is at least $n - 1$.

Proposition 2. *Suppose that the dimension of $W_L(D)$ is at least $n - 1$. Then, any $g \in \mathcal{B}_n$ such that $W_L(D) \subseteq LS(g)$ is linear or constant. As a consequence, there is no non-trivial invariant g of the S-box layer such that $W_L(D) \subseteq LS(g)$, unless the S-box layer has a component of degree 1.*

Proof. From [3, Proposition 14], it follows that

$$\dim LS(g) \geq k \Leftrightarrow \deg(g) \leq \begin{cases} n - k & \text{if } k \neq n \\ 1 & \text{if } k = n \end{cases}.$$

This implies that g must be linear or constant. Linear invariants imply the existence of a linear approximation with probability 1, or equivalently that the S-box has a component (i.e., a linear combination of its coordinates) of degree 1. □

In the rest of the paper, we will implicitly exclude the case when the S-box has a component of degree 1, as the cipher would be already broken by linear cryptanalysis.

Skinny-64. As shown before, for the untweaked version Skinny-64-64 one obtains $\dim W_L(D) = 64$. This indicates that the round constants do not allow non-trivial invariants that are invariant for both the substitution and the linear parts of Skinny-64, and this result holds for any choice of the S-box layer.

Unfortunately, the dimension of $W_L(D)$ is not high enough for the other ciphers we considered. For those primitives, we therefore cannot prove the resistance against invariant attacks based on the linear layer only.

3.2 When the Dimension Is Smaller Than $(n-1)$

Not every cipher applies round constants such that the dimension of $W_L(D)$ is larger than or equal to $n-1$. Even for Prince and Mantis, which have very dense round constants, it is not the case and we cannot directly rely on this argument. However, if $n - \dim(W_L(D))$ is small, we can still prove that the invariant attack does not apply but only by exploiting some information on the S-box layer. This can be done by checking whether there exists a non-trivial invariant g for the S-box layer which admits some given elements as 0-linear structures, in the sense of the following definition.

Definition 2. *A linear structure α of a Boolean function f is called a 0-linear structure if the corresponding derivative equals the all-zero function. The set of all 0-linear structures of f is a linear subspace of $\mathsf{LS}(f)$ denoted by $\mathsf{LS}_0(f)$. Elements β s.t. $\Delta_\beta g = 1$ are called 1-linear structures of f.*

Note that *0-linear structures* are also called *invariant linear structures*. It is well-known that the dimension of $\mathsf{LS}_0(f)$ drops by at most 1 compared to $\mathsf{LS}(f)$ [5].

Checking that all invariants are constant based on 0-linear structures. In the following, we search for an invariant g for the S-box layer S that is also invariant for the linear part of each round. Suppose now, in a first step, that we know a subspace Z of $\mathsf{LS}(g)$ which is composed of 0-linear structures only. In other words, we now search for an invariant g for S such that $\mathsf{LS}_0(g) \supseteq Z$ for some fixed Z. If the dimension of this subspace Z is close to n, we can try to prove that any such invariant is constant based on the following observation.

Proposition 3. *Let g be an invariant for an n-bit permutation S such that $\mathsf{LS}_0(g) \supseteq Z$ for some given subspace $Z \subset \mathbb{F}_2^n$. Then*

- *g is constant on each coset of Z;*
- *g is constant on $S(Z)$.*

Proof. Since $Z \subseteq \mathsf{LS}_0(g)$, for any $a \in \mathbb{F}_2^n$, we have that $g(a+z) = g(a)$ for all $z \in Z$, i.e., g is constant on all $(a+Z)$. Now, we use that g is an invariant for S, which means that there exists $\varepsilon \in \mathbb{F}_2$ such that $g(S(x)) = g(x) + \varepsilon$. Since g is constant on Z, we deduce that g is constant on $S(Z)$.   □

To show that g must be trivial, the idea is to evaluate the S-box layer at some points in Z and deduce that g takes the same value on all corresponding cosets. The number of distinct cosets of Z equals $2^{n-\dim Z}$, which is not too large when $\dim Z$ is close to n. Then, we hope that all cosets will be hit when evaluating S at a few points in Z. In this situation, g must be a constant function. In other words, we are able to conclude that there do not exist non-trivial invariants for both the substitution layer and the linear part.

In our experiments, we used the following very simple algorithm. If it terminates, all invariants must be constant. An efficient implementation in Sage of Algorithm 1 is given in Appendix D.

Algorithm 1. Checking that $\mathcal{U}(S) \cap \{g \in \mathcal{B}_n \mid Z \subseteq \mathsf{LS}_0(g)\}$ is trivial

---
1: $R = \{\}$
2: **repeat**
3:      $z \xleftarrow{\$} Z$
4:      Compute $S(z)$
5:      Add to R a representative of the coset defined by $S(z)$
6: **until** $|R| = 2^{n-\dim Z}$

Determining a suitable Z from $W_L(D)$. Up to now, we assumed the knowledge of a subspace Z of $W_L(D)$ for which $Z \subseteq \mathsf{LS}_0(g)$ for all invariants g we are considering. But, the fact that some elements are 0-linear structures depends on the actual invariant g and thus, each of the elements $d \in W_L(D)$ might or might not be a 0-linear structure. However, some 0-linear structures can be determined by using one of the two following approaches.

First approach. The first observation comes from (1) in the proof of Proposition 1.

Lemma 2. *Let $g \in \mathcal{B}_n$ be an invariant for $\mathsf{Add}_{k_i} \circ L$ for some k_i and let V be a subspace of $\mathsf{LS}(g)$ which is invariant under L. Then, for any $v \in V$, $(v + L(v)) \in \mathsf{LS}_0(g)$.*

Proof. Let $v \in V$. Similar as in the proof of Proposition 1, we use that g is an invariant for $\mathsf{Add}_{k_i} \circ L$ and see that there exists an $\varepsilon \in \mathbb{F}_2$ such that, for all $x \in \mathbb{F}_2^n$,

$$g(x) = g(x+v) + \varepsilon = g(x + L(v)) + \varepsilon.$$

We finally set $y := x + v$ and obtain

$$g(y) = g(y + v + L(v)),$$

implying that $v + L(v)$ is a 0-linear structure for g.   □

Following the previous lemma, one option is to just run Algorithm 1 on $Z = W_L(D')$ with $D' = \{d + L(d), d \in D\}$. The disadvantage is that the dimension of Z might be too low and therefore the algorithm might be too inefficient. In this case, one can also consider a different approach and run the algorithm several times, by considering all possible choices for the 0-linear structures among all elements in D. Suppose that, in the initial set of constants $D = \{d_1, d_2, \ldots, d_m, \ldots, d_t\}$, the elements $d_1, \ldots, d_m$ are all 1-linear structures for some invariant g with $\mathsf{LS}(g) \supseteq W_L(D)$. One can now consider

$$D' = \{d_1 + L(d_1), d_2 + L(d_2), \ldots, d_m + L(d_m), d_{m+1}, \ldots, d_t, d_1 + d_2, \ldots, d_1 + d_m\}$$

which increases the dimension of $W_L(D')$ by adding the sums of the 1-linear structures. We then have $W_L(D') \subseteq \mathsf{LS}_0(g)$ and we can apply Algorithm 1 on $Z = W_L(D')$. Since we cannot say in advance which of the constants are 1-linear structures, there are 2^t possible choices of such a subspace $W_L(D')$ and we run Algorithm 1 on all of them. This approach still might be very inefficient due to the smaller dimension of $W_L(D')$ and since Algorithm 1 has to be run 2^t times.

Second approach. If the S-box layer S of the cipher has an odd-length cycle (i.e., if every S-box has an odd-length cycle), we can come up with the following.

Proposition 4. *Let $g \in \mathcal{U}(S)$ where S is an n-bit permutation with an odd cycle. Then, any linear structure of g which belongs to the image set of $(S + \mathsf{Id}_n)$, i.e., $\{S(x) + x \mid x \in \mathbb{F}_2^n\}$, is a 0-linear structure of g.*

Proof. If the S-box layer has an odd cycle, then any $g \in \mathcal{U}(S)$ necessarily fulfills $g(x) = g(S(x))$ for all $x \in \mathbb{F}_2^n$. Now let $g \in \mathcal{U}(S)$ and $c \in \mathsf{LS}(g)$. This linear structure belongs to $\mathsf{Im}(S + \mathsf{Id}_n)$ if there exists $x_0 \in \mathbb{F}_2^n$ such that $S(x_0) = x_0 + c$. We then deduce that

$$g(x_0) = g(S(x_0)) = g(x_0 + c),$$

implying that c is a 0-linear structure of g.   □

Therefore, if we find enough of these $c \in W_L(D) \cap \mathsf{Im}(S + \mathsf{Id}_n)$, we can just apply Algorithm 1 on the resulting set. This approach will be used on Mantis$_7$, as explained in the next section.

3.3   Results for Some Lightweight Ciphers

Prince. For Prince, we apply the first approach to $D' = \{d + L(d), \; d \in D\}$ where

$$D = \{\alpha, \mathsf{RC}_1 + \mathsf{RC}_2, \mathsf{RC}_1 + \mathsf{RC}_3, \mathsf{RC}_1 + \mathsf{RC}_4, \mathsf{RC}_1 + \mathsf{RC}_5\}.$$

Then, $\dim W_L(D') = 51$. We run Algorithm 1 on $W_L(D')$ and the algorithm terminates within a few minutes on a standard PC. We now have proven that there are no non-trivial invariants that are invariant for both the substitution layer and the linear parts of all rounds in Prince.

Mantis. Since $\dim W_L(D) = 42$ for Mantis$_7$, applying our algorithm 2^7 times on a subspace of codimension 23 is a quite expensive task. We therefore exploit Proposition 4. Indeed, the S-box layer of Mantis is the parallel application of the following 4-bit S-box Sb.

x	0	1	2	3	4	5	6	7	8	9	a	b	c	d	e	f
$\text{Sb}(x)$	c	a	d	3	e	b	f	7	8	9	1	5	0	2	4	6
$x + \text{Sb}(x)$	c	b	f	0	a	e	9	0	0	0	b	e	c	f	a	9

The S-box layer has an odd cycle because Sb has a fixed point. Moreover, the image set of $(\text{Sb} + \text{Id}_4)$ is composed of 7 values $\{0, 9, a, b, c, e, f\}$. The $c \in W_L(D)$ for which each nibble is equal to a value in $\text{Im}(\text{Sb} + \text{Id}_4)$ is a 0-linear structure. For a random value $c \in \mathbb{F}_2^{64}$, we expect that every nibble belongs to $\text{Im}(\text{Sb} + \text{Id}_4)$ with a probability of $\left(\frac{7}{16}\right)^{16} \approx 2^{-19.082}$. In fact, one can find enough such $c \in W_L(D)$ in a reasonable time that generate the whole invariant space $W_L(D)$, implying that $W_L(D) \subseteq \text{LS}_0(g)$ for all invariants $g \in \mathcal{U}(S)$. We then run Algorithm 1 on $Z = W_L(D)$. The algorithm terminates and we therefore deduce the non-existence of any non-trivial invariant which is invariant for S and the linear parts of all rounds in Mantis$_7$.

Midori-64. For Midori-64, $W_L(D) = \{0000, 0001\}^{16}$ and has dimension 16 only. Then, there are 2^{48} different cosets of $W_L(D)$, implying that our algorithm is not efficient. Instead, we can theoretically describe the supports of all invariants of Midori-64. The proof of the following proposition is given in Appendix C.

Proposition 5. *Let S be the substitution layer in* Midori-64. *Let further $W = \{0000, 0001\}^{16}$. Let $g \in B_{64}$. Then, $g \in \mathcal{U}(S)$ and $W \subseteq \text{LS}(g)$ if and only if the support of g is defined by*

$$\text{Supp}(g) = \bigcup_{b_0 \dots b_{31} \in \text{Supp}(h)} H_{b_0 b_1} \times H_{b_2 b_3} \times \dots \times H_{b_{30} b_{31}}$$

where h is any Boolean function of 32 variables such that $\{00, 10\}^{16} \subseteq \text{LS}(h)$ and the sets H_{ab} are defined by

$$H_{00} = \{8\}, H_{10} = \{9\}, H_{01} = \{0, 3, 5, 6, b, c, f\} \text{ and } H_{11} = \{1, 2, 4, 7, a, d, e\}.$$

The invariant g_1 exploited in the invariant subspace attack described in [9] is defined by $\text{supp}(g_1) = \{8, 9\}^{16}$. In our characterization, it corresponds to

$$h(b_0, \dots, b_{31}) = \prod_{i=0}^{15} (1 + b_{2i+1}).$$

In this case, all elements in $\{00, 10\}^{16}$ are 0-linear structures for h, implying that all elements in $W_L(D)$ are 0-linear structures for g_1. If we denote the bits in the j-th cell of the Midori-64 state by $x_{j,3}, x_{j,2}, x_{j,1}, x_{j,0}$ (the lsb corresponds to $x_{j,0}$), the algebraic normal form of g_1 is

$$g_1(x) = \prod_{j=1}^{16} (x_{j,1}x_{j,2}x_{j,3} + x_{j,1}x_{j,3} + x_{j,2}x_{j,3} + x_{j,3}),$$

since $x_1x_2x_3 + x_1x_3 + x_2x_3 + x_3$ is the ANF of the 4-variable function with support $H_{00} \cup H_{10}$.

The quadratic nonlinear invariant described in [19] is given by

$$g_2(x) = \sum_{j=1}^{16} (x_{j,3}x_{j,2} + x_{j,2} + x_{j,1} + x_{j,0}).$$

It corresponds to $h(b_0, \ldots, b_{31}) = \sum_{i=0}^{15} b_{2i}$. In this second case, only the words in $W_L(D)$ with an even number of non-zero nibbles are 0-linear structures for g_2. It is worth noticing that the sum of these two invariants ($g_1 + g_2$) leads to a new invariant of degree 48 which has a linear space of dimension 32. However, as this invariant does not admit any new weak keys, it does not lead to an improved attack on Midori-64.

4   Design Criteria on the Linear Layer and on the Round Constants

In this section, we study the properties of $W_L(D)$ in more detail and explain the different behaviors which have been previously observed. Most notably, we would like to determine whether the differences in the dimensions of $W_L(D)$ we noticed are due to a bad choice of the round constants or if they are inherent to the choice of the linear layer. At this aim, we analyze the possible values for the dimension of $W_L(D)$ from a more theoretical viewpoint. We first consider the L-invariant subspace $W_L(c)$ generated by a single element c. It is worth noticing that all results obtained in this section hold for any $\mathbb{F}_q$-linear layer operating on $\mathbb{F}_q^n$, where q is any prime power. But, for the sake of simplicity, they are formulated for $q = 2$ only, which is the case of all ciphers we are considering.

4.1   The Possible Dimensions of $W_L(c)$

We show that, for a single element c, the dimension of $W_L(c)$ is upper-bounded by the degree of the minimal polynomial of the linear layer, defined as follows.

Definition 3. *(e.g., [7, p. 176]) Let L be a linear permutation of $\mathbb{F}_2^n$. The minimal polynomial of L is the monic polynomial $\mathsf{Min}_L(X) = \sum_{i=0}^d p_i X^i \in \mathbb{F}_2[x]$ of smallest degree such that*

$$\mathsf{Min}_L(L) = \sum_{i=0}^d p_i L^i = 0.$$

Moreover, the minimal annihilating polynomial of an element $c \in \mathbb{F}_2^n$ (w.r.t L) *(aka the* order polynomial of c *or simply the* minimal polynomial of c) *is the monic polynomial* $\operatorname{ord}_L(c)(X) = \sum_{i=0}^d \pi_i X^i \in \mathbb{F}_2[x]$ *of smallest degree such that*

$$\sum_{i=0}^d \pi_i(L^i(c)) = 0.$$

Proposition 6. *Let L be a linear permutation of $\mathbb{F}_2^n$. For any non-zero $c \in \mathbb{F}_2^n$, the dimension of $W_L(c)$ is the degree of the minimal polynomial of c.*

Proof. We know from Lemma 1 that $W_L(c)$ is spanned by all $L^i(c), i \geq 0$. Let d be the smallest integer such that $\{c, L(c), \ldots, L^{d-1}(c)\}$ are linearly independent. By definition, d corresponds the degree of the minimal polynomial of c since the fact that $L^d(c)$ belongs to $\langle L^i(c), 0 \leq i < d \rangle$ is equivalent to the existence of $\pi_0, \ldots, \pi_{d-1} \in \mathbb{F}_2$ such that $L^d(c) = \sum_{i=0}^{d-1} \pi_i L^i(c)$, i.e., $P(L)(c) = 0$ with $P(X) = X^d + \sum_{i=0}^{d-1} \pi_i X^i$. It follows that $d \leq \dim W_L(c)$.

We now need to prove that $d = \dim W_L(c)$, i.e., that all $L^{d+t}(c)$ for $t \geq 0$ belong to the linear subspace spanned by $\{c, L(c), \ldots, L^{d-1}(c)\}$. This can be proved by induction on t. The property holds for $t = 0$ by definition of d. Suppose now that $L^{d+t}(c) \in \langle c, L(c), \ldots, L^{d-1}(c) \rangle$. Then,

$$L^{d+t+1}(c) = L\left(L^{d+t}(c)\right) = L\left(\sum_{i=0}^{d-1} \lambda_i L^i(c)\right) = \sum_{i=0}^{d-1} \lambda_i L^{i+1}(c) \in \langle c, \ldots, L^{d-1}(c) \rangle.$$

$\square$

Obviously, the minimal polynomial of c is a divisor of the minimal polynomial of L. The previous proposition then provides an upper bound on the dimension of any subspace $W_L(c)$, for $c \in \mathbb{F}_2^n \setminus \{0\}$.

Corollary 1. *Let L be a linear permutation of $\mathbb{F}_2^n$. For any $c \in \mathbb{F}_2^n$, the dimension of $W_L(c)$ is at most the degree of the minimal polynomial of L.*

We can even get a more precise result and show that the possible values for the dimension of $W_L(c)$ correspond to the degrees of the divisors of Min_L. Moreover, there are some elements c which lead to any of these values. In particular, the degree of Min_L can always be achieved. This result can be proven in a constructive way by using the representation of the associated matrix as a block diagonal matrix whose diagonal consists of companion matrices.

Definition 4. *Let $g(X) = X^d + \sum_{i=0}^{d-1} g_i X^i$ be a monic polynomial in $\mathbb{F}_2[X]$. Its* companion matrix *is the $d \times d$ matrix defined by*

$$C(g) = \begin{pmatrix} 0 & 1 & 0 & \cdots & 0 \\ 0 & 0 & 1 & \cdots & 0 \\ & \vdots & & & \\ 0 & 0 & 0 & \cdots & 1 \\ g_0 & g_1 & g_2 & \cdots & g_{d-1} \end{pmatrix}$$

Let us first focus on the special case when the minimal polynomial of L has degree n. Then there is a basis such that the matrix of L is the companion matrix of Min_L (e.g., [11, Lemma 6.7.1]). Using this property, we can prove the following proposition.

Proposition 7. *Let L be a linear permutation of $\mathbb{F}_2^n$ corresponding to the multiplication by some companion matrix $C(Q)$ with $Q \in \mathbb{F}_2[X]$ of degree n. For any non-constant divisor P of Q in $\mathbb{F}_2[X]$, there exists $c \in \mathbb{F}_2^n$ such that $\text{ord}_L(c) = P$.*

Proof. When the matrix of the linear permutation we consider is a companion matrix $C(Q)$, then the elements in the cycle of c, $\{c, L(c), L^2(c), \ldots\}$, can be seen as the successive internal states of the n-bit LFSR with characteristic polynomial Q and initial state c. It follows that $\text{ord}_L(c)$ corresponds to the minimal polynomial of the sequence produced by the LFSR with characteristic polynomial Q and initial state c (see [16, Theorem 8.51]). On the other hand, it is well-known that there is a one-to-one correspondence between the sequences $(s_t)_{t \geq 0}$ produced by the LFSR with characteristic polynomial Q and the set of polynomials $C \in \mathbb{F}_2[X]$ with $\deg C < \deg Q$ [16, Theorem 8.40]. This comes from the fact that the generating function of any LFSR sequence can be written as

$$\sum_{t \geq 0} s_t X^t = \frac{C(X)}{Q^*(X)},$$

where Q^* denotes the reciprocal of polynomial Q, i.e., $Q^*(X) = X^{\deg Q} Q(1/X)$, and C is defined by the LFSR initial state.

Let now P be any non-constant divisor of Q, i.e., $Q(X) = P(X)R(X)$ with $P \neq 1$. Then, the reciprocal polynomials satisfy $Q^*(X) = P^*(X)R^*(X)$. It follows that, for $C(X) = R^*(X)$,

$$\frac{C(X)}{Q^*(X)} = \frac{1}{P^*(X)}.$$

Therefore, the sequence generated from the initial state defined by $C = R^*$ has minimal polynomial P. This is equivalent to the fact that the order polynomial of this initial state equals P. □

When the degree of the minimal polynomial of the linear layer is smaller than the block size, the previous result can be generalized by representing L by a block diagonal matrix whose diagonal is composed of companion matrices. It leads to the following general result on the possible dimensions of $W_L(c)$.

Proposition 8. *Let L be a linear permutation of $\mathbb{F}_2^n$ and Min_L be its minimal polynomial. Then, for any divisor P of Min_L, there exists $c \in \mathbb{F}_2^n$ such that $\dim W_L(c) = \deg P$.*
    Most notably,

$$\max_{c \in \mathbb{F}_2^n} \dim W_L(c) = \deg \text{Min}_L.$$

Proof. If P equals the constant polynomial of degree zero, i.e., $P = 1$, we choose $c = 0$. Therefore, we assume in the following that P is of positive degree.

Let us factor the minimal polynomial of L in

$$\mathsf{Min}_L(X) = M_1(X)^{e_1} M_2(X)^{e_2} \ldots M_k(X)^{e_k}$$

where M_1, ..., M_k are distinct irreducible polynomials over $\mathbb{F}_2$. From Theorem 6.7.1 and its corollary in [11], $\mathbb{F}_2^n$ can be decomposed into a direct sum of L-invariant subspaces

$$\mathbb{F}_2^n = \bigoplus_{i=1}^{k} \bigoplus_{j=1}^{r_i} V_{i,j}$$

such that the matrix of the linear transformation induced by L on $V_{i,j}$ is the companion matrix of $M_i^{\ell_{i,j}}$ where the $\ell_{i,j}$ are integers such that $\ell_{i,1} = e_i$ (the polynomials $M_i^{\ell_{i,j}}$ are called the elementary divisors of L). Let now P be a non-constant divisor of Min_L. Thus, we assume w.l.o.g that

$$P(X) = M_1(X)^{a_1} M_2(X)^{a_2} \ldots M_\kappa(X)^{a_\kappa} \text{ with } 1 \leq a_i \leq e_i.$$

Since each $M_i^{a_i}$ is a non-constant divisor of $M_i^{e_i}$, we know from Proposition 7 that there exists $u_i \in V_{i,1}$ such that $\mathrm{ord}_{L_i}(u_i) = M_i^{a_i}$, where L_i denotes the linear transformation induced by L on $V_{i,1}$. Let us now consider the element $c \in \bigoplus_{i=1}^{\kappa} V_{i,1}$ defined by $c = \sum_{i=1}^{\kappa} u_i$. Let $\pi_0, \ldots \pi_{d-1} \in \mathbb{F}_2$ such that $R(X) := X^d + \sum_{t=0}^{d-1} \pi_t X^t$ equals the order polynomial of c. In particular,

$$L^d(c) = \sum_{t=0}^{d-1} \pi_t L^t(c).$$

Using that $L^t(c) = \sum_{i=1}^{\kappa} L^t(u_i)$ and the direct sum property, we deduce that, for any $1 \leq i \leq \kappa$,

$$L^d(u_i) = \sum_{t=0}^{d-1} \pi_t L^t(u_i).$$

Then, R is a multiple of the order polynomials of all u_i. It follows that R must be a multiple of $\mathsf{lcm}(M_i^{a_i}) = P$. Since $P(L(c)) = 0$, we deduce that the order polynomial of c is equal to P. □

LED. The minimal polynomial of the linear layer in LED is

$$\mathsf{Min}_L(X) = (X^8 + X^7 + X^5 + X^3 + 1)^4 (X^8 + X^7 + X^6 + X^5 + X^2 + X + 1)^4.$$

Since its degree equals the block size, we deduce from the previous proposition that there exists an element $c \in \mathbb{F}_2^{64}$ such that $W_L(c)$ covers the whole space.

Skinny. The linear layer in Skinny with a $16s$-bit state, $s \in \{4, 8\}$, is an $\mathbb{F}_{2^s}$-linear permutation of $(\mathbb{F}_{2^s})^{16}$ defined by a (16×16) matrix M with coefficients in $\mathbb{F}_2$. Moreover, the multiplicative order of this matrix in $GL(16, \mathbb{F}_2)$ equals 16, implying that the minimal polynomial of L is a divisor of $X^{16} + 1$. It can actually be checked that $(M + \mathsf{Id}_{16})^e \neq 0$ for all $e < 16$, implying that

$$\mathsf{Min}_L(X) = X^{16} + 1 = (X + 1)^{16}.$$

It follows that there exist some elements $c \in (\mathbb{F}_{2^s})^{16}$ such that $\dim W_L(c) = d$ for any value of d between 1 and 16. Elements c which generate a subspace $W_L(c)$ of given dimension can be easily exhibited using the construction detailed in the proof of Proposition 7. Indeed, up to a change of basis, the matrix of L in $GL(16, \mathbb{F}_2)$ corresponds to the companion matrix of $(X^{16} + 1)$, i.e., to a mere rotation of 16-bit vectors. In other words, we can find a matrix $U \in GL(16, \mathbb{F}_2)$ such that $M = U \times C(X^{16} + 1) \times U^{-1}$. Let us now consider elements $c \in (\mathbb{F}_{2^s})^{16}$ for which only the least significant bits of the cells can take non-zero values. Let b be the 16-bit vector corresponding to these least significant bits, then $\dim W_L(c) = d$ where d is the length of the shortest LFSR generating $b' = U^{-1}b$. Table 1 provides some examples of such elements for various dimensions.

Table 1. Examples of $c \in (\mathbb{F}_{2^s})^{16}$ and the corresponding dimensions of $W_L(c)$.

$U^{-1} \times b$	b	$\dim W_L(c)$
1111111111111111	0011001100110011	1
1010101010101010	1111111111111111	2
1100110011001100	1001100110011001	3
1000100010001000	1011101110111011	4
1000000000000000	1111010111110001	16

Prince. The minimal polynomial of the linear layer in Prince is

$$\mathsf{Min}_L(X) = X^{20} + X^{18} + X^{16} + X^{14} + X^{12} + X^8 + X^6 + X^4 + X^2 + 1$$
$$= (X^4 + X^3 + X^2 + X + 1)^2 (X^2 + X + 1)^4 (X + 1)^4.$$

The maximal dimension of $W_L(c)$ is then 20 and the factorization of Min_L shows that there exist elements which generate subspaces of much lower dimension.

Mantis and Midori-64. Mantis and Midori-64 share the same linear layer, which has minimal polynomial

$$\mathsf{Min}_L(X) = (X + 1)^6.$$

We deduce that $\dim W_L(c) \leq 6$.

4.2   Considering More Round Constants

We can now consider more than one round constant and determine the maximum dimension of $W_L(c_1, \ldots, c_t)$ spanned by t elements. This value is related to the so-called *invariant factor form* (aka *rational canonical form*) of the linear layer, as defined in the following proposition.

Proposition 9. *(Invariant factors)* [6, p. 476] *Let L be a linear permutation of $\mathbb{F}_2^n$. A basis of $\mathbb{F}_2^n$ can be found in which the matrix of L is of the form*

$$
\begin{pmatrix}
C(Q_r) & & & \\
 & C(Q_{r-1}) & & \\
 & & \ddots & \\
 & & & C(Q_1)
\end{pmatrix}
$$

for polynomials Q_i such that $Q_r \mid Q_{r-1} \mid \cdots \mid Q_1$. The polynomial Q_1 equals the minimal polynomial of L. In this decomposition, the Q_i are called the invariant factors *of L.*

The invariant factors of the linear layer then define the maximal value of $W_L(c_1, \ldots, c_t)$, as stated in Theorem 1 which we restate below. A complete proof is given in Appendix A.

Theorem 1. *Let $Q_1, \ldots, Q_r$ be the invariant factors of the linear layer L and let $t \le r$. Then*

$$
\max_{c_1, \ldots, c_t \in \mathbb{F}_2^n} \dim W_L(c_1, \ldots, c_t) = \sum_{i=1}^{t} \deg Q_i.
$$

Most notably, the minimal number of elements that must be considered in D in order to generate a space $W_L(D)$ of full dimension is equal to the number of invariant factors of the linear layer.

Prince. The linear layer of Prince has 8 invariant factors:

$$
\begin{aligned}
Q_1(X) &= Q_2(X) = \mathsf{Min}_L(X) \\
&= X^{20} + X^{18} + X^{16} + X^{14} + X^{12} + X^8 + X^6 + X^4 + X^2 + 1 \\
Q_3(X) &= Q_4(X) = X^8 + X^6 + X^2 + 1 = (X+1)^4 (X^2 + X + 1)^2 \\
Q_5(X) &= Q_6(X) = Q_7(X) = Q_8(X) = (X+1)^2
\end{aligned}
$$

Then, from any set D with 5 elements, the maximal dimension we can get for $W_L(D)$ is $20+20+8+8+2 = 58$, while we get 56 for the particular D derived from the effective round constants $D = \{\alpha, RC_1 + RC_2, RC_1 + RC_3, RC_1 + RC_4, RC_1 + RC_5\}$. We can then see that the round constants are not optimal, but that we can never achieve the full dimension with the number of rounds used in Prince.

Mantis and Midori-64. The linear layer of Mantis (resp. Midori-64) has 16 invariant factors:

$$Q_1(X) = \ldots, Q_8(X) = (X+1)^6 \text{ and } Q_9(X) = \ldots, Q_{16}(X) = (X+1)^2.$$

From the set D of size 7 (resp. 8) obtained from the actual round constants of Mantis$_7$ (resp. Mantis$_8$), we generate a space $W_L(D)$ of dimension 42 (resp. 48) which is then optimal. We also see that one needs at least 16 round constant differences $c_1, \ldots, c_{16}$ to cover the whole input space. It is worth noticing that the round constants in Midori are only non-zero on the least significant bit in each cell, implying that $W_L(D)$ has dimension at most 16. This is the main weakness of Midori-64 with respect to invariant attacks and this explains why the use of the same linear in Mantis does not lead to a similar attack.

The maximal dimension we can reach from a given number of round constants for the linear layers of Prince and of Mantis is then depicted in Fig. 1 in Sect. 1.

4.3   Choosing Random Round Constants

Often, the round constants of a cipher are chosen randomly. In this section, we want to compute the probability that a set of uniformly random chosen elements D generates a space $W_L(D)$ of maximal dimension. Again, we first consider the case of a single constant, i.e., $D = \{c\}$.

Proposition 10. *Let L be a linear permutation of $\mathbb{F}_2^n$. Assume that*

$$\mathsf{Min}_L(X) = M_1(X)^{e_1} M_2(X)^{e_2} \ldots M_k(X)^{e_k}$$

where M_1, ..., M_k are distinct irreducible polynomials over $\mathbb{F}_2$. Then, the probability for a uniformly chosen $c \in \mathbb{F}_2^n$ to obtain $\dim W_L(c) = \deg \mathsf{Min}_L$ is

$$\Pr_{c \xleftarrow{\$} \mathbb{F}_2^n}[\dim W_L(c) = \deg \mathsf{Min}_L] = \prod_{i=1}^{k} \left(1 - \frac{1}{2^{\mu_i \deg M_i}}\right),$$

where μ_i is the number of invariant factors of L which are multiples of $M_i^{e_i}$.

Proof. We use the decomposition based on the elementary divisors, as in the proof of Proposition 8. From [11, p. 308], $\mathbb{F}_2^n$ can be decomposed into a direct sum

$$\mathbb{F}_2^n = \bigoplus_{i=1}^{k} \bigoplus_{j=1}^{r_i} V_{i,j}$$

such that the matrix of the linear transformation induced by L on $V_{i,j}$ is the companion matrix of $M_i(X)^{\ell_{i,j}}$ where, for each i, the $\ell_{i,j}$, $1 \le j \le r_i$, form a decreasing sequence of integers such that $\ell_{i,1} = e_i$. Then, the minimal polynomial of any element u in $V_{i,j}$ is a divisor of $M_i(X)^{\ell_{i,j}}$. It follows that, if $c = \sum_{i=1}^{k} \sum_{j=1}^{r_i} u_{i,j} \in \bigoplus_{i=1}^{k} \bigoplus_{j=1}^{r_i} V_{i,j}$, $\mathrm{ord}_L(c) = \mathsf{Min}_L$ if and only if, for any i, there exists an index j such that $\mathrm{ord}_L(u_{i,j}) = M_i^{e_i}$. Obviously, this situation can only occur if $\ell_{i,j} = e_i$. This last condition is equivalent to the fact that $j \leq \mu_i$, where $\mu_i = \max\{j : \ell_{i,j} = e_i\}$. Using that the invariant factors of L are related to the decomposition of Min_L by

$$Q_v = \prod_{i=1}^{k} M_i^{\ell_{i,v}}$$

where $\ell_{i,v} = 0$ if $v > r_i$, we deduce that μ_i is the number of invariant factors Q_v which are multiples of $M_i^{e_i}$. Let us now define the event

$$E_{i,j} : \quad \mathrm{ord}_L(u_{i,j}) = M_i^{\ell_{i,j}}.$$

Then, we have

$$\Pr_{c \xleftarrow{\$} \mathbb{F}_2^n}[\dim W_L(c) = \deg \mathsf{Min}_L] = \prod_{i=1}^{k} \Pr\left[\bigcup_{j=1}^{\mu_i} E_{i,j}\right].$$

It is important to note that for a fixed i, the probability of the event $E_{i,j}$ is the same for all j. This probability corresponds to the proportion of polynomials of degree less than $\deg(M_i^{\ell_{i,j}})$ which are coprime to $M_i^{\ell_{i,j}}$. Indeed, as noticed in the proof of Proposition 7, there is a correspondence between the elements in $V_{i,j}$ and the initial states of the LFSR with characteristic polynomial $M_i^{\ell_{i,j}}$. Recall that the number of polynomials coprime to a given polynomial P is

$$\phi(P) := |\{f \in \mathbb{F}_2[X] \mid \deg(f) < \deg(P),\ \gcd(f, P) = 1\}|.$$

If P is irreducible, then for any power of P we have $\phi(P^k) = 2^{(k-1)\deg P}(2^{\deg P} - 1)$. We then deduce that

$$\Pr[E_{i,j}] = \frac{\phi(M_i^{\ell_{i,j}})}{2^{\ell_{i,j}\deg M_i}} = \frac{2^{(\ell_{i,j}-1)\deg M_i}(2^{\deg M_i} - 1)}{2^{\ell_{i,j}\cdot\deg M_i}} = 1 - \frac{1}{2^{\deg M_i}}.$$

To compute $\Pr[\bigcup_{j=1}^{\mu_i} E_{i,j}]$, we use the inclusion-exclusion principle and obtain

$$\Pr\left[\bigcup_{j=1}^{\mu_i} E_{i,j}\right] = \sum_{j=1}^{\mu_i}(-1)^{j-1}\binom{\mu_i}{j}\left(1 - \frac{1}{2^{\deg M_i}}\right)^j = \left(1 - \frac{1}{2^{\mu_i \deg M_i}}\right).$$

$$\square$$

LED. The minimal polynomial of the linear layer in LED is

$$\mathsf{Min}_L(X) = (X^8 + X^7 + X^5 + X^3 + 1)^4(X^8 + X^7 + X^6 + X^5 + X^2 + X + 1)^4.$$

A single constant c is sufficient to generate the whole space. Since Min_L has two irreducible factors, each of degree 8, we get from the previous proposition that the probability that $W_L(c) = \mathbb{F}_2^{64}$ for a uniformly chosen constant c is

$$\Pr[W_L(c) = \mathbb{F}_2^{64}] = (1 - 2^{-8})^2 \approx 0.9922.$$

Probability to Generate the Whole Space with Several Random Constants. We now give a formula for the probability to get the maximal dimension with t randomly chosen round elements, when t varies. This probability highly depends on the degrees of the irreducible factors of the minimal polynomial of L. A full proof is given in Appendix B.

Theorem 2. *Let L be a linear permutation of $\mathbb{F}_2^n$. Assume that*

$$\mathsf{Min}_L(X) = M_1(X)^{e_1} M_2(X)^{e_2} \dots M_k(X)^{e_k}$$

where $M_1, \dots, M_k$ are distinct irreducible polynomials over $\mathbb{F}_2$. Then, the probability that $W_L(c_1, \dots, c_t)$ equals $\mathbb{F}_2^n$ is

$$\Pr_{c_1,\dots,c_t \xleftarrow{\$} \mathbb{F}_2^n}[W_L(c_1, \dots, c_t) = \mathbb{F}_2^n] = \prod_{j=1}^{k} \prod_{i_j=0}^{r_j-1} \left(1 - \frac{1}{2^{(t-i_j)\deg(M_j)}}\right),$$

where r_j is the number of invariant factors of L which are multiples of M_j.

It is worth noticing that, when $t < r$ with r the number of invariant factors, the product equals zero which corresponds to the fact that we need at least r constants to generate the whole space.

Prince. Recall that the minimal polynomial of the linear layer in Prince is

$$\begin{aligned}
\mathsf{Min}_L(X) &= X^{20} + X^{18} + X^{16} + X^{14} + X^{12} + X^8 + X^6 + X^4 + X^2 + 1 \\
&= (X^4 + X^3 + X^2 + X + 1)^2 (X^2 + X + 1)^4 (X + 1)^4.
\end{aligned}$$

It then has three irreducible factors

$$M_1(X) = X^4 + X^3 + X^2 + X + 1, M_2(X) = X^2 + X + 1 \text{ and } M_3(X) = (X + 1).$$

Moreover, we know that the eight invariant factors of L are

$$\begin{aligned}
Q_1(X) &= Q_2(X) = \mathsf{Min}_L(X), \\
Q_3(X) &= Q_4(X) = (X + 1)^4 (X^2 + X + 1)^2, \\
Q_5(X) &= Q_6(X) = Q_7(X) = Q_8(X) = (X + 1)^2.
\end{aligned}$$

We then deduce that $\mu_1 = 2$, $\mu_2 = 2$ and $\mu_3 = 4$. Proposition 10 then implies that $\dim W_L(c) \le 20$ and

$$\Pr[\dim W_L(c) = 20] = (1 - 2^{-8})(1 - 2^{-4})^2 \approx 0.8755$$

for a uniformly chosen c. Since L has 8 invariant factors, at least $t = 8$ elements $c_1, \dots, c_8$ are needed to reach $W_L(c_1, \dots, c_t) = \mathbb{F}_2^{64}$. The number of invariant factors in which each of the M_i appears is given by $r_1 = 2$, $r_2 = 4$ and $r_3 = 8$. From Theorem 2, we get that the probability that $W_L(c_1, \dots, c_8) = \mathbb{F}_2^{64}$ is

$$\prod_{i=0}^{1} \left(1 - 2^{-(8-i)\cdot 4}\right) \times \prod_{i=0}^{3} \left(1 - 2^{-(8-i)\cdot 2}\right) \prod_{i=0}^{7} \left(1 - 2^{-(8-i)}\right) \simeq 0.2895.$$

Mantis and Midori-64. The minimal polynomial of the linear layer of Mantis and Midori-64 has a single irreducible factor, which is $(X + 1)$. This linear layer has 16 invariant factors. Since the first 8 invariant factors equal the minimal polynomial, which has degree 6, we derive from Proposition 10 that the probability that a uniformly chosen element generates a subspace of dimension 6 is

$$\Pr[\dim W_L(c) = 6] = (1 - 2^{-8}) \approx 0.9961.$$

We need at least 16 elements $c_1, \ldots, c_{16}$ to cover the whole space and this occurs with probability

$$\prod_{j=1}^{16} \left(1 - \frac{1}{2^j}\right) \simeq 0.28879.$$

It is worth noticing that when we increase the number of random round constants from 16 to 20, this probability increases to 0.93879.

Figure 2 in Sect. 1 shows how the probability that the whole space is covered increases with the number of randomly chosen elements, for the linear layers of LED, Skinny-64, Prince and Mantis. The fact that the curve corresponding to Skinny-64, Prince and Mantis have a similar shape comes from the fact that all three linear layers have a minimal polynomial divisible by $(X+1)$, and this factor appears in all invariant factors. Then, the term corresponding to the irreducible factor of degree 1, namely

$$\prod_{j=t-r+1}^{t} \left(1 - \frac{1}{2^j}\right)$$

is the dominant term in the formula in Theorem 2. Most notably, for $t = r$, the probability is close to $(1 - 2^{-1})(1 - 2^{-2})(1 - 2^{-3})(1 - 2^{-4}) \simeq 0.3$.

5   Conclusion

For lightweight substitution-permutation ciphers with a simple key schedule, we provided a detailed analysis on the impact of the design of the linear layer and the particular choice of the round constants to the applicability of both the invariant subspace attack and the recently published nonlinear invariant attack. We did this analysis in a framework which unifies both of these attacks as so-called *invariant attacks*. With an algorithmic approach, a designer is now able to easily check the soundness of the chosen round constants, in combination with the choice of the linear layer, with regard to the resistance against invariant attacks and can thus easily avoid possible weaknesses by design. We stress that in many cases, this analysis can be done *independently of the choice of the substitution layer*. We directly applied our methods to several existing lightweight ciphers and showed in particular why Skinny-64-64, Prince, and Mantis$_7$ are secure against invariant attacks; unless the adversary exploits weaknesses which are not based on weaknesses of the underlying building blocks, i.e., substitution layer and linear layer. In fact, we are not aware of any such strong attacks in the literature.

As future work, one can think about further generalizations of invariant attacks. As it was already mentioned in [19], it would be interesting to know if one can make use of *statistical invariant attacks*, i.e., invariant attacks that only work with a certain probability instead for all possible plaintexts. A further generalization could consider different invariants for the particular building blocks in each round of the analyzed primitive.

Acknowledgements. This work was partially supported by the DFG Research Training Group GRK 1817 Ubicrypt and the French Agence Nationale de la recherche through the BRUTUS project under contract ANR-14-CE28-0015.

A   Proof of Theorem 1

In the whole section, we represent L in invariant factor form as in Proposition 9. We denote by $V_1, \ldots, V_r$ the invariant subspaces such that $\mathbb{F}_2^n = \bigoplus_{i=1}^r V_i$ and the linear transformation induced by L on V_i, denoted $L_{|V_i}$, is represented by the companion matrix $C(Q_i)$. We define $\mathbf{e_{V_i}}$ as the first unit vector in V_i, i.e., $V_i = \langle L^k(\mathbf{e_{V_i}}), 0 \le k < \deg Q_i \rangle$ and $\mathrm{ord}_{L_{|V_i}}(\mathbf{e_{V_i}}) = Q_i$. Using Proposition 7, one can prove the following lemma.

Lemma 3. *Let $t \le r$. Then*

$$\max_{c_1, \ldots, c_t \in \mathbb{F}_q^n} \dim W_L(c_1, \ldots, c_t) \ge \sum_{i=1}^t \deg Q_i.$$

Proof. We choose $c_1 = \mathbf{e_{V_1}}$ and obtain $W_L(c_1) = W_{L_{|V_1}}(c_1) = V_1$. Then $\dim V_1$ equals $\deg Q_1$. We now continue with $L_{|V_2 \oplus \cdots \oplus V_m}$ which has minimal polynomial Q_2 and choose c_2 accordingly. Iterating this until c_t, we construct $W_L(c_1, \ldots, c_t)$ as the direct sum $\bigoplus_{i=1}^t W_L(c_i)$ which has dimension $\sum_{i=1}^t \deg Q_i$. □

In order to prove equality, we need the following two lemmas.

Lemma 4. *Let c in $\mathbb{F}_2^n = \bigoplus_{j=1}^r V_j$ be represented as $c = \sum_{j \in \mathcal{J}} u_j$ with $\mathcal{J} \subseteq \{1, \ldots, r\}$ and $u_j \in V_j \setminus \{0\}$. Then $W_L(c) \subseteq W_L(\bar{c})$ with $\bar{c} := \sum_{j \in \mathcal{J}} \mathbf{e_{V_j}}$.*

Proof. Let $v \in W_L(c)$. Then

$$v = \sum_{i \in \mathbb{N}} \alpha_i L^i(c) = \sum_{i \in \mathbb{N}} \alpha_i L^i(\sum_{j \in \mathcal{J}} u_j) = \sum_{i \in \mathbb{N}} \sum_{j \in \mathcal{J}} \alpha_i L^i(u_j)$$

$$= \sum_{i \in \mathbb{N}} \sum_{j \in \mathcal{J}} \alpha_i L^i(\sum_{k \in \mathbb{N}} \beta_k L^k(\mathbf{e_{V_j}})) = \sum_{i \in \mathbb{N}} \sum_{j \in \mathcal{J}} \sum_{k \in \mathbb{N}} \alpha_i \beta_k L^{i+k}(\mathbf{e_{V_j}})$$

$$= \sum_{i \in \mathbb{N}} \sum_{k \in \mathbb{N}} \alpha_i \beta_k L^{i+k}(\sum_{j \in \mathcal{J}} \mathbf{e_{V_j}}) = \sum_{i \in \mathbb{N}} \sum_{k \in \mathbb{N}} \alpha_i \beta_k L^{i+k}(\bar{c}) \in W_L(\bar{c}).$$

□

This implies that for any $c_1, \ldots, c_t \in \mathbb{F}_2^n$, it is $W_L(c_1, \ldots, c_t) \subseteq W_L(\bar{c}_1, \ldots, \bar{c}_t)$. Thus, we can assume w.l.o.g. that all c_i are of the form $\bar{c}_i = \sum_{j=1}^r \gamma_{ij} \mathbf{ev_j}$ with $\gamma_{ij} \in \mathbb{F}_2$. Then, to any t-tuple $(c_1, \ldots, c_t) \in (\mathbb{F}_2^n)^t$ where each c_i is of the form described above, we associate a $t \times t$ matrix $\mathbf{M}_{(c_1, \ldots, c_t)} := [\gamma_{ij}]_{i,j}$ over $\mathbb{F}_2^n$.

Lemma 5. *Let* $(c_1, \ldots, c_t) \in (\mathbb{F}_2^n)^t$ *be such that* $c_i = \sum_{j=1}^r \gamma_{ij} \mathbf{ev_j}$ *and let* $\mathbf{M}_{(c_1', \ldots, c_t')}$ *be any matrix obtained from* $\mathbf{M}_{(c_1, \ldots, c_t)}$ *by elementary row operations. Then, for* $(c_1', \ldots, c_t')$ *corresponding to* $\mathbf{M}_{(c_1', \ldots, c_t')}$*, we have*

$$W_L(c_1', \ldots, c_t') = W_L(c_1, \ldots, c_t).$$

Proof. For a $t \times t$ matrix over $\mathbb{F}_2$, an elementary row operation is either

(i) a swap of two different rows or
(ii) an addition of one row to another.

Transforming a matrix $\mathbf{M}_{(c_1, \ldots, c_r, \ldots, c_s, \ldots, c_t)}$ by operation (i) results in the matrix $\mathbf{M}_{(c_1, \ldots, c_s, \ldots, c_r, \ldots, c_t)}$ and obviously $\sum_{i=1}^t W_L(c_i)$ is commutative.

We therefore only have to show that for two constants c_r, c_s the equality $W_L(c_r) + W_L(c_s) = W_L(c_r + c_s) + W_L(c_s)$ holds. Let $v \in W_L(c_r) + W_L(c_s)$. Then,

$$u = \sum_{i \in \mathbb{N}} (\alpha_i L^i(c_r) + \beta_i L^i(c_s)) = \sum_{i \in \mathbb{N}} (\alpha_i L^i(c_r) + \alpha_i L^i(c_s) + \alpha_i L^i(c_s) + \beta_i L^i(c_s))$$

$$= \sum_{i \in \mathbb{N}} (\alpha_i L^i(c_r + c_s) + (\alpha_i + \beta_i) L^i(c_s)) \in W_L(c_r + c_s) + W_L(c_s).$$

The other inclusion $\supseteq$ follows accordingly.   □

Now, we can prove the main theorem.

Proof (of Theorem 1*).* The only thing left to show is $\leq$. Given $c_1, \ldots, c_t \in \mathbb{F}_2^n$ with $t \leq r$. By Lemma 4, $W_L(c_1, \ldots, c_t) \subseteq W_L(\bar{c}_1, \ldots, \bar{c}_t)$ for appropriate $\bar{c}_i = \sum_{j=1}^r \gamma_{ij} \mathbf{ev_j}$ with $\gamma_{ij} \in \mathbb{F}_2$.

Consider the matrix $\mathbf{M}_{(\bar{c}_1, \ldots, \bar{c}_t)}$. Using elementary row operations, one can bring $\mathbf{M}_{(\bar{c}_1, \ldots, \bar{c}_t)}$ in *reduced row-echelon form* $\mathbf{M}_{(\tilde{c}_1, \ldots, \tilde{c}_t)}$. Now, by Lemma 5, the $\tilde{c}_i$ are such that $W_L(\bar{c}_1, \ldots \bar{c}_t) = W_L(\tilde{c}_1, \ldots, \tilde{c}_t)$ and, most importantly, $W_L(\tilde{c}_1, \ldots, \tilde{c}_t) = \sum_{i=1}^t W_{L_{|V_i \oplus \cdots \oplus V_r}}(\tilde{c}_i)$. This is because $\tilde{c}_i = \sum_{j=1}^r \tilde{\gamma}_{ij} \mathbf{ev_j}$ has $\tilde{\gamma}_{ij} = 0$ for all $j < i$.

Since the minimal polynomial of $L_{|V_i \oplus \cdots \oplus V_r}$ equals Q_i, one finally obtains:

$$\dim W_L(c_1, \ldots, c_t) \leq \dim W_L(\bar{c}_1, \ldots, \bar{c}_t) = \dim \sum_{i=1}^t W_{L_{|V_i \oplus \cdots \oplus V_r}}(\tilde{c}_i) \leq \sum_{i=1}^t \deg Q_i$$

□

B   Proof of Theorem 2

We now compute the probability to get the maximal dimension with t randomly chosen elements, when t varies. We need two preliminary results. The first one focuses on the case when Min_L is a power of an irreducible polynomial.

Proposition 11. *Let V be any vector space over $\mathbb{F}_2$. Let L be a linear application from V into V with exactly r invariant factors, such that the minimal polynomial of L is of the form P^e where P is an irreducible polynomial. Then, the probability that $W_L(c_1, \cdots, c_t)$ equals V is*

$$\Pr_{c_1,\ldots,c_t \xleftarrow{\$} V}[W_L(c_1, \cdots, c_t) = V] = \prod_{i=0}^{r-1} \left(1 - \frac{1}{2^{(t-i)\deg(P)}}\right)$$

Proof. Let P^{e_1}, ..., P^{e_r} with $e = e_1 \geq e_2 \ldots \geq e_r$ be the invariant factors of L. Then, $V = V_1 \oplus V_2 \oplus \cdots \oplus V_r$ where $L_{|V_i}$ is represented by the companion matrix $C(P^{e_i})$. Therefore, for each $c_i \in V$, there exist $(u_{i,1}, u_{i,2}, \cdots, u_{i,r}) \in V_1 \times V_2 \times \cdots \times V_r$ such that $c_i = u_{i,1} + u_{i,2} + \cdots + u_{i,r}$.

We first prove that if $W_L(c_1, \cdots, c_t) = V$, there exists some constant c_i, $1 \leq i \leq t$, such that $W_L(u_{i,1}) = V_1$. Obviously, the $u_{i,j}$ for $j \geq 2$ do not belong to the subspace V_1. Then, if $W_L(c_1, \cdots, c_t) = V$, $W_L((u_{i,1})_{1 \leq i \leq t})$ must cover the whole space V_1. Moreover, if $u_{i,1}$ and $u_{j,1}$ are such that $W_L(u_{i,1}) \subsetneq V_1$ and $W_L(u_{j,1}) \subsetneq V_1$, then $W_L(u_{i,1}, u_{j,1}) \subsetneq V_1$. Indeed, since $W_L(u_{i,1}) \subsetneq V_1$, the order polynomial of $u_{i,1}$ with respect to L equals P^a, for some $a < e_1$. Similarly, the order polynomial of $u_{j,1}$ equals P^b, for some $b < e_1$. Assume w.l.o.g that $a \leq b$. It is well known that, for any linear application M and any integer ℓ, we have $\ker(M^\ell) \subseteq \ker(M^{\ell+1})$. Here, we apply this to the linear application $M = P(L)$: Using that $W_L(u_{i,1}) \subseteq \ker(P^a(L))$ and $W_L(u_{j,1}) \subseteq \ker(P^b(L))$, we deduce that

$$W_L(u_{i,1}) \subseteq \ker(P^a(L)) \subseteq \ker(P^b(L)) \subsetneq V_1$$

and thus

$$W_L(u_{i,1}, u_{j,1}) \subseteq \ker(P^b(L)) \subsetneq V_1.$$

This eventually implies that at least one of the $W_L(u_{i,1})$ must cover V_1.

We now prove the result by induction on r, the number of invariant factors.

- $r = 1$. From the previous observation, $W_L(c_1, \cdots, c_t) = V$ if and only if at least one of the $c_1, \ldots, c_t$ has order polynomial P^e. We have seen in Proposition 10 that the probability that a random $c \in V$ has order polynomial P^e is

$$1 - \frac{1}{2^{\deg P}}.$$

Then, since the t constants are independent, the probability that none of the t constants has minimal polynomial P^e equals $(2^{-\deg P})^t$, implying that

$$\Pr_{c_1,\ldots,c_t \xleftarrow{\$} V}[W_L(c_1, \cdots, c_t) = V] = 1 - \frac{1}{2^{t\deg(P)}}.$$

- **Induction step.** We now assume that the result holds for any linear application with $(r-1)$ invariant factors and whose minimal polynomial is a power of an irreducible polynomial. Let us consider L with r invariant factors. If $W_L(c_1, \cdots, c_t) = V$, then at least one of the t constants satisfies $W_L(u_{i,1}) = V_1$. This occurs with probability $1 - \frac{1}{2^{t \deg(P)}}$. Once we found the constant, say c_1, such that $W_L(u_{1,1}) = V_1$, we need to focus on the application defined on the quotient space, $L' = V/W_L(c_1)$. Since the order polynomial of c_1 is the minimal polynomial of L, then the invariant factors of L' are P^{e_2}, ..., P^{e_r} (see e.g., [8, Fact 2.2]). Then we have

$$\Pr[W_L(c_1, \cdots, c_t) = \mathbb{F}_2^n] = \left(1 - \frac{1}{2^{t \deg(P)}}\right) \Pr[W_{L'}(c_2', \cdots, c_t') = V/V_1]$$

where $c_i' = (c_i)_{\mathbb{F}_2^n/V_1}$. The result then follows from the induction hypothesis applied to L', which has $(r-1)$ invariant factors. $\square$

The general case can now be tackled thanks to the following lemma.

Lemma 6. *Let L be a linear permutation of $\mathbb{F}_2^n$. Suppose that there exist two subspaces of $\mathbb{F}_2^n$, V_1 and V_2, invariant under L such that $V_1 \oplus V_2 = \mathbb{F}_2^n$ and the minimal polynomials of the linear transformations induced by L on V_1 and on V_2 are coprime. Then, for any $c_1, \dots, c_t \in \mathbb{F}_2^n$,*

$$W_L(c_1, \dots, c_t) = W_L(a_1, \dots, a_t) \oplus W_L(b_1, \dots, b_t)$$

where (a_i, b_i) is the unique pair in $V_1 \times V_2$ such that $c_i = a_i + b_i$.

Proof. First we observe that $W_L(a_1, \dots, a_t) \cap W_L(b_1, \dots, b_t) = \{0\}$. Indeed, $W_L(a_1, \dots, a_t) \subseteq V_1$ and $W_L(b_1, \dots, b_t) \subseteq V_2$ because V_1 and V_2 are invariant under L.

It is easy to check that $W_L(c_1, \dots, c_t) \subseteq W_L(a_1, \dots, a_t) \oplus W_L(b_1, \dots, b_t)$. Actually, any $x \in W_L(c_1, \dots, c_t)$ can be expressed as

$$x = \sum_{\ell \in \mathbb{N}} \sum_{i=1}^{t} \lambda_{i,\ell} L^\ell(c_i) = \left(\sum_{\ell \in \mathbb{N}} \sum_{i=1}^{t} \lambda_{i,\ell} L^\ell(a_i)\right) + \left(\sum_{\ell \in \mathbb{N}} \sum_{i=1}^{t} \lambda_{i,\ell} L^\ell(b_i)\right).$$

We now need to show that $W_L(a_1, \dots, a_t) \oplus W_L(b_1, \dots, b_t) \subseteq W_L(c_1, \dots, c_t)$. Let P_1 and P_2 respectively denote the minimal polynomials of the applications L_1 and L_2 induced by L on V_1 and on V_2. Let d_1 and d_2 denote the degree of P_1 and P_2 respectively. Let us consider the following subspace of $\mathbb{F}_2^n$:

$$W = \left\langle P_2(L^j)(c_i), 1 \le i \le t, 0 \le j < d_1 \right\rangle + \left\langle P_1(L^j)(c_i), 1 \le i \le t, 0 \le j < d_2 \right\rangle.$$

Since each $P_1(L^j)(c_i)$ (resp. each $P_2(L^j)(c_i)$) is a linear combination of elements of the form $L^\ell(c_i)$, it is clear that $W \subseteq W_L(c_1, \dots, c_t)$. On the other hand, for any $1 \le i \le t$ and any $0 \le j < d_1$, we have

$$P_2(L^j)(c_i) = P_2(L^j)(a_i + b_i) = P_2(L^j)(a_i) + P_2(L^j)(b_i) = P_2(L^j)(a_i),$$

since $b_i \in V_2$ and $P_2(X^j)$ is a multiple of the minimal polynomial of L_2. Similarly,

$$P_1(L^j)(c_i) = P_1(L^j)(b_i),$$

implying that

$$W = \Big\langle P_2(L^j)(a_i), 1 \leq i \leq t, 0 \leq j < d_1 \Big\rangle + \Big\langle P_1(L^j)(b_i), 1 \leq i \leq t, 0 \leq j < d_2 \Big\rangle.$$

Moreover, the following mapping

$$\phi_1 : V_1 \to V_1$$
$$x \mapsto P_2(L)(x)$$

is a bijection since it is linear and its kernel is equal to the all-zero vector. Indeed, if $P_2(L)(x) = 0$, then $\mathrm{ord}_L(x)$ is a divisor of P_2. But, since $x \in V_1$, we know that $\mathrm{ord}_L(x)$ is a divisor of P_1. Using that P_1 and P_2 are coprime, we get that x is the all-zero vector. Moreover, $W_L(a_1, \ldots, a_t)$ is invariant under ϕ_1. It follows that

$$\Big\langle P_2(L^j)(a_i), 1 \leq i \leq t, 0 \leq j < d_1 \Big\rangle = P_2(L)\left(\Big\langle L^j(a_i), 1 \leq i \leq t, 0 \leq j < d_1 \Big\rangle\right)$$
$$= \phi_1(W_L(a_1, \ldots, a_t)) = W_L(a_1, \ldots, a_t).$$

Similarly,

$$\Big\langle P_1(L^j)(b_i), 1 \leq i \leq t, 0 \leq j < d_2 \Big\rangle = W_L(b_1, \ldots, b_t).$$

We eventually deduce that

$$W = W_L(a_1, \ldots, a_t) \oplus W_L(b_1, \ldots, b_t).$$

Combined with the fact that $W \subseteq W_L(c_1, \ldots, c_t)$, it leads to

$$W_L(a_1, \ldots, a_t) \oplus W_L(b_1, \ldots, b_t) \subseteq W_L(c_1, \ldots, c_t). \qquad \square$$

The combination of the previous two results leads to the proof of Theorem 2.

Proof (of Theorem 2*).* Let us decompose the minimal polynomial of L as

$$\mathrm{Min}_L(X) = M_1(X)^{e_1} M_2(X)^{e_2} \ldots M_k(X)^{e_k}$$

where all M_i are irreducible. Then, from the decomposition based of the elementary divisors [11, p. 308], we know that there exist k subspaces $U_1, \ldots U_k$ invariant under L such that $\mathbb{F}_2^n = U_1 \oplus U_2 \ldots \oplus U_k$ and the minimal polynomial of the linear application L_i induced by L on each U_i equals $M_i^{e_i}$. Let us consider t randomly chosen $c_1, \ldots, c_t \in \mathbb{F}_2^n$. Then, Lemma 6 implies that

$$W_L(c_1, \ldots c_t) = \bigoplus_{i=1}^{k} W_L(u_{i,1}, \ldots, u_{i,t})$$

where $(u_{1,j}, \ldots, u_{k,j})$ is the unique k-tuple in $U_1 \times \ldots \times U_k$ such that $c_j = \sum_{i=1}^k u_{i,j}$. We deduce:

$$\Pr_{c_1,\ldots,c_t \xleftarrow{\$} \mathbb{F}_2^n}[W_L(c_1, \cdots, c_t) = \mathbb{F}_2^n] = \prod_{i=1}^k \Pr_{u_{i,1},\ldots,u_{i,t} \xleftarrow{\$} U_i}[W_{L_i}(u_{i,1}, \cdots, u_{i,t}) = U_i]$$

Proposition 11 shows that, for any $1 \leq i \leq k$,

$$\Pr_{u_{i,1},\ldots,u_{i,t} \xleftarrow{\$} V_i}[W_{L_i}(u_{i,1}, \cdots, u_{i,t}) = V_i] = \prod_{j=0}^{r_i-1}\left(1 - \frac{1}{2^{(t-j)\deg(M_i)}}\right),$$

where r_i is the number of invariant factors of L which are multiples of M_i. The result then directly follows. $\qquad\square$

C   Proof of Proposition 5 on the Invariants for Midori-64

The characterization of the invariants g of the S-box layer of Midori-64 which satisfy $\{0000, 0001\}^{16} \subseteq \mathsf{LS}(g)$ exploits the following general lemma.

Lemma 7. *Let S be a mapping from $\mathbb{F}_2^n$ to itself, and W be a linear subspace of $\mathbb{F}_2^n$. If $g \in \mathcal{U}(S)$ and $W \subseteq \mathsf{LS}(g)$, then g is constant on the sets*

$$\mathcal{E}_{S,W}(x) = \bigcup_{i \in \mathbb{N}} \tilde{S}_W^i(\{x\}), \ x \in \mathbb{F}_2^n$$

where

$$\tilde{S}_W : \mathcal{P}(\mathbb{F}_2^n) \to \mathcal{P}(\mathbb{F}_2^n)$$
$$X \mapsto \bigcup_{w \in W}\{S(S(x) + w) + w, \ x \in X\}.$$

Moreover, if S is an involution, then there exists $k \in \mathbb{N}$ such that $\mathcal{E}_{S,W}(x) = \tilde{S}_W^k(\{x\})$ for all $x \in \mathbb{F}_2^n$.

Proof. Let $g \in \mathcal{U}(S)$. Then, there exists $\varepsilon_1 \in \mathbb{F}_2$ such that $g(S(x)) = g(x) + \varepsilon_1$ for all $x \in \mathbb{F}_2^n$. Let $w \in W$. Then, w is a ε_2-linear structure of g for some $\varepsilon_2 \in \mathbb{F}_2$. It follows that, for any $x \in \mathbb{F}_2^n$,

$$g(S(S(x) + w) + w) = g(S(S(x) + w)) + \varepsilon_2 = g(S(x) + w) + \varepsilon_1 + \varepsilon_2$$
$$= g(S(x)) + \varepsilon_2 + \varepsilon_1 + \varepsilon_2 = g(x) + \varepsilon_1 + \varepsilon_2 + \varepsilon_1 + \varepsilon_2 = g(x).$$

Then, g is constant on the sets $\mathcal{E}_{S,W}(x)$. If g is an involution, then $X \subseteq \tilde{S}_W(X)$ for any set X. Indeed, since $0 \in W$, we have

$$\tilde{S}_W(X) \supseteq \{S(S(x)), x \in X\} = X.$$

It follows that the sequence $(\tilde{S}_W^i(\{x\}))_{i \in \mathbb{N}}$ is an increasing sequence for inclusion. Then, there exists k_x such that $\mathcal{E}_{S,W}(x) = \tilde{S}_W^{k_x}(\{x\})$. We get the result by choosing $k = \max_x k_x$. $\qquad\square$

In Midori-64 the sets $\mathcal{E}_{S,W}(x)$ have a simple form because S consists of 16 copies of the same 4-bit S-box, Sb, and W also corresponds to 16-th Cartesian power of a subspace of $\mathbb{F}_2^4$, namely $W = V^{16}$ with $V = \{0000, 0001\}$. Then, we can deduce the characterization given in Proposition 5.

Proof (of Proposition 5*).* Using that S consists of 16 copies of Sb and that $W = V^{16}$ with $V = \{0000, 0001\}$, we deduce that, for any $x_0, \ldots, x_{15} \in \mathbb{F}_2^4$,

$$\tilde{S}_W(\{(x_0, \ldots, x_{15})\})$$
$$= \{\text{Sb}(\text{Sb}(x_0) + w_0) + w_0, \ldots \text{Sb}(\text{Sb}(x_{15}) + w_{15}) + w_{15}, \; w_i \in V\}$$
$$= \tilde{\text{Sb}}_V(\{x_0\}) \times \ldots \times \tilde{\text{Sb}}_V(\{x_{15}\}).$$

Then, for any $k \in \mathbb{N}$,

$$\tilde{S}_W^k(\{(x_0, \ldots, x_{15})\}) = \tilde{\text{Sb}}_V^k(\{x_0\}) \times \ldots \times \tilde{\text{Sb}}_V^k(\{x_{15}\}).$$

Since the S-box layer is an involution, we deduce from the previous lemma that

$$\mathcal{E}_{S,W}((x_0, \ldots, x_{15})) = \mathcal{E}_{\text{Sb},V}(x_0) \times \ldots \times \mathcal{E}_{\text{Sb},V}(x_{15}).$$

Now, for the Midori S-box, any $\mathcal{E}_{\text{Sb},V}(x)$ correspond to one of the following sets

$$H_{00} = \{8\}, H_{10} = \{9\}, H_{01} = \{0, 3, 5, 6, \text{b}, \text{c}, \text{f}\} \text{ and } H_{11} = \{1, 2, 4, 7, \text{a}, \text{d}, \text{e}\}.$$

Moreover, all these four sets satisfy that, for any $x \in H_{ab}$, $\tilde{\text{Sb}}^k(\{x\}) = H_{ab}$ for all $k \geq 6$. Therefore, for any $x = (x_0 \ldots x_{15}) \in \mathbb{F}_2^{16}$,

$$\mathcal{E}_{S,W}(x) = H_{b_0 b_1} \times H_{b_2 b_3} \times \ldots \times H_{b_{30} b_{31}}$$

for some $b \in \mathbb{F}_2^{32}$. Since any $g \in \mathcal{U}(S)$ with $W \subseteq \text{LS}(g)$ must be constant on all $\mathcal{E}_{S,W}(x)$, we deduce that its support must be a union of such sets, i.e.,

$$\text{Supp}(g) = \bigcup_{b_0 \ldots b_{31} \in \mathcal{A}} H_{b_0 b_1} \times H_{b_2 b_3} \times \ldots \times H_{b_{30} b_{31}}$$

where $\mathcal{A}$ is a subset of $\mathbb{F}_2^{32}$. It is worth noticing that, since all the sets $\mathcal{H}_{b_0 \ldots b_{31}} = H_{b_0 b_1} \times H_{b_2 b_3} \times \ldots \times H_{b_{30} b_{31}}$ are disjoint, this equivalently means that g is a linear combination of the 2^{32} functions of 64 variables

$$g_{b_0 \ldots b_{31}} = \prod_{i=0}^{15} f_{b_{2i} b_{2i+1}} \text{ where } \text{Supp} f_{b_{2i} b_{2i+1}} = H_{b_{2i} b_{2i+1}}.$$

Let us now characterize the sets $\mathcal{A}$ which guarantee that $W \subseteq \text{LS}(g)$. Let h denote the Boolean function of 32 variables whose support equals $\mathcal{A}$. We observe that, for any $b_0 b_1 \in \mathbb{F}_2^2$, $00001 + H_{b_0 b_1} = H_{b_0 + 1 b_1}$. It follows that, for any $w \in W$ and any $b \in \mathbb{F}_2^{32}$, the image of the translation of $\mathcal{H}_b$ by w is equal to $\mathcal{H}_{b + \pi(w)}$ where $\pi(w)$ is the 32-bit word defined by $\pi(w)_i = 00$ if $w_i = 0000$ and $\pi(w)_i = 10$ if $w_i = 0001$ for all $0 \leq i \leq 15$. Therefore, if $w \in W$ is a 0-linear structure for g, we have that $b \in \mathbb{F}_2^{32}$ belongs to $\mathsf{Supp}(h)$ if and only if $(b+\pi(w)) \in \mathsf{Supp}(h)$. This equivalently means that $\pi(w)$ is a 0-linear structure for h. Similarly, if $w \in W$ is a 1-linear structure for g, we have that $b \in \mathbb{F}_2^{32}$ belongs to $\mathsf{Supp}(h)$ if and only if $(b + \pi(w)) \notin \mathsf{Supp}(h)$. This means that $\pi(w)$ is a 1-linear structure for h. We then conclude that $\pi(W) = \{00, 10\}^{16} \subseteq \mathsf{LS}(h)$.

Conversely, it is easy to check that all functions g such that

$$\mathsf{Supp}(g) = \bigcup_{b_0 \ldots b_{31} \in \mathsf{Supp}(h)} H_{b_0 b_1} \times H_{b_2 b_3} \times \ldots \times H_{b_{30} b_{31}}$$

with $\pi(W) \subseteq \mathsf{LS}(h)$ are invariants for the nonlinear layer of Midori-64. Indeed, each set $H_{b_0 b_1}$ is invariant under Sb. This property is closed under addition, implying that any such g is an invariant for S. Moreover, any $w \in \{0000, 0001\}^{16}$ is a linear structure for g because $\pi(w)$ is a linear structure for h.   □

D   Sage Code of the Algorithms

```
1  from sage.geometry.hyperplane_arrangement.affine_subspace
       import AffineSubspace
2
3  # converts an integer to a binary vector. The first bit
       represents the msb. Example:
       to_binary_vector(0xb,4) = (1,0,1,1)
       to_binary_vector(0xab,12) = (0,0,0,0,1,0,1,0,1,0,1,1)
4  def to_binary_vector(a, length):
5      ls = Integer(a).bits()[::-1]
6      return vector(GF(2), length, [0]*(length-len(ls))+ls)
7
8  # Evaluates the S-box layer with parallel application of
       S-box S (of bitlength bit_S) on vector v
9  def sbox_layer_eval(S,bit_S,v):
10     w = copy(v)
11     for i in range(len(w)/bit_S):
12         w[(i*bit_S):((i+1)*bit_S)] =
13         list(to_binary_vector(S[ZZ(list(w[(i*bit_S):((i+1)
                *bit_S)])[::-1]), base = 2)],bit_S))
14     return w
15
16 # returns complement C of V s.t. C.intersection(V) is
       trivial
17 def decomposition_complement(V):
18     L1 = list(V.basis())
19     L2 = list(V.ambient_vector_space().basis())
20     R = []
21     # basis extension
22     for v in L2:
23         if (v not in span(L1)):
24             L1.append(v)
```

```
25              R.append(v)
26          return span(R)
27
28
29  # Now, the code of the actual algorithms follows
30
31  # input: list of differences D, linear layer L as a matrix
32  # output: the subspace W_L(D)
33  def W_space(D,L):
34      R = []
35      for c in D:
36          for j in range(L.multiplicative_order()):
37              R.append((L**j)*c)
38      return span(R)
39
40  # input: S-box S, subspace Z of W_L(D)
41  # if true, the constants prevent invariant attacks
42  def check_with_sbox(S,Z):
43      bit_S = int(log(len(S),2))
44
45      # define the coset 0 + Z as an affine space (with
                offset 0) and choose a complement Q of Z
46      # Q is isomorphic to (GF(2)^n)/Z and each q in Q is a
                representative of a different coset q + Z
47      A = AffineSubspace(0,Z)
48      Q = AffineSubspace(0,decomposition_complement(Z))
49
50      # ls will indicate all cosets"hit" by the S-box layer
51      ls = set()
52      k = 2**Q.dimension()
53      print(repr(k) + ' cosets to check')
54      percent_done = 0
55
56      # repeat this until each coset is hit
57      while (len(ls) < k):
58          # every time, choose a random vector a in Z and
                    look in which coset it is mapped by the S-box
                    layer
59          a = A.linear_part().random_element() + A.point()
60          b = sbox_layer_eval(S,bit_S,a)
61          # q gives the unique representative of the coset
                    in Q
62          q = Q.intersection(AffineSubspace(b,Z)).point()
63          # we add the vector q in the set of cosets hit. We
                    represent the vector as an integer
64          ls.add(ZZ(list(q), base=2))
65          if (len(ls)/k >= (percent_done+1)/100):
66              percent_done = percent_done + 1
67              print(repr(percent_done) + ' % done')
68      return true
```

References

1. Beierle, C., Jean, J., Kölbl, S., Leander, G., Moradi, A., Peyrin, T., Sasaki, Y., Sasdrich, P., Sim, S.M.: The SKINNY family of block ciphers and its low-latency variant MANTIS. In: Robshaw, M., Katz, J. (eds.) CRYPTO 2016. LNCS, vol. 9815, pp. 123–153. Springer, Heidelberg (2016). doi:10.1007/978-3-662-53008-5_5
2. Borghoff, J., et al.: PRINCE - a low-latency block cipher for pervasive computing applications. In: Wang, X., Sako, K. (eds.) ASIACRYPT 2012. LNCS, vol. 7658. Springer, Heidelberg (2012). doi:10.1007/978-3-642-34961-4_14
3. Carlet, C.: Boolean functions for cryptography and error correcting codes. In: Crama, Y., Hammer, P. (eds.) Boolean Methods and Models. Cambridge University Press (2007)
4. Chaigneau, C., Fuhr, T., Gilbert, H., Jean, J., Reinhard, J.R.: Cryptanalysis of NORX v2.0. IACR Trans. Symmetric Cryptol. 2017(1), 156–174 (2017). doi:10.13154/tosc.v2017.i1.156-174
5. Dawson, E., Wu, C.: On the linear structure of symmetric Boolean functions. Australas. J. Comb. 16, 239–243 (1997)
6. Dummit, D.S., Foote, R.M.: Abstract Algebra. Wiley, Hoboken (2004)
7. Gantmacher, F.R.: The Theory of Matrices. Chelsea Publishing Company, New York (1959)
8. Giesbrecht, M.: Nearly optimal algorithms for canonical matrix forms. SIAM J. Comput. 24(5), 948–969 (1995)
9. Guo, J., Jean, J., Nikolic, I., Qiao, K., Sasaki, Y., Sim, S.M.: Invariant subspace attack against Midori64 and the resistance criteria for S-box designs. IACR Trans. Symmetric Cryptol. 2016(1), 33–56 (2016). doi:10.13154/tosc.v2016.i1.33-56
10. Guo, J., Peyrin, T., Poschmann, A., Robshaw, M.: The LED block cipher. In: Preneel, B., Takagi, T. (eds.) CHES 2011. LNCS, vol. 6917, pp. 326–341. Springer, Heidelberg (2011). doi:10.1007/978-3-642-23951-9_22
11. Herstein, I.N.: Topics in Algebra. Wiley, Lexington (1975)
12. Jean, J.: Cryptanalysis of Haraka. IACR Trans. Symmetric Cryptol. 2016(1), 1–12 (2016). doi:10.13154/tosc.v2016.i1.1-12
13. Lai, X.: Additive and linear structures of cryptographic functions. In: Preneel, B. (ed.) FSE 1994. LNCS, vol. 1008, pp. 75–85. Springer, Heidelberg (1995). doi:10.1007/3-540-60590-8_6
14. Leander, G., Abdelraheem, M.A., AlKhzaimi, H., Zenner, E.: A cryptanalysis of PRINTCIPHER: the invariant subspace attack. In: Rogaway, P. (ed.) CRYPTO 2011. LNCS, vol. 6841, pp. 206–221. Springer, Heidelberg (2011). doi:10.1007/978-3-642-22792-9_12
15. Leander, G., Minaud, B., Rønjom, S.: A generic approach to invariant subspace attacks: cryptanalysis of Robin, iSCREAM and Zorro. In: Oswald, E., Fischlin, M. (eds.) EUROCRYPT 2015. LNCS, vol. 9056, pp. 254–283. Springer, Heidelberg (2015). doi:10.1007/978-3-662-46800-5_11
16. Lidl, R., Niederreiter, H.: Finite Fields. Cambridge University Press, Cambridge (1983)
17. Rønjom, S.: Invariant subspaces in Simpira. Cryptology ePrint Archive, Report 2016/248 (2016). http://eprint.iacr.org/2016/248
18. Stein, W.A.: The Sage Development Team: Sage Mathematics Software (2016). http://sagemath.org
19. Todo, Y., Leander, G., Sasaki, Y.: Nonlinear invariant attack. In: Cheon, J.H., Takagi, T. (eds.) ASIACRYPT 2016. LNCS, vol. 10032, pp. 3–33. Springer, Heidelberg (2016). doi:10.1007/978-3-662-53890-6_1

Breaking the FF3 Format-Preserving Encryption Standard over Small Domains

F. Betül Durak[1]([✉]) and Serge Vaudenay[2]

[1] Department of Computer Science, Rutgers University, New Brunswick, USA
fbdurak@cs.rutgers.edu
[2] LASEC - Security and Cryptography Laboratory,
Ecole Polytechnique Fédérale de Lausanne (EPFL), Lausanne, Switzerland
serge.vaudenay@epfl.ch

Abstract. The National Institute of Standards and Technology (NIST) recently published a Format-Preserving Encryption standard accepting two Feistel structure based schemes called FF1 and FF3. Particularly, FF3 is a tweakable block cipher based on an 8-round Feistel network. In CCS 2016, Bellare et al. gave an attack to break FF3 (and FF1) with time and data complexity $O(N^5 \log(N))$, which is much larger than the code book (but using many tweaks), where N^2 is domain size to the Feistel network. In this work, we give a new practical total break attack to the FF3 scheme (also known as BPS scheme). Our FF3 attack requires $O(N^{\frac{11}{6}})$ chosen plaintexts with time complexity $O(N^5)$. Our attack was successfully tested with $N \leqslant 2^9$. It is a slide attack (using two tweaks) that exploits the bad domain separation of the FF3 design. Due to this weakness, we reduced the FF3 attack to an attack on 4-round Feistel network. Biryukov et al. already gave a 4-round Feistel structure attack in SAC 2015. However, it works with chosen plaintexts and ciphertexts whereas we need a known-plaintext attack. Therefore, we developed a new generic known-plaintext attack to 4-round Feistel network that reconstructs the entire tables for all round functions. It works with $N^{\frac{3}{2}} \left(\frac{N}{2}\right)^{\frac{1}{6}}$ known plaintexts and time complexity $O(N^3)$. Our 4-round attack is simple to extend to five and more rounds with complexity $N^{(r-5)N+o(N)}$. It shows that FF1 with $N = 7$ and FF3 with $7 \leqslant N \leqslant 10$ do not offer a 128-bit security. Finally, we provide an easy and intuitive fix to prevent the FF3 scheme from our $O(N^5)$ attack.

1 Introduction

Format-Preserving Encryption (FPE) provides a method to encrypt data in a specific *format* into a ciphertext of the same *format*. A *format* in FPE schemes refers to a finite set of characters such as the decimal (or binary) numerals or alpha-numerals along with the length of the sequence of the characters that form the plaintexts. FPE has been staging in applied cryptography community due to the desirable functionality. It secures data while keeping the database scheme intact. For instance, given a legacy database system, upgrading the database

© International Association for Cryptologic Research 2017
J. Katz and H. Shacham (Eds.): CRYPTO 2017, Part II, LNCS 10402, pp. 679–707, 2017.
DOI: 10.1007/978-3-319-63715-0_23

security requires a way for encrypting credit card numbers (CCN) or social security numbers (SSN) in a transparent way to its applications.

Brightwell and Smith [9] introduced a first known format-preserving encryption which was termed as *data-type preserving encryption* in 1997. They wanted to encrypt an existing database to let all the applications access encrypted data just as they access non-encrypted data. Their solution for this was reduced to preserve the particular datatype of entries in the databases. The term *format-preserving encryption* is due to Terence Spies from Voltage Security [21]. Though FPE dates back to late 90's, the demand to make FPE based databases has created an active area of research during last few years. There have been many techniques proposed to build FPE schemes such as prefix cipher, cycle walking, Feistel network, Feistel modes [2,4,5,7,16,20,21]. The complete list of FPE schemes for small domain size along with their description and their security level can be found in a synopsis by Rogaway [18, pp. 6, 7]. In his list, Rogaway considers the schemes that are built with pseudorandom functions (that itself might be constructed from block ciphers).

Probably, it is natural to build FPE schemes based on a Feistel network (FN) since it can be used with already existing conventional block ciphers, such as AES. Indeed, the National Institute of Standards and Technology (NIST) published an FPE standard [1] (finalized in March 2016) that includes two-approved Feistel-based FPE schemes: FF1 [5] and FF3 [8]. Both are expected to offer a 128-bit security. In this work, we are particularly interested in the attacks for breaking the FN-based standard FF3 [1] and attacks against Feistel network. The former attack utilizes the latter that is designed as a generic round-function-recovery attack.

The FF3 construction is an 8-round FN that uses a tweak XORed with a round counter as an input to the block cipher. The XOR operation guarantees that round functions are pairwise different. This is usually called "domain separation". The security of FF3 asserts that it achieves several cryptographic goals including chosen-plaintext security or even PRP-security against an adaptive chosen-ciphertext attack under the assumption that the underlying round function is a good pseudorandom function (PRF). Our work shows that its security goal has not met even when the round functions are replaced by secure PRFs and gives a round-function-recovery attack on FF3.

Our Contributions. Our work covers three significant contributions. **(a).** We give a total practical break to 8-round Feistel network based FF3 FPE standard over a small domain. Our attack exploits the "bad domain separation" in FF3. Namely, the specific design choice of FF3 allows us permuting the round functions by changing the tweak and it leads us to develop a slide attack (using only two tweaks). The attack works with chosen plaintexts and tweaks when the message domain is small. It requires $O(N^{\frac{7}{4}+\frac{1}{4L}})$ chosen plaintexts and two tweaks, with time complexity $O(N^5)$, where N^2 is input domain size to the Feistel network and L is a parameter in our attack which is typically set to $L = 3$ in experimental results. Luckily, the fix to prevent FF3 against our attack is quick and easy to maintain without changing the main structure of the scheme. **(b).** While we form our slide attack to break FF3, we develop a new generic known-plaintext attack on 4-round Feistel networks and we insert it in our slide attack. Our techniques to develop a 4-round attack is novel and different than previously known attacks on Feistel networks. In our attack, we compute the full recovery of round functions with $N^{\frac{3}{2}} \left(\frac{N}{2}\right)^{\frac{1}{2t}}$ known plaintext and time complexity $O(N^{2+\frac{3}{t}})$ for four rounds. **(c).** We utilize our 4-round FN attack to extend the round function recovery on more rounds. Due to the generic and known plaintext nature of our 4-round FN attack, we easily adapt it to a chosen-plaintext attack to apply it on 5 and more rounds Feistel structures. Our attack shows that neither FF1 with $N = 7$ nor FF3 with $7 \leqslant N \leqslant 10$ (even with our fix) offer a 128-bit security.

Overview Of Previous Works. A security for message recovery in FPE constructions along with many other notions for FPE was first defined by Bellare et al. [4]. A recent work by Bellare et al. [3] gives a practical message recovery attack on NIST standard Feistel-based FPE schemes (both FF1 and FF3) on small domain sizes. In their work, however, the security definition they consider is under the new message recovery security that they define in the same work. Briefly, consider two messages X and X' which share the same right (or left) half of the messages. In their attack, the adversary is given X' together with the encryption of X and X' under q tweaks. The adversary wins if it can fully recover X, in particular, its unknown half. The attack by Bellare et al. uses a data complexity that exceeds the message space size. Clearly stating, their work shows that Feistel-based FPE with the standardized number of rounds does not achieve good enough security on small domain sizes.

The attack by Bellare et al. works using $O(N^5 \log N)$ data and time complexity with many tweaks on eight rounds. This is quite interesting when the amount of data is limited for each tweak. It is a decryption attack. Our attack herein is more traditional. It uses only two tweaks, but $O(N^{\frac{11}{6}})$ chosen plaintexts with $O(N^5)$ time complexity. We recover the entire codebook (for both tweaks).

To apply the slide attack to recover the entire round functions of Feistel networks, we develop a generic known-plaintext attack on 4-rounds.

Since its invention, Feistel networks have created active research areas for cryptographers (both in theory and in practice) due to its applications and influence on the development of major constructions such as DES. The security for Feistel networks has been investigated for very long time and there already exist interesting results for cryptanalysis. The security of Feistel schemes aims either to distinguish a Feistel scheme from a random permutation or to recover the round functions. In their famous work [15], Luby and Rackoff proved the indistinguishability of 3-round Feistel network against chosen-plaintext attacks and 4-rounds against chosen-plaintext and ciphertext attacks for the number of queries $q \ll \sqrt{N}$, where N^2 is the size of the input domain. The directions derived from this result tried to improve the security bounds until $q \ll N$ (that is called the "birthday bound") which was a natural bound from information theory.[1]

---

[1] In an r-round FN, q samples give $2q \log_2 N$ bits of information but functions are defined by a table of $rN \log_2 N$ bits. Thus, $q = \frac{r}{2}N$ queries is enough to reconstruct the round functions, in theory.

A work by Patarin [17], using the mirror theory, showed improved proofs and stronger security bounds for four, five, and six rounds Feistel networks. Namely, for $q \ll N$, four rounds are secure against known-plaintext attacks, five rounds are secure against chosen-plaintext attacks, and six rounds are secure against chosen-plaintext and ciphertext attacks.

From an information theory viewpoint, we could recover all functions in time $N^{O(N)}$ by exhaustive search. As far as we know, there is no efficient generic attack which is polynomial in N on the Feistel scheme with $q \sim N$. Our attack uses $q \sim N^{\frac{3}{2}}$ and is polynomial in N with known plaintexts up to four rounds.

A recent work by Dinur et al. [11] gives a new attack on Feistel structures for more than four rounds to recover the round keys with a few known plaintext/ciphertext pairs when the ith round uses $x \mapsto F_i(x \oplus k_i)$, where F_i is public whereas k_i is being kept secret. Here, we focus on the case where each round function is secret in a balanced 2-branch Feistel scheme. Furthermore, we do not restrict to the XOR addition. Our results also apply to Feistel schemes with modular addition. The new cryptanalysis results against Feistel networks with modular addition for four and five rounds are presented in a recent work by Biryukov et al. [6]. For four rounds, they achieve the full recovery of round functions with data complexity $O(N^{\frac{3}{2}})$ with a guess and determine technique. However, their attack uses chosen plaintexts and ciphertexts. We summarize their results and ours on Table 1.

Table 1. Round-function-recovery attacks against balanced Feistel schemes with two branches of $\log_2 N$ bits and any addition rule (we omitted polynomial terms in $\log N$)

# rounds	Mode	Time	Data	Ref
3	Known-plaintext	N	N	Section 4.1
4	Chosen-plaintext and ciphertext	$N^{\frac{3}{2}}$	$N^{\frac{3}{2}}$	[6]
4	Known-plaintext (tested for $L = 3$)	$N^{2+\frac{3}{L}}$	$N^{\frac{3}{2}+\frac{1}{2}L}$	Section 4.2
5	Chosen-plaintext and ciphertext	$N^{N^{\frac{3}{4}}}$	N^2	[6]
5	Chosen-plaintext	$N^{O(N^{\frac{1}{2}})}$	$N^{\frac{3}{2}+\frac{1}{2}L}$	Section 4.3
$r \geqslant 6$	Chosen-plaintext	$N^{(r-5)N}$	$N^{\frac{3}{2}+\frac{1}{2}L}$	Section 4.3

Structure of the Paper. In Sects. 2 and 3, we give the details of FF3 construction and Tweakable Encryption, respectively. In Sect. 4, we develop our new generic attack for Feistel structure on specifically 4-rounds and extend it on 5 and more rounds. In Sect. 5, we give our complete slide attack to a NIST standard FF3 scheme.

2   The FF3 Scheme

A Tweakable Format-Preserving Encryption (TFPE) scheme is a block cipher that preserves the format of the domain in the output. A TFPE function E :

$\mathcal{K} \times \mathcal{T} \times \mathcal{X} \mapsto \mathcal{X}$ is defined from a key space $\mathcal{K}$, a tweak space $\mathcal{T}$, and a domain $\mathcal{X}$ to the same domain $\mathcal{X}$. We are particularly interested in a TFPE scheme by Brier, Peyrin, and Stern (depicted in Fig. 1(b)) [8] whose design is based on Feistel network depicted in Fig. 1(a). It is named as FF3 in the NIST standards.

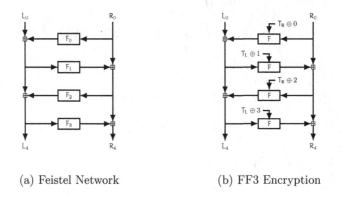

(a) Feistel Network   (b) FF3 Encryption

Fig. 1. 4-round Feistel network and FF3 encryption

We use the following notations for the rest of the paper. The domain $\mathcal{X}$ consists of strings of characters; s represents the cardinality of the set S of characters and b represents the length of the messages in the domain $\mathcal{X}$. For example, the credit card numbers (CCNs) consists of 16 digits of decimal numerals with $S = \{0, 1, \ldots, 9\}$, $s = 10$ and $b = 16$ where we have $10^{16} \cong 2^{54}$ possible distinct numeral strings. We set the minimum length of the message block $\mathsf{minlen} = 2$ and the maximum length of the message block to $\mathsf{maxlen} = \lfloor \log_s(2^{f-32}) \rfloor$, where f is the input/output size of the round function used in Feistel scheme in FF3.[2] We represent the number of rounds in the scheme with w.

Unlike standard Feistel schemes which use the exclusive or (XOR) (denoted by $\oplus$), FF3 uses the modular addition that is denoted by $\boxplus$.

We define the following notations for three functions:

STR$_s^b$: a function that maps an integer x where $0 \leqslant x < s^b$ to a string of length b in base s with most significant character first, e.g. $\mathrm{STR}_{12}^4(554) = 03A2$.

NUM$_s$: a function that maps a string X to an integer x such that $\mathrm{STR}_s^b(x) = X$. For instance, $\mathrm{NUM}_2(00011010) = 26$.

REV(X) : a function that reverses the order of the characters of string X.

The length of string X is denoted by $|X|$. The concatenation of strings is denoted by $\|$. The first (left-most) character of string X is $X[0]$. The ith one is $X[i-1]$. We denote $X[a \cdots b]$ the substring of X formed with $X[a]X[a+1] \cdots X[b]$.

The FF3 uses a tweakable block cipher as a round function, $F_K(T, X) = Y$ with $X, Y \in \{0, 1, \ldots, 2^f - 1\}$ and $T \in \{0, 1\}^{32}$, where K is a key and T is one half of the FF3 tweak with an offset.

---

[2] We consider here the FF3 block cipher. However, there is a mode of operation for FF3 allowing variable-length messages in the original paper [8].

Algorithm 1. FF3 Encryption

Input   : string X in base s of length b such that
             $b \in [minlen \cdots maxlen]$, a tweak bit string T such that
             $|T| = 64$.

Output: string Y such that $|Y| = b$

1 Let $\ell = \lceil \frac{b}{2} \rceil$; $r = b - \ell$.
2 Let $L_0 = NUM_s(REV[X[1 \cdots \ell]])$ and $R_0 = NUM_s(REV[X[\ell + 1 \cdots b]])$
3 Let $T_L = T[0 \cdots 31]$ and $T_R = T[32 \cdots 63]$
4 **foreach** $i = 0 \cdots w - 1$ **do**
5 | **if** i *is even* **then**
6 | | $L_{i+1} = L_i \boxplus F_K(T_R \oplus STR_2^{32}(i), R_i) \pmod{s^\ell}$
7 | | $R_{i+1} = R_i$
8 | **end**
9 | **else**
10 | | $R_{i+1} = R_i \boxplus F_K(T_L \oplus STR_2^{32}(i), L_i) \pmod{s^r}$
11 | | $L_{i+1} = L_i$
12 | **end**
13 **end**
14 **return** $REV[STR_s^\ell(L_w)]||REV[STR_s^r(R_w)]$

In lines 1–2, the encryption algorithm splits the input X into two substrings L_0 and R_0. In lines 5–8 (respectively in lines 10–12), the algorithm first takes the tweak T_R (respectively T_L) XORed with the encoded round index i and R_i (respectively L_i) to input tweakable PRF F_K. Second, it applies modular addition of the output of F_K to L_i (respectively R_i).

For simplicity and by abuse of notations, we say that FF3 encrypts the plaintext (L_0, R_0) into the ciphertext (L_w, R_w) with tweak (T_L, T_R), so that we only concentrate on lines 4–14. We illustrate the 4-round FF3 scheme in Fig. 1(b).

In concrete proposal, $w = 8$, $f = 128$ and

$$F_K(T, X) = NUM_2(AES_K(T \parallel STR_2^{f-32}(X)))$$

where AES maps an f-bit bitstring to an f-bit bitstring [1].

3   Tweakable Encryption

A tweakable block cipher (TBC) is a tuple $(\mathcal{K}, \mathcal{E}_K(\cdot, \cdot), \mathcal{D}_K(\cdot, \cdot))$ formed of three algorithms for key generation, encryption, and decryption with a key K; all efficiently computable algorithms. We follow the notion of security from [13] as chosen-plaintext-secure (CPA) tweakable block cipher.

Definition 1. *A TBC is a* (q, t, ϵ)-*CPA-secure cipher if for any probabilistic time adversary* $\mathcal{A}$ *limited to* t *steps and* q *oracle queries, the advantage of distinguishing TBC from* Π *is bounded by* ϵ:

$$Adv^{TBC}(\mathcal{A}) = \left| Pr\left[\mathcal{A}^{\mathcal{E}_K(\cdot, \cdot)} = 1 \right] - Pr\left[\mathcal{A}^{\Pi(\cdot, \cdot)} = 1 \right] \right| \leqslant \epsilon$$

where $K \in \mathcal{K}$ *is selected at random and* $\Pi(T, \cdot)$ *is defined as a random permutation for every* T.

In the standard model, the tweakable block ciphers [4,14] are used to construct tweakable format-preserving encryption schemes since tweakable encryptions provide better security bounds for tweakable FPE in terms of the number of chosen plaintext/ciphertext to attack the system [4].

It is underlined in [8] that using the same round function F twice during an encryption process can introduce some security vulnerability to the system. So, the domain of the tweaks in different rounds must be separated. For this, the scheme in [8] XORs tweaks with a round counters. However, this way to separate domains is not fully effective. Indeed, the tweaks are known to the adversary and are under adversary's control in chosen-tweak attacks. Consider two 4-round Feistel networks with tweaks T_R and $T_L = T_R \oplus STR_2^{32}(1)$. For the first round, we have the tweak $T_R \oplus STR_2^{32}(0) = T_R$ and the second round we have $T_L \oplus STR_2^{32}(1) = T_R$. Then, for the third round $T_R \oplus STR_2^{32}(2)$ and fourth round $T_L \oplus STR_2^{32}(3) = T_R \oplus STR_2^{32}(2)$. We observe the following behavior: round $2i$ and $2i + 1$ uses the same function $F_i = F_K(T_R \oplus STR_2^{32}(2i), \cdot)$.

For a variant of FF3 with $\oplus$ instead of $\boxplus$, we present a trivial attack: Consider an FF3 encryption with a key $K \in \mathcal{K}$, a tweak $T = T_L \| T_R \in \mathcal{T}$ and domain $\mathcal{X}$. Each round i defines a random function $F_i = F_K(T_R \oplus STR_2^{32}(i), \cdot)$ for i even ($F_i = F_K(T_L \oplus STR_2^{32}(i), \cdot)$ for i odd). We use the encryption with an input message $X = (L_0, R_0)$ and output ciphertext $Y = (L_w, R_w)$ with output X_i from each round in Fig. 2(a). We assume that b is even so that $\ell = r$. Now, we take

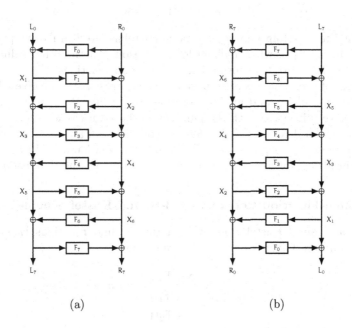

(a)   (b)

Fig. 2. Trivial attack on 8-round FF3 encryption with $\oplus$ instead of modular addition $\boxplus$.

the ciphertext Y from Fig. 2(a) and reverse it into $(L'_0, R'_0) = (R_w, L_w)$ to encrypt it with a new tweak $T' = T_R \oplus STR_2^{32}(w-1)\|T_L \oplus STR_2^{32}(w-1) \in \mathcal{T}$. We show this encryption in Fig. 2(b). We assume that w is a power of two (Fig. 2 uses $w = 8$). With given encryption, we obtain the round functions $F'_i = F_{w-1-i}$ as shown on Fig. 2(a). More precisely, the attack works as follows:

- Encrypt (L_0, R_0) with the tweak T to get (L_w, R_w).
- Encrypt (R_w, L_w) with the tweak T' to get (L', R').
- If $L' = R_0$ and $R' = L_0$, output 1. Otherwise, output 0.

The adversary always outputs 1 with $\mathcal{E}_K$. It outputs 1 with $\Pi(\cdot, \cdot)$ with probability $\frac{1}{s^b}$. Therefore, the advantage is $1 - \frac{1}{s^b}$.

4 Known-Plaintext Round-Function-Recovery Attack on Feistel Scheme

In this section, we define the Feistel network over a group of order N. Typically, this group is $\mathbb{Z}_N$. Later in Sect. 5, we assume b is even and $N = s^{\frac{b}{2}}$.

First of all, we observe that the round functions are not uniquely defined by the codebook. Namely, if $(F_0, \ldots, F_{r-1})$ is a solution to map given sample plaintexts to the corresponding ciphertexts, then we can construct many other solutions. Indeed, for any set of values $\alpha_0, \ldots, \alpha_{r-1}$ such that $\alpha_1 + \alpha_3 + \alpha_5 + \cdots = \alpha_0 + \alpha_2 + \alpha_4 + \cdots = 0$, we can define

$$F'_j(u) = F_j(u - \alpha_{j-1} - \alpha_{j-3} - \alpha_{j-5} - \cdots) + \alpha_j$$

for all j and u to obtain another solution. Therefore, we can fix one point arbitrarily in $F_0, \ldots, F_{r-3}$ when looking for a solution. All the other solutions are obtained by the above transformation of the round functions.

The rest of the section is organized as follows: in Sect. 4.1, we give a heuristic attack for 3-round FN and analyze its time complexity. We report the ratio of success recovery in Fig. 3 with the parameters the attack takes. In Sect. 4.2, we give an attack for 4-round FN that leverage our 3-round attack. The correctness and further analysis is presented with formally stated lemmas. In Sect. 4.3, we expand our attack for five rounds and more and derived the time complexities.

4.1 Round-Function-Recovery on 3-Round Feistel Scheme

Consider a 3-round Feistel Scheme with three round functions F_0, F_1, F_2 and modular addition. Given x and y in $\mathcal{X}$, we define:

$$\begin{aligned} c &= x + F_0(y), \\ t &= y + F_1(c), \\ z &= c + F_2(t). \end{aligned} \tag{1}$$

Due to the symmetry of the set of solutions (F_0, F_1, F_2) (as already observed), we can fix F_0 on one point arbitrarily. The idea of our attack is to concentrate on data for which we know how to evaluate F_0 so that we can deduce the output for the round function F_2. Then, we concentrate on data for which we know how to evaluate F_2 and we deduce more points in F_0. We continue by alternating the deduction between F_0 and F_2 until we recover them all. When we continue iterating as described, we can fully recover the tables for all three round functions (F_0, F_1, F_2). Our attack is presented in Algorithm 2 in more detail.

Algorithm 2. (F_0, F_1, F_2) Recovery Attack

---

1 Collect a set S of tuples $(xyzt)$ of size θN.
2 Take a subset $S_1 \subseteq S$ of size θ such that y is constant in S_1.
3 Fix $F_0(y) = 0$ arbitrarily and deduce θ tuples $(cyzt)$ in S_1 by
   $c = x + F_0(y)$. We collect θ equations of the form $F_2(t) = z - c$.
4 Take the subset $S_2 \subseteq S$ of all $(xyzt) \in S$ such that $\exists (x'y'z't') \in S_1$ with
   $t = t'$. The expected size of S_2 is θ^2.
5 Using the θ points of F_2, we deduce θ^2 tuples $(xyct)$ by $c = z - F_2(t)$.
   From these tuples, we obtain θ^2 equations of the form $F_0(y) = c - x$.
6 Take the subset $S_3 \subseteq S$ of all $(xyzt) \in S$ such that $\exists (x'y'z't') \in S_2$ with
   $y = y'$. The expected size of S_3 is θ^3.
7 Using the θ^2 points of F_0, we deduce from θ^3 tuples $(cyzt)$...
8 We iterate through $S_1 \subseteq S_3 \subseteq S_5 \subseteq \cdots \subseteq S$ and $S_2 \subseteq S_4 \subseteq \cdots \subseteq S$ to
   complete the tables of F_0 and F_2.

We model our set S as a bipartite graph with two parties of N vertices (one for the y's and the other for the t's) and edges for each (y, t) pair represented by tuples from S. What our algorithm does is just to look for a connected component of a random starting point y with complexity $O(\theta N)$. Following the theory of random graphs [19], we have θN random edges so that the graph is likely to be fully connected when $\theta \approx \ln(N)$. For a constant $\theta \geqslant 1$, it is likely to have a giant connected component. This component corresponds to a constant fraction of the tables of F_0 and F_2. Therefore, after $\log_\theta N$ iterations, we can reconstruct F_0 and F_2 which allow us to reconstruct F_1. For any y, we can see that it does not appear in S with probability $\left(1 - \frac{1}{N}\right)^{\theta N} \approx 1 - e^{-\theta}$. Thus, we can only hope to recover a fraction $1 - e^{-\theta}$ of the table of F_0. The same holds for F_1 and F_2. **Therefore, with data and time complexity N, we recover a good fraction of all tables. With data and time complexity $N \ln N$, we recover the full tables with good probability.**

We implemented our attack. On Fig. 3, we plot the average fraction of recovered F_0 values depending on θ for several values of N. For this, we computed an average over 10,000 independent runs. For $\theta = 1$, the fraction is about 40%. We also plot the fraction of the trials which fully recovered all functions. These two values can be taken as an approximation of the expected fraction of recovered table for F_0 and the probability to fully recover all functions, respectively. As we can see, the first value does not depend so much on N (we have a giant connected component for θ around 1), but the second one jumps for θ proportional to $\ln N$ (the graph becomes fully connected). For $\theta = \ln N$, the probability is roughly $\frac{1}{3}$.

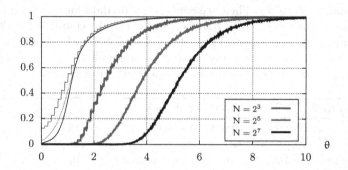

Fig. 3. Fraction of recovered F_0 depending on θ in the 3-round attack (in thin) and fraction of experiments which fully recovered all functions (in bold) over 10,000 trials.

4.2 Round-Function-Recovery on 4-Round Feistel Scheme

In this section, we give an attack to fully recover the round functions of a 4-round Feistel scheme.

Consider a 4-round Feistel scheme with round functions F_0, F_1, F_2, F_3. Given x and y in $\mathcal{X}$, we define the following equations (see Fig. 4(a)):

$$c = x + F_0(y),$$
$$d = y + F_1(c),$$
$$z = c + F_2(d),$$
$$t = d + F_3(z).$$

Assume that we collected M random pairwise different plaintext messages (xy). We collect the pairs:

$$V = \{(xy, x'y') \mid z' = z, t' - y' = t - y, xy \neq x'y'\}$$

and,

$$V_{good} = \{(xy, x'y') \mid z' = z, c' = c, xy \neq x'y'\}$$

where c, d, z, t (respectively c', d', z', t') are defined from (xy) (respectively form $(x'y')$) as above. We define $\mathsf{Label}(xy, x'y') = x - x'$.

We form a directed graph $G = (V, E)$ with the vertex set V as defined above. We take $(x_1y_1x_1'y_1', x_2y_2x_2'y_2') \in E$ if $y_1' = y_2$ (i.e. a pair of tuples $x_1y_1x_1'y_1'$ is connected to a pair $x_2y_2x_2'y_2'$ if the y_2 in the second message in former tuple is same as in the first message in latter tuple). Furthermore, we let $E_{good} = (V_{good} \times V_{good}) \cap E$ and define the sub-graph $G_{good} = (V_{good}, E_{good})$.

Then, we have the following Lemma with four properties:

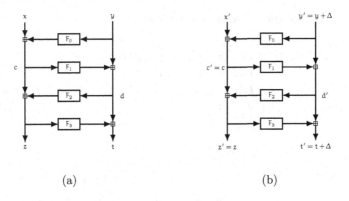

(a)   (b)

Fig. 4. 4-round Feistel scheme attack

Lemma 1. *Given a graph* G *with a vertex set* V *defined as above:*

1. $V_{good} \subseteq V$.
2. *If* $(xy, x'y') \in V$, *then* $y \neq y'$.
3. *If* $(xy, x'y') \in V_{good}$, *then* $F_0(y') - F_0(y) = Label(xy, x'y')$.
4. *For all cycles* $v_1 v_2 \cdots v_L v_1$ *of* G_{good}, $\sum_{i=1}^{L} Label(v_i) = 0$.[3]

Proof. The proofs are straightforward:

1. Clearly, $z' = z$ and $c' = c$ imply that $t' - y' = t - y$, hence $V_{good} \subseteq V$.
2. If $t' - y' = t - y$ and $y' = y$, then $t' = t$. If we further have $z' = z$, then we deduce $c' = c$. If $c' = c$, then $x' = x$, thus $xy = x'y'$. Hence, we cannot have $(xy, x'y') \in V$.
3. If $c' = c$ then $F_0(y') - F_0(y) = x - x' = Label(xy, x'y')$.
4. Let $v_i = (x_i y_i, x_i' y_i')$. If $v_i \in V_{good}$ then $F_0(y_i') - F_0(y_i) = Label(v_i)$. If we have a cycle then $y_i' = y_{i+1}$ with $y_{L+1} = y_1$. Hence, $\sum_i Label(v_i) = 0$. □

The principle of our attack is as follows: if we get vertices in V_{good}, the property 3 from Lemma 1 gives equations to characterize F_0. One problem is that we can identify vertices in V, but we cannot tell apart good and non-good (bad) ones. One way to recognize good vertices is to use property 4 in Lemma 1: to find cycles with zero sum of labels. For this, we will prove in Lemma 4 that this is a characteristic property of good cycles, meaning that all the vertices in these cycles are good vertices. First, we estimate the number of vertices and edges with the following two Lemma.

Lemma 2. *For* x, y, x', y' *random and* F_0, F_1, F_2, F_3 *random,*

$$\Pr[(xy, x'y') \in V_{good} \mid (xy, x'y') \in V] = \frac{1}{2 - \frac{1}{N}} \approx \frac{1}{2}.$$

---

[3] Note that the cycle length notation L should not be confused with the subscript L indicating the left part of a plaintext or a ciphertext.

Proof. We compute the following probabilities:

$$\Pr[xy, x'y' \in V_{good}] = \Pr[z' = z, c' = c, x'y' \neq xy]$$
$$= \Pr[z' = z, c' = c, y' \neq y]$$
$$= \Pr[y' \neq y] \Pr[c' = c \mid y' \neq y] \Pr[z' = z \mid c' = c, y' \neq y]$$
$$= \left(1 - \frac{1}{N}\right) \frac{1}{N^2}. \qquad (2)$$

$$\Pr[xy, x'y' \in V \setminus V_{good}] = \Pr[z' = z, t' - y' = t - y, c' \neq c, xy \neq x'y']$$
$$= \Pr[z' = z, d' - y' = d - y, c' \neq c, y' \neq y]$$
$$= \Pr[y' \neq y] \Pr[c' \neq c \mid y' \neq y]$$
$$\Pr[d' - y' = d - y \mid y' \neq y, c' \neq c]$$
$$\Pr[z' = z \mid d' - y' = d - y, y' \neq y, c' \neq c]$$
$$= \left(1 - \frac{1}{N}\right)\left(1 - \frac{1}{N}\right)\left(\frac{1}{N}\right)\left(\frac{1}{N}\right).$$

Hence,

$$\Pr[xy, x'y' \in V_{good} \mid xyx'y' \in V] = \frac{\Pr[xy, x'y' \in V_{good}]}{\Pr[xy, x'y' \in V]}$$
$$= \frac{1}{1 + \frac{\Pr[xy,x'y' \in V \setminus V_{good}]}{\Pr[xy,x'y' \in V_{good}]}}$$
$$= \frac{1}{2 - \frac{1}{N}} \approx \frac{1}{2}.$$

$\square$

Lemma 3. *The expected number of elements in* V_{good} *is* $\frac{M(M-1)\left(1-\frac{1}{N}\right)}{N^2} \approx \frac{M^2}{N^2}$.

Proof. We have $M(M - 1)$ possible pair of tuples $xy, x'y'$ with $xy \neq x'y'$ to construct V_{good}. From Eq. (2), the probability of each vertex in V_{good} is $\frac{1}{N^2}\left(1 - \frac{1}{N}\right)$. Thus, we expect to have $\frac{M(M-1)\left(1-\frac{1}{N}\right)}{N^2} \approx \frac{M^2}{N^2}$ elements in V_{good}. $\square$

We have the property that for each cycle $v_1 v_2 \cdots v_L v_1 \in G$, if $v_1, \ldots, v_L$ are all in V_{good}, then the sum of $\text{Label}(v_i)$ is zero due to Lemma 1, property 4. If one vertex is not good, the sum may be random. This suggests a way to find good vertices in V that is to look for long cycles in G with a zero sum of labels.

Lemma 4 (*L = 2 case*). *If* $v_1 = (x_1 y_1, x'_1 y'_1)$ *we say that* v_1 *and* v_2 *are permuting if* $v_2 = (x'_1 y'_1, x_1 y_1)$. *If* $v_1 v_2 v_1$ *is a cycle in G with zero sum of labels, and* v_1, v_2 *are not permuting, then* v_1 *and* v_2 *are likely to be good. More precisely, for* $v_1 = (x_1 y_1 x'_1 y'_1)$ *and* $v_2 = (x_2 y_2 x'_2 y'_2)$ *random, we have* $\Pr[v_1, v_2 \in V_{good} \mid v_1 v_2 v_1$ *is a cycle,* v_1, v_2 *not permuting,* $\sum_{i=1}^{2} \text{Label}(v_i) = 0] \geqslant \frac{1}{1 + \frac{10}{N-5}}$.

The proof for Lemma 4 is in Appendix A.1. We believe that Lemma 4 remains true for valid cycles of small length except in trivial cases. In Appendix A.2, we extend to $L > 2$ for cycles satisfying some special non-repeating condition [¬repeat] on the c and d values to rule out many trivial cases. However, this condition [¬repeat] cannot be checked by the adversary. Instead, we could just avoid repetitions of any message throughout the cycle (as repeating messages induce repeating c's or d's). We use the following conjecture (which is supported by experiment for $L = 3$).

Conjecture 1. *If $v_1 v_2 \cdots v_L v_1$ is a cycle of length L in G with zero sum of labels and the vertices use no messages in common, then $v_1 \cdots v_L$ are all good with probability close to 1.*

For M known plaintexts, the expected number of valid cycles in G_{good} of a given length L is $\frac{M^{2L}}{N^{3L}}$.

The aim of our attack is to collect as many F_0 outputs as possible to reconstruct a table of this function. Thus, we are interested in vertices whose labels are defined as $Label(v_i) = F_0(y) - F_0(y'), \forall i \in \{0, 1, \ldots, |V|\}$ and we generate another graph to represent the collection of many independent equations for F_0.

We have a valid cycle $v_1 v_2 \cdots v_L v_1$ of length L in G when $v_i \in V$,

$$\sum_{i=1}^{L} Label(v_i) = 0$$

and vertices use no messages in common. Now, let us define an undirected graph $G' = (V', E')$, where $V' = \{0, 1, \ldots, N-1\}$ and E' is defined as follows: for each vertex $v_i = (xy, x'y')$ in a valid cycle $v_1 v_2 \cdots v_L v_1$ of length L, add $\{y_i, y'_i\}$ as an edge in E' with label set to $Label(v_i)$. The purpose of such a graph G' is to put y values which are dependent on each other in a single connected component and put apart with independent y values in separate connected components.

When we model G' as a random graph, we can adjust M so that we can have a large connected component in G'. Given the vertex set size $|V'| = N$ and the edge size $|E'| = m$, $m = \frac{N(N-1)}{2}p$, where p is the probability that G' has an edge between two vertices. From Erdős-Rényi model [12] on random graphs, we want $Np \geqslant 1$. We know that $Np \sim 2\frac{m}{N}$. So, we want $m \geqslant \frac{N}{2}$. We have $\frac{M^{2L}}{L \cdot N^{3L}}$ expected good cycles (counted without repetition of their L circular rotations) of length L, thus $m \sim \frac{M^{2L}}{N^{3L}}$. Therefore, we need to set $M = \lambda N^{\frac{3}{2}} \left(\frac{N}{2}\right)^{\frac{1}{2L}}$ for a constant $\lambda \geqslant 1$ to have a large connected component in G'. Our attack works with $M = N^{\frac{3}{2}+\epsilon}$ for $\epsilon > 0$ small, with complexity $O(2^L N^{(1+2\epsilon)L})$ and a constant probability of success. If our attack recovers at least $\sqrt{N}$ points in F_0 correctly (which is the case when we have a large connected component in G'), we obtain $M \times \frac{\sqrt{N}}{N} \gg N$ samples to apply the attack on 3-rounds so that it recovers a good fraction of F_1, F_2, F_3. It is enough to bootstrap a yoyo attack (Steps 9–18 of Algorithm 3). And, our attack succeeds.

Now, we give the full algorithm of our attack to 4-round Feistel scheme.

Algorithm 3. (F_0, F_1, F_2, F_3) Recovery Attack (Strategy S_2)

---

1 Pick M known plaintexts and retrieve their ciphertext.
2 Create $G = (V, E)$.
3 Find valid cycles of length $2, 3, \ldots, L$ and collect the vertices in these
   cycles.
4 Create G' from $\{y, y'\}$ from the collected vertices.
5 Find the largest connected component in G'.
6 Assign one $F_0(y)$ value arbitrarily and deduce F_0 on the connected
   component.
7 For all known plaintexts using y in the connected component, evaluate
   and deduce a tuple for the 3-round Feistel scheme based on (F_1, F_2, F_3).
8 Apply the attack on 3-round Feistel scheme from Section 4.1 to recover a
   constant fraction of (F_1, F_2, F_3).
9 **while** *nothing more revealed* **do**
10   **foreach** *of the M plaintext/ciphertext pairs* **do**
11   **if** F_0 *and* F_1 *are known for this plaintext* **then**
12 | deduce one point for F_2 and F_3
13   **end**
14   **if** F_2 *and* F_3 *are known for this ciphertext* **then**
15 | deduce one point for F_0 and F_1
16   **end**
17   **end**
18 **end**

Experimentally, we noticed that $\lambda = 0.8$ is too small to obtain a large enough connected component for $L = 3$. Conversely, for $\lambda = 2$, G' is more connected but the giant component contains many bad edges that we want to avoid.

Let E_j be the event that the sizes of the j largest connected components sum to greater than $\sqrt{N}$ with no bad edges in G'. Let $E_{\leqslant j}$ be the event that either of $E_1, E_2, \ldots, E_j$ occurs. We simulated the attack for various N values and $\lambda = 1, 2, 3$ and report the numbers for $E_{\leqslant 1}, E_{\leqslant 2}, E_{\leqslant 3}$ on Table 2. When we read the table, by taking $\lambda = 1$ and $j = 3$, our attack recovers $\sqrt{N}$ points of F_0 with probability at least 23 %. In our attack, if we look at j connected components, we need to multiply the complexity by N^{j-1} (We can fix F_0 on one point for free, then all values in its connected components are inferred, but for each additional connected component, we must guess one value of F_0). It is likely that we can mitigate this N^{j-1} factor by early abort during the attack on 3-rounds.

In our experiments, we observe better success probability of our attack with $\lambda = 1$. With λ larger, the attack hardly ever succeeds. It may look paradoxical to say that if λ is too large, then the attack fails, but this is due to higher chances to collect bad edges. However, when G' is heavily connected, we could propose algorithms to eliminate inconsistencies in labels and get rid of bad edges. It means that we would have a successful attack for any $\lambda \geqslant 2$. We let it as future work.

Therefore, we have a double phase transition. The first phase transition occurs when we have enough data to be able to make the graph and find cycles. Our attack quickly succeeds after this phase transition. The second phase transition occurs when we start having bad edges in the collected cycles. Then, our attack must be enriched to be able to work any longer. We did not do it on purpose as we noticed there is a sufficient window in between these two phase transitions to break the scheme with good probability of success and without caring about possible bad edges.

In Table 3, we show the experimental results of success probability of the entire attack for various strategies. Let S_j be an event with strategy j. In S_1, we accumulate the three largest connected components and abort unless the accumulated size is at least $\sqrt{N}$ and they have no bad edges. I.e., S_1 is exactly $E_{\leqslant 3}$. In S_2, we just look at the largest connected component and fail unless it has no bad edges in G' (we remove the condition on size of the connected component that is greater than $\sqrt{N}$). In S_3 (and S_4 resp.), we look at the two largest (three largest resp.) connected components that have no bad edges. What we report in Table 3 includes the success probability Pr_{succ} of S_i and we recover the entire tables for each round function. These various strategies considered for experimental purpose even though we have the theory results that suggests to condition on the size of the connected component.

The data complexity of our attack in Algorithm 3 is $M = O(N^{\frac{3}{2}+\frac{1}{2t}})$.
We compute the time complexity for the algorithm based on the step 2, 3, 4, and 5, since the other steps are much shorter. In step 2, creating our graph G is defined as forming the vertices in G. This can be done in $M \log(M)$ time with collision detection for M known plaintext/ciphertext pairs. In step 3, we look for the cycles of length L. The cycles of length L in our graph can be found with multiplication on adjacency matrix (which is sparse). Matrix multiplication can be done in $O(|V|^2 d)$ where $d = \frac{|E|}{|V|}$ is the average degree of a vertex. Therefore, the complexity is $O(|V||E|)$. With the Floyd-Warshall algorithm, we need $(L-1)$ multiplications by the adjacency matrix in the max-plus algebra that leads us to a complexity $O(L|V||E|)$. With $|E| \sim \frac{|V|^2}{N}$, where $|V| = 2\frac{M^2}{N^2} = 2^{3-\frac{1}{t}}N^{1+\frac{1}{t}}$ and L constant, we have $O(\frac{|V|^3}{N})$ which is equal to $O(N^{2+\frac{3}{t}})$. Another method to find cycles is to enumerate all L-tuples of vertices in $O(|V|^L)$ which is $O(N^{L+1})$. Therefore, we compute the minimum between the two methods which is $O(N^3)$ for any L and it is the complexity of step 3. (It can even be lower for L > 3.) Step 4 takes N time and finally step 5 takes $\frac{M^{2L}}{N^{3L}} = \frac{N}{2}$. Since the complexity is weighted by step 3, **we have time complexity of our algorithm as $O(N^3)$ for L = 3 and a smaller $O(N^{2+\frac{3}{t}})$ for L > 3.** Instead of $L-1$ multiplications to a sparse matrix in the max-plus algebra, we could also use $O(\log L)$ general purpose matrix multiplications over the integer with the Coppersmith-Winograd algorithm [10]. We would reach a complexity of $O(|V|^{2.38} \log L)$ which is not better.

Table 2. Experimental $\Pr[E_{\leqslant j}]$ over several trials for various N, λ, and j; the number of trials correspond to the successful runs of the whole attack on FF3 in the first step out of 10 000 using L = 3.

N	M(λ)	#trials	$\Pr[E_{\leqslant 1}]$	$\Pr[E_{\leqslant 2}]$	$\Pr[E_{\leqslant 3}]$
2	2(0.71)	5022	0.00 %	0.00 %	0.00 %
4	5(0.56)	7098	1.51 %	1.51 %	1.51 %
8	15(0.53)	7010	0.36 %	4.07 %	4.07 %
16	46(0.51)	6665	0.05 %	1.23 %	1.23 %
32	144(0.50)	6103	0.02 %	0.03 %	0.16 %
64	457(0.50)	7986	0.00 %	0.00 %	0.01 %
128	1449(0.50)	7460	0.00 %	0.00 %	0.00 %
256	4598(0.50)	6879	0.00 %	0.00 %	0.00 %
512	14597(0.50)	4816	0.00 %	0.00 %	0.00 %
2	3(1.06)	4316	0.00 %	0.00 %	0.00 %
4	8(0.89)	4153	15.19 %	15.19 %	15.19 %
8	23(0.81)	6703	5.83 %	18.54 %	18.54 %
16	73(0.81)	6886	4.57 %	13.87 %	13.87 %
32	230(0.80)	6952	2.52 %	7.12 %	10.98 %
64	730(0.80)	6568	1.40 %	5.65 %	9.18 %
128	2318(0.80)	6189	0.29 %	1.13 %	2.83 %
256	7357(0.80)	7338	0.03 %	0.31 %	0.89 %
512	23355(0.80)	469	0.00 %	0.00 %	0.00 %
2	3(1.06)	4352	0.00 %	0.00 %	0.00 %
4	9(1.00)	3864	23.08 %	23.08 %	23.08 %
8	29(1.02)	5791	15.59 %	35.02 %	35.02 %
16	91(1.01)	6585	16.20 %	29.90 %	29.90 %
32	288(1.00)	6814	14.66 %	27.09 %	31.67 %
64	913(1.00)	6981	18.16 %	34.69 %	40.87 %
128	2897(1.00)	6609	16.31 %	33.53 %	40.73 %
256	9196(1.00)	6154	16.27 %	36.90 %	46.51 %
512	29193(1.00)	409	11.25 %	32.52 %	43.77 %
8	58(2.03)	988	22.77 %	23.99 %	23.99 %
16	182(2.01)	2504	6.71 %	6.79 %	6.79 %
32	575(2.00)	3425	0.53 %	0.55 %	0.55 %
64	1825(2.00)	5727	0.02 %	0.02 %	0.02 %
128	5793(2.00)	1634	0.00 %	0.00 %	0.00 %
256	18391(2.00)	107	0.00 %	0.00 %	0.00 %
512	58386(2.00)	6	0.00 %	0.00 %	0.00 %
32	863(3.00)	1389	0.00 %	0.00 %	0.00 %
64	2737(3.00)	2250	0.00 %	0.00 %	0.00 %
128	8689(3.00)	139	0.00 %	0.00 %	0.00 %
256	27586(3.00)	7	0.00 %	0.00 %	0.00 %

Table 3. Experimental $Pr[S_j]$ and success probability over many trials for various N and j using $L = 3$.

N	$M(\lambda)$	#trials	$Pr[succ, S_1]-(Pr[S_1])$	$Pr[succ, S_2]-(Pr[S_2])$	$Pr[succ, S_3]-(Pr[S_3])$	$Pr[succ, S_4]-(Pr[S_4])$
2	2(0.71)	5022	0.00 %–(0.00 %)	0.00 %–(100.00 %)	0.00 %–(49.70 %)	0.00 %–(49.70 %)
4	5(0.56)	7098	0.00 %–(1.51 %)	0.00 %–(99.42 %)	0.00 %–(36.97 %)	0.00 %–(36.97 %)
8	15(0.53)	7010	0.00 %–(4.07 %)	0.00 %–(98.49 %)	0.00 %–(36.01 %)	0.00 %–(36.01 %)
16	46(0.51)	6665	0.00 %–(1.23 %)	0.00 %–(97.99 %)	0.00 %–(38.86 %)	0.00 %–(38.84 %)
32	144(0.50)	6103	0.05 %–(0.16 %)	0.77 %–(98.33 %)	2.24 %–(45.55 %)	2.24 %–(45.53 %)
64	457(0.50)	7986	0.01 %–(0.01 %)	2.02 %–(98.32 %)	6.36 %–(53.72 %)	6.41 %–(53.72 %)
128	1449(0.50)	7460	0.00 %–(0.00 %)	2.01 %–(98.75 %)	7.02 %–(67.63 %)	7.67 %–(67.57 %)
256	4598(0.50)	6879	0.00 %–(0.00 %)	0.74 %–(98.92 %)	5.16 %–(80.23 %)	6.67 %–(80.20 %)
512	14597(0.50)	4816	0.00 %–(0.00 %)	0.29 %–(99.40 %)	2.99 %–(92.52 %)	4.94 %–(92.44 %)
2	3(1.06)	4316	0.00 %–(0.00 %)	0.00 %–(100.00 %)	0.00 %–(76.90 %)	0.00 %–(76.90 %)
4	8(0.89)	4153	0.07 %–(15.19 %)	0.07 %–(93.74 %)	1.13 %–(59.64 %)	1.13 %–(59.64 %)
8	23(0.81)	6703	3.88 %–(18.54 %)	2.27 %–(90.23 %)	4.83 %–(57.72 %)	4.85 %–(57.69 %)
16	73(0.81)	6886	10.30 %–(13.87 %)	21.71 %–(87.71 %)	29.65 %–(67.25 %)	29.67 %–(67.14 %)
32	230(0.80)	6952	10.34 %–(10.98 %)	43.18 %–(88.62 %)	57.44 %–(79.67 %)	57.44 %–(78.88 %)
64	730(0.80)	6568	8.82 %–(9.18 %)	59.10 %–(91.21 %)	75.29 %–(88.78 %)	75.21 %–(87.62 %)
128	2318(0.80)	6189	2.70 %–(2.83 %)	65.89 %–(93.89 %)	84.15 %–(93.75 %)	84.15 %–(92.39 %)
256	7357(0.80)	7338	0.87 %–(0.89 %)	67.16 %–(96.52 %)	87.79 %–(96.52 %)	88.33 %–(95.50 %)
512	23355(0.80)	469	0.00 %–(0.00 %)	66.95 %–(98.29 %)	91.04 %–(98.29 %)	91.90 %–(97.65 %)
2	3(1.06)	4352	0.00 %–(0.00 %)	0.00 %–(100.00 %)	0.00 %–(75.30 %)	0.00 %–(75.30 %)
4	9(1.00)	3864	3.03 %–(23.08 %)	3.60 %–(88.69 %)	7.27 %–(64.65 %)	7.27 %–(64.65 %)
8	29(1.02)	5791	27.65 %–(35.02 %)	29.11 %–(78.62 %)	34.31 %–(65.88 %)	34.31 %–(65.76 %)
16	91(1.01)	6585	28.44 %–(29.90 %)	49.83 %–(73.27 %)	54.08 %–(68.37 %)	54.08 %–(67.84 %)
32	288(1.00)	6814	30.69 %–(31.67 %)	62.91 %–(71.79 %)	65.17 %–(70.75 %)	65.10 %–(68.80 %)
64	913(1.00)	6981	39.52 %–(40.87 %)	73.80 %–(77.14 %)	73.24 %–(77.14 %)	72.87 %–(74.03 %)
128	2897(1.00)	6609	39.17 %–(40.73 %)	83.10 %–(83.83 %)	79.77 %–(83.83 %)	79.03 %–(79.89 %)
256	9196(1.00)	6154	45.16 %–(46.51 %)	88.53 %–(88.77 %)	85.80 %–(88.77 %)	85.00 %–(85.81 %)
512	29193(1.00)	409	42.79 %–(43.77 %)	92.67 %–(92.67 %)	90.46 %–(92.67 %)	89.73 %–(90.46 %)
8	58(2.03)	988	23.99 %–(23.99 %)	25.40 %–(25.40 %)	25.40 %–(25.40 %)	25.40 %–(25.40 %)
16	182(2.01)	2504	6.79 %–(6.79 %)	6.79 %–(6.79 %)	6.79 %–(6.79 %)	6.79 %–(6.79 %)
32	575(2.00)	3425	0.55 %–(0.55 %)	0.55 %–(0.55 %)	0.55 %–(0.55 %)	0.55 %–(0.55 %)
64	1825(2.00)	5727	0.02 %–(0.02 %)	0.02 %–(0.02 %)	0.02 %–(0.02 %)	0.02 %–(0.02 %)
128	5793(2.00)	1634	0.00 %–(0.00 %)	0.00 %–(0.00 %)	0.00 %–(0.00 %)	0.00 %–(0.00 %)
256	18391(2.00)	107	0.00 %–(0.00 %)	0.00 %–(0.00 %)	0.00 %–(0.00 %)	0.00 %–(0.00 %)
512	58386(2.00)	6	0.00 %–(0.00 %)	0.00 %–(0.00 %)	0.00 %–(0.00 %)	0.00 %–(0.00 %)
32	863(3.00)	1389	0.00 %–(0.00 %)	0.00 %–(0.00 %)	0.00 %–(0.00 %)	0.00 %–(0.00 %)
64	2737(3.00)	2250	0.00 %–(0.00 %)	0.00 %–(0.00 %)	0.00 %–(0.00 %)	0.00 %–(0.00 %)
128	8689(3.00)	139	0.00 %–(0.00 %)	0.00 %–(0.00 %)	0.00 %–(0.00 %)	0.00 %–(0.00 %)
256	27586(3.00)	7	0.00 %–(0.00 %)	0.00 %–(0.00 %)	0.00 %–(0.00 %)	0.00 %–(0.00 %)

4.3 Round-Function-Recovery on 5-Round Feistel Scheme and More

Given the 4-round full recovery attack from Sect. 4.2, we can extend it to attack 5-round Feistel network. The attack for 5-round Feistel network is straightforward; it uses chosen plaintexts and guess strategies. First of all, consider our 4-round attack and the known plaintexts from this attack. We choose plaintexts for the 5-round so that the right half of the messages have as little different values as possible then guess the corresponding images through F_0. It means that for the right halves of the messages, we generate all the possible partial tables of the first round function for these right values. Then, we guess which table is consistent after running the attack on the next 4-round. The data complexity of our 4-round attack is $\lambda N^{\frac{3}{2}+\epsilon}$, **hence our time complexity for 5-round**

recovery with chosen plaintexts is $O(N^{\lambda N^{\frac{1}{2}+\epsilon+3}})$. The data complexity is unchanged.

We can attack r**-rounds similarly with complexity** $O(N^{(r-5)N+\sqrt{N}+3})$ by guessing the round functions on the last $(r-5)$ rounds. The data complexity is unchanged. We can apply this to FF1 ($r = 10$) and FF3 ($r = 8$). We obtain a complexity lower than 2^{128} for FF1 with $N = 7$ and for FF3 with $7 \leqslant N \leqslant 10$. (For lower N, exhaustive search on either the codebook or the round functions reaches the same conclusion.) Hence, **these instances of FF1 and FF3 do not offer a 128-bit security**.

5   Slide Attack on FF3

We develop an attack on 4-round Feistel network in Sect. 4 and we deploy it as a building block for our chosen-plaintext and chosen-tweak attack to FF3 scheme. Our FF3 attack aims to reconstruct the entire codebook for a challenge tweak for a number of queries which is lower than the size of the brute force codebook attack. The main idea of the designed FF3 attack takes advantage of the flexibility to change the tweak to permute the round functions.

Consider two functions G and H, where G is a 4-round Feistel scheme using tweakable block cipher F with tweaks $(T_R \oplus STR_2^{32}(0), T_L \oplus STR_2^{32}(1), T_R \oplus STR_2^{32}(2), T_L \oplus STR_2^{32}(3))$ and H is a 4-round Feistel scheme using tweakable block cipher F with tweaks $(T_R \oplus STR_2^{32}(4), T_L \oplus STR_2^{32}(5), T_R \oplus STR_2^{32}(6), T_L \oplus STR_2^{32}(7))$. In Fig. 5, we show two runs of FF3 encryption with tweak $T = T_L \| T_R$ in (a) and tweak $T' = T_L \oplus STR_2^{32}(4) \| T_R \oplus STR_2^{32}(4)$ in (b) on two distinct plaintext. We observe that $FF3.E(K, T, \cdot) = H \circ G$ and $FF3.E(K, T', \cdot) = G \circ H$. For simplicity, we do not explicitly write $STR_2^{32}(\cdot)$ any longer. Given this permuting ability by setting the tweaks XORed with round functions, we desire to form a "cyclic" behavior of plaintext/ciphertext pairs under two FF3 encryption with sliding G and H.

We pick at random two sets of messages $X = \{xy_0^1, \ldots, xy_0^i, \ldots, xy_0^A\}$ and $\overline{X} = \{\overline{xy}_0^1, \ldots, \overline{xy}_0^i, \ldots, \overline{xy}_0^A\}$ of size A. For each message xy_0^i in X, set $xy_{j+1}^i = Enc(K, T, xy_j^i)$ with a fixed tweak $T \in \mathcal{T}$ and a fixed key $K \in \mathcal{K}$. We repeat the chain encryption of outputs B times for each message in X. Let XC be the set of chain encryption of elements of X. It contains segments of length B of cycles of $H \circ G$. Similarly, for each message $\overline{xy}_0^i$ in $\overline{X}$, set $\overline{xy}_{j+1}^i = Enc(K, T', \overline{xy}_j^i)$ with the fixed tweak $T' \in \mathcal{T}$ under the same key K. Let $\overline{XC}$ be the set of chain encryption of elements of $\overline{X}$. Apparently, we have $|XC| = AB$ and $|\overline{XC}| = AB$. Given these 2 sets XC and $\overline{XC}$, we attempt to find a collision between XC and $\overline{XC}$ such that $G(xy_j^i) = \overline{xy}_0^{i'}$ or $G(xy_0^i) = \overline{xy}_{j'}^{i'}$ for $1 \leqslant i, i' \leqslant A$ and $1 \leqslant j, j' \leqslant B$. (See Fig. 6.) Upon having a table with inputs to G and H, we can apply the known-plaintext recovery attack on 4-round Feistel networks. The concrete algorithm to collect plaintext/ciphertext pairs is given in Algorithm 4.

We, now, formally prove useful results for the analysis and success probability of the attack in Algorithm 4.

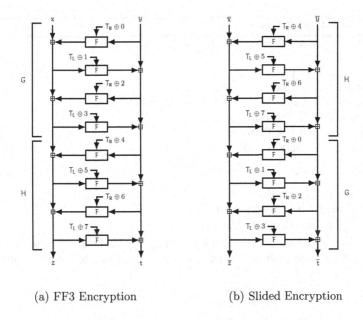

(a) FF3 Encryption   (b) Slided Encryption

Fig. 5. FF3 encryption with sliding round functions

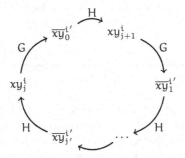

Fig. 6. Circular behavior of plaintext/ciphertext pairs.

Let Π be a random permutation on $\{0, \ldots, N^2 - 1\}$. Let c_k be the number of cycles of length k in Π. The total number of elements in a cycle of length k (for all k) is equal to N^2, meaning that $\sum_{k=1}^{N^2}(kc_k) = N^2$. It is well-known that the expected number of cycles of length k over a random Π is $\mathbb{E}_\Pi(c_k) = \frac{1}{k}$.[4]

In what follows we show two useful results.

---

[4] The probability that a given point is in a cycle of length exactly k is $\frac{(N^2-1)\cdots(N^2-k+1)}{N^2(N^2-1)\cdots(N^2-k+1)} = \frac{1}{N^2}$. Hence, the expected number of points in a cycle of length k is $1 = \mathbb{E}_\Pi(kc_k)$.

Algorithm 4. FF3 Attack

Input : a tweak bit string T such that $|T| = 64$, a key K

1 $T_L \| T_R \leftarrow T$
2 $T' \leftarrow T_L \oplus 4 \| T_R \oplus 4$
3 **foreach** $i = 1 \cdots A$ **do**
4   pick xy_0^i and $\overline{xy}_0^i$
5   **foreach** $j = 1 \cdots B$ **do**
6      $xy_j^i = \mathsf{FF3.E}(K, T, xy_{j-1}^i)$
7      $\overline{xy}_j^i = \mathsf{FF3.E}(K, T', \overline{xy}_{j-1}^i)$
8   **end**
9 **end**
10 **foreach** $i, i' = 1 \cdots A$ **do**
11   **foreach** $j = 0 \cdots B - M - 1$ **do**
12   // assume that $G(xy_j^i) = \overline{xy}_0^{i'}$
13   run attack on G with samples $G(xy_{j+k}^i) = \overline{xy}_k^{i'}$ for $k = 0 \cdots B - j$
14   if succeeded, run attack on H with samples $H(G(xy_k^i)) = xy_{k+1}^i$ for
         $k = 0 \cdots B - 1$
15   **end**
16   **foreach** $j = 0 \cdots B - M - 1$ **do**
17   // assume that $G(xy_0^i) = \overline{xy}_j^{i'}$
18   run attack on G with samples $G(xy_k^i) = \overline{xy}_{j+k}^{i'}$ for $k = 0 \cdots B - j$
19   if succeeded, run attack on H with samples $H(G(xy_k^i)) = xy_{k+1}^i$ for
         $k = 0 \cdots B - 1$
20   **end**
21 **end**

Lemma 5. *For a message xy^i picked at random, let $\mathsf{length}(xy^i)$ be the length of the cycle that contains xy^i. For two messages xy^i and $\overline{xy}^{i'}$ picked at random, let E_0 be an event that xy^i and $\overline{xy}^{i'}$ are in the same cycle. The expected value of $\mathsf{length}(xy^i)$ is $\mathbb{E}_{xy^i, \Pi}[\mathsf{length}(xy^i)] = \frac{N^2 + 1}{2}$ and the expected value of $\mathsf{length}(xy^i)$ given E_0 is $\mathbb{E}[\mathsf{length}(xy^i) | E_0] = \frac{2N^2 + 1}{3}$.*

Proof. We use the same notation for c_k as above.

$$\mathbb{E}_{xy^i, \Pi}[\mathsf{length}(xy)] = \mathbb{E}_{xy^i, \Pi}\left[\sum_{k=1}^{N^2} k c_k \frac{k}{N^2}\right] = \sum_{k=1}^{N^2} \mathbb{E}[c_k] \frac{k^2}{N^2} = \sum_{k=1}^{N^2} \frac{k}{N^2} = \frac{N^2 + 1}{2}$$

We first, observe that for any messages xy^i and $\overline{xy}^{i'}$, being in the same cycle of every possible length occurs with probability $\frac{1}{2}$. Then,

$$\Pr[E_0] = \mathbb{E}_{\Pi}\left[\sum_{k=1}^{N^2} c_k \left(\frac{k}{N^2}\right)^2\right] = \sum_{k=1}^{N^2} \frac{k}{N^4} = \frac{1}{2} + \frac{1}{2N^2} \approx \frac{1}{2}$$

$$\mathbb{E}[\text{length}(xy^i)|E_0] = \mathbb{E}_\Pi \left[\sum_{k=1}^{N^2} kc_k \left(\frac{k^2}{N^4}\right) \frac{1}{\Pr(E_0)} \right] = \frac{\sum_{k=1}^{N^2} \frac{k^2}{N^4}}{\Pr(E_0)}$$

$$= \frac{2N^2}{N^2+1} \times \frac{(N^2+1)(2N^2+1)}{6N^2} = \frac{2N^2+1}{3}$$

□

This means that if we pick xy^i and $\overline{xy}^{i'}$ at random and let $xy^j = G^{-1}(\overline{xy}^{i'})$ then xy^i and $\overline{xy}^{i'}$ are in the same cycle with probability close to $\frac{1}{2}$ and we will observe Fig. 6. One problem is that the cycle is typically long, i.e. $\frac{2N^2}{3}$ as shown in Lemma 5, but we want that two segments of length B starting from xy^i and $\overline{xy}^{i'}$ intersect on at least M points. Therefore, we need the probability of two segments overlapping in a cycle of length k on at least M points.

Lemma 6. *Let two segments* $xy^i - \Pi(xy^i) - \Pi^2(xy^i) - \cdots - \Pi^B(xy^i)$ *and* $\overline{xy}^{i'} - \Pi(\overline{xy}^{i'}) - \Pi^2(\overline{xy}^{i'}) - \cdots - \Pi^B(\overline{xy}^{i'})$ *overlap in a given cycle of length k on at least M points be the event* E_1^k. *Let* E_1 *be the union of all* E_1^k *for every possible length of k. The probability that* E_1 *occurs is equivalent to* $\frac{2(B-M)}{N^2}$ *for* $M = o(N^2)$.

Proof. We use the same notation for c_k as above.

$$\Pr[E_1] = \mathbb{E}_\Pi \left[\sum_{k=M}^{N^2} c_k \Pr[E_1^k] \right] = \mathbb{E}_\Pi \left[\sum_{k=M}^{N^2} c_k \frac{k}{N^2} \frac{\min\{k, 2(B-M)+1\}}{N^2} \right]$$

$$\sim \frac{2(B-M)}{N^2} \text{ for } M = o(N^2)$$

□

The probability of success of our FF3 attack depends on $\Pr[E_1]$ and on the success probability of our 4-round recovery attack on Feistel network. More clearly,

$$p_{success} = \left(1 - (1 - \Pr[E_1])^{A^2}\right) p_{success}^{\text{Feistel}}$$

which is equivalent to $\left(1 - e^{\frac{-2(B-M)A^2}{N^2}}\right) p_{success}^{\text{Feistel}}$. Thus, we need $A^2(B-M) \approx N^2$ to obtain a constant $p_{success}$. We can neglect the cost of the attack on H as we have plenty of samples and we only run it once G is recovered.

Our attack has 2AB data complexity. The time complexity is A^2B times the complexity of 4-round recovery attack on Feistel network. To minimize the data complexity 2AB with $A^2(B-M) = N^2$ and $B \geqslant M$, we set $B = 2M$, then $A = \frac{N}{\sqrt{M}}$. Therefore, **we have data complexity of FF3 attack as** $4N\sqrt{M}$

Table 4. Experimental probability of success in the FF3 attack for various parameters using strategy S_j

N	M	λ	A	B	#run	Pr[succ, S_1]	Pr[succ, S_2]	Pr[succ, S_3]	Pr[succ, S_4]
2	2	0.71	1	4	10000	0.00 %	0.00 %	0.00 %	0.00 %
4	5	0.56	2	10	10000	0.00 %	0.00 %	0.00 %	0.00 %
8	15	0.53	2	30	10000	0.00 %	0.00 %	0.00 %	0.00 %
16	46	0.51	2	92	10000	0.00 %	0.00 %	0.00 %	0.00 %
32	144	0.50	2	288	10000	0.03 %	0.47 %	1.38 %	1.38 %
64	457	0.50	3	914	10000	0.01 %	1.61 %	5.08 %	5.12 %
128	1449	0.50	3	2898	10000	0.00 %	1.51 %	5.25 %	5.73 %
256	4598	0.50	3	9196	10000	0.00 %	0.52 %	3.55 %	4.59 %
512	14597	0.50	3	29194	7977	0.00 %	0.18 %	1.82 %	3.00 %
2	3	1.06	1	6	10000	0.00 %	0.00 %	0.00 %	0.00 %
4	8	0.89	1	16	10000	0.03 %	0.03 %	0.48 %	0.48 %
8	23	0.81	2	46	10000	2.64 %	1.54 %	3.29 %	3.30 %
16	73	0.81	2	146	10000	7.32 %	15.34 %	21.04 %	21.05 %
32	230	0.80	2	460	10000	7.38 %	30.84 %	41.19 %	41.19 %
64	730	0.80	2	1460	10000	5.90 %	39.58 %	50.78 %	50.73 %
128	2318	0.80	2	4636	10000	1.69 %	41.36 %	53.14 %	53.16 %
256	7357	0.80	3	14714	9114	0.70 %	54.56 %	71.78 %	72.24 %
512	23355	0.80	3	46710	618	0.00 %	50.97 %	69.74 %	70.71 %
2	3	1.06	1	6	10000	0.00 %	0.00 %	0.00 %	0.00 %
4	9	1.00	1	18	10000	1.18 %	1.40 %	2.84 %	2.84 %
8	29	1.02	2	58	10000	17.24 %	17.99 %	21.46 %	21.46 %
16	91	1.01	2	182	10000	20.15 %	35.35 %	38.85 %	38.85 %
32	288	1.00	2	576	10000	22.01 %	45.89 %	48.29 %	48.24 %
64	913	1.00	2	1826	10000	28.20 %	54.14 %	54.41 %	54.15 %
128	2897	1.00	2	5794	10000	26.24 %	56.85 %	55.14 %	54.65 %
256	9196	1.00	2	18392	9961	28.10 %	55.90 %	54.65 %	54.15 %
512	29193	1.00	3	58386	500	35.00 %	77.40 %	76.20 %	75.40 %
2	6	2.12	1	12	10000	12.20 %	12.20 %	12.20 %	12.20 %
4	18	2.00	1	36	10000	14.15 %	15.62 %	16.48 %	16.48 %
8	58	2.03	1	116	10000	12.96 %	13.92 %	14.40 %	14.40 %
16	182	2.01	1	364	10000	6.10 %	7.37 %	7.65 %	7.65 %
32	575	2.00	1	1150	10000	2.20 %	3.62 %	3.80 %	3.80 %
64	1825	2.00	2	3650	10000	2.80 %	5.59 %	6.34 %	6.32 %
128	5793	2.00	2	11586	2512	2.43 %	4.34 %	4.70 %	4.66 %
256	18391	2.00	2	36782	162	1.23 %	3.70 %	3.70 %	3.70 %
512	58386	2.00	2	116772	10	10.00 %	10.00 %	10.00 %	10.00 %
2	9	3.18	1	18	10000	12.38 %	12.38 %	12.38 %	12.38 %
4	27	3.01	1	54	10000	13.92 %	15.62 %	16.46 %	16.46 %
8	86	3.02	1	172	10000	12.79 %	13.95 %	14.31 %	14.31 %
16	272	3.01	1	544	10000	5.13 %	6.56 %	6.91 %	6.91 %
32	863	3.00	1	1726	10000	2.04 %	3.25 %	3.47 %	3.46 %
64	2737	3.00	1	5474	8051	1.25 %	2.22 %	2.50 %	2.51 %
128	8689	3.00	1	17378	380	0.26 %	0.79 %	1.05 %	1.05 %
256	27586	3.00	2	55172	9	0.00 %	0.00 %	0.00 %	0.00 %
512	87579	3.00	2	175158	2	0.00 %	0.00 %	0.00 %	0.00 %

and time complexity as $2N^2$ times the complexity of 4-round recovery attack on Feistel network and $p_{success} \approx 1 - e^{-p_{success}^{Feistel}}$.

We fully implemented the attack but to test its success probability we could skip some parts of the running time we knew the attack would fail. Namely, in Algorithm 4 we can identify directly which segments overlap (using the key) and proceed directly to the 4-round Feistel attack on the right pair of segments. We show on Table 4 the experimental probability of success of the whole attack following the strategies S_j, $j = 1, \ldots, 4$. The probability was computed for 10,000 executions.[5] We also took the executions collecting less than M samples, as long as they succeed to recover all tables. Curiously, the $N \leqslant 4$ and $\lambda = 1$ cases seem to take M too low to be able to find cycles. As we can see, the success probability is pretty good (18%–77% for $8 \leqslant N \leqslant 512$) for $\lambda = 1$ and the strategy S_2 collecting the largest connected components in G'.

We conclude that the full attack succeeds with good probability.

6   Repairing FF3

As a quick fix, we can propose to change the length of the tweak in FF3 so that the adversary has no longer control on what is XORed to the round index. The same should hold if some other part of the tweak is XORed to a counter in a CBC mode, as proposed by the authors of the construction [8]. We obtain a scheme with a shorter tweak, to which we concatenate the round index instead of XORing it.

The original Luby-Rackoff results [15] was extended following this idea by Black and Rogaway [7], but the obtained security result is quite weak as we can only prove that for a number of queries $q \ll \sqrt{N}$, the cipher resists to chosen-plaintext attacks, even with only three rounds. By similarly extending the results by Patarin [17], we can obtain that for $q \ll N$, the cipher resists to chosen-plaintext and ciphertext attacks, even with only six rounds. However, this says nothing in the case $q \sim N^{\frac{3}{2}}$ which is the case of our 4-round attack.[6]

7   Conclusion

We took the NIST standard FF3 and investigated its security on small domain sizes. We started exploiting that we can permute the round functions due to a bad domain separation in the tweak scheme which uses an XOR with the round index. This permutation leads us to develop a slide attack on FF3 based

---

[5] Executions of the attack on the 4-round Feistel scheme which we used to fill our previous tables are precisely those getting the M samples in this experiment. For some rows with M too large, no experiments collected M pairwise different messages so they are not reported in the previous table. Nevertheless, our attack may still work even though we collect less than M samples. This is why they appear on Table 4.

[6] In reaction to this attack, NIST released the following announcement: https://beta.csrc.nist.gov/News/2017/Recent-Cryptanalysis-of-FF3.

on our own design for 4-round Feistel schemes attack that works with known plaintexts/ciphertexts. Our FF3 attack works with chosen plaintexts and two tweaks. It improves the recent results from Bellare et al. [3] on data and time complexity to break FF3. Our 4-round Feistel network attack is a full round-function-recovery attack that works with known plaintexts instead of chosen plaintexts and ciphertexts unlike the recent results from Biryukov et al. [6].

Acknowledgments. The work was done while the first author was visiting EPFL. It was supported by NSF grant CNS-1453132. This material is based upon work supported by the Defense Advanced Research Projects Agency (DARPA) and Space and Naval Warfare Systems Center, Pacific (SSC Pacific) under contract No. N66001-15-C-4070.

We thank Adi Shamir for the useful comments and Stefano Tessaro for the discussions.

References

1. Recommendation for Block Cipher Modes of Operation: Methods for Format Preserving Encryption. National Institute of Standards and Technology (2016)
2. Anderson, R., Biham, E.: Two practical and provably secure block ciphers: BEAR and LION. In: Gollmann, D. (ed.) FSE 1996. LNCS, vol. 1039, pp. 113–120. Springer, Heidelberg (1996). doi:10.1007/3-540-60865-6_48
3. Bellare, M., Hoang, V.T., Tessaro, S.: Message-recovery attacks on Feistel-based format preserving encryption. In: 23th CCS Proceedings (2016)
4. Bellare, M., Ristenpart, T., Rogaway, P., Stegers, T.: Format-preserving encryption. In: Jacobson, M.J., Rijmen, V., Safavi-Naini, R. (eds.) SAC 2009. LNCS, vol. 5867, pp. 295–312. Springer, Heidelberg (2009). doi:10.1007/978-3-642-05445-7_19
5. Bellare, M., Rogaway, P., Spies, T.: The FFX mode of operation for format-preserving encryption. Draft 1.1. Submission to NIST, Feburary 2010. http://csrc.nist.gov/groups/ST/toolkit/BCM/documents/proposedmodes/ffx/ffx-spec.pdf
6. Biryukov, A., Leurent, G., Perrin, L.: Cryptanalysis of Feistel networks with secret round functions. In: Dunkelman, O., Keliher, L. (eds.) SAC 2015. LNCS, vol. 9566, pp. 102–121. Springer, Cham (2016). doi:10.1007/978-3-319-31301-6_6
7. Black, J., Rogaway, P.: Ciphers with arbitrary finite domains. In: Preneel, B. (ed.) CT-RSA 2002. LNCS, vol. 2271, pp. 114–130. Springer, Heidelberg (2002). doi:10.1007/3-540-45760-7_9
8. Brier, E., Peyrin, T., Stern, J.: BPS: a format-preserving encryption proposal. http://csrc.nist.gov/groups/ST/toolkit/BCM/documents/proposedmodes/bps/bps-spec.pdf
9. Brightwell, M., Smith, H.E.: Using datatype-preserving encryption to enchance data warehouse security (1997). http://csrc.nist.gov/nissc/1997/proceedings/141.pdf
10. Coppersmith, D., Winograd, S.: Matrix multiplication via arithmetic progressions. J. Symb. Comput. **9**(3), 251–280 (1990)
11. Dinur, I., Dunkelman, O., Keller, N., Shamir, A.: New attacks on Feistel structures with improved memory complexities. In: Gennaro, R., Robshaw, M. (eds.) CRYPTO 2015. LNCS, vol. 9215, pp. 433–454. Springer, Heidelberg (2015). doi:10.1007/978-3-662-47989-6_21
12. Erdős, P., Renyi, A.: On random graphs I. Publicationes Mathematicae **6**, 290–297 (1959)

13. Goldenberg, D., Hohenberger, S., Liskov, M., Schwartz, E.C., Seyalioglu, H.: On tweaking Luby-Rackoff blockciphers. In: Kurosawa, K. (ed.) ASIACRYPT 2007. LNCS, vol. 4833, pp. 342–356. Springer, Heidelberg (2007). doi:10.1007/978-3-540-76900-2_21

14. Liskov, M., Rivest, R.L., Wagner, D.: Tweakable block ciphers. J. Cryptol. **24**(3), 588–613 (2011)

15. Luby, M., Rackoff, C.: How to construct pseudorandom permutations from pseudo-random functions. SIAM J. Comput. **17**(2), 373–386 (1988)

16. Lucks, S.: Faster Luby-Rackoff ciphers. In: Gollmann, D. (ed.) FSE 1996. LNCS, vol. 1039, pp. 189–203. Springer, Heidelberg (1996). doi:10.1007/3-540-60865-6_53

17. Patarin, J.: Security of balanced and unbalanced Feistel schemes with linear non equalities (2010). http://eprint.iacr.org/2010/293

18. Rogaway, P.: A synopsis of format preserving encryption. http://web.cs.ucdavis.edu/~rogaway/papers/synopsis.pdf

19. Saltykov, A.I.: The number of components in a random bipartite graph. Discrete Math. Appl. **5**, 515–523 (1995)

20. Schneier, B., Kelsey, J.: Unbalanced Feistel networks and block cipher design. In: Gollmann, D. (ed.) FSE 1996. LNCS, vol. 1039, pp. 121–144. Springer, Heidelberg (1996). doi:10.1007/3-540-60865-6_49

21. Spies, T.: Format preserving encryption. Unpublished white paper (2008). https://www.voltage.com/wp-content/uploads/Voltage-Security-WhitePaper-Format-Preserving-Encryption.pdf

A   Deferred Proofs

A.1   Proof of Lemma 4

Proof. Before we start computations, we let the followings:

[good]: the event that v_1 and v_2 are both in V_{good}.

[bad]: the event that v_1 and v_2 are both in V but not both in V_{good}.

[cyc]: the event that $y_1' = y_2$ and $y_2' = y_1$.

[perm]: the event that $x_1 y_1 = x_2' y_2'$ and $x_1' y_1' = x_2 y_2$.

$[\Sigma = 0]$: the event that $Label(v_1) + Label(v_2) = 0$.

$[\#\{d\} = 4]$: the event that d_1, d_1', d_2, d_2' are pairwise different.

$[\#\{d\} = j]$: the event that there are exactly j pairwise different values among d_1, d_1', d_2, d_2'.

Let $p_{good} = \Pr[good, cyc, \neg perm, \Sigma = 0]$.

Let $p_{bad} = \Pr[bad, cyc, \neg perm, \Sigma = 0]$.

We are interested in $\Pr[good \mid cyc, \neg perm, \Sigma = 0] = \frac{1}{1 + \frac{p_{bad}}{p_{good}}}$.

We want to upper bound $\frac{p_{bad}}{p_{good}}$. And, we start with the probability p_{good}.

Note that if [good], we have $[\Sigma = 0]$ and it is equivalent to $[c_1 = c_1', c_2 = c_2', d_1 \neq d_1', d_2 \neq d_2', z_1 = z_1', z_2 = z_2']$. When $[c_1 = c_1', c_2 = c_2', cyc]$ holds, [perm] is equivalent to $[c_1' = c_2]$. When $[c_1 = c_1', c_2 = c_2', y_1' = y_2]$ holds, $(d_1 - y_1) - (d_2' - y_2') = F_1(c_1) - F_1(c_2') = F_1(c_1') - F_1(c_2) = (d_1' - y_1') - (d_2 - y_2) = d_1' - d_2$. So, $y_1 = y_2'$ is equivalent to $d_1 - d_2' = d_1' - d_2$.

We let A be the event $[c_1 = c_1' \neq c_2 = c_2', \#\{d\} = 4, d_1 + d_2 = d_1' + d_2']$ which consists of only the c and d. Picking the xy is equivalent to picking the cd. So, A only depends on the c, d. We have $\Pr[A] \geqslant \frac{1}{N^3}\left(1 - \frac{1}{N}\right)^2\left(1 - \frac{3}{N}\right) \geqslant \frac{1}{N^3}\left(1 - \frac{5}{N}\right)$ (We first pick c_1 and d_1, then $c_2 \neq c_1$, $d_1' \neq d_1$, and $d_2 \notin \{d_1, d_1', 2d_1' - d_1\}$). When A holds, $[y_1' = y_2]$ only depends on F_1 and occurs with probability $\frac{1}{N}$. When A holds, $[z_1 = z_1', z_2 = z_2']$ only depends on F_2 and occurs with probability $\frac{1}{N^2}$. Therefore,

$$
\begin{aligned}
p_{\text{good}} &= \Pr[\text{good}, \text{cyc}, \neg\text{perm}, \Sigma = 0] \\
&= \Pr[c_1 = c_1' \neq c_2 = c_2', d_1 \neq d_1', d_2 \neq d_2', d_1 + d_2 = d_1' + d_2', y_1' = y_2, z_1 = z_1', z_2 = z_2'] \\
&\geqslant \Pr[c_1 = c_1' \neq c_2 = c_2', \#\{d\} = 4, d_1 + d_2 = d_1' + d_2', y_1' = y_2, z_1 = z_1', z_2 = z_2'] \\
&= \Pr_{c,d}[A]\,\Pr_{F_1}[y_1' = y_2 | A]\,\Pr_{F_2}[z_1 = z_1', z_2 = z_2' | A] \\
&\geqslant \frac{1}{N^6}\left(1 - \frac{5}{N}\right)
\end{aligned}
$$

Now, we compute the probability p_{bad}.

We know that [bad] is equivalent to $[c_1 \neq c_1'$ or $c_2 \neq c_2', F_1(c_1) = F_1(c_1'), F_1(c_2) = F_1(c_2'), d_1 \neq d_1', d_2 \neq d_2', z_1 = z_1', z_2 = z_2']$. When [cyc] occurs, [¬perm] is equivalent to $[c_1' \neq c_2$ or $c_1 \neq c_2']$. When $[F_1(c_1) = F_1(c_1'), F_1(c_2) = F_1(c_2')]$ holds, [cyc] is equivalent to $[d_1 + d_2 = d_1' + d_2', y_1' = y_2]$. When [cyc] holds, $[\Sigma = 0]$ is equivalent to $[c_1 + c_2 = c_1' + c_2']$. So, when $[\text{cyc}, \Sigma = 0]$ occurs, $[c_1 \neq c_1'$ or $c_2 \neq c_2']$ is equivalent to $[c_1 \neq c_1', c_2 \neq c_2']$.

From the symmetry, $[c_1' \neq c_2$ or $c_1 \neq c_2']$ case is at most twice the $[c_1' \neq c_2]$ case. Let B be the event $[c_1 \neq c_1' \neq c_2 \neq c_2', c_1 + c_2 = c_1' + c_2', d_1 + d_2 = d_1' + d_2', d_1 \neq d_1', d_2 \neq d_2']$ which consists of only the c and d. When B holds, $[F_1(c_1) = F_1(c_1'), F_1(c_2) = F_1(c_2'), y_1' = y_2]$ only depends on F_1. Therefore,

$$
\begin{aligned}
p_{\text{bad}} &= \Pr[\text{bad}, \text{cyc}, \neg\text{perm}, \Sigma = 0] \\
&= \Pr[c_1 \neq c_1', c_2 \neq c_2', c_1' \neq c_2 \text{ or } c_1 \neq c_2', c_1 + c_2 = c_1' + c_2', F_1(c_1) = F_1(c_1'), F_1(c_2) = F_1(c_2'), \\
&\qquad d_1 + d_2 = d_1' + d_2', d_1 \neq d_1', d_2 \neq d_2', y_1' = y_2, z_1 = z_1', z_2 = z_2'] \\
&\leqslant 2\Pr[c_1 \neq c_1' \neq c_2 \neq c_2', c_1 + c_2 = c_1' + c_2', F_1(c_1) = F_1(c_1'), F_1(c_2) = F_1(c_2'), d_1 + d_2 = d_1' + d_2', \\
&\qquad d_1 \neq d_1', d_2 \neq d_2', y_1' = y_2, z_1 = z_1', z_2 = z_2'] \\
&= 2\Pr_{c,d,F_2}[B, z_1 = z_1', z_2 = z_2']\,\Pr_{F_1}[F_1(c_1) = F_1(c_1'), F_1(c_2) = F_1(c_2'), y_1' = y_2 | B, z_1 = z_1', z_2 = z_2'] \\
&= 2\Pr_{c,d,F_2}[B, z_1 = z_1', z_2 = z_2'] \times \frac{1}{N^3}
\end{aligned}
$$

We split B following the $[\#\{d\} = j]$ cases for $j = 2, 3, 4$. Each case is denoted B_j. When we have $[d_1 \neq d', d_2 \neq d_2', \#\{d\} = 2, d_1 + d_2 = d_1' + d_2']$, we have either $[d_1 = d_2', d_1' = d_2]$ or $[d_1 = d_2, d_1' = d_2', d_1' = d_1 + \frac{N}{2}]$. When we have $[d_1 \neq d_1', d_2 \neq d_2', \#\{d\} = 3]$, we have $[d_1 = d_2$ or $d_1' = d_2']$ (If we have $[d_1 = d_2'$ or $d_1' = d_2]$, then $d_1 + d_2 = d_1' + d_2'$ and $\#\{d\} = 2$ conflicts). When we have

$[d_1 \neq d_1', d_2 \neq d_2', \#\{d\} = 4]$, we have no equality of d's. For B_4,

$$\Pr_{c,d,F_2}[B_4, z_1 = z_1', z_2 = z_2']$$

$$= \Pr_{c,d}[B_4] \Pr_{F_2}[z_1 = z_1', z_2 = z_2'|B_4]$$

$$= \Pr_{c,d}[c_1 \neq c_1' \neq c_2 \neq c_2', c_1 + c_2 = c_1' + c_2', d_1 + d_2 = d_1' + d_2', \#\{d\}=4] \Pr_{F_2}[z_1 = z_1', z_2 = z_2'|B_4]$$

$$\leqslant \Pr_{c,d}[c_1 + c_2 = c_1' + c_2', d_1 + d_2 = d_1' + d_2'] \Pr_{F_2}[z_1 = z_1', z_2 = z_2'|B_4]$$

$$= \frac{1}{N^4}$$

For each of the two cases of B_3, either $z_1 = z_1'$ or $z_2 = z_2'$ occurs with probability $\frac{1}{N}$. So,

$$\Pr_{c,d,F_2}[B_3, z_1 = z_1', z_2 = z_2']$$

$$\leqslant 2 \Pr_{c,d}[c_1 + c_2 = c_1' + c_2', d_1 + d_2 = d_1' + d_2', d_1 = d_2] \Pr_{F_2}[z_1 = z_1'|d_1 \neq d_1']$$

$$= \frac{2}{N^4}$$

For B_2,

$$\Pr_{c,d,F_2}[B_2, z_1 = z_1', z_2 = z_2']$$

$$\leqslant \Pr_{c,d}[B_2]$$

$$= \Pr_{c,d}[c_1 \neq c_1' \neq c_2 \neq c_2', c_1 + c_2 = c_1' + c_2', d_1 + d_2 = d_1' + d_1', d_1 \neq d_1', d_2 \neq d_2', \#\{d\}=2]$$

$$= \Pr_{c,d}[c_1 + c_2 = c_1' + c_2', d_1 + d_2 = d_1' + d_2', d_1 = d_2', d_1' = d_2'] +$$

$$\quad \Pr_{c,d}[c_1 + c_2 = c_1' + c_2', d_1 = d_2, d_1' + d_2', d_1' = d_1 + \tfrac{N}{2}]$$

$$= \frac{2}{N^4}$$

Therefore, $\Pr_{c,d,F_2}[B, z_1 = z_1', z_2 = z_2'] \leqslant \frac{5}{N^4}$ and $p_{bad} \leqslant \frac{10}{N^7}$.
Finally, $\frac{p_{bad}}{p_{good}} \leqslant \frac{10}{N-5}$. We deduce

$$\Pr[\text{good} \mid \text{cyc}, \neg\text{perm}, \Sigma = 0] \geqslant \frac{1}{1 + \frac{10}{N-5}}$$

$\square$

A.2 Extended Lemma 4

Lemma 7. *If* $v_1 v_2 \cdots v_i \cdots v_L v_1$ *is a cycle of length* L *in* G *with zero sum of labels and the vertices use no* d_i *or* c_i *in common, then all* v_i *are likely to be good. More precisely, for* $v_i = (x_i y_i x_i' y_i')$ *random, we have*

$\Pr[\forall i, v_i \in V_{good} \mid v_1 \cdots v_i \cdots v_L v_1 \text{ is a cycle}, (\#\{c\}=\#\{c'\}=L, \forall i \neq j \ c_i \neq c_j'), (\#\{d\}=L, \forall i, j \ d_i \neq d_j'),$
$\sum_{i=1}^{L} \text{Label}(v_i)=0)] \geqslant \frac{1}{1 + \frac{2^{L-1}}{N}}.$

Proof. We compute $p = \Pr[\text{good} \mid \text{good} \vee \text{bad}, \text{cyc}, \neg\text{repeat}_c, \neg\text{repeat}_d, \Sigma = 0]$, where we use the same notation as in Lemma 4 with new $[\neg\text{repeat}_c]$ and $[\neg\text{repeat}_d]$ notations. We define them as follows:

We note that when all v_i are vertices (good or bad), since $F_1(c_i') = F_1(c_i)$, $y_{i+1}' = y_i$ is equivalent to $d_i' - d_{i+1} = F_1(c_i) - F_1(c_{i+1})$. We further note that when this holds, then $\sum d_i = \sum d'$. To be able to compute the probability of [cyc], we introduce a condition on the non-repetition of the c and c', except for the possible equalities $c_i = c_i'$ in good vertices. Namely, we define

$$[\neg\text{repeat}_c] : \left(\#\{c\} = \#\{c'\} = L, \quad \forall i \neq j \quad c_i \neq c_j'\right)$$

When $[\neg\text{repeat}_c, \sum d = \sum d']$ holds and all v_i are vertices, [cyc] occurs with probability $\frac{1}{N^{L-1}}$. Therefore, $\Pr[\text{cyc} \mid \text{good} \vee \text{bad}, \neg\text{repeat}_c, \Sigma d = \Sigma d'] = \frac{1}{N^{L-1}}$.

The event $[\forall i \quad z_i = z_i']$ is equivalent to $c_i + F_2(d_i) = c_i' + F_2(d_i')$. To be able to compute its probability, we introduce a condition on the non-repetition of the d and d'. Namely, we define

$$[\neg\text{repeat}_d] : \left(\#\{d\} = L, \quad \forall i, j \quad d_i \neq d_j'\right)$$

Hence, when $[\neg\text{repeat}_d]$ occurs, $[\forall i \quad z_i = z_i']$ occurs with probability $\frac{1}{N^L}$: $\Pr[z' = z \mid \neg\text{repeat}_d] = \frac{1}{N^L}$. Finally, when [cyc] holds, $[\Sigma = 0]$ is equivalent to $\Sigma(c-c') = 0$, and [good $\vee$ bad] is equivalent to $[F_1(c) = F_1(c'), z' = z]$.

We define

$$p_{\text{good}} = \Pr[c=c', \neg\text{repeat}_c, \text{cyc}, \neg\text{repeat}_d, z'=z]$$

$$p_{\text{bad}} = \Pr\left[\neg(c=c'), F_1(c)=F_1(c'), \sum(c-c')=0, \neg\text{repeat}_c, \text{cyc}, \neg\text{repeat}_d, z'=z\right]$$

with obvious shorthands $[c = c']$, $[z' = z]$, $[F_1(c) = F_1(c')]$, $[\sum(c - c') = 0]$.

We upper bound $\frac{p_{\text{bad}}}{p_{\text{good}}}$ to compute p.

We have

$$
\begin{aligned}
p_{\text{good}} &= \Pr[c = c', \neg\text{repeat}_c, \text{cyc}, \neg\text{repeat}_d, z' = z] \\
&= \Pr\left[c = c', \neg\text{repeat}_c \sum d = \sum d', \text{cyc}, \neg\text{repeat}_d, z' = z\right] \\
&= \frac{1}{N^{2L-1}} \Pr[c = c', \neg\text{repeat}_c] \Pr\left[\sum d = \sum d', \neg\text{repeat}_d\right] \\
&= \frac{1}{N^{3L-1}} \frac{N(N-1)\cdots(N-L+1)}{N^L} \Pr\left[\sum d = \sum d', \neg\text{repeat}_d\right]
\end{aligned}
$$

$$
\begin{aligned}
p_{\text{bad}} &= \Pr\left[\neg(c=c'), F_1(c)=F_1(c'), \sum(c-c')=0, \neg\text{repeat}_c, \text{cyc}, \neg\text{repeat}_d, z'=z\right] \\
&= \Pr\left[\neg(c=c'), F_1(c)=F_1(c'), \sum(c-c')=0, \neg\text{repeat}_c \sum d=\sum d', \text{cyc}, \neg\text{repeat}_d, z'=z\right] \\
&= \frac{1}{N^{2L-1}} \Pr[\neg(c=c'), F_1(c)=F_1(c'), \sum(c-c')=0, \neg\text{repeat}_c] \Pr\left[\sum d=\sum d', \neg\text{repeat}_d\right]
\end{aligned}
$$

So,

$$\frac{p_{bad}}{p_{good}} = \frac{N^{2L}}{N(N-1)\cdots(N-L+1)} Pr\left[\neg(c=c'),F_1(c)=F_1(c'),\sum(c-c')=0,\neg repeat_c\right]$$

$$= \frac{N^{2L}}{N(N-1)\cdots(N-L+1)} \sum_{I\neq\emptyset} Pr\begin{bmatrix} \neg repeat_c \\ \forall i\notin I \quad c_i=c'_i \\ \forall i\in I \quad c_i\neq c'_i, F_1(c_i)=F_1(c'_i) \\ \sum_{i\in I}(c_i-c'_i)=0 \end{bmatrix}$$

$$\leqslant \frac{N^{2L}}{N(N-1)\cdots(N-L+1)} \sum_{I\neq\emptyset} Pr\begin{bmatrix} \neg repeat_c \text{ except } c'_{\max I} \\ \forall i\notin I \quad c_i=c'_i \\ \forall i\in I\setminus\{\max I\} \quad c_i\neq c'_i, F_1(c_i)=F_1(c'_i) \\ \sum_{i\in I}(c_i-c'_i)=0 \\ F_1(c_{\max I})=F_1(c'_{\max I}) \end{bmatrix}$$

$$= \frac{N^{2L}}{N(N-1)\cdots(N-L+1)} \sum_{I\neq\emptyset} \frac{N(N-1)\cdots(N-L-\#I)}{N^{2L+\#I}}$$

$$= \sum_{I\neq\emptyset} \frac{(N-L)(N-L-1)\cdots(N-L-\#I)}{N^{\#I}}$$

$$\leqslant \sum_{I\neq\emptyset} \frac{1}{N} = \frac{2^L-1}{N}$$

where $[\neg repeat_c \text{ except } c'_{\max I}]$ means

$$\begin{cases} \#\{c\} = L \\ \#\{c'_1,\ldots,c'_{\max I-1},c'_{\max I+1},\ldots,c'_L\} = L-1 \\ \forall i\forall j\neq \max I \; i\neq j \implies c_i\neq c'_j \end{cases}$$

By relaxing the constraints on $c'_{\max I}$, we can compute the probability of $\Sigma(c-c')=0$ conditioned to other events about c and c'. This probability is $\frac{1}{N}$.

Therefore,

$$\frac{p_{bad}}{p_{good}} \leqslant \frac{2^L-1}{N}$$

and we have

$$\frac{1}{1+\frac{p_{bad}}{p_{good}}} \geqslant \frac{1}{1+\frac{2^L-1}{N}}$$

$\square$

Insuperability of the Standard Versus Ideal Model Gap for Tweakable Blockcipher Security

Bart Mennink[1,2(✉)]

[1] Digital Security Group, Radboud University, Nijmegen, The Netherlands
b.mennink@cs.ru.nl
[2] CWI, Amsterdam, The Netherlands

Abstract. Two types of tweakable blockciphers based on classical blockciphers have been presented over the last years: non-tweak-rekeyable and tweak-rekeyable, depending on whether the tweak may influence the key input to the underlying blockcipher. In the former direction, the best possible security is conjectured to be $2^{\sigma n/(\sigma+1)}$, where n is the size of the blockcipher and σ is the number of blockcipher calls. In the latter direction, Mennink and Wang et al. presented optimally secure schemes, but only in the ideal cipher model. We investigate the possibility to construct a tweak-rekeyable cipher that achieves optimal security in the standard cipher model. As a first step, we note that all standard-model security results in literature implicitly rely on a generic standard-to-ideal transformation, that replaces all keyed blockcipher calls by random secret permutations, at the cost of the security of the blockcipher. Then, we prove that if this proof technique is adopted, tweak-rekeying will not help in achieving optimal security: if $2^{\sigma n/(\sigma+1)}$ is the best one can get *without* tweak-rekeying, optimal 2^n provable security *with* tweak-rekeying is impossible.

Keywords: Optimal security · Standard model · Ideal model · Impossibility · Tweakable blockciphers

1 Introduction

A blockcipher $E : \mathcal{K} \times \mathcal{M} \to \mathcal{M}$ is a family of permutations on $\mathcal{M}$ indexed by a key $k \in \mathcal{K}$. Tweakable blockciphers generalize over the classical ones by the additional input of a *tweak*. More detailed, a tweakable blockcipher $\widetilde{E} : \mathcal{K} \times \mathcal{T} \times \mathcal{M} \to \mathcal{M}$ satisfies the property that for every key $k \in \mathcal{K}$ and tweak $t \in \mathcal{T}$, $\widetilde{E}(k, t, \cdot)$ is a permutation on $\mathcal{M}$. The key is usually secret, but the tweak is a parameter that is known or even chosen by the user. In 2002, Liskov, Rivest, and Wagner [36] formalized the principle of tweakable blockciphers, and they have gained broad attention since then.

A well-established way of designing a tweakable blockcipher is by building it on top of a conventional blockcipher $E : \{0,1\}^n \times \{0,1\}^n \to \{0,1\}^n$, such

© International Association for Cryptologic Research 2017
J. Katz and H. Shacham (Eds.): CRYPTO 2017, Part II, LNCS 10402, pp. 708–732, 2017.
DOI: 10.1007/978-3-319-63715-0_24

as AES (other approaches will be discussed in Sect. 1.3). In their seminal work, Liskov et al. proposed two such constructions:

$$\mathsf{LRW1}(k, t, m) = E(k, E(k, m) \oplus t)\,, \tag{1}$$

$$\mathsf{LRW2}([k, h], t, m) = E(k, m \oplus h(t)) \oplus h(t)\,, \tag{2}$$

where for the latter scheme, h is a universal hash function taken from a family of hash functions H. Related to $\mathsf{LRW2}$ is Rogaway's XEX [50] and its generalizations by Chakraborty and Sarkar [15] and Minematsu [42]: these constructions replace the masking $h(t)$ by a tweaking function based on $E(k, \cdot)$, and therewith eliminate the use of h. All of these constructions, however, only achieve birthday bound $2^{n/2}$ security.

1.1 Quest for Beyond Birthday Bound Security

Various attempts have been made to achieve security beyond the birthday bound, and we identify two approaches: *non-tweak-rekeyable* schemes and *tweak-rekeyable* schemes. In a non-tweak-rekeyable scheme, the key inputs to the underlying block-ciphers are independent of the tweak, while in a tweak-rekeyable scheme, the tweak value may have an influence on the key input to the underlying blockcipher.

In the direction of non-tweak-rekeyable schemes, the state of the art centers around the security of $\sigma \geq 1$ round $\mathsf{LRW2}$:

$$\mathsf{LRW2}[\sigma]([\underline{k}, \underline{h}], t, m) = \mathsf{LRW2}([k_\sigma, h_\sigma], t, \cdots \mathsf{LRW2}([k_1, h_1], t, m) \cdots)\,,$$

where $\underline{k} = (k_1, \ldots, k_\sigma)$ are blockcipher keys and $\underline{h} = (h_1, \ldots, h_\sigma)$ instantiations of a universal hash function family H. Landecker et al. [35] and Procter [48] showed that this construction achieves approximately $2^{2n/3}$ security for two rounds, and Lampe and Seurin [34] proved security up to about $2^{\sigma n/(\sigma+2)}$ for an arbitrary even number of rounds. It is conjectured that this scheme achieves $2^{\sigma n/(\sigma+1)}$ security for any $\sigma \geq 1$ [34].

Tweak-rekeyable schemes on the other hand tend to achieve higher levels of security easier, but require a different model. Minematsu [43] introduced the following scheme:

$$\mathsf{Min}(k, t, m) = E(E(k, t \| 0^{n-\ell_t}), m)\,, \tag{3}$$

where ℓ_t denotes the length of the tweak, and proved that it achieves security up to $\max\{2^{n/2}, 2^{n-\ell_t}\}$. It is straightforward to derive an attack on Min matching this bound. Note that the scheme only achieves beyond birthday bound security if $\ell_t < n/2$. The tweak size can be elegantly extended using the XTX construction of Minematsu and Iwata [45] at the cost of an extra universal hash function evaluation.

Mennink [38] introduced two constructions based on one, resp. two, blockcipher calls (for $\mathsf{Men2}$ we use the adjusted function from the full version [39], see also Sect. 5.2):

$$\mathsf{Men1}(k, t, m) = E(k \oplus t, m \oplus z) \oplus z, \text{ where } z = k \otimes t\,, \tag{4}$$

$$\mathsf{Men2}(k, t, m) = E(k \oplus t, m \oplus z) \oplus z, \text{ where } z = E(2k, t)\,. \tag{5}$$

The former is proven secure up to about $2^{2n/3}$ queries, the latter approximately optimally 2^n secure. Wang et al. [56] generalized the approach of Mennink and derived a wide class of optimally secure schemes. However, on the downside, these constructions are all analyzed in the ideal cipher model, meaning that the underlying blockcipher is assumed to be perfectly random.

1.2 Optimal Security in Standard Model?

The usage of the ideal cipher model for tweakable blockciphers (and for symmetric-key schemes in general) can be considered controversial: the model is significantly stronger and allows for better security bounds, as evidenced by Mennink's and Wang et al.'s constructions. In this work, we investigate the distinction between the standard and ideal model for the case of tweakable blockciphers, and show the existence of an insuperable gap: whereas in the ideal model optimal security is possible fairly efficiently, we prove under reasonable assumptions that this cannot be achieved in the standard model.

Generic Standard-to-Ideal Reduction. All results on tweakable blockciphers in the standard cipher model [15, 34–36, 42, 43, 48, 50], implicitly rely on a generic standard-to-ideal reduction, where the keyed blockcipher calls are replaced with secret ideal permutations. This step usually costs $\mathbf{Adv}_{\Phi,E}^{\mathrm{srkprp}}(\mathcal{D})$, where $\mathcal{D}$ is some strong related-key PRP distinguisher with a certain amount of resources, usually q queries to the keyed oracle $E_{\phi(k)}$ and τ time, and Φ is the set of related-key deriving functions ϕ that $\mathcal{D}$ is allowed to choose. This reduction is in fact also broadly used beyond the area of tweakable blockciphers, such as in authenticated encryption schemes [1, 3, 11, 21, 28, 33, 37, 44, 50, 51] and message authentication codes [4, 13, 16, 24, 29, 30, 41, 47, 57–59], and in fact, we are not aware of any security result of a construction based on a standard-model blockcipher that uses a structurally different approach. Inspired by this, we investigate what level of tweakable blockcipher security can be achieved if this proof technique is employed.

Lower bound on $\mathbf{Adv}_{\Phi,E}^{\mathrm{srkprp}}(\mathcal{D})$. The generic reduction particularly means that $\mathbf{Adv}_{\Phi,E}^{\mathrm{srkprp}}(\mathcal{D})$ becomes a necessary term in the derivation, and we derive a lower bound on this advantage, i.e. to see how much the loss is.

Pivotal to the analysis is the set of related-key deriving functions Φ, which differs depending on the application. For instance, for LRW1 and LRW2 we would have $\Phi_{\mathsf{LRW}} = \{k \mapsto k\}$ and the cost of the reduction is simply the strong PRP security of E. For the cascade LRW2[σ], we would have

$$\Phi_{\mathsf{LRW2}[\sigma]} = \{\underline{k} \mapsto k_i \mid i \in \{1, \ldots, \sigma\}\}.$$

As the σ keys are independent this implies a reduction loss of σ times the strong PRP security of E (see also [34, 35]). In both cases, it is fair to assume that the strong PRP security of E is small. The situation gets more technical for tweak-rekeyable schemes. For Min and Men2 we would have larger sets of key-deriving functions:[1]

$$\Phi_{\mathsf{Min}} = \{k \mapsto E(k, t \| 0^{n-\ell_t}) \mid t \in \{0,1\}^{\ell_t}\},$$
$$\Phi_{\mathsf{Men2}} = \Phi_{\oplus} \cup \{k \mapsto 2k\} = \{k \mapsto k \oplus \delta \mid \delta \in \mathcal{K}\} \cup \{k \mapsto 2k\}.$$

If the size of Φ increases, the related-key insecurity increases. In more detail, we show that for *any* Φ and *any* E,

$$\mathbf{Adv}^{\mathrm{srkprp}}_{\Phi,E}(\mathcal{D}) \geq \Omega\left(\frac{\min\{q, |\Phi|\} \cdot r}{2^n}\right),$$

where $\mathcal{D}$ can make q related-key queries to $E_{\phi(k)}$ for random key k and has time to make r offline evaluations of E. (The bound is in fact a bit more fine-grained, cf. Proposition 1, but above simplification is adequate for a proper understanding of the result, and for $\Phi = \Phi_{\mathsf{Min}}$ and $\Phi = \Phi_{\mathsf{Men2}}$ above bound matches the one of Proposition 1.)

For Min, this bound entails a "minimal loss" of $\min\{q, 2^{\ell_t}\} \cdot r/2^n$, a term which in hindsight perfectly explains the security level of Min. For Men2 the loss is even worse: $q \cdot r/2^n$. (Also if the "subkey" $2k$ in Men2 is replaced by an independent key k', the same loss applies.) Concretely, this means that the usage of the generic standard-to-ideal reduction entails impossibility of beyond birthday bound security on Men2. Clearly, this does not invalidate the security of Men2: this negative result is purely due to the lossiness of the generic reduction.

This issue is in fact not new: already in 1998, Bellare et al. encountered it in their seminal paper on Luby-Rackoff backwards [8], and reverted to an analysis in the ideal cipher model. A formal treatment of the situation, however, has not been given. The issue also appeared for schemes based on primitives other than blockciphers. Most prominently, the security of the HMAC message authentication code is based on the PRF security of the underlying function [5,6]. As recently argued by Gaži et al. [23], this standard-model approach might be too pessimistic, and [25] approached the security of HMAC in the ideal compression function model.

Generalized Impossibility. We additionally demonstrate that the issue is not specific to Men2, but applies to a broad spectrum of schemes. In more detail, we consider a generalized construction of a tweakable blockcipher based on a blockcipher, and show that, if the generic standard-to-ideal reduction is employed, achieving optimal standard-model security *with* tweak-rekeying is at least as hard as *without* tweak-rekeying. Given the state of the art on non-tweak-rekeyable schemes, and particularly the conjecture on LRW2[σ], this shines a negative

---

[1] The generic reduction does not directly apply to Men1 as the same key is used for masking and encrypting, making the usage of the underlying cipher and the overlying mode mutually dependent. This is usually resolved by using two independent keys, such as in LRW2. In this case, $\Phi_{\mathsf{Men1}} = \Phi_{\oplus}$.

light on the possibility to find a tweakable blockcipher that is secure in the standard cipher model. Note that the result does not imply that the generic standard-to-ideal reduction is unavoidable, nor that optimal security cannot be achieved, but *if* this reduction is employed and *if* the conjecture on LRW2[σ] is true, optimality seems impossible for this generalized class of functions. The approach followed for this impossibility result may be generalizable to different types of primitives.

Discussion. It is reasonable to question the relevance of any result in any of both models (other questions are discussed in detail in Sect. 8). It appears that, while the ideal-model results may sometimes be a bit too promising, standard-model results may be extremely loose. This is for instance the case for Men2, where the ideal-model results seem more representative than the standard-model ones. A similar observation was made by Shrimpton and Terashima [55], who introduce the ideal model under key-oblivious access as a weakened version of the ideal cipher model. As a general rule, it is always wise to interpret security results in any of the models with care.

1.3   Other Ways of Tweakable Blockcipher Design

We briefly elaborate on approaches to tweakable blockcipher design, other than constructing them from conventional blockciphers. One approach is to build them "from scratch," as is done for the Hasty Pudding Cipher [53], Mercy [20], Threefish [22], and TWEAKEY [31]. This approach, however, does not allow for any reductionist security argument. Goldenberg et al. [26] and Mitsuda and Iwata [46] transformed generalized Feistel schemes into tweakable generalized Feistel schemes. These constructions only achieve birthday bound security. A novel approach is to build tweakable blockciphers from public permutations, as is done by Sasaki et al. [52], Cogliati et al. [17,18], Granger et al. [27], and Mennink [40]. This approach achieves comparable levels of security to the non-tweak-rekeyable schemes of above, but the security analysis is inherently done in the ideal permutation model.

1.4   Outline

Our model and the security of (tweakable) blockciphers are formalized in Sect. 2. In Sect. 3 we define what we consider a reduction and what we mean with optimal security. This section also includes a formalization of the generic standard-to-ideal reduction. We derive a lower bound on the strong related-key PRP security in Sect. 4. We revisit LRW2 and Men2 using these formalizations and results in Sect. 5. In Sect. 6 we present a generalized tweakable blockcipher design, and in Sect. 7 we derive our impossibility result on the optimal security of a generalized tweakable blockcipher. We present an elaborate discussion of the results in Sect. 8.

2   Notation and Model

For a positive integer n, $\{0,1\}^n$ denotes the set of bit strings of length n. If $\mathcal{X}$ is some set, $x \xleftarrow{\$} \mathcal{X}$ denotes the uniformly random drawing of x from $\mathcal{X}$. The size of $\mathcal{X}$ is denoted by $|\mathcal{X}|$.

2.1   Blockciphers

A blockcipher $E : \mathcal{K} \times \mathcal{M} \to \mathcal{M}$ is a mapping such that for every key $k \in \mathcal{K}$, $E_k(\cdot) = E(k, \cdot)$ is a permutation on $\mathcal{M}$. For fixed k, its inverse is denoted by $E_k^{-1}(\cdot)$. We denote by $\mathsf{BC}(\mathcal{K}, \mathcal{M})$ the set of all such blockciphers. Letting $\mathsf{P}(\mathcal{M})$ be the set of all permutations on $\mathcal{M}$, the strong PRP security of E is defined as

$$\mathbf{Adv}_E^{\mathrm{sprp}}(\mathcal{D}) = \left| \mathbf{Pr}\left(\mathcal{D}^{E_k^{\pm}} = 1 \right) - \mathbf{Pr}\left(\mathcal{D}^{\pi^{\pm}} = 1 \right) \right| ,$$

where the probabilities are over $k \xleftarrow{\$} \mathcal{K}$ and $\pi \xleftarrow{\$} \mathsf{P}(\mathcal{M})$, and the random coins of $\mathcal{D}$. Distinguisher $\mathcal{D}$ is typically bounded to have limited resources, such as τ time and q queries to its oracle.

We will consider a generalized security notion that captures the case where a distinguisher can perform related-key attacks. We follow the theoretical framework of Bellare and Kohno [7] and its generalization to tweakable blockciphers by Cogliati and Seurin [19]. Let Φ be a set of permitted related-key deriving functions that map $\mathcal{K}' \to \mathcal{K}$. Define the function $\mathrm{rk}[E] : \mathcal{K}' \times \Phi \times \mathcal{M} \to \mathcal{M}$ as

$$\mathrm{rk}[E](k, \phi, m) = E(\phi(k), m) .$$

Note that $\mathrm{rk}[E]$ is invertible for fixed (k, ϕ), and the inverse is defined the straightforward way. The strong related-key PRP security of E is defined as

$$\mathbf{Adv}_{\Phi,E}^{\mathrm{srkprp}}(\mathcal{D}) = \left| \mathbf{Pr}\left(\mathcal{D}^{\mathrm{rk}[E]_k^{\pm}} = 1 \right) - \mathbf{Pr}\left(\mathcal{D}^{\mathrm{rk}[rE]_k^{\pm}} = 1 \right) \right| ,$$

where the probabilities are over $k \xleftarrow{\$} \mathcal{K}'$ and $rE \xleftarrow{\$} \mathsf{BC}(\mathcal{K}, \mathcal{M})$, and the random coins of $\mathcal{D}$. Distinguisher $\mathcal{D}$ is typically bounded to have limited resources, such as τ time and q queries to its oracle.

Note that, for the sake of generality, the definition explicitly allows the domain $\mathcal{K}'$ and range $\mathcal{K}$ of the function ϕ to be distinct, although in many cases one simply has $\mathcal{K}' = \mathcal{K}$. If $\mathcal{K}' = \mathcal{K}$ and $\Phi = \{k \mapsto k\}$, the definition of related-key security boils down to the classical definition: $\mathbf{Adv}_{\{k \mapsto k\},E}^{\mathrm{srkprp}}(\mathcal{D}) = \mathbf{Adv}_E^{\mathrm{sprp}}(\mathcal{D})$. Another famous set of related-key deriving functions is $\Phi_{\oplus} = \{k \mapsto k \oplus \delta \mid \delta \in \mathcal{K}\}$. The set may also include more involved functions, e.g., ones that internally rely on evaluations of E as well [2]. Throughout, for any set Φ, we assume that it never contains two identical functions, and we denote by $|\Phi|$ the number of functions in the set.

2.2   Tweakable Blockciphers

A tweakable blockcipher $\widetilde{E} : \mathcal{K} \times \mathcal{T} \times \mathcal{M} \to \mathcal{M}$ is a mapping such that for every $k \in \mathcal{K}$ and every tweak $t \in \mathcal{T}$, the function $\widetilde{E}_k(t, \cdot) = \widetilde{E}(k, t, \cdot)$ is a permutation on $\mathcal{M}$. Like before, its inverse is denoted as $\widetilde{E}_k^{-1}(\cdot, \cdot)$. Let $\widetilde{\mathsf{P}}(\mathcal{T}, \mathcal{M})$ consist of all functions $\widetilde{\pi} : \mathcal{T} \times \mathcal{M} \to \mathcal{M}$ such that for all $t \in \mathcal{T}$, $\widetilde{\pi}(t, \cdot) \in \mathsf{P}(\mathcal{M})$. We define the *standard-model* strong tweakable-PRP security of $\widetilde{E}$ as

$$\mathbf{Adv}_{\widetilde{E}}^{\text{s-}\widetilde{\text{sprp}}}(\mathcal{D}) = \left| \mathbf{Pr}\left(\mathcal{D}^{\widetilde{E}_k^{\pm}} = 1\right) - \mathbf{Pr}\left(\mathcal{D}^{\widetilde{\pi}^{\pm}} = 1\right) \right| ,$$

where probabilities are over $k \xleftarrow{\$} \mathcal{K}$ and $\widetilde{\pi} \xleftarrow{\$} \widetilde{\mathsf{P}}(\mathcal{T}, \mathcal{M})$, and the random coins of $\mathcal{D}$. As before, $\mathcal{D}$ is typically bounded to operate in τ time and q queries to its oracle.

This definition applies to an arbitrary tweakable cipher $\widetilde{E}$. The q queries are solely made to $\widetilde{E}_k^{\pm}$ or $\widetilde{\pi}^{\pm}$, and the time τ can be spent at the distinguisher's discretion. Suppose $\widetilde{E}$ uses a blockcipher E as underlying primitive. If we denote by τ_E the uniform time needed for one evaluation of E, the distinguisher can evaluate this underlying cipher at most $r := \tau/\tau_E$ times. Assuming this blockcipher E does not show underlying weaknesses, we can consider an abstraction of the model and consider the distinguisher to be information-theoretic and to have query access to E and $\widetilde{E}_k^{\pm}$. The approach is also known as the ideal model [9,14,54]. More formally, we define the *ideal-model* strong tweakable-PRP security of $\widetilde{E}$ based on E as

$$\mathbf{Adv}_{\widetilde{E}}^{\text{i-}\widetilde{\text{sprp}}}(\mathcal{D}) = \left| \mathbf{Pr}\left(\mathcal{D}^{\widetilde{E}_k^{\pm}, E^{\pm}} = 1\right) - \mathbf{Pr}\left(\mathcal{D}^{\widetilde{\pi}^{\pm}, E^{\pm}} = 1\right) \right| ,$$

where the probabilities are over $k \xleftarrow{\$} \mathcal{K}$, $E \xleftarrow{\$} \mathsf{BC}(\mathcal{K}, \mathcal{M})$, and $\widetilde{\pi} \xleftarrow{\$} \widetilde{\mathsf{P}}(\mathcal{T}, \mathcal{M})$, and the random coins of $\mathcal{D}$. Distinguisher $\mathcal{D}$ is typically bounded to make q queries to its first (construction) oracle and r queries to its second (primitive) oracle.

3   Formalization of Reduction and Optimality

Formalization of Reduction. In order to formally argue about reductionist security of tweakable blockciphers to classical blockciphers, we first settle our definition of a reductionist proof.

Definition 1. *Let $\widetilde{E}$ be a tweakable blockcipher that internally uses a dedicated blockcipher E. We say that the strong tweakable-PRP security of $\widetilde{E}$ reduces to the strong related-key PRP security of E if for any s-$\widetilde{\text{sprp}}$ distinguisher $\mathcal{D}$ there exists an rk-sprp distinguisher $\mathcal{D}'$ with comparable resources such that*

$$\mathbf{Adv}_{\widetilde{E}}^{\text{s-}\widetilde{\text{sprp}}}(\mathcal{D}) \leq \delta \cdot \mathbf{Adv}_{\Phi, E}^{\text{srkprp}}(\mathcal{D}') + \varepsilon ,$$

where Φ is some set of related-key deriving functions depending on the design of $\widetilde{E}$, δ a small constant, and ε is a term negligible in the security parameter of $\widetilde{E}$.

All existing standard-model security proofs on tweakable blockciphers from classical blockciphers [15, 34–36, 42, 43, 48, 50] derive a reductionist bound of the form of Definition 1. Even stronger, all of these results *implicitly* rely on a generic standard-to-ideal reduction which we formalize in below lemma.

Lemma 1 (Generic Standard-to-Ideal Reduction). *Let $\widetilde{E}$ be a tweakable blockcipher that internally uses a dedicated blockcipher E. Assume that $\widetilde{E}$ makes ρ calls to its underlying E and let Φ denote the set of all related-key deriving functions under which E is evaluated. For any* s-$\widetilde{\text{sprp}}$ *distinguisher $\mathcal{D}$,*

$$\mathbf{Adv}_{\widetilde{E}}^{\text{s-}\widetilde{\text{sprp}}}(\mathcal{D}) \leq \mathbf{Adv}_{\Phi,E}^{\text{srkprp}}(\mathcal{D}') + \mathbf{Adv}_{\widetilde{E}}^{\text{i-}\widetilde{\text{sprp}}}(\mathcal{D}''),$$

where $\mathcal{D}'$ is a distinguisher making at most $\rho \cdot q$ queries and running in time τ, and $\mathcal{D}''$ is an information-theoretic distinguisher making at most q queries to its construction oracle and 0 queries to its primitive oracle.

Proof. The proof follows a simple hybrid argument: first replace the underlying blockcipher evaluations by a random blockcipher $rE \xleftarrow{\$} \mathsf{BC}(\mathcal{K}, \mathcal{M})$. This step costs us $\mathbf{Adv}_{\Phi,E}^{\text{srkprp}}(\mathcal{D}')$. For the remaining analysis of $\mathbf{Adv}_{\widetilde{E}}^{\text{s-}\widetilde{\text{sprp}}}(\mathcal{D})$ with E replaced with secret rE: the distinguisher has no access to $\text{rk}[rE]_k$ as it does not know k nor rE. Therefore, we can safely assume it has unbounded computational power, and transform it to an information-theoretic adversary that is not allowed to query the underlying primitive. Hence, we obtain the term $\mathbf{Adv}_{\widetilde{E}}^{\text{i-}\widetilde{\text{sprp}}}(\mathcal{D}'')$ where $\mathcal{D}''$ has resources $(q, 0)$. $\qquad\square$

We remark that in Definition 1 and Lemma 1, the set of related-key deriving functions Φ depends on the tweakable blockcipher. In many cases, Φ just consists of the identity function, $\Phi = \{k \mapsto k\}$, in which case the related-key security boils down to the classical strong PRP security. This is for example the case for LRW1 and LRW2, cf. Theorem 1 in Sect. 5. An example of a more elaborate set of key-deriving functions is $\Phi_{\oplus}$, cf. Theorem 3 in Sect. 5.

We furthermore remark that Lemma 1 consists of a somewhat pessimistic bounding: the distinguishers $\mathcal{D}'$ and $\mathcal{D}''$ are in fact constructed from $\mathcal{D}$, and a more accurate bounding would be of the form

$$\mathbf{Adv}_{\widetilde{E}}^{\text{s-}\widetilde{\text{sprp}}}(\mathcal{D}) \leq \mathbf{Adv}_{\Phi,E}^{\text{srkprp}}(\mathcal{D}'[\mathcal{D}]) + \mathbf{Adv}_{\widetilde{E}}^{\text{i-}\widetilde{\text{sprp}}}(\mathcal{D}''[\mathcal{D}]).$$

In the context of Lemma 1, one would usually maximize both sides of the inequality over all possible distinguishers $\mathcal{D}, \mathcal{D}', \mathcal{D}''$, while in the more accurate bounding one would simply maximize both sides over $\mathcal{D}$. In other words, the bound of Lemma 1 gives a slightly more pessimistic result, but nevertheless, it exactly covers the reduction that is implicitly used in the proofs of [15, 34–36, 42, 43, 48, 50].

Beyond this list of tweakable blockcipher results, the reduction of Lemma 1 in fact finds implicit use in myriad other blockcipher based cryptographic designs, including various authenticated encryption schemes [1, 3, 11, 21, 28, 33, 37, 44, 50, 51] and message authentication codes [4, 13, 16, 24, 29, 30, 41, 47, 57–59]. We are not aware of any security result of a construction based on a standard-model blockcipher that does not follow this reduction but that uses a structurally different approach.

Optimality. We additionally define what we mean with an optimally secure $\widetilde{E}$.

Definition 2. *Let $\widetilde{E}$ be a tweakable blockcipher that internally uses a dedicated blockcipher E. We say that it is optimally standard/ideal-model secure if for any distinguisher $\mathcal{D}$ making q queries to its construction oracle and r evaluations of the primitive (where in the standard model, $r = \tau/\tau_E$):*

$$\mathbf{Adv}_{\widetilde{E}}^{\mathrm{s/i\text{-}\widetilde{sprp}}}(\mathcal{D}) \leq \frac{const \cdot \max\{q, r\}}{\min\{|\mathcal{K}|, |\mathcal{M}|\}},$$

for some small constant const.

The term $r/|\mathcal{K}|$ corresponds to recovering the key for $\widetilde{E}$; apart from that, the bound is rather arbitrary and conservative to maintain generality. We refer to Bellare and Rogaway [10, Sect. 3.6] for an informal justification of the bound. We refer to Bernstein and Lange [12] for an interesting discussion on the heuristic existence of hard-to-find attackers.

4   Lower Bound on the Strong Related-Key PRP Security

We will derive a lower bound on the strong related-key PRP security of an arbitrary blockcipher E for any set of key-deriving functions Φ, demonstrating that it can always be distinguished from a random blockcipher up to approximately the birthday bound (apart from various technicalities). Earlier lower bounds, for instance by Bellare and Kohno [7], targeted *specific* sets Φ, but it turns out that the problem gets significantly harder if an *arbitrary* set of key-deriving functions is considered. This is in part attributed to the fact that the lower bound would depend on certain structural properties of Φ.

For a set of key-deriving functions Φ and a key $k \in \mathcal{K}$, we write $\Phi(k) = \{\phi(k) \mid \phi \in \Phi\}$. We denote by $\mathbf{Ex}\left(|\Phi(k)|\right)$ the expected size of the set $\Phi(k)$, where the randomness is taken over the choice of $k \xleftarrow{\$} \mathcal{K}$.

Proposition 1. *Consider a blockcipher $E : \mathcal{K} \times \mathcal{M} \to \mathcal{M}$, and denote by τ_E the uniform time needed for one evaluation of E. Let Φ be a set of related-key deriving functions. There exists a distinguisher $\mathcal{D}$ making q queries and operating in about τ time, such that*

$$\mathbf{Adv}_{\Phi,E}^{\mathrm{srkprp}}(\mathcal{D}) \geq \max_{\Phi' \subseteq \Phi, |\Phi'|=q'} \frac{\mathbf{Ex}\left(|\Phi'(k)|\right) \cdot r'}{2|\mathcal{K}|} - \frac{1}{|\mathcal{M}|-1},$$

where $q' = \min\{q - 1, |\Phi|\}$ and $r' = \tau/\tau_E - 1$, which are required to satisfy $q' \cdot r' \leq |\mathcal{K}|$.

Proof. Let $k \xleftarrow{\$} \mathcal{K}$ be the secret key used to instantiate the distinguisher's oracle.

Let $\Phi' = \{\phi_1, \ldots, \phi_{q'}\} \subseteq \Phi$ be any subset of Φ of size q'. We construct distinguisher $\mathcal{D}_{\Phi'}$ as follows. Denote its oracle by $\mathcal{O}_k \in \{\mathrm{rk}[E]_k, \mathrm{rk}[rE]_k\}$.

(i) Fix any $m \in \mathcal{M}$;

(ii) Let $\mathcal{K}' = \{l_1, \ldots, l_{r'}\} \overset{\$}{\subseteq} \mathcal{K}$ be a set of randomly drawn key values;

(iii) For $i = 1, \ldots, q'$, query $c_i \leftarrow \mathcal{O}_k(\phi_i, m)$;

(iv) For $j = 1, \ldots, r'$, evaluate $y_j \leftarrow E(l_j, m)$;

(v) If for some i, j we have $c_i = y_j$:

- Fix any $m' \in \mathcal{M}\backslash\{m\}$;
- Query $c_i' \leftarrow \mathcal{O}_k(\phi_i, m')$ and evaluate $y_j' \leftarrow E(l_j, m')$;
- If $c_i' = y_j'$, return 1;

(vi) Return 0.

Remains to bound the success probability of $\mathcal{D}_{\Phi'}$. Recall that

$$\mathbf{Adv}_{\Phi,E}^{\mathrm{srkprp}}(\mathcal{D}_{\Phi'}) \geq \mathbf{Pr}\left(\mathcal{D}_{\Phi'}^{\mathrm{rk}[E]_k^{\pm}} = 1\right) - \mathbf{Pr}\left(\mathcal{D}_{\Phi'}^{\mathrm{rk}[rE]_k^{\pm}} = 1\right), \tag{6}$$

and we will analyze these probabilities separately.

Starting with first probability of (6), if $\phi_i(k) = l_j$ for some (i, j), then we necessarily have $c_i = y_j$ and $c_i' = y_j'$. Therefore,

$$\mathbf{Pr}\left(\mathcal{D}_{\Phi'}^{\mathrm{rk}[E]_k^{\pm}} = 1\right) \geq \mathbf{Pr}\left(\exists l \in \Phi'(k) \; : \; l \in \mathcal{K}'\right)$$

$$= \sum_{\mathcal{L} \subseteq \mathcal{K}} \mathbf{Pr}\left(\exists l \in \mathcal{L} \; : \; l \in \mathcal{K}' \mid \Phi'(k) = \mathcal{L}\right) \mathbf{Pr}\left(\Phi'(k) = \mathcal{L}\right). \tag{7}$$

Note that two independent sources of randomness are involved: the drawing of the key $k \overset{\$}{\leftarrow} \mathcal{K}$ and the generation of random subset $\mathcal{K}' \overset{\$}{\subseteq} \mathcal{K}$. We proceed with the first probability of (7) for any fixed $\mathcal{L}$ of size at most q'. Via the inclusion-exclusion principle, Bonferroni's inequality states

$$\mathbf{Pr}\left(\exists l \in \mathcal{L} \; : \; l \in \mathcal{K}' \mid \Phi'(k) = \mathcal{L}\right)$$

$$= \sum_{\beta=1}^{q'} (-1)^{\beta-1} \sum_{\substack{\mathcal{L}' \subseteq \mathcal{L} \\ |\mathcal{L}'| = \beta}} \mathbf{Pr}\left(\forall l \in \mathcal{L}' \; : \; l \in \mathcal{K}' \mid \Phi'(k) = \mathcal{L}\right)$$

$$\geq \sum_{l \in \mathcal{L}} \mathbf{Pr}\left(l \in \mathcal{K}' \mid \Phi'(k) = \mathcal{L}\right) - \sum_{\substack{l, l' \in \mathcal{L} \\ l \neq l'}} \mathbf{Pr}\left(l, l' \in \mathcal{K}' \mid \Phi'(k) = \mathcal{L}\right) \tag{8}$$

$$= \sum_{l \in \mathcal{L}} \frac{r}{|\mathcal{K}|} - \sum_{\substack{l, l' \in \mathcal{L} \\ l \neq l'}} \frac{\binom{r}{2}}{\binom{|\mathcal{K}|}{2}} = \frac{|\mathcal{L}| \cdot r'}{|\mathcal{K}|} - \frac{\binom{|\mathcal{L}|}{2}\binom{r'}{2}}{\binom{|\mathcal{K}|}{2}} \geq \frac{|\mathcal{L}| \cdot r'}{2|\mathcal{K}|},$$

as $q', r' \geq 1$ and $q' \cdot r' \leq |\mathcal{K}|$. This gives for (7):

$$\mathbf{Pr}\left(\mathcal{D}_{\Phi'}^{\mathrm{rk}[E]_k^{\pm}} = 1\right) \geq \sum_{\mathcal{L} \subseteq \mathcal{K}} \frac{|\mathcal{L}| \cdot r'}{2|\mathcal{K}|} \mathbf{Pr}\left(\Phi'(k) = \mathcal{L}\right) = \frac{\mathbf{Ex}\left(|\Phi'(k)|\right) \cdot r'}{2|\mathcal{K}|}.$$

For the second probability of (6), focus on the indices (i, j) for which the if-clause is evaluated. We have

$$\mathbf{Pr}\left(\mathcal{D}_{\Phi'}^{\mathrm{rk}[rE]_k^{\pm}} = 1\right) \leq \mathbf{Pr}\left(c_i' = y_j' \mid c_i = y_j\right) = \frac{1}{|\mathcal{M}| - 1},$$

using that rE is a random permutation.

We thus obtain from (6):

$$\mathbf{Adv}_{\Phi,E}^{\mathrm{srkprp}}(\mathcal{D}_{\Phi'}) \geq \frac{\mathbf{Ex}\left(|\Phi'(k)|\right) \cdot r'}{2|\mathcal{K}|} - \frac{1}{|\mathcal{M}| - 1}.$$

Note that this bound holds for every choice of Φ'. The claim of Proposition 1 is satisfied for $\mathcal{D} = \mathcal{D}_{\Phi''}$, where

$$\Phi'' = \underset{\Phi' \subseteq \Phi, |\Phi'| = q'}{\mathrm{argmax}} \ \mathbf{Ex}\left(|\Phi'(k)|\right). \qquad \square$$

We remark that the bounding of $\mathbf{Pr}\left(\mathcal{D}_{\Phi'}^{\mathrm{rk}[E]_k^{\pm}} = 1\right)$ could be improved (i) by involving more terms of the inclusion-exclusion principle in (8), and (ii) for specific sets of key-deriving functions Φ, by choosing Φ' and $\mathcal{K}'$ more smartly. For instance, for $\Phi = \Phi_{\oplus}$, the bound reads

$$\mathbf{Pr}\left(\mathcal{D}_{\Phi'}^{\mathrm{rk}[E]_k^{\pm}} = 1\right) \geq \frac{q' \cdot r'}{2|\mathcal{K}|},$$

because $\mathbf{Ex}\left(|\Phi'(k)|\right) = q'$ for $\Phi' \subseteq \Phi_{\oplus}$ of size q'. It is a straightforward exercise to verify that, for a smart choice of Φ' and $\mathcal{K}'$, the probability can be pulled up to $\frac{q' \cdot r'}{|\mathcal{K}|}$. Nevertheless, the bound of Proposition 1 suffices for our purposes.

We furthermore remark that the attack of Bellare and Kohno [7] for $\Phi = \Phi_{\oplus} \cup \Phi_{+}$ is better than the one resulting from Proposition 1. In fact, their attack exploits potential collisions in Φ, rather than preimages. A generalization of Proposition 1 to cover attacks of this kind is beyond the scope of this paper. Nevertheless, we think that it is an interesting problem to derive a generalized *tight* attack on any E and for any Φ, or at least a generalized attack that covers Proposition 1, the attack of Bellare and Kohno, and more.

5   Examples

We discuss two state-of-the-art examples: one from Liskov et al. [36], and one from Mennink [38].

5.1   Liskov et al.'s Scheme

In their original work [36], Liskov et al. introduced two tweakable blockcipher constructions, both achieving approximately $2^{n/2}$ security. We consider the construction that is based on two keys: $k \in \{0, 1\}^n$ and h coming from a universal hash function family H (see also Fig. 1):

$$\mathsf{LRW2}([k, h], t, m) = E(k, m \oplus z) \oplus z, \text{ where } z = h(t).$$

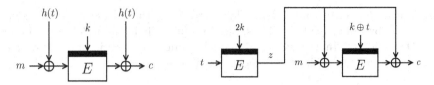

Fig. 1. Tweakable blockcipher LRW2   **Fig. 2.** Tweakable blockcipher Men2

Follow-up results analyzed the security of a cascade of more than one independent LRW2's [34,35,48]; the currently outlined example directly generalizes to these results.

Theorem 1 (Liskov et al. [36], Minematsu [42]). *Let $n \geq 1$, and let H be an ε-almost 2-XOR-universal hash function family.*[2] *Let $\mathcal{D}$ be a distinguisher making at most q construction queries and running in time τ. Then,*

$$\mathbf{Adv}_{\mathsf{LRW2}}^{\mathsf{s\text{-}\widetilde{sprp}}}(\mathcal{D}) \leq \mathbf{Adv}_E^{\mathsf{sprp}}(\mathcal{D}') + \varepsilon q^2 \,,$$

where $\mathcal{D}'$ is a distinguisher making at most q queries and running in time τ.

Note that the strong tweakable-PRP security of LRW2 reduces to the strong PRP security of E in the terminology of Definition 1. The implicit presence of the generic standard-to-ideal reduction of Lemma 1 is obvious from the bound. The term εq^2 is the security bound for LRW2 if the underlying blockcipher is replaced with an ideal secret permutation π.

5.2 Mennink's Scheme

Mennink [38,39] recently introduced two tweak-rekeyable tweakable blockciphers and analyzed them in the ideal cipher model. One of the constructions is the following (see also Fig. 2):

$$\mathsf{Men2}(k,t,m) = E(k \oplus t, m \oplus z) \oplus z, \text{ where } z = E(2k,t)\,.$$

Note that we have taken the adjusted scheme from the full version [39], where the masking is done with key $2k$ instead of k. This adjustment was introduced in order to resolve a simple oversight in the proof as pointed out by Wang et al. [56]. Mennink [39] showed that this (adjusted) scheme Men2 achieves approximately 2^n security. We remark that Wang et al. generalized the approach to designing optimally secure tweakable blockciphers. The currently outlined example directly generalizes to the constructions of [56].

Theorem 2 (Mennink [38,39]). *Let $n \geq 1$. Let $\mathcal{D}$ be a distinguisher making at most q construction queries and r primitive queries. Then,*

$$\mathbf{Adv}_{\mathsf{Men2}}^{\mathsf{i\text{-}\widetilde{sprp}}}(\mathcal{D}) \leq \frac{q+r}{2^n} + \frac{2qr}{(2^n - q)(2^n - q - r)}\,.$$

---

[2] A hash function family $H : \mathcal{K} \times \mathcal{X} \to \mathcal{Y}$ is called ε-almost 2-XOR-universal if for all distinct $x, x' \in \mathcal{X}$ and $y \in \mathcal{Y}$, $\mathbf{Pr}\left(h \xleftarrow{\$} \mathcal{K} \ : \ h(x) \oplus h(x') = y \right) \leq \varepsilon$ [32,49].

It is easy to verify that for $\max\{q, r\} \leq 2^n/4$, the advantage can be upper bounded by $4 \max\{q, r\}/2^n$. Thus, Men2 is optimally ideal-model secure in terms of Definition 2. In the standard model, using the generic transformation of Lemma 1 and the definition of Φ_{Men2} from Sect. 1,

$$\Phi_{\mathsf{Men2}} = \Phi_\oplus \cup \{k \mapsto 2k\} = \{k \mapsto k \oplus \delta \mid \delta \in \mathcal{K}\} \cup \{k \mapsto 2k\},$$

one can obtain the following result on Men2:

Theorem 3. *Let $n \geq 1$. Let $\mathcal{D}$ be a distinguisher making at most q construction queries and running in time τ. Then,*

$$\mathbf{Adv}_{\mathsf{Men2}}^{\mathrm{s\text{-}\widetilde{sprp}}}(\mathcal{D}) \leq \mathbf{Adv}_{\Phi_{\mathsf{Men2}}, E}^{\mathrm{srkprp}}(\mathcal{D}') + \frac{q}{2^n},$$

where $\mathcal{D}'$ is a distinguisher making at most $2q$ queries and running in time τ.

Proof. By Lemma 1, we have

$$\mathbf{Adv}_{\mathsf{Men2}}^{\mathrm{s\text{-}\widetilde{sprp}}}(\mathcal{D}) \leq \mathbf{Adv}_{\Phi_{\mathsf{Men2}}, E}^{\mathrm{srkprp}}(\mathcal{D}') + \mathbf{Adv}_{\mathsf{Men2}}^{\mathrm{i\text{-}\widetilde{sprp}}}(\mathcal{D}''),$$

where $\mathcal{D}'$ is a distinguisher making at most $2q$ queries and runs in time τ, and $\mathcal{D}''$ an information-theoretic distinguisher making at most q queries to its construction oracle and $r = 0$ queries to its primitive oracle. By Theorem 2, we have $\mathbf{Adv}_{\mathsf{Men2}}^{\mathrm{i\text{-}\widetilde{sprp}}}(\mathcal{D}'') \leq \frac{q}{2^n}$. $\qquad\square$

While the bound of Theorem 3 seems to improve over the one of Theorem 2, this is not the case. Indeed, by the remark *after* Proposition 1:

$$\mathbf{Adv}_{\Phi_{\mathsf{Men2}}, E}^{\mathrm{srkprp}}(\mathcal{D}') \geq \mathbf{Adv}_{\Phi_\oplus, E}^{\mathrm{srkprp}}(\mathcal{D}') \geq \frac{(2q-1)(r-1)}{|\mathcal{K}|} - \frac{1}{2^n - 1} = \Omega\left(\frac{qr}{|\mathcal{K}|}\right),$$

contradictory implying that Men2 *cannot be provably optimally standard-model secure if the standard-to-ideal reduction is used.* However, the attack of Proposition 1 to break the strong RK-security of E for related-key deriving functions $\Phi_\oplus$ *does not apply* to Men2: its in- and output of E themselves are masked via a key. A way to resolve this discrepancy would be to include the maskings *within* the definition of related-key security, say the "strong masked related-key PRP" but such a security notion would in fact be equivalent to the strong tweakable-PRP security of Men2. It would be like reducing the security of $E = \mathsf{AES}$ to the "AES-security" of E.

We note that in case one uses Men2 with two independent keys, i.e., replacing $2k$ with independent key k', a comparable reasoning to that of Theorem 3 gives bound

$$\mathbf{Adv}_{\mathsf{Men2}}^{\mathrm{s\text{-}\widetilde{sprp}}}(\mathcal{D}) \leq \mathbf{Adv}_{\Phi_\oplus, E}^{\mathrm{srkprp}}(\mathcal{D}') + \mathbf{Adv}_E^{\mathrm{sprp}}(\mathcal{D}'') + \frac{q}{2^n},$$

where $\mathcal{D}'$ and $\mathcal{D}''$ are distinguishers making at most q queries and running in time τ. The same reasoning as before subsequently applies.

6   Generalized Tweakable Blockcipher Design

We consider a generalized tweakable blockcipher $\widetilde{E}$ based on a classical block-cipher E. It follows the generic design of valid tweakable blockciphers by Mennink [38], with two differences. First, for simplicity and sake of presentation, we separate the number of calls to E into ρ message-independent calls and σ message-dependent calls, where ρ and σ are constants independent of the security parameter n. This is without loss of generality, looking back at the formalization of [38] and the assumption that $\widetilde{E}$ processes the data m "as a whole." Second, we will explicitly use two different keys k^a and k^b: k^b is only used in the key inputs to E and k^a is only used in the masking (and indirectly in the data inputs to E).[3] We remark that our description is equivalent to the one of [38] if we set $k^a = k^b$. In the generic design we consider tweaks of size n bits. The generic construction easily generalizes to arbitrarily sized tweaks, but our impossibility result of Sect. 7 assumes the tweak size to be close to n.

Formally, let $n \geq 1$ and consider a blockcipher $E : \{0,1\}^n \times \{0,1\}^n \rightarrow \{0,1\}^n$. We consider a generic tweakable blockcipher $\widetilde{E}[\rho, \sigma] : \{0,1\}^{2n} \times \{0,1\}^n \times \{0,1\}^n \rightarrow \{0,1\}^n$ based on $\rho \geq 0$ message-independent precomputation calls to E and $\sigma \geq 0$ message-dependent calls to E as follows (see also Fig. 3):

> **procedure** $\widetilde{E}[\rho, \sigma](k^a \| k^b, t, m)$
>   **for** $i = 1, \ldots, \rho$ **do**
> $x_i^{\mathrm{pre}} = A_i^{\mathrm{pre}}(k^a, t, y_1^{\mathrm{pre}}, \ldots, y_{i-1}^{\mathrm{pre}})$
> $l_i^{\mathrm{pre}} = B_i^{\mathrm{pre}}(k^b, t, y_1^{\mathrm{pre}}, \ldots, y_{i-1}^{\mathrm{pre}})$
> $y_i^{\mathrm{pre}} = E(l_i^{\mathrm{pre}}, x_i^{\mathrm{pre}})$
> $y_0 = m$
>   **for** $i = 1, \ldots, \sigma$ **do**
> $x_i = A_i(k^a, t, y_1^{\mathrm{pre}}, \ldots, y_\rho^{\mathrm{pre}}, y_{i-1})$
> $l_i = B_i(k^b, t, y_1^{\mathrm{pre}}, \ldots, y_\rho^{\mathrm{pre}})$
> $y_i = E(l_i, x_i)$
>   **return** $c = A_{\sigma+1}(k^a, t, y_1^{\mathrm{pre}}, \ldots, y_\rho^{\mathrm{pre}}, y_\sigma)$

The functions $A_i^{\mathrm{pre}} : \{0,1\}^{(i+1)n} \rightarrow \{0,1\}^n$ and $A_i : \{0,1\}^{(\rho+3)n} \rightarrow \{0,1\}^n$ compute the data inputs to E (and are keyed via k^a), while the functions $B_i^{\mathrm{pre}} : \{0,1\}^{(i+1)n} \rightarrow \{0,1\}^n$ and $B_i : \{0,1\}^{(\rho+2)n} \rightarrow \{0,1\}^n$ compute the key inputs to E (and are keyed via k^b). To guarantee invertibility of $\widetilde{E}$, we require that for fixed $k^a, t, y_1^{\mathrm{pre}}, \ldots, y_\rho^{\mathrm{pre}}$ the functions

$$A_i(k^a, t, y_1^{\mathrm{pre}}, \ldots, y_\rho^{\mathrm{pre}}, \cdot)$$

are invertible for all $i = 1, \ldots, \sigma+1$. (This is also the reason that A_i does not get inputs $y_0, \ldots, y_{i-2}$.) Apart from this condition, the functions $A_i^{\mathrm{pre}}, B_i^{\mathrm{pre}}, A_i, B_i$

---

[3] Our generalized design, as well as all follow-up results, can be easily generalized to the case of $2(\rho + \sigma) + 1$ keys (one key for every processing function).

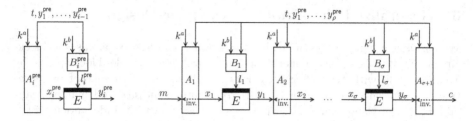

Fig. 3. Tweakable blockcipher $\widetilde{E}[\rho, \sigma]$: precomputation of y_i^{pre} (left) and processing of m (right). "inv." means that the function is invertible

can be any function, as long as they are sufficiently efficient. We put no limitation on how these functions process t; it may be split apart and processed by multiple functions separately.

Note that the message-independent precomputation calls can to a certain extent be reordered. Without loss of generality, there exists a $\rho' \leq \rho$ such that $y_1^{\mathrm{pre}}, \ldots, y_{\rho'}^{\mathrm{pre}}$ are only used as inputs to $A_i^{\mathrm{pre}}, B_i^{\mathrm{pre}}, B_i$, and that $y_{\rho'+1}^{\mathrm{pre}}, \ldots, y_\rho^{\mathrm{pre}}$ are also used as inputs to A_i. We define $\rho'' = \rho - \rho'$.

6.1 Key-Uniformity

In the remainder of this work we will require a technical condition on $\widetilde{E}$, which informally assures that $\widetilde{E}$ does not behave structurally different for different keys. For instance, it should not be the case that for some keys, l_1 can take only one value independent of the tweak, while for other keys, it can take 2^n values (one for every tweak). We will call this property "key-uniformity." Note that the condition slightly limits the generality of the scheme, but it is quite reasonable that a scheme should behave comparably for all keys.

For brevity, view the functions B_i^{pre} for $i = 1, \ldots, \rho$ as mappings $(k^a, k^b, t) \mapsto l_i^{\mathrm{pre}}$, and the functions B_i for $i = 1, \ldots, \sigma$ as mappings $(k^a, k^b, t) \mapsto l_i$. Note that, indeed, $(y_1^{\mathrm{pre}}, \ldots, y_i^{\mathrm{pre}})$, is a function of (k^a, k^b, t) for any i.

Definition 3. *We say that $\widetilde{E}$ is c-key-uniform for some $c \geq 0$, if there exist $\lambda_1^{\mathrm{pre}}, \ldots, \lambda_\rho^{\mathrm{pre}}, \lambda_1, \ldots, \lambda_\sigma$ such that for any $k^a \| k^b \in \{0,1\}^{2n}$:*

$$\text{for } i = 1, \ldots, \rho: \qquad 2^{\lambda_i^{\mathrm{pre}} - c} \leq \left| \mathsf{rng}(B_i^{\mathrm{pre}}(k^a, k^b, \cdot)) \right| \leq 2^{\lambda_i^{\mathrm{pre}}},$$

$$\text{for } i = 1, \ldots, \sigma: \qquad 2^{\lambda_i - c} \leq \left| \mathsf{rng}(B_i(k^a, k^b, \cdot)) \right| \leq 2^{\lambda_i}.$$

An observation we will use later on is that $\widetilde{E}$ calls its underlying E with key-deriving functions $\Phi = \Phi_B^{\mathrm{pre}} \cup \Phi_B$, where:

$$\Phi_B^{\mathrm{pre}} := \{(k^a, k^b) \mapsto B_i^{\mathrm{pre}}(k^a, k^b, t) \mid i \in \{\rho'+1, \ldots, \rho\}, t \in \{0,1\}^n\},$$
$$\Phi_B := \{(k^a, k^b) \mapsto B_i(k^a, k^b, t) \mid i \in \{1, \ldots, \sigma\}, t \in \{0,1\}^n\}.$$

$$(9)$$

6.2   Examples

The generalized design represents LRW2 of Fig. 1 for $\rho = 0$, $\sigma = 1$, $k^a = h$ (abusing notation), $k^b = k$, and the following processing functions:

$$A_1(h, t, m) = h(t) \oplus m \,,$$
$$B_1(k, t) = k \,,$$
$$A_2(h, t, y_1) = h(t) \oplus y_1 \,.$$

Note that LRW2 is 0-key-uniform (by putting $\lambda_1 = 0$).

The generalized design represents Men2 of Fig. 2 for $\rho = \sigma = 1$, $k^b = k$ (k^a is not used), and the following processing functions:

$$A_1^{\mathrm{pre}}(t) = t \,, \qquad\qquad A_1(t, y_1^{\mathrm{pre}}, m) = y_1^{\mathrm{pre}} \oplus m \,,$$
$$B_1^{\mathrm{pre}}(k, t) = 2k \,, \qquad\qquad B_1(k, t, y_1^{\mathrm{pre}}) = k \oplus t \,,$$
$$A_2(t, y_1^{\mathrm{pre}}, y_1) = y_1^{\mathrm{pre}} \oplus y_1 \,.$$

Also Men2 is 0-key-uniform (by putting $\lambda_1^{\mathrm{pre}} = 0$ and $\lambda_1 = n$).

7   Impossibility

We will provide a heuristic argument that if the standard-to-ideal reduction of Lemma 1 is used, optimal security in the standard model by a tweak-rekeyable tweakable blockcipher as described in Sect. 6 is at least as hard as achieving it by a non-tweak-rekeyable one. The analysis is based on below Assumption 1.

Assumption 1. *For any scheme $\widetilde{E}$ as described in Sect. 6 that is non-tweak-rekeyable (hence, l_i^{pre} and l_i are independent of t), and any $\mathcal{T} \subseteq \{0,1\}^n$ of size $|\mathcal{T}| \geq 2^{(\rho''+\sigma)n/(\rho''+\sigma+1)}$, we have*

$$\mathbf{Adv}_{\widetilde{E}}^{\text{i-}\widetilde{\mathrm{sprp}}}(\mathcal{D}) \geq \frac{q^{\rho''+\sigma+1}}{2^{(\rho''+\sigma)n}}$$

for some distinguisher $\mathcal{D}$ which only takes tweaks from $\mathcal{T}$.

The lower bound on $|\mathcal{T}|$ in Assumption 1 is argued by the observation that the bound on $\mathbf{Adv}_{\widetilde{E}}^{\text{i-}\widetilde{\mathrm{sprp}}}(\mathcal{D})$ is void for $q \geq 2^{(\rho''+\sigma)n/(\rho''+\sigma+1)}$. In other words: any attacker against $\widetilde{E}$ will make at most approximately $q \leq 2^{(\rho''+\sigma)n/(\rho''+\sigma+1)}$ queries and thus require at most that many tweaks for its attack. The assumption is discussed in further detail in Sect. 8.

Theorem 4. *Let $n \geq 1$ and let $\rho, \sigma \geq 0$. Let $\widetilde{E}$ be any tweakable blockcipher as in Sect. 6 that is c-key-uniform for some small c. Let Φ be as in (9). If Assumption 1 holds, then*

$$\max_{\mathcal{D}'} \mathbf{Adv}_{\Phi, E}^{\mathrm{srkprp}}(\mathcal{D}') + \max_{\mathcal{D}''} \mathbf{Adv}_{\widetilde{E}}^{\text{i-}\widetilde{\mathrm{sprp}}}(\mathcal{D}'')$$

$$= \Omega \left(\min \left\{ \frac{qr}{2^n}, \frac{q^{\rho''+\sigma+1}}{2^{(\rho''+\sigma)n}}, \frac{r^{(\rho''+\sigma)(\rho''+\sigma+1)}}{2^{((\rho''+\sigma)(\rho''+\sigma+1)-1)n}} \right\} \right), \tag{10}$$

where the first maximum is taken over all srkprp *distinguishers* $\mathcal{D}'$ *that make at most* $(\rho'' + \sigma) \cdot q$ *construction queries and at most* r *primitive evaluations, and the second maximum is taken over all information-theoretic* i-$\widetilde{\text{sprp}}$ *distinguishers* $\mathcal{D}''$ *that make* q *construction queries and* 0 *primitive queries.*

We give an interpretation of Theorem 4 in Sect. 7.1, and its proof in Sect. 7.2.

7.1   Interpretation of Theorem 4

Suppose our goal is to prove security of $\widetilde{E}$ against any s-$\widetilde{\text{sprp}}$ distinguisher $\mathcal{D}$, that can make q construction queries and r evaluations of the primitive. If we would opt to follow the standard-to-ideal reduction of Lemma 1, the first transition would give us an *unavoidable* bound

$$\mathbf{Adv}_{\widetilde{E}}^{\text{s-}\widetilde{\text{sprp}}}(\mathcal{D}) \leq \mathbf{Adv}_{\Phi,E}^{\text{srkprp}}(\mathcal{D}') + \mathbf{Adv}_{\widetilde{E}}^{\text{i-}\widetilde{\text{sprp}}}(\mathcal{D}''),$$

where $\mathcal{D}'$ is a distinguisher making at most $(\rho'' + \sigma)q$ queries[4] and making r primitive queries, and $\mathcal{D}''$ is an information-theoretic distinguisher making at most q queries to its construction oracle and 0 queries to its primitive oracle. Effectively, this step corresponds to replacing the ρ'' message-independent evaluations of E that are used by the masking functions $A_1, \ldots, A_\sigma$ and the σ message-dependent evaluations of E by a secret random related-key blockcipher $\text{rk}[rE]_{k^b}$. The remaining ρ' evaluations of E in the message-independent precomputation occur *indirectly* via the related-key deriving functions.

A next step in the security analysis would be to bound both terms for the strongest possible distinguishers $\mathcal{D}'$ and $\mathcal{D}''$. However, Theorem 4 shows that we can *impossibly* prove optimal security of this bound in terms of Definition 2. The theorem can henceforth be informally captured as follows.

Corollary 1. *If* $2^{\sigma n/(\sigma+1)}$ *is the best one can get* without *tweak-rekeying, optimal* 2^n *provable security with* tweak-rekeying *via the generic standard-to-ideal reduction is impossible.*

The bound of Theorem 4 is worse than the bound of Assumption 1, an unavoidable loss to cover worst-case scenarios. The loss shows that with tweak-rekeying we can get *closer to* 2^n than without tweak-rekeying, but we can never achieve optimal security. That is, the bound of (10) cannot give $2^n/const$ security provided that ρ and σ are constant.

The result leaves aside the question of whether the generic standard-to-ideal reduction is strictly necessary. We will discuss this question in Sect. 8.

---

[4] We remark that the complexity of $\mathcal{D}'$ in Lemma 1 may be optimized depending on the scheme: if ρ' out of ρ calls to the underlying E are *solely* made for the purpose of computing subkeys to later blockcipher calls, then these evaluations of E will be absorbed by the set of related-key deriving functions. This is for instance the case for Min of (3), where the set of key-deriving functions will be Φ_{Min} of Sect. 1, and $\mathcal{D}'$ can make at most q queries.

7.2 Proof of Theorem 4

Before going to the proof of Theorem 4, we will give a high-level intuition. The core idea is to consider the two terms of (10), and to make a distinction depending on how much freedom the distinguisher has in influencing the rekeying of the σ message-dependent evaluations of E. We consider two cases:

(1) Tweaks have little to no influence on the rekeying of *each* of the blockciphers. In this case, the lower bound on $\mathbf{Adv}_{\Phi,E}^{\mathrm{srkprp}}(\mathcal{D}')$ (Proposition 1) will be small and we cannot argue based on this part of the bound. On the other hand, the distinguisher can select a large set of tweaks $\mathcal{T}$ for which the blockciphers will never be rekeyed. This way, $\mathcal{D}$ would simply be considering a non-tweak-rekeyable cipher, for which Assumption 1 applies;

(2) Tweaks have a significant influence on the rekeying of *some* of the blockciphers. In this case, the lower bound on $\mathbf{Adv}_{\Phi,E}^{\mathrm{srkprp}}(\mathcal{D}')$ (Proposition 1) will be significant, and imply the impossibility of an optimal security bound.

Combining the two cases will imply the lower bound of Theorem 4. This high-level overview omits a few technicalities. Most importantly, case (1) requires an upper bound on the influence of the tweaks while case (2) requires a lower bound. This is resolved using the c-key-uniformity of Definition 3.

Proof (Proof of Theorem 4). Let k^a, k^b be two fixed secret keys. Recall that $\widetilde{E}$ is c-key-uniform for some small c. Let

$$\lambda^* = \max\{\lambda_{\rho'+1}^{\mathrm{pre}}, \ldots, \lambda_{\rho}^{\mathrm{pre}}, \lambda_1, \ldots, \lambda_\sigma\}.$$

We will derive a lower bound on

$$\max_{\mathcal{D}'} \mathbf{Adv}_{\Phi,E}^{\mathrm{srkprp}}(\mathcal{D}') + \max_{\mathcal{D}''} \mathbf{Adv}_{\widetilde{E}}^{\mathrm{i\text{-}\widetilde{sprp}}}(\mathcal{D}'') \tag{11}$$

by making a case distinction depending on λ^*.

Case $2^{n-\lambda^*(\rho''+\sigma)} \geq 2^{(\rho''+\sigma)n/(\rho''+\sigma+1)}$. For simplicity, we bound (11) as

$$\max_{\mathcal{D}'} \mathbf{Adv}_{\Phi,E}^{\mathrm{srkprp}}(\mathcal{D}') + \max_{\mathcal{D}''} \mathbf{Adv}_{\widetilde{E}}^{\mathrm{i\text{-}\widetilde{sprp}}}(\mathcal{D}'') \geq \max_{\mathcal{D}''} \mathbf{Adv}_{\widetilde{E}}^{\mathrm{i\text{-}\widetilde{sprp}}}(\mathcal{D}''),$$

and argue based on the i-$\widetilde{\mathrm{sprp}}$ security, where the maximum is taken over any information-theoretic $\mathcal{D}''$ that makes at most q construction queries and 0 primitive evaluations.

By maximality of λ^*, there is a set $\mathcal{T}' \subseteq \{0,1\}^n$ of size

$$|\mathcal{T}'| \geq \frac{2^n}{\prod_{i=\rho'+1}^{\rho} |\mathrm{rng}(B_i^{\mathrm{pre}}(k^a, k^b, \cdot))| \cdot \prod_{i=1}^{\sigma} |\mathrm{rng}(B_i(k^a, k^b, \cdot))|} \geq 2^{n-\lambda^*(\rho''+\sigma)}$$

such that $B_i^{\mathrm{pre}}(k^a, k^b, t) = B_i^{\mathrm{pre}}(k^a, k^b, t')$ and $B_i(k^a, k^b, t) = B_i(k^a, k^b, t')$ for all $t, t' \in \mathcal{T}'$. By Assumption 1, applied for this $\mathcal{T}'$, we obtain

$$\max_{\mathcal{D}''} \mathbf{Adv}_{\widetilde{E}}^{\mathrm{i\text{-}\widetilde{sprp}}}(\mathcal{D}'') \geq \frac{q^{\rho''+\sigma+1}}{2^{(\rho''+\sigma)n}}. \tag{12}$$

Note that $\mathcal{T}'$ is key-dependent and the distinguisher from Assumption 1 does not know $\mathcal{T}'$. This is not a problem, though, as in (12) we are *maximizing* over all distinguishers: the maximum over all distinguishers equals the maximum over all distinguishers that only take tweaks from $\mathcal{T}'$, maximized over all possible sets $\mathcal{T}'$.

Case $2^{n-\lambda^*}(\rho''+\sigma) \le 2^{(\rho''+\sigma)n/(\rho''+\sigma+1)}$. For simplicity, we bound (11) as

$$\max_{\mathcal{D}'} \mathbf{Adv}^{\mathrm{srkprp}}_{\Phi,E}(\mathcal{D}') + \max_{\mathcal{D}''} \mathbf{Adv}^{\mathrm{i\text{-}\widetilde{sprp}}}_{\widetilde{E}}(\mathcal{D}'') \ge \max_{\mathcal{D}'} \mathbf{Adv}^{\mathrm{srkprp}}_{\Phi,E}(\mathcal{D}'),$$

and argue based on the srkprp security, where the maximum is taken over any distinguisher $\mathcal{D}'$ that makes at most $(\rho''+\sigma)\cdot q$ construction queries and at most r primitive evaluations.

By Proposition 1,

$$\max_{\mathcal{D}'} \mathbf{Adv}^{\mathrm{srkprp}}_{\Phi,E}(\mathcal{D}') \ge \max_{\Phi'\subseteq\Phi,|\Phi'|=q'} \frac{\mathbf{Ex}\left(|\Phi'(k)|\right)\cdot r'}{2^{n+1}} - \frac{1}{2^n-1},$$

where $q' = \min\{(\rho''+\sigma)q - 1, |\Phi|\}$ and $r' = r - 1$. Note that

$$\max_{\Phi'\subseteq\Phi,|\Phi'|=q'} \mathbf{Ex}\left(|\Phi'(k)|\right) \ge \min\{(\rho''+\sigma)q - 1, 2^{\lambda^*-c}\}.$$

This maximum is achieved for Φ' being a subset of the set of key-deriving functions for which the maximum λ^* is achieved. As $2^{\lambda^*} \ge 2^{n/((\rho''+\sigma)(\rho''+\sigma+1))}$, we derive:

$$\max_{\mathcal{D}'} \mathbf{Adv}^{\mathrm{srkprp}}_{\Phi,E}(\mathcal{D}') \ge \frac{\min\{(\rho''+\sigma)q - 1, 2^{n/((\rho''+\sigma)(\rho''+\sigma+1))-c}\}\cdot r'}{2^{n+1}} - \frac{1}{2^n-1}.$$

Assuming that $\frac{2^{n/((\rho''+\sigma)(\rho''+\sigma+1))}r'}{2^{n+1+c}} \le 1$ (otherwise the term will not influence the bound), above term is lower bounded by

$$\max_{\mathcal{D}'} \mathbf{Adv}^{\mathrm{srkprp}}_{\Phi,E}(\mathcal{D}') \ge \min\left\{\frac{((\rho''+\sigma)q - 1)r'}{2^{n+1}}, \frac{2^n r'^{(\rho''+\sigma)(\rho''+\sigma+1)}}{2^{(n+1+c)(\rho''+\sigma)(\rho''+\sigma+1)}}\right\} - \frac{1}{2^n-1}.$$

Conclusion. We get for (11):

$$\max_{\mathcal{D}'} \mathbf{Adv}^{\mathrm{srkprp}}_{\Phi,E}(\mathcal{D}') + \max_{\mathcal{D}''} \mathbf{Adv}^{\mathrm{i\text{-}\widetilde{sprp}}}_{\widetilde{E}}(\mathcal{D}'')$$

$$= \Omega\left(\min\left\{\frac{qr}{2^n}, \frac{q^{\rho''+\sigma+1}}{2^{(\rho''+\sigma)n}}, \frac{r^{(\rho''+\sigma)(\rho''+\sigma+1)}}{2^{((\rho''+\sigma)(\rho''+\sigma+1)-1)n}}\right\}\right),$$

assuming that c is a small constant. This completes the proof. □

8   Discussion

The results shine a negative light on optimal standard-model security of tweakable blockciphers and give rise to multiple questions.

What are the implications of the negative standard-model result on Men2 *of Theorem 3?* Despite what the lower bound of Theorem 3 suggests, the gap is mainly caused by the estimation in the hybrid step. More detailed, the step where E is replaced with $\mathbf{Adv}^{\mathrm{srkprp}}_{\Phi_{\mathsf{Men2}},E}(\mathcal{D}')$ is extremely loose, and an attacker $\mathcal{D}'$ that maximizes its success probability in breaking the related-key security of E is not transformable to an attacker on Men2. Concretely, standard-model security derivations simply *cannot confirm* this.

How do the standard and ideal model compare, and what are the implications of results in both models? This question is not easy to answer. Results in the ideal cipher model are likely to be over-optimistic, while the standard-model results are too loose, mainly due to the seemingly necessary generic reduction of Lemma 1. Intuitively, the "real" security of a scheme satisfies

ideal-model security $\leq$ "real" security $\leq$ standard-model security.

The question is, which of the estimates is tighter? In the ideal-model versus standard-model results on Men2, Theorem 2 versus Theorem 3, the standard-model bound seems to be too loose. For different schemes, it may be the other way around. A potential approach to go is to weaken the ideal-model, an approach for instance followed by Shrimpton and Terashima [55], yet, this approach is ultimately still an ideal-model approach.

In either situation, the findings of this work contribute to a better understanding of how both models compare, and demonstrate that results in the two models should be interpreted with care. We believe that, taking these issues into account, the ideal-cipher security model is still reasonable to consider.

Is Assumption 1 reasonable? Recall that Lampe and Seurin [34] conjectured that the cascade of σ LRW2's achieves $2^{\sigma n/(\sigma+1)}$ security (for the cascade of LRW2's we have $\rho = \rho' = \rho'' = 0$). Assumption 1 suggests that this is the best possible for non-tweak-rekeyable tweakable blockciphers. Regardless of this, it is merely used as starting point: if the assumption holds, then tweak-rekeying will not help in achieving optimal security. Assumption 1 allows for some stretch: if it is not true and a slightly more secure tweakable blockcipher can be constructed, the results (and in particular Theorem 4) generalize accordingly.

The heuristic bound in Theorem 4 is better than the one of Assumption 1, which indicates that tweak-rekeyability *may* result in a better bound than non-tweak-rekeyability (but no optimal one). However, the derivation of the bound of Theorem 4 is very conservative. For instance, it relies on the superset bound $\Phi \supseteq \Phi_B$ of (9) and on a lower bound on $|\Phi_B|$, both of which are loose. Tighter bounds for Theorem 4 may be achieved if more properties of $\widetilde{E}$ are taken into account.

Can we Salvage the Generic Standard-to-Ideal Reduction? Theoretically, Theorem 4 gives a lower bound on an upper bound argued via the generic reduction of Lemma 1. This is in itself little informative, yet it shows us that *if* this classical first-step reduction is used, we cannot get optimal security. Note that we do not claim that the standard-to-ideal reduction is unavoidable, but that *if* this reduction is applied, the term of (10) is unavoidable. A way to circumvent the usage of the reduction and the strong (related-key) PRP security definition as formalized in Sect. 2.1 may be by using a generalized security model for blockciphers, such as the "strong masked related-key PRP security." Such a generalized security model would, however, only absorb various design properties of the tweakable blockcipher, and shift the problem instead of solving it.

Acknowledgments. Bart Mennink is supported by a postdoctoral fellowship from the Netherlands Organisation for Scientific Research (NWO) under Veni grant 016.Veni.173.017. The author would like to thank the anonymous reviewers of CRYPTO 2017 for their comments and suggestions.

References

1. Abed, F., Fluhrer, S., Forler, C., List, E., Lucks, S., McGrew, D., Wenzel, J.: Pipelineable on-line encryption. In: Cid, C., Rechberger, C. (eds.) FSE 2014. LNCS, vol. 8540, pp. 205–223. Springer, Heidelberg (2015). doi:10.1007/978-3-662-46706-0_11
2. Albrecht, M.R., Farshim, P., Paterson, K.G., Watson, G.J.: On cipher-dependent related-key attacks in the ideal-cipher model. In: Joux, A. (ed.) FSE 2011. LNCS, vol. 6733, pp. 128–145. Springer, Heidelberg (2011). doi:10.1007/978-3-642-21702-9_8
3. Andreeva, E., Bogdanov, A., Luykx, A., Mennink, B., Tischhauser, E., Yasuda, K.: Parallelizable and authenticated online ciphers. In: Sako, K., Sarkar, P. (eds.) ASIACRYPT 2013. LNCS, vol. 8269, pp. 424–443. Springer, Heidelberg (2013). doi:10.1007/978-3-642-42033-7_22
4. Andreeva, E., Daemen, J., Mennink, B., Van Assche, G.: Security of keyed sponge constructions using a modular proof approach. In: Leander, G. (ed.) FSE 2015. LNCS, vol. 9054, pp. 364–384. Springer, Heidelberg (2015). doi:10.1007/978-3-662-48116-5_18
5. Bellare, M.: New proofs for NMAC and HMAC: Security without collision-resistance. In: Dwork, C. (ed.) CRYPTO 2006. LNCS, vol. 4117, pp. 602–619. Springer, Heidelberg (2006). doi:10.1007/11818175_36
6. Bellare, M., Canetti, R., Krawczyk, H.: Keying hash functions for message authentication. In: Koblitz, N. (ed.) CRYPTO 1996. LNCS, vol. 1109, pp. 1–15. Springer, Heidelberg (1996). doi:10.1007/3-540-68697-5_1
7. Bellare, M., Kohno, T.: A theoretical treatment of related-key attacks: RKA-PRPs, RKA-PRFs, and applications. In: Biham, E. (ed.) EUROCRYPT 2003. LNCS, vol. 2656, pp. 491–506. Springer, Heidelberg (2003). doi:10.1007/3-540-39200-9_31
8. Bellare, M., Krovetz, T., Rogaway, P.: Luby-Rackoff backwards: Increasing security by making block ciphers non-invertible. In: Nyberg, K. (ed.) EUROCRYPT 1998. LNCS, vol. 1403, pp. 266–280. Springer, Heidelberg (1998). doi:10.1007/BFb0054132

9. Bellare, M., Rogaway, P.: Random oracles are practical: A paradigm for designing efficient protocols. In: ACM Conference on Computer and Communications Security, pp. 62–73. ACM, New York (1993)
10. Bellare, M., Rogaway, P.: Introduction to Modern Cryptography, Pseudorandom Functions (2005). http://cseweb.ucsd.edu/~mihir/cse207/classnotes.html
11. Bellare, M., Rogaway, P., Wagner, D.: The EAX mode of operation. In: Roy, B., Meier, W. (eds.) FSE 2004. LNCS, vol. 3017, pp. 389–407. Springer, Heidelberg (2004). doi:10.1007/978-3-540-25937-4_25
12. Bernstein, D.J., Lange, T.: Non-uniform cracks in the concrete: the power of free precomputation. In: Sako, K., Sarkar, P. (eds.) ASIACRYPT 2013. LNCS, vol. 8270, pp. 321–340. Springer, Heidelberg (2013). doi:10.1007/978-3-642-42045-0_17
13. Black, J., Rogaway, P.: CBC MACs for arbitrary-length messages: the three-key constructions. In: Bellare, M. (ed.) CRYPTO 2000. LNCS, vol. 1880, pp. 197–215. Springer, Heidelberg (2000). doi:10.1007/3-540-44598-6_12
14. Black, J., Rogaway, P., Shrimpton, T.: Black-box analysis of the block-cipher-based hash-function constructions from PGV. In: Yung, M. (ed.) CRYPTO 2002. LNCS, vol. 2442, pp. 320–335. Springer, Heidelberg (2002). doi:10.1007/3-540-45708-9_21
15. Chakraborty, D., Sarkar, P.: A general construction of tweakable block ciphers and different modes of operations. In: Lipmaa, H., Yung, M., Lin, D. (eds.) Inscrypt 2006. LNCS, vol. 4318, pp. 88–102. Springer, Heidelberg (2006). doi:10.1007/11937807_8
16. Chang, D., Dworkin, M., Hong, S., Kelsey, J., Nandi, M.: A keyed sponge construction with pseudorandomness in the standard model. In: NIST's 3rd SHA-3 Candidate Conference 2012 (2012)
17. Cogliati, B., Lampe, R., Seurin, Y.: Tweaking even-mansour ciphers. In: Gennaro, R., Robshaw, M. (eds.) CRYPTO 2015. LNCS, vol. 9215, pp. 189–208. Springer, Heidelberg (2015). doi:10.1007/978-3-662-47989-6_9
18. Cogliati, B., Seurin, Y.: Beyond-birthday-bound security for tweakable even-mansour ciphers with linear tweak and key mixing. In: Iwata, T., Cheon, J.H. (eds.) ASIACRYPT 2015. LNCS, vol. 9453, pp. 134–158. Springer, Heidelberg (2015). doi:10.1007/978-3-662-48800-3_6
19. Cogliati, B., Seurin, Y.: On the provable security of the iterated even-mansour cipher against related-key and chosen-key attacks. In: Oswald, E., Fischlin, M. (eds.) EUROCRYPT 2015. LNCS, vol. 9056, pp. 584–613. Springer, Heidelberg (2015). doi:10.1007/978-3-662-46800-5_23
20. Crowley, P.: Mercy: A fast large block cipher for disk sector encryption. In: Goos, G., Hartmanis, J., Leeuwen, J., Schneier, B. (eds.) FSE 2000. LNCS, vol. 1978, pp. 49–63. Springer, Heidelberg (2001). doi:10.1007/3-540-44706-7_4
21. Datta, N., Nandi, M.: ELmE: A misuse resistant parallel authenticated encryption. In: Susilo, W., Mu, Y. (eds.) ACISP 2014. LNCS, vol. 8544, pp. 306–321. Springer, Cham (2014). doi:10.1007/978-3-319-08344-5_20
22. Ferguson, N., Lucks, S., Schneier, B., Whiting, D., Bellare, M., Kohno, T., Callas, J., Walker, J.: The Skein Hash Function Family, submission to NIST's SHA-3 competition (2010)
23. Gaži, P., Pietrzak, K., Rybár, M.: The exact PRF-security of NMAC and HMAC. In: Garay, J.A., Gennaro, R. (eds.) CRYPTO 2014. LNCS, vol. 8616, pp. 113–130. Springer, Heidelberg (2014). doi:10.1007/978-3-662-44371-2_7
24. Gaži, P., Pietrzak, K., Tessaro, S.: The exact PRF security of truncation: Tight bounds for keyed sponges and truncated CBC. In: Gennaro, R., Robshaw, M. (eds.) CRYPTO 2015. LNCS, vol. 9215, pp. 368–387. Springer, Heidelberg (2015). doi:10.1007/978-3-662-47989-6_18

25. Gaži, P., Pietrzak, K., Tessaro, S.: Generic security of NMAC and HMAC with input whitening. In: Iwata, T., Cheon, J.H. (eds.) ASIACRYPT 2015. LNCS, vol. 9453, pp. 85–109. Springer, Heidelberg (2015). doi:10.1007/978-3-662-48800-3_4

26. Goldenberg, D., Hohenberger, S., Liskov, M., Schwartz, E.C., Seyalioglu, H.: On tweaking luby-rackoff blockciphers. In: Kurosawa, K. (ed.) ASIACRYPT 2007. LNCS, vol. 4833, pp. 342–356. Springer, Heidelberg (2007). doi:10.1007/978-3-540-76900-2_21

27. Granger, R., Jovanovic, P., Mennink, B., Neves, S.: Improved masking for tweakable blockciphers with applications to authenticated encryption. In: Fischlin, M., Coron, J.-S. (eds.) EUROCRYPT 2016. LNCS, vol. 9665, pp. 263–293. Springer, Heidelberg (2016). doi:10.1007/978-3-662-49890-3_11

28. Hoang, V.T., Krovetz, T., Rogaway, P.: Robust authenticated-encryption AEZ and the problem that it solves. In: Oswald, E., Fischlin, M. (eds.) EUROCRYPT 2015. LNCS, vol. 9056, pp. 15–44. Springer, Heidelberg (2015). doi:10.1007/978-3-662-46800-5_2

29. Iwata, T., Kurosawa, K.: OMAC: One-key CBC MAC. In: Johansson, T. (ed.) FSE 2003. LNCS, vol. 2887, pp. 129–153. Springer, Heidelberg (2003). doi:10.1007/978-3-540-39887-5_11

30. Iwata, T., Kurosawa, K.: Stronger security bounds for OMAC, TMAC, and XCBC. In: Johansson, T., Maitra, S. (eds.) INDOCRYPT 2003. LNCS, vol. 2904, pp. 402–415. Springer, Heidelberg (2003). doi:10.1007/978-3-540-24582-7_30

31. Jean, J., Nikolić, I., Peyrin, T.: Tweaks and keys for block ciphers: The TWEAKEY framework. In: Sarkar, P., Iwata, T. (eds.) ASIACRYPT 2014. LNCS, vol. 8874, pp. 274–288. Springer, Heidelberg (2014). doi:10.1007/978-3-662-45608-8_15

32. Krawczyk, H.: LFSR-based hashing and authentication. In: Desmedt, Y.G. (ed.) CRYPTO 1994. LNCS, vol. 839, pp. 129–139. Springer, Heidelberg (1994). doi:10.1007/3-540-48658-5_15

33. Krovetz, T., Rogaway, P.: The software performance of authenticated-encryption modes. In: Joux, A. (ed.) FSE 2011. LNCS, vol. 6733, pp. 306–327. Springer, Heidelberg (2011). doi:10.1007/978-3-642-21702-9_18

34. Lampe, R., Seurin, Y.: Tweakable blockciphers with asymptotically optimal security. In: Moriai, S. (ed.) FSE 2013. LNCS, vol. 8424, pp. 133–151. Springer, Heidelberg (2014). doi:10.1007/978-3-662-43933-3_8

35. Landecker, W., Shrimpton, T., Terashima, R.S.: Tweakable blockciphers with beyond birthday-bound security. In: Safavi-Naini, R., Canetti, R. (eds.) CRYPTO 2012. LNCS, vol. 7417, pp. 14–30. Springer, Heidelberg (2012). doi:10.1007/978-3-642-32009-5_2

36. Liskov, M., Rivest, R.L., Wagner, D.: Tweakable block ciphers. In: Yung, M. (ed.) CRYPTO 2002. LNCS, vol. 2442, pp. 31–46. Springer, Heidelberg (2002). doi:10.1007/3-540-45708-9_3

37. McGrew, D.A., Viega, J.: The security and performance of the galois/counter mode (GCM) of operation. In: Canteaut, A., Viswanathan, K. (eds.) INDOCRYPT 2004. LNCS, vol. 3348, pp. 343–355. Springer, Heidelberg (2004). doi:10.1007/978-3-540-30556-9_27

38. Mennink, B.: Optimally secure tweakable blockciphers. In: Leander, G. (ed.) FSE 2015. LNCS, vol. 9054, pp. 428–448. Springer, Heidelberg (2015). doi:10.1007/978-3-662-48116-5_21

39. Mennink, B.: Optimally secure tweakable blockciphers. Cryptology ePrint Archive, Report 2015/363 (2015). Full version of [38]

40. Mennink, B.: XPX: Generalized tweakable even-mansour with improved security guarantees. In: Robshaw, M., Katz, J. (eds.) CRYPTO 2016. LNCS, vol. 9814, pp. 64–94. Springer, Heidelberg (2016). doi:10.1007/978-3-662-53018-4_3

41. Mennink, B., Reyhanitabar, R., Vizár, D.: Security of full-state keyed sponge and duplex: applications to authenticated encryption. In: Iwata, T., Cheon, J.H. (eds.) ASIACRYPT 2015. LNCS, vol. 9453, pp. 465–489. Springer, Heidelberg (2015). doi:10.1007/978-3-662-48800-3_19

42. Minematsu, K.: Improved security analysis of XEX and LRW modes. In: Biham, E., Youssef, A.M. (eds.) SAC 2006. LNCS, vol. 4356, pp. 96–113. Springer, Heidelberg (2007). doi:10.1007/978-3-540-74462-7_8

43. Minematsu, K.: Beyond-birthday-bound security based on tweakable block cipher. In: Dunkelman, O. (ed.) FSE 2009. LNCS, vol. 5665, pp. 308–326. Springer, Heidelberg (2009). doi:10.1007/978-3-642-03317-9_19

44. Minematsu, K.: Parallelizable Rate-1 authenticated encryption from pseudorandom functions. In: Nguyen, P.Q., Oswald, E. (eds.) EUROCRYPT 2014. LNCS, vol. 8441, pp. 275–292. Springer, Heidelberg (2014). doi:10.1007/978-3-642-55220-5_16

45. Minematsu, K., Iwata, T.: Tweak-length extension for tweakable blockciphers. In: Groth, J. (ed.) IMACC 2015. LNCS, vol. 9496, pp. 77–93. Springer, Cham (2015). doi:10.1007/978-3-319-27239-9_5

46. Mitsuda, A., Iwata, T.: Tweakable pseudorandom permutation from generalized feistel structure. In: Baek, J., Bao, F., Chen, K., Lai, X. (eds.) ProvSec 2008. LNCS, vol. 5324, pp. 22–37. Springer, Heidelberg (2008). doi:10.1007/978-3-540-88733-1_2

47. Mouha, N., Mennink, B., Herrewege, A., Watanabe, D., Preneel, B., Verbauwhede, I.: Chaskey: An efficient MAC algorithm for 32-bit microcontrollers. In: Joux, A., Youssef, A. (eds.) SAC 2014. LNCS, vol. 8781, pp. 306–323. Springer, Cham (2014). doi:10.1007/978-3-319-13051-4_19

48. Procter, G.: A note on the CLRW2 tweakable block cipher construction. Cryptology ePrint Archive, Report 2014/111 (2014)

49. Rogaway, P.: Bucket hashing and its application to fast message authentication. In: Coppersmith, D. (ed.) CRYPTO 1995. LNCS, vol. 963, pp. 29–42. Springer, Heidelberg (1995). doi:10.1007/3-540-44750-4_3

50. Rogaway, P.: Efficient instantiations of tweakable blockciphers and refinements to modes OCB and PMAC. In: Lee, P.J. (ed.) ASIACRYPT 2004. LNCS, vol. 3329, pp. 16–31. Springer, Heidelberg (2004). doi:10.1007/978-3-540-30539-2_2

51. Rogaway, P., Bellare, M., Black, J., Krovetz, T.: OCB: a block-cipher mode of operation for efficient authenticated encryption. In: ACM Conference on Computer and Communications Security, pp. 196–205. ACM, New York (2001)

52. Sasaki, Y., Todo, Y., Aoki, K., Naito, Y., Sugawara, T., Murakami, Y., Matsui, M., Hirose, S.: Minalpher v1, submission to CAESAR competition (2014)

53. Schroeppel, R.: The Hasty Pudding Cipher, submission to NIST's AES competition (1998)

54. Shannon, C.: Communication theory of secrecy systems. Bell Syst. Tech. J. **28**(4), 656–715 (1949)

55. Shrimpton, T., Terashima, R.S.: Salvaging weak security bounds for blockcipher-based constructions. In: Cheon, J.H., Takagi, T. (eds.) ASIACRYPT 2016. LNCS, vol. 10031, pp. 429–454. Springer, Heidelberg (2016). doi:10.1007/978-3-662-53887-6_16

56. Wang, L., Guo, J., Zhang, G., Zhao, J., Gu, D.: How to build fully secure tweakable blockciphers from classical blockciphers. In: Cheon, J.H., Takagi, T. (eds.) ASIACRYPT 2016. LNCS, vol. 10031, pp. 455–483. Springer, Heidelberg (2016). doi:10.1007/978-3-662-53887-6_17

57. Yasuda, K.: The sum of CBC MACs is a secure PRF. In: Pieprzyk, J. (ed.) CT-RSA 2010. LNCS, vol. 5985, pp. 366–381. Springer, Heidelberg (2010). doi:10.1007/978-3-642-11925-5_25

58. Yasuda, K.: A new variant of PMAC: Beyond the birthday bound. In: Rogaway, P. (ed.) CRYPTO 2011. LNCS, vol. 6841, pp. 596–609. Springer, Heidelberg (2011). doi:10.1007/978-3-642-22792-9_34

59. Zhang, L., Wu, W., Sui, H., Wang, P.: 3kf9: Enhancing 3GPP-MAC beyond the birthday bound. In: Wang, X., Sako, K. (eds.) ASIACRYPT 2012. LNCS, vol. 7658, pp. 296–312. Springer, Heidelberg (2012). doi:10.1007/978-3-642-34961-4_19

Author Index